AUSTRALIAN DICTIONARY

OF BIOGRAPHY

General Editors
BEDE NAIRN
GEOFFREY SERLE

AUSTRALIAN DICTIONARY OF BIOGRAPHY

VOLUME 9 : 1891-1939

Gil-Las

General Editors
BEDE NAIRN
GEOFFREY SERLE
Deputy General Editor
CHRISTOPHER CUNNEEN

Section Editors
G. C. BOLTON
K. J. CABLE
R. J. O'NEILL
J. R. POYNTER
HEATHER RADI

MELBOURNE UNIVERSITY PRESS

First published 1983
Typeset by Dovatype, Melbourne
Printed in Australia by Griffin Press Limited
Netley, South Australia, for
Melbourne University Press, Carlton, Victoria 3053
U.S.A. and Canada: International Scholarly Book Services, Inc.,
P.O. Box 1632, Beaverton, OR 97075
United Kingdom, Ireland and Europe: Europa Publications Limited
18 Bedford Square, London WC1B 3JN

National Library of Australia Cataloguing-in-Publication entry

Australian dictionary of biography.
  Volume 9. 1891-1939, Gil-Las.
  ISBN 0 522 84273 9.
  ISBN 0 522 84236 4 (set).

  1. Australia — Biography. 2. Australia — History — 1891-1901.
3. Australia — History — 1901-1945. I. Nairn, Bede, 1917-   .
II. Serle, Geoffrey. 1922-   . III. Cunneen, Christopher, 1940–
920'.094

CORRIGENDA
to accompany volume 9

Australian Dictionary of Biography

Volume 1: 1788-1850 A-H

Volume 2: 1788-1850 I-Z

Volume 3: 1851-1890 A-C

Volume 4: 1851-1890 D-J

Volume 5: 1851-1890 K-Q

Volume 6: 1851-1890 R-Z

Volume 7: 1891-1939 A-Ch

Volume 8: 1891-1939 Cl-Gib

This list includes only corrigenda discovered since volume 8 was published in 1981.

Note that only corrections are shown; additional information is not included; nor is any re-interpretation attempted. The only exception to this procedure is when new details become available about parents or births, deaths and marriages.

Documented corrections are welcome from readers. Additional information, with sources, is also invited and will be placed in the appropriate files for future use.

N.B. Copies of cumulative corrigenda up to volume 7 and the list published with volume 8 are available on request from the publishers at cost of postage.

1983

Volume 1: 1788-1850 A-H

61b BARRALLIER
line 6 *for* 1764-1832 *read* 1749-1809
line 7 *for* nephew *read* relative

63b BARRINGTON
bibliog line 2 *for* 1830 *read* 1930

105a BIRNIE
lines 42-3 *for* considered . . . Gipps
read not confirmed until 1838
line 47 *delete* also

176a BUNCE
line 5 *for* 1835 *read* 1833

201b CAMPBELL, P. L.
line 2 *after* public servant, *insert*
son of Ronald Campbell and his
wife Charlotte, née Cloeté,

Volume 2: 1788-1850 I-Z

96a LAWSON
line 35 *for* next year *read* in January 1812
lines 36-7 *for Admiral* . . . place
read Guildford

153b MACARTHUR
line 1 *after* 1767 *insert* ?
line 5 *after* second *insert* surviving

213b MASON
line 1 *delete* (d. 1821)

214a line 4 *insert* , but went ashore at
Portsmouth and disappeared.
after Mary

231b MILLS, J. B. and C. F.
line 35 *for* 1849 *read* 1852

348a POWELL
lines 21-22 *for* administered . . .
1818. *read* died in August 1836,
having married James Moore in
June 1829.

403a ROWLEY
line 13 *for* Piper *read* Townson

623a WOOLLEY
line 28 *delete* first

Volume 3: 1851-1890 A-C

27a ALLEYNE
lines 24-5 *for* also . . . administer
read administered

49a ARMITAGE
line 17 *for* In July 1855 *read* That year
line 19 *after* Wales. *insert* He
arrived in Sydney in January 1855.

351a CARANDINI
line 11 *for* 1814? *read* 1803

452a COOPER
line 40 *for* 1855 *read* 1855-56

486b COX
line 9 *for* education *read* Church schools

Volume 4: 1851-1890 D-J

2a D'ALBERTIS
line 12 *for* 1876 *read* 1872

67b DIBBS
line 16 *for* February *read* January

299a GRIBBLE
line 7 *for* at 20 *read* on 4 February 1868

305a GROOM
line 62 *for* 1859 *read* 1860

362a HAY
line 4 *insert* . *after* runs
lines 5-6 *delete* and as . . . district.

386b HERZ
line 2 *delete* the first committee of
line 3 *for* Musical Association *read*
Association of Professional
Musicians,
lines 6-8 *for* the twenty-five . . .
founding of *read* twelve who founded

414a HOLT, T.
line 8 *for* 1822-32 *read* 1832-42

Volume 5: 1851-1890 K-Q

24b KIDD
line 10 *for* June *read* August

61b LANGRIDGE
line 3 *for* William *read* John

172b MACKIE
line 50 *delete* where *insert* . *after*
Horsham
line 51 *for* in December 1860 *read*
In September 1861
line 52 *after* Lyon *insert* Williamson at Geelong

182a McLAURIN
line 3 *for* 2 *read* 20

211b MARKS
line 4 *for* eldest *read* second

270b MONTEFIORE
line 26 *for* B. *read* R.

349b OAKES
lines 43-7 *delete* By 1854 . . . 4000
sheep. *insert* In the 1850s he had

four runs in the Wellington District amounting to some 132 400 acres and capable of carrying 3560 cattle.

Volume 6: 1851-1890 R-Z

59a ROSEBY
line 59 *for* 83 *read* 82

65a ROUSE
line 18 *for* runs *read* properties

73b RUSDEN
line 6 *for* Townshend *read* Townsend

74a lines 51-2 *for* first . . . Victoria in *read* Victorian Cremation Act,

127a SIMPSON
line 44 *for* 1888 *read* 1889

170a SPENCE
lines 20-21 *for* International *read* Industrial

219b SUMMERS
line 1 *for* 1827 *read* 1825
line 2 *for* 1827 *read* 1825
line 3 *after* Charlton *add* Mackrell

220a line 2 *for* 1852 *read* 1854

280a TODD
line 4 *for* eldest *read* second

365a WATT
line 30 *for* 1863 *read* 1866

Volume 7: 1891-1939 A-Ch

2b ABBOTT, P. P.
lines 5-6 *delete* , and grandson of Edward Abbott [q.v.1]

114a ASHTON, J. R.
line 5 *delete* Florentine
line 6 *insert* Carlo *before* Rossi *insert* , a Sardinian diplomat *after* Rossi

123a AUSTIN
line 58 *for* 1913-25 *read* 1910-25

240a BECKETT
lines 52-4 *delete* held . . . Works *insert* was honorary minister

274b BERNACCHI, A.
line 1 *for* GUILIO *read* GIULIO

275b BERNACCHI, L.
line 4 *for* Guilio *read* Giulio

342a BONYTHON
line 57 *for* Kim *read* Kym

609a CHANTER
line 36 *delete* and agriculture

Volume 8: 1891-1939 Cl-Gib

12b CLARK, R. M.
lines 13-14 *delete* and . . . stamp

28a CLENDINNEN
lines 40-44 *delete* Both . . . Paris.

135a CRAIGIE
bibliog line 1 *delete* NSW Public Service Board, *insert* (Melb) *after* Progress

140b CRAWFORD, T. S.
line 5 *for* eldest *read* youngest *for* fifth *read* ninth

168b CULLEN
line 26 *delete* the McGowen . . . government's *insert* acting Premier W. A. Holman's [q.v.]
line 28 *for* dissolved. *read* prorogued.

196a DALLAS
line 35 *for* 279 cm *read* 188 cm

265a DE BERNALES
line 17 *for* Hill *read* Bill

374b DUNN, W. F.
line 48 *for* August *read* July

393b DYER
line 16 *for* 1933 *read* 1932
line 23 *for* taught at *read* attended

402a EARP
line 5 *for* Shetton *read* Shelton

468a FARNELL
line 20 *for* 1891 *read* 1894

528a FLIERL
lines 3-4 *for* Wilhelm Kelhofer *read* Georg Pilhofer

574b FRANKLIN, S.
line 33 *for* Adams *read* Addams

598b FULLWOOD
line 9 *for* 1881 *read* 1883

622b GARRAN
lines 29-32 *delete* He . . . matters.

640b GEPP
line 17 *for* nights *read* mornings
line 23 *for* 1896 *read* 1898

660b GIBSON
lines 11-12 *delete* began the teaching *insert* became the first full-time teacher

PREFACE

This volume of the *Australian Dictionary of Biography*, containing 678 entries by 460 authors, is the third of six for the 1891-1939 section. The two volumes of the 1788-1850 section and the four of the 1851-1890 section have already been published. The late Douglas Pike was general editor for volumes 1 to 5 and Bede Nairn for volume 6 and Nairn and Geoffrey Serle for volumes 7 and 8. The chronological division was designed to simplify production, for more than 7000 entries will be included in volumes 1-12. (Volumes 1-2, for 1788-1850, had 1116 entries; volumes 3-6, for 1851-1890, 2053; and 4000 are planned for volumes 7-12). The placing of each individual's name in the appropriate section has been determined by when he/she did his/her most important work (*floruit*). A general index volume will be prepared when the three sections are completed.

The selection of names for inclusion required prolonged consultation. After quotas were estimated, working parties in each State and the armed services working party prepared provisional lists, which were widely circulated and carefully amended. Many of the names were obviously significant and worthy of inclusion as leaders in politics, business, the armed services, the professions, the arts, the labour movement, etc. Many others have been included as representatives of ethnic and social minorities and of a wide range of occupations, or as innovators, notorieties or eccentrics. Many had to be omitted through pressure of space or lack of material, and thereby joined the great mass whose members richly deserve a more honoured place; however, many thousands of these names, and information about them, are accumulating in the biographical register at the *Dictionary* headquarters in the Australian National University.

Most authors were nominated by working parties. The burden of writing has been shared almost equally by university staff and by a wide variety of specialists in other fields.

The *Australian Dictionary of Biography* is a project based on consultation and co-operation. The Australian National University has borne the cost of the headquarters staff, of much research and of some special contingencies, while other Australian universities have supported the project in various ways. Its policies were originally determined by the national committee, composed mainly of representatives from the departments of history in each Australian university. At Canberra the editorial board has kept in touch with all these representatives, and with the working parties, librarians, archivists and other local experts, as well as overseas correspondents and research assistants in each Australian capital. With such varied support the *Australian Dictionary of Biography* can truly be called a national project.

ACKNOWLEDGMENTS

Special thanks are due to Professor K. S. Inglis and Dr A. Barnard for their guidance as chairman and acting chairman of the editorial board and to Professor G. M. Neutze, director of the Research School of Social Sciences, Australian National University, and Mr P. Grimshaw, business manager of the research school. Those who helped in planning the shape of the work have been mentioned in earlier volumes.

Within Australia the *Dictionary* is greatly indebted to many librarians and archivists in Canberra and in each State; to the secretaries of many historical and genealogical societies; to the Australian War Memorial, Australian National Gallery and Department of Veterans' Affairs, in Canberra; to the registrars of probates, in the various States, and of Supreme and Family Courts, whose generous co-operation has solved many problems; and to the Department of Defence for authenticating many details. Warm thanks for the free gift of their time and talents are due to all contributors and to all members of the national committee, editorial board, and the working parties. For particular advice the *Dictionary* owes much to M. Austin, Margaret Brennan, B. Gandevia and T. G. Vallance.

Essential assistance with birth, death and marriage certificates has been provided by the generous co-operation of registrars in New South Wales, Queensland, South Australia, Tasmania, Western Australia, the Northern Territory, the Australian Capital Territory and Norfolk Island and by the government statist, Victoria; by the Alexander Turnbull Library, Wellington, New Zealand; by the General Register Office, Edinburgh, Scotland; by Bureaux of Vital Statistics in State Health departments in California, Connecticut, Florida, Hawaii, Illinois, Iowa, Louisiana, Massachusetts, Michigan, Mississippi, Ohio, Pennsylvania and South Carolina in the United States of America; by registrars-general in Fiji and Trinidad and the principal civil status officer, Port Louis, in Mauritius; by the mayors of Cannes, Pau, St Jean-de-Luz and Strasbourg in France; by the mayor of Bochum and the director, city archives, Braunschweig, Federal Republic of Germany; by the civil status officers, Genoa and Milan, Italy; by the archivist, Lund, Sweden; by the department of Internal Affairs, South Africa; by the mayor of Noumea, New Caledonia; and by the Royal Danish Embassy and the Embassy of the Federal Republic of Germany.

For assistance overseas, thanks are due to Sean Murphy, Dublin, and Ignatius Cleary, Corofin, Ireland; to Information Systems Consultants Inc., Bethesda, Maryland, in the United States of America; to the archives and/or libraries of the universities of Birmingham, Cambridge, Durham, Leeds, London, Manchester and Oxford and of the Imperial College of Science and Technology, King's College and University College, London, in England, of the universities of Edinburgh and Glasgow, in Scotland, of Queen's University of Belfast, in Northern Ireland, and of Trinity College, University of Dublin, in Ireland, and of Stanford, California, Yale, Connecticut, and New York universities in the United States of America.

Thanks are also due to the British Architectural Library, the Chamberlain's Court, Guildhall, the Geological Society of London, the Institution of Civil Engineers, the Institution of Mechanical Engineers, the Linnean Society of London, the Public Record Office, the Royal Academy of Arts, the Royal Academy of Music, the Royal College of Veterinary Surgeons, the Royal Geographical Society and the Royal Philatelic Society, all in London, to Marlborough College, Wiltshire, and the Ministry of Defence, Middlesex, in England; to the National Archives, Indonesia; to Los Angeles Public Library, California, and Concordia Historical Institute and the National Personnel Records Centre, Missouri, in the United States of America; the Dictionaries of Canadian and South African Biographies; and other individuals and institutions who have co-operated with the *Dictionary*.

The *Dictionary* deeply regrets the death of such notable contributors as J. J. Auchmuty, K. A. Austin, W. Bossence, A. R. Chisholm, Rev. H. Condon, E. G. Coppel, Sir William Crowther, Monsignor J. H. Cullen, Alan Dougan, Philip Geeves, Helen Haenke, Morton Herman, K. Hindwood, H. T. E. Holt, T. S. Louch, Austin McCallum, C. A. McCallum, G. R. Manton, Jean Martin, Leslie Moorhead, E. J. R. Morgan, Barbara Penny, Father E. Rowland, H. E. Rundle, Alfred Stirling and Fred Williams.

Grateful acknowledgment is due to the director and staff of Melbourne University Press; to the editorial and research staff in Canberra: Frank Brown, Martha Campbell, Suzanne Edgar, James Gibbney, Helga Griffin, Diane Langmore, Merrilyn Lincoln, Sally O'Neill, Ann Smith and Margaret Steven; to Barbara Dale, Ruth Frappell and Michal Bosworth in Sydney, Betty Crouchley in Brisbane, Joyce Gibberd in Adelaide, Wendy Birman in Perth, Margaret Glover in Hobart, Mimi Colligan in Melbourne and Léonie Glen in London; and to the administrative staff: Helen Bankowski, Marion Consandine, Bronwyn Dingwall, Frances Dinnerville, Dianne Mahalm, Ivy Meere and Carolyn Page.

COMMITTEES

COMMITTEES

WORKING PARTIES

New South Wales
B. G. Andrews; J. M. Bennett; K. J. Cable; F. K. Crowley; C. Cunneen; R. F. Doust (chairman); R. Else-Mitchell; F. Farrell; B. H. Fletcher; Baiba Irving; Hazel King; Beverley Kingston; W. G. McMinn; B. E. Mansfield; B. A. Mitchell; Heather Radi; J. A. Ryan; G. P. Walsh; J. M. Ward.

Queensland
R. J. N. Bannenberg; Nancy Bonnin; E. Clarke; F. S. Colliver; J. C. H. Gill; Lorna McDonald; D. J. Murphy (chairman); Mary O'Keeffe; Margaret O'Hagen; S. J. Routh; C. G. Sheehan, P. D. Wilson.

North-Queensland sub-committee
D. W. Hunt; K. H. Kennedy; I. N. Moles (convener); R. J. Sullivan.

South Australia
C. R. Bridge; D. A. Dunstan; R. Gibbs; P. A. Howell; Helen Jones; J. Love; J. D. Playford (chairman); J. M. Tregenza.

Tasmania
G. P. R. Chapman; Margaret Glover; Elizabeth McLeod; Mary McRae; I. Pearce; J. Reynolds (chairman); O. M. Roe; G. T. Stilwell.

Victoria
W. A. Bate; G. J. Davison; J. B. Hirst; S. M. Ingham; J. F. Lack; S. Murray-Smith; J. R. Poynter (chairman); J. D. Rickard; Judith Smart; F. Strahan.

Western Australia
D. Black; Wendy Birman (chairman); G. C. Bolton; P. J. Boyce; C. Coggin; B. K. de Garis; Rica Erickson; Alexandra Hasluck; J. H. M. Honniball; Lyall Hunt; D. Hutchison; Lenore Layman; Mollie Lukis; Toby Manford; Margaret Medcalf; R. W. Reece; C. T. Stannage; A. C. Staples; Mary Tamblyn; Merab Harris Tauman.

Armed Services
M. Austin; F. H. Brown; P. Burness; C. D. Coulthard-Clark; A. J. Hill (chairman); Merrilyn Lincoln; J. McCarthy; G. Odgers (now retired); R. J. O'Neill (former chairman); A. J. Sweeting.

AUTHORS

ADLAM, Harry:
Hogan, P.
ALBISTON, Harold E.:
Kendall.
ALEXANDER, Alison:
Johnson, J. A.
ALLEN, Margaret:
Gooch.
AMOS, Keith:
Gillespie.
ANDREWS, B. G.:
Gould, N.; Gregory, J. M.; Jeffery; Kippax.
ANSTEY, Cris:
Henley, F.
ARNOT, Jean F.:
Ifould; Kibble.
ASHWORTH, Phyllis:
Johnston, G.
ATCHISON, John:
Halloran; Hardie, J. J.; Johnstone, J.; Lang-well.
AUSTIN, A. G.:
Greeves.

BAINTON, *Helen:*
Hutchens.
BAKER, J. S.:
Kraegen.
BALDERSTONE, Susan M.:
Henderson, K.
BALMFORD, Peter:
Ham.
BAMBRICK, Susan:
Knibbs.
BARNARD, Alan:
Guthrie, J.; Kelly, Sir G.
BATE, Weston:
Kirton.
BEBBINGTON, Warren A.:
Keats.
BENNETT, Bruce:
Hayward.
BENNETT, J. M.:
Heydon; Irvine, W.; Jordan.
BENNETT, Scott:
Grant, C; Hayes.
BERESFORD, Quentin:
Jensen, J. A.; Keating.
BERGMANN, G. F. J.*:
Jacobs, J.
BIRMAN, Wendy:
Jackson, Sir C.
BISHOP, Geoffrey C.:
Hamilton, H.
BLACKBURN, C. R. B.:
Lambie.
BLAINEY, Geoffrey:
Hannan, P.

BLAKE, L. J.:
Hansen.
BLEWETT, Neal:
Gunn, John; Kneebone.
BLUNT, Michael J.:
Hunter, J. I.
BOLTON, G. C.:
Green, A. E.; Illingworth, F.; Johnston, E.; Keenan; Kingsmill.
BOLTON, H. C.:
Grayson.
BORCHARDT, D. H.:
Knox, Sir R.
BOSSENCE, W. H.*:
Goddard, B.
BOSWORTH, Michal:
Innes-Noad.
BOUGHEN, Robert K.:
Jefferies.
BOURKE, Helen:
Heaton.
BRADLEY, David:
Hart, A.
BREMNER, J.:
Heagney.
BRIDGE, Carl:
Giles; Holden, L.; Jarvis.
BRIDGES, Doreen:
Ives.
BRIGGS, B. E.:
Holden, F.
BROADHEAD, H. S.:
Kellow, H. B.
BROOME, Cecil:
Horniman.
BROOME, Richard:
Griffiths, A.; Horniman; Jackson, P.
BROOMHILL, Ray:
Hill, L.
BROWN, Judith M.:
Horn.
BROWN, Margaret:
Holman, M.
BROWNE, Geoff:
Goudie; Hutchinson; Kennedy, T. J.; Kiernan; Knox, Sir G.; Langdon.
BROWNFOOT, Janice N.:
Goldstein.
BURCHILL, Sandra:
Jeffery.
BURGIS, Peter:
Hall, E.
BURKE, Keast*:
Kerry.
BURNESS, Peter:
Goddard, H.
BURNET, Macfarlane:
Kellaway, C. H.

* deceased

xi

AUTHORS

BUTLER, Graeme:
Irwin.
BYGOTT, Ursula:
Haugh.

CABLE, K. J.:
Kirkby.
CAMPBELL, Ruth:
Greig; Jenks.
CARDELL-OLIVER, John:
Henn.
CARMENT, David:
Groom, Sir L.
CARMODY, John:
Griffen Foley; Kelly, F.
CARNELL, I. G.:
Greene; Hungerford.
CARRON, L. T.:
Lane-Poole.
CARTLAND, George B.:
Havelock.
CHAMBERS, Don:
Harper, A.
CHAN, Adrian:
Kwok Bew.
CHAPMAN, R. J. K.:
Israel.
CHISHOLM, Patricia:
Joseland.
CHURCH, Patricia Sholl:
Jull, R.
CLARKE, E.:
Goddard, E.
CLARKE, Joan:
Herz.
CLELAND, K. W.:
Hill, J.
CLOSE, Cecily:
Hoare; Knowles, M.; Laby.
COLE, Keith:
Lamble.
COLLIGAN, Mimi:
Goll; Hanna.
CONNELL, W. H.:
Harry; Howell, G.
CONROY, Denise K.:
Graham, A.
COOK, Peter:
Guthrie, R.; Harper, R.
COOKE, T. H.:
Howell, C.
COPE, Graeme:
Hirst.
CORBETT, Arthur:
Harricks; Julius; Kneeshaw.
CORRIS, Peter:
Hardwick.
COSTAR, B. J.:
Kirwan, M.
COULTHARD-CLARK, C. D.:
Glasfurd; Grant, D.; Harrison, E. F.; Holdsworth; Irving, G.; James, T.; Jess.
COURTNEY, James W.:
Gordon, B.

COWDEN, Victoria:
Harper, M.
COWEN, Zelman:
Isaacs.
COWLEY, R. E.:
Gordon, G.; Herrod.
CREELMAN, A. E.:
Hobler.
CRIBB, Margaret Bridson:
Gledson; Hunter, J. A. J.
CROFT, Julian:
Idriess.
CROUCHLEY, Betty:
Gray, G.; Lahey, R.
CUBIS, Richmond:
Hurst; Kyngdon.
CUNNEEN, Chris:
Gorman; Gowrie; Hampden; Hennessy, A.; Hopetoun; Horder; Houghton, T.; Huie; Jersey; Larkin.

DALE, B.:
Kopsen.
DALY, John A.:
Grimmett; Hill, C.
DANIELS, Louis V.:
Hay, R.
DARRAGH, Thomas A.:
Hall, T.
DAVIES, Helen M.:
Hunt, A.
DAVIES, Peter:
Gregory, H.
DAVIS, J. M.:
Halcomb.
DAVIS, R. P.:
Gormanston.
DAVISON, Graeme:
Judkins.
DAW, E. D.:
Jones, L.
DE GARIS, B. K.:
Howitt.
DE SERVILLE, P. H.:
Hood, R. & R.; Huntingfield.
DOCHERTY, J. C.:
Hollis.
DOLAN, David:
Howie, L.
DONOVAN, Peter:
Gsell.
DREYFUS, Kay:
Grainger, G.
DUNSTAN, David:
Gillott; Hennessy, Sir D.; Irvine, H.
DUNSTAN, Douglas A.:
Hassell.
DUNSTAN, Keith:
Judkins.
DUPLAIN, R. C.:
Hall, J.
DURWARD, E. L. D.:
Gill, T.

AUTHORS

HARPER, Norman:
Hughes, E.
HARRIS, W. J. H.:
Hoolan.
HARRISON, Peter:
Griffin.
HARRY, Ralph:
Glasgow; Holder.
HASLUCK, Alexandra:
Hackett, D.
HASLUCK, Sally Anne:
Lapsley.
HAWKER, G. N.:
Gullett, H.; Johnson, Sir W. E.
HAZELL, T. A.:
Kenny, A.
HEAP, Grenfell:
Kenniff.
HENN, Wilfrid E.:
Goldsmith.
HICKS, Neville:
Hone.
HIGGINS, Matthew:
Kenny, T.
HILL, A. J.:
Grant, W.; Gullett, Sir H.; Hobbs; Howse;
Hutton, Sir E.
HILLIARD, David:
Harmer.
HODDINOTT, Ann:
Harper, N.
HOGAN, Janet:
Hall, F.
HOHNEN, Peter:
Innes.
HOLT, H. T. E.*:
Hamilton, H. M.
HOPGOOD, Donald J.:
Lacey.
HOPLEY, J. B.:
Jeffries, C.
HOPPER, J. R.:
Kruttschnitt.
HORNER, D. M.:
Howell-Price.
HOWARD, Frederick:
Kingsford Smith.
HOWARD, Rod:
Hennessy, J.
HOWELL, P. A.:
Hague; James, F.
HUGHES, J. Escourt:
Johnson, E.
HUNT, Arnold D.:
Howard, H.; Jenkin.
HUNT, D. W.:
Hynes.
HUNT, Lyall:
Hackett, Sir J.;
James, Sir W. H.
HUNTER, Roslyn F.:
Haddon.
HUTCHISON, Noel S.:
Hoff; Illingworth, N.

HUTLEY, F. C.:
Harvey, Sir J.
HYSLOP, Anthea:
Kirk.
HYSLOP, Robert:
Hyde.

INGLIS, Amirah:
Hargrave.
ISAACS, Keith:
Hart, W.; Jones, A. M.

JACOBS, Marjorie:
Hentze.
JACOBS, S. J.:
Jacobs, S.
JAENSCH, Dean:
Hudd; Jenkins, Sir G. F.; Jenkins, J. G.;
Kirkpatrick. A.
JAMES, G. F.:
Gilpin.
JARROTT, J. Keith:
Groom, A.
JENKINS, C. F. H.:
Glauert.
JOHNSON, Donald H.:
Gunter.
JOHNSON, K. A.:
Jones, N.
JOHNSTON, W. Ross:
Hancock, J. H.; Harrington; Hawthorn.
JONAS, Pam:
Hogan, E.
JONES, Helen:
Jacob.
JORDAN, Ellen:
Hopkins.
JOSKE, Prue:
Hancock, W. J.
JOYCE, R. B.:
Griffith, S.; Lamington.

KATZMANN, Anna:
Herring.
KEARNS, R. H. B.:
James, D.
KELLY, Farley:
Guerin.
KENNEDY, B. E.:
Jamieson.
KING, Hazel:
Hall, W. & E.; King, Sir G. E.; King, O.
KING, Richard:
King, H.
KINGSTON, Beverley:
Golding.
KIRKBY, Diane:
Henry, A.
KIRKPATRICK, Rod:
Groom, H.

* deceased

xiv

KLOOT, Tess:
Hull; Iredale, T.
KNIGHT, Allan:
Gillies, J. H.
KNIGHT, Stephen:
Hornung.
KRAEHENBUEHL, Darrell N.:
Holtze.
KWAN, Elizabeth:
Halley.

L'ESTRANGE, P.:
Jerger.
LACK, John:
Goble, J.; Hoadley, A.; Hoadley, C.; Kinnear.
LAMB, Lesley:
Harford.
LAMONT, R.:
Jose.
LAND, William A.:
Hamilton, J.
LANGMORE, Diane:
Howard, A. C.; Jeffries, M.
LANSBURY, Coral:
Lamond.
LARACY, Hugh:
Grimshaw.
LAVERTY, John:
Jolly, W.; Jones, A. J.
LAWSON, Elaine:
Harrison, Sir J.
LEGGETT, C. A. C.:
Hirschfeld.
LEWIS, N. B.:
Jolly, N.
LINCOLN, Merrilyn:
Graham, M.; Gray, E.; Kirkcaldie, R.
LINDESAY, Vane:
Jonsson.
LINN, R. W.:
Keynes.
LIPKE, Ian:
Glassey.
LOGAN, G. N.:
Hardacre; Huxham.
LOMAS, L.:
Hill, W. C.
LONG, Gavin*:
Gwynn.
LOUGHEED, A. L.:
Gow.
LOUGHLIN, Graham:
Gordon, Sir J.
LOVE, Peter:
Hannan, J.
LOVERING, J. F.:
Gregory, J. W.
LUDBROOK, N. H.:
Howchin.
LYNCH, A. J.:
Kruttschnitt.
LYONS, Mark:
Green, D.; Jessep; Kethel.

MacAULAY, Bettina:
Harvey, L.
MacCALLUM, M.:
Jones, F.
McCALLUM, Austin*:
Greenfield.
McCARTHY, Dudley:
Keysor.
McCARTHY, John:
Goble, S.; Harrison, E.
McCARTHY, Perditta M.:
Gould, E.
McCONVILLE, Chris:
Green, S.
McCREDIE, Andrew:
Hill, A.
McDONALD, Lorna L.:
Grant, K. M.; Kellow, H. A.
McEVEY, Allan.
Keartland.
McFARLANE, B. J.:
Irvine, R.; Jensen, H.
McINTYRE, Darryl:
Grieve; Ingram.
McKEOWN, Malcolm:
Hewlett.
McKERNAN, Michael:
Gillison; Green, J.; Kennedy, J. J.
McLAREN, Ian F.:
Gye; Holden, A.
McMINN, W. G.:
Gould, Sir A.; Lamaro.
McNICOLL, Ronald:
Hill, T.; Kenyon.
MAIN, J. M.:
Hills.
MALONE, Stephen:
Kirkpatrick, J.
MANION, Jim:
Green, W.; Hodel.
MANNING, K. W.:
Johnson, G.
MANSFIELD, Joan:
Hammond, R.
MARKS, E. N.:
Hamlyn-Harris.
MAYNARD, Margaret:
Jenner; Lahey, F.
MENGHETTI, Diane:
Heron.
MERRETT, D. T.:
Healy, G.
MERRILLEES, P. H. & R. S.:
Keys.
MIGUS, Michael:
James, W. E.
MITCHELL, A. G.:
Holme, E.
MITCHELL, Ann M.:
Gullett, L.; Holmes à Court; Hood, Sir A.; Kellett.

* deceased

MITCHELL, Bruce:
Gocher; Kilgour.
MITCHELL, Elyne:
Hogue, O.
MITCHELL, L. M. M.:
Jones, K.
MOORE, Andrew:
Goldfinch; Hardy.
MOORHEAD, Leslie M.*:
Groom, A. C.
MORISON, Patricia:
Haswell; Kelly, R. V. & R. H.
MORLEY, I. W.:
Jackson, C. F.
MORRIS, Deirdre:
Gowrie.
MOSS, Stan:
Hancock, W.
MOSTERT, Chris:
Heyer.
MUECKE, I. D.:
Hay, W.
MULVANEY, D. J.:
Gillen, F.
MURPHY, D. J.:
Gillies, W.; Givens; Goold-Adams; Hunter, J. McE.; Kidston.
MURPHY, Leonard J. T.:
Harris, S.
MURRAY-SMITH, S.:
Kernot.

NAIRN, Bede:
Griffith, A.; Hall, D.; Hickey; Holman, W.; Jackson, A.; Lang.
NASH, George H.:
Hoover.
NETHERCOTE, B. W.:
Hamilton, W.
NEWTON, G.:
Kauffmann.
NEWTON, L. G.:
Irving, J. & J. W.

O'COLLINS, Gerald:
Glynn.
O'FARRELL, Patrick:
Holland; Kelly, M.
OGILVIE, June:
Holmes, M. & M.
O'NEILL, Sally:
Grover; Gunn, Jeannie; Haynes, T.; James, W. L.; Knox, Sir E. G.
OSBORNE, Graeme:
Higgins, E., T. & A.
OWEN, Selwyn M.:
Girdlestone.

PAGE, K. R.:
Heathershaw.
PAHL, P. D.:
Graebner.
PARSONS, George:
Hoskins.

PATRICK, Ross:
Jackson, E.; Kenny, E.
PAULE, Bruce:
Jones, J.
PEARCE, B.:
Gruner.
PEOPLES, Kevin:
Lansell.
PERRY, Warren:
Gordon, J. M.; Griffiths, T.; Hoad; Johnston, C.
PERVAN, Ralph:
Kenneally.
PESCOTT, R. T. M.:
Kershaw.
PHILLIPS, Nan:
Hunt, J. & A.
PHILLIPS, Walter:
Kiek.
PIKE, A. F.:
Hurley.
PLAYFORD, John:
Kingston.
PORTER, Anne:
Lane, Z. & Z. B.; Langler.
POWELL, Alan:
Gilruth.
POYNTER, J. R.:
Grimwade.
PRICE, John E.:
Kelly, N.
PROUD, J. C.:
Hanran.

RADCLIFFE, John C.:
Goodman.
RADI, Heather:
Henley, Sir T.; Hinder; Holman, A.; Kay, A.; Keegan.
RADIC, Maureen Thérèse:
Hart, F.
RAMSLAND, John:
Grasby.
RANK, Benjamin:
Hailes.
READ, Peter C.:
Gratton.
REDDROP, B. H.:
Hart, J.
REEVES, Andrew:
Laidler.
REFSHAUGE, W. D.:
Kay, W.
REYNOLDS, John:
Jones, Sir H.
RICHARDS, Eric:
Holden, H. & Sir E.
RICHMOND, Merle:
Hunt, P.
RICKARD, John:
Hancock, J.; Higgins, H.

* deceased

TREMBATH, Richard:
  Henderson, J. I.
TROLLOPE, D. H.:
  Hawken.
TYERS, Judith:
  Grice.

UNSWORTH, Barrie:
  Kavanagh.

VALLANCE, T. G.:
  Laseron.
VAN DEN HOORN, Rob:
  Gillen, P.; Gordon, Sir D.; Hawker, E.;
  Howe, J. H.
VAN DISSEL, Dirk:
  Hawker, C.; Kelly, R. & W.
VASEY, Katherine:
  Gordon, Sir T.; Grimley; Howie, Sir A.
VERNEY, Guy:
  Harper, R. R.
VERNON, P. V.:
  Granville.
VINTER, Mary:
  Greville.
VOGT, A. E.:
  Lade.

WALKER, D. R.:
  Kesteven.
WALKER, J. D.:
  Kirkcaldie, D.
WALLACE, R. L.:
  Handcock.
WALSH, G. P.:
  Godfrey; Governor; Grace; Harrison, L.;
  Hartigan; Healy, C.; Hunt, H.; Iredale, F.;
  Kaleski; Kieran; Kirkpatrick, J. S.; Koerstz;
  Lane, F.; Jones, E.; Kellermann; Lasseter.
WARD, Russel:
  Kidman.
WARDEN, Alan:
  Holyman.
WATEN, Judah:
  Goldhar.
WATSON, Jack:
  Hay, C.; Hayes-Williams; Holme, J.
WATSON, T.:
  Kerr, J.
WATT, Alan:
  Hodgson.

WEBBER, Kimberley:
  Hill, W. D.
WEBSTER, D. B.:
  Heath.
WEBSTER, Hilary:
  Hebblethwaite.
WELBORN, Suzanne:
  Kelly, A.
WETTENHALL, R. L.:
  Johnston(e), R.
WHEELER, Doreen:
  Kelly, A. E.; Knox, W.
WHITE, Anthony D.:
  Horsfall.
WHITE, K. R.:
  Imlay.
WHITELAW, J.:
  Hawker, J.
WHITLAM, E. G.:
  Knowles, Sir G.
WHITTLE, Nancy Robinson:
  Lake.
WILDE, W. H.:
  Gilmore.
WILLIAMS, J. G.:
  Heane; Lalor.
WILLIAMSON, Noeline:
  Kirkpatrick, M.
WILSON, Paul D.:
  Goodwin.
WINTER, W. G.:
  Jones, William.
WIXTED, E. P.:
  Hinkler.
WOOD, Christine:
  Joyce.
WORRALL, Airlie:
  Hirsch.
WRIGLEY, C. W.:
  Guthrie, F.
WYND, Ian:
  Hitchcock; Holden, G. F.

YOUNG, J. McI.:
  Hodges; Hood, Sir J.

ZAINU'DDIN, A. G. Thomson:
  Krome.
ZWILLENBERG, H. J.:
  Jensen, J. C.

A NOTE ON SOME PROCEDURES

Among our authors and readers and, indeed, on the editorial board, there is strong disagreement on whether certain facts should normally be included—such as cause of death, burial or cremation details, and value of estate. In this volume our practices have been as follows:

Cause of death: include, except usually in the case of the very old; in practice we include in about two-thirds of the entries.

Burial/cremation: include when details available.

Value of estate: normally include for certain categories such as businessmen, and when the amount is unusually high or low. In recent years, when the practice developed of early distribution of assets in order to avoid estate and probate duties, the sum is not always meaningful; moreover it is not always possible to ascertain the full facts. Hence we have resorted to discretionary use.

Some other procedures require explanation:

Measurements: as the least unsatisfactory solution, we have used imperial system measurements (as historically appropriate), followed by the metric equivalent in brackets. Round metric figures are used when the number is clearly approximate, e.g., 500 miles (800 km).

Money: we have retained £ for pounds for references prior to 14 February 1966 (when the conversion rate was A£1 = A\$2).

Religion: stated whenever information is available, but often there is no good evidence of actual practice, e.g., the information is confined to marriage and funeral rites.

[q.v.]: the particular volume is given for those included in volumes 1-8 but not for those in this and future volumes. Note that the cross-reference [q.v.] now accompanies the names of all who have separate articles in the *Dictionary*. In volumes 1-6 it was not shown for royal visitors, governors, lieut-governors and those Colonial Office officials who were included.

Small capitals: used for relations and others when they are of substantial importance but not included in their own right.

Five-year rule: a few men and women, whose *floruit* was pre-1940 but who lived to an advanced age, have been excluded on the ground that they died too recently for proper historical consideration. No one is included who died less than five years before date of publication, except some sportsmen whose years of fame were long ago.

CORRIGENDA

Every effort is made to check every detail in every article, but inevitably a work of the size and complexity of the *Dictionary* includes some errors.

Corrigenda have been published regularly with each volume and a list is included with Volume 9 showing corrections made since the publication of Volume 8 (1981).

Only corrections are shown; additional information is not included; nor is any reinterpretation attempted. The only exception to this procedure is when new details become available about parents or births, deaths and marriages.

Documented corrections are welcomed. Additional information, with sources, is also invited and will be placed in the appropriate files for future use.

A copy of cumulative corrigenda up to Volume 7 and the list published with Volume 8 are available from the publishers at cost of postage.

REFERENCES

The following and other obvious works of reference have been widely used but not normally acknowledged:

Australian encyclopaedia, 1-2 (Syd, 1925), 1-10 (1958)

Biographical register for various Australian parliaments: (A. W. Martin & P. Wardle *and* H. Radi, P. Spearritt & E. Hinton—New South Wales; G. C. Bolton & A. Mozley—Western Australia; K. Thomson & G. Serle—Victoria; D. B. Waterson—Queensland; S. & B. Bennett—Tasmania; and J. Rydon—Commonwealth)

D. Blair, *Cyclopaedia of Australasia* (Melb, 1881)

B. Burke, *A genealogical and heraldic history of the colonial gentry*, 1-2 (Lond, 1891, 1895)

O'M. Creagh and E. M. Humphris (eds), *The V.C. and D.S.O.: a complete record* . . . 1-3 (Lond, 1934)

Dictionary of national biography (Lond, 1885-1971)

H. M. Green, *A history of Australian literature*, 1-2 (Syd, 1961, 2nd edn 1971)

C. A. Hughes and B. D. Graham, *A handbook of Australian government and politics 1890-1964* (Canb, 1968); *Voting for the Australian House of Representatives 1901-1964*, with corrigenda (Canb, 1975), for *Queensland Legislative Assembly 1890-1964* (Canb, 1974), for *New South Wales* . . . (1975), *Victoria* . . . (1975), and *South Australian, Western Australian and Tasmanian Lower Houses* . . . (1976)

F. Johns, *Johns's notable Australians* (Melb, 1906), *Fred Johns's annual* (Lond, 1914); *An Australian biographical dictionary* (Melb, 1934)

A. McCulloch, *Encyclopedia of Australian art* (Lond, 1968)

E. M. Miller, *Australian literature* . . . *to 1935* (Melb, 1940), extended to 1950 by F. T. Macartney (Syd, 1956)

W. Moore, *The story of Australian art*, 1-2 (Syd, 1934)

P. C. Mowle, *A genealogical history of pioneer families in Australia* (Syd, 1939; 5th edn Adel, 1978)

P. Serle, *Dictionary of Australian biography*, 1-2 (Syd, 1949)

Who's who (Lond), and *Who's who in Australia* (Syd, Melb), present and past editions.

xxi

ABBREVIATIONS USED IN BIBLIOGRAPHIES

AAA	Amateur Athletic Association		Fr	Father (priest)
AAO	Australian Archives			
ABC	Australian Broadcasting Commission		G, Geog	Geographical
			Govt	Government
ACT	Australian Capital Territory			
Adel	Adelaide		HA	House of Assembly
Agr	Agriculture, Agricultural		Hist	History, Historical
AIF	Australian Imperial Force		HO	Home Office, London
ALP	Australian Labor Party		Hob	Hobart
ANU	Australian National University, Canberra		HSSA	Historical Society of South Australia
ANU Archives	ANU Archives of Business and Labour		IAN	Illustrated Australian News
ANZAAS	Australian and New Zealand Association for the Advancement of Science		Inst	Institute, Institution
			introd	introduction, introduced by
			ISN	Illustrated Sydney News
A'sian	Australasian			
Assn	Association		J	Journal
Aust	Australia, Australian		JCU	James Cook University, Townsville
AWM	Australian War Memorial, Canberra			
			LA	Legislative Assembly
			LaTL	La Trobe Library, Melbourne
Basser Lib	Adolph Basser Library, Australian Academy of Science, Canberra		Launc	Launceston
			LC	Legislative Council
Battye Lib	J. S. Battye Library of West Australian History, Perth		Lib	Library
			Lond	London
Bd	Board			
BHP	Broken Hill Proprietary Co. Ltd		Mag	Magazine
			Melb	Melbourne
bibliog	bibliography		MDHC	Melbourne Diocesan Historical Commission (Catholic), Fitzroy
biog	biography, biographical			
Brisb	Brisbane			
			MJA	Medical Journal of Australia
c	circa		ML	Mitchell Library, Sydney
CAE	College of Advanced Education		MS	manuscript
			mthly	monthly
Canb	Canberra			
cat/s	catalogue/s		nd	date of publication unknown
CO	Colonial Office, London		NL	National Library of Australia, Canberra
C of E	Church of England			
Col Sec	Colonial Secretary		no	number
Com	Commission		np	place of publication unknown
comp	compiler		NSW	New South Wales
CSIRO	Commonwealth Scientific and Industrial Research Organization		NSWA	The Archives Authority of New South Wales, Sydney
			NT	Northern Territory
cttee	committee		NZ	New Zealand
Cwlth	Commonwealth			
			Oxley Lib	John Oxley Library, Brisbane
Dept	Department			
DNB	Dictionary of National Biography		p	page, pages
			pc	photocopy
			PD	Parliamentary Debates
			PP	Parliamentary Papers
ed	editor		PRGSSA	Proceedings of the Royal Geographical Society of Australasia (South Australian Branch)
edn	edition			
Edinb	Edinburgh			
Eng	England		priv print	privately printed

ABBREVIATIONS

PRO	Public Record Office	SLNSW	State Library of New South Wales
Procs	*Proceedings*	SLSA	State Library of South Australia
pt	part, parts		
PTHRA	*Papers and Proceedings of the Tasmanian Historical Research Association*	SLT	State Library of Tasmania
		SLV	State Library of Victoria
pub	publication, publication number	*SMH*	*Sydney Morning Herald*
		Soc	Society
		supp	supplement
Q	*Quarterly*	Syd	Sydney
QA	Queensland State Archives, Brisbane		
		TA	Tasmanian State Archives, Hobart
Qld	Queensland	Tas	Tasmania, Tasmanian
RAHS	Royal Australian Historical Society (Sydney)	*T&CJ*	*Australian Town and Country Journal*
RG	Registrar General's Office	*Trans*	*Transactions*
RGS	Royal Geographical Society		
RHSQ	Royal Historical Society of Queensland (Brisbane)	UK	United Kingdom
		UN	United Nations
RHSV	Royal Historical Society of Victoria (Melbourne)	UNSW	University of New South Wales
Roy	Royal	UNE	University of New England, Armidale
RWAHS	Royal Western Australian Historical Society (Perth)	Univ	University
		UPNG	University of Papua New Guinea
1st S	First Session		
2nd S	Second Session		
2nd s	second series	*V&P*	*Votes and Proceedings*
SA	South Australia	*VHM(J)*	*Victorian Historical Magazine (Journal)*
SAA	South Australian Archives, Adelaide	v, vol	volume
Sel	Select	Vic	Victoria
		WA	Western Australia

Gil

GILBERT, CHARLES MARSH (NASH) WEB (1867-1925), sculptor, was born on 18 March 1867 at Cockatoo, near Maryborough, Victoria, third child of William Gilbert, engine driver from Cornwall, and his wife Nasaretha, née Jackson, of Sydney. Two months after Gilbert's birth his father died, leaving the family in financial difficulty. At 9 the boy was apprenticed to T. F. Gunsler, proprietor of the Vienna Café, Melbourne. He was taught to model icing-sugar cake decorations and, presumably to improve this skill, he attended drawing lessons given by Mr Sayer in South Yarra. After four years he graduated, eventually becoming chef at Parer's restaurant, where he remained until 1914. His marriage on 17 March 1887 to Alice Rose Eugenia Daniell ended in divorce in 1911; they had no children.

Meanwhile Gilbert had developed an interest in sculpture that grew to be all absorbing. From 1888 to 1891 he attended part time as a drawing student at the National Gallery school under G. F. Folingsby [q.v.4], Bernard Hall and F. McCubbin [qq.v.]. At that time there was no instruction in sculpture at the school and Gilbert had to teach himself. At life classes at the Victorian Artists' Society he met the sculptor C. D. Richardson [q.v.] who gave him advice and sympathetic encouragement. In 1898 he was an original member of the Yarra Sculptors' Society and showed work at its first exhibition, held that year.

Gilbert slowly learned the technique of marble carving and was able to translate his first large work, 'The Vintage Offering' (1897), from plaster into this more permanent medium. He also established a studio off Collins Street, in which he conducted art classes.

About 1905 the liveliness and sense of immediacy obtainable through direct casting in bronze encouraged him to set about mastering the complexities of bronze founding. In a new studio at 59 Gore Street, Fitzroy, he built his own foundry and by trial and error made himself proficient in all aspects of the craft. He regularly exhibited with the Victorian Artists' and Yarra Sculptors' societies, arranging his work as a chef so that more time could be given to his art.

Aided by the patronage of Hugo Meyer, in 1914 Gilbert went to Europe, arriving in London in May. Stranded in England when war broke out, too old for military service or to enrol at any London art school, he resumed making sculpture. He was encouraged by his meeting with eminent sculptors Alfred Drury and Gilbert Bayes and in 1915 sent two works to the Royal Academy exhibition. He exhibited again next year and in 1917 his marble bust, 'The Critic', was purchased for the Tate Gallery under the terms of the Chantrey Bequest. 'The Sun and the Earth' (National Gallery of Victoria) was exhibited at the Royal Academy in 1918; this is perhaps his finest work in marble and most clearly proclaims his debt to Rodin and to late nineteenth-century English sculpture. On 7 May 1917 at Chelsea registry office he had married Mabel Annette Woodstock.

Late in 1917 Gilbert joined the Australian Imperial Force as a sculptor in the War Records Section, and after the war travelled throughout France gathering information to make accurate models of the battlegrounds, now in the Australian War Memorial, Canberra. In 1920 he returned with his family to Melbourne where he reoccupied his studio and began work on the memorial to the A.I.F. 2nd Division for Mont St Quentin, France. His work for the rest of his life was predominantly commemorative.

In 1923 Gilbert won the commission for the Anzac memorial to be erected at Port Said, Egypt. Concurrently he worked on the large memorial to Matthew Flinders [q.v.1], for Melbourne. Cast in France, it was unveiled in November 1925 after the sculptor's death of cardiovascular disease at Fitzroy on 3 October. Gilbert was survived by his wife, twin sons and a daughter and was buried in Coburg cemetery. His Anzac memorial, which had proceeded only as far as the full-scale model, was completed by Paul Montford and Sir Bertram Mackennal [qq.v.].

In addition to many portrait busts in marble or bronze, work by Gilbert includes 'The Wheel of Life' (University of Melbourne), 'Grief', a tomb for Sir Samuel Gillott [q.v.], Melbourne; World War I memorials for the Chamber of Manufactures, Melbourne, the Malvern Town Hall, the British (Australian) Medical Association, Parkville, Shepparton, and Burnside, Adelaide, and the huge 'Australian Soldier', Broken Hill, New South Wales. A portrait drawing of Gilbert by Will Dyson [q.v.8] is in *Art in Australia*, No.14, 1925.

Poorly educated and largely self-taught, Gilbert achieved remarkable work. Unfortunately the time-consuming nature of his occupation, the interruptions of war, and later the almost exclusive demand for memorials served both to dissipate his energies and to divert him from more creatively profitable areas.

W. Moore, *A jubilee volume; studio sketches* (Melb, 1906); Ballarat Fine Art Gallery, *Early Australian sculpture*, catalogue (Ballarat, 1976); G. Sturgeon, *The development of Australian sculpture, 1788-1975* (Lond, 1978); K. Scarlett, *Australian sculptors* (Melb, 1980); *Lone Hand*, Oct 1908, Apr 1910; *Studio* (Lond), 67 (Feb 1916); *Argus*, 14 July 1909; *Herald* (Melb), 3 Jan 1920, 15 Aug 1924, 15 Oct 1925; O. Cohn, Me in the making (MS, LaTL).

G. STURGEON

GILBERT, DAVID JOHN (1873-1950), journalist and comptroller of repatriation, was born on 18 December 1873 at Minchinbury, New South Wales, son of John Gilbert, vigneron, and his wife Margaret, née Hanna, both Irish-born. After a state school education Gilbert accepted a cadetship on the *Daily Telegraph*, although he had earlier hankered after a naval career. Later, during four years on the editorial staff of the Sydney *Bulletin*, he became an active Federationist, forming friendships with Henry Lawson [q.v.], William Astley [q.v.3] and (Sir) Edmund Barton [q.v.7]. He was appointed assistant to the secretary of the Australasian Federation League of New South Wales, Atlee Hunt [q.v.], and in 1899 campaigned strenuously with Barton, Hunt and Leopold Broinowski [q.v.7] in Queensland.

Gilbert worked briefly for the Brisbane *Courier* in 1900 before returning to Sydney as general reporter and editor of the agricultural section of the *Daily Telegraph*. He married Lilian Ethel Lewington, eight years his senior, at St Philip's Church of England, Sydney, on 13 April 1901; they had two sons and one daughter. In 1907 he joined the *Sydney Morning Herald* as leader-writer, remaining until 1911 when he founded the *Land* as a weekly mouthpiece of the Farmers and Settlers' Association of New South Wales. With a reputation as a clear, concise writer, Gilbert also acted briefly as Australian correspondent for the London *Times*.

He did not complete the law studies which he began in 1909 at the University of Sydney, and in 1912 he left journalism to work for a gas-light company in Queensland. Then, in 1913, he became secretary to the Commonwealth royal commission on Northern Territory railways and ports. Declining a subsequent government invitation to write a book on the Territory, in April 1914 he accepted J. C. Watson's [q.v.] offer of the editorship of a new Labor newspaper, the

World. The outbreak of World War I, however, precluded publication and Gilbert followed Watson into repatriation work when the latter was appointed honorary organizer of the State War Councils in 1915.

As secretary of the State War Council in Sydney Gilbert helped draft the report on which the system of soldier land settlement was founded. Next year he became secretary of the board of trustees of the Australian Soldiers' Repatriation Fund which was authorized to appeal to the public for money to be distributed through the war councils. Gilbert was also general secretary of the National Referendum Council in 1916. In August 1917 the Australian Soldiers' Repatriation Act abolished the inefficient Repatriation Fund and provided for a Repatriation Department. Gilbert, as deputy to the comptroller (Sir) Nicholas Lockyer [q.v.], supplied the basic drafts for the creation of the department which began operation in April 1918. He became comptroller in June and, with (Sir) Robert Gibson [q.v.8], formulated the principles of a repatriation scheme afterwards acknowledged as the most generous and comprehensive of that of any country engaged in the war. In 1931 Lockyer paid tribute to Gilbert's 'rare intellectual ability', his 'genius and singular foresight' in developing the system.

Gilbert retired from the comptrollership in June 1920 and spent the following two years recuperating from a period of strain. In 1922 he moved to Adelaide as secretary to J. E. Davidson's [q.v.8] newly founded News Ltd, becoming manager and director, and finally general manager. From there he went to Perth as managing director of the *Daily News* in 1931-32. His wife had died in 1925 and on 19 September 1932 at St George's Cathedral, Perth, he married Florence Emily Western Hodgetts. A member of the National Party, Gilbert was perturbed by the Western Australian secession movement and in 1933 he became publicity officer for the Federal League. He wrote *A word to the wheatgrowers* before the April referendum and, after the affirmative vote for secession, was one of the Federal committee in Canberra which prepared *The case for union* (1934). At this time he also submitted a scheme to the Federal government for rural debt adjustment.

Big, heavy and solemn-looking, but witty, a warm-hearted family man and well-respected journalist, Gilbert worked with passion for interests dear to him, especially Federation, repatriation and the welfare of rural workers; he was indifferent to the personal accumulation of material goods. He spent the 1940s in Melbourne and died of coronary occlusion at Toorak Gardens, Adelaide, on 13 May 1950, survived by his second wife and the children of his first marriage. He was buried in St Saviour's cemetery, Glen Osmond.

E. Scott, *Australia during the war* (Syd, 1936); *Newspaper News*, 1 Apr 1931; *Daily Telegraph* (Syd), 12 Aug 1907; *Punch* (Melb), 23 Apr 1914, 23 July 1918; Pearce papers, MS 213/16/543, 213/17, 1927/3/796 (NL).   ANN G. SMITH

GILBERT, EDWARD (d. 1978), cricketer, was probably born in 1905 or 1906 at Durundur Aboriginal reserve near Woodford in south-eastern Queensland. His birth was not registered and his parents are unknown but came from North Queensland. While still an infant Eddie and his brother were separated from their parents when Durundur was abolished. He was incarcerated in the children's dormitory on Barambah (later Cherbourg) reserve near Murgon, and tribal influences were replaced by an inferior form of primary schooling to grade four. Gilbert was then contracted out by the reserve superintendent as an unskilled labourer in seasonal occupations.

He probably began to play cricket during 1917, under the inspiration of Jack Daylight, when the Barambah Aboriginal cricket club was formed; in 1922 he was a slow to medium-paced bowler. Developing a unique style of fast bowling, he was coached by the new Barambah schoolmaster, Robert Crawford.

By 1929 news of Gilbert's phenomenal success in local matches reached Brisbane and the Queensland Cricketing Association brought him to Woolloongabba for a demonstration. Despite his remarkably short approach run, his 5 ft. 7 ins. (170 cm) stature and his slight nine stone (57 kg) frame, his muscular physique and a reach some 4 ins. (10 cm) beyond the normal powered a whip-like wrist action which released the ball like a stone from a catapult. Chosen in 1930 for Queensland against New South Wales Colts, he captured six wickets. Critics now began to question his bowling style: the *Brisbane Courier*'s 'Long On' first described his action as almost a throw. He was nevertheless picked for the Queensland Sheffield Shield team against South Australia and was named bowler of the match. When Queensland beat New South Wales in November, the Queensland selectors responded to New South Wales complaints by filming his arm action in slow motion; they found no irregularities. In January 1931 Gilbert took 7 West Indian wickets for 91 runs.

Gilbert's most memorable bowling performance occurred against New South Wales on 6 November 1931. His first ball, a bumper, had the opening batsman caught behind. The first of the three following balls to Donald Bradman knocked the bat from his hands, the next made him fall backwards on the pitch, and the third had him caught behind. The Barambah Aboriginals listening to the game relayed through Crawford's radio joined the Brisbane crowd of 7000 in cheering themselves hoarse.

Because of assertions by the New South Wales manager and the team that he threw, Gilbert narrowly avoided being dropped from the Queensland team to meet South Africa; he took five wickets in the match. A month later during the match against Victoria in Melbourne, he was repeatedly 'no-balled' for throwing. He was filmed again from four angles by slow-motion cameras.

It was suggested that Gilbert might provide a freak response to the English 'bodyline' tactics in 1932-33 but, suffering from an inflamed shoulder socket, he was barely bowling above medium pace. Moreover, responding to constant criticism, he was attempting to eradicate his 'snappy wrist action' and had lost pace. Suggestions began to be made that he was a spent force. Gilbert did not play in the 1933-34 season but in 1934-35 he topped the Queensland bowling figures with an average of 18.43. During his last season he confronted Bradman again in January 1936 and took his wicket; his bumpers had injured three New South Wales players in an earlier match when he had again been 'no-balled'. A new Marylebone Cricket Club ruling later in the year against 'intimidatory' bowling effectively ended his career. Although he took five Victorian wickets in the first innings of his last match, he was retired in November 1936 on the ground of his 'hopelessly bad' form, and returned to Cherbourg. He had taken 87 wickets in first-class cricket at an average of 29.21.

Controversy still rages over the question of possible racial discrimination relating to Eddie Gilbert's career. There seems little doubt that he was discriminated against as an Aboriginal. He was escorted constantly by white bureaucrats and cricket officials and the constant slurs on his bowling style are reminiscent of similar innuendoes against the earlier Aboriginal cricketers Jack Marsh and Albert Henry. Though one of the finest Australian fast bowlers, Gilbert never played for Australia and was regarded by the crowds more as a novelty than as an exceptional sportsman.

Back at Cherbourg, Gilbert resumed the mundane routine of reserve existence, doing menial odd-jobs. He revived interests in music and boxing but played little cricket. Remembered as quiet and courteous, he married Edith Owens of Pialba on 9 March

1937. While working as a hospital orderly Gilbert began to exhibit signs of increasing mental instability. Admitted to Goodna Psychiatric Hospital on 8 December 1949, he remained there until his death on 9 January 1978. Leading sportsmen including Sir Donald Bradman attended his large Cherbourg funeral. His son Eddie Barney became a professional boxer.

Eddie Gilbert was perhaps the only hero detribalized Aboriginals had in the 1930s.

Cricketer, Nov 1972, p 33, Feb 1978, p 19; *Aboriginal and Islander Identity*, Jan 1978, p 30; *Brisbane Courier*, 27, 29 Oct, 4, 10 Dec 1930, 7, 12, 13, 14, 25 Nov 1931, 24 Jan, 4 Feb 1933, 2, 13 Jan, 13 Nov 1936; *Southern Burnett Times*, 9 Jan 1931; *Townsville Daily Bulletin*, 9 Feb 1933; personal information.

RAYMOND EVANS

GILES, CLEMENT (1844-1926), pastoralist, merchant and politician, was born on 21 February 1844 in Adelaide, son of William Giles [q.v.1], manager of the South Australian Co., and his second wife Emily Elizabeth, née McGeorge. He was the twelfth of his father's fifteen sons and had six sisters. Giles was educated at John Lorenzo Young's [q.v.6] Adelaide Educational Institution. At 15 he went to the South-East to learn sheep and cattle droving on various stations there and in Victoria till, in 1864, he rode alone 500 miles (800 km) to manage Yanyarrie station north of Melrose, South Australia, which was part-owned by his brother-in-law F. W. Stokes. He did well and learned the valuable skills of woolclassing and scouring. In 1866 he rented nearby Haverhill farm from C. H. Pearson [q.v.5] and, with two bullock teams, carted chaff as far north as Blinman. He also began a wool-wash and built a flour-mill as a member of his brother's stock and station firm Giles & Smith. In 1871 Giles purchased his own farm near Melrose, which he called Rookwood. On 7 August 1872 he married Isabella Begbie Cockburn of Beaumont, Adelaide, sister of the future premier, (Sir) John Cockburn [q.v.8].

Like his father, Giles's interest was not just in working his own estate; full of intense nervous energy, he itched to be a merchant and developer. So he accepted a partnership in Giles & Smith and moved with his family to Adelaide in 1882, though he kept Rookwood. That year he joined twelve other merchants and farmers to form the Willowie Land & Pastoral Co. which bought J. H. Angas's [q.v.3] large Mount Remarkable estate for £310 000.

In 1887 Giles was elected to represent Frome in the House of Assembly; he held it until 1902 when, after a redistribution, he failed to win Burra. Giles was energetic on behalf of his district and spoke often on land and education questions. He had been chairman of a land commission in 1888 which led to considerable modification of the Land Act so that wheat-farmers in low rainfall areas could purchase land at less than £1 an acre and, if necessary, use it for pastoral purposes and not reside on it. He successfully opposed free education for the rich beyond the compulsory standard, but failed to secure grants for private schools. Over probate and succession duties, he was a radical, but he defended the restricted franchise of the Upper House. A careful thinker, he was very much his own man and did not take any party whip.

Costly and unsuccessful litigation with Angas over the Mount Remarkable estate, plus the droughts and bank collapses of the early 1890s, resulted in Giles losing half his assets. Consequently in 1895 he became manager-secretary of the South Australian Farmers' Co-operative Union, formed by mid-northern wheat-farmers in 1888. Giles expanded the union by introducing wool and spread its operations to other parts of the colony. He became a director in 1904. In 1909 he resigned to represent the union's interests in London. He returned after the outbreak of World War I and was elected sole growers' representative on the Commonwealth government's Australian Compulsory Wheat Pool Board in 1917. When compulsory pooling ended in 1921, Giles retired to Chivery Hall, near Tring, in England. He died on 19 July 1926, survived by his wife, three sons and two daughters. One son farmed Rookwood till 1961; another was mayor of Westminster, London, in 1943.

J. J. Pascoe (ed), *History of Adelaide and vicinity* (Adel, 1901); C. Hill, *Fifty years of progress* (Adel, 1938); G. L. Buxton, *South Australian land acts 1869-1885* (Adel, 1966); J. Faull (ed), *Melrose: child of the mountain* (Melrose, 1979); *Pictorial Australian*, Feb 1891; *Observer* (Adel), 4 Jan 1890; *Quiz* (Adel), 25 Sept 1891; *Register* (Adel), 28 July 1926; Giles papers (held by Mrs W. Warburton, Magill, SA).

CARL BRIDGE

GILL, HARRY PELLING (1855-1916), art curator and teacher, was born on 9 March 1855 at Brighton, Sussex, England, son of Alfred Gill, master dairyman and his wife Frances Elizabeth, née Pelling. He was educated at Brighton, Hove and Sussex Grammar School and at the local art school as an evening student. In 1877 he won a scholarship to the National Art Training School, South Kensington, London (Royal College of Art), which he held for five years and combined with teaching. In 1882 the Board of Governors of the South Australian Institute (from 1884 the Public Library, Museum and Art Gallery of South Australia) chose Gill as master of the school of design, one of its two art departments, at a salary of £300 and some fees. He arrived in Adelaide in September and organized elementary and advanced classes, instruction in crafts, teaching of drawing and correspondence lessons. He also gave instruction to trainee teachers. On 29 April 1886 at North Adelaide he married Annie Waring Wright; they had two sons.

In 1889 Gill became director for technical art at twice his former salary. He published books on geometrical drawing and design and *The straight and crooked paths of studentship* (1894). In 1892 he was appointed honorary curator of the art gallery and, following the resignation in December of Louis Tannert as master of the school of painting, Gill assumed control of all the board's art teaching activities.

As honorary curator he advised the board on gallery matters and on the acquisition of works of art; he discouraged the buying of paintings by historic masters or copies of them. Following the 1897 bequest of £25 000 from Sir Thomas Elder [q.v.4] Gill advised on the use of the money, instituting an adventurous policy of regular spending on Australian works and recommending purchase of the works of contemporary overseas artists. Among the important Australian paintings, now regarded as masterpieces, acquired were works by Louis Buvelot [q.v.3], Tom Roberts, Sydney Long, Fred McCubbin, Hans Heysen, John Longstaff, Walter Withers, W. Lister Lister and Blamire Young [qq.v.]. In 1899 Gill visited England and Europe to make purchases and among the eighty-eight works by living artists that he recommended were works by Frank Brangwyn, Alma-Tadema, Fantin-Latour, Giovanni Segantini, Emile Claus and Aubrey Beardsley. Gill helped to design the first section of the art gallery building (opened 1900) and in 1903 initiated the formation of an art museum and applied arts collection. He compiled the first official catalogue of the gallery's paintings (1903) and also arranged and described some of the board's coin collection.

Gill had shown promise as an artist and hoped to win repute in Australia. However, teaching and administration had left little time for his painting. His rare decorative and aesthetic compositions, and also his landscapes, are painted with meticulous detail without sacrificing the overall unified effect. This is a quality passed on to some of his students, including the Hambidge sisters and Gustave Barnes [q.v.7] in his early work. Gill's landscapes and some of his interiors show that he was interested in the accurate rendering of light—a rare quality

in Adelaide before 1900. Although he was mainly a water-colourist, the Art Gallery of South Australia holds two of his oils and some etchings as well as a number of water-colours. Gill was a disciplinarian, but his students found his help had been sound and 'true to the best traditions of English art'. His administration was efficient, painstaking and dedicated, and his constant advocacy of drawing as an important school subject led to its inclusion in public examinations.

His growing authority in art matters, his self-confidence and abrasive manner and his attitude toward other art schools, led to criticism. The sale of art work through the school of design provoked parliamentary questions in 1907 and later a lengthy board enquiry into Gill's conduct of the school. No impropriety was discovered, but even the favourable minority report concluded that Gill had been somewhat injudicious. The majority recommendation that the board's art teaching be transferred to the Education Department, was adopted and in 1909 Gill became principal and examiner of the new Adelaide School of Arts and Crafts, but he did not remain as gallery curator. He retired in 1915 and died at sea next year, on 27 May, during a voyage to England for health advice.

Critics found Gill a vain man who controlled lucrative and influential art offices and who disdained the democratic brotherhood of art. His supporters admitted that he could be uncompliant and disagreeable, but said that he had worked hard, was a good judge of the monetary value of pictures, saved the board expense, and was a courageous and incorruptible curator. He supported and reorganized the South Australian Society of Arts and was its first president elected from the fellows (1909-11). He was an Associate of the Royal College of Art, London, and a Freemason. The Art Gallery of South Australia holds his portrait, by Millicent Hambidge, and a self-portrait. A medal, awarded by the South Australian School of Art, commemorates his name.

Advertiser (Adel), 31 May 1916; SA Public Lib, Museum and Art Gallery Bd, Records, GRG19 (SAA).   G. L. FISCHER

GILL, THOMAS (1849-1923), public servant, was born on 23 February 1849 at Glen Osmond, South Australia, son of Thomas Gill, labourer and surveyor, and his wife Marie, née Selby. He was educated locally and in 1865 became a messenger with the Volunteer and Reserve Forces. Gill then worked at the Destitute Asylum, the Audit

Office from 1871, in the Agent-General's Office, London, in 1879-80 and from 1883 at the South Australian Treasury as accountant; in 1894 he became under treasurer of South Australia; although due to retire in 1919, he was asked to continue for another year. On 5 October 1874 at Port Wakefield he had married Louisa Jane Bristow.

Gill suffered only one major set-back in his career: his failure to become deputy commissioner of taxation in 1884. He has been regarded as a major influence on the formation of the Civil Service Association in South Australia in 1885; he was a member of its first council and one of the honorary secretaries in 1888-94. A loyal public servant, he was nevertheless critical of low salaries and unsatisfactory junior appointments.

Thorough, dedicated and tireless as under treasurer, Gill was also comptroller of Imperial pensions, public debt commissioner, executive officer of the Public Service Superannuation Fund and active on several boards. After retiring he was government representative on the Municipal Tramways Trust and chairman of its finance committee; he was made a trustee of the Savings Bank of South Australia in 1920. That year his appointment to a royal commission to investigate the public service aroused some criticism.

Gill was an enthusiastic collector of Australiana, reflecting his interest in Australian history and geography, Aboriginals, exploration and the history of his State. He compiled his *Bibliography of South Australia* (1886) and *Bibliography of the Northern Territory* (1903) largely from his own library. He was made an honorary fellow of the Royal Australian Historical Society in 1921.

Gill was also a governor of the Public Library, Museum and Art Gallery of South Australia from 1896 until his death, and a member of the Library Association of Australasia. The *Transactions and proceedings* of the association's Adelaide meeting include a paper by him, 'A few notes respecting the statistics of suburban and country Institutes of South Australia' (1901). He wrote *The History and topography of Glen Osmond* (1905) for the Glen Osmond Institute. Gill was treasurer of the South Australian branch of the Royal Geographical Society of Australasia from its inception in 1885 until his death. The society's acquisition of the valuable York Gate Library was largely due to his energy and enthusiasm. His library was sold to the society for £300 as his will directed. The society's *Proceedings* contain several of Gill's papers, some of which were also published separately, including an enlarged edition of *A biographical sketch of Colonel William Light* (1911). His paper, 'Phenomenal sounds in the in-

terior of Australia' (1913), was published in the *Report* of the Melbourne meeting of the Australasian Association for the Advancement of Science, of which he was also a member.

Gill was kind, courteous and unassuming. He was appointed a companion of the Imperial Service Order in 1903 and C.M.G. in 1918. He died on 21 July 1923 after being knocked down by a tram-car on the previous day and was buried in Glen Osmond cemetery. Predeceased by his wife (d. 1915), he was survived by three daughters and two sons. The premier, Sir Richard Butler [q.v.7] commented that 'South Australia never had a more loyal, devoted and trustworthy public servant'.

W. F. Morrison, *The Aldine history of South Australia*, 2 (Syd, 1890); H. T. Burgess (ed), *Cyclopedia of South Australia* 1 (Adel, 1907); P. Mander-Jones, *Catalogue of the manuscripts in the library of the Royal Geographical Society of Australasia (South Australian Branch) Inc.* (Adel, 1981); *PRGSSA* (Index v 1-40, 1885/86-1938/39); *Public Service Review* (SA), 1 (Feb 1893), no 7, p 60; *Observer* (Adel), 27 Feb 1915; *Chronicle* (Adel), 8 June 1918; *Advertiser* (Adel), 23 July 1923; G. N. Hawker, The development of the South Australian civil service 1836-1916 (Ph.D. thesis, ANU, 1967); Gill family records, PRG 170 (SAA).   E. L. D. DURWARD

GILLEN, FRANCIS JAMES (1855-1912), ethnologist, was born on 28 October 1855 at Little Para, South Australia, eldest son of Thomas Gillen, agricultural labourer, and his wife Bridget, née McCan. His Irish parents had migrated to Australia in the year of his birth and settled at Clare. One of his brothers, Peter Paul Gillen [q.v.], became commissioner of crown lands.

Gillen joined the public service in 1867 as a postal messenger at Clare. He was transferred to Adelaide in 1871, combining work as a telegraph operator with evening study at the South Australian School of Mines and Industries. He was the duty operator in 1874 when news was transmitted from Barrow Creek telegraph station of the fatal Aboriginal attack there. Gillen began work on the overland telegraph line in 1875, culminating with his appointment as Alice Springs post and telegraph station master in 1892. On 5 August 1891 he married Amelia Maude Besley at Mount Gambier; they had six children.

Gillen's boisterous Irish humour, his championship of Home Rule, his genial administrative efficiency in the Centre's senior command, combined with a sense of justice for Aboriginals, made him a celebrity. He hosted the earl of Kintore [q.v.5] during his 1891 journey, and assisted the

Horn [q.v.] Scientific Expedition to Central Australia in 1894. An inveterate gambler in mining shares, he promoted the Arltunga goldfield, but his Wheal Fortune syndicate lost heavily and share losses explain the sale of his ethnographic collection to the National Museum of Victoria in 1899. He donated further material in 1902.

As Alice Springs special magistrate and Aboriginal sub-protector, Gillen strove to ameliorate racial issues at a time when 'dispersal' was a convenient euphemism for murder: he travelled unarmed, and charged the notorious mounted Constable W. H. Willshire [q.v.] with Aboriginal homicide. Although Willshire was acquitted, he did not return to Alice Springs.

Gillen met the anthropologist (Sir) Baldwin Spencer [q.v.] in 1894, when Spencer was his guest after the Horn expedition departed. In Gillen's convivial, smoke-filled den, Spencer absorbed the protector's ethnographic lore. As editor of the Horn expedition volumes, Spencer prompted Gillen to contribute, and later urged fuller publication.

During the summer of 1896-97, Spencer returned to Alice Springs, where Gillen 'arranged' the performance of complex Aboriginal ceremonies. Their book, *The native tribes of Central Australia* (1899), won them acclaim overseas and influenced contemporary anthropological theory. (Sir) James Frazer became their patron and, following his petition to the South Australian and Victorian premiers in 1900, Gillen and Spencer obtained a years leave. Next year they crossed the continent and attracted popular interest. Their last joint field-work occurred during a brief trip in 1903, north-west of Lake Eyre. These expeditions were published as *The northern tribes of Central Australia* (1904). The success of their anthropological team had depended initially upon acceptance by Aranda elders of Gillen's authority and paternalism.

Gillen wrote over 150 lengthy letters to Spencer by 1903, mostly ethnological in content and now in the Pitt-Rivers Museum, Oxford. Spencer adapted this discursive material and stimulated Gillen to crosscheck and supplement it. Although four titles were published under their joint authorship, Spencer was sole author and all the theory was his. At the 1900 Australasian Association for the Advancement of Science congress, Gillen was ethnology and anthropology section president; he also delivered several public lectures in South Australia and his important ethnographic photographs are in the South Australian Museum.

Family considerations forced his reluctant transfer as postmaster to Moonta in 1899 and to Port Pirie in 1908. His health failed and, from 1911, he was confined to an invalid chair. He died at Woodville on 5 June 1912, from a neurological disorder, aggravated by depression following the fatal accidental shooting of his eldest son. A Catholic, Gillen was buried in Sevenhill College cemetery near Clare.

W. F. Morrison, *The Aldine history of South Australia* (Syd, 1890); W. B. Spencer and F. J. Gillen, *Across Australia* (Lond, 1912); *Gillen's diary; the camp jottings . . .* (Adel, 1968); D. J. Mulvaney and J. H. Calaby, *'So much that is new'—Sir Baldwin Spencer, a biography* (forthcoming); *Quiz* (Adel), 11 Sept 1903; *Advertiser* (Adel), and *Register* (Adel), 6 June 1912; F. J. Gillen, 1875 diary (SA Museum).

D. J. MULVANEY

GILLEN, PETER PAUL (1858-1896), shopkeeper and politician, was born on 7 July 1858 at Golden Grove, Adelaide, second son of Thomas Gillen, labourer, and his wife Bridget, née McCan, both formerly of Cavan, Ireland. They moved up-country to Clare in 1862 where Peter attended R. Graham and L. W. Stanton's schools. An early bout of rheumatic fever left him weak, with a heart malfunction. He worked at Andrew Clarke's general store and on 24 May 1881 married Mary Gertrude Cousins at St Aloysius Church, Sevenhill. Later he partnered his uncle Philip in a general storekeeping business, P. & P. P. Gillen. An active debater and land reformer, in 1882 he became secretary of the Irish Land League committee. Although never a shearer, he helped form the local branch of the Amalgamated Shearers' Union of Australasia. He was committed to his depressed district's development, and urged farmers to diversify. In 1887 he was elected a town councillor.

Gillen was also actively involved in the Hibernian Australasian Catholic Benefit Society, several Adelaide Catholic literary societies, the Catholic *Southern Cross*, the Australian Natives' Association and several Western Australian mining companies.

Disregarding medical advice, he won the House of Assembly seat of Stanley, at a by-election in 1889, supported by the Catholics and the Licensed Victuallers' Association (although he was a teetotaller). In parliament his aggressive, excitable nature, rapid speech, and uncompromising attitude drew criticism. He favoured protection, Federation, the expansion of South Australia's rural industries and the resumption of large estates for small farmers, although he opposed the single tax. He soon lost his stridency, became very popular, and aligned himself with the radical liberals.

In 1892 Gillen was minister of crown lands

and immigration in the short-lived Holder [q.v.] ministry, and he held the same portfolio with C. C. Kingston [q.v.] next year. He sponsored village settlements, a device to place unemployed men on the land which was seen by conservatives as socialistic. At his death he was working on a major revision of pastoral legislation and on a speech for the new bill's second reading (passed in December).

Gillen's doctor had warned him against excitement; he did not expect to live long. On 22 September 1896 he suffered a heart attack during a cabinet meeting and died. He was survived by his wife (d. 1929), five sons and a daughter and, after a state funeral, was buried at Sevenhill, near Clare. His colleagues' eulogies stressed Gillen's love for the poor and Kingston recalled that his last words had been 'benevolent counsels for the aid of the necessitous'. Gillentown near Clare and Gillen on the River Murray were named after him. His brother, Francis James Gillen [q.v.], was a prominent ethnologist and explorer.

W. F. Morrison, *The Aldine history of South Australia*, 2 (Adel, 1890); *PD* (SA), 1896, p 434; *Quiz* (Adel), 23 Oct 1891, 21 Oct 1892; *Pictorial Australian*, June 1892; *Public Service Review* (SA), Sept 1896; *JHSSA*, no 6 (1979); *Observer* (Adel), 3 May, 13 Sept 1890, 17 Oct 1891, 10 June, 1 July 1893, 26 Sept, 3 Oct 1896; *Register* (Adel), 25 Apr 1890; *Northern Argus* (Clare), 25 Sept 1896; *Chronicle* (Adel), and *Weekly Herald* (Adel), 26 Sept 1896.

ROB VAN DEN HOORN

GILLESPIE, SIR ROBERT WINTON (1865-1945), flour-miller, was born on 3 July 1865 at St Kilda, Melbourne, fourth son of Scottish parents, George Gillespie, produce and grain merchant, and his wife Margaret, née Thompson. Educated privately he then worked for Gibbs, Bright & Co., merchants, later becoming a flour-miller. At Brighton on 11 November 1903 he married Jessie Jean Binnie. He moved to Sydney to join his brothers John and George in Gillespie Bros & Co. (later Gillespie Bros Ltd), proprietors of the Anchor Flour Mills.

For over thirty years Gillespie's main business interest was in flour-milling: he was chairman of the N.S.W. Flour Millers Produce Co. Ltd in 1909-19, and a director of Pardey & Co. Ltd, Temora, and M. McLeod Ltd, Wellington, and in the 1920s, chairman of the National Export Committee. Chairman of the Flour Millowner's Association of New South Wales in 1939-45, he was a founder and chairman of the N.S.W. Flour Millers' Trade Council in 1942-45. He told the 1919 royal commission into the George Georgeson wheat contract that he

had advised the minister W. C. Grahame [q.v.] to get rid of the inferior wheat (sold to Georgeson) as it was rapidly deteriorating. In 1923 he became a director of the Bank of New South Wales and influenced its expansion into the wheat-growing areas of Western Australia. He was also a director of the Colonial Sugar Refining Co. (1929-40), and the Queensland Insurance Co. Ltd, as well as chairman of Ball & Welch Ltd, Melbourne softgoods merchants.

A staunch Presbyterian, Gillespie was influenced by the Scottish tradition of support for kirk and school, inculcated by his parents. He was an elder of Wahroonga Presbyterian Church, a director of the Scottish Hospital, chairman of the council and benefactor of the Presbyterian Ladies' College, Pymble, and in 1924 a founder, benefactor and first chairman of the council of Knox Grammar School. He also founded a Presbyterian Church educational trust with an initial gift of £9000, gave generously to St Andrew's College, University of Sydney, and donated the Deissmann collection of ostraca to the university's Nicholson [q.v.2] Museum of Antiquities. An active board-member of the Burnside Presbyterian Orphan Homes, he was also a founder of the Fairbridge [q.v.8] Farm Schools in New South Wales. He was a founder and president of the Avondale Golf Club, Pymble—golf was his main leisure interest.

Alarmed by the Depression and the election of J. T. Lang's [q.v.] government, in November 1930 Gillespie became chairman of the central committee of 'the Movement' or Old Guard, founded by a vigilante group of businessmen, ex-officers and graziers, including (Sir) Philip Goldfinch, Lieut-Colonel G. C. Somerville and Brigadier General James Heane [qq.v.]. Although prepared to act forcibly to maintain essential services and defend property rights in crisis involving disorder, it melted quietly away after Lang's dismissal by the governor Sir Philip Game [q.v.8].

In 1937 Gillespie attended the ninth congress of the International Chamber of Commerce in Berlin and later expressed pro-Fascist sympathies. In November he succeeded Sir Thomas Buckland [q.v.7] as president of the Bank of New South Wales. For ten years he had worked closely with its general manager (Sir) Alfred Davidson [q.v.8], but now tried to exercise more control over him, particularly in staff appointments, and there was increasing friction between them. Gillespie was knighted in 1941 and retired as president of the bank in 1945.

Gillespie died at his Wahroonga home on 2 August 1945 and was cremated with Presbyterian forms. He was survived by his wife and an adopted daughter. His estate was valued for probate at £232 601 in New South Wales and £33 173 in Victoria, a figure not accepted by the commissioner of taxation. An appeal by his executors to have the death duties reduced by the amount levied on the R. W. Gillespie Trust was upheld in 1951 by the Privy Council.

E. Campbell, *The rallying point* (Melb, 1965); R. F. Holder, *Bank of New South Wales: a history*, 2 (Syd, 1970); K. Amos, *The New Guard movement 1931-1935* (Melb, 1976); P. J. Cochrane, *Industrialization and dependence* (Brisb, 1980); *SMH*, 10 Aug, 27 Nov 1937, 12 June 1941, 26 Mar, 3 Aug 1945, 19 Aug, 17 Dec 1949, 12 Dec 1951; Chief general manager correspondence file GM/302/361 (Bank of NSW Archives, Syd).   KEITH AMOS

GILLIES, JAMES HYNDS (1861-1942), inventor and industrialist, was born on 11 November 1861 at Millers Forest, New South Wales, son of Malcolm Gillies, farmer, and his wife Margaret, née McPherson, migrants from the Isle of Skye, Scotland. With a strong Presbyterian upbringing, Gillies intended to study for the ministry; but instead, from about 1887 until 1894 he sold real estate through the Eastern Suburbs Agency Co. at Paddington, Sydney. On 25 August 1886 at East St Leonards he married Annie Griffiths with Congregational forms; they had six children.

In the mid-1890s Gillies qualified as a metallurgist in Sydney, and spent several years working on various mining fields. In 1905 he became manager of the Gillies Sulphide Concentrating Machine Ltd. The company erected a plant, including mechanical patents invented by Gillies, to treat tailings from the Block 10 Mine at Broken Hill, using the (C.V.) Potter [q.v.] process: the attempt failed. Next year Gillies moved to Melbourne and in 1907 took out patents in the United States of America, Germany, Belgium, Mexico and Australasia for an electrolytic process for the treatment of refractory zinciferous ores. After an experimental plant in Melbourne succeeded he floated the Complex Ores Co. in 1908 and proposed to set up a full-scale works in Tasmania, utilizing hydro-electric power from the waters of the Great Lake and the Ouse and Shannon rivers.

The hydro-electric scheme had been suggested to Gillies by Harold Bisdee and Professor Alexander McAulay [q.v.] and was the subject of negotiations with the Tasmanian government in 1908 and 1909. Gillies's original proposal was for the government to harness the power and sell it to the Complex Ores Co. at a cheap rate; when this proved unacceptable he sought the right for the company to generate the elec-

tricity itself at Waddamana. Gillies had to contend with much local opposition: although he insisted that he needed the cheap power only in order to operate his metallurgical reduction works, he was attacked as a monopolist, especially by the Hobart Gas Co. and Edward Mulcahy, later minister for lands and mines; the Hercules Mining Co. also withdrew support for the scheme in favour of its own proposed method of zinc extraction. The requisite authority was granted in the Complex Ores Act of 1909, which allocated a site at Electrona, a deep-water port on North West Bay, for the proposed refining plant, but clauses were inserted requiring completion of the scheme by January 1914 and the company's continuous use of 3000 horsepower in metallurgical works.

To finance the hydro-electric development the Complex Ores subsidiary Hydro-Electric Power and Metallurgical Co. Ltd was formed in January 1911. Gillies, who travelled to London to raise the capital, found it expedient to include a calcium carbide works in the scheme as added security to shareholders. He was later to argue, successfully, that completion of these works, even without the zinc treatment plant, would fulfil the requirements of the Act. Work began in August and contracts were let for the lighting of Hobart streets and the operation of flour and woollen mills.

By the end of 1912 an expansion of the original hydro-electric project, coupled with bad weather and trouble with carriage, trade unions and the contracting engineers from British Westinghouse Co., plunged the company into serious financial difficulty. Gillies believed that matters were worsened by adverse publicity and that the parliamentary resolution setting up a select committee of inquiry that year was prejudicial to the company: 'It is not advisable when a man is hard up to advertise it from the housetops'. An intransigent man, he reacted violently against attempts by Henry Jones [q.v.] to gain control of the company. Unexpectedly, Gillies could not raise further capital in London and in May 1914 the hydro-electric undertaking was purchased by the Earle [q.v.8] Labor government at cost price and a State Hydro-Electric Department established.

After the sale of the concession Gillies abandoned his zinc extraction scheme and concentrated on his carbide enterprise at Electrona; but difficulties in obtaining materials retarded progress and it was not until after World War I that production began. In 1921 Gillies was managing director of Carbide & Electro Products Ltd with his eldest son Percy McPherson manager of the works. Meanwhile, in 1916, the government, with surplus electricity supply on its hands, entered into a contract with Amalgamated Zinc (De Bavay's [q.v.8]) Ltd to produce zinc at Risdon.

In 1924 Gillies's company went into receivership and was taken over by the Hydro-Electric Department. Gillies moved to Sydney where he continued to exercise his inventive bent, taking out patents for improved car lighting, sound-proofing with diatomaceous earth and for a new type of refrigeration using dry ice. In 1935, when virtually bankrupt, he was granted an annual pension of £350 by the Tasmanian government for services rendered to the State. He died, 'disillusioned ... frail, disappointed', on 26 September 1942 at South Camberwell, Melbourne, and was cremated, survived by his wife, three sons and a daughter. Gillies was a member of the Royal Society of Tasmania from 1920. Ida McAulay described him in his younger days as 'a sanguine, enthusiastic little man with bright eyes', 'an inventor and a dreamer—a gentleman who took no account of the ways of big business and men with financial power'.

Hydro-Electric Dept (Tas), *Souvenir programme ... inauguration of the Tasmanian hydro-electric power scheme* ... (Hob, 1916); *V & P* (HA Tas), 1909 (38), 1912 (45), 1914 (9) (10); *PTHRA*, 6 (1957), no 2, 8 (1959), no 1, 8 (1960), no 4; Inst of Engineers, Aust, *Transactions*, 7 (1926), p 3ff; *Mercury*, 28 Sept 1942; *Examiner* (Launc), 14 Sept 1951; Gillies papers (Univ Tas Archives); I. McAulay, Kanna Leena (transcript, NS 374/14, TA); information from C. R. Gillies, Hob.   ALLAN KNIGHT
                                                 ANN G. SMITH

GILLIES, JOHN (1844-1911), newspaperman and politician, was born on 6 March 1844 at Airdrie, Lanarkshire, Scotland, son of John Gillies, shepherd and later tailor, and his wife Janet, née Mathison. Arriving in Sydney in the *General Hewett* on 13 November 1848, the family settled at West Maitland, where Jack was educated by Rev. W. McIntyre [q.v.5]. At 13 he was apprenticed as a compositor on the *Maitland Mercury*, becoming so proficient at his trade that he won intercolonial speed contests. A part-owner and business manager of the paper from 1874, he made it a daily in 1893.

On 11 March 1865 Gillies had married Margaret Frost Mair with Primitive Methodist forms. An active sportsman and committee-member of the Northern Hunt Club in his youth, Gillies was for many years secretary and treasurer of the Maitland Volunteer Water Brigade, which operated during floods. By the late 1880s he held many public offices—including president of the Rowing Club and of the Maitland Rugby Football Club, vice-president of the Northumberland Football Club, committee-member of the hospital, the West Maitland School of Arts, the Northern Jockey Club, the Hunter River Agricultural and Horticultural Association, and a trustee of a building society and the Maitland branch of the Savings Bank of New South Wales. In 1883 he was appointed a justice of the peace and sat regularly on the bench. He served on the Maitland Municipal Council and was mayor in 1888-90; his name was carved on the corner-stone and over the porch (misspelled 'JONH') of the new Town Hall. He was an active Freemason and a teetotaller, a member of the Order of the Sons of Temperance.

Elected to the Legislative Assembly for West Maitland in 1891, Gillies easily held his seat until 1911 (Maitland from 1904). The key to his parliamentary career was popularity and service to the city; he secured several impressive public buildings —a court house, the hospital, technical college, the boys' high school, and a river embankment. In a period when conservative groups were consolidating a non-Labor party, Gillies's frank pursuit of local public works precluded ministerial office. Nominally a free trader in the 1890s, he also supported the Protectionist ministries of Sir George Dibbs [q.v.4] and (Sir) William Lyne [q.v.]. After 1905 he supported the revived Liberal party under Sir Joseph Carruthers [q.v.7] and in November 1910 declared himself a member of an independent third party.

In his maiden speech Gillies had drawn attention to the neglect by past governments of the floods that periodically ravaged the lower Hunter; flood mitigation was his perennial cause. Justifying his defection in 1899, with A. Edden [q.v.8] and others, he attacked Reid's government for its neglect of Newcastle and Maitland—local folk, he said, would long remember the record flood of 1893.

Gillies died suddenly from heart disease at his Maitland home on 23 September 1911. In the impressive funeral cortège, his coffin was born by the flood-boat, the *Jack Gillies*, mounted on wheels and drawn by the Water Brigade in uniform. He was buried with Masonic rites and Presbyterian forms in West Maitland cemetery. His wife, a son and four daughters survived him. In 1968 his name was commemorated when the township of East Greta, near Maitland, became Gillieston Heights.

E. Digby (ed), *Australian men of mark*, 2 (Syd, 1889); *Maitland Mercury*, 4 Mar 1890, 22 July 1904, 23 Sept 1911; *Newcastle Morning Herald*, and *SMH*, 25 Sept 1911.   L. E. FREDMAN

GILLIES, WILLIAM NEIL (NEAL) (1868-1928), farmer, premier and industrial arbitrator, was born on 27 October 1868 at Eccleston, New South Wales, son of Dougald Gillies, farmer, and his wife Mary, née Gillies; they were Scottish migrants. In 1882 he went with his parents to a Richmond River sugar-farm. There, his father founded an Anti-alien League, dedicated, like his own later New South Wales Sugar Growers' Defence League, to keeping the industry white. About 1900 he married Margaret Smith; they had a son and a daughter. Before inspecting land being opened for settlement near Atherton in Queensland in 1908, Gillies had worked in timber, sugar and dairying. A member of the Tintenbar Shire Council, he stood unsuccessfully as a Labor candidate for both the State and Federal seats of Richmond in 1910.

Late in 1910 Gillies selected a block at Atherton but was soon in business there as a commission agent and bought shares in the Labor-oriented *Tableland Examiner*. When the new Queensland Legislative Assembly seat of Eacham was created, he won it for the Labor Party in 1912, despite a charge of falsely stating his period of residence on an electoral claim. In the successful 1915 electoral campaign, T. J. Ryan [q.v.], the Labor party leader, placed great emphasis on winning the votes of sugar-growers. Trusted by growers and a participant in their meetings with the Colonial Sugar Refining Co., Gillies gave valuable advice to Ryan on what legislation the growers wanted.

Gillies retained his seat easily in 1915 and, being a hard worker, advanced rapidly in the party. He was a member of the Australian Workers' Union, and his fierce opposition to non-European labour earned him the support of both the union and Labor members in sugar seats. His suspicion of and public animosity to big corporations won him backing also from small selectors. A conciliator in other respects, Gillies became a trusted supporter of both Ryan and his deputy E. G. Theodore [q.v.]. As chairman of the Public Works Commission recommending the Brisbane-Kyogle railway, he saw the obligation of central government to undertake road construction and, when a minister in 1919, he established the Main Roads Board. The Gillies Highway was named for him.

Gillies was elected to cabinet on 25 April 1918 after the general election. As assistant minister for justice under Ryan, he negotiated with the Legislative Council over rejected bills and with North Queensland railway employees during a rail strike in 1918. When Ryan decided to enter Federal politics, Gillies gained the important post of sec-retary for agriculture and stock, and lost the deputy premiership to John Fihelly [q.v.8] by only two votes; he won it, however, when Fihelly became agent-general in 1922. Gillies was an able minister for agriculture and stock. The new legislation creating commodity boards and co-operative marketing schemes was largely Theodore's but the conciliatory Gillies administered it sympathetically. His farming legislation consolidated the party's rural vote won under Ryan.

In February 1925 Theodore resigned as premier and Gillies narrowly defeated the more able but more truculent William McCormack [q.v.] for the premiership. Gillies won support because of his seniority, but also from the caucus militants; the latter feared that McCormack would clash with the left-wing unions and wanted more legislation based on radical policies. A bitter wrangle inherited from Theodore between the government and the militants, particularly the Australian Railways Union, erupted into a strike in August. Gillies settled it by bypassing the Arbitration Court and conceding the union's demands; but he had not consulted cabinet and his caucus friends deserted him. When the Industrial Arbitration Act was amended to provide for the appointment of non-legal members to the court, Gillies accepted one of the positions in October rather than be deposed.

Though an able administrator, Gillies was not a leader and McCormack's biographer aptly summed up the Gillies dilemma. 'The qualities which had won Gillies the leadership—his personal kindness, his freedom from spleen, his ability to co-operate with all factions—did not fit him for the position of Premier'. On the Board of Trade and Arbitration which replaced the Industrial Court, Gillies was overshadowed by his other lay colleague, W. J. Dunstan [q.v.8]. Nevertheless, he was regarded as a fair commissioner by employers and warmly remembered by the militant unions for his 1925 decision. On 9 February 1928 he died suddenly in Brisbane of hypertensive heart disease and was buried in Toowong cemetery. His estate was valued at £5321 in Queensland and £1410 in New South Wales. His brother, Robert Towers Gillies, represented Byron Bay in the New South Wales Legislative Assembly in 1925-27.

J. W. Collinson, *Tropic coasts and tablelands* (Brisb, 1941); D. J. Murphy and R. B. Joyce (eds), *Queensland political portraits 1859-1952* (Brisb, 1978); D. J. Murphy et al (eds), *Labor in power . . . Queensland 1915-1957* (Brisb, 1979); K. H. Kennedy, The public life of William McCormack: 1907-1932 (Ph.D. thesis, James Cook Univ, 1973).

D. J. MURPHY

GILLISON, ANDREW (1868-1915), Presbyterian minister and military chaplain, was born on 7 June 1868 at Baldernock, Stirling, Scotland, son of Rev. John Gillison, minister of the Free Church of Scotland, and his wife Jane, née Broatch. He was educated in Edinburgh, at Watson's College and the University of Edinburgh (M.A., 1889; B.D.). Having studied theology at New College, Edinburgh, in 1890-94 he accepted a call to the ministry in the United States of America and gained further experience in Edinburgh and England before he was called to the Free Church at Maryhill, Glasgow, in 1897. He had married Isobel Napier in 1895. He accepted a call in 1903 to St Paul's Presbyterian Church, Brisbane, and in 1909 became minister at St George's Church, East St Kilda, one of the most important Presbyterian charges in Victoria.

Gillison had served as a private in the Queen's Edinburgh Rifle Volunteer Corps in 1885-87, and had maintained close contact with soldiers in Glasgow where his church adjoined the military barracks. He became a part-time chaplain to the Australian Military Forces on 9 November 1906, and from 1909 was chaplain to the Victorian Scottish Regiment. He was appointed chaplain-captain (4th class) in the Australian Imperial Force on 23 October 1914 and applied for the 14th Battalion out of respect for its commander, Lieut-Colonel R. E. Courtney.

As one of the few A.I.F. chaplains with any previous military experience Gillison introduced some British customs to his battalion. On 13 December 1914 the governor-general Sir Ronald Munro Ferguson [q.v.] presented the unit with its colours, which Gillison consecrated, and next Sunday the battalion paraded at his church to witness the consignment of the colours 'until our return'. Gillison spoke to the men 'about the responsibility of having colours, and what these meant'. His parishioners farewelled him warmly and generously, presenting him with two cameras, field-glasses, an automatic pistol, a wristlet watch, an attaché case and a purse of twenty guineas. They also donated £250 and sports equipment for the use of the battalion.

They sailed on 22 December and Gillison devoted himself to routine troopship tasks. He censored the mail, visited the hospital and detention cells each day, and conducted two services on Sundays. Arriving in camp at Heliopolis, Egypt, on 3 February 1915, he took part in many of the training exercises and attended lectures. While he mixed with the elite of British society in Cairo and, co-incidentally met acquaintances from his Edinburgh days, the troops found entertainment elsewhere. 'I fear the character of the city has to some extent reflected on the

character or rather the reputation of the troops', he wrote. In camp he was mess secretary and treasurer of the battalion's fund.

Gillison had a good view of the Anzac landing from his destroyer; he wrote that the Australians showed 'a dash characteristic of the finest British traditions'. He landed on 26 April at about 11 p.m. but the message ordering him ashore was a mistake and he returned to his ship where he cared for the wounded and buried eight men at sea. He landed on the third morning, the second chaplain ashore he believed, and took up duty at a dressing station. He consoled the wounded and buried the dead, praying over men of all denominations and sharing the work with all chaplains, even saying of the Catholic service that it 'may not be all that we would desire, but it is simple and we can all join in it'.

Gillison found the burial of the dead, on the day of the truce arranged for that purpose, a gruesome task. 'I never beheld such a sickening sight in my life and hope it may not be my lot again'. His diary ends on that sad note. He died on 22 August 1915 of wounds received during the advance on Hill 60. The official historian, C. E. W. Bean [q.v.7], records that while Gillison was waiting to read the burial service for men who had fallen in this action he heard someone groaning in the scrub nearby. He had been warned against moving onto the ridge in daylight but he went forward far enough to see that a wounded man was being troubled by ants, and called on two men to help him drag the wounded soldier out. When a Turkish sniper opened fire Gillison was severely wounded and died that day. He was mentioned in dispatches and tributes to his work showed what a popular and respected chaplain he had been.

His wife, three sons and a daughter survived him. One son, Douglas Napier, wrote the World War II official history of the Royal Australian Air Force in 1939-42.

C. E. W. Bean, *The story of Anzac* (Syd, 1924); R. S. Browne, *A journalist's memories* (Brisb, 1927); N. Wanliss, *The history of the Fourteenth Battalion, A.I.F.* (Melb, 1929); M. McKernan, *Australian churches at war* (Syd, 1980); *London Gazette*, 28 Jan 1916; Presbyterian Church of Australia, *Year book*, 1902-10 (Melb); *Messenger of the Presbyterian Church of Vic*, 10 Sept 1915; *Argus*, 28 Aug 1915; A. Gillison diary, Dec 1914-Aug 1915, file 12/11/5409, War records section (AWM).

MICHAEL MCKERNAN

GILLOTT, SIR SAMUEL (1838-1913), lawyer and politician, was born on 29 October 1838 at Sheffield, Yorkshire, England, son of Joseph Gillott, corn-miller, and his wife Elizabeth, née Whitehead. He was educated at Sheffield Grammar School.

Gillott arrived in Melbourne in 1856 and obtained employment with the legal firm of Vaughan, Moule & Seddon. Later he was articled to Thomas O'Brien. Gillott studied law at the University of Melbourne, securing the Chancellor's exhibition in 1860-61 and a gold medal in 1861-62. He was admitted to practise in 1863 and was straightway taken into partnership by his employer. On 26 September at St James' Church, Melbourne, he married Elizabeth Jane Hawken, London-born daughter of a builder; they had no children. For some years Gillott practised on his own before joining forces with (Sir) Arthur Snowden in the mid-1870s. In 1886 the firm became Gillott, Crocker & Snowden. Snowden left in 1894 and Gillott continued with various partners. He was essentially a lawyer.

Until the early 1890s Gillott had a very large police court practice, though his firm did act in the celebrated *Speight* v. *Syme* [qq.v.6] libel case. Gillott's industry was rewarded with wealth which he increased considerably by shrewd investment, principally in city property. In 1896 he followed the example of his former partner, Snowden, and gained election to the Melbourne City Council. In 1899 he lost the mayorship by one vote. The next year he was elected without opposition and held the position for the following two terms. Meanwhile, in November 1899 he was elected to the Legislative Assembly seat of East Melbourne. In 1900 he was president of the Law Institute, having served on the committee for a number of years.

As mayor Gillott proved to be very much the man of the hour. With the visit of the duke and duchess of Cornwall and York and the advent of Federation, 1901 was a year in which Melbourne was in the limelight. Gillott 'had the money to spend, and he entertained royally'. He 'just turned on the champagne, cut the bands of his cigar-boxes and welcomed all the globe-trotters'. In return the office was distinguished by the title lord mayor and in May 1901 he was knighted.

In 1900 Gillott was nominated an honorary minister in the second Turner [q.v.] government and remained in the subsequent Peacock [q.v.] ministry. From June 1901 until June 1902 when the ministry fell he was attorney-general. Under (Sir) Thomas Bent [q.v.3] he became chief secretary and minister for labour from February 1904. By this stage he had cultivated an image as a mild and respected urban liberal. However, his fall was to be dramatic. In May 1906 he was attacked by the demagogue reformer W. H. Judkins [q.v.] who held him, as chief secretary, responsible for illegal off-course gambling, the most conspicuous instance of which was John Wren's [q.v.] Collingwood tote, which Judkins held to be prima facie evidence of a corrupt administration and police force. In response Gillott asked for proof of either his department's incompetence or police corruption. Judkins, however, had tapped a reserve of public concern on the gambling issue and Bent announced that he was prepared effectively to prohibit off-course betting. Responsibility for this devolved on Gillott who in August introduced the gaming suppression bill. It was on the way to becoming law when John Norton's [q.v.] *Truth* published an attack on Gillott entitled 'Lechery and lucre' accusing him of lending money to Caroline Pohl, or 'Madam Brussels', Melbourne's leading madam, and detailing financial dealings between them dating back to 1877. The same information reached Judkins, who denounced Gillott from his Sunday platform with devastating effect. Protesting that the worries and troubles of public life were too much for his health, on 4 December Gillott announced his resignation from both the ministry and parliament. Soon afterwards he left for England where he remained for nearly a year.

Although Norton delivered the telling blow, Judkins had presented the more sustained and coherent argument and Gillott's demise has been seen largely in a light Judkins created, that of the immoral plutocrat posing as a respectable figure in front of vice and corruption. It may be that Gillott is more appropriately seen as a sharp lawyer and man of the world, but a poor politician grown uncommonly fond of pomp in his old age. Out of his depth in the world of real politics he retreated when caught in a crossfire, simply leaving the stage wounded.

On his return to Melbourne Gillott resumed his seat on the city council and continued his work on the committee of the (Royal) Melbourne Hospital. He was a councillor and in 1911 president of the Working Men's College. While on another visit to England with his wife, he died on 29 June 1913 at Sheffield after falling down a flight of stairs at night. His body was returned to Australia for burial in Melbourne cemetery. He left an estate valued for probate at £291 864, much of which was bequeathed to the University of Melbourne and to charitable institutions.

J. Smith (ed), *Cyclopedia of Victoria*, 1 (Melb, 1903); C. Pearl, *Wild men of Sydney* (Lond, 1958); *J. of Religious Hist*, June 1978; *Leader* (Melb), 27 July 1901; *Punch* (Melb), 17 Sept 1903, 7 June 1906; *Truth* (Vic edn), 1 Dec 1906; *Age*, 1 July 1913.

DAVID DUNSTAN

GILMORE, DAME MARY JEAN (1865-1962), writer, was born on 16 August 1865 at Mary Vale, Woodhouselee, near Goulburn, New South Wales, eldest child of Donald Cameron, a farmer, born in Inverness-shire, Scotland, and his native-born wife Mary Ann, née Beattie. Her father had migrated to Australia in 1838 from Fort William, and her mother's family had come from County Armagh, Ireland, in 1842. The Camerons and Beatties owned adjoining properties.

Donald Cameron, a wanderer by nature, was in turn farmer, mail contractor, property manager, carpenter, innkeeper and builder, moving with his family around south-western New South Wales. Later Mary's mother lived in Sydney and wrote for the *Australian Town and Country Journal* and the *Daily Telegraph*. At 7 Mary went to school briefly at Brucedale near Wagga Wagga and at 9 to Wagga Wagga Public School. In 1877 the family moved to Houlaghan's Creek and she attended the school at Downside. For the next four years she was an unofficial pupil-teacher in small schools at Cootamundra, Bungowannah and Yerong Creek. At 16 she passed a formal entrance examination and began as a probationary pupil-teacher at the Superior Public School, Wagga Wagga. After a period of ill health and failure in a teacher's examination in December 1884, she resigned, but was re-employed in May 1886 at Beaconsfield Provisional School. She was transferred in March 1887 to Illabo Public School. After passing the IIIA teachers' examination, Mary was appointed in October 1887 as temporary assistant at Silverton Public School near Broken Hill. She remained there until December 1889 spending the Christmas vacation of 1888-89 in Sydney with her mother. Mary was transferred to Neutral Bay Public School in January 1890.

Her relationship with Henry Lawson [q.v.] probably began in 1890: in 1923 she recalled that 'It was a strange meeting that between young Lawson and me. I had come down permanently to the city from Silverton'. Her account of an unofficial engagement and Lawson's wish to marry her at the time of his brief trip to Western Australia (May-September 1890) could be accurate regarding dates, but there is no other corroborative evidence. There was clearly, however, a close relationship between them in 1890-95, but it was broken by his frequent absences from Sydney. Mary's later comments on his career were always somewhat proprietorial but the extent of her influence on his literary talents and her contribution to his literary education remain unsubstantiated.

In May 1891 Mary was transferred to Stanmore Superior Public School. She had become involved in the increasing radicalism of the day, supporting the maritime and shearers' strikes as actively as possible for a schoolteacher subject to the strict rules of the Department of Public Instruction. It was her lifelong claim that she had, under her brother John's name, been co-opted to the first executive of the Australian Workers' Union. She assisted William Lane [q.v.] and the New Australia movement, and was largely responsible for overcoming the financial difficulties that threatened to prevent the departure for Paraguay of the *Royal Tar* on 16 July 1893. On 31 October 1895 she resigned from teaching and sailed from Sydney in November in the *Ruapehu*, arriving at the Cosme settlement in Paraguay in January 1896. She married fellow-colonist, a Victorian shearer, William Alexander Gilmore (1866-1945), at Cosme on 25 May 1897 and their only child William Dysart Cameron Gilmore (1898-1945) was born on 21 August 1898 at Villarica, near Cosme. In August 1899 the Gilmores resigned from Cosme and Will left the settlement to work at various jobs. In November 1900 the family went to Rio Gallegos in southern Patagonia where Will worked on a ranch and Mary gave English lessons. On 1 April 1902 they reached England, stayed briefly with Lawson and his family in London, and arrived in Australia in the *Karlsruhe* in July.

Back in her familiar Sydney environment Mary was attracted to the busy literary and political scene but, acknowledging her family responsibilities, went with her husband to Strathdownie, near Casterton in western Victoria, where Will's parents had a property. Life there was far from congenial but she had a long-sustained correspondence with A. G. Stephens [q.v.] of the *Bulletin* and was delighted to have her life and work featured in the 'Red Page' on 3 October 1903. In 1907 they moved into Casterton where Billy attended school. Mary's long connexion with the *Australian Worker* began in 1908 when, in response to her request for a special page for women, the editor Hector Lamond [q.v.] invited her to write it herself. She was to edit the 'Women's Page' until 11 February 1931. Mary also began campaigning for the Labor Party, helping to have its candidate for the Federal seat of Wannon elected in 1906 and 1910. Her first collection of poems, *Marri'd, and other verses*, simple colloquial lyrics, written mainly at Cosme and Casterton, commenting on the joys, hopes, and disappointments of life's daily round, was published in 1910 by George Robertson [q.v.6] & Co. Pty Ltd of Melbourne, on the advice of Bernard O'Dowd [q.v.] who professed to be 'simply enraptured with their lyric magic'.

The Gilmores left Casterton in 1912, Mary and her son going to Sydney where she had the security of her *Worker* position and Billy the opportunity of a secondary education, while Will joined his brother on the land in the Cloncurry district of Queensland. They were rarely reunited in the years that followed, but, loose and impersonal as the husband-wife relationship must have appeared to outside observers, it was always characterized by affection, respect, and abiding mutual interest.

Mary was soon involved in literary activities. A staunch supporter of journals such as the *Bulletin*, the *Lone Hand* and the *Bookfellow*, she invested her own (borrowed) money in the latter to prevent its closure through bankruptcy. The accounts in 1913-16 of Mary Gilmore trading as the *Bookfellow* and her correspondence with Stephens indicate the scope of her participation. Her second volume of poetry, *The passionate heart* (1918), reflected her horrified reaction to World War I. Poems such as 'The measure' stress the futility and waste of war, while 'Gallipoli', a deeply felt, imaginative account of that famous battlefield with its scars covered by the recurring miracle of spring, offers consolation to those grieving for the loss of loved ones. She gave the royalties from *The passionate heart* to the soldiers blinded in the war. In 1922 her first book of prose, a collection of essays entitled *Hound of the road*, was published. In the early 1920s her health, never robust, became a problem. High blood pressure and heart trouble led to a stay in hospital in Sydney in 1920; she was sent to Goulburn by her doctor to escape the pressure of city life at different times between 1921 and 1924. In 1925 a third volume of verse, *The tilted cart*, appeared; the poems were accompanied by copious notes indicating her keen interest in recording the minutiae of the pioneer past.

Mary Gilmore's final years with the *Worker* were not placid: she resigned at the end of January 1931. Her book of verse, *The wild swan*, had been published in 1930, its radical themes, together with its anguish over the ravaging of the land by white civilization and the destruction of Aboriginal lore, making it her most impressive work to that point. It was followed in 1931 by the book of largely religious verse, *The rue tree*, which she claimed was a tribute to the Sisters of the Convent of Mercy at Goulburn, and in 1932 by *Under the wilgas*. Her twin books of prose reminiscences, *Old days, old ways: a book of recollections* and *More recollections* were published in 1934 and 1935. In them she recaptures the spirit and atmosphere of pioneering. These anecdotal accounts which present 'Australia as she was when she was most Australian' are lively and attractive examples of her skill as a prose writer and, although unreliable and romanticized, have become invaluable sources of the legend of the pioneer days.

Over the years Mary Gilmore campaigned in the *Worker* and any other available forum for a wide range of social and economic reforms, such as votes for women, old-age and invalid pensions, child endowment and improved treatment of returned servicemen, the poor and deprived and, above all, of Aboriginals. She wrote numerous letters, as well as contributing articles and poems, to the *Sydney Morning Herald* on these causes and such diverse subjects as the English language, the Prayer Book, earthquakes, Gaelic and the immigration laws, the waratah as a national emblem, the national anthem and Spanish Australia. All her life she encouraged young writers and enthused over their work. She carried on a prolific correspondence with many friends including Dowell O'Reilly, Hugh McCrae, Nettie Palmer, George Mackaness [qq.v.], A. H. Chisholm and R. D. FitzGerald. In 1980 a selection of her letters was published posthumously. She was a founder of the Lyceum Club, Sydney, a founder and vice-president in 1928 of the Fellowship of Australian Writers, an early member of the New South Wales Institute of Journalists and life member of the Royal Society for the Prevention of Cruelty to Animals.

To mark the considerable public acclaim for her literary and social achievements, she was appointed D.B.E. in 1937. Thereafter she was a celebrated public figure. She published a new volume of poems, *Battlefields*, in 1939. The title referred to her own radical campaigns. During World War II, perched in her Kings Cross flat at 99 Darlinghurst Road, she anathematized German and Japanese ambitions of world domination. She recognized the growing threat to Australia in her stirring call to Australian patriotism, the poem 'No Foe Shall Gather our Harvest', while she castigated Allied incompetence and corruption in the poem 'Singapore', just after its fall. In 1945 her husband and son both died in Queensland.

From 1952 Mary Gilmore was associated with the Communist newspaper *Tribune*, largely because of her pacifism and her anger at the government's attitude to the Youth Carnival for Peace and Friendship then being staged in Sydney. Her *Tribune* column 'Arrows' appeared regularly until mid-1962, commenting on contemporary Australian and world affairs. In 1954, as she approached her ninetieth year, she published her final volume of poetry, *Fourteen men*. The Australasian Book Society commissioned William Dobell to paint her portrait for her 92nd birthday in 1957. She strongly defended the controversial portrait because she felt it captured something of her ancestry; she donated it to the Art Gallery of New South Wales.

Her last years were made memorable by ever-increasing signs of public esteem. Her birthdays were celebrated publicly by Sydney literati and ordinary folk alike; streets, roads, schools, old people's homes were named after her; literary awards and scholarships were given in her name; visitors from Australia's literary and political world, and overseas admirers, made regular pilgrimages to her; her pronouncements were highlighted by the media; she made television and radio appearances; she led May Day processions as the May Queen. She died on 3 December 1962 (Eureka Day) and, after a state funeral at St Stephen's Presbyterian Church, Macquarie Street, was cremated, her ashes being buried in her husband's grave in the Cloncurry cemetery, Queensland; she was survived by a grandson. Her estate was valued for probate at £12 023.

Mary Gilmore's significance is both literary and historical. As poet and prose writer she has drawn considerable praise from such connoisseurs of literature as McCrae, FitzGerald, Judith Wright, Douglas Stewart and T. Inglis Moore. She wrote too much (often on ephemeral trivia) and too hastily, but her best verse—brief lyrics such as 'Nationality', 'Eve-Song', 'The Tenancy', 'Never Admit the Pain', 'Gallipoli', 'The Flight of the Swans'—are among the permanent gems of Australian poetry. As patriot, feminist, social crusader and folklorist she has now passed into Australian legend.

Besides the Dobell portrait of Dame Mary Gilmore, the Art Gallery of New South Wales holds one by Joshua Smith and a bronze head by Rayner Hoff [q.v.]; portraits by Eric Saunders and Mary McNiven are held by the National Library of Australia, Canberra.

D. Cusack et al (eds), *Mary Gilmore* (Syd, 1965), and for bibliog; S. Lawson, *Mary Gilmore* (Melb, 1967); W. H. Wilde, *Three radicals* (Melb, 1969); W. H. Wilde and T. I. Moore (eds), *Letters of Mary Gilmore* (Melb, 1980); *Meanjin Q*, 1960, no 4, 1973, no 4; *Southerly*, 3 (1949), 4 (1965); *Age*, 15 Aug 1959; *Bulletin*, 22 July 1980; Mary Gilmore, *and* Nettie Palmer papers (NL).   W. H. WILDE

GILPIN, OLIVER (1874-1942), chain store proprietor, was born on 8 July 1874 at Seven Creeks near Euroa, Victoria, fourth child and second son of William Gilpin, farmer, and his wife Dinah, née Barton, both from Tyrone, Ireland. He was educated at local state schools and became a draper's assistant at Euroa. A testimonial as 'an energetic, pushing salesman, a careful stock-keeper . . . honest and industrious' gained him city experience with Ball & Welch Ltd, drapers, in their Carlton store.

He used an inheritance to open a drapery store at Korumburra, south Gippsland, in 1895, moving to Rutherglen in the upper Murray valley in 1899. Frustrated by irregular stock deliveries, he moved to Fitzroy, Melbourne, in 1902, seeking a warehouse and the benefits of combined supplies for effective development of country trading. By 1905 he was producing many stock items at Northcote and had established retail outlets at Bendigo and Warracknabeal. Branches at Echuca, Numurkah and Yarrawonga followed in 1906, with ten more in 1907. He moved his city establishment to East Malvern in 1911, and had opened forty shops by 1920 and seventy-four by 1928. All were managed by women, on a strictly cash basis. Drapery remained the main line, supplemented by ironmongery, crockery, school requisites and toys.

Gilpin saw the Depression years as a challenge. Between 1928 and 1931 he established eighteen new branches, including two in Tasmania, at Devonport and Ulverstone. The chain included South Australian branches at Mount Gambier, Millicent and Renmark, twenty-five stores in southern and western New South Wales, and ten in suburban Melbourne. Gilpin's *Chain Store News* was issued monthly.

A fleet of twenty motor trucks, with trailers, Australia's largest privately owned diesel fleet, ensured prompt deliveries and ready transfers between branches. Containers expedited loading and unloading, and minimized damage. The trucks also occasioned clashes with State governments, intent on maintaining rail haulage of commercial freight. In 1929 Gilpin challenged charges on goods taken across the Murray River, and unsuccessfully appealed to the Privy Council. In 1924 his business became a proprietary company and in 1931 a limited company.

At Euroa on 26 January 1897 with Wesleyan forms, Gilpin had married Annie Pease, a local dressmaker; she divorced him for desertion in 1920. There were three daughters and two sons of the marriage. On 25 February 1921 he married Ruby Gertrude Brewer of Williamstown, a former branch manager who was daughter of a Congregational minister. Gilpin divorced her in May 1926; there were no children. On 17 February 1928 according to Methodist forms, he married Muriel Doris Round, formerly a director of the company; a son Oliver was born in 1930.

In later years Gilpin lived extravagantly. He owned two Rolls-Royces. He built a two-storey luxury mansion, Idylwylde, in Balwyn, and intended to extend it to eight storeys. The 20-acre (8 ha) garden included an artificial lake, huge aviaries and a zoo of Australian animals.

Gilpin died of cancer on 19 October 1942 and was cremated. Idylwylde was bought by the Missionary Sisters of the Sacred Heart in 1945 and by the Wesleyan Central Mission in 1978. In 1944 Foy [q.v.4] & Gibson [q.v.8] acquired a controlling interest in Gilpin's business and in 1951 the chain was bought by G. J. Coles & Co. Ltd for £1 250 000. Gilpin's estate had been sworn for probate at £157 472.

Argus, 16 July 1929, 18 Feb 1939, 1 July 1944; *Sun-News Pictorial*, 4 Oct 1949; *Daily Mirror* (Syd), 2 Mar 1945; *People*, 22 July 1959; *Age*, 22 May 1951, 9 Sept 1978; *Bulletin*, 3 Oct 1978.   G. F. JAMES

GILRUTH, JOHN ANDERSON (1871-1937), veterinary scientist and administrator, was born on 17 February 1871 at Auchmithie, a fishing village near Arbroath, Forfar, Scotland, second child of Andrew Gilruth and his wife Ann, née Anderson. His father was a tenant farmer of the Carnegie family, the earls of Northesk. His mother, a teacher before marriage, was a woman of character and intellect; John always considered her to be the major influence upon his life. The boy attended the village school at Auchmithie, where, according to his recollections late in life, reading and writing were confined to the Bible and early Scottish history which left him with a fixed impression that Robert Bruce was the father of Queen Victoria.

Gilruth went on to high school at Arbroath and, briefly, Dundee. During holiday periods he spent much time with Jamie Macdonald, a perceptive shepherd who inspired his interest in the problems of animal management and disease. Under family pressure Gilruth spent two years as clerk to an Arbroath solicitor before his father agreed to let him go to Glasgow Veterinary College in 1887. In his first year he took medals in botany and anatomy and went on to sweep the board in all subjects at the examinations of the Royal College of Veterinary Surgeons, London, before being admitted to membership of that institution in 1892. Soon afterwards he applied for and received appointment as a government veterinary surgeon in New Zealand.

Gilruth arrived there late in 1893 and spent three years investigating stock diseases. In 1896 the government sent him to study bacteriology at the Pasteur Institute in Paris. Upon his return in 1897 he became chief veterinarian and government bacteriologist. A pioneer of his profession in New Zealand, he proved a vigorous and able leader both in research and in the movement for upgrading standards of meat inspection and slaughtering. In 1900 he was appointed a member of the royal commission on public health in New Zealand and a year later became pathologist to the newly formed Health Department. In appreciation of his work with that department the New Zealand branch of the British Medical Association made him an honorary member in 1902. His career prospered to the extent that in 1904 the government blocked a move to offer him a lucrative post in South Africa, on the ground that New Zealand could not afford to lose his services. In 1907 he became a fellow of the Royal Society of Edinburgh.

Gilruth usually preferred directness to diplomacy. It is said that a well-known sheep-breeder once asked him why his young ewes would not thrive, whereupon Gilruth replied, 'Why don't you feed your bloody sheep?'. In this case he was right and friendship resulted. But his forthrightness in pressing for improvements in research facilities and health measures raised tensions with government officials and the minister for lands. He became increasingly frustrated, despite the warm support of his colleagues and farmers' organizations, and when the University of Melbourne offered him the newly created chair of veterinary pathology in 1908 he accepted. With characteristic energy, he turned to building up the veterinary faculty and its associated research institute. His teaching methods, unorthodox at the time, aimed to stimulate students' curiosity; Gilruth set a fine example by his own passion for his work which, during this period, included investigations of fundamental importance into black disease and entero-toxaemia. In 1909 the university awarded him an honorary doctorate of veterinary science.

In 1911 Prime Minister Andrew Fisher [q.v.8] invited him to join a scientific mission to investigate the potential of the Northern Territory. The leader of the mission, Professor (Sir) Baldwin Spencer [q.v.], was his colleague and friend and, as first Commonwealth-appointed protector of Aborigines, later his adviser. Gilruth's northern expedition fired him with enthusiasm for economic development of the Territory by means of mining, crop-growing and pastoralism. In February 1912 he accepted from the Fisher government the post of administrator of the Northern Territory. Two months later he arrived in Darwin, confident of his own leadership ability and of strong government support for his developmental plans.

From the beginning his plans went awry. Territorians and the Federal government alike held unrealistically high hopes for economic development, yet half expected failure because such was seen to have been the result of all earlier efforts by South Australia in the Territory. Thus every set-back was doubly condemned. Gilruth did his best to promote agriculture, mining and, after initial doubts, the development of meatworks in Darwin by the giant English firm, Vesteys. All proved disappointing. With the outbreak of World War I in August 1914, an already wavering Commonwealth government lost interest in Territory development. The one great hope, Vesteys' meatworks, closed in 1920 after a consistent history of industrial unrest and cost inflation.

The weight of public frustration fell upon Gilruth, quite unjustly. Yet his own character helped to bring about that result. Among scientists of similar background and interests, his blunt, dynamic style of leadership was respected and he was able to show best the personal kindliness and loyalty which endeared subordinates to him. Among the heterogeneous population of the Northern Territory he was seen as arrogant and insensitive. Tutored by Spencer, he went to Darwin predisposed to treat the Chinese with reserve, the Aboriginals with heavy-handed paternalism and the white trade unionists with suspicion. In June 1913 the real wages of government field-survey hands were arbitrarily reduced. When the fledgling Amalgamated Workers' Association staged a strike over the matter Gilruth crushed it ruthlessly and earned the enduring enmity of the union leaders.

Harold Nelson [q.v.], the able organizer (later secretary) of the Darwin branch of the Australian Workers' Union, skilfully used the antagonism to isolate Gilruth while he built his union into the great industrial power of the Territory. Gilruth's response was hindered by the Commonwealth government which neither gave him the powers he needed to rule effectively nor evolved consistent policies for the region. His own officers clashed with him over industrial matters and he upset the small group of Darwin employers over his attitude to town lands and the abolition of the Palmerston Council. Only among the graziers did he find sympathy. His greatest pleasure was to take long drives through the outback in his Talbot, the first car seen in nearly all the areas he visited.

On 17 December 1918 public discontent peaked in a confrontation between Gilruth and townspeople which became known as the 'Darwin Rebellion'. Gilruth, with the courage which never failed him, faced an angry mob demanding that he leave Darwin. In February 1919 the government recalled him for consultation and eight months later some of the Darwin citizenry forced the departure of three of his close associates, H. E. Carey, director of the Northern Territory, J. D. J. Bevan, judge of the Supreme Court, and R. J. Evans, government secretary. Reacting sharply, the Hughes [q.v.] ministry appointed Mr Justice N. K. Ewing [q.v.8] as royal commissioner to investigate the causes of these events. Ewing immediately cast doubt on his impartiality by hiring Nelson as 'representative of the citizens of the Northern Territory' to assist at the hearings. Ewing's report, completed in April 1920, accused Gilruth of allowing irregular practices in the courts and Aborigines Department and of personal impropriety in land and mining deals. Mr Justice Kriewaldt later described the report as 'a shoddy piece of work', with some justification since the evidence does not support any of these findings, but Ewing was right in believing that, for all his great abilities, Gilruth was not fitted 'to rule a democratic people'.

Sir Robert Garran [q.v.8], Commonwealth solicitor-general, absolved Gilruth from Ewing's charges of impropriety, but the government treated him shabbily, evading the promise of a post with the Institute of Science and Industry. Gilruth battled through the 1920s as a private consultant, but in 1929 became consultant to, and next year acting chief of, the newly formed division of animal health within the Council for Scientific and Industrial Research; he became chief of the division in 1933. He regained his zest for research and under his inspired guidance the scattered activities of existing organizations working on animal health were co-ordinated. To facilitate the study of problems associated with cattle raising in tropical and sub-tropical Australia, Gilruth arranged the temporary transfer to C.S.I.R. in September 1931 of the Queensland government's Stock Experiment Station at Oonoonba, Townsville; on his recommendation Zebu cattle were later introduced for cross-breeding. In November the (Sir Frederick) McMaster [q.v.] Animal Health Laboratory was opened in Sydney. The same year Gilruth was appointed chairman of a committee consisting of representatives of C.S.I.R. and the New South Wales Department of Agriculture to direct the study of fly-strike in sheep, and in 1933 he was appointed to a committee to survey coast disease in South Australia. In 1934 Gilruth reported on the beef-cattle industry in northern Australia and on the general possibilities of the north; he also conducted an inquiry into the organization of the Tasmanian Department of Agriculture. During his period in charge of the division of animal health many of the problems on which he had personally worked were brought nearer solution.

Gilruth's retirement in 1935 was regretted by his senior colleagues, many of whom had been his students and by whom he was regarded with respect and affection. In 1933 he was elected to the presidency and in 1936 to honorary membership of the Australian Veterinary Association. His publications on veterinary research in the professional journals were voluminous. He died of a respiratory infection on 4 March 1937 at his home at South Yarra, Melbourne, and was cremated. His wife Jeannie McLean, née McLay, whom he had married on 20 March 1899 at Dunedin, New Zealand, a son and two daughters survived him. His name is commemorated in Gilruth Plains, a research station near Cunnamulla, Queensland, and by the Gilruth prize of the Australian Veterinary Association. Darwin remembers him in the name of an avenue. His portrait by Longstaff [q.v.] hangs in the Animal Health Laboratory, Parkville, Melbourne.

CSIR, *Reports*, 1930-35; *Aust Veterinary J*, June 1937; *Labour Hist*, Nov 1966; F. X. Alcorta, A history of the social and economic development of the Northern Territory, 1911-1914 . . . (M.A. qual. thesis, Univ Qld 1981); A. W. Powell, Gilruth vs Ewing: The Royal Commission on Northern Territory administration (paper delivered to ANZAAS Congress, 1980, held by author, Winnellie, Darwin); Gilruth papers (Basser Lib, Canb).

ALAN POWELL

GIRDLESTONE, HENRY (1863-1926), Anglican clergyman and headmaster, was born on 5 July 1863 at Penkridge, Staffordshire, England, eldest son of Henry Girdlestone, clergyman, and his wife Eliza Jane, née Webb. He grew up at the rectory of Bathampton, where he acquired a love of the country and where respect for Anglican principles and traditions was instilled in him by his father. He attended Bath College for eight years before going to Magdalen College, Oxford, where he took a third-class degree in natural science (M.A., 1889) and stroked his college eight for three years and the university crew in 1885 and 1886. After a short period tutoring the Irish baron, Lord Ashtown, Girdlestone became assistant master and chaplain at his old school, in 1890-93; he was ordained in 1892.

In 1894 he arrived in Adelaide as headmaster of the Collegiate School of St Peter.

Bishop Kennion [q.v.5], after interviewing the applicants in England, had cabled: 'Excellent man, Girdlestone, Stroke Oxford Eight, Honours, Maths and Science'. Intending to stay only two years, he remained for twenty-two, and 'raised St. Peter's from a small struggling school (170 boys) to a large and prosperous College (475 boys)'. A shy man, 'a man's man', he proved one of its greatest headmasters and organized the school 'to fit a man to take his part in the civil work of the State'. Six feet (183cm) tall and broad-shouldered, he had a commanding presence, a friendly disposition and a conviction that firm discipline and thoroughness produced good character and were the prerequisites for a life of Christian service. His sermons in the school chapel were inspiring: he distrusted mysticism and emotion. He avoided 'cramming' and was sceptical of the value of excessive practical work in science teaching. He instilled in the school a spirit of cohesion and loyalty to the British Empire.

Girdlestone co-founded the school mission at St Mary Magdalene's Church, Adelaide, in 1908. The school's preparatory department was opened in 1910, and he strengthened the Old Collegians' Association. He sat on the council of the University of Adelaide from 1901, was a vice-president of the Classical Association of South Australia, president of the Adelaide Rowing Club and an honorary canon of St Peter's Cathedral from 1912. In 1916 he resigned from the school, as he felt that a younger man was required and he doubted his own ability to continue to inspire loyalty and devotion. He helped to run a small school at Hunters Hill, Sydney, and in 1917-19 was acting headmaster of Melbourne Church of England Grammar School while R. P. Franklin [q.v.8] saw military service overseas.

Next year Girdlestone returned to England and was licensed to officiate in the diocese of Bath and Wells in 1922. On 17 September 1900, in Adelaide, he had married Helen Joanna Crawford in his school's chapel. When he died from intestinal neoplasm at his home Hillcote, Lansdown, near Bath, on 29 June 1926, she survived him with their daughter and son; he was buried in Lansdown cemetery.

Melbourne C of E Grammar School, *Liber Melburniensis*, centenary ed (1965); *St Peter's College Mag*, May 1916, Aug 1926; *Mail* (Adel), 14 Dec 1912; A. Grenfell Price, The Collegiate School of St Peter 1847-1947 (SAA); P. C. Girdlestone, Canon Henry Girdlestone (MS), *and* Council of Governors, St Peter's College, Minutes, 1893-1916, *and* Collegiate School of St Peter, School List, 1900, 1905, 1911 (St Peter's College Archives).

SELWYN M. OWEN

GIVENS, THOMAS (1864-1928), miner, sugar worker, newspaper editor and politician, was born on 12 June 1864 at Cappagh White, Tipperary, Ireland, son of Robert Givens, farmer, and his wife Mary Ann, née White. In 1882 he arrived in Queensland and, after a brief period on the North Queensland sugar plantations, spent the following sixteen years on the Charters Towers and neighbouring goldfields, with sorties to New South Wales and Victoria. At Eidsvold he formed a miners' union of which he was successively secretary and president; but as the gold petered out at Eidsvold in the late 1880s he returned to Charters Towers where he became an Australian Workers' Union organizer.

In 1893 the new Labor Party was contesting its first election. Givens was typical of the early Labor candidates. He nominated against S. W. Griffith's [q.v.] protégé and solicitor-general, T. J. Byrnes [q.v.7], for Cairns, where he had established a branch of the A.W.U., and campaigned on an anti-'Kanaka' platform. Byrnes won by 416 votes to 311. Givens contested the seat against another Liberal in 1896 but was again beaten, by 43 votes. In 1898 he established and edited the *Cairns Advocate* and next year, when the Liberals did not field a candidate, won Cairns against the former Labor leader John Hoolan [q.v.]. He married Katie Allen at St John's Church of England, Cairns, on 6 April 1901; they had three sons and three daughters.

Givens's speeches in the Queensland parliament were not notable apart from those on Pacific islands labour. He was strongly opposed to the use of black labour in the canefields and advocated a restriction on the employment of Pacific islanders in factories or within five miles of a factory. During his term in the Queensland parliament, he established a friendship with Andrew Fisher [q.v.8] that was to assist him in his later career. On his defeat at the 1902 State election he returned to the editorship of the *Trinity Times* with which the *Advocate* had merged, but in 1903 he won a Senate place and remained a professional politician for the following twenty-five years.

In Federal politics, although never a possibility for cabinet, Givens was considered a 'good party man'. Melbourne *Punch* described him in 1910 as a pugnacious man with a marked Irish brogue, 'over six feet tall, limbed and muscled on a colossal scale'. From 1908 he was a Queensland delegate to the Labor Party's Interstate (Federal) Conference. In 1912 his compromise proposal to have the conference structured on a basis similar to that of the House of Representatives rather than on a strictly Federal basis was defeated by one vote; the idea waited seventy years for implementation. In 1909 Givens was a member of the Senate select committee on the press cable service; he was temporary chairman of committees in 1910-12 and served on the 1912-13 royal commission on the pearl-shelling industry. When Henry Turley [q.v.], a Queenslander and president of the Senate, stood down after the 1913 election, Givens was elected in his place and held the presidency until 1926. His decisions in the chair revealed a wide knowledge of the standing orders and rules of debate.

As the first Federal president of the Labor Party when the Federal Executive was formed in 1915 Givens gave loyal support to Hughes [q.v.]. Following the withdrawal of the proposed prices referendum in November 1915, he played a major part in having the censure motion against Hughes recommitted and dropped. After Hughes had lost the conscription referendum in October 1916, it was to Givens and (Sir) George Pearce [q.v.] that he turned for advice. Givens left the Labor Party with Hughes and became a Nationalist. He retained the presidency of the Senate and wore the president's wig, in contrast to Turley's practice of appearing bareheaded.

Givens did not attract the same opprobrium from his former Labor colleagues as did some others who left the party over conscription. On his death at Canterbury, Melbourne, of cardiac disease, on 19 June 1928, the Labor newspapers in Queensland were generous about his early role in the party. After a state funeral he was buried in Box Hill cemetery. He was survived by his wife and children and left an estate valued for probate at £9986.

L. F. Crisp, *The Australian Federal Labour Party 1901-1951* (Lond, 1955); D. J. Murphy et al (eds), *Prelude to power* (Brisb, 1970); L. F. Fitzhardinge, *The little digger* (Syd, 1979); *V&P* (LA Qld), 1897, 4, p 253; *British A'sian*, 21 June 1928; *Worker* (Brisb), 14 Jan, 1, 8 Apr 1893, 22 Jan 1910; *Punch* (Melb), 22 Sept 1910; *SMH*, 20 June 1928.

D. J. MURPHY

GLASFURD, DUNCAN JOHN (1873-1916), soldier, was born on 23 November 1873 at Matheran, India, second son of Major General Charles Lamont Robertson Glasfurd of the Bombay Staff Corps, and his wife Jane Cunningham, née Cornwall. His brother Alexander (1870-1942), C.M.G., D.S.O., became a colonel in the Indian Army.

Raised at Altnaskiach, Inverness, Scotland, Glasfurd was educated in Edinburgh—probably at Blairlodge School—and at the Royal Military College, Sandhurst, England. In October 1893 he was commissioned in the 2nd Battalion, Argyll and Sutherland Highlanders, and served as adjutant of the 1st Battalion in South Africa in 1899. He had married Agnes Guinevere Gilmour at Eaglesham, Renfrewshire, on 20 December 1898.

In South Africa Glasfurd was promoted captain in January 1900 and took part in operations in the Orange Free State, receiving slight wounds at Paardeberg; he then saw action in the Transvaal and Orange River Colony until severely wounded in October. In April 1901 he went to British East Africa on operations against the Ogaden Somalis in Jubaland until November. Service in India followed, with an interval in 1903-04 when he served in Somaliland, commanding the 4th Somali Camel Corps; he was mentioned in dispatches.

In June 1908 Glasfurd became staff captain for coast defences, Scottish Command, and that year was selected to attend the Staff College, Camberley, England. He graduated in 1909 and joined his regiment in Malta in May 1910; in November he was appointed brigade major to the Lothian Infantry Brigade. On 24 June 1912 he was seconded to the Australian Military Forces and appointed director of military training at Army Headquarters with the temporary rank of captain, A.M.F. His main duties involved inspection of compulsory training under the cadet scheme, and although enthusiastic over the military potential of Australian youths, he was reportedly dissatisfied with the perfunctory training which many cadets received. Glasfurd was promoted major, British Army and A.M.F., on 20 September 1913.

On the outbreak of war he sought to rejoin his regiment which had been sent to France. Instead, on 15 August 1914, he was appointed by Major General (Sir) William Bridges [q.v.7] to the Australian Imperial Force as a general staff officer with the 1st Division. In Egypt he was largely responsible for training the division at Mena Camp. At Gallipoli he went ashore at 5.35 a.m. on the day of the landing, distinguishing himself by his work in establishing the firing line at Anzac, and served throughout the whole of the campaign. He proved himself, according to the official historian, 'one of the bravest and most conscientious officers upon the Staff' and rose to chief of staff of the division. He was mentioned in dispatches and promoted lieut-colonel, A.I.F., on 1 October 1915 and for outstanding service in the field was made brevet lieut-colonel in the British Army in January 1916.

Next month Glasfurd was given temporary command of the 12th Australian Infantry Brigade; the appointment was con-

firmed in March with promotion to colonel and temporary brigadier general, A.I.F. His brigade was sent to France in June and on 4 July moved into the Fleurbaix sector, where Glasfurd was slightly wounded on 7 July. He was mentioned in dispatches four days later. Early in August the 12th Brigade went into action at Pozières Heights and later at Vierstraat and Diependal. On 12 November 1916 it relieved the 2nd Brigade at Dernafay Wood. That morning Glasfurd was wounded by shell-fire in Cheese Road while reconnoitring the trenches. After a ten-hour stretcher journey from the front line he died at the 38th Casualty Clearing Station at Heilly, though not before his brother—serving with the British 48th Division—found him in a dressing station at Becordel and spoke with him. He was posthumously mentioned in dispatches. His qualities of courage, unselfishness and devotion to duty were highly regarded within his brigade and division. The official historian described him as 'boyish, loyal and devoted, if somewhat old-fashioned', and as 'an able officer with a profound knowledge of his profession, capable of brain, slow of thought but sound of judgement and possessed of . . . hard pluck'.

Glasfurd and his wife had been divorced in October 1914 and when he went on active service their three sons were at Geelong Church of England Grammar School. Charles Eric (1902-1940) joined the Royal Navy in 1916 and was captain of the destroyer *Acasta* during the battle of Narvik; he went down with his ship. Duncan Angus (1905-1980) and Divie Colin Peter (1906-1941) took up sheep-farming in Western Australia. The latter was killed at Tobruk while serving as a captain with 9th Division Headquarters.

C. E. W. Bean, *The story of Anzac* (Syd, 1921, 1924), and *The A.I.F. in France*, 1916 (Syd, 1929); R. C. B. Anderson, *History of the Argyll and Sutherland Highlanders, 1st Battalion, 1909-1939* (Edinburgh, 1954); A. L. Glasfurd, *The Glasfurd family, 1550-1972* (np, nd, c. 1972); *London Gazette*, 2 Sept 1904, 5 Aug 1915, 2 May, 11 July 1916, 2 Jan 1917; *British A'sian*, 23 Nov 1916; *Argus*, 16 Nov 1916; *The Times*, 20 Nov 1916; War diary, 12th Infantry Brigade, A.I.F. (AWM); information from Mrs E. Glasfurd, Claremont, W.A., and Mr A. L. Glasfurd, Lewes, Sussex, England.

C. D. COULTHARD-CLARK

GLASGOW, SIR THOMAS WILLIAM (1876-1955), soldier, politician and diplomat, was born on 6 June 1876 at Tiaro, near Maryborough, Queensland, fourth child and third son of Samuel Glasgow, a farmer from Northern Ireland, and his wife, Mary Margaret Trotter, née Anderson, an English-woman of Scottish descent. 'Bill' Glasgow was educated at the One-Mile State School, Gympie, and Maryborough Grammar School. In 1893 he started work as a junior clerk in the office of a mining company at Gympie and later became a clerk in the Queensland National Bank there. (Sir) Brudenell White [q.v.], a clerk in a rival bank, was among his friends.

While still in his teens Glasgow joined the Wide Bay Regiment, Queensland Mounted Infantry, giving up most of his week-ends to soldiering. In 1897, with nineteen other volunteers he represented Queensland at the diamond jubilee of Queen Victoria in London. He served in the South African War as a lieutenant with the 1st Q.M.I. Contingent, participating in the relief of Kimberley, the capture of Cronje's laager on the Modder and the occupation of Bloemfontein in 1900; on 16 April 1901 he was mentioned in dispatches and awarded the Distinguished Service Order.

Back in Australia Glasgow formed a partnership, T. W. & A. Glasgow, with his younger brother Alexander, and took over his father's Gympie grocery store. On 21 April 1904 at Gympie, with Presbyterian forms, he married Annie Isabel, daughter of Jacob John Stumm, Federal member for Lilley. His dedication to military service continued: in 1903 he organized the 13th Light Horse Regiment at Gympie; he was promoted captain in the Australian Military Forces (militia) in 1906 and major in 1912.

Having relinquished storekeeping, Glasgow had just bought a cattle station in central Queensland when World War I broke out. However he immediately enlisted in the Australian Imperial Force and was appointed major in the 2nd Light Horse Regiment. Three of his six brothers also enlisted. He embarked for Egypt on 24 September 1914 and landed at Gallipoli on 12 May 1915. He succeeded Lieut-Colonel F. M. Rowell as acting commandant of Pope's Hill and from there on 7 August he led 200 New South Wales Light-horsemen in an attack on Dead Man's Ridge. All but 46 were killed or wounded. Glasgow was among the last to retire, carrying with him one of his wounded troopers. Next day he was given command of the 2nd Light Horse and held that appointment, as lieut-colonel, until after the evacuation.

In March 1916 when the 4th and 5th Divisions were formed, Glasgow was promoted temporary brigadier and given the task of raising and commanding the 13th Infantry Brigade. He led his men in many important actions including those at Pozières, Messines, Passchendaele, Mouquet Farm and Dernancourt. He was appointed C.M.G.

in June 1916 and C.B. in December 1917.

On 25 April 1918 the 13th Brigade, together with Brigadier General H. E. Elliott's [q.v.8] 15th Brigade, recaptured the town of Villers-Bretonneux after the Germans had overrun the 8th British Division under General Heneker. It was a feat subsequently described by Lieut-General Sir John Monash [q.v.] as the turning-point of the war, and there was disappointment in 1938 when Glasgow was not present at the opening of the memorial at Villers-Bretonneux. Before the counter-attack Glasgow, having reconnoitred the position, demurred at British orders to attack across the enemy's front. 'Tell us what you want us to do Sir', he said to Heneker, 'but you must let us do it our own way'. He refused to attack at 8 p.m.: 'If it was God Almighty who gave the order, we couldn't do it in daylight'. They attacked successfully at 10 p.m.

On 30 June Glasgow was promoted major general and appointed commander of the 1st Division in Flanders. On 8 August, the fourth anniversary of Glasgow's enlistment, his division rejoined the Australian Corps on the Somme and participated in the massive offensive in August and September. He led the 1st Division with distinction in its major successful engagements at Lihons, Chuignes and Hargicourt.

Glasgow remained with the 1st Division until the end of the war, embarked for Australia on 6 May 1919 and was demobilized on 19 August. He was appointed K.C.B. in recognition of his outstanding war service and was nine times mentioned in dispatches; the French government awarded him the Légion d'honneur and the Croix de Guerre; he also won a Belgian Croix de Guerre. Back in Queensland Glasgow continued on the reserve of officers of the 1st Military District with command (from 1921) of the 4th Division. Then he became honorary colonel of the 5th Light Horse and the 1st Battalion. For twenty years he led the Anzac Day parade in Brisbane as general officer commanding the parade.

C. E. W. Bean [q.v.7] described him as 'the most forcible of the three strong brigadiers of the 4th Division. With keen blue eyes looking from under puckered humorous brows as shaggy as a deer-hound's; with the bushman's difficulty of verbal expression but sure sense of character and situations; with a fiery temper, but cool understanding and a firm control of men; with an entire absence of vanity, but translucent honesty and a standard of rectitude which gave confidence both to superiors and subordinates, he could—by a frown, a shrewd shake of the head, or a twinkle in [the eye] ... awaken in others more energy than would have been evoked by any amount of exhortation'. According to Monash, 'Glasgow succeeded not so much by exceptional mental gifts, or by tactical skill of any very high order, as by his personal driving force and determination'. (Sir) Robert Menzies later described Glasgow as 'the complete personal embodiment of the A.I.F.'.

Glasgow was a stern man in his military views. He joined Brigadier General William Holmes [q.v.] in 1917 in requesting an amendment of the Defence Act to bring it into line with British and New Zealand law so that it would be possible to inflict the death penalty in a few flagrant cases of desertion. In 1918, when 119 men of the 1st Battalion were found guilty of desertion, he refused to recommend remission of the sentences which were, however, not exacted because the war ended. But he was at the same time a great battler for the welfare of his men. Just before the end of the Gallipoli campaign he took 'French leave' from Lemnos, where he had been sent for a few days' rest, to return to Gallipoli to take away the remnants of his regiment; his inspiring voice and wise guidance were valued during those anxious hours. After the war he was an equally stern fighter for the rights of soldiers, though he deprecated extravagant claims to privileges.

In 1919 Sir William Glasgow was elected to the Senate as a Nationalist. He was no orator but his rugged common sense was appreciated and he quickly made his mark in Melbourne. In February 1923 he reluctantly refused the leadership of the non-Labor forces in Queensland with the prospect of becoming premier. He succeeded (Sir) George Pearce [q.v.] as minister for home and territories in the Bruce-Page [qq.v.] government on 18 June 1926. From April 1927 until October 1929 he was minister for defence. In 1928 Glasgow led an Australian delegation to the Empire Parliamentary Association conference in Canada and visited England to study modern war methods. In this period the government completed its five-year defence programme which increased the citizen army to 45 000 and modernized and expanded the Royal Australian Air Force.

During the Scullin [q.v.] government Glasgow was deputy leader of the Opposition in the Senate. He saw his role as that of frustrating Labor's attempt to force its inflationary policy on the nation. But in 1931 Labor polled well in Queensland against the national landslide and Glasgow lost his seat in the Senate. Next year he resumed his pastoral interests in Queensland where he became a director of several companies and, in January 1936, a member of the Queensland board of advice of the National Bank of Australasia Ltd. President of the Queens-

land branch of the United Australia Party, he stressed the necessity for unity among the parties opposed to the 'extremists'.

On 24 December 1939 Glasgow was appointed first Australian high commissioner to Canada where he arrived late in March 1940. His work included negotiation on matters of policy regarding the Empire Air Training Scheme and he regularly visited the far-flung camps and schools in Canada where Australians were training or awaiting embarkation. He made sure the airmen had good conditions and that mail and other amenities were promptly distributed. He established Anzac clubs in Ottawa and Halifax and during his tours publicized the Australian war effort. The University of Manitoba awarded him an honorary LL.D. in 1942.

Glasgow's direct and frank approach won the trust of Prime Minister Mackenzie King and the ministers for external affairs, defence, and munitions and supply. From the time of his arrival he advocated much closer liaison on Pacific strategy and dispositions. He was not so successful in enlisting Mackenzie King's support for Prime Minister Curtin's idea of a British Commonwealth Council and secretariat. In March 1944 an agreement was concluded for 'mutual aid' between Australia and Canada and a mission set up under Glasgow's supervision. The Canadians provided two merchant ships, one of which, the *Taronga Park*, was launched by Lady Glasgow. In August 1943 and September 1944 Glasgow attended the Quebec conferences between Churchill and Roosevelt to be briefed by Churchill and his staff and to register Australian interests. Canadian government advisers recommended Glasgow for consideration as governor-general.

He returned to Australia in 1945 and resumed his pastoral and business interests in Queensland. His last years were spent in Brisbane where he died on 4 July 1955, survived by his wife and two daughters. He was given a state funeral after a service at St Andrew's Presbyterian Church, and was cremated. In 1966 a bronze statue of Glasgow by Daphne Mayo was unveiled at the junction of Roma and Turbot streets in Brisbane. At the ceremony Sir Arthur Fadden described him as 'one of the most distinguished soldiers of our age and generation'.

J. Monash, *The Australian victories in France in 1918* (Lond, 1920); C. E. W. Bean, *The story of Anzac* (Syd, 1921, 1924), and *The A.I.F. in France*, 1916-18 (Syd, 1929, 1933, 1937, 1942); *Reveille* (Syd), 1 Jan 1937; *JRHSQ*, 11 (1979-80), no 1; *Table Talk*, 25 July 1929; *Herald* (Melb), 19 June 1926, 2 May 1931; *Telegraph* (Brisb), 5 July 1955; *SMH*, 9 July 1955.

RALPH HARRY

GLASS, BARNET (1849-1918), rubber manufacturer, was born in March or April 1849 at Walkivich, Russia (Poland), son of Jacob Glass and his wife Sarah, née Tafilstein. As a young man he worked in Manchester, England, where he learned the processes of manufacturing waterproof clothing. On 1 September 1869 at Manchester he married Esther Frazensky; they had two sons and three daughters.

Glass arrived in Victoria probably in 1876 and, unable to establish himself, enlisted the support of Frank Stuart [q.v.] who was then connected with L. Stevenson & Sons, traders in softgoods. Glass imported materials and began manufacturing about 1878 in Carlton. In 1882 he bought land in Queensberry Street, North Melbourne, where he built a factory and employed about twenty-five people. He first manufactured rubberized coats and capes for mounted troopers but soon supplied a variety of rubber garments and accessories including 'Baptist trousers', used by ministers when baptizing by total immersion. By the end of the decade the business had two departments: general clothing and waterproof garment manufacture. In 1890 Glass went to England to buy modern plant and machinery, but had to cancel his orders. However, his business prospered despite the depression and in 1894 an office was opened in London and a branch factory, the Pioneer Rubber Co., in Adelaide. In 1893 Glass patented in England, the United States of America and the Australian colonies, a rubber garment called the Hercules.

Two sons, Jacob and Ernest Ezekiel, were already employed in the business, while a son-in-law, F. S. Ornstein (afterwards Ormiston), went to England in the late 1890s for further experience. Barnet's nephew and son-in-law, Philip Joseph Glass, took charge of the Adelaide branch and organized the shipment of plant and machinery for the new Pioneer Rubber Factory of Australia, opened at Kensington, Melbourne, in August 1899.

In October 1900 Glass converted his business into a company, Barnet Glass & Sons Pty Ltd, and became its managing director at a salary of £500 for an agreed period of ten years. In 1905 the Dunlop Pneumatic Tyre Co. (Dunlop Rubber Co. of Australasia) bought the business. In the preliminary negotiations Glass stipulated that he be retained as managing director for the unexpired term of his contract, but on completion of the transfer he was offered only an insecure post as manager of the waterproof clothing department. He refused the post, sued the Dunlop Co. and was awarded, with costs, £1000 of the £3000 sought. Glass claimed in his evidence that he would find it difficult to establish himself again in competition with Dunlop's, which had acquired not only the factory but his trained staff and customers. However he soon bought land at Footscray, built a factory and plant and, with his two sons and his sons-in-law, began work as Glass & Co. In 1908 the firm was converted into a public company, Barnet Glass Rubber Co. Ltd. As well as manufacturing rubber, the company were agents for Michelin motor tyres. By 1918 Glass had branches in every Australian State and in New Zealand. His tyres had early won distinction—'miles cheaper and Australian' —while his Boomerang anti-skid tread tyres were famous by 1917. In 1929 the company merged with its old rival the Dunlop Rubber Co. Barnet Glass Co. manufactured and traded as a separate organization until 1937, when its manufacturing activities at Footscray were transferred to the Dunlop factories.

Glass took an active part in Jewish communal affairs as a member of the executives of the East Melbourne synagogue, the Jewish Philanthropic Society and the Jewish Education Board. His first wife had died on 26 June 1910. On 16 November that year at St Kilda he married Esther Moses. She survived him, together with the children of his first marriage, on his death on 18 March 1918 at St Kilda. He was buried in Melbourne general cemetery. His estate was sworn for probate at £12 874.

A. Sutherland et al, *Victoria and its metropolis*, 2 (Melb, 1888); J. Smith (ed), *Cyclopedia of Victoria*, 1 (Melb, 1903); H. Michell (ed), *Footscray's first fifty years* (Footscray, 1909); *Vic Law Reports* (1906); *A'sian Manufacturer*, 16 Mar 1918; *Aust Storekeepers & Traders J*, Mar 1895, Sept 1899, Mar, May, Aug 1906; *Sluyter's Mthly*, Jan 1922; *Jewish Herald*, 23 Mar 1918; Barnet Glass Co., Records (LaTL, *and* Univ Melb Archives).

KATHLEEN THOMSON

GLASSEY, THOMAS (1844-1936), politician, was born on 26 February 1844 at Markethill, Armagh, Ireland, son of Wilhelm Glassey, mill hand, and his wife Susannah, who died when Thomas was an infant. First employed at 6 in linen mills, he became a letter-carrier and then at 13 left an unhappy home to live with a married sister in Scotland and work in coal-mines. Self-educated, he became a trade-union activist, was blacklisted and was forced in 1867 to move to Bedlington in Northumberland, England. At Airdrie, Scotland, on 3 August 1864, he had married Margaret White; they had six sons and four daughters. Overwork in organizing a franchise reform campaign sent him into a Dublin hospital in 1877. He then worked in a Bedlington co-operative store, became an auctioneer and was a member of the Bedlington Local Board in 1881-83.

Glassey and his family sailed for Queensland in the *Merkara* on 23 September 1884. Settling first at Bundaberg, he soon moved to Brisbane, joined the Post Office briefly, then became an auctioneer in Fortitude Valley. At the request of coalminer friends, he called the meeting in 1886 at Bundamba which created the Ipswich Coal Miners' Mutual Protective Association of which he became secretary.

Elected to the Legislative Assembly in May 1888 as a trade union candidate supporting the Liberals, he was soon respected for his pugnacity and devotion to principle. Although his zealous moralizing irritated other members, it won votes from newspaper readers who did not have to listen to him. His radical notion that only those few with capital had the opportunity to practise the classical liberal creed and that *laissez faire* liberalism merely gave ideological legitimacy to the maintenance of social and moral evils, was premature in Queensland.

Accepted by the Australian Labor Federation, Glassey accompanied Gilbert Casey [q.v.7] and Albert Hinchcliffe [q.v.] on a triumphant organizing trip in the north and west. His effective membership of a factories and works commission ensured radical recommendations, and his defence of union interests after the shearing strike of 1891 made him the idol of unionists but most unpopular in parliament. When three more Labor members were elected, the party held its first convention in August 1892; Glassey presided as central executive chairman.

At the 1893 election he joined Sir Charles Lilley [q.v.5] in an attempt to unseat Sir Thomas McIlwraith [q.v.5] from North Brisbane. It was a miscalculation. Glassey himself was defeated and failed again when he tried Bundamba. Financed by a public subscription, he toured New Zealand and the United States of America for his health. On his return John Plumper Hoolan [q.v.] resigned his Burke seat in May 1894; Glassey won it and succeeded Hoolan as Labor leader. Slightly built, with a loud voice, he was eminently honest and respectable, yet lacked ability as leader. He abandoned Burke in 1896 to challenge a ministerial supporter in Bundaberg, won easily and for some time was able to pacify the opposing factions. In 1898 the Labor Party finally became the formal parliamentary Opposition and in his role as leader he represented Queensland on the Federal Council of Australasia. He was now increasingly falling out with his party colleagues.

Following the death of his wife in 1899

Glassey declined nomination as leader and began to urge the unpopular causes of Federation and support for the British in South Africa. He refused to join the short-lived ministry of Andrew Dawson [q.v.8], then resigned as Labor member for Bundaberg, renominated as an Independent and resoundingly defeated Hinchcliffe, the endorsed Labor candidate.

Standing as a Protectionist Glassey became a senator for Queensland in 1901. Although his White Australia speech was one of the most effective delivered in the new parliament, he was defeated in 1903. Inclined now to rural populism, he maintained a keen interest in reform, contested Bundamba and Fortitude Valley in 1904 and 1907 and tried again for the Senate in 1910, but was always defeated. He served the State government in 1911-12 as an immigration officer in England, and in 1917 was a founder of the Nationalist Party in Queensland. A director of the New Aberdare Colliery Ltd from 1913, he lived simply, died in Brisbane on 28 September 1936 and was buried in Toowong cemetery with Presbyterian forms.

JRHSQ, 4 (1946), no 2; *Brisbane Courier*, 21 May 1886, 27 Feb 1891, 16 Aug, 8, 12, 15, 17 Sept 1894; *Courier Mail*, 26 May 1886, 2 Mar 1896, 27 Feb 1934; *Qld Times*, 26 Apr, 10 May 1888; *Boomerang*, 23 June 1888; *Worker* (Brisb), 2 May, 25 July 1891, 3 Dec 1892, 22 Apr, 13 May 1893, 15 Sept 1894, 12 Dec 1903; I. Lipke, Thomas Glassey . . . (M.A. qual thesis, Univ Qld, 1975); S. A. Rayner, The evolution of the Queensland Labor Party to 1907 (M.A. thesis, Univ Qld, 1947); Glassey papers (Oxley Lib).
                                                          IAN LIPKE

GLAUERT, LUDWIG (1879-1963), museum curator, was born on 5 May 1879 at Ecclesall Bierlow, Yorkshire, England, son of Johann Ernst Louis Glauert, merchant and cutlery manufacturer, and his wife Amanda, née Watkinson. He was educated in Sheffield at the grammar school, Firth (University) College and the Technical School; he trained as a geologist. In 1900 he became a fellow of the Geological Society of London. He worked as a demonstrator for four years at the college and then for his father. In 1908 he migrated to Western Australia with his wife Winifrede Aimée, née Berresford.

In July Glauert joined the Geological Survey in Perth as a palaeontologist, and helped to arrange the collections of the Western Australian Museum: for two years he identified, classified and described material collected by his superiors in the field. In 1910 he joined the permanent staff as the director's scientific assistant and was promoted in 1914 to keeper of geology and ethnology. In 1909-15 he carried out field-work on the Pleistocene limestone of the Margaret River Caves, investigating the discovery there of the remains of several species of the extinct marsupial and monotreme fauna and the remains of Victorian and Tasmanian mammals, whose presence in Western Australia had never been suspected. Sir Winthrop Hackett [q.v.] commented 'they had got a little gold mine out of the block of limestone on which Mr Glauert's hands had wrought such marvellous results'. He was also interested in the Aboriginals, was a conservationist, and as 'Jay Penne' contributed to the *West Australian*.

On 3 October 1917 Glauert enlisted in the Australian Imperial Force and served briefly overseas. After the war he lectured to servicemen on scientific subjects and studied Australian natural history material in the British Museum. On returning to Perth in 1920, he became keeper of the biological collections at the Western Australian Museum; during this period he described a new phreatoicid isopod which stimulated interest in the group. In 1927 he was appointed curator (director from 1954) of the museum.

Glauert completed an arts degree at the university in 1928. He was an indefatigable collector in his spare time and produced many papers on fields as diverse as stratigraphical geology, palaeontology, zoogeography, entomology, carcinology, mammalogy, herpetology, ornithology, arachnology and ethnology. However, field-work and the acquisition of specimens for the museum by direct collecting in the years between the wars was virtually suspended because of pitifully inadequate funding and staff: for years Glauert was the only scientist, with a taxidermist and one technical assistant. He used his private means to purchase books for the museum.

He made a zoological survey at Rottnest Island, however, and in 1930, with C. F. H. Jenkins, described for the first time the breeding habits of the banded stilt; he did valuable work on Australian scorpions and became an acknowledged authority on Western Australian reptiles. In 1938, funded by the Carnegie Corporation of New York, he toured overseas museums. This resulted in his modernizing the display areas of the Perth museum, but World War II checked these developments. In 1945 Glauert received the Royal Society of Western Australia's medal; he was president of the society in 1933 and 1947.

Glauert's principles of museum management were to instruct and inspire the amateur; to build up a store of research material for the professional biologist; and to educate and hold the interest of the general public. His enthusiastic approach, especially with young people, made him a catalyst; he was sanguine, bold and optimistic. The museum became a meeting-place for the Royal Society, the Western Australian Naturalists' Club and the Western Australian Gould League, in all of which he was active. His articles, lectures and broadcasts ensured that the institution received a constant flow of specimens. In 1948 he was awarded the Australian Natural History medallion and he was appointed M.B.E. after retiring in 1956.

Glauert published handbooks on the snakes and lizards of Western Australia in 1950 and 1961. In retirement he continued work on reptiles and scorpions. Survived by three daughters and a son, he died in Perth on 1 February 1963 and his ashes were scattered at sea off his home beach at Cottesloe. Glauert's oil portrait by E. Buckmaster hangs in his old museum.

PP (LA WA), 1909, 1 (6); Roy Soc WA, *J*, 31 (1944-45), p vi, 62, (1979), p 33; *WA Naturalist*, 5 (1957), p 148, 8 (1963), p 189; *Emu* (Melb), 63 (1963), p 74; *Daily News* (Perth), 10 Dec 1928; *Countryman* (Perth), 20 Feb 1963.

C. F. H. JENKINS

GLEDSON, DAVID ALEXANDER (1877-1949), trade union leader and politician, was born in 1877 at Saintfield, Down, Ireland, son of William Gledson, miner, and his wife Mary, née Magill. Migrating to Queensland in 1885, the family settled at Bundamba where David was educated at the local state school. Going to work early in the Bundamba mine, he was inspired with union ideals by Gilbert Casey [q.v.7]. Blacklisted and dismissed from Bundamba, he followed his father into the Tivoli pit. After a strike in 1905, he helped to found the Queensland Colliery Employees' Union.

Active in union and Labor politics, he qualified as an accountant in night classes at the Ipswich Technical College, won a certificate of competency as a mine-manager, and in 1908 was appointed first full-time secretary of his union at £150 a year. Under his lead the union embarked on a period of expansion and consolidation and, after he became a district check-inspector in 1910, on a programme to improve conditions in Queensland mines. A strong supporter of the federation of State mining unions, Gledson represented Queensland at the 1915 meeting in Sydney which brought the Australasian Coal and Shale Employees' Federation into being. Shortly afterwards, he resigned as Q.C.E.U. secretary but remained on the executive for some time as treasurer.

Unsuccessfully contesting the State seat of Bundamba for the Labor Party in 1908 and 1909, Gledson won Ipswich in 1915 and became a back-bencher in T. J. Ryan's [q.v.] victorious party. Representing small unions on the Queensland central executive in 1916-20 and as an elected convention delegate in 1920-32, he was also a member of the A.L.P.'s inner executive in 1926-28. Elected to the cabinet on 21 October 1925, he was minister without portfolio till 6 September 1926, then secretary for labour and industry. When the government was defeated in May 1929 Gledson also lost Ipswich but both he and the A.L.P. were returned at the general election of June 1932. In the Forgan Smith [q.v.] ministry of 1932-42 he was additional member of the Executive Council and assistant secretary for agriculture and stock in February-July 1939, secretary for mines in 1939-41 and attorney-general from 8 December 1941. He retained this portfolio in the Cooper and Hanlon ministries, dying in office of cerebro-vascular disease at Ipswich on 14 May 1949. He was buried in Ipswich cemetery with Methodist forms. A son and four daughters were issue of his marriage at Bundamba on 24 February 1904 to Susannah Jane Bird.

Like so many Ipswich workers and their families at that period, Gledson was a staunch and active Methodist. While his tenure as a parliamentarian and minister was long, he was best remembered for his service to the trade union movement. As the champion of their cause, 'Davie' Gledson won the abiding loyalty and allegiance of the miners of the West Moreton field.

E. Ross, *A history of the Miners' Federation of Australia* (Syd, 1970); D. J. Murphy, R. B. Joyce and C. A. Hughes (eds), *Labor in power... Queensland 1915-1957* (Brisb, 1979); *Daily Standard*, 18 May 1915.   MARGARET BRIDSON CRIBB

GLENCROSS, ELEANOR (1876-1950), feminist and housewives' advocate, was born on 11 November 1876 at 61 Cleveland Street, Sydney, eldest daughter of Angus Cameron [q.v.3], carpenter, trade unionist and politician, and his native-born wife Eleanor, née Lyons. Educated at Cleveland Street Public School and Miss Somerville's Ladies' College, she gained an early political education assisting her father. She later worked for the Liberal and Reform Association.

Noted for her eloquence, Eleanor in 1911 became general secretary, chief speaker and organizer of the Australian Women's National League in Melbourne. Next year she worked for the rival People's Liberal Party, returning to Sydney in 1913 to become women's organizer for the Liberal Association of New South Wales. At St Stephen's Presbyterian Church, she married Andrew William Glencross, a grazier, on 14 March 1917. She moved to Stawell, Victoria, and later that year helped in the pro-conscription campaign in Melbourne.

At the end of World War I Eleanor Glencross became an honorary director of the Strength of Empire Movement, which advocated prohibition. Like her father, she had a lifelong interest in liquor reform, working at various times for the Woman's Christian Temperance Union, the Victorian Prohibition League and the temperance committee of the Presbyterian Church of Victoria. In 1920 she became president of the Housewives' Association of Victoria, which had been formed by Ivy Brookes [q.v.7 H. Brookes] to educate working-class women in thrifty housekeeping. Under Glencross in the 1920s the association aimed at lowering the cost of living by political lobbying and co-operative stores. In 1923 she became president of the Federated Housewives' Association of Australia.

An executive-member in 1918-28 and president in 1927-28 of the National Council of Women of Victoria, Glencross lobbied for support for female candidates for public office and in 1922 encouraged the formation of the Victorian Women Citizens' Movement. She failed three times to enter parliament as an Independent: the Federal seat of Henty in 1922, the Victorian seat of Brighton in 1928 and the Federal seat of Martin in 1943. In 1923 she served on the Victorian royal commission on the high cost of living; her minority report called for prices legislation. In 1927 she was among the first female justices of the peace appointed in Victoria.

On her appointment to the Commonwealth Film Censorship Board in December 1928, Glencross transferred her activities to Sydney, but was not reappointed by the incoming Labor government. Later she was an active president of the Good Film and Radio Vigilance League of New South Wales. On the death of her husband in 1930 she was left economically insecure. Next year she joined the staff of the National Association of New South Wales and later worked for the women's section of the United Australia Party. In 1938 she became salaried chairwoman of directors of the Housewives' Association of New South Wales and henceforth frequently clashed with Portia Geach [q.v.8]. As the result of an inquiry into the association's administration in 1941 and its alleged arrangement with the Meadow-Lea Margarine Co., it was reorganized, but increasingly Glencross was accused of 'dictatorship'.

During World War II she was prominent in patriotic activities as a member of the State advisory committee of the Commonwealth prices commissioner, the council of the Lord Mayor's Patriotic and War Fund and of the executive of the Women's Voluntary National Register. In 1946 she was bankrupted by a defamation suit brought by Mrs Margaret Simson, whom she had expelled from the Housewives' Association. However Glencross remained chairwoman of the association until she died, childless, at her home at Cremorne on 2 May 1950. She was buried in the Presbyterian section of Rookwood cemetery.

Forthright in her speech and opinions, an inveterate letter-writer and often the centre of turbulence, Eleanor Glencross had devoted her life to improving the conditions of women and children in the home. Described as 'truly feminine' by her supporters, she seemed never to have seen any contradiction between her own public career and the domestic role that she enhanced and exalted as the true occupation for Australian women.

Report of Roy Com into the high cost of living, *V&P* (LA Vic), 1923-24, 2 (38), 1924, 1 (3) (5) (6); *Housewife* (Melb), 5 Sept, 5 Nov 1929; *Progressive J* (Syd), 1 June 1935; *Argus*, 3 Jan, 1 Aug 1911, 1 Feb 1912, 5 Mar 1930; *SMH*, 22 Oct 1927, 18, 21 Jan 1930, 31 Mar 1931, 10 Sept 1941, 9-11 Oct 1941, 18 Mar 1942, 29 Oct 1946, 5 May 1950; National Council of Women (Vic), Executive *and* Council minutes (NL); Brookes papers (NL).

MEREDITH FOLEY

GLOSSOP, JOHN COLLINGS TASWELL (1871-1934), naval officer, was born on 23 October 1871 at Twickenham, Middlesex, England, son of George Goodwin Pownall Glossop, vicar of Twickenham, and his wife Eliza Maria, née Trollope. Passing out of H.M.S. *Britannia* in 1887, he served for a short time in the Channel Fleet. His lifelong association with Australia began in 1888 when he arrived as a midshipman in H.M.S. *Orlando*, flagship of the Australian Squadron. He was then transferred to H.M.S. *Calliope* and to H.M.S. *Egeria*, both serving in the Pacific. Promoted sublieutenant in 1891 and lieutenant in 1893, he specialized in navigation, returning to the Australia Station in 1896 as navigating officer of H.M.S. *Royalist*.

Glossop returned to England in 1900 and after two years as an instructor in *Britannia* was given his first command, H.M.S. *Lizard*, in June 1902. This gunboat had only a short commission in Australian and New Zealand waters before being sold in 1904. Promoted commander in June, he was appointed draft-

ing commander at the Royal Naval Barracks, Chatham. He came back to Australia in 1908 in command of H.M.S. *Prometheus*, a protected cruiser. Much of the next two years was spent in the Pacific Islands. From *Prometheus* he returned to England and was promoted captain in June 1911. Officially reported by the Australian naval representative in London as being 'anxious to command a ship of the R.A.N.' and 'in entire sympathy with the Australian Navy movement', he was given command of the new light cruiser, H.M.A.S. *Sydney*, in June 1913; he had held the R.A.N. rank of captain since March. *Sydney* sailed for Australia in company with the new flagship, the battle-cruiser H.M.A.S. *Australia*, and received a tumultuous welcome on arrival in Sydney in October.

In the early months of World War I, *Sydney* searched for enemy warships off northern New Guinea and took part in the capture of Rabaul. She then proceeded to Albany, Western Australia, to escort the first Australian and New Zealand troop-convoy to Egypt. On 9 November 1914 the convoy was some fifty miles (80 km) off the Cocos Islands when the wireless station there reported the presence of a German cruiser. *Sydney* was detached to investigate. The raider, the light cruiser *Emden*, stood out to sea and engaged *Sydney* at extreme range, killing four sailors and destroying the range-finder before *Sydney* opened fire. However, *Sydney*, with the advantage in speed and armament, thereafter stayed out of *Emden*'s range, reducing her to a blazing shambles and driving her aground. *Sydney* left to pursue the fleeing collier, *Buresk*, took off her crew and watched her sink, then returned to *Emden* to find her ensign still flying. Glossop's demands for surrender were ignored; he fired two salvos after which the ensign came down and white flags were shown. No assistance could be given to *Emden* immediately as the German landing-party on Direction Island had to be dealt with. Glossop was unaware that they had escaped in a schooner after destroying the wireless station but *Sydney*'s diversion to the island meant that medical aid was not given to *Emden* until late next day. With the last survivors, including Captain von Müller, transhipped, *Sydney* made for Colombo to rejoin the convoy.

Emden had cut a swathe of destruction through British and allied shipping in the Indian Ocean and the news of her end was received with jubilation. Glossop was congratulated by the Australian Naval Board but has been criticized since both for being caught by *Emden*'s first salvo and for firing on the wreck. Basing his assessment of *Emden* on the standard references, he was unaware of modifications to her guns which increased their range, and was initially caught by surprise; he correctly fought the remainder of the action out of his enemy's reach. The final shots at *Emden*, provoked by the defiant flying of her battle ensign and the possibility that she could still resist with torpedoes and rifle-fire, were necessary to compel a definite sign of surrender, namely, the white flag. Glossop cannot be reproached for doing his duty according to the usages of naval warfare even though he himself, a genuinely humane man, found it very painful—'it makes me feel almost like a murderer'.

Although they were arduous years of command for Glossop, the remaining war service of *Sydney* patrolling in the Caribbean, the Atlantic and the North Sea was in a sense a protracted anticlimax. On 9 February 1917 he was relieved by Captain J. S. Dumaresq [q.v.8] and sailed for Australia to take up the three-year appointment of captain-in-charge of naval establishments, Sydney. This post, third in importance in the Australian Navy, brought him into sustained contact with civilian attitudes to the war; deeply patriotic himself, he was upset by the slowness of recruiting and the difficulties involved in dealing with unions in the manning and coaling of ships.

Glossop was promoted commodore second class on 1 March 1919 and in June presided over the controversial court-martial of mutineers of H.M.A.S. *Australia*. The severity of the sentences caused a political uproar and he was attacked in the Federal parliament. He was defended by the acting navy minister but the affair may have contributed to his failure to be appointed Australian naval representative in London, a post for which he was recommended by the Naval Board. He reverted to the Royal Navy in October 1920, and after a short period as coast guard captain at Queenstown, Ireland, was promoted rear admiral on 20 November 1921 and retired next day. He became a vice admiral on the retired list in 1926.

Glossop had been mentioned in dispatches early in 1914, was appointed C.B. after destroying the *Emden* and in 1917 was awarded the Japanese Order of the Rising Sun and the Légion d'honneur. On 19 January 1918 he had married Ethel Alison McPhillamy at All Saints Anglican Cathedral, Bathurst, New South Wales. They had a daughter and a son who became a Royal Navy officer. In retirement Glossop lived near Bridport, Dorset, England, and was active in the Anglican Church, local hospital and British Legion affairs; he relaxed with fly-fishing and philately. Survived by his family, he died of septicaemia at Weymouth on 23 December 1934 and was cremated. He

is commemorated by tablets in Bothenhampton Church, Dorset, and in the naval chapel, Garden Island, Sydney. A portrait by James Quinn [q.v.] is in the Australian War Memorial.

Described by the *Bulletin* as a 'suave, bald, soft-voiced little man who looked the antithesis of a fire-eater', and to his officers 'the embodiment of the true English gentleman', Glossop exemplified the best type of naval officer of his generation. Dedicated to his profession, respected and well-liked by his men, and chivalrous to the defeated, he has an enduring place as commander in the first sea battle of the Royal Australian Navy.

A. W. Jose, *The Royal Australian Navy 1914-18* (Syd, 1928); E. Scott, *Australia during the war* (Syd, 1936); R. Hyslop, *Australian naval administration 1900-1939* (Melb, 1973); *Reveille* (Syd), Feb 1935; *SMH*, 13 Apr, 15, 16, 25 May, 28 June, 31 Aug, 25 Sept, 22 Dec 1917, 1 May 1918, 13 Apr 1920, 26 Dec 1934, 4 Nov 1935; *The Times*, 24 Dec 1934; *Bridport News*, 27 Dec 1934; *Bulletin* (Syd), 2 Jan 1935; MP 427, 525, 124/6, 1587, *and* SP 339/1 (AAO); *Sydney-Emden* file (AWM); family papers held by Lt Cdr J. J. Glossop, St Ives, Syd; information from Mr E. C. Boston, Croydon, Syd, *and* Mr R Hyslop, Yarralumla, Canb.

DENIS FAIRFAX

GLOVER, CHARLES RICHMOND JOHN (1870-1936), lord mayor, public benefactor, businessman and book collector, was born on 3 May 1870 at Richmond, Surrey, England, son of Charles Peter Glover, publican, and his wife Hannah, née Shortland, who were holidaying in Britain. His father had migrated to Adelaide in 1855 and his mother in 1859. Together they took over the Plough & Harrow Hotel in Rundle Street. Charles was educated at Prince Alfred College in 1882-87 and then qualified as a pharmaceutical chemist, having been articled with F. H. Faulding [q.v.4] & Co. For six years from 1898 he was a sharebroker on the Adelaide Stock Exchange. On 17 May 1900, at St John's Church, Adelaide, he married Elizabeth Maude Hannam. In 1903 the Plough & Harrow (later Richmond) Hotel was transferred to him and on his mother's death in 1913 he inherited half her estate of £32 000.

Glover had begun a career on the Adelaide City Council in 1906. He was an alderman from 1909 to 1917 when he became mayor. In 1919 he became Adelaide's first lord mayor, a position he also held in 1923-25 and 1930-33, when he retired. His period as a civic father saw the development from a geometric village to a consciously beautiful city. Glover held *ex officio* positions on numerous civic bodies including the board of management of the Adelaide Hospital, the Metropolitan County Board, the Botanic Garden Board and the Municipal Tramways Trust. He was active in a bewildering variety of charitable, philanthropic, public utility, cultural and sporting bodies. In 1919 he initiated and donated part of the cost for the War Memorial Drive on the northern banks of Torrens Lake and he presented three children's playgrounds to the city. He was a patron of many local sporting clubs. Hardly a day passed without meetings. His business positions included chairman of directors of the Imperial Building Society, and director of the Bank of Adelaide, the United Insurance Co. and the South Australian Gas Co.

Glover visited England in 1891, 1904, 1921 and 1933. He published in the church paper 'A brief history of the Church of St John the Evangelist, Adelaide, 1839-1909' and *A history of the first fifty years of Freemasonry in South Australia, 1834-84* (1916). He had been a devoted Freemason: after being deputy, in 1909 he was elected grand secretary of the Grand Lodge, a position he held until 1936.

After his purchase in 1914 of St Andrews, a spacious mansion in North Adelaide, Glover developed his library and ethnological collection. He specialized in books on Australasia and the South Sea, largely acquired between 1912 and 1934, keeping thorough records of his purchases from Australian booksellers and on his overseas trips; he had his own bookplate. The greater part of his library, one of the major Australian collections, was sold at auction in Melbourne in 1970. Many of his Aboriginal artefacts had originally been collected by Charles Chewings [q.v.7] on his travels between Alice Springs and Newcastle Waters, and by George Aiston, protector of Aboriginals. Glover ceased acquiring ethnological material about 1920. Most of it was sold by auction in Sydney in 1970.

Of medium height, bespectacled, and with dark hair that receded early, Glover was a meticulous hoarder of receipts, invitations, menus and ephemera invaluable to historians. He maintained detailed inventories of his furniture, pictures and other possessions. He is privately remembered as being generous, considerate, tolerant, a very good employer, and one who conducted all his duties honourably and thoroughly. But this quiet person of high ideals, who embodied the concepts of duty and civic responsibility, was never formally honoured for his assiduous service to his State. Survived by his wife, a son and a daughter, he died of cancer on 27 October 1936 and was buried in the family vault in West Terrace cemetery. His estate was sworn for probate

at £27 737. An oil portrait of Glover by Alfred Gant is in the Adelaide Town Hall where his son John also served as lord mayor in 1960-63.

Universal Publicity Co., *The official civic record of South Australia* (Adel, 1936); Adel City Council, *Annual Report*, and *Notice Papers*, 1906-36; *Year book of the City of Adelaide*, 1919, 1924; *Aust Book Review*, Oct 1970, p 325; *Advertiser* (Adel), 28 Oct 1936; Glover papers, PRG 310 (SAA).

VALMAI A. HANKEL

GLYNN, PATRICK McMAHON (1855-1931), Federationist, politician and lawyer, was born on 25 August 1855 at Gort, Galway, Ireland, third of the eleven children of John McMahon Glynn (1824-1879), who ran a large general store in the town square, and his wife Ellen, née Wallsh (1835-1918). Glynn received his primary education at Gort from the Sisters of Mercy whose convent superior, Mother Mary Aloysius, had nursed with Florence Nightingale in the Crimea. From February 1869 he boarded for three and a half years at French (later Blackrock) College, conducted by the Holy Ghost Fathers on the outskirts of Dublin, and won prizes in French, Greek and Latin before being articled to James Blaquiere, a Dublin solicitor. In 1875 Glynn entered Trinity College, Dublin, and in 1876-77 was also enrolled at the King's Inns. After graduating B.A. from Trinity in July 1878, he studied law at the Middle Temple in London, and was called to the Irish Bar in April next year. But he confided to his diary: 'the good opinion' of many friends, 'the flattering hopes of others, and a not altogether empty brief bag during ... sixteen months membership of the Irish Bar' did not prove 'a sufficient inducement to remain at home'. On 4 September 1880 he sailed from London to Melbourne where he obtained temporary admission to the Victorian Bar.

In Melbourne, however, attendance at the courts, the publication of a thirty-two page pamphlet (*Irish state trials*) and speeches for political societies brought him not a single brief. 'Trying to get business here as a stranger', he wrote to his brother James, 'is like attacking the devil with an icicle'. In January 1882 he eventually got some work—as a travelling agent for the Mutual Life Assurance Society and Singer sewing-machines. Six months later the Adelaide law firm of Hardy & Davis brought him to South Australia to open a branch office at Kapunda. The chance came through Glynn's aunt, Grace Wallsh, who had migrated to Australia in the 1860s and was one of the first companions of Mother Mary McKillop [q.v.5] in founding the Sisters of St Joseph.

On 21 July 1883 Glynn was admitted as a practitioner of the South Australian Supreme Court (he took out his LL.B. from Trinity in December), and by 1886 had done well enough to buy the Kapunda practice for £155. He retained it when he moved to Adelaide in 1888 and opened a practice in Pirie Street. In 1883-91 he was also editor of the *Kapunda Herald*. Alongside his legal and editorial work, he entered quickly into the political life of the colony, and in 1884 helped to found the South Australian Land Nationalisation Society, for which he himself wrote a manifesto. The basic views, taken from Henry George [q.v.4], involved land nationalization, complete free trade, and a single tax, namely the land-tax. He became for many years president of the Irish National League in South Australia.

In April 1887 Glynn was elected to the House of Assembly as junior member for Light. During his first term, by advocating free trade he aligned himself with the conservatives; by supporting payment of members, female suffrage and reform of the Upper House, he found himself with the liberals and radicals; while his championing of land nationalization tended to isolate him. He lost his seat in 1890—partly through the farming community's dislike for his philosophy of land tenure. In 1893 he stood again for Light without success, but in 1895 he was returned in a by-election for North Adelaide—the first election in Australian history to be held under adult suffrage. He was a close friend of the premier, C. C. Kingston [q.v.], though they differed on many political issues. Glynn lost his seat at the election next year, but won it back in a by-election of 1897 and, retaining it in 1899, became attorney-general in the short-lived V. L. Solomon [q.v.] government.

In 1897 'Paddy' Glynn was elected as one of the ten South Australian delegates to the federal convention. At the first session in Adelaide he established a reputation for his knowledge of constitutional law, thorough research into the topic under discussion, rapid delivery, broad brogue and general learning. Alfred Deakin [q.v.8] believed that 'if not the best-read man of the Convention', Glynn 'certainly carried more English prose and poetry in his memory than any three or four of his associates'. With H. B. Higgins and (Sir) Josiah Henry Symon [qq.v.], Glynn led the judiciary committee, which together with the constitutional and finance committees prepared a draft bill. During the Sydney session of the convention in September he brightened proceedings by what the *Bulletin* called his 'meteor-like rush into matrimony'. Within a week he wrote a letter of proposal, was accepted by telegram, slipped down to Melbourne, married Abigail Dynon

on 11 September at St Francis Church and returned to Sydney. King O'Malley [q.v.] was his best man. At the final session of the convention in Melbourne next year Glynn made his best-known contribution to the Constitution, a reference to God in the preamble ('humbly relying on the blessing of Almighty God').

Elected to the House of Representatives as a Free Trader in 1901, Glynn began two decades of service in the Commonwealth parliament. He was returned unopposed for the division of Angas in 1903, won easily against a Labor candidate in 1906, was unopposed again in 1910, 1913 and 1914, just got home against a Labor candidate in 1917, and lost his seat to Labor in December 1919. Glynn served as attorney-general in Deakin's Fusion government (1909-10), minister for external affairs in the Cook [q.v.8.] (Liberal) administration (1913-14), and minister for home and territories in W. M. Hughes's [q.v.] Nationalist government from 1917.

The control and use of Australia's inland rivers proved Glynn's most enduring political interest. He doggedly contributed to that cause from his membership in 1889-94 of the South Australian royal commission on the Murray waters through to the Commonwealth River Murray Waters Act (1915). In 1905 he prepared for the South Australian government two volumes of legal opinion on the Murray riparian rights. He was appointed K.C. in July 1913. Glynn vigorously supported Australia's role in World War I; Home Rule for Ireland (in the mitigated form of a local parliament with limited powers); the welfare of the New Hebrideans under the Anglo-French Condominium; (Sir) Hubert Murray's [q.v.] policies in Papua; fair treatment of enemy aliens during and after World War I; the proper administration and development of the Northern Territory under Commonwealth control; and decimal coinage. In 1918-19 he had the unhappy task of handling the Darwin rebellion. At the invitation of the Empire Parliamentary Association he had visited France and the United Kingdom in 1916.

After his defeat in 1919 Glynn resumed full-time legal work. He had taken (Sir) Herbert Angas Parsons [q.v.] as partner in 1897 and George McEwin and (Sir) Mellis Napier later joined the firm. He was the last of the 'founding fathers' to sit in the Commonwealth parliament and in 1927 attended the opening of the new parliament house in Canberra as one of the three survivors of the 1901 session.

A non-smoker and from 1883 a teetotaller, Glynn was a dapper man about 5 ft. 4 ins. (163 cm) tall who wore a bushy moustache. At hunts he was a fearless rider and his reputation as a sportsman contributed to his political success. A person of extraordinary integrity and industry, his oratorical powers, humour and learning made him a consistently popular speaker for literary and national societies. The more eloquent his speech, the thicker became his brogue. He could quote Shakespeare to illuminate any political, legal, business or social occasion. His letters to his family, edited by G. O'Collins and including a bibliography of his published works, were published in 1974.

He died of pneumonia on 28 October 1931 at North Adelaide and was buried in West Terrace cemetery; he was survived by two sons and four daughters, his wife having predeceased him in 1930. His estate was valued for probate at £30 022. Two brothers, Eugene and Robert, had migrated to South Australia and practised as doctors at Kapunda and Riverton. Another brother, Sir Joseph, was chairman of the Irish insurance commissioners in Dublin, 1911-33.

A. Deakin, *The Federal story*, H. Brookes ed (Melb, 1944); G. O'Collins, *Patrick McMahon Glynn, a founder of Australian Federation* (Melb, 1965); R. G. Ely, *Unto God and Caesar* (Melb, 1976); *Bulletin*, 25 Sept 1897, 22 Mar 1961; *Punch* (Melb), 31 Aug 1905, 2 Dec 1909, 12 Dec 1912; *SMH*, 29 Oct 1931; Glynn papers, MS 4653 (NL).

GERALD O'COLLINS

GOBLE, JOSEPH HUNTER (1863-1932), Baptist pastor, was born on 17 February 1863 at Rosebrook, near Belfast (Port Fairy), Victoria, son of Joseph Goble and Maria Anne Ballentine. His English father arrived in Belfast in the 1850s, prospered as a mill engineer and flour-miller, and was a borough councillor in 1883-89. His Irish mother disembarked at Geelong in 1856 as a domestic servant.

Joseph Hunter Goble appears to have moved to Melbourne with his mother in the mid-1870s. They lived in poverty at Sandridge, Emerald Hill and Fitzroy. Joseph left school and worked in factories and on the railways. Finally he served an apprenticeship as a compositor. From 1885 he was a member of the Melbourne Typographical Society; in 1889 he was elected to its board of management, from 1894 to 1896 he was a vice-president, and in 1897 he became president.

Goble had become a devout Christian in his mid-teens, and ascribed his conversion to the kindly reception accorded him at the Seamen's Bethel at Fishermen's Bend. Beginning as a cleaner and bell-ringer, he became a Sunday School teacher and open-air worker, then in 1884 student pastor at the

Baptist church in Footscray. His ministry was successful, but his health collapsed and in 1886 he had to withdraw. On 17 August he married Mary Adelaide Wouldham, a mission worker, in Holy Trinity Church of England, Port Melbourne, and a son was born in 1888. The Gobles were received into the fellowship of the Albert Park Baptist Church in 1892, and when the Baptist cause began at Port Melbourne in 1894, Joseph was one of the first Sunday school teachers. The following year a deputation from Footscray waited on him at his workplace and implored him to come as their preacher. On 3 March 1895 he began his remarkable pastorate. His wife died from typhoid fever in 1897; he never remarried. He resumed his studies and was ordained in 1900.

Joe Goble's rapport with working men and women made his ministry one of the most outstanding in Australia. By 1902 the local membership roll had trebled to over 200, the Paisley Street church had been twice enlarged, and the Sunday school was the largest in the denomination. Evening services held in the Federal Hall attracted congregations in excess of 2000. A red-brick church was built in 1904 to seat 700. Baptist services began at Yarraville in 1903, and a branch church at Footscray seated 250 in 1909, and 500 in 1914.

Goble was a stirring preacher—simple, direct, at times dramatic, and above all conveying his immense sincerity, honesty and affection. Reverent but possessing a sense of fun, serious but incapable of pomposity, he was widely revered, even among workers indifferent to religion. Despite his opposition to strong drink Goble was never labelled a 'wowser'. He was a keen supporter of the Footscray Football Club, and was prominent in local Masonic circles. He was a great visitor of the troubled and the poor, churchgoers and non-churchgoers alike, and championed the right of ordinary people to a decent standard of living. Before World War I he denounced the existence of unemployment as a national disgrace, and attacked jingoism, the arms race and compulsory military training.

Goble refused to accept a stipend greater than the average working wage, and gave most of his money to the needy. An imposing man—6 ft. 4 ins. (193 cm) and large of frame—he became a familiar figure on his specially reinforced bicycle and by the 1920s he was identified widely as 'Goble of Footscray'. His steadfast loyalty was vital to a district with a fragile sense of its worth.

In Baptist circles his duties were extensive: examiner at the training college, member of council, vice-president and president of the Union, country visitor for the Home and Foreign Mission, chairman for many years of the Baptist Foreign Missionary Society and subsequently of the Australian Board of Baptist Foreign Mission, and from 1913 chairman of the advisory board of the Union. In 1926-29 Goble was first president of the Baptist Union of Australia. He laid the foundation stone of the Canberra Baptist Church, and presided at the dedication. While no theologian, his plain evangelism inspired many, including his son, to enter the ministry.

By 1930-31 Goble was an exhausted man. Following his death on 31 January 1932, thousands lined the route of the funeral to the Footscray cemetery. The Baptist Union erected a Goble Memorial Hall in East Melbourne, the Footscray congregation unveiled in the Paisley Street church a mosaic tablet bearing his portrait and a stained glass window of the Good Samaritan, and the citizens of Footscray erected on the Geelong Road an elevated, life-size statue in marble.

J. McDonald Martin, *The life of a great and worthy Freemason* (Melb, 1937); F. J. Wilkin, *Baptists in Victoria . . . 1838-1938* (Melb, 1939); *Southern Baptist*, 1 Jan 1905, 3 Dec 1907, 1 Dec 1908; *Aust Baptist*, 31 Aug 1926, 27 Mar 1928, 26 Feb 1929, 9 Feb 1932; *Propagandist*, 5 Mar, 5 Apr 1930; *Vic Baptist Witness*, 5 Mar 1932; *Footscray Advertiser*, 21, 28 Apr 1900, 1 Mar, 25 Oct 1902, 1 Aug 1903, 13 Aug 1904, 21 Nov 1908, 1 July 1911, 11 Mar, 4 Nov 1916, 26 Jan 1929, 6, 13 Feb 1932.

JOHN LACK

GOBLE, STANLEY JAMES (1891-1948), air vice marshal, was born on 21 August 1891 at Croydon, Victoria, son of George Albert William Goble, a Victorian-born stationmaster, and his wife Ann Elizabeth, née Walton, from England. At 16 he joined the transportation branch of the Victorian Railways and by 1914 was working as a relieving stationmaster. On the outbreak of war he tried to enlist in the Australian Imperial Force but was twice rejected on minor medical grounds. Determined, however, to follow his three brothers into active service, he paid his own passage to England. On 13 July 1915 he was accepted as a trainee airman with the rank of temporary flight sublieutenant in the Royal Naval Air Service. After training at Chingford Air Station, Essex, he was confirmed in rank on 20 October and posted to Dover Air Station where he was employed in test-flying new aircraft and in carrying out brief anti-submarine patrols over the English Channel. He was then moved to the Royal Naval Air Service Base at Dunkirk from which he flew the single-seater Sopwith Pup. From Dunkirk

he shot down a German L.V.G. two-seater in September 1916.

The battle of the Somme in 1916 led to the formation, with the most experienced pilots available, of No. 8 Squadron, R.N.A.S. Goble, a foundation member, flew the Pup and the French Nieuport fighter, combating not only German aircraft but the appalling westerly gales which blew throughout most of the battle. On 1 October he was promoted flight lieutenant and later that month was awarded the Croix de Guerre, and won the Distinguished Service Cross for attacking two enemy aircraft near Ghistelles, France, bringing one down in flames.

On 1 February 1917 Goble was posted to No. 5 Squadron, R.N.A.S., which, newly equipped with the D.H.4 day and night bomber, was operating from Petite Synthe, France. He was appointed acting flight commander and on 17 February was awarded the Distinguished Service Order for 'conspicuous bravery and skill in attacking hostile aircraft on numerous occasions'. On 30 June his appointment as flight commander was confirmed and from July he was acting squadron commander; this rank became substantive on 1 January 1918. The potentially difficult transition from flying single-seater fighter sorties to leading two-seater bombing raids was carried out successfully. With No. 5 Squadron Goble planned and led, in the first instance, attacks mainly aimed at German naval targets and aerodromes. When General Ludendorff launched his offensive in March 1918, Goble's squadron was committed in front of General Gough's Fifth Army and its targets shifted to bridges, railway sidings and columns of advancing enemy infantry. Such objectives were attacked from heights of between 15 000 feet (4597 m) and 800 feet (244 m) in the face of intense German land and air opposition. The rapid German advance once brought Goble's aerodrome under shell-fire from medium-range artillery and he was forced to conduct a hurried evacuation. When the R.N.A.S. lost its separate identity on 1 April 1918 and merged with the Royal Flying Corps to form the Royal Air Force, Goble was appointed major in the new service. He returned with his squadron to England on 15 May. He was appointed M.B.E. in 1917, O.B.E. in 1918 and was twice mentioned in dispatches.

The experience of war had proved Goble to be a gallant and distinguished leader. He had also been fortunate in that, although twice shot down, he escaped the war unwounded. In 1919 his prospects as a regular officer in the Royal Air Force were most satisfactory. He returned to Australia with the rank of lieut-colonel and was asked by the chief of the Australian Naval Staff to act as adviser on the formation of the Australian air force. Thus, although he received a permanent commission in the Royal Air Force as a squadron leader on 1 August 1919, he was at once made an honorary wing commander and seconded for service with the Royal Australian Navy. The navy, anxious to gain control of a substantial portion of Australia's air resources and defence vote, nominated Goble for the position of chief of the air staff. This fact, together with the inter-service disputes which marked the creation of the air force, led Goble into serious conflict with the ultimately successful candidate, Wing Commander (Sir) Richard Williams [q.v.]. When the (Royal) Australian Air Force officially came into existence on 31 March 1921 Goble resigned his R.A.F. commission, was appointed to the Australian Air Force and next November was made second member of the Air Board and director of personnel and training under Williams. It quickly became an established practice to ensure that these two officers served as little together as possible. Goble was sent to the United Kingdom in October 1921 to undertake a marine observer's course. On 25 April 1922, at the Church of St Martin in the Fields, London, he married Kathleen Doris Latitia Wodehouse, and soon returned to Australia. Williams then attended the British Army Staff College, Camberley, while Goble was appointed acting chief of the air staff. While holding this position he advocated the creation of a fleet air arm, a project which Williams was quick to discredit.

On 7 April 1924 Goble left Melbourne with Flying Officer I. E. McIntyre in a Fairey IIID seaplane on what became the first successful attempt to fly around Australia. The flight, carried out in often hazardous conditions, covered 8500 miles (13 680 km) in some ninety hours flying time before arriving back in Melbourne on 19 May. Acclaimed as a great achievement in the history of aviation, the flight won the coveted Britannia Trophy for 1924 and Goble was appointed C.B.E. On Williams's return to Australia in 1926, Goble left for the United Kingdom to attend the Royal Air Force Staff College at Andover and the Imperial Defence College at Camberley. While in Britain he acted between May 1926 and September 1927 as air liaison officer in the high commissioner's office in London. He was promoted group captain on 1 April 1928 and temporary air commodore in 1932. During Williams's absence from Australia in 1933-34, he was acting chief of the air staff. In 1935-37 he was seconded to the R.A.F. where he served as deputy director of air operations in the Air Ministry and then commanded a bomber group based at Abingdon,

Berkshire. He was promoted temporary air vice marshal on 28 February 1937.

In June 1938 Goble was back in Australia when Sir Edward Ellington, a former chief of the air staff in the Royal Air Force, arrived to carry out an inspection and report on the Australian service. He commented adversely on the causes of several flying accidents and drew the conclusion that flying training was deficient. Goble, as air member for personnel, was responsible for manning and training, but he pointed out to the minister for defence that Williams had made himself responsible for operational training. The government removed Williams from his post as chief of the air staff and on 28 February 1939 Goble was appointed to act in that capacity with the rank of air vice marshal. An R.A.F. officer, Air Commodore J. C. Russell, was seconded to fill the position of air member for personnel.

This period proved an unhappy one for Goble. His relations with Russell rapidly became strained, and once war had broken out it became necessary to plan not only for Australia's local defence but for the contribution to be made towards Imperial defence. Goble initially was unenthusiastic about the Empire Air Training Scheme and preferred to concentrate upon increasing local air power and sending overseas a self-contained Australian air expeditionary force. However, the government, without his knowledge, was negotiating with Britain's Air Ministry to secure the services of a British officer as chief of the air staff. In December 1939 Goble told the prime minister that he wished to resign not only as chief executive officer but also his commission in the Royal Australian Air Force on the grounds that Russell had been undermining his authority. When he attempted to withdraw both resignations he was unsuccessful. Although allowed to retain his commission, he was told that he would be replaced. This difficult situation was only resolved when he accepted the offer to act in Canada as Australian liaison officer to the Empire Air Training Scheme; he served in this capacity until 1945. He played a part in negotiating the Joint Air Training Plan in 1942. In April 1946 he retired from the Royal Australian Air Force with the rank of air vice marshal.

The promise shown by Goble's operational leadership in World War I was not realized in the inter-war years. Partly it was blighted by his relationship with his immediate superior, and by the suspicion held by some in earlier years that he was too eager to foster the interests of the navy to the detriment of those concerns peculiar to an independent air force. His contribution to the defence debate was marginal. His advice to the government during his tenure as acting chief of the air staff in 1939 was largely ignored and in this period of stress he clearly lacked the political skill to be an effective head of an armed service. For many years he was a member of the Institute of Aeronautical Engineers and the Athenaeum Club in Melbourne.

Goble died of hypertensive cerebrovascular disease on 24 July 1948 in the Repatriation General Hospital, Heidelberg, Melbourne, survived by his wife and three sons. He was cremated with Anglican rites.

H. A. Jones, *The war in the air*, II (np, 1924), IV (np, 1934); D. Gillison, *Royal Australian Air Force 1939-1942* (Canb, 1962); J. McCarthy, *Australia and imperial defence* (Brisb, 1976); R. Williams, *These are facts* (Canb, 1977); *British A'sian*, 5 Aug 1915, 2 Nov 1916; *Sea, Land and Air*, 2 Oct 1922; *Reveille* (Syd), Jan 1937, Feb 1939; *Mufti*, March 1939; *Table Talk*, 12 Apr 1928; *SMH*, 27 Sept 1921, 1, 7 Apr, 21 May, 3 June 1924, 10 Feb, 23 July 1925, 30 June 1926, 24 Feb 1928, 10 June 1936, 21, 22, 23, 28 Dec 1939, 3 May 1940, 3 July 1945, 25 Feb 1946, 26 July 1948; *Argus*, 26 July 1948; PRO, DO 35/1003/1.   JOHN MCCARTHY

GOCHER, WILLIAM HENRY (1856-1921), artist, bimetallist and pioneer daylight surfer, was born on 20 March 1856 at Ipswich, Suffolk, England, son of Charles Gocher, salesman, and his wife Louisa, née King. He was educated at St John's College, Hurstpierpoint, Sussex. He and several of his four brothers and five sisters were converted to Roman Catholicism. Each son was given £1000 and three of them came to Australia, William Henry about 1872. From about 1884 he worked in Sydney as an artist, painting portraits (sometimes of the famous), religious pictures and racehorses.

In the 1890s Gocher was caught up in the bimetallic movement. Vice-president of the Bimetallic League of New South Wales, he published in 1897 a pamphlet, *Australia, the light of the world*, which urged the creation of a national, state-owned bank, the closing of private banks, the coining of silver and the issue of a ten-shilling note. He greatly admired William Jennings Bryan and looked to Federation to save Australia from the 'jeers of Jews, capitalists and the press'. He stood for the Senate in 1901, coming forty-ninth out of fifty candidates—he failed similarly at State elections in 1901 and 1904. Retaining his enthusiasm for bimetallism when the movement waned, he was president of the Australian Currency League in about 1912-18. In 1918 he published *Australia must be heard*, a pamphlet which incorporated some earlier writings in an appeal to the Pope to bring about an armistice.

For some years Gocher wrote for John Norton's [q.v.] *Truth*; when he inherited money in 1900 he moved his family to Manly and established a short-lived newspaper, the *Manly and North Sydney News*. Through this paper he staged the scene at Manly for which he is remembered. He determined to expose the irrelevance of the local government regulations which forbade sea-bathing in daylight hours. The issue was one of public decency as there were no changing sheds and swimming costumes were rare. Clad in a neck-to-knee costume, Gocher in October 1902 swam at midday after announcing his intentions in his paper. Twice ignored by the authorities, he duly criticized their lack of zeal; on a third occasion he was escorted from the water and interviewed by the police who brought no charges. In November 1903 the reluctant Manly council resolved to allow all-day bathing, rapidly growing in popularity, provided that a neck-to-knee costume was worn. Gocher claimed a triumph and in 1907 friends presented him with a gold watch and a purse of fifty sovereigns.

In 1906 Gocher sold for £500 a block of land bought at Manly cheaply in 1900 and returned to the city to launch the short-lived *Balmain Banner*, 'a democratic journal . . . brisk and fearless'. At Surry Hills on 2 May 1888 he had married Elizabeth Josephine Storm who was born at Balmain. She was well educated, played the piano and taught in Catholic schools. Gocher was slightly built, 5 ft. 6 ins. (167 cm), wore glasses and smoked a pipe. Greatly distressed by a son's death at Gallipoli, he had a stroke in 1917. He died on 18 August 1921 of arteriosclerosis and chronic nephritis and was buried in Waverley cemetery. He was survived by his wife (d. 1937), four sons and two daughters.

P. W. Gledhill, *Manly and Pittwater, its beauty and progress* (Syd, 1948); *Table Talk*, 28 Mar 1901; information from Mrs R. Mahoney, Brighton-Le-Sands, Syd.   BRUCE MITCHELL

GODDARD, BENJAMIN (1834-1912), leader in the Kyabram reform movement, was baptized on 7 December 1834 at Shabbington, Buckinghamshire, England, son of Thomas Goddard, publican, and his wife Elizabeth, née Kimble (Kimbell). He had had some experience in the bakery and confectionery trade in London before migrating to Australia, arriving in Melbourne on 5 January 1853. After working in Sydney for a time, he returned to Victoria and prospected for gold on the Ballarat fields. He worked for a wholesale merchant in Melbourne before moving to McIvor (Heathcote) about 1856. On 10 October 1857 with Church of England rites he married 31-year-old Mrs

Louisa Nicolls, née Kerr, a schoolmistress; Goddard was then working as a baker at Heathcote. He managed a store for Moore, Christie & Spinks for five years before going on a trip to England in 1869.

Goddard sold out at Heathcote in 1872 and joined Clements Mumford in a general storekeeping business with shops at Rushworth and Murchison. He also set up a store and hotel at Tatura, with Mumford, Angus Ross and Robert Currie; from 1876 the partnership traded as Ross & Co. Goddard lived at Murchison and acted as post and telegraph master.

In 1873 he explored the country north of Murchison and selected allotments at Taripta, north-east of present Kyabram, under the terms of the 1869 Land Act. He gave up storekeeping and farmed the property for some ten years before moving to Kyabram in 1889 to set up again as a storekeeper and wheat-buyer.

As secretary of the Goulburn Valley (West Side) Railway League, Goddard had given evidence at the bar of the Legislative Council in support of the railway. In September 1879 he was appointed secretary-treasurer of a Kyabram movement agitating for a line from Tatura to Echuca (opened 1887). Known affectionately as 'B.G.' throughout the Goulburn valley, he promoted the merits of irrigation in the *Australasian* (1894) and 'stumped the electorate eight or nine times in the interests of political aspirants and . . . nearly every man he "ran" got into Parliament'.

Goddard supported Federation of the Australian colonies and Church union, but within months of the inauguration of Federation he and other electors became alarmed at the cost of government. Goddard sounded the keynote at a meeting which predated the foundation of the Kyabram Reform League, when he called for drastic economies in government. At the founding meeting of the league on 13 November 1901 he moved the first motion and was appointed joint-secretary, S. Lancaster [q.v.] becoming president. More than two hundred branches were formed and at the Citizens' Reform League's conference in April 1902, Goddard was elected vice-president. In 1902 the league swept all before it: the Peacock [q.v.] ministry fell, the subsequent Irvine [q.v.] ministry easily won the election, and the number of parliamentarians was considerably reduced.

Goddard's first wife had died in 1897 and on 11 December 1901 he married 33-year-old Ann Bevan of Merrigum. After retiring to Heathcote for four years he returned to Kyabram where he died on 26 October 1912. He was survived by two sons and a daughter of his first marriage and three sons and two daughters of his second; their ages ranged from 54 to 1½ years. He was buried in Kyabram cemetery.

H. L. Nielson, *The voice of the people* (Kyabram, 1902); J. Smith (ed), *Cyclopedia of Victoria*, 3 (Melb, 1905); W. H. Bossence, *Kyabram* (Melb, 1963), and *Murchison* (Melb, 1965); *Kyela*, 1970, p 71, 74; *Kyabram Free Press*, 6, 13 Jan 1905, 8 Nov 1912.

W. H. BOSSENCE*

GODDARD, ERNEST JAMES (1883-1948), professor of biology, was born on 10 March 1883 at Newcastle, New South Wales, son of Alfred Russell Goddard, coachpainter, and his wife Elizabeth Jane, née Cowan. Educated at Maitland High School and the University of Sydney (B.A., 1904; B.Sc. 1906, with honours in zoology and palaeontology) he was appointed demonstrator in biology on graduation. As Linnean Macleay [q.v.5] research fellow in 1908 he carried out superficial work on the Hirudinea and Oligochaeta for which he received in 1910 the university's first doctorate in zoology. His thesis was published as a series of papers in the *Journal of the Linnean Society of New South Wales*. At Petersham on 28 April 1910 Goddard married Sarah May Morris of Goulburn; they had no children. Appointed to the chair of zoology in Victoria College (later the University of Stellenbosch), Cape Province, South Africa, by 1922 he had made his department the largest in the country.

Professor of biology at the University of Queensland from 1922, Goddard became in 1927 the first dean of the faculty of agriculture. Active in establishing faculties of agriculture, dentistry, veterinary science and medicine, he also chaired many societies including the Royal Society of Queensland, the Queensland Naturalists' Club, the Queensland branch of the Australian Institute of Agricultural Science, the Entomological Society of Queensland and the Australian-American Association. In 1936-39 he was seconded to the State Department of Agriculture and Stock as science co-ordinating officer.

Goddard believed that education should foster individualism and develop the maximum capability allowed by heredity. He was also influenced by the achievements of some American universities in combining theory and practice, and therefore encouraged close co-operation between the university and the agricultural department, advocated close links between the university and the farmer, and promoted extramural education. In newspaper articles, interviews, radio talks and well-attended public lectures, he popularized scientific developments, especially in biology, applicable to primary industry. He urged public support for the University of Queensland and emphasized its importance. He was a member of the Council for Scientific and Industrial Research from its foundation in 1926 until 1941. Public life left little time for personal research though he did supervise important investigations including work on the banana disease, bunchy top.

Short, with piercing eyes and an unruly forelock, Goddard had enormous physical energy and a wide range of enthusiasms. An incisive and forthright lecturer, he was popular both with students and extramural audiences. While setting up a marine research station at Heron Island on the eve of retirement, he died of coronary occlusion on 17 January 1948, and was cremated after a Methodist service.

E. Marlay, *A history of dental education in Queensland, 1863-1964* (Brisb, 1979); *Univ Qld Gazette*, 9 (1948), p 3; *Brisbane Courier*, 7 July 1923, 10 June 1925, 14 Dec 1926; *Telegraph* (Brisb), 3 May 1930; *Daily Standard*, 16 June 1932; *Courier Mail*, 17 Jan 1948.   E. CLARKE

GODDARD, HENRY ARTHUR (1869-1955), merchant, company director and soldier, was born on 13 December 1869 at West Hackney, Middlesex, England, son of Henry Goddard, insurance clerk, and his wife Elizabeth, née Simmons. He migrated to Australia in 1890 and settled in Brisbane.

Goddard had been a sergeant in the Essex Rifle Volunteers and took a keen interest in military matters. In 1899 he was commissioned in the Queensland Defence Force and by 1913 had risen to command the 7th Infantry (Moreton) Regiment. On 28 June 1897, describing himself as a clerk, he married Elizabeth Maud Morrow at All Saints Anglican Church, Brisbane, and gradually established a successful importing business with offices interstate. He was interested in growing malting barley and experimented with this crop on the Darling Downs. In 1906-15 he was also the consul for Paraguay in Brisbane. His business interests required extensive travel overseas, affording him the opportunity to attend military manoeuvres in England and to observe developments on the Continent. Although not a professional soldier, he developed a wide knowledge of military affairs and on the outbreak of war in 1914 was placed in command of the Brisbane defences.

Putting his business affairs in order, Goddard joined the Australian Imperial Force with the rank of lieut-colonel on 16 March 1915 and was appointed to command the 25th Battalion. When changes were made to commands in the 2nd Division he was transferred to the 17th Battalion, which he joined as it embarked from Sydney on the troopship *Themistocles* on 12 May 1915, bound for Egypt. From there the battalion sailed for Gallipoli in August but without Goddard who was in hospital. He was on the *Southland* sailing to rejoin the unit when the ship was torpedoed on 2 September. Rescued by a Royal Navy vessel he was taken to Lemnos and finally landed on Gallipoli on 6 September. He took command of his battalion next day in the trenches at Quinn's Post, one of the most dangerous positions on the peninsula. He served there until the evacuation and remained behind until the last parties of the unit were ready to move out on 20 December 1915. The 17th Battalion sailed to Lemnos, then to Alexandria, Egypt, where orders were received to proceed to Tel el Kebir. Goddard's health had suffered on Gallipoli and he was admitted to hospital with dysentery on 18 January 1916. In April he was invalided to Australia.

In mid-July he again embarked for overseas service. He reported to A.I.F. Headquarters in London and was appointed commander of the recently raised 35th Battalion (part of the new 3rd Division) in October. He arrived in France with his new command on 22 November. After serving in a quiet sector at Armentières the battalion took part in the battle of Messines on 7 June 1917. For his work at Messines and his contribution to the efficiency of the brigade Goddard was awarded the Distinguished Service Order. The battalion was heavily committed in the battle of Broodseinde Ridge on 4 October and in the attack on Passchendaele Ridge a week later. Weary and depleted, the 3rd Division was eventually sent back to the quieter sector in the north where it remained until early in 1918.

In appearance Goddard was tall and spare with a lean countenance behind a heavy dark moustache. 'A quiet, witty, scholarly man, far removed from the mud and blood of Flanders' trenches', he soldiered with quiet efficiency. 'With his intellectual and military qualifications he combined the attributes of sincerity, courtesy, a dry humour and natural dignity in his relations with superiors and subordinates alike'.

Although never robust, Goddard performed outstanding work during the great German offensive near Amiens in March-April 1918. With the enemy advancing on the city the 9th Brigade was detached from the division and rushed to reinforce the defences in front of Villers-Bretonneux. In the brigadier's absence Goddard established headquarters in the town and took temporary command of the brigade. On 4 April the

Germans commenced a devastating bombardment. The infantry fell back on the town and Goddard found his headquarters in the front line. The situation was desperate but Goddard acted promptly and decisively, bringing all his reserves forward and ordering the commanding officer of the 36th Battalion to counter-attack immediately. Under strong leadership the Australians rallied and, assisted by the British cavalry and some infantry, held the line and repulsed the enemy. Early next morning Goddard ordered his weary troops to attack again. The enemy was taken by surprise and driven back from the town and for the moment Amiens was saved.

On 5 May Goddard's battalion played the major role in the successful attack at Morlancourt. Next month he was promoted colonel and temporary brigadier general and appointed to command the 9th Brigade which he led during the British Somme offensive until the end of the war. Important actions included the battle of Bray-sur-Somme and the attack on the Hindenburg line. Goddard was mentioned in dispatches three times, and after the Armistice the awards of the C.M.G. and the Belgian Croix de Guerre were announced.

Goddard returned to Australia in 1920 and resumed his business and militia interests. He moved to Sydney and in 1921-26 commanded the 14th Infantry Brigade, A.M.F., with the rank of honorary brigadier general; he was placed on the retired list in 1931. For twenty-one years, until 1947, he was president of the Imperial Service Club. He was joined in his importing company (H. A. Goddard Pty Ltd) by his son Horace Leopold who had served as a private in his father's battalion during the war (a second son had died in infancy). Goddard continued to travel, was commercial representative of *The Times* in Australia, and remained active in business until his death.

Survived by his wife, son and daughter, he died in Concord Repatriation Hospital, Sydney, on 24 October 1955 and was cremated with Anglican rites. His estate was sworn for probate at £3156.

C. E. W. Bean, *The A.I.F. in France*, 1918 (Syd, 1942); K. W. Mackenzie, *The story of the Seventeenth Battalion A.I.F. in the great war 1914-1918* (Syd, 1946); *Reveille* (Syd), Aug 1938; *SMH*, 26 Oct 1955; Goddard papers (AWM).

PETER BURNESS

GODFREY, SIDNEY GEORGE (1897-1965), boxer, was born on 20 August 1897 at Raglan near Bathurst, New South Wales, sixth child of Joseph Godfrey, farmer, and his wife Lillian, née Jones. He began boxing at 12 in a barn on his father's farm and at 14 went to Sydney where he worked for a blacksmith at Auburn for 5s. a week. He did well in amateur bouts and greatly improved after taking lessons at Redfern from Jim Barron, a former heavyweight. After some notable amateur successes, he attracted the attention of R. L. 'Snowy' Baker [q.v.7], who in 1916 arranged twelve professional fights, six of which he won by quick knockouts. In 1917 he won the Australian featherweight title from Vince Buckley and next year sixteen fights out of eighteen; he was dubbed the 'K.O. King' and was one of boxing's greatest drawcards.

In the Philippines in 1919 Godfrey drew with Francesco Flores over fifteen rounds and in a second bout was knocked out in the first round by Cabanello Dencio. Back in Australia in 1920 he lost his featherweight title on points to Jackie Green, but defeated such first-class fighters as Englishman Joe Symonds and Belgian Arthur Wyns, European featherweight champion.

By 1921 Godfrey was in the lightweight division and was trained by Arthur Hennessy [q.v.]. He reduced his weight to 9 st. (57 kg) to fight Frenchman Eugène Criqui, later world featherweight champion, for a purse of £800: on 21 February before a crowd of 15 000 (with thousands turned away), on one of the wildest nights ever seen at Sydney Stadium, Godfrey made the weight at the ringside and fought well until his drastic dieting reduction took its toll and he was knocked out in the tenth round. Criqui refused a challenge to fight him at 9 st. 5 lbs. (59 kg). In Brisbane on 10 August Godfrey lost on points to Archie Bradley, 'the Gympie Tiger', in a bout according to the perplexed Godfrey fought on 'the Marquis of Queensland Rules'. Later that year he knocked out the Filipino Dencio in Sydney. In 1921 he won the Australian lightweight title from Hop Harry Stone; Godfrey's challengers included Stone and Bert Spargo; but he lost it to Hughie Dwyer in 1922. He retired in 1924; making a come-back next year, he lost a bout for the welterweight title.

A deadly puncher with a trip-hammer right as his speciality, Godfrey, with his aggressive ringcraft, delighted the crowds and earned £20 000 prize money. Out of 109 professional fights he won 79 (41 by knockout) and drew 12. On retiring he managed some hotels and became the well-liked and genial host at the Horse and Jockey, Homebush. He retired from business in 1957 and lived at Bronte. He died of heart disease in the Mater Hospital, North Sydney, on 22 February 1965 and was cremated with Anglican rites. He was survived by his wife Eva Margaret, née Pettingell, whom he had married at the Methodist parsonage, Auburn, on 13 March

1917, and by their two sons and five daughters. His estate was sworn for probate at £66 630.

J. Blanch (ed), *Australian sporting records* (Melb, 1981); *Parade*, Nov 1973; *SMH*, 6 Feb 1949, 27 Apr 1950, 21 July 1957; *Truth* (Melb), 7 Dec 1952; *Daily Examiner* (Grafton), and *Daily Telegraph* (Syd), 23 Feb 1965; *Sun* (Syd), 24 Mar 1975, 14 May 1980.

G. P. WALSH

GOE, FIELD FLOWERS (1832-1910), Anglican bishop, was baptized on 10 February 1832 at Louth, Lincolnshire, England, only son of Field Flowers Goe, solicitor, and his wife Mary Jane. He was educated at King Edward's Grammar School, Louth, and after reading law for a time he proceeded to Oxford, matriculating at St Edmund's Hall in 1853 and graduating from Magdalen Hall (later Hertford College) B.A. (3rd class honours) in 1857 and M.A. in 1860.

Goe was ordained deacon and priest in 1858 by Archibishop Thomas Musgrave of York and appointed curate of Christ Church, Kingston-on-Hull. In the same year he was appointed incumbent of this parish and on 5 June 1861 married Emma Rodgers, daughter of William Hurst, architect, of Doncaster. He remained at Hull until 1873 when Bishop Baring of Durham presented him to the important rectory of Sunderland. In 1877 he was presented by Lord Chancellor Cairns to St George's rectory, Bloomsbury, where his preaching talents and organizing ability had greater scope. He was in demand as a missioner, participated in several Church congresses, and, although an Oxford man, was appointed in 1884 one of the select preachers to the University of Cambridge.

In 1886 the appointment of a successor to James Moorhouse [q.v.5] as bishop of Melbourne was remitted to an English committee comprising the archbishops of Canterbury and York, the bishops of Durham and Manchester and Bishop Perry [q.v.5]. Goe was appointed in September, awarded an honorary D.D. from Oxford, consecrated bishop on 24 February 1887, and installed at Melbourne on 14 April.

Goe succeeded to an unfinished cathedral and an unwieldy diocese in a rapidly expanding metropolis. He quickly decided that priority must be given to St Paul's Cathedral which was completed, apart from spires and tower, and consecrated on 22 January 1891. However, metropolitan extension and creation of country dioceses had to be postponed when diocesan and parochial income contracted following the collapse of the land boom. Not until 1901, when on 3'October the Church Assembly passed an Act creating three new dioceses at Bendigo, Gippsland and Wangaratta, was subdivision achieved.

Goe was an Evangelical churchman but this was apparent more in support for activities than in discouragement of other schools of thought in the diocese. He promoted a mission to the diocese by the Irish evangelist, George Grubb, in 1891 and in 1892 encouraged the formation of a local association for the Church Missionary Society; but he also gave strong support to the 'deaconesses' of the high church Mission to the Streets and Lanes. While the alleviation of social evils of the time, such as the problem of sweated labour in factories, concerned him, he believed that 'salvation ought to come first'.

Goe was contrasted unfavourably with his eloquent and forceful predecessor, Moorhouse, and was characterized as cautious and colourless. But he displayed an exemplary devotion to duty and, in the dark days of depression, courage in adversity. His sincerity was never questioned.

Goe's wife accompanied him on his extensive travels and was especially active in the Church's work among women and children. On her death on 24 July 1901 the *Australasian* wrote that 'memories will be cherished in many a bush vicarage of the quiet lady with the sympathetic voice, chatting away cheerfully and hopefully under the grand old gum tree at Bishopscourt'. Her death, and increasing ill health, led Goe to resign in October of that year. He left Melbourne on 7 April 1902 and accepted a brief appointment as assistant bishop of Durham. He retired to Wimbledon where he died on 25 June 1910. A portrait by J. C. Waite [q.v.6] is in the Chapter House of St Paul's Cathedral, Melbourne.

Church of England Messenger (Vic), 7 Oct 1886, 4 Oct 1901, 1 May 1902; *Australasian*, 5 Oct 1895, 27 July 1901; *Argus*, 30 June 1910; *Guardian* (Lond), 1 July 1910.

JAMES GRANT

GOLDFINCH, SIR PHILIP HENRY MACARTHUR (1884-1943), businessman and politician, was born on 13 April 1884 at Gosport, Hampshire, England, son of Lieutenant Henry Goldfinch, Royal Navy, and his wife Elizabeth Maria, née King, daughter of Philip Gidley King [q.v.5]. He spent much of his childhood in New South Wales at Dunheved, the King family property at St Marys, and was educated at Sydney Grammar School. In 1902 he enlisted as a trooper in the South African War but arrived after the war was over. His marriage to Mary Medora Cowper, great-granddaughter of Sir Charles Cowper [q.v.3], on 7 March 1911 at St John's Anglican Church, Camden, further cemented his ties with colonial patrician families.

Goldfinch had joined the Colonial Sugar Refining Co. in 1902. He gained practical experience of its affairs in Queensland in 1911-13 as a cane inspector at Macknade and in 1914-18 at the Homebush plant near Mackay, where in 1915 he was appointed manager. In 1919 he returned to C.S.R.'s head office in Sydney, his zest and energy impressing E. W. Knox [q.v.], to whom he became personal adviser. In 1928 Goldfinch became general manager. He was more inclined to seek expert advice and more subject to the opinions of the board of directors than previous general managers, but he remained an implacable opponent of government interference and public accountability in the industry. He steered the company towards diversification, mainly the manufacture of building materials. It is a tribute to his business acumen that though sugar consumption declined significantly during the Depression, C.S.R. paid its customary dividends and bonuses.

Goldfinch's interest in political affairs gradually developed. In the late 1920s and early 1930s he was associated with the Constitutional Association of New South Wales, the All for Australia League and the Primary Producers' Advisory Council. In November 1930 he helped to form a secret counter-revolutionary organization, the Old Guard, which maintained a discreet vigil lest a serious disturbance should swamp the police and the armed forces. The Old Guard came perilously close to mobilizing, but the dismissal of the Lang [q.v.] government by the governor, Sir Philip Game [q.v.8], dissipated much of the political tension. Except for a curious article which appeared in *Smith's Weekly* in 1936, headlined 'Sir Philip Goldfinch's Secret Service', the organization disappeared without leaving a trace. In June 1934 he had been appointed K.B.E.

In November 1935 Goldfinch won Gordon in the Legislative Assembly for the United Australia Party. He intended to prove that it was possible for someone with 'a man sized job in civil life to take on politics'. But his spirited maiden speech was reviled by Lang who suggested that, 'the "boss" himself was coming on the job' and that the 'fountain head of the great octopus, the sugar combine' had no right to sit in parliament. This set the pattern for a brief and inglorious political career, Goldfinch defending the profits of C.S.R. and criticizing unemployment relief, family endowment and other welfare enterprises, the Labor Opposition finding the titled 'sugar daddy', with his spats and monocle, an easy target for sarcastic criticism. In July 1937 he resigned.

His experience as an overseer was called upon in World War II when, in 1940, he was appointed chairman of the Board of Area Management for New South Wales, Ministry of Munitions, responsible to Essington Lewis [q.v.] for the planning and production of munition projects and supplies. Again Goldfinch instigated a minor controversy by attacking the 'red-tape' of officialdom, the lack of decentralization of munition factories and the propensity of politicians to pester him about allocating defence projects to their electorates. During World War II Goldfinch became president of the Union Club; he was also a member of the Australasian Pioneers' Club and of Royal Sydney Golf Club. He had bought a property at Sutton Forest near Moss Vale but he did not live to enjoy its rural charm. On 7 April 1943 he died of cardiovascular disease at Roseville and was cremated with Anglican rites. He was survived by a son and two daughters. His estate was valued for probate at £36 284, and included pictures and antique furniture, some belonging to the King family.

Goldfinch was an archetypal Anglo-Australian. As chairman of the British Settlers' Welfare Committee he was keenly interested in Empire migration. His speeches and radio addresses reveal an intelligent grasp of world affairs although his attitude to the Fascist powers was somewhat ambivalent. He enjoyed club life, golf, fishing, tennis and rifle-shooting. But essentially he was a serious man, unsympathetic to frivolous behaviour, straight laced and conservative. Throughout his career and particularly during the Depression, Goldfinch served the state and the employing class in a loyal, untiring and uncompromising fashion.

A. G. Lowndes (ed), *South Pacific enterprise* (Syd, 1956); R. Goddard, *The Union Club 1857-1957* (Syd, 1957); D. P. Mellor, *The role of science and industry* (Canb, 1958); E. Campbell, *The rallying point* (Melb, 1965); *PD* (NSW), 1936, p 145, 538; *SMH*, 4 June 1934, 19 Mar, 28 May, 5, 17 Nov 1935, 5 June 1940, 22 Apr 1941, 8 Apr 1943; *Smith's Weekly* (Syd), 22 Aug 1936; *Sun* (Syd), 2 Feb 1941; Col Sec file B32/2669 no 2082 (NSWA); CSR Archives (Syd); information from Mrs N. Mannix, Hunters Hill, NSW.   ANDREW MOORE

GOLDHAR, PINCHAS (1901-1947), writer, was born on 14 June 1901 at Lodz, Russia (Poland), son of Jacob Goldhar, dyer, and his wife Rachael, née Hirshkowitz.

Goldhar published his first stories in Yiddish publications in Warsaw and in Lodz, where in 1922 he worked for the daily *Lodzer Tageblatt*. Having studied German and French language and literature at the University of Warsaw, from which he graduated, he translated a number of French and German novels and stories into Yiddish. His translation of *The weavers*, by the German dramatist Gerhart Hauptmann, became a favourite on the Yiddish stage.

Yiddish literature in the Polish Republic in the early 1920s experienced a minor renaissance; Goldhar was one of a highly talented group of writers which included the Singer brothers. Yiddish was still the vehicle of political and cultural expression of Jews in Poland who wanted an autonomous Jewish community with minority rights and a national language, within the confines of the Polish state. However this view was challenged by the Zionists who advocated the establishment of a Jewish state in Palestine and the use of Hebrew rather than Yiddish, and by many educated Jews who had adopted Polish as their language. As the possibility of earning a living from writing in Yiddish diminished, many writers migrated, mainly to the United States of America.

Goldhar, because of family connexions, came to Australia, arriving in Melbourne in 1926. His father, brother and sisters also migrated, and his father set up a small dyeing business in Carlton known as Jacob Goldhar & Sons. Pinchas Goldhar worked in the factory as a dyer.

In 1928 he became the first editor, for about three years, of the first Yiddish newspaper in Australia, the weekly *Yiddish News*. He turned to exploring the fate of Polish Jewish migrants transplanted to a new land with different customs and language. His first stories of Jewish life in Australia were concerned with the theme of disintegration and doom. One of his most celebrated stories, 'The last minyan', tells of the break-up of a Jewish community in a gold-mining town, while the rabbi carries on his synagogue even though there is no longer a minyan, the ten men required by Jewish law to hold a religious service.

In 1939 Goldhar published *Stories from Australia*, the second Yiddish book to be published in Australia. Some of the stories were translated into English: Vance Palmer [q.v.] included 'The funeral' in *Coast to coast*, 1944, and 'Café in Carlton' was published in *Southern stories* (1945) and included in *Shalom*, a collection of Australian Jewish stories compiled by Nancy Keesing (1978). Goldhar admired Australian literature and in 1944 published here and abroad translations into Yiddish of stories by Henry Lawson [q.v.], Vance Palmer, Frank Dalby Davison and Alan Marshall. His essay on Australian literature was translated by Nita Bluthal and Stephen Murray-Smith and published in *Melbourne University Magazine* in 1947.

On 24 June 1934 in the Carlton synagogue Goldhar married Ida Shlezynger, also from Poland; they had a son and twin daughters.

He died at Belgrave of coronary thrombosis on 25 January 1947 and was buried in Fawkner cemetery.

As a writer Goldhar was influenced by Western literary modernism but Chekhov remained his model. His best stories are distinguished by their tightness of structure and power of compressed metaphor. While many of them deal with everyday Polish-Jewish life in Australia, they are far removed from the folk manner of classical Yiddish literature.

H. Brezniak, 'Pinchas Goldhar', *Bridge*, 3 (1967), no 2; *Aust Jewish Hist Soc J*, 7 (1973), no 4; *Aust Jewish News*, 31 Jan 1947.   JUDAH WATEN

GOLDIE, Dulcie; *see* DEAMER

GOLDING, ANNIE MACKENZIE (1855-1934), feminist teacher, and ISABELLA THERESA (1864-1940), public servant, were born at Tambaroora, New South Wales, on 27 October 1855 and 25 November 1864, eldest and third daughters of Joseph Golding (d. 1890), gold-miner from Galway, Ireland, and his Scottish wife Ann (d. 1906), née Fraser.

In 1874 Annie began teaching at Sallys Flat Provisional School, near Bathurst. Thereafter she slowly acquired training, qualifications and experience, first at Catholic schools at Paddington and Waverley, then at the Asylum for Destitute Children, Randwick, later at Esk Bank (Lithgow). In 1886 her family moved to Newcastle and she taught at New Lambton and Cooks Hill Public schools. Back in Sydney she taught at Macdonaldtown (Erskineville) and Croydon. She worked mainly with infants and girls. Although she often failed to obtain the promotions or qualifications she sought, by 1900 Annie Golding was mistress in charge at West Leichhardt (Orange Grove) Public School. She retired in 1915.

In the 1890s she became active in the new Teachers' Association of New South Wales. In 1897-1915 she was a member of the committee of the Public School Teachers' Institute and of the council of the New South Wales Public School Teachers' Association.

With their sister Kate Dwyer [q.v.8], Annie and Belle were members of the Womanhood Suffrage League of New South Wales from about 1893. Their branch at Newtown with Annie as secretary offered something of a working woman's challenge to Rose Scott's [q.v.] presidential view of the suffrage question from Woollahra; in 1902 the branch was expelled for its defiance of the central council. Thereafter the Golding sisters and some of their friends who were

Labor supporters formed the Women's Progressive Association with Annie as president from 1904; small but persistent, it lobbied for women's equality before the law. She often organized or led deputations for equal pay, the removal of the sex barrier in employment and the appointment of women as justices of the peace and police officers.

Annie Golding kept female education and employment conditions before sections of the Labor Party and Catholic organizations. Her association responded to (Sir) Charles Mackellar's [q.v.] request for support for his reform of the child welfare law. She served as a member of the State Children Relief Board from May 1911 which led her eventually to concern for the welfare of Aboriginal children. She also supported the University of Sydney reforms introduced by the McGowen [q.v.] government in 1912.

Neither Annie nor Belle married. They shared a house in Annandale close to Kate and Michael Dwyer. Belle seems to have been less political than Annie—her life is even less documented, but she started work in the public schools. In May 1900 she became the first female inspector under the Early Closing Act of 1899. On 1 December 1913 she transferred to the inspectorate under the Factories and Shops Act as senior (women) inspector; she retired in 1926. Her reports reveal a passion for the health, welfare and just treatment of women in their employment. It seems likely that much of Annie's knowledge and understanding of employment conditions among women was in fact collected and passed on by Belle.

Annie Golding died on 28 December 1934, the day after she had slipped while alighting from a tram. She was buried in her mother's grave in the Catholic section of Waverley cemetery, after a service at St Brendan's Catholic Church, Annandale. Belle died on 11 December 1940 and was buried in the Catholic section of Waverley cemetery. Both sisters were practising Roman Catholics—hard-working, respectable and evidently lacking in frivolity. (Annie's recreations were 'reading, writing, lecturing'.) Their feminism was of an earnest, practical kind.

B. A. Mitchell, *Teachers, education, and politics* (Brisb, 1975); J. Mackinolty and H. Radi (eds), *In pursuit of justice* (Syd, 1979); *Aust Worker*, 5 Jan 1927; *SMH*, 29 Dec 1934; NSW Dept of Labour and Industry, Annual Reports, 1900-26, *V&P* (LA, NSW), 1900-04, and *PP* (NSW), 1904-28; Register of teachers, Education Dept Archives (Syd); Scott family papers, v34 (ML). BEVERLEY KINGSTON

GOLDING, KATE; *see* DWYER, CATHERINE WINIFRED

GOLDSMITH, FREDERICK WILLIAM (1853-1932), Anglican bishop, was born on 3 August 1853 in London, eldest son of Frederick William Goldsmith and his wife Dorothy, née Watkins. His father taught at the Merchant Taylors' School where Frederick was educated in 1864-72. He won a scholarship to St John's College, Oxford (B.A., 1876; M.A., 1879).

Goldsmith was ordained priest in 1877 in the diocese of Rochester, to a curacy at Old Charlton. On 22 April 1880 he married Edith Emma Frewer; they had no children. Next year they moved to St Philip's, Cheam Common; he was vicar of Halling, Kent, in 1885-87.

In April 1888 Goldsmith came to Western Australia as dean of Perth, where he served under Bishops Parry [q.v.5] and C. O. L. Riley [q.v.] till 1904. He also managed the Girls' Orphanage and administered the diocese after Parry's death. There seems to have been friction between him and Bishop Riley. They both had strong characters and guarded their own spheres, and their churchmanship was very different, but Goldsmith served loyally, without resentment.

In 1903 the Perth synod set up the southwestern corner of the State as the new diocese of Bunbury and next year, on 17 July, Goldsmith became its first bishop, and was awarded an honorary doctorate by Lambeth. He also had missionary jurisdiction over the North-West, a huge area which, until 1910, when Bishop Trower [q.v.] was appointed, he faithfully administered in addition to his own large diocese.

In Bunbury he had to contend with the poverty of the diocese, its rapid and unexpected growth in population and industry and, later, World War I. He travelled incessantly and constantly sought men and money to develop the work: he went three times to England. In twelve and a half years he obtained the site and started a building fund for a suitable cathedral, established the itinerant Bush Brotherhood of St Boniface at Williams, organized new parishes as railways and land opened up, created a sound central administration, and established the new diocese of North-West Australia in 1909.

Worn out by the responsibility and the travelling, Goldsmith resigned in 1917 to take up the living of St John's, Hampstead, London. Bronchitis forced him latterly to winter in southern Europe. On retirement in 1926 he lived in London and Eastbourne. He died at St Leonards on 7 July 1932 and his ashes were buried in the Hampstead parish churchyard. He was survived by his wife, whose nephew, Rev. G. Frewer, was bishop of the North-West in 1929-61.

Goldsmith was most remembered for his energy, organizing ability and hard work, but also for his care for people, courage, dominating personality, cultured mind and deep piety. He published *Humble access* (1899) and *Home reunion papers* (1902), and played the violin and the organ. 'He developed the Diocese [of Bunbury] tenderly, wisely and well', fostering missionary work, education, and social work. His churchmanship was Tractarian, coupled with a sense of the importance of beauty in worship. Although 'very definite as to his own religious beliefs', he was tolerant. Bunbury continued in the Tractarian tradition that he established.

C. L. M. Hawtrey, *The availing struggle* (Perth, 1949); F. Alexander (ed), *Four bishops and their see* (Perth, 1957); St George's Cathedral Vestry, Perth, *Minute-books*, 1880-91, 1891-99; *Perth Q Mag*, 1889-90, 1891-92, 1895-96; C of E, *Diocese of Perth Year Book*, 1888-1905, *and* Diocese of Bunbury, *Occasional Papers*, Sept 1904-Feb 1917, and *Diocese of Bunbury Year Book*, 1904-18; *The Times*, 8 July 1932; Goldsmith papers and letters (held by author, Darlington, WA).   WILFRID E. HENN

GOLDSTEIN, VIDA JANE MARY (1869-1949), feminist and suffragist, was born on 13 April 1869 at Portland, Victoria, eldest child of JACOB ROBERT YANNASCH GOLDSTEIN and his wife Isabella, née Hawkins. Jacob, born at Cork, Ireland, on 10 March 1839 of Polish, Jewish and Irish stock, arrived in Victoria in 1858 and settled initially at Portland. He was commissioned a lieutenant in the Victorian Garrison Artillery in 1867 and rose to the rank of colonel. On 3 June 1868 he married Isabella (1849-1916), eldest daughter of Scottish-born squatter Samuel Proudfoot Hawkins.

After living at Portland and Warrnambool, where Jacob ran a general store, the Goldsteins moved to Melbourne in 1877. There Jacob worked as a contract draughtsman. He was a Unitarian, but the family attended Scots Church and later the Australian Church where Dr Charles Strong [q.v.6] encouraged a deep involvement in social welfare work. A founding member of the Melbourne Charity Organisation Society, its honorary treasurer and later honorary secretary, Goldstein believed that charity and poor relief should be scientifically organized, not handed out indiscriminately. He was a member of the Women's Hospital Committee for many years and also helped to promote the Cheltenham Men's Home. With Strong, Dr Bevan [q.v.7] and others Goldstein assisted with the project which began in 1892 for forming labour colonies, notably at Leongatha. Described by

some as irascible, domineering and opinionated, he became estranged from his feminist wife, although they lived under the same roof. He died at their apartment in Bank Place in the city on 21 September 1910.

Although an anti-suffragist, Jacob Goldstein encouraged his daughters to be economically and intellectually independent. Vida and her sisters were all well educated by a private governess; from 1884 Vida attended Presbyterian Ladies' College where she matriculated in 1886. An attractive girl, always well dressed, she led, for a time, a light-hearted social life. In 1892-98, when the family income was affected by Melbourne's bank crashes, she conducted with her sisters a co-educational preparatory school in Alma Road, St Kilda. Of the four sisters, Lina in 1892 married a banker H. J. Henderson, son of Rev. W. Henderson [q.v.4]; Elsie married H. H. Champion [q.v.8] in 1898; Aileen and Vida did not marry, though Vida had many proposals. Selwyn, their only brother, became a mining engineer.

Vida's mother was a confirmed suffragist, an ardent teetotaller and a zealous worker for social reform. Vida's own public career began about 1890 when she helped her mother collect signatures for the huge Woman Suffrage Petition. In the 1890s she also became involved in the National Anti-Sweating League, the Criminology Society and various social welfare activities, particularly those promoted by Strong and by her close friend Annette Bear-Crawford [q.v.7], with whom she helped to organize the Queen Victoria Hospital Appeal for the Queen's jubilee in 1897. She read widely on political, economic and legislative subjects and attended Victorian parliamentary sessions where she learned procedure while campaigning for a wide variety of reformist legislation. In 1899 after the death of Mrs Bear-Crawford, she was undisputed leader of the radical women's movement in Victoria, and that year made her first public-speaking appearance to advocate the vote for women. Trained initially by her friend, Vida quickly became a remarkably capable and impressive speaker with the ability to handle wittily even the most abusive of hecklers.

Between 1899 and 1908 Vida's first priority was the suffrage. In 1902 she travelled to the United States of America to speak at the International Woman Suffrage Conference, was elected secretary, gave evidence in favour of woman suffrage to a committee of the United States Congress and attended the International Council of Women Conference. Australian women had been granted the Federal vote in 1902 and on her return from America she became the first woman in the British Empire to be nominated and to stand for election to a national parliament. In her first bid as an Independent candidate for the Senate in 1903, she was proposed and assisted by the Women's Federal Political Association. This association had been formed to organize the women's vote for the first Federal elections, but by July 1903 with Vida as president it had become a vehicle for her platform and opinions. Despite ridicule of her candidacy, at the December election she polled 51 497 votes. Concluding after her defeat that women needed greater organization, she began educating female voters through the renamed Women's Political Association (W.P.A.), through her paper the *Woman's Sphere* which she owned and edited between September 1900 and March 1905, and by lecture tours around Victoria. She also campaigned untiringly for the State suffrage.

Once the State franchise was won in 1908 Vida returned to national politics and made four more attempts to gain election to Federal parliament: in 1910 and 1917 for the Senate and in 1913 and 1914 for the House of Representatives, always as an Independent Woman Candidate. She polled well except in 1917 when she lost her deposit, partly because of her uncompromising position on pacifism during the war. But there were other reasons for her failures. Her rigidly independent status alienated party supporters, and the press was either antagonistic to her, misrepresented her or ignored her. Yet it is clear that Vida was a candidate of sincerity and integrity. Her beliefs are revealed in her election manifestos between 1903 and 1917. Although they changed in detail, she consistently supported the principles of compulsory arbitration and conciliation, equal rights, equal pay, the appointment of women to a variety of official posts, and the introduction of legislation which would redistribute the country's wealth. She was outspokenly opposed to capitalism, supporting production for use not profit, and public control of public utilities. She opposed the White Australia policy in principle although she believed alien immigration should be restricted until equal pay for equal work had been achieved. Her desire to enter parliament and her avowed ambition to become prime minister were based on her determination to put her ideals into practice.

Vida actively promoted women's rights and emancipation in many other ways over the years from 1891 to 1919. She helped to found or supported many women's organizations including the National Council of Women, the Victorian Women's Public Servants' Association and the Women Writers' Club. She also worked for many social reforms including equal property rights for man and wife and raising the age of marriage and consent, while advocating new laws on land taxation, food adulteration and the sweating of women workers. Her methods included lobbying politicians to urge amendments to proposed legislation; she directly influenced many Acts. In December 1906, for example, she had the satisfaction of seeing passed into law her long-demanded Children's Court Act, the terms of which she had helped to draft. In her article 'Socialism of today—An Australian view' in the September 1907 issue of *Nineteenth Century and After*, she included in cost-of-living tables her findings on the lowest wage that a man and his family needed to pay for the barest necessities; this information, it is claimed, influenced Mr Justice Higgins [q.v.] in handing down his famous Harvester Judgment which established the legislative concept of a basic wage. In August 1909 Vida launched her second paper, the weekly *Woman Voter*, of which she was owner-editor.

Of the Australian women connected with the emancipation and suffrage movements of the day Vida Goldstein was the only one to gain a truly international reputation. In February 1911 she visited England at the invitation of the Women's Social and Political Union and her speeches drew huge crowds. Alice Henry [q.v.] wrote that Vida 'was the biggest thing that has happened to the woman movement for some time in England'.

During World War I Vida was uncompromisingly pacifist. She became chairman of the Peace Alliance, formed the Women's Peace Army in 1915, and was involved in much valuable social work including the organization of a women's unemployment bureau in 1915-16 and a Women's Rural Industries Co. Ltd. In 1919, with Cecilia John [q.v.], she accepted an invitation to represent Australian women at a Women's Peace Conference in Zurich: she was away three years. This trip signalled the end of her active public involvement in Australian feminist and political work: the Women's Political Association was dissolved, the *Woman Voter* ceased publication and Vida turned her attention increasingly to promoting more general causes, particularly pacifism and an international sisterhood of women.

Throughout the inter-war years, although no longer publicly prominent, Vida continued to lobby for social reforms such as improved provision of birth control and equal naturalization laws, and urged both women and men to support disarmament and to oppose war. She was now deeply committed to internationalism. Among the recurrent themes in her writings were her visionary suggestions for a new social order which was to have a spiritual foundation and be based on the 'brotherhood of man' concept of true socialism and on Christian ethics. Indeed, although she had always refused to join a party, Vida sympathized deeply with labour and the cause of working peoples. Most press reports called her a socialist, but she described herself as a democrat with a vision of society which would enable the complete equality of women with men and decent standards of living for all. She maintained her belief that women had special talents and needs, were potentially the world's civilizers, and therefore had contributions to make to political and international affairs.

In later life, while realizing that people might scoff at her 'simple faith in moral force' and her constant promotion of spiritual solutions for national and world problems, Vida became rather obsessive about the belief which had once been her motivation—that 'Righteousness exalteth a Nation'. In some disillusion, she became increasingly involved in Christian Science as a practitioner or healer, and at one time was a reader and president of its church in Melbourne which she had helped to found. Vida and her mother had first chosen to follow this religion about 1899. In her last years Vida lived quietly with her sisters Elsie and Aileen, who was also a practitioner.

Although Vida Goldstein may appear to have been a visionary idealist, yet by her pioneering efforts, her successes and her failures, she was a trail-blazer who provided leadership and inspiration to innumerable people. Vida summarized her basic attitude to politics and public life as: 'In essentials unity; in non-essentials liberty; in all things charity'. She was humane, kind and sincere, genuinely concerned for the underdog of whatever race or nationality. Charming, public-spirited and believing in Christian principles which she consistently practised, she was a born reformer, though she promoted simple solutions to complex social problems. According to a testimonial from her supporters, she 'offered to the people the wit and eloquence of an orator, the knowledge and foresight of a statesman, and the devotion and courage of a brave woman'. She died of cancer at her home in South Yarra on 15 August 1949 and was cremated. Her death passed almost unnoticed. A portrait of her, painted by Phyl Waterhouse from a photograph, is in Parliament House, Canberra.

L. M. Henderson, *The Goldstein story* (Melb, 1973); S. Encel et al, *Women and society* (Melb, 1974); J. Brownfoot and D. Scott, *The unequal half* (Syd, 1976); *New Idea*, 1 Oct 1902; *Imperial Review*, 1904, no 39; *Votes for Women* (Lond), 4 (Mar 1911), no 159; *Aust J of Politics and Hist*, Nov 1960; *Labour Hist*, May 1968, no 14; *Table Talk*, 27 Oct 1899; J. N. Brownfoot, Women organisations . . . in Victoria c.1890 to c.1908 (B.A. Hons thesis, Monash Univ, 1968), and for bibliog; Goldstein papers (Fawcett Lib, Lond); Alice Henry papers, *and* Leslie Henderson collection, MS 1637, *and* Rischbieth collection (NL).   JANICE N. BROWNFOOT

GOLL, EDWARD (1884-1949), pianist and music teacher, was born on 4 February 1884 at Kaaden, Bohemia, Austria-Hungary, son of Edward Goll, teacher, and his wife Aloysia, née Schmitt. Introduced to the piano by his father, he learned violin with Otakar Sevčík, making a first concert appearance at 9. At the Prague Conservatorium he decided on the piano, became one of the five pupils of the composer Antonín Dvořák and studied in 1899-1904 under Emil Sauer, a pupil of Franz Liszt. In 1904 he went to Paris to play concertos under the conductor Arthur Nikisch, then to England to work with Hans Richter and (Sir) Henry Wood. In 1909 he toured Europe in a trio with Jan Kubelík and Leopold Schwab. A friend of Queen Marie of Romania, he received the Romanian Order of Merit for the Arts.

Goll came to Melbourne in September 1911 as accompanist to the Welsh tenor Ben Davies. During the tour he met Julia O'Brien, née Walsh, a 45-year-old widow with one child, and they were married in St Mary's Catholic Church, Hawthorn, on 13 February 1912. After honeymooning in England they settled in Melbourne in October 1912. Goll gave some private concerts but by December 1914 had joined the staff of the Albert Street Conservatorium of Music. After a concert tour in September 1915 with Henri Verbrugghen [q.v.], he was offered a post in the new Sydney Conservatorium but, in November, accepted appointment in the Melbourne University Conservatorium as piano soloist (for recitals) and chief study teacher of pianoforte. Soon after, he was appointed musical director of Presbyterian Ladies' College.

Though naturalized on 15 August 1914 Goll, like many other enemy aliens, was under suspicion in World War I. A bitter campaign of vilification in the *Graphic of Australia* led in November 1916 to a petition from 110 ardent patriots asking the Presbyterian Assembly to dismiss him from the college. The assembly rejected it indignantly.

In 1922-23 Goll visited Europe, took refresher lessons under Eugene D'Albert and toured professionally in the United

States of America with the Minneapolis Symphony Orchestra and Verbrugghen. Returning full of enthusiasm for British music, he declared that (Sir) Arnold Bax was greater than Brahms and that John Ireland was a musical 'landscape painter'. He predicted rapid oblivion for Debussy, Stravinsky and Scriabin with permanent fame for Ravel and Franz Schreker.

As a teacher Goll stressed sight-reading, proper listening and constant, unremitting practice. 'Technique', he said, '*is* interpretation' and for his own performances he was known to practise five weeks on one line. A contemporary called him 'the best practiser I ever heard'. Prominent pupils included the composer Margaret Sutherland and the pianist Nancy Weir. After a disagreement with the conservatorium authorities in the early 1930s he taught mainly at home.

Short and stocky with a marked physical resemblance to Beethoven (noted by many in the bust by Nelson Illingworth [q.v.] at the Melbourne Conservatorium), Goll was a popular teacher who inspired many. He recorded frequently from 1902 and surviving discs are held by record collector L. Gravino of Sydney and by the National Library of Australia. Goll's wife died in 1927. A diabetic from about 1931, he resigned from P.L.C. in 1935. He abandoned plans for another American tour after World War II and died at his home in Mont Albert of cerebro-vascular disease on 11 January 1949. He was buried in Melbourne general cemetery.

M. O. Reid, *The ladies came to stay* (Melb, 1960); K. Fitzpatrick, *PLC Melbourne* (Melb, 1975); *Aust Musical News and Musical Digest*, 1 Mar 1924, 1 July 1931; *Music and the Teacher*, June 1981; *Punch* (Melb), 2 Nov 1911, 30 Jan, 27 Mar 1913; *Australasian*, 21 Mar, 5 Dec 1914; *Argus*, 16 June, 17 Nov 1916; *Age*, 29 Jan 1949; University of Melbourne Conservatorium records (Univ Melb Archives); A1 22/16261 (AAO, Canb); information from A. Corder, Hawthorn East, Vic.

H. J. GIBBNEY
MIMI COLLIGAN

GOOCH, WALTER (1842-1918), merchant and conservationist, was born on 10 November 1842 near Paradise, Adelaide, youngest son of Charles Gooch, merchant and farmer, and his wife Georgiana, née Hayward. He was educated at Rev. E. K. Miller's school and J. L. Young's [q.v.6] Adelaide Educational Institution and joined the National Bank of Australasia at 17. In 1867 he began work with his brother-in-law Henry Scott, a wool merchant, agent and trustee of Eagle Chambers. Scott, later a member of the Legislative Council, had been associated with Gooch's brothers Douglas and George in the northern pastoral industry. On 31 October 1871 Gooch married Elizabeth Jessy Samson (d. 1905) in Trinity Church, Adelaide; they had two daughters and four sons.

In 1877 when he moved to Belair, in the hills eight miles from Adelaide, Gooch decided that the 'setting apart of the property then known as Government Farm as a recreation ground for the people of Adelaide would be a great benefit'. In 1881, when the government seemed likely to divide the farm at Belair and sell it, he organized a picnic there to arouse publicity. Next year he obtained 213 influential signatures to a memorial urging that the farm be kept for the public. A number of possible uses were listed: a water or forest reserve, experimental farm, acclimatization station, zoological gardens, and national recreation ground. As a consequence, an Act was passed in 1883 which prevented the government from selling the farm without parliament's sanction.

In 1888 the new flora and fauna protection committee of the field naturalists' section of the Royal Society of South Australia criticized the Act's meagre scope. They claimed that since 1883 the government had cut down many magnificent trees and that the farm's subdivision into working men's blocks was being considered. They joined with Gooch and others whose objective was a people's park, in applying pressure through numerous deputations on government. They succeeded and a new Act was passed in 1891. Gooch was a foundation commissioner of the National Park and actively fostered its good management and development. But to the chagrin of the naturalists, under Gooch and like-minded commissioners the park's recreational aspect was developed at the expense of its natural resources. This area was the second national park established in Australia.

Gooch had been a member of the local board of the National Bank in 1881-83. He was also chairman for sixteen years of the Unley school board of advice and an active Anglican. A member of the Australian Natives' Association from 1889, in 1892 he became a trustee, member of the local board of directors and president of the Adelaide No. 1 branch. He was admired for his integrity and straightforward dealing as a businessman and never retired. He died of cerebro-vascular disease at his home Tooroo, Belair, on 10 October 1918 and was buried in the Anglican cemetery at Mitcham.

H. T. Burgess (ed), *Cyclopedia of South Australia*, 1 (1907); *Quiz* (Adel), 18 Sept 1901; Roy Soc SA, *Trans*, 35 (1911); *Advertiser* (Adel), 11 Oct 1918; Some information about origin of National Park (D4556 (L), SAA).   MARGARET ALLEN

GOODE, AGNES KNIGHT (1872-1947), social and political activist, was born on 31 January 1872 at Strathalbyn, South Australia, daughter of James Fleming, storekeeper and customs official, and his wife Charlotte, née Knight. Agnes taught school before marrying, on 11 July 1896, William Edward Goode, a sheep-farmer from Port Lincoln; they had a daughter and two sons. In 1915 she moved the family to Adelaide, perhaps partly because her husband was an unreliable manager.

In World War I Agnes Goode was founding vice-president of the Women's State Recruiting Committee; she was a forceful speaker and organized a rousing march by women through Adelaide streets. She was secretary from 1916 and president in 1921-22 of the Liberal Women's Educational Association. In 1916 she became a justice of the peace and member of the State Children's Council; from 1919 she presided over the State Children's Court, showing little leniency. She made a 12-year-old boy, convicted of stealing six bicycle chains, a state ward for six years; when his father protested, Goode responded that 'the theft would be the stigma; not the sentence'. From 1917 she had been a censor of cinematograph films.

In 1918-24 she edited the women's page of the *Liberal Leader* which she headed with the Shakespearian couplet:

Do you know I am a woman?
When I think I must speak.

She covered such topics as: women police; the need for the guardianship of children to be vested equally in their mothers; representation by women on government boards and juries; careers and equal pay for women; prices regulation; probation; and the National Council of Women (to which she belonged). She believed that the different, feminine virtues were needed in the councils of the state.

Goode opposed the controversial A. A. Edwards [q.v.8] and stood against him, as a Liberal, twice unsuccessfully in 1924 in the State and Adelaide City Council elections. She was president of the Adelaide women's branch of the Liberal Federation and next year won a seat on the St Peters Corporation which she held until she stood unsuccessfully for mayor in 1935. In 1926 she criticized Edwards's performance as a visiting justice, but a royal commission exonerated him. He then publicly attacked the State Children's Council and Goode's refusal to increase the children's weekly wage. She declared to the 1926 royal commission on law reform that she 'had never yet known a child brought up in an institution who was not exceedingly wasteful'. Despite an active campaign by women, the council was replaced by a new board of which Goode was not a member. She announced that she was leaving party politics but stood, again unsuccessfully, as a representative of the Women's Non-Party Association at a by-election for Adelaide in September. Next year she again failed to win the same seat for the Liberal Federation; she complained that her character had been 'been torn to bits' by Edwards.

Her husband died of cancer on 14 November 1929, but Goode remained indefatigable. She had been an official visitor to Parkside Mental Hospital and to the Adelaide Gaol and its Convicted Inebriates Institution and was busy in innumerable groups advancing the interests of poetry, theatre, Aboriginals, housewives, unemployed women, travellers, local industries and kindergartens. A pre-school named for her was opened at Stepney in 1949.

Although this rotund, ample-bosomed public figure was a devoted family woman, her life illustrated her conviction that woman's voice should be heard throughout the community. She died of coronary occlusion on 20 February 1947 at Toorak Gardens and was privately cremated.

Universal Publicity Co., *The official civic record of South Australia* (Adel, 1936); *PP* (SA), 1926 (54); *Housewife* (Adel), 5 June 1935; *Daily Herald*, 9 Jan 1919; *Liberal Leader*, Mar, Apr, Aug 1920, 1 Jan 1924; *Observer* (Adel), 22 Mar 1924; *Advertiser* (Adel), 29 Mar 1924, 16, 24, 26, 30 Mar 1927, 21 Feb 1947; *Australasian*, 29 Oct 1927; *Chronicle* (Adel), 19 June 1930; information from B. Clark, Paradise, *and* J. Churchett, Edwardstown, SA.

SUZANNE EDGAR

GOODISSON, LILLIE ELIZABETH (1860?-1947), racial hygienist, was born at Holyhead, Wales, daughter of John Richard Price, physician, and his wife Frances Elizabeth, née Roberts. She trained as a nurse and aged 19 married Lawford David Evans, physician, in London. They migrated to Auckland, New Zealand, where their two children were born in 1881 and 1883. Lillie Evans had moved to Melbourne by 1895 and about 1897 set up Myrnong private hospital at St Kilda. Widowed in 1903, in the early 1900s she went to Western Australia. At East Fremantle she married 33-year-old Albert Elliot Goodisson, business manager, on 11 June 1904. They lived at Geraldton until Albert Goodisson went to Batavia in September 1913 for 'health reasons'. Lillie visited him there, before he died on 4 February 1914, in the lunatic asylum where he had been committed for 'general paralysis' and derangement. Emotionally and financially bereft, Lillie, with the aid of a loan from her friend Ivy Brookes [q.v.7 H. Brookes], returned to Melbourne.

During World War I she worked as a secretary for the women's division of the People's Liberal Party, the Empire Trade Defence Association and various patriotic causes. By 1919 she was also secretary of the women's section of the Australian Industries Protection League. Her finances remained a problem, and in 1921 Ivy Brookes again came to her aid, establishing her in a small library at Elwood, Melbourne. Mounting debts and ill health forced its liquidation in 1924.

In 1926 Lillie Goodisson moved to Sydney, where her daughter was living. With the Women's Reform League she founded the Racial Hygiene Association of New South Wales, to promote sex education, the prevention and eradication of venereal disease and the education of the public in eugenics. As general secretary she advocated the selective breeding of future generations for the elimination of hereditary disease and defects. With some vice-regal, political and clerical patronage she campaigned unsuccessfully for the segregation and sterilization of the mentally deficient and for the introduction of pre-marital health examinations. In 1933 the association established the first birth-control clinic in Sydney—it was for married women with hereditary, economic or health problems. In response to her critics, Goodisson maintained that judicious birth control would eradicate inheritable disease, diminish maternal mortality (by discouraging abortion) and result in an increased and healthier population.

A woman of unusual force of character, Lillie Goodisson in her seventies and eighties was still dedicated and active; she was also an outspoken executive member of the National Council of Women of New South Wales, the Travellers' Aid Society, the Good Film League of New South Wales, the Sydney Health Week and Mental Hygiene Council. For the last twenty years of her life her work and that of the Racial Hygiene Association were inseparable; a fellow-worker noted that 'she is the Society and without her there would be no Society'. She died on 10 January 1947 at Cremorne Point and was cremated. Her son and daughter survived her.

Progressive J (Syd), 1 Aug, 5 Nov, 5 Dec 1935; National Council of Women (NSW), *Biennial Report*, 1921-34; Racial Hygiene Assn of NSW, *Annual Report*, 1928-48; *Bowyang*, 6, 1981; *West Australian*, 5, 11 Feb 1914; *Argus*, 30 Apr 1915, 25 Jan 1918; *SMH*, 7 Jan 1935, 25 Nov 1937, 11 Jan 1947; Brookes papers (NL).   MEREDITH FOLEY

GOODMAN, SIR WILLIAM GEORGE TOOP (1872-1961), engineer, was born on 14 March 1872 at Ramsgate, Kent, England, son of William Henry Goodman, carpenter, and his wife Emma Ann, née Limeburner. After attending St George's Boys' Central School, Ramsgate, he joined Poole & White, engineers, London. On 7 January 1893 he married Florence Letitia Attreed. In Tasmania in 1895 Goodman installed the first electric plant at the Mount Lyell mine. He then became assistant electrical engineer in the tramway construction branch of the Department of Public Works, New South Wales, in 1897-1900, before joining the firm Noyes Brothers Pty Ltd, which built the tracks of New Zealand's first electric tramway at Dunedin. In 1903 he became that city's electrical engineer and inspected tramway systems around the world.

In 1907 when Adelaide's new Municipal Tramways Trust was formed, Goodman became chief engineer; from next year he was also general manager. He was to hold this joint-appointment for forty-two years and his policies were to have a major influence on the development of metropolitan Adelaide. His proposals to open the grassed city squares and sacrosanct parklands and to remove 150 trees for laying tracks embroiled him in controversy, but he won. Contracts were let for 56 miles (90 km) of track, a depot, 100 trams, an administrative building at Hackney and a power station. Despite delivery delays, electric trams were running by November 1908 and the formal opening took place on 9 March 1909. Electrification was completed by 1914 and a separate Port Adelaide system was opened in 1917.

That year Goodman was commissioned by the Federal government to visit Britain, Europe and the United States of America to investigate munitions factories. While there he learned to fly. In 1921 he reported on Brisbane's electric tramway system. In the early 1920s returned servicemen began to operate buses in competition with the Adelaide trams. To counter this Goodman purchased forty American Mack buses in 1925; although his choice was criticized, they lasted twenty-five years. From 1927 he sat on the Metropolitan Omnibus Board which licensed private bus operators; he circumvented further competition by buying eighty-two private buses for the M.T.T. In 1929 the trust took over the two Adelaide-Glenelg steam railways: Goodman converted the southern line to a high-speed, reserved track, electric tramway which still operates in the 1980s in its original form and with the same cars.

Goodman's decisions were often opposed by the Adelaide City Council, but his view usually prevailed as, for example, when he sought to build an additional tramway depot in the city's heart—Victoria Square. In 1928 he served in Auckland on a royal commission into its transport and next year he was a member of a Commonwealth-States inquiry into the Hume Reservoir. In 1931 he chaired the important royal commission on the South Australian railways which reviewed Commissioner W. A. Webb's [q.v.] era. Next year Goodman's services to Adelaide were recognized by a knighthood.

Goodman replaced Port Adelaide's trams with double-deck trolleybuses in 1938; a complementary service in Adelaide's eastern suburbs had already begun. In 1937-44 he was chairman of the new and successful South Australian Housing Trust which provided small homes at low rents. He was a director of several companies and a member of the council of the University of Adelaide in 1913-54: he played a valuable role on its finance committee. In 1945 Goodman received the Peter Nicol Russell [q.v.6] memorial medal from the Institution of Engineers, Australia. He retired in 1950.

Goodman's managerial style was strict—coats were never removed in the office and there was no smoking on duty—and direct. His skill in all aspects of his work ensured respect from his men. His fairness is illustrated by the occasion when a motorman, charged with having driven the first tram of the day off the end of the Henley Beach line, was instructed to wait until 'The Chief' tried the terminus, in the dark, next morning. When Goodman also drove the tram off the line (the terminus's street light was broken) the charge was dropped and an apology extended. He advanced the employment opportunities of returned servicemen after both world wars. An accomplished organist and drummer, Goodman, when young, enjoyed dancing, the cinema and deep-sea diving. He belonged to the Adelaide Club, and was an Anglican.

Following three years in hospital, Goodman died at College Park on 4 February 1961 and was buried in North Road cemetery, Nailsworth. Predeceased by his wife (d. 1956), he was survived by four daughters and two sons. His estate was sworn for probate at £123 083. A portrait by G. R. Shedley is held by the South Australian Housing Trust.

R. I. Jennings, *W. A. Webb, South Australian Railways commissioner, 1922-1930* (Adel, 1973); G. Stewart, *The end of the penny section* (Wellington, 1973); J. C. Radcliffe and C. J. M. Steele, *Adelaide road passenger transport, 1836-1958* (Adel, 1974); *PP* (LA Vic), 1912, 3 (16), p 660, 676; *Advertiser* (Adel), 29 Nov 1950, 6 Feb 1961; *News* (Adel), 29 Nov 1950.   JOHN C. RADCLIFFE

GOODWIN, SIR THOMAS HERBERT JOHN CHAPMAN (1871-1960), soldier, medical practitioner and governor, was born on 24 May 1871 at Kandy, Ceylon (Sri Lanka), eldest son of Surgeon Major John Kilealy Goodwin and his wife, Melbourne-born Marion Agnes, née Power. Educated at Newton College, Devon, and St Mary's Hospital, London, Goodwin graduated M.R.C.S. and L.R.C.P. in 1892. Commissioned in the British Army Medical Service on 29 July 1893 as surgeon lieutenant, he served in the United Kingdom for three years, then was posted to India where he saw active service on the North-West Frontier in 1897-98 and won the Distinguished Service Order.

On 29 December 1897 at Simla, he married Lilian Isabel Ronaldson; they were childless. Returning to Britain in 1902 as a medical officer at the Royal Military College, Sandhurst, he went back to India in 1906-11 as surgical specialist to Western Command.

From 1914 Goodwin served in France and was mentioned in dispatches three times. He accompanied the Balfour Mission to the United States of America in 1917 as assistant director, medical services. Returning to the War Office in January 1918, he was appointed director general, Army Medical Services in June. He retired as lieut-general in July 1923 after serving as honorary surgeon to the King.

Appointed governor of Queensland on 19 February 1927, Goodwin reached Brisbane on 13 June. Described as 'tall, with grey hair and a closely clipped moustache', he and Lady Goodwin travelled extensively and took a lively interest in the welfare of British migrants.

Despite the governor's reputation as a keen shot and fisherman, they were interested in wild-life preservation; they also followed racing enthusiastically and enjoyed inspecting rural industries. Goodwin took a professional interest in the health of Europeans in the tropics and in the campaign against eye disease in western Queensland, especially among children. He strongly supported moves for a Queensland medical school. He faced no constitutional problems, the change of government in May 1929 being handled by William Lennon [q.v.] while Goodwin was on tour in Torres Strait. When insults to the Italian coat of arms by Innisfail pranksters at Christmas 1928 brought angry diplomatic protests, he strongly urged the McCormack [q.v.] government to respond calmly. Goodwin's quiet term of office expired on 7 April 1932, when he returned to England.

He was appointed C.M.G. (1915), C.B. (1918), K.C.B. (1919) and K.C.M.G. (1932)

and was awarded many foreign honours and honorary degrees. Predeceased by his wife, he died at Oxford on 29 September 1960.

Queenslander, 5 Feb, 16 June 1927; GO, Correspondence, 1927-32 (QA).   PAUL D. WILSON

GOOLD-ADAMS, SIR HAMILTON JOHN (1858-1920), soldier and governor, was born on 27 June 1858 at Jamesbrook, Cork, Ireland, fourth son of Richard Wallis Goold-Adams, later high sheriff of the county, and his wife Mary Sarah, née Becher. Apprenticed on a training ship, he changed his mind and was commissioned in the Royal Scots Regiment in 1878. Promoted captain in 1885 and major in 1895, he served principally in southern Africa in 1884-1901. He led several expeditions into the interior, one of which almost proved fatal. He was deputy commissioner of the Orange River Colony and was its lieut-governor in 1901-07. He was appointed C.M.G. in 1902 and G.C.M.G. in 1907. In the South African War he was mentioned in dispatches and helped to defend Mafeking. He returned to England and on 4 July 1911 married Elsie Riordan of Montreal, Canada; they had two children. Appointed high commissioner to Cyprus in 1911, he became governor of Queensland in 1914.

The reserved and somewhat dour Goold-Adams arrived in Brisbane on 15 April 1915 two months before the election of T. J. Ryan's [q.v.] Labor government. The first elected Labor government in Queensland, it began state enterprises and introduced radical labour and farming legislation which affronted Goold-Adams. In his first dispatch to the secretary of state, he objected to the 'mass of undigested legislation' being introduced, but reported favourably on the cabinet and referred to Ryan as 'a gentleman of high standing, courteous and always ready to oblige'.

In the turbulent years 1916-18 when Ryan was faced with an intransigent Legislative Council and an irascible William Morris Hughes [q.v.], he found Goold-Adams a good friend and counsellor who defended his government to the Colonial Office and to the governor-general, Sir Ronald Munro Ferguson [q.v.]. In 1917 Goold-Adams seemed to exercise his own judgment about the appointment of thirteen new legislative councillors, but actually followed the advice of Ryan. In 1918, however, when the Legislative Council continued to defeat government money bills and Ryan sought further Labor appointments to the Council, Goold-Adams refused.

When he was to retire in 1919, he advised the Colonial Office to accept the appointment of William Lennon [q.v.], Speaker of the Legislative Assembly, as lieut-governor while a new governor was found. The appointment partly satisfied local aspirations for an Australian governor, and gave Lennon the opportunity to appoint a majority of Labor nominees to the legislative council; in 1921 they voted for the abolition of the Council.

Goold-Adams left Brisbane in January 1920 to retire in England. He contracted pleurisy on the ship and died in Capetown on 12 April.

C. A. Bernays, *Queensland—our seventh political decade 1920-1930* (Syd, 1931); D. J. Murphy, *T. J. Ryan* (Brisb, 1975); D. J. Murphy et al (eds), *Labor in power . . . Queensland 1915-1957* (Brisb, 1979).
                                                      D. J. MURPHY

GORDON, BERNARD SIDNEY (1891-1963), soldier and dairy farmer, was born on 16 August 1891 at Launceston, Tasmania, son of Charles Gordon, cabman and later hotel proprietor, and his wife Mary, née Rowlands. After schooling at Deloraine and Devonport he worked as a cooper's machinist at Beaconsfield. He later went to Townsville, Queensland, where he was in charge of remounts en route to India.

Gordon enlisted in the Australian Imperial Force at Townsville on 27 September 1915 and joined the 41st Battalion as a private, embarking for overseas service on the *Demosthenes* in May 1916. He remained with the battalion throughout the war, serving in France and Belgium where he was first wounded on 5 October 1917. In June 1918 he was promoted lance corporal.

In July 1918 the 41st Battalion, as part of the 11th Infantry Brigade, was involved in an attack on Hamel, and Gordon was awarded the Military Medal for gallant conduct. He was later awarded the Victoria Cross, for 'most conspicuous bravery and devotion to duty on 26th-27th August, 1918, east of Bray'. In this action, the citation stated, Gordon displayed 'a wonderful example of fearless initiative'. He led his section through heavy shell-fire to its objective, which he consolidated. 'Single-handed he attacked an enemy machine-gun which was enfilading the company on his right, killed the man on the gun and captured the post, which contained one officer and ten men. He then cleaned up a trench, capturing twenty-nine prisoners and two machine-guns . . . Practically unaided, he captured, in the course of these operations, two officers and sixty-one other ranks, together with six machine-guns'.

Gordon was again wounded on 1 September while the battalion was advancing in the Mont St Quentin area. He returned to Australia in January 1919, and was discharged in Queensland in April. He ran a grocer's shop at Clayfield but then took up a dairy farming and Jersey stud property, Lincolnfield, near Beaudesert, where he farmed for forty-three years. A keen amateur rider, he was also a good horse-breaker and keen sportsman, a promoter of racing, cycling, boxing and football; he won many amateur boxing tournaments and medals for his achievements. He was a popular man in any company, with a ready wit and a keen sense of humour, and was well known for his stories and anecdotes. In 1956 he attended the Victoria Cross centenary celebrations in London, and in 1960, in his honour, the Gordon Soldiers' Club was opened at Cabarlah, Queensland.

Gordon remained at Lincolnfield until ill health forced him to move to Hervey Bay early in 1962. He had suffered for years from pulmonary tuberculosis. He died at Torquay, Queensland, on 19 October 1963, and was cremated in Brisbane with Methodist forms. Gordon had married Evelyn Catherine Lonergan on 29 December 1915 at Launceston, with Catholic rites; there were six children of this marriage. He was a widower when he married Caroline Edith Manley, née Victorsen, a widow, on 15 September 1938, at Ann Street Presbyterian Church, Brisbane; they had two sons and one daughter. Gordon was survived by his second wife and eight of his children.

C. E. W. Bean, *The A.I.F. in France*, 1918 (Syd, 1942); L. Wigmore (ed), *They dared mightily* (Canb, 1963); *London Gazette*, 24 Dec 1918, 21 Jan 1919; *Reveille* (Syd), Dec 1963; Records (AWM); information from Mrs C. E. Gordon, Caboolture, Qld.

JAMES W. COURTNEY

GORDON, SIR DAVID JOHN (1865-1946), journalist and politician, was born on 4 May 1865 at Riverton, South Australia, son of Thomas Gordon, carpenter, miller and farmer, and his wife Ann, née Stewart; they were both from Scotland. David received an elementary education at J. S. C. Cole's [q.v.8] Stanley Grammar School, Watervale. His family moved to Yorke Peninsula and at 11 he was on a farm working large teams of horses. He then took a job with the Port Adelaide branch of John Darling [q.v.4] & Son, grain merchants and shipping agents. He also became a deacon of the Port Adelaide Congregational Church.

On 4 April 1888 Gordon married Anna Louisa Peel, a pianist and accompanist at his church. From that year he managed the local branch of the daily newspaper, the *South Australian Register*. He became known as a tenacious newshound by interviewing passengers on ships docking at the port. In 1891 the paper had him accompany Clement Giles [q.v.] into Central Australia and Gordon returned enthusiastically committed to development of the country's resources: he published numerous articles and pamphlets on the subject over the next twenty years.

In 1893 he became the *Register*'s financial and commercial editor and agricultural editor of its weekly, the *Observer*, often writing under the pseudonym 'Wuronga'. Six years later he was promoted to the daily's editorial staff, becoming in turn leader-writer, acting associate editor, chief of literary staff and chief of Hansard staff. Gordon travelled his State extensively and became a popular advocate for the improvement of the farming and pastoral industries—production, transportation and sales. With his friend George Riddoch [q.v.] he persuaded the government to establish a freezing works at Port Adelaide and he was a vice-president of the River Murray League.

Gordon had spent considerable time in State and Federal press-galleries and around 1908 began to advance the affairs of the Australian National League. Next year he negotiated the fusion of this group with the remaining two anti-socialist groups in State politics. He was active on the executive of the Liberal Union and, after standing unsuccessfully for the Senate, in 1911 he was elected to the House of Representatives seat of Boothby. He continued to press for increased exploitation of South and Central Australia's resources and sat on the royal commission on the fruit industry. In 1913 he was defeated, but won the State Legislative Council seat of Midland.

In July 1917 Gordon was minister of education and repatriation in the Peake [q.v.] government, but he resigned next month after its coalition with the National Party. His distaste for Peake's action ran deep, for he rejected two subsequent offers of a post. In 1918 he became Liberal leader in the council and was its president in 1932-44. He was knighted in 1934.

A highly principled man with a strong personality, Gordon was a friend of Herbert Brookes [q.v.7] and supported his propaganda campaign waged via the *Australian Liberal*. Gordon's liberal individualism permeated his publications, nearly all of which were concerned with resource development. They include *The central State* (1903) and *The 'Nile' of Australia* (1906), numerous pamphlets, and several annual editions of the *Handbook of South Australia* (1908).

Gordon was an inveterate committeeman. In 1927 he chaired the Australian delegation to the International Economic Conference, Geneva. He was president of the Australian Liberal Union (1932-34), the Associated Chambers of Commerce of Australia (1921-22), and in South Australia the Adelaide Chamber of Commerce (1919-21), Toc H, and the Sailors' and Soldiers' Fathers' Association. His directorships included the Adelaide Electric Supply Co. Ltd, Broken Hill South Ltd, North Broken Hill Ltd, Broken Hill Associated Smelters Pty Ltd, and the local branch of Goldsbrough Mort [qq.v.4,5] & Co. Ltd. He joined the Adelaide Club in 1922.

He retired from the council in 1944 and died on 12 February 1946 at his home in Victoria Avenue, Unley Park, survived by two sons and two daughters. His wife had predeceased him in 1933. Gordon was buried in Mitcham cemetery. One son, Douglas Peel Gordon, was a legislative councillor for Midland in 1947-48 and the other, John Rutherford Gordon, in World War I was awarded the Military Cross as a pilot. An oil portrait of their father by George Webb hangs in the South Australian houses of parliament.

R. Rivett, *Australian citizen: Herbert Brookes* (Melb, 1965); *Daily Herald*, 10 June 1910; *Mail* (Adel), 17 May 1913; *Liberal Leader*, 1, 21 Feb 1923; *Advertiser* (Adel), 13 Feb 1946; H. and I. Brookes papers, MS 1924 (NL).   ROB VAN DEN HOORN

GORDON, GROSVENOR GEORGE STUART (1877?-1955), soldier, is said to have been born on 7 February 1877 at Bangalore, India, son of George Charles Gordon, soldier, and his wife Marie Louise. Nothing is known of his early life. As a youth he served in England with the City of London Rifle Battalion and the 17th Lancers and then spent sixteen months with the East Origaland Defence Force. He saw active service with the British Army in 1896 during the Matabele War in operations around Bulawayo and Salisbury. By 1900 he had migrated to Australia and on 15 June that year married Mary Jane Hooper in Melbourne with Free Christian Church rites. On his marriage certificate he gave his age as 34 and his occupation as actor.

During the South African War Gordon enlisted as a corporal in the 5th Victorian (Mounted Rifles) Contingent in February 1901 and served in Cape Colony, Orange River Colony and Eastern Transvaal. He was promoted to sergeant and returned home in April 1902. On 7 March 1910 he was commissioned as a second lieutenant in the Citizen Military Forces and posted to the Australian Corps of Signallers (Victoria), and in 1913 was promoted lieutenant in the 26th Signal Company, Australian Engin-

eers. On the outbreak of World War I he was appointed to the Australian Imperial Force as a lieutenant with the 1st Divisional Signal Company and embarked for Egypt in October 1914. He served at Gallipoli from the landing on 25 April 1915 until the evacuation and from 9 September commanded the signal company. He was promoted captain on 3 November and played an important part in the planning and execution of line communications vital to the successful withdrawal of the 1st Division, the last message being received by line at Divisional Headquarters on 20 December, just two hours before the last boat left Anzac Cove. For his work at Gallipoli he was mentioned in dispatches.

Gordon embarked for France on 21 March 1916, was promoted major on 3 August and commanded the 1st Divisional Signal Company for the rest of the war and beyond. For his personal courage and tireless efforts in maintaining line communications in the front line, particularly during the shell-fire and barrages at Pozières, he was awarded the Distinguished Service Order in December 1916. He was also twice mentioned in dispatches in 1917. His A.I.F. appointment ended in July 1920 and in 1920-30 he was 'a mechanical expert and sales manager' with the Dunlop Rubber Co. in Sydney. In 1931-39 he owned a milk bar at Randwick and from August 1948 received a Totally and Permanently Incapacitated pension. After World War I he served with the citizen forces, in 1921-27 commanding the 1st Divisional Signals as lieut-colonel. Brigadier J. H. Thyer, historian of the signals corps, recalled that 'he appeared at camps always immaculately dressed in faultlessly starched drill, beautifully polished leather, a pith helmet and, above all, an eyeglass. He impressed'.

Known by his contemporaries as a colourful, cheerful and efficient officer, Gordon helped to lay the foundations of the modern Royal Australian Corps of Signals. In World War I, when radio was in its infancy, and rarely seen on the battlefield, his determination and courage in providing and maintaining line communications, often with horse-drawn cable teams under shell-fire, significantly contributed to the operational success of the 1st Division.

Survived by his wife and son, Gordon died at Concord on 15 July 1955 and was cremated with Anglican rites. His death certificate stated that he was 81.

Aust Defence Dept, *Official records of the Australian military contingents to the war in South Africa*, P. L. Murray ed (Melb, 1911); C. E. W. Bean, *The A.I.F. in France*, 1916 (Syd, 1929); R. R. McNicoll, *The Royal Australian Engineers 1902 to 1919* (Canb, 1979); *London Gazette*, 28 Jan, 29 Dec

1916, 2 Jan, 28 Dec 1917; *Reminder*, July 1955; *SMH*, 1 Aug 1938; J. H. Thyer, Royal Australian Corps of Signals, Corps history 1906-1918 (MS, 1974), *and* War diary, 1st Divisional Signal Company, AIF (AWM); information from Dept of Veterans' Affairs, Canb.   R. E. COWLEY

GORDON, SIR JOHN HANNAH (1850-1923), politician and judge, was born on 26 July 1850 at Kilmalcolm, Renfrewshire, Scotland, eldest son of Rev. James Gordon, preacher of the Free Church, and his wife Margaret, née Leonard. In 1859 the family migrated to South Australia where James Gordon became pastor of Presbyterian churches at Mount Barker and Gawler. John was educated privately and at Rev. J. Leonard's school. His first employment was with W. Duffield & Co., merchants, followed by a term with Dunn & Co., millers, before studying theology fop two years. In July 1871 he was articled to J. J. Bonnar, whose Strathalbyn law practice he acquired upon admission to the Bar in 1876. On 4 January 1877 at the Presbyterian church, Strathalbyn, he married Ann Wright Rogers; they had two sons and two daughters. In 1879 he was elected mayor of Strathalbyn and served in this office for one year. He transferred his practice to Adelaide in 1887.

At the 1888 election Gordon, later described as 'a consistent Liberal, with a tendency . . . towards the left', entered the Legislative Council as member for Southern District. In June 1889 he was appointed leader of the government in the council and minister of education and of the Northern Territory, holding these offices for the remaining term of the Cockburn [q.v.8] ministry until April 1890. Gordon also served as president of the 1890 Intercolonial Post and Telegraph Conference in Adelaide and as a delegate to the 1891 Federal convention where he favoured a loose confederate type of union; his introduction of the subject of preferential railway rates led ultimately to the inclusion of the interstate commission clause in the Constitution. In June 1892 he was reappointed minister of education in the Holder [q.v.] ministry but resigned from parliament just four months later when on the verge of bankruptcy. The principal sources of Gordon's financial difficulties were his partnership in Crown Point cattle-station in the Northern Territory and ownership of nearly all shares in the ailing West Australian Timber Co. Ltd. He avoided official insolvency by assigning all of his prop-

erty by deed and thereby maintained his parliamentary eligibility.

Gordon was re-elected to the council for Southern District in June 1893 and was appointed chief secretary in the Kingston [q.v.] ministry. At the height of the Adelaide Hospital dispute in February 1896 he resigned this office in the wake of claims that he had improperly aided his sister's promotion to a senior nursing post. This charge was not substantiated by the royal commission which preceded his resignation but rumours continued to appear in the press. His resignation was further precipitated by the refusal of the hospital board of management to comply with recommendations of the royal commission which he had endorsed.

In 1897 Gordon was elected as a South Australian delegate to the Australasian Federal Convention and served as a member of the important constitutional committee. On the conference floor, together with Patrick McMahon Glynn [q.v.], he led and won the case for South Australia's equal access to River Murray water. From December 1899 until December 1903 Gordon was attorney-general in the Holder and then in the Jenkins [q.v.] ministries; he also held the education portfolio from April 1902. In these final parliamentary years he was appointed Queen's Counsel in July 1900, was a delegate to the 1902 Corowa conference on water conservation which recommended the appointment of a royal commission into navigation and irrigation of the River Murray, and served as president of the South Australian Law Society.

In December 1903, despite his absence from legal practice for many years, Gordon was appointed to the Supreme Court and for a time administered its wage-determining jurisdiction. He was knighted in 1908. He was chairman of the Commonwealth royal commission into the sugar industry in 1911 but soon resigned because of ill health; in February 1913 he declined an invitation from W. M. Hughes [q.v.] to move to the High Court.

Gordon had suffered since a child from a rheumatic heart condition. He died in Adelaide of cardiac disease on 23 December 1923, survived by his wife and daughters. Throughout his parliamentary and judicial career he was praised for his courtesy, generosity and superb oratory; as a judge he was industrious and conscientious. A brother, William Beattie, was a member of the Western Australian Legislative Assembly in 1901-11.

L. F. Fitzhardinge, *William Morris Hughes*, 1 (Syd, 1964); H. J. Stowe, *They built Strathalbyn* (Adel, 1973); *Qld Hist Review*, 1 (1968), p 49; *Observer* (Adel), 1 July, 5 Dec 1903; *Register* (Adel),

28 Feb 1927; M. A. Heaney, The Adelaide Hospital dispute 1894-1902 (B.A. Hons thesis, Univ Adel, 1980); G. Loughlin, South Australian Queen's Counsel 1865-1974 (B.A. Hons thesis, Univ Adel, 1974); GRG/14/4300 (SA). GRAHAM LOUGHLIN

GORDON, JOSEPH MARIA (1856-1929), army officer, was born on 18 March 1856 at Jeréz de la Frontera, Andalusia, Spain, son of Carlos Pedro Gordon and his wife Elena, née Prendergast. He was baptized José Maria Jacobo Rafael Ramon Francisco Gabriel del Corazon de Jesus Gordon y Prendergast. Little is known of his childhood; he left Spain with his parents, probably in 1867, for Scotland where the family settled on an inherited property known as Wardhouse in Aberdeenshire. Before becoming a boarder in 1868 at the Oratory School, Edgbaston, Birmingham, he had to learn to speak English. He later attended Beaumont College, a Jesuit school at Old Windsor.

Gordon entered the Royal Military Academy, Woolwich, in March 1874 and in February 1876 became a lieutenant in the Royal Artillery. He was stationed in Ireland in 1877-78, then contracted rheumatic fever and resigned his commission on 16 August 1879. For health reasons he sailed to New Zealand where he became a drill instructor in the armed constabulary. Gordon then went to Melbourne, and while trying to obtain military employment entered two unsuccessful business ventures and for a few months went on the stage. His expectations of a commission in Victoria's permanent artillery were not realized, but through the influence of the governor of South Australia, Sir William Jervois [q.v.4], he was employed as a mounted constable in Adelaide in June 1881, then in December was offered an artillery appointment. He began duty in January 1882 as a subaltern on the permanent staff. He had come to South Australia just when a permanent artillery unit was first being raised; his promotion was rapid and by May 1892 he was a lieut-colonel. That year, on 29 February, he married Eleanor Fitzgerald (d. 1910) at St James Catholic Church, Elsternwick, Melbourne. In July 1893 he was appointed commandant of the military forces of South Australia vice Major General M. F. Downes [q.v.4] and, from 2 August, held the rank of colonel.

When the South African War began in October 1899 Gordon had been serving temporarily in London for over a year as inspector of warlike stores for South Australia and other Australian colonies. After returning to Adelaide he sailed for Cape Town in January 1900 as a special service officer and was appointed chief staff officer for Overseas Colonial Forces. Gordon took part in military operations in Cape Colony, the Orange Free State and the Transvaal but was recalled after nine months by the South Australian government. For his work in South Africa he was appointed C.B. and mentioned in dispatches.

In December 1900 Gordon was granted the 'local and temporary' rank of brigadier general. Federation brought no immediate change in his career, except that after 1 March 1901 he became responsible to the Federal minister for defence, and in the long run it brought him no promotion. In 1902 he was transferred to Victoria where, from July 1902 to January 1905, he commanded the Commonwealth Military Forces in that State; he held the same post in New South Wales in 1905-12.

Gordon was passed over for the post of inspector general and for that of chief of the General Staff. Colonel (Major General Sir) J. C. Hoad [q.v.] was appointed C.G.S. in 1909 despite the fact that General Sir Edward Hutton [q.v.] had made a more favourable report on Gordon. In May 1912 Gordon became C.G.S. but without promotion to major general—probably to avoid extending his age for retirement. Early in 1914 the inspector general of British Overseas Forces, General Sir Ian Hamilton, reported on Australia's military forces and, pending the completion of his inspection, the Federal government deferred Gordon's relinquishment of the post of C.G.S. until 31 July 1914. He was at sea on his way to England for a holiday when World War I broke out. He offered his services to the Australian government but the offer was refused. In the United Kingdom he commanded the 92nd Brigade and the 10th Reserve Division, British Army, in 1914-15, was an inspector in the Ministry of Munitions in 1916-17, and in 1919 was with the army of occupation in Cologne, Germany. On 1 November 1921 he was placed on the retired list of the Australian Military Forces with the honorary rank of major general.

After the war Gordon lived in England and in 1921 his autobiography, *The chronicles of a gay Gordon*, was published in London. Survived by his son and daughter, he died of cancer on 6 September 1929 at Egham, Surrey, and was buried in the Catholic section of Old Windsor cemetery, Berkshire.

Gordon was a keen, energetic and tenacious officer who made the best of the scant means at his disposal to keep himself professionally informed and efficient. None of the governments he served in Australia sent him to courses of training in England. He was, moreover, an officer with ideas. He was an early exponent of universal training and was active in the early development of military aviation in Australia and in the creation of the Small Arms Factory at Lithgow, New South Wales. But officers with ideas gather enemies as well as friends in seats of power and Gordon's fate in this respect, especially after Federation, seems to have been no exception.

Aust. Defence Dept, *Official records of the Australian military contingents to the war in South Africa*, P. L. Murray, ed (Melb, 1911); *London Gazette*, 29 Nov 1900, 16 Apr 1901; *Vic Hist J*, 47 (1976), no 2; *Sabretache*, Mar-June 1979; *Bulletin*, 28 June 1902; *Australasian*, 27 Apr 1912; *Punch* (Melb), 2 May 1912; *Herald* (Melb), 9 Sept 1929; *The Times*, 10 Sept 1929.   WARREN PERRY

GORDON, MARGARET JANE (1880-1962), singer, was born on 3 March 1880 at New Quay, Cardiganshire, Wales, daughter of Thomas Thomas, master mariner, and his wife Anne. Educated privately, she studied singing with Madame Clara Novello at Cardiff and at the Royal Academy of Music, London. In 1904 she made her debut in London and was engaged by J. C. Williamson [q.v.6] to tour Australia with the Parkina-Földesy Concert Company in February-March 1905. A mezzo-soprano, she charmed audiences with the 'beautiful timbre' of her voice and her vivacity.

When the tour ended in Perth, Miss Thomas joined Williamson's Royal Comic Opera Company. Opening in Sydney on 6 May as Nanoya in *The Cingalee*, she surprised 'her most hopeful admirers by her aptitude as an actress'. She visited Perth and Adelaide with the company and in Melbourne in September delighted as Hélène de Solanger in *Véronique*. She returned to Sydney with the company in December.

Petite, with wavy, brown hair and large, expressive, yellow eyes, Margaret Thomas captivated (SIR) ALEXANDER GORDON (1858-1942), a leading barrister, who visited the theatre every Saturday night, anonymously sending her large bunches of violets. Eventually they met and she left the professional stage in May 1906. They visited Britain and were married with Calvinist Methodist forms at New Quay on 26 September. The Gordons returned to Sydney and lived at Elizabeth Bay, where their children were born in 1908 and 1912. Gordon shared his wife's musical interests and was a vice-president of the Sydney Madrigal and Chamber Music Society and the Royal Philharmonic Society of Sydney.

During World War I Mrs Gordon aided the Red Cross Society and regimental and battalion comforts funds, by singing at concerts and matinées, helping at innumerable fêtes, playing in bridge tournaments and running a flower stall on Saturday mornings. On 23 June 1915 she was chief organizer of a concert at the Town Hall featuring Antonia Dolores, and herself sang 'some melodious little Welsh songs'; over £1000 was raised for the Red Cross. As the 'singing voice', she and Ethel Kelly [q.v.], as the 'speaking voice', staged Henri Murger's 'La Ballade du Désespéré', set to music by Herman Bemberg, on several occasions.

Between the wars Margaret Gordon worked on committees for many worthy causes, particularly for hospitals, children and the St John Ambulance Association (she was appointed an officer of the Order of St John of Jerusalem in 1937). Becoming totally deaf, she no longer sang in public, but remained 'interested in everything'. She loved arranging amateur theatricals—including 'Violet Matinées' for the Women's Hospital and three performances of *Berkeley Square* at the Palace Theatre in June 1930 for the Karitane mothercraft training centre. She was also 'an indefatigable worker for the arts' and a strong supporter of the Sydney Symphony Orchestra. Among the young musicians she aided was Joan Hammond, for whom she organized a popular concert in 1936. She loved gardening and had a self-confessed passion for jam-making. Bilingual all her life, she kept up with the local Welsh societies.

A vice-president of the Australian Red Cross Society in 1940-47, Lady Gordon again threw herself into fund-raising during World War II. After the war she went to England, where her daughter had married. She died on 23 September 1962 at Savernake near Marlborough, Wiltshire. Her son and daughter survived her.

Her husband, Alexander Gordon, was born on 22 May 1858 in Sydney, son of Alexander Gordon [q.v.4], London-born barrister, and his wife Annie, née Chambers. Educated privately and in England at Repton School, Derbyshire, he returned to Sydney in 1878 to read for the Bar with Gateward Coleridge Davis and C. B. Stephen [q.v.]. He was associate to Judge J. F. Hargrave [q.v.4] and was admitted to the Bar on 31 July 1882.

For many years Gordon attended the Northern Circuit and built up an extensive practice in equity, probate, bankruptcy and company law. He took silk in March 1904. Appointed to the Supreme Court Bench on 27 April 1910, he became judge in divorce and successfully put the practice of that court on a sound footing. 'One of the most able and popular judges', he was noted for his humanity. He retired in April 1928 and was knighted in 1930.

A practising Anglican, Gordon was a member of the councils of Cranbrook School and St Luke's Hospital, chairman of the Hospital Saturday Fund, a vice-president of the St John Ambulance Association and a member of the advisory board of Karitane. Dignified, with a domed forehead and a walrus moustache, he belonged to the Union and Australian clubs and, a keen sportsman, was president of the Sydney Lawn Tennis Club and a vice-president of the New South Wales Cricket Association. He died in Sydney on 7 January 1942 and was cremated with Anglican rites. His estate was valued for probate at £48 967.

Cyclopedia of N.S.W. (Syd, 1907); *SMH*, 15, 23 Feb, 29 Apr, 8 May 1905, 1 June, 4 Dec 1918, 9 Oct 1925, 17 Apr 1928, 3, 27 June 1930, 19 Apr 1934, 12 Mar 1936, 14 July 1937, 31 May 1940, 9 Jan 1942; *Bulletin*, 16 Feb, 11 May 1905, 17 May 1906; *Australasian*, 11 Mar, 22 Apr, 7 Oct, 18, 25 Nov, 23 Dec 1905, 19 May 1906, 19 Sept 1914, 10 July, 28 Aug, 11, 18 Sept 1915, 26 Aug 1916, 12 Apr, 8 June 1918, 1, 15, 22 July 1922; information from Mrs R. Lloyd, Wiltshire, England.

MARTHA RUTLEDGE

GORDON, SIR THOMAS STEWART (1882-1949), businessman, was born on 26 April 1882 at Ardrossan, Yorke Peninsula, South Australia, eldest son of William Gordon, farmer, and his wife Alice, née Wicks; he was a nephew of Sir David Gordon [q.v.]. The family moved to Broughton in the Wimmera district of Victoria where Thomas was educated before attending the Commercial College, Adelaide. In 1900 he was employed by George Wills & Co., merchants and shipping agents at Fremantle, Western Australia. In 1902 he joined Birt & Co. Ltd, shippers and merchants, and next year moved to Sydney. He represented that firm in New Zealand in 1908-11, returning to Sydney as shipping manager.

Like many up-and-coming businessmen of his day, Gordon took an interest in politics, serving as an alderman on the Mosman Municipal Council in 1925-28, and was active in the National Party. In September 1928, as chairman of the Oversea Shipping Representatives' Association (of which he was a founder), he denounced the Waterside Workers Federation of Australia's strike. Next year, Gordon succeeded Sir Owen Cox [q.v.8] as chairman and managing director of Birt & Co. and in 1929-34 was a council-member of the Australian Oversea Transport Association.

Gordon was also chairman of the Darling Island Stevedoring and Lighterage Co. Ltd, Australian director of the Federal Steam Navigation Co. Ltd of London, the Newstead Wharves & Stevedoring Co. Pty Ltd of Brisbane, and a director of the Royal Exchange of Sydney, Australian General Insurance Co. Ltd, Bellambi Coal Co. Ltd, Cockatoo Docks & Engineering Co. Pty Ltd, Ready Mixed Concrete Ltd and Lapstone Hotel Ltd. He was a council-member of the Sydney Chamber of Commerce and a member of the Swedish Chamber of Commerce for Australia, New Zealand and South Sea Islands, and president of the Belgian Chamber of Commerce for Australasia; on a visit to Brussels in 1937 he was presented with the Order of Leopold. He was knighted in 1938.

In 1932 Gordon had been nominated to the Legislative Council to ensure the passage of legislation to reform the Upper House and to protect it against the danger of abolition by a 'revolutionary party' in the Lower House. He did not seek election to the reconstituted council in 1933.

From the outbreak of World War II until 1947, Gordon was a member of the Shipping Control Board and from December 1939 the representative in Australia of the British Ministry of Shipping (War Transport). He became chairman of the Allied Consultative Shipping Council in May 1942. The shipping crisis in 1942 led to the creation of the Department of Supply and Shipping and to Gordon's appointment in October as director of shipping. Responsible directly to the minister, he controlled all shipping in Australian waters, including Australian, British, American, Dutch and Norwegian ships and later Canadian and Swedish. Gordon exercised his powers discreetly and efficiently. By 1944 available tonnage had increased and the volume of essential cargo fell, but these gains were offset by a decline in efficiency on the waterfront. When he resigned as director in October 1945 Prime Minister Chifley praised his public spirit and ability.

Among the many charitable institutions for which he worked, Gordon was chairman of several relief funds for seamen and of the Corps of Commissionaires, New South Wales, president of the Adult Deaf and Dumb Society of New South Wales, a committee-member of the Sydney Industrial Blind Institution and vice-president of the Japan-Australia Society. In his off-duty moments he was a keen golfer and belonged to the Royal Sydney Golf and the Elanora Country clubs.

Ill health forced Gordon to retire from public life in February 1948. He died of cerebral haemorrhage on 5 July 1949 at his Point Piper home and was cremated after a Presbyterian service. He was survived by his wife Victoria, née Fisher, whom he had married in Sydney on 11 September 1909, and by his three daughters. His sizeable estate was valued for probate at £76 856.

S. J. Butlin, *War economy, 1939-42*, 1 (Canb, 1955); S. J. Butlin and C. B. Schedvin, *War economy 1942-1945*, 2 (Canb, 1977); *United Aust Review*, 21 Sept, p 14, 21 Oct 1932, p 16; *Pastoral Review*, 16 July 1938, p 758; *World* (Syd), 17 Sept 1932; *Chronicle* (Adel), 22 Sept 1932; *SMH*, 27 Sept 1928, 13 Apr 1929, 1 Jan 1930, 14 Sept 1932, 12 Nov 1937, 9 June 1938, 19 Feb, 13 Dec 1940, 28 Feb 1946, 17 Mar 1948, 6 July, 28 Sept 1949.

PETER SPEARRITT
KATHERINE VASEY

GORMAN, JOHN THOMAS (1901-1978), footballer, was born on 6 June 1901 at Mackay, Queensland, eldest son of William Gorman, native-born soft-drink maker, and his Irish-born wife Elizabeth Bridget, née Maher. About 1906 he moved with his parents to Toowoomba, where he attended the Christian Brothers' school. An outstanding schoolboy footballer, at 16 he represented Toowoomba against an army side and played for the local Brothers Rugby Union team. With the collapse of amateur rugby football in Queensland, he and the Brothers team in the 1920 season switched to Rugby League, and Gorman became a member of the Queensland team during that season.

From 1920 Tommy Gorman played as centre three-quarter for what became an incomparable Toowoomba team (dubbed 'the galloping Clydesdales') boasting also fellow three-quarter E. S. 'Nigger' Brown, forward Herb Steinohrt and half-back Duncan Thompson [q.v.]. In 1922 at Sydney Gorman was one of the Queensland team which defeated New South Wales for the first time since the establishment of the code in 1908. He represented his State for the remainder of the 1920s—palmy days for the 'Reds', as they won seventeen of the following twenty-four interstate encounters, a Queensland domination never since repeated. In 1926 Gorman had transferred, for £200, to Brisbane Brothers club, becoming its coach and first paid player.

Gorman first represented Australia against a touring English team at Sydney Cricket Ground on 23 June 1924. He played in ten consecutive tests between the two countries, captaining Australia both in the 1928 home series and on the fourth Kangaroo tour of England in 1929-30. He retired upon returning to Brisbane. He is the only Queenslander selected while playing for that State to lead Australia on an English tour.

An elusive centre, Gorman was a sure handler of the ball, who gave a perfect pass and was adept at the art of short kicking. Moreover, he was able to draw opponents, give his side the overlap, and set up tries. A sure but not a rugged tackler, he sought the ball rather than the man. With 'nothing showy or false about him' he was an unselfish player, who seldom scored himself and never in a test. Sandy-haired in his youth, he was 5 ft. 8 ins. (173 cm) tall, and his playing weight was 11 st. 10 lbs. (74 kg).

On 22 August 1932 at Annerley, Brisbane, Gorman married Agnes Josephine McCrystal, a barmaid. He was, by then, publican of the Exhibition Hotel, Brisbane, and subsequently managed five hotels successively in Fortitude Valley and the city. A popular and successful publican, he retired in 1962.

Gorman died on 22 June 1978 at Mater Misericordiae Hospital, South Brisbane, and was buried in Nudgee cemetery after Catholic rites. In 1980 an old colleague recalled that Gorman needed 'no praise. Was the perfect footballer'.

Redcap Rugby League Annual, 1926; *Telegraph* (Brisb), 24 June 1978.

CHRIS CUNNEEN

GORMANSTON, JENICO WILLIAM JOSEPH PRESTON, 14th VISCOUNT (1837-1907), governor, was born on 1 June 1837 at Gormanston Castle, Meath, Ireland, son of Edward Anthony John Preston, 13th Viscount Gormanston and his wife Lucretia, née Jerningham. In August 1855 Preston joined the 60th King's Rifle Corps and saw action as a lieutenant in the Indian Mutiny campaigns of 1857-58. He left the army in 1860 and married Ismay Louisa Ursula Bellow at Barmeath, County Louth, on 8 January the following year. From July 1866 to December 1868 Preston was chamberlain to the lord lieutenant of Ireland. In 1876 he succeeded his father as Viscount Gormanston in the Irish peerage and Baron Gormanston in that of the United Kingdom. The Salisbury [q.v.3, Cecil] Conservative government in 1885 appointed him governor of the Leeward Islands and transferred him two years later to the larger colony of British Guiana where he remained in office till 1893. Gormanston's next post was governor of Tasmania; he presided there for an extended term from 8 August 1893 until August 1900.

As Ireland's premier viscount, Gormanston was honoured as befitted his rank: high sheriff for Dublin (1865) and Meath (1871); deputy lieutenant for Dublin; K.C.M.G. (1887) and G.C.M.G. (1897). As governor, he proved no cipher. In British Guiana, despite the concession in 1891 of directly elected members on the executive council, he was not afraid to act against the wishes of the majority and quelled unrest by strength rather than persuasion. In Tasmania, despite its well-established tradition of self-government, he refused to support recommendations for knighthoods, lectured his ministers on defence needs, and strongly opposed the appointment of a chief justice. He was uneasy about the rise of a Labor Party, and Tasmanian radicals were correspondingly dubious about naming a west-coast mining township Gormanston.

In general, however, Gormanston was satisfied with Tasmanian society at the turn of the century. While disappointed at the island's lack of enthusiasm for Federation, he heartily approved of its fervent loyalty during the Queen's jubilee and positive response to the South African War. He was a Catholic; his piety encouraged his co-religionists in the colony, though they were warned in 1895 by the visiting Irish Nationalist leader, Michael Davitt, that Gormanston was a bad Irishman and one of the worst landlords.

Gormanston's first wife died without issue in 1875. The governor's amiable consort in Tasmania was Georgina Jane, née Connellan. Marrying on 29 October 1878 at Coolmore, County Kilkenny, the couple had three sons and a daughter. Gormanston stood 6 ft. 2 ins. (188 cm) and enjoyed field sports till increasing weight restricted his movement. Troubled by ill health in Tasmania he died in Dublin of cerebral haemorrhage on 29 October 1907. He was buried in the family vault at Stamullen, near Gormanston, survived by his wife and children and succeeded by his eldest son, Jenico Edward Joseph. Although Gormanston could pass as a conscientious governor in the 1890s, the Imperial ideal of this Irish Catholic aristocrat, whose title dated back to 1370, was already an anachronism.

Mercury, 7 Aug 1893; *Australasian*, 6 Oct 1894; *Clipper*, 20 May 1899; Letter-books of despatches, *and* confidential despatches, to Secretary of State, 16 Jan 1821-21 Jan 1911, GO 25, 21 Apr 1869-29 Dec 1913, GO 27 (TA).   R. P. DAVIS

GOUDIE, SIR GEORGE LOUIS (1866-1949), farmer, grazier, storekeeper and politician, was born on 30 April 1866 at Homebush, near Avoca, Victoria, third child of George Goudy, Scottish-born schoolteacher and later railways official, and his wife Caroline, née Ashton, of Adelaide. He always spelt his name as Goudie.

After education at state schools, in 1888 Goudie took up farming at Birchip; he was one of the first users of superphosphate in the Mallee. From 1904 he combined farming with storekeeping as a partner in the firms of Goudie, Young & Sanders at Birchip, and Goudie Williams & Co. at Hopetoun. He later owned a grazing property at Egerton, and a wheat farm at Hopetoun before moving to Elsternwick, Melbourne, about 1920.

Before entering politics Goudie had acquired formidable experience of local government. He was a member of three shire councils, Birchip (1895-1910), Ballan (1914-16) and Karkarooc (1917-22), and was president of Birchip Shire in 1898-99 and 1907-08. In May 1919 he was elected unopposed as a Victorian Farmers' Union (Country Party from 1926) member of the Legislative Council for North-Western Province, the first V.F.U. candidate to be elected to the council. He held the seat until his death in 1949 and had the singular record of never having to contest an election.

He served as commissioner of public works and minister of mines in the Lawson [q.v.]-Allan [q.v.7] ministry from September 1923 to March 1924 and held the same portfolios under Allan from November 1924 to May 1927. In (Sir) Stanley Argyle's [q.v.7] ministry he held the portfolios of water supply from May 1932 to March 1935 and of labour from May 1932 to July 1934; he was also in charge of electrical undertakings from July 1934 to March 1935. Together with Allan he argued strongly against the decision to withdraw Country Party support from Argyle's ministry in March 1935. Nonetheless, he served in the resulting Dunstan [q.v.8] Country Party ministry as commissioner for public works and minister of immigration from April 1935 to September 1943 and was government leader in the Legislative Council in 1942-43.

Goudie never pretended to brilliance, but was a 'good solid plodder' who became a highly competent administrator, noted for his practical contributions to debates on rural issues. He chaired the Employment Council for six years and, in 1942, was appointed chairman of the Air Raids Precautions Shelters Committee. He was knighted in 1939.

On 9 September 1890 at Birchip Goudie had married Alice Maud Watson with Presbyterian forms; they had five sons. A tall, large-framed man, he was 'hard but just', patient and very likeable. He was a keen gardener, enjoyed reading, and taught himself French. Survived by his wife and sons he died at Elsternwick on his eighty-third birthday, 30 April 1949, and was cremated after a state funeral.

L. G. Houston, *Ministers of water supply in Victoria* (Melb, 1965); J. E. Senyard, *Birchip—essays on a shire* (Birchip, 1970); *PD* (Vic), 1949, p 597; *Age*, 23 June 1938, 2 May 1949; information from Mr J. A. Goudie, Elsternwick, Victoria.

GEOFF BROWNE

GOULD, SIR ALBERT JOHN (1847-1936), lawyer and politician, was born on 12 February 1847 in Sydney, son of John Morton Gould, solicitor, and his wife Anne, née Livingstone. After attending Rev. Dr William Woolls's [q.v.6] school at Parramatta he studied law at the University of Sydney without taking a degree, served his articles with his father and was admitted as a solicitor in December 1870. Next year he began work at Singleton for a Sydney legal firm and by 1887 had established his own practice both there and in Sydney. He entered partnership with A. G. Y. Shaw about 1889 and moved to Sydney in 1897.

While at Singleton Gould was active in local affairs: he was president of the mechanics' institute, vice-president of the Northern Agricultural Association, served on the hospital committee and pressed for the construction of a railway from Sydney. In 1882 he was elected to the Patrick's Plains (Singleton from 1894) seat in the Legislative Assembly, retaining it until 1898. He entered parliament as an opponent of the Parkes-Robertson [qq.v.5,6] coalition but supported the Robertson government in 1885-86 and became a great admirer of Parkes. As a Free Trader he served as minister for justice under Sir Henry Parkes (1889-91) and (Sir) George Reid [q.v.] (1894-98). During his first period in office he embarrassed Parkes by quarrelling with the chief justice, Sir Frederick Darley [q.v.4], over what he considered harsh punishment for contempt of two witnesses and over Darley's requests for improved court accommodation. But his friendship with Parkes survived this and also Parkes's later bitter denunciations of the Reid government. For more than thirty years after Parkes's death Gould venerated his memory, speaking frequently at the annual commemoration of his birth by the National Club.

As minister for justice Gould showed himself to be an energetic administrator, with a strong interest in the consolidation of the law and in the reform of legislation relating to police-court matters. He also worked to tighten the licensing laws. He built up in parliament a reputation as a skilful, but always judicious, debater. Melbourne *Punch* described him as a balding, tall, slender man with a pale face and tired eyes, his demeanour forever serious and his speeches delivered in a high, thin voice. He opposed the 1898 Federation bill in the belief that New South Wales was not receiving adequate recognition.

He lost his assembly seat in 1898 but the following year Reid nominated him to the Legislative Council. In 1901 Gould was elected as one of the first six-year-term senators for New South Wales. Re-elected in 1906, he was president in 1907-10 in succession to Sir Richard Chaffey Baker [q.v.7] and was knighted in 1908. He remained a member until 1917 when the National Party failed to endorse his candidature, although he was a strong supporter of conscription. He was seriously offended at being the only sitting government supporter not to receive endorsement, but he refused to split the Nationalist vote by standing as an independent.

Although he was occasionally treated by the press as an elder statesman, Gould devoted the rest of his life to his extensive business, charitable and church interests. An original member of the Great Cobar Copper Mining syndicate formed in 1876, he was reputed to have early made his fortune. He was chairman of the Sydney Electric Light and Power Supply Corporation and a director of the City Bank of Sydney from 1899. He was also a director of the Royal Prince Alfred Hospital and the Royal Alexandra Hospital for Children. A devout Anglican, he served as a member of the Sydney and Newcastle synods, in the latter case for nearly sixty years, and was chancellor of both dioceses. In his earlier years he had been a supporter of the Volunteer movement, enlisting as a private in the West Maitland company in 1865 and retiring with the Volunteer Officers' Decoration and the rank of lieutcolonel in the 4th Regiment Volunteer Infantry in 1902. A Freemason from 1879, he was master of the Lodge St Andrew in 1883; he was also a Mark Mason and a Royal Arch Mason. He was a member of the Australian Club, Sydney, and of the Melbourne Club.

Gould died in Sydney on 27 July 1936; after a state funeral he was buried in South Head cemetery. His estate, valued at £12 459, was divided among his two sons and three daughters. His wife Jeannette Jessie, née Maitland, whom he had married on 12 September 1872 in St Paul's Church of England, Maitland, had died in 1928. Competent if undistinguished as both minister and presiding officer, Gould was one of the many late nineteenth century liberals who could find no secure place in the polarized politics of the next generation.

Cyclopedia of N.S.W. (Syd, 1907); A. P. Elkin, *The diocese of Newcastle* (Syd, 1955); *T&CJ*, 4 June 1887; *Punch* (Melb), 3 Jan 1907, 5 Sept 1912; *Fighting Line*, 19 Apr 1913; *SMH*, 31 Dec 1928, 28, 29 July 1936; McMillan papers, *and* Parkes correspondence (ML).

W. G. McMINN

GOULD, ELLEN JULIA (1860-1941), nurse, was born on 29 March 1860 at Aberystruth, Monmouthshire, Wales, daughter of Henry Gould, agent, and his second wife

Sarah, née Baker. Sarah Gould died in childbirth when Ellen was 18 months old; she was 4 when the family moved to Portugal, where the young children were cared for and given early tutoring by their father. At 10 she attended a Portuguese school to learn languages and her stepsister Emily came from England to supervise her English education. After ten apparently happy years the family returned to London, where Ellen attended Mildmay Park College; she passed the senior local Cambridge examination in 1876, remained on the teaching staff until 1879 and then worked in Hamburg, Germany, as a governess for four and a half years.

In 1884 'Nellie' and her stepsister visited relatives in New South Wales. She then began a two-year training course at Royal Prince Alfred Hospital, Sydney, on 19 January 1885. On its completion she remained on the staff for two years. She was then appointed matron of St Kilda Private Hospital at Woolloomooloo and in 1891 became matron and superintendent of the training school of Sydney Hospital where her skill as an administrator and teacher was recognized. She resigned in October 1898 to join the New South Wales Public Health Department and was matron of the Hospital for the Insane at Rydalmere in 1898-1900.

In February 1899 Colonel, later Surgeon-General, (Sir) W. D. C. Williams [q.v.] asked her help to form an Army Nursing Service Reserve attached to the New South Wales Army Medical Corps, and in May twenty-six nurses were sworn in. Miss Gould was appointed lady superintendent. On 17 January 1900, in charge of thirteen nursing sisters, she left in the *Moravian* for the South African War, with the 2nd New South Wales Army Medical Corps Contingent. She served first at a stationary hospital at Sterkstroom and later at No. 3 British General Hospital, Kroonstad, No. 6 British General Hospital, Johannesburg, and No. 35 Stationary Hospital, Ermelo, returning to Australia in August 1902. With her friend, Sister Julia Bligh Johnston, she then opened Ermelo Private Hospital at Newtown, Sydney, and for the next ten years her energy and initiative were devoted to the welfare of nurses and the enhancement of the status of the profession. She also organized the Army Nursing Service Reserve in New South Wales and was appointed principal matron of the 2nd Military District. Ermelo was sold in 1912 and Ellen Gould and Julia Johnston joined the Public Health Department.

On 27 September 1914 Miss Gould enlisted in the Australian Imperial Force and was appointed matron of No. 2 Australian General Hospital. With six other nurses she left Australia on 20 October, disembarking at Alexandria, Egypt, on 4 December. The hospital unit arrived later and she took up her duties as matron on 21 January 1915. The staff were established at Mena House when, a few months later, casualties from Gallipoli made necessary the preparation of a second hospital at Ghezireh Palace; the two hospitals had a total of 1500 beds. In April 1916 No. 2 A.G.H. was transferred to France and established at Wimereux, arriving on 30 June, the eve of the advance on the Somme.

In 1917, after a long period of arduous duty, Miss Gould was posted to England to No. 1 Australian Auxiliary Hospital (Harefield). In November she was transferred to Cobham Hall, an Australian convalescent hospital. She returned to Australia in January 1919 and was discharged from the A.I.F. on 3 March. Her health was broken and she was unfit to take up nursing duties again; from 1920 she received a war service pension. Her distinguished service was recognized by the award of the Royal Red Cross (1st class) in 1916.

Ellen Gould had a great influence on the development of professional nursing in Australia; she was involved in founding the Australasian Trained Nurses' Association and was a council member from its inception in 1899 until her retirement in 1921. She instigated the publishing of the A.T.N.A. journal in 1903 and served on the editorial committee.

She was a woman of vision and energy, an excellent nurse, an able administrator and highly professional. Of good appearance, impeccable manners and gentle humour, she set and maintained standards which have left their mark on generations of Australian nurses. After her retirement she lived quietly with Julia Johnston at Miranda, Sydney. She died in hospital at Neutral Bay on 19 July 1941 and was privately cremated.

Aust Defence Dept, *Official records of the Australian military contingents to the war in South Africa*, P. L. Murray, ed (Melb, 1911); A. G. Butler (ed), *Official history of the Australian Army Medical Services . . . 1914-19*, 1, 3 (Melb, 1930, Canb, 1943); D. M. Armstrong, *The first fifty years: a history of nursing at the Royal Prince Alfred Hospital, Sydney, 1882 to 1932* (Syd, 1965); *London Gazette*, 14 Jan 1916; *A'sian Nurses' J*, July 1904, Apr 1907, Jan 1909, Mar 1910, July 1912, Aug, Nov, Dec 1914, June 1916, Aug 1941; Sydney Hospital, *Annual report*, 1891, 1898; Council of N.S.W. Trained Nurses' Association, Minute-book, 1899-1905; *SMH*, 23 July 1941; papers by E. J. Gould, MS 4364/34/6 (AWM); family papers, and information from Mrs G. R. Lamont, Manly, NSW, *and* the director of nursing, Roy Prince Alfred Hospital, Syd, *and* the Dept of Veterans' Affairs (Syd).

PERDITTA M. MCCARTHY

GOULD, NATHANIEL (1857-1919), journalist and novelist, was born on 21 December 1857 at Cheetham, Manchester, Lancashire, England, only son of Nathaniel Gould, tea merchant, and his wife Mary, née Wright; both parents came from Derbyshire yeomen families. Known as Nat, Gould was educated at Brooks Bar and Strathmore House, Southport, and was then apprenticed to the tea trade, but he found the business irksome and went farming with his uncles. At 20 he answered an advertisement for a position on the *Newark Advertiser*, where he worked for seven years as a reporter and as correspondent for Nottingham and London newspapers, and became interested in the turf. He decided to visit Australia, arriving in 1884. He was employed on the *Brisbane Telegraph* in its shipping, commercial and racing departments, and was correspondent for the *Sportsman* and the Sydney *Referee*. On 14 April 1886 he married Elizabeth Madelaine Ruska at the Ann Street Presbyterian manse, Brisbane; they had three sons and two daughters.

Late in 1887 Gould quarrelled with the *Telegraph* management and moved to Sydney to become turf editor for the *Referee*. Under the pseudonym 'Verax' he wrote a weekly column which established his reputation as a tipster, a series of special articles and the racing serial 'Blue and White' (8 March-3 May 1888). In 1888 he moved to Bathurst to edit the *Bathurst Times*, but retained his link with the *Referee* through another racing serial, 'With the Tide', commonly thought his first; by the time it was completed in May 1890 he had rejoined the *Referee*. Published in London in 1891 under the title of *The double event*, it was a success on railway bookstalls in England and sold widely in Australia, partly because of its release at the time of the 1891 Melbourne Cup. The stage adaptation by George Darrell [q.v.4] in 1893 was climaxed by a cup scene with twenty horses filling the stage.

Living in Sydney in 1890-95, Gould combined journalism and fiction: he continued as 'Verax' in the *Referee*, wrote as 'Old 'Un' for the *Sunday Times* and the *Bird O' Freedom*, and completed eight more stories which were serialized in the *Referee* before being published by Routledge in London. In January 1895 he resigned from the *Referee* and left Australia in April in the *Orizaba* with the champion racehorse Carbine; he tipped the winner of the next Victoria Derby as the ship pulled away from the wharf.

Gould settled near Staines, Middlesex. For the next twenty-five years he found time to enjoy the theatre, travel and antiquarian history and to turn out annually four or five sporting and adventure novels. The basis of his success was his ability to blend a sporting subject with elements of the detective story and the popular romance: his heroes and heroines characteristically overcome obstacles such as corrupt bookmakers and win important races climaxed by a thrilling finish. Gould became a household name and sales of his 'yellowbacks' have been estimated in tens of millions; *The double event* sold upwards of 100 000 copies in its first ten years and was still in print in 1919. Preferring the security of regular payment, he sold outright the copyright of each novel; this meant, with his punting, that he left only £7797 after he died from diabetes at Newhaven Bedfont, Staines, on 25 July 1919. He was buried at Ashbourne, Derbyshire.

In all Gould wrote some 130 novels, including twenty-two released posthumously; three dozen or more are set in Australia. His recipe to aspiring writers was, 'write about men and things you have met and seen; take your characters from the busy world, and your scenes from Nature'. He followed this prescription best when depicting racecourse, cricket and theatrical scenes, but was less adept in his sentimental portraits of the colonial and English aristocracy, to which class he aspired. He was a political conservative, a staunch Imperialist patronizing about Chinese, Indians and Aboriginals, and something of a wowser despite his gambling. These qualities emerge not only in his novels but also in his three autobiographical works: *On and off the turf in Australia* (1895), *Town and bush* (1896) and *The magic of sport, mainly autobiographical* (1909).

A short, tubby, jovial man who sported a twirling moustache in later life, Gould was described, after a surprise victory in a handicap sprint at the 1888 picnic of *Referee* staff, as having 'attained that comfortable rotundity that tells of luxurious living and a good digestion'. His experiences in Australia during one of its golden ages of sport changed his life, and he retained a great affection for the country, particularly for Brisbane. He inaugurated the Australian sporting novel, rivalled only by his imitator Arthur Wright, but he has been claimed just as enthusiastically as a representative Englishman. More accurately, he should be seen as an archetypal Anglo-Australian Imperialist sportsman at the turn of the century.

R. Cashman and M. McKernan (eds), *Sport in history* (Brisb, 1979), and *Sport: money, morality and the media* (Syd, 1981); *London Mag*, Aug 1967; *Bird O' Freedom*, 25 Apr 1891, 26 Aug 1893; *The Times*, 26, 28 July, 15 Sept 1919; *Bulletin*, 28 July, 4 Aug 1927, 18 Dec 1957; *Sporting Globe*, 28 Oct 1950-17 Feb 1951; George Routledge & Co. Archives, 1853-1902 (mfm G 14808-13, NL); MS and printed cats under Gould (ML).

B. G. ANDREWS

GOVERNOR, JIMMY (1875-1901), outlaw, was born on the Talbragar River, New South Wales, son of Sam (later Thomas) Governor (or Grosvenor), bullock-driver, and his wife Annie, née Fitzgerald. He received his schooling at a mission school and at Gulgong. Short, good-looking and part-Aboriginal with reddish hair, Jimmy worked at Wollar before becoming a police tracker at Cassilis from 15 July 1896 to 18 December 1897. He returned to Wollar and, after woodcutting at Gulgong and woolrolling at Digilbar, married on 10 December 1898 Ethel Mary Jane Page, a 16-year-old white woman, at the Church of England rectory, Gulgong.

In April 1900, after a variety of jobs, Jimmy got a contract for fencing (splitting and erecting posts earning 10s. and 12s. a hundred respectively) from John Thomas Mawbey at Breelong, near Gilgandra. Conscientious and anxious to prove himself in white society, Jimmy was on good terms with his employer, obtaining his rations from him and playing cricket with his small sons. Jimmy and Ethel were joined by his brother Joe and Jacky Underwood (alias Charlie Brown), a full blood, who both helped in the work, and later by Jacky Porter, another full blood, and Jimmy's nephew Peter Governor. All claimed rations from Jimmy Governor.

Strains emerged in the marriage. Ethel, who did housework for the Mawbeys, grew unhappy; after a dispute with Mawbey, Jimmy and his friends talked of taking up bushranging. Touchy about his colour, Jimmy was stung by reports that Mrs Mawbey and Helen Josephine Kerz, a schoolteacher who lived with the Mawbeys, had taunted his wife for marrying a blackfellow. With Underwood he confronted the women, who were alone in the house with seven children and Mrs Mawbey's 18-year-old sister Elsie Clarke, on the night of 20 July 1900. Jimmy alleged that the women laughed at him and Helen Kerz said: 'Pooh, you black rubbish, you want shooting for marrying a white woman'. Losing all control, the two, with nulla-nullas and tomahawk, killed Mrs Grace Mawbey, Helen Kerz, and Grace (16), Percival (14) and Hilda Mawbey (11); Elsie Clarke was seriously injured.

Underwood was quickly caught but Jimmy and Joe Governor, calling themselves 'bushrangers', went on a fourteen-week, 2000-mile (3220 km) rampage, terrorizing a wide area of north-central New South Wales. Seeking revenge on persons who had wronged them, they killed Alexander McKay near Ulan on 23 July, Elizabeth O'Brien and her baby son at Poggie, near Merriwa, on 24 July, and Keiran Fitzpatrick near Wollar, on 26 July. After committing numerous robberies as far north as Narrabri, and in the Quirindi district, they moved into the rugged headwater country of the Manning and Hastings rivers, pursued by Queensland black trackers, bloodhounds and hundreds of police and civilians. Exulting in outwitting their pursuers, the Governors blatantly broadcast their whereabouts and wrote derisive notes to the police. On 8 October the government offered a reward of £1000 each for their capture.

After several close escapes Jimmy was shot in the mouth by Herbert Byers, a hunter, on 13 October; in a weakened condition he was captured by a party of settlers at Bobin, near Wingham, on 27 October. Joe was shot dead by John Wilkinson north of Singleton on 31 October. They had been outlawed on 23 October.

Jimmy stood trial on 22-23 November in Sydney for the murder of Helen Kerz. He was defended by Francis Stewart Boyce [q.v.7] who raised the defence of *autrefois aquit* and *autrefois attaint*, arguing that as a result of outlawry Governor had already been attainted and could not be tried for the same crimes. These pleas in bar of trial were rejected and Governor was convicted. An appeal was dismissed, and he spent his last days reading the Bible, singing native songs and blaming his wife. He was hanged at Darlinghurst Gaol on 18 January 1901 and buried in an unmarked grave in the Anglican section of Rookwood cemetery; Underwood had been hanged in the Dubbo gaol four days before. Governor was survived by his wife and son; on 23 November Ethel Governor married Francis Joseph Brown by whom she had nine more children. She died in Sydney on 31 December 1945.

Jimmy Governor's ravages, in the context of Aboriginal dispossession and white racism, were the subject of Thomas Keneally's novel *The chant of Jimmy Blacksmith* (1972), which was made into a film in 1978.

F. P. Clune, *Jimmy Governor* (Syd, 1959); E. C. Rolls, *A million wild acres* (Melb, 1981), and for bibliog; *Government Gazette* (NSW), 2, 8, 23 Oct 1900; *NSW Law Reports*, 21 (1900), p 278; *Sydney Mail*, 28 July, 4 Aug, 3 Nov 1900; *SMH*, 23 July, 23 Aug, 3 Oct, 23, 24 Nov 1900, 19 Jan 1901; *Quirindi Advocate*, 28 July, 4, 11 Aug 1944; *Sunday Telegraph* (Syd), 20 Apr 1980; 6/1029 (NSWA).

G. P. WALSH

GOW, ROBERT MILNE (1868-1948), businessman, was born on 9 April 1868 at Newcastle, New South Wales, son of Scottish-born James Falconer Gow, saddler, and his wife Jane Strachan Dickson, née

Barry, from Manchester, England. Educated at Newcastle Public School, he began his commercial career with Frank Gardiner, insurance and shipping agent of Newcastle; in 1888 he transferred to (F. A.) Wright [q.v.6] Heaton & Co. Ltd. After a short period in their Sydney office he went to Brisbane in 1897 to manage the Queensland branch. Recognizing the opportunities for enterprise in Brisbane, he left Wright Heaton in 1900 to open his own business on the corner of Edward and Mary streets as a customs agent, carrier, mercantile broker and produce merchant. Starting with three employees, Gow quickly obtained the Queensland distribution rights of Arnott's [q.v.3] biscuits and Foster Clark products. He arranged the first shipment of Queensland wheat to England in August 1904 in the *Banffshire*. By 1912, as a large shipper of butter and frozen products to Britain, Gow was a strong advocate of improved shipping facilities for Brisbane. In 1901 he took a partner, E. C. Chambers, but bought him out in 1909.

The firm prospered and spread its activities across the wholesale merchandizing of foods and household requisites. Before R. M. Gow & Co. Ltd became a private company in 1921, Gow's four sons had joined the firm but he remained as governing director until his death. In 1926 the firm began manufacturing the 'Gold Crest' range of food products; the name was derived from the golden crest on the family emblem. Despite the many problems of the depressed 1930s, the firm continued to prosper. Gow was able to enlarge sales by introducing an ingenious system of marginal cost pricing; in 1938 it celebrated its first annual turnover exceeding £1 million. After becoming a public company in March 1951, the firm expanded considerably. Much of its success was due to the enterprising founder who was always ready to undertake new ventures. Those family members who succeeded him shared his attitude.

A member of the Brisbane Chamber of Commerce for many years and its president in 1926-27, Gow was also well respected as a sportsman. A keen golfer and yachtsman and a patron of the Queensland Game Fishing Association, he had represented Queensland in both Rugby Union and bowls. On 27 April 1892, at Newcastle, he had married Agnes Mary Jones. When he died on 20 May 1948 at Gowanbrae, his Hamilton home, he left his sons in charge of the firm. His estate was valued for probate at £47 389. He was buried in Toowong cemetery with Congregational forms.

Courier Mail, 21 May 1948; *Aust Financial Review*, 30 Apr 1981; Gow family records.

A. L. LOUGHEED

GOWRIE, SIR ALEXANDER GORE ARKWRIGHT HORE-RUTHVEN, 1st EARL (1872-1955), governor-general, was born on 6 July 1872 at Windsor, England, second son of Walter James Hore-Ruthven, 8th Baron Ruthven, and his wife Lady Caroline Annesley, née Gore, daughter of the 4th Earl of Arran. The family was Scottish. Registered as Alexander Harry Gore Ruthven and known throughout his life as 'Sandie', Alexander was educated at Winchester and Eton. In 1892 he joined the militia (3rd Battalion Highland Light Infantry), in 1893 visited Canada and in 1898 travelled to Egypt. Temporarily attached to the Egyptian Army, he commanded the Slavery Department Camel Corps and for rescuing a wounded Egyptian officer from the Dervishes on 22 September he won the first Victoria Cross to be awarded to a militia officer. In May next year he was gazetted to the Cameron Highlanders but remained in Egypt for the Sudan campaign —he was mentioned in dispatches three times. He was special-service officer in Somaliland in 1903-04, then rejoined the Cameron Highlanders in Dublin. In 1904-08 he was military secretary to the lord lieutenant of Ireland, Lord Dudley [q.v.8], and his successor Lord Aberdeen.

On 1 June 1908 at St George's, Hanover Square, London, he married ZARA EILEEN (1879-1965), daughter of John Pollok and his wife the Honourable Florence Madeline, née Bingham. Zara had been born at Lismany, Galway, Ireland, on 20 January 1879. Her family opposed the marriage, regarding Hore-Ruthven, he later wrote, as 'the impecunious son of an impoverished family, with indifferent prospects'. In July 1908 as military secretary, he rejoined Dudley, newly appointed governor-general of Australia. They arrived in Sydney in September.

In 1909 Hore-Ruthven returned to England to join Kitchener's staff and accompanied him on his tour of Australia. Next year he was appointed to Quetta Staff College in India. When war was declared in 1914 he became Arabic interpreter to the Meerut Division which sailed to France. A major in the Welsh Guards from April 1915, he fought at Gallipoli, was severely wounded at Suvla in August and returned to England. In 1917 he served in France, joining the Guards division. Next year he was brigadier-general, 7th Army Corps, until its decimation in March 1918, and in July he took command of the Highland Brigade of the 9th Division. He was awarded the Distinguished Service Order with Bar, was appointed C.M.G. in 1918 and C.B. in 1919 and was mentioned in dispatches five times.

In 1920-24 Hore-Ruthven commanded the Welsh Guards, and in 1924-28 the 1st Brigade of Guards at Aldershot. In May 1926 his troops were stationed in London during the general strike.

Retiring from the army in 1928, Hore-Ruthven became governor of South Australia, and was appointed K.C.M.G. He arrived in Adelaide in May. Active and enthusiastic, he travelled the State by Moth aeroplane. He was an enthusiast for the Boy Scout and his wife for the Girl Guide movements. She was also president of the State branch of the Red Cross Society and was associated with the Victoria League. In a 1930 Anzac Day speech Hore-Ruthven expressed sympathy for returned soldiers 'suffering hardship and deprivation owing to the misguided leadership of a few hot-headed irresponsible [strikers]'. The United Trades and Labor Council censured him. As early as February 1931 he privately urged Governor Game [q.v.8] of New South Wales to dismiss J. T. Lang [q.v.]. In London on leave during 1933 he helped mediate in the cricket 'body-line crisis'.

Hore-Ruthven's term of office, extended to April 1934, saw the rise and fall of the L. L. Hill [q.v.] government. In 1934 the British secretary of state for the Dominions J. H. Thomas, observing that Hore-Ruthven had 'done extremely well' in Adelaide, claimed that Hill's 'firm attitude' during the financial crisis had been 'largely due to the Governor's influence'. Hill and his followers were expelled from the Labor Party; the governor's speeches commonly expressed the need for politicians to rise above party.

On his return to England Hore-Ruthven was selected as governor of New South Wales and arrived in Sydney on 21 February 1935. But while in London he had already been sounded by the King about appointment as governor-general, and on 23 January 1936 he assumed that office, succeeding Sir Isaac Isaacs [q.v.]. At the suggestion of Prime Minister J. A. Lyons [q.v.] he had been created Baron Gowrie of Canberra and Dirleton; in December 1935 he was appointed G.C.M.G. Gowrie was conscious that as an 'imported' governor-general following an Australian his exercise of office would be under intense critical scrutiny. He believed that he should 'try and reestablish the dignity of the office and ensure the proper performance of the social and official duties without causing undue criticism on account of the extra expense involved'. Possessing only a small, private income, he found the cost a strain. He faced no constitutional crises until the death of Lyons in April 1939, when Gowrie's action in commissioning Sir Earle Page [q.v.], after having obtained privately the advice of W. M. Hughes [q.v.], was uncontroversial. He planned to relinquish office in September, and the duke of Kent was named as his successor. But on the outbreak of war Gowrie's appointment was continued, in the first instance for an additional year.

In 1941 Gowrie was privately apprehensive of the new Curtin government, but he quickly became close to the prime minister. His military experience enabled him to contribute to discussions of Australia's conduct of the war and he was closely involved with the visits, sometimes clandestine, of military figures. During both General MacArthur's and Mrs Roosevelt's visits he took part in briefings. H. V. Evatt, later paying tribute to Gowrie's 'great strength', observed that he was 'a splendid counsellor to Cabinet Ministers during World War II'.

Lady Gowrie, too, was tireless in her work. She organized concerts and Government House fêtes to raise money for the war effort, set up a soldiers' club in Canberra and lent her support to the establishment of what became known as the Lady Gowrie kindergartens. Her 1941 New Year's Day radio broadcast to the women of Australia calling for 'hope and courage' was followed by a similar message next year from Lord Gowrie. Their only surviving son Patrick was killed in action in 1942; next year a collection of his poetry was published. Despite Gowrie's ill health and their desire to see their grandsons they were persuaded to stay on for another two years. In 1943 a Gowrie scholarship trust fund was set up for ex-service personnel and their children.

They left Australia on 10 September 1944; officially his appointment continued until he was succeeded by the duke of Gloucester on 30 January 1945. Gowrie's nine years is a record term as governor-general. In 1945 he was created earl, and until 1953 was deputy constable and lieut-governor of Windsor Castle. He was president of the Marylebone Cricket Club in 1948. 'Tallish and spare of build, lightly moustached, with a soldier's trimness without a general's portentous carriage', Gowrie had an attractive personality and a capacity for getting on with fellows who were useful to know. Though he had sailed close to the wind in Adelaide at a time of political turmoil, his term in Canberra, particularly during war years when patriotism ran high, was dignified and successful. Gowrie died in Gloucestershire on 2 May 1955, survived by his wife, who died on 19 July 1965, and by two grandsons. A portrait by Charles Wheeler [q.v.] hangs in Parliament House, Canberra.

Advertiser (Adel), 25 Apr, 3, 6 May 1930; *SMH*, 12 Feb 1933, 18 Jan 1945, 4 May 1955; *Herald* (Melb), 15 Aug 1935; *The Times*, 4 May 1955; Gowrie papers, MS 2852, *and* DO 35/444/20110A/9 (NL).

DEIRDRE MORRIS
CHRIS CUNNEEN

GRACE, JOSEPH NEAL (1859-1931), retailer, was born on 10 September 1859 at Winslow, Buckinghamshire, England, son of John Grace, schoolmaster, and his wife Sarah, née Neal. After being indentured to a small retail drapery firm at Notting Hill, London, and working for Crisp & Co. Ltd, and Jones & Higgins Ltd in London, he migrated to Australia in about 1880 and became a retail assistant with Farmer [q.v.4] & Co. Ltd in Sydney.

About 1883 Grace bought a horse and cart and took out a hawker's licence to sell drapery and other stock. Exposure to the keen bargaining of the housewife in the inner industrial suburbs of Sydney made him a first-class trader. Soon taking about £30 a week he was advised by a warehouseman to open a store. In 1885, borrowing £500, he and his brother Albert Edward (d.1938), who had arrived from Boston that year, bought the premises, fittings and stock of John Kingsbury, draper, at 5-7 George Street, West (Broadway), Glebe. Business prospered: in 1891-92 the brothers took over three adjacent shops and four years later had a four-storey building erected at the rear in Grose Street. Further extensions with clock tower, globe and an electricity power house were built in 1904; the Broadway front was rebuilt in 1906.

Grace knew the importance of service and a good window display and it was not long before the slogan 'Be sure and get it at Grace Bros' was deeply embedded in the minds of faithful shoppers. The slogan was parodied by his staff, 'Be sure you'll get it at Grace Brothers—the sack at 21!';—the firm relied heavily on junior sales assistants. The removal, storage and shipping division emerged out of the firm's retail furniture business to become the largest of its type in Australia. In 1917 the partnership was incorporated as a private company, Grace Bros Ltd, with all the shares owned by members of the family; Grace became governing director.

Quiet and unobtrusive socially, Grace was, however, active in employer and business organizations. He was president of the Retail Traders' Association of New South Wales, and member of the Employers' Federation of New South Wales and Sydney Chamber of Commerce. In 1926 he opposed the introduction of the Workers' Compensation Act. Work was Grace's joy in life; he took great pleasure in displaying the slogan 'There's no fun like work' given him by Gordon Selfridge of London. He claimed that 'Work is quite as interesting as golf or billiards, or any other game . . . I will slip out of business as quietly as I came into it, and fill in my days in my garden or with an occasional game of golf'.

Grace died suddenly at his residence, Yasmar, Parramatta Road, Haberfield, on 5 July 1931 and was cremated with Anglican rites. He was survived by his wife Sarah Selina, née Smith, whom he had married at St Aiden's Chapel, Ballarat, Victoria, on 20 December 1911. His estate was valued for probate at £636 156.

Under the chairmanship (1931-38) of A. E. Grace the firm expanded to the suburbs. One of Australia's largest retail businesses, Grace Bros Pty Ltd became a public company on 7 October 1960. In 1979 the firm took over J. B. Young Ltd, giving it a chain of over 130 stores.

Rydge's, 1 June 1929, p 436; *Wireless Weekly*, 2 Aug 1935; *SMH*, 7 July 1926, 17 May 1930, 6 July 1931, 21 Mar 1938, 3 Oct 1981, 1 Apr 1982.

G. P. WALSH

GRAEBNER, CARL FRIEDRICH (1862-1949), clergyman and educationist, was born on 8 October 1862 at St Charles, Missouri, United States of America, son of Pastor J. Henry Philipp Graebner and his wife Jacobine, née Denninger. Pastor Graebner, a Franconian missionary, had helped to establish Lutheran colonies in Michigan. Carl was educated at a private school, at Northwestern University, Wisconsin (B.A., 1882), and at Concordia Seminary, St Louis. He was ordained at Sedalia, Missouri, his first parish, in 1885. Next year on 12 August at Washington, Missouri, he married Charlotte Stoeppelwerth. From 1889 to 1903 he served at Topeka, Kansas, and Bay City, Michigan.

In 1902 Professor A. L. Graebner, Carl's brother, travelled to Murtoa, Victoria, to settle differences at the local Concordia College and seminary, formed from the school founded by T. W. Boehm [q.v.7]. On returning home, he sought a professor for the college. Carl Friedrich accepted. He arrived at Murtoa in August 1903 to find that the college had closed again. He revived the parish's support, and Concordia reopened in April next year. In December it moved to Unley, Adelaide, where it resumed as Concordia College and Seminary in February 1905, with Graebner as headmaster. He remained pastor of Murtoa parish and president of the synod's eastern district. He and his wife, matron at Concordia from 1905, were naturalized soon after arriving in Australia. A benign teacher, in the college he conducted services and taught Latin; in the seminary he taught Hebrew, Old Testament, dogmatics and minor disciplines. In 1927 Concordia took the novel step of enrolling girls.

Graebner was bilingual and he influenced Lutheran pastors at a time when the Evangelical Lutheran Synod in Australia was changing from the predominant use of German to the exclusive use of English. This was partly a response to the hostility directed at Australian Lutherans of German descent in World War I. In 1915 the South Australian parliament debated a bill for German schools to be scrutinized and registered by government inspectors, and to limit teaching in the German language. In June Graebner headed a deputation to parliament from E.L.S.A. which withdrew their opposition to the bill. He emphasized E.L.S.A.'s loyalty to the Empire and insisted that their schools' concern was educational and religious. He welcomed government visitors, so that citizens might be reassured of the sincerity of the schools, but begged that any school deemed 'inefficient' under the Act might be dealt with by synod.

Graebner worked with Lutheran War Relief and on the board of the Myrtle Bank Soldiers' Home. After the war he helped to produce a Lutheran hymn-book in English and for a time he edited the first English language church newspaper, the *Australian Lutheran*. These activities stressed the internationalism of E.L.S.A. and helped to dissociate it from the idea that Lutheran meant German. In 1925 he received an honorary doctorate of divinity from his old seminary.

In 1935 Graebner's wife died. Four years later he retired from the headmastership, although he remained president of the seminary until 1941. He died at Prospect on 5 June 1949, survived by two sons, both Lutheran pastors, and four of his six daughters, and was buried in West Terrace cemetery.

A. Brauer, *Under the Southern Cross* (Adel, 1956); Concordia College, *Brown and Gold*, 1924-1939; *Aust Lutheran Almanac*, 1934; *Aust Lutheran*, 5 July 1935; *Advertiser* (Adel), 19 June 1915; *Germans in SA*, 1914-18 (SA Collection, SLSA); C. F. Graebner file, Lutheran Church Archives (North Adel).   P. D. PAHL

GRAHAM, ARTHUR ERNEST JAMES CHARLES KING (1876-1938), public servant, was born on 19 June 1876 at Wagga Wagga, New South Wales, son of James Graham, publican, and his wife Mary Ann, née King. Ernest (as he was known) was educated at the Bega Public School and Grammar School and passed the public service examination, but instead of entering the service he took up dairy production. After private study he became butter and cheese maker in 1893 at the N.S.W. Creamery Butter Co.'s Bega factory and manager of the Wandella cheese factory in 1894. Two years later he was appointed manager of the cheese factory at Mogilla. In 1894-1903 he worked at the company's Cobargo butter and cheese factory, as manager from 1899. Employed as a judge of dairy produce at agricultural shows in the Bega district from 1900, from 1903 he leased a Tilba Tilba farm where he milked 130 cows as well as another 56 at Cobargo. On 21 November 1900, at Cobargo, he married Annie Ellen Engstrom.

Graham moved to Queensland in 1906. Dairy instructor at the Queensland Agricultural College, Gatton, for one year, he then became manager of the Queensland Farmers' Co-operative Co. Ltd at Booval for eighteen months prior to his appointment on 1 November 1908 as dairy expert in the Department of Agriculture and Stock. Chief dairy expert from October 1915, he became director of dairying and cold storage in September 1922 and then under secretary for agriculture and stock in January 1925. In addition, he was director of marketing from March 1930.

Graham's most notable work in the department was the framing of the Margarine Act of 1910 and of the Dairy Produce Act of 1920 which was designed mainly to regulate the industry in the interests of public health. Much legislation in Australia and overseas, particularly in the provinces of the Union of South Africa, has been based on this Act. He was keenly interested too in the pooling of commodities under the Primary Producers Organization and Marketing Acts, supervising closely the necessary machinery. As permanent head he represented the State government on numerous extra-departmental bodies such as the Australian Agricultural Council and the State committee for the British Empire Exhibition of 1924. He attended every annual conference of ministers of agriculture from 1913 till his death. A board member of the faculty of agriculture of the University of Queensland, he published numerous articles in the *Queensland Agricultural Journal* and elsewhere on aspects of rural production. With a background of practical experience which inspired confidence among farmers, he was closely connected with Lewis Richard Macgregor [q.v.] in the formulation and promulgation of the State's orderly marketing legislation which enshrined the principle of grower control. The legislation was widely copied.

Graham was an omnivorous reader and something of an authority on English and classical literature. He died in office on 1 May 1938 of cerebro-vascular disease after several years ill health. Survived by his wife, eight daughters and three sons, he was buried in Bulimba cemetery after a service in St John's Anglican Cathedral.

Government Gazette (Qld), 29 July, 12 Aug 1922, 6 Dec 1924, 19 Apr 1930; *Qld Agricultural J*, Jan 1925, p 7, May 1938, p 510; *Qld Producer*, 4 May 1938, p 6; *Daily Mail* (Brisb), 19, 20 Mar 1930; *Daily Standard*, 19 Mar 1930; *Brisb Courier*, 19, 20 Mar, 6 Dec 1930; *Courier Mail*, 2 May 1938; *Telegraph* (Brisb), 4 May 1938; Personnel file, Dept of Public Service Bd, *and* Dept of Primary Industries (QA).

DENISE K. CONROY

GRAHAM, GEORGE (1838-1922), farmer and politician, was born on 16 August 1838 at Linlithgow, West Lothian, Scotland, son of George Graham, farmer, and his wife Ellen, née Hardy. Graham's parents migrated to Victoria to take up land near Ballarat, leaving George junior to follow later. He took part in a sealing venture in Greenland before returning to Linlithgow, where he was a tenant farmer. He arrived in Melbourne in 1856.

After working on the Eureka, Ararat and Pleasant Creek goldfields, Graham was a pioneer of the bogus Port Curtis rush in Queensland in 1858. But he had no success as a digger, and returned to the family farm at Miners Rest, where he worked as a contractor with his father. On 14 July 1863 with Presbyterian forms he married Hannah Welch, a dressmaker, born in Northamptonshire, England; they had five children.

In 1873-74 Graham selected land in the Goulburn Valley, near Numurkah, and developed the Wunghnu Park estate. He became the first president of the Shepparton Shire Council, 1879-81, and president of the Farmers' Union at Wunghnu. His interest in fostering the area led him into politics and after an unsuccessful attempt in 1883, he was elected member for Moira in the Legislative Assembly at a by-election in May 1884. He continued to represent the district until his retirement in 1914, as member from 1889 for Numurkah and Nathalia, and from 1904 for Goulburn Valley.

Graham's original campaign was based on getting a 'practical farmer' to represent the district. His main interests were the development of country railways and water conservation, especially the Goulburn levee scheme. He was a member of Alfred Deakin's [q.v.8] royal commission into water-supply in 1884-85. He was also concerned to promote the power of country members in defence of rural interests, and was involved with a number of country factions. In November 1890 he became minister of water supply in the 'National Liberal' Munro [q.v.5] ministry, and from April 1891 minister of agriculture as well, retaining these posts in the Shiels [q.v.] ministry until it fell in January 1893. He was important in winning country support for the Liberal government of (Sir) George Turner [q.v.] formed in September 1894, but refused an offer to join it. By the 1897 election, however, Graham had moved into Opposition, and used his considerable weight with country members to help to defeat the Turner ministry in November 1899. He then became minister of agriculture, commissioner of public works and, in October-November 1900, minister of labour, in the subsequent 'country' ministry led by A. McLean [q.v.].

In 1902 Graham was again important in organizing a group of country members, this time to dismiss the Liberal Peacock [q.v.] government. However he again declined to participate in the resulting Irvine [q.v.] ministry. Even when party lines became much more rigid under the impact of the National Citizens' Reform League's support of the government in the 1902 elections, he still exercised considerable independence.

Although formed in 1904 without reference to country factions, the Bent [q.v.3] government was sympathetic to rural interests. Graham gave it good support, and for most of its life held the powerful position of chairman of the Railways Standing Committee. However by 1907 country members within government ranks again found it necessary to form a 'country party' to counterbalance any concessions to the Liberals, with whom Bent formed a coalition in 1907. Elements of this country faction were responsible for Bent's defeat on a motion of no confidence in 1908. Although Graham had supported Bent, and stood as a ministerialist in the ensuing elections, he represented the country faction in the new ministry formed by John Murray [q.v.], becoming minister of water supply and of agriculture. He continued to hold these portfolios in the Watt [q.v.] ministry in 1912-13, until it was defeated by the defection of a new country faction and replaced by the Elmslie [q.v.8] Labor ministry. He did not contest the 1914 election.

Wunghnu Park was taken over by Graham's two sons. Graham, who was in poor health and becoming senile, continued to live in the Numurkah district. He was a firm Methodist, a strong supporter of the temperance movement, and a Freemason. He died on 22 July 1922 at his daughter's home at Numurkah, and was buried in Wunghnu cemetery.

G. M. Hibbins, *A history of the Nathalia Shire* (Melb, 1978); *Punch* (Melb), 3 Aug 1905; *Argus*, 24 July 1922; K. Rollison, Groups and attitudes in the Victorian Legislative Assembly 1900-1909 (Ph.D. thesis, La Trobe Univ, 1972).

KAY ROLLISON

GRAHAM, MARGARET (1860-1942), nursing sister and army matron, was born on 15 February 1860 at Carlisle, Cumberland, England, daughter of John Graham, journeyman house-painter, and his wife Margaret, née Farrer. Nothing is known of her early life or of the circumstances which brought her to Australia. She entered the (Royal) Adelaide Hospital as a probationer on 2 April 1891, was recommended for promotion to charge nurse on 22 October 1894 and acted in this position until 15 February 1895 when her promotion was cancelled for alleged insubordination; she was later dismissed.

On 5 January Nurse Graham had signed a letter sent by five other charge nurses to Premier C. C. Kingston [q.v.], requesting an independent inquiry into 'unjust treatment' of Charge Nurse Louise Hawkins by the hospital board. Nurse Hawkins had protested against the promotion, over better-qualified and more efficient nurses, of Nurse A. H. Gordon, sister of the colony's chief secretary, (Sir) J. H. Gordon [q.v.]. The board considered the letter 'disrespectful' and urged the nurses to withdraw their statements. The other five did so, but although she had had nothing to gain personally by signing the letter Margaret Graham 'refused to retract', insisting that an injustice had been done to fourteen senior nurses. She remained intransigent and was dismissed on 4 March. The chief secretary and the hospital's medical superintendent then offered her positions in other hospitals which she denounced publicly as 'bribes for silence'. She attacked the chief secretary in a public letter dated 6 March imputing improper motives to the hospital board, the medical superintendent and the matron, and calling for an independent inquiry. A long and bitter public controversy followed which resulted in a royal commission into the management of the Adelaide Hospital. In evidence before the commission in March Graham described Nurse Gordon's appointment as 'a glaring piece of favoritism', asked why no members of the hospital board had spoken out against the 'tomfoolery' surrounding her own dismissal, and attacked the premier for his 'meally-mouthed utterances' during the dispute. The commission's progress report, issued in April, recommended her reinstatement. The government accepted this recommendation, whereupon the medical superintendent and the matron resigned. The reinstatement also contributed to the resignation of the entire honorary medical staff, the dismissal of the hospital board and the disruption of all clinical teaching at the hospital. J. H. Gordon resigned his office at the same time.

Margaret Graham was appointed charge nurse by the government in March 1896 and, because of her competence, dedication and high principles, quickly lived down her reputation as a rebel. On 1 January 1898 she was promoted matron, a position which she held with distinction until 1920. She was an excellent nurse and trainer of nurses but an indifferent administrator and left most of her book-work to her superintendent of night nurses. She was a foundation member of the South Australian Branch of the Royal British Nurses' Association and was its elected lady consul in 1900-20; she was also active in the Australasian Trained Nurses' Association.

In 1904 she had become the first lady superintendent in the State of the Australian Army Nursing Service and in August 1914 enlisted in the A.A.N.S., Australian Imperial Force, as a matron. One of the first three nurses to leave Australia on active service, she embarked at Melbourne in December and served in Egypt in 1915-16 at the 1st Australian General Hospital, Heliopolis, and at Ghezireh and Choubra. She also worked on hospital ships carrying wounded from Gallipoli. She was mentioned in dispatches in October 1916 and awarded the Royal Red Cross, 1st class, in December. In January 1917 she left Suez for Australia on transport duty on a troopship, reembarked in May, and in July was attached to the 3rd Australian Auxiliary Hospital at Dartford, England. She served there until January 1918 when she was posted to the medical offices at A.I.F. Headquarters, London. She was discharged, medically unfit, from the A.I.F. on 28 August. She returned to the Adelaide Hospital as matron but after May 1919 was transferred temporarily to the Exhibition Building, Adelaide, to superintend the nursing of pneumonic influenza cases. She resigned her matronship in December 1920 and left Australia early next year to settle in England.

Margaret Graham was a spirited, forthright, highly intelligent woman with a ready wit and strong leadership qualities. During her matronship nearly 3000 nurses came under her care and she won the 'esteem and affection' of most of them. On her resignation the *Australasian Nurses' Journal* praised her 'breadth of mind and unfailing justice'. She died, unmarried, at Carlisle, England, on 4 July 1942.

Aust Trained Nurses' Centenary Cttee, *Nursing in South Australia 1837-1937* (Adel, 1939); A. G. Butler (ed), *Official history of the Australian Army Medical Services . . . 1914-19*, 3 (Canb, 1943); J. E. Hughes, *A history of the Royal Adelaide Hospital* (Adel, 1967); *PP* (SA), 1896 (20, 21); *A'sian Nurses' J*, Oct 1909, Apr 1917, Dec 1919, Apr, May, Dec 1920, Aug 1942; *London Gazette*, 1, 29 Dec 1916; *Register* (Adel), Oct 1896-Jan 1897; *Herald* (Melb),

23 Feb 1917; *Observer* (Adel), 11 Dec 1920; *Advertiser* (Adel), 7 Jan 1921; Press cuttings file, Adelaide Hospital dispute (held by SA Branch, Aust Medical Assn, Adel); M. A. Heaney, The Adelaide Hospital dispute 1894-1902 (B.A. Hons thesis, Univ Adel, 1980); records (AWM).

MERRILYN LINCOLN

GRAHAME, WILLIAM CALMAN (1863-1945), politician, was born on 3 February 1863 at West Maitland, New South Wales, eldest surviving son of Scottish parents, William Graham(e), farmer, and his wife Isabella, née Calman. His father, a Protectionist, represented Newcastle in the Legislative Assembly in 1889-94. Grahame had little formal education while working on his father's farm, and was later apprenticed in the family jewellery business at Newcastle; he was a good athlete, with an impressive physique. Describing himself as a bookmaker living at Maitland, he married Leona Angelina Blanch at Wallsend on 27 February 1884; she died childless on 21 April next year. Grahame had returned to Newcastle and was a watchmaker when he married with Wesleyan Methodist rites Emily Smith on 27 October 1886.

Encouraged by his father to enter public life, Grahame was a member of Wickham Municipal Council in 1900-07. In the 1907 Legislative Assembly elections he ran for Labor, emphasizing that he was a total abstainer and with impeccable turf connexions (he was also a past president of Tattersall's Club); he defeated the formidable J. L. Fegan [q.v.8] for Wickham. In 1912, as a member of the select committee on the Newcastle iron and steel works bill, he favoured the Broken Hill Proprietary Co. Ltd's proposal despite strong party opposition.

After assisting the secretary for lands from March 1915, Grahame became minister for agriculture in June under W. A. Holman [q.v.] and was beset by administrative problems with the war-time wheat pool. He opposed conscription in 1916-17 but was loyal to Holman and expelled from the Labor Party. As minister he was at the centre of three scandals which were to undermine the government. The John Brown [q.v.7] coal contract that Grahame negotiated with the Victorian government was the subject of a censure motion in January 1918 when it was alleged that he had secured special favours for Brown, who was his racing associate, very unpopular in Labor ranks. Soon after cabinet split over the omission of safeguard clauses in a wheat-silo contract with H. Teasdale Smith [q.v.]. Meanwhile the minister and his department were trying to cope with a big surplus from the deteriorating wheat crop, and he jumped at the chance to sell a large amount to a speculator George Georgeson without tender or approval from State or Federal wheat boards.

The resignation of G. Beeby [q.v.7] from cabinet in July 1919 led to the appointment as royal commissioner of Mr Justice R. D. Pring [q.v.] who, in his second report, attacked the incompetence of the State Wheat Office. Georgeson failed to give evidence because of illness, and late in 1920 Pring returned his commission leaving in suspense imputations against Grahame's honesty. Meanwhile Grahame, pressed to resign in January, had met constant noise and innuendo when he stood as an Independent for Newcastle in March; he was defeated. He also lost at Hawkesbury in 1927.

Grahame was deeply hurt by the circumstances that ended his parliamentary career. After the death of his wife in 1921, he moved to the Brisbane Water district where his sons were orchardists. On 23 October 1925 at Hazelbrook, with Catholic rites, he married a 30-year-old widow Myra Lascelles White, née Campbell. He established a garage, and timber businesses, and was a member of Erina Shire Council in 1933-36. He was mayor of Gosford in 1936-40; Grahame Park alongside Brisbane Water was named after him. He died at Gosford on 15 September 1945 and was buried in the Methodist section of Point Clare cemetery. He was survived by four daughters and one of his three sons of his second marriage, and by his third wife and their two sons.

H. V. Evatt, *Australian Labour leader... W. A. Holman* (Syd, 1940); J. T. Lang, *I remember* (Syd, 1956); C. Swancott, *The Brisbane Water story* (Gosford, NSW, 1953); *PP* (NSW), 1919, 1, p 179, 1920, 2, p 219; *Newcastle Morning Herald*, 20 Aug 1907, 6 Mar 1917, 21 Feb 1920, 17 Sept 1945; *SMH*, 13 Mar 1915; family information. L. E. FREDMAN

GRAINGER, GEORGE PERCY (1882-1961), musician, was born on 8 July 1882 at Brighton, Melbourne, only child of John Harry Grainger, architect, and his wife Rosa (Rose) Annie, née Aldridge, of Adelaide.

John Grainger (1855-1917) came originally from Durham, England, and was educated there and in London and France. He migrated to Adelaide in February 1877 to take up a post in the Engineer-in-Chief's Office; he resigned in mid-1878 to concentrate on his extensive private practice. Soon after his marriage to Rose on 1 October 1880 he set up in private practice in Melbourne, where he had made a name for himself in 1879 as winner of a competition for the design of the new Princes Bridge. Later, as chief architect in the Western Australian Department of Public Works in 1897-1905, he was responsible for sections of the Perth Art Gallery, the Museum and Public Library, the Perth Law Courts, and for the first stage of Parliament House. The fine Wardens' Court in Coolgardie was designed by him. A close friend of David Mitchell [q.v.5] and his family, he designed Melba's [q.v.] Coombe Cottage, built at Coldstream near Melbourne in 1912.

Percy Grainger's parents, his mother particularly, had little doubt that he would be 'an artist'. The boy obliged by showing precocious talent in both graphic and musical arts, the first of which developed under his father's, the second under his mother's tutelage. He had three months formal schooling at the Misses Turner's Preparatory School for Boys in Caroline Street, South Yarra, probably in 1893 or 1894. His piano studies continued from 1892 with Louis Pabst, then, after Pabst's departure for Europe in 1894, with his pupil Adelaide Burkitt. He studied harmony for a brief period, possibly with Julius Herz [q.v.4]. His first composition, a birthday gift for his mother, dates from 1893.

In September 1890 John Grainger had returned home to England on a visit, leaving his wife and son in Melbourne. Though he was back in Australia by the end of that year, he did not rejoin his family. Thereafter they met only occasionally, in Europe and Australia.

Percy first came before the public eye as a pianist at a Risvegliato concert in the Masonic Hall, Melbourne, on 9 July 1894. Various other public performances included three appearances at W. J. Turner's People's Promenade Concerts at the Exhibition Building in October 1894. The boy's 'exceptional talent' was repeatedly noted.

In May 1895, following a benefit concert in the Melbourne Town Hall under the direction of G. W. L. Marshall-Hall [q.v.], Grainger left with his mother to further his musical studies in Germany. He never returned to Australia to live but retained a ferocious nationalism, an intense love of the landscape and a rather quixotic view of the virtues of the Australian character.

Grainger entered Dr Hoch's Conservatorium in Frankfurt-am-Main at the minimum age of 13. Over the next four and a half years he studied piano with James Kwast, taking counterpoint and composition classes with Iwan Knorr. Several compositions date from these years, including the earliest of his settings of Kipling. He continued his lessons in painting and drawing, but the name of his teacher is not known. A Frankfurt graphic artist and amateur musician, Karl Klimsch, had a profound influence on Grainger, who later described him as 'my only composition teacher'.

A solo recital given in Frankfurt on 6 December 1900 marked the end of Grainger's student years and the beginning of a long and arduous concert career which took him first to London, where he lived with his mother from May 1901 to August 1914. Grainger benefited greatly from the close-knit strength of the Anglo-Australian community in London in the first years, but he was soon accepted by the best society. He played several times before royalty, accumulating an impressive collection of aristocratic tie-pins and cuff-links. His 1907 solo recital enjoyed the patronage of Queen Alexandra.

Various landmarks highlight the growth of his pianistic career through these London years: his tour of the English provinces with Adelina Patti in 1902; his studies in Berlin with Ferruccio Busoni in 1903; his tour of Australasia and South Africa as a member of Ada Crossley's [q.v.8] concert party in 1903-04; further extensive tours with Crossley of the English provinces in 1907, and of Australasia in 1908-09. His career as a virtuoso was enhanced by the publicly expressed admiration of Grieg, who selected Grainger to play his concerto under his baton at the Leeds Festival in 1907. Though Grieg died before the festival, Grainger's reputation as 'the greatest living exponent' of Grieg's piano music was established. That year, also, began a close friendship and professional association with Frederick Delius.

From his first Danish engagements of 1904, Grainger's European touring circuit grew annually to include regular appearances throughout Scandinavia, as well as in Holland, Germany and Switzerland. In 1913 he gave concerts in Finland and Russia. Between times, in London, he took pupils, played at 'at homes' and went about in society in the way Rose considered essential to 'getting on'. The pace was relentless and the financial pressures considerable, especially since from about 1906 he was supporting both his parents. Grainger was a man who could not afford to fail. In later years, although his earning power was immense, this financial pressure was exacerbated by an almost self-destructive generosity.

Although there were performances of his music from as early as 1902, the Balfour Gardiner Choral and Orchestral Concerts of 1912 and 1913 really brought Grainger before the public as a composer, and as conductor of his own music. Success was instantaneous. Schott & Co., London, began publishing his music as fast as he could prepare it. There were numerous performances throughout Britain and in Europe, and he began to add conducting to his concert activities. In October 1911 he took the professional name of 'Percy Aldridge Grainger'.

The Graingers' sudden departure for the United States of America at the beginning of September 1914, traumatic in its immediate effects and later repercussions, cost them the goodwill of many of their patriotic upper-class British friends. This hostility was to some extent ameliorated when Grainger joined the U.S. Army as a bandsman in June 1917. He did not see active service, but he did appear a number of times in uniform at concerts in aid of the Red Cross and other wartime charities. He became a naturalized American citizen on 3 June 1918.

On being discharged from the army in February 1919, Grainger embarked on what was perhaps the most flamboyant decade of his career. Lionized as a pianist and fêted as a composer, he was acclaimed as 'a latter-day Siegfried' and a worthy successor to Paderewski. Essentially the pattern of constant touring, teaching and composing did not change. Financial security came gradually: in 1921 he bought the house at White Plains, New York, in which he lived until he died. Much of his music was now published by the firm of G. Schirmer Inc., New York. His record-breaking piano piece *Country gardens*, a piece which most music-lovers associate above all else with his name, was published by Schirmer's in 1919.

Grainger's father had died in Melbourne of syphilis on 13 April 1917. His mother's suicide in April 1922, from despair at rumours of incest and gathering effects of syphilis, was a crushing blow. She had been his constant companion, 'managed' his business, social and emotional affairs, guided his career with single-minded purpose. Her influence was definitive; her death left Grainger with a lifetime legacy of guilt and remorse.

Grainger visited Australia twice during the 1920s, privately in 1924 to see his mother's family, then in 1926 on a concert tour for J. C. Williamson's [q.v.6]. Both tours marked new departures.

On the 1924 tour he began to present, albeit privately, a new type of 'lecture recital', concerts in which he talked as much as he played and in which his choice of music was determined primarily by his own cultural interests, however much these might go against the mainstream of audience taste. The results were often controversial.

The 1926 tour was significant more for personal reasons. Returning home from Australia to the United States he met on board ship a Swedish-born poet and painter, Ella Viola Ström. They were married on 9 August 1928 at a public ceremony at the con-clusion of a concert in the Hollywood Bowl, Los Angeles. Ella was Grainger's 'Nordic Princess', a woman of outstanding beauty, 'generosity, joy-in-life and commonsense'. The marriage restored to Grainger the kind of exclusive companionship he had had with Rose. There were no children.

Grainger returned to Australia in 1934-35, touring for the Australian Broadcasting Commission. Income from this tour established the 'Music Museum and Grainger Museum' in the grounds of the University of Melbourne. He also gave a series of twelve radio talks called 'A commonsense view of all music'. Museum and broadcasts sprang from a single impulse: the desire to educate the Australian musical public to a 'universalist' view of music, celebrating the superior achievements of the composers of the 'Nordic group', but also embracing a selection of the world's musics, folk and art, Western and non-Western, 'primitive' and 'sophisticated', ancient and modern.

In these activities Grainger was projecting the universalism of his outlook. His musical eclecticism and aesthetic curiosity opened his mind to the beauties of an extraordinarily wide range of music which he variously collected, transcribed, edited, arranged, taught, performed and wrote about. The impulse to explore other cultures led him to the study of languages. He was fluent in some half-dozen European languages and their dialects, and read and studied as many more. His idiosyncratic and vigorous English prose style, exemplified in his enormous correspondence, shows the same fresh approach to language. An obverse of this eclecticism was a rather cranky concentration on notions of Nordic racial superiority and language purification. The letters also document Grainger's complex sexuality, his regular practice of flagellation, and his private absorption with what he called his 'cruelty instincts'—which were tempered in reality by an intense and tender approach to human relationships.

In the latter part of his life, Grainger's surplus energy and time were directed into two large-scale projects: the completion and arrangement of his museum in Melbourne, and his White Plains-based experiments in what he called 'free music'. In pursuit of the imagined sound of his free music, a music unconstrained by fixed pitch, regular metre and human performance, he built mechanical music machines which combine the makeshift and the futuristic. The museum building was finished and opened on a return trip to Melbourne in 1938. His concert activity continued on a reduced scale through the 1940s and 1950s. He even began to enjoy the special advantages that came with age. 'When I take part in a concert', he wrote in 1951, 'the concert-givers are only glad that one doesn't have a stroke on stage, and they don't expect one to play the right notes any more'.

The last decade of Grainger's life was shadowed by illness, and he underwent major surgery several times. Overwhelmed by a sense of his failure as a serious composer, his habit of bitter introversion intensified. Despite these inhibitions he continued his work, visiting Australia and his museum for the last time in 1955-56 and giving his last public concert performance on 29 April 1960. He died of cancer in the White Plains hospital on 20 February 1961. His gross estate was valued in the United States at $208 293. His remains were brought to Australia for burial in the Aldridge family grave in Adelaide, where his mother was also buried. His wife died at White Plains on 17 July 1979.

Of Grainger the pianist the *New York Times*'s music critic Harold Schonberg wrote, 'He was one of the keyboard originals —a pianist who forged his own style and expressed it with amazing skill, personality and vigor'. This opinion may be measured against the many gramophone records Grainger made in a long recording career from 1908 to 1957. He also cut Duo-Art piano rolls with the Aeolian Co. in the United States, though these are generally regarded as less reliable guides to an artist's playing because of the possibilities of editorial interference. Something of his style at the keyboard and on the conductor's rostrum can be seen in a short silent film, probably made by Schirmer's for promotional purposes in 1920.

His reputation as a composer was indelibly stamped by the success of *Country gardens*, and he became known primarily as the composer of cheerfully extroverted piano pieces. In fact, he wrote very little originally for the piano. In recent years, as the growing number of recorded performances draws attention to the quantity and variety of his output, his reputation has revived and grown again. His compositions for military band are regarded as classics of the genre; his settings of British and Danish folksongs are acclaimed for their sensitivity and appropriateness.

The fact that Grainger's appearance matched his talent was a not insignificant component of his success. As a young man, his Byronic good looks and his golden hair were almost as much admired and as often remarked as was the strength and vigour of his playing. In later years he affected a markedly eccentric presentation, a personal style which, if nothing else, made for good 'copy'. Grainger's pianistic feats were complemented by a vigorous athleticism;

long-distance walking was a favourite if intermittent pastime. Throughout his life he abstained from alcohol and tobacco and in his middle years he became a vegetarian.

There are several portraits, most notably two by Rupert Bunny [q.v.7] (1902 and 1904) and one by Jacques-Émile Blanche (1906) in the Grainger Museum, and a charcoal sketch by John Singer Sargent (1908) in the National Gallery of Victoria.

H. C. Schonberg, *The great pianists* (NY, 1966); R. Covell, *Australia's music* (Melb, 1967); T. Balough (ed), *A complete catalogue of the works of Percy Grainger* (Perth, 1975), and *A musical genius from Australia* (Perth, 1982); J. Bird, *Percy Grainger* (Lond, 1976); F. Callaway and D. Tunley (eds), *Australian composition in the twentieth century* (Melb, 1978); K. Dreyfus, *Percy Grainger music collection*, 1 (Melb, 1978), and *Percy Grainger's Kipling settings* (Perth, 1980); P. Cahn, *Das Hoch'sche Konservatorium in Frankfurt am Main (1878-1978)* (Frankfurt, 1979); S. Sadie (ed), *The new Grove dictionary of music and musicians* (Lond, 1980); *Studies in Music*, 10 (1976), 12 (1978); *Current Musicology* (NY), 15, 16 (1973), 17 (1974); *Music and Musicians*, 18 (1970); Grainger Museum collections (Univ Melb).   KAY DREYFUS

GRAINGER, HENRY WILLIAM ALLERDALE (1848-1923), politician, journalist and stockbroker, was born on 7 August 1848 in Cumberland, England, son of Henry Grainger, a businessman who was interested in the colonization of South Australia and who owned land in Adelaide. Henry junior went to Rugby School in 1861-66; a possible career in finance on the London Stock Exchange was cut short by the depression of 1866, which ruined his father. He worked in North America as a journalist, then moved to Melbourne and to Adelaide in 1876.

It was said that he was 'a man whose capital is his brains': with his City experience, Grainger offered himself as a financial expert and journalist. From 1877 he ran the *Australian Star*, a weekly penny paper expressing protectionist and 'reforming' views, including restriction of Chinese immigration and the establishment of employers' liability. When the paper failed in 1881 he turned to freelance journalism and stock-market speculation, especially in copper and silver lead shares. He wrote for the South Australian *Register* and ran an agency business.

Allerdale Grainger's public advocacy of protection and reform and his experience in finance and as a journalist led him into politics. After three unsuccessful contests he was elected as one of the two House of Assembly members for Wallaroo in 1884 and became conspicuous for his outspoken independence. However insolvency caused him to resign next year. After four more attempts to return in 1885 and 1887 he was re-elected in 1890 for Wallaroo which he held until 1901. In 1890-97 he was a council-member of the School of Mines and Industries; he was secretary of the Mining Commission and controlled several early Western Australian goldmining companies.

In the assembly, Grainger was a moderate Liberal. He opposed a progressive land tax in favour of a flat rate of tax on agricultural land held unused in large estates. He was more radical in other financial matters, supporting a state bank capable of raising local capital instead of relying on the London market. He continued to favour protection and unrestricted mining on private land. As distinct liberal and conservative groupings emerged in the assembly from 1893, Grainger continued to support the Liberal Kingston [q.v.] ministry. It was, however, his political style, rather than his political views, which made him notable. A tall, commanding figure, and a vigorous though not polished debater, he incessantly criticized all governments, earning the title of 'interjector-general'. This stance won him no political friends and, despite his ability, he was never offered a ministerial position.

In 1901 the Holder [q.v.] government offered him the State's agent-generalship in London. With Federation, the position was being downgraded but Grainger accepted. He was a successful though not remarkable agent-general until 1905. He then returned to South Australia and lived quietly in North Adelaide. He was appointed secretary of the South Australian Liquor Trades' Defence Association and in 1907-20 was a trustee of the Savings Bank of South Australia. The debonair 'Ally' was said to be a 'brilliant raconteur' and a 'thorough Bohemian'. From 1920 he lived with his sister at Leamington, Warwickshire, England, where he died on 17 December 1923. He had been married and had at least one son.

Pictorial Australian, May 1890, July 1891; *Quiz and the Lantern*, 17 Oct 1890, 6 June 1901; *Australasian*, 8 June 1901; *Advertiser* (Adel), 7 Aug 1919; *Register* (Adel), 21 Dec 1923.

KAY ROLLISON

GRANO, PAUL LANGTON (1894-1975), journalist and poet, was born on 22 October 1894 at Ararat, Victoria, fifth child of Theodore George Grano, barrister, and his wife Kate Cecilia, née Patten, both of whom were born in Victoria. He was educated at Ararat and at St Patrick's College, Ballarat. Matriculating at the University of Mel-

bourne on 27 March 1912, he entered on a law course and graduated LL.B. on 20 December 1916.

For a time Grano practised law at Stawell. On 11 December 1919 he married at St Mary's, Hawthorn, Violet Irene Galloway, a professional musician, by whom he had a son and twin daughters. Early in the 1930s, probably in 1932, he moved to Brisbane, where his literary life really began. He became friendly with Father A. J. Mills of St Vincent's Hostel, editor of *Australia*, to which he contributed. He also wrote for the Brisbane *Catholic Advocate*. At that period there were writing in Brisbane several poets—though they never formed a school—among whom were James Picot, Brian Vrepont, Martin Haley, Frank Francis and James Devaney; Grano was a respected voice among them. In 1944 he was the chief mover in establishing in Brisbane the Catholic Readers' and Writers' Society which, apart from purely religious aims, tried to encourage young writers and published the periodical *Vista*. In 1946 he edited *Witness to the Stars*, an anthology with notes on living Australasian Catholic poets.

His own poetry was published in several volumes: *Poems personal and otherwise* (1933), *The roads, and other poems* (1934), *Quest* (1940), *Poet's holiday* (1941), *Poems, new and old* (1945), *Selected verse of Paul Grano* (1976).

Grano joined the public service and in 1939 began as a tally clerk with the Queensland Main Roads Commission. In October 1950 he moved to Townsville, where he was employed, still in the Main Roads Commission. Refused a transfer to Brisbane when his health broke down in February 1953, he was retrenched in May and returned to Brisbane. These three years in the north he looked back on with some detestation. From 1954 until 1960 he worked for the Queensland Housing Commission. On 5 December 1959 he married Bobs Victoria, née Sears; they had one daughter.

As a poet Grano was minor, as he admitted to his son. He was always a devoted son of the Church, and much of his verse concerned religious faith and religious themes. Here the influence of Gerard Manley Hopkins was sometimes obtrusive. And unfortunately Grano's professions were often expressed in abstractions, terms which poetry for the most part does not readily assimilate. Fortunately, as he continued he turned more to the concrete, the visual, and some of the images in his later verse have an immediacy that can help preserve his name. So it is not surprising that poems of locality are among his best work.

Grano was always a man of independent mind—he did not wait for others to act on his behalf. When he felt himself failing, he put himself into Canossa, a Catholic institution at Oxley, Brisbane. There for some years he was ailing, and there he died on 11 January 1975. He bequeathed his body to the medical faculty of the University of Queensland.

Meanjin Q, Dec 1973; *Courier Mail*, 12 Jan 1975; information from Qld Main Roads Dept, *and* P. Grano, Ararat, Vic, and T. Grano, Graceville, Brisb.

CECIL HADGRAFT

GRANT, ALEXANDER CHARLES (1843-1930), pastoralist and businessman, was born on 12 August 1843 at Inverness, Scotland, son of Peter Grant, sugar merchant of Demerara, West Indies, and his wife Jessie, daughter of John Macdonald of Ness Castle, Inverness. He was educated at the Royal High School, Edinburgh, the Royal Academy of Halle, Germany, and Montgrennan House, near Irvine, Scotland. Early in 1861 Grant arrived in Queensland to work for his uncle Chesborough Claudius Macdonald on Cadarga in the Burnett district. At first an unpaid jackeroo, then superintendent of the store and the cattle, he also drove 20 000 sheep north to Macdonald's Logan Downs, near Clermont. In 1868 Grant and his brothers bought Dartmoor, inland from Mackay, but sold out in 1870 when the country proved unsuitable for sheep. He established Wrotham Park on the Mitchell River in 1874. Although he sold meat to the Normanby and Palmer goldfields, he failed to find a partner for a wholesale meat concern. This failure and severe malaria led him to sell his share of Wrotham Park in 1878.

While seeking health in travel overseas, Grant wrote a fictionalized account of his experiences, published in *Blackwood's Magazine* in 1879-80 and reprinted as *Bush life in Queensland* or *John West's colonial experiences* (Edinburgh, 1881); there were two later editions. Returning to Queensland in 1879, he married Sarah Elizabeth North at Ipswich on 28 November and joined the mercantile and pastoral firm, B. D. Morehead [q.v.5] & Co. His practical background soon made him indispensable and he was rapidly promoted to manager of the stock and station business and to a junior partnership. Through the senior partners, Morehead and William Forrest [q.v.8], he made valuable political and financial contacts. In great demand as an assessor in hearings before the land boards inaugurated by the Crown Lands Act of 1884, he travelled widely throughout Queensland, seeking lower valuations for pastoralists. Although the firm was old and respected, it was badly shaken by the Queensland National Bank crash which brought not only deflated land values and bankruptcies but also a whiff of scandal since Morehead had been a director of the bank. In the resultant reshuffle Grant emerged as managing director of the new company, Morehead's Ltd, with a 30 per cent shareholding. Morehead & Co. had sponsored the Queensland Meat Export and Agency Co. Ltd which allowed Queensland to enter the frozen meat trade. From the 1880s Grant campaigned for local sale of wool rather than sending the clip to Sydney or London. In spite of opposition the Brisbane wool sales were successfully established in 1898.

A captain in the Queensland Scottish Volunteers until 1890, Grant was also a trustee of the Brisbane Public Library in 1896, a member of the Johnsonian Club and vice-president of the Queensland Stock Breeders and Graziers' Association in 1898. In the drought of 1900-01 he lost heavily. Convinced that the best days of pastoralism were over, fearful of radical political trends and concerned about his children's prospects, he decided to seek refuge in the United States of America. Selling up all his Queensland interests in 1902, he took his wife, three sons and eight daughters to California. He died in Los Angeles on 8 January 1930.

Alcazar Press, *Queensland*, 1900 (Brisb, nd); *Government Gazette* (Qld), 3 May 1890, 3 Jan 1891; *V&P* (LA NSW), 1901 (4), 365; *Queenslander*, 17, 31 May, 1 June 1902, 16 Jan 1930; J. L. F. Mitke, The history of our race (1969, MS, held by Dr Peter Grant, Indooroopilly, Qld); MS and correspondence FM4/3653, 6463 (ML); Groom papers (NL); ANU Archives, 167 Box 59.   CHRIS TIFFIN

GRANT, CHARLES HENRY (1831-1901), engineer, businessman and politician, was born on 9 November 1831 at Great Marlow, Buckinghamshire, England, son of William Grant, linen draper, and his wife Mary Ann. After education in applied sciences at King's College, London, in 1847-50, Grant worked until 1866 in the London engineering office of Robert Stevenson. In the late 1860s he worked on railway construction in the United States of America.

On 19 April 1872 Grant was appointed engineer to the Tasmanian Main Line Railway Co. and arrived from London in July to superintend construction of the line between Hobart and Launceston. After completion of the railway in 1876 he served as general manager until the line's purchase by the government in 1890. In March 1892 he floated the Hobart Electric Tramway Co. in London. He was himself a director and had charge of the construction of the tramways in 1892-93, having been consulting engineer to the project as early as 1888. As a director of the Zeehan Tramway Co. he was also responsible for construction of the tramway there in 1893. The Victorian government appointed him a member of a board to investigate the Victorian Railways in 1895.

Grant's business activities also included directorships of Cascade Brewery, Perpetual Trustees, Executors and Agency, Hobart Gas, Hobart Coffee Palace and Parattah Hotel companies, and of several mining bodies. He was said to draw some £12 a week in director's fees, and was described as 'pre-eminently a money making machine and successful speculator'.

In 1892-1901 Grant was a member of the Legislative Council and served until 1894 as minister without portfolio under Henry Dobson [q.v.8]. As a Tasmanian delegate to the 1897 Federal Convention he confined himself mainly to railway matters. Most active in local government, he was chairman of the Road Trust (1886-92), Town Board (1889-1901) and Board of Health (1888-1901) at Glebe, where his home, Addlestone, still stands. He was also a member of the Metropolitan Drainage Board (1893-1901), the Queen's Domain Committee (1891-1901) and the Board of Immigration (1883-85), and was a trustee of the Tasmanian Museum, Art Gallery and Botanical Gardens. He was president of the Hobart Chamber of Commerce in 1896 and of the Hobart Horticultural Society. He became a fellow of the Royal Society of Tasmania in 1874.

Grant died from diabetes in Hobart on 30 September 1901 after attending the Sydney celebrations for the inauguration of the Commonwealth. He was buried in Cornelian Bay cemetery, survived by his wife Mary Ann Jane, née Nicholls, two daughters and two sons. His estate was valued for probate at about £48 000. During his time with the Main Line Co. Grant was noted as a 'good boss', being 'always mindful of the comfort and prosperity of the railway man'. The Hobart *Mercury* described him as possessing 'a power of mind not to be trifled with. His *bonhomie* was invariable, but his kindly disposition was not weakness'. In 1914 the hamlet of South Bridgewater, north of Hobart, was renamed Granton in his honour.

CHARLES WILLIAM (1878-1943), Grant's elder son, was born on 24 April 1878 in Hobart. Educated at The Hutchins School, he worked on mainland sheep stations before becoming a Hobart merchant in 1901 and eventually chairman of directors of several companies. On 10 June 1903 at Wagga Wagga, New South Wales, he married Charlotte Bell. Member for Denison in the House of Assembly in 1922-25 and 1928-32, he was

honorary minister in the McPhee [q.v.] government. He was a Nationalist and United Australia Party senator in 1925 and 1932-41. He died on 14 December 1943 in Hobart, survived by one son and three daughters. His estate was sworn for probate at £112 603.

Cyclopedia of Tasmania, 1 (Hob, 1900); *V&P* (HA Tas), 1873 (26), papers 86, 112; *Mercury*, 1 Oct 1901, 15 Dec 1943; *Australasian*, and *Clipper*, 5 Oct 1901; *Examiner* (Launc), 18 June 1896, supplement.

SCOTT BENNETT

GRANT, DONALD McLENNAN (1888-1970), agitator and politician, was born on 26 February 1888 at Inverness, Scotland, son of Donald Grant, insurance agent, and his wife Mary, née McLennan. Educated at the High School, Inverness, he was apprenticed to a dental mechanic but, unhappy with his prospects, he migrated to Australia, reaching Sydney in 1910; he found work in a paper mill.

Opposed to the growing Imperialist militarism, Grant joined the Australian Freedom League in 1912 and became its joint treasurer with P. J. Minahan [q.v.]. He also became associated with the Industrial Workers of the World and, after the outbreak of World War I, emerged as a prominent anti-war speaker; in 1916 he was dismissed from his job for his activities.

Meanwhile Grant, tall, with his flaming red hair brushed back, drew record crowds to the I.W.W.'s regular Sunday meetings at the Sydney Domain, and in Melbourne. A fiery mob orator, with a thick Scots burr, he inveighed against conscription and expounded the I.W.W.'s opposition to the war through industrial action, including sabotage. After the arrest of Tom Barker [q.v.7], Grant informed a Domain meeting that 'for every day that Barker is in gaol, it will cost the capitalists ten thousand pounds'. This statement was an important part of the case against him when, on a visit to Broken Hill in October 1916, he was charged, with eleven other I.W.W. members, with treason, later altered to conspiracy to defeat the ends of justice and to commit arson, and incitement to commit sedition. Grant was convicted on all three counts and sentenced to fifteen years.

The campaign to free the 'I.W.W. Twelve' began in December 1916, when Grant's friend H. E. Boote [q.v.7] started widespread agitation. Eventually N. K. Ewing's [q.v.8] royal commission overturned most of the convictions. Grant was released in August 1920. At a meeting in Sydney Town Hall on May Day 1921 his criticism of Australian soldiers aroused wild anger in the conservative press, and allegations that he had said that he was 'glad' the soldiers had died haunted his later political career.

Grant became associated with the 'Trades Hall Reds' of the Labor Council of New South Wales and broke with the 'anti-political' I.W.W. in 1923 over the issue of joining the Labor Party. In 1922 he lost in the State seat of Sturt for the Industrial Socialist Labor Party, and in 1925, running for Labor, failed in the Senate elections. He was gaoled over unauthorized street demonstrations against the execution of Sacco and Vanzetti in 1927. Elected to the Sydney Municipal Council in 1931, he represented Phillip Ward until 1944. In 1930-33 he was also a member of the socialization committee of the State Labor Party. Appointed to the Legislative Council in November 1931, he was elected to the reconstituted council in April 1934; in 1940 he refused to seek re-election, declaring the council to be 'the bulwark of vested interests, and even worse than the House of Lords'.

During the early years of World War II Grant worked as a dental mechanic. On 3 November 1943 at his home at New South Head Road, Double Bay, he married a librarian Elizabeth Jane Dowse with Presbyterian forms. Earlier that year he had been elected to the Senate, and became an adviser to the minister for external affairs Dr H. V. Evatt. In 1946 he was an Australian representative to the Paris Peace Conference and a delegate to the International Labour Organization conference at Montreal, Canada. While overseas he was entertained by the provost and Town Council of Inverness. He also attended the Commonwealth Parliamentary Association conference at Nairobi in 1954. Grant lost Senate pre-selection in 1959 after attacking his old friend Evatt: 'If Machiavelli were alive today he wouldn't qualify to hand out leaflets at an Evatt meeting'. His parliamentary speeches had been generally well informed and carefully reasoned, and as the capitalist system evolved after World War II, he moved towards a left-Keynesian reformist approach as an alternative to communism.

Grant died in hospital at Darlinghurst on 9 June 1970 and was cremated without a religious service. He had suffered for some time from emphysema, which had hindered his performance in parliament towards the end. He was survived by his second wife, Marjorie Frances, née Templeton, whom he had married at his Double Bay home on 18 August 1955. His estate was valued for probate at $55 342.

H. E. Boote, *The case of Grant* (Syd, 1917); I. Turner, *Sydney's burning* (Syd, 1969); R. Cooksey, *Lang and socialism* (Canb, 1971); *Labour Hist*, Nov 1970, no 19; Grant papers (ML, *and* NL).

FRANK FARRELL

GRANT, DOUGLAS (1885?-1951), draughtsman and soldier, was a full-blooded Aboriginal born about 1885 in the Bellenden Ker Ranges, Queensland. In 1887 his parents were killed, apparently in a tribal fight although some accounts claim it was during a punitive action launched from Cairns, and he was rescued by two members of a collecting expedition from the Australian Museum, Robert Grant and E. J. Cairn. The former sent the infant to the Lithgow (New South Wales) home of his parents and later adopted him. As Douglas Grant the child was raised with Robert Grant's own son Henry, received a good education at Annandale, Sydney, and trained as a draughtsman. He became a clever penman and sketch artist and at the Queen's diamond jubilee exhibition of 1897 won first prize for a drawing of the bust of Queen Victoria; in addition he learned taxidermy from his foster-father.

For ten years Grant was a draughtsman at Mort's [q.v.5] Dock & Engineering Co. in Sydney. About 1913 he resigned to work as a woolclasser at Belltrees station, near Scone. In January 1916 he enlisted as a private in the 34th Battalion, Australian Imperial Force, but when his unit was about to leave for overseas service he was discharged because of regulations preventing Aboriginals leaving the country without government approval. He again enlisted and in August embarked for France to join the 13th Battalion. On 11 April 1917, during the 1st battle of Bullecourt, he was wounded and captured. He was held as a prisoner of war in a camp at Wittenberg, and later at Wünsdorf, Zossen, near Berlin. He became an object of curiosity to German doctors, scientists and anthropologists—the sculptor Rudolf Markoeser modelled his bust in ebony—and was given comparative freedom.

Grant was repatriated to England in December 1918, and visited his foster-parents' relatives in Scotland where his racial features, combined with a richly burred Scottish accent, attracted attention. In April 1919 he embarked for Australia and after demobilization on 9 July returned to work at Mort's Dock. Several years later he moved to Lithgow, where he was employed as a labourer at a paper products factory and a small-arms factory. He was active in returned servicemen's affairs in this period and conducted a 'Diggers session' on the local radio station. In the early 1930s, by which time both his foster-parents and his foster-brother had died, he returned to Sydney. He worked as a clerk at the Callan Park Mental Asylum and lived there, constructing in his spare time a large ornamental pond spanned by a replica of the Sydney

Harbour Bridge. After World War II he lived at the Salvation Army's old men's quarters in Sydney and after 1949 at La Perouse. He died of a subarachnoid haemorrhage in Prince Henry Hospital, Little Bay, on 4 December 1951 and was buried in Botany cemetery. He was unmarried.

A popular member of his battalion, Grant had also impressed his German captors as a man of superior intellect; to his fellow prisoners he was aggressively Australian. His attainments included a wide knowledge of Shakespeare and poetry and considerable skill as an artist and bagpipe-player. Despite his acceptance of white culture, in later life he suffered rejection and frustration on account of his race, and developed an alcohol problem. He was nonetheless an exceptional man.

T. A. White, *The fighting Thirteenth*, (Syd, 1924); H. Gordon, *The embarrassing Australian* (Melb, 1965); *J* (LC NSW) 1888-89, 1, p 185; *British A'sian*, 2 Nov 1916; *Army J*, Mar 1973; *Reveille* (Syd), Dec 1931, Jan 1932, Feb 1952; *Sydney Mail*, 20 Mar 1918; Grant papers, MS 2766 (ML).

C. D. COULTHARD-CLARK

GRANT, KENNETH McDONALD (1869?-1922), businessman and politician, was born about 1869, probably in Scotland, son of William Grant, farmer, and his wife Jessie, née McDonald. They had migrated to Victoria about 1863, gone back to Scotland, and then returned to Australia, arriving in Brisbane in March 1883. After attending briefly Brisbane Normal School, Grant was appointed a telegraphist in the Brisbane Telegraph Office on 1 November 1883. Next year he moved to the Rockhampton railway traffic office. After some years he returned to the Telegraph Department and was second-in-charge at Rockhampton when he resigned in 1902 to stand for the Queensland parliament.

Teamed with the experienced Labor leader William Kidston [q.v.], Grant was elected as one of the two members for Rockhampton, defeating G. S. Curtis [q.v.8] in a remarkably restrained and fair campaign. When Grant made it clear that he represented the whole city, the *Capricornian* announced that he carried 'the goodwill of his opponents equally with that of his supporters'. After Kidston became premier in January 1906 he voluntarily undertook as much as possible of Kidston's electorate work. Like Kidston, Grant fell under the liberalizing influence of John Blair [q.v.7] and in January 1908 abandoned the Labor Party by nominating as a 'Kidstonian' candidate.

Soon afterwards, he established K. M. Grant & Co., commission agents, and launched out on a private business career. When Kidston resigned as premier, Grant became secretary for public instruction in the Denham [q.v.8] ministry on 7 February 1911. In September 1912 he left the ministry on principle. Denham, who had recently announced publicly the continuation of work on railway extensions, decided that the only exception would be the Mount Morgan to Dawson Valley extension in Grant's electorate. Grant realized that, as a director of the Blair Athol Coal & Timber Co. and as its business agent, he could be accused of trying to smother the competition of struggling coal companies in the Dawson Valley and, failing to dissuade his colleagues from the decision, resigned in protest. 'I am only a poor man', he said; 'my only asset is my good name and that I am going to jealously guard'.

In April 1912 the Rockhampton electorate was divided and Grant won the new seat of Fitzroy. He won office again as home secretary and secretary for mines in February 1915 but in May the government was crushingly defeated: Grant lost his seat by a narrow margin and failed to regain it in 1918. Having opened a Brisbane branch of K. M. Grant & Co. some time before, he settled there after his defeat. He died at Windsor on 13 August 1922 and was buried in Toowong cemetery after a Presbyterian service. He had never married.

P. J. Gribble, *What hath God wrought: the story of the electric telegraph, Queensland* (Brisb, 1981); *Morning Bulletin*, 11 July 1899, 8 Oct 1906, 15, 20 Jan 1908, 17 Jan 1911, 3, 5, 7 Sept 1912, 19 Aug 1922; *Capricornian*, 22 Mar 1902, 31 Aug, 3 Sept 1912, 19 Aug 1922; family information from Mr H. C. Grant, Rockhampton, Qld.

LORNA L. McDONALD

GRANT, SIR KERR (1878-1967), physicist and professor, was born on 26 June 1878 at Bacchus Marsh, Victoria, elder of two sons of William Grant, a Scottish flour-miller and grazier and his wife Janet Langlands, née Kerr. Kerr Grant won a scholarship to J. B. O'Hara's [q.v.] South Melbourne College and in 1897 entered the University of Melbourne with a residential scholarship to Ormond College. He enrolled in engineering, but specialized in mathematics and won first-class honours (B.Sc., 1901; M.Sc., 1903). After lecturing at the Ballarat School of Mines for two years he returned to Melbourne as a tutor at Ormond. In 1904 he studied at the University of Göttingen where he mastered German, attended Felix Klein's lectures and was paired with Irving Langmuir in H. W. Nernst's practical classes. On vacation, he cycled from Paris to Rome.

Returning to Melbourne, Kerr Grant joined the university's natural philosophy department where he collaborated with B. D. Steele [q.v.] in the construction of a micro-balance sensitive to one-millionth of a milligramme. An account of this fine work was communicated to the Royal Society of London by Sir William Ramsay who built a Steele-Grant balance and used it to determine the atomic weight of radon. In 1909 Kerr Grant became acting professor of physics at the University of Adelaide following the resignation of W. H. Bragg [q.v.7] and in 1911 he became Elder [q.v.4] professor. A year earlier he had married Kate Macaulay Moffatt and they settled permanently in a large house in the suburb of St Peters.

During his long tenure of the chair, Kerr Grant established himself primarily as a teacher and a public figure. Among his students were (Sir) Hugh Cairns [q.v.7], H. W. (Lord) Florey and (Sir) Mark Oliphant. He wrote in his *Life and work of Sir William Bragg* (Brisbane, 1952) that research was 'regarded as a natural and unforced product of academic employment and intellectual interest; subordinate nevertheless, to the performance of the professor's contractual obligation to train his students in the discipline of his special science, and to serve the general public as an authority and consultant on whom reliance could be placed for trustworthy information or wise counsel in all matters relating to his particular province of expert knowledge'. This aptly summarizes his own credo. But he also engaged in several minor researches of which the most interesting was the organization, with G. F. Dodwell, the government astronomer, of an expedition to Cordillo Downs in northeast South Australia to observe the 1922 total solar eclipse, for the further verification of Einstein's theory of the deflection of light in a gravitational field. Although not entirely successful, the astronomer royal wrote of it that 'under the difficult conditions, you have every reason to be satisfied, and I offer heartiest congratulations'.

The most significant original work done in Kerr Grant's department stemmed from the year he spent in 1919, at Langmuir's invitation, in the laboratories at the General Electric Co. at Schenectady, United States of America. Kerr Grant was intrigued by Langmuir's work on molecular films and, on his return to Adelaide, successfully urged R. S. Burdon to study such films on mercury. In 1927 he visited Europe and Britain to inspect laboratories and universities, and purchased modern equipment for Adelaide. He was particularly impressed by the Radium Institute of the Vienna University. He went abroad again in 1931 and investigated developments in radium therapy for the treatment of cancer. On his return he reported his findings to the cancer research committee at the university.

In World War II some of his department's resources were directed to war work and Kerr Grant became chairman of the Scientific (physics) Manpower Advisory Committee, controller of the Adelaide branch of the Army Inventions Directorate, a member and later chairman of the Optical Munitions Panel (of the Ordnance Production Directorate), and a member of the physical and meteorological sub-committee of the Chemical Defence Board. In 1947 he was appointed K.C.B. Later that year he took part in a symposium on atomic energy at the Australian and New Zealand Association for the Advancement of Science congress in Perth, and he also went with Sir John Madsen [q.v.] and others on an Australian scientific mission to India. Next year he retired and was created emeritus professor. In 1951 he presided over the A.N.Z.A.A.S. meeting in Brisbane and he continued his service on the council of the South Australian Institute of Technology (formerly School of Mines and Industries) until 1960, having been president in 1942-58. The institute holds his portrait bust by John Dowie.

Although Kerr Grant was not and would never have claimed to be an outstanding physicist, he had an alert and penetrating mind as is illustrated by two remarkably prescient addresses: 'Things unattempted yet' (university commemoration address, Adelaide, 1924) and 'Atomic transmutation' (A.N.Z.A.A.S. *Reports*, 1926) in which he anticipated developments in nuclear physics and space flight. But it was not his way to constrain his wide-ranging intellect into the narrower paths of definite research projects. Rather he enjoyed the role of departmental autocrat, who nevertheless won his students' affection and was respected by the public. He contributed a regular column in the local press which answered citizens' questions on scientific affairs, and his door was always open to back-yard inventors. He looked the part: he had a heavy walrus moustache, thick shaggy eyebrows and an unruly mop of iron-grey curly hair. He was everyman's idea of the absent-minded professor, partly through nature's art and, one suspects, not a little through his own: many amusing stories grew up around him. He read widely and could quote freely from literature: Byron was a favourite poet and his final lecture each year traditionally concluded with a spirited rendering of Kipling's 'If'. Brought up a Presbyterian, he became a tolerant agnostic with a strong sense of humour. He was a member of the Savage Club.

He was admitted to hospital with a fractured hip and died of pneumonia on 13 October 1967, survived by his wife and three sons who pursued medical and scientific careers.

W. G. K. Duncan and R. A. Leonard, *The University of Adelaide, 1874-1974* (Adel, 1973); *SA Homes and Gardens*, 1 Mar 1949; Univ Adel Graduates' Union, *Mthly Newsletter and Gazette*, Mar 1968; *Aust Physicist*, 4 (1977); *Mail* (Adel), 6 June 1914; *Observer* (Adel), 20 Dec 1924, 28 Jan 1928; *Chronicle* (Adel), 25 Feb 1932; Personalities remembered, ABC radio script, 8 Nov 1970, D5390, misc (SAA).   S. G. TOMLIN

GRANT, WILLIAM (1870-1939), grazier and soldier, was born on 30 September 1870 at Pleasant Creek (Stawell), Victoria, son of Scottish-born Edmund Craigie Grant, miner and later mine-owner and grazier, and his wife Elizabeth Ann, née Parkinson, from England. He was educated at Brighton Grammar School and Ormond College at the University of Melbourne from which he graduated B.C.E. in 1893 and received a rowing blue. He was employed on railway construction in New South Wales in 1894, but after his father's death that year he gave up engineering for the land and bought Bowenville station on the Darling Downs, Queensland, in 1896. He married Eveline Ryan Woolcott at All Saints Anglican Church, St Kilda, Melbourne, on 21 July 1897; they had three sons and two daughters.

In 1901 Grant was commissioned as a lieutenant in the Queensland Mounted Infantry (militia). He was old for his rank but education and a flair for soldiering made up for this. 'He was a typical light horse subaltern', according to General Sir Harry Chauvel [q.v.7], 'tall, lithe and wiry, and full of dash and energy, and I early had my eye on him as a possible leader'. Promotion came quickly; as a major he took command of the 14th Light Horse in 1910 and was made lieut-colonel next year. In the reorganization of 1912 his regiment became the 3rd (Darling Downs) Light Horse.

It was not until March 1915 that Grant was offered command of the 11th Light Horse Regiment in the Australian Imperial Force. The unit went to Egypt with the 4th Light Horse Brigade only to be disbanded and dispatched to Gallipoli late in August as reinforcements to other light horse regiments. Grant, with one of his squadrons, was allotted to the 9th Light Horse who were engaged in the futile struggle for Hill 60; when the commanding officer of the 9th was killed Grant took command on 29 August, remaining with the regiment until the evacuation when it returned to Egypt. He resumed command of the 11th Light Horse when it was re-formed early in 1916 but served under British command. That year he took part in a number of successful minor operations in Sinai where he quickly won a reputation for his 'phenomenal sense of locality and direction'. In a raid on Maghara in October he led the column across trackless dune country and through fog so accurately that 'as daylight was breaking, the advanced screen was fired on by a Turkish outpost'. He was awarded the Distinguished Service Order in December.

After the 4th Light Horse Brigade had been re-formed as part of the Imperial Mounted Division, Grant led his 11th Regiment in the abortive 2nd battle of Gaza in April 1917. In August he was promoted brigadier general and given command of the 3rd Light Horse Brigade but a month later transferred to the 4th Light Horse Brigade on the eve of the 3rd battle of Gaza. In that battle Grant was set the task of galloping the Turkish defences to the east of Beersheba and seizing the wells which were believed to be vital to any further advance of the Desert Mounted Corps. That bold thrust in the gathering dusk suited his impetuous temperament and provided a chance for his brigade to prove itself. The charge of the 4th and 12th Light Horse Regiments, with Grant initially at their head, was one of the most brilliant feats of the campaign. Driven home at no great cost to the Australians, it was completely successful. All the wells but two were captured intact while the Turks fled in disarray. The commander-in-chief, General Sir Edmund Allenby, personally decorated Grant with a Bar to his D.S.O., the day after the charge.

Grant was prominent in the battles of 1918. In the 2nd battle of the Jordan (30 April-4 May) his task was to cover the left flank of the Desert Mounted Corps while other troops captured Es Salt and attacked the main Turkish position. In spite of a rapid advance he failed to reach and seize the main crossing of the Jordan at Jisr ed Damieh. Next morning the Turks attacked him in overwhelming strength. His brigade fell back, losing nine of the twelve guns supporting it; however, when reinforced, it prevented the enemy from cutting off the rest of the Australian Mounted Division in Es Salt. Allenby acknowledged that Grant's withdrawal was ably conducted but considered that his defensive layout had been faulty, blaming him for the loss of the guns, the only guns which Australians lost to the enemy in the whole war except for those deliberately abandoned in the evacuation of Anzac. Grant had been sufficiently concerned about his defences to ask for an additional regiment before the Turkish attack but owing to the shortage of troops his request was refused.

In the triumphant battles of September 1918, presaging the collapse of Turkey, Grant led his brigade with success, notably in the fight for Semakh. The village was held by a strong garrison of German and Turkish troops. Riding by night with less than half the brigade, Grant surprised the defenders, the 11th Light Horse charging in the moonlight with swords drawn. They were surprised in their turn by the obstinate resistance of the enemy, forcing them to clear houses with the bayonet room by room, an experience probably unique in the campaign. The garrison of over 500 was killed or captured except for a handful who fled. Grant was awarded the Order of the Nile, 3rd class, in 1918 and appointed C.M.G. in 1919; he was mentioned in dispatches four times. For a brief period at the end of 1918 he commanded the Australian Mounted Division.

Grant returned to his property on the Darling Downs in August 1919 and within a year was appointed to command the 1st Light Horse Brigade in the Citizen Military Forces. In May 1921 this was designated 1st Cavalry Brigade and he remained in command until June 1925. He was placed on the retired list in 1928.

Colonel P. J. Bailey, who knew Grant better than most, described him as 'one of nature's gentlemen, a fine soldier and a firm friend of all Diggers'. He was known for his fairness and reliability and for his attention to every aspect of his command.

Grant sold Bowenville in 1931 and lived in Brisbane but in 1934 he bought Corack, a property near Dirranbandi in southern Queensland. He died suddenly of heart failure at Southport on 25 May 1939 and was cremated with military honours in Brisbane. He was survived by his wife and children. A pencil sketch of Grant by George Lambert [q.v.] is held by the Australian War Memorial.

H. S. Gullett, *The A.I.F. in Sinai and Palestine, 1914-18* (Syd, 1923); E. W. Hammond, *History of the Eleventh Light Horse Regiment* (Brisb, 1942); G. W. Nutting, *History of the Fourth Light Horse Brigade* (Brisb, 1953); A. J. Hill, *Chauvel of the Light Horse* (Melb, 1978); *London Gazette*, 1, 29 Dec 1916, 12, 18 Jan, 9 Nov 1918, 3, 5 June 1919, 11 June 1920; *Reveille* (Syd), June, July 1939; War diaries, 11th Light Horse Regiment, *and* 4th Light Horse Brigade, Australian Mounted Division (AWM).

A. J. HILL

GRANVILLE, CECIL HORACE PLANTAGENET (1877-1969), soldier and farmer, was born on 26 January 1877 at Aberystwyth, Wales, son of Frederick John Gran-

ville, gentleman, and his wife Cecilia Anne, née Hook. His mother died when he was twelve days old, and his father six years later. He was brought up by an aunt, widow of Rev. Lord Charles Paulet. His brother, Charles Delabere Granville, became a rear admiral in the Royal Navy.

Granville was educated at Repton School and raised as an Anglican. As a young man he came to Sydney to stay with Lady Paulet's son-in-law, Major General E. T. H. Hutton [q.v.], and then bought a small property near Scone, New South Wales. He joined the Scone Troop of the 1st Australian Horse and served as a trooper in the South African War with that regiment, taking part in actions at Driefontein, Poplar Grove, Bloemfontein and Karee Siding. He was invalided home in August 1900, resumed farming and continued his service with the 1st Australian Horse; after Federation the Scone Troop was placed in the 6th and later in the 4th Australian Light Horse (Hunter River Lancers). He was commissioned in 1904.

In 1910 Granville, who had not distinguished himself as a farmer, took up full-time work with the Australian Military Forces as an area officer at Grafton. He was promoted captain in the 6th L.H.R. in November 1912 and next year was transferred to the area office at West Maitland. After the outbreak of war he enlisted in the Australian Imperial Force on 14 September 1914 and was given command of 'C' Squadron, 1st Light Horse Regiment; he was promoted major in October. The regiment reached Egypt in December and in May 1915 was sent to Gallipoli as part of the 1st Light Horse Brigade, to serve in an infantry role. The 1st L.H.R. fought at Quinn's Post and Pope's Hill until September and was then moved to No. 1 Outpost. Granville temporarily commanded the regiment on 6-19 November and during the evacuation was in charge of its rear party.

Once re-horsed in Egypt, the 1st L.H.R. was employed in operations against the Senussi in Upper Egypt; in May 1916 it crossed the Suez Canal and from then on was engaged in Sinai, Palestine, the Jordan Valley and Amman. Granville was awarded the Distinguished Service Order in June 1916, was temporarily in command during the battle of Romani in August, and was appointed commanding officer of the regiment in September. He was promoted lieut-colonel in February 1917 and commanded the 1st Light Horse Brigade for two periods in 1918. In the enemy attack on Abu Tellul in the Jordan Valley in July 1918, Granville's 1st L.H.R. was in reserve. Brigadier General C. F. Cox [q.v.8], on realizing that a strong German and Turkish force had penetrated far into his brigade's position, reacted swiftly. 'Get to them Granny', was his brief but comprehensive order and Granville's squadrons' 'slashing work with the bayonet' and the fire from Cox's posts brought the fight to a close.

Granville was a good horseman and horse-master and the horses of his regiment were always one of his first concerns. He was liked as a commanding officer because of his calm, 'unflappable' temperament, and was respected as a man of courage. He would often be up with the troops when they were in action; at Romani, for example, he would stand up under machine-gun fire and walk around the positions. Apart from receiving the D.S.O. he was mentioned in dispatches and awarded the Order of the Crown of Romania. On 30 November 1916, at the British Consulate, Port Said, he married Louisa Theresa Beveridge, of Junee, New South Wales, who was serving with the Red Cross Society.

On returning to Australia he became A.M.F. area officer at Granville, Sydney, in July 1919 but resigned in March 1920 and was awarded the Volunteer Officers' Decoration in 1924. He took up poultry farming near Epping, but this was unsuccessful and in the 1920s he worked for the Yellow Cab Company as a taxi-driver in Sydney. In the 1930s he bought into a timber-yard at Camden. His last years were spent at the Masonic Homes, Glenfield, Sydney. He died on 12 December 1969, his wife having pre-deceased him, and was cremated with Anglican rites. His only child, Richard, was killed in action in Papua in 1942 while serving as a fighter pilot with the Royal Australian Air Force.

Aust Defence Dept, *Official records of the Australian military contingents to the war in South Africa*, P. L. Murray ed (Melb, 1911); H. S. Gullett, *The A.I.F. in Sinai and Palestine, 1914-18* (Syd, 1923); P. V. Vernon (ed) *The Royal New South Wales Lancers, 1885-1960* (Syd, 1961); *London Gazette*, 3 June, 11 July 1916, 20 Sept 1919; information from Captain C. Upton, Lindfield, *and* Lieut-Colonel P. H. Treasure, Balgowlah, *and* Miss P. White, Woollahra, *and* Mrs H. Clark, Warrawee, NSW, *and* Mrs J. J. Thorne, Canb, ACT; album of press cuttings held by Mrs Thorne.

P. V. VERNON

GRASBY, WILLIAM CATTON (1859-1930), agricultural journalist and educationist, was born on 2 October 1859 at Balhannah, South Australia, third son of William Grasby, farmer and Methodist lay preacher, and his wife Frances, née Catton; both were from Yorkshire. On his parents' mixed farm Grasby developed an interest in agriculture and horticulture. He was largely educated at home by his father and developed a love of literature and European culture; at 13 he became a pupil-teacher for six years, but later described this system as barbarous. In 1881 he travelled in Europe. He then taught in state primary schools where he introduced libraries and nature museums and experimented with nature study, drawing and science. At Payneham in 1887 he founded the Boys' Field Club for Saturday nature excursions. He became profoundly dissatisfied with the Education Department's policies.

In 1889 Grasby studied educational innovations in North America, Britain and Europe and published his findings in *Teaching in three continents* (1891); the first major work of comparative education published by an Australian, it was well reviewed in London. He then campaigned to improve the local state school system at a time when reforms were unlikely because of recession. The polemic *Our public schools* (1891) outlined his proposals: kindergartens; manual, agricultural and horticultural training for primary schools; the abolition of school fees; payment of teachers by results and the pupil-teacher system. He advocated employing adult teachers with at least two years full-time, pre-service training, free state secondary schools and agricultural colleges, and changes in school building and furniture design. The pamphlet was hotly discussed by teachers and in newspapers. Grasby also edited the twelve issues of the journal the *Educator* (1893-94). Although his reform campaign achieved no tangible result, it foreshadowed innovations in most Australian States by the 1920s.

In 1892-94 Grasby was director of agronomy and manual training at the progressive Way College, Unley, where his teaching methods won repute. He attended a government conference on agricultural education in 1892 and chaired the committee appointed to implement its recommendations. In 1894-96 he taught at Roseworthy Agricultural College and from 1894 was a member of the Central Bureau of Agriculture. On 13 October 1896 he married Hannah Propsting, a Tasmanian Quaker. He then toured Mediterranean countries as honorary government commissioner reporting on fruit-growing techniques. His observations of cincturing currant vines in Greece assisted the South Australian dried fruit industry. He returned to Way College in 1897-98, frequently speaking publicly on agricultural matters, often for the agricultural high school movement. In 1900 he gave valuable and humane evidence to the Victorian royal commission on technical education and recommended a system of agricultural high schools which was subsequently adopted. In 1896-1904 Grasby owned and edited the *Australian Garden and Field*. He had stood unsuccessfully for the colonial and Federal parliaments in 1887 and 1890 and in 1903.

In 1904 he reported prophetically on agricultural and fruit-growing possibilities for the Western Australian government and from 1905 he was the agricultural editor of the *Western Mail* and *West Australian*. He gained a huge following for his weekly advice column for farmers, 'Mutual Help', and taught agriculture at Perth Technical School and Guildford Grammar School. In 1912 he published an important textbook, *Principles of Australian agriculture*. He advocated tertiary education for Western Australia, in 1912-14 was a member of its university's first senate, and sat on the extension lectures committee (later the Workers' Educational Association). He helped to found the State's Kindergarten Union in 1911, was on its executive, lectured on nature study in the union's first training programme and examined candidates for its training colleges. He was an admirer of Froebel.

With his friend Charles Harper [q.v.4], Grasby developed the first Western Australian wheat varieties: 'Gresley' and 'Wilfred'. He was an ardent conservationist, and in his chapter in Sir James Barrett's [q.v.7] *Save Australia* (1925) attacked the killing of animals for scientific collections as 'inimical to the survival of fauna'. He was a fellow of the Linnean Society of London, and president of the Royal Society of Western Australia in 1929-30.

In 1928 Grasby had retired; he died at his East Guildford home on 26 October 1930 of diabetes and gangrene of the leg, survived by his wife, a daughter and son, and was buried in the Anglican section of Guildford cemetery. (Sir) Walter Murdoch [q.v.] wrote of him that he 'combined a rare simplicity of character with a rare sagacity of intellect'.

C. Turney (ed), *Pioneers of Australian education*, 2 (Syd, 1972); N. Hall, *Botanists of the eucalypts* (Melb, 1977); *Way College Boomerang*, Sept 1896, July 1897, Dec 1900; Boys' Field Club (Adel), *Procs*, 1893-1902; Roy Soc WA, *J*, 17 (1930-31); *South Australiana*, 18 (1979), no 1; *Advertiser* (Adel), 24 Jan 1893, 27 Oct 1930; *West Australian*, 27, 29 Oct 1930; J. Ramsland, The life, work and contribution of William Catton Grasby (MS, Fisher Lib, Univ Syd); Grasby papers held by and information from Ms N. Grasby, Kalamunda, WA.

JOHN RAMSLAND

GRATTON, NORMAN MURRAY GLADSTONE (1886-1965), schoolmaster, was born on 21 July 1886 at Richmond, Melbourne, elder son of Joseph Gladstone Gratton, a grocer from England, and his Victorian-born wife Annie May, née Carlin. His father died in 1888, his mother when he was 12. Educated at North Melbourne State School, he then attended Melbourne Teachers' College and, with a scholarship, the University of Melbourne (Dip.Ed., 1913; B.A., 1915). He taught in various Victorian state schools. On 31 December 1912 Gratton married a teacher, Jeannie Gordon Tweedie.

He held a commission in the Victorian Rangers but was rejected for service in the Australian Imperial Force. After joining the Collegiate School of St Peter in Adelaide in 1916 as senior master to establish a curriculum for non-academic senior boys, in 1918 he was appointed founding headmaster of a Presbyterian school to be established as a memorial to the sons of Scotland who had fallen in World War I.

Next February Scotch College, with an enrolment of 72 boys (12 boarders), was opened in small premises at Unley Park formerly occupied by Kyre College. At the end of 1919 Scotch moved to Torrens Park, the former home of Robert Barr Smith [q.v.6] on its present site, Carruth Road, Mitcham. The daunting task of turning an elegant but run-down Victorian mansion into a first-class boys' college was a challenge that Gratton met. Under his energetic leadership classrooms and dormitories were created, army huts were converted to classrooms or workshops, the coach-house became a science block and the stables a gymnasium. Ovals and tennis courts were established. By 1928 there were over 300 boys. The Depression led to a dramatic fall in numbers, but the college survived. In 1942 the Torrens Park property was compulsorily acquired by the American Army, and it was later occupied by the Royal Australian Air Force. Through Gratton's determination the college survived in temporary quarters at Belair until 1944. He then initiated a programme of expansion and development on the Mitcham site: in 1946 the college built a junior school, Gratton House.

When he retired in 1951 there were over 400 pupils. No more popular figure had ever trod the school grounds. As Mr Justice Bright said: 'None could doubt the total involvement of Mr Gratton in the School ... he was an unquestioned leader. I never heard him raise his voice in anger, or saw him lose control. Boys who towered over him physically obeyed him without thinking ... He lived for the School'. He was concerned with educational principles, disapproved of fierce competition and his voice carried weight in professional conferences. Gratton had been a member of the South Australian Public Examinations Board and of the English and Australian Headmasters' conferences, and chairman of the local Headmasters' Association. He was chief commissioner of the Boy Scouts' Association of South Australia in 1931-34. An elder of the Presbyterian Church, he had been president of the Presbyterian Men's League. He was appointed C.B.E. in 1952.

In 1955 his Adelaide Hills home and possessions were destroyed by a bush fire. Norman Gratton died on 1 January 1965, survived by his wife and two sons. His ashes were scattered in the college grounds and his portrait, by Nora Heysen, hangs in the school chapel.

Scotch College Mag (SA), 48 (1965); *Advertiser* (Adel), 13 Dec 1948, 2 Jan 1965; R. N. Gilchrist, History of Scotch College Junior School (typescript held by school Archives); *Scotch Reports,* 1964-81.   PETER C. READ

GRAVES, JAMES JOSEPH (1882-1964), fitter, trade union official and politician, was born on 23 June 1882 at Waverley, Sydney, eldest son of native-born parents James Joseph Graves, book-keeper, and his wife Elizabeth, née Dobson. He attended the Marist Brothers' College, Darlinghurst, and at 15 was apprenticed as a fitter. He joined the Political Labor League of New South Wales in 1900 and on 21 February 1901 married Edith May Sessle; they had two sons and eight daughters.

In 1906 Graves was a foundation member of the Stove and Piano-Frame Moulders' and Stovemakers' Employees' Union. In 1912 he became industrial advocate for the stovemakers before the Commonwealth and State courts of conciliation and arbitration, a role he was to continue until 1930. The same year he joined the executive of the Labor Council of New South Wales; soon he left the metal trades to become full-time secretary of the Stovemakers' Union —he later became general president.

After the Labor Party split over conscription, Graves followed the executive of the Labor Council in a swing to the left, which was greatly accelerated by the débâcle of the 1917 transport strike. In 1919 he joined the breakaway Industrial Socialist Labor Party formed following the narrow defeat of left-wing efforts to convert the State Labor Party into a revolutionary socialist re-

flex of the One Big Union. He was closely associated with the 'Trades Hall Reds' led by J. S. Garden [q.v.8]. In 1922 a writer in the *Communist* described Graves as 'solid', 'silent' and 'thoroughly dependable' and, when elected to the State A.L.P. executive in 1923, he was described in the Communist press as one of 'the Red . . . Comrades' who, with other leftists, held the balance of power at the conference.

Like Garden, and many other 'Trades Hall Reds', Graves began to distance himself from the Communist Party of Australia as the 1920s progressed. He was president of the Trades Hall Association (1923-24) and of the Eight Hour Committee (1927), and a delegate to the founding congress of the Australasian Council of Trade Unions in 1927. He also supported J. T. Lang [q.v.]. President of the State (Lang) party from 1927 to 1930, he became general secretary in 1930 and a key figure in the notorious 'Inner Group', a coterie of Lang's personal aides and party officials who controlled policy in the 1930s. Graves remained in his salaried position despite the dramatic split between Garden and Lang over control of radio station 2KY in 1936. A delegate to the Federal Labor conferences in 1930, 1936 and 1939, he was vice-president of the federal executive in 1936-38. When Lang was deposed as State parliamentary leader in 1939, Graves narrowly lost his position as general secretary. During World War II he worked for the Australian Red Cross Society.

Graves was nominated to the Legislative Council in November 1931 and was re-elected after its reconstitution in 1934 until he was defeated, after being placed last on the Labor Party ticket in April 1961. He was a member of the Empire Parliamentary Association in 1933. In 1946 he was expelled by the A.L.P. State executive for his absence from the council during a vital vote. The party's annual conference readmitted him the next year, but his performance in the council continued to provoke criticism within the party. Graves died on 23 January 1964, in hospital at Kirrawee, after collapsing at his nearby home some days before. Survived by his wife, seven daughters and a son, he was buried in Botany cemetery after a service at St Patrick's Roman Catholic Church, Sutherland.

J. T. Lang, *I remember* (Syd, 1956); R. Cooksey, *Lang and socialism* (Canb, 1971); M. Dixson, *Greater than Lenin?* (Melb, 1977); *Communist* (Syd), 8, 15 June 1923; *SMH,* 23 Jan 1964; H. Boote, Diary (MS 2070/2, NL).   FRANK FARRELL

GRAY, EDMUND DWYER; *see* DWYER-GRAY

GRAY, ETHEL (1876-1962), nursing sister and army matron, was born on 24 April 1876 at Carlton, Melbourne, eldest of the eight children of Samuel Gray, clothing manufacturer from Cavan, Ireland, and his English-born wife Amelia, née Bird. Educated at Lee Street State School, East Melbourne, and the Presbyterian Ladies' College, she entered (Royal) Melbourne Hospital as a probationer in March 1900, gained her certificate on 12 March 1903 and was promoted staff nurse two days later and sister on 29 May. A supervisor described her as 'most satisfactory, very quick and observant, reliable and thoroughly conscientious in her work, also a favourite with the patients'. She remained on the staff until 1908 when she was appointed matron of the Queen's Memorial Infectious Diseases Hospital, Fairfield. She returned to Melbourne Hospital as house matron in July 1909 and in February 1911 became assistant lady superintendent.

Sister Gray became matron of Perth Public Hospital in January 1913. In January 1915 she volunteered for the Australian Army Nursing Service and, having been asked to take charge of a convalescent depot for Australian troops in England, enlisted in the A.A.N.S., Australian Imperial Force, on 9 February as a matron. She embarked ten days later with five sisters who were to form the nucleus of the depot's nursing staff. On reaching England she discovered that the hospital, Harefield Park House, Middlesex, was not ready for occupation. Her first tasks were to advise on alterations necessary 'to make the place capable of holding 150 convalescent patients' and to purchase equipment and furnishings. Before the first intake of patients in June, she was told that Harefield was to become the 1st Australian Auxiliary Hospital. The rapid expansion and the changing role of the unit placed heavy strains on the staff but 'great unity' existed and 'the spirit of the hospital was good'. Matron Gray, already showing the dedication and the exceptional organizing and administrative skills which were to make her one of the most highly decorated members of the A.A.N.S., supervised the general running of the hospital and the management of the nursing staff until 30 November 1916. By this time Harefield had 1000 beds. Next June she received the Royal Red Cross, 1st class, for her work there.

On 9 December 1916 she joined the 2nd Australian General Hospital at Wimereux, France, retaining charge of the nursing staff until March 1919 when the hospital closed. The 'rush of work' which began with the battle of Vimy Ridge in April 1917 continued until October 1918. She was mentioned in dispatches in 1917 and 1919,

appointed C.B.E. in 1919 and awarded the Medaille de la Reconnaissance Française in 1920, being the only Australian woman to receive this honour. On 19 March 1919 she assumed duty with the 1st A.G.H. at Sutton Veny, England, and embarked for Australia on 22 January 1920. She was discharged from the A.I.F. a month later. Soon after demobilization she became the first matron of Epworth Intermediate Hospital, Richmond, Melbourne, a hospital founded by the Methodist Church, and remained in charge until her retirement in 1939. She died in Epworth on 22 July 1962 and was buried in Melbourne general cemetery. Her estate was sworn for probate at £30 997.

Ethel Gray was a woman of great constitutional stamina and forceful, sometimes domineering, personality. A staunch adherence to Methodism influenced her whole life. Totally dedicated to the nursing profession, she expected the same singlemindedness from her colleagues and, though generally considerate of others, was a firm disciplinarian. A strong sense of duty, instilled by both family and church, never left her. She was 5 ft. 4½ ins. (164 cm) tall, carried herself well, and usually wore her dark hair parted in the centre. A fresh complexion softened her strong, rather angular features. Her portrait, by Ernest Buckmaster, is in Epworth Hospital. A niece remembers her as 'a lovable person' to whom 'everything was of absorbing interest and worthy of comment'. From her personal diaries, faithfully kept throughout 1915-19, she emerges as a capable, energetic woman with rigid standards of personal morality and compassion and concern for her patients and staff.

Una, July 1903, June 1906, June 1908, Jan 1913, May 1915, June, Dec 1916, Mar 1917, Oct 1962; *A'sian Nurses J*, May, June 1913, Apr, Sept 1917, May 1918; *London Gazette*, 3 June 1916, 28 Dec 1917, 3 June, 11 July 1919; *Spectator* (Melb), 11 Oct 1939; *Age*, 23 July 1962; records, and information from the Roy Aust Nursing Federation, Vic Branch, *and* Roy Melb Hospital; family papers held by, and information from, Mrs R. Brown, Canterbury, Melb; E. Gray, Personal diaries 1915-19, donated records section, no 1326, and notes prepared for collator of medical records, World War I, no 1326, file AO 419/40/6 (AWM).

MERRILYN LINCOLN

GRAY, GEORGE WILKIE (1844-1924), businessman, was born on 3 August 1844 in Sydney, son of Alexander Gray, licensed victualler, and his wife Margaret, née Hall. Leaving school early he studied accountancy at night and went in 1863 to Queensland where he was a clerk at Ipswich until made manager of the Brisbane branch of

Clarke, Hodgson & Co., merchants, in 1867. Becoming friendly with Michael Quinlan, a mercantile shipping agent, he joined Quinlan Donnelly & Co. shortly before marrying on 11 February 1871 Mrs Quinlan's niece Maria Emma Boulderson, with his cousin C. S. Mein [q.v.5] as witness.

After Quinlan died in 1878 Mrs Quinlan made Gray managing partner in the renamed Quinlan Gray & Co. They ratified an agreement made before Quinlan's death, with E. and N. Fitzgerald [q.v.] of Victoria, to establish a brewery at Milton. The two businesses amalgamated in 1887 into a public company, Castlemaine Brewery and Quinlan Gray & Co. Brisbane Ltd, Gray being managing director until 1924. The Fourex brew was introduced in 1916 and the company restricted its interests to the liquor trade. E. G. Theodore [q.v.] appointed Gray, who was regarded as a good employer, to the Brewing Malting and Distilling Industry Board in 1916.

Gray the entrepreneur had 'coined money' with his schooner *Monarch* and other vessels on the Ipswich-Moreton Bay run from 1866 to 1872. Other investments included Barron River cedar, coastal shipping, the Bendigo pottery, land in Melbourne and Brisbane, hotel properties, mining, cotton growing and, in 1867-1907, the sugar industry. He was managing director of the Queensland Sugar Company Ltd and advocated 'Kanaka' labour. Innovative and receptive to new ideas, he installed the first telephone in Queensland in 1880, and pioneered the use of artesian bores. Chairman of directors of the National Mutual Life Association of Australasia Ltd (Queensland) and the *Daily Mail*, he held directorships in the Queensland National Bank, Millaquin Sugar Co., Queensland Insurance Co. Ltd, and Queensland Trustees Ltd. Many of the politicians and commercial leaders whom he entertained at his Hamilton home, Eldernell, were his business partners: a member of the Queensland Club from 1871, he had a talent for friendship as well as business.

A convert to Roman Catholicism, Gray was trustee and adviser to the Sisters of Mercy on their sugar lands and Brisbane properties and also a trustee of the Hospital for Sick Children, Brisbane. The Sisters found him a man of 'large hearted generosity' especially towards causes concerned with children; for many years at Christmas he gave a present to every child in the Nudgee orphanage. The controversy over the extension of scholarship benefits to Catholic schools led to his joining a private deputation to the premier in 1899.

While Gray's primary concerns were not with politics, he was a member of the Legislative Council from August 1894 until its abolition in 1921. When Dickson [q.v.8] appointed him minister without portfolio in October 1898 a storm of protest resulted, mainly from opponents of over-representation of business interests; to J. T. Bell [q.v.7] Gray was 'a mere sprat thrown out to catch the Roman Catholic vote'. In the subsequent Philp [q.v.] ministry until 1903 as an adviser on commercial matters, he was a proponent of States' rights and blamed the Commonwealth for the government's financial troubles. Too conservative for the 'Lib-Lab' coalition, Gray led council opposition to Kidston [q.v.], became disillusioned with Denham [q.v.8] because his handling of the Liquor Bill 'injured our vested interests and favoured the Labour party', and made his last speech in November 1917 opposing Ryan's Sugar Prices Act amendment bill.

A slightly built energetic man, Gray was a liberal patron of sport, particularly athletics, bicycling, sailing and cricket. He played in the first two intercolonial cricket matches between Queensland and New South Wales in 1864-65 and in the first match at the Brisbane Cricket Ground, of which he was honorary treasurer and later a trustee.

Gray died on 24 September 1924 at Eldernell and was buried in Nudgee cemetery. His first wife had died in 1916 and he married in Sydney in 1919 a widow, Lilian Eleanor MacDonnell, daughter of Patrick Perkins [q.v.5]. She and two sons of his first marriage survived him. Having assigned his life insurance policies to the Sisters of Mercy, enabling them to build the Mater Children's Hospital, he left to relatives his estate valued for probate in Queensland at £37 268.

Fifty years in retrospect: the story of Castlemaine Perkins Ltd (1887-1937) (Brisb, 1937); D. Jones, *Hurricane lamps and blue umbrellas* (Cairns, 1973); H. J. Summers, *They crossed the river* (Brisb, 1979); *V&P* (Qld), 1889, 4, p 184, 352; *PD* (LC Qld), 1898, p 758; Commercial Publishing Co. of Sydney, Ltd, *Annual Review of Qld*, 1 (1902), no 1; *Fourex News*, March, Aug 1976; *Queenslander*, 22 Oct 1898, 27 Sept 1924; SCT/T259, 1035/1888 (QA); family papers held by Mr G. H. B. Gray, Ascot, Qld.

BETTY CROUCHLEY

GRAY, ISABEL (1851?-1929), hotelier and storekeeper, was the daughter of James Richardson, army captain, and Priscilla Wright. On her first marriage certificate in April 1869 she was recorded as being born eighteen years before in England. When she married again in 1871 she claimed to have been born in Mauritius. Said to have been well educated in Switzerland, she was sent to Australia, probably in 1868. On 29 April

1869 at Warialda, New South Wales, Isabella Richardson married the 32-year-old Scots superintendent, James McIntosh. He died soon after. On 2 March 1871 at Roma, Queensland, Isabel McIntosh, widow and governess, married Richard William Robinson, station-manager of Spring Grove, Surat.

The Robinsons remained in south-west Queensland. By 1886 they were hotel-keepers at Eulo, on the Paroo River, an important staging post between Cunnamulla and Thargomindah and coach junction from Hungerford. Eulo was thus a gathering-place for travellers and others. On 1 September 1889 Robinson acquired the freehold and hotel and billiard licences of the Royal Mail Hotel, Eulo. The Robinsons also conducted a store and butcher's shop.

About this time the legend of the 'Eulo Queen' began. Although short, Isabel probably possessed some personal beauty with the physical sumptuousness so esteemed by contemporary males, and a complaisant husband enabled her to operate as a successful courtesan. Her bedroom was a scene of great activity. A stock of liquor there helped her to entertain groups of gentlemen with conversation and gambling. More intimate entertainment was available. Opals were the key to her heart; she was captivated by these fiery gems. She used them as currency and for adornment, including a fantastic girdle of alternate large opals and nautilus shells. Some say she styled herself 'Queen of Eulo', but others consider admirers conferred the title. The 1893 financial crisis and the 1896 failure of the Queensland National Bank reduced her wealth.

On 18 October 1902 Robinson died at Cunnamulla. On 31 October 1903 Isabel married, at Eulo, a 29-year-old Tasmanian, Herbert Victor Gray. The bride was about 53 but claimed she was 35. She recouped her fortunes and in 1913 went to Europe where she lived lavishly. On her return she quarrelled with Gray; he beat her, and was charged with assault, convicted and fined £25. Isabel paid the fine but thereafter she denied Gray her bed and board. He joined the Australian Imperial Force, but died before going to France.

World War I ended with Eulo's importance lost to railways and better roads, the opal industry in deep recession and the young men away on war service, many never to return. The Eulo Queen's remaining enterprises withered on the vine. By 1926 she was living in poverty at Eulo, the military pension as Gray's widow her sole support. Later she was admitted to Willowburn Mental Hospital at Toowoomba and died there on 7 August 1929. Buried in Toowoomba cemetery, she left an estate of £30.

Isabel Gray could be hard in her business dealings but, if the mood moved her, kind to genuine cases of distress. Self-willed and self-indulgent she was, but the Eulo Queen will live as one of the characters of south-west Queensland history.

F. C. Folkard, *The rare sex* (Syd, 1965); Warrego and South West Qld Hist Soc, *A collection of papers prepared by members . . . on the history and other subjects relating to Cunnamulla and district*, 1 (Cunnamulla, 1970?); T. W. Blake, *Cunnamulla, a brief history of the Paroo Shire* (Cunnamulla, 1979); *People* (Syd), 7 Jan, 15 Apr, 30 Sept 1959; Roy Automobile Club Qld, *Road Ahead*, Sept 1968; *SMH*, 22 Jan 1976; *Sun* (Syd), 24 June 1977; *Sunday Mail* (Brisb), 17 Aug 1980, supp; S. W. Jack's cutting book, no 41 (Oxley, Lib).   J. C. H. GILL

GRAYNDLER, EDWARD (1867-1943), trade unionist and politician, was born on 12 October 1867 at One Tree Hill near Mount Victoria, New South Wales, fourth son of John Grayndler, a Canadian migrant, and his Irish wife Johanna, née Maloney. He attended Home Rule (Mobellah) Public School and as a youth worked in outback New South Wales and Queensland in various jobs ranging from fencing, droving and shearing to mining; in 1886 he became a foundation member of the Amalgamated Shearers' Union of Australasia (later part of the powerful Australian Workers' Union). In 1895 he was appointed shearers' union organizer for the A.W.U. in New South Wales. In 1900 he became secretary of the Victoria-Riverina branch with headquarters at St Arnaud, Victoria, and from 1905 at Ballarat. At Coonamble Wesleyan Church, New South Wales, he married Margaret Tamar Welsh on 12 February 1901. After the shearers' strikes of the 1890s Grayndler became an early and staunch advocate of the settlement of industrial disputes through arbitration. At the 1906 Federal election he failed to win the Victorian seat of the Grampians for the Labor Party.

In ill health, he left his union job in 1909 to become a travelling salesman for a British firm; but he continued to enjoy the patronage and support of A.W.U. leaders such as Donald Macdonell [q.v.]. Grayndler, cured after eighteen months, set up on his own account in Victoria, but soon afterwards he agreed to Macdonell's request to represent the A.W.U. at the Commonwealth Court of Conciliation and Arbitration. In 1912 he became general secretary of the A.W.U., and moved to Sydney. Until 1940 he prepared all Federal Arbitration Court cases for the union and became a formidable industrial advocate.

Grayndler was a hard-headed bureaucrat. He opposed attempts to have the A.W.U.

support W. M. Hughes's [q.v.] Labor government's pro-conscription policy in 1916. He supported H. E. Boote [q.v.7], editor of the *Australian Worker*, in his anti-conscription crusade and campaigns against the severe restraints of wartime censorship. In 1915-18 he was a member of the Commonwealth Repatriation Commission.

The failure of the arbitration system to safeguard living standards during World War I produced massive discontent in the A.W.U., especially among shearers and miners. Although at first diverted by the conscription issue, the rank and file put increasing pressure on the union leadership after 1916. Grayndler was a target of some criticism and, with Arthur Blakeley and John Bailey [qq.v.7], he was a leading strategist of the conservative response to the post-war radical trend in the labour movement.

Appointed O.B.E. in 1920, Grayndler was nominated to the Legislative Council in August next year but was defeated in 1934, when the council was reconstituted. However, he was elected to a casual vacancy in November 1936 and remained a member until 1943. His political career suffered considerably from the decline of A.W.U. influence on the New South Wales Labor Party in the 1920s, and in 1931 he criticized J. T. Lang [q.v.], voting against his wages-tax bill. He was a member of the Bruce [q.v.7]-Page [q.v.] government's Industrial Delegation to the United States of America in 1927, and served on the Commonwealth Wool Inquiry Committee in 1932.

Ted Grayndler was a keen sports fan and a convivial drinker, thoroughly absorbed in Sydney's suburban culture. In his mid-sixties he had a 'burly figure' and curly dark hair. He lived for much of his life in Canterbury, but died of broncho-pneumonia on 12 March 1943 in hospital in Melbourne and was buried in Melbourne general cemetery after a service at St Ignatius Roman Catholic Church, Richmond. He was survived by his wife, two sons and two daughters.

V. G. Childe, *How Labour governs*, 2nd edn, F. B. Smith ed (Melb, 1964); F. Farrell, *International socialism and Australian labor* (Syd, 1981); *Aust Worker*, 5, 19, 26 Aug, 2, 23 Sept 1915; *SMH*, 16 Oct 1920; *Bulletin*, 8 July 1931; *Argus*, 13 Mar 1943; H. Boote, Diary (MS 2070/2, NL).

FRANK FARRELL

GRAYSON, HENRY JOSEPH (1856-1918), nurseryman and inventor, was born on 9 May 1856 at Worrall, near Sheffield, Yorkshire, England, son of Joseph Grayson, master cutler, and his wife Fanny, née Smith. By 1861 Henry was probably living with his mother and maternal grandfather, George Smith, a nurseryman at nearby Rotherham. Henry began training as a gardener at an early age. He took up the study of botany and bought his first microscope. In the early 1880s he went to New Zealand; in 1884-85 he was listed as a member of the Philosophical Institute of Canterbury (Christchurch). He returned to England, visiting Victoria on the way, and on 11 August 1886 in the Wesleyan Chapel at Davyhulme, near Manchester, married 37-year-old Elizabeth Clare, daughter of a blacksmith. Soon afterwards the couple migrated to Melbourne and for some years Grayson worked in the nursery of Brunning [q.v.3] & Sons.

Grayson became acquainted with William Stone [q.v.] and the architect James Fawcett, both amateur scientists and his lifelong friends and eventual executors. He attended meetings of the (Royal) Microscopical Society and the Field Naturalists' Club of Victoria. In 1889 he visited Christchurch again and on his return exhibited New Zealand diatoms and some botanical preparations at the Field Naturalists' Club; his paper on the subject, delivered in September 1892, was published in the *Victorian Naturalist* the following month. He was elected to the club in May 1901.

Meanwhile Grayson's talent in preparing microscope slides, both biological and petrological, had brought him to the notice of Rev. Walter Fielder, university demonstrator in histology and a keen microscopist. Through Fielder, Grayson obtained a rock-sectioning machine and he relied largely on this and a lathe as his equipment in his home workshop. He used glass where others with more mechanical training and equipment would have used steel.

In microscopy, calibration of the field of view and the quantitative test of objectives require test rulings. Grayson made an entirely new micro-ruling machine in order to have better rulings than those available. The early version of this machine was mainly of glass and wood. It ruled excellent lines, up to 40 000 an inch (25.4 mm), using a diamond fragment and did not show the irregularities of those of his only rival, the French physicist Nobert. For the improved version of the machine, Stone designed and made the central components. Grayson did not publish an account either of this particular machine or of his techniques, but Stone and W. M. Holmes wrote accounts after his death. Grayson's test rulings rapidly achieved international fame and Carl Zeiss commissioned a plate with rulings up to 120 000 an inch to test Abbe's theory of the microscope. In 1894 Grayson had exhibited rulings from 5000 to 120 000 an inch.

In 1898 Grayson was appointed as laboratory assistant in physiology (also designated physiological school porter) at the University of Melbourne. On the arrival of Professor J. W. Gregory [q.v.] in 1900, he was transferred to geology and in 1901-02 was a member of Gregory's expedition to Lake Eyre. He was elected associate member of the Royal Society of Victoria in 1902. His work in geology and his reputation in microscopy gained him support in 1909 from professors (Sir) T. R. Lyle, E. W. Skeats and (Sir) D. O. Masson [qq.v.] for a bursary. His election that year to the science faculty was supported by an article in the *Argus* and he was given an assistant.

Under the stimulus of Stone, Grayson in 1909-10 began the ruling of diffraction gratings, installing his grating-ruling engine under the floor of his workshop at home. In 1912 Lyle arranged for Grayson and his grating-ruling engine to be transferred to the natural philosophy department. In 1913 he was working full time on the grating project under Lyle's guidance. Grayson wrote an article on the engine in the *Proceedings* of the Royal Society of Victoria (1917) and was awarded the David Syme [q.v.6] research prize in 1918. His optical blanks were probably not sufficiently flat to rule a grating of the six inches (152 mm) width for which the engine was designed.

Grayson died of heart disease at Clyde on 21 March 1918 and was buried in Boroondara cemetery, Kew. He was survived by his wife (d. 1926); they had no children. Grayson's research notes and papers were collected by Stone but were accidentally burnt. Lyle bought the micro-ruling machine and the ruling-engine from his estate. A test in 1972 of one of the gratings made on the engine showed that its performance was good by any standard. Grayson's abilities were acquired by long personal experience, aided by high standards of self-discipline. The quality of his optical work was unsurpassed anywhere in his day.

Industrial Aust and Mining Standard, 64 (1920), p 63; Institute of Physics (Lond), *J of Scientific Instruments*, 11 (1934), p 1, 14 (1937), p 8; J. J. McNeill, 'Diffracting grating rulings', *Records of the Aust Academy of Science*, 2 (1972), no 3, p 18, 3 (1974), no 1, p 30; *A'sian Radiology*, 19 (1975), p 216; H. C. Bolton and J. J. McNeill, 'H. J. Grayson. A pioneer ruler of diffraction gratings', *VHJ*, 52 (1981), no 1, p 63; Grayson papers (Univ Melb Archives).

H. C. BOLTON

GREAVES, EDWIN (1846-1934), pastoralist, was born on 25 June 1846 at Arncott, Oxfordshire, England, youngest child of John Greaves of Biddlesden, Buckingham-shire, and his wife Elizabeth, née Holt. He accompanied his mother and nine other children to Port Phillip in the *Louisa Bailie* to join his father who had taken up land at Nillumbik on the River Plenty. When they arrived on 12 October 1849 they discovered that John Greaves had died. Three of the older sons became prominent settlers near Melbourne: Richard (1831-1913) of Cranbourne and Heidelberg, James (1832-1919) of Dandenong, and William (1834-1919) of Lyndhurst.

After his mother's death on 26 September 1859 Edwin worked with James who established a butchery at Dandenong in 1860. In 1869 Edwin went into business at Berwick with his friend Alexander Crighton (later Crichton). In the early 1870s Edwin became manager of the extensive W. J. T. Clarke [q.v.1] estate at Berwick which adjoined his brothers' property at Cranbourne. He bought the homestead section of the estate, since known as The Springs, in 1901. Edwin and his family established a reputation for horse-breeding especially draughthorses, trotters, Shetland ponies and his own Dandy breed of ponies. He became widely known as a judge of stud-stock. The ploughing matches of the Mornington Farmers' Society were held on the property. Although possessed of a strong community spirit, a characteristic of the family, Edwin held office only as justice of the peace. He and his brother James were described as 'broad shouldered solid men, reserved in manner but wise in all stock matters, splendid and deservedly trusted advisers to young men'.

On 30 January 1874 Edwin married Margaret McDonald, daughter of Robert White of Janefield, and had a son and a daughter. His wife died in 1876 and on 19 June 1886 he married Margaret, daughter of Charles Forrester of Brighton. Their three sons were prominent in rural and equestrian affairs. He died at The Springs on 6 May 1934.

Edwin's nephew WILLIAM CLEMENT GREAVES (1866-1936), eldest son of William and his wife Margaret Elizabeth, née Payne (who claimed to be the sixth white child born in Victoria), was born on 22 March 1866 at Bittern and raised at Lyndhurst. In 1883 he took up land at Wonthaggi, but settled at Monomeith in 1887 and, in 1890, obtained the lease of the extensive 'College' lands on Western Port Bay belonging to the Council of Agricultural Education. Like his uncles he acquired the best land of the old pastoral runs in the district—Warrook, formerly a property of William Lyall [q.v.5] in 1904, and later Caldermeade, the Macmillan estate. He was a successful breeder and judge of livestock, and served as federal president of the Australian Society of Breeders of British Sheep in 1928-32. An advocate of producer co-operatives, he was a founder and leading shareholder of Gippsland & Northern, stock and station agents. He was also chairman of the syndicate which opened up the Kyogle estate, Richmond River, New South Wales, and Merrimac, Queensland, for settlement from 1903 onwards. He was three times shire president and was a councillor of the Royal Agricultural Society of Victoria from 1908. He was a forceful personality and his views carried much weight: he once told Carlo Catani [q.v.7] that one of his drainage schemes was 'public money wasted'. He supported the Presbyterian Church, maintained an Edwardian brick villa and, a methodical man, kept a diary. On 21 January 1892 he had married Mary Flora, daughter of Donald McLellan of Lyndhurst; she was a noted horsewoman. Greaves died at Warrook, Monomeith, on 2 September 1936, survived by a son and three daughters.

T. W. H. Leavitt and W. D. Lilburn (eds), *The jubilee history of Victoria and Melbourne* (Melb, 1888); H. H. Peck, *Memoirs of a stockman* (Melb, 1942); N. E. Beaumont et al, *Early days of Berwick and its surrounding districts . . .* (Melb, 1948, *and* 3rd ed 1979); N. Gunson, *The good country: Cranbourne shire* (Melb, 1968); H. B. Ronald, *Hounds are running* (Kilmore, 1970); *Dandenong Advertiser*, 4 Sept, 16 Oct 1919; *Argus*, 7 May 1934; *Gippsland and Northern Co operator*, 10 Sept 1936, 22 July 1965; Mrs D. N. Gunson diaries, *and* G. Brownfield notes (held by Dr W. N. Gunson, ANU, Canb); Greaves family information.

NIEL GUNSON

GREEN, ALBERT ERNEST (1869-1940), politician, was born on 21 December 1869 at Avoca, Victoria, youngest of four children of Thomas Green, builder, and his wife Mary, née Marshall. His mother was a strong-minded personality who, although in her eighties before she learned to read, encouraged her children to take an interest in literature and the labour movement. After a local primary education Albert Green worked for a Ballarat telephone company and then entered the family's bricklaying business. Between 1889 and 1895 he travelled extensively and adventurously in the United States and Central America, returning with socialist ideals and the lifelong nickname of 'Texas'.

In June 1895 Green followed his brother to the gold rushes in Western Australia, where he established a branch of the Australian Natives' Association in Perth. Qualifying for the public service, he became a clerk at the Coolgardie post office in November 1895, and was soon transferred to Kalgoorlie. There he founded branches of the A.N.A. and the Post and Telegraphists'

Union and threw himself into local Labor politics. A strong supporter of Federation, he was Western Australian president of the A.N.A. for several years. With Charles Lee and Julian Stuart [qq.v.] he helped found the Amalgamated Workers' Association in 1897 and in 1904-11 was vice-president of the Kalgoorlie branch of the Australian Labor Federation. In 1906 he was foundation president of the Social Democratic Association, an organization for the discussion of economic and social questions and the grooming of Labor speakers. A popular and energetic figure in the goldfields community, he was endorsed for Kalgoorlie at the 1911 State elections, winning the seat in a landslide from (Sir) Norbert Michael Keenan [q.v.].

Green served in the Legislative Assembly from October 1911 to December 1913, when he resigned to seek pre-selection for the Federal seat of Kalgoorlie but was beaten by Hugh Mahon [q.v.]. Re-elected to his State seat in October 1914 he sat until defeated in March 1921 by John Boyland [q.v.7]. A strong advocate of state industries and a persistent though unsuccessful champion for a rail link between Kalgoorlie and Esperance, Green survived the conscription split although his support of the 'No' case placed him in opposition to his colleagues in the A.N.A.

Between March 1921 and December 1922 Green was goldfields business manager for the *Westralian Worker*. At the Federal elections of 1922 he won back Kalgoorlie for the Australian Labor Party and retained the seat easily for the rest of his life. In Australia's largest electorate he was a tireless local member, travelling vast distances to maintain touch with his constituents, at first by camel, later over execrable roads by motor. An early campaigner for a strong Australian air force, he was minister for defence in the Scullin [q.v.] government from 22 October 1929 to 4 February 1931, and despite the Depression managed to implement a training scheme for Australian pilots and the purchase of a few aircraft. Compulsory military service was abolished and economies imposed on the army and navy. Between February 1931 and January 1932 he was postmaster-general and minister for works and railways. He was greatly distressed by the defection of Lyons [q.v.], and of Fenton [q.v.8] (whom he had known since schooldays). When Lyons left Canberra railway station to begin the discussions which led to his change of party allegiance, Green ran alongside the departing train calling out 'For God's sake, don't do it, Joe!'. Subsequently he took a major part in promoting the claims of John Curtin to whom he brought the offer of support for the Federal leadership of the party in 1935.

Well-read, generous, and extrovert, Green was an apt representative for Labor's outback supporters in the early twentieth century: a strong nationalist, limitlessly confident in Australia's developmental potential, but concerned that economic development should foster social justice and greater egalitarianism. He was affectionately remembered on the goldfields for many years after his death on 2 October 1940 at East Coolgardie. He was buried at Kalgoorlie after a state funeral, survived by his wife Emily Elenor, née Berry, whom he had married on 25 January 1899 at St John's Church of England, Kalgoorlie, and by three sons and a daughter.

J. S. Battye (ed), *Cyclopedia of Western Australia*, 1-2 (Adel, 1912, 1913); *Aust Worker*, 18 Dec 1929; *West Australian*, 2, 3 Oct 1940; family papers held by Mrs G. S. Pestell, Dalkeith, WA.

G. C. BOLTON

GREEN, ARTHUR VINCENT (1857-1944), Anglican bishop, was born on 31 October 1857 at Albury, Surrey, England, son of Rev. Samuel Dutton Green and his wife Eliza, née Dutton. Much of his childhood was spent travelling between England, Australia and New Zealand: his father was appointed to the parish of Penwortham and Clare in the diocese of Adelaide in 1861 and in the next ten years lived variously in Wales, Scotland and New Zealand. After Arthur's mother died in New Zealand in 1872, his father took up an appointment at Kangaroo Flat, Victoria, before returning to England for the sake of the boy's schooling.

Matriculating in 1874 from the College of St Andrew and St Edmund, Salisbury, Arthur apparently studied law at the University of Durham before joining his father at Cape Town; there he worked as a junior master at the Diocesan College, Rondebosch. He then accompanied his father (d. 1879) to Victoria.

Green planned to complete his law course, but first had to matriculate at the University of Melbourne. However, on meeting Bishop Moorhouse [q.v.5], he offered himself for ordination. He obtained a stipendiary readership under Archdeacon J. K. Tucker and took services from Benalla to Yarrawonga whilst lodging at Wangaratta. At the same time he studied for his matriculation examination, which he passed in mid-1877; four months later he completed the first year of his arts degree. Moorhouse offered him a scholarship at Trinity College, University of Melbourne, and he graduated B.A. with honours in 1879 (M.A., 1883). In 1880 he was ordained as curate of St Andrew's, Brighton,

and on 28 December at Avenel, married Matilda, daughter of Archdeacon Tucker, then in her early thirties. After a trip to Europe Green returned to assist H. H. P. Handfield [q.v.4] at St Peter's, East Melbourne, and in 1885 was appointed vicar of Maldon, having meanwhile enrolled for a law degree at the University of Sydney (LL.B., 1885; LL.D., 1887). He was appointed to St Martin's, Hawksburn, in 1887 and a year later to St Paul's, Geelong. In 1890 he became archdeacon of Ballarat, vicar of Christ Church and examining chaplain to Bishop Thornton [q.v.6] for whom he had high regard.

Green was elected bishop of Grafton and Armidale, New South Wales, in 1894, the first Victorian-trained clergyman to become an Australian bishop. During his seven-year episcopate he doubled the staff of the clergy, dedicated over eighty new churches, established a theological college for the training of local clergy and built a registry office and bishop's house at Armidale. He travelled widely throughout his diocese, often camping out in primitive conditions.

In December 1900 Green was translated to Ballarat as its second bishop, his diocese comprising the western half of Victoria. He set out to augment the Home Mission Fund to assist payment of poorer clergy, to establish St Aidan's Theological College and to make a beginning on Christ Church Cathedral. In 1903 the Synod of Brisbane elected him as bishop but he declined the invitation. In 1908 he began plans for establishing Ballarat Church of England Grammar School for Boys which opened in 1911. In 1910 he delivered the Moorhouse lectures on 'The Ephesian Canonical Writings' (published that year in London); his *Australian sermons* (1914), were extensively used by the lay readers in his diocese. On medical advice he resigned in 1915 and moved to Heidelberg, but continued for eight years as a canon of St Paul's Cathedral and a lecturer at Trinity College. He died on 24 September 1944, predeceased by his wife and survived by his son, Rev. Walter Green.

Green was described as a man of 'unquenchable vitality', tall and slender, with blue eyes and classic, well-modelled features; he was always immaculately dressed. An able scholar with a passion for education, he had a personal magnetism which drew large crowds wherever he preached.

His elder sister Agnes was a religious of the Community of St Denys in Wiltshire, England. His younger sister FLORENCE EMILY (1862-1926) was born on 12 April 1862 at Oamaru, New Zealand. She was educated by her parents and at a private school, Sorbonne, at South Yarra, Melbourne. Although one of the first women to sign the University of Melbourne's matriculation register, she did not take a degree there. She was, however, a Th.A. of the Australian College of Theology with first class honours.

Florence's life was devoted to her religion, to her brother Arthur and to the education of young women. In the early 1880s she paid for the boarding and tuition fees of young Ettie (Henry Handel) Richardson [q.v.], who later caricatured her maliciously but accurately as 'Miss Isabella' in *The getting of wisdom*; Arthur was the irritable 'Mr Shepherd'.

Florence moved to Maldon with Arthur in 1885 and in 1886 helped to found Trinity Church High School. She remained headmistress until 1889 and when Arthur moved to Geelong, she founded the Girls' High School there, the forerunner of The Hermitage. In 1895 she was first headmistress of the New England Girls' School; under her guidance it became one of the largest girls' boarding schools in Australia. In 1907 the diocese purchased the school from her and she went abroad, returning to Victoria in 1910. After acting as caretaker headmistress of Firbank Church of England Girls' Grammar School, Brighton, in 1911, in failing health she went to Ballarat and later lived at Greensborough, Ivanhoe and Murrumbeena.

Florence Green was deeply religious. The basis of her life was prayer. She was also very practical and, like Arthur, a born teacher. Pedagogically she stressed good reading, religion and 'current affairs'; she was interested in the public questions of the day and up to the minute in her own reading. She possessed boundless mental and physical energy and determination. Brisk and cheerful, she had a warm smile and even at 50 her skin was unlined and her hair thick and shiny; her eyes were 'quite startlingly blue'. By nature however she was an ascetic.

Florence Green never married. She died of Parkinson's disease at Murrumbeena on 5 April 1926 and her ashes were interred in Warringal cemetery, Heidelberg.

J. Forster, *Address on Florence Emily Green's death, St Peter's Cathedral, 11 April 1926* (Armidale, 1926; *Ballarat Church Chronicle*, July 1915; New England Girls' School, *Chronicle*, June 1926; *Overland*, 72 (1978), p 24; *Ballarat Courier*, 3, 5 July 1915; *Armidale Chronicle*, June 1926; *Argus*, 26 Oct 1944; *Armidale Express*, 11 Dec 1946; W. Green, Memorandum on New England Girls School and Florence Emily Green (MS, c 1965), *and* E. Summons, Memories of Florence Emily Green, *and* C. Wellard, An appraisal of the ideology of Florence Emily Green (copies held by Dr K. Grose, UNE).

A. DE Q. ROBIN
KELVIN GROSE

GREEN, DANIEL COOPER (1869-1939), commission agent and promoter, was born on 18 June 1869 at Surry Hills, Sydney, third son of Thomas Hyndes Green, coal-trader and ship-owner, later a forest ranger at Casino, and his first wife Alexandrina, née Patison. He began work as a clerk in a bank and then in the Customs Department, but soon found the discipline of regular work irksome. His wits found more of a challenge on the street and as a runner for law firms. In 1895 he persuaded at least one Crown witness to holiday in Brisbane, helped R. D. Meagher [q.v.] to procure witnesses for the royal commission into the case of George Dean [q.v.8], arranged Meagher's election campaign and appeared in court on two charges of conspiracy arising from the above and for fighting. He was cleared on all charges. All of this provided him with a working knowledge of many aspects of the law. As well, he found time to attend sheep and wool classes at Sydney Technical College.

Retaining his link with Meagher and his partner W. P. Crick [q.v.8], Green played a wonderfully devious role when Arthur Coningham [q.v.8], a noted cricketer, sued his wife for divorce naming Fr. Denis O'Haran [q.v.] as co-respondent. Though not a Catholic, Green enthusiastically procured evidence to discredit the Coninghams. In one role he impersonated a secret informant, known only as 'Zero', who was feeding Coningham information about O'Haran's movements. As the second 'Zero', Green supplied the unsuspecting Coningham with much false information. A year later Green published a detailed account of the case, though somewhat exaggerating his role in it: *The secret history of the Coningham case* (1901), complete with photographs and facsimiles of documents.

In 1904 Green began a betting club and in 1905 moved to larger premises, occupying three floors in Pitt Street. Within a few months the club had over 6000 members. It was backed by John Wren's [q.v.] brother Joseph. But the 1906 Gaming and Betting Act put Green's establishment outside the law. After two police raids he sought refuge in bankruptcy in 1907; his stepmother bought his household furniture, his only possessions.

Although never a member of the Labor Party, Green had developed links with the movement since 1904, and for a time sold advertising for the *Australian Worker* and performed other electoral and legal tasks for the Australian Worker's Union. Generous and romantic, with an easy manner and a carefully cultivated anonymity, Green became a valued confidant and fixer for many prominent Labor and later non-Labor politicians. About 1910 he moved his main residence to Melbourne, to be near Federal parliament. Although more circumspect, he retained a certain larrikin streak: during the second conscription referendum (1917), which he opposed, he provoked the Melbourne police by hanging from his window what appeared to be a red flag, but which proved on closer inspection to be a small portion of a huge Union Jack. On one occasion, he reputedly entertained at dinner the commissioner for police and the notorious 'Squizzy' Taylor [q.v.] for whom the police had been searching.

Long interested in literature and theatre, in good food and literate company, Green became a well-known man about town after returning to Sydney in the 1920s. Always working with others, often with his friends E. J. and Dan Carroll [qq.v.7], he backed or promoted boxing events, circuses, theatrical and concert ventures and films. He was often retained by promoters for advice and to entertain visiting celebrities. In 1925 he helped E. J. Carroll to promote a concert tour by Kreisler; it was reputedly financed by Wren. He had rooms in the Australia Hotel, and flats in Melbourne and Brisbane. He unsuccessfully dabbled in the 1920s oil search boom.

In the 1930s Green reduced his activity, though still occasionally entertaining and advising his wide range of acquaintances from his flat in Kings Cross. He suffered from bad eyesight and frequent pain from a duodenal ulcer. He died in hospital on 11 July 1939 of cerebro-vascular disease and was buried in the Anglican section of South Head cemetery. He had never married. His old friend Hugh McCrae [q.v.] described him as a 'mystery man', who had been for two decades the man 'behind the scenes' in many important political developments. Always generous to the poor, he died owing nearly £5000.

H. I. Jensen, *Dan Green* (Brisb, 1948); J. T. Lang, *I remember* (Syd, 1956); F. P. Clune, *Scandals of Sydney town* (Syd, 1957); C. Pearl *Wild men of Sydney* (Melb, 1965); *V&P* (LA NSW), 1895, 2, p 1213, 1901, 2, p 841; *SMH*, 16 Dec 1895, 12, 29 July 1939; *Truth* (Syd), 16 July 1939; *Bulletin*, 19 July 1939; Bankruptcy file, 1907, no 17355 (NSWA).

MARK LYONS

GREEN, JAMES (1864-1948), clergyman and military chaplain, was born on 14 October 1864 at Newcastle upon Tyne, England, son of William Green, journeyman mason, and his wife Isabella, née Palmer. He was educated at Rutherford College, Newcastle upon Tyne, and was a teacher before migrating to New South Wales in 1889 and entering the ministry of the Primitive Methodist Church. He served in parishes in the Newcastle area, married Caroline Jane Atkinson on 19 April 1893 at Annandale, Sydney, and was appointed to Marrickville in 1894. In February 1900 he sailed as Wesleyan chaplain to the New South Wales Citizens' Bushmen, raised for service in the South African War. When the contingent returned home in June 1901 he served with troops in training before re-embarking with the 1st Australian Commonwealth Horse.

At Eland's River, Green was captured by the Boers but his imprisonment was short lived. Following the death, illness or evacuation of many newspaper correspondents he became the sole Australian correspondent, sending regular reports to the *Sydney Morning Herald*. These became the basis of *The story of the Australian bushmen* (1903), his first book, which was a straightforward account of service, somewhat romanticized, but sensitive to the evils of warfare. Of Eland's River he wrote: 'It is easy to … throw a glamour over an engagement, but the truth should be told. One has to be in an engagement to see what "the glorious death of the soldier" really is in these times of modern artillery. One man was lying with an arm blown away, and a great hole in his side such as is made in the earth with a shovel'. He returned to Sydney in 1903 and after three country postings was appointed to Newtown in 1912. He also acted as a part-time chaplain to the Commonwealth Military Forces.

Green was a logical choice for the senior Methodist chaplaincy on the formation of the Australian Imperial Force in August 1914. He was appointed chaplain colonel with the 1st Battalion. He claimed to have landed at Anzac Cove on 25 April 1915. This is unlikely; however, he was one of the first chaplains ashore and probably conducted the first formal burial party. His service at Gallipoli impressed on him the 'bedrock simplicity' of the men. With A. E. Talbot [q.v.], an Anglican, he conducted a joint communion service, a rare event because communion was reckoned as a sign of membership of a particular church. He left Gallipoli on 29 June, returning to Egypt to take charge of hospital visitations and continued to exercise the practical ecumenism learnt at Gallipoli.

Green worked with the Red Cross and comforts funds authorities in Egypt to secure supplies for the troops at Gallipoli, such as the first consignment of mosquito netting and crude petroleum. He considered this 'one of the most useful things done during [his] chaplaincy' as the supplies saved many lives by preventing the spread of disease. He returned to Gallipoli on 9 November but was soon evacuated when he injured his knee. He reached the 3rd Australian General Hospital, Lemnos, and, although a patient, resumed duty because there was no other chaplain available. He served with the 55th Battalion from its formation and accompanied his men in the trenches in France in 1916 and through the battle of Fromelles and the first battle of the Somme. Then from December 1916 to April 1917 Green was attached to A.I.F. Headquarters in London. Moved by the sight of Australians loitering on the streets, he gained the co-operation of the Australian Young Men's Christian Association and the Wesleyan Army and Navy Board, and opened a recreation centre in Horseferry Road which became a focal point of A.I.F. life in London.

Green returned to the front regularly but became seriously ill in November 1917 and was invalided to Australia. He had been awarded the Distinguished Service Order for tending wounded men 'under a barrage . . . in the front line trenches, Fleurbaix', in September-October 1916 and for similar work previously at Fromelles. He was appointed C.M.G. in 1918 and twice mentioned in dispatches. As one of the longest-serving A.I.F. chaplains he was recognized by the New South Wales Methodist Conference which elected him president for 1918. He devoted this year to establishing the Church's War Memorial Hospital at Waverley. He published two books arising from his experiences at the front: *News from no man's land* (1917) and *The year of Armageddon* (1919). His letters home, in which he strove for realism, were published in the *Methodist*.

Green's war experience left a permanent mark on his ministry. He was a very approachable man who hated aloofness or snobbery of any kind. He asserted that institutional Christianity had 'humbugged' men and interfered with the relationship between man and God. His ministry continued in Sydney, first at Paddington, then at Croydon Park. In 1927 he became commissioner for Leigh College, the Methodist theological institution. He retired from active ministry in 1934 and in 1935 wrote *From my hospital window*, a series of essays on 'sane democracy'. This book is his best: he emerges as a good-natured, tolerant, faithful man, compassionate towards the unemployed and other victims of economic crisis. His other books were *The selector* (1907) and *The lost echo* (1910).

Survived by his wife and two sons, Green died on 6 November 1948 at Waverley and was buried in Rookwood cemetery.

M. M. McKernan, *Australian churches at war* (Syd, 1980); *Methodist*, 6, 27 Mar, 10 Apr, 14 Aug 1915, Nov-Dec 1948; *SMH*, 31 Mar, 2 Apr 1934; James Green file, War Records Section (AWM).

MICHAEL McKERNAN

GREEN, PERCY GORDON (1889-1972), printer and typographer, was born on 6 March 1889 at Akaroa, New Zealand, eldest child of Edward Charles Green, carpenter and farmer, and his wife Emma Lucretia, née King, both New Zealand-born. While attending schools at Ashhurst and Woodville he helped his father on a farm and delivered the tri-weekly Woodville *Examiner*. After about a year at High School, he became a 'printer's devil' at Palmerston North.

In 1912 Green migrated to Toowoomba, Queensland, and worked for the Harrison Printing Co. Ltd. Soon he began to study lettering and printing design by a correspondence course run by the *Inland Printer*, the 'Bible' of self-improving printers in the United States of America. At the Wesley Church, Kangaroo Point, Brisbane, he married Clementina Margaret Dunstan (d. 1961) on 25 January 1916. Both were musical: he played several instruments, and also conducted; she sang in church choirs.

Moving to Sydney in 1918 as a factory manager, Green saw that specially designed lettering could be combined with illustrations within one block to much better effect in advertisements. This led to the founding of the Green Press Ltd at Glebe, as a letterpress printing firm, working in close collaboration with firms of commercial artists, notably (S. Ure) Smith [q.v.] & Julius. But Green also wished to demonstrate his artistic talent by printing limited editions. In 1921 he produced *The Windsor book*, largely an essay by J. H. M. Abbott [q.v.7] with etchings by Lionel Lindsay [q.v.] and Ure Smith. He hand-set the type and used an Albion hand-press. In the 1920s and 1930s Green produced other prestigious books including *A century of journalism*, the centenary history of the *Sydney Morning Herald*. Hardy Wilson's [q.v.] *Grecian and Chinese architecture*, limited to an edition of 100, was illustrated with copper half-tone blocks, set in Caslon type and printed on goatskin parchment paper.

A foundation member of the Australian Limited Editions Society's technical committee from 1936, Green produced his most famous book for the society in 1938—Watkin Tench's [q.v.2] *Narrative of the expedition to Botany Bay*, originally published in 1789. Green set the book in Caslon Old Face, in the manner of Caslon's original 'English' face, manufactured about 1730; it was exhibited at the San Francisco World Fair as one of the best fifty books of the year. He also designed an edition of Henry Lawson's [q.v.] *Romance of the swag* for the society but during its production the Green Press was reorganized; Green was 'shunted' and took the book to Waite & Bull to print and bind.

The episode distressed Green and he moved to Melbourne where he continued to work as a compositor and typographer, sporadically with the *Age*. In 1940 he published *A sentimental story* and in his eightieth year, he set and hand-printed fifty copies of *I am evergreen*, a brief history of his family. He died in hospital at Camberwell on 28 August 1972 and was cremated. Two sons and two daughters survived him.

Aust Ltd Edns Soc, *Prospectus* (Syd, 1936); *Aust Book Review*, Sept 1972; *Graphic Arts*, 20 Sept 1972.

J. HAGAN

GREEN, SOLOMON (1868-1948), book-maker and philanthropist, was born on 1 August 1868 at Mile End, London, son of Judah Green, publican, and his wife Elizabeth, née Jacobs. As he later put it, 'I was born in England of poor but very worthy and charitable parents'. He was apprenticed to upholstery but at 15 set off for Australia. He spent his first colonial years working around Melbourne's wharves or buying and selling about the streets. In 1887 he commenced bookmaking, on the Flat at Flemington, suffered some heavy losses and was reduced to pencilling for former rivals. In 1891, after a visit to England, he again tried his skill with odds, taking bets on the Adelaide Cup. He extended his betting to the goldfields in Western Australia and began a mail-order doubles book which, despite initial legal problems, became a huge success. At the turn of the century he operated the Melbourne Tattersall's Club.

Profits from his bookmaking were invested in pastoral property and in city and suburban real estate. Green also bred race-horses at his Shipley stud, near Warrnambool. His horses won several of Australia's major races. In 1910 Comedy King won the Melbourne Cup. Among other successes were the 1927 and 1928 Newmarket Handicaps with Gothic; Strephon, perhaps his best horse, won the Victoria Derby in 1928 and the St Leger in 1929. But his investments in breeding never won consistent success. He sold Shipley but later bought studs at Underbank and Parwan Park, near Bacchus Marsh.

Green retired from bookmaking in 1913. His mail-order betting had become too extensive; before popular meetings he no longer knew his full liabilities. He owned the Victoria Buildings and the Swanston Buildings in central Melbourne as well as two pastoral estates in Queensland: Dynevor Downs and Llanrheidol. Green's family also held shares in the Glenesk pastoral company, New South Wales, and he had interests in the plastics industry in that State.

When Comedy King won the Cup, Green donated £500 to local charities. His reputation for philanthropy grew with his fortune. He began an annual appeal for blankets for the poor with a donation of £1000. He sponsored several funds to assist victims of World War II bombing in England. His Sol Green Trust bought land at Sandringham and Black Rock to build cheap housing for ex-servicemen but the scheme was hampered by irregular payments. Green bought land for a children's playground in South Melbourne. He gave constantly to Melbourne's public hospitals and in 1947 donated £40 000 to the Royal Melbourne Hospital.

'Sol Green—sufficient address, Melbourne' (or Sydney) enlivened the racing world. Sharp with his odds, he covered some huge doubles bets on the Caulfield and Melbourne Cups. A big man, always with his hat, spats and Havana cigar, Sol Green arrived at race meetings in a gold-plated Rolls Royce. His dry wit and quick patter established a unique reputation.

On 3 February 1892 at Albert Park, Melbourne, he had married Rebecca Mendes; they had three sons. Green died on 11 May 1948 after several years illness. He was 'always proud' of being a Jew and was associated with the Alma Road Jewish Temple. Many hospitals and charities benefited from provisions in his will, valued in Victoria for probate at £481 721.

E. H. Buggy, *The real John Wren* (Melb, 1977); *Punch* (Melb), 2 Nov 1911; *Herald* (Melb), 12 May 1948, 24 Nov 1979; *Age*, 12 May 1948; *Truth*, 15, 22 May 1948; information from N. Cooper, *and* Sir L. Pyke (Melb).

CHRIS MCCONVILLE

GREEN, WILLIAM HERBERT (1878-1968), businessman and philanthropist, was born on 11 October 1878 in Brisbane, son of Charles Green, ironfounder, and his wife Eliza, née Welding or Vaughan. After his father became a partner in a Mackay foundry in 1881, he was educated at Mackay public school and sent to Way College, Adelaide, for a Methodist education. Apprenticed in 1896 to a Townsville pharmacist, Cromwell Ridgley, in 1901 he completed his professional education at the Queensland College of Pharmacy, Brisbane. Registered on 22 January 1902, he returned to Townsville and bought Ridgley's business. He owned four shops by 1914, and by 1920 W. H. Green Ltd controlled eight branches in North Queensland. Eventually there were at least sixteen pharmacies in the chain but the requirement in the Pharmacy Act 1933 for professional managers forced the company to disband.

On the outbreak of World War I in 1914 Green served for three and a half months on Thursday Island as sergeant-compounder with the Kennedy Regiment of the Citizen Forces.

In 1920 Green both became mayor and was elected to the Legislative Assembly for Townsville. A member of the Northern Country Party and deputy leader of the United Party of Queensland in the assembly, he was principally an advocate of northern interests and northern separation. His election, however, had been an aberration of the city's predominantly Labor electorate and in 1923 he was defeated; a bid for the Federal seat of Kennedy in 1926 failed.

A Methodist lay preacher like his father for over fifty-five years and superintendent of a Sunday school for thirty-five, Green served on most of the committees administering the Methodist Church in Queensland and was secretary or treasurer of many of the Queensland Methodist loan funds. He was treasurer of the Methodist King's College at the University of Queensland for twenty-five years and a foundation member and president of the interdenominational Queensland Council of Churches. His lifelong support of the temperance movement stemmed no doubt from his mother's pioneer involvement at Mackay. Treasurer of the Queensland Temperance League to 1940, then chairman to 1965, he represented Australia at international temperance conferences, including Lucerne in 1948 and Paris in 1952, and was vice-president of the World International Bureau against Alcoholism. He was chairman of temperance private hotels in Sydney, Brisbane and Toowoomba.

Green lived entirely in Brisbane from 1930. He was chairman of the Equitable Probate and General Insurance Co. Ltd and the Indooroopilly Toll Bridge Co., and was a director of the Atlas Insurance Co. and Busby's Ltd. A Freemason from 1905, he was district grand master of North Queensland in 1922 and State grand master in 1929-30 and 1932-33; in 1931 and 1935-45 he was pro-grand master under the governor. He was appointed O.B.E. in 1958 in recognition of his numerous church projects, charitable works and donations.

On 29 October 1903 at Townsville, Green married Clara Cockerill; they had five children. After she died in 1930, he married her sister Frances Gertrude on 13 July 1933 at Hamilton, Brisbane. When she too died, he married Georgina Singleton at Glasgow, on 4 October 1948 during a visit to Scotland. Green died in Brisbane on 18 March 1968 and was cremated. He left to his family an estate valued for probate at $75 925 with instructions to trustees not to invest in mining companies. His son-in-law Rev. Arthur Preston summed up his work: 'A life that was so full, a life that was so useful, a life that was so dedicated to humanity'.

Methodist Church jubilee souvenir (Townsville, 1926); B. A. Hedges, *The Methodist Church in Townsville* (Townsville, 1976); *Chemist and Druggist of A'sia*, 2 Dec 1901, 1 Feb 1902, 1 Sept 1914, 1 Jan, 1 Feb 1915; United Grand Lodge of Qld, *Ashlar*, 5 June 1968; *A'sian J of Pharmacy*, May 1968; *Townsville Daily Bulletin*, 4 Feb 1904, 23 Feb 1920, 1 Jan 1958, 19 Mar 1968; *Aust Temperance Advocate*, Feb, Apr 1968; The activities of William Herbert Green (MS, nd, held by Qld Temperance League, Brisb).   JIM MANION

GREENE, GEORGE HENRY (1838-1911), pastoralist, wheat-grower and politician, was born on 20 July 1838 at Collon, Louth, Ireland, fifth son of Lieutenant William Pomeroy Greene, R.N., and his wife Anne, née Griffith. In 1842 William chartered the *Sarah* to convey an extensive household to Port Phillip, including his sons Molesworth [q.v.4] and George, and (Sir) William Stawell [q.v.6] who married daughter Mary. Soon after arriving on 1 December, the Greenes settled at Woodlands, near Melbourne. George was educated at Mr Trollope's Collingwood school, the Melbourne Diocesan Grammar School and the Richmond Grammar School; in 1855 he enrolled at the University of Melbourne. In 1858 he was one of the first five students to graduate B.A.

Greene acquired pastoral experience in southern New South Wales on Billabong station, in which he held a share, and later was part-owner of Tooma and Marogle stations. He was appointed a magistrate in 1867. On 26 July 1870 at New Town, Tasmania, he married Ellen Elizabeth (Nelly), daughter of Lieut-Colonel Andrew Crawford [q.v.3]. They travelled around the world for two years after selling their station interests in 1875.

On his return to New South Wales Greene bought Iandra, a 32 600 acre (13 200 ha) estate near Grenfell, in 1878 and began grazing and wheat-growing. He was a member of the Young Pastures and Stock Protection Board in 1881-84 and chairman in 1885-88. An early advocate of netting to control the spread of rabbits, he attended various conferences and, despite scepticism from his neighbours, had his property fully netted at an early date. Later he was vindicated. In 1888 Greene called the meeting at which the

Young and Lachlan District Sheepowners' Association was formed, and on 9 July 1890 became a foundation member of the Pastoralists' Union of New South Wales. He favoured conciliation with the Amalgamated Shearers' Union of Australasia; unlike many other pastoralists, he was not opposed to unionism itself. In 1893 he was a commissioner for the World's Columbian Exposition at Chicago.

Greene's wheat-growing gradually met with success and in 1893 he introduced share-farming, which soon proved very popular. By 1911 Iandra had some fifty share-farmers working 18 000 acres (7300 ha); with another 5000 acres (2000 ha) fallow and 20 000 sheep being run. The farmers supplied the labour and machinery, while Greene provided land cleared for ploughing, the seed and some fertilizer, and closely controlled the farming practices. In 1903 Greene was the first to grow W. J. Farrer's [q.v.8] 'Federation' wheat commercially.

Elected as a free trader, Greene represented Grenfell in the Legislative Assembly in 1889-91, from July to October 1894 (when he was unseated on a recount after a petition) and in 1895-98. In the House he was progressive and independent, and successfully advocated a branch railway line from Koorawatha to Grenfell. Always an ardent supporter of Federation, he was nominated to the Legislative Council in April 1899 to facilitate passage of a bill to have the Constitution put to a referendum. He was a member of the Union Club, Sydney.

As Iandra prospered, Greene in 1908 started building a village at the Iandra rail siding that became known as Greenethorpe. In 1910 he completed an ornate Edwardian mansion costing an estimated £63 000; it was built of reinforced concrete and featured towers and a mock-Tudor courtyard. He died on 22 December 1911 and was buried with Anglican rites at St Saviour's Church, Iandra. The share-farmers placed a plaque there to his memory. His estate was valued for probate at £83 937. He was survived by his wife (d. 1921), three daughters and a son Captain William Pomeroy Crawford Greene, who represented Worcester in the British House of Commons in 1923-45.

Methodist Dept of Christian Citizenship, *The Iandra story* (Cowra, NSW, nd); M. F. E. Stawell, *My recollections* (Lond, 1911); W. A. Bayley, *Golden granary* (Grenfell, 1954); *PP* (NSW), 1917-18, 1, p 190; *Agricultural Gazette* (NSW), 19 (1908); *Pastoralists' Review*, 15 Jan 1912, p 1151; F. S. Piggin, 'NSW pastoralists and the strikes of 1890 and 1891', *Hist Studies*, 56, April 1971; *Daily Telegraph* (Syd), 2 Aug 1894, 12 Nov 1910; *T&CJ*, 13 Apr 1889; *SMH*, 23, 25 Dec 1911; *Grenfell Record*, 29 Dec 1911; information from the National Trust of Australia (NSW).

I. G. CARNELL

GREENE, SIR WALTER MASSY; *see* MASSY-GREENE

GREENFIELD, ALEXANDER MACKAY (1839-1922), merchant, citizen-soldier and sportsman, was born on 5 February 1839 at Auchencrow, Berwickshire, Scotland, son of John Greenfield, merchant, and his wife Janet Cora, née Mackay. When Alexander was 7 his father died. It is believed that he then came under the care of a guardian, completing his schooling at 15 when he was articled to a Berwick solicitor. He began to study law at Edinburgh before deciding to seek his fortune on the Victorian goldfields. After disembarking on 14 September 1857 he walked first to the Ararat field and then to Pleasant Creek (Stawell). He had no luck and, after working on a sheep-station, secured a clerk's position in Melbourne with the London Chartered Bank of Australia.

Greenfield impressed his employers: in 1860 he was sent to the important Ballarat branch as its accountant and immediately became involved in sporting activities. Tall, strong and athletic, Alex Greenfield was first captain of the Ballarat Football Club. His togs and his portrait are enshrined in its clubrooms. He also succeeded as a high and long jumper and hurdler, winning many local and colonial events.

In 1866 he established his own business, A. M. Greenfield & Co. In commodious premises in Doveton Street, the company dealt with farm produce, land and property sales, auctioneering and sales of machinery and fertilizers in the heyday of the district's farming development. His many business interests included chairmanship of Permewan [q.v.5] Wright & Co. Ltd and Brind's Pty Ltd, distillers. He also opened offices in South Africa and New Zealand. Although he suffered severe financial losses in the 1890s, he paid off his creditors to the sum of £40 000 within a promised ten years.

In 1861 Greenfield had joined the Ballarat Volunteer Rifle Rangers. In 1866 he was commissioned and retired in 1877 as captain. When the 3rd, or Ballarat Battalion, Victorian Rifles, was set up in 1884 he returned to the force and was promoted major and adjutant; five years later he became lieut-colonel commanding the battalion. R. E. Williams [q.v.] remembered him as 'A gentleman ... and a bitter foe to humbug and pretence'. A fine marksman, in 1876 he commanded a team of Victorian riflemen which competed in England and the United States of America with notable success. He retired from the reserve of officers in 1902. In 1914, 'The Colonel' was prominent in forming a citizen defence corps, becoming president.

Greenfield was president of the Ballarat Club in 1891-95 and of the Ballarat Agricultural and Pastoral Society, and after terms as secretary was president for many years of the Ballarat Turf Club. He helped to found the Ballarat Agricultural High School and the Fish Acclimatization Society, and was an active member of the orphanage committee. He was a justice of the peace for thirty years and, as a regular member of the bench, was known for kindness, tolerance and good humour.

On 27 July 1871 with Presbyterian forms, Greenfield had married Jessie, daughter of James Williamson, a bank-manager and a defendant in the Mount Egerton mine case. Greenfield died on 29 October 1922 and was buried in Ballarat new cemetery, leaving an estate valued for probate at £15 227. He was survived by five of his six daughters and by his son Angus (1875-1951) who took over control of the firm. Angus surpassed his father's achievements as an athlete; he was also captain of the Ballarat Football Club and played for Geelong while still at Geelong Church of England Grammar School. After leaving school, during the football season he cycled from Ballarat to Melbourne or Geelong and back every Saturday. He won national cycling championships and State championships in pole-vaulting and weight-putting, was an outstanding rower, and was probably Ballarat's best athlete.

A portrait in oils by J. Oldham of 'The Colonel' in uniform is at the Ballarat Club.

M. M. McCallum, *Ballarat and district citizens and sports at home and abroad* (Ballarat, 1916); W. Bate, *Lucky city* (Melb, 1978); *Ballarat Star*, 15 Jan 1921; private papers and information from Messrs A. and H. Greenfield, Ballarat, Vic.

AUSTIN MCCALLUM*

GREENWELL, SYBIL ENID VERA MUNRO; *see* MORRISON

GREEVES, EDWARD GODERICH ('CARJI') (1903-1963), footballer, was born on 1 November 1903 at Warragul, Victoria, son of Edward Goderich Greeves, farmer, and his wife Frances Adaline, née Nasmith. He was nicknamed 'Carji', derived from 'Carjillo, the Rajah of Bhong', a character in a popular play. After the family returned to the Geelong district, Greeves attended Geelong College in 1916-23 where he showed outstanding prowess as an all-round sportsman. As captain of cricket he was a useful bowler and a dashing left-hand bats-

man; he won the school tennis championship; he stroked the crew and won golden opinions as a footballer.

Geelong Football Club was keen to secure his services even before his schooldays were over, but the principal refused him permission to play. After leaving school in May 1923 he was quickly snapped up by the club and he began his illustrious career, first as a rover and on the forward line, then in the centre which he soon made his own—a position which had been held with distinction, for Geelong, by his father.

In 1924, to honour the memory of Charles Brownlow, an early player for Geelong and long an administrator, the Victorian Football League created the Brownlow medal for the fairest and best player in the league. Greeves won the first award, and was runner-up in 1925 to Colin Watson (St Kilda) and in 1926 and 1929 to Ivor Warne-Smith (Melbourne). The sight of Greeves (in guernsey number 20) playing his 137 games in ten years, as an amateur, was always memorable; at 5 ft. 9 ins. (175 cm) and 12 stone (76 kg) he was never very fast but had a remarkable sense of anticipation, was an excellent mark and a devastating kick with either foot, though favouring his right. He never wore football boots, preferring ordinary boots of very soft leather, suitably stopped. He played in the premiership teams of 1925 and 1931, and was four times a member of interstate teams.

In the American winter of 1928-29 he was invited as specialist coach of the University of Southern California football team by Andrew Chaffey (son of George Chaffey [q.v.7]) who was treasurer of the university and was anxious to improve his team's kicking and marking. Greeves spent a happy time in Southern California, was widely fêted, gave several famous demonstrations of his kicking ability, and noticeably improved his charges by insisting that they drop-kick using the instep instead of the toe.

In the early 1930s Greeves worked as a contractor in the Inglewood district. On 9 April 1934 at St David's Presbyterian Manse, Newtown, Geelong, he married Alma Catherine Condie. Later he went to Ararat, where he took charge of the spare-parts section of a garage; he coached the Warracknabeal and Ararat football teams until a cartilage operation forced him to give up the game.

From the 1930s Greeves suffered from pulmonary tuberculosis and emphysema. He died on 15 April 1963, survived by his wife and two daughters; he was cremated at Ararat. His image is kept alive in Geelong by the award of the football club's annual best and fairest trophy—the Carji Greeves medal—and in Harold Freedman's mural of the Western District in the State Public Offices.

J. Dunn and J. Main (eds), *Footy annual* (Melb, 1968); 'Carji' Greeves scrapbook (held by Mrs A. C. Greeves, Anglesea, Vic); information from Geelong Football Club officials.   A. G. AUSTIN

GREGORY, HENRY (1860-1940), farmer and politician, was born on 15 March 1860 at Kyneton, Victoria, son of Thomas Mamby Gregory, storekeeper, and his wife Catherine, née Kelleher. Educated at Kyneton, he opened a tinsmithing business at Rochester at the age of 16 and subsequently ran an ironmonger's store. On 21 October 1885 at Sandhurst (Bendigo) he married Sarah Richards with Catholic rites; she died the following year, and on 10 February 1891 at St Kilian's Church, Sandhurst, Gregory married Ruth Belinda Cartmell. There were four sons and two daughters of the second marriage.

Almost bankrupt in 1892, Gregory moved to Western Australia where, unsuccessful as a gold prospector, he worked for the storekeepers Askin & Nicholson at Ninety Mile, near Coolgardie, in 1893. He then opened what Melbourne *Punch* later termed 'an unimpressive public house of corrugated iron and mulga rafters' at Menzies. In January 1896 he was elected mayor of Menzies and appointed justice of the peace. In March he forestalled a move by W. E. Clare of the *Coolgardie Miner* to found a paper in Menzies and established the *North Coolgardie Herald & Menzies Times*. In so doing he earned the lifelong enmity of Hugh Mahon [q.v.], the proprietor of the *Menzies Miner* which Gregory and his co-directors bought out in August 1898. Gregory and Mahon also clashed over Gregory's flotation of two mining companies in 1896, the Menzies Compass and the Menzies Tornado. The bitterness reached a peak during the 1897 elections when both men, although of similar political views, stood for the Legislative Assembly seat of North Coolgardie (Menzies from 1900). Gregory won by sixty votes, and was the only Liberal to gain a mining seat. He supported Federation and payment of members and was for many years a popular spokesman for the goldfields. However, he grew more conservative and lost to Labor in 1911 amid claims from the *Kalgoorlie Miner* that he had 'forgotten his origins'. After his defeat he moved to his property at Wickepin.

Gregory was minister for mines, with one brief interval, in the Leake and James [qq.v.] ministries from May 1901 to August 1904, and minister for mines and railways in the Rason, Moore and Wilson [qq.v.] ministries

from August 1905 until October 1911; he was acting premier and acting treasurer in 1910-11. His best work was done in consolidating and reforming the mining laws. The 'Gregory Act' (1904) was described by a visiting American mining commissioner as the 'most evenly balanced mining enactment in the world'; its basic principles were retained in the Mining Act of 1978. Gregory placed the granting of exemptions on a sound basis and stopped the practice of giving away Crown land in return for the conditional surrender of gold mining leases. He established state batteries and the system by which a miner could hold eighteen acres (7 ha) of mineral country without rent provided he developed it. He also initiated the Inspection of Machinery Act (1904) and the Mines Regulation Act (1906).

In 1913, now ultra-conservative, Gregory won the Federal seat of Dampier; he held Swan from 1922. He proved a well-informed, independent although prolix spokesman of inflexible principles who believed in a balanced budget and found excessive expenditure intolerable. He was admirably suited to the Joint Committee on Public Works of which he was a member in 1914-26 and 1929-31 and chairman in 1917-26. He also served conscientiously on the royal commissions on the pearling industry (1913), powellized timber (1914) and the Australian moving picture industry (1927-28). Throughout World War I Gregory actively represented the interests of the Western Australian Farmers and Settlers' Association, though he refused to sign a pledge and was never endorsed by that organization. Following the introduction of preferential voting in 1919 he became involved in the formation of the Country Party. He was deputy leader from January 1920 until November 1921 when he resigned after an argument with (Sir) Earle Page [q.v.] over the party's failure to form a coalition with the Nationalists. He was unopposed by the Nationalists at the 1922 election, but when the Bruce [q.v.7]-Page ministry was formed the following year he was precluded from membership by his implacable opposition to the Nationalist tariff policy.

Gregory had always been a keen Statesrighter and his dislike of protection was reinforced by Western Australia's dependence on imported manufactured goods. He led an attack on the (Sir) W. Massy Greene [q.v.] tariff introduced by the Hughes [q.v.] government in 1921 and he remained Western Australia's chief advocate in the various tariff battles which lasted until World War II. Supported by John Prowse, Percy Stewart and E. A. Mann [qq.v.], Gregory fought his lonely battle with dogged determination and lengthy speeches; his arguments for lower duties on fencing wire earned him the nickname 'Barbwire Harry'. In September 1932 he moved for a referendum on the question of altering the Constitution to allow Western Australia power over its own customs and excise laws for twenty-five years. When his motion, based on the findings of the 1924-25 Commonwealth royal commission on the finances of Western Australia as affected by Federation, was set aside by the Lyons [q.v.] government, he embraced the secessionist cause. In 1933 he published 'Why Western Australia should secede' in the *Australian Quarterly*.

Despite advancing old age and indifferent health, Gregory remained a forthright representative of his adopted State; he was last elected in September 1940 at the age of 80, the oldest member of parliament. A small man with determined features, he felt no compunction in attacking his colleagues in debate and was frequently censured in the party room. However, despite his intransigence on matters of principle he was generally liked by his peers for his otherwise congenial nature. Always interested in defence, he was awarded the certificate of merit by the Western Australian branch of the Returned Sailors' and Soldiers' Imperial League of Australia for his work on behalf of returned servicemen. In 1935 he represented Australia at the jubilee of King George V in London. He was the Western Australian member of the Australian Cricket Board of Control for many years. In 1907, for his part in saving the life of an Italian miner, he had been appointed Chevalier of the Crown of Italy.

Gregory died on 15 November 1940 at Fitzroy, Melbourne, survived by his wife, three sons and a daughter, and was buried in the Catholic section of Fawkner cemetery after a state funeral. His estate was valued for probate at £2341.

U. R. Ellis, *A history of the Australian Country Party* (Melb, 1963); F. C. Green, *Servant of the House* (Melb, 1969); *PD* (Cwlth), 1940, 165, p 17, 32; *Kalgoorlie Miner*, 3 Oct 1911; *Primary Producer* (Perth), 8 Aug 1924; *Punch* (Melb), 23 Apr 1925; *West Australian*, 16 Nov 1940; *Argus*, 16 Nov 1940; H. J. Gibbney, Hugh Mahon (M.A., ANU, 1969). P. Davies, Henry Gregory and the Australian tariff 1921-1933 (B.A. Hons thesis, Univ NSW, Duntroon, 1981).   PETER DAVIES

GREGORY, JACK MORRISON (1895-1973), cricketer, was born on 14 August 1895 at North Sydney, third son and sixth child of native-born parents Charles Smith Gregory (1847-1935), accountant, and his wife Jessie Anne, née Morrison. The Gregorys [q.v.4] were long established in Australian cricket. Jack was educated in 1907-12 at Sydney Church of England Grammar School (Shore), where he showed promise as a hurdler. He was a lower grade player with the North Sydney Cricket Club when he enlisted as an artillery gunner in the Australian Imperial Force in January 1916. Promoted sergeant in December, second lieutenant in September 1918 and lieutenant in December, he had two tours of duty in France. In 1919 he joined the A.I.F. cricket team in England.

Under the leadership of H. L. Collins [q.v.8], Gregory developed into an all-rounder whose spectacular hitting was matched by fearsome fast bowling and prehensile slip fielding. On the A.I.F. tour of England and South Africa in 1919-20 he scored 1352 runs at 31 and took 178 wickets at just under 17. The team returned to Australia to play their last matches; Gregory scored a stunning century in each innings and took eight wickets against New South Wales.

Discharged from the A.I.F. in March 1920, Gregory played a leading part next summer in the recovery of the Ashes from England, with 442 runs at 73 in the five matches, including a century at Melbourne, 23 wickets at 24, and 15 catches. Touring England in 1921 under the captaincy of Warwick Armstrong [q.v.7], Gregory and E. A. McDonald [q.v.] formed the first major opening bowling partnership based on speed. The explosive action of Gregory complemented perfectly the smoothness of McDonald. Between them they took 46 of the 71 English wickets that fell to bowlers in the Test matches; in first-class matches Gregory took 116 wickets at 16, scored 1135 runs at 36, and was named among *Wisden*'s cricketers of the year. *En route* home, he scored a century against South Africa in seventy minutes which has remained the fastest century in Test cricket.

After 1922 Gregory was hampered by injuries and diverted by work commitments and other sporting interests. He did not play in the 1922-23 or 1923-24 seasons, but returned for the Test matches in 1924-25; used as a stock bowler, he took 22 wickets at 37. In the 1925-26 season, now playing for Paddington, he topped the Sydney first-grade averages with 34 wickets at 13 and was chosen for the 1926 tour of England, but took only three Test wickets. After this tour, he played little cricket. In December 1928 he broke down with a knee injury in the first Test against England and retired. In 24 Test matches he had taken 85 wickets at 31, made 1146 runs at just under 37, and taken 37 catches. In first-class cricket his figures were 504 wickets at 21 and 5661 runs at 36.

Gregory stood well over six feet (183 cm), was strongly built and, although possessed of an outswinger, relied more for his effect on pace and bounce. As a left-handed batsman, he attacked the bowling and scorned protective gear like gloves, cap and box. A popular figure wherever he played, he was seen as a symbol of Australian manhood in the years after World War I. In 1936 he shared a benefit match with Warren Bardsley [q.v.7].

At Launceston, Tasmania, on 26 June 1928, Gregory had married Phyllis Ethel von Alwyn, 'Miss Australia' for 1927, who had appeared at an Atlantic City pageant in the United States of America. They lived at Woollahra until the early 1950s. He had joined Kavanagh & English Pty Ltd, sheet metal manufacturers, in the mid-1920s and was a director by 1928. A trustee of the Sydney Cricket Ground in 1947-65, he was a member of the Royal Motor Yacht Club. In retirement at Narooma he fished and played bowls. Predeceased by his wife, he died at Bega on 7 August 1973 and was cremated with Anglican rites; he was survived by a son and daughter. His estate was valued for probate at $43 386.

R. Barker and I. Rosenwater, *England v Australia . . . 1877-1968* (Melb, 1969); R. Mason, *Warwick Armstrong's Australians* (Lond, 1971); D. Frith, *The fast men* (Lond, 1975); P. Derriman, *The grand old ground* (Syd, 1981); NSW Cricket Assn, *Annual Report*, 1914-15; *Wisden Cricketers' Almanack*, 1920-29; *Aust Cricket*, Oct 1973; *Mercury* (Hob), 27 June 1928; *SMH*, 13 Feb, 18 July, 24 Nov 1923, 5 Dec 1928, 10 Oct 1936, 14 Oct 1947, 16 Aug 1965, 8 Aug 1973.   B. G. ANDREWS

GREGORY, JOHN WALTER (1864-1932), geologist, geographer and explorer, was born on 27 January 1864 at Bow, London, only son of John James Gregory, wool merchant, and his wife Jane, née Lewis. After education at Stepney Grammar School, at 15 he became a clerk at wool sales in the City of London. His growing interest in the natural sciences led him to attend evening classes at the London Mechanics' Institute (Birkbeck College). He matriculated in 1886 and graduated B.Sc. with first-class honours in 1891 and D.Sc. (London) in 1893. Meanwhile in 1887 he was appointed assistant in the geological department of the British Museum (Natural History), replacing Robert Etheridge [q.v.8].

In 1891 Gregory made his first journey outside Europe, studying the geological evolution of the Rocky Mountains and the Great Basin of western North America. In 1892 he was seconded as naturalist to a large expedition to British East Africa; when this collapsed he set out on his own with a party of forty Africans. In five months he completed scientific observations in fields ranging from structural geology and physical geography to anthropology, and from mountaineering and glacial geology to the malarial parasites. His major success was the study in this region of the volcanic rocks and structural features of what he termed the 'Great Rift Valley'. His conclusions were summarized in two classic books—*The great rift valley* (1896) and *The rift valleys and geology of East Africa* (1921). Other major scientific expeditions were the first crossing of Spitsbergen with Sir Martin Conway (1896); in the West Indies (1899) with his wife Audrey, née Chaplin, whom he had married on 6 June 1895; and a 1500-mile (2400 km) walk with his son through Burma to southwestern China and Chinese Tibet (1922). In 1908 and 1912 he headed expeditions to Cyrenaica (in Libya) and southern Angola, inquiring into the suitability of these areas for Jewish colonization.

On the death of Sir Frederick McCoy [q.v.5], the University of Melbourne decided to create a new chair in geology and mineralogy. Gregory was attracted to the possibility of creating a new geology department in a region rich in mineral resources. He applied and was appointed in December 1899. His arrival in Melbourne in February 1900 was heralded by the *Age* as opening a 'new era in the popularizing of University teaching in Victoria'. For his part Gregory called for new courses with 'field work, camping out, the linking of theoretical study with mining work, the advancement of the mineralogical features of the science'. Unfortunately the university then lacked the resources to enable him to carry out his relatively modest requests for accommodation and for funds to cover operating costs. Even the teaching collections had been spirited away to the National Museum in the city, leaving him with just one specimen.

In conjunction with his university appointment, in 1901-04 Gregory was director of the Geological Survey of Victoria, and in this role visited most of the mining areas; in January and May 1903 he gathered information for his book *The Mount Lyell mining field, Tasmania* (1905). In the summer of 1901-02 he led a student scientific expedition around Lake Eyre. The resulting book, *The dead heart of Australia* (1906), was remarkable for the coining of the evocative phrase 'dead heart' for the central deserts of Australia, and for the proposition (now discredited) that the hot waters of the Great Artesian Basin were of 'juvenile' or deep-seated, as distinct from atmospheric, origin.

With university permission, Gregory also

accepted the directorship of the civilian scientific staff of the 1901-04 British National Antarctic Expedition commanded by Commander R. F. Scott. However he resigned (1901) when 'representatives of the Royal Geographical Society... and of a few scientific men belonging to the Navy' opposed the agreement that he would have charge of the landing party's scientific programme. Yet he gave generous praise to the scientific observations of Scott and his colleagues when reviewing the expedition's accomplishments in *Nature*, 25 January 1906.

At the request of the director of education, Gregory wrote a series of small geographical textbooks for primary schools and also gave classes in physical geography for secondary teachers, publishing the first general textbook on the geography of Victoria in 1903.

Despite his known ambition to stay in Victoria and help the development of an Australian school of mining geology, Gregory finally realized that the university was not going to provide him with the laboratory facilities for which he had continued to argue. In May 1904 he successfully applied for the new chair of geology at the University of Glasgow and on 16 September he left from Adelaide. His final shot, 'The mining policy for Victoria' (*Age*, 19 September), made a strong case for the importance to the mining industry of adequately supported practical geological training and for proper quarters for geological survey, and expressed concern for miners' working conditions.

In Glasgow Gregory soon built up a vigorous department and established himself as a formidable teacher, administrator and researcher. His informal manner, his stimulating lectures, his entire accessibility and readiness to discuss any subject at any time endeared him to his students until he retired to Essex in 1929.

An extremely facile and interesting writer, Gregory published twenty books and over 300 papers. In 1901 he was elected a fellow of the Royal Society. Many awards and honours were showered upon him, including medals of various societies and honorary degrees of the universities of Melbourne (D.Sc.) and Liverpool and Glasgow (LL.D.).

At 68 Gregory joined an expedition to Peru. On 2 June 1932 he was drowned when his canoe overturned in the Urubamba River in northern Peru. He was survived by his wife, a son and a daughter. A memorial to him is in Woodham Walter Church, Maldon, Essex.

Most who knew him were charmed by his diffident manner, enthusiasm and geniality and all were overwhelmed by the breadth and depth of his knowledge in virtually all subjects. Although rather small, he was exceptionally forceful and energetic. If there was a chink in his armour it was a tendency to elaborate theories after paying flying visits to regions of complex geology. Two critics in New South Wales were E. F. Pittman [q.v.] and J. B. Jaquet, who took issue with Gregory's hastily proposed 'saddle reef' theory for the origin of the Broken Hill ore lodes. Nevertheless most would view Gregory as an exceptional scientist whose greatest achievements straddled the shadow line between geology and geography. Gregory did much to counteract the parochialism of British geology and achieved for himself a world-wide reputation unequalled by any other British geologist of his time.

C. J. Gregory, *J. W. Gregory—a sketch* (priv. pub., Chelmsford, 1977, copy Univ Melb Archives); *Nature* (Lond), 16 May 1901, 25 June 1932, 27 Aug 1932; *Obituary Notices of Fellows of the Roy Soc*, 1 (1932); Geological Soc of Lond, *Quarterly J*, 89 (1933); *Age*, 26 Feb 1900; *Argus*, 3 Oct 1904; *The Times*, 14 June 1932; E. Lim, Professor Gregory ... (MS, Univ Melb Archives, 1975).

J. F. LOVERING

GREIG, JANE STOCKS (1872-1939) and JANET LINDSAY (1874-1950), medical practitioners, CLARA PUELLA (1877-1957), tutor, GRATA FLOS MATILDA (1880-1958), barrister and solicitor, and STELLA FIDA (1889-1913), law graduate, were the daughters of Robert Lindsay Greig (1845-1904), merchant, and his wife Jane Stocks, née Macfarlane (1848-1902). The family included three sons, James Arthur (1882-1935), merchant, Ernest Howard (1884-1972), mining engineer, and Hector Maximus (1887-1979), merchant.

In 1889 Robert Greig and his family migrated to Australia from Scotland, arriving in Melbourne in the *Parramatta* on 20 April. With his younger brother James Patrick (1855-1917) who had arrived in 1886, Robert founded the textile firm of Greig Bros. Robert Greig was an ardent advocate of higher education for both sexes, and succeeded in imparting this ambition to his children. As early as 1887, when his daughters were still at school in Dundee, he wrote to James asking about the prospect of Jane and Janet studying medicine in Melbourne, and received an encouraging reply.

Jane Stocks Greig, known as Jean, was born on 12 June 1872 at Cupar, Fife, Scotland. After arriving in Melbourne she and her sister Janet attended Brunswick Ladies' College. They both entered the University of Melbourne to study medicine in 1891;

Jean graduated M.B. in 1895 and B.S. in 1896, with honours. She carried on a general practice for some years, mainly in Brighton and Fitzroy, and was appointed to the medical staff of the Citizens' Life Assurance Co. Ltd. A founder of the Queen Victoria Hospital in 1896, she was a member of the honorary medical staff until 1910. However, her main interests were in the field of public health. She received the diploma of public health at the University of Melbourne on 16 April 1910, the first woman to do so. On 1 November she was one of the first three medical officers appointed to the Victorian Education Department, and in 1929 became chief medical officer. She retired in 1937. Untiring in her efforts to improve the standards of health of Victorian schoolchildren, she played a key role in the introduction of regular dental inspection and treatment, and of special services for handicapped children. She was widely recognized as an excellent organizer and administrator. In 1925 the Commonwealth government appointed her a member of the royal commission on health; in 1929, with official accreditation, she visited New Zealand, North America and Britain, to report on methods of medical and dental inspection. She lectured on hygiene at the university and the Teachers' Training College in 1916-39.

Jean Greig was one of the founders of the Victorian Medical Women's Society (1896) and represented that body on the council of the Victorian branch of the British Medical Association. She was president of the Victorian Women Graduates' Association, secretary of the Victorian branch of the Health Association of Australasia, and active in the Town Planning Commission, the Victorian Baby Health Centres Association, the Victorian Bush Nursing Association, the Midwives' Board and the Council of Public Education. Her reports and articles, published in the *Medical Journal of Australia* between 1919 and 1937, received favourable overseas notice. She died of cancer in hospital at Richmond, Melbourne, on 16 September 1939.

Janet, known as Jenny, was born on 8 August 1874 at Broughty Ferry, Scotland. She graduated M.B., B.S. with honours in 1895. Her high place in the honours list would normally have entitled her to an appointment to the resident staff of the (Royal) Melbourne Hospital, but there was much opposition to the appointment of women. The question was hotly debated, and finally Janet Greig and Freda Gamble were appointed. After the successful completion of her residency Janet commenced private practice in Fitzroy, where she lived for many years. Later she practised as a consulting physician in Collins Street for over thirty years. She was a founder of the Queen

Victoria Hospital and when she retired in 1948 had been an active member of the honorary medical staff for fifty-two years. In 1937 the hospital named its new pathology block after her.

Janet Greig is recognized as the first woman anaesthetist in Victoria: she was honorary anaesthetist at the Women's Hospital in Melbourne from 1900 to 1917, honorary assistant anaesthetist at the Melbourne Hospital in 1903 and was admitted as a member of the Royal Australasian College of Physicians in 1940. She was a foundation member of the Lyceum Club in 1912. She demanded high standards of herself, and did not spare herself in her work. Forthright and determined, she was uninterested in frivolities or luxuries, but was always generous and kind and devoted to her patients. She died in London on 18 October 1950 while on a visit.

Clara Puella was born on 23 December 1877 at Broughty Ferry. She was educated at Presbyterian Ladies' College, Melbourne and matriculated in 1897. She studied for the degree of B.Sc. at the university from 1898 to 1901 but did not complete the course. In 1904 she opened a coaching college for university students in The Block, Collins Street, and engaged the services of her women graduate friends as specialist tutors. Later she was joined by her friend Jessie Webb [q.v.]. On 11 October 1910 at Brighton, with Presbyterian forms, she married Clement Alfred Hack (1877-1930) patent attorney, grandson of J. B. Hack [q.v.1]. She died at Brighton on 9 June 1957 survived by one of her two sons and a daughter.

Grata Flos Matilda, known as Flos, was born on 7 November 1880 at Broughty Ferry. She attended P.L.C. between 1894 and 1896 and, having decided on a legal career when still at school, enrolled at the university in 1897 for arts and law, the first woman to enter the law faculty. Male law students greeted her advent with some raillery, but voted in her first year that women should be admitted to practice. Completing her pass arts degree in 1900 (and formally graduating in 1904), she graduated LL.B. on 28 March 1903, the first woman in Victoria to do so, with third class honours, second in her year. In April, through her efforts and those of her friends, the Victorian parliament passed what was dubbed the 'Flos Greig Enabling Bill', to remove 'some anomalies in the law relating to women' thus permitting her (and subsequent women) to be admitted to legal practice. After thorough articles with Frank Cornwall, she was admitted on 1 August 1905 thus becoming the first woman to enter the legal profession in Australia.

Her realism led her, as a pioneer, to practise as a solicitor rather than a barrister. Self-employed in her early professional years, Flos drafted for the Woman's Christian Temperance Union amendments to the bill which passed into law as the Children's Court Act, 1906. She apparently worked later as an employee solicitor, and spent some dozen years in the office of Paul Mc-Swiney at Wangaratta before her retirement in 1942.

In her years at Wangaratta, from which she explored the countryside in a 'Baby' Austin tourer, she actively supported the extension of adult education facilities to the area. In the 1930s, through altruism and dissatisfaction with the existing economic order, she was a serious student and advocate of Douglas Credit. A frequent and intrepid Eastern traveller from an early date, Flos Greig developed an interest in Asian religions and customs, and lectured with lantern slides about her journeys. She lived in retirement at Rosebud for some years before her death at Moorabbin on 31 December 1958. Kindly, involved and articulate, Flos Greig was an important trail-blazer.

Stella Fida, known as Fida, was born on 3 December 1889 at North Carlton, Melbourne. She graduated from the University of Melbourne with a pass LL.B. degree on 8 April 1911. Unhappily, she died of tuberculosis on 4 December 1913, aged 24.

G. H. Swinburne, *The Queen Victoria Memorial Hospital* (Melb, 1951); M. O. Reid, *The ladies came to stay* (Melb, 1960); Education Dept (Vic), *Vision and realisation*, L. J. Blake (ed) (Melb, 1973); R. Campbell, *A history of the Melbourne Law School, 1857 to 1973* (Melb, 1977); M. Hutton Neve, *This mad folly* (Syd, 1980); *MJA*, Feb 1940, May 1953; *Law Inst J*, Dec 1975; *Weekly Times* (Melb), 15 July 1899; *Table Talk*, 8, 14 Dec 1899, 16 Apr 1903, 18 May 1905; *Australasian*, 5 Aug 1905; *Age*, 19 Sept 1939, 21 Oct 1950, 3 Jan 1959; *Argus*, 3 Aug 1937, 19 Sept 1939; G. Wilson, Dr Janet Lindsay Greig (paper delivered to Roy Aust College of Surgeons, Melb, May 1967); family information.

RUTH CAMPBELL
J. BARTON HACK

GRESSWELL, DAN ASTLEY (1853-1904), public health administrator, was born on 11 September 1853 at Louth, Lincolnshire, England, second of eight sons and seven daughters of Dan Gresswell, veterinarian, and his wife Ann, née Beastall. Six of the sons became prominent in medicine or the veterinary profession. Dan senior was elected fellow of the Royal College of Veterinary Surgeons for original researches and was active in local politics promoting sanitary improvements.

Dan Astley matriculated in 1871 at Oxford and won a scholarship to Christ Church to read physical sciences (B.A., 1875). After studying physiology in Germany at Würzburg and Bonn, he entered St Bartholomew's (Bart's) Hospital and in 1881 graduated M.B. (Oxon.) and M.R.C.S. (London); he gained the Cambridge Sanitary Science Certificate in 1884.

After graduation in 1881 he spent nine months at Stockwell Asylum Board Hospital (returning in 1886-87) and a year as house physician at Bart's. Then, to determine the effects of climate on the communicable diseases, he visited South Africa. Next he became surgeon-superintendent to the South Australian Emigration Service and spent three months in 1883 visiting the chief cities of Australia. On 27 November 1883 at Christ Church, Adelaide, he married Agnes Neill.

On his return to England Gresswell was an assistant demonstrator at Bart's, then worked as temporary medical inspector for the Local Government Board before investigating the sanitary state of the major cities of Europe. In 1889 he was awarded M.D. (Oxon.) for his thesis, 'A contribution to the natural history of scarlatina . . .', with a recommendation, acted on by the university in 1890, that it be published. He received M.D. (Melb.) *ad eund.* in 1891.

In 1889 he was appointed medical inspector of the new Victorian Board of Public Health, established as the outcome of a royal commission into the sanitary state of Melbourne. Under the amending Public Health Act of 1889 responsibility for health matters devolved on the local councils. As the source of the board's expertise Gresswell came to the job supremely well trained and with the highest recommendations. His handling of the influenza epidemic raging in Victoria when he arrived in March 1890, won him the gratitude of the premier, the respect of the medical profession and the lasting confidence of the public.

In October he presented his 'Report on the sanitary condition and sanitary administration of Melbourne and its suburbs', showing Melbourne to be most insalubrious. A key concept of the report was the employment by local authorities of salaried full-time medical officers of health. Major objectives were the establishment of at least one infectious diseases hospital; control of tuberculosis through elimination of tubercular cattle by veterinarians; isolation and treatment of patients in special sanatoriums (the first was established in 1903); and education in management of sputa. The DO NOT SPIT signs built into the walls of many public buildings and the Gresswell Sanatorium are memorials to his campaigns. Gresswell had used his inquiry to meet and educate the local councils because he be-

lieved in education rather than legal coercion. He made effective use of widely distributed pamphlets to achieve sanitary reform. The report also stressed the need for
a pure water-supply, underground sewerage (with a double pan system in the interim) and specific measures to ensure un-
adulterated food and drink. From the mid-
1890s he drafted a series of bills to achieve
these purposes, including the Meat Supervision (1900), Wine Adulteration (1900) and
Pure Food (1905) Acts, which when enacted
made Victoria a leader in this area. Some
of his recommendations for milk handling
(1896) were passed in 1905 but compulsory
pasteurization against tuberculosis and typhoid was delayed until 1943.

The 1889 Health Act had excluded any
doctor from chairmanship of the Board of
Public Health. The 1894 debates to amend
the Act and allow for Gresswell's appointment reveal him as outstandingly competent and efficient, unfailingly courteous
and humane, and very highly esteemed by
all those who knew or worked with him.

The decline in Victorian death rates between 1890 and 1904 must be attributed in
part to Gresswell. In addition, Victoria's
relative immunity to the 1900 plague outbreak also testified to his foresight and efficiency. He demonstrated what an exceptional administrator could achieve despite
defective legislation. In spite of his youthful
appearance the medical profession acknowledged his zeal and special knowledge
and, impressed by his clear, incisive and
eminently practical remarks and his sanitary inventions, elected him president of the
British Medical Association, Victorian
branch, as early as 1893.

In 1896 Gresswell initiated and chaired
the first of the intercolonial quarantine conferences. He co-authored the Royal Society
of Victoria's 1892 report on cremation and
on 11 December ignited the first authorized
cremation in the colony, the body of a Chinese leper. His work was so very much his
life that he took no holidays. Yet he possessed a gentle sense of humour. His only
relaxations seem to have been music and
various hospital balls, although at Oxford
he had been a noted sculler. After smelling
the Yarra he forswore further rowing.

In November 1898 Gresswell suffered a
severe attack of jaundice from which he
never fully recovered. He died of septicaemia on 10 December 1904, survived by
his wife; they had no children. He was buried
in the Anglican section of Boroondara cemetery.

E. Ford, *Bibliography of Australian medicine
1790-1900* (Syd, 1976); Roy Com on charitable insti-
tutions, *PP* (Vic), 1892, 4, p 497, 1457; Procs of the
A'sian quarantine conference of Melb, Vic, *PP*
(Vic), 1896, 4; *PD* (Vic), 1894, p 889, 958; *A'sian
Medical Gazette*, and *Intercol Medical J of A'sia*, 20
Dec 1904; *Health*, 2 Jan 1924; *Age*, and *Argus*, 12
Dec 1904; *Weekly Times*, 17, 24 Dec 1904.

DIANA DYASON

GREVILLE, HENRIETTA (1861-1964),
labour organizer, was born on 9 October
1861 at Dunedin, New Zealand, fourth child
of Australian-born parents Henry Wyse and
his wife Rebecca, née Hutchinson. Henry,
son of ex-convict Isaac Wyse, had taken his
wife and family to New Zealand in a vain
search for gold. In 1866 they moved to Victoria, settling at Howlong, New South
Wales, in 1868. Although with very little formal education, Henrietta at 17 was briefly
a schoolteacher, and helped in her aunt's
hotel at Albury, until she married John
Collins, jeweller, at Albury Registry Office
on 3 August 1881. The marriage failed and
in 1889 she returned with her four children
to her parents' farm at Temora. Her husband died later in Western Australia.

To support her family Henrietta worked
as a seamstress, later establishing refreshment rooms in the town. Forced by the depression of the 1890s to close, she took her
family to the goldfields at West Wyalong;
she pegged out a claim, sold meals to the
miners and helped to establish a branch of
the Political Labor League.

Here at the registry office on 30 July 1894
she married Hector Greville, a miner and
union organizer. A well-educated socialist,
he supported her political activity, and the
marriage was a very happy one. Lack of permanent work kept them moving through
the mining districts of western New South
Wales, Henrietta helping to support them
by cooking and sewing. She became an organizer for the Australian Workers' Union;
later she organized the Women Workers'
Union and for some time acted as its delegate at the Trades and Labor Council. In
1902 the family spent some time in Sydney
and Henrietta became part of the radical
group centred around Bertha McNamara's
[q.v.] bookshop in Castlereagh Street. In
1908 she became an organizer for the White
Workers' Union and attacked the working
conditions and wages of female shirt-
makers. For many years she was an organizer for the Labor Party, a member of the
Labor Women's Central Organising Committee and the Labor Women's Advisory
Council. In 1916-17 she campaigned against
conscription. As a Labor candidate she was
defeated for the Federal seat of Wentworth
in 1917 and the State seat of Vaucluse in
1927. From the mid-1920s she was closely
associated with Marion Piddington [q.v.]
and sex education.

In 1914 Henrietta had joined the first tutorial class of the Workers' Educational Association of New South Wales and studied economics for two years. She became branch secretary at Lithgow in 1918, a member of the executive in 1919 and the first woman president in 1920. She remained active in the association and when aged 94 directed a group of women studying sex hygiene.

Hector Greville died in Sydney in 1938, but Henrietta continued her political activities. In 1945 she became a life-member of the Union of Australian Women. In her later years she identified more with the Communist Party of Australia, managing one of its bookshops at Rockdale and helping on the Release Sharkey Committee. In the 1940s she also worked for the Rockdale branch of the Original Old Age and Invalid Pensioners' Association. In January 1958 she was appointed M.B.E.

Henrietta Greville died in hospital at Lakemba on 29 August 1964 and was cremated without religious rites. She was survived by two sons and a daughter of her second marriage. Full of energy and vitality, her life was dedicated to making 'a better world . . . a world of peace'. Her work was commemorated when a block of pensioners' units was named after her in 1964.

Henrietta Greville: veteran Labor pioneer (Syd, 1958); J. Tabberer, *The times of Henrietta* (Syd, 1970); *Aust Highway*, May 1920, Apr, June 1921, Feb 1924, May, Dec 1925; *Aust Worker*, 3 May, 19, 26 Apr 1917; *West Wyalong Advocate*, 6 Jan 1947, *SMH*, 22 Oct 1949, 6 Nov 1955, 1 Jan, 1 Oct 1958, 1 Oct 1961, 31 Aug, 1 Sept 1964; Workers Educational Assn of NSW, Annual Report, 31 Dec 1917-23 (held at head office, Syd).

MARY VINTER

GRICE, SIR JOHN (1850-1935), businessman, was born on 6 October 1850 in Melbourne, fourth son of Richard Grice [q.v.4] and his wife Anne Lavinia, née Hibberson. He was educated at Melbourne Church of England Grammar School in 1861-66 and then at the newly opened Wesley College, where he won a prize as the first boy from Wesley to matriculate with credit at the University of Melbourne.

Grice graduated LL.B. in 1871 and B.A. in 1872. He founded the University Boat Club, rowed in the first intervarsity boat race (1870) and was a member of an intercolonial four-oared crew in 1872. Although he was admitted to the Bar in 1872 he joined the family firm of Grice, Sumner & Co. He spent some nine years in South Australia as director of the shipping firm Ormerod & Co.

of Robe, Kingston and Naracoorte (from July 1878 known as John Grice & Co.). On 8 May 1878 at St John's Church, Toorak, he married Mary Anne, daughter of David Power of Moorak, Mount Gambier, South Australia.

After his father's death in 1882 Grice returned to Melbourne and the family business. In 1887 he joined the board of the National Bank of Australasia. He was active in the crisis of 1893 when the bank's payments to depositors were suspended for eight weeks, salaries reduced and staff retrenched. As chairman from 1906 he combined constant demands for caution in the bank's activities with a strong nineteenth-century commitment to *laissez-faire* economics. He was completely opposed to the establishment of a central banking authority. He resented the power given to the Commonwealth Bank in 1929 to acquire compulsorily all the gold reserves of the trading banks. In 1932 he resigned as chairman but remained on the board until his death.

As chairman of directors of the Metropolitan Gas Co. from 1901, Grice also attracted publicity. In the 1920s he was prominent in combating threats to nationalize the company. During a protracted strike of 1920 the company took a strong stand, articulated in the press by Grice, against the striking workers over a pay claim. His attitude to employees' demands, which was also reflected in his attempts to prevent the formation of a bank officers' union in 1920, did not make him popular with those who worked for the companies he directed. As a fellow board-member, however, he was considered an honest, astute advocate who could drive a hard bargain, yet command respect.

Grice was also chairman of directors of the Dunlop Rubber Co. of Australasia Ltd (later Dunlop Perdriau [q.v.] Rubber Co.), the Trustees, Executors & Agency Co. Ltd, the Emu Bay Railway Co. Ltd, North British & Mercantile Insurance Co. Ltd, Howard Smith [q.v.6] Ltd, the New Zealand Loan and Mercantile Agency Co. Ltd and the Australian Glass Manufacturers Co. Ltd. He had interests in Queensland as director of the Portland Downs and Malvern Hills pastoral companies.

In 1888 Grice had been elected to the Council of the University of Melbourne. He became vice-chancellor in 1918 at a time when the council felt his business experience would be useful in the task of overcoming financial difficulties. He donated £2000 to the university in 1920 and later gave gifts to the school of architecture; his portrait, painted by Longstaff [q.v.] in 1927, now hangs in that department.

Like his father, Grice was long associated

with the (Royal) Melbourne Hospital. He took an active part in its affairs as a member of its committee of management from 1886 and as president in 1905-18. As the first voluntary treasurer of the Victorian branch of the Red Cross, Grice contributed to the war effort; these services were recognized by his knighthood in 1917. He remained interested in Wesley College; when in 1918 he was elected president of the old boys' association he marked the occasion by establishing the Grice scholarship for sons of officers who had been killed in World War I.

Family life was centred on Coolullah, South Yarra, and Coolangatta, his holiday home at Mount Macedon. Of his six surviving children, the eldest son was killed in the South African War and another died of wounds in World War I. Twins John and James entered the medical and engineering professions. Elsa helped to found the Country Women's Association in Australia after World War I.

Grice is remembered by his descendants as fairly remote and rather stern. No doubt time spent with family was reduced by work commitments, although friends were frequently contacted at the Melbourne Club, either for formal dinners, or to play a rubber or two of bridge.

After a period of slowly failing health, Sir John Grice died at South Yarra on 27 February 1935 and was buried in St Kilda cemetery. His wife had predeceased him. His estate was sworn for probate at about £40 000.

A. Henderson (ed), *Early pioneer families of Victoria and Riverina* (Melb, 1936); G. Blainey, *Gold and paper* (Melb, 1958); *Age*, 18 June 1920, 28 Feb 1935; *Argus*, 28 Feb 1935; Grice papers (Univ Melb Archives); family information. JUDITH TYERS

GRIEN, HENRI; *see* DE ROUGEMENT, LOUIS

GRIEVE, ROBERT CUTHBERT (1889-1957), soldier and businessman, was born on 19 June 1889 at Brighton, Melbourne, son of John Grieve, clerk and later warehouseman, and his wife Annie Deas, née Brown, both Victorian-born. Educated at Caulfield Grammar School and Wesley College, he became an interstate commercial traveller in the softgoods trade. On enlistment in the Australian Imperial Force on 16 June 1915, after nine months service in the Victorian Rangers, he was posted to the 37th Battalion. He was commissioned as a second lieutenant on 17 January 1916 and promoted lieutenant on 1 May; a month later the bat-

talion embarked for training in England. When the 10th Light Trench Mortar Battery was organized there Grieve was seconded to it in January 1917 but on 19 April he rejoined the 37th Battalion in France, receiving his captaincy and the command of 'A' Company. The appointment was well received by his fellow soldiers who respected his quiet, understanding style of command.

The 37th Battalion took part in no major action, although its strength had been tested in several sharp raids, until the battle of Messines in June. Grieve was to receive the Victoria Cross for gallantry in this attack. Before the battle the unit made a detailed study of its role and Grieve ensured that his men were as fully informed as possible. On the night of 6 June the 37th began its approach march and soon suffered an intensive gas-attack. Just before dawn it reached its assembly trenches, moved about 11 a.m. towards its objective and came under heavy shell-fire; the resulting casualties, with those of the previous night, seriously depleted its strength.

In the afternoon of 7 June, Grieve's company was in position on the battalion's left flank. In front of its objective lay a thick band of wire and as the company ran through several gaps it came under intense fire from a German pillbox. An attempt to mortar this strong point was unsuccessful. Grieve, the only unwounded officer in 'A' Company, decided to attack the pillbox alone. Taking a supply of Mills bombs he dashed forward, taking cover wherever possible. His well-aimed grenades silenced some of the gunners, allowing him time to reach the nearby trench and bomb the rest of the machine-gun crew. His company was then able to advance and had scarcely gained its objective when a sniper's bullet severely wounded Grieve in the shoulder. He was the first member of the 3rd Division to win the Victoria Cross.

He was evacuated to England and returned to his unit on 29 October but soon afterwards suffered acute trench nephritis and double pneumonia and was invalided to Australia in May 1918. On 7 August, at Scots Church, Sydney, he married Sister May Isabel Bowman of the Australian Army Nursing Service who had nursed him during his illness. She died some years later and there were no children of the marriage. After demobilization Grieve established the business of Grieve, Gardner & Co., softgoods warehousemen, in Flinders Lane Melbourne, and was managing director until 4 October 1957 when he died of cardiac failure; he had suffered from nephritis since 1917. He was buried with military honours in Springvale cemetery. He was a staunch supporter of Wesley College to which his Victoria Cross was presented in 1959.

The history of Wesley College 1865-1919 (Melb, 1921); C. E. W. Bean, *The A.I.F. in France, 1917* (Syd, 1933); N. G. McNicol, *The Thirty Seventh: history of the 37th Battalion AIF* (Melb, 1936); L. Wigmore (ed), *They dared mightily* (Canb, 1963); *London Gazette*, 2 Aug 1917; *Reveille* (Syd), June 1937, Sept 1968; *Mufti*, Oct 1937, Nov 1957; *Sydney Mail*, 14 Aug 1918; *Age*, 5 Oct 1957; War diary, 37th Battalion AIF, *and* Personal narrative of R. C. Grieve (A. G. Butler Collection, AWM).

DARRYL MCINTYRE

GRIFFEN FOLEY, JAMES JOSEPH (1872-1924), journalist, singer and music critic, was born at Hyderabad, India (Pakistan), only son of Patrick James Foley, Indian army, and his wife Catherine, née Griffen—both from Templemore, Tipperary, Ireland. Brought up and educated in Ireland, he studied music in England, where he had experience in cathedral work, and in Italy, becoming fluent in Italian. A bass, he reputedly came to Australia about 1894, with a visiting opera company and had to abandon the stage after an accident during a performance.

Settling in Sydney, Griffen Foley taught singing and voice production; his most noted pupil was Alfred O'Shea [q.v.]. On 3 April 1904, he married Mary Theresa Donnelly. He continued to sing in concerts, often with his wife, his pupils and various small ensembles which he formed and trained, such as the Griffen Foley choristers and the Euterpean Society. A devout Catholic, he was an authority on ecclesiastical music, especially the masses of Palestrina, Gregorian chant and plain-song. He devoted much effort to raising the standard of church music, and was choirmaster to several churches, including All Saints Anglican Church, Woollahra. His wife died childless in 1908; on 28 December 1910 he married a Canadian typist, Lilla Louise Lebrun Marsh.

In 1909 Griffen Foley had become music critic for the *Star* and was employed by the *Sun* from its foundation in 1910. For it he wrote the popular columns 'Crotchets and Quavers' and 'Plays and Players' and, with Howard Ashton [q.v.7] and Henry Pryce, contributed to the regular popular comedy feature 'The Moving Picture Show'. Griffen Foley was also the Sydney correspondent for the *Australian Musical News*, and Australian correspondent for the English *Musical Times* and the American *Musical Courier*. His friends included the singers Antonia Delores (Trebelli), John McCormack and Melba [q.v.], who claimed that Griffen Foley 'was more than a critic: he was an inspiration. When I read what Griffen Foley had to say about me I used to feel as though he had, in some subtle way, himself thrown a new light on my own interpretations'. Fellow critic G. de Cairos Rego believed that Griffen Foley 'did a world of good in peppering away at the professional voice-destroyer; of the blind leading the blind'. Since some of the 'destroyers' were prominent in Sydney musical education—and he made no secret of their identity—he had enemies; they were compounded when on Melba's advice he declined to join the staff of the New South Wales State Conservatorium of Music.

Griffen Foley died of cancer at his home at Chatswood on 12 May 1924 and was buried in the Catholic section of Northern Suburbs cemetery. He was survived by his second wife, and their son and three daughters, for whom Melba organized a benefit concert. His wife studied beauty culture and the treatment of hair with the Ogilvie sisters in New York and as 'Louise Le Brun' opened an American-style beauty and hair-dressing salon next door to the Hotel Australia in 1926. His son John Raymond was well known as a journalist and film and theatre critic. His sister Agnes (1865-1932), as Mother St John of the Cross, was prioress of the Convent of Carmel in Sydney and later founded and directed the Order's Melbourne house.

Aust Musical News, 2 June 1924, p 25; *Woman's World*, 1 Apr 1926, p 279; *SMH*, 7 Mar 1903, 14, 15 May 1924; *Sun* (Syd), 13, 14, 17 May, 2 Aug 1924; family information.

JOHN CARMODY

GRIFFIN, WALTER BURLEY (1876-1937), architect, landscape architect and designer of Canberra, was born on 24 November 1876 at Maywood, near Chicago, United States of America, eldest of four children of George Walter Griffin, insurance agent, and his wife Estelle Melvina, née Griffin. Griffin attended high school at Oak Park, graduated B.Sc. from Nathan Ricker's renowned school of architecture at the University of Illinois in 1899 and was admitted as an associate of the American Institute of Architects.

He first worked as a casual employee of Dwight Heald Perkins and other architects in Chicago's Steinway Hall, then in 1901-06 as an associate of Frank Lloyd Wright at Oak Park. He also undertook private commissions, the most notable of which were the Emery house (1903) and the landscape designs for the grounds of the state normal schools of Eastern Illinois (1901) and Northern Illinois (1906). Griffin started his own practice in Steinway Hall in 1906 and by 1910, when his work was featured in the *Architectural Record*, was becoming recognized as a practitioner of what eventually became known as the Prairie School of architecture.

On 29 June 1911 Griffin married 40-year-old MARION LUCY MAHONY (1871-1961), daughter of an Irish-born schoolteacher. They had no children. Tall, with a tomahawk profile and theatrical demeanour, she was the second woman to graduate in architecture from the Massachusetts Institute of Technology, in 1894. Wright, with whom she worked until 1909, had a high regard for her talents as a draughtsman, illustrator and designer of furnishings. After Wright absconded to Europe with Mrs Cheney, Marion joined the office of Hermann von Holst, with responsibility for Wright's uncompleted commissions. Her hero-worship of Wright was transferred to Griffin.

They were married two months after the international competition for the design of the new Federal capital of Australia was announced. Assisted by others in Steinway Hall, including Roy Alstan Lippincott—who soon married Griffin's sister, Genevieve—and George Elgh (all of whom joined the Griffins in Australia in 1914), Marion produced the elegant set of drawings illustrating Griffin's ideas. He won the competition in May 1912. She later claimed that it was only her importunings that persuaded him to complete the design, a grandly conceived arrangement for a national capital of 75 000, by the time required. Taking advantage of the topography within and around the splendid site, the plan is a masterly derivation from—and an extension of—the design ideas which Griffin had observed in the Chicago Fair (1893), the McMillan plan for Washington (1901), the Burnham and Bennett plan for Chicago (1909) and other work of their principal author, the Chicago architect Daniel Hudson Burnham, an outstanding figure in the City Beautiful movement.

Griffin and his winning design generated prolonged and bitter controversies. King O'Malley [q.v.], the fustian minister for home affairs, appointed a reviewing board of departmental officers who produced their own plan, a grotesque scheme that was widely condemned. In 1913 after the fall of the Fisher [q.v.8] government, W. H. Kelly [q.v.], acting minister for home affairs, invited Griffin to consult with the board. Kelly was completely won over by Griffin's missionary zeal and in October had him appointed Federal capital director of design and construction, a half-time post, for three years. The terms of the contract, drawn up by Griffin himself and intended to place him

in effective control, were humiliating to the officers of the former departmental board, in particular the chairman, Colonel David Miller, head of the Department of Home Affairs and Lieut-Colonel Percy Thomas Owen [qq.v.], director-general of Commonwealth works. Believing that many features of Griffin's plan were vastly extravagant and incapable of realization, they nevertheless pressed on, to Griffin's chagrin, with the design and construction of the engineering works to serve the future city. In September 1914 when the Fisher government returned to power, another new minister, W. O. Archibald [q.v.7], baffled by having to deal with 'two staffs of experts', demanded from Griffin, whom he described as a 'Yankee bounder', his long-promised 'amended plan', which was presented in March 1915. That month the Parliamentary Standing Committee on Public Works rejected Griffin's peculiar proposals for the sewerage system, and in November 1916 his extensive lakes scheme was rejected in favour of the more feasible proposals recommended by Owen. Griffin's railway proposals were not opposed, but no railway through the city was ever built.

The return of O'Malley as minister for home affairs under Hughes [q.v.] in October 1915, this time as a friend and ally, had improved Griffin's prospects. In April 1916 O'Malley persuaded cabinet to renew Griffin's contract for a further three years. With O'Malley's connivance, William Webster [q.v.], the postmaster-general, made a virulent attack in parliament on the officers responsible for the project. A royal commissioner, Wilfred Blacket [q.v.7], K.C., was appointed to inquire. For seven months from July 1916 Webster himself conducted what amounted to a case for the prosecution; Owen was, perforce, counsel for the defence. The commissioner's findings, presented in six reports in March and April 1917, were more remarkable for their discursiveness than their prudence. Blacket held Griffin blameless and found the former minister, Archibald, and certain unnamed officers guilty of forming 'a combination . . . hostile to Mr Griffin and to his design for the city'. He judged that many engineering decisions on water supply and sewerage were wrong, and made scathing observations about inefficient management and wasteful expenditure. He held the extreme view that Archibald should have 'either cancelled Griffin's contract and reverted to the design of the Departmental Board, or else have allowed Mr Griffin's contract to be performed and his design carried out'.

Prime Minister Hughes and his new Nationalist government, more concerned with Australia's wartime problems, ap-

peared unimpressed with Blacket's findings. The works branch of Home Affairs had
already been made a separate Department
of Works and Railways (with Miller as its
permanent head) during the course of the
inquiry and the political career of O'Malley,
Griffin's strongest supporter, had ended
with his electoral defeat in May 1917. That
year Griffin had the survey of the main axial
lines of the city completed and in 1918 produced his final plan, showing the lakes
exactly as he wanted them. But apart from
tree-planting, little work was carried out on
the site in the remaining years of Griffin's
directorship. By 1920, when the Hughes
government was importuned to meet the
constitutional requirement to establish Canberra as the seat of government, it had become apparent that by training and temperament Griffin could not fulfil the
executive role required. Offered a place on
the Federal Capital Advisory Committee
under the chairmanship of (Sir) John Sulman [q.v.], he printed a resounding statement of the reasons for his refusal and circulated it, with copies of the findings of the
Blacket commission and his correspondence
with the prime minister, to newspapers and
periodicals throughout Australia.

The Sulman committee was instructed by
the minister for works, Littleton Ernest
Groom [q.v.], to proceed 'on the basis of the
acceptance of the plan of the lay-out of the
Federal Capital by Mr W. B. Griffin'. In
1925, when an independent Federal Capital
Commission was established with (Sir) John
Henry Butters [q.v.7] as chairman (and
Owen as its chief engineer), Groom, then
attorney-general, introduced the requirement that Griffin's plan should be published
in the *Government Gazette*, and any variation to it be open to disallowance by parliament. In 1928 Griffin asserted that the commission 'had violated the aesthetic, social
and economic principles in almost every act
and [his] details for roads and services had
not even been referred to in the actual work'.
But Griffin's ideas were respected to the extent that they were judged feasible. The
lakes scheme, as completed in 1964, designed without regard to the conflicts of
fifty years before, conforms closely to the
proposals of the otherwise discredited
board's plan.

Throughout his seven turbulent years as
part-time Federal director Griffin was active in private practice: for three years from
1914 in a long-distance Chicago partnership
with Francis Barry Byrne, a former Oak
Park colleague; until June 1915 in a short-
lived partnership with J. Burcham Clamp
[q.v.8] in Sydney; and from 1915 in his own
office in Melbourne, with Marion, Lippincott and Elgh, who was soon to be replaced

by an Australian, Edward Fielder Billson.
Griffin's letterhead from that time carried
the legend, 'Architect and Landscape Architect — Sydney - Melbourne - Chicago'. He
undertook numerous site-planning commissions in the United States and Australia,
only a few of which were carried out. The
most notable were the Rock Crest-Rock
Glen community in Mason City, Iowa,
where Griffin designed some distinguished
houses, the town plans for Griffith and Leeton, New South Wales, and the Summit and
Glenard estates at Eaglemont, Melbourne.
At Eaglemont the Griffins built the only
house designed for themselves, a modest
'one-room' dwelling constructed in Knit-
lock, a precast concrete building block,
which Griffin had patented in 1917.

His first successful architectural commission in Australia was a reconstruction,
in 1916, for the Café Australia, Melbourne,
a *tour de force* in interior design with furniture and decoration designed by Marion.
The most notable building completed in
these early years was Newman College, University of Melbourne, in 1917, a design in
which Lippincott played a major part. At the
end of his Federal capital appointment in
1920 Griffin remained in practice in Melbourne. His most important commissions
were a seven-storey office building, Leonard
House (1924), notable for its glazed curtain-
wall facade, and the Capitol Theatre (1924),
a richly ornamented cinema within an
eleven-storey office block. Capitol House
was the most substantial and most celebrated building of his career. The cinema,
with its geometrically modelled ceiling,
richly illuminated with concealed lighting,
was saved from demolition and partly restored in 1965.

In 1920 Griffin formed the Greater Sydney Development Association Ltd to build
residential estates on three picturesque
headlands on Sydney's Middle Harbour.
The first estate, Castlecrag, designed to retain the character of the natural landscape,
was begun in 1921 with several of Griffin's
distinctive houses of rock and concrete intended to demonstrate the style of house lot-
purchasers would be required to build.
Although revered by later generations, the
houses at the time were widely regarded as
eccentric; they tended to leak. By 1937 only
nineteen houses, sixteen of them designed
by Griffin, had been built on the 340 lots.
Griffin moved from Melbourne to Castlecrag in 1924, and his junior partner, Eric
Milton Nicholls, followed in 1932. From
1929 the partnership survived almost
entirely on commissions for the design of
municipal incinerator buildings for the
Reverberatory Incinerator & Engineering
Co. Twelve were completed in the four east-

ern States. All were of distinctive design and two have been preserved by conversion; one near Castlecrag is a restaurant, another at Ipswich, Queensland, a community theatre.

Marion throughout encouraged Griffin in the role of a missionary, claiming the divine right of the gifted designer to have his own way. From time to time she produced superbly presented decorative drawings, colour-rendered on fabric, of his building designs; but her principal role at Castlecrag was as a community leader, organizing a variety of cultural activities from ballet classes to classical drama, staged in a rock-gully adapted to serve as an amphitheatre. Both Walter and Marion were interested in Theosophy until, in 1930, they were attracted to Anthroposophy, Rudolf Steiner's science of the spirit, which Marion extended to highly personal forms of mysticism.

Griffin was invited to design a library for the University of Lucknow and left for India in October 1935. Nothing came of this project but he was engaged as the designer of the United Provinces Exhibition of Industry and Agriculture in Lucknow and ran into troubles similar to those he had encountered with Canberra. Only a small part of his imaginative and extravagant scheme was carried out. But he and Marion were entranced by India and enthusiastically worked together on numerous designs for palaces and bungalows. Few of them were used, but one building commissioned to house the *Pioneer* newspaper was completed after his death.

Griffin died of peritonitis on 11 February 1937 in Lucknow five days after an operation, and was buried there. Marion, dissuaded from an attempt to carry on his work in India, returned briefly to Castlecrag where it was established that Griffin had left heavy debts. While unsuccessfully attempting to practise in Chicago, she wrote a disjointed account of her life with Griffin. The book-length typescript, 'The Magic of America', is in four parts, 'The Empirial [sic] Battle' (India), 'The Federal Battle' (Canberra), 'The Municipal Battle' (Castlecrag) and the 'Individual Battle'. It unwittingly helps to explain how her influence contributed to the difficulties Griffin had in his dealings with people and why he remained an expatriate.

Although at the time of his death Griffin might have been judged a failure, later generations regard his designs and ideas with a respect which would have astounded his contemporaries, and his surviving buildings are valued as part of Australia's architectural history. In 1963, the fiftieth anniversary of the naming of Canberra, a commemorative postage stamp was issued with his portrait. The Canberra lake, built in the

form to which he was so strongly opposed, was given his name in 1964. A competition for the design of a memorial, on Mount Ainslie overlooking the city, to mark the centenary of his birth was won by an American entry, but following a change of government in 1975, and with strong echoes of similar changes fifty years earlier, the project was 'deferred'.

D. L. Johnson, *Canberra and Walter Burley Griffin: a bibliography of 1876 to 1976 and a guide to published sources* (Melb, 1980).

PETER HARRISON

GRIFFITH, ARTHUR HILL (1861-1946), teacher, politician and patent attorney, was born on 16 October 1861 at Gortmore Hall, Westmeath, Ireland, son of Arthur Griffith, solicitor, and his wife Hannah, née Cottingham. He migrated with his family to Melbourne in 1871 and went to Scotch College, matriculating in 1877. Self-reliant, he moved to Sydney in 1880, attended arts lectures at the university and taught at Sydney Grammar School in 1884-94. He excelled at sport: swimming, heavyweight boxing and rowing. He was awarded the medal of the National Shipwreck Relief Society of New South Wales for rescuing a man from the sea. In 1890-93 he was secretary of the New South Wales Lawn Tennis Association. In 1895 he founded the patent attorney firm of Griffith, Hassel & Griffith, and on 4 May 1899 he married Mildred Carrington Smith at All Saints Anglican Church, Petersham.

Griffith read much progressive literature and perceived the basic social problem of the late nineteenth century as 'the upheaval . . . against the grinding tyranny of industrial monopoly'. He wrote several letters to newspapers on it. By 1890 he was both a socialist and a republican; next year he welcomed the new Labor Party and soon joined it as its best-known representative of professional, middle-class colonists. In 1893 he published *The Labor platform: an exposition*, arguing that the programme was 'the only firm foundation . . . amid a wilderness of shifting creeds and jarring factions'. He demonstrated that the party had a place for educated radicals. Next year, answering a call for candidates in the country, he won the mining seat of Waratah in the Legislative Assembly; he was then an unequivocal 'Labor man', his commitment reinforced by his prickly, stiff-necked manner, combined paradoxically with much panache and some 'Celtic' romanticism. Sporting a full, aggressive moustache, he became one of Labor's best speakers, sarcastic and vigorous. He was a formidable man.

Griffith contributed to the structural growth of the Labor Party, and represented the parliamentarians at the conference in May 1895 that set up the Political Labor League to settle the competing claims for control of the Australian Labor Federation and the Labor Electoral League. He made his mark in parliament, debating with great skill, asking many questions, submitting private members' bills (having success with the Patents and Trade Marks Act, 1897). He became the party's expert on education. He helped Labor to retain its identity in its support of the Reid [q.v.] government in 1894-99; as secretary of caucus, he negotiated with (Sir) William Lyne [q.v.] in the deposition of Reid. Griffith was one of the unsuccessful ten Laborites nominated for the 1897 Federal Convention. At the 1899 party conference at Woonona he backed J. C. Watson [q.v.] to ensure that Labor would support the submission of the Federal Constitution to a referendum. Militarism was one of Griffith's aversions; with W. A. Holman [q.v.] he courted social and political disapproval in opposing the South African War, 1899-1902.

In 1903 Griffith resigned his seat to run for the Federal Senate. He failed but next year won the State seat of Sturt, a far-western mining electorate. The 1908-09 Broken Hill strike provoked him into strong protest in parliament, and he was suspended; whereupon he resigned on 3 November 1908, to be returned unopposed at the by-election on 13 November. Labor's need for suburban seats persuaded him to run for Annandale in 1913. He had become minister for public works in the first Labor cabinet in 1910, under J. S. T. McGowen [q.v.].

With Griffith taking the lead, the government began to set up state enterprises and to expand public works. Although several changes unsettled the cabinet, he retained his portfolio until March 1915 and inaugurated works worth over £4 million in his first eighteen months—compared to about £2.5 million in the three years of the preceding Wade [q.v.] ministry. Emphasis was put on the duplication of railway tracks. Reflecting his vision of development through enlightened and practical socialism, Griffith initiated state industries, including brick and pipe works, quarries, an engineering works and a building construction unit; and foreshadowed state monopolies in meat, bread, fish, liquor and petrol. In 1912 he prepared legislation to set up an iron and steel works in accordance with the Labor platform, but opposition in the Legislative Council, where the government, led by F. Flowers [q.v.8], was outnumbered by 70 to 13, and scarcity of finance held it up. Subsequently G. D. Delprat [q.v.8], on behalf of the Broken Hill

Proprietary Co. Ltd, negotiated successfully with Griffith to establish a works at Newcastle. The 1913 party conference censured the cabinet for it, but it proved a success.

With J. D. Fitzgerald [q.v.8], he complemented advanced professional opinion in proposals for a greater Sydney and for improved city traffic engineering. In 1913 he promoted J. J. C. Bradfield [q.v.7] as chief engineer for metropolitan railway construction.

The range and vigour of Griffith's activities disturbed those whose financial interests were affected, part of the general fears felt by conservatives at the government's programme. He became their main target. In parliament Wade and (Sir) T. Henley [q.v.] were the spearhead of the reaction, and Griffith developed a bitter distaste for them. Many charges of corruption were made against Griffith, two of which resulted in royal commissions, in 1912 and 1916, but nothing was proved. He interpreted the cause of the latter inquiry as the attempt of powerful international groups to prevent the State from forming a monopoly in oil. In 1916 he unsuccessfully sued a publican, H. Combellack, for libel.

In 1915 Griffith became minister of public instruction in Holman's cabinet. He introduced H. Verbrugghen [q.v.], the first director of the New South Wales State Conservatorium of Music, at a concert in November, and announced the provision of musical scholarships—he had made it possible for Verbrugghen to bring his own string quartet. Confronting the New South Wales branch of the British Medical Association, he improved the school clinic system; and in 1916 took the initiative in the passage of the Public Instruction (Amendment) Act. He planned the extension of the teaching of agriculture in high schools, and presciently fostered the training of aeroplane pilots, opening the State Aviation School at Richmond on 28 August.

Griffith saw World War I as a crusade against Germany for the preservation of civilization, demanding total support. He joined the Universal Service League in 1915 and next year refused to accept the Labor conference's direction to oppose conscription for overseas service, arguing that, as he had been elected on a party platform that was silent on it, he had the right to private judgment. But he was expelled. With his radicalism undimmed, he refused to consider joining Holman's National government, a coalition with Wade's Liberals. Griffith contested seats in 1917 and 1920 as independent Labor, but lost.

He did not agree that his expulsion was valid, nevertheless he applied for readmission at several annual conferences in the 1920s. In 1930 he was allowed back, but the 'militants', headed by J. S. Garden [q.v.8] and D. M. Grant [q.v.], whom Griffith had never conciliated, had the motion rescinded. When the State and Federal Labor branches split in 1931 he joined the latter as an executive member; he ran unsuccessfully for the Federal seat of Gwydir in 1934.

Originally a prohibitionist, Griffith came to champion Australian wines, and in 1932 was buying 'excellent claret and hock' for 5 s. per gallon. He retained his patent attorney business; he had set up the Patents Investigation Board in 1916; he became a full member of the Chartered Institute of Patent Agents, London, in 1917; president of the Institute of Patent Attorneys of Australia, in 1929 he was appointed to the Board of Examiners of Patent Attorneys for the Commonwealth. He was the first chairman (1911) of the Murrumbidgee Irrigation Trust and the town of Griffith was named after him. In the 1930s he was writing stiff letters to the newspapers on the iniquity of J. T. Lang [q.v.], 'basher-gangs', drugs and other social and political problems.

Griffith died at his home at Jannali on 1 September 1946 and was cremated with Anglican rites. He was survived by his second wife, Elsie Marion, née Edwards, whom he had married at Ashfield with Church of Christ forms on 22 October 1932, by one son of his first and a son and daughter of his second marriage.

H. V. Evatt, *Australian Labour leader... W. A. Holman* (Syd, 1943); P. Ford, *Cardinal Moran and the A.L.P.* (Melb, 1966); B. Nairn, *Civilising capitalism* (Canb, 1973); Roy Com of inquiry into charges preferred against the minister for public works, *PP* (NSW), 1912, 3, p 489; Roy Com of inquiry into ... proposed state monopoly of petrol industry, *PP* (NSW), 1916, 6, p 765; *Daily Telegraph*, 21 July 1894; *Newcastle Morning Herald*, 20 May 1898; *SMH*, 12 Oct 1915, 15 Mar, 18 July, 29 Aug, 2 Oct, 4 Nov 1916, 12 Oct 1928, 28 Apr 1930, 3 Sept 1946; *Sunday Sun*, 5 Nov 1916.   BEDE NAIRN

GRIFFITH, SIR SAMUEL WALKER (1845-1920), chief justice and premier, was born on 21 June 1845 at Merthyr Tydfil, Glamorganshire, Wales, second son of Rev. Edward Griffith (1819-1891), Independent minister, and his wife Mary, née Walker. Edward served at Portishead and Wiveliscombe, Somerset, after his first pastorate at Merthyr. Then in 1853 an invitation from the Colonial Missionary Society, supported by the prominent colonists John Fairfax [q.v.4] and David Jones [q.v.2], took him with his wife and family of two sons and three daughters to Australia. He became Congregational minister at Ipswich, Queensland (1854-56); Maitland, New South Wales (1856-60); and Wharf Street, Brisbane (1860-89). Samuel, despite the brevity of his sojourn in Wales, regarded himself as Welsh; his romanticizing ignored the reality of his English background. He drifted from his father's fundamentalism, as a politician becoming embarrassed by Edward's presence in Brisbane, and joined the more fashionable Church of England after his father died in 1891.

Samuel was educated at Ipswich (1854-55), Woolloomooloo, Sydney (1855-56), and Rev. William McIntyre's [q.v.5] school at Maitland (1856-59). McIntyre failed to pass on his rabid Presbyterianism but inspired Samuel's love of the classics. He was dux and gained the nickname 'Oily Sam' from his 'ability to argue on any side of any subject'. Continuing his education in a brilliant arts course at the University of Sydney (B.A., 1863; M.A., 1870), he earned first-class honours in classics and mathematics. In 1862 he won the (Sir Daniel) Cooper [q.v.3] scholarship in classics (Professor Woolley [q.v.6] assessing him as one of the four best students of his decade), and the (Thomas) Barker [q.v.1] scholarship in mathematics. He also studied law, taking general jurisprudence as an extra university course, and on 11 May 1863 became an articled clerk under Arthur Macalister [q.v.5] at Ipswich. He was vain enough, when only 18, to apply in July 1863 for the headmastership of Ipswich Grammar School, and was already interested in politics, attending the debates in the Queensland parliament and publishing in 1862 a series of twenty-five critical articles on its members in the *Queensland Guardian*. He proved a successful articled clerk, accepting increasing responsibilities and representing his master solicitor on circuit in Rockhampton.

In 1865 when he was awarded the highly competitive Mort [q.v.5] travelling fellowship from the University of Sydney the Queensland Supreme Court allowed him to interrupt his articles. Chief Justice Cockle's [q.v.3] 'peculiar pleasure' in discharging this duty indicated how well known Griffith was in Queensland's small legal fraternity. He arrived in England on 20 January 1866 and spent a month there, visiting art galleries and relatives, before undertaking a 'grand tour' of Europe and then returning to England for a further six months. He had begun learning Italian and was reading French and English works, including Shakespeare. Conscientiously he sought understanding of paintings, claiming that by the end of his stay his taste had become 'strongly set' although his praise covered a wide spectrum including Rubens, Ruysdael, Brueghel and Landseer. In sculpture he gave highest appreciation to the 'wonderful and accurate tension of all the muscles' in the Laocoön group at the Vatican; in architecture he found Paris the most impressive. Politically his visit coincided with the Austro-Prussian War and Italian moves towards unification, and he enjoyed talking with a man who had served 'with Garibaldi against the Papal government'. He was often broke, unrepentant about his drinking and a past liaison with a married woman, and his family saw him as irresponsible, his brother refusing to lend him money.

Griffith's romanticism, which had already prompted him to propose to Brisbane's 'loveliest daughter', Etta Bulgin, now led to involvement with three female cousins, aged 25, 20 and 18, and he proposed marriage to the youngest. Her father objected and Samuel remained single. Yet it was serious, for his mother, in whom he rarely confided, intuited that he had left his 'heart behind'. Perhaps Samuel realized that this journey was to be his last chance of carefree enjoyment, before resuming his legal career. As well he was already contemplating entering politics, his father pointedly telling him that four Queensland parliamentarians had begun study for the Bar: '*you see your competition*'.

Back in Queensland Griffith completed his articles at the end of September 1867, immediately sat and passed Bar examinations, and was admitted on 14 October. He was soon busy with briefs, first appearing in a Supreme Court action in 1867 and taking silk in 1876. By 1893 he had appeared in 280 recorded cases; he travelled frequently on circuit to Ipswich, Toowoomba, Rockhampton and Maryborough, and his returns rose rapidly. He had been paid £200 by Macalister in 1867, by 1870 his annual receipts had reached £1000, by 1893 his legal earnings were at least £3500. He appeared in widely varying fields of law, including criminal, property, company and probate.

Socially he had close friends such as C. S. Mein [q.v.5] and led an active physical life. He was a Freemason (later a grand master), and prominent in intellectual societies. He became involved again with Etta, but soon after she became engaged he visited Maitland and began courting Julia Janet Thomson. Their marriage was celebrated in St Stephen's Presbyterian Church, East Maitland, on 5 July 1870. The union provided a stable social life for Samuel, especially as their family increased. The couple were rarely separated, but Griffith's letter of 9 November 1873, when Julia took their son and daughter south for seven weeks, reveals beneath his increasingly aloof and cold exterior an emotionally deeply involved husband and father, very conscious of loneliness.

Another change coincided with the marriage; a week after he returned from Maitland in July 1870 Griffith was asked to enter politics. He was closely involved in the Reform League later in that year, and while he declined to contest a seat in April 1871, stood successfully for the seat of East Moreton next year. His political career was to be combined with his work as a barrister until 1893.

His 1872 electoral speech promised legal reform and opposition to (Sir) Arthur Palmer's [q.v.5] squatter-biased legislation. Griffith also advocated European immigration, more expenditure on public works, the setting up of rural boards and the encouragement of municipal government. During his first two years in Opposition he was responsible for legal reform, introducing as a private member the Telegraphic Messages Act (1872), which he had drafted, as he did the Equity Procedure Act (1873). In debates on the legal practitioners bill he consistently argued that barristers should be separate and superior to solicitors. He was returned unopposed to the new seat of Oxley in November 1873 and did not hide his disappointment at not being appointed to the Macalister ministry; his trenchant criticisms of the new attorney-general E. O. MacDevitt [q.v.5] made the latter's 'life not worth the living'. After MacDevitt resigned, Griffith served as attorney-general from 3 August 1874 to 7 December 1878. He was also implicated in the resignation of (Sir) Thomas McIlwraith [q.v.5] from the ministry in 1874 and for the next sixteen years McIlwraith and Griffith represented the opposing poles of Queensland politics.

Griffith was thrice disappointed in his ambition to lead the Liberal Party: in 1876 when George Thorn [q.v.6] was preferred by the governor (Sir) William Cairns [q.v.3]; in 1877 when Thorn was succeeded by John Douglas [q.v.4]; and in 1878 when Governor Sir Arthur Kennedy [q.v.5] refused Douglas's offer to resign if replaced by Griffith. The Liberal Party lost its majority to McIlwraith in the elections of November 1878, although Griffith polled higher than his opponent Palmer in North Brisbane. Griffith finally replaced Douglas as party leader in May 1879. During this calculated and determined rise within the hierarchy Griffith held three portfolios: attorney-general, secretary for public instruction (1876-79) and secretary for public works (1878-79). He proved his ability in each, assiduously drafting bills and supervising administrative details. Among the most contentious of the problems he dealt with were his efforts to have the evidence of Aboriginal witnesses admissible in legal proceedings; his attempts to limit legally the flood of Chinese (when Cairns reserved assent to a statute he angrily offered his resignation); legalistic rulings on the increasingly disputed use of Pacific island labourers; methods of controlling the clash between squatters and selectors; implementing the provisions of the free, compulsory and secular Education Act (1875); beginning moves to establish a university in the colony; and assessing rival claims for public works.

As leader of the Opposition in 1879-83 Griffith proved far more successful than his predecessors: C. H. Buzacott [q.v.3] praised his 'brilliant fight ... [He] proved himself as parliamentary leader unsurpassed in Australian history'. The major clash with McIlwraith was the 'steel rails affair', the allegation that the premier, when issuing governmental contracts, had favoured certain firms, including the shipping company McIlwraith, McEacharn [q.v.] & Co. After a Queensland select committee in 1880 found no corruption, splitting on party lines, an enquiry was begun in London, where both McIlwraith and Griffith appeared early in 1881. Griffith was disappointed even before its decision reaffirmed the Queensland negative finding: 'The people called', he told his wife, 'refused to tell all the truth so I fear the enquiry will not result in discovering all the truth'. On his return to Brisbane Griffith was fêted, greeted by an enormous crowd which left him 'excited and sleepless'. Compulsively, he persisted in debating the affair, once speaking in the House for seven hours, but a censure motion was lost on party lines by 27 to 20. Despite these defeats Griffith had succeeded politically by raising the slogan of clean government against the suspicion of corruption.

Griffith made other challenges against McIlwraith, alleging in 1882 corruption in land sales, and increasingly criticizing the labour traffic, particularly for the supply of firearms to islanders returning to their villages. He claimed that McIlwraith's main motive in annexing New Guinea was to obtain more cheap labour. The McIlwraith government was defeated on 5 July 1883 on its ambitious plan to build a transcontinental railway on the land-grant principle and in the subsequent election Griffith's followers won easily. His personal leadership, backed by the well-organized internal party machinery with its increasingly regular caucus meetings, was aided by close attention to the electoral rolls by Robert Bulcock [q.v.3] and the active extra-parliamentary Liberal Association. Griffith exercised his plural voting rights in four electorates. He

and William Brookes [q.v.3] won the two North Brisbane seats against their erstwhile leader Douglas.

Griffith was premier from 10 November 1883 to 13 June 1888, and was appointed K.C.M.G. in 1886. Despite his assiduous country electioneering tours, his support was still dominantly from Brisbane and southern electorates. He advocated the continued unity of Queensland, opposing the developing regional separation movements in both the northern and central parts of the colony. In 1883 his party was close knit and strictly controlled, showing 92.6 per cent cohesion in divisions in the House. By 1888 this figure had declined but so had that of his opponents; the differences between the two leaders were becoming outdated by social and economic changes, particularly the clashes between employers and employees and the end of the long period of economic expansion.

As premier Griffith maintained a close personal supervision over his ministry, often working over eighty hours a week. In contrast to McIlwraith's brief minutes on dispatches, Griffith frequently wrote at length after detailed study of the issues. A reluctance to delegate authority was his weakness, even if he could argue that there were few reliable administrators in his small public service. He was accused of patronage, a charge supported by an 1887-89 royal commission on the civil service. His excuse was the need for efficiency and his dislike of the seniority principle. He appointed supporters to prominent positions and followed McIlwraith's precedent by pruning on political grounds the list of magistrates, so winning the support of the Protestant newspaper, the *Queensland Evangelical Standard*, which believed some magistrates had proved corrupt and that Griffith had 'erred on the side of mercy'. His father, associated with this newspaper, was appointed to the Brisbane Hospitals' Board, and his brother made honorary commissioner to the Melbourne Centennial Exhibition and chairman of the Brisbane Licensing Board (Division of Balmoral). A shortage of other suitable candidates enabled both to keep their positions even after the royal commission's findings were published.

Griffith remained critical of political patronage by his opponents, notably the two appointments in September 1883 to the Legislative Council which threatened to frustrate his legislative programme. He was, however, able to fulfil his electoral promise to end McIlwraith's scheme of introducing labourers from India, and to prevent any revival of transcontinental railway schemes. He did not abolish the use of Pacific island labourers, but insisted on careful surveillance, immediately ending the supply of arms and ammunition to those returning to their islands. In March 1884 he legislated to restrict their labour to field-work on sugar plantations, and to introduce more stringent controls on recruiting, which he forbade from the New Guinea area. His policies disclosed abuses, especially on some recruiting voyages and led to his criticism of planter attitudes as displayed in the Mackay riot of Christmas 1883.

The trial of members of the *Hopeful* crew in December 1884 was followed by an emotional public debate on the two death sentences, and eventually all the Executive Council except Griffith and Mein voted for commutations. The case almost converted Griffith to abolition of recruiting but before taking this drastic step, feared by the sugar industry, he appointed a royal commission on recruits from New Guinea and other islands. Its findings condemned the recruiting methods of most captains, and recommended the return of all these islanders. This was carried out despite objections from employers, against whom Griffith's instructions were definite: 'Take no notice of protests. Remove the men and use force if necessary to overcome resistance'. In November 1885 Griffith decided to end the traffic: his bill providing that no more islanders were to be introduced after 31 December 1890 was accepted by both Houses. He planned central governmental mills supplied by small blocks, so limiting the dominance of large plantations and reducing the need for cheap labour.

Griffith's opposition to the growing movements to divide Queensland was related to his fears that any new colonies would be dominated by sugar planters. He attacked campaigners, arguing that petitions were unrepresentative of the majority. Political leaders, particularly J. M. Macrossan [q.v.5], bitterly denied his criticisms, and Griffith eventually accepted some validity to arguments based on distance. In 1887 he introduced a financial districts bill, seeking some devolution of power and a more equitable distribution of funds, but it, like other separation proposals, was defeated in parliament.

The changing emphasis of Griffith's government, giving more opportunity than McIlwraith's to agriculturalists rather than sugar-planters and pastoralists, was emphasized in C. B. Dutton's [q.v.4] 1884 Crown Lands Act. Its basis was leasehold rather than freehold, and its provisions were to be administered by a land board. Subsequent amending Acts of 1885 and 1886 followed the same principle, but these measures did not end the dominance of pastoralists. Griffith's government continued major expenditure on public works but conflicting priorities led to stress in his ministry, as in 1885 when W. Miles [q.v.5], secretary for public works, threatened to resign. Griffith flatly refused to compensate the Australian Transcontinental Railway Syndicate, suspecting close liaison between it and the bank McIlwraith supported, the Queensland National. Its manager E. R. Drury's [q.v.4] fear that Griffith in power would 'clip our wings' was justified, in so far as in February 1886 Griffith founded the Royal Bank of Queensland—its second manager was his brother and its auditor his brother-in-law.

Nevertheless the Liberals also came to rely on the Queensland National Bank. One loan was raised without its assistance, but it was partly involved in a proposal of December 1884 to obtain £10 million, and was by 1886 at the centre of financial negotiations. In 1887 when Griffith proposed a land tax his treasurer (Sir) James Dickson [q.v.8] resigned, as did the postmaster-general, Macdonald-Paterson. Griffith became treasurer and dealt directly with Drury in attempting to raise further loans in 1888. Although Griffith was to blame 'disloyal financial organizations' alliance with opposition' for his 1888 election defeat, when he came second to McIlwraith in a bitter fight in North Brisbane, no clear evidence exists against Drury or his bank.

Griffith continued previous government encouragement of immigration from Britain and Europe, strictly controlling abuses on migrant ships or at depots. He saw agricultural workers from Europe as eventually replacing Pacific islanders. He maintained restrictive policies on Chinese, increasing the poll tax and limiting the number allowed to be carried on migrant ships. His objections to Chinese stressed differences between their civilization and that of Queensland: 'they cannot be admitted to an equal share in the political and social institutions of the colony'. He believed the 1887 Chinese commissioners appreciated these arguments. Griffith increased Aboriginal evidential rights, and passed a Native Labourers' Protection Act dealing with fisheries in 1884. He also took action on difficulties with the native police. Although Aboriginal problems were not central to his administration, he was more humanitarian than most Queenslanders; indeed a press report wrote of 'Mr Griffith and the black sympathisers'.

His humanitarian concern spread to white victims, including orphans, lepers, the insane and the poor. Public charitable institutions were controlled more effectively after his 1885 Charitable Institutions Management Act. His 1884 Health Act recognized government responsibility, forming a central board which uncovered many serious defects. During a debate urging repeal of the Contagious Diseases Act (1868) Griffith revealed how he reconciled state intervention with his liberalism. The Act was 'an infringement of ... liberty ... and so is every law relating to the public health, but we have for many years adopted the principle that in [such] matters ... the comfort of the individual must yield to the good of the public'. He saw no contradiction in his involvement in many individual cases seeking justice even if this meant overruling previous decisions, whether of judges, ministers or civil servants. His continuing interest in legal reform was apparent when in 1886, influenced by Howard Vincent, he introduced probation for first offenders.

As unemployment increased after 1886 Griffith showed sympathy with the emerging labour movement. He introduced a statute to legalize trade unions, and an Employers' Liability Act (1886), and in his 1888 election manifesto declared that 'the great problem of this age is not how to accumulate wealth but how to secure its more equitable distribution'.

After his government's defeat in 1888 Griffith strengthened his relationship with the emerging Labor Party. At William Lane's [q.v.] invitation he published in the *Boomerang* of 17 December 1888 an article 'Wealth and want' deploring the domination of the weak by the strong, and stressing as a function of government the protection of the weak. Lane urged Griffith to lead Australian radicals: 'What Pericles was to Athens and Greece such a leader could be to Australia and Queensland'. As a private member Griffith introduced an eight-hours bill in 1889, and a year later two bills comprising an elementary property law seeking to ensure a 'proper distribution of the products of labour'.

After only twenty-two months in Opposition, Griffith became premier again in August 1890 in an unlikely alliance with McIlwraith, the so-called 'Griffilwraith'. Hints of this unlikely alliance had begun in March 1889, related to the splits in McIlwraith's party and the worsening economic situation and in retrospect the sincerity of Griffith's support for Labor must be queried. Certainly he was to compromise during the thirty-two months of the 'Griffilwraith', and during the bitter strikes of 1891 he lost any remaining support from the labour movement. Within the government he was a moderating influence, trying to keep it neutral in upholding the rule of law, and he criticized both labour and employer extremists; yet his government was to use the military and to arrest, try and imprison some of the strikers.

Eventually Griffith declared that he had no sympathy with 'men who endeavour to bring about reforms ... by crime and violence'. Lane now wrote of him as a 'fraud' whose previous radical writings were merely 'wordy tommyrot'. During the strikes Griffith gave evidence to a New South Wales royal commission urging reform by legislation such as that proposed by his elementary property bills. He continued to hold that employers and employees should not regard each other as hostile enemies; he published similar sentiments in 1919. In 1891-93 his government ran a labour bureau to aid the unemployed, but it was also used to spy on labour agitators.

An even greater apparent change was his manifesto of 13 February 1892, prolonging the use of Pacific island labourers for another decade. He argued that this was temporary, justified by the industry's worsening economic crisis, exacerbated by competition from European subsidized beet sugar. Before so deciding he had personally visited most of the sugar areas and had sought information on alternative sources of labour. Delighted planters gave him champagne receptions, replacing the 'Damn Sam Griffith' toasts of the 1880s. Labor's hostility was typified by hooting at Bundaberg as he proceeded to his champagne. Abolitionists were shocked, however much Griffith tried to justify his decision, and he was denounced by previous supporters such as Brookes and Rev. J. G. Paton [q.v.5]. Griffith introduced even more stringent methods of controlling the revived island labour traffic and promised 'constant watchfulness' against any abuses.

Another apparent change of policy was his 1890 proposal to divide Queensland into three provinces, although arguably this was only an extension of his 1887 financial districts bill. Provocatively, in the parliamentary debate he challenged members to show any inconsistency between any two speeches he had made on any subject. Griffith used the planned division of powers as a model when discussing Australian Federation. He was surprised when his provincial scheme was defeated in 1891, though well aware of the rivalries between the northern and central groups. In September 1892 Griffith changed policy in another area, allowing the private building of railways on the land-grant principle. He justified this change by the degenerating financial situation as marked by crises, such as the involvement of the Queensland National Bank in an action taken against Samuel Grimley and others by the Queensland Investment & Land Mortgage Co. Ltd in 1891-92.

Griffith was sometimes consistent: anti-Chinese regulations were strictly enforced;

some care was expressed for the Aboriginals, as in the strong response to criticisms by the Presbyterian Church alleging neglect, though Griffith shared prevailing views that they were a dying race.

Throughout his political career Griffith was interested in external affairs. Immediately after forming his 1883 ministry he had attended the Intercolonial Convention, Sydney, where he persuaded his fellow members to support the annexation of New Guinea rather than the New Hebrides. He was prominent in the formation of the Federal Council of Australasia, drafting the bill for its constitution. Although this proved a weak body, and a false start towards Federation, its regular meetings gave delegates such as Griffith, who was thrice president, an opportunity to discuss mutual legal and security problems. He remained involved in intercolonial negotiations particularly concerning New Guinea, New Caledonia and the New Hebrides. As a Queenslander and Imperialist he was interested in moves to strengthen Australian defences. Although he did not, unlike Mein, join the volunteer forces he regularly attended their camps. As premier he introduced the 1884 Defence Act which strengthened the army and created a navy. In the Sudan crisis of February 1885 he made an imperialistic speech at Warwick and offered Britain a Queensland contingent. In the 1885 Russian scare, when Queensland was close to a war footing, he tried to spread scarce resources of men and materials along the coast.

On the arrival of Queensland's two naval ships *Paluma* and *Gayundah* Griffith insisted on colonial control in line with his plans, first formulated in June 1885, for an Australasian auxiliary squadron of six cruisers supplemented by torpedo boats, partly manned by Australian cadets and flying the white ensign with a distinguishing mark. He developed a close relationship with Admiral Tryon [q.v.6], the British commander of the Australian squadron, culminating in a somewhat abortive conference in Sydney in April 1886. In debating the bizarre incident when Captain Wright the British senior naval officer, turned the guns of the *Gayundah* on the Queensland parliament, Griffith reiterated his view that the mere flying of the white ensign did not give Wright immunity.

At the 1887 Colonial Conference in London, where agreement was reached on strengthening the Australian naval squadron, Griffith was regarded as the senior Australian representative. He drafted the legislation for the new colony of British New Guinea and was a key figure in the choice of its first administrator, (Sir) William MacGregor [q.v.5]. After the conference he succeeded in persuading the Queensland parliament to support New Guinea with financial and administrative aid, although he was less successful in convincing Governor Musgrave [q.v.5], who was sure the system of divided control could not work. Nor did Griffith succeed in having the naval agreement accepted by the Queensland parliament. For this defeat he blamed an Australian sentiment 'of want of regard for the Empire and a disposition to look for causes of difference with the Mother Country with the ultimate object of separating altogether'.

Griffith was not opposed to Australian nationalism but hoped it would occur within the Imperial framework, seeing no incompatibility in being loyal to Queensland, Australia and Britain (or Wales). After his 1888 electoral defeat he contemplated moving to Britain, seeking a seat in the House of Commons for a constituency in North Wales, with the hope of influencing Imperial policy.

His vague plans were postponed by the 1890s moves for Federation. His speech at the 1890 Melbourne conference accurately represented him as a cautious lawyer and practical politician. He was particularly influential in the 1891 Sydney convention where he admitted he dominated the discussions: 'my work ... was very hard, for it fell to my lot to draw the Constitution, after presiding for several days on a Committee, and endeavouring to ascertain the general consensus of opinion'. Deakin [q.v.8] agreed: 'as [a] whole and in every clause the measure bore the stamp of Sir Samuel Griffith's patient and untiring handwork, his terse, clear style and force of expression ... few even in the mother country or the United States ... could have accomplished ... such a piece of draftsmanship with the same finish in the same time'. Griffith defended this draft constitution in his July 1891 presidential address to the Queensland branch of the Royal Geographical Society of Australasia on the grounds of patriotism: 'In spirit I am as much an Australian as any man'.

By the time constitutional discussion was resumed in 1897 Griffith was out of politics, but he continued to advocate Federation. In 1896-1900 he wrote extensively on the subject and corresponded with many delegates to the 1897-98 convention, sending detailed comments to (Sir) Robert Garran [q.v.8], secretary of the drafting committee. 'It is fitting' writes Professor La Nauze 'that the final form of the Constitution contains not only much of Griffith's text of 1891, but his lofty corrections of the words of the later and lesser draftsmen of 1897'. Griffith, in Melbourne during the premiers' conference of January 1899, saw all the representatives and travelled back to Sydney with (Sir) George Reid [q.v.], perhaps assisting in drafting the decisions. His address in May to the Queensland Federation League had the avowed object of influencing Queenslanders to vote for Federation. (Sir) John Quick [q.v.] was sure this intervention had been crucial, telegraphing Griffith: 'I congratulate you on Federal Voting in Queensland. Thus crowning your long sustained and patriotic labours in the cause of Australian unity'.

Griffith was consulted by (Sir) John Forrest [q.v.8] about Western Australia joining as an original State, a question eventually left to the London constitutional deliberations in 1900 when Griffith, as acting governor, suggested amendments. Although he refused a request from the British government to try to persuade the delegates to accept changes, his support for wider rights of appeal to the Privy Council placed him in a 'distinctly equivocal' position. His redrafting of the appeals clause caused bitter clashes with Deakin, (Sir) Edmund Barton [q.v.7], C. C. Kingston and (Sir) Josiah Symon [qq.v.].

Frustrated, disappointed and confused during his second premiership Griffith had welcomed his translation to the judiciary. He served as Queensland's chief justice from 13 March 1893 to 6 October 1903, a most peaceful decade, during which he was appointed G.C.M.G. in 1895 and to the Privy Council in 1901. He restored the prestige of the Supreme Court by his many judgments, over 400 being reported, of which the majority involved the interpretation of statutes closely followed by practice decisions. He presided over the Kenniff [q.v.] murder trial of 1902, the winding-up of companies such as the Darling Downs brewery and the 1900 James Tyson [q.v.6] case. Generally he worked well with his fellow judges, despite disagreements with G. R. Harding [q.v.4], who had hoped to be appointed chief justice, and in the Kenniff case, with Patrick Real [q.v.].

Griffith made a lasting professional contribution by codifying the Queensland criminal law, a massive task which occupied much of his spare time in 1896-99, Deakin wondering how he had found 'leisure for such a feat while discharging the onerous duties of your office'; he also revised the Supreme Court rules and those for matrimonial and probate cases.

A tall, spare figure, of fair complexion, his full beard late in becoming grey, Griffith served several times as deputy and lieutenant-governor. He was head of the trustees of both Brisbane grammar schools, where his children were educated, a trustee of the Queensland Art Gallery, and was involved with the university extension movement and with various intellectual and financial societies. He used his 'leisure' to translate parts of Dante which he published in 1898, 1907, 1912 and 1914. These included the three parts of the *Divine comedy* and a series of love poems, the *Vita nuova*. Although critics justifiably complained that his English versions were too literal, reflecting his own object of presenting 'a true photograph of the original', Griffith's interest also reflected his continued romanticism. His personal life was mostly stable; he lived in a luxurious home, Merthyr, on the Brisbane River. His tranquillity was shattered in December 1901 by the death after a long illness of his beloved eldest son, Llewellyn. His wife took three of their children to Tasmania for three months during which Griffith's correspondence reveals how little satisfaction he obtained from his routine work; his Dante translation was one of his only consolations.

In 1903 after considerable political debate the Judiciary Act (drafted by Griffith) was passed, so inaugurating the High Court of Australia, and he was chosen as first chief justice. He had contemplated returning to politics in 1901, being approached by both Barton and Sir William Lyne [q.v.], but his hints at having a guarantee for the Federal chief justiceship weakened his cause. His closest rivals were Barton and Symon. The latter's disappointment was manifest in his clashes as attorney-general with the High Court in 1904. Griffith's original colleagues were Barton, who asked Deakin 'will it be easy to make Griffith laugh', and R. E. O'Connor [q.v.]; the triumvirate agreed constitutionally, being determined to perpetuate Federalism by limiting the effect of central over State powers. This harmony was disturbed by the 1906 appointments of (Sir) Isaac Isaacs and H. B. Higgins [qq.v.] who wanted the Federal government to exercise fuller powers. O'Connor died in 1912; and in 1913 (Sir) Charles Gavan Duffy [q.v.8], (Sir) Charles Powers and (Sir) George Rich [qq.v.] were appointed. Legal and personal clashes between Griffith and his colleagues increased with time, although Duffy, seeing the judges as 'a set of feudal barons', praised Griffith's role: 'among the many characteristics of greatness which you possess is the capability of forgetting little irritations'. The Griffith line of constitutional interpretation mainly prevailed until his retirement; the Engineers' Case, a triumph of the Isaacs-Higgins line, was decided on 31 August 1920, just after Griffith's death.

During his sixteen years (1903-19) on the bench Griffith sat on some 950 reported cases, the highest annual number being 90 in 1906. In 1913 he visited England and sat on the Privy Council. He was not over-impressed by the law lords, and renewed his arguments for the appointment of more judges from the Dominions to overcome 'the old insular doctrine of the essential difference in quality between English and Colonial persons'.

Griffith had aged markedly and he was plagued with ill health. Prime Minister Hughes [q.v.] urged him to go slower: 'be a little kind to your poor flesh'. On 16 March 1917 he suffered a stroke while on the bench and was temporarily retired till February next year. His desire to pay off his home forced him, aged 72, to return, but he heard few cases, only 19 in 1918 and 4 in 1919. Cases interpreting sections of the Constitution were fewer than 8 per cent of those he heard. The majority were appeals on matters familiar from his experience on the Queensland Supreme Court: interpretations of other statutes (Federal and State) dominated with 13 per cent, closely followed by contracts, practice and procedure, property and probate. Griffith's judgments in all legal fields reveal the breadth of his contribution, and why Barton saw him as 'the greatest lawyer in the Commonwealth'.

Successive governors-general had sought his advice even beyond the limits of constitutional propriety. When Prime Minister Fisher [q.v.8] sought a dissolution in May 1909 Griffith 'wrote notes' for Dudley [q.v.8] on which basis the request was refused. The newly appointed Munro Ferguson [q.v.], facing a request for a double dissolution from Cook [q.v.8] in June 1914, also relied heavily on Griffith whom he described as 'by far the most outstanding personage that I have met' in Australia. When Fisher planned to resign in 1915 Griffith again advised Munro Ferguson that he could appoint the new ministry on the advice of another member of parliament. Griffith firmly considered that a governor-general had a 'duty to dismiss his ministers' if he believed their actions were 'detrimental to the welfare of the Empire or State'. He was also consulted by prime ministers. He offered to act for Hughes as conciliator in the coal strike of 1916; was appointed by Hughes, after the second conscription referendum, as royal commissioner to inquire as to reinforcing the Australian Imperial Force; and was consulted in proceedings against Sinn Feiners in June 1918.

From 1903 Griffith had lived in the heart of Sydney. He continued and varied his wide outside interests. He was an active member of the Senate of the University of Sydney in 1904-17; was appointed a vice-president of the Royal Colonial Institute in 1909 and an honorary fellow of the British Academy in 1916; and was awarded honorary doctorates of law by the University of Queensland in 1912 and the University of Wales in 1913.

He established the practice of extensive circuits of the High Court, with regular sittings in every capital city. But he remained a Queenslander. He retired to Brisbane where he died at Merthyr on 9 August 1920. Survived by his wife, four daughters and a son, he was buried in Toowong cemetery. His estate was valued for probate at £27 335. Fittingly, Griffith's portrait now hangs in the High Court in Canberra where a suburb also bears his name. His intellectual brilliance and achievements especially in law are unchallengable, and despite the equivocacy of parts of his political career he made vital contributions to Queensland and Australia.

D. J. Murphy and R. B. Joyce (eds), *Queensland political portraits 1859-1952* (Brisb, 1978); *Hist Studies*, Oct 1974, no 63; Griffith papers (Dixson Lib, *and* ML).   R. B. JOYCE

GRIFFITHS, ALBERT (1871-1927), boxer, was probably born on 23 July 1871 at sea, son of Charles Griffiths, London-born seaman and wharf labourer, and his first wife. The family arrived in Victoria and moved to Sydney in the mid-1870s. Albert, after the death of his mother, was brought up by the Allner and Horner families at Millers Point and went briefly to St Patrick's school. A street-fighting newsboy in the Rocks area, he worked for a tailor, the *Sydney Morning Herald* and a racehorse trainer, before progressing to professional boxing. About 1886 he went to Larry Foley [q.v.4] for tuition and guidance.

Known as 'Griffo' he won the Australian featherweight title on 27 December 1889 from Nipper Peakes. He and the Australian boxing *cognoscenti* claimed with good reason that he won the world title from Billy Murphy in September 1890, but this was unacknowledged elsewhere. Fighting in the days when boxing was still less than respectable, he dominated his opponents with fast footwork, masterly evasion, quick leads and lightning combinations. Despite being a 5 ft. 4 in. (162 cm), 120 lb (54 kg) featherweight, he defeated men up to 6 ft. (185 cm) and 160 lbs (72 kg). Joe Pluto was the only Australian featherweight whom 'Griffo' failed to defeat; they drew five times in Melbourne.

Increasingly, 'Griffo' neglected his training for 'grog' and the good life, but still remained undefeated in at least 79 bouts. However, he was only saved from certain defeat by the Negro Jerry Marshall in December 1892, when his supporters from the Rocks invaded the ring and intimidated Marshall and the referee. A crowd of 4000 witnessed the return match at Darlinghurst. Again the ring was invaded and an unnerved Marshall lost the fight on a foul—a low blow perhaps deliberately thrown.

After an official ban on boxing contests, 'Griffo' left for the United States of America on 15 May 1893 in the *Alameda*. Once there, he slipped further into hopeless alcoholism, exacerbated by poor and irresponsible management. He was always unfit, often fought while intoxicated, and even drank during fights. Jack McAuliffe was given an unpopular decision over 'Griffo' in their world lightweight title fight in 1894 and 'Griffo' drew three times in title fights against the featherweight champion George Dixon. He outlived all in reputation as 'the cleverest boxer of all time', yet, penniless and always in strife, he had numerous encounters with the police for drunkenness and resisting arrest. In April 1896 he narrowly avoided a manslaughter charge when an opponent died and in August he was gaoled in New York for a year, charged with assaulting a 12-year-old boy while drunk. In 1898 the 26-year-old 'Griffo' was admitted to an inebriates' home.

Thereafter he had few fights and survived by performing stunts. Later he relied on free meals and board from former admirers, although at times he was forced to beg, for which offence he was arrested in 1912. In the 1920s a grey-haired, overweight, but sober and content 'Griffo', sat each night on the steps of the Rialto Theatre on Broadway and watched the passing parade. He died at 466 West Forty-third Street, New York, on 7 December 1927 of apoplexy and was buried in Woodlawn cemetery with Baptist forms; his coffin was carried by boxing greats.

K. Roberts, *Captain of the push* (Melb, 1963); P. Corris, *Lords of the ring* (Syd, 1980); *Sporting Standard*, 9 Sept 1890, 17 Mar 1891, 27 Dec 1892, 7 Mar 1893; *New York Times*, 14 Aug 1896, 8-12 Dec 1927; *SMH*, 9 Dec 1927; *Referee*, and *Sporting Globe*, 14 Dec 1927; Boxing statistics compiled by M. Williams, held by J. Thompson, Alphington, Vic.   RICHARD BROOME

GRIFFITHS, GEORGE WASHINGTON (1844-1924), foundry proprietor, was born on 24 March 1844 at Bristol, England, son of Thomas Griffiths, accountant and Congregational minister, and his wife Elizabeth, née Hawkins. The family moved to London in 1846 and to Manchester in 1848 where Thomas became a junior partner in A. & S. Henry, cotton merchants; he became

wealthy from contraband cotton during the American Civil War. George was educated at Dr Clark's Boarding School, Brill, Buckinghamshire, and briefly at Manchester Mechanics' High School. Hoping to become an architect, he left school in December 1857 and worked briefly in building, engineering and haberdashery before joining A. & S. Henry. On 31 July 1867 George was married by his father to Isabella Park Atherton. With his wife, children and brother-in-law William Atherton, he sailed for Queensland on 2 October 1870.

Griffiths and Atherton bought a small ironmongery and mechanical repair shop at Toowoomba late in 1871; Atherton soon left and, after the arrival of a brother, John Alfred Griffiths [q.v.], and two sisters, the firm became Griffiths Bros & Co. early in 1873. Moving to a larger site in 1874, they built a foundry and made their first casting in February 1876. They survived by making some of Australia's earliest metal windmills until their first contract for railway rolling-stock in 1881. In 1884 Griffiths bought out his family partners and formed the Toowoomba Foundry and Rolling Stock Manufacturing Co. Ltd with himself as quarter stockholder and managing director. To make steel sleepers for the Normanton-Croydon Railway, a plant was opened in Brisbane. When the railway contracts expired in 1892, the firm was saved by an accommodation with the Queensland National Bank and by the purchase in Griffiths's wife's name of some £5000 worth of shares held outside the family. Saved again by railway contracts in 1895-1902, the firm then began to produce the famous 'Southern Cross' windmill. It contracted in 1910 and 1914 to build thirty-five locomotives for Queensland but, after a loss on a Commonwealth contract, it abandoned railway work. After a trip to England in 1903-04 Griffiths began transferring control to his two youngest sons. He retired in 1911.

Griffiths himself was not an engineer and did not employ designers and engineers, preferring to rely on imported designs or the patterns provided with the precarious railway contracts. When necessary, he hired his brother John Alfred. A good estimator and manipulator of money, Griffiths removed competition by ruthless price-cutting. Essentially he was a salesman rather than a manager and often relied on injections of capital by his wealthy father in difficult times. Generous in large matters but parsimonious in small, he loved reading novels and history and devoted much leisure to a large garden. An active Freemason, he turned from the Congregational to the Anglican Church. He served briefly on the Toowoomba Municipal Council.

Following his wife's death in 1910, Griffiths married Margaret Ann Hunt on 7 March 1911 at Mosman, Sydney. He died on 27 August 1924 at Rose Bay, Sydney, survived by his wife and four daughters and three sons of his first marriage.

His third son ALFRED ATHERTON GRIFFITHS (1879-1948) was born on 5 March 1879 at Toowoomba. Educated at Toowoomba Grammar School, he joined the foundry in January 1895 as a storeman but soon unofficially assumed many of his father's managerial duties. He became a director in 1900, *de facto* managing director in 1908 and joint managing director in 1911 with his brother GEORGE HERBERT GRIFFITHS (1881-1977), born on 17 April 1881 at Toowoomba. Educated at J. A. Baxendall's Downs School, Toowoomba, Bert joined the firm in 1898. More technically minded than his brother, he started on the works floor, is credited with developing the 'Southern Cross' windmill, became a director in 1904 with the unofficial title of works manager and joint managing director in 1911. From the mid-1920s both brothers delegated their routine duties to other directors but retained overall control. Atherton became the first president of the Southern Cross group of companies and was succeeded by Bert.

Under their direction branches were established all over Australia. They took over the Eclipse Windmill Co. in 1925, created an export division in 1939 and established a subsidiary in South Africa. They also diversified into south-west Queensland pastoral properties. During World War II the Toowoomba foundry employed over 1000 men on shell-primers, engines and other equipment for the Australian and allied forces. In peace, the firm concentrated on water-supply systems and, more recently, automotive castings. Industrial Investments Pty Ltd was formed in 1949 (renamed Industrial Enterprises in 1952) to coordinate all Australian operations.

The two brothers had an amicable, complementary but distant relationship. Atherton, like his father, was the manager and salesman with a head for figures and minute detail. Like his uncle, Bert was inventive, even visionary, and usually initiated major developments. From 1904 the two gradually bought shares held outside the immediate family and ensured that the company remained a family business.

Much more outgoing than Bert, Atherton was an alderman of Toowoomba, intermittently in the 1920s and consistently in 1930-48. A football enthusiast, he was one of the oldest practising Rugby referees in the world when he retired in 1943. He married Evelyn Hamilton at Toowoomba on 20 June 1907; they had five children. Divorced on 12 September 1934, he married Marjorie Jessie Nankervis in 1937. He died of cancer at Toowoomba on 25 June 1948 and was cremated. Bert, who served in France as a sapper in 1918, was a crack rifle shot. He had an alert, retentive mind, and in retirement made extensive notes on the firm's history. He married Agnes McIntyre at Sandgate on 10 October 1917; they had three children. Three more children resulted from his marriage to Margaret Walton Kent at Inverell, New South Wales, on 4 November 1933. He died at Toowoomba on 8 July 1977 and was cremated.

M. J. Fox (ed), *The history of Queensland*, 1 (Brisb, 1919); South-West Qld Railway Hist Soc, *Pony Express*, Oct 1973; *Darling Downs Gazette*, 21 July 1884; *Toowoomba Chronicle*, 28 Aug 1924, 26 June 1948, 9 July 1977; Griffith family register and papers, *and* notes on the history of Toowoomba Foundry, 5 vols (typescript, held by Toowoomba Foundry Archives); Foundry records (Darling Downs Institute of Advanced Education Archives).   M. FRENCH

GRIFFITHS, JOHN ALFRED (1848-1933), engineer, was born on 26 January 1848 at Bethnal Green, London, son of Thomas Griffiths, accountant, and his wife Elizabeth, née Hawkins. He was a younger brother of George Washington Griffiths [q.v.]. Educated at Owens College, Manchester, in 1865-68, he sat for the examinations of the Royal College of Chemistry, completing the practical part of his training with Gregson, Brown & Son, toolmakers, of Middleton, Lancashire. He took further examinations in mining and metallurgy from the Royal School of Mines in 1872-73 and obtained associateships of both institutions which gave him the right to a B.Sc. Winning a Whitworth scholarship in mechanical engineering in 1872, he worked with the London & North Western Railway till 1873 when he went to Queensland to join his brother in establishing the foundry of Griffiths Bros & Co. at Toowoomba. A partner in 1873-76, he was probably responsible for the design of the company's famous 'Southern Cross' windmill.

Griffiths left the firm in 1876 but remained a shareholder till 1884. He worked as a draughtsman and engineer for the Queensland Government Railways, then briefly in Western Australia on railway construction, leaving for England in December 1879. After a short engagement as a lecturer at Owens College, he managed the plant of the Waste Water Meter Co. at Liverpool in 1881-84. At Blackley, Lancashire, on 14 February 1884, he married Caroline Alexandra Brooks; two daughters survived them.

After manufacturing bicycles at Coventry in 1885-87, Griffiths returned to Australia in 1888. He worked on water-supply in Victoria, then in North Queensland on the Normanton-Croydon railway. In 1895 he entered the Queensland Public Service as an inspector of bores in the water-supply branch of the Public Works Department engaged on a survey of the artesian basin. In 1900 he transferred to the Queensland Patent Office as an examiner and, when the function of registering patents was transferred to the Commonwealth in 1904, became a Commonwealth public servant. He remained in the Brisbane office until he was promoted to Melbourne about 1909. He retired at the beginning of 1913, worked briefly as acting engineer for the Glenelg Shire Council, then returned to Brisbane. He died on 30 March 1933 and was buried in Bulimba cemetery with Methodist forms.

Griffiths was an authority on wind power and won both the James Watt medal and the Crampton prize of the Institution of Engineers, London, which he had joined in 1873. A paper by him on windmills is quoted in the 11th edition of the *Encyclopaedia Britannica*. He was also a member of the Institution of Mechanical Engineers, London, and joined the Victorian Institute of Engineers in 1910.

T. G. Chambers, *Register of the associates and old students of the Royal College of Chemistry . . .* (Lond, 1896); Roy Soc, *Catalogue of scientific papers, 1884-1900*, 15 (Cambridge, UK, 1916); Inst of Mechanical Engineers, *Procs*, June 1933; *Government Gazette* (Cwlth), 1 Feb 1913; *Queenslander*, 1 Feb 1913.   H. J. GIBBNEY

GRIFFITHS, PHILIP LEWIS (1881-1945), jurist, was born on 30 June 1881 at Stony Creek, near Talbot, central Victoria, sixth son and eighth surviving child of Thomas Griffiths and his wife Sarah, née Jones, both natives of South Wales who migrated with fellow villagers in the 1870s. Philip learned the grinding labour of a dairy farm and attended local state schools before winning a scholarship to Caulfield Grammar School (1894). Dux in 1897, he went on further scholarships to the University of Melbourne and its Trinity College. He performed brilliantly in classics and philology, taking a first-class M.A. (1903).

In July 1902 Griffiths went to Hobart to teach at Queen's College. Eighteen months later he turned to journalism, working for the *Mercury* both in Hobart and Launceston (1908-10). During the latter sojourn he studied law, graduating LL.B. (Tasmania) in

June 1910, again with distinction. The previous year he had been foundation secretary of a 'Writers' and Artists' Association', which soon transformed itself into the Tasmanian chapter of the nascent Australian Journalists' Association.

Griffiths began legal practice in Hobart in July 1912. From 1913 (to 1930) he was also lecturer in law at the University of Tasmania, most importantly in 'wrongs' (covering both torts and criminal law). As a barrister he specialized in civil matters. His scholarship was always apparent. Students, colleagues, and even judges found Griffiths demanding; conversely, his closest friend was R. L. Dunbabin [q.v.8], the two supporting each other in classical studies against the barbarian world. Yet Griffiths essentially was a humble man who upheld the simple virtues: Hobart folklore remembers him leading a cow to milk at his suburban home, reading all the while. He served the Church of England, so breaking from his parents' Primitive Methodism (although otherwise he honoured his Welsh heritage).

In September 1930 Griffiths became solicitor-general of Tasmania. Thereby ended his business partnership with H. S. Baker (then attorney-general; future chancellor of the University of Tasmania), but the two continued close friends. In his new role, Griffiths embellished his record of scholarship and efficiency. He became King's Counsel in August 1933, but chances for promotion to the bench lessened with the premiership (from June 1934) of A. G. Ogilvie [q.v.].

From August 1938 to March 1939 Griffiths was acting chief judge of the Mandated Territory of New Guinea, and on 1 July 1939 became second judge there. When (Sir) Frederick Phillips [q.v.] went on war leave in 1940, Griffiths again was acting chief judge from October. Few records of this work survive. Griffiths appreciated the difficulties of applying European law in an exotic situation. True to his philology, he took care to improve translation of statements by accused natives. He believed that Australia at least had done no irreparable harm in New Guinea.

On leave in Hobart when the Japanese captured Rabaul, he thereafter served as Tasmania's deputy-director of security. While not a sinecure, the post offered little scope. Griffiths died of coronary occlusion on 4 June 1945 and was buried in Cornelian Bay cemetery. He had married Ethelinda Maud Archibald on 18 November 1914, and fathered three daughters and two sons.

Cyclopedia of Tasmania (Hob, 1931); *Rabaul Times*, 29 Sept 1939; *Examiner* (Launc), and *Mercury*, 5 June 1945; Aust Journalists' Assn records (held by the Assn); personal information.
MICHAEL ROE

GRIFFITHS, THOMAS (1865-1947), army officer and civil servant, was born on 29 September 1865 at Presteigne, Radnor, Wales, son of James Griffiths, builder, and his wife Mary Ann, née Knowles. Educated at the Old Vicarage, Wrexham, Denbighshire, he migrated to Australia as a young man and enlisted as a gunner in the Victorian Permanent Artillery on 22 July 1886. In March 1890 he was appointed to the headquarters of the Victorian forces as a military staff clerk and next year, on 7 October, married Delia McNamara at the Church of the Immaculate Conception, Hawthorn. He was promoted in October 1894 to regimental quartermaster sergeant and a year later became chief clerk of the Victorian forces, with the rank of warrant officer. After Federation he was appointed, in April 1902, to Headquarters, Australian Military Forces, as a superintending clerk in the adjutant general's branch. In September 1908 he was appointed secretary of the military board, A.M.F., with the honorary rank of lieutenant in the Corps of Military Staff Clerks. He was granted the honorary rank of captain next August and five years later became an honorary major.

When the Australian Imperial Force was raised in August 1914 Griffiths joined as an original officer with the rank of captain. Although his first posting was that of general staff officer, 1st Australian Division, he performed the duties of assistant military secretary to the general officer commanding the A.I.F., Major General (Sir) William Bridges [q.v.7], who was aware of his ability and experience and wanted him on his staff. Griffiths sailed with the first contingent. In Egypt, in January 1915, he was officially posted to Bridges's A.I.F. Headquarters staff as assistant military secretary and retained this appointment until 28 March when he became deputy assistant adjutant general of 1st Division. He was D.A.A.G. at the Gallipoli landing on 25 April and remained at Anzac until the evacuation. On 2 May he was made temporary deputy assistant adjutant and quartermaster general to the division and in August was confirmed in this appointment; in June he had been promoted major. At Gallipoli he was mainly concerned with personnel movements and in almost nightly duty was to supervise the landing of reinforcements, frequently under shell-fire, and the evacuation of the wounded. In October he was transferred to Headquarters, Australian and New Zealand Army Corps, nominally as military secretary to the corps commander Lieut-General Sir William Birdwood [q.v.7], and was charged with all details concerning promotion; in effect he was adjutant general to the A.I.F. He was mentioned in dispatches and awarded the Distinguished Service Order for his work at Gallipoli and in the reorganization of the A.I.F. in Egypt.

From May 1916 Griffiths served in France as a lieut-colonel and A.A.G. at A.I.F. Headquarters and was attached for duty to the Headquarters of Birdwood's 1st Anzac Corps. Much against his will he left France in April 1917 to become acting commandant of A.I.F. Headquarters, London, and under the direction of Birdwood and Brigadier General (Sir) Brudenell White [q.v.] drafted the orders for administration of the A.I.F. In May he was promoted colonel and confirmed as commandant. In June 1918 he became a temporary brigadier general and remained A.I.F. commandant in London until the end of the war. His tasks included servicing the divisions in the field, recording deaths, casualties and promotions, liaising with the Department of Defence in Australia, and being administratively responsible for A.I.F. personnel in the United Kingdom. In October 1918, with Major General Sir Neville Howse [q.v.] and Lieut-Colonel A. G. Butler [q.v.7], he returned to Australia to discuss medical policy with the minister for defence. The Armistice made this mission unnecessary and in December Griffiths re-embarked for London where he resumed duty at A.I.F. Headquarters. Five months later he sailed for home, reaching Melbourne on 4 September 1919.

'No praise can be too high for Griffiths', Brudenell White concluded. 'The administration of nearly half a million men in war conditions, without much guide and precedent, was no mean task, and its successful accomplishment was mainly due to Griffiths'. C. E. W. Bean [q.v.7] described him as 'One of the great figures in the Australian Army', 'responsible for a great part of what is noble' in its traditions. He was known throughout the force as industrious, indefatigable, capable but unobtrusive. He was mentioned in dispatches in 1916, and appointed C.M.G. in January 1917 and C.B.E. in January 1919.

In March 1920 Griffiths became inspector general of administration in the Department of Defence, Melbourne, but in April he was appointed administrator of the former German territory of New Guinea. He was a popular and sound administrator but after the first few months of his term, a period of preparation for the expropriation of German interests, the post of administrator lost much of its significance. In October 1920 he applied for reappointment in the coming civil government but the position went to Brigadier General E. A. Wisdom [q.v.] who took over in March 1921. That year Griffiths became administrator of Nauru and during his six years in office the island made steady progress. He relinquished office in June 1927 but in 1929 came out of retirement to become deputy chairman of the Commonwealth War Pensions Entitlement Appeal Tribunal. Three years later he returned to New Guinea where in 1932-33 he was acting administrator and from July 1933 to September 1934 administrator. He then retired to Melbourne; in 1938 he applied, unsuccessfully, for the post of administrator in Nauru. During World War II he served briefly in the Department of Defence Co-ordination, then located in Melbourne.

Survived by his two daughters, Griffiths died on 16 November 1947 at Toorak, and was buried with military honours in Melbourne general cemetery after a requiem Mass in St Colman's Church, Balaclava. His portrait, by George Coates [q.v.8], is in the Australian War Memorial, Canberra.

C. E. W. Bean, *The story of Anzac* (Syd, 1921, 1924), and *The A.I.F. in France*, 1916-18 (Syd, 1929, 1933, 1937, 1942); C. D. Rowley, *The Australians in German New Guinea, 1914-1921* (Melb, 1958); *Encyclopaedia of Papua New Guinea*, 1, (Melb, 1972); *London Gazette*, 5 Nov 1915, 3 June, 11 July 1916, 24 Jan 1917, 1 Jan 1919; *Reveille* (Syd), Jan 1934; *Pacific Islands Monthly*, Dec 1947; *Argus*, 18 Nov 1918, 4 Sept 1919, 17 Nov 1947; *SMH*, 18 Nov 1947; CRS A518, items 852/1/451, 118/12, 518, 432, 29/1581 (AAO); records (AWM); information from Mrs D. Hyslop, Yarralumla, ACT.

WARREN PERRY

GRIMLEY, FRANK (1853?-1930), hardware merchant and coachbuilder, was born at Birmingham, Warwickshire, England, son of Edwin Grimley, saddler and coachbuilder, and his wife Mary, née Benton. Educated at King Edward's School, Grimley joined the Birmingham firm of Insole & Grimley in 1867, receiving a training in the coach and saddler's ironmongery business.

In 1880 Grimley came to Australia as a manufacturer's agent. Soon after he bought the saddlery branch of E. Williams & Co., Sydney, and in 1883 began his own business. By the late 1880s he had built a five-storey warehouse in Clarence Street and in the early 1890s he took over two coachbuilding firms. By 1895 Frank Grimley, saddlers and coachbuilders, were one of the largest wholesalers in the trade, holding agencies for a number of related products. That year the *Australasian Coachbuilder and Saddler*, with whom he advertised regularly, described him as 'one of the most aggressive and progressive coach-ironmongers in Australia'.

Like many successful entrepreneurs Grimley bitterly opposed government intervention in business. He railed against the 1(per cent tax which the New South Wales government placed upon coachbuilders materials in the early 1890s. In 1895 he urged cab-drivers in Sydney to reduce their charges to stimulate trade, which he claimed would benefit them, coachbuilde: and the public alike. He advocated standard ization of vehicle parts and served for a time as the treasurer of the Freetrade and Land Reform League. In 1897 he failed to be elected as a member of the Federal Convention. He also found time to devote to volun tary welfare, being a founder of the Queen Victoria Homes for Consumptives and of the Hospital Saturday Fund of New South Wales in 1894 and sometime director of the New South Wales Institution for the Dea and Dumb and the Blind.

He retired from active control of his firm in 1907 but remained on the board. Grimley Ltd was registered in May 1920 with Grimley as first chairman. The early 1920s were good years for the company but in 192: the directors explained that falling profi was due to 'the rapid displacement of horse carriages by motor transport'. By 192: Grimley Ltd managed to get a toe-hold in the motor accessory trade and this proved profitable, but losses were still incurred in liquidating unsaleable old stock. By the early 1920s Grimley was also a director o Marcus Clark [q.v.8] & Co. Ltd, and its off shoots Bon Marche Ltd, and Craig, William son Pty Ltd (Melbourne), the Australian Linoleum Co. Ltd, Clyde Brick Co. Ltd, and Cumberland Paper Board Mills Ltd.

Now calling himself a Nationalist Grimley persisted with his long-held abhor rence of taxation. In 1928 he wrote to the *Sydney Morning Herald* attacking any form of levy on the rich on the grounds that i 'diminishes enterprise and production by taking unduly from the funds of the em ployers of labour'. He became a keen collec tor of Australian paintings, including Conder [q.v.3] and Streeton [q.v.].

At St Peter's Anglican Church, Sydney on 19 September 1887 Grimley had married Amy Sparrow. He died, aged 77, in hospita at Stanmore on 1 June 1930 and was crema ted with Anglican rites; he was survived by a son and three daughters. His estate wa valued for probate at £195 015 in New Soutl Wales and £10 041 in Victoria.

A'sian Coachbuilder and Wheelwright, 5 (1895) no 10, p 147, 19 (1908), no 2, p 31; *SMH*, 10 Au; 1922, 7 Jan 1928, 3 June, 10 Oct 1930; *Heral* (Melb), 26 Feb 1946.   PETER SPEARRITT
KATHERINE VASEY

GRIMMETT, CLARENCE VICTOR (1891-1980), cricketer, was born on 25 December 1891 at Caversham, Dunedin, New Zealand, son of Richard James Grimmett, bricklayer, and his wife Mary, née McDermott. They moved to Wellington where Grimmett was educated at the Mount Cook Boys' School; at 15 he was apprenticed to a signwriter. He began playing senior district cricket for Wellington East and, later, for Wellington Province in Plunket Shield matches. In 1914 he moved to Sydney where as a wily leg-break bowler he played for Leichhardt, Paddington and the Sydney Districts clubs. Three years later he settled in Melbourne and played for South Melbourne and Prahran. He practised assiduously in his backyard with a fox-terrier that he trained to retrieve balls. On 1 November 1919 at Prahran, with Catholic rites, he married Elizabeth Annie Egan (d. 1968).

Playing for Victoria in Adelaide in the 1923-24 season, 'Clarrie' Grimmett was spotted by a South Australian who found him work in Adelaide. He also became a cricket writer for the *South Australian Register*. In 1925 he was chosen to play in the fifth Test against England in Sydney, and proved a match-winner, taking 5 wickets for 45 and 6 for 37. In 1926 in England he captured 5 for 88 runs and 2 for 9 in the third Test at Leeds.

Completely dedicated, he became renowned for his accuracy and nagging persistency—'a master of length, able to spin and flight the ball with infinite variation'—especially in England. Grimmett's age, almost frail stature, and determined, enthusiastic personality excited the press: they nick-named him 'the gnome', 'the fox', and 'Scarlet' (after the heroic 'Pimpernel'). Neville Cardus described him as 'an unobtrusive little man ... a master of surreptitious arts'.

Overall, Grimmett took 1424 first-class wickets at 22 runs apiece and was the first bowler of any country to capture 200 Test wickets. In 1924-36 he played in 37 Tests for Australia, taking a record 216 wickets at 24 runs; he was a useful late-order batsman. In 1936-37 and 1938 he was omitted from the Test sides against England. Grimmett never overcame his chagrin. In 1938 he was guest of the Maharajah of Jath in India; and in the Australian season of 1938-39 he took a record total of 73 wickets.

In 1941 Grimmett played his last big match. After that he coached at many schools and worked as an insurance salesman. He published three books: *Getting Wickets* (1930), *Tricking the batsman* (1932) and *Grimmett on cricket* (1948). He described how he got his 'sympathy with the ball': before bowling he would interlock 'the fingers on both hands, then pull and stretch the fingers as hard as I could'. Then when he took hold of the ball, 'it nestled in my hand and felt so much smaller'.

Grimmett played tennis and golf as he grew older. On 28 May 1971 with Anglican rites he married Gwenyth Montgomerie Beeton. Survived by her and a son from his first marriage, he died on 2 May 1980 and was buried in Centennial Park cemetery.

G. Tebbutt, *With the 1930 Australians* (Lond, 1930); A. G. Moyes, *Australian cricket* (Syd, 1959); S. Downer, *100 not out* (Adel, 1972); C. Martin-Jenkins, *The complete who's who of test cricketers* (Adel, 1980); *News* (Adel), 30 Dec 1961; *Advertiser* (Adel), 30 Nov, 16, 23 Dec 1938, 19 Sept 1963, 23 Dec 1965; *Sun-Herald*, 17 Feb 1980; *SMH*, 4 May 1980.

JOHN A. DALY

GRIMSHAW, BEATRICE ETHEL (1870-1953), writer, was born on 3 February 1870 at Cloona, Antrim, Ireland, daughter of Nicholas William Grimshaw, merchant, and his wife Eleanor Thomson, née Newsam. Her early life was comfortable and her education desultory. Tutored privately, she went to school at Caen in France, and later attended Bedford College, University of London (1887), and Queen's College, Belfast (1890-91). She did not take a degree and never married but saw herself as a liberated 'New Woman'.

A Dublin journalist from 1891, she displayed her independence in 1894 by leaving the Church of Ireland to become a Catholic. In 1897 she published her first novel, *Broken Away*, a romance about an assertive young woman rather like herself. She was interested in competitive cycling and showed her tendency to romanticize herself by claiming a world record for a 24-hour ride; experts doubt the claim.

Grimshaw worked for various shipping companies in the Canary Islands, the United States of America and England, then in 1902 became publicity manager in the Liverpool head office of the Cunard Line. Resigning in 1903 to report on the Pacific for the *Daily Graphic*, she accepted government and company commissions in 1904 and 1905 to write tourist publicity for the Cook Islands, Tonga, Samoa, Niue and New Zealand, and on the prospects for settlers in Fiji. She completed three books in Europe before returning to the Pacific. Commissioned by *The Times*, London, and the *Sydney Morning Herald*, she sailed late in 1907 to report on Papua, intending to stay only two or three months; in fact she lived in Port Moresby for most of the next twenty-seven years. A close friend of the acting administrator, (Sir) Hubert Murray [q.v.], she became his unofficial publicist and in 1908 urged Prime Minister Alfred Deakin [q.v.8] to make his temporary position permanent. Commissioned by Deakin to advertise Papua's need for white settlers and capital, pamphlets published in 1909 were followed in 1910 by a book, *The new New Guinea*.

Thereafter, Grimshaw concentrated on fiction. Her forty-two books included a part-autobiography, *Isles of Adventure*, and thirty-eight volumes of novels and stories. Most were escapist, outdoor romances with a Pacific setting. *Conn of the Coral Seas* (1922) was filmed by Hollywood as *Adorable Outcast*. Written to supply the popular market, her works have little literary merit but *The Times* obituarist justly acknowledged her 'high competence'. Her prose is often lively and the variations on her standard plot-formula are occasionally ingenious. In her New Guinea stories particularly, the backgrounds reflect her considerable knowledge of the country and its European inhabitants. Her fiction therefore constitutes a useful source of information on the attitudes, values and fantasies of settlers, especially their profound sense of racial superiority.

Grimshaw managed a plantation near Samarai in 1917-22. She accompanied exploring parties up the Sepik and Fly rivers in 1923 and 1926, and in 1933 she took up tobacco-growing near Port Moresby with her brother Ramsay. Then in 1934 she left Papua with Ramsay and another brother, Osborne, who was retiring from government service. She again visited Fiji, Samoa and Tonga before retiring in 1936 to Kelso, near Bathurst, New South Wales. She died on 30 June 1953 and was buried in Bathurst cemetery.

J of Pacific Hist, 12 (1977), and for bibliog; *New Literature Review*, (1977); *Adorable outcast*, film collection, *and* Deakin papers (NL).

HUGH LARACY

GRIMWADE, EDWARD NORTON (1866-1945), HAROLD WILLIAM (1869-1949), and SIR WILFRID RUSSELL (1879-1955), businessmen, were sons of Frederick Sheppard Grimwade [q.v.4] and his wife Jessie Taylor, née Sprunt, of Launceston. Felton [q.v.4] Grimwade & Co., wholesale druggists formed in 1867, developed into firms manufacturing acids, salt, glass bottles, fertilizers and eucalyptus oil. Grimwade left a considerable business empire to his sons.

Edward Norton, the eldest of nine children, was born at St Kilda on 25 May 1866. After attending Melbourne Church of England Grammar School, Norton went 'home' in 1883 to be apprenticed to a firm of London druggists. In 1886, before he had qualified, he was recalled to Melbourne to assist the firm. He completed his apprenticeship in Melbourne, winning the president' prize in his final year at the College of Pharmacy. In 1889 he was admitted partner in Felton Grimwade & Co. On 2 December 1891 at St Mary's Church of England, Caulfield, he married Phelia Whittingham and established a home, Drusilla, at Macedon. A formidable man of business with an easy mastery of financial detail, Norton could be roused to unexpected enthusiasms by travel, photography, the works of Shakespeare, and his family.

Harold, born on 18 May 1869 at St Kilda, went from Melbourne Grammar to Queen Elizabeth School at Ipswich, Essex, England, before serving his apprenticeship in London. He returned to Melbourne as a qualified pharmacist and became Felton Grimwade's warehouse manager; admitted a partner in 1893, he showed as much talent for the management of men as Norton for books of account. In 1891 he joined the Victorian forces. On 19 August 1896 at St Paul's Church, Camperdown, he married Winifred Thornton and built Marathon, near Frankston. Yachting on Port Phillip Bay joined golf, shooting and military exercises as his chief diversions.

Wilfrid Russell was born on 15 October 1879 at Harleston, the mansion F. S. Grimwade built at Caulfield and which his sons were to present to Melbourne Grammar after their mother's death in 1916. Russell went from Melbourne Grammar to Ormond College, University of Melbourne, graduating B.Sc. in 1901. After a period in London observing recent work in chemistry, he joined Felton Grimwade's in 1903 as director of the new research laboratory. He was admitted a partner in 1907. On 12 October 1909 at Toorak Presbyterian Church he married Mabel Louise, daughter of George Kelly and elder sister of (Sir) George Dalziel Kelly [q.v.]. A year later he bought Mieguryah in Orrong Road as a wedding present for his wife.

On their father's death in 1910 the three brothers inherited the original partnership and substantial interests in Felton Grimwade & Bickford's of Perth, J. Bosisto [q.v.3] & Co., Cuming [q.v.8] Smith & Co. Ltd, the Adelaide Chemical and Fertilizer Co. Ltd and the Melbourne Glass Bottle Works Pty Ltd. Norton and Harold were well established as leaders of Melbourne business life, Norton becoming president of the chamber of commerce in 1912. The family's next venture, the establishment of the Australia Oxygen Co. in June 1910, arose from Russell's lifelong interest in industrial gases and became his particular responsibility;

vied with a new Sydney company as pioneer of large-scale oxygen production in Australia. Russell's interest in forests and their products led him to persuade Bosisto's to experiment with the extraction of oils and compounds from indigenous plants. It proved an interesting failure, though sales of eucalyptus oil sustained the company.

When war broke out in 1914 Harold quit business to become chief embarkation officer for the Australian Imperial Force in Victoria, before forming, in August 1915, the 4th Field Artillery Brigade and taking it to Egypt and France. In 1916 he took command of the 3rd Division Artillery with the rank of brigadier general, and at the end of the war was appointed general officer commanding Artillery, Australian Corps. A forceful leader, he was four times mentioned in dispatches, was appointed C.M.G. in 1917 and C.B. in 1918, and received a Croix de Guerre. He also earned two nicknames: in the army 'Grim Death' and in the Grimwade firms in later years 'the General'. From 1926 to 1930 he commanded 4th Division, Australian Military Forces.

Despite vicissitudes, war strengthened the Grimwade enterprises. Russell took Harold's place on the boards of Cuming Smiths and the Melbourne Glass Bottle Works. In 1915 the latter became Australian Glass Manufacturers Ltd, with Norton as chairman and W. J. 'Gunboat' Smith [q.v.] as managerial genius. Felton Grimwade's itself lost overseas sources of supply, leading Russell to experiment with local production of tar derivatives and with drug-growing. His scientific ingenuity was challenged further by his membership of the advisory council set up in 1916 (forerunner of the Commonwealth Scientific and Industrial Research Organization) on which he joined Professor (Sir) David Orme Masson [q.v.] and others in some remarkable scientific improvisations.

In 1920 Felton Grimwade and other Grimwade partnerships were reorganized as proprietary companies. Alfred Sheppard Grimwade (1874-1941), a surgeon, joined his three brothers as director of the new Australian Oxygen and Industrial Gases Pty Ltd, with Russell as chairman. A new venture, the Felton Grimwade Scientific Instrument Co., failed within a year; and indeed the new structure of Felton Grimwade's itself was short lived. In 1929 local competition forced a merger with Duerdin & Sainsbury Pty Ltd; in the same year threats from overseas persuaded the Grimwades to take their pharmaceutical and dental companies into a new national structure, Drug Houses of Australia Ltd. Norton became D.H.A.'s first chairman, and Harold a board member; Russell joined the board when Norton retired

from it in 1937, he and Harold both serving several terms as chairman. The Grimwades regretted the passing of earlier, more intimate styles of business leadership. Russell celebrated life in the firm's old bluestone headquarters in his *Flinders Lane: recollections of Alfred Felton* (1947); five years later he wrote a further nostalgic note when Felton Grimwade & Duerdins Pty Ltd became simply D.H.A. (Vic) Pty Ltd. He did not live to see D.H.A. itself fall prey to international asset-strippers.

The Grimwade brothers were very successful in the new environment. As chairman of Cuming Smiths from 1920 until 1945, Norton helped that remarkable company maintain profitability by shedding functions. He also presided over the opposite process in the glass industry, the conglomerate Australian Consolidated Industries Ltd replacing Australian Glass Manufacturers in 1939. Russell was forced to see his beloved Australian Oxygen merge with British and Sydney interests to form Commonwealth Industrial Gases Ltd in 1935, but he rightly foresaw C.I.G.'s future strength. He consoled himself by nurturing the sickly Carba Dry Ice (Australia) Ltd, formed on his initiative in 1929.

Norton remained chairman of A.C.I. until he died at Macedon on 29 April 1945. Of his five sons, one died as a stretcher-bearer on Gallipoli, another was a prisoner in Germany; Geoffrey Holt Grimwade (1902-1961) was the only one to persist in a business career. Norton provided Melbourne Church of England Girls' Grammar School with Phelia Grimwade House in honour of his wife, and was quietly generous to a number of other causes.

Harold succeeded Norton as chairman of A.C.I. and of Felton Grimwade & Duerdins. He died at Marathon on 2 January 1949, survived by two sons and a daughter. His estate was sworn for probate at £239 381. Russell succeeded Harold as chairman of Felton Grimwade & Duerdins, and continued as a director of C.I.G. until 1953, when he also relinquished chairmanship of Carba. Bosisto's, of which he had long been chairman, at last became a subsidiary of D.H.A. in 1951.

The brothers shared in succession membership of the Felton Bequests Committee. Norton succeeded his father in 1910, and as chairman steered the committee through its frequently turbulent relations with the National Gallery of Victoria, deserving more credit than he was usually given. Harold succeeded him briefly. Russell was chosen to succeed Harold in 1949, and became chairman in 1952. (Sir) Daryl Lindsay [q.v.], director of the National Gallery, was a close friend and Frankston neighbour, and

Russell set out to strengthen both the London and Melbourne operations of the committee, inspired by his personal admiration for its founder.

Russell's other interests and commitments outside business were extraordinarily diverse. Like his brothers he loved travel, and recorded in diary and in photographs the leisurely expeditions undertaken by the rich of his generation. He was an early motoring enthusiast, the first to drive from Melbourne to Adelaide. He financed and organized an expedition to Goondiwindi, Queensland, to observe the eclipse of the sun in 1922 and another in 1947 to follow Eyre's [q.v.1] route across the Nullarbor. His most frequent trips were into the forests; and the development of his remarkable garden at Miegunyah was but part of his life-long passion for plants and trees. He read widely in botanical literature, and published in 1920 *An anthography of the Eucalypts*, a survey illustrated with his own photographs. He campaigned tirelessly for the conservation of forests as an office-bearer of the Australian Forest League and a contributor to its journal *Gum Nut*. He supported the opening of the Australian Forestry School, under his friend C. E. Lane Poole [q.v.], at Canberra in 1927, endowing the Russell Grimwade prize to encourage scientific forestry. At home, in his workshop, he developed cabinet-making skills of a very high order, using native timbers. (In 1939 the workshop became a crutch factory, Russell and his friends producing 3000 pairs by 1941, to his own improved design.) He gave financial support to the forest products division of the Council for Scientific and Industrial Research, as well as involving himself, for forty years, in C.S.I.R.'s advisory councils.

Russell's interest in drug growth and manufacture involved him in medical research, and he was a member of the board of the Walter and Eliza Hall [qq.v.] Institute of Medical Research from 1935 and its chairman in 1942-48. In 1950 the Victorian branch of the British Medical Association admitted him to honorary membership, a rare distinction. An active member of the Royal Australian Chemical Institute, he was especially concerned to bring science and industry into closer relationships; in 1938 he was elected a fellow of the institute, and in 1939 president of the chemistry section of the Australian and New Zealand Association for the Advancement of Science. His presidential address on 'The atmosphere as a raw material', was a remarkable synthesis of his preoccupations as industrial chemist and naturalist, earning him a place in the history of the conservation movement in Australia.

He was concerned also to conserve the works of man. He acquired a strong collection of Australian prints and books and some notable pictures, chief among them Strutt's [q.v.6] 'Bushrangers on the St Kilda Road'. Sharing his generation's admiration for the explorers and settlers he made Cook [q.v.1] a particular hero, and in 1934 donated the so-called Cook's Cottage to the people of Victoria as a centenary gift. He believed in progress, in civilization as in science, and celebrated white exploration and settlement without much concern for antecedent cultures. In campaigning to preserve relics of the past at a time when Australians commonly despised everything old, however, he anticipated the aims of the National Trust.

Russell also belonged to the advisory committee for the Botanic Gardens, the board of the National Museum of Victoria and the Council of Melbourne Grammar School. A member of the Council of the University of Melbourne from 1935, and deputy chancellor in 1941-43, he was active on its buildings committee and was one of those responsible for the appointment of (Sir) J. D. G. Medley as vice-chancellor in 1938. Generous to many causes, Russell's largest gift during his lifetime was of £50 000 to the university in 1944, towards the building of the Russell Grimwade School of Biochemistry.

Russell Grimwade was appointed C.B.E. in 1935 and knighted in 1950. Severe illnesses in 1950 and 1953 were followed by his death from coronary vascular disease on 2 November 1955. His estate was valued for probate at almost £1 million. His wife, who died on 6 September 1973, left a further $2 million. Between them they left Miegunyah and a substantial endowment to the University of Melbourne, for its general benefit. They had no children.

J. R. Poynter, *Russell Grimwade* (Melb, 1967), and *Alfred Felton* (Melb, 1974); Felton Grimwade, Russell Grimwade and DHA papers (Univ Melb Archives); H. W. Grimwade papers (AWM); family information.   J. R. POYNTER

GROOM, ARTHUR (1904-1953), conservationist and author, was born on 11 December 1904 at Caulfield, Melbourne, son of Arthur Champion Groom [q.v.] and Eva Rosabelle Groom. His parents moved to Longreach, Queensland, about 1911 and to Julia Creek about 1916. Arthur finished his schooling as a boarder at the Southport School near Brisbane. He was a jackeroo at Lake Nash cattle-station on the Northern Territory border in 1922-25, then went to Brisbane in 1926 to write for the *Sunday Mail*. He won second prize in a *Bulletin* story competition in the late 1920s and in 1930 published his first book, *A merry Christmas*, in London. The story was set in Brisbane and far western Queensland.

In 1927-32 Groom worked as a salesman, first for the Engineering Supply Co. of Australia Ltd in Brisbane and then for Underhill, Day & Co. Ltd, engineers. At week-ends and on holiday, he headed with pack and camera into the rain forest from O'Reilly's [q.v.] guest-house on the edge of Lamington National Park. He was a founder in May 1930 and for four years honorary secretary of the National Parks Association of Queensland. In 1933 he helped to form Queensland Holiday Resorts Ltd and henceforth managed their Binna Burra guest-house on the north-east border of Lamington Park. He had to be jack of all trades—guide, entertainer, mechanic, builder of slab huts and sometimes cook. For many years everything was brought into the guest-house by flying fox up a steep hill.

Groom was an excellent outdoor photographer and, during World War II, lectured on survival in the jungle to the 50 000 Australian and American troops who passed through the Canungra jungle training centre. He continued to write, but abandoned fiction. *One mountain after another* (1949) told the story of the border-survey between New South Wales and Queensland, and of Lamington Park and Binna Burra, and pleaded for protection of 'The Scenic Rim' as he called a proposed reserve along McPherson Range and the Great Dividing Range. *I saw a strange land* (1950) covered his extensive walks with pack-camels in Central Australia. His posthumous publication, *Wealth in the wilderness* (1955), dealt with the Northern Territory and its future.

Groom was a remarkable walker. About 1930 he walked across country by moonlight from O'Reilly's to Mount Barney, selected a camp-site, talked to landowners and returned, covering seventy miles (112 km), midnight to midnight. He died in Melbourne of coronary vascular disease on 14 November 1953 while engaged in tourist promotion, and was buried in Box Hill cemetery. He had married three times. His first wife, Catherine Edith, née Nicoll, whom he married in Brisbane on 6 June 1931, died four months later. His second marriage, in Brisbane on 16 January 1936 to Marjorie Edna Dunstan, ended in divorce in 1949; they had three sons. His third wife Isla Hurworth, née Madge, whom he married at Surfer's Paradise on 22 August 1949, survived him with their daughter.

Southerly, 15 (1954), no 3, p 219; *Sunday Mail*, 15 Nov 1953; *Courier Mail*, 15 Nov 1956; personal information.   J. KEITH JARROTT

GROOM, ARTHUR CHAMPION (1852-1922), politician and land and stock agent, was born on 26 November 1852 at Harefield, near Fingal, Van Diemen's Land, fifth son of Francis Groom, who had settled at Harefield in 1843, and his wife Matilda Emma, née Minnett. He was educated at Horton College, Ross.

In September 1872 Groom arrived in Victoria. He was managing a station, probably near Geelong, at the time of his marriage on 8 January 1877 at All Saints' Church of England, Geelong, to Gertrude Rudge; they had a daughter and three sons. About 1878 he joined William Hamilton & Co., stock and station agents. In May 1881 he took over the goodwill of the firm, retaining its name until about 1903, when it became known as Hamilton, Groom & Co. The head office was in Queen Street, Melbourne, but it operated mainly in south Gippsland and sales were held monthly and fortnightly at the firm's yards at Leongatha, Poowong, Loch, Korumburra and other townships.

As the firm's principal and a well-known auctioneer, Groom became identified with many interests in the Gippsland district. He turned his attention to politics and in March 1886 defeated the sitting member F. C. Mason [q.v.5] for the seat of South Gippsland in the Legislative Assembly. After a redistribution in 1889 he won Gippsland West, but lost the seat in April 1892; another attempt in 1897 was unsuccessful. Groom had been involved with Sir Matthew Davies [q.v.4] in Country Estates Ltd, an attempt to subdivide land at Neerim South. In 1889 he was a member of the royal commission on the coal industry of Victoria, which issued three reports between 1889 and 1891, and in 1890 he was a member of the Railways Standing Committee. He was also closely involved in the late 1880s in the movement towards a closer organization of rural members as a 'country party'.

Transferring his ambitions to the Federal sphere, in March 1901 Groom won Flinders in the House of Representatives. However he retired from politics at the next election in December 1903. R. A. Crouch [q.v.8] described him as one of the few Victorian free traders in the first Federal parliament, a 'quick nervous speaker' who attended rarely, claiming that his business as stock agent was quite as important as parliament.

Groom's term in Federal parliament coincided with his part as originator and moving spirit of a venture which united a number of Gippsland landowners and businessmen in a syndicate to buy Kyogle, a property on the Richmond River in northern New South Wales. Groom became managing director and W. C. Greaves [q.v.] chairman of the company formed in November

1903 to make the purchase. Shareholders and buyers made large profits from the subsequent subdivision, improvement and resale of the land.

The success of the Kyogle venture encouraged Groom to look further north, and in 1908 he set himself up as a special agent for the Queensland government for the sale of land. In 1910 he managed a large sale at Merrimac (near Surfers Paradise). He decided to settle in Queensland, first at Rosabel station, near Arrilah, Longreach, in 1911-14 and later at Rosabel Downs, Julia Creek.

He died on 22 March 1922 in hospital at Cloncurry, survived by his second wife Eva Rosabel, née Groom, and their three daughters and four sons, of whom the eldest was Arthur [q.v.]. A daughter of his first marriage also survived him.

J. Smith (ed), *Cyclopedia of Victoria*, 3 (Melb, 1905); H. Copeland, *The path of progress* (Warragul, Vic, 1934); H. H. Peck, *Memoirs of a stockman* (Melb, 1942); B. D. Graham, *The formation of the Australian Country Parties* (Canb, 1966); Crouch memoirs (LaTL).   LESLIE M. MOORHEAD*

GROOM, HENRY LITTLETON (1860-1926), newspaper proprietor and politician, was born on 4 January 1860 at Toowoomba, Queensland, eldest son of William Henry Groom [q.v.4] and his wife Grace, née Littleton. Educated at St Mary's School, Ipswich, and Brisbane Grammar School, he entered the office of the *Toowoomba Chronicle* which his father owned solely from 1876. Although he soon rose to become business manager, he knew the workings of the paper from front to back and could 'get things going if there was an early-morning press breakdown'. As W. H. Groom's political activities increasingly took him away from Toowoomba in the late 1880s and the 1890s, Henry became the backbone of the *Chronicle* enterprise. When his father relinquished sole proprietorship in November 1900 with the formation of W. H. Groom & Sons Ltd, he became a director. On his father's death in August 1901, he became managing director and administered the *Chronicle* until the Dunn family [q.v.8] took over in June 1922. He contributed greatly to the country press as a whole through his presidency of the Queensland Country Press Association from 1912 to 1923.

The take-over marked the saddest day of Henry Groom's life. Although it had been W. H. Groom's express wish that the family should not sell, Henry's brother William, who was accountant at the *Chronicle* and held power of attorney for other family shareholders, is said to have secretly arranged the sale. Henry stayed on as business manager until June 1925.

Groom had been an enthusiastic supporter of the closer settlement policy championed by his father and unsuccessfully contested Drayton and Toowoomba in a 1904 by-election for the Legislative Assembly. On 12 July 1906 he was appointed to the Legislative Council by the Kidston [q.v.] ministry and held his seat until 23 March 1922. He made one major speech on closer settlement, but spoke rarely and made little impression. Politically, Henry was always overshadowed by his younger brother Littleton Ernest [q.v.], a Commonwealth minister to whom he gave valuable service as a reporter on his electorate.

In early manhood Groom joined the Queensland Defence Force and rose to the rank of lieutenant in the 4th (Darling Downs) Infantry. He accompanied the Toowoomba detachment sent to the Charleville district during the shearers' strike in 1891 and retired in 1896. He was active in patriotic organizations during the South African War and in World War I was one of the principal workers for the Toowoomba Patriotic Fund.

On 30 November 1898 at Toowoomba Groom had married Marion Flora Black. Of their four children, William Henry George built up his own daily newspaper at Innisfail, while a daughter Marion Flora, known as Dolly, was also a journalist. Groom died at Toowoomba on 4 January 1926 and was buried in Toowoomba cemetery with Church of England rites.

Government Gazette (Qld), 28 Sept 1889, 18 Dec 1896; *A'sian Journalist*, 15 Nov 1926; *SMH*, 5 Jan 1896; *Toowoomba Chronicle*, 1 Dec 1898, 7 Oct 1899, 3 Oct 1922, 5 Jan 1926; *Bulletin*, 31 May 1923; *Bundaberg Daily Times*, 16 Aug, 2 Nov 1926; Groom papers (NL).   ROD KIRKPATRICK

GROOM, SIR LITTLETON ERNEST (1867-1936), barrister and politician, was born on 22 April 1867 at Toowoomba, Queensland, third son of William Henry Groom [q.v.4] and his wife Grace, née Littleton. A brilliant student, winning many prizes, he was educated at Toowoomba North State School, Toowoomba Grammar School and the University of Melbourne (M.A., 1891; LL.M., 1892). While at Ormond College, Melbourne, he participated in a range of journalistic and cultural activities, exposing himself to ideas which would later emerge in his political career. In 1891-1901 he combined a barrister's practice in Brisbane with involvement in Church and educational ventures. An active and devout

Anglican, he felt that Christians should make practical efforts to help the less fortunate. He worked for the Brisbane Literary Circle and the Brisbane School of Arts and was a leading figure in the Queensland University Extension Movement. He collaborated in the authorship or preparation of legal reports and texts and in 1900 was appointed a deputy District Court judge. On 4 July 1894 at South Melbourne he married Jessie, daughter of Charles Bell, a Presbyterian minister of Wagga Wagga, New South Wales.

William Groom had been elected to the first Commonwealth House of Representatives as member for the Darling Downs in 1901 but died on 8 August of that year. At the request of his father's supporters, Groom stood at the subsequent by-election; he received the endorsement of the Barton [q.v.7] government and despite a strong opponent was elected with a substantial majority on 14 September. He soon became identified in the House of Representatives with the more radical Protectionists. An enthusiastic convert to the 'New Liberal' ideology, he was also a fervent Australian nationalist who believed that the Commonwealth rather than the States should become the focus of popular loyalties. He argued for a drastic extension of Commonwealth powers, particularly in regard to industrial relations. Because of his views on Commonwealth conciliation and arbitration he supported the short-lived Labor administration of 1904 and entered the alliance formed between Labor and some Protectionists.

On 5 July 1905 Alfred Deakin [q.v.8] appointed Groom minister for home affairs in the new Liberal Protectionist administration. The appointment revealed that Groom had emerged as an energetic and forceful politician. Just as important, though, were his links with the Labor caucus as the Deakin government was dependent on Labor support. Groom saw as his main task the expansion of Commonwealth activity. Almost inevitably this involved him in clashes with the States such as the disputes with New South Wales over the proposed Commonwealth Bureau of Census and Statistics and the site for a Federal capital. His greatest success in overcoming State objections concerned Commonwealth involvement in meteorology and the transfer to the Commonwealth of State properties. Promoted to attorney-general on 12 October 1906, Groom was for the next two years closely involved with most aspects of government policy. He defended New Protection which he saw as an attempt to raise the tariff so that it could cope with a range of community needs; he introduced bounties legislation, helped enforce H. B.

Higgins's [q.v.] 'Harvester Judgment', attempted to control the operations of large trusts and represented the Commonwealth in the High Court when its Excise Tariff (Agricultural Machinery) Act (1906) came under challenge. His last major achievement during the Deakin administration was the drafting and carrying of legislation to provide Commonwealth invalid and old age pensions.

Groom had reservations about the Fusion of non-Labor parties in 1909 yet in the end saw no realistic alternative, given the announced Labor intention to stand candidates against Liberal Protectionists. He was also concerned that Labor was moving towards more doctrinaire socialism; for him the stage had been reached where governments should consolidate on previous reforms rather than introduce new ones. One of only three Liberal Protectionists included in the Fusion government of 2 June 1909, he served for the next eleven months as minister for external affairs. However, much of his legislation was blocked in the House of Representatives, and even his high commissioner bill, which was ultimately successful in establishing Australian representation in London, received much criticism.

In the election of April 1910 Groom was one of the few former Liberal Protectionists to hold his seat against Labor. Thereafter he became a prominent opponent of Labor's socialistic measures. He attacked such proposals as the establishment of a Commonwealth bank and the attempts to gain Commonwealth control over monopolies, which he now argued were designed only to appeal to trade unionists or unnecessarily interfered with individual rights. He was once more in office, as minister for trade and customs, in (Sir) Joseph Cook's [q.v.8] Liberal government between 24 June 1913 and 17 September 1914. The policy to reverse Labor's achievements, however, frustrated whatever desire he had for positive initiatives. Along with Cook, he often declared that the Liberals could achieve little while Labor controlled the Senate.

After Labor's victory in the double dissolution election of September 1914 Groom devoted himself to the national war effort. He constantly stressed the righteousness of the allied cause and was active in the pro-conscription campaign before the 1916 referendum. From 17 February 1917 he served in the Nationalist government of W. M. Hughes [q.v.] as assistant minister for defence until 16 November when he became vice-president of the Executive Council. He was prominent in the second conscription referendum of 1917 and remained a strong supporter of Hughes's prosecution of the war.

The war turned Groom back to being an advocate of increased Commonwealth powers. In 1919, unlike many Nationalists, he supported Hughes's proposals to further strengthen the Commonwealth's powers in industry, trade and commerce. He felt that the war had accustomed people to the idea of extended national authority, and maintained that the Commonwealth government was the only instrumentality able to cope with the perplexing problems of the immediate post-war years. As minister for works and railways from 27 March 1918 he pushed for a vigorous development programme. He supervised increased Commonwealth involvement in the Murray Waters conservation scheme and the start of new construction at Canberra where, according to W. D. Bingle [q.v.7], he was 'the man who lifted the whole business out of the bog'.

On 21 December 1921 he again became attorney-general, retaining the post for four years. Although the most senior minister in the House of Representatives, he was passed over for the Nationalist leadership on Hughes's resignation when the Nationalist-Country Party coalition under (Viscount) Bruce [q.v.7] was formed. He was not happy with the coalition agreement, nor did he like Bruce, but the relationship between the two started amicably enough. Bruce respected Groom's experience and was no doubt largely responsible for the latter's appointment as K.C.M.G. in January 1924. From 29 May until 13 June 1924 Groom was also minister for trade and customs and for health. He had become K.C. in 1923.

As attorney-general Groom's record was mixed. On the positive side, he presided over the introduction of a new public service superannuation scheme and replaced the public service commissioner with a board of three. He encountered problems in his attempts to extend the Commonwealth's industrial powers. During 1924 he served as leader of the Australian delegation to the Fifth Assembly of the League of Nations in Geneva. As a committee chairman he helped formulate a protocol which aimed to establish a more concrete system of international arbitration. He was later disappointed when most League members, including Britain and Australia, rejected the protocol: instructed to abstain, Groom voted for the measure.

Perhaps of most significance was his role in deportation proceedings. He had a deep and sincere, if exaggerated, concern that 'foreign' radical agitators posed a threat to Australia. It was largely on his initiative that two Irish republican spokesmen were deported early in 1923 and he participated in the unsuccessful attempt to deport two overseas-born leaders of the Australian Seamen's Union during 1925. Partly because of his handling of the latter case and also from dissatisfaction with his general performance, Bruce demanded Groom's resignation as attorney-general which took effect on 18 December.

In compensation for his removal from the ministry Groom became Speaker of the House of Representatives the following January. On 10 September 1929 he refused to use his casting vote to save the government from defeat over its maritime industries bill, which proposed to remove the Commonwealth from most areas of conciliation and arbitration. His notion of an independent speakership, opposition to the bill itself and resentment at his forced resignation in 1925 were the main reasons for this crucial decision. He was subsequently denied Nationalist endorsement for the Darling Downs and on 12 October lost his seat to the official Nationalist candidate following a very bitter campaign. His defeat brought to an end nearly seventy years continuous parliamentary representation of the Toowoomba district by the Groom family.

Groom returned to the Bar in Brisbane but won back the Darling Downs as an Independent on 15 December 1931. He joined the United Australia Party in August 1933. For the remainder of his life, however, he was not as active as hitherto in parliament. Instead, he used his prestige to aid particular causes. He was president of the Australian branch of the League of Nations Union, remained a leading lay member of the Church of England and forcefully argued for a national university in Canberra. He died there on 6 November 1936 of coronary vascular disease, survived by his wife and one of their two daughters. A well-attended funeral service was held at Parliament House and he was buried in the grounds of St John's Church of England. There is a portrait of Groom by Fred Leist [q.v.] in Parliament House and a memorial spire stands in Toowoomba.

Throughout his career Groom followed a routine which differed little from year to year. In addition to his political duties he led an active social life, spent considerable time working for the Church of England, at one stage being a member of its Australian Synod, and wrote dozens of articles and pamphlets on legal, political and religious subjects. He was joint author, with Sir John Quick [q.v.] of *The judicial power of the Commonwealth* (1904). At Toowoomba he resided in a comfortable home overlooking the Great Dividing Range, and was a conscientious local member, whose short and always well-dressed figure was a familiar sight. What leisure time he had was spent in gardening, photography and reading.

Groom has sometimes been viewed as a rather dull politician of only moderate ability. Certainly he was not a gifted orator nor was he in the limelight as often as some of his contemporaries. Yet he was a generally sound administrator who left a distinct mark on Australia. Hard-working and honest, he was responsible for a variety of reforms and was among the first to realize that many political problems could only be treated in a national context. He also stands out as the representative of a significant mode of non-Labor political thought, though his concept of the active social role of the state differed from the Labor view only in degree. On occasions he went so far as to justify the limitation of individual liberties if the interests of the majority were at stake. In his speeches and writings he always portrayed himself as a liberal in the evident belief that the word had a consistent, if developing, meaning. The striking feature of his life was not only the continuity of his beliefs but the frequency with which he acted on them over a very long period after their first formulation.

L. F. Fitzhardinge et al, *Nation building in Australia; the life and work of Sir Littleton Ernest Groom* ... (Syd, 1941); D. Carment, Australian liberal; a political biography of Sir Littleton Groom, 1867-1936 (Ph.D. thesis, ANU, 1975), and for bibliog.

DAVID CARMENT

GROVER, MONTAGUE MacGREGOR (1870-1943), journalist, was born on 31 May 1870 at West Melbourne, son of Harry Ehret Grover, old Etonian and former gold escort officer, from Hertfordshire, England, and his wife Jessie, née McGuire, of Melbourne, for many years a contributor to Melbourne *Punch* and the *Bulletin*'s 'Red Page'. Monty was educated at Melbourne Church of England Grammar School (1881) and Queen's College, St Kilda, and attended art school for two years. In 1888-92 he was articled to a firm of architects.

From about 1890 he wrote short pieces for the *Bulletin*. When the depression ended hopes of a career in architecture he decided to try newspaper work. An introduction to David Syme [q.v.6] of the *Age* led to casual reporting assignments and in August to October 1894 he also worked on the short-lived labour weekly, the *Boomerang*. Late that year he was offered a permanent job with the *Age*; in 1896 he joined the *Argus*. Always fascinated by the theatre, in 1902-03 he travelled to England as secretary to J. C. Williamson [q.v.6].

On 29 May 1897 at Holy Trinity vicarage, Coburg, Grover had married Ada Goldberg; they had two sons and five daughters, one

of whom died in infancy. The family settled at Bondi in 1907 when Grover joined the *Sydney Morning Herald* as sub-editor.

Grover maintained that a newspaper should sell news, not mould public opinion. His unorthodox views were appreciated by (Sir) Hugh Denison [q.v.8] who in 1910 invited him to rejuvenate the evening *Star*. Grover renamed the paper the *Sun* and even designed the new mast-head. Many of the features he incorporated in the *Sun* were new to Australian journalism: bold, expanded heading types, lively headlines and brisk, tersely written news stories. Long-winded reports were out. Other innovations included crosswords and, in late 1921 in the Sunday edition, colour comic-strips featuring the work of his protégé Jim Bancks [q.v.7]. The *Sun*'s circulation soared; Grover's name became a synonym for news enterprise. As a colleague later observed, he 'found the newspapers of the Commonwealth rather stodgy and complacent; he left them awakened and aggressive'.

After editing the Sunday issue of the *Sun* from 1917, Grover represented the paper in London for a year, returning to Sydney in 1921. In 1922 he was appointed to launch the *Evening Sun* in Melbourne, Denison's rival to (Sir) Keith Murdoch's [q.v.] afternoon *Herald*. When Murdoch blocked production by flaunting a territorial agreement that had six months to run, Grover persuaded Denison to publish a completely new style of morning paper, the *Sun-News Pictorial*; it proved highly successful. The *Evening Sun* was launched by Grover in April next year and also sold well but when Murdoch bought it in 1925, he closed it down. Grover supervised the minor publications of the Herald and Weekly Times Ltd before leaving on a world tour. He returned to the *Herald* in 1929-30 as its magazine editor but found the post unchallenging. In September 1931 he was first editor of the Sydney labour daily, the *World*, which ceased publication fourteen months later.

Apart from writing verse and stories for the weekly press, Grover published *The minus quantity and other short plays* (1914); 'Gib it tshillin' was included in *Best Australian one-act plays* (1937). Both pro-socialist ('before I had even heard of Marx') and passionately pro-Australian, he outlined his views in a popular treatise, *The time is now ripe* (1937). Earlier, his reminiscences had appeared in *Lone Hand*, July-November 1914. He was remembered for his unquenchable humour and puckish wit, his honesty, his hatred of opportunism and compromise, and his insistence that every person, regardless of status, sex or race, was worthy of respect. He was a teetotaller, but loved good company and talk.

Grover divorced his wife in 1914 and on 14 September 1915 at Hampton, Melbourne, he married 24-year-old Regina Roseville Varley; they had three children. His health was not good from the early 1930s; he died of hypertensive cardiovascular disease on 7 March 1943 at his South Yarra home and was cremated. He was survived by his second wife and seven children, three of whom were journalists. The Montague Grover memorial prize competition for cadet journalists is held annually.

R. B. Walker, *The newspaper press in New South Wales*, 1803-1920 (Syd, 1976); J. Ryan, *Panel by panel* (Syd, 1979); *Journalist*, 15 May 1925, May 1973; *Newspaper News*, 1 May 1929, 1 Apr 1930, 1 Sept 1931, 1 Apr 1943; *Bulletin*, 31 Dec 1903, 16 July 1930; *Punch* (Melb), 20 Nov 1919; *Aust Worker*, 2 Sept 1931; *Argus*, and *Herald* (Melb), 8 Mar 1943; information from H. Grover, Blairgowrie, D. Parker, Frankston, K. Grover, Sth Yarra and M. Cannon, Main Ridge, Vic.

SALLY O'NEILL

GRUNER, ELIOTH (ELLIOTT) LAURITZ LEGANYER (1882-1939), landscape artist, was born on 16 December 1882 at Gisborne, Poverty Bay, New Zealand, younger son of Elliott Grüner, bailiff, and his Irish wife Mary Ann (d. 1922), née Brennan. His father was born of German parentage in Christiania (Oslo) and later migrated to New Zealand. In 1883 the family settled in Sydney, where Gruner from 1894 had drawing lessons from Julian Ashton [q.v.7]. At 14 he became a draper's assistant, and attended classes at Ashton's art school, where he met George Lambert [q.v.], who remained a lifelong inspiration.

From October 1901 Gruner exhibited regularly with the Society of Artists, Sydney, and from 1907 attracted serious attention. An important admirer was Norman Lindsay [q.v.]; from about 1913 he frequently visited Lindsay at Springwood, where he painted with Harley Griffiths.

Despite the responsibility of supporting his mother, Gruner left his job in 1912 to manage the Fine Arts Society's Bligh Street gallery and shop, dealing solely with Australian art. In 1914 he became an assistant at Ashton's Sydney Art School, but did not like teaching. In 1915 he visited Melbourne and painted with Griffiths and with Max Meldrum [q.v.], whose tonal theories strongly affected his vision and technique; he also visited the National Gallery of Victoria to see Corot's 'The Bent Tree'. He assisted with the organization in 1916 of an exhibition of the work of J. J. Hilder [q.v.], whose influence was also important. Until the end of the decade Gruner produced his finest

work, arising out of an intense lyrical preoccupation with the effects of, and even the very substance and nature of, light. His almost pantheistic obsession, which manifested itself mainly around Emu Plains and Windsor in the *plein air* style he had learned from Ashton, inspired Lindsay to the most extravagant praise in print. Gruner was awarded the Wynne prize for 1916 for the painting 'Morning Light' (and was to win six more times—1919, 1921, 1929, 1934, 1936 and 1937).

Deeply disturbed by Australia's involvement in World War I, he fretted about being safely home when others were suffering; and in October 1917 told Hans Heysen [q.v.] that 'I cannot hope for any peace of mind until I am trying to do something to repair the damage done the unfortunate victims of the ghastly tragedy'. He enlisted in the Australian Imperial Force on 4 June 1918, went into Liverpool camp and was discharged on 31 December.

In 1919 Gruner's acceptance by the official art world was further confirmed when the trustees of the National Art Gallery of New South Wales commissioned a painting, 'Valley of the Tweed'. In 1923 his friend Howard Hinton [q.v.] paid his passage overseas. In London Gruner reluctantly agreed to manage the Society of Artists' exhibition of Australian art at Burlington House. Sir William Orpen, unaware that he was being escorted around the exhibition by the artist, pungently criticized Gruner's paintings; embarrassed, Orpen later made more constructive comments that were to change Gruner's style dramatically. He spent two years in Europe and was impressed by the paintings of Cézanne and Gauguin. When he returned to Sydney early in 1925, he accepted Orpen's advice to make smaller pictures, thin down his paint and achieve a drier, pastel-like surface; he steered towards an English style of modernism, interpreting the rhythmic anatomy of the earth as seen from a higher vantage-point, which tended to flatten forms. His tonality grew even more sombre in the 1930s. In the late 1920s his paintings sold extremely well and a large loan exhibition of his work was mounted by the Art Gallery in Sydney in 1932.

Of medium height and weight, Gruner 'was fair, with a slight squareness of face from his Nordic father, and a faintly humorous twitch up at the corners of lips ... He was slow-moving and slow-spoken, with a well modulated voice'. Beneath the surface of his success and recognition he was desperately unhappy and in later years drank more and more. According to Jack Lindsay, 'He could not achieve a settled love-relationship and remained at an uneasy bisexuality'. Shy and reticent, he was painfully sensitive to the smallest criticism of his work, destroying many pictures which caused him dissatisfaction. Gruner was fearful of persecution and occasionally prone to frustrated outbursts of anger. He also felt uncomfortable when overpraised. His double existence—long periods of painting in the field while living in primitive conditions contrasted with the fastidious and stylish social life he led in the city—underscored his final despair of identity and purpose.

Suffering from chronic nephritis, Gruner died at his home at Waverley on 17 October 1939 and was cremated with Anglican rites. Next year the Art Gallery mounted a memorial exhibition of his work. A self-portrait is privately owned.

J. Ashton and N. Lindsay, *The art of Elioth Gruner* (Syd, 1923); N. Lindsay, *Elioth Gruner* (Syd, 1947); J. Lindsay, *The roaring twenties* (Lond, 1960); J. Hetherington, *Norman Lindsay* (Melb, 1973); Bernard Smith, *Australian painting 1788-1970* (Melb, 1971); L. Rees, *The small treasures of a lifetime* (Syd, 1969); Cats and biog files, Art Gallery of NSW, Syd; Heysen papers (NL); H. Hinton *and* L. Lindsay *and* S. Ure Smith papers (ML).

B. PEARCE

GSELL, FRANCIS XAVIER (1872-1960), missionary and bishop, was born on 30 October 1872 at Benfeld, Alsace-Lorraine, Germany, son of Laurent Gsell, spinner, and his wife Josephine, née Jehl. He grew up in Sainte-Croix-aux-Mines where he was apprenticed as a cotton-spinner. From 15, at Issoudin, he studied for six years at Le Petit-Oeuvre, run by the Missionaries of the Sacred Heart. In 1892 he took his vows and entered their society, after which he studied theology and philosophy at the St Apollinaire University in Rome. Eugene Pacelli, the future Pope Pius XII, was a colleague. Gsell was ordained in 1896.

Next year he went to Sydney and taught future missionaries at the Order's motherhouse at Kensington. He was relieved to begin active missionary work in 1900 in Papua. His next appointment was as apostolic administrator of the Northern Territory at Palmerston (Darwin) in 1906, where he re-established the Catholic Church. In 1909 Gsell became a naturalized Australian. At first he concentrated on the Christian education of Catholic children; he then took up the conversion of the Aboriginals. He had the humility to become his own anthropologist: 'I had to establish contact with the natives, alone, slowly, prudently; I had to . . . learn gradually their habits and customs so as to penetrate into their minds without hurt or shock'.

He persuaded the South Australian government to grant him 10 000 acres (4000 ha) for an Aboriginal mission on Bathurst Island in 1910. He studied the intricate laws and customs of the local Aboriginals and carefully chose for his central site an area which none of them claimed. In 1912 the island was proclaimed an Aboriginal reserve, and Gsell lived and worked here, apart from a visit to Europe in 1920, until 1938. He understood Aboriginal life, spiritual values and rituals and sought the people's advancement; at this time even some anthropologists believed that they would become extinct. He worked patiently: during fifteen years the mission performed only 113 baptisms; after thirty years he did not claim a single adult convert.

He was concerned to alter the polygamous nature of Tiwi society. Once, to save a girl from having to live unwillingly with an old man to whom she had been promised at birth, Gsell was inspired to 'buy' her. Thereafter he 'bought' 150 wives and, through their education and marriage to young men who accepted the Christian concept of marriage, he spread his religion. However he knew the Tiwi too well to entertain illusions. Their comprehension of the new marriage pattern probably represented a modification of traditional ways, but not a fundamental break.

In 1936 Gsell was appointed O.B.E. Two years later he left Bathurst Island to be consecrated bishop of Darwin. He established a mission at Arltunga in Central Australia, and a settlement for part-Aboriginals at Garden Point, Melville Island. His imperturbability belied his tenacity and forcefulness. In 1946 the Commonwealth government sought to resume all freehold land in Darwin and to remove the Catholic cathedral and school to another site. He fought the move—and won.

Next year he visited Rome. In 1950 he was awarded the Légion d'honneur; he retired to the Sacred Heart Monastery, Kensington, Sydney. Here he dictated his perceptive autobiography, *The bishop with 150 wives*; this was published in French in 1954, and in translation next year. In 1951 Pope Pius XII created him bishop assistant at the pontifical throne. He died on 12 July 1960 at Kensington and was buried in the Catholic cemetery, Douglas Park.

F. Flynn, *Distant horizons* (Syd, 1947) and *Northern gateway* (Syd, 1963); C. W. M. Hart and A. R. Pilling, *The Tiwi of north Australia* (New York, 1960); *NT News*, 12 July 1960 supplement, 24 June 1971; V. Krastins, The Tiwi. A culture contact history of the Australian Aborigines on Bathurst and Melville islands, 1705-1942 (B.A. Hons thesis, ANU, 1972); J. O'Carrigan and J. Morris, Christian marriage and family life on Bathurst Island mission [1964] *and* J. F. Murphy, 'Bathurst Island. A mission station for the Aborigines', *Australia*, Mar 1920 (typescript and pc held by Aust Inst of Aboriginal Studies); AA 20/21513 (AAO).

PETER DONOVAN

GUERIN, JULIA MARGARET (BELLA) (1858-1923), feminist, political activist and teacher, was born on 23 April 1858 at Williamstown, Victoria, daughter of Patrick Guerin, penal sergeant, later governor of gaols, and his wife Julia Margaret, née Kearney, both from Ireland.

Having studied at home to pass matriculation in 1878, Bella became the first woman to graduate from an Australian university when she gained her B.A. from the University of Melbourne in December 1883, becoming M.A. upon application in 1885. She taught first at Loreto Convent, Ballarat, urging higher education scholarships for Catholic girls to produce 'a band of noble thoughtful women as a powerful influence for good'; then as lady principal of Ballarat School of Mines university classes, resigning upon marriage to civil servant and poet Henry Halloran [q.v.4] at St Patrick's Cathedral, Melbourne, on 29 June 1891. Halloran, then aged 80, had addressed a laudatory poem to her after seeing a graduation portrait in 1884. He died in Sydney on 19 May 1893, leaving her with an infant son, Henry Marco. A second marriage at Christ Church, St Kilda, Melbourne, on 1 October 1909 to George D'Arcie Lavender, thirty years her junior, was apparently short lived. For much of her life she lived with her brother Marco Guerin, also a teacher.

Returning to teaching from financial necessity, Bella taught in Sydney, then Carlton, Prahran and East Melbourne. From the mid-1890s she frequented suffragist circles, becoming office-bearer in the Bendigo Women's Franchise League while running University College, Bendigo, in 1898-1903. From 1904 to 1917 she taught at Camperdown and in a succession of small Melbourne schools at South Yarra, St Kilda, Parkville and Brunswick with diminishing success. Her increasing political activity and disputes over conditions with the Education Department probably contributed to this outcome.

As vice-president of the Women's Political Association in 1912-14 Bella Guerin co-authored Vida Goldstein's [q.v.] 1913 Senate election pamphlet, but dual membership of non-party feminist and Labor Party organizations proved untenable. From 1914 she wrote and spoke for the Labor and Victorian Socialist parties and the Women's League of Socialists, and was recognized as a 'witty,

cogent and instructive' commentator on a range of controversial social issues; they included the rights of illegitimate children, 'brotherhood and sisterhood without sex distinction' and defence of English militant suffragettes. An ardent anti-war propagandist, she led the Labor Women's Anti-Conscription Fellowship campaign during the 1916 referendum and spoke in Adelaide, Broken Hill and Victorian metropolitan and country centres against militarism and in defence of rights of assembly and free speech.

Appointed vice-president of the Labor Party's Women's Central Organizing Committee in March 1918, she aroused censure and controversy for describing Labor women as 'performing poodles and packhorses' under represented in policy decisions and relegated to auxiliary fund-raising roles. Henceforth she organized for Labor 'only so far as it stands for those principles represented by the Red Flag', believing in the parliamentary system but desiring capitalism's elimination.

In religion she moved from Catholicism to rationalism. She described her political evolution as from 'Imperialistic butterfly' to 'democratic grub' and experienced continual tensions as a socialist feminist within the Labor Party. Her son, who practised as a doctor in Adelaide from 1915, described her as 'the kindest and most gentle of women'; she saw herself as a 'national idealist' and an 'incorrigible militant', promoting women's participation in public life. She was regarded as an orator of 'unique talents'.

She died in Adelaide on 26 July 1923 of cirrhosis of the liver and was buried in the Catholic cemetery, West Terrace.

I. Selby, *The old pioneers' memorial history of Melbourne* (Melb, 1924); Loreto Convent, *Eucalyptus Blossom*, 10 Dec 1886, p 8; *A'sian Schoolmaster*, 16 Mar 1904, p 171; *T&CJ*, 3 May 1884; *Woman Voter*, 13 May 1912; *Socialist*, 24 July 1914, 7 July, 22 Dec 1916, 24 May, 16 June, 5 July 1918, 7, 21 Nov 1919, 9 Jan 1920; *Labor Call*, 27 June 1918; family information and letters in possession of Mrs F. Halloran, Tranmere, SA.   FARLEY KELLY

GULLETT, HENRY (1837-1914), journalist and politician, was born on 20 January 1837 at Newton-Bushell, near Teignmouth, Devon, England, eldest child of Henry Gullett, stonemason, and his wife Isabella, née Keats (who was a cousin of the poet). He was educated at sundry schools in London and the provinces, wherever his father found work, then did odd jobs and assisted his father. The family reached Melbourne in the *Emigrant* on 29 April 1853. Henry junior spent the next three years working as a mason and a goldminer, and in 1856 went to his father's small farm at Mount Macedon.

An omnivorous reader, Gullett sailed for England in July 1861 in a fruitless search for a literary career. He returned to Melbourne in February 1863 and was employed as a court reporter on the *Argus* by Edward Wilson [q.v.6]. He represented the paper in Ceylon in 1869 and on his return to Melbourne next year became a sub-editor. At Williamstown on 25 November 1872 Gullett married his first cousin Lucinda (d. 1900), née Willie. That year he became editor of the *Australasian*; his wife, under the pseudonym 'Humming Bee', contributed to its women's pages.

In 1885 Gullett became associate editor of the Sydney *Daily Telegraph*, in which he had acquired an interest. In June 1890 he and its editor, F. W. Ward [q.v.], now a close friend, resigned over the question whether the directors or the editors should determine policy. Gullett moved to the *Sydney Morning Herald* as associate editor. A free trader, he absorbed the ideas of his friend Sir Henry Parkes [q.v.5] on Federation and combined them with his own belief in the iniquity of new States, outlined in his pamphlet, *Tropical New South Wales* (1887). In the 1890s Gullett fervently advocated Federation and supported a White Australia, better treatment of Aboriginals and rapid expansion of public works. Appointed acting editor of the *Herald* during the Constitution campaign of 1898, he gained much credit for the success of the referendum next year.

After his return from a tour of England in 1899, Gullett tried to retire from journalism but in 1901 was induced to edit the *Daily Telegraph*. By February 1903, when he finally retired, he was the largest shareholder in the Daily Telegraph Newspaper Co. Ltd, and remained a director until he was nominated to the Legislative Council in 1908. He attended regularly but he was nervous of making 'extempore speeches'; his only legislative contribution was the Defamation Amendment Act of 1909.

Gullett found writing difficult and his journalism was subdued and reflective. He had a literary outlet for his scholarly inclinations in the Shakespeare Society of New South Wales; its president in 1904-11, he published two booklets, the *Making of Shakespeare and other papers* (1905) and the *Study of Shakespeare* (1906). He was an enthusiastic member of the Sydney branch of the Royal Astronomical Society, a vice-president of the New South Wales Institute of Journalists and a director of the Mutual Life & Citizens Assurance Co. Ltd in 1908-14.

Placid and usually methodical, Gullett was rather dapper in appearance and enjoyed his large home and garden, Hindfell, Wahroonga, where he entertained often but quietly. He died there on 4 August 1914 and was buried in the Anglican section of Gore Hill cemetery. He was survived by four daughters including Dr Lucy Gullett [q.v.] and Amy, who married T. W. Heney [q.v.], his successor at the *Herald*; Sir Henry Somer Gullett [q.v.], was a nephew. His estate was valued for probate at £137 831. The Art Gallery of New South Wales holds his portrait by Julian Ashton [q.v.7].

C. B. Fletcher, *The great wheel* (Syd, 1940); R. B. Walker, *The newspaper press in New South Wales, 1803-1920* (Syd, 1976); *Daily Telegraph* (Syd), 5 Aug 1914; *SMH*, 5, 15 Aug 1914; Parkes letters, *and* Gullett papers (ML).

G. N. HAWKER

GULLETT, SIR HENRY SOMER (1878-1940), farmer, journalist, historian and politician, was born on 26 March 1878 at Toolamba West, Victoria, son of London-born Charles William Gullett, farmer, and his wife Rose Mary, née Somer, born in Victoria. He was educated at state schools and learned milking, ploughing, harvesting and horsemanship even as he received his schooling. Only 12 when his father died, Gullett left school to help his mother on the farm. He soon began to write on agriculture for the *Geelong Advertiser*. His uncle, Henry Gullett [q.v.], who had been editor of the *Sydney Morning Herald*, encouraged him to pursue journalism and in 1900 he joined the staff of that paper.

Having quickly become established in his profession, in 1908 Gullett went to London where he worked as a freelance but also wrote for the Sydney *Daily Telegraph* and *Sun*. He took up intensive study of migration, believing it to be the key to the development and defence of Australia. He became closely involved in the immigration work of Australia House and in 1914 published in London *The opportunity in Australia*, an illustrated, practical handbook on Australian rural life. Its first chapter was autobiographical. Gullett married Elizabeth Penelope Frater, daughter of Barbara Baynton [q.v.7], at a civil ceremony in Marylebone, London, on 2 October 1912; they had a son and a daughter.

In 1915 Gullett was appointed official Australian correspondent with the British and French armies on the Western Front. After a year in France he returned to Australia to lecture on the war, then in July 1916 enlisted in the Australian Imperial Force as a gunner. His return to England early in 1917 coincided with the organization of the Australian War Records Section designed by C. E. W. Bean [q.v.7] as a preliminary to the foundation of an Australian war museum. Bean selected Gullett to command the sub-section to be set up in Egypt and had him commissioned in August 1917. After a few weeks in France with Bean, Gullett sailed for Egypt in November. However, his work in the field for War Records was brief, as the A.I.F. in Palestine saw in him what they had so long been denied—their own Australian war correspondent. Bean gladly recommended him and he took up this appointment in August 1918, just in time for the final offensive. He was joint editor of *Australia in Palestine* (Sydney, 1919), an outstanding record of the campaign by participants.

Early in 1919, before returning to London, Gullett showed moral courage by confronting the commander-in-chief, General Sir Edmund Allenby. Since the Surafend incident when angry Anzacs had avenged the murder of a New Zealander by an Arab thief, Allenby had not only punished the Anzac Mounted Division but had pointedly ignored the Anzacs on public occasions when praising other troops. Gullett convinced him of the wider repercussions of his attitude and persuaded him to issue to every soldier a generously worded order of the day before they left for home.

Gullett attended the peace conference in Paris as press liaison officer on the staff of Prime Minister Hughes [q.v.]. He was so impressed by 'the lust of territory' which he saw as 'the sinister and dominating note of the proceedings' that he wrote a pamphlet, *Unguarded Australia* (London, 1919), in which he argued that 'immigration means defence'. In this cause he was as tireless as he was persuasive. On return to Australia he was briefly the first director of the Australian War Museum (now Memorial) but in 1920 he readily accepted the invitation of Hughes to be director of the Australian Immigration Bureau. He also wrote volume VII of *The official history of Australia in the war of 1914-1918*, recounting the exploits of the A.I.F. in Sinai, Palestine and Syria. It was 'a dog of a job', he told a friend, but it was completed by the end of 1922 and published the following year. By 1940 it had been reprinted eight times and was hailed by Bean as 'the most readable and most read' of all the volumes of that history.

Disagreements with Hughes over immigration policy led to Gullett's resignation in February 1922 and his return to journalism with the Melbourne *Herald* after rejecting the offer of a post on *The Times*. An attempt to enter Federal politics in the election of 1922 failed but in 1925 he was elected as a Nationalist for Henty, a seat he held for the rest of his life. He became minister for trade

and customs in November 1928, a most exacting portfolio at a time when world trade was declining and the Nationalist-Country Party government was in difficulties. After the defeat of the coalition in October 1929, Gullett sat on the Opposition benches until the fall of the Labor government in December 1931. For a time he was deputy leader of his party and of the Opposition but, on the formation of the United Australia Party under J. A. Lyons [q.v.], he stood aside for (Sir) John Latham [q.v.]. Having resumed his former portfolio in January 1932, Gullett accompanied (Viscount) S. M. Bruce [q.v.7] to the Imperial Economic Conference at Ottawa. Bruce recalled that he put Gullett's fiery temper to good use towards the end when, after informing him of matters in which the British delegation might have been more generous, Gullett 'went completely off the handle' and was granted 'all sorts of little concessions at the last moment'. His work at Ottawa was recognized by his appointment as K.C.M.G. in January 1933 but his health had so deteriorated that he resigned his portfolio the same month.

By October 1934 he was well enough to become minister without portfolio but with responsibility for trade treaties. He travelled extensively in Europe in 1935 and was successful in concluding several trade agreements. Gullett resigned again in March 1937 after differences with his colleagues over trade policy. When (Sir) Robert Menzies formed his first government in April 1939, Gullett returned to office as minister for external affairs. After the outbreak of war with Germany in September he became, in addition, minister for information with the task of creating the new department. He was also a member of the War Cabinet from 15 September 1939 to 13 March 1940.

His tenure of both ministries was short and troubled. When Menzies formed a coalition with the Country Party in March 1940, Gullett became vice-president of the executive council, minister in charge of scientific and industrial research and minister assisting the minister for information. The intensification of the war effort, following the invasion of France in May, caused Menzies to appoint Sir Keith Murdoch [q.v.] director general of information, an arrangement scarcely feasible but for the long-standing friendship between Gullett and Murdoch.

Gullett's career ended tragically on 13 August 1940 when the aircraft in which he was travelling crashed near Canberra. After a service at St Paul's Cathedral, Melbourne, with state and military honours, his remains were cremated. He was survived by his wife and children. His estate was valued for probate at £13 265. His son Henry Baynton Somer Gullett served with distinction in the Second A.I.F. and became a member of the House of Representatives and ambassador to Greece.

Sir Henry Gullett was passionately concerned with the development and safety of his country and of the British Empire. In politics he showed vigour and courage even to the point of voting against his party when he saw that course as his duty. Similarly, no pressure from senior officers could persuade him to deviate from the lines he had chosen when writing the history of the A.I.F. in Palestine. As a minister his policies were sometimes controversial but he was constructive and he bore no grudges. He made many friends in many lands and the Gulletts' home in Toorak was for long the resort of leaders in art, literature, politics, journalism and the army.

P. Hasluck, *The government and the people, 1939-1941* (Canb, 1962); R. M. Younger, *Australia and the Australians* (Adel, 1970); *PD* (Cwlth), 1940, 164, p 374; *Reveille* (Syd), Sept, Dec 1940; *Stand-To*, Jan-Feb 1962; *Punch* (Melb), 29 Oct 1925; *SMH*, 15 Aug 1940; Gullett collection (AWM), *and* papers (MS 3078, NL).   A. J. HILL

GULLETT, LUCY EDITH (1876-1949), medical practitioner and philanthropist, was born on 28 September 1876 at Hawthorn, Melbourne, third daughter of Henry Gullett [q.v.], journalist, and his wife Lucy, née Willie. She was educated at Sydney Girls' High School and the University of Sydney (M.B., 1900; Ch.M., 1901). In 1901-02 she was first resident medical officer at the Women's Hospital, Crown Street, and in 1902-03 was resident surgeon at the Hospital for Sick Children, Brisbane. In 1906 her father bought her a general practice at Bathurst, New South Wales, but in 1911 she returned home to Wahroonga to provide company for her unmarried sister Minnie. In 1922-33 the Gullett sisters lived in a waterfront house built for them at Kirribilli. Their last home was in Wyagdon Street, North Sydney.

Minnie Gullett was a Shakespeare 'buff', an enthusiastic member of the Lunacy Reform League of Australia, and a generous supporter of stray animals, drunks and ex-patients from lunatic asylums to whom she devoted most of her inheritance. Dr Gullett publicly shared Minnie's concern for mental health reform. Together they also persuaded their reluctant sisters to commission from Bertram Mackennal [q.v.] the Shakespeare memorial that their father had proposed just before he died in 1914. Costing

some £10 000, the six-figure group was installed in February 1926 on a prominent site near the Mitchell Library.

The expectation of financial independence had sapped Lucy Gullett's medical ambition. Her private practice in North Sydney from 1912 was modest and reputedly adjourned on major race days. She spent many afternoons playing bridge at the Queen's Club of which she was an early member (1912). During 1915-16 she went at her own expense to Europe and served in a French Red Cross military hospital at Lyons. In 1919 during the influenza epidemic she was medical officer at the City Road emergency hospital, Sydney—a harrowing experience that gave rise to her only significant scientific paper. She was honorary outpatients physician to the Renwick Hospital for Infants (Benevolent Society of New South Wales) in 1918-32, and attached to a government baby health centre at about the same time. She was on the council of the Sydney District Nursing Association in 1934-49.

Inspired by the success of the Queen Victoria Memorial Hospital, Melbourne, run by women for women, Lucy Gullett founded the New South Wales Association of Registered Medical Women in 1921 and was honorary secretary, with Dr Harriet Biffen as president. Plans for a hospital dominated association business. A house in Surry Hills was opened as an outpatient dispensary on 3 January 1922 and known as the New Hospital for Women and Children. Drs Biffen and Gullett shouldered most of the early financial responsibility. The hospital moved to Redfern and was renamed the Rachel Forster Hospital for Women and Children in 1925. Dr Gullett resigned as secretary in 1926 but remained on the hospital committee and was vice-president in 1932-49. She was also life governor, trustee, honorary physician until 1935 (consultant thereafter), and first chairman of the medical board until 1942. Hers was the decisive voice when the board of directors hesitated over its expansion programme in 1940: 'Well, I think we should go on with the building of the new hospital. If the British Empire falls, it won't matter on what we have spent our money; but if it doesn't, we will have our hospital'. In December 1941 she announced a convalescent home as her next target: the Lucy Gullett Convalescent Home at Bexley was opened on 9 November 1946.

In 1932 Lucy Gullett stood as an Independent Women's candidate for the Legislative Assembly seat of North Sydney. She lost her deposit. At Jessie Street's instigation she was elected to the executive committee of the United Associations of Women in 1935 and was vice-president in 1936-38 and 1943.

The family holds a charming portrait of

the young Lucy (1887) by Julian Rossi Ashton [q.v.7]. In appearance she was dark, later grey-haired, short and thickset like her father. She 'knew everyone' and was a gifted hospital canvasser with ready access to the press. Unfailingly kind-hearted she had instant rapport with the working-class women who were her patients. On 29 December 1943 Minnie Gullett died. Thereafter Lucy, who suffered from nephritis, relied on her friend, the cellist Julia (June) Holland, for comfort and support. After a stroke in mid-1949, Dr Gullett died in the Rachel Forster Hospital on 12 November 1949. She was buried with Anglican rites in the family grave in Gore Hill cemetery. Her estate, valued for probate at £15 918, was left mostly to her family.

MJA, 30 Aug 1919, 11 Feb 1950, 13 Sept 1958; *SMH*, 27 Aug 1912, 30 Jan, 4 Feb 1926, 14, 18 Nov 1949; Minutes, NSW Assn Registered Medical Women, *and* Rachel Forster Hospital, *and* United Assn of Women (ML); information from Mr S. Garton, Miss H. and Mr J. H. W. Heney, Syd.

ANN M. MITCHELL

GUNN, JEANNIE (1870-1961), author, was born on 5 June 1870 at Carlton, Melbourne, fifth child and fourth daughter of Thomas Johnstone Taylor, from Chapelton, Scotland, and his wife Anna, née Lush, from Ilchester, Somerset, England. Jeannie's father and grandfather were ordained Baptist ministers; her father served at Sandhurst (Bendigo) and Melbourne, but later went into business, and for some twelve years before his death in 1909 was on the staff of the *Argus*.

Jeannie was educated at home by her mother and at 17 matriculated at the University of Melbourne. In 1889 she and her sisters opened 'Rolyat' school at the family home in Creswick Street, Hawthorn. When it closed in 1896 Jeannie became a visiting teacher; her subjects included gymnastics and elocution. She was tiny, about 5 ft. (152 cm), energetic and determined. Former pupils recalled listening for her light, springing step; outings with her were as 'exciting as setting off to the moon'.

In the late 1890s she met Aeneas James Gunn, eight years her senior; they were married with Presbyterian forms at Rolyat on 31 December 1901. Son of Rev. Peter Gunn (d. 1864), who had migrated from Scotland in 1841 to minister to the Gaelic settlers around Melbourne, Aeneas was running the Prahran Free Library and writing articles for the *Prahran Telegraph* when Jeannie met him, but he had spent most of the 1890s in northern Australia. With his cousin Joseph Bradshaw ('a buccaneer of the old

school') he had helped to establish sheep and cattle stations on the Prince Regent and Victoria rivers. He had explored the coast by sea and contributed his findings to scientific and geographical journals; in 1896 he was made a fellow of the Royal Geographical Society, London. Just before his marriage he had become a partner in Elsey cattle station on the Roper River, some 300 miles (483 km) south of Darwin. He was to be the station's new manager, and on 2 January 1902 the couple sailed for Port Darwin.

In Palmerston (Darwin), Jeannie was assured that as a woman she would be 'out of place' on a station such as the Elsey, where news of the boss's marriage had already caused alarm. Nevertheless she insisted on accompanying her husband. Her pluck in tackling the journey, her sense of humour and her fine horsemanship won her the admiration and friendship of the stockmen. Unfortunately outback life lasted only thirteen months for the Gunns. On 16 March 1903 Aeneas died of malarial dysentery. In April Jeannie returned to Melbourne, where she lived with her father at Hawthorn.

In the next few years Jeannie wrote the two books that made her famous. Encouraged by friends who had read her letters and heard her tell stories to their children, she wrote (as Jeannie Gunn) *The little black princess: a true tale of life in the Never-Never land*, about Bett-Bett, an Aboriginal child at the Elsey. The book was published in London and in Australia in 1905, with a new and revised English edition in 1909. In 1908 she published (as 'Mrs Aeneas Gunn') *We of the Never-Never*. Although entitled a novel, it was a re-creation of actual events; her main concession to fiction was the use of stylized names to veil the identity of her characters. It remains a fresh, affectionate and minutely observed account of tropical outback life which Australian readers readily assumed as part of their heritage. By 1945, 320 000 copies had been sold. In a plebiscite reported by the Melbourne *Herald* in 1931, Jeannie Gunn was ranked third among Australian novelists after Marcus Clarke [q.v.3] and Rolf Boldrewood [q.v.3, T. A. Browne].

Both her books were adapted for schools; *We of the Never-Never* was translated into German in 1927. Over the years newspapers and magazine articles chronicled the fortunes of the Elsey characters; Jeannie outlived all but Bett-Bett. She wrote no more books although she planned one on the Aboriginal John Terrick and another on the Monbulk district of the Dandenongs, where she often stayed. In 1909-12 she travelled overseas, returning to live with her sisters at East Melbourne and later Hawthorn. During World War I and after, she was active in welfare work for soldiers, ex-servicemen and their families, especially those of the Monbulk area. She was patron of many fund-raising activities associated with ex-servicemen and in 1946 she helped to organize a club room and library for the Monbulk sub-branch of the Returned Sailors', Soldiers' and Airmen's Imperial League of Australia. In 1939 she was appointed O.B.E.

Jeannie Gunn died at Hawthorn on 9 June 1961 and was buried in Melbourne general cemetery after a service at Scots Church. Her estate, which included substantial royalties from her books, was valued for probate at £12 181.

I. Nesdale, *The little missus* (Adel, 1977); *Woman's World*, 1 Sept 1927; *Walkabout*, 1 Nov 1944; *Argus*, 2 Dec 1905, 13 Nov 1908, 2 Feb 1909; *Herald* (Melb), 2 June 1931, 29 Jan 1940, 9 Oct 1948; *Sun-Herald*, 11, 18 June 1961; *Advertiser* (Adel), and *Age*, 12 June 1961; Mrs Aeneas Gunn papers (NL).   SALLY O'NEILL

GUNN, JOHN (1884-1959), premier, was born on 16 December 1884, at Rheola, near Bendigo, Victoria, second of nine children of William Gunn, a Scottish miner, and his Victorian-born wife Mary Ann, née Wayman. When his father died he began work as a butcher's boy before moving to Melbourne in 1901 to take jobs as a tea-packer and trolley-driver. He then worked briefly in Western Australian timber-mills. He was devoted to self-education, particularly in public speaking and economics, and was influenced and encouraged by Tom Mann [q.v.]. On 8 September 1908 Gunn married Labor co-worker Haidee Smith at Collingwood, Melbourne. John's sister Ethel married Frank Hyett [q.v.] in 1910.

The Gunns moved to Adelaide where he worked as a horse-lorry driver and became president of the State branch of the Federated Carters and Drivers' Union in 1909. Next year, as union secretary, he led the drivers' strike which won reduced working hours. Gunn was president of the United Trades and Labor Council in 1911 and in 1914-16 was on the Adelaide City Council. In 1916 he became federal president of his union.

A pale, thin, serious young man, he had entered the House of Assembly as one of the United Labor Party representatives for Adelaide in March 1915 when the Vaughan [q.v.] Labor government took office. Soon he was embroiled in the bitter conscription debate that wracked and wrecked the party for a time. Reflecting the view of the extra-parliamentary wing, Gunn was fervently anti-conscriptionist, but caucus was not. He resigned to contest unsuccessfully the Federal seat of Boothby as an anti-conscription-ist in the election of 1917. However, he regained an Adelaide seat in the 1918 State election.

The State parliamentary party had lost its entire leadership following the split and the untried Gunn was elected leader in the new parliament. With tact and perseverance he rebuilt the shattered party by restoring its majority in metropolitan Adelaide by 1921 and, for the next three years, by wooing country voters. He presented the Labor and Country parties, the producers, as sharing a community interest against exploitative middlemen—the Liberals. In 1924 Gunn received a sympathetic coverage in the rural press, while Liberal and Country party antagonisms, which he had exacerbated, led to split non-Labor votes in many rural seats. As a result, Labor won seven country seats, giving it an Assembly majority of eight. He became premier and treasurer on 16 April, at 39. He was also minister for irrigation and repatriation, although he relinquished these portfolios next year on taking over as minister for railways.

Gunn accepted phlegmatically the predictable defeat of his government's constitutional proposals—a redrawing of Assembly electorate boundaries, a proportional representation electoral system, and adult franchise for the Upper House—by the conservative-dominated Legislative Council. But he was piqued by its rejection of a measure to establish a State government insurance commission, and sought to outflank his opponents by administrative fiat. And he succeeded with another allegedly 'Socialist proposal'—establishing a state bank, mainly to provide rural credit, with whose help he built his own Hawthorn home. He was closely involved in the imaginative but controversial project to provide 1000 homes a year for needy families: one of the first fully planned suburbs in an Australian city, Colonel Light Gardens. Expenditure on education was increased markedly, particularly on teachers' salary rises, expanded medical support for schools, more scholarships and the establishment of new junior technical schools. He also reformed public service working conditions.

Gunn embarked on an ambitious road programme, completed the dilatory negotiations with the Commonwealth on the northern railway, and carried out massive afforestation. His government inquired into rural settlement and the pastoral industry and expanded access to bore water; it strengthened the agricultural departments' scientific resources and set up the model Urrbrae Agricultural High School. Although Gunn delegated responsibility in a cabinet which remained harmonious, he developed the main lines of government policy and actively defended his ministers when they were entangled in controversy. He won his colleagues' affection, his opponents' respect, the grudging commendation of the press, and a public popularity rarely achieved before or since by a Labor leader in South Australia.

It came then as a shock when, on 9 August 1926, he announced his impending resignation to join the Commonwealth Development and Migration Commission. At 41 he was apparently at the height of his political power and influence. The decision was puzzling and, for Gunn, fateful. It was alleged that the Nationalist prime minister (Viscount) S. M. Bruce [q.v.7], had engineered the appointment to lure a skilled opponent from the South Australian political scene. The £2500 offered was double Gunn's salary as premier; his wife urged acceptance. Political reasons doubtless added their weight. Gunn's authority within the Labor movement had recently been undermined because of his lack of sympathy for 44-hour week proposals and his attitude to the Bruce-Page [q.v.] attempt by referendum to establish effective Commonwealth control over industrial legislation. Gunn followed the Federal Labor Party's support for the referendum, whereas the local party was moving towards opposition. Whatever the mixture of motives, Gunn resigned on 28 August and left for Melbourne.

The Development and Migration Commission failed to realize its potential and was terminated by the Scullin [q.v.] government in June 1930. Gunn was transferred to the Prime Minister's Department as director of development at £1800 a year but the Lyons [q.v.] government put his job under scrutiny. Much of his time in it was spent on the royal commission on mineral oils and petrol and other products, which reported in 1935. In May that year the government decided not to renew his contract. Gunn's life disintegrated. He was separated from his wife, two sons and two daughters, who had remained in Adelaide; he had a nervous breakdown and there is a hint of financial trouble. His pathetic letter to the prime minister requesting re-employment was ignored. At 50 his career had ended. He disappeared from public sight and died in poverty in hospital at Waterfall, New South Wales, on 27 June 1959; he was cremated. His death was so obscure that no obituary was published in the South Australian press until a fortnight later.

Gunn was short and slightly built but was 'well set-up and as straight-backed as a military man who wore corsets'. He was a lucid and forceful speaker although he lacked eloquence and colourful phrasing. He developed rapidly from a rather embittered young radical to a political moderate who as premier impressed all by his courtesy and patience. His political rise was as fortunate as it was meteoric. The one election in modern South Australian history in which the non-Labor forces were seriously split gave him the premiership in 1924. A booming economy helped it to be productive but his talents, courage, and vision in government enabled him to capitalize on his good fortune. Political leadership would have been more demanding for Gunn after 1926 with the erosion of his own authority and the comparative unity of the non-Labor forces. Whether flaws in character would have ruined him, or his enemies destroyed him had he remained in active political life, is unknowable. In 1917-18 he had taken the flood which led on to fortune; in 1926, after taking the less obviously hazardous choice, the remaining voyage of his life was 'bound in shallows and in miseries'.

ALP, *Labor's 30 years record in South Australia 1893-1923* (Adel, 1923); T. Sadler, *Some annals of Adelaide* (Adel, 1933); S. McHugh, *My life and work* (priv print Adel, 1950); A. Wildavsky and D. Carboch, *Studies in Australian politics* (Melb, 1958); *Labour Hist*, 1969, no 17, 1976, no 31; *Advertiser* (Adel), 15, 16 Apr 1924, 11 Aug 1926, 20 Oct 1928; D. Hopgood, A psephological examination of the South Australian Labor Party from World War One to the Depression (Ph.D. thesis, Univ Adel, 1974); Gunn papers, CP314/3 item 14 (AAO).

NEAL BLEWETT

GUNTER, HOWEL (1844-1902), regular soldier, was born on 9 May 1844 at Fulham, Middlesex, England, son of John Gunter, gentleman, and his wife Lucy Jane, née Picard. He was commissioned from the Royal Military College, Sandhurst, into the 73rd Regiment of Foot on 8 July 1862 as an ensign, without purchase, and on 23 June 1865 purchased promotion to lieutenant. After service in China in 1866-68 the regiment was transferred to the Straits Settlement in December 1868 and to Ceylon in March 1869. Gunter served as adjutant in 1866-67 and 1870-74. On 2 February 1871, at Christ Church Cathedral, Colombo, he married a widow, Mary Alice Sinclair MacLagan, née Wall. They had four sons.

After six months home leave in 1873 Gunter returned to India and on 7 July 1874 was promoted captain, without purchase. He qualified at the Garrison School of Instruction, Umballa, in 1876, with distinguished results in fortifications, military law and tactics and became a specialist in these fields, lecturing as assistant garrison instructor at Sialkot in 1876-78 and garrison instructor at Agra in 1878-85. After the

Cardwell reforms the 73rd Regiment had become the 2nd Battalion, the Black Watch, Royal Highlanders. Gunter was promoted major in this unit on 10 July 1881, remained in India until 1885 and served in England for the next six years. Although appointed to command the Black Watch in January 1891 with the rank of lieut-colonel, he exchanged to command the Norfolk Regiment next November. He landed in Burma with the Norfolks in December 1891, took the regiment to India in 1893 and relinquished command on 19 August 1894; he then went on half-pay in the British Army.

Gunter was rescued from the limbo of half-pay curry colonels by the Queensland government. That colony had maintained local volunteer and militia forces almost since its inception and until 1884 the Queensland Defence Force had been commanded by local officers. That year, an Imperial officer, Colonel (Sir) George French [q.v.8] took command and was succeeded by Major General John Fletcher Owen. Gunter became commandant in April 1895 with the local rank of major general. At least one contemporary source suggests that he was not quite the success his predecessors had been. In *A journalist's memories* (Brisbane, 1927), Major General R. Spencer Browne [q.v.7] alleges that he 'did not quite catch the Australian spirit' and that the Queensland government accepted him on the misunderstanding that it was getting a 'writer on Tactics of the same surname and didn't discover the mistake until it was too late to remedy it'. Spencer Browne acknowledged that the story was 'rather apocryphal'. Gunter was an expert in fortifications and, since a large proportion of Queensland's defence vote in the 1890s went towards the maintenance of a garrison on Thursday Island, it is reasonable to assume that he was appointed because of his qualifications.

Gunter had a comparatively tranquil tour of command, being largely occupied with intercolonial conferences concerning the amalgamation of the colonies' forces in a Commonwealth army. In July 1899, on Gunter's recommendation, Queensland was the first colony to offer troops for service in South Africa. On 22 September he attended a meeting of Australian commandants in Melbourne to organize an Australian contingent. He left for England on leave in December and was placed on the unattached list, British Army, next April. He was colonel commanding the 63rd Regimental District, Ashton-under-Lyne, when he died of cardiac disease at Kensington, London, on 2 August 1902. A *Times* obituary paid tribute to his work in Queensland. He had done 'good service in the practical training in camp of the colonial troops. He was a strong advocate of thorough company training, and the good service done by the Queensland contingent in the late war in South Africa bore testimony to his efforts'. He was also 'much esteemed for his amiable disposition'.

D. H. Johnson, *Volunteers at heart* (Brisb, 1974); *British A'sian*, 14 Mar, 4 July 1895; *The Times*, 9 Aug 1902; Gunter papers, BP 133, Series 1 (AAO); Service record, H. Gunter, WO 76/383 (PRO, Lond).
DONALD H. JOHNSON

GUTHRIE, FREDERICK BICKELL (1861-1927), agricultural chemist, was born on 10 December 1861 in Mauritius, son of Frederick Guthrie, and his wife Agnes, née Bickell. His father, a fellow of the Royal Society, was professor of chemistry in Mauritius and later became professor of physics at the Royal School of Mines, London. Frederick junior was educated at University College, London. After two years study for a doctoral degree under Professor Zincke at the University of Marburg, Germany, in 1882 he became demonstrator in chemistry at Queen's College, Cork, Ireland. In 1888 he was appointed demonstrator in chemistry at the Royal College of Science, South Kensington, London, under (Sir) Thomas Thorpe.

Guthrie came to Australia in 1890 to take up duties as demonstrator in chemistry at the University of Sydney under Archibald Liversidge [q.v.5]. Although he occupied this position briefly, his association with the university continued throughout his career—he served as acting professor of chemistry in 1896-97, 1904-05 and 1908-09.

Guthrie's main contributions to science were made as chemist with the Department of Agriculture. He was appointed on 1 January 1892, shortly after the formation of the department; he retired in January 1924. In his first job, assisting the wheat-breeder W. J. Farrer [q.v.8] with his experimental cross-breeding, Guthrie devised models of mill and bakery conditions suitable for 50 to 100 gramme samples—at a time when wheat-breeding was in its infancy and when selection for suitable grain quality was hardly considered by overseas breeders. This kind of scientific co-operation was unique at the time, though it has later become an integral part of wheat-breeding.

As a result of Guthrie's work, the suitability of potential parent wheats could be assessed, and newly produced cross-bred lines could be tested early. Farrer and Guthrie used Indian wheats to confer early maturity and tolerance to drought, combined with Canadian Fife parents which contributed good baking quality. Later they incorporated wheats that had been selected for suitability to the Australian climate. The many successful varieties that resulted helped to improve the quality and production of wheat early in the twentieth century and have formed the basis of subsequent breeding of quality wheats for Australia.

Guthrie also added to the knowledge of the chemical composition of wheat flour in relation to quality. His duties with the Department of Agriculture involved many other branches of agricultural chemistry—particularly soil and fertilizer analyses, and even the possible preparation of alcohol from prickly pear or water hyacinth. Guthrie was author or co-author of 180 scientific articles. He was president of the Royal Society of New South Wales in 1903-04 (and joint honorary secretary in 1906-10) and of the State branch of the (Royal) Australian Chemical Institute in 1920-21. He presided over the chemical section in 1901 and the agricultural section in 1913 of the Australasian Association for the Advancement of Science, served on the council of the Royal Agricultural Society of New South Wales from 1910, was an original member of the Commonwealth Advisory Council of Science and Industry from 1916, a member of the Australian National Research Council from 1921 and a fellow of both the (Royal) Institute of Chemistry and the Chemical Society of London.

Occasionally Guthrie wrote verse for the *Bulletin* and 'was happiest in the company of artists'—'Hop' [q.v.4 L. Hopkins] was a close friend. On 15 November 1890 at Neutral Bay he had married Ada Adams; their two sons Frederick and Malcolm gave their lives in World War I. Survived by his wife and daughter, Guthrie died from cancer at Moss Vale on 7 February 1927 and was cremated with Anglican rites. His memory is perpetuated in the Guthrie medal, awarded every three years by the Royal Australian Chemical Institute.

Agricultural Gazette of NSW, 6 (1895), p 159, 9 (1898), p 363; Dept of Agriculture (NSW), *Science Bulletin*, 1912, no 7, 1914, no 11; Roy Aust Chemical Inst, *Procs*, 40 (1973), p 368; *Records of the Aust Academy of Science*, 4 (Nov 1978-Apr 79), no 1, p 7, and for bibliog; *SMH*, 20 Apr 1923, 8 Feb 1927; *Bulletin*, 10 Feb 1927; Dept of Agriculture (NSW), Staff file.   C. W. WRIGLEY

GUTHRIE, JAMES FRANCIS (1872-1958), stock-breeder, woolbroker and senator, was above all else a 'wool man'. He was born on 13 September 1872 at Rich Avon, near Donald, Victoria, youngest son of Thomas Guthrie [q.v.4] and his wife Mary, née Rutherford. After attending Geelong College he joined the Geelong branch of Dalgety [q.v.4] & Co. Ltd in October 1891 as a junior clerk, initially unpaid. His preferment in the next fifteen years was rapid, assisted by the influence of his father and E. T. Doxat, Dalgety's chairman. Six years of branch experience were followed by about two years working in textile mills in England, at Bradford and elsewhere. He rejoined Dalgety's in 1900 as wool expert and traveller at Geelong, valuing for the company's New Zealand sales as well. In the 1904-05 season he became head valuer for Australia, based in Melbourne.

At Dunedin, New Zealand, he met and on 5 March 1902 married Mary Isobel, daughter of John Thomas Wright, founder of one of Dalgety's strongest competitors in that country. Next year, while examining sheep there Guthrie contracted anthrax and lost his left leg above the knee. Crutches diminished neither his activity nor his avid interest in sport and he later served on the executives of various racing, coursing and cricket clubs, including the Melbourne Cricket Club. A recuperative trip to England and the United States of America also extended his knowledge of wool.

Guthrie's unpredictable, insurbordinate behaviour made his Melbourne service increasingly unhappy despite his pleasure in compiling *Dalgety's Annual Wool Review*. In 1915 he was moved sideways to the Geelong managership rather than to the Melbourne sub-managership. Service as a member of the Victorian State Wool Committee and as the first chairman of the Wool Export Advisory Committee, during Britain's wartime purchase of the clip, soon diminished his branch work. Then in 1919 Dalgety's London board, with mixed feelings, approved his nominating for the Senate, as a National Party candidate, and retaining the Geelong management if elected. He took his seat on 1 July 1920. Tensions soon developed between Guthrie's two occupations. His large plans for the Geelong business produced no profits and by 1926 there were hints of his retirement. When parliament moved to Canberra in May 1927 he neglected it, boasting of an attendance totalling two and a half hours over seven months. He concentrated on business, but his assertive temperament upset an already demoralized staff. Early in 1928 the executive determined he must go. A generous pension and a special retainer as Australian wool adviser to the London board, both continued at the board's pleasure until his death, retained his extensive personal influence among woolgrowers for the company.

Guthrie held his Senate seat until June 1938, being defeated at the 1937 election.

His record was undistinguished. He served on the Senate select committee on beam wireless charges (1929) and was a delegate to Empire Parliamentary Association conferences in 1924 and 1937. His speeches sometimes pursued quite idiosyncratic interests. A self-professed hater of profiteers and Bolsheviks, from the first he also criticized the 'bush capital' and lobbied for the Limbless Soldiers' Association. He bitterly deplored the degradation of British cultural standards in Australia resulting from America's stranglehold on cinema showings. He actively assisted the British National Film League in Melbourne and became a shareholder in British Dominion Films Ltd that issued from it. As a founding director in 1923 of Federal Woollen Mills Ltd, Guthrie castigated the 'machinations of the Flinders-lane mob' of woollen wholesalers and advocated free trade in woollen cloths. Indeed, though a protectionist, Guthrie would have exempted from tariffs not only fencing wire, cars and other goods used in rural production but also goods whose protection led to 'fattening the already over-fat and over-rich'.

By background, connexion and inclination, Guthrie spoke for big grazing and woolbroking interests. As wool prices fell to Depression levels and competition from synthetic fibres increased, he worked behind the scenes to secure legislation establishing the Australian Wool Board and imposing a wool levy so that the board could fund promotion of wool and further research. As the government's sole representative on the board from its establishment in 1936 until 1945 he had a hand in the formation of the International Wool Secretariat in 1937. He was appointed C.B.E. in 1946.

Guthrie listed fishing, flying and stud stock-breeding as his recreations. But sheep-breeding was a passion. He was a director of the family company formed in 1906 to operate his father's stations and in 1910-21 was managing director of the company that bought one of them, Avon Downs, in the Northern Territory. In 1912 he established a Corriedale stud on portions of Borambola and Book Book stations (renamed Corriedale Park and Colongolong) near Wagga, New South Wales. He later sold those properties, had an interest in numerous others until the 1950s but concentrated his Corriedale and thoroughbred horse studs at Bulgandra near Albury, New South Wales (1923-50), and Elcho and Coolangatta near Geelong (1926-52). In 1912 Corriedales were not well known in Australia. As founder of the Australian Corriedale Sheepbreeders' Association in 1914, as owner of a stud that won international success and through often flamboyant promotion, he did

much to publicize them. By 1951, they formed the most significant non-merino pure breed of sheep in Australia.

In 1952 Guthrie retired to his small farm, Pidgeon Bank at Kangaroo Ground near Melbourne, to indulge his lifelong interest in the history of his industry. He had published a history of Australian wool-selling in Professor R. P. Wright's *The standard cyclopedia of modern agriculture and rural economy* (London, 1911). In 1927 he sketched the history of Australian sheep and wool to the (Royal) Historical Society of Victoria and again in the official publication commemorating the Victorian centenary in 1934. The culmination of his research was *A world history of sheep and wool* published privately in 1957. Almost encyclopedic in its approach, the book epitomized Guthrie's qualities as a devotee and a publicist. He died on 18 August 1958, predeceased by his wife (1946) and son (1935) and survived by his daughter. His estate was valued for probate at a modest £40 516.

Pastoral Review, 16 Dec 1927, 18 Sept 1958; *Punch* (Melb), 6 Nov 1919; *Geelong Standard*, 18 Aug 1923; *Table Talk*, 23 June 1927; *Age*, 20 Aug 1958; Guthrie, *and* Dalgety & Co papers (ANU Archives).

ALAN BARNARD

GUTHRIE, ROBERT STORRIE (1857-1921), seaman, trade unionist and politician, was born on 17 November 1857 at Patrick, near Glasgow, Scotland, son of Andrew Guthrie, joiner, and his wife Elizabeth, née Storrie. He was educated at Glen's School, Glasgow, and in 1872 became a ship's apprentice; in later years he spoke with nostalgia of his long experience as a seaman, albeit with bitterness at the appalling conditions. In July 1878 Guthrie transferred to the South Australian coastal trade. He married Janet Deer on 8 November 1881 at Port Adelaide and left the sea to settle there in 1887.

Guthrie became secretary of the South Australian branch of the Federated Seamen's Union of Australasia in January 1888 and was later federal president for many years. A delegate to the United Trades and Labor Council of South Australia, he served on its executive in 1889-91 and was also president of the South Australian Maritime Council in 1890. That year he was a delegate to the Sydney conference of unionists on the maritime strike and in 1902 was made secretary and treasurer of the newly formed Federated Council of Australasian Labor Unions. Guthrie was elected to the South Australian Legislative Council as a Labor representative for Central District in 1891 and retained his seat until 1903 when he won election to the Senate. Re-elected as a Labor senator in 1910 and 1914, he won as a Nationalist in 1917 and 1919 after leaving the Labor Party, and earning expulsion from the Seamen's Union, over conscription.

Throughout his political life Guthrie pursued two main interests: the trade union movement, in whose cause he frequently negotiated during strikes; and the maritime industry, where his concern for working conditions was intense almost to the point of obsession. His most notable contribution to politics was made as a member of the royal commission on the navigation bill, 1904-07; the resulting Act was sometimes spoken of as the 'Guthrie Act' and Guthrie himself called 'the Australian Plimsoll'. He also served on select committees on the press cable service (1909) and the Fitzroy Dock, Sydney (1913); he was a member of the parliamentary delegation to the coronation of George V in 1911 and Australian representative at the second International Labour Conference at Genoa, Italy, in 1920.

'Bob' Guthrie was short, and spoke with a distinct Scots burr. His close friend, W. M. Hughes [q.v.], described him as 'a shellback—a real sailor' who still 'woke . . . at 4 a.m. . . . rolled heavily in his gait', and retained 'the poorest opinion of steamships'. He always wore a square pilot coat and billowy pants. A sociable, unpretentious man, he was given to forceful and plain expression of his views. It was said of him that 'he was true to his mates' and that he had many of them. He was a Presbyterian and a district ruler of the Independent Order of Rechabites in Adelaide.

On 19 January 1921 Guthrie was knocked down by a tram in Melbourne and died next day. After a state funeral his body was taken to Adelaide and buried in Cheltenham cemetery. He was survived by his wife, three daughters and two sons; two sons were killed in action in World War I.

H. T. Burgess (ed), *Cyclopedia of South Australia*, 1 (Adel 1907); T. H. Smeaton, *The people in politics* (Adel, 1914); W. M. Hughes, *Policies and potentates* (Syd, 1950); *Observer* (Adel), 30 May 1891; *Age*, 21 Jan 1921; *Bulletin*, 27 Jan 1921; *Westralian Worker*, 4 Feb 1921; United Trades and Labor Council of South Australia, Minutes, 1888-91, 1903 (microfilm M15, ANU Archives).

PETER COOK

GWYNN, SIR CHARLES WILLIAM (1870-1963), soldier, was born on 4 February 1870 at Ramelton, Donegal, Ireland, son of Rev. John Gwynn, sometime professor of divinity at Trinity College, Dublin, and his wife Lucy Josephine, née O'Brien. His brothers were Stephen, scholar and author; Robert, who became professor of Hebrew at Trinity College; Edward, provost of Trinity College; and John Tudor, a writer on Indian affairs.

Gwynn was educated at St Colomba's College, Dublin, and the Royal Military Academy, Woolwich, was commissioned in the Royal Engineers on 15 February 1889, and in 1893-94 took part in operations against the Sofas in West Africa; he was wounded three times and was awarded the Distinguished Service Order and mentioned in dispatches. In 1897-1901 he worked in the geographical section of the intelligence branch at the War Office and in the Sudanese-Abyssinian frontier, and in 1901-04 was attached to the Egyptian Army. In 1900 he was promoted captain and brevet major. The reconquest of the Sudan had involved much surveying and Gwynn was employed on delimiting the wild Sudan-Abyssinian frontier; for this work he was appointed C.M.G. in 1903. Next year he returned home and married Mary, widow of Lieutenant Lowry Armstrong, R.N.; they had no children. After graduating at the Staff College, Camberley, in 1906 he studied for a year at the London School of Economics, and in 1908-09 was a commissioner of the Abyssinian and East African Boundary Commission. He was promoted major in 1908.

When the Royal Military College at Duntroon, Federal Capital Territory, was opened in June 1911 with Brigadier General (Sir) W. T. Bridges [q.v.7] as commandant, Gwynn, as director of military art and with local rank of lieut-colonel, was the senior of a small group of outstanding British Army officers appointed to key posts. This learned and widely experienced soldier made an immediate impact on the young Australian cadets as their first instructor in strategy, tactics and military history. His influence on the college was the greater because Bridges, always a remote figure, was absent visiting military academies in Europe in 1911-12; thus for more than half of the college's first year Gwynn acted as commandant.

His four-year term was cut short by the outbreak of war in August 1914. When the 1st Division of the Australian Imperial Force was formed with Bridges as its commander, Gwynn was by far the best qualified officer available for the post of senior staff officer, but his relations with Bridges had not been entirely harmonious and the appointment went to a promising Australian, Major (Sir) C. B. B. White [q.v.]. 'Much as I should have wished to join the A.I.F.', Gwynn recalled in 1932, 'it was pretty apparent that there was no immediate chance of my finding a niche in it'.

Though urged by the governor-general Sir Ronald Munro Ferguson [q.v.] to remain in Australia, Gwynn was in England by the end of September, but was told at the War Office that there was no chance of his getting to France. After serving with a Territorial division he was sent to the Middle East in July 1915, and was ordered to Gallipoli to become G.S.O.1 to Major General J. G. Legge [q.v.] of the 2nd Australian Division; he served with the division until the evacuation, temporarily commanding the 5th and 5th Brigades. His hopes of leading the 6th Brigade in France were dashed in February 1916 when he was appointed chief of staff to Lieut-General Sir Alexander Godley, commanding II Anzac Corps; in this post Gwynn served until after the Armistice.

Thus he headed the staff of the corps at the battle of Messines in June 1917 when it played the leading part in the first thoroughly planned offensive carried out by the British Army in France. In this and later operations (at the end of 1917 the corps was renamed the XXII British Corps) the support of a talented chief of staff was needed by Godley, who was more at home in colonial campaigning or on the hunting field than in large-scale European warfare. In 1918 Gwynn was appointed C.B. and during the war was mentioned in dispatches six times, received the brevet ranks (British Army) of lieut-colonel and colonel, and was awarded the Belgian Croix de Guerre and the Légion d'honneur. In a *Reveille* article in 1932 he wrote of the Australian soldiers: 'No troops showed greater appreciation of the value of training or more care to work out the details of every operation—great or small. Although no troops showed more desire to kill the enemy, few showed as much determination to keep alive themselves in the process'.

In 1919, after six months commanding a brigade with the army of occupation on the Rhine, he was appointed G.S.O.1 of the 1st Division at Aldershot, was promoted colonel in 1920, and in 1920-24 was on the staff of Eastern Command. In January 1925 he was promoted major general and in May 1926 was made commandant of the Staff College, Camberley. In his five years there he had as instructors or students the future field marshals Wilson, Brooke, Montgomery and Alexander and as students several Duntroon graduates destined for high appointments in 1939-45, notably Lieuts-General (Sir) Sydney Rowell and (Sir) Frank Berryman. He retired in 1931 and was appointed K.C.B. His book, *Imperial policing*, was published in London in 1934. In his retirement he also wrote military articles for *The Times, Daily Telegraph* and *Morning Post*. He died in Dublin on 12 February 1963.

Gwynn was of medium height, spare, and had a slight stammer, which, as Rowell remembered, was 'intensified after the third glass of port'. At Duntroon he won esteem by his learning, high standards of discipline and behaviour and impartiality. His influence on the college after its establishment was as potent as that of Bridges. In action he proved one of the outstanding staff officers of the British Army, and in peace a notable trainer of future senior commanders.

A. J. Godley, *Life of an Irish soldier* (Lond, 1939); J. E. Lee, *Duntroon* (Canb, 1952); S. F. Rowell, *Full circle* (Melb, 1974); *Roy Engineers*, June 1963; *The Times*, 13 Feb 1963.   GAVIN LONG*

GYE, HAROLD FREDERICK NEVILLE (1888-1967), artist and writer, was born on 22 May 1888 at Ryde, Sydney, son of Walter Neville Gye from London, and his second wife Priscilla Theodosia, née Warr. A descendant of the Devonshire branch of the French Huguenot family of De Rohan-Gyé, Walter Gye worked as a builder in Sydney before moving with his family to Black Range (Lavington) near Albury, where he took up land and prospected optimistically for gold. Hal completed his education at the local bush school.

When he was 12 the family moved to Melbourne. Hal worked in a city architect's office for about two years before becoming a law clerk, during which time the Sydney *Bulletin* published his first verse, 'Mrs. Melba's motor car'. He was an omnivorous reader of books on drawing and joined the art class of Alek Sass. Gye was one of the Melbourne Bohemian group which met at the Mitre Hotel and Fasoli's.

When he found he could make a living out of drawing, Gye left the law firm. He contributed political cartoons, illustrated jokes, caricatures and paragraphs to the *Bulletin*, and in 1910 inherited the theatrical cartoons when his friend Will Dyson [q.v.8] went to London. He provided cartoons for the Melbourne *Herald, Weekly Times, Weekly Times Annual, Sporting Globe, Punch* and *Table Talk*, the Sydney *Arrow* and *Referee* and *Smith's Weekly*, as well as decorative pieces for the *Lone Hand*. He produced, with T. M. Hogan, *The tight little island* (c. 1912), and is also represented in *Melba's gift book* (1915) and *Art in Australia*.

C. J. Dennis [q.v.8], as editor of the Adelaide *Gadfly*, had accepted contributions from Gye during 1906-07. They met later in Melbourne and when Dennis requested 'decorations' for *The songs of a sentimental bloke* (1915), a most successful collaboration followed. Gye stayed with Dennis at Toolangi, producing the whimsical 'bloke cupids'; he was to provide the illustrations for most of Dennis's works until the author's objection to a direct arrangement between Angus [q.v.7] and Robertson [q.v.] and Gye for *Rose of Spadgers* (1924) terminated the partnership. Angus and Robertson commissioned book illustrations from Gye for works by Henry Lawson, Will Ogilvie and A. B. Paterson [qq.v.]. The originals, and drawings published in the *Bulletin*, are held at the Mitchell Library, Sydney.

During the war years Gye shared a studio in Collins Street, Melbourne, with David Low [q.v.], who later recalled his association with both Gye and Dennis: 'Here were a couple of characters in whose company I found rest and understanding. We could laugh, shout, sing, exult, mourn, curse the wrongdoer in the open, as we wrestled with our work ... Even on the blackest days I found relief in that pool of goodwill'. At Flemington on 15 November 1916 Gye married with Methodist forms Alice Clara Gifford, one of the famous J. C. Williamson [q.v.6] front-row chorus girls.

In the 1920s Gye sold 'hundreds of oils', exhibited paintings and held a one-man show of monotypes. A painter of delicate water-colours and a talented black-and-white artist, he is represented in several State galleries, and by mounted oils of 'The Glugs of Gosh' in the State Library of South Australia. He designed the costumes for a ballet based on the 'Sentimental Bloke' in 1952. In 1963 he unveiled the Dennis memorial plaque at the Southern Cross Hotel, Melbourne.

After a serious motor accident in the early 1930s, Gye concentrated on writing and in 1937 began his humorous 'Father' and 'Jules' short stories in the *Bulletin* under the pseudonym of 'James Hackston'. His stories were included four times in *Coast to coast* and were later collected, and illustrated by 'Hal Gye', in *Father clears out* (1966) and the posthumous *The hole in the bedroom floor* (1969). In the 1940s and 1950s he published verse in the *Bulletin* under the pseudonym 'Hacko'. His facility for writing vernacular verse in the Dennis style is evidenced in *The sentimental bloke and the Burnie Mill* (1959) which he also illustrated.

Gye was described by John Hetherington in 1966 as a 'small, slim, quick-moving man pink-faced and ageless, a birdlike man with delicate hands and light step, who might have stepped, alive, from the pages of his own sketchbook'. J. K. Moir of the Bread and Cheese Club, said of him: 'He's rare. Men like to knock a bottle off with him; women love him; and artists admire his work'. He had a high sense of fun, and humour was an important ingredient in his work.

Hal Gye worked at his home at Armadale in his latter years. He died, survived by his son, at Beaumaris on 25 November 1967, and was cremated.

D. Low, *Autobiography* (Lond, 1956); D. Stewart, foreword in J. Hackston, *Father clears out* (Syd, 1966); *People* (Syd), 28 July 1954; *Bulletin*, 6 Oct 1954; *Sun-News Pictorial*, 3 Nov 1956; *Age*, 24 Sept 1966; *Herald* (Melb), 25 Nov 1967; Hal Gye's association with C. J. Dennis (MS, McLaren collection, Baillieu Lib, Univ Melb).

IAN F. McLAREN

H

HACKETT, DEBORAH VERNON (1887-1965), mining company director and welfare worker, was born on 18 June 1887 at West Guildford, Western Australia, daughter of Frederick Slade Drake-Brockman [q.v.8], surveyor, and his wife Grace Vernon, née Bussell, the heroine of the shipwreck in 1878 near the mouth of the Margaret River. Of their seven children, Deborah was the third daughter and middle child. She was unusual: 'an individualist from an early age'. She was educated at the Guildford Grammar School for boys, which then took a few girls from surrounding homesteads, and she spent much time at Wallcliffe, exploring caves, riding, learning to know the Aboriginals.

The Drake-Brockmans were a good-looking family. Deborah too possessed a most pleasing delicacy of feature, and dark blue eyes and raven hair. She also had 'fire' and a quick mentality. Despite family disapproval, at St Mary's Anglican Church, Busselton, on 3 August 1905, aged 18, she married an Irishman, (Sir) John Winthrop Hackett [q.v.], forty years her senior. They had four daughters and a son, all of whom were particularly gifted; the son General Sir John Hackett, commander-in-chief of the British Army on the Rhine, became principal of King's College, University of London, on his retirement from the army.

Lady Hackett became a society hostess and worked strenuously for the war effort during World War I. The French government rewarded her with La Medaille de la Reconnaissance Française. She edited a tome, *The Australian household guide* (Perth, 1916), which purported to contain everything that an Australian housewife might want to know. Profits went to charities and a second edition in 1940 again raised large sums for the Red Cross Society.

Sir Winthrop Hackett had died in 1916. On 10 April 1918 Lady Hackett married (Sir) Frank Beaumont Moulden [q.v.] in Adelaide and moved there to live. As his lady mayoress in 1920-22, she raised £100 000 for Adelaide charities, besides re-establishing the South Australian branch of the National Council of Women, of which she was president in 1921, and becoming first State commissioner of the Girl Guides' Association.

In 1923 Lady Moulden became interested in some rare Australian minerals, specifically tantalite in the Northern Territory and at Wodgina in Western Australia. This was scarce throughout the world. She visited the desolate areas in which it was found, chartering a small single-engine plane, trudging over sandy wastes in desert heat or bumping along in trucks, descending mines in a bosun's chair. By 1925 she was convinced of the wealth tantalite could bring Australia if developed. She went to the United States of America and made a contract with the Fansteel Metallurgical Corporation for the supply of ore for tantalite concentrates; she soon realized that at the enormous price of tantalum it would be advantageous to have the ores processed within Australia or elsewhere in the British Commonwealth. So she moved to London in 1927 and in 1932 Tantalite Ltd was incorporated. It was difficult, however, to persuade governments to process the mineral in its country of origin. Returning to Australia to live, she formed a syndicate to mine wolfram in Central Australia. In World War II her tantalum was used in developing radar. The need for the minerals in various fields became so obvious that the Commonwealth government resumed Tantalite Ltd, which had taken over the wolfram mines, for the duration of the war.

In 1932 the University of Western Australia had honoured its benefactor's widow when the Winthrop Hall was opened by conferring on her the degree of Doctor of Laws, *in absentia* because of the recent death of Sir Frank Moulden. On 27 June 1936 in St Patrick's Cathedral, Melbourne, she married Basil Buller Murphy, a barrister nine years her junior; she became known as Dr Buller Murphy. She supported the women's auxiliaries of Melbourne's hospitals and welfare committees, and proffered untiring hospitality. Intrepid, with superabundant energy and inquiring mind, she was in every way an unusual woman of strong character. After the war she moved from Toorak to an orchard property in the Dandenongs. During the 1956 Olympic Games in Melbourne Dr Buller Murphy prepared an alfresco Australian luncheon for 200 visitors: Darwin barramundi, Onslow oysters, Geraldton crayfish, wild turkey from Carnarvon and venison from the Victorian Alps. Two years later she published *An attempt to eat the moon*, a book of legends of the Dordenup tribe of Aboriginals that she had known when young. Predeceased by her third husband (d. 10 March 1963), she died at her home Lordello, Kilsyth, on 16 April 1965 and was buried in Karrakatta cemetery, Perth. Her estate was sworn for probate at about £88 000.

A portrait of her in oils by James Govett,

is at St George's College in the University of Western Australia.

B. Buller Murphy, *A lady of rare metal* (np, 1949); G. Drake-Brockman, *The turning wheel* (Perth, 1960); F. Alexander, *Campus at Crawley* (Melb, 1963); M. L. Skinner, *The fifth sparrow* (Lond, 1973); *People* (Syd), 16 Aug 1950; *Daily Mirror*, 3 Mar 1969.
ALEXANDRA HASLUCK

HACKETT, SIR JOHN WINTHROP (1848?-1916), editor and politician, was born probably on 4 February 1848 (his baptismal record shows 1847) near Bray, Wicklow, Ireland, eldest son of Rev. John Winthrop Hackett of the Church of Ireland, and his wife Jane Sophia Monck, née Mason. Educated at Trinity College, Dublin (B.A., 1871; M.A., 1874), he was called to the Irish Bar in 1874. He migrated to Sydney in 1875 and settled in Melbourne next year as vice-principal of Trinity College, University of Melbourne, and tutor in law, logic and political economy. He contributed to the *Age* and *Melbourne Review* and made two unsuccessful attempts to enter parliament.

Hackett went to Western Australia in 1882 to manage a sheep station in the Gascoyne district. Next year he joined Charles Harper [q.v.4] as partner and business manager of the *West Australian*, a Perth triweekly newspaper committed to conservative politics and the rural hegemony. From 1885 it was published daily and the *Western Mail* was launched as a weekly journal of condensed news and advice for farmers. In 1887 Hackett became editor of the *West Australian* when Sir Thomas Cockburn-Campbell [q.v.3] resigned. He was slow to settle into the role. Racial intolerance was displayed in attacks on Rev. John Gribble [q.v.4] who exposed the exploitation of Aboriginals in the pastoral and pearling industries. The paper's image suffered when Hackett sided with Governor Broome [q.v.3] in the fracas between governor and officials which saw Chief Justice Onslow [q.v.5] suspended. Irresponsible editorials by Hackett led to conviction of the paper's proprietors for defamation. Popular pressure then forced Hackett to take stock. Controversy was inimical to the organic view of society that he wished to project. Henceforth he avoided disputation. His editorials became didactic statements in which it was sometimes difficult to discern a clear line.

Hackett was on safer ground in reversing the paper's policy to argue for responsible government for Western Australia. In a period of rising population, agitation, focused by the Reform Association of which Hackett was a committeeman, saw the Colonial Office yield in 1890. Responsible government confirmed Hackett's rising stature when Premier (Sir) John Forrest [q.v.8] proposed him for nomination to the Legislative Council in December. He remained a councillor until his death—consistently returned unopposed for South-West Province after the council became elective in 1894.

Hackett described himself as an 'advanced liberal': he was progressive, for example, on education, female suffrage and lunacy reform. He believed in the freedom of the individual to exploit talents uninhibited by regulation. Hence his approach to industrial regulation was *laissez-faire*. However on constitutional questions he was conservative. His fears of democracy were confirmed by a radical candidate's success in a Perth electorate in 1888, despite strong advice from the *West Australian*. The 1890 constitution, as prompted by Hackett, established a bicameral legislature with the Legislative Council controlled by rural interests. This bias was confirmed in provisions for the election of councillors from 1894 which enshrined a propertied franchise and a rural gerrymander. The council had co-ordinate powers with the popular house, the Legislative Assembly, except for the origination of money bills. Even here, the right to 'request' amendments, added to the constitution in 1893 at Hackett's instigation, gave it virtually co-ordinate powers. The responsibility of the executive to both houses was central to Hackett's thinking. Councillors, acting independently, would guard the State against democratic excesses. Hackett always defended this Burkeian concept of the independent member: the *West Australian* even avoided identifying party affiliations of legislative councillors until 1912.

He cemented his position in Western Australian society through personal links. Some spoke of a triumvirate of Hackett, Forrest and Bishop C. O. L. Riley [q.v.]. Hackett preceded Riley as grand master of the Grand Lodge of Freemasons of Western Australia in 1901-03. He was diocesan registrar of Perth and chancellor of St George's Cathedral and always reported the bishop's sermons verbatim. The premier and the editor, despite occasional differences politically, co-operated. Hackett joined Forrest's confidants who met most Sunday mornings at the premier's home. He refused a position in the ministry, but served as mentor to Forrest and publicist of his policies.

The great theme was development. The gold rush trebled Western Australia's population between 1892 and 1900. Posts and telegraphs, railways, hospitals, harbours, water supplies, schools had to be provided, and Hackett gave consistent publicity. His backing was crucial in winning parliamentary approval in 1896 of C. Y. O'Connor's [q.v.] plan to pump water to the eastern goldfields from the Darling Range. Detractors derided 'the Forrest-Hackett curse' until silenced by its successful completion in 1903. Forrest's other grand scheme—to use the men and monies of the gold rush to settle a 'bold yeomanry' on the land—also had Hackett's support. His paper backed the Homestead Act (1893) and Land Act (1898), the Agricultural Bank Act (1894), and the Bureau of Agriculture which provided land, capital and scientific advice for farmers. Meanwhile the *Western Mail* prospered as the man on the land's bible. Ironically, Hackett's own rural investments failed.

Hackett considered education the key to society's improvement. He gave long service to Perth High School as chairman and later he led the crusade for a university. In the 1890s, despite Forrest's doubts, he orchestrated the abolition of grants to private schools through the dual system which had provided funds to both government and church schools. *West Australian* editorials, from 1892 to 1895, focused opposition to this arrangement, which mainly benefited the Roman Catholic Church. Within synod Hackett worked to align the Church of England with opponents of the system. His motives included sectarianism, a desire to improve educational standards in government schools, and a commitment to the separation of church and state. Forrest gave way in 1895. Hackett had been the central figure and the *West Australian* the instrument of the change, which led to the emergence of free, compulsory and secular education in Western Australia in 1899.

Civic and cultural improvements benefited from Hackett's encouragement and leadership. He advocated the preservation of Queen's Gardens and King's Park and later chaired the King's Park Board. He proposed a deep drainage and sewerage scheme for Perth and the relocation of the city cemetery at Karrakatta; afterwards he chaired the Karrakatta Cemetery Board. The observatory and mint had his backing. In 1897, as chairman of the Acclimatisation Committee, he persuaded Premier Forrest to establish zoological gardens and then nominated the South Perth site, selected Ernest Le Souef [q.v.] as first director, and presided over the Zoological Gardens Board. Similarly he spurred on the commission responsible for opening up scenic caves in the south-west. He helped to establish the Victoria Public Library (1889) and the Western Australian Museum (1895). At his invitation J. S. Battye [q.v.7] came to Perth as librarian in 1894. New buildings were opened in 1903 and Hackett remained library chairman until 1913, arranging the merger of the library, museum and art gallery under joint trustees in 1911.

Events modified his *laissez-faire* attitudes. In 1890, for example, he had opposed industrial arbitration as 'placing too great a limitation on individual freedom'. By 1900, after waterfront strikes, he asserted pragmatically that an arbitration court would 'get rid of strikes'. Yet he could also sympathize with the working man. When it became apparent that timber workers in his electorate were being exploited, he lashed the mill-owners and supported the Truck Act (1899) which ensured that workers received cash wages instead of credit at a company store. However Hackett spoke rarely in parliament on industrial matters. He accepted reluctantly the necessity for major intervention by the Forrest government between master and servant, and then only after the need was apparent and there was wide community support.

Competition from a new daily, the *Morning Herald*, faced Hackett from 1896. He met it by keeping advertising rates low and by installing the latest linotype and printing machinery. The *West Australian* was expanded to twelve pages—half of them advertisements—and the *Western Mail* was illustrated. He established useful contacts with (Sir) John Kirwan [q.v.] of the *Kalgoorlie Miner* to share reporting and news services. Although Hackett encouraged correspondence and aired divergent views, he ignored local writing and literature reflecting working-class values. He drew inspiration from Britain and maintained contacts while attending the Imperial Press Conference in London in 1909. At home he kept a tight rein on policy, writing most editorials himself in a clear style which contrasted with his prolix and over-qualified speeches. He was firm with staff but progressive on working conditions: the *West Australian* was said to have been the first Perth firm to introduce the eight-hour day, and it recognized union labour. Yet Hackett opposed the emergence of the political labour movement and election of the first Labor Party members in 1901 because of their sectional interest.

As politician-confidant-editor, Hackett was at the centre of debate over Western Australia's entry into Australian Federation. He supported Australasian co-operation but saw no urgency. At the 1891 federal convention he predicted: 'either responsible government will kill federation, or federation in the form in which we shall, I hope, be prepared to accept it, will kill responsible government'. The epigram pinpointed the difficulty of grafting responsible government on to a Federal system in which a Senate, representing the States equally, would exercise co-ordinate powers with the popular house. Hackett was the only Westralian delegate to support the 'compromise of 1891', which modified the Senate's co-ordinate powers by denying its right to amend money bills, while conferring a power to 'request' amendments. His intention was not to tip the scale in favour of responsible government but to effect a compromise which would stop short of rendering a Federal government responsible only to the lower house.

By 1895 Hackett had decided that Western Australia's entry into the Federation would have to be delayed until its industries were developed behind tariff walls, which would not be permitted after union. That remained his belief throughout the Federal campaign. He attended the Federal Council of Australasia meetings of 1895, 1897 and 1899 and the more important convention of 1897-98 that set the stage for Federation. He spoke rarely but, in divisions, was one of the more liberal Westralians on social questions. He talked generally of Western Australia's need for concessions in the Constitution but, significantly, abstained on the vote for the protection of the colony's customs revenue through section 95. Some historians have assumed that he contributed crucially behind the scenes through legal skills, influence on Forrest and acquaintance with Federalists, particularly Alfred Deakin [q.v.8].

By 1898 Hackett and Forrest were diverging: Hackett opposed immediate Federation; Forrest heralded a Federal referendum. Both were to be overwhelmed by events. Under pressure from conservatives, including Hackett, Forrest reversed his decision. In turn, Hackett found that popular agitation for Federation could not be contained, despite it being played down in the West Australian. In 1899 both men agreed to seek concessions, including five years complete customs freedom, as the price of Federation. They failed in this endeavour, despite joint approaches to the eastern capitals in January 1900. Reluctantly, Hackett recommended support for Federation on the eve of the referendum, which was carried decisively. He did this, despite Harper's contrary advice, believing that Federation was inevitable and the terms the best available. In the most important issue of his editorial and political career, he had influenced significantly neither the form nor the timing of Federation.

After 1901 Hackett lost his direct access to State premiers and contacted Forrest mainly to assist anti-Labor candidates during Federal elections. Locally, progressive politicians held sway for four years. The most serious challenge came from the government of (Sir) Walter James [q.v.] of 1903-04, when it determined to democratize parliament. Bills to redistribute electorates, extend the franchise and provide deadlock machinery, were anathema to Hackett and the Legislative Council. Protracted wrangling was reported by the West Australian. Finally the Upper House permitted only minor amendments and a redistribution. Hackett was the key to this failure to achieve a democratic constitution for Western Australia.

On 3 August 1905 Hackett married eighteen-year-old Deborah Vernon Brockman [q.v. Hackett] at Busselton. With conservative governments in office in 1905-11 he could be less assiduous in his parliamentary duties. The couple travelled widely and entertained lavishly, inhibited only by Hackett's ill health. A wealthy man, he was said to draw £9500 annually from the West Australian. When Harper died in 1912 Hackett acquired full ownership for £88 000. Soon afterwards the paper was converted into a public company.

From the 1880s Hackett had looked to a university as the coping-stone of the education system and open to all who might benefit. He educated the public to the idea through his newspaper. In 1909 he chaired the royal commission that recommended the establishment of the University of Western Australia; lectures began in 1913. A decision to charge no fees was made by the senate on his casting vote as chancellor and he endowed the chair of agriculture.

Distinguished in appearance by meticulous dress and clipped beard and moustache, Hackett was not handsome, being gaunt with prominent eyes, one of which was defective. He was not robust but highly strung. Aloof and imperious, with a strong sense of duty, he yet could charm with his melodious Irish voice.

Hackett was made an honorary doctor of laws by the University of Dublin in 1902; he was knighted in 1911 and appointed K.C.M.G. in 1913. Having suffered from Parkinsonism, he died in Perth on 19 February 1916 of a heart condition and was buried in Karrakatta cemetery. After providing for his wife, son (later General Sir John Hackett) and four daughters, and adding many bequests to charitable and public institutions including the State Library (where a marble bust of Hackett by E. E. Benson is displayed), he made the University of Western Australia and the Church of England residuary legatees. The estate was realized in 1926 after £700 000 had derived from Hackett's interest in the West Australian Newspaper Co. The university received £425 000 which it used principally to establish Hackett studentships and bursaries, and to construct Winthrop Hall and the Hackett Build ngs at Crawley. The Church used its £138 000 to build St George's College. Hackett had given his adopted country a university, a powerful press and an entrenched Legislative Council. His posthumous portrait by William Dargie hangs in the university.

F. Alexander, *Campus at Crawley* (Melb, 1963); P. Loveday et al (eds), *The emergence of the Australian party system* (Syd, 1977); L. Hunt (ed), *Westralian portraits* (Perth, 1979); C. T. Stannage, *The people of Perth* (Perth, 1979), *and* (ed), *A new history of Western Australia* (Perth, 1981); *Aust Economic Hist Review*, pt 3, 1968; *Hist Studies*, Oct 1968; *Studies in WA Hist*, Mar 1978; *West Australian*, 21 Feb 1916, 5 Jan 1933; R. Gore, The Western Australian Legislative Council, 1890-1970—aspects of a House of review (M.A. thesis, Univ WA, 1975).　　　　　　　　　　　LYALL HUNT

HACKETT, WILLIAM PHILIP (1878-1954), priest, teacher and propagandist, was born on 2 May 1878 at Kilkenny, Ireland, son of John Byrene Hackett, medical practitioner, and his wife Bridget, née Doheny. The Hacketts, a family of writers and bibliophiles, could trace their Irish patriotism to the battle of the Boyne (1689). Educated at St Stanislaus, Tullamore and Clongowes Wood colleges, William entered the Society of Jesus in 1896 and studied in France and Holland where he found his 'nerves' intolerable and theology intractable. He taught at Clongowes for six years and, after ordination in 1912, at Crescent College, Limerick, for nine. His friendship with participants such as Eamon de Valera in the 1916 rebellion, his republicanism and ardent loquacity influenced his removal in 1922 to Australia.

After teaching in Sydney at St Aloysius College and then in Melbourne at Xavier College, he was appointed parish priest of St Ignatius, Richmond, in 1925. Meanwhile his reputation for Irish patriotism, scholarship and energy had endeared him to Archbishop Daniel Mannix [q.v.], who encouraged him to found the Central Catholic Library. It opened in May 1924 and by 1937 more than 2000 borrowers had access to about 60 000 books. Hackett's axiom was: 'a country that does not read does not develop; a community without spiritual ideas cannot survive'. Though he lacked business or administrative sense, he triumphed over financial problems owing to his humorous and courtly personality, and a showmanship backed by a wide-ranging acquaintance with literature. The library became a centre for discussion groups of graduates of Catholic secondary schools and at Newman College, University of Melbourne. Hackett

fostered the emergence of an intelligentsia in the Campion Society, founded in 1931. As chaplain he took a heuristic line; laymen, he felt obliged to say, were not the clergy's inferiors.

Appalled by the Depression and the growth of communism, he helped to launch the influential Sunday Catholic Hour broadcast (3AW) in 1932 and was a frequent commentator; he watched over the foundation of the monthly *Catholic Worker* in 1936 and the national secretariat of Catholic Action in 1937 of which he became ecclesiastical assistant from 1943. While condemning both Nazis and Spanish socialists and extolling constitutional freedoms, he praised the pro-family and anti-communist policies of Fascist régimes. He helped to foster the Catholic Women's Social Guild, addressed the inaugural meeting of the Australian section of St John's International Alliance and supported the innovation of the Grail lay female institute.

Hackett's zeal did not make him generally popular during his rectorship of Xavier College in 1935-40. He ridiculed the emphasis on competitive sport (though he enjoyed vigorous bush-walking), joked about social committees, caused resignations from the Old Xaverians' Association by putting liturgical study groups before conviviality and, forming an élite student Catholic Action group, invited Campions to inspire students to reform capitalism as well as fight communism. In spite of a huge school debt he responded to Mannix's urging to found a second preparatory school, Kostka Hall, in Brighton and was held responsible for a later cheap sale of choice Xavier land to clear liabilities. His concern was less with curriculum and instruction than with activities such as the revival of the cadet corps. He farewelled the class in 1939: 'Keep fit. Don't grumble. Shoot straight. Pray hard'.

This militancy, and a vein of conspiracy, flowed through his later years. His health had been precarious: in the early 1940s he was confined to light parish work and from 1943 counselling at Xavier, then from 1948 at Kostka Hall. In 1952, however, he was appointed first superior of the pro-'Movement' Institute of Social Order. He wrote a pamphlet *Why Catholic Action?* in 1949, itemizing its official bodies but failing to mention 'the Movement'. He voted for the Communist Party dissolution bill of 1951, admired John Wren's [q.v.] simple faith and marvelled at his ill-repute. He was a founder of the Aisling Society which propagated Irish culture, and he had a special knowledge of illuminated manuscripts. In 1942 he became a trustee of the Public Library, Museums, and National Gallery of Victoria.

Obliged as a confidant to consult with and

entertain Mannix on Monday evenings and to accompany him on his annual vacations at Portsea, Hackett appeared to relish both these privileges and the role of court jester but his letters show he disliked being 'a quasi-episcopal hanger-on'. A man of 'gasps, grunts and angular gestures', he was a facile butt for Mannix's friendly if sharp jibes, but he was revered by Catholic intellectuals for his kindliness, enthusiastic piety, scrupulous poverty and scattered erudition. He boasted of his schooldays acquaintance with James Joyce and then castigated himself in private for such vanity. On retreat he complained of spiritual emptiness, occasionally scourged himself lightly but wondered if this were not self-indulgence. A feckless jaywalker, he died on 9 July 1954, a week after being hit by a car on a rainy Melbourne night. He was wearing a penitential hair shirt. In his panegyric Mannix called Hackett the founder of Catholic Action in Australia, praised his vibrant humour and said he was the humblest man he had ever known. He was buried in Boroondara cemetery.

G. Dening, *Xavier* (Melb, 1978); U. M. L. Bygott, *With pen and tongue* (Melb, 1980); *Catholic Worker*, Aug 1954; *Irish Province News* (Dublin), Oct 1954; Xavier College, *Xaverian*, 1954; *Herald* (Melb), 28 Jan, 4 Feb 1935; *Argus*, 10 July 1954; *Advocate* (Melb), 15 July 1954; C. H. Jory, The Campion era: the development of Catholic social idealism in Australia (M.A. thesis, ANU, 1974); Hackett papers (Society of Jesus Provincial Archives, Hawthorn, Melb); personal information.

JAMES GRIFFIN

HADDON, ROBERT JOSEPH (1866-1929), architect, was born on 25 February 1866 in London, son of Joseph Haddon, carpenter, and his wife Elizabeth, née Switzer. After serving his articles in 1881-84 with F. Templeton Mew of London, he was employed as an assistant to T. H. Watson for four years. In 1889 Haddon came to Melbourne, joined the firm Sydney Smith & Ogg and was elected to the Victorian Architectural and Engineering Association and the Victorian Artists' Society.

In 1892 Haddon settled in Hobart, where he was appointed an architectural instructor at the Government Technical School and designed some houses before moving to Adelaide in 1894. On 21 January 1896 he married Ada Templer of North Adelaide. They went to Perth where Haddon worked as a first-class draughtsman with the Department of Public Works for two years. While in Perth, Haddon was the secretary of the Western Australian Society of Arts; he had also become a member of the South Aus-

tralian Institute of Architects and a fellow of the Royal Victorian Institute of Architects in 1896. He returned to Melbourne in 1899 and set up his own practice in August 1901. By then he had established his name as an architectural artist; his work for other architects included coloured and line perspectives and the design of building façades. By 1904 his new office was known as the Central Drawing Office and Haddon called himself a consulting architect. In this way his name can be associated with such architects as G. B. Leith and Sydney Smith & Ogg of Melbourne, Laird and Barlow of Geelong and Michael McCabe of Camperdown.

In 1902 he had become head of the department of architecture at the Working Men's College. He influenced many architects through his teachings, and some who were articled in his office later became principals of their own firms. These included Percy Oakley, A. C. Leith, E. M. Nicholls and Eric Hughes. William Alexander Henderson joined Robert Haddon's practice in 1903 and in 1919 became a partner of the firm Haddon & Henderson. His practical interests complemented Haddon's flair for design and architectural drawing.

Haddon was a council-member of the Royal Victorian Institute of Architects in 1902-05, and over his lifetime was involved with both writing and drawing for the institute. In 1907 he became a fellow of the Royal Institute of British Architects. He was a founding vice-president of the Arts and Crafts Society of Victoria in 1908.

In his designs for offices, residences, churches and other public buildings, Haddon attempted to realize the principles so strongly propounded in his writings. In addition to delivering papers, he wrote a section on 'Australian Planning and Construction' in volume 5 of *Modern buildings: their planning, construction and equipment* edited by G. A. T. Middleton (London, 1905-06). His book, *Australian architecture*, was published in Melbourne in 1908. Haddon argued that originality in design was made possible by responding to the unique Australian conditions and by the use of local materials. Each design had to be conceived anew. His aim therefore was to design for each individual client, and to produce a harmonious, balanced composition. He emphasized simplicity in design, stating that ornament should be applied only for a specific purpose, and must fully utilize Nature and its play of light and shadow.

The façades of Milton House, Flinders Lane (1901) and Eastbourne House, Wellington Parade (1901), are composed of carefully placed elements and ornament on plain surfaces, producing overall balanced designs. These two private hospitals were rec orded as designed by Sydney Smith & Ogg but contain elements which suggest that Haddon was largely responsible.

His design for his own residence, Anselm, 4 Glenferrie Street, Caulfield (1906), combined elements characteristic of much of his work; balanced asymmetry, the use of towers, bays and bull's-eye windows, steep roofs, attic rooms, open planning and applied decoration in the form of terracotta patterned tiles and florid wrought iron. His principles were closely allied with those of the English Arts and Crafts architects who were propounding simplicity, originality, craftsmanship, structural honesty and a national sentiment.

Haddon's designs became typified by the simplicity of plain façades and the careful use of ornament and positioning of elements to produce a distinctive, and often delicately balanced, composition. This is seen in his house at 9 Sydney Road, Brunswick (1906); his North Melbourne picture theatre, Errol Street (1913); his remodelling of two city office façades, the Fourth Victorian Building Society office at Collins Street (1912) and the Wharf Labourers' building, Flinders Street (1915-16, demolished); and his design for the Swinburne Arts School, Hawthorn (1917). The plain façade of the Collins Street office was contrasted by the use of two large lions' heads and their slavering vertical streams, and by projections placed to catch the northern sun and cast shadows to form an integral part of the façade.

Haddon drew upon both English and American sources. His three Presbyterian Church designs—Malvern (1906), St Stephen's, Caulfield (1926) and St Andrew's, Oakleigh (1928)—were based on Gothic principles but used a more liberal and individual approach. In all he favoured the use of colour: red brick, terracotta ornament and green tiles being frequently used. Haddon's often florid treatment of ornament and his approach to composition have led him to be compared with architects like C. R. Mackintosh of Glasgow who were broadly linked with the art nouveau movement in Europe and Britain. Inasmuch as this style signified an individual relaxation of past forms of composition and decoration and a turning to Nature for inspiration, Haddon was working within its context.

Haddon was admired in professional circles although such work as the Fourth Victorian Building Society offices and the Wharf Labourers' Union building provoked hostile criticism. He was a vocal, dominating figure within his profession but appeared restrained in his private life, spending much time travelling and painting. He produced many sketch-books which remain unpublished.

He died at Caulfield of cardiac disease on 16 May 1929 and was buried in the Presbyterian section of Box Hill cemetery. He was survived by his wife; they had no children. Haddon's estate was valued for probate at £7715. In his will he made provision for a travelling scholarship to be known as the Robert and Ada Haddon architectural bequest, which was the richest of its kind when first awarded in 1934. His practice was absorbed by A. C. Leith.

Building, Engineering and Mining J, 9, 16 Dec 1893; *Roy Vic Inst of Architects J*, Nov 1903; *Vic Architectural Students Soc J*, Mar 1909; *Building* (Syd), 11 Nov 1916; *Real Property Annual*, 1917; *Argus*, 18 May 1929; D. K. P. Wee, Robert Haddon (B. Arch report, Univ Melb, 1966); Letter by Haddon 11 June 1902 to secretary, Vic Artists' Soc, (LaTL).   ROSLYN F. HUNTER

HAGELTHORN, FREDERICK WILLIAM (1864-1943), stock and station agent and politician, was born on 23 January 1864 at The Whim Holes, Ballarat, Victoria, son of Frederick Hagelthorn, a Swedish seaman who had jumped ship in Melbourne to head for the Ballarat diggings, and his Irish wife Mary, née Robertson. She brought her son up in the Catholic faith. After attending the Sebastopol State School Hagelthorn worked for several years at mining until the family moved to Allendale. He welcomed the opportunity for further education and spent a year at Creswick Grammar School where (Sir) Alexander Peacock [q.v.] was an assistant teacher.

Matriculating in 1880, Hagelthorn found employment in stores in the Stawell and Horsham districts. Briefly, he had his own general store. Then, after managing a store at Portland for several years, he set himself up as a stock and station agent. The business prospered and by 1900 the firm of F. Hagelthorn & Co. had substantial property holdings. About 1904 Hagelthorn formed a partnership with a banker, W. C. Bolton, and, operating from Horsham, launched into larger enterprises, particularly the purchase, subdivision and sale of land near the Murray. At 40 Hagelthorn was wealthy, respected and well known throughout the Mallee and Wimmera. He helped to found the Horsham branch of the Australian Natives' Association and the Horsham Working Men's College; he endowed scholarships for schoolchildren and awarded prizes for educational attainment. On 9 February 1905 at the Horsham Catholic Church he married Sarah Newton.

In 1907, standing as a Liberal for the North-Western Province, Hagelthorn was elected to the Victorian Legislative Council.

In his maiden speech he advocated the opening for settlement of Crown lands, particularly in the Mallee, water conservation schemes and construction of railways. Reforms to the education system and establishment of agricultural high schools were also part of his platform. In June 1909 he was appointed honorary minister in charge of immigration in the Murray [q.v.] government and held this post in the succeeding Watt [q.v.] ministry until June 1913 when he was made minister of public works and of public health and vice-president of the Board of Lands and Works. Following the short-lived Labor ministry in December, Hagelthorn resumed the vice-presidency of the Board of Lands and Works and was also commissioner of public works in the second Watt and the Peacock ministries until his appointment as minister for agriculture in November 1915.

Hagelthorn was a man of great persuasive influence who sought not plaudits but results. During his ministerial career, which lasted until November 1917, he steadily championed farming interests and steered bills dealing with closer settlement, railways, water distribution and education through the ponderous deliberations of the Legislative Council whose members objected to his barn-storming tactics. He worked closely with departmental heads, encouraging new ventures, and particularly promoted the work of Elwood Mead [q.v.] of the State Rivers and Water Supply Commission, William Calder [q.v.7] of the Country Roads Board and Drs T. Cherry, S. S. Cameron [qq.v.7] and A. E. V. Richardson [q.v.] of the Department of Agriculture.

The establishment of the Commonwealth Advisory Council of Science and Industry in March 1916 owed much to Hagelthorn's efforts. Inspired by a British White Paper of July 1915 on the national organization and development of scientific and industrial research, he brought together an influential lobby to gain the support of Prime Minister Hughes [q.v.] for a similar venture in Australia. Earlier in 1915 Hagelthorn had persuaded Hughes to adopt his wartime plan for marketing wheat. The Australian Wheat Harvesting Scheme, which came into effect on 1 December, set up State and Commonwealth wheat boards; growers pooled their wheat and the Commonwealth arranged for its shipping and sale. Hagelthorn, aptly termed 'Minister for Wheat' by Melbourne *Punch*, during this period was vice-president of the Commonwealth Wheat Board. Under his careful nurture the scheme prospered and the Victorian pool continued after the war as the Victorian Wheat-Growers' Corporation.

However, following criticism of the oper-ations of the wheat-pooling scheme by a small but significant minority of wheat-growers, Hagelthorn declined to stand for the North-Western Province in the 1919 council elections. Instead he contested the South-Eastern Province and was defeated with only one-fifth of the electors voting; he retired bitter and broken to lose again in 1924 when he stood for the Legislative Assembly seat of Mornington.

In his remaining years Hagelthorn campaigned actively for tariff reforms and against socialism. He became a trustee of the Henry George [q.v.4] League in 1922 and was subsequently vice-president and president: free trade formed part of the single-tax doctrine. In 1925 he helped found the Town and Country Union of Victoria, a non-political organization whose objectives were the reduction of customs duties, opposition to socialism and the development of 'national efficiency'; as vice-president he issued over the secretary's name a spate of leaflets on tariff anomalies. In 1931 he formed the Tariff Reform League which called for a return to the 1912 tariff. The union and the league shared the same office and secretary and survived through the 1930s; they had little impact on government policies.

Hagelthorn died at East Melbourne on 21 July 1943 and was buried in Brighton cemetery. He was survived by four of his five daughters.

E. Scott, *Australia during the war* (Syd, 1936); G. Currie and J. Graham, *The origins of CSIRO* (Melb, 1966); W. S. Robinson, *If I remember rightly*, G. Blainey ed (Melb, 1967); L. F. Fitzhardinge, *The little digger* (Syd, 1979); *Punch* (Melb), 8 Apr, 18 Nov, 9 Dec 1915, 6, 27 Jan, 3 Feb 1916, 22 May 1919; *Horsham Times*, 23 May 1943; *Herald* (Melb), 21 July 1943; *Age*, and *Argus*, 22 July 1943; F. Pilgrim [Hagelthorn], The beloved minister (typescript, c.1950, NL).　　　　J. W. GRAHAM

HAGUE, WILLIAM (1864-1924), storekeeper and politician, was born on 8 March 1864 at Angaston, South Australia, eldest son of James Hague, storekeeper, and his wife Patience, née Taylor. James, the son of a Congregationalist minister in Manchester, England, had migrated to South Australia in 1855. He opened general stores at Angaston, Truro and Sedan in partnership with his brother Edward, and represented Barossa in the House of Assembly from 1890 to 1902.

William was educated at Rev. James Leonard's private school at Angaston. After five years in the shipping and customs section of an Adelaide warehouse, he entered the family firm in 1885 and, when it was restructured in 1902, took charge of the Angaston store, trading as Wm. Hague & Co. from 1904. He expanded the business by buying and marketing considerable quantities of wheat, dried fruits and dairy produce. As secretary of the local agricultural society he organized Angaston's annual show. He became chairman of the Angaston District Council, president of the local nursing and benevolent society, the literary society and other groups, and master of the Barossa Masonic Lodge.

Elected to the House of Assembly in 1912 as one of the members for Barossa, Hague was soon appointed to the Standing Committee on Railways and became its chairman in 1918. This committee exposed scandals in railway management and checked the mania for building uneconomic 'developmental' lines which had saddled South Australia with relatively high interest bills and taxation. Newspapers hailed him as 'one of the few honest politicians'. Although he criticized some of the policies of fellow Liberals A. H. Peake [q.v.] and Sir Richard Butler [q.v.7], he was elected chairman of the coalition parties in 1917 and of the parliamentary wing of the Liberal Union in 1919; in April 1920 Peake offered him office as commissioner of public works, minister of railways and minister of industry. On Peake's death a few days later, the new premier, (Sir) H. N. Barwell [q.v.7], confirmed Hague in these posts and fully supported his proposals for a mammoth reorganization and rehabilitation of the railways, carried out by a new chief commissioner, W. A. Webb [q.v.]. Hague also sponsored water conservation, irrigation and better methods of roadmaking. In November 1922 he exchanged the works portfolio for the Treasury. He doubled the allowances for dependent children and legislated to end the tax exemption for interest on government bonds, arguing that it had unfairly benefited the rich. He retained his seat when Labor won the 1924 elections.

Hague died from cerebro-vascular disease at Henley Beach on 9 October 1924. He was given a state funeral and buried in Mitcham cemetery with Congregational rites. He was survived by his wife Elizabeth Maud, née Weller, whom he had married at Norwood on 3 December 1885, and by a son and two of their three daughters. His estate was sworn for probate at £9120.

'Painstaking rather than brilliant', Hague was a lovable and humane politician. During World War I he resisted legislation designed to degrade the many South Australians of German ancestry. As a minister he had some success in preventing further parliamentary discrimination against Aboriginals, maintaining that many were 'really decent fellows, and I do not think a slur should be cast upon them'. Yet he tended to view issues with a businessman's eye, and was fond of remarking that 'the pioneers had succeeded through energy and industry, and not through strikes and a go-slow policy'.

H. T. Burgess (ed), *Cyclopedia of South Australia* 2 (Adel, 1909); R. I. Jennings, *W. A. Webb, South Australian railways commissioner, 1922-1930* (Adel, 1973); *Critic* (Adel), 18 June 1919; *SA Freemason* (Adel), 10 Nov 1924; *Chronicle* (Adel), 25 Sept 1915; *Observer* (Adel), 19 Aug 1916; *Evening Journal* (Adel), 29 Aug 1918; *Sun-News Pictorial*, 2 Feb 1924; *Register* (Adel), 10, 11 Oct 1924; *Advertiser* (Adel), 12 Oct 1923, 10, 11 Oct 1924; *Barossa News*, 16 Oct 1924; Hague papers, PRG84 and A441 (SAA); family papers held by Mrs P. Reid, Hazelwood Park, SA.   P. A. HOWELL

HAILES, WILLIAM ALLAN (1891-1949), surgeon, was born on 9 June 1891 at Moonee Ponds, Melbourne, son of Walter Crossdell Hailes, commercial traveller and later manufacturer, and his wife Isabel McDonald, née Smith, both Melbourne-born. At Essendon Grammar School, and later at Scotch College, he established a fine record as a scholar and sportsman which he continued at the University of Melbourne (M.B., Ch.B., 1914). Cricket remained his first love in sport; he gained his university blue in 1911 and after World War I captained Essendon in district cricket.

His early professional interests focused on medicine and paediatrics but, after one year as a hospital resident, in January 1915 he was commissioned a captain in the Australian Army Medical Corps, Australian Imperial Force, and in November embarked for overseas. With the 20th Battalion, he was twice mentioned in dispatches and won the Distinguished Service Order in November 1917. In January next year he transferred to the 1st Australian General Hospital at Rouen and was then attracted to a career in surgery.

After the armistice Hailes stayed on in London to gain his F.R.C.S. in 1919. He returned to Melbourne in January 1920 and on 29 March at Malvern Presbyterian Church married Mary Maud Whitfield, a nursing sister at the (Royal) Melbourne Hospital. He set up in general practice at Moonee Ponds but was soon appointed honorary out-patient surgeon and clinical lecturer in surgery to the Melbourne Hospital. Many stories are told of how he rode his bicycle from Moonee Ponds to the hospital at all hours of day and night, conscious only of his duties and obligations to his hospital appointment and his general practice. He quickly established a high reputation as a consulting surgeon in the keen competition of the time.

In 1934 Hailes became honorary surgeon to in-patients at the hospital and relinquished his general practice. He had rapidly earned popularity as a devoted teacher with a gift of making students feel that he was 'on their side'. In 1936 he became dean of the hospital clinical school, and in 1937 Stewart lecturer in surgery at the university.

In December 1940 Hailes was appointed consulting surgeon to the A.I.F. with the rank of colonel. In this role he was never tied to base headquarters but was out seeing the units at work; he knew his men and their capabilities, and ensured that the right officers got appropriate postings, being always ready to circumvent or breach the rules of 'seniority'. In October 1942 he became director of surgery, with promotion to brigadier in February 1944.

His attitudes towards fostering the young and the place of apprenticeship as opposed to 'teaching' are well set out in his George Adlington Syme [q.v.] Oration (1947). It was a thesis he had scrupulously applied as censor-in-chief (1943) and as councillor (from 1944) of the Royal Australasian College of Surgeons.

Hailes died of hypertensive cerebrovascular disease on 22 January 1949 at East Melbourne. Survived by his wife and three daughters, he was cremated. A memorial fund in his name set up and furnished the 'Hailes Room' at the R.A.C.S.

A naturally friendly person, Bill Hailes never lost the common touch or forgot that he himself was once a student and novice helped along by others. He was blessed with the rare hallmark of true greatness—humility. There was no trace of flamboyance or false pride in his make-up. He attracted loyalty not only among his students because of his standard of teaching but also from the many who had the good fortune to come within his orbit throughout his personal and professional life.

B. Rank, *Jerry Moore and some of his contemporaries* (Melb, 1975); *Aust and New Zealand J of Surgery*, 19 (1949), 1, p 1.   BENJAMIN RANK

HAIN, GLADYS ADELINE (1887-1962), lawyer, journalist and housewives' association president, was born on 1 July 1887 at West Shelbourne, near Maldon, Victoria, eldest child of John Wightman Taylor, teacher, and his wife Adeline Landsborough, née Nicholl, both Victorian-born. After education at state and private schools at Castlemaine, she studied arts and law at the University of Melbourne (B.A., 1908; LL.B., 1910; M.A., 1912) winning the Bowen [q.v.3] prize in 1909. She also qualified for a diploma of education. After serving articles with (Sir) James McCay [q.v.], she was admitted to the Bar in May 1912 and set up on her own as a solicitor in Melbourne.

On 25 April 1915 at St Martin's Church of England, Hawksburn, she married Reginald (Rex) Edric Hain, a barrister, whom she had first met 'with some indignation' after he had published a skit on one of her political speeches in *Melbourne University Magazine*, which he edited. A week after their marriage he embarked as a lieutenant in the 23rd Battalion, Australian Imperial Force, serving on Gallipoli and in France before being invalided to England. Gladys sailed for England in 1916 where she did voluntary war work and began writing for a living. Her book of short stories, *The Coo-ee contingent*, was published in 1917. The Hains had two daughters; the first was born in England in 1919 and the second in Melbourne in 1921.

Once her children had reached kindergarten age Mrs Hain took up journalism: her husband, never well after the war, did not want her to practise law. She joined the staff of the Argus and Australasian Ltd, becoming social editress of the *Star* (1933-36) and later of the *Argus*. She was also for some years Melbourne correspondent for the Tasmanian *Mail*. With her wide general knowledge and ability of total recall, she proved a talented and successful interviewer; notable subjects included Chico Marx, Harry Lauder and Archbishop Mannix [q.v.]. She wrote articles on art and during World War II acted as music critic for the *Argus*.

Shortly before her husband's death in 1947 Gladys Hain retired from the *Argus* but continued to contribute in 1948-53. She resumed her law practice, first as a solicitor and from 1955 as a barrister. At the same time she became more actively involved in women's organizations. As a journalist she had been radical in politics, a 'fighter for the ordinary people'. Just after her marriage she had delivered a paper on the legal status of women to the National Council of Women. In the 1920s she campaigned for standardization of divorce laws in Australia. Over the years she acted as legal adviser to women's groups on such subjects as the adoption of children, prostitution and the problems of venereal disease. Despite her forthright opinions, and capacity to 'get tough if they asked for it', she was described as a softly spoken and gentle woman.

In 1952 Mrs Hain was elected fourth president of the Housewives' Association of Victoria and was for six years federal president of the Federated Housewives' Association of Australia. She campaigned for better conditions for housewives, lobbying producer and government groups for better prices and quality of essential food items such as bread. She was a representative of the Dairy Products' Board and in 1956 was appointed to the royal commission on the Victorian Housing Commission.

Mrs Hain had undergone an operation for cancer and later broke her leg in a street accident. She died in hospital at Carlton on 6 March 1962 and after a service conducted at the College Presbyterian Church, Parkville, was buried with her parents at Campbell's Creek cemetery, near Castlemaine. Her daughters survived her.

A. M. Norris, *Champions of the impossible* (Melb, 1978); *Age*, 7 Mar 1962; *Sun-News Pictorial*, 7, 8 Mar 1962; *Herald* (Melb), 1 May 1954; *Argus*, 23 Dec 1954; information from Mrs M. Couchman, Ferntree Gully, Vic.

HALCOMB, FREDERICK (1836-1919), parliamentary officer, was born on 25 July 1836 at High Trees farm near Marlborough, Wiltshire, England, fourth son of Thomas Halcomb, landlord, and his wife Emma Susan, née Worthington. He was educated at Macclesfield and at King Edward VI Grammar School, Bath, before matriculating on an open scholarship to Wadham College, Oxford in 1855 (B.A., 1859; M.A., 1878). In 1860 Halcomb left for South Australia in the *Morning Light* and arrived early next year. He joined the Gilbert [q.v.4] family at Pewsey Vale and later spent two years at Booborowie. With Thomas McTurk Gibson he opened up country north-west of Port Augusta for sheep-raising, at Yudnapinna, but the disastrous droughts of 1864-66 thwarted them. Halcomb moved to Henry Holroyd's Duck Ponds near Port Lincoln, and in 1866 married Henry's sister Margaret.

He entered the parliamentary service as librarian in 1870, but transferred in 1874 to clerk-assistant and sergeant-at-arms in the Legislative Council and became clerk of the House of Assembly in 1887. His career culminated in the appointment in 1901 as clerk of the parliaments and of the Legislative Council, where he succeeded E. G. Blackmore [q.v.3]. In 1918 Halcomb retired, having been associated with twenty-four ministries. He was somewhat reserved, but his genial courtesy made him many friends. He prepared a new code of standing orders for the Upper House, as well as revising the *Statistical record of the legislature* and Blackmore's *Parliamentary procedure*. It was said in the council that 'to know him was to respect, to honour, and to love the old gentleman ... there was never any semblance of

party feeling shown by him ... a safe and reliable counsellor ... a real English gentleman ... he had all the points of Parliamentary procedure at his fingers' ends'.

Halcomb was a member of the Senate of the University of Adelaide from 1877. In earlier days he had been an enthusiastic oarsman and later became captain of the university boat club. At public examinations he was an examiner in Latin and Greek and he was also a governor of the Collegiate School of St Peter. From 1872 he lived in the Walkerville district and his *Short history of St Andrew's Church, Walkerville by a warden* was published in 1914. An amateur painter, he executed in the church, by the light of a candle, a hand-painted reredos. He also kept a sketch-book diary and a delightful record exists of his family's holiday at Victor Harbour in 1878.

Halcomb's first wife died in 1882 and on 27 July 1895 he married Angela Hilda Cornish, who had migrated from England to marry him. He died on 20 October 1919 at his home, The Gables, Gilberton, and was buried in the Anglican North Road cemetery. He was survived by his second wife and two sons from the first marriage.

H. T. Burgess (ed), *Cyclopedia of South Australia* 1 (Adel, 1907); *PD* (SA), 1919, p 1276; Statistical record of the legislature, 1836-1977, *PP* (SA), 1978-79 (116); *Advertiser* (Adel), and *Register* (Adel), 21 Oct 1919.

                                              J. M. DAVIS

HALES, ALFRED ARTHUR GREENWOOD (1860-1936), author, war correspondent, miner and adventurer, was born on 21 July 1860 at Kent Town, Adelaide, son of Frederick Greenwood Hales, gold-digger and wood-turner, and his wife Sarah Leigh, née Veal, 'staid, respectable God-fearing folk'. Not so Hales, who recalled his mother's hope that he would get a 'call' and 'let light into the heathen. I've done it too [he wrote]— with a rifle'. He attended Burgoyne and Hosking's and R. C. Mitton's grammar schools in Adelaide and was briefly apprenticed to a carpenter, but he left home and school at 13. At 16 his first published story appeared in *Frearson's Weekly*. He read compulsively and widely and worked at fossicking, timber-splitting, droving, dingo-trapping and storekeeping. He studied assaying at the Ballarat School of Mines, Victoria, became athletics editor for the Sydney *Referee*, then was a mining reporter for the *Barrier Miner* and the *Silver Age* at Broken Hill, New South Wales, in 1886-89 where he exposed fraudulent sales of 'salted' mines and worthless shares. He also went to the United States of America as manager for the Australian boxer F. P. Slavin. In London when news of the Western Australian gold discoveries arrived, he 'went homewards like a homing bird'.

'The man with the chronic smile' arrived at Coolgardie in 1894 and, during the next five years, became one of the most colourful of those eastern goldfields literati who divided their time between the pick and the pen. His first newspaper job there was with the *Coolgardie Miner*. Billy Clare, the owner, recalled this 'dashing, picturesque looking chap', whom 'so many on the field had mentioned in connection with journalistic exploits and coups in Broken Hill, Adelaide, Sydney . . . He was dynamic . . . His ready pen and readier imagination suited the goldfields readers . . . to a degree which probably no other newspaper man in Australia could have attained'. Hales founded his own weekly, the *Coolgardie Mining Review*, and later the daily Boulder *Miner's Right*. He also managed a hotel, organized fortnightly boxing bouts and stood unsuccessfully for parliament in 1897 when president of the Coolgardie branch of the Amalgamated Workers' Association of Western Australia.

In 1899 Hales went to the South African War as a correspondent. His dispatches to the London *Daily News* and *John Bull* won him a reputation as a critical and daring front-line reporter which was enhanced after his wounding and capture by the Boers at Rensburg. He was commissioned by the *Daily News* in 1903 to report the Macedonian rebellion against Turkish control; two years later he was at some of the major Russo-Japanese battles. He spent about four years in South America. In World War I Hales enlisted in the Serbian Army and acted as a freelance journalist for London papers; he claimed that the first report ever made of an air fight was written by him for the *Evening News*.

He travelled the world, lectured, crossed the Gobi desert on horseback, did 'some gun-running and [was] mixed up in a couple of revolutions'; he explored most of the world's great mineral fields, owned several mines and wrote over fifty books. His first, a best-seller and the only one published in Australia, was *The wanderings of a simple child* (1890), a highly coloured mixture of reportage and fiction informed by 'an almost ferocious patriotism'; *Campaign pictures of the war in South Africa* appeared in 1900. Then came the first of the many McGlusky novels written between 1902 and 1935, which made their author a popular writer of light fiction in Britain, North America and Australia. McGlusky was a tough, adventurous Scot who roamed the world 'with a Bible in one hand and a brick in the other'. His creator wrote of himself in *Broken trails* (1937): 'A man cannot write . . . fifty novels and at the same time leave his foot-trails over four-fifths of the globe, and be blown aside like last year's leaves'. He also wrote historical novels, exotic stories set in Africa, Arabia, Japan and South America, books of poems and ballads, plays, and a string of loosely organized autobiographies: a mixture of recollection, fantasy and prophecy.

Despite his nickname, 'Smiler' Hales was a heavily jowled man whose sagging pouches underlined a rather belligerent gaze and a jutting jaw. He died on 29 December 1936 at Herne Bay, Kent, and was buried there. He was survived by the daughter and four sons of his first marriage on 15 May 1886 to Emmeline Pritchard (d. 1911), and by his second wife Jean Reid, a Scotswoman whom he had married in 1920.

L. W. Matters, *Australians who count in London . . .* (Lond, 1913); P. Depasquale, *A critical history of South Australian literature, 1836-1930 with subjectively annotated bibliographies* (Adel, 1978); *British A'sian*, 23 Aug, 18 Oct, 15 Nov 1900; *Tocsin*, 26 Sept 1901; *Golden West* (Perth), 1917, 1921; *All About Books*, 1 Dec 1931; *To-day* (Melb), 1 Aug 1933; *Morning Herald* (Perth), 12 Jan 1897; *Kalgoorlie Miner*, 16, 20 Jan 1897; *Western Argus*, 15 Jan 1901; *Sunday Times* (Perth), 21 July 1907; *Observer* (Adel), 29 Nov 1924; *The Times*, 30 Dec 1936; *West Australian*, 31 Dec 1936; D5390 (SAA).

DONALD GRANT

HALL, ARTHUR CHARLES (1896-1978), soldier and grazier, was born on 11 August 1896 at Granville, Sydney, eldest son of Charles Hall, grazier, of Glenelg station near Nyngan, and his wife Emma Jane, née King. He attended All Saints' College, Bathurst, in 1909-12 and became an overseer on his father's properties.

Hall enlisted in the Australian Imperial Force at Dubbo on 3 April 1916 and was posted to the 6th Reinforcements for the 54th Battalion, embarking in October. After further training in Britain, he joined his battalion on 8 February 1917 at Montauban, France. He received a severe leg wound on 30 March but returned to his unit on 21 April, and fought in the 2nd battle of Bullecourt in May and at Polygon Wood in September; he was promoted lance corporal in June and corporal in October. In 1918 his battalion returned to the Somme to fight at Villers-Bretonneux in April, Morlancourt in July, and in the general offensive from August.

On 1 September, while the 54th Battalion was engaged in an attack on Péronne, a machine-gun post was checking the advance. Single-handed, Hall 'rushed the position, shot four of the occupants and captured nine others and two machine-guns.

Then crossing the objective with a small party, he afforded excellent covering support for the remainder of the company'. He was continually in advance of the main party, located many points of resistance and personally led parties to attack them. Next day, while his unit mopped up at Péronne, Hall rescued a wounded mate under shell-fire. For his actions on 1 and 2 September he was awarded the Victoria Cross. On 11 October he was transferred to the 56th Battalion and on 6 March 1919 was promoted temporary sergeant, a rank he retained until his discharge from the A.I.F. on 3 August in Sydney.

After demobilization Hall returned to the Nyngan district where he bought a pastoral property, Gundooee station, near Coolabah. On 26 April 1927 he married Catherine Jessie Hemington Harris at the Union Church, Lahey's Creek, with Anglican rites. In 1942 he served as a lieutenant in the 7th Garrison Battalion and on returning to Gundooee carried on his pastoral activities, running sheep and building up a fine herd of Poll Devon cattle. He was president of the Nyngan Picnic Race Club for twenty years and was a foundation member and keen competitor in the Coolabah District Rifle Club; he was also active in the Nyngan District Historical Society.

Survived by his wife, a daughter and three sons, Hall died in Nyngan District Hospital on 25 February 1978. He was buried at the tiny Anglican Church of St Matthew's, West Bogan, which had been built from timber cut and milled on his property. His estate was sworn for probate at $160 191. He left his Victoria Cross to the Australian War Memorial.

C. E. W. Bean, *The A.I.F. in France*, 1917-18 (Syd, 1933, 1937, 1942); L. Wigmore (ed), *They dared mightily* (Canb, 1963); W. A. Steel and J. M. Antill, *The history of All Saints' College, Bathurst, 1873-1963* (Syd, 1964); *Mufti*, Apr 1939; *Reveille* (Syd), Apr 1978; *Despatch*, May 1978; Country Women's Assn of NSW (Syd), *Country Woman*, May 1978; *SMH*, 27, 28 Feb 1978; records (AWM).

GEORGE HALL

HALL, DAVID ROBERT (1874-1945), lawyer and politician, was born on 5 March 1874 (and registered as Thomas) at Harrietville, Victoria, son of Thomas Hall, farmer, and his wife Marion, née Hutchinson, both Scottish born. His family moved to New South Wales in December and he went to public schools at Cooma, where his father was a road-worker, and Forest Lodge, Sydney. In the 1890s he worked in various clerical positions with Goldsbrough Mort [qq.v. 4, 5] & Co. Ltd, the Sun Insurance Co., James Sandy & Co. and Foley Bros. In 1899-1901 he was private secretary to J. H. Young [q.v.6] and T. H. Hassall, ministers for lands. He studied law with W. A. Holman and W. M. Hughes [qq.v]. An unmatriculated student in 1902 at the University of Sydney, he was admitted to the Bar on 19 November next year. Dapper and enterprising, by 1900 Hall sported a flowing moustache and displayed striking buttonholes. A Freemason, he was the very model of the efficient clerk, with professional ambitions. In Sydney on 8 February 1905, with Church of Christ forms, he married Catherine Amelia Jackes.

He was attracted by the fresh radicalism of the Labor Party and joined it in the early 1890s. In 1901 he was on the executive of the party and won the State seat of Gunnedah. Hall made good use of his parliamentary experience, polishing his speaking and debating skills and observing the implications of the novel relationship between legislation and public administration, with its portents of a new role for government in the early twentieth century. In 1902 he became a justice of the peace, and was one of the first to raise doubts about the administration of the Department of Lands by W. P. Crick [q.v.8]. His association with Holman grew into a warm friendship; but he lacked Holman's style and charisma.

Back on the party executive in 1904, Hall failed to be re-elected to parliament. He took an interest in Labor's Federal branch and in November was in touch with its caucus regarding party organization. He acted as Holman's 'junior counsel' in the famous debate on socialism with (Sir) George Reid [q.v.] in 1906. The same year Hall won Werriwa in the Commonwealth House of Representatives. His nationalism was strengthened but his expectations were frustrated in the Federal arena; and he resigned his seat to accept Holman's invitation in March 1912 to return to the New South Wales parliament to join the McGowen [q.v.] government as solicitor-general and minister of justice with a place in the Legislative Council.

Hall came into his own as the government's administration expert, helping to balance on the executive in 1913-15 the residual force of reformist socialism against the growing power of trade union, industrialist pragmatism, which was threatening Holman's position. In parliament Holman formed his first ministry in June 1913 and next year Hall relieved him as attorney-general, allowing him to move more on to the national stage. Hall won Enmore in the Legislative Assembly in November, and could then operate as the premier's trouble-shooter, especially aware of the politics of rising prices as war came next year. He administered the Necessary Commodities Control Act, 1914, with some success in price-fixing; he also organized the acquisition, as a war measure, of the State's wheat crop. With Holman he published *Cost of living* in 1915.

The industrialists controlled the 1916 Labor Party conference. They opposed conscription and directed the parliamentarians to do likewise. Meanwhile, Hall, stirred by the war, in 1915 had been a foundation member of the Universal Service League; early next year he was rejected for service with the Australian Imperial Force. With Holman and many others he refused to obey conference and was expelled from the party. Holman formed a National ministry with the Liberals on 15 November 1916; Hall relinquished the justice portfolio, but remained as attorney-general. He bitterly criticized Hughes's conduct of the two national referendums on conscription in 1916-17. Retaining some of his radicalism as minister for housing in 1919-20, he was also vice-president of the Executive Council in that period.

By 1920 Hall cut a fine figure; he had shaved his moustache and acquired a confident style. Sensing that the days of the National government were numbered, he obtained Holman's approval to become State agent-general in London, where he would have shone. He set out for England, but Labor won the March 1920 general election and, as memories of 1916 were sharp and bitter, Hall's appointment was cancelled. He returned to Sydney, was admitted as a solicitor on 24 February 1921 and embarked on what was to prove a successful and lucrative legal career.

Hall kept up his interests, especially in prison reform, giving many lectures and engaging in many debates in the 1920s and 1930s: in 1935 he contributed to *Trends in Australian politics*. He had shared the enthusiasm of N. R. W. Nielsen [q.v.], Labor minister for lands 1910-11, for the preservation of harbour foreshores, and was a vigorous and effective trustee of the Nielsen-Vaucluse Park trust in 1915-44, president four times. In the 1930s he invested with his sons in catering. He was a member of the New South Wales council of the United Australia Party in 1932-40 and ran unsuccessfully as its candidate for the Senate in 1937. He gave an eloquent and moving panegyric on Holman's death in 1934.

Hall's wife died in 1928. He was made a freeman of the City of London in 1943. He married Myra Isobel Johnstone Perkins in London on 22 March 1944, and was survived by her and two sons of his first marriage when he died in Sydney on 6 September 1945; he was cremated with Church of

Christ forms. His estate was sworn for probate at £5522.

H. V. Evatt, *Australian Labour leader... W. A. Holman* (Syd, 1942); L. F. Fitzhardinge, *The little digger* (Syd, 1979); *Daily Telegraph* (Syd), 5 July 1901; *SMH*, 9 July 1901, 19 Oct 1915, 14 Mar, 16 Nov 1916, 21 Mar, 4 May, 9 Aug 1917, 24 Apr 1919, 16 Jan, 27 Mar 1920, 13 Apr 1922, 1 Oct 1929, 1 Apr 1931, 2 Feb 1935, 17 July 1937; *T&CJ*, 30 Apr 1919; *Australasian*, 15 Jan 1921, 20 Sept 1924.

BEDE NAIRN

HALL, ELSIE MAUDE STANLEY (1877-1976), pianist, was born on 22 June 1877 at Toowoomba, Queensland, elder daughter of William Stanley Hall, reporter, and his wife Mary Ann, née Sadgrove, piano-teacher. The family moved to Sydney in 1882 when her father was appointed mining editor with the *Sydney Morning Herald*. Taking to the piano before she was 3, Elsie proved a child prodigy and by 1884 was appearing in concerts. From the age of 5 she was taught by Josef Kretschmann, a fine German violinist; her first major recital was on 16 October 1886 when she played the Beethoven C Minor Concerto at the University of Sydney.

In 1888 Elsie, with her mother and sister Muriel, travelled to Germany where she enrolled at the Stuttgart Conservatorium. In 1889 she performed at the Australian kiosk at the Paris exhibition and next year moved with her family to London where she won a pianoforte scholarship at the Royal College of Music. Anticipating a return to Australia, she declined the award and when her trip home was cancelled she became a pupil of John Farmer at the Harrow Music School. Through the patronage of Mendelssohn's eldest daughter, Marie Benecke, she subsequently attended the Royal High School for Music in Berlin, studying under Ernst Rudorff and Rudolf Joachim; in 1895 she won the coveted Mendelssohn State Prize and next year made her public début playing Chopin's E Minor Concerto with the Berlin Philharmonic Orchestra.

In November 1897 Miss Hall returned to the Australian colonies in spite of a warning from Ada Crossley [q.v.8] that to do so would be 'suicide'. Accompanied by Muriel, now a proficient violinist, she toured outback and cities for several years before accepting a teaching appointment at the Elder [q.v.4] Conservatorium of Music, Adelaide. About 1903 she returned to her concert career in England; in 1908 she pioneered classical entertainment at the Coliseum and Hippodrome theatres, London. She also did a little teaching, her most notable pupils being Princess Mary (aged 14) and George

Lambert's [q.v.] sons, Maurice and Constant.

On 22 November 1913 Elsie married Frederick Otto Stohr whose medical career took him to South Africa where the couple made their permanent home; they had one daughter and two sons. During World War I Miss Hall served at the Anzac Buffet, London, and toured the French war zone with Lena Ashwell's entertainment party. In 1919 she gave her first recital with the Cape Town Symphony Orchestra and continued to play with leading South African orchestras until she was 93. An outstanding interpreter of Beethoven, Tchaikovsky, Mozart, Schumann and Chopin, she periodically returned to Europe to work and made occasional visits to Australia. In June 1957 she was awarded an honorary doctorate of music from the University of Cape Town. Her autobiography, *The good die young*, was published in 1969. Miss Hall made broadcasts for both the South African and British Broadcasting Commissions and gramophone records for the Pathé company (1910), His Master's Voice (early 1930s) and Decca (late 1930s); a limited edition long-playing record was issued in South Africa in 1970. Well into old age, she performed on television. She died at Wynberg, South Africa, on 27 June 1976 in her one hundredth year and was buried in Hout Bay cemetery; ne son survived her.

Argus, 8 Feb, 12 Apr 1890; *Sydney Mail*, 25 Dec 1897, 22 May 1935; *Cape Times* (South Africa), 1 July 1976; *The Times* (Lond), 28 July 1976.

PETER BURGIS

HALL, FRANCIS RICHARD (1862-1939), architect, was born on 9 February 1862 in Brisbane, son of John Hall, architect, and his wife Philadelphia, née Starr. His mother died when he was 2. Educated at Brisbane Grammar School from 1876, he joined his father's architectural practice, renamed John Hall & Son. When his father died in January 1883, he became head of the firm.

With Robin S. Dods [q.v.8] as partner in 1896-1913, the firm became known as Hall & Dods; about 1923-27 with Alan Devereux a partner, it was Hall & Devereux; and from about 1928 Hall & Cook, with Harold M. Cook. In these partnerships Hall was largely the administrator, businessman and job-getter. He chose his design partners carefully; that they proved extremely capable is a tribute to his sound judgement and foresight. He delighted in supervisory work and as always scrupulously fair and impartial in the administration of building contracts. He was conservative, however, in the use of new building materials and methods. He enjoyed his professional life and at the time of his death was the oldest practising architect in Australia.

Through Dods's appointment as architect to the Anglican diocese of Brisbane, the firm secured the supervision of construction of the Anglican Cathedral of St John, opened in 1910. Later they carried through the Cathedral School and church offices, and the chapel at the archbishop's residence, Bishopsbourne. For the Catholic diocese, they undertook St Brigid's Church and the Mater Misericordiae Hospital. Other projects included the nurses' home at the Royal Brisbane Hospital, the Maryborough Town Hall, and buildings for the Bank of New South Wales and the Australian Mutual Provident Society, including their main Brisbane offices.

A large and generous man, Hall was a keen photographer and race-goer; Hall & Cook were architects to the Queensland Turf Club. He died on 18 March 1939 of coronary vascular disease at the Ascot racecourse during the running of a welter handicap. His estate, valued for probate at £4637, was left to his wife Anna Katherina, née Tranberg, whom he had married at Trinity Church of England, Fortitude Valley, on 30 January 1884, and to their two surviving children.

THOMAS RAMSAY HALL (1879-1950), his stepbrother, was born on 2 January 1879 in Brisbane, son of John Hall and his third wife Charlotte, née Whiteway. Educated at Brisbane Grammar School from 1891, he won the Francis memorial prize for mathematics. On leaving school he studied accountancy and architecture, became an approved valuer and in 1907 was town clerk of Sandgate. He practised as an architect independently of his brother from 1913 in Hall & Prentice and Hall & Phillips (1930-50). His firms designed the Brisbane City Hall, Tattersall's Club, Ascot Chambers and Shell House. He was involved in racing through Tattersall's and the Queensland Turf clubs, and his name is commemorated in the T. R. Hall Handicap. When he died on 15 December 1950 of coronary vascular disease he left an estate valued for probate at £21 114 to his widow Emma, née Lingley, whom he had married at Sandgate on 9 March 1910, and to their four children.

Notable Queenslanders (Brisb, 1915, 1928, 1936-37, 1950); Roy Aust Inst of Architects, Qld chapter, *Buildings of Queensland* (Brisb, 1959); *Architecture, Building, Engineering*, 29 (1 Feb 1951), p 29; *Daily Mail* (Brisb), 28 July 1926; *Brisbane Courier*, 14, 20 Apr 1928, 24 Oct 1929, 18 Mar 1939; *Telegraph* (Brisb), 16 Mar 1939; J. Capper, Thomas Ramsay Hall (MS, 1979?, held by Brisb Civic Art Gallery and Museum), *and* Letters to Janet Hogan

(National Trust of Qld, Brisb, 1981), who also holds F. R. Hall, *Memories of my architect grandfather and family* (MS, 1980); J. V. Coutts, *Early Queensland architects* (MS held by Roy Aust Inst of Architects, Qld chapter).   JANET HOGAN

HALL, GEORGE WILLIAM LOUIS MARSHALL; *see* MARSHALL-HALL

HALL, JOHN JOSEPH (1884-1949), journalist and rural politician, was born on 18 February 1884 at Eaglehawk, Victoria, sixth child of Joseph Hall, goldminer and later tea merchant, and his wife Isabella, née Gray, both from northern England. Of their seven children, only John and a sister survived to adulthood. John's father was a Primitive Methodist lay preacher who imbued his son with a sense of service to others and of the need to uphold principles.

Educated at the local state school and by reading in mechanics' institutes, Hall joined the Victorian Railways as a booking clerk at 15. He taught himself shorthand and became a cadet with the *Bendigo Advertiser*. His rounds in the north-west of the State gave him an empathy with small farmers and townspeople. Through association with John Allan [q.v.7] he became interested in the Kyabram reform movement. This populist revolt of the rural quarter against the State government taught the young Hall the importance of founding a separate rural political party. He married Clarissa Jessamine Snell, dressmaker, on 26 December 1907 at Bendigo; they had four sons and two daughters. Hall's *Advertiser* salary was supplemented by his appointment as *Argus* mining correspondent in the Bendigo region. He developed a vigorous writing style and a vast knowledge of rural matters.

When Bowser's [q.v.7] 'Economy Party' emerged in 1916 from within the Liberal Party, Hall urged primary producers to take direct political action. In April a meeting at Fern Hill had brought Hall together with Isaac Hart and led to amalgamation with P. G. Stewart's [q.v.] Mallee movement. Through press campaigns and rural gatherings, in September this threesome established the Victorian Farmers' Union (after 1926 known as the Victorian Country Party). Hall constantly demanded that members 'stick to principles': farmer representation on marketing boards and endorsed farmer candidates pledged to the V.F.U. platform. He moved his family to Melbourne and became an estate agent in Collins Street before becoming first editor of the V.F.U. journal, the *Farmers' Advocate*, in January 1917. His stirring editorials and his work as general secretary of the V.F.U. made the union a serious political threat.

Hall won Kara Kara in November 1917 by a narrow margin but lost the seat after a recount. Undaunted, he contested the Flinders Federal by-election against S. M. (Viscount) Bruce [q.v.7] in 1918 and by withdrawing his candidature at the last minute secured a deal from W. M. Hughes [q.v.] for the V.F.U. He ran unsuccessfully for Kara Kara in 1920 and Benambra in 1924.

When the *Advocate* folded in 1924, Hall became managing editor of the *Morning Post*. This paper was incorporated with the *Sun-News Pictorial* in 1927 and Hall was made country editor and State political reporter, a post he held until 1946. He was a close adviser to (Sir) Keith Murdoch [q.v.] and (Sir) Albert Dunstan [q.v.8] during these years. His colourful editorials focused on 'The exploitation of the primary producer', 'Who are the profiteers?' and 'The metropolis gaining over the country'. For three years before his death he was editor of the *Leader*.

Hall was a bookish man and serious when discussing politics and newspapers. He mellowed in later life, held a part-ownership in a racehorse and enjoyed spectator sports. He died at Richmond on 30 June 1949 after an ulcer operation and was cremated. One son became editor of leading country newspapers.

U. R. Ellis, *A history of the Australian Country Partry* (Melb, 1963); B. D. Graham, *The formation of the Australian Country Parties* (Canb, 1966); *Age* 2 July 1949; *Countryman* (Melb), 28 Sept 1956; information from Mr J. Hall, Ballarat, Mrs N Gledhill, Dromana *and* Mr F. Louch, Murrumbeena, Vic.   R. C. DUPLAIN

HALL, LINDSAY BERNARD (1859-1935), artist, teacher and gallery director, was born on 28 December 1859 at Garston, Liverpool, England, son of Lindsay Hall, broker of Scottish descent, and his wife Emily Margaret, née Brugheer Herrmann. Bernard was brought up in an affluent, well educated, cultured circle. He was educated at Kensington Grammar School, London, and Cheltenham College.

Hall was very musical but decided upon art as a career. In 1874 he began four years at the School of Design (Royal College of Art), South Kensington, under the French trained Edward Poynter who stressed drawing skills, especially nude studies. Hall's choice of continental postgraduate study after he had gained his teacher's certificate reflected his respect for technical skill. Throughout his life he was to prize craft manship, technical understanding and manual skill very highly, believing that individuality could never be taught but that, if it were already there, it would develop naturally in an artist's work. In Antwerp he studied under the Belgian master Charles Verlat, renowned for his history paintings, portraits and animal studies. Verlat was a leader in the revival of interest in the graphic arts in Antwerp and this may have been where Hall gained his strong interest in graphic art. In Munich he studied under Professor Ludwig von Loefftz, a history and landscape artist; and at this period the famous Karl von Piloty was director of the Munich academy. A studentship under von Piloty, a remarkable teacher, forms a link between Hall and his predecessor at the National Gallery of Victoria, George Frederick Folingsby [q.v.4].

In 1882 Hall returned to London where he worked as a painter and black and white artist for the illustrated press. In 1883 his first picture was accepted by the Royal Academy where he subsequently had works hung several times. Others, mainly portrait and genre studies, were exhibited with the Society of British Artists. He was a foundation member of the New English Art Club, formed in 1886, but seems not to have kept up the association.

On Folingsby's death in 1891 Hall was appointed director of the National Gallery of Victoria and head of the Art School. He arrived in Melbourne early in 1892.

Hall was also expected 'to advise the Trustees in regard to the purchase of works of Art'. This proved a thorny task. No guidelines were set and although his first recommendations were accepted Hall was increasingly frustrated by the lack of an overall purchasing policy for the gallery and by the prevailing low aesthetic standards. In 1900 he submitted a report to the trustees on a future purchasing policy. Although this was initially received with hostility it was a major factor in changing the trustees' attitude; in 1905 he was appointed first Felton [q.v.4] Bequest buyer and was sent to Europe.

Hall brought high standards of aesthetic merit and craftsmanship to the Melbourne artistic community. One of his most famous phrases was that there was no immorality in art other than faulty or bad technique—a belief that places him firmly in the context of aesthetic London of the 1880s and 1890s. He was strong minded and sure of his own judgement. Many of his purchases for the Felton Bequest such as the J. M. W. Turner 'Okehampton', Rodin's 'Minerve sans Casque' and bust of Jean Paul Laurens, and Pissarro's 'Boulevard Montmartre', all purchased on the 1905 trip, and the Rembrandt 'Two Philosophers' which he acquired in 1934, are among the great treasures of the National Gallery of Victoria.

As a teacher Hall left unchanged much of what Folingsby had initiated. He continued to teach the Munich system of highly structured pictures conceived tonally, working outwards from a dark background to a middle ground and then setting silvery lights and reflected highlights at crucial points on the plastic objects carefully built up within the illusory space. Not all his students agreed with his teaching, especially towards the end of his career, but important artists trained under him, including James Quinn, Hugh Ramsay, W. B. McInnes, Charles Wheeler and Margaret Preston [qq.v.]. His own painting typifies his system and pays particular homage to Vermeer, Velasquez and Whistler. His preferred subjects were nudes and still life. Although his duties at the gallery left him little time, he did exhibit at times with the Victorian Artists' Society and hold one-man exhibitions which were respectfully, if not rapturously, received. He was described as dark, thin and reticent, always faultlessly dressed. Arnold Shore [q.v.] remembered him as 'upright in carriage, straight-laced, eagle-eyed, with hair cut "en brosse" '; his somewhat cold and reserved manner concealed a shy, sensitive nature.

On 18 December 1894 at St George's Church of England, Malvern, Hall had married Elsinore Mary Shuter, who died in 1901 leaving a son. On 16 April 1912 at Malvern he married Harriet Grace Thomson, a 27-year-old nurse. In February 1934 he went to London to take up the post of buyer of works of art for the gallery, but died on 14 February 1935, survived by his wife, two sons and a daughter.

Principal works by Hall in public collections include 'The Model', 'Coyness', 'The Marble Staircase', 'An Interior' (Art Gallery of New South Wales); 'Sleep', 'Processional', 'A Studio Party', 'The Giant Crab' (National Gallery of Victoria); and 'After Dinner', 'Still Life' (Art Gallery of South Australia).

U. Hoff, *The National Gallery of Victoria, Melbourne* (Lond, 1973); E. D. Lindsay, *The Felton Bequest, an historical record 1904-1959* (Melb, 1963); L. B. Cox, *The National Gallery of Victoria, 1861 to 1968* (Melb, 1970); *Lone Hand*, 1 Apr 1908, p 613; *Argus*, 19 Mar 1892, 23 Feb 1935; *Herald*, 29 June 1945; *Age*, 28 Oct 1961; H. L. Saunders, Bernard Hall and his influence on the National Gallery of Victoria and Associated School until 1917 (B.A. Hons thesis, Univ Melb, 1979); Trustees of the National Gallery of Victoria, Minute-book, *and* Reports (held by Administrative Section, SLV); Directors' Reports, 1908-35 (files of National Gallery of Vic, PRO, Vic); Bernard Hall papers (LaTL).

ANN E. GALBALLY

HALL, ROBERT (1867-1949), ornithologist, was born on 19 October 1867 at Lal Lal, Victoria, third son of Isaac Jones Hall, railway stationmaster from Cork, Ireland, and his English wife Eleanor, née Fisher. Educated at Scotch College, Melbourne, Hall in the 1890s set up in Melbourne as a tea merchant and cartage contractor. But his great interest was ornithology. After 'some biological work' at the University of Melbourne he travelled through the north and west of Australia before accompanying a Norwegian expedition to Kerguelen Island, as naturalist, in 1897. Two years later he made a bird-collecting trip to the Houtman Abrolhos. His major expedition outside Australia was with R. E. Trebilcock to Siberia, via Japan and Korea, in February-December 1903 to collect specimens and eggs of Siberian birds known to migrate to Australia in summer. He travelled 3000 miles (4800 km) along the Lena River to its mouth, collecting 90 species totalling 401 specimens; when he failed to raise sufficient funds from Australia to cover his expenses he sold the skins to the Rothschild Museum at Tring, Hertfordshire, England.

Hall returned impressed by overseas museum technology and became an influential advocate of nature study in schools: 'Nature is the true foundation of the finest education'. Already the author of *A key to the birds of Australia and Tasmania* (1899) and *Insectivorous birds of Victoria* (1900), the latter a standard Victorian Department of Education issue to state schools, he wrote, with William Gillies, *Nature studies in Australia* (1903) and gave evening lectures to metropolitan teachers. *Some useful birds of southern Australia* followed in 1907.

In January 1908 Hall succeeded Alexander Morton [q.v.] as curator of the Tasmanian Museum and Botanical Gardens. He had worked briefly for the Queensland Museum in 1901 and claimed experience at the National Museum, Melbourne. Although well over six feet (183 cm) tall and craggy in build, he had a cherubic expression and appeared to the *Mercury* on the day he commenced duties as an intensely shy man; he needed much prompting to expound his idea of creating attractive and realistic displays of fauna in simulated natural surroundings and so bringing 'nature . . . to the people who will not go to Nature'. Himself a skilled preserver of birds, he regarded the taxidermist as the 'mechanical pulse' of the museum.

Hall's plans were not realized and he resigned in 1912 after disagreeing with the museum trustees over the possible purchase of some Tasmanian Aboriginal skulls; he also relinquished the secretaryship of the Royal Society of Tasmania. He became an orchardist at Bellerive, then at Cygnet and Sandy Bay; describing himself as 'nature scientist', he promoted various short-lived, eccentric schemes including the production of fish meal, and possum-farming. He remained always helpful to students and until the 1920s continued as a prolific contributor to nature journals. In 1922 he published *Australian bird maps*. A foundation member of the (Royal) Australasian Ornithologists' Union (1901) and president in 1913; he was also a corresponding member of the Zoological Society of London (1903), a fellow of the Linnean Society (1903) and a colonial member of the British Ornithologists' Union (1908). He died on 19 September 1949 at New Norfolk, and was cremated. His wife Edith Mary, daughter of W. R. Giblin [q.v.4] and sister of L. F. Giblin [q.v.8], whom he had married on 17 September 1908 at St David's Cathedral, Hobart, survived him; they had no children. Parts of his private bird and egg collections are held at the Tasmanian Museum and the National Museum, Melbourne.

L. J. Blake (ed), *Vision and realisation*, 1 (Melb, 1973); Tas Museum, *Minute-books*, 1912; *Emu*, Oct 1949; Roy Soc Tas, *Procs*, 1949; *Aust Bird Watcher*, Sept 1978; *Sun-News Pictorial*, 4 June 1927; *Mercury*, 3 Jan 1908, 20 Sept 1949.   ANN G. SMITH

HALL, THOMAS SERGEANT (1858-1915), scientist, was born on 23 December 1858 at Geelong, Victoria, son of Thomas March Hall, draper from Lincolnshire, England, and his wife Elizabeth, née Walshe, from Dublin. He was educated at Geelong Church of England Grammar School in 1867-77 where he was greatly influenced by J. L. Cuthbertson [q.v.3]. Hall matriculated at the University of Melbourne on 11 August 1879, but taught at Wesley College and Hawthorn College before entering the university in 1883. He graduated B.A. in 1886 and was awarded the scholarship in natural science. His interest in natural history, fostered by his father, was reflected in the subjects studied for his degree: comparative anatomy, zoology, botany, geology and palaeontology, all taught by Professor Frederick McCoy [q.v.5]. After a year teaching at Girton College, Sandhurst, Hall returned to the university (M.A. 1888). In 1889 he studied under Professor (Sir) Baldwin Spencer [q.v.] and passed in Spencer's new subjects of biology and systematic zoology. From 1889 Hall's excursions with the Melbourne University Science Club resulted in the first of a series of papers describing in detail the complex sequence of Tertiary rocks in central Victoria. He undertook this work with his friend and

olleague G. B. Pritchard [q.v.]; together
hey published twelve papers between 1892
nd 1904.

In 1890 Hall was appointed director of the
Castlemaine School of Mines. Little money
was available for the school, but his time at
Castlemaine enabled him, with consider-
ble encouragement from Spencer, to press
n with his first papers on graptolites and
Tertiary stratigraphy. More importantly,
e was able to examine the Ordovician rocks
f the district in considerable detail, thus
urthering his interest in graptolites which
ad been kindled at Sandhurst and on Sci-
nce Club excursions to Lancefield. His
work at Castlemaine led him in 1893 to sug-
est a preliminary subdivision of the Lower
Ordovician rocks based on the order of suc-
ession of certain graptolites which was elab-
rated in more detail the next year, when
even zones were proposed. In 1899 he again
xtended this work and attempted to corre-
ate the Victorian Ordovician rocks with
nose of other parts of the world. In recog-
ition of his achievement in this field he was
warded 'The Balance of the Murchison
und' for 1901 by the Geological Society of
ondon. His published work on graptolites
eighteen papers) was submitted for a doctor-
te of science in the University of Melbourne
> which he was admitted in April 1908.

In December 1893 Hall had succeeded A.
endy [q.v.8] as lecturer and demonstrator
biology, and he was thus able to pursue
is research interests more fully. In April
399 he and Pritchard were appointed to
arry on the work of the natural science
chool during Professor McCoy's illness,
ntinuing after his death until Professor
W. Gregory [q.v.] took up his position in
ebruary 1900.

In 1890 Hall was elected to the Royal
ociety of Victoria and in 1896 became a
ouncillor. He served as honorary librarian
1897-99, as secretary in 1899-1914 and as
resident in 1914-15. He contributed thirty-
ve papers to the *Proceedings* of the society
etween 1889 and 1914 on a wide range of
eological and palaeontological subjects.
e was also closely involved with the work
the Australasian Association for the Ad-
ancement of Science, editing the reports
the Melbourne meetings in 1900 and 1913;
acted as local secretary in Victoria in
07-15 and was president of the geology
ction in 1902. He published five papers in
e reports of the association, including one
th Pritchard, and contributed to the hand-
ok for the Melbourne meetings. He was
so secretary for Victoria of the zoological
ction of the British Association visit in
14.

Hall was active in the Field Naturalists'
ub of Victoria which he had joined in 1888.

From 1895 to 1910 he was a member of the
committee, serving as vice-president from
1897 to 1900 and president from 1901 to
1903. Between 1890 and 1914 he contributed
forty articles on a variety of topics to the
Victorian Naturalist. He was involved in the
movement to secure Wilson's Promontory
as a National Park and later served on the
park's committee of management. His term
of office as librarian to the Royal Society of
Victoria led him in 1897 to compile a *Catalogue of the scientific and technical periodical
literature in the libraries in Melbourne*. It
was published in 1899, reissued in an enlarged form in 1911 with the assistance of
E. R. Pitt [q.v.] and was the forerunner of
the modern union catalogue of scientific
serials.

Hall was a well-known contributor of
popular scientific articles to newspapers, in
particular to the Science Notes column of
the *Australasian* under the nom de plume
'Physicus'. His popular series of geological
articles published in the *Argus* in 1905-06
were collected and republished with additional matter in 1909 as *Victorian hill and
dale*. He also contributed the article on Victorian geography, geology and fauna in the
Victorian year book for 1904 and subsequent
years to 1915-16.

Hall was the first Australian-born palaeontologist to achieve an international reputation and is arguably the most talented
palaeontologist to work in Victoria. His
work on Tertiary stratigraphy but more especially on graptolites and his discovery of
the key to the unravelling of the complex
Ordovician sequence are his lasting
achievements which form the foundations
for those who follow in these fields.

Hall died of chronic nephritis at Camberwell on 21 December 1915 and was buried
in Boroondara cemetery, Kew. He had married Eva Lucie Annie Hill on 21 December
1891 at All Saints' Church, Bendigo, and was
survived by three sons and a daughter. His
extensive collection of graptolites and Tertiary fossils are housed in the National
Museum of Victoria. His memory is perpetuated in the annual T. S. Hall memorial lecture sponsored by the Melbourne University Science Club and in a brass tablet on
the wall of the foyer of the university's zoology department building.

F. A. Cudmore, *Author index to the publications
of the Royal Society of Victoria . . . 1855-1934* (Melb,
1934); J. A. Baines, *The Victorian Naturalist author
index 1884-1975* (Melb, 1976); *Scientific Australian*, 11 (1905), no 1; *Geological Mag* (Lond), 3
(1916), no 3; Roy Soc Vic, *Procs*, 28 (1916), no 2;
Vic Naturalist, 32 (1916), no 9; Hall papers
(National Museum of Vic, *and* LaTL); Pritchard
papers (National Museum of Vic).

THOMAS A. DARRAGH

HALL, WALTER RUSSELL (1831-1911), businessman, and ELIZA ROWDON (1847-1916), philanthropist, were husband and wife. Walter was born on 22 February 1831 at Kington, Herefordshire, England, eldest son of Walter Hall, glover and later miller, and his wife Elizabeth Carleton, née Skarratt. Educated at Kington and Taunton, Somerset, he arrived in Sydney in 1852 with very little money. For a short time he was employed by David Jones [q.v.2], retailer, but soon left for the Victorian goldfields. At Ballarat at the time of the Eureka rebellion in 1854, he was said not to have been within the stockade, as was his brother Thomas. Walter moved on to Bendigo and the Ovens goldfields but had little success. For a time he ran a carrying service between Ballarat and Melbourne, became agent for Cobb [q.v.3] & Co. at Woods Point and, in 1861, with James Rutherford [q.v.6] and others, formed a partnership to take over that firm. Later Hall acted as its Sydney agent. He travelled extensively in New South Wales and Queensland to open new lines and on inspections. He left the firm in the mid-1880s.

Hall was already wealthy when his brother Thomas, who was manager of the Rockhampton branch of the Queensland National Bank, invited him to join the syndicate formed to develop the Mount Morgan mine. The Halls and their associates resisted nine attempts to jump their claim, two of which reached the Privy Council. On 1 October 1886 the Mount Morgan Gold Mining Co. Ltd, with capital of £1 million, was registered in Queensland. The mine yielded gold and copper worth over £19 million and paid £8 079 166 in dividends by 1913. Hall was a major shareholder, a director of the company and chairman of the Sydney board. He was also a director of the Mercantile Mutual Insurance Co. Ltd, and the Sydney Meat Preserving Co. Ltd, and engaged briefly with associates in unprofitable railway contracting.

Hall never attempted to make a splash in Sydney society, did not entertain lavishly, and was regarded as rather mean in this regard, but he liked 'to give the boys a good time' on his annual visits to Mount Morgan (which he continued until 1910). Irrespective of rank he welcomed employees at dinners and convivial gatherings and also entertained the Mount Morgan children, in whom he took a great interest. He gave generously to the town's educational and other institutions.

When in Sydney Hall seldom missed a race meeting. He was a committee-member of the Australian Jockey Club in 1873-1911; his horses included the Sydney winners: Garfield (Sires' Produce Stakes, 1884), Dela-

ware (Doncaster, 1895) and Reviver (Champagne Stakes, 1899). When Reviver won the Metropolitan in 1900, Hall anonymously gave £1000 to charities. He also engaged in coursing. Benevolent and generous, he made large donations to public institution and also helped individuals; many of his benefactions were anonymous, but not the £5000 he contributed to the Patriotic Fund during the South African War and the £10 000 which he gave to the Dreadnought Fund.

At St Paul's Anglican Church, Melbourne, Hall had married Eliza Rowdon Kirk on 15 April 1874. She was born on 2 November 1847 in Melbourne, eldest daughter of George Kirk, a Yorkshire-born butcher, and his wife Elizabeth, née Wippell, from Devon. George Kirk, after engaging in various pursuits, had acquired large pastoral interests in partnership with Richard Goldsbrough [q.v.4] and represented East Bourke in the Legislative Assembly of Victoria in 1861-64. In 188 Walter and Eliza Hall visited England and remained away for over a year.

Wildfell, their home at Potts Point, Sydney, was a large two-storeyed house with the garden extending to the water. Eliza, who loved good jewellery, filled the house and her Melbourne residence with pictures among them landscapes by Bernard Evans and Alfred Breanski and portraits by Hoppner, Romney and, reputedly, Gainsborough—bronzes, marble statues, chinand glass. In the large entrance hall live an enormous, colourful Brazilian macaand a chatty cockatoo. Mrs Hall took daily 'carriage exercise'. Childless, she undertoo the care of two young orphaned cousin sending them to boarding schools and in th holidays making them feel that Wildfell wa their home.

Walter Hall died at Wildfell on 13 Octobe 1911 and was buried in Melbourne gener cemetery with Anglican rites. His esta was valued for probate at £2 915 513 in thre States, his principal beneficiary being h wife. Soon after his death she set aside million in order to commemorate him an to do something for the benefit of the com munity and was finally persuaded that he own name should be linked with her hu band's. On her instructions, the trust dee of the Walter and Eliza Hall Trust wa drawn up with Richard Gardiner Case [q.v.3], (Sir) John French [q.v.8], (Si George Kelso King, and (Sir) Adrian Kn [qq.v.] as the original trustees. Its term were made public on Empire Day (24 Ma 1912 and it came into operation on 1 Janua 1913: half of the income was to be spent New South Wales, the State in which Ha had first made his wealth, one quarter

Queensland, where he had greatly increased it, and one quarter in Victoria, his widow's home State. It was to be used for the relief of poverty, the advancement of education, the advancement of religion in accordance with the tenets of the Church of England, and for the general benefit of the community not falling under the preceding heads. As far as was practicable, one third of the income in each State was to be used for the benefit of women and children.

Many individuals have benefited from the trust, not least those who obtained postgraduate travelling and research fellowships—some have had distinguished careers and made valuable contributions to the Australian community. A large part of Victoria's share of trust funds was spent in establishing in 1916 the Walter and Eliza Hall Institute of Research in Pathology and Medicine in Melbourne. Bequests and donations from other sources greatly enlarged this institute which over the years has made notable contributions to medical knowledge.

A diabetic, Eliza Hall died of cancer at Wildfell on 14 February 1916 and like her husband was buried in Melbourne general cemetery with Anglican rites. Her estate in three States was valued for probate at £1 180 059; in her detailed will she left generous bequests and annuities to her own and to her husband's numerous relations, to friends and to servants. Her large collection of jewellery was divided among her female relatives, and she left some pictures and statues to the Melbourne and Sydney art galleries.

There is a tablet in memory of Walter and Eliza Hall in St Paul's Cathedral, Melbourne. Their portraits by F. McCubbin [q.v.] are on loan to the Walter and Eliza Hall Institute of Medical Research; another portrait of Mrs Walter Hall by McCubbin is held by the National Gallery of Victoria; and marble busts of both by Bertram MacKennal [q.v.] were given to the institute by the Art Gallery of New South Wales.

R. R. Jones, *Gold mining in central Queensland and the Mount Morgan mine* (Rockhampton, 1913); K. H. Finn, *The Walter and Eliza Trust* (Syd, 1939); K. A. Austin, *The lights of Cobb and Co.* (Adel, 1973); *Austral Briton*, 19 Feb 1916; *Daily Telegraph* (Syd), and *Morning Bulletin*, 14 Oct 1911; Trust deed of the Walter and Eliza Trust, 27 Mar 1912 (RG, Syd); family information.

HAZEL KING

HALLAHAN, WALTER REWI (1889?-1918), soldier and metallurgist, was born probably on 2 August 1889 at Westport, New Zealand, son of James Patrick Hallahan and his wife Janet. He studied metallurgy at Westport and, after his family moved to Western Australia, attended the Kalgoorlie School of Mines. He began work on the assay staff of various local gold-mines and later became an amalgamator. In 1909 he joined the 84th Infantry (Goldfields) Regiment, trained as a machine-gunner and in July 1914 was commissioned as a second lieutenant.

Hallahan enlisted as a private in the Australian Imperial Force on 18 August 1914 and was posted to the 11th Battalion; by 9 September he had been promoted sergeant because of his militia experience. In November he embarked for Egypt and trained with his machine-gun section before sailing for Gallipoli. He showed great courage and dash during the Anzac landing on 25 April 1915 as he led his section to the top of Shrapnel Gully to mount their guns. That evening the Turks attacked their position but under Hallahan's leadership his men drove them back. During this engagement he received a flesh wound in the neck; for forty-eight hours after the landing he had 'kept his machine gun in action until the firing line was established, although subjected to heavy shrapnel and rifle fire'. Afterwards he was hospitalized and resumed duty on 9 May.

The Turks launched a massive attack along the Australian front ten days later and Hallahan stood on the parapet to make the most effective use of his machine-gun—he is said to have prayed aloud that it would not jam. He remained there even when the enemy were only fifty yards (46 m) away, and he inflicted heavy losses and helped to bring 'a determined attack to a standstill'. On 1 August he was noted for gallantry at Leane's Trench when he led his detachment across open ground under heavy rifle-fire; soon after occupying the captured trench he was wounded. He was commissioned second lieutenant on 4 August and remained at Gallipoli until 16 November when his battalion was sent to Lemnos for rest and was later shipped to Egypt. For distinguished service at Gallipoli, especially for gallantry at the landing and on 19 May and 1 August, he received the Military Medal (although the award was not gazetted until October 1916) and was mentioned in dispatches.

In April 1916 the 11th Battalion reached France and Hallahan was promoted lieutenant on 8 May; his unit went into the line at Fleurbaix twelve days later, then moved to Pozières on the Somme on 19 July. In the battle for Pozières, when almost half the battalion became casualties, Hallahan took temporary command of his company. On 19-20 August the 11th became the carrying battalion for the 3rd Brigade at Mouquet Farm; after carrying all day on the 20th Hallahan, with another officer, was chosen to lead an attack aimed at establishing the brigade's flank. The daylight attack, which they launched under cover of an Australian artillery barrage, gained ground. Exploding shells buried Hallahan twice but even after the ordeal of being dug out he refused to leave the line. For 'daring and capable leadership' at Pozières and Mouquet Farm he was awarded the Military Cross. He fought at Hill 60 and Flers later in 1916 and on 26 December was promoted captain.

The 11th Battalion saw action at Tailloy, Lagnicourt, Bullecourt and Ypres between February and September 1917, and Hallahan commanded 'D' Company until 30 September when he was posted to the A.I.F. 2nd and 3rd Training Battalions in England. He rejoined his unit in May 1918 for the assault on Mont de Merris where he was wounded but remained on duty and then moved to Cérisy. In August he received orders to take up transport duty to Australia but after reaching England he was recalled to his battalion on 15 September, the day before his intended marriage to a nurse. He returned to the 3rd Brigade front opposite Villeret and prepared for the battalion's final operation of the war—the attack on the Hindenburg outpost-line. On 18 September the battalion moved forward rapidly in three waves, closely following the barrage. Hallahan commanded the third wave, whose task was to mop up; his company was caught by the German counter-barrage and he was killed instantly. He was buried in Tincourt cemetery. C. E. W. Bean [q.v.7] wrote that he was 'a beloved officer . . . a tall, thin, gentle looking chap with a refined face, a gallant man with a quiet manner'. Three of his brothers, two of whom were killed in action in 1916, served with the A.I.F.

C. E. W. Bean, *The story of Anzac* (Syd, 1921, 1924), and *The A.I.F. in France*, 1916-18 (Syd, 1929, 1933, 1937, 1942); W. C. Belford, *Legs-eleven: the 11th Battalion A.I.F.* (Perth, 1940); *London Gazette*, 24 Mar, 27 Oct, 29 Dec 1916; *Reveille* (Syd), Jan 1936; *Western Argus*, 1 Oct 1918.

ANTHONY ELLIS

HALLEY, IDA GERTRUDE MARGARET (1867-1939), medical officer and feminist, was born on 1 August 1867 at Ballarat West, Victoria, daughter of Rev. Jacob John Halley [q.v.4] and his wife Margaret, née Fletcher. Educated at the Presbyterian Ladies' College, she was among the first women medical students at the University of Melbourne (M.B., B.S., 1896). After graduation she practised with Dr Kent Hughes of Melbourne and was active as a founder and treasurer of the Queen Victoria Hospital for Women. She became honorary surgeon there and a specialist in eye and ear work, a field she had researched in London and Shanghai, China.

In 1906 Halley was appointed to assist the chief health officer in Tasmania as medical inspector of schools. With Dr Hogg of Launceston she devised an eye test for children which was adopted throughout Australia and in other parts of the British Empire. In 1910 she moved to Sydney to a similar appointment, which also involved lecturing Teachers' College students on hygiene and teaching older schoolgirls the care of infants. Early in 1913 Halley was chosen to establish the long-awaited medical branch of the Education Department in South Australia. Accompanied initially by one school nurse, she began the examination of 50 000 children at the rate of one hundred per day. She made extensive use of the parents' meeting since, like her closest friend and colleague Lydia Longmore [q.v.], inspector of infant schools, she believed that educating mothers and fathers was one of the best means of improving children's health. They pioneered the use of intelligence tests in South Australian schools. From the beginning Halley argued for separate and skilled teaching for mentally retarded children. She also promoted model playgrounds for children. Appointed vice-chairman of the playgrounds section of the interstate Town Planning Exhibition in Adelaide, she was later an Education Department representative on the playground committee of the Town Planning Association. Within the department Dr Halley continually pressed for better school medical facilities and more staff. By 1925 she headed a staff of sixteen, including three dentists, five medical assistants, three nurses and a psychologist, Dr Constance Davey [q.v.8]. The press commented that she 'had been fighting against heavy odds with skill, enthusiasm and courage' to get her 'forward' policies accepted.

Her impressive professional achievement until her retirement in 1931 was matched by her activities in the wider society. Within a few months of her arrival in Adelaide, she became a leading member of the Women's Non-Party Political Association (later League of Women Voters), which sought to mobilize women politically on a variety of social issues. As chairwoman of the League of Loyal Women (in 1916-22) she sought to unite South Australian women of all classes in war work. In 1920 Gertrude became a founding member of the South Australian branch of the National Council of Women, was a committee-member for the first ten years and was convener of its standing committee on public health from 1927 to 1929.

These commitments reflected Dr Ialley's endorsement of contemporary feminists' contention that women could contribute much to the wider society; they also related to her religious beliefs. Raised in a Congregational manse, she had been encouraged to develop a concern for reform. She was an active member of the Clayton Church and the Congregational Church Women's Society of South Australia.

After some years' ill health, Gertrude Ialley died of hypertensive cardiovascular disease at her home at Maylands on 1 October 1939; she was cremated. A portrait by her friend Marie Tuck [q.v.] is held by the Queen Victoria Memorial Hospital, Melbourne.

C. M. Davey, *Children and their law-makers* (Adel, 1956); Annual Reports of the Medical Inspector in the Annual Reports of the Minister Controlling Education, *PP* (SA), 1914-31; Roy Com on Education, *PP* (SA), 1913 (75); *Lone Hand*, 1 Feb 915; *Advertiser* (Adel), 2 Oct 1939; Records, National Council of Women in SA, *and* League of Women Voters, *and* League of Loyal Women SAA).   ELIZABETH KWAN

HALLIGAN, GERALD HARNETT (1856-1942), hydrographer and civil engineer, was born on 21 April 1856 at Glebe, Sydney, son of Irish parents Gerald Halligan, clerk, and his wife Mary Ann, née Harnett. His father later became under secretary of the Department of Public Works. Gerald junior was probably educated at Fort Street Model School and on 1 August 1871 joined the Department of Public Works. In July 1889 he was appointed chief surveyor of the harbours and rivers navigation branch and was for many years in charge of all borings relating to harbour and bridge construction works in the colony. He introduced practical innovations to improve techniques in boring.

At the invitation of the Royal Society, London, in 1898 he joined the third scientific expedition to the Pacific atoll of Funafuti in the Ellice Islands. Assisted by two experienced departmental foremen, he supervised deep borings into the coral from a stage rigged over the bows of H.M.S. *Porpoise*. In 1899 he was appointed hydrographic surveyor and in 1911 inspecting engineer (later reclassified as supervising engineer), in which capacity he served the department until he retired in 1918.

Halligan made a lifetime study of tides and currents and their effects. He was particularly knowledgeable on the formation of sand dunes and on the control of movements of sand and sediment in channels and harbours, becoming an international authority

in oceanography. He was a member of the Royal Society of New South Wales in 1880-1942 and of the Linnean Society of New South Wales from 1897, and a fellow of the Geological Society of London in 1900-29. In 1911 he was one of three Australians to address the Institution of Civil Engineers in London on the bar harbours of New South Wales, and put forward several novel theories which aroused considerable interest.

His advice was sought outside New South Wales—in 1918 Halligan advised the Tasmanian government on the problem of sand drift on to agricultural land on the northeast coast. In 1922, on the suggestion of his friend Professor Sir Edgeworth David [q.v.8], he made a hydrographical examination from the air of Lake Eyre in South Australia. He compiled a number of maps for the oceanographic section of Pan Pacific Science congresses in 1923 and 1929. He published many papers, some in association with Edgeworth David, in scientific journals.

He had married Harriet Victoria, sister of the artist W. C. Piguenit [q.v.5], at Petersham, Sydney, on 3 November 1881. She died in 1919 and on 26 April 1922 at St Peter's Church of England, Wahroonga, he married Sarah Albina, née Genders, the widow of W. H. Twelvetrees, geologist to the Tasmanian Mines Department; both marriages were childless. For much of his life he lived at Hunters Hill. Halligan died on 23 November 1942 in hospital at Killara and was buried in the Roman Catholic section of Northern Suburbs cemetery.

V&P (LA NSW), 1901 (2), p 965; Roy Soc NSW, *J*, 77 (1943), p 173; *Australasian*, 25 Feb 1922.
       H. VAUGHAN EVANS

HALLORAN, HENRY FERDINAND (1869-1953), realtor, was born on 9 August 1869 at Glebe, Sydney, eldest child of Edward Roland Halloran, a native-born bank clerk and later architect, and his English wife Adeline Burgess, née Reuss. A grandson of Henry Halloran [q.v.4] and great-grandson of Laurence Halloran [q.v.1], Henry was educated at Petersham Public School, Newington College and Sydney Boys' High School. Reuss family background influenced his career in land development.

Articled to Arthur Stephen at Blue Gum Flat, near Ourimbah, Halloran became a licensed surveyor (1890), valuer (1895) and conveyancer (1896). By 1897 he had set up in Sydney as Henry F. Halloran & Co., specializing in land and property dealings. His *Property owners guide* (1900) epitomized the entrepreneurial verve that made his firm prominent. On 23 December 1903 in Sydney he married a divorcee Alice Mabel Cobcroft (d. 1921), née Chowne.

His 1906-08 subdivisions at Seaforth, Cronulla Highlands, Warriewood, Stanwell Park, Avoca and Yow Yow (near Gosford) emphasized Halloran's predeliction for coastal waterways. One of the earliest practitioners of the American manner of real estate development, he used colourful brochures and high-pressure salesmanship. Halloran's preliminary artistic layout of estates was praised by the Town Planning Association of New South Wales (of which he was a fellow and later a vice-president). In his paper at the second Australian Town Planning Conference and Exhibition in Brisbane in 1918, he stressed the necessity of zoning cities and towns 'in the interest of property values'. Halloran represented New South Wales at the 1923 international conference on town planning at Gothenburg, Sweden, and, with Sir John Sulman [q.v.], the Commonwealth at the 1924 Amsterdam conference. He was a member of the Royal Institution of Chartered Surveyors, London, and of the American Institute of Planners, and a fellow of the Royal Society of Arts, London, and the Institution of Surveyors, New South Wales.

An unassuming but independent man of small build, Halloran embarked on a number of long-range plans, focusing on Canberra, Port Stephens and Jervis Bay; they were thwarted by the Depression. He had established Canberra Freehold Estates after the proclamation of the Jervis Bay Act (1915) and laid out various subdivisions on Canberra approaches. Environa, the most ambitious, was sited on the Queanbeyan-Cooma railway and included clear views of the capital. Its circular and radiating features recalled W. Burley Griffin's [q.v.] 1912 plan, and with Tanilba Bay and Stanwell Tops, reflected his interest in rustic stone for pillars, archways and rotundas. He also subdivided numerous estates at Lake Macquarie, the Blue Mountains and the central coast. Realty Realizations Ltd was incorporated on 5 June 1930 to take over real estate agency activities, leaving Henry F. Halloran & Co. to act as advisers, conveyancers, surveyors and town planners.

A Freemason, Halloran was a member of the Royal Society and of several clubs and groups. A liking for local history led him to join the Royal Australian Historical Society and enjoy the Australasian Pioneers' Club. He died suddenly on 22 October 1953 at Bellevue Hill and was cremated with Anglican rites. He was survived by three sons of his first marriage, by his second wife Amy Gwendoline, nèe Powell, whom he had mar-

ried at Manly on 26 March 1924, and by thei two sons and two daughters. His probate was sworn at £70 389. A portrait by Josepl Wolinski is held by the family and he is com memorated by the Halloran fund of the New South Wales branch of the Institution of Sur veyors, Australia.

Volume of proceedings of the Second Australian Town Planning Conference ... (Brisb, 1918); L Sandercock, *Cities for sale* (Melb, 1975); L Halloran (comp), *An imaginative speculator* (Syd 1980); *Architecture*, 20 Apr 1920; *SMH*, 23 Oc 1953; H. F. Halloran & Co., Subdivision brochure (ML); information from L. Halloran, Epping, ane W. Halloran, Syd, and Inst of Surveyors, Aust NSW.
JOHN ATCHISON

HAM, WILBUR LINCOLN (1883-1948) barrister, was born on 14 November 1883 a Armadale, Melbourne, third son and tenth child of Cornelius Job Ham [q.v.4] and hi. wife Hattie White, née Latham. He wa: brought up in the beliefs of the Baptis Church and attended Melbourne Church o England Grammar School (1895-96) and Toorak Grammar School. From 1901 he studied law at the University of Melbourne residing in Ormond College. He wa: awarded a university scholarship and the Supreme Court prize, graduating LL.B. ir 1905 and LL.M. in 1906. In June 1905 he wa: articled to James Cooper Stewart of Mal leson, England & Stewart, solicitors of Mel bourne; and on 1 August 1906 was admitted to practise as a barrister and solicitor. He signed the roll of the Victorian Bar on 1: February 1907, thus joining about ninety others who practised exclusively as barris ters.

After enlisting, in March 1915 Ham wa: commissioned as a second lieutenant in the 13th Australian Light Horse Regiment, Aus tralian Imperial Force. He served in Egyp from July, at Gallipoli from September unti the evacuation, and in France from June 1916. For six months in 1917 he was adjutan of the 1st Anzac Mounted Regiment. On 1 November he was promoted from captain to major but on 9 November his horse slipped on ice and the resulting injury to his kneecap left him with a permanent limp. He was men tioned in dispatches in 1917. He returned to Australia in May 1918 and on 30 November married Aileen Marjorie, only child of Charles William Wren, general manager for Australasia of the English, Scottish and Australian Bank.

Ham resumed legal practice; he was appointed K.C. in February 1927, and is said to have refused appointment to the Supreme Court in 1934. He was active in the affairs of the Bar, being chairman of the Committee

Counsel in 1930-32, 1933-34, 1937-38 and 939-46. He was president of the Medico-egal Society of Victoria in 1933-34. He gave p practice because of ill health in 1947, hen according to the *Law List* there were 16 barristers in practice in Victoria of hom five were his seniors by date of admission.

Ham was troubled by poor eyesight for any years before an operation restored his ision, and suffered from pernicious anemia. He spoke with a 'highly cultured accent' and his manner, according to Sir Arthur Dean, was rather patrician. Yet he was he 'kindest of men' and a most industrious worker. He had a fund of Rabelaisian stories nd Sir Robert Menzies remembered him as a master of polished profanity'. A very able awyer, Ham enjoyed an enormous practice n the Supreme Court and the High Court n the 1930s and 1940s. Of the cases reported n twelve of the twenty-five volumes of the *Commonwealth Law Reports* between 1933 nd 1945, over a hundred (nearly 30 per ent) of them emanated from Victoria. Ham as engaged in over a third of these and ocasionally in one from elsewhere; about half f them were concerned with taxation or onstitutional law. Well-known cases in hich he appeared were *Clements* v. *Ellis* 1934) (Torrens [q.v.6] system), *Grant* v. *Australian Knitting Mills Ltd* (1936) (negligence) and *South Australia* v. *Commonvealth* (1942) (constitutional law).

Ham had three sons and a daughter. The hildren were enrolled at school with the urname 'Wilbur-Ham' and retained it subsequently. Predeceased by his wife (1946) nd a son (1939) Ham died from bronchopneumonia on 30 January 1948 and was remated.

J.B. Kiddle (ed), *War services of Old Melburnians* Melb, 1923?); A. Dean, *A multitude of counsellors* Melb, 1968); R. G. Menzies, *The measure of the ears* (Melb, 1970); *Vic Law J*, July 1932, p 131; *Argus*, 14 Nov 1934, 31 Jan 1948.

PETER BALMFORD

HAMILTON, ALEXANDER GREEN-LAW (1852-1941), schoolteacher and naturalist, was born on 14 April 1852 at Bailie-borough, Cavan, Ireland, son of Alexander Greenlaw Hamilton, later a quarantine supervisor, and his wife Joyce, née Wynne. Migrating to New South Wales early in 1866, the family was living at Fish River Creek, near Oberon, by Christmas. Mrs Hamilton opened a school on 1 July 1867 with her son as honorary assistant, whom he local inspector ascertained had 'had some experience as a monitor or pupil teacher in Model Schools at Belfast, Ireland & elsewhere'. Alexander junior seemed to be responsible for much of the instruction. In mid-1869 the family moved to Meadow Flat, east of Bathurst, where Mrs Hamilton ran the school until October 1870.

In February Hamilton had been 'appointed temporarily assistant' at St Mary's Church of England school, South Creek (St Mary's). After three months at Fort Street Training School, in October he was sent to Guntawang Public School near Gulgong at £96 a year. On his twenty-first birthday (14 April 1873) he married Emma Thacker at St John the Baptist's Anglican Church, Mudgee. During seventeen years at Guntawang, Hamilton devoted himself to teaching, preparing (with varying results) for teachers' examinations, studying the natural history of the area, ministering to local first-aid needs and serving as librarian of the local School of Arts that he had helped to establish. In 1885 he joined the Linnean Society of New South Wales and published the first of many papers in its *Proceedings*. J. J. Fletcher [q.v.8] in 1887 named one of Hamilton's discoveries in his honour—the earthworm now known as *Spenceriella (Spenceriella) hamiltoni*, not refound.

An ardent microscopist (which contributed to failing sight in his later years), Hamilton published frequently on the processes of pollination and fertilization, the morphology of xerophylic and insectivorous plants and botanical and ornithological check-lists; studied bird-calls; and with Fletcher compiled an article on Australian land planarians. Most of his scientific papers appeared in the *Proceedings* of the Linnean Society but he also published in the *Sydney Quarterly Magazine, Australian Naturalist, Public Instruction Gazette* and in the *Reports* of the Australasian Association for the Advancement of Science. His paper on 'The effect which settlement in Australia has produced on indigenous vegetation' won the bronze medal of the Royal Society of New South Wales. In 1937 he republished articles written for the *Sydney Quarterly* as *Bush rambles*.

In October 1887 Hamilton was transferred to Mount Kembla Public School as headmaster. Here he investigated the fascinating rain forest ecology. He could now attend lectures at the University of Sydney and meetings of the societies with which he was associated. He was a council-member in 1906-39 and president in 1915-16 of the New South Wales Linnean Society, president of the Australian Naturalists' Society of New South Wales in 1913-14 and 1920-21, and a member of the Royal, Microscopical and Royal Zoological societies of New South Wales, the Wild Life Preservation Society of Australia and of the Gould [q.v.1] League of Bird Lovers.

Granted six months leave in 1902, Hamilton visited Western Australia. Refreshed, and enjoying 'better health than I have had for years', he was soon faced with the turning-point in his career. At a conference, following the 1903 report by G. H. Knibbs and J. W. Turner [qq.v.] on primary education, he successfully pleaded for greater emphasis on nature study in schools. By the end of 1904 he was involved in promoting the subject in accordance with Peter Board's [q.v.7] new syllabus, lecturing to teachers at many centres. His influence on its teaching long before the 'environment movement' would be impossible to assess.

In March 1905 Hamilton became headmaster of Willoughby Public School and lecturer in nature study at Blackfriars and Hurlstone Training colleges. Although formally appointed to Teachers' College, Sydney, on 1 January 1907 at a salary of £350, he was still performing his dual function in May, working six days a week. He was appointed senior lecturer in botany and nature study in July 1919 but retired next year.

A tall, active, rather spare man, Hamilton considered himself 'immense' when he was 'nearly 12 stone'. Although naturally shy, he could be induced to play the piano and organ, and to sing. He was an enthusiastic amateur photographer, an accomplished natural history artist, a collector of orchids, horticulturist, an inveterate bush-walker, bibliophile, golfer and, certainly whilst at Guntawang, a cricketer. He admitted to being a 'wretched speaker' and 'frightfully nervous', but others enjoyed his 'never failing humour' and found him an inspiring teacher. His astonishing industry and dedication were widely acknowledged, if not fully understood.

Hamilton died at his home Tanandra, Chatswood, on 21 October 1941 and was cremated with Anglican rites. He was survived by two of his three sons and by a daughter.

Aust Naturalist, June 1942; Linnean Soc NSW, *Procs*, 69 (1944); A. G. Hamilton, Letters to J. D. Cox (ML); School records (NSWA, *and* NSW Education Dept); Syd Teachers' College, Records; information from Mrs T. Y. Stead, Watson's Bay, Syd.   L. A. GILBERT

HAMILTON, HENRY (1826-1907), grapegrower and wine-maker, was born on 6 January 1826 at Dover, Kent, England, son of Richard Hamilton, farmer, and his wife Ann, née Holmes. In 1837 his father bought a land order for eighty acres (32 ha) in South Australia, which he took up next year; his

Curtis Farm was on the Sturt River, si miles south of Adelaide. Henry remained t attend school at Christ's Hospital, Londor before migrating in 1841. After workin near Burra he joined his father in 1848 an began to extend his vine plantings. On 5 A gust 1851 at St Mary's Church, South Roac Adelaide, he married Mary Elizabeth Bel they had eight sons and a daughter.

After his father's death in 1852 Henr worked Curtis Farm for his mother. In 185 he bought forty-seven acres (19 ha) adjoir ing the property and named it Ewell Farr after the village of Temple Ewell near hi birthplace. By the 1860s he was a wel established grape-grower and farmer, usin a rotation of wheat, hay and fallow ever three or four years. In 1860-62 he was chai man of Brighton District Council and i 1866 president of his district's first horticu tural society. Henry's wife died in 1870 an on 28 March 1872 he married Sarah Glove but in December she also died. On 2 Febri ary 1878 he married Mary, née Schrode widow of Captain John Finlay Duff.

After Mrs Hamilton senior's death in 188 Curtis Farm was divided among her nin children and Henry acquired a further forty six acres (19 ha) from his siblings. In 189 he transferred management of the Ewe farm and winery to his son Frank. That yea and again next year, Ewell Vineyards wo the Royal Agricultural and Horticultura Society of South Australia's Angas [q.v.3 award for the best farm under 200 acres (8 ha). The report stated that 'The vineyar consists of . . . 20 acres of Pedro Ximene vines . . . and 20 acres of good wine and tabl grapes . . . The wine-making plant an buildings were very good, and some fin large casks . . . are full of wine, and if equa to the samples we tasted is of most excellen quality. The vineyard is well kept and fre from weeds'.

On 10 February 1907 at Ewell Vineyard Henry Hamilton died and was buried in North Brighton cemetery.

His third surviving son FRANK HAMILTON (1859-1913) was born on 5 February 1859 a Ewell Vineyards, and was educated at Glen elg Grammar School. On 17 September 189 at St Mary's Church, South Road, he mar ried Violet Elsie Mabel Ayliffe. By 1897 h had purchased the remainder of the origina Hamilton property and over the next decad expanded the wine business considerably Most of the wines produced were fortifiec styles but there was limited production o a dry white Chablis-type wine. Frank Hamil ton was chairman of the Marion Distric Council in 1896-97. In 1910 his eldest sor Eric joined the business which operated a F. Hamilton Ltd. On 13 June 1913 Frank diec from septicaemia at Ewell Vineyards and as buried in North Brighton cemetery; he ad been a quiet, hard-working, intelligent nan. The business continued under family ontrol until 1979. Portraits of Henry and 'rank Hamilton painted by Rex Wood from hotographs are at the winery, Morphett coad, Warradale.

B. M. Burton, *Joseph Bell—the pathfinder in Australia 1833* (Adel, 1973); G. C. Bishop, *The ineyards of Adelaide* (Adel, 1977); A. Dolling, *The istory of Marion on the Sturt* (Adel, 1981); *PP* (SA), 868 (20); Roy Agricultural and Horticultural Soc f SA, *Procs*, 1890, p 61, 1891, p 65; *Aust Wine, 'rewing and Spirit Review*, Apr 1960; *Register* \del), 13 Feb 1907, 14, 16 June 1913; *Observer* \del), 27 Feb 1909; *Chronicle* (Adel), 29 Mar 1919; A. Hamilton, The story of the Ayliffe family his- ory (pc of typescript, Adel, c. 1978); Lands Dept :cords, Adel; MRG 36/4/1854-55 (SAA); infor- iation from A. J. Ludbrook, Toorak Gardens, M. . Ragless, Clovelly Park, H. A. Laffer, Happy Val- ·y, SA.   GEOFFREY C. BISHOP

HAMILTON, HUGH MONTGOMERIE 1854-1930), judge, was born on 26 June 1854 t Parramatta, New South Wales, son of lugh Hamilton, a pastoralist from Ayr- hire, Scotland, and his native-born wife 1argaret Clunes, née Innes, of Tomabil and ovd stations, Forbes; she was a niece of .. C. Innes [q.v.2]. Educated at Geneva, :dinburgh, and Marlborough College, .ngland, in 1868-72, he became head of that ollege's modern side, captained its Rugby ootball team, and later played for the Lon- on club, Marlborough Nomads. Selected by .ngland and Scotland to play in the same 1atch, he elected to play for Scotland, ,hich he represented in 1874 and 1875; with iir) William Milton, he introduced the ·assing game' into Rugby Union. He was lso a good athlete and boating enthusiast.

After failing in one subject for the Indian :ivil Service, Hamilton took up law at the Jniversity of London, passing the inter- nediate examination in 1878, and com- leted his studies at the University of Heid- lberg. He was called to the Bar from the mner Temple on 15 May 1878, practised on he northern circuit and was counsel to the 'reasury in 1884-89. On 18 March 1880 at horley, Cheshire, he married Adelaide :liza Margaret Northcott. He returned to ydney in 1889 and was admitted to the New outh Wales Bar on 18 November.

On visits to New Zealand, Hamilton took art in the first exploration of the Murchi- on Glacier in January 1890, and in Decem- er next year tried unsuccessfully to climb 1t Darwin and Mt De La Bêche in the outhern alps—Mt Hamilton, 9915 ft (3023 1), in the Malte Brun Range was named

after him. He was a good golfer and in 1893 one of the founders of the Sydney Golf Club at Dame Eadith Walker's [q.v.] Yaralla es- tate at Concord; it became the Royal Sydney Golf Club, Rose Bay. Hamilton served on its committee for thirty years.

Draftsman for the Statute Law Consoli- dation Commission in 1893, Hamilton later acted as parliamentary draftsman during the absence of J. L. Watkins. With G. C. Addison he published *The Crimes Act, 1900 . . . and Piracy Punishment Act, 1902*. It be- came a standard textbook as *Criminal law and procedure, New South Wales* and was re- vised from time to time. Hamilton had drafted both Acts. On many occasions from 1901 he acted as a judge of the District Court and chairman of Quarter Sessions, and sat in every court of the State except Broken Hill, Bourke and Cobar. On 15 May 1914 he was appointed a permanent District Court judge and chairman of Quarter Sessions, serving in the Northern District, then from 1918 in the Southern and Hunter District. A capable, fearless and kindly judge, he was prone to sit for long hours and in civil cases tried to eliminate technicalities and ab- struse legal questions. Well-versed in crimi- nal law, 'he had almost a Dickensian charac- ter, looking older than his years, having a pronounced limp'. On four occasions be- tween 1902 and 1917 he acted as a royal com- missioner and in 1920 was appointed chair- man of the Compensation Assessment Board under the Liquor (Amendment) Act, 1919.

Hamilton was grand master of the United Grand Lodge of New South Wales in 1909. He held high offices in other branches of Masonry including sovereign grand inspec- tor-general of the Rose Croix, grand master of the Master Mark Masons in 1912-13 and 1926-27 and first grand principal of Royal Arch Masons in 1910-11, 1912 and 1924, and was involved with the Knight Templars and Ark Mariners. As well he was an honorary life-governor of Royal Prince Alfred Hospi- tal, chairman of the United Charities Fund and of the Australian Metropolitan Life As- surance Co. Ltd; he was also president of the Sydney Mechanics' School of Arts, the Hor- ticultural Society, the Poultry Club and the Kennel Association (all of New South Wales) and a vice-president of the Royal Agricultural Society, Furlough House, the New South Wales Rugby Union, and the local Philatelic Society and a member of the Australian Club from 1890. He built up a fine collection of antique china and was a keen judge of dogs. His postage stamp collection was celebrated particularly for its New South Wales and New Zealand sections.

In 1924 Hamilton retired and continued to live at his home Tomabil, Strathfield, where he died on 11 August 1930. He was survived by two sons and a daughter by his second wife Minnie (d. 1924), née Redfearn.

G. E. Mannering, *With axe and rope in the New Zealand Alps* (Lond, 1891); *Cyclopedia of N.S.W.* (Syd, 1907); W. F. L. Owen, *A short history of the Royal Sydney Golf Club* (Syd, 1949); H. T. E. Holt, *A court rises* (Syd, 1976); *Geog J*, 1 (Jan 1893); *Magistrate* (Syd), 1 June 1914, p 164, 172; *SMH*, 12 Aug 1930.   H. T. E. HOLT

HAMILTON, JOHN (1896-1961), soldier and wharf labourer, was born on 24 January 1896 at Orange, New South Wales, son of William Hamilton, butcher, and his wife Catherine, née Fox. Nothing is known of his schooling but he described himself as a butcher when he enlisted as a private in the Australian Imperial Force on 15 September 1914; he had had prior service in the militia. He was posted to the 3rd Battalion, 1st Brigade, and embarked from Sydney in October. After training in Egypt his battalion sailed for Gallipoli and took part in the Anzac landing on 25 April 1915. A month later he was evacuated with influenza and did not resume duty until 2 June.

At 4 a.m. on 9 August, during the battle of Lone Pine, the Turks launched a bomb attack followed by a violent general assault with intense rifle and machine-gun fire. Near Sasse's Sap the 3rd Battalion counter-attacked and drove them back but soon afterwards Turkish soldiers again streamed down the sap. Lieutenant Owen Howell-Price [q.v.], adjutant of the 3rd Battalion, ordered several men, including Hamilton, to scramble onto the parapet and fire on the enemy in the trenches while he confronted those advancing along the sap. Exposed to intense fire and protected only by a few sandbags, Hamilton lay out in the open for six hours telling those in the trenches where to throw their bombs while he kept up constant sniper fire. A dangerous assault was thus halted. For his 'coolness and daring example' he received the Victoria Cross, the only one awarded to his unit during the war. The 3rd Battalion was decimated at Lone Pine but, after reorganization in Egypt, left for France in March 1916 and went into the line at Armentières. Hamilton was promoted corporal on 3 May and fought at Pozières in July, Mouquet Farm in August and Flers in November. He was promoted sergeant in May 1917 and that year his battalion served at Bullecourt, Menin Road and Broodseinde.

On 5 July 1918 Hamilton was posted to No. 5 Officer Cadet Battalion at Cambridge,

England; he was commissioned secon lieutenant in January 1919 and promote lieutenant next April. He rejoined a much depleted 3rd Battalion in France late tha month and returned to Australia in August His A.I.F. appointment ended on 12 Septem ber. After demobilization he lived at Tempe Sydney, and was a wharf labourer for ove thirty years; he also worked as a shippin clerk, storeman and packer. He was an ac tive member of the Waterside Workers Federation and was Labor nominee for th position of Sydney branch secretary in 1952 During World War II he served as a lieuten ant with the 16th Garrison Battalion an several training battalions. In 1942 he wer to New Guinea with the 3rd Pioneer Ba talion, then served with Australian Labou Employment Companies until 1944 when h transferred to the Australian Army Labou Service. He was promoted captain in th Australian Military Forces in October 1944 He returned to Sydney in April 1946.

Hamilton died of cerebro-vascular di ease in the Repatriation General Hospita Concord, Sydney, on 27 February 1961 an was buried in Woronora cemetery. He wa survived by his wife and one son.

C. E. W. Bean, *The story of Anzac*, 2 (Syd, 1924 and *The A.I.F. in France*, 1916-17 (Syd, 1929, 1933 E. Wren, *Randwick to Hargicourt . . ., 3rd Ba talion, A.I.F.* (Syd, 1935); L. Wigmore (ed), *The dared mightily* (Canb, 1963); *London Gazette*, 1 Oct 1915; *Reveille*, Dec 1930; *SMH*, 1, 6, 7 July 195 19 May 1956, 28 Feb 1961; records (AWM).
                                        WILLIAM A. LAND

HAMILTON, WILLIAM (1858?-1920 trade union leader and politician, was bor probably in 1858 in Melbourne, son c George Hamilton, miner, and his wife Mar Ann, née Richardson. In 1860 his parent took him to the McIvor Creek goldfiel (Heathcote) where, after a rudimentary edu cation, he began work as a miner. He wer to New South Wales in 1875 as an itineran bushworker and moved to Queensland as shearer in 1882. Three years later, minin lured him to Croydon, Queensland, to th Kimberleys, Western Australia, and t Broken Hill, New South Wales, before he re turned to the shearing sheds of wester Queensland in 1888.

During the shearers' strike of 1891 Hami ton led a strike camp at Clermont. On March some of his men jostled and abuse members of the pastoralists' executive an threw stones at their police escort. Althoug Hamilton sought to restrain illegal acts, h was arrested with other union leaders an charged with criminal conspiracy under tatute of 1825, already repealed in England. Convicted and sentenced by a hostile judge to three years imprisonment, he refused proposed release unless his innocence was acknowledged. Declaring 'I will see you in Hell before I'll scab on my mates', he served his full sentence on the penal island of St Helena in Moreton Bay. Following his release, Hamilton returned to western Queensland and on 8 June 1896, at Rockhampton, married Mary Ann Mitchell, daughter of a Longreach grazier who in his youth had participated in the Eureka rebellion.

As Labor member for Gregory in the Queensland Legislative Assembly in 1899-1915, Hamilton secured enactment of the Shearers' and Sugar Workers' Accommodation Act in 1905. When T. J. Ryan's [q.v.] Labor government took office in May 1915, Hamilton's seniority and his reputation as a martyr of the early labour movement ensured his election to the ministry. He was appointed on 8 June as minister without portfolio but when Ryan persuaded caucus of the need for a minister in the Upper House, Hamilton became minister for mines and was appointed to the Legislative Council on 10 July.

Opposition to Queensland's first 'socialist' government was entrenched in the council where Hamilton faced the toughest challenge of his political career; his response was competent but not brilliant. Though an adept tactician and a forcible speaker, he lacked the legal background to counter attacks on Labor's legislative programme. As the council rejected twenty-seven major bills in his twenty months as government leader, the pressures on Hamilton were immense and his work-load as mines minister was heavy. When the president of the council Sir Arthur Morgan [q.v.] died, Hamilton was appointed on 15 February 1917 to preside over his erstwhile political opponents. Firm and dignified, he was so impartial that some believed he had lost his Labor sympathies. He died on 27 July 1920 of cardiac disease at his South Brisbane home and was buried in Toowong cemetery after a state funeral with Anglican rites. His wife, three daughters and a son survived him.

The keynote of Hamilton's career was his enduring faith in the capacity of Labor to capture control of the political system by constitutional means and to use parliamentary power as an instrument of social change.

J. Stuart, *Part of the glory*, foreword L. Hadow (Syd, 1967); D. J. Murphy, *T. J. Ryan* (Brisb, 1975); *PD* (Qld), 1891, p 102, 1920, p 28; *Daily Standard*, 28 July 1920; *Queenslander*, 31 July 1920; *Worker* (Brisb), 5 Aug 1920; PRI 2/7/259, Col Sec A/4829 (QA).   B. W. NETHERCOTE

HAMLYN-HARRIS, RONALD (1874-1953), entomologist, was born on 1 September 1874 at Eastbourne, Sussex, England, son of Hamlyn Huntingdon Harris, retired lieutenant of the 18th Hussars, and his wife Sarah Wheeler, née Smith. Educated in Germany and England, he trained in estate management and, while managing his father's Gloucestershire orchard, became an expert apiarist. Research in Naples, Italy, in 1901, won him a D.Sc. from the Eberhard Karl University, Tübingen, Germany, in 1902 for a thesis on 'The Statocysts of Cephalopoda'.

Hamlyn-Harris arrived in Sydney in May 1903 and next month became science and German master at Toowoomba Grammar School, Queensland. He revitalized science teaching, raised funds for a new laboratory, gave popular lectures at the technical college and in 1908 became foundation president of the Toowoomba Field Naturalists' Club.

In October 1910 he became director of the run-down Queensland Museum. Reorganizing its scientific work and the presentation of collections, he expanded its publications and arranged an extensive programme of public lectures. His exhibition of Sir William MacGregor's [q.v.5] New Guinea artefacts won the governor's praise. In 1911 Hamlyn-Harris gave the first lectures in biology at the University of Queensland and in 1912-18 published twenty anthropological papers. President of the Royal Society of Queensland in 1916, he accomplished much, but overwork and problems at the museum affected his health. In August 1917 he resigned to grow fruit at Stanthorpe. As foundation president in 1919-21 of the Stanthorpe Entomological Society he urged the need for an experimental field station. In 1922 he took charge of the Australian Hookworm Campaign's central laboratory in Brisbane, undertaking malaria/filaria and mosquito field-surveys. After the campaign was discontinued in 1924 he taught at The Southport School.

The first city council under the City of Brisbane Act, 1924, opened a department of health and created an entomological section in 1926 to control mosquitoes. Hamlyn-Harris's appointment as city entomologist with a staff of fourteen remains the only such appointment ever made in Australia. Organizing laboratories and field teams, he advised on engineering measures and carried out an intensive educational campaign and published twenty papers. His pioneering investigations of biological control are again relevant since residual insecticides have become unpopular. By 1934 when the council abolished his office dengue had not recurred since 1926 and filariasis had almost disappeared from Brisbane, largely due to his work. He concluded his scientific career as a full-time lecturer in zoology at the university in 1936-43.

Hamlyn-Harris died in Brisbane on 26 June 1953 and was cremated. He was survived by his wife Bertha Hamlyn, née Harris, whom he had married at Tumut, New South Wales, on 30 December 1908, and by three sons and three daughters.

Of medium height and fair complexion with a shiny bald pate from middle age, Hamlyn-Harris was kindly, courteous, hospitable and a versatile practical scientist. His infectious enthusiasm inspired many young people with a love for science. He especially enjoyed playing the role of Charles Dickens at gatherings of the Brisbane Dickens Fellowship, of which he was president.

R. D. Goodman, *Toowoomba Grammar School 1875-1975* (Toowoomba, Qld, 1976); *Toowoomba Grammar School Mag*, 1 (1904), 2 (1905), 3 (1906), 4 (1907); Qld Museum, *Memoirs*, 13 (1956); Entomological Soc of Qld, *News Bulletin*, 9 (1982).

E. N. MARKS

HAMMOND, GEORGE MEYSEY (1892-1918), soldier, was born on 3 July 1892 at Handsworth, Staffordshire, England, son of George Richard Hammond, grocer, and his wife Emily, née Roberts. Educated privately and from 13 at the National School, Pershore, Worcestershire, he was briefly secretary to a vicar and then apprenticed himself to a grocer. The sea and the prospect of escape from a humdrum existence appealed strongly to him and when, to his mortification, he twice failed to pass the test for colour-blindness with a shipping line he decided to migrate to Australia.

Hammond arrived in Western Australia in February 1911 and, having refused all aid from his father, was employed as a labourer on a wheat farm near Moora and then as a boundary rider on the Upper Gascoyne and in the De Grey district. With two 'chums' he bought a 6000-acre (2430 ha) farm but this venture failed and in mid-1913 he signed on at Fremantle as a seaman on the schooner *Penguin*. After one voyage to the East Indies, full of hardship, danger and excitement (vividly described in a narrative written soon afterwards), he was put ashore at his request on the Western Australian coast near Dongara with no boots and little more than the nondescript clothes he was wearing. He worked briefly on a dairy farm, then sat for the qualifying examination for entry into the Commonwealth Public Service. He was working as a post-office assistant at Broome when war broke out in August 1914. On 25 February 1915 he enlisted in the Australian Imperial Force and was posted to the

28th Battalion. He was promoted corporal on 24 May and sailed for Egypt in June. On 6 August he was promoted sergeant and on 10-11 September disembarked at Anzac where the 28th Battalion moved into trenches near Rhododendron Ridge.

During thirteen weeks under fire on Gallipoli Peninsula Hammond distinguished himself in patrol work and won a reputation for absolute fearlessness. He was sent off just before the evacuation in December, but was specially mentioned for his work and awarded the Military Medal. He rejoined his unit in March 1916, just before it left Egypt for France. He was wounded in the leg during heavy fighting north of Pozières on 29 July; in hospital he learned that he had been promoted second lieutenant on that date. In fact he should not have been in the fighting; he had been ordered to remain at Albert with a nucleus group but had disobeyed.

Hammond rejoined his unit at Ypres in September and next month accompanied it to the Somme. Just before the attack on the German trenches at Flers on 5 November his left arm was shattered by a bullet—so badly that from then on it was useless and had to be carried in a sling; a glove covered the skin discolouration which developed. A medical board recommended his return to Australia, but he pleaded so strongly that in May 1917 he was back with his battalion. He had been promoted lieutenant five months earlier and on resuming duty was appointed intelligence officer—doubtless with the intention of keeping him out of the fighting. He was prominent in action at Polygon Wood in September, capturing twenty Germans and winning the Military Cross, and in the attack in October on Broodseinde Ridge, where he and the signals officer were observed well ahead of the advancing infantry, exuberantly charging pillboxes.

Early in 1918 A.I.F. Headquarters decided to send an officer to Palestine to take control of the War Records Section from Captain (Sir) Henry Somer Gullett [q.v.] who had been appointed official war correspondent with the Light Horse. The choice fell on Hammond who joined the War Records Section in London in April with obvious reluctance. When, soon afterwards, letters began to arrive from his mates on the Somme, he begged to be allowed to return to his unit and rejoined it in mid-May as a company commander with the rank of captain. On 10 June the 28th attacked the German lines at Morlancourt. Hammond, knowing that the eager Australians were in danger of advancing too quickly and being caught in the supporting shell-fire, walked ahead of his men, checking the bounds of the barrage with watch in hand, all the time upright, frequently with his back to the enemy, straightening out the line with an occasional motion of his walking-stick, halting it and ordering it to ground whenever it moved too close to the bursting shells. He was the first man into the enemy trenches and a dozen or so Germans had surrendered to him before the rest of the troops arrived. He was wounded while visiting his outposts next day. He died on 14 June and was buried in Viquacourt cemetery. His deeds at Morlancourt resulted in the award of a Bar to his Military Cross.

Tall and rather thin, with an exceptionally deep voice, Meysey Hammond was an unconventional soldier and an unusually brave one. His speech was studded with nautical expressions and his cap and clothing were freakish and sometimes disreputable. It was a tribute to his character that in an army where a 'new chum' was often regarded with amusement, and unorthodoxy with suspicion, Hammond was held by his men in esteem verging on worship. His renown as a fighting man spread far beyond the bounds of his unit.

H. B. Collett, *The 28th: a record of war service A.I.F. 1915-1919* (Perth, 1922); C. E. W. Bean, *The A.I.F. in France*, 1918 (Syd, 1942); *London Gazette*, 27 Oct 1916, 26 Oct 1917; *Anzac Bulletin*, July 1918; *Reveille* (Syd), Oct, Nov, Dec 1938, Jan, Feb, Mar 1939; records (AWM).   A. J. SWEETING

HAMMOND, ROBERT BRODRIBB STEWART (1870-1946), Anglican clergyman, evangelist and social reformer, was born on 12 June 1870 at Brighton, Melbourne, third son and seventh of ten children of Robert Kennedy Hammond, a New South Wales-born stock and station agent, and his Scottish wife Jessie Duncan, née Grant. He was educated at Melbourne Church of England Grammar School where he was school captain in 1888, and exhibited the sporting prowess which later took him into the Essendon football team that won the premiership in 1897.

Hammond was made a deacon by the bishop of Melbourne on 20 May 1894 and ordained priest in 1896. His early ministries included Omeo (1894-97), St Mary's, Caulfield (1897-98), and Walhalla (1898). He moved to Sydney in 1899 and was curate of St Philip's, Church Hill (1901-04); he married Jean Marion Anderson there on 9 June 1904. He was organizing missioner for the Mission Zone Fund of the Church Society in 1904-11 working within the congested areas of Waterloo, Woolloomooloo, Surry Hills, Redfern and Darlington. His vigorous programme of pastoral care and evangelism

made him familiar with the social problems of Sydney's slums. In 1909-18 he was rector of St Simon's and St Jude's Church, Surry Hills (from 1913 also of St David's, Arthur Street), in 1918 becoming the rector of St Barnabas, Broadway, where he remained until 1943. He was a canon of St Andrew's Cathedral in 1931-44, and archdeacon of Redfern in 1939-42. Hammond restored St Barnabas from decline to vigorous life. The Wednesday night men's meetings proved popular, while the notice-board fronting Broadway became famous for the weekly 'sermon-in-a-sentence': 'Drink promises you heaven, but gives you hell!'.

One of the best-known Australian churchmen of his day, Hammond regarded himself primarily as an evangelist, and his zeal, commanding presence, compelling oratory and gift of repartee led many to Christian commitment. His concern for the 'whole man' and his knowledge of life in the slums convinced him that spiritual welfare was intimately related to general well-being. Appalled by problems associated with alcohol, he became an advocate of total prohibition and a leader of the temperance movement, revelling in the nickname of 'the Wowser'. He served as president of the Australasian Temperance Society in 1916-41 and of the New South Wales Alliance in 1916-25 and again from 1929 after some differences had been composed. In 1907 he founded *Grit*, a weekly devoted primarily to the temperance cause, editing it until 1942.

Another striking personal initiative took Hammond daily for years to the 'drunks' yard' at Central Police Court, where, from 1912, he was permitted to talk to those awaiting appearance in court. Before handing over to a special missioner he had personally interviewed over 100 000 people, of whom 20 000 had signed the pledge. As a temperance leader, Hammond was well known beyond Australia. In 1911 he helped in New Zealand campaigns, and in 1917, 1919 and 1922-23 travelled extensively and attended international conferences on alcoholism in North America. His experiences led to the publication of *With one voice: a study in prohibition in the U.S.A.* (Sydney, n.d.).

Also known as 'Mender of Broken Men', Hammond in 1908 established, in an old warehouse at Newtown, his first Hammond Hotel to rehabilitate some of Sydney's destitute. By 1933 there were eight (and a family 'hotel' at Glebe). Deploring cold charity, he aimed at restoring hope and self-esteem to his 'guests' as well as providing temporary assistance. The diverse forms of relief organized at St Barnabas in the Depression were placed under its registered charity, Hammond's Social Services, which by the time of his retirement administered relief,

Hammond

A.D.B.

Police Court work, and a Children's Court and Family Welfare Bureau.

His greatest single achievement in social reform was Hammondville. Suspicious of radical ideology, Hammond saw in the 'back to the land' movement a partial solution to the steep rise in homelessness, a means of encouraging independence and self-esteem through home ownership, and a bulwark against communism. In 1933 a company, Hammond's Pioneer Homes Ltd, was set up and by 1937, on land purchased near Liverpool, 100 homes had been built to house families with at least three children and a father unemployed at time of settlement. Settlers were helped to find employment, could buy their homes by easy instalments, and supplement wages by home-grown food. Hammondville won recognition as an important model for small-scale land settlement. In 1937 he was appointed O.B.E.

Hammond was actively concerned with Aboriginal welfare, the Father and Son Welfare Movement of Australia and both State and Church housing committees. He was first president of the Pedestrians' Road Safety League of Australia and one of the founders of 'Boys on Farms', a rural employment scheme.

Hammond's wife died on 3 June 1943, when his own health was deteriorating, with evidence of Parkinson's disease. He resigned from St Barnabas on 10 November and three days later married 39-year-old Audrey Spence, who resigned her position as nursing sister to devote herself to his care. He died of cardiac failure on 12 May 1946, at his Beecroft home, bought for him by public fund. After cremation, his ashes were buried at St Andrew's Cathedral. A memorial tablet was erected in St Barnabas in 1947.

A 'loner' following his own lights, Hammond was impatient of committees: 'If Noah had had a committee he would never have built the Ark'. He was tolerant of other persuasions and critical of 'party' manipulation of synod elections. He was a man of enormous energy, intensity and complexity of character. Deeply compassionate and capable of great patience, he could also erupt in bursts of anger, but he had pre-eminently the gift of appealing to a diversity of people, from the destitute and struggling to civic and business leaders who supported his projects with money and expertise.

B. G. Judd, *He that doeth—the life story of Archdeacon R. B. S. Hammond, O.B.E.* (Lond, 1951); G. M. Dash, *Hammondville 1932-1937* (Syd, 1938); and *The radiations of a Church* (Syd, nd); C of E, Diocese of Syd, *Yearbook*, 1938, 1947; *SMH*, 25 Mar 1924, 7 May, 2 Aug 1929, 13 May 1946; *Grit*, 20 Oct 1942; *Church Standard*, 17, 24 May 1946.

JOAN MANSFIELD

HAMPDEN, Sir HENRY ROBERT BRAND, 2ND VISCOUNT (1841-1906), governor, was born on 2 May 1841 at Government House, Devonport, Devon, England, eldest son of Henry Bouverie William Brand, army officer, later Speaker of the House of Commons and 1st Viscount Hampden, and his wife Elizabeth Georgina, née Ellice. Educated at Rugby, he entered the army in December 1858, serving, as had his father and grandfather, in the Coldstream Guards. In 1862 he was aide-de-camp to Viscount Monck, governor-general of Canada. On 21 January 1864 at Bray in Berkshire he married Victoria Alexandrina Leopoldina Van de Weyer (d. 1865); he retired from the army in October 1865. At Pimlico, London, on 14 April 1868, he married Susan Henrietta Cavendish, niece of the 7th Duke of Devonshire; they had six sons and three daughters.

A Liberal, Hampden possessed 'the serious introspective air which marks the Whig when under forty', with 'a deliberatedness in his movement and a gravity in his manner', emphasized by his domed forehead and a drooping moustache, partly concealing rather full lips. He sat for Hertfordshire in the House of Commons in 1868-74, and for Stroud in 1874 (until unseated by petition) and in 1880-86. In 1883-85 he was surveyor-general of ordnance. Joining the Liberal Unionists over Irish Home Rule, he was defeated for Cardiff in 1886. He succeeded to the viscountcy and as 24th Baron Dacre in 1892.

In June 1895, refusing a K.C.M.G., Hampden was appointed governor of New South Wales, succeeding Sir Robert Duff [q.v.8]. With his wife, a son and three daughters, he arrived in Sydney on 21 November. His term was remarkable as one of political calm, as the colony was led adroitly for the whole time by (Sir) George Reid [q.v.]. The governor faced no political or constitutional crises, but was an interested observer of the emerging Labor Party, of the constitutional conventions leading to Federation and of colonial restrictive immigration legislation. In November 1896 he visited Norfolk Island on instructions from the British government and next year government of the island was vested in him under advice from his ministry. He had hoped to see Federation accomplished but resigned office prematurely due to his eldest son's contemplated marriage. The Hampdens' departure from Sydney on 5 March 1899 was a quiet affair, shadowed by the recent death in England of their youngest son. He was appointed G.C.M.G. in June and retired into private life.

A member of Brooks' and the Travellers Club and a keen sportsman, he had observed that, lacking good hunting, shooting and

180

fishing, 'New South Wales cannot be called a sporting country', though he noted that Australians were 'passionately attached to horse-racing' and superior to England in the cricket field. Hampden died of chronic Bright's disease on 22 November 1906 in London. His portrait by Tom Roberts [q.v.] is at Government House, Sydney.

Anthony Hampden, *Henry and Eliza* (priv print, Haywards Heath, England, nd); *Referee*, 7 Dec 1898; *SMH*, 26 Feb 1899; *The Times*, 23 Nov 1906; Barton papers (NL); Carruthers papers (ML).

CHRIS CUNNEEN

HANCOCK, JOHN (1846-1899), trade unionist and politician, was born on 21 April 1846 at Clerkenwell, London, son of Alexander Hancock, clerk, and his wife Elizabeth, née Russell. After six years schooling, in the course of which he was much influenced by a teacher with Chartist leanings, he went into the printing trade. His first job was as a 'reading boy': he was required to read aloud to the proof-reader Charles Dickens's [q.v.4] *All the year round*. He was apprenticed as a compositor with the *British Medical Journal* and later worked for various newspapers and journals; in 1867 he had some months in Paris as assistant reader for the *Paris American*.

On 15 October 1870 at St Giles-in-the-Fields, London, Hancock married Charlotte Jackson, daughter of a carpenter. In 1884 he and his family migrated to Melbourne where he worked as a reader for Sands [q.v.6] and MacDougall. He spent a probationary period on David Syme's [q.v.6] *Leader*; his failure to secure an appointment seems to have contributed to his later hostile relationship with the *Age*.

Hancock's wide London experience in the trade helped to gain him prominence in the Melbourne Typographical Society. In 1889 he not only became the society's secretary and the editor of its journal (retaining the latter position until his death) but also president of the Melbourne Trades Hall Council. During his presidency he did his utmost to reassure employers. He told a chamber of commerce dinner that the country needed 'not socialism but capital and stability'; like most Victorian trade unionists he loyally defended tariff protection; he even urged employers to follow the trade unions' example in combination. On the eve of the 1890 maritime strike he joined with James Service [q.v.6] in a vain attempt at conciliation.

Hancock was involved in the strike's management as chairman of the Melbourne committee of finance and control. The crushing defeat suffered by the unions in some measure radicalized him. He was very conscious of the isolation of the labour movement, and he saw an alliance of parliament and press, not to mention pulpit, bench and army, as contributing to the unions' humiliation. He was soon active in moves to launch labour into parliament. Although at first reluctant, he agreed to contest in the Labor interest a by-election for Collingwood in April 1891. His success, in the face of the *Age*'s opposition, was widely hailed as an augury of Labor's coming triumph in the eastern colonies.

Hancock's initial term in parliament was brief. In his maiden speech he was prescient in urging reform of the banking system. He was hounded for his tactless criticism; it was even claimed that his speech had had an adverse effect on the colony's credit in England. This incident hardly mattered in an electorate like Collingwood, but the trade unions' political organization, the Progressive Political League, was making little impact and Hancock could not even enthuse his own printing union in the cause of labour representation. In the 1892 elections he failed to win the second Collingwood seat by twenty-five votes.

In 1894 he was returned as Labor candidate for Footscray and retained his seat in 1897. Although he dutifully supported the Liberal Turner [q.v.] government, and the social reforms it introduced, Hancock grew impatient with the Labor members' subservience to the Liberal alliance. He was increasingly critical of W. A. Trenwith's [q.v.] leadership of the Labor group, particularly when Trenwith, out of step with the Trades Hall, campaigned for acceptance of the Federal Constitution in 1898.

Although a moderate, Hancock was more interested than many of his colleagues in developing an independent Labor Party. *Tocsin* described him as a Labor member who 'never compromised his principles, and never lost the faith of the workers'. He had a particular aversion to military display, and once told parliament that he hated the sight of a soldier. Hancock was, however, a genial, witty and convivial figure. Indeed it was said of him that had he been less popular he would have been more powerful.

Hancock died at his home at Footscray on 22 November 1899 after a bronchial illness which led to heart and kidney complications. He was buried in Melbourne general cemetery, the cortège journeying from Footscray past the Trades Hall. Although he had not been a church-goer he was also accorded a memorial service at St John's Church, Footscray. He was survived by his wife and five of his seven children, on behalf of whom the Melbourne Typographical Society launched an appeal.

J. Hagan, *Printers and politics* (Canb, 1966); F. T. Fitzgerald, *The printers of Melbourne* (Melb, 1967); *A'sian Typographical J*, Dec 1899; *Footscray Advertiser*, and *Independent* (Footscray), 25 Nov 1899; *Tocsin*, 30 Nov 1899; J. F. Lack, Footscray: an industrial suburban community (Ph.D. thesis, Monash Univ, 1976).   JOHN RICKARD

HANCOCK, JOSIAS HENRY (1875-1945), timber merchant, was born on 14 October 1875 at Ipswich, Queensland, son of Josias Hancock, timber miller, and his wife Emily, née Traveskas. His Cornish grandfather had been a timber man and his father had opened a mill in Stanley Street, Brisbane, which became Hancock & Gore in 1898 and was converted to a limited company in 1904. After education at Ipswich Grammar School, Josias Henry joined the board, soon became managing director and dominated the firm until his death.

Under his lead the company expanded rapidly, building mills at thirteen rural centres, five points in the Brisbane metropolitan area and at Rosebery and Lismore in New South Wales. A case mill was added to the Ipswich Road mill in Brisbane and a joinery about 1920. A veneering plant installed in 1930-31 had become Australia's largest producer of plywood by 1945. Besides the logging mills of Hancock & Gore, Hancock headed seven subsidiary companies including Brown & Broad Ltd, the Timber Corporation Ltd, Burt's Transport Ltd and Hancock & Gore Homes Ltd. He was also a director of Yarraman Pine Pty Ltd and a member of the Queensland Export Association and the Rural Fires Board.

World War I created a heavy demand for timber but by the late 1920s housebuilding had slumped and the industry was depressed. As chairman of the Timber Merchants' Association, Hancock proposed that the government reduce royalties on timber exports; the idea was accepted and recovery followed. In 1932-33 he participated in the purchase by a consortium of Brisbane timber men of the unprofitable state-owned mills in Brisbane and at Yarraman. He believed it 'undignified' for the government to trade. In 1933-34 he was one of a group seeking government help for the veneer and plywood industry which was experiencing heavy competition; the government created the Plywood and Veneer Board, which Hancock joined. At its peak Hancock & Gore, with over 2000 employees on the payroll, was Queensland's largest employer other than the railways.

Because of the intense competition for diminishing timber resources, Hancock entered into an arrangement with Edward Farrell late in 1944 to purchase a large concession in New Guinea. He acted against the advice of his solicitor, the proposition turned out to be a massive confidence trick with political ramifications, and the reputation of his firm suffered in the subsequent royal commission.

A sociable man, known usually as Harry, Hancock was a deacon of the City Congregational Church, a vice-commodore of the Royal Queensland Yacht Club and a member of numerous societies. Intending to retire after a bad car accident, he died of apoplexy during a visit to Townsville on 24 April 1945 and was buried in South Brisbane cemetery. His estate, valued for probate at £51 521, was left to his wife, Mary Isabella, née Peel, whom he had married on 18 June 1902, and their four sons; their only daughter had predeceased him.

M. J. Fox (ed), *The history of Queensland*, 1 (Brisb, 1919); *Queensland and Queenslanders* (Brisb, 1936); Commercial Publishing Co. of Sydney, *Annual Review of Qld*, 1 (1902) no 1; *Government Gazette* (Qld), 5 May 1934; *Aust Timber J*, May 1945, p 149; Roy Soc Qld, *Procs*, 67 (1955); *RHSQJ*, 9 (1969-70); *Courier Mail*, 26 Apr 1945; Company records, Qld Commissioner of Corporate Affairs (Brisb); information from E. S. Hancock, Norman Park, Brisb.   W. ROSS JOHNSTON

HANCOCK, WILLIAM (1863-1955), clergyman, was born on 14 April 1863 at West Geelong, Victoria, sixth child of Daniel Hancock, a brick manufacturer from London, and his wife Margaret, née Higgins, from Londonderry, Ireland. His mother died in tragic circumstances in October 1878; in November, helped by his father, William gained employment in Melbourne as a clerk in the Audit Office. He gave up a promising civil service career when in 1882 he responded to a call by Bishop Moorhouse [q.v.5] to join the ordained ministry. After eight months part-time study, he matriculated and was subsequently accepted by Trinity College at the University of Melbourne. He graduated B.A. in 1887 (M.A., 1900) and gained first-class honours in theology at Trinity.

Hancock was deaconed in 1887 and priested in 1888. After a stint as assistant chaplain of Melbourne hospitals in 1887, he was appointed to Nathalia, a large, sparsely settled parish in the north of Victoria. In 1889 he returned to Melbourne as curate of Christ Church, St Kilda. On 5 June 1890 at St Paul's Church, Camperdown, he married Elizabeth Katharine McCrae, daughter of a builder; they had been engaged since 1886. After being locum tenens of St Paul's, Bendigo, for a year, in 1892-96 Hancock was minister of Euroa. He was inducted to St Mark's, Fitzroy, in 1896 but in 1900, for the sake of his wife's health, moved back to a country parish as rector of St John's, Bairnsdale, where he was collated archdeacon of Gippsland. When that diocese was formed in 1902, he was asked to raise £10 000 to help secure its financial base, an objective he achieved in twelve months. His next appointment was St Thomas, Essendon, in 1908-18, and while there he acted as rural dean of Melbourne North.

St Andrew's, Brighton, of which he was incumbent in 1918-28, was the climax of his parochial ministry. He took the lead in acquiring Brighton Grammar School for the Church in 1924; under his chairmanship of the council in 1925-35 the first buildings of the present school were erected. Hancock was also a member (1918-37) and chairman (1927-36) of the council of Firbank Church of England Girls' Grammar School.

His commitment to diocesan affairs expanded: he was a canon of St Paul's Cathedral in 1912-28, chaplain to the archbishop in 1924-26 and warden of the Community of the Holy Name in 1927-40. After his retirement from parochial ministry at 65, he undertook more diocesan administrative responsibilities. In 1928 he was archdeacon of Geelong and also of Melbourne (1928-35). He also became organizing secretary of the Bishop of Melbourne's Fund and acting administrator of the diocese. He was appointed archdeacon of Dandenong in 1932 and in 1930-33 was warden of the Diocesan Mission to Streets and Lanes. Archbishop Booth wrote of him that probably no man ever rendered greater service to the Church in Victoria.

In his prime, Hancock was regarded as a distinguished preacher, a lucid writer, especially on the subject of his experiences in country parishes, and an effective administrator. In churchmanship, he was considered a liberal catholic. His son, the historian Sir Keith Hancock, wrote of his father as 'confident and serene', with a highly developed sense of private duty, and common sense, humour and a 'natural genius for finance'. Archdeacon Hancock died on 29 October 1955 at Brighton and was buried in Box Hill cemetery. Two daughters and two sons survived him: his eldest son was killed in World War I.

W. K. Hancock, *Country and calling* (Lond, 1954); *C of E Messenger* (Vic), 1928, 1929; *Geelong Advertiser*, 14, 15 Oct 1878; *Australasian*, 30 May 1903; *Herald* (Melb), 29 Oct 1955; *Age*, 31 May 1955.

STAN MOSS

HANCOCK, WILLIAM JOHN (1864-1931), electrical engineer and radiologist, was born on 2 May 1864 in Dublin, eldest son of William John Hancock, actuary, and his wife Annette Dickson, née Bowdler. He studied engineering for two years at the University of Glasgow under his uncle by marriage, Professor James Thomson whose brother became Lord Kelvin.

After experience with the Dublin Telephone Exchange, Hancock came to Western Australia in 1885, as superintendent of telephones. He installed the first line between Government House and the Colonial Secretary's Office in 1886 and the Perth exchange in 1887, and supervised the construction of the Perth to Fremantle line. In 1890 he was appointed superintendent of telegraphs, and was responsible for the extension of lines to the goldfields and the remote north. There were difficulties due to the distance, termites, lack of water, heat, bushfires and damage by Aboriginals.

Hancock became government electrical engineer in 1894, a post he retained until his poor health forced his retirement in 1920: he supervised all electrical works in Western Australia, including submarine cables and tramways.

Röntgen's discovery of X-rays was published in 1895. Hancock obtained the apparatus from London and demonstrated its use in Perth in August. The Perth Public Hospital allocated him a small room and appointed him honorary radiographer in 1898. For the next twenty-two years he worked as an engineer by day and contributed his services and equipment, valued at £500, to public patients on several afternoons and evenings each week: it is estimated that he handled over 30 000 exposures. He was assisted in this work by his brother Neilson, secretary to the Perth Public Hospital, 1897-1913, secretary to the Western Australian branch of the British Medical Association, 1918-44, and registrar of the Medical Board 1927-49.

Hancock married Ida Helen, daughter of Dr T. H. Lovegrove, on 1 December 1910, in St George's Anglican Cathedral. They had no children.

In 1915 he was honorary radiologist at the Fremantle Base Hospital, where his apparatus and skills were invaluable in detecting bullets and shrapnel in wounded returned soldiers. The danger of prolonged exposure to bare X-ray tubes was not initially understood, and Hancock had suffered mutilations and ulceration to his hands by 1903. He was a semi-invalid on his retirement, although he continued as honorary consulting radiologist to Perth Hospital until 1930. He received a government pension of £369 a year from 1922.

Hancock was awarded the first Kelvin gold medal by the Royal Society of Western Australia in 1924. In 1915-27 he was a member of the Senate of the University of Western Australia which conferred on him an honorary doctorate of science in 1925. A member of many scientific, engineering and radiological societies, he had advocated the use of solar energy in Australia in 1918. He was a member of the British Medical Association and of the Weld Club.

During his later years he lived for long periods in the south of France and spent the last year of his life in various London hospitals. Hancock died on 26 August 1931. He was cremated and his ashes were scattered in the grounds of the University of Western Australia. A stained glass window was dedicated to him in the University's Winthrop Hall in 1934 and a memorial plaque at the Institute of Anatomy in Canberra also commemorates him. His wife, who died in 1943, left £1000 to the Royal Perth Hospital whose Hancock Memorial Museum of Radiology was opened in 1957.

A tall, handsome man, noted for his gentleness, patience and tact with the sick, Hancock was an avid philatelist and notoriously vague about money. His dedicated service, freely given at the cost of his own health, mark him as a martyr to medical science in Australia.

Roy Soc WA, *Procs*, 3 (1916-17), p 17, 10 (1923-24), p xv; *MJA*, 2, 1931, p 465; Roy Perth Hospital, *J*, 8 (1954), no 6, p 30, 9 (1956), no 6, p 259, 10 (1957), no 3, p 118, 17 (1972), no 5, p 293; *West Australian*, 8 Mar 1886, 31 Aug, 18 Dec 1931, 10 Feb 1934, 22 Oct 1957.
                                        PRUE JOSKE

HANDCOCK, PETER JOSEPH (1868-1902), soldier and blacksmith, was born on 17 February 1868 at Peel, New South Wales, third of eight surviving children of English-born William Handcock, farmer and carrier, and his Irish wife Bridget, née Martin. His father died when he was 6 and as a youth he worked at Bathurst as a blacksmith. When he married Bridget Alice Mary Martin on 15 July 1888 in the Catholic cathedral, Bathurst, he described himself as a labourer from Dubbo.

In 1899, when a railwayman, Handcock enlisted for the South African War as a shoesmith in the 2nd Contingent of the 1st New South Wales Mounted Rifles. Reaching Cape Town in February 1900 he was promoted farrier sergeant before transferring to the Railway Services Police. In February 1901 he joined the Bush Veldt Carbineers as a veterinary lieutenant. Raised for guerilla warfare, the B.V.C. operated from headquarters at Pietersburg, northern Transvaal.

In June Handcock joined a detachment under Captain Robertson, a British officer, at Fort Edward in the Spelonken district where the fighting was bitter and brutal. Robertson's detachment lacked discipline and shot prisoners and he was dismissed by Colonel F. H. Hall, the B.V.C.'s Pietersburg area commandant. By late July Captain P. Hunt, also British, was in command. Lieutenant H. H. Morant [q.v.], a close friend of Hunt, was also at Fort Edward. Hunt was killed in action and his body mutilated. Left in command, Morant ordered all Boer prisoners to be shot from then on. He and his men afterwards swore that Hunt had received verbal orders from Lieut-Colonel H. Hamilton, General Kitchener's military secretary, not to take prisoners and that Hunt had reprimanded them for disobeying. The B.V.C. rigorously hunted Boers; prisoners and those who surrendered were shot. Morant praised the work of Handcock, and Hall congratulated Morant for his detachment's success.

In August 1901 a German missionary, C. A. D. Heese, was murdered near Fort Edward; he had been seen talking to Boer prisoners who may have told him that they were afraid they would be shot. The murder attracted the close scrutiny of British Intelligence. Kitchener ordered a full investigation. In October certain B.V.C. officers, including Handcock and Morant, were arrested pending a court of inquiry into the murder of Heese and the shooting of prisoners.

Before general courts-martial proceedings began, Colonel Hall was transferred to India out of the way. Morant accepted full responsibility for the shooting of twelve prisoners, saying that the others had carried out his orders. Hamilton denied having given Hunt instructions regarding prisoners. Handcock and Morant were found guilty of murdering twelve prisoners, inciting to murder and of manslaughter. The charges against Handcock for Heese's murder and against Morant for instigating the crime failed. Both officers were shot by firing squad in Pretoria gaol on 27 February 1902 and were buried in a single grave in Pretoria cemetery.

Other British units were known to have shot Boer prisoners without being brought to trial. This may explain the widespread belief that the sentences took into account Heese's murder. Opinions of contemporaries on whether Handcock murdered Heese are divided. Lieutenant G. R. Witton, a B.V.C. officer sentenced to penal servitude at the same time, later wrote in *Scapegoats of the Empire* (1907) that Handcock 'was

simply the chosen tool of unprincipled men
... He never initiated any outrage, but he
had a keen sense of duty, and could be absolutely relied upon to fulfil it'. However, in
1929 Witton wrote to Major J. F. Thomas,
defence counsel for Handcock, Morant and
himself, that Heese's murder was 'a most
cold blooded affair. Handcock . . . described
it all to me'. Witton's letter was not made
public until 1970. In 1902 Captain F. R. de
Bertodamo, the Intelligence officer whom
Kitchener had ordered to investigate the
Heese case, had referred to 'that poor fool
Handcock' who apparently had a reputation
for blindly obeying orders. During his trial
Handcock testified: 'I have had a very poor
education. I never cared much about being
an officer; all I know is about horses, though
I like to fight ... I did what I was told to
do, and I cannot say any more'. In a farewell
letter to his sister he wrote: 'If I overstepped
my duty I can only ask my People & Country
for forgiveness'.

Handcock was survived by his wife and
by two sons and a daughter. He was the first
Australian national executed for war crimes
and his sentence, which had been carried out
without the knowledge and consent of the
Australian government, aroused bitter
public controversy.

Aust Defence Dept, *Official records of the Australian military contingents to the war in South Africa*, P. L. Murray, ed (Melb, 1911); F. M. Cutlack,
Breaker Morant (Syd, 1962); H. J. May, *Music of
the guns* (Johannesburg, 1970); R. L. Wallace, *The
Australians at the Boer War* (Canb, 1976); *Dictionary of South African biography*, 3, (Cape Town,
1977); M. Carnegie and F. Shields, *In search of
Breaker Morant* (Melb, 1979); *National Advocate*,
29 Mar 1902; 'The Bushveldt Carbineers', Marquis
del Moral (F. R. Bertodamo) papers, National Archives, Rhodesia; P. J. Handcock papers (AWM);
J. F. Thomas papers, AM 77/8 (ML); information
from Mr T. Barker, *and* Bathurst Hist Soc *and*
Catholic Archives Office, Bathurst.

R. L. WALLACE

HANKINSON, ROBERT HENRY (1877-
1953), storekeeper and politician, was born
on 11 October 1877 at Edenhope, Victoria,
son of Robert Hankinson, labourer, and his
wife Alice, née Davies. He left Edenhope
State School at 13, and worked as a hotel
yardsman and farm labourer before moving
to Narrandera in the New South Wales Riverina as a shop assistant with H. S. Rich &
Co. in November 1898. On 16 October 1901
at Germanton (Holbrook) he married Beatrice Mary Klimpsch; they had three daughters.

Lean and dark with a Henry Lawson [q.v.]
moustache, affable, forthright and talkative, by 1915 Hankinson owned stores at
Narrandera, Grong Grong, Matong, Gan-
main and Leeton; they prospered with local
expansion of closer settlement and irrigation before World War I. Later he dealt
successfully in land and as a moneylender,
was a pioneer rice-grower, and in 1935
helped convert the failing Leeton fruit cannery into a successful co-operative. He became a generous patron, among other gifts
donating Narrandera's town clock and its
valuable Royal Doulton fountain, and he
helped some men establish themselves on
the land or in business, and several Narrandera students on to higher education.

Although an alderman on Narrandera
Municipal Council in 1911, Hankinson first
threw himself into public affairs in 1915,
raising patriotic funds and men for the war
effort. For the next forty years he was involved in every public movement in Narrandera. He was twelve times mayor, the last
time in 1950-51, president or patron of
numerous local committees and charities, a
Presbyterian elder for fifty-one years, first
chairman of the Rice Marketing Board in
1928-31 and a co-opted member of the Primary Producers' Advisory Council.

Hankinson was typical of intelligent Riverina conservatives of his time. His Riverina
was dominated by Victoria, and had a long
tradition of resentment of the Sydney government. By the early 1920s Hankinson and
others felt keenly that the population drift
to the cities would undermine both rural
business and the pioneer and British virtues
which they believed were best expressed in
country life, and on which Australia's
national strength depended. In 1920 he
helped to organize the first Bush Week in
Sydney, the forerunner of Country Week,
and to found the Country Promotion
League, which campaigned with the Commonwealth Immigration Office to attract
British migrants to the Narrandera-Yanco
area. In April 1928 he helped form the Riverina Development League, which advertised
the area's economic attractions and the
moral advantages of the country.

These activities led Hankinson to the Riverina Movement, which with Charles Hardy
[q.v.] and others he launched in 1931. They
wanted not a new State but greater local
government powers for country areas: the
movement spoke for country-town businessmen rather than being truly rural. Hankinson carried its concerns into the Country
Party. Narrowly defeated for the Federal
seat of Riverina in 1932, he won the State
seat of Murrumbidgee later that year and
held it for the Country Party until he retired
in 1941. His 1932 campaign speech spoke of
a State government composed of city men
who neglected the country, and of disloyal
men influenced by Communists who were

betraying those British virtues for which 60 000 Australians had died in the war. When he died at Narrandera on 25 October 1953 the council flew the Union Jack from its chambers, to mark the passing of its most generous citizen, and one who did much to win the mighty bush for the conservatives. His wife and two daughters survived him.

PD (NSW), 1953, p 1396; *Aust Q*, 3 (June 1931), no 10, p 58; *Narrandera Argus*, 20 Apr 1928, 10 Mar 1931, 27 May 1932, 18 Oct 1951, 26 Oct 1953; Charles Hardy correspondence, MS 3775 (NL).

BILL GAMMAGE

HANNA, GEORGE PATRICK (PAT) (1888-1973), entertainer, was born on 18 March 1888 at Whitianga, New Zealand, son of Patrick Hanna, hotelkeeper, of Downpatrick, Ireland, and his wife Mary Jane, née Carnie, of Sandhurst (Bendigo), Victoria. He was educated at Wanganui High School. A talent for drawing led to a signwriting apprenticeship, and he worked as a cartoonist in Wellington on the *Free Lance* while conducting a commercial art and signwriting business. He was also a champion diver.

On 15 August 1914 Hanna enlisted as a private in the New Zealand Expeditionary Force, in the Samoan Advance Party which took over the German Territory. In March 1916 he left for Europe in the Otago Regiment. By 1918 he held the rank of lieutenant. At the end of the war Hanna was appointed recreational and entertainment officer for the New Zealand division which was part of the army of occupation. He introduced a new game, 'Batinton', an adaptation of badminton. More importantly he organized the Diggers Concert Party, writing, acting in and producing the shows. Led by Hanna, they performed in France, England and North America. In 1919 they toured New Zealand and in 1920 appeared in the principal Australian cities for J. C. Williamson [q.v.6] Ltd. Augmented by Australian soldier talent they called themselves 'The Diggers' or 'Pat Hanna's Famous Diggers', and toured Australasia for the next ten years. The Cremorne Theatre, Brisbane, and Arcadia, an open-air theatre on the Esplanade, St Kilda, in Melbourne were notable venues. Hanna's shows were noted for their topical, witty writing, which was never *risqué* at a time when 'blue' humour was popular. His versatile characterizations and lightning sketching were among the main attractions.

On 8 April 1922 at St Kilda Hanna married Jessie Meadows who with her sister Hilda formed a musical 'sister act' in the show. By the 1930s the success of the troupe, and in particularly his own comedy sketches, encouraged Hanna to use the Diggers as the basis of a series of films. *Diggers* (1931) was produced by Efftee Films, directed by F. W. Thring [q.v.] and scripted and supervised by Pat Hanna. After quarrelling with Thring, Hanna formed his own production unit and in 1933 he made *Diggers in Blighty* and *Waltzing Matilda*. Although popular, the films were not a financial success, largely because of distribution problems. Hanna made gramophone records of his humorous monologues, including 'The Gospel According to Cricket', and 'Mademoiselle from Armentières'. In 1937 he also broadcasted on 3LO.

In 1934 he went overseas promoting the films and discs. In the United States of America he was called the 'Down Under Will Rogers'. During World War II Hanna invented an igniter for petrol grenades, became an honorary bomb instructor, and devised a bomb training manual.

Hanna typified the ideal digger in his stage and screen characterizations. He was a man of boundless energy and enthusiasm but, while his abilities as a graphic artist, actor, film producer, inventor and sports promoter were undoubted, he was not a good businessman and few of his ventures were financially successful.

After the war he resumed his 'Batinton' promotion and in 1961 took it to England, where he and his wife settled. The last twelve years of his life were devoted to his interest in the Scottish Hanna clan and his successful efforts to help to secure its ruined ancestral home, Scorbie Tower, Galloway. He died at Ampthill, Bedfordshire, on 24 October 1973, survived by his wife, a son and a daughter. His portrait by Esther Paterson is held by the family.

Theatre Mag (Syd, Melb), 1 May 1920; *Footlight Star*, Jun-July, Oct-Nov to Xmas 1920, Jan-Feb to Apr-May 1921; *Cinema Papers*, Apr 1974; *Evening Post* (Wellington, NZ), 31 Jan 1974; information from Mrs J. and Ms P. Hanna, Middle Park, and Mr I. Hanna, Balaclava, Vic.   MIMI COLLIGAN

HANNAFORD, GEORGE (1852-1927), and ERNEST HAYLER (1879-1955), farmers, were father and son. George was born on 4 January 1852 at Hartley Vale, South Australia, third son of George Williams Hannaford, farmer, who had migrated in 1840 from England, and his wife Ann, née Cornish. He helped his parents grow fruit and as a youth farmed with his three brothers at Riverton, Yorke Peninsula. He founded the peninsula's agricultural society, and was a member of Riverton's first school board and of the main roads board, before becoming overseer of the Government Experimental Farm at Mannahill.

On 3 February 1876 he married a widow, Bertha Hayler Whibley, née Linfield.

Hannaford later moved to Cudlee Creek in the Adelaide Hills where he grew apples and pears, which, in 1896, he was the first South Australian to export to England and Germany, and engaged in forestry and wattle and hop-growing. He also developed the Gipsy apiary, several hundred hives to house the queen bees which he imported from Italy. Hannaford was well read and was a public speaker, contributor to the press and lay preacher in the Baptist Church. In 1907 he moved to Kent Town. He died there from cancer on 7 November 1927. After a funeral at Cudlee Creek he was buried in the family vault at the local cemetery.

Ernest Hayler, eldest surviving son of George and Bertha's three sons and three daughters, was born on 21 June 1879 at Mannahill and, after private tuition, ran his father's large bee-farm at Bonney Flat near Mount Crawford. He then bought The Briars at Millbrook where he built up an orchard of fifty acres (20 ha) of plums, pears and apples, exporting Cleopatra, Jonathan, Dunn's Seedling, Rome Beauty and Stone Pippin apples. He also maintained 360 colonies of bees, yielding ten tons of honey annually, and wattle groves for bark tanning. Responsible for the planting of pine forests surrounding the Millbrook reservoir, he accompanied the surveyor who created the siting for the beautiful Gorge Road through the River Torrens valley. He served terms as secretary of his district branch of the South Australian Farmers and Producers' Association and as president of the Beekeepers' Association. On 20 April 1904 Hannaford married Florence Elizabeth Pool at Cudlee Creek. They had two daughters and two sons.

Hannaford was a member, and chairman for seven years, of the Talunga District Council, then spent over ten years on the St Peters Town Council, for two periods of which, in 1926-28 and 1937-42, he was mayor. In 1927-30 he was a conservative member of the House of Assembly for Murray. His approach to the Depression and unemployment was to increase production via reduced costs and to strive for peace in industry; Hannaford believed that 'strikes had done incalculable harm to Australia and the Arbitration Courts seemed to have caused more harm than good'. He was defeated in a bid to re-enter the House for Torrens in 1938.

Like his father, Hannaford was a Baptist preacher; he also supported the Methodist Church after his marriage. Survived by his wife, two daughters, and two sons, he died on 21 December 1955, following surgery, and was cremated. His estate was sworn for probate at £51 185. St Peters Council has named a reserve, the land for which he had donated, after him.

H. T. Burgess (ed), *Cyclopedia of South Australia*, 2 (Adel, 1909); Universal Publicity Co, *The official civic record of South Australia* (Adel, 1936); *Advertiser* (Adel), 8 Nov 1927, 2 Apr 1930, 22 Dec 1955; *Observer* (Adel), 12 Nov 1927.

ROBERT F. G. SWINBOURNE

HANNAN, JOSEPH FRANCIS (1875?-1943), trade unionist and politician, was born probably in Yorkshire, England, son of Scottish parents James Hannan, pipemoulder, and his wife Jane, née Hay, a nurse. He migrated to Victoria with his parents in 1888.

Hannan worked for two years in a racing stable before following his father's trade, finding employment in Melbourne's booming economy just before the onset of the depression and strikes of the early 1890s. He took an active interest in union affairs which provided both a career and a higher education. He was a delegate to the Melbourne Trades Hall Council before the turn of the century and was a member of its committee in 1900 that worked to establish the Political Labor Council of Victoria. During his career he was associated with such diverse unions as the Ironfounders, Fuel and Fodder, Pantrymen, Coopers and Cycle Trades.

Hannan held an extraordinary number of positions within the labour movement. He became a member of the executive of the T.H.C., vice-president in 1912 and president in 1913. He served on the Victorian central executive of the Labor Party for many years, taking his turn as president in 1911. As a Victorian delegate to several Australian Labor Party Commonwealth and State conferences he counselled moderate reform. At the 1921 Commonwealth conference he observed that the socialization objective would 'hang like a millstone around the neck of the Movement' and become an electoral liability. Between 1924 and 1928 he reached the pinnacle of the party machine when he was elected federal president. He was also appointed a justice of the peace in 1925.

Tall, with a commanding appearance, Hannan was described as 'a good platform man'. In 1910 he stood unsuccessfully against (Sir) George Fairbairn [q.v.8] for the seat of Fawkner in the House of Representatives. He won it in 1913 and again in 1914 but was defeated in 1917 after resolutely opposing conscription. Although he had defended W. M. Hughes [q.v.] against criticism within caucus in mid-1916, he proved his loyalty to the party by seconding the no confidence motion which provoked Hughes's defection in November 1916. His parliamentary speeches reflected deep knowledge of union affairs and scrupulous regard for party principles and policy. In 1918 he won a by-election for the Victorian Legislative Assembly seat of Albert Park, but resigned in 1919 to contest his old seat of Fawkner. He lost. However, he was compensated in 1924 with an appointment to fill a casual Victorian vacancy in the Senate. In 1925 he was defeated again. He contested the assembly seat of Castlemaine and Kyneton in 1927, and that of Albert Park in 1932, and stood for the Federal seats of Kooyong and Flinders in 1934.

After leaving politics he worked as a traveller until his death at Black Rock on 14 March 1943. On 17 March 1903, aged 27, he had married Agnes Theresa Phelan at St Peter and Paul's Roman Catholic Church, South Melbourne. Survived by two daughters and a son, he was buried in Coburg cemetery. He was remembered as 'genial Joe' Hannan who gave a lifetime of faithful service to the labour movement during some of its most difficult years.

ALP (Vic), *Central Executive Report* (Melb, 1943); L. F. Crisp, *The Australian Federal Labour Party 1901-1951* (Lond, 1955); P. M. Weller (ed), *Caucus minutes, 1901-1949* (Melb, 1975); P. Weller and B. Lloyd (eds), *Federal executive minutes, 1915-1955* (Melb, 1978); *Labor Call*, 4 July, 29 Aug 1912, 26 June 1913, 17 Oct 1918, 30 Aug 1934, 18 Mar 1943; *Argus*, 24 July 1916, 15 Mar 1943; *Herald* (Melb), 19 Mar 1927; *Age*, 15 Mar 1943; Trades Hall Council (Melb), Minute-books, 1890-1940, *and* Executive Minute-books, 1904-27 (LaTL).

PETER LOVE

HANNAN, PATRICK (1843-1925), prospector, was baptized on 26 October 1843 at Quin, Clare, Ireland, son of Patrick Hanneen and his wife Catherine, née Gleeson. He arrived in Victoria in December 1862 and worked underground at Ballarat. In the period 1868 to 1880 he spent six years on New Zealand goldfields, but where he spent the other six years is unknown. Probably he was on Australian goldfields: the search for gold infatuated him.

As the spearhead of prospecting moved from the well-watered slopes of the Great Dividing Range to the dry plains, a new breed of prospector was needed. Paddy Hannan exemplified that breed. He learned how to find water before looking for gold, to travel lightly, and to operate far from the nearest supply base. He was one of the first men at various gold rushes in dry terrain: Temora in New South Wales in 1880, Teetulpa in South Australia in 1886, and the gold camps around Southern Cross, Western Australia, in 1889. He joined the rush to remote Coolgardie where, in 1893, he won enough alluvial gold to finance further prospecting trips.

In June 1893 Hannan and Thomas Flanagan and Dan O'Shea (their names have various spellings) followed a new rush to the east of Coolgardie. Along the track on 10 June, they found gold near the surface of the dry red soil. Working in secret, each man won the equivalent of several years wages in the space of a week. On 17 June Hannan rode his horse to Coolgardie with about 100 ounces (2.8 kg) of gold and broke the news. The next morning the rush to Kalgoorlie began.

Hannan's fame as the discoverer of the richest goldfield in Australia came rather easily. His find was not as difficult or as courageous as the earlier Coolgardie find. An unassuming man, he did not claim that he was the sole discoverer. Moreover he did not initially recognize the value of the geological formation—the Golden Mile Dolerite—which has yielded most of Kalgoorlie's gold. Even the popular picture of him as a lonely walker carrying swag and water-bag is romantic: he travelled in company, and with horses. But he deserved his success. He had boldly prospected in new territories for a quarter of a century. Above all, his discovery came in the depth of a national depression: never was a goldfield so timely.

In 1894 Hannan saw the sea for the first time in five years, and then returned to seek new goldfields. Mostly camping on his own, sometimes earning money by prospecting for syndicates, he did not entirely give up the search until his visit to the Bullfinch rush in 1910. By then he was living comfortably on a compassionate allowance of £150 a year from the Western Australian government.

Hannan was short and slight and his face was weather beaten. A photograph in old age shows a bald head, wispy beard, strong nose and sad, searching eyes. He was not gregarious or talkative: loneliness and secrecy were the hallmarks of many fine prospectors. His last years were spent with two female relatives in the Melbourne suburb of Brunswick where he died on 4 November 1925. He left an estate valued for probate at £1402. His grave in the Catholic section of the Melbourne general cemetery attracts many pilgrims from the West. His Kalgoorlie statue, complete with water-bag, is one of the nation's most appealing monuments and the town's main street is named after him.

J. Raeside, *Golden days* (Perth, 1929); J. Kirwan, *My life's adventure* (Lond, 1936); M. Uren, *Glint of gold* (Melb, 1948); C. Turnbull, *Frontier: the story of Paddy Hannan* (Melb, 1949); G. Blainey, 'Patrick

Hannan', in L. Hunt (ed), *Westralian portraits* (Perth, 1979); *Chronicle* (Adel), 16 Sept 1893.

GEOFFREY BLAINEY

HANRAN, PATRICK FRANCIS (1831-1916), merchant and politician, was born on 16 September 1831 at Limerick, Ireland, son of Corporal Francis Hanran (Hanrahan) of the 28th Regiment and his wife Bridget, née Hayes. His parents reached Sydney in 1834, presumably in a troop-ship. His father served at Bowen's Hollow (Bowenfels) guarding convicts, then sailed for England in the *Trusty* on 21 March 1840. Taking his discharge there, he returned to Sydney and began business as a commission agent. Patrick went to the Christian Brothers' School on the corner of Kent and Argyle streets.

Failing to maintain the family business after his father's death in 1851, Hanran went prospecting with some success in New South Wales and Victoria. Working successively at Turon, Louisa Creek, Bendigo and Ballarat, he was an eye-witness of the fight at the Eureka Stockade. In New Zealand in 1861 he followed the gold rushes at Gabriels Gully, Tuapeka and the west coast though with less success than in Australia.

After returning to Sydney in 1864, he probably spent a little time at Ipswich, Queensland, before establishing himself as a storekeeper at Townsville in March 1866, seventeen months after the town's foundation. Despite ups and downs which included an insolvency on his own petition in December 1874, he carried on the business for the rest of his life. First elected to the Townsville Municipal Council in 1868, he was an alderman for twenty-seven years and mayor nine times between 1871 and 1896. His long civic service also included membership of the board of health, the fire brigade board, the harbour board, the Cleveland Bay Immigration Board, the hospital, state school and orphanage committees and the council of the Northern Separation Movement.

Hanran was elected to the Queensland Legislative Assembly as junior member for Townsville in 1899. Overshadowed by his colleague (Sir) Robert Philp [q.v.] throughout, he retired from parliament in 1909. He had a reputation for taciturnity and newspapers dubbed him the most silent member of his day. In State politics his career was insignificant, but in a long and productive municipal career he helped to guide Townsville from a struggling settlement of about 100 people on a muddy creek to a thriving city and port with a population of about 10 000 in the 1890s. His well-documented generosity and kindness, while not conducive to commercial success, endeared him to the local citizens. He boasted proudly that in his long career as a general storekeeper he had never sued for a debt. He and his publican brother John were among the best-known racehorse owners in the district.

By his marriage in Sydney on 17 September 1864 to Mary Ann Ogle, born in Drogheda, Ireland, there were five daughters and two sons. His wife and a daughter predeceased him. Hanran died at Townsville on 8 August 1916 and was buried in the Catholic section of Townsville cemetery.

W. F. Morrison, *The Aldine history of Queensland*, 2 (Syd, 1888); W. J. Doherty, *The Townsville book* (Brisb, 1919); *Government Gazette* (Qld), 1874, p 2433; *Townsville Herald*, 24 Dec 1887; *Queenslander* (Brisb), 6 Jan 1894; *Sun* (Brisb), 26 Jan 1908; *Nth Qld Register*, 14 Aug 1916; Townsville City Council Minutes, 1876-96 (held by Council).

J. C. PROUD

HANSEN, MARTIN PETER (1874-1932), educationist, was born on 24 January 1874 at Crosbie, Victoria, third surviving child of Hans Truelsen Hansen, farmer, and his wife Caroline, née Hollander, both from Schleswig (Prussia). Educated at Toolleen primary school, he won a scholarship to Scotch College, Melbourne, where he boarded in 1887-89. He matriculated in November 1890. An unpaid junior teacher from August 1891 at Abbotsford primary school, he qualified as a teacher of military drill before entering on 18 July 1892 the Teaching Institute, where he obtained his Trained Teacher's Certificate and won the Gladman [q.v.4] prize for teaching.

Hansen was appointed in July 1893 as head teacher at Cochranes Creek near Bealiba. Before he resigned in February 1895, he was commended for having greatly improved his school. After teaching at University High School for two years he rejoined the Education Department in December 1896 as assistant at Warrnambool. Next year he began duty as head teacher at Ripplebrook, Gippsland. In November he took charge of St Leonards and Paywit North schools on the Bellarine Peninsula but by 1898 was teaching full time at Paywit North.

While in the country he pursued university studies, graduating B.A. (1898), LL.B. (1899) and M.A. (1900), and winning the Bowen [q.v.3] prize in 1898. On 5 February 1900 he resigned from the department to accept a position at Wesley College and, on 11 July at Woodford, he married Margaret Morgan, manager of a coffee palace at Warrnambool; they had a son. At Wesley

Hansen began as a sports master and then became noted as a teacher of natural science. As first assistant master he did much of the organizing of the school and from April to November 1907 served as headmaster while Adamson [q.v.7] was overseas. Hansen helped to found the (Incorporated) Association of Secondary School Teachers of Victoria in 1904. He produced two successful textbooks on physics for schools and with Alfred Hart [q.v.] published *English ideals* (1903) and *Typical selections in prose and poetry* (1912); he collaborated with D. McLachlan in the 1912 publication of *An Austral garden: an anthology of verse*.

On 10 February 1909 Hansen rejoined the Education Department as inspector of registered teachers and schools and began his valuable association with Frank Tate [q.v.]. On 8 August he became chief inspector and chairman of classifiers of secondary schools. He went overseas in 1922-23 and on his return urged in a report on education in Britain and America the trial of the 'platoon' or notary system of organization in schools. He deplored the emergence in Victoria of a dual system of secondary and technical schools instead of one secondary multicourse establishment for each area.

Hansen was assistant director of education from 1925 and acting director from 1927; on 25 June 1928 he succeeded Tate as director. Early next year he set up committees to plan the co-ordination of postprimary education but the antipathy of the minister, John Lemmon [q.v.], who refused approval for multi-purpose schools, combined with the onset of the Depression with harsh financial cut-backs, effectively destroyed the proposals. During 1930 Hansen set up a committee to investigate teaching techniques for use with visual education equipment. To a board of inquiry in 1931 he proposed the consolidation of schools in both city and country, the creation of separate classified rolls for primary, secondary and technical teachers, and the abolition of the time-honoured Merit Certificate. His term as director, however, was marked by a bitter ideological conflict with Donald Clark [q.v.8], chief inspector of technical schools, his opposition to the appointment of Julia Flynn [q.v.8] as chief inspector of secondary schools, and growing disharmony with his minister. His health suffered. But his last book, a collection of lectures delivered in Australia and New Zealand, *Thoughts that breathe* (1932), gave emphasis to the numerous educational reforms that he sought and to his belief that 'a spirit of joint responsibility, the sense of partnership, and the practice of mutual consultation' must be developed by teachers and students. He argued the need for 'the

suppression of class consciousness and of individual greed'.

Hansen had been appointed to the Council of the University of Melbourne in 1923. R. H. Croll [q.v.8] described him as an 'absolutely just person, sympathetic, firm in his judgments but a patient listener, a delightful companion, but never more ... than when the conversation took a bookish turn'.

Over the years Hansen had kept up his interest in athletics. He had been president of the Wallaby Club, a member of the Beefsteak and Boobook clubs and for some ten years from 1905 secretary of the Melbourne Shakespeare Society.

Hansen became ill in April 1932 but recovered and returned to work. After a relapse he died from duodenal haemorrhage at his home at Toorak on 11 December 1932 and was buried in Boroondara cemetery.

R. J. W. Selleck, *Frank Tate: a biography* (Melb, 1982); Education Dept (Vic), *Vision and realisation*, L. J. Blake ed (Melb, 1973); *Age*, 28 June 1928; *Herald* (Melb), 30 June 1928; Education Dept (Vic), Records (History section, Education Dept, Melb), *and* PRO (Vic).   L. J. BLAKE

HANSON-DYER; *see* DYER

HARDACRE, HERBERT FREEMONT (1861-1938), politician, was born probably on 7 March 1861 at Dayton, Ohio, United States of America, son of English migrants James Hardacre, mechanic, and his wife Sarah Ann, née Butterfield. A veteran of Chartism and the Anti-Corn-Law League, his father fought for the North in the American Civil War. When he died in 1865, Herbert and his mother moved back to Keighley, Yorkshire, England. He supported her while still at school by part-time work in a worsted factory and left school at 9 to work full time in the mill. Trained as a butcher, he was second butcher on the troopship *Catalonia* during the Egyptian War of 1882.

Hardacre migrated to Queensland in the *Nowshera* in 1883 and roved Queensland and New South Wales for six years as a butcher. Sometimes unemployed, he became acutely aware of the uneven distribution of Australia's growing wealth which he believed was a consequence of land monopoly. In Sydney in 1886 he was in touch with the incipient land and labour reform movement which advocated the ideas of Henry George [q.v.4].

As secretary of the Brisbane Butchers' and the Brisbane Tramways Employees unions in 1890-93, Hardacre participated in the Australian Labour Federation formed in 1890. Reading widely, he remained a disciple of Henry George and opposed further alienation of crown land. His famous gridiron map showing the extent of alienation possible under the revived land-grant railway scheme of Sir Thomas McIlwraith [q.v.5] contributed to the election to the Legislative Assembly in 1893 of sixteen Labor members including himself as member for Leichhardt. While minister for lands and agriculture in Dawson's [q.v.8] six-day Labor ministry of 1899, he began selecting agricultural land in County Denison. He relinquished part of this in the 1902 drought and the rest in 1906. On 30 April 1901 at Alpha he married with Anglican rites Alice Beatrice Maynard; they had three sons.

To his great disappointment Hardacre was appointed to public instruction instead of lands in the first Ryan [q.v.] ministry of June 1915. Despite wartime restrictions he began to reform vocational, secondary, health and rural education. Trade education was expanded and reorganized after 1915, rural schools introduced in 1917, and extra state scholarships gave easier access to secondary schools. Hardacre's detestation of child labour, his attempted abolition of homework, his introduction of seaside camps for rural children and his abolition of 'quarter money' reveal a compassion born of his own difficult childhood. Though a thorough and conscientious administrator, he sometimes seemed bumbling. Confronted by such controversial issues as sex education, wartime 'jingoism' in schools and proposals to teach political economy, he cautiously and methodically fostered public debate, used trial periods before deciding and sometimes then did nothing. *Truth* compared him to a man watching a train leave while debating which carriage to enter. Nevertheless his interest in the teaching of political economy led to government subsidies in 1915 for the new Queensland Workers' Educational Association and to the publication in 1926 of his *The dawn of settlement in Australia*.

Though a slow speaker and an unconvincing debater, Hardacre was respected in the House for his knowledge of parliamentary practice. Originally a supporter of conscription, he allowed himself to be persuaded by Ryan whose efforts to avoid a party split he loyally supported. He resigned from parliament on 23 October 1919 to join the Land Court as one of three judges created under the Crown Lands Act 1910-18. Immediately on his compulsory retirement in 1931, he unsuccessfully contested the Federal seat of Capricornia. He continued to speak and write on land issues until his death in Brisbane on 5 March 1938. He was buried in Bulimba cemetery.

The Labour government of Queensland (Brisb, 1915); *Administrative actions of the Labour government in Queensland 1915-23* (Brisb, c. 1924); E. W. Culley, *This struggle* (Melb, 1939); D. J. Murphy, *T. J. Ryan* (Brisb, 1975); *Brisbane Courier*, 29 Mar 1893, 15 May 1907; *Queenslander*, 23 Sept 1893; *Truth* (Brisb), 25 Feb 1917; *Daily Mail* (Brisb), 4 Sept 1919; *Telegraph* (Brisb), 11 Sept 1919; *Courier Mail*, 5 Mar 1938.

G. N. LOGAN

HARDIE, SIR DAVID (1856-1945), medical practitioner, was born on 4 June 1856 at Elgin, Morayshire, Scotland, son of John Hardie, farmer, and his wife Margaret, née Mason. Educated at the University of Aberdeen (M.B., Ch.B., 1878), he worked there for two years as a demonstrator in anatomy, then started general practice in 1880 at Forres, Morayshire. In 1883 he married Marianne Jeans at Nairn.

Gaining an Aberdeen M.D. in 1887, Hardie took his family to Melbourne on the advice of Australian friends. He decided to settle in Brisbane and was registered in Queensland on 5 May 1887. Living initially at Stanley Villa on the south bank of the Brisbane River, he settled finally, after several moves, in Wickham Terrace. There he specialized in the diseases of women and children, particularly those arising from climate. In 1893 he became president of the Medical Society of Queensland which later became the Queensland branch of the British Medical Association. On a visit to Europe in 1895 he investigated Röntgen's work on X-rays but although he brought radiology equipment to Australia he did not pursue the work. In 1902 he built Firhall in Wickham Terrace where he resided and practised. A sound and capable family physician, popular with patients in all levels of society, Hardie won many distinctions. He was Queensland president of the British Medical Association in 1910 and 1920. A foundation member of the University Senate in 1911-16, he chaired the Emmanuel College Council in 1911-40. On the recommendation of the Denham [q.v.8] ministry, he was appointed K.B. in the New Year honours list for 1913 and thus became Queensland's first medical knight.

Hardie joined the Royal Army Medical Corps and served with it in France in 1915-16. On his return to Brisbane he became the first chairman of the Presbyterian and Methodist Schools Association. After retiring from active practice in 1922, he was commissioned by the Queensland government to investigate the treatment of tuberculosis in England and Switzerland in 1922-23. A staunch Presbyterian, he was active from 1928 in the formation of Rev. John Flynn's [q.v.8] Aerial Medical Service of the Australian Inland Mission and fostered the development of Traeger's [q.v.] pedal wireless. An honorary physician for years to the Hospital for Sick Children, the Lady Bowen Hospital and the Lady Lamington Hospital, he served also on the Central Board of Health in 1894-1915 and the Medical Board of Queensland in 1894-1934. He published numerous journal articles and one book in 1893, *Notes on some of the more common diseases in Queensland in relation to atmospheric conditions.* In 1919 the University of Aberdeen awarded him an honorary LL.D. and in 1927 he became a founding fellow of the (Royal) Australasian College of Surgeons.

Hardie died in Brisbane on 11 November 1945, full of years and honours, and was cremated. His patients had ranged from the vice-regal to the humblest citizen. His capacity for work had been great, but he had remained warmly human. His wife, two daughters and a son survived him.

W. Watson & Sons Ltd, *Salute to the X-ray pioneers of Australia* (Syd, 1946); *MJA*, 12 Oct 1946, p 507; *Brisbane Courier*, 2 Jan 1913; *Courier Mail*, 13 Nov 1945; P. D. Robin, The British Medical Association in Queensland (B.A. Hons thesis, Univ Qld, 1966); J. Hardie, Early reminiscences of Brisbane's first medical knight (MS F1431, Fryer Lib); Governors secret despatches (GOV/68, QA).

J. C. H. GILL

HARDIE, JOHN JACKSON (1894-1951), rural adviser and author, was born on 8 November 1894 at Troon, Ayrshire, Scotland, son of James Hardie, master mariner, and his wife Agnes Hawthorn, née Johnstone. Educated at Troon and at the Royal Academy, Irvine, he migrated to Australia in 1911 and jackerooed at Avon Downs, Northern Territory.

On the declaration of war Hardie rode to Cloncurry, Queensland, to enlist in the Light Horse. Rejected, he reached Townsville and shipped to England to join the 2nd King Edward's Horse in April 1915. He served in France from July until August 1917 and was attached to the 59th Training Battalion from October. Commissioned as temporary second lieutenant in March 1918, he joined the Indian Army in September and served with the 3rd Skinners Horse on the North-West Frontier, in the 3rd Afghan War. He returned to Australia in 1920.

From 1921 to 1925 Hardie grew bananas at Highfields, Terranora Broadwater, near Tweed Heads, New South Wales. Driven out by bunchy-top infestation, he learned wool-classing and, in 1926, joined the Graziers' Co-operative Shearing Co. Ltd. He joined the company permanently in 1938 as technical services officer and was responsible for checking wool purchases in New South Wales and Queensland. Well-liked and widely known, he had a sound grasp of stockowners' and breeders' problems and bridged effectively the traditional gap between pastoral research and rural practitioner. His articles in agricultural journals and the *Bulletin*'s 'Man on the Land' page were expanded into three practical manuals.

Hardie wove his experiences into four well-written and popular minor novels. All relayed an authenticity which gained him a wide readership. *Cattle camp* (1932) is the romance of a Scots-born bushman and his war experiences; it won third prize in the *Bulletin*'s novel competition; its two main characters reappear in *Lantana* (1933). The other novels are *The bridle track* (1936) and *Pastoral symphony* (1939), the first of an unfinished trilogy.

At St Patrick's Vestry, Sydney, on 30 November 1935 Hardie married a typist Margot (Marguerite) Ernestine Daly, from New Caledonia; they lived at Neutral Bay. Hardie's knowledge of cattle and fluency in French enabled him to act as agent for the French government between the Noumea veterinary office and Australian stockbreeders for bulls to improve New Caledonian livestock. An initial draft of stud cattle was selected at the Sydney Royal Show (1940).

In November 1940 Hardie was placed on the Reserve of Officers as a captain. He joined the Volunteer Defence Corps in 1942 as a private and was promoted lieutenant (1942) and captain (1943). In September 1945 he was discharged and returned to his previous status in the reserve. While Hardie recuperated from heart trouble, he and Marguerite decided to visit New Caledonia. Hardie suffered an attack on the flying boat and died immediately after transfer to Noumea hospital on 26 September 1951.

G. W. L. Nicholson, *Canadian Expeditionary Force 1914-1919* (Ottawa, 1962); *Pastoral Review* 16 Oct 1951; *SMH*, 22 Feb 1940, 2 June 1950, Oct 1951; information from Mrs D. Maze and M. N. Daly, Noumea, New Caledonia.

JOHN ATCHISON

HARDIE, JOHN LESLIE (1882-1956), soldier, was born on 20 March 1882 at Ballarat, Victoria, eldest of the six children of native-born John Hardie, draper, and his English wife Anne, née Reddall. He attended Hawthorn College and then studied medicine at the University of Melbourne but did not complete his course. In July 1903 he was commissioned lieutenant in the 6th Australian Infantry Regiment and in March 1908 was promoted captain.

Hardie developed a keen interest in the army and on 1 May 1909 was appointed a lieutenant on the Administrative and Instructional Staff of the Australian (permanent) Military Forces. He married Lena Elizabeth Wentworth at Holy Trinity Church, Kew, Melbourne, on 16 June 1910 and next year was promoted captain. In 1911-13 he was a general staff officer in Western Australia and South Australia and became deputy assistant adjutant general in South Australia from October 1914. He was promoted major in June 1916.

On 9 December Hardie was appointed to the Australian Imperial Force and embarked for France ten days later. As brigade major, 1st Australian Infantry Brigade, 1st Division, he served with distinction during the attack at Hermies and Demicourt on 9 April 1917 and during the defence of Lagnicourt a week later. He showed the same qualities of leadership during the 2nd battle of Bullecourt in May when his brigade dug a 1200-yard (1100 m) communication trench for the 2nd Division's attacking troops. The brigade then fought in this battle and in the subsequent German counter-attack. It also took part in the battle of Menin Road in September. For his ability and constant devotion to duty during these operations Hardie was awarded the Distinguished Service Order and after the Australian attack on Broodseinde Ridge in September-October was mentioned in dispatches.

On 1 April 1918 he was appointed D.A.A.G. on 1st Division Headquarters. A fortnight later the division halted a strong German attack between Armentières and Béthune. From May to July its battalions conducted demoralizing raids and small, set-piece attacks on the enemy and played a major part in the preliminary operations and the assault on the Hindenburg line in September. On 16 November Hardie was appointed assistant adjutant and quartermaster general with the temporary rank of lieut-colonel and in April 1919 embarked for Australia. For arranging the provision of ammunition during wartime operations and supplies to units after the Armistice he was appointed O.B.E. in June; next month, when his A.I.F. appointment ended, he was again mentioned in dispatches.

After demobilization Hardie resumed duty with the A.M.F. in South Australia, and in October 1920 was transferred to the Staff Corps. In 1921-31 he held senior staff appointments in Sydney, Melbourne and Perth and was promoted lieut-colonel in March 1923 and colonel in August 1930. In

September 1931 he was appointed commandant in South Australia with the rank of brigadier and in June 1935 he became commandant in New South Wales. As the international situation deteriorated he encouraged service in the militia and school cadet units and, as president of the United Service Institution of New South Wales, also encouraged discussion on defence issues. He was promoted major general in July 1937. Next year, under his supervision, recruiting for the militia increased markedly.

On the outbreak of war in 1939 Hardie implemented arrangements for extended recruiting for militia units. Though due for retirement he served as inspector general in the Department of Defence Co-ordination in 1939-40 and inspector of administration at Army Headquarters in 1940. He retired with the honorary rank of major general on 20 March 1942. Hardie had been vice-president of, and an active worker for, the St John Ambulance Association and now became commandant general of the Corps of Commissionaires. Survived by his wife and son, he died with Parkinson's disease at the Repatriation General Hospital, Concord, Sydney, on 21 July 1956 and was privately cremated.

Hardie was a man of high professional and personal standards. Lieut-General S. F. Rowell describes him as 'a staff officer of rare ability'. His orders and instructions reveal his attention to detail and also a full understanding of matters of policy. A strict disciplinarian, he was held in awe by some young officers, yet he was a compassionate man. He had a high regard for the ordinary soldier, who affectionately nicknamed him 'Bull'.

C. E. W. Bean, *The A.I.F. in France*, 1917-18 (Syd, 1933, 1937, 1942); S. F. Rowell, *Full circle* (Melb, 1974); *London Gazette*, 25, 28 Dec 1917, 3 June, 11 July 1919; *Bulletin* (Syd), 1 Aug 1956; *SMH*, 1, 7 June, 4, 17, 19 July, 10 Aug, 16 Oct 1935, 13 Jan 1936, 27 Nov 1937, 15, 16, 24 Aug, 29 Nov 1939, 25 July 1956; War diaries, Headquarters, 1st Division, *and* 1st Infantry Brigade, AIF (AWM); Records, Dept of Veterans' Affairs, Canb, *and* The United Service Institution of NSW, *and* the University of Melbourne; information from Brigadier M. Austin, Braddon, ACT, Brigadier G. Adams, Chatswood, NSW, Lieut-Colonel H. Hartnett, Arncliffe, NSW, Lieut-Colonel A. Seymour, Maroubra, NSW, Mr B. Hardie, Hampton, Vic.
R. SUTTON

HARDWICK, ARTHUR ERNEST (1906-1976), boxer known as Jack Carroll, was born on 3 February 1906 at Kensington, Melbourne, seventh child of Thomas Hardwick and his wife Elizabeth, née Boland, both Victorian-born. His father was a lorry driver, Kensington was a working class suburb and the boy received a basic state school education. He was at work in the local abattoir in his early teens.

In the 1920s West Melbourne Stadium operated two fight programmes a week throughout the year. 'Jack Carroll' was the real name of a friend who fought as 'Charlie Ring' and Hardwick assumed it to mislead his father who disapproved of fighting. As a youth he was simply a walk-up, tough slugger trained by Billy McWilliams of Carlton who was no devotee of style. Carroll transferred to Bill O'Brien of Flemington who completely changed his approach. 'Red' Carroll, who became known as 'the red fox', emerged as an unorthodox, perplexing fighter who baffled his opponents with his speed and variety of punches. Flicking, slapping, evasive and aggressive by turns, Carroll put together a series of long winning streaks. He won the Australian welterweight title from Al Burke in Sydney in March 1928 and, although this title was claimed by others after Carroll lost a nontitle bout to Charley Purdy in December, he remained the effective champion until he 'regained' the title in 1933. Carroll's loss to Fred Henneberry by thirteen-round knockout in February 1932 was the last defeat he suffered. He beat Henneberry twice subsequently and many leading welterweights and middleweights, winning thirty of his last thirty-three fights (one draw, two no contests).

Abstemious and always fit, Carroll was undoubtedly a world-class fighter. In 1934 he beat Billy Townsend who claimed the world junior welterweight title and he defeated world-ranked welterweights Bep Val Klaveran (twice), Jimmy Leto (three times) and Izzy Jannazzo to become the number one contender for the world title held by Barney Ross. Whether Carroll could have beaten Ross is still debated. A match between them was seriously mooted but promotional difficulties prevented it. In the later stages of his career Carroll had difficulty in making the welterweight limit of 10 stone 7 pounds (67 kg) and his punching technique would have been penalized in America. Carroll himself did not think an all-out pursuit of the title worthwhile: 'I'm such a bad traveller that I'm sick from the time I start travelling to the time I finish'.

Carroll retired in 1938 with a house, a car and savings—one of the few Australian boxers to achieve financial stability through the sport. He returned to manual work on the Melbourne wharves, trained fighters without notable success and was a skilled referee. He had married Doreen Mary Thomas on 9 June 1931 and had two daughters and a son. He died of hypertensive cardiac disease on 14 September 1976, and was cremated.

Homely in appearance, reserved by temperament and not a knock-out puncher, Jack Carroll nevertheless became a legendary figure in Australian boxing, probably because he symbolized the virtues of the 'battler' in an era of limited opportunities.

J. Pollard, *The Ampol book of Australian sporting records* (Syd, 1968); P. Corris, *Lords of the ring* (Syd, 1980); *People* (Syd), 22 Apr 1953; *Sporting Globe*, 11 Apr 1928; information from Mr H. Orford, North Fitzroy, Melb.   PETER CORRIS

HARDY, CHARLES DOWNEY (1898-1941), timber merchant and politician, was born on 12 December 1898 at Wagga Wagga, New South Wales, son of Charles Hardy junior, contractor, and his wife Mary Alice, née Pownall. The Hardy family was well known in the Riverina. Charles Hardy senior had settled at Wagga in 1862 and established the firm C. Hardy & Co. which supervised the construction of many public buildings and bridges in the area. His son Charles junior (d. 1934) took over the firm; deeply religious, he was known locally as 'the white man of the Riverina'. Charles, the grandson, was educated at Wagga High School and at the Geelong Church of England Grammar School. He returned to Wagga in 1915 where he trained as an apprentice carpenter. On 2 January 1917 he enlisted as a sapper in the Australian Imperial Force, serving in the 1st Pioneer Training Battalion and 1st Field Company, Australian Engineers, before being gassed in March 1918. One month before the Armistice he was promoted lance corporal. On his discharge in September 1919 he returned to the family firm, having gained experience of concrete engineering and draughting with Trollope Colls Ltd of London. On 11 July 1922 at St Hilary's Anglican Church, Kew, Melbourne, he married Alice Margaret Ann Trim.

Hardy was an energetic and ambitious businessman. He formed Hardy's Ltd in 1920. In 1924 he visited the United States of America to study afforestation, timber-handling techniques and industrial relations, and spent £35 000 on modern timber-dressing machinery which was put to use processing logs brought from Tumbarumba; this project also entailed the construction of a railway four miles (6.4 km) into precipitous mountain terrain. Hardy also acquired contracts to supply timber for Canberra's housing. The firm survived 'financial adversity' during the Depression although in 1934 Alpine Ash (Pty Ltd from 1937) was formed to take over its assets. By

)40 Hardy had also established a third com-
any, Bogo Timbers Pty Ltd.

Throughout the 1920s Hardy was active
local affairs. He was a mainstay of the
'agga sub-branch of the Returned Sailors'
id Soldiers' Imperial League of Australia.
1928 he proposed the formation of the Riv-
ina Development League, concerned
rgely with local matters such as irrigation,
id in 1930 he became a member of
ie United Australia Association. Hardy
hieved national prominence next year as
ader of the Riverina Movement which had
s main centres at Wagga and Narrandera;
was strongly supported by the prominent
arrandera storekeeper and rice-grower,
obert Henry Hankinson [q.v.]. Hardy
lvocated the replacement of State parlia-
ents with provincial councils and threat-
ied that the Riverina would secede. He
valled the leader of the New Guard, Eric
ampbell [q.v.7], for intemperate criticism
the New South Wales government of J. T.
ang [q.v.]. R. C. Packer, managing editor
Associated Newspapers Ltd, and other
embers of an employing class which had
ecome disillusioned with parliamentary
emocracy, championed Hardy as the
romwell of the Riverina', a Mussolini-
yle Messiah, who, like another 'lowly car-
enter', had returned to his earthly kingdom
r the day of judgment. With a campaign
ounted and co-ordinated by the O'Brien
ublicity Co., Hardy swooped around New
outh Wales in an aeroplane, delivering
emagogic speeches as part of his 'message
hope'. He did not shrink from describing
mself as a Fascist and referred obliquely
a 'Silent Division' within the movement,
hich he termed 'the country method of up-
olding law and order', but which others
ave interpreted as a secret paramilitary
m not unlike the New Guard.

Hardy's truculent oratory generated in-
rest among the police and the Common-
ealth Investigation Branch and conster-
ation from the leaders of the United
ountry Party, who, while involved in
iother, hardly less militant rural separatist
ganization, the New England New State
ovement, perceived Hardy to be a threat
their leadership. The Riverina Movement
as gradually subsumed by the parliamen-
iry party; in August 1931 Hardy became
iairman of the jointly formed United
ountry Movement and was elected to the
enate as a United Country Party candidate
December. Nevertheless, in May 1932,
iring the final tempestuous days of the
ang government, he was 'theatrical' in
rging that the country movements step
itside the constitution and set themselves
p in office. It was later alleged that he had
rivers ready to rush proclamations to four

hundred rural centres, a twelve-man emergency junta ready to assume office and a military organization prepared to defend these
leaders against arrest.

After the demise of the Lang government
Hardy's political career followed more orthodox lines until his defeat in the 1937 general elections. He took an active and important part in the administration of the Country
Party. Several times leader of its Riverina
division during the 1930s, he was the party's
leader in the Senate from October 1935 until
June 1938. During World War II Hardy
served as honorary co-ordinator of works
with the Royal Australian Air Force and as
liaison officer to the business member of the
Air Board supervising constructional expenditure, until being seconded to the Department of Defence Co-ordination. He died
on 27 August 1941 in an air crash at Coen,
Queensland. Survived by his wife and two
sons, he left an estate valued for probate at
£16 653.

U. R. Ellis, *The Country Party* (Melb, 1958); E.
C. G. Page, *Truant surgeon*, A. Mozley ed (Syd,
1963); *Table Talk*, 2 Apr 1931; *SMH*, 28 Aug 1941;
W. A. Beveridge, The Riverina movement and
Charles Hardy (B.A. Hons thesis, Univ Syd, 1954);
C. L. A. Abbott, Family background. The Upper
Hunter Abbotts, Abbott papers (MS 4744, NL);
Charles Hardy scrapbook (Riverina CAE Ar-
chives); Hardy letters (MS 3775, NL); Intelligence
reports, CRS A367 item C94121 (AAO).

ANDREW MOORE

HARFORD, LESBIA VENNER (1891-
1927), poet, was born on 9 April 1891 at
Brighton, Melbourne, daughter of Edmund
Joseph Keogh, a well-to-do financial agent,
and his wife Helen Beatrice, née Moore, both
born in Victoria. Her mother was related to
the earl of Drogheda. About 1900 the
Keoghs fell on hard times and in an effort
to retrieve the family fortunes Edmund
went to Western Australia, where he
eventually took up farming.

Lesbia was born with a congenital heart
defect which restricted her activity
throughout her life. Nettie Palmer [q.v.] remembered her at a children's party as 'a
dark-eyed little girl who sat quite still, looking on'. She was educated at Clifton, the
Brigidine convent at Glen Iris, and Mary's
Mount, the Loreto convent at Ballarat, but
she rebelled against the family's staunch
Catholicism: in 1915 she conducted services
for F. Sinclaire's [q.v.] Fellowship group.

In 1912 she enrolled in law at the University of Melbourne, paying her way by coaching or taking art classes in schools. She
graduated LL.B. in December 1916 in the
same class as (Sir) Robert Menzies. During

her undergraduate years she had become embroiled in the anti-war and anti-conscription agitation, forming a close friendship with Guido Baracchi (son of Pietro Baracchi [q.v.7]) who claimed later that 'she above all' helped him to find his way 'right into the revolutionary working class movement'.

On graduation she chose what she considered to be a life of greater social purpose and went to work in a clothing factory. Much of her poetry belongs to this phase of her life and she shows a growing solidarity with her fellow workers and an antagonism towards those whom she saw as exploiters. She became involved in union politics and like her brother Esmond (later a Melbourne surgeon) joined the Industrial Workers of the World. She went to Sydney where she lived with I.W.W. friends and worked, when strong enough, in a clothing factory or as a university coach. On 23 November 1920 in Sydney she married the artist Patrick John O'Flaghartie Fingal Harford, a fellow I.W.W. member and clicker in his father's boot factory: they moved to Melbourne where he worked with W. Frater [q.v.8] in Brooks Robinson & Co. Ltd and was a founder of the Post-Impressionist movement in Melbourne.

For many years Lesbia had suffered from tuberculosis. She tried to complete her legal qualifications but died in hospital on 5 July 1927. She was buried in Boroondara cemetery.

Lesbia transcribed her poems into notebooks in beautiful script; she sang many of her lyrics to tunes of her own composing. Some she showed to friends or enclosed in letters. She was first published in the May 1921 issue of *Birth*, the journal of the Melbourne Literary Club, and then in its 1921 annual. She provoked much interest at the time and Percival Serle [q.v.] included some of her poems in *An Australasian anthology* (Sydney, 1927). In her review of the anthology, Nettie Palmer singled out Lesbia's poetry for special praise, and in September and October 1927 published four of her poems in tribute to her. Lesbia mistrusted publishers, explaining that she was 'in no hurry to be read'. In 1941 a collection edited by Nettie Palmer was published with Commonwealth Literary Fund assistance. No complete collection exists. On her death her father took custody of her notebooks and they were lost when his shack was destroyed by fire.

The poems of Lesbia Harford, introd. N. Palmer (Melb, 1941); *Melb Univ Mag*, Aug 1914, 1947; Prime Minister's Dept correspondence files, Cwlth Literary Fund, 1941 (AAO, Brighton, Melb); Baracchi, *and* Palmer papers (NL); Higgins papers (ML); P. Serle papers (LaTL).   LESLEY LAMB

HARGRAVE, LAWRENCE (1850-1915 aeronautical pioneer and inventor, was bor on 29 January 1850 at Greenwich, Englan second son of John Fletcher Hargrave [q.v. and his wife and cousin Ann, née Hargrav In 1856 J. F. Hargrave, leaving his wife ar three younger children, sailed for Ne South Wales with his eldest son Ralph ar brother Edward, to join another broth Richard, a member of the Legislative A sembly for New England. Ann Hargrav with her children Lawrence, Alice and G bert, moved to Keston, Kent. Lawrent went to Queen Elizabeth's School at Kirkl Lonsdale, Westmoreland. When he was 1 his father sent Ralph back to England fetch him.

They reached Sydney in the *La Hogue* c 5 November 1865; Lawrence moved in Rushcutters Bay House which his father ha had built. Destined for the law, he was p to a tutor, but when he was offered a tr on the schooner *Ellesmere* to the Gulf of Ca pentaria, his father consented. They calle at Somerset on the tip of Cape York ar islands in the Torres Strait, sailed into tl Albert River and circumnavigated the Au tralian continent.

Hargrave failed his matriculation exar ination and in 1867 was apprenticed in tl engineering workshops of the Australasia Steam Navigation Co. where he worked f five years, learning design and other pract cal skills which would be invaluable to hi later. His appetite for exploration, whette by the *Ellesmere* expedition, responded the colonizing and gold-feverish atmo phere of the 1870s. He joined J. D. Lang [q.v.2] New Guinea Prospecting Associatic and was among those who sailed for Ne Guinea on 25 January 1872 in the unse worthy brig *Maria*; she struck Bramble re and sank with great loss of life. Three yea later Hargrave joined (Sir) Willia Macleay's [q.v.5] *Chevert* expedition, lea ing it after six months to join the more inte esting Octavius Stone in the *Ellengowan*: the three months he spent exploring tl area around Hanuabada with Rev. W. (Lawes [q.v.5], Hargrave took detailed note and drawings of Papuan people, homes ar technological devices with which he wa much taken. He returned to Sydney at th end of February 1876, but was soon o again; joining Luigi D'Albertis [q.v.4], tl Italian naturalist, he sailed from Somersε in the *Neva*.

He made a chart of the Fly River and i tributary the Strickland and, as the ship engineer, a post he had also filled in the pr vious two expeditions, Hargrave showed th resourcefulness, mechanical skill an powers of observation which were to remai characteristic of him. But he found person;

relations difficult. Unassertive, softly spoken and gentle by temperament, and shocked by D'Albertis's looting of sacred objects, food and artefacts, Hargrave said nothing to him. Only in his letters, diary and journal did he display his disapproval and distaste. Leaving the *Neva* without recompense or recognition, he attempted unsuccessfully to correct D'Albertis's chart of the Fly and always considered that he had been shabbily treated. He was, however, elected a member of the Royal Society of New South Wales in July 1877.

Back in Sydney, Hargrave worked in the foundries of Chapman & Co., then spent five years from 1 January 1879 as extra observer (astronomical) at Sydney Observatory, working with H. C. Russell [q.v.6]. He observed the transit of Mercury in 1881, made observations of the Krakatoa explosion which led him to a theory linking it with the brilliant sunsets seen at the time, assisted Russell to measure double stars, and designed and built adding machines to facilitate their calculations.

Thanks to Judge Hargrave's prudent and extensive land purchases, his sons were well provided for. Lawrence, with part of his land at Coalcliff leased out for coal-mining, found himself with a comfortable income before he was 30 and by 1883 his income from land and coal was about £1000 a year. That year, he gave up paid employment and became a gentleman-inventor.

His observation of waves and of the motion of fish, snakes and birds had led Hargrave to consider flight. His theoretical approach was based on the necessity to 'follow in the footsteps of nature'. He expounded the theory in a long paper, 'Trochoided plane', to the local Royal Society on 6 August 1884, the first of a series of reports on experiments in the construction of machines for flying that he carried out both at Rushcutters Bay and later at Hillcrest House, Stanwell Park, the house he inherited from his brother Ralph and to which he moved in 1893. Hargrave's early experiments were with the means of propulsion; his goal, the flapping motion of birds' wings, hamstrung his aeronautical work throughout his life'. Experiments on the shape of supporting surfaces followed and on their soaring behaviour in different winds. His early models were monoplanes, powered by clockwork or rubber bands. From June 1887, when he began to work on the problem of a machine heavy enough to carry a man's weight, he constructed several types of engines, powered by petrol and compressed air. In 1889 he built the compressed air engine powered by an arrangement of three rotating cylinders which was one of the great inventions of his career.

From 1893 Hargrave began the investigations which led him to his second great invention, the box kite. He had begun experiments into the behaviour of curved surfaces for the wings of his flying machines in 1892, inspired by the work of the American engineer Octave Chanute, but had given them up. Now, further research convinced him that cellular or box kites had greater stability and lift than monoplanes. Corresponding with aeronautical experimenters in Europe and the United States of America, Hargrave was fired with the prospect of himself flying in one of his machines and, after a number of trials, on 12 November 1894, lifted himself from the beach at Stanwell Park in a four kite construction, attached to the ground by piano wire. When the first European aircraft were built, they too used Hargrave-type box kites for their supporting surface.

Hargrave had continued to seek an engine that would be light and powerful enough to get his flying machines into the air, keep them there and propel them in a horizontal direction. From February to August 1892 he had doggedly built seventeen steam engines —all unsuccessful. Defeated, both by the lack of engineering skill in Sydney, by a shortage of money and by the solitary nature of his work, he never built a satisfactory engine; nor were his soaring machine or flying boat experiments any more successful. At the end of 1903, when he again turned to work on an engine for his flapping wings, he heard the news of the Wright brothers' flight. Hargrave continued to work on engines and to experiment with the curvature of supporting surfaces in order to produce absolute stability. He became first vice-president of the New South Wales section of the Aerial League of Australia in 1909. But his important work was done.

From the early 1900s Hargrave was writing to institutions in Australia and overseas, offering them his models. Motivated by a desire to have his work recognized and by an understanding of its historical importance, he responded bitterly to the rejection of his gift by Australian institutions which could not, they said, afford to display the models as Hargrave demanded. At the end of 1909, the models were accepted by the Bavarian government for display in the Deutsches Museum at Munich.

A man of determined public views, Hargrave wrote many letters to the daily press proclaiming the principles of free competition and survival of the fittest, Darwinian theories of the evolution of species which he believed applied to all aspects of human society. But his strongest arguments were directed against the patenting system. He published all his theoretical work and divulged the results of all his experiments in the *Journal and Proceedings* of the Royal Society of New South Wales with the deliberate intention of foiling a 'master patent thereby throwing back our work for years'. In 1909 he presented to the Royal Society his elaborately constructed, circumstantial and obsessively held Lope de Vega theory, many years in the forming, that two Spanish ships, the *Santa Ysabel* and *Santa Barbara*, had found their way into Sydney Harbour, stayed several years and left in 1600, only to be wrecked on their voyage home.

Hargrave's social Darwinism and his literal engineer's mind refused to entertain the use of flying machines for war. When hostilities began in 1914, he returned the Bavarian award which he had received in recognition of his pioneering aeronautical work and, even before Australia declared war, reported himself for service; he was then almost 65.

On 7 September 1878 Hargrave had married with Presbyterian forms Margaret Preston, daughter of David Johnston, a Sydney shipping clerk; the marriage seems to have been devoid of romance in its beginning and short on pleasure or comradeship. Seven children were born, two of whom died in infancy; and their only son Geoffrey was killed in action at Gallipoli in May 1915. Hargrave died on 14 July at Darlinghurst from peritonitis following an operation for appendicitis and was buried in Waverley cemetery. Survived by his wife and four daughters, he left an estate valued for probate at £20 489. Margaret took her youngest daughter and her husband's papers, diaries and journals to England, where she settled.

During his life, Hargrave felt isolated from his surroundings and unrecognized. 'You cannot understand' he wrote to George Augustine Taylor [q.v.] in 1909, 'the bedrock feelings of Sydney people to one who has lived among them for 42 years and yet is not of them'. Today, his surviving models have returned to Sydney (the Museum of Applied Arts and Sciences), his name is commemorated in many places and his 'dark, austerely bearded features' framed by his box-kites, are engraved on every $20 note.

N. Lindsay, *Bohemians of the Bulletin* (Syd, 1965); Roy Soc NSW, *A century of scientific progress* (Syd, 1968); W. H. Shaw and O. Ruhen, *Lawrence Hargrave* (Syd, 1977); E. Grainger, *Hargrave and son* (Brisb, 1978); A. Inglis, 'Trials of an inventor in New South Wales: the case of Lawrence Hargrave', *Records of the Aust Academy of Science*, 1 (Dec, 1966), no 1, and for bibliog; *RAHSJ*, 64 (1978); Hargrave papers (Museum of Applied Arts and Science, Syd, *and* NL).

AMIRAH INGLIS

HARGREAVES, WILLIAM ARTHUR (1866-1959), chemist and government analyst, was born on 29 October 1866 at Ipswich, Queensland, son of Ebenezer Watson Hargreaves, ironmonger, and his wife Sarah née Horne. He was educated at Ipswich Grammar School and the University of Melbourne (B.A., 1890; B.C.E., 1891; M.A., 1892) where he won the university prize in natural sciences. A part-time instructor in geology and mineralogy at the Working Men's College, Melbourne, in 1889-91, he was director of the Gordon Technical College, Geelong, from 1891. Two years later he returned to Queensland to teach science at Brisbane Grammar School but found science held in low esteem: he discovered that he 'was the lowest paid master on the staff, and held no hope of advancement in status'. So in 1897 he left to become assistant government analyst in the Queensland Mines Department. While working in Brisbane he taught courses in science at the Pharmacy College and the Technical College, and as an extension lecturer for the University of Sydney. On 27 June 1894 in Melbourne he had married Camilla Maude Nicholls; they had one daughter.

In 1899 Hargreaves moved to South Australia as government analyst and chief inspector of explosives. In 1916 he became director of the State's new Department of Chemistry, established by R. P. Blundell [q.v.7]. While continuing routine chemical analyses the department performed tasks recommended to the government by a State advisory committee on scientific research as part of a nation-wide attempt to harness science more efficiently during World War I. An important aim was to link industry and pure science; investigations would be commercially based and provide research assistance for smaller manufacturers. In a 1917 public lecture Hargreaves emphasized that universities should train scientists more practically so that they could be employed in industry rather than pure science: he outlined a curriculum for such a technologically oriented course. Hargreaves published the results of his chemical investigations into foodstuffs, drinks, and explosives in official South Australian series and chemical and engineering journals; he also submitted some results of his research to the University of Adelaide (D.Sc., 1916). From 1916 until 1940 he was a member of the State committee of first the Commonwealth Advisory Council of Science and Industry and then the Council for Scientific and Industrial Research.

Hargreaves was a foundation member of the (Royal) Australian Chemical Institute in 1917 and of the Institution of Engineers, Australia, in 1920. From 1927 he sat on the

Australian National Research Council and he was a member of the science faculty of the university (1918-49) and of the council of the South Australian School of Mines and Industries (1936-50). The proud holder of the first driver's licence issued in South Australia (30 August 1906), he studied the problem of alternative fuels during both world wars and drove his car on a mixture of molasses and petrol at the end of World War.

Hargreaves retired in 1931, but continued to practise as a chemical analyst. He was an Anglican. Predeceased by his wife and daughter, he died on 31 March 1959 at his St Peters home and was buried in North Road cemetery.

H. T. Burgess (ed), *Cyclopedia of South Australia*, 1 (1907); D. C. Winterbottom, *Weevil in wheat and storage of grain in bags* (Adel, 1922); *Public Service Review* (SA), 23 Mar 1934; *South Aust Motor*, Apr-May 1959; Roy Aust Chemical Inst, *Procs*, 26, 1959, no 5; Hargreaves personal papers (PRG 64, SAA).   LYNDSAY FARRALL

HARKER, CONSTANCE ELIZABETH (1875-1964), headmistress, was born on 1 April 1875 at Fitzroy, Melbourne, eldest child of John Harker, manufacturer, and his wife Priscilla Matilda, née Boase, both Australian-born. Constance attended private schools until the family moved to Petersham, Sydney, where she entered Normanhurst school, Ashfield. Matriculating at 16, she became one of the four original members of the Women's College, University of Sydney. Her B.A. (1895) included first-class honours in English and history.

After teaching at Kambala, Bellevue Hill, Constance was senior English and classics mistress at Presbyterian Ladies' College, Croydon, where she met her future co-principal Marjorie Kate Jarrett. She studied languages and educational methods in England, France and Germany in 1905-08, then became acting head of the Brisbane High School for Girls with an option to buy it from the founder Miss Fewings [q.v.8]. She and Miss Jarrett purchased the school in 1909 and began their long partnership as co-principals. They gained little income from the school: teacher-proprietors could not hope to finance a modern expanding school, especially one which provided boarding facilities. In 1918 they transferred ownership to the newly formed Presbyterian and Methodist Schools Association while retaining their principalship. In 1920 the school moved from Wickham Terrace to Vulture Street, South Brisbane, took the name Somerville House and opened with an enrolment of 225 pupils. The boarding school occupied Cumbooquepa, former home of Thomas Blacket Stephens [q.v.6]. Over the next two decades the school carried out a major building programme and established a high reputation.

Constance Harker occupies an illustrious position in the annals of education in Queensland. The academic achievements of Somerville House during her co-principalship were due largely to her inspired teaching and supervision of class work. She widened the interests of her pupils by encouraging visitors who were authorities on literature, music, art and international affairs. She fostered ideals of good citizenship and social service, and during World War I she formed the first school branch of the Red Cross Society in Queensland. The school subsequently had branches of the Australian Student Christian Movement and the League of Nations Union, two companies of Girl Guides, and a Cot Fund which supported the ill and disabled. The Queensland Girls' Secondary Schools' Sports Association, initiated by her, still functions. Constance herself, when time permitted, transcribed for the Braille-Writers' Association.

She retired in 1931 but continued to live at the boarding school until Miss Jarrett's retirement in 1940. The two ladies frequently made camping expeditions to the Lamington Plateau and elsewhere and were enthusiasts for wild life; they made a motor trip to the Northern Territory in 1938. After Miss Jarrett's death in Sydney in 1944, Constance lived at Toowoomba. In 1963 she was appointed M.B.E.; the governor of Queensland travelled to Toowoomba especially to perform the investiture. She died on 16 December 1964 in Wesley Hospital, Toowoomba.

Miss Harker has been remembered by the Women's College, Sydney, where a room bears her name. At Somerville House in 1934 she laid the foundation stone of the library building, a gift of the old girls' association to commemorate the work of the two principals. Harker Hall, the school auditorium, also honours her.

P. G. Freeman, *History of Somerville House* (Brisb, 1949); R. Goodman, *Secondary education in Queensland, 1860-1960* (Canb, 1968); *Somerville House Mag*, 1963; *Courier Mail*, 17 Dec 1964.
    K. E. GILL

HARMER, JOHN REGINALD (1857-1944), Anglican bishop, was born on 11 July 1857 at Maisemore, Gloucestershire, England, son of Rev. George Harmer and his wife Kate, née Kitching. He was educated at Eton, where he was school captain and

Newcastle scholar, and at King's College, Cambridge (B.A., 1881; M.A., 1884; D.D., 1895), where he had a distinguished scholastic career. He was a fellow of King's College in 1883-89. After a year as curate at Monkwearmouth, Durham, in 1884 he was ordained priest by and appointed domestic chaplain to Bishop J. B. Lightfoot of Durham, a noted biblical scholar and historian of the early church. At the episcopal residence, Auckland Castle, Harmer supervised the theological studies of university graduates (the Auckland Brotherhood) preparing there for ordination under Lightfoot. After Lightfoot's death in 1889, Harmer returned to Cambridge to edit the bishop's unpublished works, but he made no original contribution to theological scholarship. He was a fellow of Corpus Christi College in 1889-99, dean 1893-95, and honorary fellow 1905-44. In 1891-92 he was also vice-principal of the Clergy Training School, Cambridge. On 3 January 1895, at St Augustine's, South Kensington, London, he married Mary Dorothy Somers Cocks who had been born in India and whose family had many aristocratic connexions.

In March 1895 Harmer was appointed bishop of Adelaide, to succeed G. W. Kennion [q.v.5], by the archbishop of Canterbury and four bishops to whom the synod of the diocese of Adelaide had delegated its right of election. Consecrated bishop in Westminster Abbey on 23 May, he reached Adelaide on 2 July and was enthroned in St Peter's Cathedral two days later. Harmer's appointment aroused little enthusiasm in Adelaide because he had 'no impressive presence' and lacked parish experience. To some extent he was successful in winning respect. His manner was genial and unassuming. Describing himself as a 'moderate High Churchman', he avoided religious controversy and, unlike his predecessors, established good relations with the leaders of other denominations. He proved to be a capable administrator, but was criticized for failing 'to inspire the energies of his flock'.

Harmer saw his chief tasks as the completion of St Peter's Cathedral and an increase in the number of clergy. A collection of funds to finish the nave of the cathedral and to build twin towers and spires was successful, due largely to gifts of £4000 from Sir Thomas Elder [q.v.4] and £10 000 from Robert Barr Smith [q.v.6], so that by 1904 the building's exterior was substantially complete. Although Harmer recognized the need for the Church of England in Australia to adapt to its environment, and the eventual necessity of a local ministry, he found it easier to obtain clergymen from England. In 1895-1905 he recruited thirty-seven English clergymen for the diocese, of whom twenty-seven were graduates of Oxford or Cambridge. The only political issue in which he became deeply involved was the unsuccessful campaign to introduce religious instruction in South Australian state schools. He was deeply disappointed by the failure of an official referendum on this issue in 1896, and in 1902 he became first president of the interdenominational Religious Education in State Schools League. Initiated into Freemasonry while in Adelaide, he was master of Lodge St Alban in 1903-04.

Harmer visited England in 1897 to attend the Lambeth Conference, and again in 1903 when he declined the mastership of Pembroke College, Cambridge, and the suffragan bishopric of Southampton. It therefore came as no surprise in South Australia when in 1905 he accepted nomination to the see of Rochester, Kent. He left Adelaide on 4 May and was enthroned in Rochester Cathedral in July. Harmer's episcopate in Rochester was quiet, and he played little part in national church affairs. When he resigned the see in 1930 he was remembered chiefly for his tolerant leadership, his kindness, and his avoidance of controversy. In World War I he was active on behalf of Belgian relief for which in 1919 he was appointed Commander of the Order of Leopold II.

He died at Marine Cottage, Instow, Devonshire, on 9 March 1944, survived by his wife and a daughter. His ashes were interred in Rochester Cathedral. There are oil portraits at Bishop's Court, Adelaide, and at Bishopscourt, Rochester.

G. H. Jose, *The Church of England in South Australia, 1882-1905* (Adel, 1955); *Treasury* (Lond), July 1905; *Adel Church Guardian*, Nov, Dec 1948, Feb, May, June, Aug 1949; *Register* (Adel), 3 July 1895, 3, 5 May 1905, 30 Apr, 8 May 1925; *The Times*, 10 Mar 1944.   DAVID HILLIARD

HARPER, ANDREW (1844-1936), college head and biblical scholar, was born on 13 November 1844 in Glasgow, Scotland, son of Robert Harper, merchant, and his wife Elizabeth, née Calderwood. Before arriving in Melbourne in 1856 with his parents and brother Robert [q.v.] he was educated at Glasgow Academy. He attended Scotch College in 1857-59 and matriculated at the University of Melbourne in 1864, graduating B.A. in 1868 (M.A., 1878) while a part-time student working as an articled clerk in the Office of the Government Shorthand Writer. With the help of James Balfour [q.v.3] he returned to Edinburgh in 1868 to study theology at New College (B.D., 1872) where he was influenced by A. B. Davidson

Old Testament, and awarded the Cun-
ingham fellowship. Deeply impressed by
two summer sessions at Berlin University,
nder August Dillmann in Old Testament,
he went via Alexandria to Damascus in
872-73 for first-hand experience of Eastern
thought and languages. 1872 was his 'crisis
year' when he gave up thoughts of the Pres-
yterian ministry, seeing all 'higher regions' as equally valid and feeling unable
to subscribe to the Westminster Confession.

Nevertheless, in Melbourne in September
873 Harper was welcomed by his old
teacher, Rev. Adam Cairns [q.v.3], to be assistant at Chalmers Church, Eastern Hill.
His 'doubts' influenced him to take up
schoolteaching and he joined the new Pres-
yterian Ladies' College in 1875 as English
master. He replaced his friend Charles Pear-
on [q.v.5] as headmaster in 1877 and became principal in 1879. Harper encouraged
his students to sit for the university matricu-
ation examinations; his high standards of
scholarship largely set the tone for P.L.C.
In 1882-86 he was warden of the Melbourne
university senate and was a member of the
council in 1886-1901. On 23 October 1875 at
Albert Street, East Melbourne, he had married Agnes Marion, daughter of Rev. George
Craig of Kelso, Scotland; she died in 1885
leaving a son and three daughters including
Margaret Hilda [q.v.].

Harper developed an international repu-
ation in the 1880s as an Oriental linguist
and Old Testament scholar. In 1888 he resigned from P.L.C. to become lecturer in
Hebrew and Oriental languages at the Pres-
yterian Theological Hall, Ormond College.
Ordained in March 1893, he became reverend professor of Hebrew and Old Testament
there, and received a D.D. from the Univer-
ity of Edinburgh in 1901. In 1892 he had
been a close contender for the Old Testament chair, Trinity College, Glasgow. In
Edinburgh on 8 December 1892 he married
Barbara Harriet, daughter of his former
principal, Dr Robert Rainy of New College;
they had one son, Robert Rainy [q.v.], and
three daughters.

Harper's critical approach to Scripture
made him a controversial figure in British
church circles, his impact spreading to the
Melbourne press by 1890. Public addresses
on 'the Higher Criticism' drew fierce clerical attacks thereafter, and some critics explicitly compared his stance to that of
Charles Strong [q.v.6]; supported by J. L.
Rentoul [q.v.], Harper maintained his position. His insistence that the religious revelation of Scripture and Christian faith were
not dependent upon the historical infalli-
bility of biblical statements became accept-
ble: his staunchly evangelical teaching and
practice, and overseas standing, over-

powered his critics. In 1895 the Presbyterian
Church appointed him editor of the *Messenger*, whose columns had previously carried
many attacks on his ideas.

Convinced that a nation without religious
belief was doomed to disintegration, Harper
argued strongly for religious teaching in
schools. He also led Protestant agitation for
a 'Godly contribution' during the Federation debate. He was deeply influenced by
nationalistic German theologians and,
though he denied 'racist' attitudes, his spirited defence of the White Australia policy
and his attitude to Aboriginals were based
on rigid notions of European cultural superiority, as well as desire to maintain living
standards for Australian workers of any colour. Genuine concern at human suffering
was tempered by conviction of the inevita-
bility of the labourer's hard lot, but he
dreamed the Australian dream of a southern
paradise sharing its common wealth.

In 1902 Harper resigned his Ormond chair
and took up duties as principal of St
Andrew's College within the University of
Sydney. At the same time he was appointed
to the college's Hunter Baillie professorship
of Oriental and Polynesian languages and
to its theological faculty's chair of Hebrew
and exegetical theology of the Old Testament. He moved his large family to Sydney
but retained his seaside home at Lorne.

During his years at St Andrew's, academic standards were raised and student
numbers grew considerably, while his status as a scholar enhanced the reputation of
the college within the university. Benefactions increased and Harper brought about
several building extensions. He had supported the union of the Australian Presbyterian Churches in 1901 and in the following
years promoted union with Methodists and
Congregationalists. His influence was also
felt in the community through his lectures
for the Workers' Educational Association of
New South Wales, and he was active in the
work of the Sydney University Extension
Board.

Harper resigned the principalship in 1920
and his academic posts in May 1924, returning to Scotland later that year. He died in
Edinburgh on 25 November 1936, near
blind, after being injured by a car.

A handsome and austere man of firm principles, Harper was respected rather than
loved by many colleagues; but loved and admired by many students who saw his more
human side, including a sense of humour.
His publications include *The book of Deuter-
onomy* (London, 1895), *Australia without
God* (Melbourne, 1897), *The Song of Solomon*
(Cambridge, 1902), *The Honourable James
Balfour M.L.C.* (Melbourne, 1918), *Christian
essentials* (Melbourne, [1914]) and polemical

pamphlets on the relationship between religion and education. Portraits are at P.L.C. and Ormond College, and at St Andrew's College where the Harper building is named after him.

C. A. White, *The challenge of the years* (Syd, 1951); A. R. Chisholm, *Men were my milestones* (Melb, 1958); M. O. Reid, *The ladies came to stay* (Melb, 1960); A. A. Dougan, *The Andrew's book; being a book about St. Andrew's College within the University of Sydney* (Syd, 1964); K. Fitzpatrick, *PLC Melbourne* (Melb, 1975); *Vic Presbyterian Messenger*, 20 Nov, 4 Dec 1936; *Argus*, 2 Dec 1936; *SMH*, 21 May 1920, 17 May 1928, 28 Nov, 2 Dec 1936; J. Balfour papers (held by Mrs J. W. Read, Camberwell, Vic).   DON CHAMBERS

HARPER, CHARLES WALTER (1880-1956), orchardist and co-operator, was born on 27 January 1880 at Guildford, Western Australia, eldest of the ten children of Charles Harper [q.v.4] and his wife Fanny, née de Burgh. Walter was educated at the High School, Perth, and Guildford Grammar School. Later he shared his father's interests in agricultural experimentation and co-operation, working with him and W. Catton Grasby [q.v.]. As a young man Walter studied fruit-growing and marketing among the orchardists of California and also analysed the needs of British and European markets. He then managed his family's Woodbridge estate and joined the co-operative movement and the Farmers' and Settlers' Association.

On 8 October 1910 he married Margaret Rose Maxwell Drummond, a great-granddaughter of Western Australia's first government naturalist James Drummond [q.v.1]; they had four daughters and two sons. In March 1913 a Farmers' and Settlers' Association meeting accepted Harper's policy of establishing a new co-operative and next year he successfully moved that the Westralian Farmers Ltd ('Co-operative' was added in 1946) be registered; he became a director. An accident of Nature released him from management of the Woodbridge estate so that he could devote almost his full time to the welfare of farmer organizations. The tremendous floods of 1917 had severely damaged the Woodbridge orchards and other Harper properties. In 1918 Harper attended the first Australia and New Zealand-wide conference of producers' co-operative societies, instigated by the Western Australian movement. It formed Australian Producers' Wholesale Co-operative Federations Ltd which decided to establish a selling floor in London for Australian, New Zealand and South African growers, to be known as Overseas Farmers' Co-operative

Federations Ltd. Next year Harper becam the first chairman of the Co-operative Fe eration of Western Australia.

He kept himself above party politics. H was wary of political schemes for solvin economic problems after his chairmanshi of the 1924-25 royal commission into th group settlement scheme in Western Au tralia. In the course of this inquiry Harpe journeyed widely, despite rough tracks an the administrative problems which atter ded the hearings. He wrote the con mission's report. In 1934 he was a membe of the Commonwealth royal commission o the wheat, flour and bread industries.

Throughout the 1920s, as Co-operativ Federation chairman, board member of Pro ducers' Markets Co-op Ltd and office-beare of the Fruit Growers' Association, Harpe travelled throughout the south-west of th State. He was a trustee of the first Co operative Wheat Pool of Western Australi in 1922 and that year became chairman c directors of Westralian Farmers. In th 1920s and 1930s, supported by compan leaders like Basil Murray and John Thom son, he took the firm into the wheat busines as a buyer and broker and later as a founde of Co-operative Bulk Handling. Harper ha difficulty convincing farmers that the were to own Co-operative Bulk Handlin directly, and not through their shareholdin in Westralian Farmers, but his objectiv was achieved with the setting up of Co operative Bulk Handling Ltd in 1933. H helped Thomson develop it to become Aus tralia's cheapest and most efficient grair handling authority.

Harper had been chairman of Westralia Farmers when the company established th State's first radio station (6WF) in 1924 Next year they built the State's first pasteur ized milk plant. In 1926 the company lifte the first wheat shipment from Esperanc and formed a honey pool. Harper was als vice-chairman of Producers' Markets and member of the Metropolitan Market Trust In 1927 he brought farmers into th superphosphate business, as one-third owners of Cuming [q.v.8] Smith & Moun Lyell Farmers Fertilisers Ltd; with hi father and Grasby he had discovered tha most Western Australian soils would ben efit from additional soluble phosphate.

Harper supported his general manage Thomson in efforts to win realistic freigh rates for the transport of Western Aus tralian produce to London in the 1920s an 1930s. In taking on the British shipping com panies, they attracted the Federal govern ment's ire; Prime Minister S. M. (Viscount Bruce [q.v.7], referred to them as 'pirates These freight-rate advantages had a shor life because of the outbreak of World Wa

II, but Westralian Farmers' Transport Ltd was established in London in 1937 as the company's shipping arm. Next year Harper joined the delegation representing the Australian Producers' Wholesale Co-operative Federation Ltd to England. On his return, in support of the war effort, he served on the Western Australian District Contracts Board.

Harper's influence was most apparent in the almost Spartan way in which Westralian Farmers Co-operative Ltd was run. Despite primitive conditions in country towns, the firm attracted excellent staff who assisted the organization's growth to become (in 1982) one of the fifty largest companies in Australia. In Harper's time it went into trading in the North-West with the acquisition of the Ashburton Transport Co. This was allied with the formation of a trading co-operative, initially for plantations on the Gascoyne River at Carnarvon, which later prospered as the North-West developed.

In 1953 Harper retired as company chairman. He died on 1 July 1956 and was cremated. Sir John Teasdale concluded that 'he, more than anyone else, fostered and cared for' the Western Australian co-operative movement which would 'remain his monument'.

Harper had been a frugal, abstemious, reserved man, and a talented cricketer and golfer. He was admired for his lucid, analytical thinking, his conservatism and his selfless service: as a director of Westralian Farmers his fees had generally been a guinea for a meeting and, for a long time, his remuneration as chairman was only £600 a year.

J. Sandford, *Walter Harper and the farmers* (Perth, 1955); F. R. Mercer, *The life of Charles Harper* (Perth, 1958); family papers (held by Mrs J. Hamersley, Guildford, WA). KEVIN P. SMITH

HARPER, HERBERT REAH (1871-1956), electrical engineer, was born on 23 June 1871 in London, son of James Harper, commercial traveller and his wife Hannah, née Reah. He studied engineering at the City and Guilds Technical College, Finsbury, after attending Dulwich College. At 20 he was apprenticed to the Tyneside firm of Rennoldson and in 1893 he joined the Brush Electrical Engineering Co. In 1895 the company sent him to Malta to supervise the installation of an electricity supply system and he remained a second year as the chief engineer of the power authority. He returned to England to supervise the extension of town lighting and tramway systems. In 1899 the company sent Harper as assistant to F. W. Clements at its Melbourne sub-

sidiary, the Electric Light and Traction Co.

In 1901 Harper replaced A. J. Arnot [q.v.7] as electrical engineer to the Melbourne City Council. He extended and improved generation, establishing a new unit at Spencer Street, introducing three-phase transmission, and maintaining low production costs despite the rising price of imported black coal. Harper, a widely read and active professional (he was correspondent to the Institution of Electrical Engineers, London, and the American Institute of Electrical Engineers), became convinced that cheap electrical power must be the corner-stone of Victoria's industrialization.

He now joined Hyman Herman [q.v.] of the Department of Mines in the cause of Victorian brown coal. On an overseas tour in 1911 Harper had been impressed by Germany's use of brown coal in power generation and, during the recurring interruptions to black coal supply, he experimented with the coal on a commercial basis. In 1917 he devoted his presidential address to the Victorian Institute of Engineers to the urgent need to build a modern electricity supply system fuelled from brown coal. He recommended the establishment of a public utility similar to the Ontario Hydro Electricity Commission (which he had also visited in 1911). Harper's address attracted widespread interest and he was appointed a member of the government's brown coal advisory committee chaired by Herman. This committee's report became the blueprint for the brown coal-mining and power generation scheme at Yallourn in the La Trobe valley.

In 1919 Harper successfully applied to become the first chief engineer of the State Electricity Commission of Victoria. Much of his early work was in evaluating consultants' reports on proposed developments. He persuaded the commissioners to resist excursions into hydro power until after Yallourn had commenced operations. He also proposed extensions to the Newport powerstation and the retention of city powerstations to provide an alternative base load, if Yallourn could not meet capacity. This proved sound advice because the Yallourn scheme ran into difficulties burning a wetter coal than expected. In later years Harper worked on projects to increase the generating capacity at Yallourn, the introduction of rural electrification and the first hydropower scheme in the Rubicon valley.

In 1935 the S.E.C. sent him on a world tour. On retiring next year he continued to serve the community as before: as churchwarden of twenty-eight years' standing to East St Kilda Anglican Church, and as member of the Melbourne Church of England Girls' Grammar School council, the university's faculty of engineering, and Rotary. As a consultant to the New South Wales government in 1937-38 he endorsed the notion of a Snowy Mountains hydro-power project; he was also a member of the Army Mechanization Board in 1941-45. 'H.R.H.' was an inspirational figure, whether as the campfire aesthete, or as the energetic, loyal engineer despite being denied twice the S.E.C.'s highest post. A fitness enthusiast, he could be seen daily riding his bicycle to a polar swimming club or marching to the railway station dapperly dressed, 'head thrown back, cane swinging'. He was an active member of the Wallaby Club (president 1923).

A proud, old-school engineer, Harper was also an effective advocate and professional leader. He was elected first president of the Electrical Supply Association of Australia (1918), president of the Institution of Engineers, Australia (1933) and was a recipient of the Kernot and (Sir) Peter Nicol Russell [qq.v.5,6] medals. The Harper Power Laboratory at Monash University was named after him. He rightly saw himself as one of the champions of Victoria's industrialization based on cheap power. He also knew that he was one of only two engineers (with Herman) who had turned personal dreams into permanent reality.

On 11 January 1902 Harper had married his English fiancée, Eva Beatrice Ellis, at St Alban's Church, Armadale, Melbourne. Although both clung to Old Country ways, they and their four children came to love the Australian bush. Harper died at Toorak on 27 July 1956, survived by his wife, two daughters and a son.

C. Edwards, *Brown power* (Melb, 1969); *SEC Mag*, Sept 1936, Aug-Sept 1956; T. C. McCredden, The impact of electricity on Victoria 1880-1920 (B.Com. thesis, Univ Melb, 1977); Electricity Supply Dept, Melb City Council, Annual Report, papers and newspaper cuttings (held by ESD); information from Mr J. Harper and Mrs C. Kirkhope, Toorak, Melb.   ANDREW SPAULL

HARPER, MARGARET HILDA (1879-1964), paediatrician, was born on 4 April 1879 in Melbourne, third child of Rev. Andrew Harper [q.v.], principal of the Presbyterian Ladies' College, and his first wife Agnes Marian (d. 1885), née Craig. Brought up by aunts and housekeepers until her father remarried in 1892, Margaret was a half-sister of Robert Rainy Harper and niece of Robert Harper [qq.v.]. She was educated at P.L.C. and matriculated at the University of Melbourne in 1899, sharing the W. T. Mollison [q.v.2] scholarship for a year of study in Italy. She began medicine in 1901, but next year transferred to the University of Sydney (M.B., Ch.M., 1906) when her father became principal of St Andrew's College. She worked briefly as an honorary medical officer at the Sydney Medical Mission and as a resident at the Queen Victoria Memorial Hospital, Melbourne.

In 1907 Dr Harper returned to Sydney to the Royal Hospital for Women, Paddington, and from 1910 was at the Royal Alexandra Hospital for Children. She was honorary physician at the first Baby Health Centre opened at Alexandria in 1914, a council-member of the Royal Society for the Welfare of Mothers and Babies and medical director of its Mothercraft Homes and Training Schools (Tresillian) in 1919-49, a founder of the Rachel Forster Hospital for Women and Children in 1922, and first honorary doctor to care for new-born babies at the Royal Hospital in 1926. She supplemented her income from her small practice in Macquarie Street by administering anaesthesia until she developed diabetes in 1929.

Recognizing the need to simplify and demystify the formulas for infant care, Margaret Harper resisted the commercialization of infant food preparations and, after a visit to New Zealand in 1919, quietly but firmly rejected the 'Plunkett system' devised by Dr Truby King. She painstakingly experimented with infant diets and won international repute for discovering the difference between coeliac disease and cystic fibrosis of the pancreas in 1930.

In 1926 Margaret Harper published *The parents' book* on child care, which ran to twenty editions over some thirty years. In 1930-38 she lectured to medical students on mothercraft at the university and in 1933-36 as 'The Lady Doctor' broadcast weekly fifteen-minute sessions for the Australian Broadcasting Commission. She served on the Hospitals Commission of New South Wales in 1936-44 and the Child Welfare Advisory Council from 1949. She was a foundation fellow of the Royal Australasian College of Physicians in 1939, and an honorary member of the Australian Paediatric Association from 1952. Analytical and forthright, she was outstanding in her dedication and benevolence. Although sometimes impatient, she inspired confidence in her patients and their parents.

A tall, dignified and beautiful woman, Margaret Harper was proud of her Scots heritage and adhered to the Presbyterian faith. She enjoyed golf and read widely in medicine, religion and literature. For over fifty years she lived at Wollstonecraft with her close friend Helen Wark, lecturer in art at the Teachers' College, Sydney. She died in hospital at Chatswood on 2 January 1964 and was cremated. A ward at the Rachel Forster Hospital and a diet kitchen at the Royal Alexandra Hospital were named after her.

L. R. Cohen, *Dr. Margaret Harper* (Syd, 1971); *MJA*, 28 Oct 1939, 2 May 1964; Roy Soc for the Welfare of Mothers and Babies, Minutes, and Annual Reports (Syd); Margaret Harper papers (held by Mr I. R. L. Harper, Syd); information from Mr I. R. L. Harper, Syd, and Dr Grace Cuthbert-Browne, Waverton, Syd.   VICTORIA COWDEN

HARPER, NATHANIEL WHITE (1865-1954), mine-manager and investor, was born on 18 March 1865 at Tullynewy, Antrim, Ireland, son of John Harper, farmer, and his wife Margaret, née White. During his childhood he went to school for six months in the year and in the other half helped his father in the potato fields.

In 1883 Harper migrated to New Zealand where he worked in a gold-mine and gained his first experience of hydraulic sluicing in Otago. He moved in 1887 to Broken Hill, New South Wales, where he rose to mines foreman with the Broken Hill Proprietary Co., and in 1889 to Zeehan, Tasmania, where he managed his first mine but was also vice-president of the local miners' union. On 19 September 1891 at Naseby, New Zealand, he married Margaret Jane Thomas. Next year he went to Western Australia as manager of Fraser's mine at Southern Cross, moving in 1895 to Kanowna where he managed the White Feather Main Reef. He also became owner-manager of the Koh-I-Nor in 1898 and manager of the Golden Pile in 1903-10. An efficient manager, skilled in hydraulic problems, he was a fair employer. Although he failed in a bid to become first mayor of Kanowna in 1896, he succeeded next year and was also chairman of the local hospital board, justice of the peace, and acting coroner. In 1897 he stood for the Legislative Assembly seat of North-East Coolgardie as an advanced democrat but was beaten by F. C. B. Vosper [q.v.]. Harper could be cantankerous: in 1901 a newspaper referred to his reputation for being 'one of the solidest "stoushers" in Western Australia'.

By 1900 he was diversifying his interests. On the Swan River foreshore he built Perth's Esplanade Hotel, an elegant red-brick building noted for its interior panelling; for half a century it was Perth's best hotel. It was the centre of a big strike against the employment of Chinese waiters in 1921. He also bought a farm near Beverley and in 1910 became Liberal member of the Legislative Assembly for the district, defeating Sir Walter James [q.v.]; but although he succeeded in securing a branch railway for his electorate he was burnt in effigy by his constituents after delays in its construc-

tion and lost his seat in 1914. Next year he was in Siberia and Japan promoting English and Western Australian mining interests. Later he provided financial backing for W. J. Winterbottom, who had the local franchise for several makes of motor car, including Dodge, Chrysler and Austin; they founded the Winterbottom Motor Co. in 1927. It prospered, and Harper also became a director of Wentworth Motors and Harper Motors. At the time of his death at his home in West Perth on 3 January 1954 his estate was valued at £384 428. His major philanthropy had been the foundation in 1947, in conjunction with the State government, of the Nathaniel Harper Homes for mentally retarded children at Guildford and Bassendean; one of his sons was handicapped. Harper was buried in Karrakatta cemetery with Presbyterian forms.

His first wife had died in 1921. They had two sons who predeceased him and a daughter Ethel May, who became the mother of W. L. Grayden, a Western Australian cabinet minister (1974-78, 1980-83). On 5 February 1924, in Scots Church, Melbourne, Harper married Olive Estelle Story. By her he had a daughter and a son who survived him.

Harper's strongest claim to fame arose from his persistent belief that he was responsible for convincing Sir John Forrest [q.v.8] of the feasibility of the Coolgardie goldfields water pipeline scheme, which was constructed under C. Y. O'Connor [q.v.] between 1896 and 1903. From 1910 until his death he pressed his case with characteristic tenacity, in old age even commissioning the writing and production of a play setting out his account of events. It is unquestionable that when Forrest visited Kanowna on 24 November 1895 he was present at a dinner when Harper made a speech urging the pumping of water from the Avon River to the eastern goldfields, and later that night spent some time discussing Harper's ideas with him. At that date O'Connor was already collecting data in support of a long-distance pipeline, but he never claimed to have originated the scheme and there is no evidence that Forrest was then committed to supporting it. The debate centres around the extent to which he was convinced by the arguments of Harper, an expert on the water question, whom Forrest is known to have consulted on other occasions. The controversy preoccupied Harper's old age and has overshadowed his other achievements.

F. Alexander et al, *The origins of the eastern goldfields water scheme in Western Australia* (Perth, 1954); *West Aust Mining and Commercial Review*, Oct, Nov 1938; *T&CJ*, 29 Dec 1915; *West Australian*, 25, 27, 28 June 1921, 28 Oct 1936, 5 Jan 1954; family information.   ANN HODDINOTT

HARPER, ROBERT (1842-1919), businessman and politician, was born on 1 February 1842 in Glasgow, Scotland, son of Robert Harper, merchant, and his wife Elizabeth, née Calderwood, and elder brother of Andrew Harper [q.v.]. Educated at Glasgow Academy until 13, Robert was employed in Glasgow until he migrated to Melbourne with his family in August 1856. He worked for J. F. McKenzie & Co., roasting and grinding millers, and became a partner about 1863. In 1865 the partnership was dissolved and Harper established Robert Harper & Co., trading in tea, coffee and spices from the East Indies and later in oatmeal and flour.

The business prospered; the firm established a factory to process and package its goods and also large rice-dressing mills. By the mid-1870s Harper was a leading Melbourne merchant. His brother William became a partner and another brother John joined them about 1883. Branches were established in Sydney (1877), Adelaide (1882), Brisbane (1887) and later in the other colonies including New Zealand.

From the mid-1870s Harper diversified, investing in banking, land, sugar, coal and timber. President of the Victorian Chamber of Manufactures in 1877-78, he was regarded as one of the most astute businessmen of his day and, although he caught the speculative fever of the late 1880s, his business acumen and caution were such that his integrity and fortune remained intact in the collapses of the early 1890s. He was a long-standing director of the Kauri Timber Co. (chairman in 1890-94), of several insurance companies and of the Commercial Bank of Australia. He also owned a sheep-station, Dhurringhile, in Gippsland.

On 21 January 1868 at Chalmers' Church, East Melbourne, Harper married Jane Ballingall, youngest daughter of Rev. Dr Cairns [q.v.3]. His wife, credited with a keen sense of humour and a love of dancing, bore him seven children and became a prominent Melbourne philanthropist. At her death in 1924 she had been president of The Spinners for thirty-three years and of the Ministering Children's League for twenty-six; she had also held high office in the Young Women's Christian Association, the Free Kindergarten Union and the Ladies' Work Association.

Harper was a founder of the Toorak Presbyterian Church and its senior elder. His firmly held religious beliefs strongly influenced the manner of his business dealings and his political and social attitudes. He took a strong stand against the secularization of state schools; he opposed the Sunday opening of the National Gallery; in the early 1880s he took a prominent part in the schism in his Church over the liberal theological views of Dr Charles Strong [q.v.6]; and in 1883 he and others purchased the *Daily Telegraph* and the *Weekly Times* as avenues for their strict views on social issues.

Harper took no part in politics until 1878 when his alarm at the radical Berry [q.v.3] government and the events leading up to 'Black Wednesday' led him in February 1879 to contest a by-election for the Legislative Assembly seat of West Bourke where he had a country house at Mount Macedon and was a shire councillor. His opponent, Alfred Deakin [q.v.8], was successful by a narrow margin but after a heated dispute about irregularities at one polling booth Deakin resigned the seat and in a second contest in August Harper defeated him. Berry's controversial constitutional reform bill was subsequently defeated by one vote, with Harper voting against, after which parliament was dissolved. In the ensuing election in February 1880 Harper again defeated Deakin, but the verdict was reversed in an election next August. In his memoir of these four contests Deakin said of Harper that he was a man 'with means, some leisure, and good natural capacity... A man of keen intelligence, well-informed on political questions, of strong character, great persistency, marked resoluteness and untiring energy'.

Harper won the seat of East Bourke in 1882 and held it until 1889. He was re-elected in 1891, the year in which the first Labor member was elected to the assembly and the Progressive Political League of Victoria established. Harper was prominent among those Melbourne merchants who founded in July the National Association of Victoria with the object of unifying the non-Labor groups to resist the agent of 'class politics' and the party of 'anarchy'. The Labor threat, however, was short-lived and the association subsided to continue through the 1890s as a platform to rally the Conservatives against the Liberals. In 1894 Harper sat on the royal commissions on constitutional reform and state banking.

Harper was defeated in the election of September 1897 but in 1901 won, and held in three later elections, the seat of Mernda in the House of Representatives. He was now a Protectionist, and a follower of Deakin; otherwise his deeply conservative, inflexible outlook remained unchanged. R. A. Crouch [q.v.8] observed that a droop in his eye and an 'almighty style' gave him a supercilious air. In 1909-10 Harper was the successful defendant in a bitter lawsuit with Rev. J. B. Ronald who sued him for slander over a charge of improper language ('dirty talk', Crouch called it) in parliament.

Harper believed that men were not equal, that enterprise and industry should be rewarded with special privileges and that 'natural economic laws' should be allowed to operate without restriction. However his switch from the free-trade to the protectionist camp called forth the accusation that his main political principle was that of whatever ensured maximum profit. It was because of his attitudes, as much as his devotion to business, that although an able debater and a competent politician he never became a minister. Nevertheless he was a respected figure in the Victorian and Commonwealth parliaments and a power in his party.

Harper retired from parliament in 1913 and died at his home in South Yarra on 9 January 1919. Survived by his wife, one of his two daughters and four of his five sons, he was buried in Boroondara cemetery. His estate in Australia was valued for probate at £175 239 and left to his family.

A. Sutherland et al, *Victoria and its metropolis*, 2 (Melb, 1888); *Vic Law Reports*, 1909; *British A'sian*, 28 July 1910; *Industrial Aust and Mining Standard*, 16 Jan 1919; *Retailer of Qld*, 26 Mar 1962; *Table Talk*, 28 Aug 1891; *Punch* (Melb), 4 June 1908, 16 May 1912, 21 July 1921; *Argus*, 10 Jan 1919; *Australasian*, 26 July 1924; Crouch memoirs (LaTL).   PETER COOK

HARPER, ROBERT RAINY (1894-1941), soldier and business manager, was born on 18 February 1894 at Toorak, Melbourne, son of Rev. Andrew Harper [q.v.], professor of Hebrew and Old Testament studies at Ormond College, University of Melbourne, and his second wife Barbara Harriet, daughter of Dr Robert Rainy, principal of New College, Edinburgh. He was a half-brother of Margaret Hilda Harper and nephew of Robert Harper [qq.v.]. His father resigned his chair in 1902 to become principal of St Andrew's College, University of Sydney, and Robert attended Sydney Grammar School in 1907-12 and the university in 1913-14, studying arts. Awarded blues in Rugby football and rowing, he also reached the rank of sergeant in the Sydney University Scouts and in December 1914 joined the 26th Infantry Regiment (militia), Australian Military Forces, as a second lieutenant. In January 1915 he enlisted in the 18th Battalion, Australian Imperial Force, but on 10 May was commissioned in the 20th Battalion. He embarked for Egypt in charge of the unit's 1st Reinforcements in June, and served on Gallipoli from August until the evacuation. He was promoted lieutenant in November.

Harper sailed from Egypt for France in March with the 20th Battalion. Though wounded in action at Bois Grenier on 5 May,

he remained on duty and on 26 July, while participating in the taking of Pozières, was promoted captain. He led one of four parties in an attack aimed at capturing the Old German lines south of Pozières and, although the other parties were checked, he and his men took their objective and held it for an hour under heavy fire. Harper was wounded in the head and leg but continued to direct his troops until they ran out of grenades; his party then retreated across no man's land with Harper refusing to be removed until he had seen all his men to safety. He was evacuated to England late in August. For his leadership at Pozières he received the Distinguished Service Order, a decoration rarely awarded to a lieutenant; he also received the French Croix de Guerre and was mentioned in dispatches. He was invalided to Australia in December 1916.

Harper's A.I.F. appointment ended on 1 May 1917. By this time he had recovered sufficiently to join the staff at Liverpool camp near Sydney and trained reinforcements for the Western Front. He also commanded the Sydney University Company of A.I.F. Reinforcements. In 1919-21 he studied medicine at the university but did not complete his degree. He became a captain in the Sydney University Scouts in February 1921 but in 1922 was placed on the A.M.F. reserve of officers when he moved to Melbourne to work for Holden's [q.v.] Motor Body Builders; he was sales manager by 1924. That year, on 28 May, he married Sylvia Lance at St Stephen's Presbyterian Church, Sydney. He was manager of Holden's Melbourne branch from 1928 until his death from meningitis on 2 May 1941. He was cremated. His wife and son survived him.

C. E. W. Bean, *The A.I.F. in France*, 1916 (Syd, 1929); G. E. Hall and A. Cousins (eds), *Book of remembrance of the University of Sydney . . . 1914-1918* (Syd, 1939); St Andrew's College, Univ Syd, *The Andrew's book* (Syd, 1964); *London Gazette*, 26 Sept, 8 Dec 1916, 2 Jan 1917; *Argus*, 3 May 1941; information from Mr I. R. L. Harper, Syd.
           GUY VERNEY

HARRAP, GEORGE EDWARD (1856-1937), merchant and soldier, was born on 18 August 1856 at Westbury, Tasmania, only son of Alfred Harrap [q.v.4] and his wife Amelia, née Tobin. Educated at the Launceston Church Grammar School, he was in later life a member, and several times chairman, of its board of management. After leaving school he entered the service of the Commercial Bank of Tasmania and then joined the Bank of Australasia, gaining experience in Victoria and New South Wales before returning to Launceston in the late 1880s to his father's woolbroking, grain and produce business. In 1887 the business was divided into two sections with Harrap father and son managing the Cameron Street headquarters and J. A. Bain the shipping end at Queen's Wharf. On the death of his father in 1893 George became head of the firm, registered in 1900 as Alfred Harrap & Son. When the company was incorporated in 1924 Harrap and Bain both became directors and the business passed to the Bain family when Harrap died.

George also succeeded his father, in 1891, as vice-consul for Norway and Sweden and was subsequently appointed Knight (1st class) of the Order of St Olaf by the King of Norway. He was a justice of the peace from 1894. Again, like his father, he had a distinguished career in the Launceston Volunteer Artillery. A lieutenant in 1881, he received the Volunteer Officers' Decoration for long service in 1898 and retired in 1913 from command of No. 1 Tasmanian Battery, Australian Field Artillery, with the rank of lieut-colonel, having acted as honorary aide-de-camp to several governors. In 1915 he attempted to enlist but served instead as district censor for Tasmania until October 1916.

In 1900-37 Harrap was an executive-member and for varying periods chairman of the general committee of the Launceston Bank for Savings. An original subscriber in 1901 to the Tasmanian Permanent Executors and Trustees' Association, he was chairman in 1926-37. He was president of the Launceston Chamber of Commerce in 1909-10, of the National Agricultural and Pastoral Society in 1926 and several times of the Launceston Club. He supported the Victoria League, was a member of St John's Anglican Church and a foundation member of the Launceston Bowling Club.

Harrap loved the theatre, particularly light English opera, and had a meticulous regard for the proper use of the English language. He was president of the Launceston Players when it was formed and a member until he died, unmarried, on 21 June 1937 at Launceston. His three sisters received the bulk of his estate, valued for probate at £87 202, but friends, employees and benevolent institutions were remembered.

Cyclopedia of Tasmania, 1 (Hob, 1900); *Alfred Harrap and Son Pty Ltd* (priv print, Launc, 1957); Minutes, *and* records, Launc Bank for Savings, *and* Tasmanian Permanent Executors Ltd; personal recollections of R. J. Bain, Launceston, *and* R. A. Ferrall, Dilston, Tas.   R. A. FERRALL

HARRICKS, DUDLEY FRANCIS JOHN (1880-1960), engineer, was born on 6 February 1880 at Maryborough, Queensland, third son of John Hugh Harricks, surgeon, who had migrated from Liverpool, England, in 1874, and his Sydney-born wife Christmas Anne, née Vokes-Dudgeon. Educated at Maryborough Grammar School, Dudley was apprenticed to Walkers Ltd, engineers, in 1896. On completing his articles he joined the Colonial Sugar Refining Co. in Sydney. A Rugby Union enthusiast, he captained the Maryborough team and in his early days in Sydney was a part-time actor under the stage name of 'Leonard Dale'.

In 1905 Harricks was given charge of the drawing office and in 1918 became engineer-in-chief (until he retired in 1939) with responsibility for the wide range of mechanical, electrical and marine engineering in the company's mills in New South Wales, Queensland and Fiji, large workshops at Pyrmont, Sydney, and a fleet of ships. A staunch conservative in matters affecting the company, Harricks required apprentices to study outside working hours, but encouraged them by founding, and serving as president of, the Engineering Apprentices and Old Boys Club. For those who attained professional qualifications he obtained staff status in the company. He worked assiduously to raise the standing of engineers in the community.

A member of the Engineering Association of New South Wales from 1906, Harricks contributed papers to its meetings and acted as honorary secretary and editor of its *Minutes and Proceedings*. During World War I he and the association gave a lead to local manufacture of munitions by publishing information collected world wide. He also stressed the responsibility of engineers for the aesthetic qualities of their designs and for minimizing pollution. As president of the Engineering Association from 1916, Harricks was the driving force behind the amalgamation of the foundation societies to form the Institution of Engineers, Australia, in 1920. He could have been first president of the new body, but instead supported Professor W. H. Warren [q.v.6]. He was a foundation council-member until 1938, president in 1929 and was awarded its (Sir) Peter Nicol Russell [q.v.6] memorial medal in 1939.

In 1917 Harricks had advocated a 'Science House' to bring together Sydney's learned societies: when the government granted land he organized finance for the building, which was opened in 1931. He was a council-member of the Standards Association of Australia, a member of the government's Housing Improvement Advisory Committee and of the Institution of Mechanical Engineers, London. In his later years he enjoyed tennis and motoring.

At St James's Anglican Church, Melbourne, Harricks had married Mary Geraldine Smyth on 18 September 1907; they lived at Wollstonecraft, Sydney, and had a daughter and three sons, two of whom were employed by C.S.R. Predeceased by his wife, he died in hospital at Kirribilli on 8 March 1960 and was cremated with Christian Science forms. The Sydney division of the Institution of Engineers has honoured him with the annual Harricks address and in 1961 C.S.R. established the Harricks memorial medallion.

A. H. Corbett, *The Institution of Engineers, Australia* (Syd, 1973); Inst of Engineers, Aust, *J*, 1 (1929), 2 (1930), 32 (1960); Engineering Assn of NSW, *Minutes*, 30 (1914-15), 34 (1918-19) (copies held ML, and Inst of Engineers, Aust, Library (Canb)); Harricks papers (Colonial Sugar Refining Co. Lib, Syd).   ARTHUR CORBETT

HARRINGTON, WILLIAM FREDERICK (1840-1918), company manager, was born about 16 April 1840 at Kingland, Roscommon, Ireland, son of Thomas Harrington, farmer, and his wife Eleanor, née Cullinan. Educated at a private school, he was employed at 15 in the counting-house of a large firm of merchants in western Ireland. Arriving in Melbourne in September 1864 in the *Great Victoria*, he worked as an accountant with a Ballarat mining agency and in August 1865 became accountant and financial manager in the Union Foundry of John Walker & Co. When a branch of the firm opened in 1868 at Maryborough, Queensland, appeared shaky, Harrington was sent to inspect it in 1870. Impressed by the potential of Wide Bay in particular and Queensland in general, he urged that the branch be given more time to settle down.

The Maryborough foundry, established to make mining machinery for Gympie, now turned to sugar-milling plant. On a second visit in 1872 Harrington sought orders as far north as Mackay. In December he became the firm's fourth partner and in 1873 went to England for new tools and equipment to improve the capacity at Maryborough. On his return he arranged the sale of a half-share in the Ballarat business. The proceeds were used to expand at Maryborough and Harrington settled there. The remainder of the Ballarat business was sold in 1879 and the other partners also moved to Maryborough. In 1884 the business became a public company under the name John Walker & Co. Ltd with Harrington as chairman and managing director, which he remained until his death.

A centre of engineering in Queensland, the company kept diversifying its activities and eventually began ship-building. A. J. Goldsmith, an engineer with the Harbours and Rivers Department, was recruited in 1881 and numerous ships were built in the 1880s under his management. A locomotive-building section turned out its hundredth unit in 1909 and by 1912-13 averaged more than one a week. Meanwhile, the production of mining and sugar-milling equipment for Australia, New Zealand, Borneo and the Straits Settlements continued steadily. In 1912 the company began producing its own steel.

Harrington several times refused nomination for a seat in parliament. He was a member of the Maryborough Municipal Council in 1876-79, an active member and president of the chamber of commerce, and took part in such movements as the resuscitation of the School of Arts and the erection of new buildings for the Wide Bay Pastoral and Agricultural Society. The Albert State School, created principally for the benefit of company employees, owed much to him and he was both a founder and long-term trustee of the Maryborough Boys' and Girls' Grammar schools.

Harrington died at Maryborough on 8 March 1918 leaving two children of his marriage to Jemima Ross at Heidelberg, Victoria, on 11 April 1874. A grandson, Vice Admiral Sir Wilfred Hastings Harrington, was chief of the Australian Naval Staff in 1962-65.

Alcazar Press, *Queensland*, 1900 (Brisb, nd); A. J. Goldsmith, *Reminiscences of an old engineer* (Syd, 1926); R. S. Maynard, *Sugar, ships, locomotives* (Syd, 1946); *A'sian Hardware and Machinery*, 1 Apr 1918, p 86; Roy Soc Qld, *Procs*, 67 (1955); *Aust Railway Historical Soc Bulletin*, Oct 1968; *Brisbane Courier*, 28 July 1924; John Walker & Co., Annual Report and Balance Sheet, 1884-88 (Oxley Lib).   W. ROSS JOHNSTON

HARRIS, ALFRED (1870-1944), journalist, was born on 7 August 1870 in Melbourne, eldest son of Prussian-born parents Henry Harris (d. 1923), storekeeper and printer, and his first wife Johanna, née Levy. After his mother's death Alfred and his infant sister Amelia were taken in by a family related to Sir Isaac Isaacs's [q.v.] wife.

In 1881 Alfred, against his will, joined his father and worked in his store at Jerilderie, New South Wales, until, aged 14, he ran away. During the next decade Harris gained experience, largely in newspaper work, in different parts of Australia including Brisbane, where he founded and edited a Masonic journal, the *Keystone*. Moving to Sydney, he rejoined his father who had established a printery, Harris & Son, at 249 George Street. Alfred became editor of the Sydney *Freemason's Chronicle of Aus-*

tralasia, published and printed by Harris & Son until 1909, and helped to found the Country Press Association of New South Wales.

On 1 November 1895 Harris edited and printed the first issue of the *Hebrew Standard of Australasia*: it failed but was re-established on 23 July 1897; Harris remained editor until May 1908. On 28 October at the Great Synagogue, Sydney, he married Celia Esther Harris (no relation), a Hebrew schoolteacher from a prosperous Anglo-Jewish family. Since neither family approved of the match, Harris and his wife left Sydney for Yerranderie in the Burragorang valley where he became a storekeeper. In 1914, after a brief return to Sydney, they moved to Brisbane where he joined the staff of the *Brisbane Courier* and published the *Keystone*. In 1920 he went to Toogoolawah, Queensland; in 1921-24 he owned the *Brisbane Valley Advertiser* and a printery.

Returning to Sydney, in January 1925 Harris took over management of the printery at Harris & Son and, persuaded by Rabbi F. L. Cohen [q.v.8], resumed editorial control of the *Hebrew Standard*, now owned by his sister Amelia. Self-educated and an avid reader, Harris was more of a theist than an ultra-orthodox Jew. Throughout his life he was an altruist, helping those in need, but was not adept at business. He became dependent on the moral and financial support of the conservative Anglo-Jewish leadership emanating from the Great Synagogue and was influenced by Cohen, with whom he shared the belief that Jews owed their national allegiance to Australia alone, not to Zionism. His anti-Zionist policies were supported by Isaacs, a close friend. Harris's conviction that Zionism was a negative force brought him into increasing conflict with some fellow Jews, especially refugees from Nazism. He was unable to attract their support, and the *Standard* declined towards the end of his life.

During World War II, Harris continued to publish the *Standard*, almost single-handed. He died from coronary occlusion on 25 January 1944 at his residence at Darling Point and was buried in Rookwood cemetery. He was survived by his wife, and by two sons and a daughter, all of whom became medical practitioners.

S. D. Rutland, *Seventy-five years; the history of a Jewish newspaper* (Syd, 1970); Aust Jewish Hist Soc, *J*, 2 (July 1944), pt 1, p 52; *Hebrew Standard of A'sia*, 1 Nov, 6 Dec 1895, 23 July 1897, 23 Jan, 27 Feb 1925, 22 Sept 1938, 27 Jan, 3 Feb 1944, 4 July 1952; S. D. Rutland, The Jewish community in New South Wales, 1914-1939 (M.A. Hons thesis, Univ Syd, 1978); information from Drs L. L. Harris, Rose Bay, and I. J. Segal, Darling Point, Syd.

SUZANNE D. RUTLAND

HARRIS, SIR JOHN RICHARDS (1868-1946), medical practitioner, vigneron and politician, was born on 24 January 1868 at Chiltern, Victoria, second son of Cornish parents Thomas Henry Harris, miner, and his wife Mary Richards, née Hollow. He was educated at Rutherglen State School, Grenville College, Ballarat, the Ballarat School of Mines, and the University of Melbourne, where he completed medicine with outstanding results (M.B., 1890; B.S., 1891; M.D., 1902). He returned in 1892 to Rutherglen where he established a successful general practice and, later, a private midwifery hospital. On 16 December 1896 with Presbyterian forms he married Jessie Lily Prentice, daughter of a local vigneron. In 1909 he bought a farming, grazing and vine-growing property east of Rutherglen.

Believing his eldest son too frail for active service, Harris represented the family in the Empire's cause when he enlisted in the Australian Army Medical Corps on 9 August 1917. On arrival at Cairo on 20 October he served as medical officer of No.1 (initially No.67) Squadron, Australian Flying Corps. He became ill in late 1918 and was repatriated, arriving in Melbourne in January 1919. He subsequently resumed practice at Rutherglen.

On 2 September 1920 Harris was elected to the Legislative Council for North-Eastern Province. One of few representatives in the council of the Victorian Farmers' Union (later the Country Party), he rose rapidly to prominence and influence, becoming an honorary minister in the Allan [q.v.7]–Peacock [q.v.] ministry from July 1925 to May 1927. He was unofficial leader of the House from November 1928 to April 1935, apart from a brief period in May 1932, when he resigned in protest at his failure to gain selection in the Argyle [q.v.7] ministry and then accepted the unanimous request of a meeting of members to resume the office. While unofficial leader he asserted that he was independent of party loyalties; in 1934 he refused to take the pledge required by the Country Party's new constitution. However, he took the pledge before he was appointed minister of public instruction and public health under (Sir) Albert Dunstan [q.v.8] and government leader of the House from April 1935 to January 1942. He was chairman of the State Emergency Council for Civil Defence from October 1939 to January 1942, and a member of the Council of Agricultural Education in 1925-45. In May 1937 he was knighted. Harris was returned unopposed from 1928 to 1946, when he was defeated by another Country Party candidate.

Diligence and a driving ambition for advancement, influence and honours, together with what he called 'old-fashioned conservatism', characterized Harris's political career. He astounded the council with his authoritative addresses on a range of subjects and is said to have shown 'phenomenal' ability in the management of business.

As minister of public health his most valuable achievements were his sponsorship of the Anti-Cancer Council (1936) and, following a visit to inner-Melbourne slums in 1935, his strong support for the health amendment bill of 1937. As minister of public instruction he took a special interest in technical and agricultural education, the work of the curriculum and research officer (1938) and the Australian Council of Education (1936). Probably his most constructive decision was the appointment of a departmental advisory committee in 1939. On balance, however, he must be held responsible for his government's failure to repair the damage inflicted on the state system of education by the drastic economies of the Depression budgets and to adopt policies to extend educational opportunities.

Dr Harris was a competent medical practitioner who served his district conscientiously. He was active in local affairs as a member of the Australian Natives' Association, district medical officer and also as a prominent Freemason. As a vigneron he made the sweet red and white fortified wine of the district and had unorthodox views on the propriety of adding as a preservative salicylic acid, forbidden by the Wine Adulteration Act of 1900. In the 1920s he experimented with a dry sherry style made from Palomino grapes, and his 'Dr John' sherry, made in the Spanish manner, won many show awards.

In his prime Harris was a large man, with broad face, high forehead, dark eyebrows and small, quick eyes. He was irascible, brusque and domineering, except with his wife and friends who agreed that his bark was worse than his bite. Predeceased by his wife in 1937 and survived by his three sons, Sir John died on 16 September 1946 and was buried in Carlyle cemetery, Rutherglen. His estate was sworn for probate at £16 327.

P. Hasluck, *The government and the people, 1939-1945*, 2 (Canb, 1970); Education Dept (Vic), *Vision and realisation*, L. J. Blake ed (Melb, 1973); G. C. Bishop, *Australian winemaking, the Roseworthy influence* (Adel, 1980); *PD* (LC Vic), 1945-47, p 224, 2202; *Age*, 11 May 1937, 17 June, 17 Sept 1946; *Table Talk*, 27 May 1937; *Argus*, 17 Sept 1946; *Herald* (Melb), 15 Nov, 4, 9 Dec 1939, 17 June 1946; *Weekly Times* (Melb), 18 Sept 1946; J. B. Paul, The premiership of Sir Albert Dunstan (M.A. thesis, Univ Melb, 1961); Harris letters and diary, Army Medical Corps, Aug 1917-Dec 1918 (held by Mrs W. Salway, Elsternwick, Vic); Harris papers (LaTL); family information.   LLOYD EVANS

HARRIS, LAWRENCE HERSCHEL LEVI (1871-1920), radiologist, was born on 8 December 1871 at Kensington, London, son of Bernard Levi, merchant, and his wife Elizabeth, née Harris. Brought to Australia as an infant, he was educated at Sydney Grammar School, and in 1890 enrolled in arts at the University of Sydney. From 1891, when he transferred to medicine, he used Harris as his surname. He graduated M.B., Ch.M., in 1896 and was resident medical officer in 1896-97 and senior resident in 1897-1900 at Sydney Hospital.

A keen photographer, Harris became interested in X-rays in the second half of 1896, one year after Röntgen's discovery, and founded an X-ray unit at Sydney Hospital. In 1900 he became honorary skiagrapher (later radiographer) there and was also assistant surgeon for a time. He also became honorary radiographer for the Royal Alexandra Hospital for Children in 1902 and the Royal Prince Alfred Hospital in 1911, and was connected with other institutions.

Herschel Harris became a leading figure in radiology in New South Wales. He won international repute, maintained worldwide contacts with experts, and published some twenty-eight articles on radiology. He was one of the first to use opaque meal for the examination of gastric and intestinal diseases and initiated the use of X-rays to treat keloid scars. He sought more efficient units in hospitals, advocating specific training of sisters.

In England in 1914 for the annual meeting of the British Medical Association, Harris volunteered soon after the outbreak of World War I. As a captain in the Royal Army Medical Corps he joined the Australian Voluntary Hospital under Lieut-Colonel W. Eames [q.v.8], as radiologist. At Wimereux, France, he set up his X-ray equipment within seven hours of landing. Promoted major in May 1915, he was transferred to the 3rd Australian General Hospital at Lemnos, where he was hindered by the difficult climate and surroundings and by dermatitis of the hands (pioneer radiologists were unaware of the danger of unshielded X-rays). After the evacuation of Gallipoli he was invalided to England, before returning to Australia through the United States of America where he was made life member of the American Roentgen Ray Society.

Kindly, generous and popular, Harris was ready to share his knowledge and experience. He was handsome with dark wavy hair and a handle-bar moustache, and known for his consideration for nurses: during the war, he had devoted part of his military pay to assist them and at Lemnos spent much of his off-duty time trying to find extra rations for them.

On 13 September 1920 Harris died at his home at Macquarie Street, Sydney, from encephalitis following influenza and was buried with military honours in the Jewish section of Rookwood cemetery. A bachelor, he was survived by two sisters; Dr S. Harry Harris [q.v.] was a cousin. His estate was valued for probate at £71 128. Harris had contributed significantly to the development of radiology. His name, with that of F. J. Clendinnen [q.v.8] of Melbourne, is honoured in the Centre Antoine Béclère in Paris.

W. Watson & Sons Ltd, *Salute to the X-ray pioneers of Australia* (Syd, 1946); P. L. Hipsley, *The early history of the Royal Alexandra Hospital for Children 1880-1905* (Syd, 1952); D. G. Hamilton, *Hand in hand* (Syd, 1979); Syd Hospital, *Annual Report*, 1896-1915; *MJA*, Sept 1920; *SMH*, 14 Sept 1920; *Hebrew Standard of A'sia*, 17 Sept 1920.

SUZANNE D. RUTLAND

HARRIS, SIR MATTHEW (1841-1917), alderman, was born on 18 September 1841 at Magherafelt, Londonderry, Ireland, third son of John Harris (d. 1846), merchant, and his wife Nancy, née McKee. On inheriting part of his great-uncle John Harris's [q.v.1] estate, his father migrated to New South Wales with his family, including Matthew and John [q.v.4], and reached Sydney probably in August 1844. Matthew was educated at the Normal Institution, Sydney Grammar School and the University of Sydney (B.A., 1863). On 4 August 1868 in Sydney he married Frances Lane (d. 1915) with Free Church of England rites.

On reaching the age of 21 Harris had inherited considerable property including some twenty acres (8 ha) in the Sydney suburb of Ultimo. Like his three brothers and sister, he built a big house, Warrane, at Crown Road, and surrounded it with terraces, and spent his time managing his real estate.

In 1883-1900 Harris represented Denison Ward on the Sydney Municipal Council. A free trader and staunch supporter of (Sir) George Reid [q.v.], he represented Sydney-Denison in the Legislative Assembly in 1894-1901. In the House he rarely spoke, but in 1896 carried the Municipal Council of Sydney Electric Lighting Act. He was mayor of Sydney in 1898, 1899 and 1900 but faced with a large deficit—including that on the Queen Victoria Building (which he opened in July 1898)—and allegations that the council was inefficient, he was unable to introduce reforms (or electric lighting) and complained that the council lacked the power to sweep away slums. In mid-1899 he put forward a unitary plan for a 'Greater Sydney' in which a metropolitan council would replace existing authorities and be given the power to control water supply, sewerage, abattoirs, traffic, building regulation, parks, libraries, art galleries and fire prevention. While mayor he became a friend of the governor Earl Beauchamp [q.v.7], helped to organize the Commonwealth inaugural celebrations and welcomed the governor-general Lord Hopetoun [q.v.].

A director from 1896, Harris was president of Sydney Hospital in 1912-17, and regularly attended its weekly house committee meetings. He was also a vice-president of the Royal Agricultural Society of New South Wales and president of the Wentworth Park trust and of the Australasian Pioneers' Club (1912). Knighted in 1899, he had bought Etham, Darling Point, in 1900. He built up a fine library with many rare Australiana books and was a notable collector of *objets d'art*, particularly Japanese. Bearded and handsome, if somewhat solidly built, he was apt to 'roar like a lion' at his family.

On 8 June 1917 Harris died in hospital at Potts Point and was buried in the family vault at Rookwood cemetery with Presbyterian forms. He was survived by six sons (two of whom served with the British Army in World War I) and by two daughters; the elder, Mary, married Dr C. Carty Salmon [q.v.], the younger, estranged from her father, challenged his will in the Supreme Court. His estate was valued for probate at £32 792—he had given some £250 000 to his children in 1913.

His portrait, painted posthumously by Herbert Beecroft, is in Sydney Town Hall.

F. A. Larcombe, *The stabilization of local government in New South Wales* (Syd, 1976), and *The advancement of local government in New South Wales 1906 to the present* (Syd, 1978); John Harris, 'Governor's errors, silly, but colossal', *Canberra Historical Journal*, Mar 1981; *Daily Telegraph* (Syd), 14 July 1894; *Sydney Mail*, 25 Dec 1897; *T&CJ*, 10 June 1899, 13 June 1917; *SMH*, 9 June 1917, 5 July 1918, 8 Oct 1919, 18 Mar 1937; Sir Matthew Harris papers (ML); information from John Harris, Syd.

MARTHA RUTLEDGE

HARRIS, SAMUEL HENRY (1881-1936), urological surgeon, was born on 22 August 1881 in Sydney, second son of Sydney-born parents Henry Harris, custom-house agent, and his wife Hannah, née Solomon. Always known as Harry, he was educated at Sydney Grammar School, where he was school captain in 1900, and at the University of Sydney (M.B., Ch.M., 1906), where he won a blue for cricket. He was resident medical officer at Sydney Hospital in 1906-07.

Starting general practice at Enmore, Harris was early attracted to gynaecology and was appointed to the South Sydney Women's Hospital. In 1914 his thesis 'Ureteral Catheterisation in Obstetrics' gained him his M.D. The cystoscopic and radiographic studies required for this work made him realize the challenge of the newly emerging speciality of urology. That year he was appointed honorary urologist to the Lewisham Hospital where he carried out almost all his surgery; he was also consultant urologist to the Marrickville Cottage Hospital. At the Scots Church, Sydney, he married New Zealander Isabel Alison Aitken on 15 April 1920; they lived at Double Bay.

When Harris began his work, suprapubic prostatectomy was hazardous with high mortality, except in the hands of a few experts. By 1922 his first major paper on the operation reported that he had used the accepted technique on 146 patients, with a mortality rate of 3.4 per cent. Modifying this method in 1927 he recorded 433 operations with a rate of 3.6 per cent, reduced to 2.8 per cent over the last 245 patients. His third technique was the 'Harris prostatectomy' on which his fame rests. He devised an operation of precision which, if his prerequisites of meticulous haemostasis by suture, reformation of the posterior wall of the urethra and obliteration of the prostatic cavity were achieved, would allow primary bladder closure. He designed a lighted bladder retractor and other instruments for this purpose. In 1934 his mortality rate was 2.7 per cent in 413 such operations.

These unparalleled successes aroused little interest, especially abroad, and probably were simply not believed. Harris visited Britain in 1935 to demonstrate the advantages of his technique, and had to overcome 'a definitely hostile school of opinion' which, after his demonstrations, was followed by a wave of enthusiasm. Most surgeons, however, found that they could not reproduce his success. The operation continued to be practised in Sydney, Glasgow, Auckland and Vienna.

It is apparent that Harris's technique was not an important factor in his results. The basis of his success lay primarily in his surgical skill. First gaining his patients' confidence, he closely supervised their postoperative recovery, under the care of the dedicated and experienced Nursing Sisters of the Little Company of Mary. His surgery was made easier by his expert team. Harris published many papers on various aspects of urology, usually displaying originality and his inventive mind. He was a foundation fellow of the College of Surgeons of Australasia (later Royal Australasian College of Surgeons), and a member of the Inter-

national Society of Urology and the editorial committees of the *British Journal of Surgery* and the *Australian and New Zealand Journal of Surgery*. In 1936 he was involved in the transformation of the Sydney Urological Association into the Urological Society of Australasia.

Harris had returned from Britain a sick man, and he performed only a few more operations before he died of pneumonia on Christmas Day 1936 in Lewisham Hospital; he was cremated. He was survived by his wife and son, to whom he left his estate, valued for probate at £29 588. In 1968 the Urological Society of Australasia established the Harry Harris memorial oration.

Had Harris lived and continued to demonstrate that suprapubic prostatectomy could be a relatively safe operation, many lives would have been saved. With the advent of antibiotics, blood transfusion and advances in anaesthesia in the post-war years, Harris's advanced technique lost much of its importance.

L. J. T. Murphy, 'Harry Harris and his contribution to suprapubic prostatectomy', in H. Attwood and G. Kenny (eds), *Festschrift for Kenneth Fitzpatrick Russell* (Melb, 1978); *British Medical J*, 1 (1937), p 304; *Lancet*, 1 (1937), p 412; *MJA*, 1 (1937), p 522; *Aust Catholic Hist Soc J*, 4 (1973), pt 2, p 1; *SMH*, 28 Dec 1936; information from Sr M. Jeanne Hyland, LCM, Lewisham Hospital, and Dr G. H. Harris, Syd.   LEONARD J. T. MURPHY

HARRIS, VIDA; *see* JONES, Nina Eva Vida

HARRIS, WILLIAM (1867-1931), civil rights leader, was born in 1867 in Western Australia, one of seven children of convict William Harris (alias William Paulet), a tramper from Wales, and his wife Madelaine whose mother was Aboriginal. He was a private pupil at the Swan Native and Half-Caste Mission, Perth. Harris mined at Paynes Find and Yalgoo, and farmed in the Morawa district for over forty years. He fought the issue of Aboriginal civil rights for some twenty-two years in the face of the Aborigines Act, 1905, which restricted civil liberties of those classified on the basis of proven or assumed, total or partial, Aboriginal descent.

In 1906 Harris argued with the premier for government assistance to Aboriginals on the north-eastern goldfields. He claimed that the Aboriginals' economic dependency resulted from the denudation of native game by miners, and demanded provision of food and medicine from monies designated for Aboriginal use under the Federal Constitution.

In 1913 in a local newspaper he again denounced depressed conditions. He particularly objected to an incident near Paynes Find in which police, apparently unprovoked, had shot some Aboriginals' dogs which were essential for hunting kangaroos, whose skins were a major source of income. During the subsequent debate Harris denounced the 1905 Act in the *Sunday Times* on 6 April.

The Act's provisions were being extended to the South-West, and affected people of mixed descent not previously regarded as having Aboriginal affiliations, because of their education and lifestyle. Harris described 'half-castes and others brought up and educated on the same lines as whites, who pay taxes, and whose ideals of life are the same as those of a white man. Yet by law these people are denied the suffrage, and further are not allowed to enter a public house'. Without the right to enter a hotel Aboriginals were virtually excluded from a district's social life and the opportunity for contacts leading to employment. But their civil liberties were increasingly eroded by the Act and its 1911 amendment, producing many disgruntled disadvantaged people. This culminated in November 1926 in Harris's formation of an Aboriginals' union. It was the work of one man and a few local followers, but it was intended to unite similar groups throughout the South-West. The union's aims included: voting rights for southern Aboriginals, a uniform law for Aboriginals and whites, and 'justice and fair play'.

Next year, on 18 March, central Perth was prohibited to Aboriginals. This stirred Harris's nephew Norman Cleaver Harris to employ a lawyer. On 9 March 1928 William Harris led a representative deputation to the premier of those who had suffered under the Act. Edward Jacobs and Arthur Kickett, successful farmers, had long fought the Education Department for the right to send their children to state schools. At the meeting Harris concentrated on the demoralizing Government Native Settlement at Moore River where families were split and people of varying cultural backgrounds grouped under police control. Despite the recognition by Premier Collier [q.v.8] of 'a great obligation to do justice to the Aboriginal, because [the white man] had deprived him of his country', legislative change did not occur until after World War II.

Harris died, unmarried, on 13 July 1931 and was buried in the Aboriginal cemetery at Utacarra, Geraldton. He had remained undaunted by the task of confronting public dignitaries and seeking to redress injustice. His tenacity and strength were remarkable.

P. Biskup, *Not slaves, not citizens* (Brisb, 1973); *West Australian*, 9 Feb 1906, 14 Mar 1913, 10 Mar 1928; *Sunday Times* (Perth), 6 Apr 1913, 26 Nov 1927, 11 Mar 1928; *Mirror* (Perth), 10 Mar 1928; P. Biskup, Native administration and welfare in Western Australia, 1897-1954 (M.A. thesis, Univ W.A., 1965); Aborigines Dept, Files AD 955/1899 and AD 94/1928 *and* Native Union Newsletter, 1970 *and* Education Dept, File 4259/14/1915 (Battye Lib); South West Aboriginal Studies oral history collection (Western Australian College).

LOIS TILBROOK

HARRISON, AMY ELEANOR; *see* MACK

HARRISON, ERIC (1886-1945), aviator and regular air force officer, was born on 10 August 1886 at Clinkers Hill, near Castlemaine, Victoria, fourth son of Victorian-born Joseph Wilkinson Harrison, printer and stationer, and his wife Ann Eliza, née Ingamels, from Yorkshire, England. Educated at Castlemaine Grammar School, he became a motor mechanic. After witnessing a flight by a representative of the Bristol Aircraft Co., he left for England in March 1911 to learn to fly. Accompanying him were three friends who were also to make their mark in Australian aviation: H. A. Kauper, H. G. Hawker [qq.v.] and H. Busteed. Harrison trained on the Bristol Boxkite at the company's flying school at Salisbury Plain and in August qualified as a pilot after, he later said, some thirty minutes tuition; he was awarded the Royal Aero Club's pilot certificate no. 131 on the world register. He was employed by Bristol as a flying instructor, taught for them at the Spanish Army School and then in Italy, and was chief instructor at the Bristol flying school at Halberstadt, Germany, where he also acted as examiner of German military pilots.

In 1912 the Australian government advertised in the British press for two 'mechanists and aviators'. H. A. Petre [q.v.], who was at that time employed by the British Deperdussin School, and Harrison were appointed. On 16 December he was made an honorary lieutenant on the Aviation Instructional Staff, Australian Military Forces, and after overseeing the construction of the training aircraft purchased by the government, joined Petre at the newly formed flying instructional centre at Point Cook, Victoria, in January 1914; the two were to establish the Central Flying School there and on 1 March

Harrison made the first flight from Point Cook in a Bristol Box-kite. On 29 June, at St Mary's Catholic Church, West Melbourne, he married Kathleen, daughter of George Michael Prendergast [q.v.].

After the outbreak of war he was commissioned lieutenant on the permanent staff, A.M.F., and by 17 August was training Australia's first military pilots who comprised the half-flight sent to Mesopotamia under Petre's command in 1915. In September 1914 Harrison was placed in charge of the flying unit sent to German New Guinea with the Australian Naval and Military Expeditionary Force but enemy resistance was slight and the aircraft were not uncrated. On returning to Australia he remained at Point Cook and was responsible for training the first three Australian squadrons to be sent overseas. In 1916 he pioneered the building of aircraft engines in Australia and was promoted temporary major in June 1917 and officer-in-charge, Central Flying School; he was appointed major in the Australian Imperial Force on 9 September 1918. When Point Cook was closed at the end of the war he was sent to the United Kingdom on attachment to the Aeronautical Inspection Directorate. He was transferred to the Royal Australian Air Force on its formation in 1921 and, with the rank of squadron leader, was its liaison officer with the Air Ministry in London until 1925.

In 1927 Harrison returned to Australia as assistant director, technical services, R.A.A.F., and in May became a foundation member of the Air Accident Investigation Committee. He was also appointed director of aeronautical inspection and on 1 July 1928 was promoted wing commander. He travelled extensively in Australia probing into aircraft crashes and inspecting air force equipment. On 1 January 1935 he was promoted group captain and in 1937 visited the United Kingdom to study air accident investigating procedures and aircraft production methods. He was retired from the R.A.A.F. on 12 March 1938 but retained his appointment as director of aeronautical inspection in a civilian capacity. During World War II the development of the local aircraft industry led to an expansion of his highly technical work and by 1945 he was directing a staff of over 1200.

Survived by his wife and daughter, Harrison died on 5 September 1945 from hypertensive cerebro-vascular disease at his home in Brighton, Melbourne, and was cremated. He has been called the 'Father of the R.A.A.F.', a title which he should share with Petre. A Deperdussin monoplane which was part of the original equipment at Point Cook and which Harrison helped to erect is on display at the Australian War Memorial.

M. Hawker, *H. G. Hawker, airman* (Lond, 1922); F. M. Cutlack, *The Australian Flying Corps . . . 1914-1918* (Syd, 1923); Dept of Air, *The golden years; the Royal Australian Air Force 1921-71* (Canb, 1971); R. Williams, *These are facts* (Canb, 1977); *Aircraft* (Melb), Oct 1945; *Punch* (Melb), 9 July 1914; *SMH*, 10 Jan, 17 May 1927, 7 Sept 1945; *Herald* (Melb), 23 Feb 1927, 9, 13 Jan, 17 July 1936, 24 Sept, 4 Oct 1937; *Argus*, 7 Sept 1945.

JOHN McCARTHY

HARRISON, ERIC FAIRWEATHER (1880-1948), soldier and politician, was born on 16 April 1880, at Stanmore, Sydney, son of English-born James Start Harrison, accountant, and his Australian wife Jane Ann, née Crane. He was educated at Sydney Church of England Grammar School (Shore) and Bedford Grammar School, England. In 1898 he entered Trinity College, Cambridge (B.A., 1901; M.A., 1902); he rowed in a Trinity crew which won the Thames Cup at Henley Royal Regatta.

Harrison returned to Australia and in 1903 was appointed second lieutenant in the militia garrison artillery in New South Wales. On 1 April 1904 he was commissioned lieutenant in the Royal Australian Artillery, Australian Military (permanent) Forces, and in 1906 was sent to Thursday Island and in 1908 to Western Australia. In January 1910 he became the first Australian to attend the Staff College at Quetta, India, and was promoted captain in March 1911. He then served on the general staff at Kohat for three months and on the headquarters staff until December 1912. He was appointed to the district staff in Victoria in January 1913 and was promoted major in May 1914.

As the duty staff officer at Army Headquarters on the outbreak of war Harrison gave the order to the fortress commander at Port Phillip Heads to fire across the bows of the German steamer *Pfalz* and prevent its escape. Shortly afterwards he was appointed director of military training at Army Headquarters, then in October 1915 director of military art at the Royal Military College, Duntroon, with temporary rank of lieut-colonel. When, in March 1916, a school was established there to train junior officers for the Australian Imperial Force he also became chief instructor. He ended his term at Duntroon in October 1917 and next month joined the A.I.F. as a major and served in France with 1st Division Headquarters during operations at Hazebrouck, Strazeele, Flêtre and on the Somme. In September 1918 he joined the staff of the 3rd Division and took part in operations against the Hindenburg line. He was made brevet lieut-colonel in January 1919 and mentioned in dispatches in March.

After the war Harrison served as a staff officer in Tasmania for nine months in 1919-20 and was acting commandant for four months. Further appointments followed on the district staff in Victoria and at Army Headquarters. He married Roma Wingfield Zilla Clarke at St John's Anglican Church, Toorak, on 9 November 1920. In 1925 and from 1927 he was director of military operations and intelligence until appointed commandant of the R.M.C. in January 1929; in July he was promoted colonel and temporary brigadier. He considered the move of the college to Sydney in 1930, as an economy measure, a severe blow to the 'Duntroon spirit'. He was transferred to Army Headquarters in January 1931, placed on the un-attached list in March, and then retired to Clondrisse, his farming property on the Mornington Peninsula, Victoria. At the 1931 Federal elections he won Bendigo as United Australia Party candidate and in parliament spoke frequently on defence issues and matters affecting rural industry; he took a strongly anti-communist stance. Re-elected in 1934, in 1937 he unsuccessfully sought party endorsement for the new seat of Deakin.

In 1936 Harrison had been a government delegate to the International Labour Conference in Geneva and in 1937-43 was president of the Australian Council of Employers' Federations. As chairman of the Victorian branch of the Australian Defence League he was involved in the 1938 campaign to stimulate voluntary recruitment for the Citizen Military Forces. In World War II he was called from the reserve of officers and again appointed commandant of the R.M.C. on 1 August 1940 as an honorary brigadier; was also responsible for a school for trainees seeking A.I.F. commissions. One of the Duntroon cadets named him 'Banana Body': it 'may have been irreverent but it was apt; in profile Brigadier Harrison, an imposing figure, was not fat but noticeably convex'. He retired from the R.M.C. on 15 January 1942. In 1944 he became president of the Victorian Employers' Federation and represented employers as a member of the Discharged Servicemen's Employment Board. He was still holding these posts when he died in Melbourne on 15 April 1948; he was cremated with Anglican rites.

Harrison was survived by his wife (d. 1974), a son and a daughter. His son Alastair Brian, a captain in the 2nd A.I.F., in 1946 inherited a family estate in England and was Conservative member for Maldon (Essex) in the House of Commons in 1955-74.

Who's who in the world of women (Melb, 1930, 1934); J. A. Venn, Alumni Cantabrigiensis, Pt II, Vol II (Cambridge, 1947); J. E. Lee, Duntroon (Canb, 1952); G. D. Solomon, A poor sort of memory (Canb, 1978); Roy Military College, Duntroon, Dec 1950; Roy Military College, Duntroon, Reports 1915-17, 1930, 1940, 1941; SMH, 19 Apr 1880, Argus, 1, 17, 29 Dec 1931, 24 Aug, 26 Sept 1934, 3 July, 12 Aug 1937, 30 Nov 1938, 16, 17 Apr 1948, Evening News (Lond), 12 Nov 1938; The Times, 16 Apr 1948; Bulletin, 21 Apr 1948; E. F. Harrison file, War Records Section (AWM); information from Mr A. B. C. Harrison, Kojonup, WA.

C. D. COULTHARD-CLARK

HARRISON, SIR JOHN (1866-1944), building contractor, was born on 1 July 1866 at Shildon, Durham, England, son of John Christopher Harrison, mason, and his wife Jane, née March. He was educated at the Shildon Church of England National School, and privately at Bishop Auckland. Aged 16 he was apprenticed to Thomas Richardson & Sons, engineers, where he remained until he sailed for Australia with his parents in the Liguria, arriving in Sydney on 30 June 1885. The firm of John C. Harrison & Son, master builders, was soon established and constructed several large buildings in Sydney.

Harrison's business interests took second place to community works from the outbreak of World War I in 1914. He organized transport and outings for disabled soldiers and his sympathy for the problems of returned servicemen led him to support a proposal by the Voluntary Workers' Association of New South Wales to establish the Matraville Garden Village for disabled soldiers and the widows of soldiers. After he became chairman of the board of control Harrison's leadership, enthusiasm and professional building skills helped to transform seventy-five acres of sandy coastal country eight miles from Sydney into a model suburb. He personally supervised both the paid and voluntary workers, and obtained donations of £27 000 for the scheme. The premier John Storey [q.v.] made labour available for the construction of roads and by 1920 the project was completed—it was a great personal triumph for Harrison. He was a member of the board of control of the Matraville Garden Village in 1917-30, and also on the Subsidiary Disposals Board, War Service Homes, in 1921-23. He was appointed K.B.E. in 1923.

A member of the Federal Capital Commission in 1924-29, Harrison was directly involved with the planning of Canberra after the departure from Walter Burley Griffin's [q.v.] original plan. Parliament House, the Commonwealth offices, the Hotel Canberra, Telopea Park High School, the arcaded shopping blocks at Civic, the prime minister's lodge and the remodelling of Government House, Yarralumla, were all either begun or completed during his term on the commission.

A man of considerable height and bulk, Harrison was well liked by his colleagues, although he displayed an abundance of nervous energy which some found exhausting. Keenly interested in sport, he had been president of the Ashfield Bowling Club, Sydney, and a state selector; he was also first patron of the Canberra Bowling Club. His fondness for cigars, bridge and billiards was well known, as were such idiosyncrasies as his determination to have wax matches banned in Canberra because he considered them dangerous.

At Armadale, Melbourne, Harrison had married with Wesleyan forms Edith Avice Moran on 20 September 1899. He was, however, a supporter of the Church of England throughout his life. He died at his home, Chandos Street, Ashfield, on 22 June 1944 and was cremated. A son and a daughter survived him. His estate was valued for probate at £89 321 in two States; he left £2000 (stg) to found a scholarship at his old school at Shildon.

Canberra Community News, July 1926, Apr 1927; *Aust National Review*, Dec-Jan 1923; *SMH*, 1, 2 Jan, 14 Mar 1923, 18 Oct 1924, 4 Jan 1929, 23 June 1944; *Canb Times*, 29 Jan 1966; information from Mr J. I. Harrison, Syd.

ELAINE LAWSON

HARRISON, LAUNCELOT (1880-1928), zoologist, was born on 13 July 1880 at Wellington, New South Wales, son of Thomas Harrison, medical practitioner, and his wife Elizabeth Maria, née Round. He was educated at The King's School, Parramatta, where for two years he was head of the school and Broughton [q.v.1] scholar. He matriculated in 1900 and joined the Citizens' Life Assurance Co. A champion schoolboy athlete, he represented New South Wales in Rugby football against Queensland and New Zealand in 1901. At North Sydney on 29 February 1908, with Methodist forms, he married Amy Eleanor Mack [q.v.]; they had no children.

A keen amateur naturalist from boyhood, Harrison became prominent in the Wild Life Preservation Society of Australia and the Naturalists' Society of New South Wales. In 1911 he went up to the University of Sydney where he was a distinguished prizeman and graduated B.Sc. with first-class honours and the University medal in zoology in 1914. In 1913-14 he was junior demonstrator in zoology and botany and in 1914 won the John Coutts scholarship and an Exhibition of

1851 scholarship on which he went to Emmanuel College, Cambridge, England (B.A. (Research), 1916). He was president of the Cambridge Natural History Society and a vice-president of the Cambridge Union Society.

After about fifteen months postgraduate work and after having previously been rejected for military service, Harrison was appointed advisory entomologist to the British Expeditionary Force in Mesopotamia with the rank of lieutenant. His preventive work on insect-carried diseases saved many lives, although he himself contracted both typhus and malaria. He was promoted captain on the special reserve list of officers.

Appointed lecturer and demonstrator in zoology at the University of Sydney while on active service in 1918, Harrison took up duty in July 1919; next year he was appointed acting professor and lecturer in veterinary parasitology; in 1922 he became Challis [q.v.3] professor of zoology. An excellent and enthusiastic teacher, he made his department one of the most active and progressive in the university; he restructured the courses and encouraged a wide variety of research. His students found zoology a dynamic force for the discovery of new knowledge.

Harrison published mainly on Mallophaga and the relations between host and parasite on which he was a world authority, but he was also an expert on frogs, interested in zoogeography and the Wegener hypothesis (the theory of continental drift), especially in relation to the origin of the Australian fauna. His historical and anatomical research was used by H. J. Burrell [q.v.7]. In 1925 he organized a successful interdisciplinary scientific reconnaissance of the Barrington Tops and in 1926 began a university tutorial class on the biological basis of sociology and visited Perth for the Australasian Association for the Advancement of Science congress.

A popular public lecturer and publicist on such topics as evolution and heredity, Harrison was president of the Royal Zoological (1923-24), and the Linnean (1928) societies of New South Wales and a trustee of the Australian Museum, Sydney, from 1924. He was president of the Sydney University Union (1920-21) and active in university science and dramatic societies. Despite poor health as a result of his war experiences and severe arthritis, Harrison was always cheerful and optimistic. He wrote and published clever children's verse under the pseudonym 'Alter Ego' including the delightful *Tails and tarradiddles: an Australian book of birds and beasts* (1925), which he illustrated himself.

Harrison died suddenly of a cerebral

haemorrhage while holidaying at Narooma on 20 February 1928 and was cremated with Anglican rites. His wife survived him.

H. J. Carter, *Gulliver in the Bush* (Syd, 1933); *Aust Zoologist*, 5 (1928), p 132; Linnean Soc NSW, *Procs*, 53 (1928), p 6; *Aust Mus Mag* (1928), p 191; *Syd Univ Medical J* (1928), p 125; *Hermes* (Syd), 34 (1928), p 3; *SMH*, 22 Jan 1918, 19 July 1923, 20 June 1924, 10 Jan, 9 Feb 1925, 20 May, 6 June, 26 Aug 1926, 22, 23, 25 Feb 1928. G. P. WALSH

HARRY, GILBERT (1893-1931), soldier and farmer, was born on 21 February 1893 at St Peter Port, Guernsey, Channel Islands, son of Samuel Harry, Primitive Methodist minister, and his wife Sarah Ida, née Bleathman. He migrated to Queensland shortly before World War I and when he enlisted in the Australian Imperial Force on 13 May 1915 gave his occupation as gunsmith and settler. He had been working his own land at Milwerran.

Harry was allotted to the 26th Battalion and because of his knowledge of firearms and service with the Derbyshire Volunteers was soon posted to unit headquarters as armourer sergeant. The battalion sailed for Egypt in June and landed at Gallipoli on 11 September; five days later Harry was transferred to Ordnance, Anzac Corps. On 29 October he returned to his battalion which remained at Gallipoli until evacuation in December. It embarked from Egypt for France on 15 March 1916; from May to August Harry was attached to 2nd Divisional Armoury but he rejoined his battalion in time for the terrible fighting around Pozières in August. There, during the 26th's fifty hours in the trenches, he won his first decoration, the Military Medal. Although a non-combatant attached to battalion headquarters, he pleaded to take part in the attack. When the officer commanding the battalion ammunition dump became a casualty he took over and 'despite the fact that he was once completely buried and later was severely shaken by a high explosive shell stuck to his job gamely'. At great personal risk, he guided carrying parties across the open from the dump to the captured trenches. Commissioned as a second lieutenant on 16 August, he was appointed sniping officer to the 7th Brigade in September; he was promoted lieutenant on 9 December and attended a staff course at Clare College, Cambridge, from February to April 1917.

Harry was awarded the first of his Military Crosses in September for 'courage, devotion to duty and plucky and clever reconnaissance' as brigade intelligence officer before the attack on Westhoek Ridge, near Ypres, Belgium. Because of his work, which involved being under continuous heavy shell-fire, the battalions of the 7th Brigade suffered no casualties while they were assembling for the assault. On 4 October he was wounded during the fighting around Broodseinde. He was awarded a Bar to his Military Cross for 'fine courage and determination' south of Framerville, France, on 11 August 1918; as brigade intelligence officer he obtained required information even though he was caught in a barrage and 'his clothing was pierced by enemy snipers' fire'. He was wounded again at Mont St Quentin on 1 September but remained on duty; that month he was made a temporary captain in the 26th Battalion but remained on secondment for brigade intelligence work for the rest of the war. He embarked for Australia in June 1919 and his A.I.F. appointment ended on 19 September.

Little is known of Harry's post-war civilian life. In 1922-30 he was dairy farming at Kanyan near Gympie, Queensland; a nearby storekeeper recalled that his agricultural career was dogged by misfortune. He died, unmarried, at Gympie on 21 March 1931 of acute respiratory illness and was buried in an unmarked grave in Gympie Anglican cemetery. Harry was reserved by nature, dapper and small in stature. He was one of only nine members of the A.I.F. to win the Military Medal and Military Cross and Bar.

C. E. W. Bean, *The A.I.F. in France*, 1916 (Syd, 1929); *London Gazette*, 19 Sept 1916, 28 Dec 1917, 5 Nov 1918; Embarkation roll, 26th Battalion, AIF, *and* War Diary, 26th Battalion, AIF (AWM); information from Mr A. W. Nahrung, Gympie, Qld.
W. H. CONNELL

HART, ALFRED (1870-1950), scientist, educator and Shakespearean scholar, was born on 5 December 1870 on a farm in Cedar County, Iowa, United States of America, son of Frederick Hart, farmer, and his wife Ellen, née Latham; his parents were on a visit from Birmingham, England, and shortly returned there. Alfred arrived at Melbourne with his father, brother and sister in September 1879. He won a scholarship to Melbourne Church of England Grammar School in 1884, carrying off the Agar Wynne [q.v.] prizes for Latin in 1885 and Greek in 1886.

Despite a period of residence in Trinity College (1888-89) Hart did not complete a B.A. at the University of Melbourne until 1896. Reluctant to seek support from his family, he had gone schoolteaching in northeast Victoria and in Gippsland, finally becoming headmaster of St James's Grammar School, Melbourne. There he also conduced adult evening classes. Having taken his M.A. in 1901, he enrolled in natural philosophy, and next year was appointed science master at Melbourne Grammar, at the same time teaching English and business communication at the Working Men's College. On 20 February 1903 he married Teresa Jane Tucker of Bendigo and marked the year with his first publication, an anthology of extracts for schools, *English ideals*, edited with M. P. Hansen [q.v.]. (A companion volume appeared in 1912.) Now a B.Sc. (1904), he joined the Working Men's College full time, first as instructor in mathematics, his salary supplemented by part-time tutoring at Catholic teachers' colleges, and then, in 1908, as head of the department of mathematics and physics. He retired in 1935. He devoted some of his leisure to chemistry, winning the Dixson Research Scholarship in 1906 and taking his M.Sc. in 1911. He enjoyed a small private practice as a chemical analyst for many years.

Hart was active in the post-Federation debates over technical training and state funding of secondary schools. His submission to the parliamentary inquiry into the Working Men's College (1911) illustrates his characteristic appeal for proper academic standards of technical teaching within a liberalized syllabus and he succeeded in increasing the humanities content of the curriculum of the new junior technical colleges. He was, on the other hand, convinced that the extension of technical training was a prime responsibility for a modern state, and published two pamphlets on the subject, in 1915 and 1917. As member of the standing committee of Convocation representing graduates in arts in 1924-50 he organized the Melbourne University Association, and published under its auspices a scathing attack on government parsimony: *University reform and finance . . .* (1936).

In 1940 a grateful university conferred a Litt.D. upon Hart, but this rare distinction was won by examination and was a recognition of his eminence in what had been a beloved pastime—the study of Shakespeare. He was at various times secretary and president of the Melbourne Shakespeare Society and one of its most regular speakers. Thirty-eight of his addresses survive. Five were collected and revised in *Shakespeare and the homilies* (1934). In the remainder, seeking for 'more facts and fewer guesses' in Shakespearean scholarship, he set out to test the then current theories of the provenance of a variety of sound and suspect Shakespearean texts by arithmetical calculations of their line-lengths and vocabularies. Later in *Stolne and surreptitious copies* (1942) he argued an impressive case for the unorthodox view that the 'bad' Quartos must

have originated from a double process of theatrical cutting and memorial reconstruction. Both books made lasting contributions to the international debate on the principles of Shakespearean editing, but Hart never went abroad, and his work, hampered by isolation, had been overtaken, even in 1942, by scholars overseas. A later study of Shakespearean vocabulary, the labour of six years, remains in manuscript, irrelevant now in the age of computers.

His last published work was a genial *History of the Wallaby Club* (1944), a record of forty-two years of companionship in that exclusive rambling and dining society. Hart died on 6 October 1950, predeceased by his wife in 1938 and by a son and a daughter, and survived by a daughter. He was buried in Fawkner cemetery. Hart had had no religious affiliation.

Education Dept (Vic), *Vision and realisation*, L. J. Blake ed (Melb, 1973); *PP* (LA Vic), 1911, 2 (14); *Univ of Melb Gazette*, Nov 1950; S. Murray-Smith, A history of technical education in Australia (Ph.D. thesis, Univ Melb, 1966).

DAVID BRADLEY

HART, FRITZ BENNICKE (1874-1949), composer, conductor and teacher, was born on 11 February 1874 at Greenwich, England, eldest child of Frederick Robinson Hart and his wife Jemima (Jemmima) Waters, née Bennicke. His father, a commercial traveller, directed the parish choir in which Hart sang from the age of 6. His Cornish mother taught pianoforte. Both sides of the family claimed musical distinction as performers and minor composers.

Hart became a chorister at Westminster Abbey where he remained for three years under the directorship of Sir Frederick Bridge. In 1893-96 he was a student at the Royal College of Music. His friends there included the composers Gustav Holst, Coleridge Taylor, William Hurlstone; later friends were Ralph Vaughan Williams and John Ireland.

After graduating Hart toured and acted for eighteen months with a dramatic company; this led to writing incidental music for *Julius Caesar*. His first opportunity to conduct came at Eastbourne where he directed his own music for *Romeo and Juliet*. His next few years as musical director with various touring companies gave him a range of experience from operettas and musical comedy to dramatic incidental music and opera. On 4 September 1904, at Bristol, he married Jessie Florence Glover Beattie; their only child, Basil, was born in 1905.

In 1909 Hart came to Australia when J. C. Williamson [q.v.6] offered him an engagement for twelve months. It was extended to four years. In 1913, when G. W. L. Marshall-Hall [q.v.] went to London, Hart assumed his lecturing duties at the Conservatorium of Music, Melbourne. A year later Marshall-Hall sent instructions to close the conservatorium, but the remaining staff refused to resign and made Hart their director. In 1915 Marshall-Hall was reinstated as Ormond [q.v.5] professor of music at the University of Melbourne, thus returning as a rival to his former institution. Amalgamation proved impossible, even after Marshall-Hall's death in July 1915. Anti-German feeling provoked by World War I isolated Marshall-Hall and his largely German-born staff from the popular Albert Street conservatorium under Hart, whose extravagantly pro-British ally (Dame) Nellie Melba [q.v.] threw in her lot with Albert Street, founding there her school of singing.

Melba and her pupils shaped Hart's work as a composer in his choice of vocal forms, though the Celtic revival and the poetry of Herrick also influenced him. Eighteen of his twenty-two operas, 267 of his 514 listed songs (he destroyed several hundred more) and three of his four large choral works were composed in Melbourne. Fifteen orchestral works, including one symphony, numerous chamber and solo instrumental works, unaccompanied choruses, part-songs, transcriptions and arrangements are among his remaining output.

In 1913 Hart and Alfred Hill [q.v.] founded the short-lived Australian Opera League whose first programme on 3 August 1914 included the first performance of Hart's opera *Pierrette*. Six other operas were staged in his lifetime, all in multiple performances: *Ruth and Naomi* (7 July 1917, Melbourne); *Malvolio* (5 December 1918, Melbourne), *Deirdre in exile* (22 September 1926, Melbourne); *The woman who laughed at Faery* (25 September 1929, Melbourne); *St George and the dragon* (10 July 1931, Melbourne); *Even unto Bethlehem* (20 December 1943, Honolulu). The choral first performances in Melbourne include *New Year's eve* and *Salve caput cruentatum* (6 July 1925); *O gloriosa Domina* (28 November 1925); *Natural magic* and *The gilly of Christ* (3 June 1927) and *Joll's credo* (1934).

In March 1924 Hart was made a fellow of the Royal College of Music, London. In 1927 he became acting conductor for the Melbourne Symphony Orchestra, and in 1928 permanent conductor. Late in 1932 the Melbourne University Conservatorium Orchestra and the M.S.O. amalgamated under the joint conductorship of Hart and Professor Bernard Heinze.

Meanwhile in December 1931 Hart was

invited to Hawaii as guest conductor of the Honolulu Symphony Orchestra. He returned annually, remaining there from December to April. In 1937 he accepted the post of permanent conductor of the Honolulu Symphony Orchestra and first professor of music at the University of Hawaii. Hart's wife had died in 1935 and on 16 September 1937 he married Marvell Newman Allison, an American. He visited Melbourne only once thereafter—for the jubilee of the Albert Street conservatorium in July 1945 when he conducted several of his works. He returned to Hawaii in November where he continued to compose, paint and write no fewer than twenty-three unpublished novels.

As described by his contemporaries, Hart was quick in all his movements and had a deep, resonant voice; he was a skilled raconteur. He died on 9 July 1949 at Honolulu of cardiac disorder and was cremated, survived by his son and his second wife.

T. Brentnall, *My memories* (Melb, 1938); E. Blom (ed), *Grove's dictionary of music and musician* (Lond, 1961); G. McInnes, *Goodbye, Melbourn town* (Lond, 1968); *Aust Musical News*, 1 July 1920; Melba Conservatorium (Melb), *Con Amore*, (1932?), 10 (1943), 16 (1949?); *ABC Weekly*, 28 July 1945; *Honolulu Today*, Oct 1947, Aug 1975; *Table Talk*, 26 May 1927; *Argus*, 17 July 1946; Hart collection, MS 9528, *and* Melba memorial book, 1871-1931 (typed news items), McEwen collection (LaTL); Prospectuses of Conservatorium of Music, Melb, 1900-37, *and* Faculty of Music, Univ Melb Records (Univ Melb Archives); Programmes, S. F Schneider collection (Grainger Museum, Univ Melb); Melba letters, 1915-26 (Performing Art Museum, Melb); Procs of Arbitration Court 1933 on MSO, USO and ABC (Univ Melb Archives); Brookes papers (NL).

MAUREEN THÉRÈSE RADIC

HART, JOHN STEPHEN (1866-1952), Anglican bishop, was born on 27 December 1866 at Caulfield, Melbourne, eldest son of John Hart, accountant, and his wife Mary Anne Sibella, sister of J. W. Stephen [q.v.6]. His younger brother was Thomas Stephen Hart [q.v.]. He was educated at East St Kilda Grammar School and the University of Melbourne where he graduated B.A. with first class honours in natural science in 1887, and B.Sc. and M.A. in 1889. Hart then taught matriculation classes at Tintern Ladies College, Hawthorn, where the principal told him he was a born teacher. Believing that 'there is only one thing I consider worth teaching for the rest of my life', he offered himself for ordination to Bishop Goe [q.v.] and was made deacon in 1893 and ordained priest in 1894.

He served his title at St Paul's, Geelong

1893-96, and a second curacy at Christ Church, South Yarra. After his marriage on 18 September 1900 to Catherine Lucy Buckhurst he was appointed incumbent of Holy Trinity, Benalla (1900-03), St Anselm's, Middle Park (1903-07), and St Martin's, Hawksburn (1907-14), where he became well known for his lucid preaching and High Church sympathies. Hart headed the first Th.L. list of the Australian College of Theology in 1898, and gained his Th.Schol. with first-class honours in 1901 and a fellowship in 1907. He was then appointed visiting lecturer at St John's College, East St Kilda, which prepared non-matriculants for ordination, and in 1914 became warden and chaplain. However, falling wartime enrolments and the suspicion, quite unfounded, that Hart and St John's were producing ordinands in the mould of Fr Cyril Barclay, the militant Anglo-Catholic missioner at St John's, La Trobe Street, resulted in the college's unceremonious closure at the end of 1919.

Hart had been a canon of St Paul's Cathedral from 1908 and was elected dean in September 1919. Though the dean's position provided honour and influence, Hart had to find his own living. In his own words he survived 'on the rental from the Deanery, my Pharmacy College' (where he was examiner and later lecturer in botany between 1895 and 1927) 'and Trinity College Lectureships and my wife's money'. Hart used the cathedral pulpit effectively as teacher and apologist and entered vigorously into debates on ecclesiastical, social and political issues. He had been an active member of the diocesan Social Questions Committee since its inception and soon acquired a reputation at the hands of the *Argus* as the 'Labour Dean'. In fact his main concern, as in his defence of Fr Barclay and his vehement efforts on behalf of striking police in 1923, was to ensure that individuals and causes be judged on the merits of their case and not on the distortions and prejudices of their opponents.

Hart was elected bishop of Wangaratta in 1927, being consecrated on 29 June. The diocese was small and rural and, though he ministered faithfully as pastor and teacher, his gifts were clearly appropriate to a wider sphere. Thus, in General Synod he succeeded Bishop G. M. Long [q.v.] of Bathurst as leader of the movement to secure constitutional authority for the Church of England in Australia. In 1932, at the special Constitutional Convention, Hart, though a leading Anglo-Catholic, succeeded in gaining the confidence and adherence of the diocese of Sydney, only to have his draft rejected by the diocese of Brisbane. At the time he was described as 'a little man in spectacles', with 'a mild manner, a certain whim-

sical humour—and a mind like a knife'. But Hart's brusque and distant manner and thin piping voice precluded a wide or easy popularity and, contrary to expectations, he was not translated to a larger diocese.

His literary output was considerable, including in addition to articles, sermons and pamphlets, his two Moorhouse [q.v.5] lecture series—*Spiritual sacrifice* (1915) and *The Gospel foundations* (1928)—and *A companion to St John's Gospel* (1952).

Hart's wife died in August 1942, and in December he retired to Glen Iris where he died on 29 May 1952, survived by one son. He was buried in St Kilda cemetery.

T. B. McCall, *The life and letters of John Stephen Hart* (Syd, 1963); Archives, Mollison Lib, Trinity College, Univ Melb.   B. H. REDDROP

HART, THOMAS STEPHEN (1871-1960), scientist, was born on 30 March 1871 at Caulfield, Melbourne, sixth child of John Hart, a London-born accountant and secretary to the Shire of Caulfield, and his wife Mary Anne Sibella, née Stephen, sister of J. W. Stephen [q.v.6]. Thomas's elder brother was John Stephen Hart [q.v.].

Thomas attended East St Kilda Grammar School and completed his secondary education at John Craig's Toorak College in 1886. He studied at the University of Melbourne, graduating B.A. in 1890 and M.A. in 1892. He was awarded first-class honours in mathematics and natural philosophy and the Wyselaskie [q.v.6] scholarship in mathematics. Hart's university studies also included Latin, Greek, comparative philology, mining and engineering. He completed practical requirements for an engineering degree in 1895-96, but did not graduate B.C.E. formally until 1901.

In July 1896 Hart was appointed lecturer in geology, mineralogy, mining and botany as well as curator of the museum at the Ballarat School of Mines which in 1908 conferred on him the title of professor. In May 1913 he was appointed first senior master in charge of the Creswick School of Forestry. He joined the Education Department and became a member of the foundation staff of Footscray Technical School in 1916. The next year he took an appointment at the Bairnsdale School of Mines where he taught mathematical, geological, and botanical subjects. In 1931 he transferred to Brighton Technical School and later that year to the Correspondence School in Melbourne from which he retired in 1936.

Hart had a lifelong interest in science, especially natural history. In 1886-87 he read papers to the Hart family 'Natural History

Society and Saturday Club'. In 1887 he joined the Field Naturalists' Club of Victoria and in 1894 the Royal Society of Victoria. He was elected a fellow of the Geological Society of London in 1901. He attended the congresses of the Australasian and British associations for the advancement of science when they were held in Melbourne. He contributed over fifty papers to the *Victorian Naturalist* between 1892 and 1954 and ten to the *Proceedings* of the Royal Society of Victoria between 1899 and 1913, most of them descriptive accounts of botanical and geological features in Victoria. Hart became well known among Australian naturalists for his wide knowledge of Victorian plants about which he carried on a vigorous correspondence with both expert and novice.

He loved cycling and combined this with his favourite recreation of botanical and geological rambles through the Victorian countryside. An orchid which he discovered near Bairnsdale in 1925 was named *Prasophyllum Hartii* by R. S. Rogers [q.v.] in his honour. He was a foundation and long-serving member of the committee of management for the Lakes National Park at Sperm Whale Head and a member of the Victorian Plant Names Committee of the Field Naturalists' Club.

Hart had married Ethel Jane, daughter of Rev. James Rickard, at Brighton Congregational Church on 14 December 1898. They had no children but adopted three Rickard nephews and a niece. He was an active Christian. While living in Ballarat he was secretary of the Sebastopol Congregational Church and vice-president of Christian Endeavour. In Bairnsdale, where there was no Congregational church, he acted as a Presbyterian lay preacher. Predeceased by his wife in 1940, Hart died at Croydon on 26 June 1960. He was buried in Box Hill cemetery according to Congregational forms.

M. M. McCallum, *Ballarat and district citizens and sports at home and abroad* (Ballarat, 1916); Ballarat School of Mines, *Students Magazine*, Sept 1899; *Vic Naturalist*, 77 (1960); *Taxon*, 23 (1977); *Ballarat Courier*, 19 Jan 1905; *Age*, 10 Feb 1914, 20 Apr 1929, 27 June 1960; *Sun-News Pictorial*, 27 June 1960; *Ringwood Mail*, 7 July 1960; Hart papers (LaTL, *and* Herbarium, Melb); information from Dr E. Turner, Roy Children's Hospital, Parkville, Melb and Mrs W. Knapton, Pakenham, Vic.

LYNDSAY FARRALL

HART, WILLIAM EWART (1885-1943), airman and dentist, was born on 20 April 1885 at Parramatta, New South Wales, third of nine children of William Hart, timber merchant, and his wife Maria Alice, née Gazzard, both born at Parramatta. Educated locally, Bill was apprenticed at 16 to a dentist and was registered on 26 June 1906. He practised at West Wyalong, Newcastle and Sydney.

Mechanically minded, Hart was interested in aviation. In September 1911 he bought, for £1333, a Bristol Box-kite from Joseph Hammond, who was touring Australia as a demonstration pilot for the British & Colonial Aeroplane Co. Ltd. Hart received some tuition from Hammond's mechanic and first flew solo on 3 November. By 16 November he had completed flying tests conducted by the Aerial League of Australia. Presented with Australian aviator's licence no. 1, dated 5 December 1911, he was the first airman to qualify as a pilot in Australia. This licence was superseded by the Fédération Aéronautique Internationale's certificate no. 199, issued by the Royal Aero Club of the United Kingdom on 29 March 1912.

Meanwhile on 18 November 1911 Hart had flown 47 miles (75 km) from Penrith, via St Marys to Sydney, completing the first cross-country flight in New South Wales in 55 minutes; he was awarded a special plaque. On 3 January 1912 the postmaster-general C. E. Frazer [q.v.8] opened Hart's aviation school at Penrith; in March he transferred his operations to Ham Common (now Richmond aerodrome). On 29 June he won Australia's first air race when he defeated the American A. B. Stone (who lost his way) over a 20-mile (32 km) course from Botany to Parramatta Park. During the year the cinematographer Ernest Higgins [q.v.] made eighteen flights with Hart and obtained enough footage for three movies, *The camera in the clouds* (1912), *Among the clouds with a camera* (1912) and *Australia calls* (1913).

In August 1912 Hart constructed a two-seat monoplane which he successfully tested at Wagga Wagga, but wrecked it in a serious accident at Richmond on 4 September. He was badly injured and never flew again. In January 1916 he enlisted in the Australian Imperial Force, and as a lieutenant in No. 1 Squadron, Australian Flying Corps, he went to Egypt and Britain, where he was an instructor but, found medically unfit, he returned to Australia and was discharged on 11 September.

Resuming his career as a dentist Hart opened spacious new surgeries on a whole floor of Boomerang House, King Street, in 1918. At St Philip's Anglican Church, Sydney, he married Thelma Clare Cock on 10 August 1929; they lived at Cheltenham. In the 1930s he visited Britain and the United States of America where he observed the latest developments in dentistry. On his return he introduced several new dental theories. In World War II he was rejected, as medically unfit, for the Royal Australian Air Force.

On 29 July 1943 Hart died in Sydney from heart disease. He was cremated with Methodist forms as the R.A.A.F. flew overhead in salute. His wife and son survived him. At the time of his death Hart was vice-president of the Air Force Association; its minutes recorded that he was a 'resourceful, courageous pioneer, soldier, airman, loyal friend and good citizen, lovable personality and gallant gentleman'. A memorial to him in Parramatta Park was unveiled in 1963.

S. Brogden, *The history of Australian aviation* (Melb, 1960); N. Ellison, *Wings over the north* (Newcastle, NSW, 1938); W. Joy, *The aviators* (Syd, 1965); E. Reade, *Australian silent films* (Melb, 1970); R. J. Gibson, *Australia and Australians in civil aviation 1823 to 1920* (Syd, 1971); *Wings* (Melb), 31 Aug 1943; RAHS, *Newsletter*, June 1970; *14-18 J*, 1975.   KEITH ISAACS

HARTIGAN, PATRICK JOSEPH (1878-1952), priest and poet, was born on 13 October 1878 at O'Connell Town, Yass, New South Wales, eldest surviving son of Patrick Joseph Hartigan, produce merchant, and his wife Mary, née Townsell, both from Lisseycasey, Clare, Ireland. After attending the convent school at Yass, he entered St Patrick's College, Manly, in February 1892 but, uncertain of his vocation for the priesthood, left for St Patrick's College, Goulburn, where he studied under the noted classicist Dr John Gallagher, later bishop of Goulburn. He returned to Manly in 1898 and was ordained priest on 18 January 1903. After a curacy of seven years at Albury, he became inspector of schools for the vast diocese of Goulburn in 1910 and was based at Thurgoona near Albury. He was one of the first curates in the State with a motor car; in 1911 he took the last sacraments to Jack Riley of Bringenbrong, said to have been A. B. Paterson's [q.v.] 'The man from Snowy River'. In 1916 he was appointed priest-in-charge of Berrigan and next year parish priest of Narrandera.

All this time Hartigan was a keen student of Australian literature. In 1906 he began publishing verse in such journals as the *Albury Daily News, Catholic Press* and the *Bulletin* under the pen-name 'Mary Ann'. Encouraged by George Robertson [q.v.], C. J. Dennis [q.v.8] and others, he published *Around the boree log and other verses*, under the pseudonym 'John O'Brien', in November 1921. Recording with humour and pathos the lively faith, solid piety and everyday lives of the people around him, Hartigan successfully combined the old faith of Ireland with the mateship and ethos of the bush, towards the end of an age when the small selectors and squatters went by sulky or 'shandrydan' to 'The Church Upon the Hill'.

> 'We'll all be rooned', said Hanrahan,
>   In accents most forlorn,
> Outside the church, ere Mass began,
>   One frosty Sunday morn.

'Said Hanrahan' and the other poems were an instant success. Dennis hailed them in the *Bulletin* as in 'the direct Lawson [q.v.]-Paterson line mainly—unaffected talk about Australians, much as they would naturally talk about themselves'. *Around the boree log* ran to five editions and 18 000 copies by 1926, was widely popularized throughout eastern Australia by the recitations of John Byrne ('The Joker'), acclaimed in Ireland and the United States of America, and made into a film in 1925. Twenty poems were set to music by Dom S. Moreno of New Norcia, Western Australia, in 1933.

Hartigan was a popular figure in the town and community. His years at Narrandera were happy if arduous, disturbed only perhaps by the sectarianism engendered by the Sister Ligouri [q.v. Partridge] case. His poems and short stories regularly appeared, many in the religious journal, *Manly*. Advancing age, ill health and a desire to carry out more historical research led Hartigan to retire as pastor of Narrandera in 1944; he became chaplain of the Convent of the Sacred Heart, Rose Bay. In Sydney he was a familiar figure in the Mitchell Library and wrote a series of articles, 'In Diebus Illis', recording the struggles of the pioneer clergy, published in the *Australasian Catholic Record* in 1943-45 and posthumously in book form as *The men of '38 . . .* (Kilmore, 1975). Still much in demand as occasional speaker and preacher, in 1947 he was appointed domestic prelate with the title of right reverend monsignor in October 1947. His main comforts in his semi-retirement were the love of his near relations, receiving visitors (especially from Narrandera) and watching the shipping on the harbour. Ill with cancer from 1951 he completed *On Darlinghurst Hill* (Sydney, 1952), written for the centenary of the Sacred Heart Parish.

Hartigan died in Lewisham Hospital on 27 December 1952 and, after a requiem Mass in St Mary's Cathedral, was buried beside his parents in North Rocks cemetery.

Tall, handsome in his young days, and impressive always, Hartigan for all his broad humanity and kindliness was shy and somewhat detached. Possessed of a dry humour underlain by a touch of wistfulness, he was a good conversationalist and raconteur:

literature, art, cricket, horses, the land and cars were ready subjects. He was an excellent, yet undemonstrative preacher—his addresses, including panegyrics on his friends, with their pervading poetic imagery, sense of history and heartfelt sincerity are beautiful examples of Irish-Australian oratory.

Much of 'John O'Brien's' unpublished verse appeared in *The parish of St. Mel's* (Sydney, 1954). A selection of his poems, illustrated by the paintings of Patrick Carroll, was published as *Around the boree log* (Sydney, 1978). A portrait by E. M. Smith is at St Patrick's College, Manly.

F. A. Mecham, *John O'Brien and the boree log* (Syd, 1981) and for bibliog; *Catholic Weekly* (Syd), 8, 15, 22 May 1952, 1 Jan 1953, 9 Sept 1971; *SMH*, 6 Mar 1976.   G. P. WALSH

HARVEY, SIR JOHN MUSGRAVE (1865-1940), judge, was born on 22 December 1865 at Hampstead, London, second son of Rev. Charles Musgrave Harvey, prebendary and vicar of Hillingdon, and his wife Frances Harriet, née Brewster. Educated at Marlborough College in 1878-84 on a Foundation scholarship, he was a prefect, member of the Rugby team and won a classical scholarship to Keble College, Oxford (B.A., 1888).

On the voyage from England in 1889 as a tutor to the children of J. W. Johnson, a Sydney solicitor, Harvey met (Sir) Langer Owen [q.v.] who interested him in the law. He was associate to Sir William Owen [q.v.], chief judge in Equity, in 1890-93 and was admitted to the Bar on 21 March 1892. He soon made his mark and appeared in many important cases, principally in Equity; a number of pupils read with him. From 1893 to 1900 he was a reporter for the *New South Wales Law Reports* and the *New South Wales weekly notes*. At Woollahra he married Pauline Beatrice Ward, daughter of the registrar-general, on 4 January 1895. In 1898 Harvey published *Service of equitable process* and in 1902, with (Sir) George Rich and Arthur Newham [qq.v.], *The practice in equity*, an annotated edition of the Equity Act, 1901, and other relevant statutes.

Although still at the junior Bar, Harvey was appointed on 15 April 1913 to the Supreme Court bench, becoming probate judge in 1918 and chief judge in Equity on 10 February 1925. He disposed of an immense volume of work with courtesy and efficiency. A master of technicality, he used his skill to cut through it to reach the heart of the problem. He was an acknowledged master in probate, construction of wills, administration of estates and conveyancing of real property, but he delivered important judgments on the law of trusts, of charities, company law and crown lands, and as a member of the Full Court dealt with the law generally. He believed that the law 'should be kept as a well tempered and sharp instrument for doing the business of the community'. Forward-looking, he advocated the bringing of all land under the Torrens [q.v.6] system.

From February to November 1918 Harvey served as royal commissioner inquiring into the terms and provisions of a bill to amend and consolidate the law of property and to simplify and improve the practice of conveyancing. Although many of his recommendations were copied from the United Kingdom and other States, the Conveyancing Act, 1919, contained many original ideas and remains the statutory framework for the law of real property in New South Wales. The complex measure was carried in parliament virtually without debate or amendment. The Act was Harvey's greatest achievement and an astonishing one as he continued to sit as a judge, carried out his duties as official visitor to the prisoner of war internment camps and, in August-September, inquired into the detention of the Irish Republican Brotherhood internees. As royal commissioner Harvey also inquired into the administration of the New South Wales Child Welfare Department in 1927, and next year into the contract entered into by the Municipal Council of Sydney for the steam-raising plant at Bunnerong power house; in his report he censured A. J. Arnot [q.v.7] and revealed corruption among officers and members of the council. Harvey was remarkable for the promptitude with which he produced his reports as royal commissioner.

His leisure was devoted to religion and music, with a little tennis and trout fishing. A devoted Anglican, Harvey was for twenty-eight years a warden of St Mark's Church, Darling Point, a member of the choir and a parish nominator. He was foundation chairman of the council of Cranbrook School, Bellevue Hill, in 1918-38, and in 1931 initiated the opening of the law year by religious services. Chancellor of the diocese of Sydney in 1934-38, he supported the provision of a constitution for the Church of England in Australia and served on important diocesan committees. He was president of the Sydney Madrigal and Chamber Music Society in the 1920s.

Knighted in June 1933, Harvey was appointed as acting chief justice on 30 June but he suffered failing eyesight and retired from the bench in December next year. He died at his Double Bay home with cerebral thrombosis on 13 June 1940 and was cremated. He was survived by his wife, son and

224

hree daughters. His estate was sworn for probate at £22 225.

Nothing has happened to diminish the regard in which Harvey was held as a dispenser of justice to litigants or the respect for his work as a law reformer, but he has not worn as well as an articulator of legal doctrine. The sheer speed with which he worked was not conducive to the production of polished judgments.

His portrait by Harold Abbott is held by Cranbrook School.

Cyclopedia of N.S.W. (Syd, 1907); A. C. Child, *Cranbrook; the first fifty years 1918-1968* (Syd, 1968); *Magistrate*, 1 May 1913, p 146; *Aust Law*, 7, 15 July 1933, p 133, 8, 15 Jan 1935, p 317; *SMH*, 3 June 1933, 14, 15, 18 June 1940.

F. C. HUTLEY

HARVEY, LEWIS JARVIS (1871-1949), craftsman and teacher, was born on 16 June 1871 at Wantage, Berkshire, England, son of Enos James Harvey, moulder, and his wife Eliza, née Jarvis. Migrating with his family to Brisbane in 1874, he attended the Kangaroo Point State School and began work as a telegraph messenger. From about 1887 he studied art at Brisbane Technical College under Joseph Augustine Clarke. He was probably apprenticed about 1886 to woodcarver Edward G. Madeley, then to Cuthbert Vickers. In 1888-90 Harvey won first and special prizes for carved wood panels in competitions restricted to apprentices. He regarded Vickers as 'a great carver' and worked for him until about 1895 when he started his own business in part of his father's Elizabeth Street foundry.

Brisbane Technical College appointed Harvey a part-time instructor in wood-carving and chip-carving on 10 January 1902. From August 1916 to December 1937 he was a full-time applied arts teacher of modelling, wood-carving and pottery at the college. In 1915 he designed a new system for teaching pottery and used it for the rest of his career. Experimenting with glazes, emphasizing Australian motifs, researching and exploiting local clays, he attracted students from other States even though his fondness for Renaissance Classical revival traditions sometimes resulted in over-decorated formal pieces. Among sculpture students whom he encouraged to study abroad were Daphne Mayo and William Bowles [q.v.7]. Lloyd Rees, who spent a year as a day student with him believed that Harvey was content to be a "medium" . . . or the great ones of the past . . . [he] was not a creative artist of importance but he was a creative influence'.

Harvey excelled as a wood-carver and had wide local impact on furniture design and manufacture. His best apprentice, John Adamson, working for the important Brisbane furniture manufacturer Edmund Rosenstengel, closely followed Harvey's use of motifs, timbers and grains to achieve special decorative effects. His two sons began making art furniture, and in 1938 Harvey himself opened an applied art school in Adelaide Street.

In 1938-45 he was a member of the Queensland Art Gallery's art advisory committee. During both World Wars, as a member of the Arts and Crafts Society, he taught disabled service personnel. Major works by him include the stone carvings on the Elizabeth Street façade of the Brisbane General Post Office (c.1908), a St John's Cathedral side-chapel altar (1910) and high altar communion rails (1929), and statue of St Brigid and high altar crucifix, St Brigid's Church, Red Hill (1914). He exhibited widely, winning a gold medal at the Franco-British Exhibition (1908) and bronze medals at the British Empire Exhibition, London (1924-25). His work is represented in the Australian National Gallery, the Queensland Art Gallery, and the Museum of Applied Arts and Sciences, Sydney. In the 1940s he began oil painting, exhibiting with the Queensland Art Society.

Harvey collapsed and died at a Royal Queensland Art Society meeting on 19 July 1949 and was cremated with Anglican rites. He was survived by his wife Fanny Ellen, née Keal, whom he had married in Brisbane on 5 January 1898, and three of their five children. A bust of Harvey by Daphne Mayo is in the collection of his son E. B. Harvey, and his name is commemorated by the L. J. Harvey memorial prize for drawing awarded biennially by the Queensland Art Gallery.

R. Free, *Lloyd Rees* (Melb, 1972); M. Y. Graham, *Australian pottery of the 19th and early 20th century* (Syd, 1979); K. W. Scarlett, *Australian sculptors* (Melb, 1980); Half Dozen Group papers (Fryer Lib, Univ Qld); L. J. Harvey papers (held by E. B. Harvey, Wynnum, Brisb); Roy National Assn papers (Oxley Lib, Brisb); Brisb Technical College, and Brisb Central Technical College Minutes and records (Oxley Lib, *and* QSA).

BETTINA MACAULAY

HASSELL, GEORGE FREDERICK (1869-1945), printer, was born on 22 February 1869 at Leicester, England, eldest son of George Hassell, printer, and his wife Emma, née Buckley. In 1883 the family migrated to Adelaide and two years later re-established the printing business, G. Hassell & Son, in Victoria Square. In 1887 it moved to Franklin Street and in 1910 transferred to 104 Currie Street. At 14, while still at Leicester, George had induced his father to buy some new decorative initial letters to embellish a particular piece of typography. After his father retired in 1900, and George and his brother Frank took over, a higher standard of work was produced. In 1904-53 the firm printed for the University of Adelaide. On 12 November 1890 Hassell had married Agnes Anna McLeish; they were Methodists.

He was more than a mechanical printer. He was a true bibliophile who loved literature and music and eventually owned over 1200 classical records. These interests led him into publishing, between 1900 and 1935, nearly seventy works. They included Theocritus's *The feast of Adonis* (1910), translated by Hassell's close friend R. J. M. Clucas [q.v.8]. Hassell personally handset this text, which was printed with the Greek and English versions on facing pages; a leather-bound, hand-tooled copy is in the Mitchell Library, Sydney. He compiled a tiny booklet, *Those shadowy recollections* (1915), a collection of poetry on the theme of lost youth. The beautiful anthology of Australian prose, poetry, art and photography, *Art and letters, Hassell's Australian miscellany*, appeared in 1921. The firm now had a branch in Melbourne and from 1922 was known as The Hassell Press. That year the brothers' partnership was dissolved and Hassell's son, Frederick William, whose wife was also a printer, entered the business.

Other books to appear under their imprint covered art, economics, law, philosophy, poetry and science. They published Henry Lawson, Sir Douglas Mawson, Professor W. Howchin, Dr T. Brailsford Robertson, Simpson Newland [qq.v.], (Viscount) S. M. Bruce [q.v.7] and (Sir) A. Grenfell Price. George Robertson [q.v.] of Sydney correctly predicted that works from the Hassell Press would become collector's items; Lawson's *Joseph's dream* (1923) and *The auld shop & the new* (1923), printed for Robertson, are among them.

Hassell's involvement in publishing, as distinct from printing for other publishers, was comparatively rare then or now. In his dedication to fine typography he adopted a restrained, formal, classical approach and abhorred the flamboyant garishness of many of his contemporaries. He studied and followed the Oxford University Press style and returned twice to England in 1926 and 1936. He had few contemporary Australian competitors in typographical design and printing quality; many of his peers were content with the mediocre and few were skilled typographers. Although his conservative approach achieved some fame early in this

century, today his meticulous attention to detail might be considered unimaginative His work, however, won repute throughout Australia and brought Adelaide to the fore in the field.

Hassell was a genial, lovable man formed by his reading—he was 'one of the best-read men in Adelaide, and one of the more modest'. His enthusiasm led him to form the Book Club and he was a president of the Adelaide Dual Club.

Survived by his second wife, Ida Frances and two sons, he died of cancer at his Wayville home on 2 November 1945. His estate was sworn for probate at £13 573. His work lived on in the high standards maintained by his son, at whose request the firm in 1953 merged with Griffin Press Ltd. Continuation of the family name in the printing world was prevented when Fred's son Geoffrey was killed in action in World War II.

W. H. Langham, *The Hassell press 1885-193*. (Adel, 1935); *Newspaper News*, 15 Dec 1945; *A'sian Printer*, Nov 1951; *Advertiser* (Adel), 8 Nov 1945.
DOUGLAS A. DUNSTAN

HASWELL, WILLIAM AITCHESON (1854-1925), biologist, was born on 5 August 1854 at Gayfield House, Edinburgh, one of a large family of James Haswell, banker, and his wife Margaret, née Cranston. He was educated at the Edinburgh Institution and the University of Edinburgh (M.A., 1877 B.Sc., 1878; D.Sc., 1887). He also studied science for some months at the University of Leipzig, Germany, in 1877. Broadly cultivated, neat and shy in demeanour, a meticulous prize-winning scholar, he was inspired by the teaching of T. H. Huxley [q.v.1] and C. Wyville Thompson, who directed his aptitude for natural history into marine zoology

In 1878, for health reasons, Haswell visited Australia. Welcomed as a kindred spirit in Sydney by (Sir) William Macleay [q.v.5] he began work in a small marine zoological laboratory at Watson's Bay on a long series of important researches on the collections from the *Chevert* expedition to New Guinea and on the marine fauna of Port Jackson and the adjacent coast; in 1897 he was elected a fellow of the Royal Society, London. Curator of the Queensland Museum during 1880, he returned to Sydney, and in 1881 joined H.M.S. *Alert* on a surveying cruise of the Great Barrier Reef, studying especially crustaceans. In 1882 he was appointed demonstrator in comparative anatomy and physiology and histology at the University of Sydney, and from 1884 lecturer in zoology and comparative anatomy and demonstrator in histology. In 1890 he became first Challis [q.v.3] professor of biology (restyled zoology in 1915).

Haswell significantly helped to stimulate recognition for science at the university 'against the entrenched forces of Arts', and more widely in Australasia. He was a council-member from 1881 and president in 1892 and 1893 of the Linnean Society of New South Wales, an active member of the local Royal Society (which awarded him the (W.B.) Clarke [q.v.3] medal in 1915), a trustee of the Australian Museum, Sydney, in 1891-1923 and a contributor to meetings of the Australasian Association for the Advancement of Science and of the British Association for the Advancement of Science in 1914. Between 1916 and 1919 he advised the Commonwealth government on insect damage to wheat, fisheries and a proposed marine biological station in Sydney.

Although Haswell's most valuable work related to the Crustacea, Annelida and Bryozoa of the Australian seas, he is best remembered for *A text book of zoology* (London, 1897), 'a monument of scholarship', written with Professor T. Jeffrey Parker of the University of Otago, New Zealand; it ran through four editions by 1928, was translated into Russian in 1908 and abridged as *A manual of zoology* in 1913. Parker died shortly before its first publication, but Haswell retained the joint authorship in honour of his friend. At Christchurch, New Zealand, on 28 August 1894 he married a former pupil of Parker, Josephine Gordon Rich of Toi Toi, New Zealand, who assisted him in his work.

Haswell died of heart disease on 24 January 1925 at his home at Point Piper, Sydney, and was buried with Presbyterian forms in the Anglican section of Waverley cemetery. His wife and only daughter Mary survived him.

A. M. Moyal (ed), *Scientists in nineteenth century Australia* (Melb, 1975); Linnean Soc Lond, *Procs*, 1924-25, p 74; Roy Soc Lond, *Procs*, 1925, p xii; Linnean Soc NSW, *Procs*, 1928, p 485, and for publications; *SMH*, 26, 27 Jan, 9 Feb 1925; J. T. Wilson papers (Basser Lib, Canb); CSIRO Archives (Canb); family information.

PATRICIA MORISON

HATFIELD, WILLIAM (1892-1969), writer, whose original name was Ernest Chapman, was born on 18 March 1892 at Nottingham, England, son of Joseph Chapman, policeman, and his wife Mary, née Cudworth. After education at a Nottingham council school, he briefly attended Nottingham University and was articled to a solicitor. He decided to migrate, however, worked his passage as a steward and jumped ship at Port Adelaide in January 1912. Setting off

on foot for 'the interior', by the evening he had reached Glenelg.

Hatfield soon became a first-rate bushman. For many years he worked in the north of South Australia, Central Australia, the Northern Territory and Queensland as a station-hand, stockman, drover, cook, horse-breaker, kangaroo-shooter, dingo-trapper, book-keeper, seaman, miner, fruit-picker, painter and timber-worker. In 1915 he attempted to join the Light Horse but was rejected because of injuries. Over the years he sympathetically studied Aboriginal languages and customs.

Hatfield had always been ambitious to write but for twelve years accumulated rejection slips. While unemployed in Sydney, however, he wrote the successful *Sheepmates* (1931), a novel about a Central Australian station. In 1931 he made a car trip to Darwin and another round Australia in 1932, reporting on the way, which won him some celebrity. The trips were the basis for *Australia through the wind screen* (1936). Angus [q.v.7] & Robertson [q.v.] published seven more novels, of which *Desert Saga* (1933) about an Aboriginal boy was the most serious, and three children's stories.

During a visit to England Hatfield finally adopted his pen-name by deed poll in 1938. He was proud when Oxford University Press published his autobiographical *I find Australia* (1937), a lively account which fully displays his energy, vitality and willingness to tackle any occupation. He had made a fair living from writing during the Depression, but on returning to Australia in 1939 he was soon destitute in Perth with a young family. He was awarded a Commonwealth Literary Fund grant, but in 1940 joined the Australian Military Forces, serving in 1942-43 as a lieutenant in the Army Education Service.

During the 1940s and later, Hatfield's interests concentrated on conservationist issues. He lectured as a declared Communist and wrote, notably in *Australia reclaimed* (1944), on water conservation, irrigation, soil erosion and reafforestation, holding similar views to J. J. C. Bradfield's [q.v.7] on a possible water-diversion scheme in Queensland. He argued vigorously in favour of breaking up pastoral leaseholds in northern Australia and promoting agricultural settlement.

After some years of ill health Hatfield died, intestate, at Concord, Sydney, on 2 February 1969 and was cremated. He was married three times: on 6 November 1916 at Townsville, Queensland, to Constance Jean Ferguson (d. 1923); on 16 July 1930 in Sydney to a divorcee Winifrid Josephine Finlayson Lofting, née Wilson (they were divorced in 1937); and on 15 November 1937 at Bridport, Dorset, England, to Janet Guthrie Fulton who survived him with a daughter and a son.

G. Disher, 'Before the age of hurry-up . . .' Australian landscape writing 1925-1950 (M.A. thesis, Monash University, 1978); *Overland*, no 9, Apr 1957.   GEOFFREY SERLE

HAUGH, DENIS ROBERT (1872-1933), Catholic philanthropist and tea merchant, was born on 20 July 1872 in County Clare, Ireland, son of James Haugh, grazier, and his wife Mary, née Collins. When he was a baby the family migrated to Toowoomba, Queensland, where he was educated. He early became interested in the work of the Society of St Vincent de Paul in Australia and in the mid-1890s moved to Sydney.

Residing in the parish of St Francis, Haymarket, Haugh soon came under the influence of the society's founders in Sydney, Charles O'Neill [q.v.5] and L. F. Heydon [q.v.]. His literary interests led to his involvement in Irish affairs; he was secretary and, reputedly, later editor and part-owner of the *Sydney Irish World*, edited in 1894-95 by H. Foran [q.v.8]. In 1903 Haugh was caretaker at St Francis Girls' School; by 1908 he had set up as a tea merchant, but devoted more time to the Society of St Vincent de Paul. Well-known in the area for his devotion to the poor, especially Chinese, and to children, he was president of the society's Haymarket conference in 1907-19, when he moved to Carlton, and of its Metropolitan Central Council of Sydney in 1915-30.

In constant attendance at the Children's Court and children's shelter, Haugh in the 1920s represented the Catholic Church in all dealings with the Child Welfare Department. He appealed to families to adopt orphaned children and, while still a bachelor, adopted a 4-year-old boy, who was cared for by his half-sister Mary. At St Mary's Cathedral on 24 October 1918 he married Kathleen Griffin (d. 1957), a 26-year-old music teacher.

For many years secretary of St Margaret's Hospital, Haugh had deep sympathy for girl-mothers and their babies, and helped Gertrude Abbott [q.v.7] to place the young women. From 1916 he began working for the establishment of St Anthony's Home for neglected and abandoned infants and children; it was started in a house at St Peters, later at Petersham (1922). St Anthony's Foundling Home at Croydon, opened in 1925, was a work of the Society of St Vincent de Paul. As president, Haugh used his literary and oratorical powers to gain widespread support for the home.

Mischievous and wild in his youth, Haugh in later years was quiet, reserved and deeply compassionate: few knew the extent of his charitable labours. He received the papal Cross 'pro Ecclesia et Pontifice' in December 1920. He was a champion tea-taster and draughts player, and acted as presiding officer in all municipal and parliamentary elections in the Haymarket area. He died of cancer in the Sacred Heart Hospice, Darlinghurst, on 23 January 1933 and was buried in Woronora cemetery. He was survived by his wife, two sons and two daughters. In February the D. R. Haugh memorial fund was set up to raise money for his wife and children, who were also assisted by the Society of St Vincent de Paul.

St Anthony's Home, Croydon, Silver Jubilee, 1922-47 (Syd, 1947); *Freeman's J* (Syd), 16 Dec 1920, 26 Jan, 2, 9 Feb, 9 Mar 1933; *Catholic Press*, 15 Dec 1932; *Daily Telegraph* (Syd), and *SMH*, 24 Jan 1933; St Anthony's Foundling Home, Croydon, NSW, Fifteenth Annual Report, 1938, *and* Society of St Vincent de Paul, Superior Council Report, 1933 (ML); information from Miss P. Haugh, Braidwood, NSW.   URSULA BYGOTT

HAVELOCK, SIR ARTHUR ELIBANK (1844-1908), governor, was born on 7 May 1844 at Bath, Somerset, England, third son of Lieut-Colonel William Havelock of the 14th Light Dragoons and his wife Caroline Elizabeth, née Chaplin. Arthur was a nephew of Major General Sir Henry Havelock. He was educated at private schools in India and England and in 1860 entered the Royal Military Academy, Sandhurst. He was gazetted ensign in the 32nd Cornwall Light Infantry on 14 January 1862, was promoted lieutenant in 1866 and served as aide-de-camp to the governor of Mauritius in 1873. In 1874-75 he acted as chief civil commissioner of the Seychelles, later becoming colonial secretary and receiver-general of Fiji.

Havelock returned to England in 1876, retired from the army in March 1877 with the rank of captain and joined the colonial service. After two years in the West Indies he returned to the Seychelles as chief civil commissioner and was appointed C.M.G. in 1880. In 1881 he became governor of the West African settlements and consul-general in Liberia where he was engaged in the settlement of the colonial boundaries. Appointed governor of Trinidad and promoted K.C.M.G. in 1884, he became governor of Natal and Zululand in 1885. He returned to Europe in 1889 to join the international anti-slavery commission, was appointed governor of Ceylon the following year and in 1895 governor of Madras. He was promoted G.C.M.G. in 1895, G.C.I.E. in 1896 and G.C.S.I. in 1901 when he left Madras. Because of ill health he refused the governorships of the Straits Settlements and Victoria, but later accepted appointment as governor of Tasmania.

Sir Arthur arrived in Tasmania on 8 November 1901, but did not complete his term. He notified the premier, W. B. Propsting [q.v.], on 6 January 1904 of his decision to retire and left the State on 16 April. He returned to England and settled at Torquay, Devon. He died at Bath on 25 June 1908, six months after the death of his wife Anne Grace, née Norris, whom he had married on 15 August 1871 at Kensington, London. He was survived by a daughter.

Havelock spent nearly thirty years in a variety of colonial posts and appears to have been a devoted and hard-working administrator. He demonstrated tact, firmness and a measure of diplomatic skill in the Liberian boundary situation. He also showed a humane feeling for the populations under his care, particularly in Ceylon, where he abolished the 'paddy' or rice tax, and again in Madras where his firm but sympathetic handling of affairs earned him high regard. But his years of executive responsibility in tropical climates undermined his health. This legacy cut short his service in Tasmania to a bare two and a half years and also probably accounts for the fact that he seems not to have made any significant mark as a constitutional governor there.

DNB, 1901-1911; *Cyclopedia of Tasmania* (Hob, 1931); *The Times*, 26 June 1908.

GEORGE B. CARTLAND

HAWES, JOHN CYRIL (1876-1956), architect and priest, was born on 7 September 1876 at Richmond, Surrey, England, third son of Edward Hawes, solicitor, and his wife Amelia Mariana, née Boult. Educated at Brighton and at the King's School, Canterbury, he was greatly influenced by the splendour of Canterbury Cathedral and showed an early talent for drawing. In London in 1893 he was articled to Edmeston & Gabriel, architects, and attended lectures at the Architectural Association School and at the Central School of Arts and Crafts under Professor W. R. Lethaby. There he came under the influence of the Arts and Crafts movement: the work of Ninian Comper and Charles Voysey, and the writing of John Ruskin.

In 1897 Hawes started practice, designing his first domestic buildings at Bognor, Sussex. In 1898 he created a scale-model church for the Royal Academy summer exhibition (the first year that architectural models were permitted) which brought him a commission to design a church for Bishop Hornby at Gunnerton, Northumberland (1899). About this time he experienced a strong religious conversion and, largely under Hornby's influence, entered Lincoln Theological College. He was ordained an Anglican priest in 1903 in London and was curate at the Church of The Holy Redeemer, Clerkenwell, in 1903-06. Hawes chose a High Church stronghold for he was committed to the Catholic Movement in the Church of England, and later joined Dom Aelred Carlyle's Benedictine community on Caldy Island, South Wales, and was architect for the project. His monastery guest-house and some of his restoration work still exist, although the grandiose plans for the monastery proper were abandoned after disagreements with Dom Aelred culminating in Hawes leaving Caldy in 1907.

In 1909 Hawes was invited by Bishop Hornby to join the Church of England mission in the Bahama Islands where many churches had been damaged by a hurricane. On Long Island he ministered to his native parishioners, repaired the churches, and designed and built St Paul's, Clarence Town. After several years dissatisfaction with High and Low Church divisions, Hawes experienced a second conversion in 1911 and left the Bahamas for New York to become a Roman Catholic. Then followed three years of indecision and wandering, mainly in Canada, where he worked as a teamster and labourer on the Canadian Pacific Railway. He entered The Beda College, Rome, in 1913 and was ordained priest two years later.

In Rome Hawes met Bishop William Bernard Kelly from Western Australia and was recruited for his Geraldton diocese. The dual role of outback missionary and architect with a commission to design a cathedral appealed strongly to Hawes's two major enthusiasms. Arriving in Geraldton in November 1915, he took up a temporary appointment in the Murchison goldfields parish of Mount Magnet and Cue, but started work on his Geraldton cathedral next June. By August 1918 the nave was opened for services but the Cathedral of St Francis Xavier was not completed until 1938, owing to lack of funds and the hostility of Dr Richard Ryan who succeeded Bishop Kelly in 1923. The cathedral is Hawes's most important building: frankly eclectic, a mixture of Romanesque and Californian Spanish Mission styles, but with a roughcast simplicity and dignity totally in harmony with the surroundings.

Of Hawes's other buildings in Western Australia, the most interesting include his highly individual parish church of Our Lady of Mount Carmel, Mullewa, again largely Romanesque and built of local stone mainly through the architect's own labours, and the adjoining priest's house (1927). There are also churches at Morawa (1932), Carnarvon (1934), Northampton and the Utakarra cemetery chapel (1935), and Perenjori (1936); and he designed chapels at Yalgoo, Bluff Point, Nanson and Melangatta homestead.

In 1922 Archbishop Clune [q.v.8] commissioned Hawes to design a new cathedral for the Perth diocese, but while Hawes was in England ordering stained glass and mosaics for the project his plans were rejected and the choice of architect switched to M. F. Cavanagh. Bitterly disappointed, Hawes was later befriended by his next bishop, James Patrick O'Collins, who greatly valued his work and arranged in 1937 for him to receive the Papal title, monsignor.

Throughout most of his life Hawes was attracted by the eremitical ideal: in 1939 he returned, via England, to the Bahamas where he built a hermitage on Cat Island and attempted to live as a hermit under the name of Fra Jerome. But his architectural talents were soon sought and he spent much time designing churches and supervising building on Cat Island, Long Island, and in Nassau where a convent, a boys' college, and the Benedictine Monastery of St Augustine brought him fame. Worn out through hard work and a severe regimen, he died in St Francis Hospital, Miami, Florida, United States of America, on 26 June 1956. He was buried in the cave he had prepared for himself below his hermitage on the hilltop of Cat Island.

P. F. Anson, *Abbot extraordinary*, and *The hermit of Cat Island* (Lond, 1958); J. M. Freeland, *Architecture in Australia* (Melb, 1968); *Westerly*, Nov 1963, Sept 1976; J. C. Hawes diaries and letters (St Augustine's Monastery, Foxhill, Nassau, Bahama Islands, *and* Bishop's House, Geraldton, WA).   A. G. EVANS

HAWKEN, ROGER WILLIAM HERCULES (1878-1947), civil engineer, was born on 12 May 1878 at Darlington, Sydney, son of Nicholas Hawken, merchant, later a member of parliament, and his wife Mary Jane, née Vance. Educated at Newington College and the University of Sydney (B.C.E., 1900; B.A., 1902), he worked as an engineering assistant, first on the Tamworth–Manilla railway and in 1901-03 on an early abortive design for a Sydney harbour bridge.

A short term as acting professor at the Ballarat School of Mines, Victoria, preceded appointment in 1905 as director of public works for the Federated Malay States; there he developed an interest in hydrology and earth pressures which led later to major research. Returning to Australia in 1909, Hawken was successively engineer to the shires of Ashford, New South Wales, and Yalleroi, Queensland. After a brief period as locum tenens for Professor W. H. Warren [q.v.6] at the University of Sydney, he became in October 1912 the first lecturer in civil engineering in the new University of Queensland. When his professor A. J. Gibson [q.v.8] was called for service as a reserve officer in World War I, Hawken became professor of engineering *de facto* in 1916 and *de jure* in 1919 when Gibson resigned.

Hawken's academic bent was evident by 1903 in a remarkably advanced paper to the Sydney University Engineering Society on the structural analysis of bridges. He graduated M.C.E. from Sydney in 1918 after submitting a thesis on column design, a frontier topic of the period, and appears to have had slightly the better of a lively argument with the eminent English engineer, E. H. Salmon, who had written an authoritative text on the subject. In the 1920s he turned again to earth pressures and the stability of slopes; he thus was one of the pioneers of the study of soil mechanics, a subject generally neglected until the 1950s. In later work on rainfall run-off and flooding potential and the economic appraisal of engineering schemes, his ideas were well ahead of his time.

Hawken was reserved and excessively formal, with a wry, sometimes biting sense of humour; engineering and the university made up his life. He saw the complete engineer as a combination of wide experience and wide culture, encouraged originality in his students, called himself 'the senior student', and was known as 'Hanks'. A founder of the Institution of Engineers, Australia, in 1919, he was its president in 1923 and a councillor until his death. In 1931 he was awarded the (Sir) Peter Nicol Russell [q.v.6] memorial medal. At his suggestion in 1928, Queensland became the first State to legislate for compulsory registration of consulting engineers. Hawken was commissioned by the government in a number of investigations.

On 18 October 1947, fifteen days after his retirement was announced, Hawken died of cerebro-vascular disease at his home, and was cremated. He was survived by his wife Adelaide Margrette, née Mott, whom he had married at Black Mountain, New South Wales, on 17 January 1912, and by five daughters. The main engineering building on the St Lucia campus of the University of Queensland is named after him and contains a portrait by Dorothy Coleman. The annual Hawken address, presented by the Queensland division of the Institution of Engineers, is usually held in its Hawken Auditorium.

A. H. Corbett, *The Institution of Engineers, Australia* (Syd, 1973); Univ Qld, *Calendar*, 1911-47; *Univ Qld Gazette*, Dec 1947; D. H. Trollope, 'Engineering—the makings of man', inaugural Hawken address, 1973 (held by Qld division, Institution of Engineers, Aust).   D. H. TROLLOPE

HAWKER, CHARLES ALLAN SEYMOUR (1894-1938), politician and pastoralist, was born on 16 May 1894 at Bungaree homestead, near Clare, South Australia, second son of Michael Seymour Hawker, manager of the Hawker family stations, and his wife Elizabeth Begg, née McFarlane, and grandson of George Charles Hawker [q.v.4]. From his family Charles inherited a tradition of patriotism, loyalty to the Crown, attachment to Great Britain and parliamentary service. He was educated at Geelong Church of England Grammar School where he distinguished himself as a scholar and athlete, and from 1913 at Trinity College, Cambridge (B.A., 1919; M.A., 1922), where he read history.

In 1914 he enlisted in England and was commissioned as a temporary lieutenant in the 6th (Service) Battalion, Somerset Light Infantry (Prince Albert's), on 1 August 1915. He served on the Western Front in the Ypres salient from May 1915 and was wounded on 16 August and again on 25 September at Loos, as a result of which he lost an eye. After recuperating from fourteen operations he was attached in 1917 to the regiment's 1st (Regular) Battalion in England. Although classified unfit for active service, Hawker insisted on returning to the front with his battalion in May 1917 in command of a company, with the rank of captain. On 4 October 1917, at Broodseinde during the 3rd battle of Ypres, he was again severely wounded, and paralysed from the waist down. After a series of operations, and through sheer determination, he was able to walk with two sticks, although his legs were in surgical irons to the end of his life.

Hawker returned to South Australia in 1920, studied woolclassing, forestry and botany and took an increasing interest in the family properties. In 1921 he joined the State council of the Returned Sailors' and Soldiers' Imperial League of Australia and served as vice-president. His father gave him Warrakimo, a run in the Flinders Ranges and in 1925 he bought himself Dillowie, a property near Hallett where he shared a galvanized iron cottage with his manager. That year he also travelled to England for a further operation, taking the opportunity to visit woollen mills at Bradford and return via the United States of America to examine rural industries. His knowledge of marketing problems led to him becoming in February 1928 the South Australian member of the Commonwealth Board of Trade. Hawker's economic thinking, as the Depression deepened, was coloured by his conviction that the countries of the British Empire should act as an economic unit and by his opposition to sectional and State interests in Australia. He believed that Australia's prosperity depended on the export value of its primary produce, but he pleaded for equality of sacrifice throughout the nation and strongly opposed any selfish national policies which might embarrass Great Britain.

From September 1927 to 1930 Hawker had been president of the new Liberal Federation of South Australia. During this time he worked hard to unite the anti-Labor forces in South Australia, but although he made many overtures to the Country Party the breach was not healed till 1932 when the Liberal Country League was formed. In 1929 he entered the House of Representatives as member for Wakefield, when in the Australia-wide landslide to Labor the prime minister, S. M. (Viscount) Bruce [q.v.7], lost his seat. Hawker offered to resign in his favour. In January 1932 at (Sir) John Latham's [q.v.] request, and despite his own misgivings about Hawker's individualism, Prime Minister Lyons [q.v.] appointed Hawker minister for markets and repatriation. The Country Party was not represented in the cabinet, so Hawker was the only expert on rural affairs. When the markets portfolio was renamed in April 1932 he became the first minister of commerce, until he resigned on 23 September over the issue of reduction of members' salaries, to which he was committed. In the debate on the financial emergency bill he crossed the floor to vote in a minority of eight, 'the hardest walk in my life' and one that caused political consternation. His detractors asserted that as a 'rich man' he could easily afford the reduction, but, in fact, he had lost heavily by drought and low prices and carried a mortgage on Dillowie. The act cost Hawker dearly in political terms.

In November 1932, in a widely acclaimed speech, he forcefully defended the provisions of the Ottawa Agreement, for which as minister he had helped to prepare the Australian case. He continued to monitor the government's failure to implement the agreement or to reduce tariffs and in 1933 denounced what he saw as a policy of 'government of the feeble for the greedy'. A recognized spokesman for the primary producer, he argued constantly for reduced costs and charges and for stabilized prices, as expounded in his pamphlet *Problems of the wheatgrower* (1934). The development and improvement of the viticulture and fruit-growing industries were also among his crusades. In the 1934 election he was a highly successful campaign director for the Liberal Country League, promoting the composite Lyons-Page [q.v.] ministry that resulted. His own election margin was greatly increased in his wheat-growing electorate.

Hawker travelled widely, often in his own specially adapted car but increasingly by air. In 1935 he toured England, France and Germany to investigate livestock and agricultural conditions and marketing arrangements. At Lyons's request he acted as consultant to the negotiations on meat at the Imperial Trade Conference. The growing anxiety about Hitler heightened his interest in Empire unity and defence and precipitated him into an examination of modern military equipment and organization. He also spent three weeks travelling in the Soviet Union, publishing his observations in a pamphlet *An Australian looks at Russian farms* (1936). Hawker visited Japan in 1936 and was drawn into the negotiation of a new Australian trade policy that severely strained relations with Japan. He favoured a more generous understanding with Japan in the interests of security as well as marketing and contributed an article to the *Australia Asiatic Bulletin* (April 1937) on the dispute. Hawker also visited Peking and Shanghai and was able to bring a wealth of first-hand information to parliamentary debates. Generous-minded and charming he was appreciated as a convincing speaker with a comprehensive grasp of national and international issues.

At the British Commonwealth Relations Conference in September 1938 at Lapstone, New South Wales, he delivered a paper on 'Australia's foreign trade treaties'. In 1937 Hawker unsuccessfully led the 'Yes' case in South Australia in the referendum for Commonwealth control of marketing and aviation. He advocated the development of north Australia as crucial to Australia's future, and during 1938 spoke repeatedly on defence, urging some form of universal military training. Believing war inevitable he criticized inadequate defence votes and castigated isolationists in speeches that led to further press support for his reinclusion in cabinet.

Hawker was killed on 25 October 1938 when the aircraft *Kyeema* crashed into Mount Dandenong in Victoria. His untimely death was sharply felt. He had been an outstanding and respected figure in the Federal parliament, whom some of his own party would have supported as prime minister. John Curtin, the Opposition leader, believed he had been on the threshold of great achievements. His patrician politics, as well as his courage and determination, had already given rise to what was to become a 'Hawker legend'. He reassured and influenced those who met him. 'It wasn't so much that he displayed physical courage', wrote one of them, 'what struck me most deeply about him was that the light never went out inside him'. His friend (Sir) Keith Hancock discerned in him 'the best that an Australian can do or be'.

A state memorial service was held at St Peter's Cathedral in Adelaide. His ashes were buried privately in the churchyard of St Michael's, Bungaree. Hawker was a practising Anglican. Unmarried, he had a large number of god-children. He was short, with brown hair and blue eyes, and had the neat head of his family. He was active in the establishment of St Mark's College, University of Adelaide, and a council-member till his death. Buildings at St Mark's and the Waite [q.v.] Institute in Adelaide, a library at Geelong Grammar School and a room in Burgmann College, Canberra, perpetuate his memory. In 1968 a new Federal electorate was named in his honour. A portrait by J. Hanson Walker is held by the family and another by W. A. Dargie is in Parliament House, Canberra.

W. K. Hancock, *Country and calling* (Lond, 1954); D. Pike, *Charles Hawker* (Melb, 1968); L. Needham, *Charles Hawker; soldier-pastoralist statesman* (Adel, 1969); *PD* (Cwlth), 1937-39, p 1041; *Aust Q*, Sept 1937, Dec 1938; *Pastoral Review*, 48 (Nov 1938); *Aust J of Politics and Hist*, vol 27 (1981), no 2; *SMH*, 17 Oct 1929; *Advertiser* (Adel), 24 Sept 1932, 26 Oct 1938; J. Lonie, Conservatism and class in South Australia during the depression years 1929-1934 (M.A. thesis, Univ Adel, 1973); M. Williams, C.A.S. Hawker (B.A. Hons thesis, Univ Adel, 1982); Hawker-Needham papers *and* Hawker papers and correspondence (NL).

DIRK VAN DISSEL

HAWKER, EDWARD WILLIAM (1850-1940), barrister, grazier, politician and metallurgist, was born on 14 January 1850 at Bungaree near Clare, South Australia, eldest of fifteen children of George Charles Hawker [q.v.4], grazier, and his wife Bessie, née Seymour. Hawker was educated at the Collegiate School of St Peter, Adelaide; Harrow; and Trinity College, Cambridge (B.A., 1874; LL.B., 1873; M.A., LL.M., 1890). In 1874 he was called to the Bar at the Inner Temple. Returning to South Australia in 1875, he had difficulty in settling down; next year he joined (Sir) Richard Chaffey Baker's [q.v.7] law firm but soon left for New Zealand. In 1879 he was admitted to the South Australian Bar and began to practise, eventually in Nicholson & Hawker.

In 1884 Edward became member for Stanley in the House of Assembly as a representative of the conservative pastoral interest. In 1889 he resigned and sailed for England. After a year at Cambridge pursuing law, he studied mining and metallurgy at the Mountain Academy, Clausthal, Germany. He returned home in 1892 with his wife Mary Letitia, daughter of Sir William Stawell [q.v.6], whom he had married in London on 14 May 1890. Hawker began work as a metallurgist and in 1893 regained his seat in the assembly where he occasionally felt handicapped by his father's presence. Assisted by his wife in preparing speeches and analysing new legislation, he was considered to be never more than an earnest, persevering, rather prosy politician, who favoured rigid economy and retrenchment. He lost his seat in 1896 and became a lecturer in mining at the South Australian School of Mines and Industries. He enjoyed teaching and often took his students on trips to mines throughout the colony.

Hawker was the first president of the South Australian branch of the Australian Natives' Association in 1888; a member of the Public Library Board (1894-1910); a council-member of the School of Mines (1893-96); a member of the State Children's Council (1898-1909); and president of the Adelaide Club (1925-27). He belonged to the British Institution of Mining Engineers and the American Institute of Mining Engineers, and was also a fellow of the Geological Society of London. He presided over the Australasian National League (1905-07) and was active in the Liberal Union (later Liberal Federation) and the Liberal and Country League. He was a prodigious letter-writer and compiler and distributor of extracts from Hansard; his wife (d. 1938) was also articulate and active in the anti-Labor cause.

In 1895 Hawker inherited a large estate at East Bungaree; in 1907 he began grazing there full time and energetically cultivated suitable African and Asian grass strains. His hobbies included bookbinding, shooting and billiards. He died at Bungaree on 20 September 1940, survived by three daughters and two sons. Charles Seymour Hawker [q.v.] was a nephew.

T. Sadler, *Some annals of Adelaide* (Adel, 1933); *Quiz* (Adel), 2 Dec 1892; *Observer* (Adel), 10 June 1893, 28 Apr 1894; *South Australian*, 18 Feb 1926, 10 Feb 1927; *Advertiser* (Adel), 21 Sept 1940; E. W. Hawker, Diaries and digest of diaries, *and* political correspondence, *and* G. C. Hawker, Letters to E. W. Hawker (SAA).   ROB VAN DEN HOORN

HAWKER, HARRY GEORGE (1889-1921), aviator, was born on 22 January 1889 at South Brighton, Melbourne, son of George Hawker, blacksmith, and his wife Mary Ann, née Anderson, both Victorian-born. He attended schools to the age of 12 at Moorabbin, East Malvern, St Kilda and Prahran.

As a young boy Hawker studied the flight of birds and announced his intention of becoming an aviator. In 1901 he became a trainee mechanic at the Melbourne branch of Hall & Warden bicycle depot, where in 1903 he road-tested Oldsmobile cars. In 1905 he joined the Tarrant [q.v.] Motor and Engineering Co. as a qualified mechanic, gaining a reputation as an expert trouble-shooter. He also became an enthusiastic and skilful motor cyclist. About 1907 he set up his own workshop at Caramut, western Victoria, where he serviced a small fleet of cars owned by the de Little family. He saved most of his earnings and in 1911 left for England where he hoped to become an aviator. Of slight build and only 5 ft. (152 cm) tall, he looked much younger than his 22 years; shy and quietly spoken, usually forgetting to carry references, Hawker was often brushed aside as an over-ambitious child.

He was about to return home when in July he gained a position with the Commer Car Co. which allowed him to show his all-round ability as a tradesman. In early 1912 he worked for the Mercedes Co. and then the Austro-Daimler Co. In June Australian friends introduced him to Fred Sigrist, foreman of the Sopwith Aviation Co. Ltd, who engaged him to work on the Sopwith-Wright biplane. He again showed outstanding ability as a tradesman and spent his first wages in enrolling in a flying school where his new employer, (Sir Thomas) Sopwith, gave him personal tuition. Hawker proved to be a natural pilot, and after only three lessons flew solo for 50 minutes. In October he gained his Royal Aero Club licence, No. 279.

After logging only 24 hours flying time he took part in competitions with the Sopwith-Wright. His first major win was the Michelin Cup No. 1 for 1912 when he remained aloft for 8 hours, 23 minutes, and created a new British duration record. Sopwith appointed him as test pilot, gave him free rein as a designer, and in 1913 was rewarded with several ideas destined to improve world aviation standards. Among these was a move by Hawker to eliminate roof-top crashes by encouraging airmen to fly at higher altitudes; he set an example by taking part in high altitude competitions. In June he created a new British height record for a solo flight at 11 450 ft. (3490 m), then another with one passenger at 13 400 ft.

(4080 m). In August, with Harry Kauper [q.v.] as his mechanic, he made two attempts for the *Daily Mail* Round Great Britain prize of £5000, in a seaplane. The second attempt ended near Dublin after they had flown 1043 miles (1678 km) in 21 hours, 44 minutes flying time. Acknowledging that this was the first time that 1000 miles (1609 km) had been flown over an outwards course, the *Daily Mail* management presented Hawker with a special prize of £1000.

During November Hawker produced the Sopwith Tabloid, a revolutionary short-winged biplane which emerged as the fastest and most manoeuvrable aeroplane in the world and led to biplanes gaining preference over monoplanes as combat aircraft during World War I. Following test flights at Brooklands, Hawker shipped the plane to Australia and gave Australians their first practical flying exhibitions when between January and April 1914 he flew at Melbourne, Sydney, Albury and Ballarat. During the tour he carried many notable citizens as passengers, including the governor-general and minister of defence. Dubbed the country's 'first real apostle of flight', he greatly boosted Australia's confidence in the aeroplane.

Back in England in June, Hawker found aviation set back because of the number of airmen being killed in tail-spin crashes. He developed a method of recovering from a tail-spin which became standard training practice. In June he also completed a record twelve loops in succession in a Tabloid. At the beginning of World War I he enlisted with the Royal Naval Air Service but was withheld from active service to continue his design work at Sopwith's and to serve as a general test pilot. In the first two years of the war he tested 295 planes over 199 flying days and advised various aircraft manufacturers, checking for inherent structural faults and recommending modifications where necessary. Later in the war he visited aerodromes in England and France on trouble-shooting missions. On 14 November 1917 at St Peter's Anglican Church, Ealing, he married Muriel Alice Peaty.

After the war Hawker renewed his interest in long-distance flying and in May 1919, with Commander Kenneth MacKenzie-Grieve, attempted to fly the Atlantic Ocean from Newfoundland to England. They took off on 18 May but an icy storm caused the plane to drift off course with its engine developing radiator trouble, and eventually Hawker had to ditch in the mid-Atlantic. They were picked up by a Danish tramp steamer which did not carry wireless. The men were posted missing, presumed dead. King George V sent a message of condolence to Hawker's wife, but after learning of the rescue announced that both men would be presented with the first Air Force Crosses ever to be awarded. The *Daily Mail* acknowledged Hawker as the first pilot to fly over 1000 miles (1609 km) of water without touching down, and awarded him a prize of £5000.

With a lull in aircraft production, in 1919 Hawker participated in speedboat and motor racing events and tried to revive the Sopwith Aviation Co. which had closed down. In November 1920, with the aid of Sopwith and Sigrist, he formed the H. G. Hawker Engineering Co. which built the H. G. Hawker two-stroke motor cycle. He also bought and modified a sports car prototype from the A.C. Co. which he drove as the first car to reach 100 miles (161 km) an hour. In 1921 he again turned his ambitions towards winning the Aerial Derby. He was killed while flying a French Goshawk on a trial run near Hendon, England, on 12 July 1921. Survived by his wife and two daughters, he was buried in Hook cemetery. An inquest revealed that he had lost control of the plane through paralysis caused by a sudden haemorrhage of an abscess on the spine. He had also been suffering from tuberculosis, and his licence had expired at the end of June.

Dept of Civil Aviation, *Harry George Hawker* (np, nd); M. Hawker, *H. G. Hawker, airman* (Lond, 1922); C. Kingston, *It don't seem a day too much* (Adel, 1971); *Flight* (Lond), 30 Aug 1913; *Aircraft* (Melb), Jan, Feb 1962; *Argus*, 28 Jan 1914; *Daily Telegraph* (Syd), 23 Feb 1914; *Albury Daily News*, 9 Mar 1914; *Punch* (Melb), 26 Mar 1914; *Ballarat Courier*, 6 Apr 1914; *Manchester Guardian*, 13 July 1921; information from Mr H. Miller, Broome, WA.   THOMAS SHEEHY

HAWKER, JAMES CLARENCE (1859-1951), soldier, was born on 8 May 1859 in Adelaide, second son and fifth child of James Collins Hawker, tide surveyor and later pastoralist and stock and station agent, and his wife Louisa, née Lipson, both English-born. James Collins Hawker was a son of Vice Admiral Edward Hawker, Royal Navy, and his brother George Charles [q.v.4] became a South Australian cabinet minister. They founded the famous Bungaree grazing property near Clare.

Although there were naval antecedents on both sides of his family James Clarence chose the army and on 17 October 1881 was commissioned in the Adelaide Rifles, a volunteer unit. After becoming adjutant and being promoted captain in 1883, he was appointed a lieutenant in the Permanent Artillery of South Australia on 4 April 1885.

In 1886 he took charge of Fort Largs where he commanded a detachment of thirty men. He was promoted captain in 1891. In March 1893 he sailed for Albany, Western Australia, in charge of a party of South Australian gunners; their task was to form the new garrison and mount the guns as part of an arrangement whereby the several Australian colonies had agreed to co-operate in defence matters. Hawker supervised the mounting of three six-inch breech-loading guns at Albany before returning to Adelaide in June; in August he became commander of the Permanent Artillery in South Australia. He was promoted major in 1896.

During the South African War Hawker served as a major with the 4th (South Australian) Imperial Bushmen as second-in-command and adjutant. He saw operations in the Transvaal, Orange Free State and Cape Colony, including the action at Wittebergen, before being invalided home on 28 February 1901. He resumed command of the Permanent Artillery in South Australia on 1 May after the formation of the Commonwealth Military Forces. In May 1903 he was posted to Sydney as a company officer, Royal Australian Artillery, 2nd Military District. A succession of staff and regimental appointments followed in Victoria, New South Wales and Western Australia until his promotion to lieut-colonel on the Administrative and Instructional Staff and his appointment as assistant adjutant general, Victoria, in 1911. He was promoted colonel on 1 May 1914. In World War I he remained A.A.G. in Victoria, having his retirement date extended until 1 November 1918. His retirement, with the honorary rank of brigadier general, ended thirty-seven years of continuous service in the military forces of Australia. He was one of the first Australian-born soldiers to reach high rank.

Hawker had married Agnes Maud Phillips on 2 April 1887 at Trinity Church, Adelaide; the marriage was later dissolved. They had two sons and a daughter. The younger son, Godfrey Carew Hawker, served in the Royal Field Artillery in France in World War I, in the 3rd Afghan War in 1919 and with the Australian Imperial Force in World War II. Survived by his sons, James Clarence Hawker died at Mornington, Victoria, on 9 November 1951 and was cremated with Anglican rites. His estate was sworn for probate at £27 203. Edward William Hawker, South Australian grazier and politician, and Charles Allan Seymour Hawker, Federal parliamentarian [qq.v.], were his cousins.

Aust Defence Dept, *Official records of the Australian military contingents to the war in South Africa*, P. L. Murray ed (Melb, 1911); *South Australian Artillery 1840-1966* (Adel, 1968).

J. WHITELAW

HAWKINS, HERBERT MIDDLETON (1876-1939), real estate agent and politician, was born on 29 October 1876 at Brixton, London, son of Thomas Richardson Hawkins, accountant, and his wife Ann, née Butters. Educated in London, he migrated to Sydney about 1895 and by 1897 was city manager of the Vacuum Oil Co. Ltd. At Stanmore on 4 November 1899 he married Beatrice Buchanan (d. 1935).

Soon prominent in Methodist circles, Hawkins was organizing secretary of the Sydney Central Methodist Mission (later honorary treasurer and a member of the executive until 1939), a lay representative at the Methodist Jubilee Conference in 1905 and a circuit steward from 1907. From about 1911 he was also manager of Spencer's [q.v.] Pictures Ltd and a director of the firm.

During and after World War I Hawkins set up as an agent and auctioneer (1916) and later joined H. W. Horning & Co. Ltd, auctioneers and real estate agents, one of Sydney's biggest firms, becoming joint managing director. He actively promoted the Real Estate Institute of New South Wales, of which he was an early secretary and president in 1926-29. In the 1920s he moved for a federal organization, the Associated Real Estate Institutes and Agents Association of Australia, and was its president in 1928-39. He found that real estate gave ample space for his 'mental and physical and moral powers'.

Such capacity was extended by philanthropic labours: he was honorary treasurer of the non-denominational United Charities Fund, vice-president of the New South Wales Alliance for the Suppression of Intemperance in 1918-25 and a founder and honorary secretary of the War Memorial Hospital, Waverley. When appointed in June 1932 to the Legislative Council and an honorary minister assisting the minister for labour and industry (assistant colonial secretary from 1933), he spoke authoritatively on food relief frauds. Although apparently a political unknown Hawkins had been a council-member of the National Party for most of the 1920s and represented the All for Australia League at the formation of the State branch of the United Australia Party, later joining its finance and convention committees.

An articulate parliamentarian, able to both represent and lead the government in the Upper House, Hawkins attained full ministerial responsibility in the second Stevens [q.v.]-Bruxner [q.v.7] cabinet as minister for social services in 1935-38; from June to December 1936 he was also acting minister for education and from October 1938 minister for labour and industry. His portfolios encompassed well-established charitable concerns, hospitals, children, outdoor relief and, notably, housing reform. This involved him in responses to anti-slum campaigners, a fact-finding world tour in 1937 and support for housing improvement schemes.

At Woollahra on 21 July 1938 Hawkins married Gwendoline, née Jupp, widow of G. H. Bosch [q.v.7]. On 16 June 1939 he fell to his death from the window of his ministerial office. His demise was inexplicable, and the coroner brought in a finding of accidental death. After a state funeral in St Andrew's Anglican Cathedral, Hawkins was buried in the Methodist section of Northern Suburbs cemetery. He was survived by his second wife and by a son and two daughters of his first marriage. His estate was valued for probate at £20 652.

Theatre Mag (Syd), 2 Dec 1912; Real Estate Institute of NSW, *J*, 1 (Aug 1939), no 1; *SMH*, 1 Jan 1920, 17, 19 June 1939, 6 July 1939.   J. I. ROE

HAWTHORN, ARTHUR GEORGE CLARENCE (1859-1934), solicitor and politician, was born on 31 October 1859 in Hobart Town, son of George Hawthorn, shipmaster, and his wife Isabella Marie Louise, née Steele. Educated at the Hobart High School, he was later articled to three different legal firms. Admitted as a solicitor in 1884, he was immediately persuaded by Thomas Macdonald-Patterson, a Brisbane solicitor, to move to Queensland as a partner in Macdonald-Patterson, Fitzgerald & Hawthorn, later Hawthorn & Byram (1900), Hawthorn & Lightoller (1916) and A. G. C. Hawthorn & Co. (1931).

Elected to the Ithaca Shire Council in 1899, he was president in 1901 and in 1901-04 was on the executive of the Local Authorities' Association of Queensland. He was a delegate of the association in 1901-02 lobbying the government about new local government legislation. In 1902 Hawthorn won the Legislative Assembly seat of Enoggera as an Independent Ministerialist, defeating the sitting Labor member Matt Reid [q.v.]. Joining the Morgan [q.v.] Liberal group in 1903, he helped to bring down the conservative Philp [q.v.] government. A popular local member, Hawthorn was unopposed in 1904. He believed in progressive reform: the vote for women, and legislation against sweated labour and for wages boards; he was also interested in farming, irrigation and local government and took a sound critical interest in financial debates. Though often asserting his independence, Hawthorn was by 1907 in basic agreement with William Kidston [q.v.] and supported his increasingly independent stand against Labor organization. He be-

came Kidston's home secretary from 3 July to 19 November 1907 and again from 18 February 1908. From 29 October 1908 to 7 February 1911 he was Kidston's treasurer.

Hawthorn easily withstood bitter campaigning by Philp's supporters who raised the socialist bogey. Presenting himself as a democrat and supported by capable electorate committees, he secured easy majorities: much of his support came from women and Labor voters. As home secretary he legislated in 1908 for old-age pensions, electoral reform and a referendum on religious instruction in state schools. As treasurer in 1909 he initiated a scheme to provide cheap houses for low-income workers. Five days after Kidston's resignation in February 1911 Hawthorn was appointed to the Legislative Council. He unsuccessfully sought re-election for Ithaca in 1912, then became increasingly conservative after the advent of the Labor government in 1915. In 1916-21 he stoutly resisted Labor's attacks on the council, extended his opposition to almost every aspect of its policy, and tried to form a combined anti-Labor Liberal party. When the council went out of existence in 1922 his political career ended.

On 12 December 1894 at Ashgrove, Brisbane, Hawthorn had married Mary, daughter of Alexander Stewart [q.v.]; they had two daughters. Quiet, reserved and a thoughtful, careful speaker, he was a popular member of numerous sporting bodies. He died with leukaemia in Brisbane on 6 May 1934 and was buried in Toowong cemetery after a Presbyterian ceremony.

Brisbane Courier, 29 Apr 1907, 7 Feb 1911; *Courier Mail*, 7 May 1934; *Daily Standard*, 8 May 1934; Local Authorities Assn, Minutes (Local Government Assn of Qld, Brisb); information from Mrs D. Hill Smith and Miss D. Hawthorn, Ashgrove, Brisb.   W. ROSS JOHNSTON

HAY, CLIFFORD HENDERSON (1878-1949), public servant, was born on 22 April 1878 in Adelaide, son of Thomas Davidson Hay, English-born marine engineer and later secretary of the Australasian Institute of Marine Engineers, and his wife Mary Ann, née Green. The family moved to Sydney in 1884. After attending Croydon Park and Crown Street Public schools, Hay entered a mercantile office. He joined the public service in 1896 and by 1901 was a clerk in the taxation branch of the Colonial Treasurer's Department. At St Clement's Anglican Church, Mosman, on 12 February 1907 he married Lucille Florence May Westcott. Later that year he was appointed senior clerk in the newly formed Premier's Department; on 15 March 1916 he became secretary and permanent head.

Hay's department administered the affairs of Government House, both branches of the Legislature, the Agent-General's Office in London, foreign consuls and the State's representation abroad; it was the channel of communication with the Commonwealth and other State governments. In World War I Hay 'worked almost continuously day and night in the discharge of additional duties devolving upon him as a result of war conditions'. As general secretary to the Conference of Premiers of the Australian States, he had 'a tremendous amount of clerical labour' with 'responsibility for securing legislative and administrative effect' to the conference's decisions. Hay ran his department with 'conspicuous ability and great tact'.

From April until October 1917 he proved an efficient aide to the premier, W. A. Holman [q.v.], on an official mission to Britain, Europe and North America. He also accompanied Premiers Storey [q.v.] to England, America and Japan in 1921 and Sir George Fuller [q.v.8] overseas in 1923.

A conspicuous public figure, Hay was identified with the organization of state occasions, notably the visits to Sydney of the French mission (1918); Admiral the Earl Jellicoe (1919) and General Sir William Birdwood [q.v.7] (1920); the victory celebrations (1919); the tour of the prince of Wales (1920), for whom he arranged a special aerial mail service from South Australia to Sydney; and the visits of the Royal Navy in 1924 and the American fleet in 1925. Hay was appointed M.V.O. (1920), C.M.G. (1921) and, after the visit of the duke and duchess of York in 1927, C.B.E. (1928). In recognition of his increased status and responsibilities, he was appointed under-secretary on 1 July 1924.

In the 1930s Hay was State organizer for the opening of the Sydney Harbour Bridge on 19 March 1932 and, with characteristic efficiency, was able to provide a replacement ribbon after the unscheduled activities of Captain de Groot. He managed the visit of the duke of Gloucester (1934), and was executive member of Australia's 150th Anniversary Celebrations Council. In May 1938 Hay was appointed agent-general for New South Wales in London, but suffered a stroke late next year and was recalled. In 1940-43 he was president of the State Superannuation Board.

Very tall and straight-backed, Hay was a fine-looking man, always impeccably dressed. Good-humoured, with unfailing courtesy, he was at home in any company. An able and tireless worker, attentive to detail, he engaged in a wide range of outside interests: cycling, tennis, bowls, Free-

masonry, fishing and gardening. He was a fellow of the Queensland branch of the Royal Geographical Society of Australasia and the New South Wales branch of the Royal Empire Society, and for some years was chairman of the board of trustees of St Margaret's Hospital.

Hay died from cerebral thrombosis at his home at Cremorne on 16 December 1949 and was cremated with Anglican rites. His wife and three sons survived him. Although frequently mentioned for appointment to other positions, Hay had remained chief official associate of seven premiers, Holman, Storey, Dooley [q.v.8], Fuller, Lang [q.v.], Bavin [q.v.7] and Stevens [q.v.]. Many of the measures and statements for which they were applauded originated with Hay.

Smith's Weekly, 29 Dec 1921, 11 July 1925; Sunday Times, 16 Apr 1925, 17 July 1927; SMH, 30 Dec 1924, 18 Dec 1949; CO 448/23, p 175 (PRO, Lond); information from and newspaper cuttings held by Mrs P. M. Hay, Chatswood, and Mr R. H. Hay, Killara, Syd.   JACK WATSON

HAY, JAMES (1865-1962), Salvation Army officer, was born on 25 May 1865 at Govan, Scotland, son of Samuel Hay, blacksmith, and his wife Mary, née Barnes. After primary schooling he worked as a grocer but in September 1881 was converted by the Salvation Army and decided to become an officer. Entering the new training college at Clapton, London, in November 1882, he was commissioned and served seven years in various corps in England and Ireland. At Dumfries, Scotland, about 1885 he married a fellow officer, Jeannie Gwen Waugh; they had a daughter and four sons.

Promoted to the staff in 1890, Hay became field secretary, then chief secretary for Great Britain and, after promotion to commissioner, principal of the Clapton International Training College. In 1909 he was appointed territorial commissioner for Australia and New Zealand and arrived in Melbourne with his wife on 6 September. He immediately began to tour his vast command by rail until eventually given a motor car by (Sir) Sidney Kidman [q.v.]. An enthusiastic Puritan, he deplored the régime of his recalcitrant predecessor Herbert Booth [q.v.7], ordered the removal of his name from foundation stones and closed down his motion-picture work. In 1912 his load was reduced by the establishment of a separate territorial command in New Zealand.

Hay went to the army's international conference in London in 1914 and was returning to Australia when war was declared. On arrival he launched a campaign of work with the troops which burgeoned later into the extensive Red Shield organization. He became well known to most of the nation's political leaders and in 1918 was appointed O.B.E. During 1921 he carried out the separation of the Australian administration into two territorial commands. Promoted to British commissioner that year, Hay left an organization which had been immeasurably strengthened by his land dealings, the purchase of 426 new buildings and the creation of forty new institutions. Some of his subordinates later achieved high command, notably George Carpenter, the army's commanding general in 1939-46.

Soon driven out of Britain by ill health, Hay commanded South Africa and Rhodesia in 1922-26, New Zealand in 1926-29 and Canada and Newfoundland until his retirement in 1934. He chose to retire to Melbourne, built a house called Clydebrae in Camberwell, and became an elder statesman of the army in Australia. He wrote a great deal and was in constant demand as a speaker in Sydney, Melbourne and New Zealand. His wife died on 16 October 1951 and was commemorated by the building of a Jeannie Hay Memorial Wing in the Bethany Eventide Home for Women which Hay had founded. In the same year he published an autobiography, *Aggressive Salvationism*. He had been the first officer in the world to receive the badge marking fifty years service but he lived on long after and won world-wide interest as the oldest officer in the army. On the eve of his ninety-sixth birthday he delivered a public lecture but died in Melbourne some months later on 22 March 1962. He was buried in Box Hill cemetery.

Salvation Army, *Property souvenir, Australia* (Melb, nd); B. Bolton, *Booth's drum* (Syd, 1980); *War Cry* (Melb), 30 June, 7, 14, 21, 28 July 1962.
· H. J. GIBBNEY

HAY, ROBERT SNOWDON (1867-1943), bishop, was born on 24 September 1867 at Bishop Auckland, Durham, England, youngest son of James Hay, house-painter, and his wife Elizabeth, née Blair. Robert adhered throughout his life to his mother's strict Sabbatarianism. He was educated at Bishop Barrington Preparatory School, James I Grammar School, Durham, and Hatfield Hall, Durham University (L.Th., 1888; B.A., 1891), where he showed outstanding ability as a student and athlete. He led the Bishop Auckland soccer team to victory over several seasons. After a period as classics master at Durston House School, Ealing, London, Hay was ordained deacon at Auckland in 1891 and appointed curate of St Ives, Leadgate; in 1895 he was curate at South Hylton, Sunderland.

In 1897 Bishop W. T. T. Webber [q.v.] of Brisbane visited England to recruit clergy and offered Hay a parish. On 10 November at St George's Parish Church, Bloomsbury, he married Maud Caroline Glenny, a trained nurse, and three days later sailed for Queensland with his wife, to be incumbent of the parish of Laidley. Originally intending to remain in Australia only five years, in 1903 he moved to Bundaberg, then to St Mark's, Warwick, in 1907, and St Andrew's, South Brisbane, in 1911. Among his many community activities he formed the Lockyer Cricket Association and the Bundaberg Gordon Club and took an intense interest in Pacific islanders and Chinese in the Bundaberg district. He established a large branch of the Church of England Men's Society in Warwick. His success as a parish priest resulted in his election as an honorary canon of St John's Cathedral, Brisbane, in 1909.

In 1916 Hay succeeded Joseph Bertram Kite as dean of Hobart and in 1919, when Bishop Reginald Stephen unexpectedly resigned, he was unanimously elected seventh bishop of Tasmania by a special session of synod. He was consecrated on St Bartholomew's Day by the primate of Australia, Archbishop J. C. Wright [q.v.], in St Andrew's Cathedral, Sydney, and enthroned in Hobart on 9 September. During the troubled inter-war period Hay offered security to the diocese through firm leadership and loving pastoral care. An active champion of the cause of Church reunion, he strongly supported the United Social Services Committee, a body that drew the Protestant denominations closer together. During his episcopate St Wilfrid's College at Cressy was closed, and a new Christ College opened on the Queen's Domain in Hobart. Five new urban parishes were created, St David's Cathedral was completed, and St John's Hospital in Hobart and Broadland House Girls' Grammar School in Launceston were founded.

In August 1942, although ill, Hay presided over the centenary celebrations for the diocese. A holiday followed, but his health did not improve and after an operation he died at East Melbourne on 3 February 1943. His had been the longest term of any bishop of Tasmania. His body was sent back to Hobart for burial in Cornelian Bay cemetery. Predeceased by his wife in 1940, he was survived by three sons and four daughters. A portrait by Florence Rodway [q.v.] hangs in the board room of Church House, Hobart.

W. R. Barrett, *History of the Church of England in Tasmania* (Hob, 1942); *Church News* (Hob), July, Sept 1916, July, Sept, Oct 1919, May, Dec 1920, Dec 1921, Aug 1939, Sept 1942, Aug 1973; *Mercury*, 4 Feb 1943.   LOUIS V. DANIELS

HAY, WILLIAM GOSSE (1875-1945), author and essayist, was born on 17 November 1875 at Linden, Hazelwood Park, Adelaide, son of Alexander Hay [q.v.1] and his wife Agnes Grant, née Gosse, cousin of (Sir) Edmund Gosse, literary critic and essayist, and sister of William Christie Gosse [q.v.4]. Hay was educated privately in Adelaide and from 1889 at Melbourne Church of England Grammar School before in 1895 entering Trinity College, Cambridge (B.A., 1898). At Cambridge he became interested in Australian history and wrote a novel about convict transportation to New South Wales. His father's death in 1898 released him from an obligation to study law and allowed him to devote himself to writing. Early poems and short stories were unsuccessful but in 1901 his Cambridge novel, *Stifled laughter: a melodrama (time 1834)*, was published through the agency of London literary friends and with the financial support of his mother, herself a minor biographer and novelist.

Having inherited independent means, Hay returned thankfully to South Australia in 1901, married Mary Violet Williams on 26 October and settled down to become a 'man of letters'. His seriousness was misunderstood by his relatives and acquaintances, and his response to their dismissive attitude was to withdraw into an intensive study of literary and historical accounts of the convict era in New South Wales and Tasmania. Slowly and painstakingly, he also sought to develop a distinctive style, using for models such writers as R. L. Stevenson, Charles Dickens [q.v.4], George Meredith and Henry James. In 1901 he began, but did not finish, a light satire on South Australian society. He then returned to convict history and wrote his three best-known novels: *Herridge of Reality Swamp* (1907), *Captain Quadring* (1912) and *The escape of the notorious Sir William Heans . . .* (1919). The last most effectively expresses his preoccupation with an individual's struggle to maintain his identity in circumstances hostile to his moral values and social standards. He pursued this theme indirectly in *An Australian Rip Van Winkle and other pieces* (1921), a miscellany of historical studies, literary essays and autobiographical short stories, and again in his last two novels, *Strabane of the Mulberry hills . . .* (1929) and *The mystery of Alfred Doubt . . .* (1937), where the theme becomes subordinate to a more melodramatic affirmation of the triumph of good over evil.

Hay's books were published in London where they attracted favourable reviews. Little critical interest was aroused in Australia where he was barely known in literary circles. His claim to merit as a serious and innovative writer was recognized by very few until the republication of *Sir William Heans* in 1955 led to a controversial revaluation. Critical commentary has since focused chiefly on his style, his historical interpretation of the convict system and the extent to which he objectified personal conflicts within that context. This body of criticism has given him significant status as an Australian novelist.

From 1925 Hay lived in seclusion near Victor Harbor. Although he held liberal views in religion and politics, describing himself as an Anglican of the Low Church and a 'conservative democrat', his less flexible adherence to the social attitudes of his youth led to exaggerated accounts of eccentricity. Those who knew him, including his publisher Sir Stanley Unwin, allowed that he was obsessed with his objectives as a writer and intensely sensitive to critical and personal affront; but also found him aware of his foibles and not without humour. He died on 21 March 1945 after illness attributed to over-exertion in fighting a bush fire. He was buried at Victor Harbor and was survived by his wife and three sons.

F. Gosse, *The Gosses, an Anglo-Australian family* (Canb, 1981); I. D. Muecke, The life and novels of William Hay (M.A. thesis, Univ Adel, 1965); S. J. Way, Letterbooks, 1897-1910 (SAA); Hay papers (Baillieu Lib, Univ Melb).   I. D. MUECKE

HAYES, JOHN BLYTH (1868-1956), farmer and premier, was born on 21 April 1868 at Bridgewater, Tasmania, son of Joshua John Hayes, schoolmaster, and his schoolteacher wife Elizabeth, née Blyth. His grandfather, John Hayes, was member of the House of Assembly for Brighton in 1882-86. Hayes was educated by his mother. At some time in the late 1880s or early 1890s he joined the mining rush to Western Australia. Details of his early career are lost, though it is known that he managed an ore-reduction and cyanide works at Wiluna. He returned to Tasmania about 1906 and purchased Burnside, Scottsdale, to which he took his bride Laura Linda, née Blyth, a cousin whom he married with Anglican rites on 22 January 1907 at St David's Cathedral, Hobart. For most of his life he was active in local farming affairs; in 1912-20 he was secretary of the Scottsdale Board of Agriculture and in 1911 president of the North-Eastern Agricultural and Pastoral Association.

Hayes entered politics at the January 1913 Tasmanian election on the Liberal ticket for Bass. During the campaign he made much of his farming background, speaking almost exclusively of rural matters as 'the farmers' candidate'. Helped by the largest vote in the Scottsdale subdivision, he was one of three Liberals returned for the electorate. Hayes was fortunate to win his seat during a time of political upheaval. During his first three years both the Solomon [q.v.] and Earle [q.v.8] governments fell, and in (Sir) Walter Lee's [q.v.] first Nationalist government of April 1916 he became minister for lands and works and minister responsible for agriculture and for the Hydro-Electric Department; in 1919-22 he was minister for works. He was a competent administrator, winning plaudits from rural interests for his support, as well as for his work in soldier settlement. He was appointed C.M.G. in 1921.

The emergence of the Country Party, antagonistic to Lee, and led by Ernest Frederick Burns Blyth who, as a Liberal, had followed his cousin and brother-in-law Hayes into the House in June 1913, led to a bitter election battle in June 1922. The contest split the anti-Labor vote and gave the Country Party the balance of power. It was clear that any attempt to reconcile the conservative parties would fail while Lee remained premier and, although a vote of no confidence in August failed, Lee resigned, advising the governor to send for Blyth. Blyth arranged a meeting of both parties and a unanimous vote elected Hayes as premier of Tasmania's first coalition government; he also became minister for works, with Lee as treasurer and Blyth minister for lands and mines.

The Hayes ministry was never allowed to settle into the job, largely because of the 'financial bog' it inherited. Tasmania had borrowed heavily during and after the war and by 1922 was faced with a huge interest bill which swallowed over one-third of the annual revenue. The State also suffered from a particularly low return on its public services: in 1922-23 over £350 000 was lost in the politically sensitive areas of railways, soldier settlement and shipping. The report of a government-appointed Economy Board recommended heavy retrenchments in all sections of the bureaucracy. Little was done, other than to reduce teachers' salaries, and the call was taken up by the ministry's critics who also seized on a condemnatory Railways Commission report.

Demands for the premier's resignation began in mid-1923. In August Hayes used a meeting of dissident government politicians, convened to discuss the government's future, as sufficient reason to resign, and despite invitations to reconsider he stood aloof, refusing also to contemplate joining any new ministry. J. C. Newton was elected Nationalist leader but failed to gain adequate support, and Hayes performed a last service for his party by securing the re-election of Lee. He then moved promptly to nominate for a Senate vacancy in September 1923 and at a joint sitting of the Tasmanian parliament was narrowly elected.

As a Nationalist and United Australia Party senator Hayes usually spoke on rural affairs, especially as they related to Tasmania. Another matter of great concern to him was the effect of Federation on the Tasmanian economy, and he argued strongly for generous Commonwealth assistance. In 1927 he spoke at length in support of changes in the *per capita* arrangements, and next year he attacked the Navigation Act for its restriction of Tasmanian shipping. He was a member of the Joint Committee of Public Accounts in 1926-32 (chairman in 1932), and temporary chairman of committees in 1932-38. President of the Senate in 1938-41, and known to his friends as 'J.B.', he was described as 'a tall handsome man with quiet dignity' and was noted for his non-provocative attitude to the party battle; after his death he was praised by Labor premier Cosgrove for his Senate work for Tasmania.

Hayes retired from parliament in 1947. At the same time he left farming and moved to Launceston. A devout Anglican, he was a trustee and churchwarden at Scottsdale, was on the diocesan council, and served as chairman of committees of the Tasmanian Synod. He died at Launceston on 12 July 1956 and after a service at St Aidan's Church was buried in Carr Villa cemetery. He was survived by his wife; they had no children.

F. C. Green (ed), *A century of responsible government 1856-1956* (Hob, 1956); *PD* (Senate, Cwlth), 1927, 115, p 661, 1928, 119, p 6373, 6588, 1956, 9, p 9; *Examiner* (Launceston), 18 Jan 1913, 6 Feb 1923, 13, 17 July 1956; *North-Eastern Advertiser*, 17 July 1956.   SCOTT BENNETT

HAYES-WILLIAMS, WILLIAM GORDON (1862-1934), registrar-general, was born on 4 November 1862 at Otahuhu, near Auckland, New Zealand, son of John Radcliffe Hayes-Williams, schoolteacher, and his wife Maria Eliza, née Garty. He arrived in Sydney in 1868 with his mother, who opened a 'ladies school' at Newtown and whose self-sacrifice and determination enabled her son to be prepared for his future career. Educated privately and at St Stephen's Denominational School, Newtown, William entered a mercantile office. On 16 October 1883 at the Wesleyan parsonage, Forest Lodge, he married Annie Glover, daughter of James Lister Laurence, chief clerk of the District Court. He was soon bound to William Cope [q.v.8], solicitor. While still articled he became managing clerk for his brother-in-law Charles Laurence and, on being admitted to practice on 7 June 1890, became a partner in Laurence, (J. C.) McLachlan [q.v.] & Williams. At the end of 1894 he joined E. W. Perkins.

Hayes-Williams was appointed registrar-general on 18 October 1898. The office was one of heavy responsibility in the field of registration: patents and trade marks (transferred to the Commonwealth in 1904 and 1906 respectively), births, deaths and marriages, companies, firms, stock mortgages, liens on crops and wool, deeds affecting land and titles to land. Hayes-Williams reorganized the department and diligently set about providing premises and practices appropriate to the needs of the twentieth century. A site near Queen's Square was provided and he witnessed the erection of a substantial building for the department—it had been hampered by the occupation of separate and inadequate premises. In 1904 the Deeds Registry and the Births, Deaths and Marriages Registry occupied part of the west wing and eventually all branches were located in the new building.

A man of outstanding ability with sound legal knowledge, Hayes-Williams was a wise and firm administrator and his advice was a significant factor in the drafting and implementation of many new Acts, administered by the department, which simplified practices and were to public advantage. As registrar of joint stock companies, he dealt with the steady increase in the number of limited companies and firm names. He retired on 3 November 1927 after a term as yet unequalled. A memorial plaque in the departmental building aptly records: *Si monumentum requiris circumspice.*

A tall and stately man, with a flowing moustache, very reserved, Hayes-Williams nevertheless was a sociable person within the family circle. A lover of gadgets and inventions, he always had some novelty to show his grandchildren. His diverse interests included motoring, tennis, rifle-shooting, art, philately, Freemasonry, Esperanto and the construction of crystal sets in the early days of wireless.

Upon retirement Hayes-Williams resumed practice as a solicitor. He died in his office on 13 March 1934 of cerebro-vascular disease and was cremated after a service at St Thomas Anglican Church, North Sydney. He was survived by his wife and two sons. His intestate estate was sworn for letters of administration at £447.

Cyclopedia of N.S.W. (Syd, 1907); *SMH*, 15 Mar 1934; information from M. Hayes-Williams, King's Lynn, UK, *and* J. D. Hayes-Williams, Wheeler Heights, *and* J. Matthews, Artarmon, NSW.　　　　　　　　　JACK WATSON

HAYNES, RICHARD SEPTIMUS (1857-1922), lawyer and politician, was born at Picton, New South Wales, youngest son of John Joseph Haynes, civil servant, and his wife Margaret, née Daly. At Morpeth Haynes senior taught Richard before sending him to Sydney Grammar School. In 1873 Haynes was articled, first in Sydney and then at Armidale, and in 1880 was admitted to the New South Wales Bar. On 27 December next year in Sydney he married Marion Adelaide Goodwin; they had six daughters and five sons.

In 1885 Haynes moved to Perth to represent the interest of Anthony Hordern [q.v.4] in the Great Southern Land Co. Next year he formed with John Horgan [q.v.] the Eight Hours Association, was elected to the Perth City Council and became chairman of the Local Board of Health. After three years he resigned from the council and board because the city's police magistrate (later premier), G. W. Leake [q.v.5], was not enforcing the health regulations. Haynes rejoined the council in 1891-94. He formed and chaired the Municipal Association in 1894 and in 1901 was mayor of North Perth.

'Dickie' Haynes's radicalism had been obvious in the late 1880s when he supported Chief Justice Onslow [q.v.5] in his dispute with Governor Broome [q.v.3] and convened public meetings to protest over Broome's failure to relieve unemployment. He backed Horgan in his successful battle with Septimus Burt [q.v.7] for the seat of Perth in 1888 and, as organizer and chairman of the Central Reform League, he led the democratic movement. At the first election under responsible government, in December 1890, Haynes stood for, but lost, the Legislative Assembly seat of West Perth on a radical platform. He won Central Province in the Legislative Council in 1896; his seat embraced the Murchison goldfields and he kept it until 1902. An uncompromising critic of (Sir) John Forrest's [q.v.8] government, he was a powerful advocate for reforms such as manhood suffrage, payment of members, and the abolition of property qualifications and plural voting. He remained an independent, a natural oppositionist and individualist. In 1905 his wife died and on 6 October 1908 he married Anastasia D'Arcy in Sydney.

Haynes's large legal firm was at 66 St George's Terrace. In the late 1880s he had ably defended the bushranger Edward Hughes. Another important case in that period was that of Rev. J. B. Gribble [q.v.4] versus the *West Australian*, in which Haynes defended the *West* from a libel charge. He fought an extradition order against the murderer, F. B. Deeming [q.v.8], in 1892. In 1902 he was appointed K.C.

Legally, he was regarded as a 'last ditcher', possessing a caustic, witty tongue.

Haynes was vice-president of several football and cricket clubs and in the 1880s appeared frequently in amateur theatricals. He was small and solid, clean-shaven, with a perky demeanour and pugnacious jaw: bewigged he looked formidable.

In 1921 he contracted diabetes and part of his right leg was amputated. While recuperating he fell, weakened further, and died on 20 February 1922. He was buried in the Roman Catholic section of Karrakatta cemetery.

W. B. Kimberly (ed), *History of West Australia* (Melb, 1897); P. W. H. Thiel & Co., *Twentieth century impressions of Western Australia* (Perth, 1901); Truthful Thomas, *Through the spy-glass* (Perth, 1905); J. S. Battye (ed), *Cyclopedia of Western Australia*, 1 (Adel, 1912); J. G. Wilson (ed), *Western Australia's centenary, 1829-1929* (Perth, 1929); *Magistrate* (Perth), 1916, 1922; *West Australian*, 21 Feb 1922; *Call* (Perth), 24 Feb 1922; C. T. Stannage, Electoral politics in Western Australia 1884-1897 (M. A. thesis, Univ WA, 1967).

TOM STANNAGE

HAYNES, THOMAS WATSON (1878-1963), chartered accountant and company director, was born on 10 May 1878 at South Melbourne, fifth child of Robert Haynes, warehouseman, from Staffordshire, England, and his Scottish-born wife Margaret, née Watson. He was educated at state schools in Ballarat, then supported his widowed mother by working as a telegraph boy. In 1892 he joined the Broken Hill Proprietary Co., but after an attack of sunstroke at Broken Hill in 1896 returned to Melbourne as assistant accountant to the Mount Lyell Mining & Railway Co. Ltd. By 1904 he was listed as an associate of the Incorporated Institute of Accountants of Victoria. On 7 September 1905 at Holy Trinity Church, Balaclava, he married Ethel Constance Timmins, daughter of a civil engineer.

Haynes served with the Mount Lyell Co. until 1910, when he left his position as sales manager of the chemical works department and set up his own company, Paterson, Haynes & Co., in Melbourne. In May 1911 he rejoined Mount Lyell as officer in charge of the chemical works department, with responsibility for the Yarraville plant and development of the chemical works at Fremantle in Western Australia. From 1929 Haynes was general manager of Commonwealth Fertilisers & Chemicals Ltd, a new amalgamation, and of Cuming [q.v.8] Smith and Mount Lyell Fertilisers Ltd (W.A.) until October 1930, when he resigned to carry on business as legal manager and accountant

in Melbourne. He continued to act as a consultant to his former employers.

In January 1931 Haynes became director in charge of the Melbourne office of Kelly & (E.P.) Lewis [q.v.] Pty Ltd, engineers, and later joined the board of Sydney Cotton Mills. Haynes joined Parbury Henty [q.v.1] & Co., merchants, in April 1932 as managing director until 1943 and chairman until 1956. He was chairman of Parbury Henty Holdings Ltd from 1956 to 1960. He was remembered as far-seeing and calm, a businessman of 'absolute integrity'. In 1938-39 he was president of the Melbourne Chamber of Commerce and in 1940 junior vice-president of the Associated Chambers of Commerce of Australia.

Rejected for active service in World War I, Haynes was a member of several official bodies in connexion with wartime administration. He was effective in work on behalf of soldiers' wives and families and in gaining employer and government support for retraining returned servicemen. He served on the State War Council on employment for returned soldiers from 1915 and on the State Repatriation Board (1917-20). He was also a member of the Federal Prices Commission Advisory Board of Victoria.

In 1922 Haynes visited Nauru and Ocean Island with the British Phosphate Commission. He was inspired to write a novel, *Our daily bread* (London, 1933), an account of political and financial intrigue involving American agents bent on cornering the world's phosphate supply.

A member of the Melbourne, Australian and Royal Melbourne Golf clubs, Haynes was especially fond of golf, and enjoyed a game of bridge. He died on 29 August 1963 at his home in Monomeath Avenue, Canterbury, survived by his wife, two sons and four daughters, and was buried in Box Hill cemetery with Methodist forms.

Industrial Aust and Mining Standard, 9 Oct 1930; *Argus*, 8 Sept 1915, 3, 12 July 1929, 25, 27 Mar 1939; *Age*, 4 Oct 1930, 12 Sept 1931, 25 May 1938, 4 Sept 1963; *Times Literary Supp*, 27 Apr 1933; family information.   SALLY O'NEILL

HAYWARD, CHARLES WILTENS ANDRÉE (1866-1950), journalist and writer, was born on 21 July 1866 at Court Huntington, Herefordshire, England, second son of Johnson Frederick Hayward (1822-1912), gentleman, and his wife Ellen Margaret, née Litchfield. Johnson Hayward had migrated to South Australia in 1847, and had prospered on the northern sheep runs; he returned to England in 1864, revisiting the colony in 1869. Andrée was educated at Rugby

School and matriculated to Exeter College, Oxford, in 1885 (B.A., 1888). He was called to the Bar of the Inner Temple in 1890. After working in South Africa he moved to the Western Australian goldfields in 1894.

Hayward was briefly at Cue before starting as a reporter on the *Geraldton Express*; he was sub-editor in 1896-98 under John Drew [q.v.8]. In 1897 his *Along the road to Cue; and other verses* was published under the pseudonym 'Viator'. From 1898 he edited the *Murchison Advocate* at Cue, from 1901-02 the Kalgoorlie *Sun* and in 1902-04 the Perth *Sunday Times*. In 1905 he returned to the *Express* for twelve months before re-joining the *Sunday Times* under his close friend J. E. Webb's editorship. In Perth, on 7 November 1900, Hayward had married Elizabeth Marie Dunn. In 1922 he moved to Sydney and joined the *Bulletin*, where he wrote light satirical verse and topical articles under the pseudonyms 'T the R' Thomas the Rhymer', 'Midford', 'Oxmead', 'Victor', 'Iford' and 'Pipards'. He died at Crenorne, Sydney, on 10 August 1950, survived by his wife, a daughter and two sons.

Hayward was a 'tall, willowy and soft spoken' man. He was a leading figure in the group of Western Australian goldfield writers whom A. G. Stephens [q.v.] praised for their vigorous, versatile and 'manly' verse. Hayward had read widely in the classics but admired contemporary writers such as Calverley of *Punch*, J. K. Stephen, Kipling and Bret Harte. He had read some Australian writers in England, and after migrating he became a devotee of Henry Lawson, 'Banjo' Paterson [qq.v.], E. G. Dyson [q.v.8] and other *Bulletin* contributors. After the nostalgia for England of his early work, Hayward's editorials, articles and poems soon supported the populist, patriotic strain in Australian literature and life. He saw verse as 'an essential ingredient of journalism' and espoused Labor on the goldfields, as in 'The Sneer of Septimus Burt' [q.v.7] (1895), in which he ridicules the attorney-general's opposition to votes for miners:

'Tis a voice that has rung aforetime, since
    the days when the world was new,
Wherever the sweating thousands have
    toiled for the favoured few,
'Tis the horsehair wig that is speaking to the
    roofing of cabbage tree,
Stiff broadcloth and speckless linen to mole-
    skin and dungaree, ·
The puny quill to the pickaxe, the gown to
    the clay-stained shirt,
The man of words to the worker—the voice
    of Septimus Burt.

Hayward relished the goldfields' comradeship and vigorous language and his writing reflects respect for those prospec-tors and miners who survive, with a sense of humour, their harsh surroundings. Coupled with this social concern is an Anglo-Saxon superiority and a fear, common then, of an influx of 'alien bands ... from Asian lands'. His influence on literary policies and journalism in the West deserves comparison with A. G. Stephens's role in Sydney: both significantly affected the development of a distinctively Australian literature.

V. Courtney, *All I may tell* (Syd, 1956); J. E. Webb, *Alms for oblivion* (priv print, Syd, 1966); *Leeuwin*, 1 (1910), no 1, 2, 3, (1911), no 4, 5; *PRGSSA*, 29 (1927-28); *Univ Studies in History*, 4 (1963-64), no 2; *Westerly*, Sept 1976; *Spectator* (Perth), 2 July 1903; *Bulletin*, 16, 30 Aug 1950.

BRUCE BENNETT

HAZON, ROBERTO (1854-1920), conductor and music teacher, was born on 25 September 1854 at Borgotaro di Parma, Italy, son of Eugenio Hazon, Crown barrister, and his wife Ottavia, née Devoti. He was educated at the Scuola del Carmine at Parma and at the Royal Conservatory of Music, Milan. At Milan he was a pupil of Franco Faccio, conductor at La Scala, then for six years conducted opera at the Teatro Dal Verme. On 9 February 1879 he married Clotilde Capredoni.

Engaged by Martin Simonsen as musical director for his New Royal Italian Opera Company, Hazon arrived in Melbourne in the *Lusitania* on 27 November 1886. Throughout 1887 the company played in Melbourne and Sydney and visited other capitals: Hazon conducted many operas, some for the first time in Australia. The *Australasian*, commenting on Verdi's *Un ballo in maschera*, claimed that 'Signor Hazon ... has infused the whole performance with his own enlightenment, enthusiasm, and good taste'. In 1888 Hazon decided to remain in Melbourne and was joined by his wife and son. In July before an audience of 2000 at the town hall he conducted Berlioz's *Symphonie fantastique*.

Hazon was engaged by George Rignold [q.v.6] for concerts at Her Majesty's Theatre, Sydney, in May 1889. In July he became conductor of the (Royal) Sydney Philharmonic Society, and on 2 October he skilfully directed the English baritone (Sir) Charles Santley and 450 performers in Mendelssohn's *Elijah*. Settling happily in Sydney, Hazon taught 'singing, harmony, and orchestration' and by 1902 lived at Strathfield. From 1889 to 1895, when he visited Italy, he also conducted the Metropolitan Liedertafel. The Philharmonic Society, under Hazon's baton, gave notable performances of many popular oratorios and of less well-known works by Australians Charles Packer [q.v.5] and Alfred Hill [q.v.] and, for the first time in Sydney, Berlioz's *La damnation de Faust*.

Efforts between 1889 and 1891 to found a permanent professional orchestra failed, but late in 1891 Hazon founded the Sydney Amateur Orchestral Society. 'Night after night this fierce-eyed man was bathed in perspiration, gesticulating almost madly, shouting encouragement in English and swearing in unintelligible Italian'. At his annual concert series he introduced many new works (occasionally his own compositions) to the public and was associated with the distinguished musicians who visited Sydney, notably Johann Kruse in 1895 and Paderewski in 1904.

In 1901 Hazon visited Italy to engage singers and the orchestra for the J. C. Williamson [q.v.6] Italian Opera Company; he was musical director and conductor for the season. The company staged many old favourites and presented for the first time in Australia Puccini's *La Bohème*, Verdi's *Otello* and Giordano's *Fedora*. On the opening night in Melbourne on 1 June, Hazon conducted *Aida* with such gusto that he built up 'as it were, a wall of sound between the hearers in front and singers on the stage'.

With a black, curling moustache and neatly trimmed beard, Hazon had a 'high-spirited almost boyish gaiety of exuberance' as well as temperament (rehearsals were often stormy). He was always willing to help young musicians, to conduct at charity matinées or to judge competitions. In May 1907 he resigned because of increasing ill health. At his emotional farewell concert in the Sydney Town Hall on 24 September he was presented with a testimonial and £600 by the governor Sir Harry Rawson [q.v.]. Hazon returned to Milan and conducted at La Scala for a time. In 1910 he visited Australia as conductor and director of Williamson's Grand Opera Company with the French soprano Bel Sorel and Amy Castles [q.v.7] singing *Madame Butterfly*, in English, on alternate nights.

Hazon died at Milan on 9 September 1920; he was survived by his wife (d. 1921), a son and two daughters, who were harpists.

J. K. Gill, *A souvenir of the golden jubilee of the Royal Philharmonic Society of Sydney 1885-1935* (Syd, 1935); R. H. Todd, *Looking back* (Syd, 1938); W. A. Orchard, *Music in Australia* (Melb, 1952); *A'sian Manufacturer*, 2 Apr 1927; *Australasian*, 4 Dec 1886, 29 Jan 1887, 21 Jan, 7 July 1888, 14 Dec 1894, 8 June 1901, 3 Dec 1910; *SMH*, 3 Oct 1889, 14 Dec 1894, 2 Nov 1895, 26 Sept 1907, 28 Mar 1910, 30 Sept, 2 Oct, 6 Nov 1920; *Catholic Press*, 2 May 1907, 17 Feb 1910; *Punch* (Melb), 28 July 1910; theatre programmes, *and* Syd Philharmonic Soc papers (NL)   MARTHA RUTLEDGE

HEAD, FREDERICK WALDEGRAVE (1874-1941), Anglican archbishop, was born on 18 April 1874 at Tollington Park, London, son of the Reverend George Frederick Head, later canon of Bristol, and his wife Mary Henrietta, née Bolton. He was educated at Alton School, Plymouth, Windleshan House, Brighton, and Repton School, Derbyshire. In 1893 he entered Emmanuel College, Cambridge, and graduated in 1896 (M.A., 1900), with a first class in the historical tripos. He was awarded the Lightfoot and Whewell scholarships and in 1900 was appointed to a junior fellowship at Emmanuel.

Head was ordained deacon in 1902 and priest in 1903 by Bishop Alwyne Compton of Ely; he returned to Emmanuel that year as dean and tutor, and in 1907 was appointed senior tutor and chaplain. As a Cambridge don, Head exercised an important though restricted ministry, known, respected and appreciated within his university and college communities.

In 1915, feeling too old to serve as a chaplain, he volunteered for service in France with the Young Men's Christian Association. However, his effectiveness was such that in 1916 he was appointed to a chaplaincy with the Guards' Division. He finished as senior chaplain and was awarded the Military Cross and Bar.

He resumed his Cambridge appointments in 1919 but in 1922 became vicar of Christ Church, East Greenwich. This was a large working-class parish, very different from a Cambridge college, but Head quickly commended himself by his genuine friendliness. In 1922, also, he was appointed chaplain to King George V and preached regularly at Buckingham Palace and Sandringham. After four hectic years at Greenwich he moved to Liverpool as canon and sub-dean of the cathedral, charged with breathing life into Scott's monumental new edifice. In addition to these ministries, Head served as examining chaplain to the bishops of Southwark and Peterborough, and proctor in the convocations of both Canterbury and York, and lectured in pastoral theology at Cambridge.

In August 1929 he was elected archbishop of Melbourne and accepted, seeing the unexpected invitation as a clear call to serve God. He was consecrated in Westminster Abbey on 1 November and enthroned in Melbourne on 23 December.

Head came to a diocese that was in good

heart, that had shared in the expansion of the 1920s, and whose cathedral spires were then being built. But his arrival coincided with the onset of the Depression which crippled parochial work and created immense social problems. Head believed that his diocese's major contribution to recovery lay in strengthening parochial life. By preaching, teaching and visitation, by regular meetings with country bishops and with his own archdeacons and rural deans, and by the appointment of J. J. Booth as the first Melbourne coadjutor bishop in 1934, he strove to equip clergy and parishes for more difficult times. Church societies received his active encouragement, particularly the Boys' Society for its camping programme and the Men's Society for its evangelistic and beach missions. The Brotherhood of St Laurence moved to Melbourne from Newcastle, New South Wales, in 1933 at his invitation, and R. G. Nichols [q.v.], 'Brother Bill', was strongly supported in his settlement work at St Mark's, Fitzroy. In the referenda on prohibition held in 1930 and 1938 Head joined Protestant leaders in campaigning unsuccessfully for a 'Yes' vote. A scholar himself, Head invited a series of overseas scholars to Melbourne and spoke frequently on platform and radio on historical and apologetical subjects. Ecumenically, Head was chairman of the local committee of the world Faith and Order movement and initiated a series of conversations with Victorian Methodists.

Grave but kindly, gentle but fearless and strong in character, Head, while lacking the bubbling *bonhomie* of his predecessor, Harrington Clare Lees [q.v.], was held in high regard in every section of his diocese and the Victorian community. Despite his Establishment background, he knew no distinction of class or education and impressed as a man of engaging modesty and unfailing courtesy. He believed wholeheartedly in the British Empire, declaring at his welcome by 10 000 Anglicans in the Exhibition Building, 'I love the Empire, I want to serve it and keep it Christian'. However, his outspoken support for the Premiers' Plan in 1931 drew criticism and this intervention in politics was not repeated.

Head's major publications comprise *The fallen Stuarts* (1900) and *Six great Anglicans* (1929), together with contributions to *The heart of the Empire* (1901). In 1927 he was appointed a life fellow of Emmanuel College, Cambridge, and in 1929, when visiting Canada, he received the honorary degree of D.D. from Emmanuel College, Saskatoon.

Head died on 18 December 1941, following injuries received in a motor accident, and his ashes are interred in St Paul's Cath-

edral, Melbourne. He was survived by his wife, Edith Mary, née Colman, whom he had married on 30 August 1904, and a son. A memorial bronze by Andor Meszaros is in St Paul's Cathedral, and a portrait by Aileen Dent, painted posthumously from a photograph, is in its chapter house. Other memorials are the Archbishop Head flats for retired clergy at Oakleigh, and the Edith Head Hostel for country girls at North Melbourne.

E. Head, *F. W. Head, Archbishop of Melbourne. A sketch for those who loved him* (Lond, 1943); *Table Talk*, 23 Jan 1930; *Argus*, 19 Dec 1941.

JAMES GRANT

HEAD, WALTER ALAN; *see* WOODS, Walter Alan

HEADLEY, BARBARA (LADY); *see* BAYNTON

HEAGNEY, MURIEL AGNES (1885-1974), trade unionist and feminist, was born on 31 December 1885 in Brisbane, daughter of PATRICK REGINALD HEAGNEY (1858-1922), publican and later a carpenter, and his wife Annie Agnes, née Currie. Muriel was raised in a Labor atmosphere. Her maternal grandfather, an Irish immigrant, was a friend of Peter Lalor [q.v.5]. Her father, born in 1858 at Bacchus Marsh, Victoria, was the son of Martin Heagney, farmer, and his wife Catherine, née Hogan, both from Ireland. Patrick went to Queensland in the 1880s, became an early member of the Australian Workers' Union and contributed to the *Worker* and the *Bulletin*. He married on 9 February 1885 at Isisford and moved his family to Melbourne in the late 1890s.

In 1902 he founded the Richmond branch of the Political Labor Council. He was secretary of the central executive of the P.L.C. in 1904-10 and attended the Commonwealth Political Labor conferences of 1905 and 1908. He was defeated as Labor candidate for Bulla in the Legislative Assembly elections of 1907 and also in a by-election for Mornington next year. Heagney was a member of the Richmond Council in 1908-11. With his daughter he attended the Australian Trade Union Congress in Melbourne in 1921 and that year published the pamphlet *Social reconstruction: plans and specifications*. He died on 7 December 1922 at St Kilda.

Muriel was educated at a Richmond convent and later trained as a primary school teacher, a vocation she abandoned in 1915. A member of the Richmond branch of the P.L.C. from 1906, she was a delegate to the Women's Central Organizing Committee in

245

1909 and attended the first Victorian Labor Women's Conference. During World War I she worked as the only female clerk in the Defence Department and, significantly, received equal pay. She was active in the anti-conscription campaigns and in 1915 was a committee-member of the Workers' Educational Association.

Secretary of the Australian Relief Fund for Stricken Europe in 1921-23, she spent the following two years overseas; she visited Russia, worked briefly for the International Labour Organization in Geneva, and in London in 1925 represented the Melbourne Trades Hall Council at the first British Commonwealth Labour Conference. Returning to Melbourne, she was a member of the Victorian central executive of the Labor Party in 1926-27, when she also helped establish the Labor Guild of Youth, and was an unsuccessful candidate in the Boroondara by-election of 1933.

Heagney's main endeavour was to establish equal pay for women; she saw wage inequality as the major obstacle to the achievement of equality of status and opportunity. In 1919-20 she worked as an investigator for the Federated Unions of Australia in their submission to the Commonwealth royal commission on the basic wage and in 1923 and 1927 she prepared cost-of-living schedules for the Clothing Trades Union in its submissions to the Commonwealth Court of Conciliation and Arbitration for a uniform basic wage for both sexes. In 1928 she presented a paper 'The trade union women' at the first Pan-Pacific Women's Conference, Honolulu.

Alarmed at the plight of jobless women during the Depression, Heagney in 1930 formed the Unemployed Girls' Relief Movement which established sewing centres where women worked for unemployed families in return for a relief allowance. She also set up a jam factory. To counter propaganda against employment of women in the 1930s, she undertook a survey for the Victorian branch of the Open Door Council and published *Are women taking men's jobs?* (1935); the book made equal pay a serious national issue, but brought no practical results.

In 1937 Heagney helped to found the Council of Action for Equal Pay under the auspices of the New South Wales branch of the Federated Clerks' Union, and was honorary secretary until 1949. A witness in basic wage hearings before the Arbitration Court in 1937 and 1949, she appeared before the New South Wales Industrial Commission in support of the Clerks' Union's case for equal pay in 1940. By 1941, the year she attended the International Labour Organization conference in New York as an observer, she believed victory on female wages was immi-

nent. But while the Women's Employment Board awarded a high percentage of the male rate of pay to women in 'male' industries for the duration of the war, women in the traditional female sector remained disappointingly on 54 per cent.

In 1936-42 Muriel made a living as a travel organizer for the Queensland Tourist Bureau in Sydney. In 1943-47 she was women's organizer there for the Amalgamated Engineering Union. She wrote *Equal pay for the sexes* in 1948. In 1950 she returned to Melbourne where she wrote the condemnatory *Arbitration at the cross roads* (1954). Her Labor Party activities continued: in September 1955 she became secretary of the Women's Central Organizing Committee and an *ex officio* member of the party's central executive. She began to write a history of the labour movement, but was unsuccessful in her application for a Commonwealth Literary Fund grant. She died in poverty at St Kilda on 14 May 1974, and was cremated. A week earlier the National Wage Case decision had granted women an adult minimum wage.

M. Bevege et al (eds), *Worth her salt* (Syd, 1982); *Refractory Girl*, Autumn 1974; *LaTLJ*, 4 (1975), no 15; Labour Hist, Melb, *Recorder*, June 1974; *Argus*, 19 June 1930, 1 Feb 1935; *Truth* (Syd), 12 July 1936; *Labor*, 27 June 1974; P. Ranald, Feminism and class ... (M.A. thesis, Univ Adel, 1980); Clothing and Allied Trades Union of Aust, Equal pay records (Trades Hall, Melb); A. T. Brodney papers *and* M. A. Heagney papers (LaTL).

J. BREMNER

HEALY, CECIL PATRICK (1881-1918), swimmer and commercial traveller, was born on 28 November 1881 at Darlinghurst, Sydney, third son of native-born parents Patrick Joseph Healy, barrister, and his wife Annie Louisa, née Gallott, late Girard. He was educated at J. Lee Pullings's school at Bowral and in 1895 won a 66-yard handicap race at the old Sydney Natatorium. He joined the East Sydney Amateur Swimming Club, steadily improved, and in 1901 with F. C. V. Lane [q.v.] and others won the 500 yards flying squadron teams race in the New South Wales Championships for the first of many times.

In 1902-04 Healy was frequently placed in sprint and middle-distance races, often second to Dick Cavill [q.v.7, F. Cavill], and in 1905 at Balmain won the 100 yards State championship in 61.1 seconds, came third in the 220 yards freestyle and was a member of the victorious flying squadron (world record time) and water polo teams. At the Australasian championships in Melbourne the same year he won the 100 yards freestyle title in 58.0 seconds, equalling the world record.

Retaining his Australasian 100 yards title in 1906, Healy finished third to C. Daniels and Z. Halmay in the 100 metres final at the unofficial Olympics at Athens. On a successful tour of Britain and Europe he won the 220 yards Amateur Swimming Association championship of England in 2 minutes, 37.4 seconds, came second in the English 100 yards title and won the 100 metres and Kaiser's cup at Hamburg.

At the Australasian titles in 1908 Healy regained the 100 yards freestyle title in the record time of 57.2 seconds (not equalled until 1922 and not bettered in the event until 1927) and the 220 yards title in 2 minutes, 34.2 seconds. He retained the 100 yards championship in 1909 and 1910 and in 1911-12 had some interesting contests and wins against (Sir) Frank Beaurepaire [q.v.7] and Bill Longworth. At the Stockholm Olympics in 1912 he finished a close second to Duke Kahanamoku in the 100 metres final and won a gold medal in the 4 x 200 metres relay.

Short and stocky with powerful arms and shoulders, Healy developed the two-beat Australian crawl and was famed for his brilliant finishes. He contributed articles on swimming and other subjects to the press and was a fluent speaker, often for the Liberal political interest. He was vice-president of the New South Wales Amateur Swimming Association and of the Surf Bathing Association of New South Wales. An excellent surfer, he was a founder, captain and gold honour badge holder of the Manly Surf Club and prominent in the fight to deregulate bathing laws. A paradigm of the true sportsman, he received the silver medal of the Royal Shipwreck Relief and Humane Society of New South Wales in 1911.

On 15 September 1915 Healy enlisted in the Australian Imperial Force and after service as a quartermaster sergeant in the Army Service Corps in Egypt and France he transferred to the infantry officer school at Trinity College, Cambridge, where he swam, rowed, boxed and played Rugby. On 1 June 1918 he was commissioned second lieutenant in the 19th (Sportsman's) Battalion and was killed in his first action in the battle for Mont St Quentin on 29 August. A requiem Mass for him was celebrated in St Mary's Cathedral, Sydney, on 23 September. He was unmarried. He is commemorated by the Healy shield for life-saving in New South Wales and in 1981 was honoured by the International Swimming Hall of Fame at Fort Lauderdale, Florida, United States of America.

H. Healy, *Cecil Healy: in memoriam* (Syd, 1919); *Forbes Carlisle on swimming* (Lond, 1963); J. Blanch (ed), *Australian sporting records* (Melb, 1981); *Lone Hand*, 1 Mar 1916; *T&CJ*, 15, 22 Aug, 12 Sept 1906, 18 Sept 1918; *Freeman's J* (Syd), 18 Aug 1906; *Referee*, 12 Mar 1913; *SMH*, 24 Sept, 30 Oct 1918, 2 Jan, 18 July 1919.   G. P. WALSH

HEALY, GEORGE DANIEL (1872-1967), banker, was born on 11 August 1872 at Maryborough, Victoria, son of Joseph Austin Healy, a Dublin-born clerk of the local mining board, and his wife Ann, née Spence, from Aberdeen, Scotland. In 1889 he joined the Mercantile Bank of Australia, then in 1892 the British-owned Bank of Australasia as clerk in its Australian headquarters at 394 Collins Street, Melbourne. He married Florence Mabel Young at Scots Church, Melbourne, on 10 April 1909; they had two sons and a daughter.

In 1910 Healy was promoted confidential clerk to the newly appointed superintendent, C. J. Henderson. By 1914 he had become an inspector. Immediately after the war he took charge of the day to day negotiations with the newly formed Bank Officials' Association, and argued the banks' case before various industrial tribunals, often interstate. Henderson sent him to London for further experience in 1922. The Court of Directors recognized his potential and urged that he be appointed manager of the Melbourne branch. He took up this post on his return from London and became superintendent on Henderson's retirement in October 1926.

Healy was a conservative banker who followed his often expressed motto of 'safety first'; under his stewardship the bank followed a cautious lending policy. Some expansion occurred in the form of a short-lived search for new accounts, the opening of new branches, and of new activities such as small personal loans, the issue of travellers' cheques, and the creation of a Ladies Banking Department in the remodelled building in Collins Street. These developments owed more to the promptings of the directors and pressure from aggressive competitors than to his own inclinations.

Like most senior bankers Healy believed that regulation by a central bank was unnecessary and dangerous if the central bank was not independent of the government. He was prepared to co-operate to a degree with the Commonwealth Bank of Australia and the Commonwealth and State governments during the Depression and with the New Zealand government during its exchange crisis of 1938-39, but only on stringent conditions.

As chairman of the Associated Banks of Victoria in 1931-32 Healy spoke for the five Melbourne-based trading banks during the formulation of the Premiers' Plan and negotiations with the Commonwealth Bank concerning the exchange rate and other matters. Chairman again in 1935-36, he played a full part in the royal commission on money and banking as a witness and behind the scenes. His last term as chairman in 1941-42 coincided with the far-reaching National Security (War-time Banking Control) Regulations of November 1941 that gave the Australian government complete control over banking. During the war he became a senior spokesman for the business community as president of the Melbourne Chamber of Commerce in 1939-43 and as president of the Associated Chambers of Commerce of Australia in 1941-43. In 1942-57 he was a director of the Colonial Mutual Life Assurance Society.

In 1933 the directors asked Healy, who had reached the age of retirement, to stay on as superintendent. However, by the early 1940s they were becoming increasingly concerned about the bank's lack of progress and reluctantly invited him to retire in April 1944. Healy died in Brisbane on 20 November 1967.

Healy was a tireless worker who set himself the highest standards of professional and personal conduct and expected no less from his staff. Tall and powerfully built, he impressed those about him as a commanding and rather intimidating figure. He was a highly disciplined man, though given to occasional bursts of temper, and his austere personal manner set him apart from his staff and all but the most important of the bank's customers.

S. J. Butlin, *Australia and New Zealand Bank* (Melb, 1961); Aust and NZ Banking Group Ltd Archives, Melb, *and* information from Mr F. S. Holt, archivist.   D. T. MERRETT

HEANE, JAMES (1874-1954), soldier and orchardist, was born on 29 December 1874 in Sydney, son of James Heane, grazier and commission agent, and his wife Emily Sarah Parsons, née Tuting, both English-born. He was educated at Dubbo Superior Public School and Sydney Boys' High School, becoming a certificated auditor and then a farmer in the Dubbo district. After serving for five years in the Cadet Forces he was commissioned second lieutenant in the 3rd Australian Infantry Regiment (militia) in February 1899. In 1903 he transferred to the 2nd Light Horse Regiment (which later became the 9th) as a lieutenant and in 1910, on the introduction of compulsory military training, he was appointed area officer at Dubbo.

When war came in 1914 Heane joined the Australian Imperial Force on 3 September as a captain in the 4th Battalion. It was as a major commanding 'D' Company at the Gallipoli landing that he earned his nickname 'Cast Iron Jimmy' for he showed no fear as he moved among his men under heavy fire. For gallantry on 1 May, when he led a company 'to support a small, isolated force in a trench without means of retreat' he was awarded the Distinguished Service Order; he also received the first two of seven mentions in dispatches for his work at Gallipoli. While there he was wounded three times: first, in the thumb on 2 July, later in the mouth, and in the charge at Lone Pine on 6 August was so badly wounded that he was evacuated and hospitalized. He rejoined his unit at Tel-el-Kebir, Egypt, in January 1916; shortly afterwards he was promoted lieut-colonel and transferred to command the 1st Battalion which moved to the Western Front.

On 30 June 1916 Heane's battalion conducted a very successful raid on the German trenches at Sailly and he was later appointed C.M.G. for distinguished service at Pozières. Twice in 1916 he held temporary command of the 1st Brigade and on 3 December was promoted colonel and appointed to command the 2nd Brigade. Four days later he was again wounded, this time in the head and was evacuated to England. He rejoined his brigade at Buire in January 1917 and took part that year in the battles of the Hindenburg line, Menin Road, Broodseinde Ridge and Passchendaele. His brigade performed particularly well in August-September 1918 during the attacks on Lihons, Herleville and St Martin's Wood. At the height of these battles it was not uncommon for Heane to take short cuts across open ground raked by fire. He remained in command until the Armistice. For his command of the 2nd Brigade he was appointed C.B. and in 1917-19 was mentioned in dispatches five more times; in 1918 he received the Belgian Croix de Guerre.

After the Armistice Heane was one of the first Australians to visit Alsace-Lorraine and the occupied territory along the Rhine. He transferred to England in March 1919 and commanded the 1st Division Demobilization Group at Tidworth for the next three months. After leaving the A.I.F. on 7 January 1920 he commanded the 11th Brigade, Australian Military Forces, from July 1920 until April 1921, then the 5th Brigade until June 1926. On 4 April 1923 at St John's Anglican Church, Beecroft, Sydney, he married Edna Dulcie Martyn, of Narrabri. He was honorary colonel of the 4th Battalion from 1926 until he transferred to the retired list as an honorary brigadier in 1935. In 1931 and possibly from the movement's foun dation, he held overall command of the Sydney-based Old Guard.

Strict, serious, energetic, Heane was popular with his men. He was an archetype of the higher level Australian commander of World War I and 'one of the great field successes of the war'. He became an orchardist soon after returning to Australia and settled on a large citrus orchard at West Pennant Hills. He was president of the Fruitgrowers' Federation of New South Wales in 1922-41. He remained actively associated with the army and in World War II commanded the State Volunteer Defence Corps until 1942.

Survived by his wife and two daughters, 'Cast Iron Jimmy' died of cerebral thrombosis at Collaroy on 20 August 1954 and was cremated with Anglican rites. His estate was sworn for probate at £31 138. A portrait of Heane by James Quinn [q.v.] is in the Australian War Memorial.

C. E. W. Bean, *The story of Anzac* (Syd, 1921, 1924), and *The A.I.F. in France*, 1916-18 (Syd, 1929, 1933, 1937, 1942); K. Amos, *The New Guard movement 1931-1935* (Melb, 1976); *London Gazette*, 1 June, 3 Aug 1915, 29 Dec 1916, 2 Jan, 1 June, 25, 28 Dec 1917, 28 May, 12 July, 31 Dec 1918, 11 July 1919; *Reveille* (Syd), Mar 1937; *T&CJ*, 30 Jan 1907, 14 May 1919; *SMH*, 5 July 1915, 1 Jan 1917, 1, 15 Jan 1918, 28 Mar, 25 Oct 1919, 1 May 1926, 21 Aug 1954; *Bulletin*, 1 Sept 1954; War diary, 1st, *and* 4th Battalion, *and* 1st, *and* 2nd Brigade AIF (AWM); J. Heane file, War Records Section (AWM).

J. G. WILLIAMS

HEATH, ALBERT EDWARD (1887-1955), timber merchant, was born on 9 November 1887 at Maryborough, Queensland, eldest child of Queensland-born parents Henry Arthur Heath, grocer, and his wife Emily Evelyn, née Lockyer. He went to the Albert State School, but his education was interrupted when he was bitten by a snake, which affected his heart. He started work in a furniture factory at 5s. a week, but in 1905 went to Tasmania where he qualified as a chartered accountant.

Moving to Sydney in 1909, Heath worked for two firms of accountants and in 1912 set up on his own. At Hurstville he married Minnie Eastmure Swanton on 17 June 1911. In World War I he enlisted in the Australian Imperial Force, was commissioned in the 18th Battalion but, contracting enteric fever, was invalided out. In 1916 he became secretary of A. C. Saxon & Sons, timber merchants, a director in 1920 and, on the death of Saxon in 1926, general manager. Interested in business politics, Heath was president of the Sydney and Suburban Timber Merchants' Association in 1928-33; he was also

a council-member of the Sydney Chamber of Commerce and of the Employers' Federation of New South Wales, a member of the Council for the Prevention and Relief of Unemployment in 1930, vice-chairman of the Metropolitan Transport Trust in 1930-31 and in 1932 chaired a Federal conference on transport. He was on the council of the Primary Producers' Advisory Council, and was an original member of the executive of the All for Australia League, but resigned in May 1931 'as a protest against machine politics'.

After the abolition of the position of agent-general by the Stevens [q.v.] government, Heath was appointed the New South Wales government's official representative in London on 15 February 1934; he had the task of restoring British and European confidence in the security of investments in New South Wales. He was a firm admirer of S. M. (Viscount) Bruce [q.v.7], with whom he established a close working relationship. Appointed C.M.G. in 1935, he regularly visited the Continent and attended congresses of the International Chamber of Commerce in Vienna (1933), Paris (1935), Berlin (1937) and Montreux (1947), where he expressed his vigorous opposition to tariffs, quotas and economic nationalism; in Berlin his views conflicted with Goering's opening address.

In 1937 Heath was appointed agent-general but resigned next year to become secretary of the Sydney and Suburban Timber Merchants' Association Ltd. He reorganized the industry which he considered 'a rabble', and established associations for different sections. Under his guidance member companies negotiated price-fixing agreements and set quotas. He was described as 'a sort of benevolent dictator' of the State timber industry. In 1955 an Industrial Commission inquiry found that these arrangements were monopolistic, returning members a higher profit margin and generally favouring large firms; it recommended voluntary reform of these objectionable features, and that the government should reintroduce price control.

Meanwhile Heath had been president of the Sydney Chamber of Commerce in 1940-42, 1944-46 and 1947-49; he was chairman of Babcock & Wilcox of Australia Pty Ltd and a director of the Union Trustee Co. of Australia Ltd, Beard Watson & Co. Ltd, Allen Taylor [q.v.] & Co. Ltd and of several timber companies. He was a director of the Institute of Public Affairs, New South Wales, from 1943, a trade adviser at the International Trade Organization conference at Geneva in 1947 and was appointed to the Capital Issues Board in 1951. Interested in Australian history, he and his friend M. H. Ellis arranged for the maintenance of Governor Macquarie's [q.v.2] tomb on Mull. He was a member of the Australasian Pioneers, and Union clubs and of the Royal Sydney Yacht Squadron; he enjoyed fishing and motoring.

Heath died of myocardial infarction in hospital on 27 December 1955 and was cremated with Anglican rites. He was survived by his wife and daughter, who inherited his estate, valued for probate at £27 240 in New South Wales and £3862 in Victoria.

PP (NSW), 1955-56, 3, p 884; *Commerce* (Syd), 6 Sept 1937; *SMH*, 10 Mar, 20 May 1931, 22 June 1932, 11 Jan, 9 Mar 1934, 27 Jan 1937; *Bulletin* (Syd), 4 Jan 1956; DO 35/450/20254/5 (NL); information from Miss R. Todhunter, Edgecliff, Syd.

D. B. WEBSTER

HEATHERSHAW, JAMES THOMAS (1871-1943), public servant, was born on 7 May 1871 at Beaufort, Victoria, twelfth child and fourth surviving son of Rev. Henry Heathershaw from the Isle of Man, and his wife Amelia Nancy, née Robilliard, from the Island of Jersey, Channel Islands, who migrated after their marriage in 1853. Henry served in the Victorian Primitive Methodist ministry until 1899 as 'an old-time popular preacher'.

The boys shared a patient industriousness and respectable rewards: for forty-two years Henry Robilliard (1855-1933) worked for the London Chartered Bank, retiring as a branch manager in 1915; William Philip (1868-1929) toiled as a clerk in the Chief Secretary's Office of the Victorian Public Service in 1884-1901, then rose steadily to become under-secretary in 1924; Sydney Arthur (Sid) (1870-1947) followed William into the public service in 1887, received his first promotion in 1902 and was secretary of the police department in Victoria in 1920-35.

James, educated at Flinders School, Geelong, entered the Victorian Treasury as a clerk in March 1889, transferring to the Federal Treasury in 1902. Ledger-keeper in 1904, he was sub-accountant in 1907 and accountant in 1916. In 1926 he became acting assistant secretary and, following the departure to London of J. R. Collins [q.v.8], acting secretary. He was appointed secretary to the Treasury, the head of the department, on 3 August and was appointed C.B.E. in June next year.

Most of Heathershaw's career was concerned with the administrative responsibilities of the Treasury. However, in a memorandum to Lyons [q.v.] on the economy in September 1930 he stressed the need for 'equality of sacrifice by the whole com-

munity' and on his retirement he asserted that some Commonwealth treasurers had not an idea of their own. (The treasurers whom he did admire were S. M. (Viscount) Bruce [q.v.7], E. G. Theodore and (Sir) Walter Massy-Greene [qq.v.].) Described as a 'courteous gentleman' Heathershaw worked harmoniously with his juniors S. G McFarlane and (Sir) Henry Sheehan [q.v.] the latter succeeding him. In April 1932 deteriorating health prevented Heathershaw continuing as secretary and led him to accept transfer to the position of assistant secretary (pensions, etc.) at a salary reduced from £1700 to £994. He retained the increasingly important office of Commonwealth pensions commissioner, superintending the payment of invalid and old age pensions and maternity allowances, and also dealt with Commonwealth workers' compensation and insurance matters.

After staying on beyond the normal date of retirement in May 1935 to complete a reorganization of the pensions area of the department, Heathershaw retired in December, returning thankfully to Elwood Melbourne, to practise his recreations of golf and gardening and to deplore the increasingly partisan character of political life. He died on 25 July 1943 at Oakleigh railway station of coronary vascular disease and was buried in Kew cemetery. His estate was sworn for probate at £646. His wife Rosa Ethel, née Rodway, whom he had married at the Primitive Methodist Church, Carlton on 7 March 1901, predeceased him; he was survived by a son and a daughter.

To-day (Melb), 14 May 1932; *Punch* (Melb), and *Sun-News Pictorial*, 13 Sept 1927; *Argus*, 28 Nov 1903, 25 Nov 1929, 25 Mar 1933, 28 Feb 1935, 26 July 1943; MS 4851, box 2, folder 14 (NL).

K. R. PAGE

HEATON, HERBERT (1890-1973), economic historian and educationist, was born on 6 June 1890 at Silsden, Yorkshire England, son of Fred Heaton, blacksmith and his wife Eva, née Waterhouse. Educated at Batley Grammar and Morley Secondary schools, he studied history and economics at the University of Leeds (B.A., 1911; M.A. 1912; D.Litt, 1921). He worked on industrial life in eighteenth-century Yorkshire at the London School of Economics in 1911-12 for his M.A. thesis, and was appointed assistant lecturer in economics under (Sir) William Ashley at the University of Birmingham (M.Comm., 1914). He received his doctorate for his work *The Yorkshire woollen and worsted industries* (Oxford, 1920). Through the Co-operative movement, Heaton had been introduced to the Workers' Educational Association and its founder Albert Mansbridge, and at Birmingham had lectured for the W.E.A. He was chosen by Mansbridge and Ashley to follow Meredith Atkinson [q.v.7] to Australia to organize tutorial classes: his post was lecturer in history and economics at the University of Tasmania. He arrived in mid-1914, having married Ellen Jane Houghton at St Paul's Church, Cheltenham, Gloucestershire, on 11 April.

Within the university, Heaton developed the study of economics and encouraged research into Australian economic history. However his extramural lectures for the W.E.A., particularly his objective comments on the war, provoked the censure of conservative sections of the Tasmanian press and public. In 1917 he was appointed director of tutorial classes and lecturer in history and economics at the University of Adelaide. There he expanded the infant discipline of economics and developed the diploma of commerce. His W.E.A. lectures were published in his *Modern economic history with special reference to Australia* (Adelaide, 1921). Again his forthright comments on contemporary issues sparked continual controversy. Adelaide businessmen regarded his left-liberal position on the war and the peace, and his expositions of socialist theory, as evidence of the danger of teaching economics. Heaton argued that 'all the evils and aches of individual and corporate life [had] their ultimate cause in capitalism' which, he predicted, would 'give place naturally to socialism'. Consequently, the university refused to establish a degree in economics, and by implication a chair, while Heaton led the discipline. Appreciating the forces against his advancement in Australia, Heaton accepted a chair of economic and political science at Queen's University, Kingston, Ontario, Canada. His departure in August 1925 caused considerable public comment and regret.

He had been one of the founders of the modern social sciences in Australia. His pioneering research on Australian economic history appeared in the *Economic Journal* and the *Quarterly Journal of Economics*. In Australia he had contributed with great heart to many causes, such as the Co-operative Union and the League of Nations Union; in Adelaide he was the founder of the community singing movement and a member of repertory theatre. Australia could ill afford to lose such a vigorous citizen, progressive teacher and active intellectual.

In 1927 Heaton moved to the University of Minnesota, United States of America, where he pursued a distinguished career as professor of economic history until he retired in 1958. His works include *Economic history of Europe* (1936), long *the* standard text, and his tribute to Edwin Gay, *A scholar in action* (1952). On 24 January 1973 he died in Minneapolis, survived by his three Australian-born children and his second wife Marjorie Edith Ronson whom he had married in London on 6 August 1959.

American Hist Review, 78 (1973), p 1171; *Mercury*, 16 Sept 1915; *Register* (Adel), 17 June 1925; *Advertiser* (Adel), 10 Aug 1925; Heaton papers (Univ Minnesota Archives); Files of Univ Adel 1917-25, *and* Bd of Commercial Studies, Univ Adel 1917-25.   HELEN BOURKE

HEBBLETHWAITE, JAMES (1857-1921), poet, teacher and clergyman, was born on 22 September 1857 at Preston, Lancashire, England, son of William Hebblethwaite, corn miller, and his wife Margaret, née Cundall. Educated largely by means of scholarships, Hebblethwaite spent five years as a pupil-teacher before attending Battersea Training Institute for Schoolmasters, London, in 1877-78. He spent the next twelve years as headmaster of Lancashire schools and part-time lecturer in English literature at the Harris Institute, Preston. In 1890 he travelled to Hobart in search of health and taught at The Friends' School and Buckland's School for several years until illness forced his resignation. He married Mary Browne, a spinster ten years his senior, on 22 April 1895 in Hobart, according to Congregationalist forms.

Although a certified teacher for Anglican schools, Hebblethwaite entered the Congregational ministry in 1898, serving in the parishes of Bream Creek and Latrobe; he was principal of Queen's College, Latrobe, in 1899. In 1903 he forsook Congregationalism to become a deacon in the Church of England; he was ordained in 1904. Curate of Holy Trinity, Hobart, in 1903-05, he was vicar of George Town in 1905-08, Swansea in 1908-09 and The Channel in 1909-16 when he retired. Mary Hebblethwaite died in 1909 and on 20 April 1914 at Woodbridge he married Lucy Mabel Turner; they had one son.

During his early years in Hobart, Hebblethwaite contributed verse to various newspapers and journals including the Sydney *Bulletin* and the *Mercury*. In 1895 his only novel, *Castlehill, or a tale of two hemispheres*, was published in London; it is stilted and melodramatic, the Australian scenes particularly unconvincing. A small volume, *Verse*, containing nineteen poems mainly on classical themes, was published in 1896; only one poem, addressed to A. B. Paterson [q.v.], had any Australian content. In 1900

A. G. Stephens [q.v.] produced *A rose of regret* as number two of the *Bulletin* booklet series. *Meadow and bush* appeared in 1911 and *The poems of James Hebblethwaite* (1920) was followed by his last volume, *New poems of James Hebblethwaite* in 1921.

Contemporary critics described his poetry as wistful, romantic, scholarly and lacking force: Nettie Palmer [q.v.] averred his poetry 'seldom startles'; 'Furnley Maurice' [q.v. F. L. T. Wilmot] acknowledged his charm but was critical of his preoccupation with literary themes from the old world. Nostalgia is characteristic of Hebblethwaite's poetry and the language is often archaic and strained, although occasional stanzas attain a simple nobility. Hebblethwaite's last poems, philosophical and religious in tone, have no more Australian content than his earlier work. Yet some, using the device of an Australian setting in the first stanza, present the voice of an individual devoted to the culture of Europe making an earnest attempt to appreciate and love the antipodean environment: this kind of pioneering may also be seen as heroic.

Hebblethwaite was a dreamy, romantic man; a teetotaller, he was stocky, untidy, a man more at home in his private world than the practical one, but nevertheless a conscientious, liked and respected clergyman. His wide reading and keen interest in art made him a pleasant companion. He died on 13 September 1921 in Hobart and was buried in Cornelian Bay cemetery, survived by his wife and son.

F. Maurice, *Romance* (Melb, 1922); N. Palmer, *Modern Australian literature, 1900-1923* (Melb, 1924); W. N. Oats, *The rose and the waratah* (Hob, 1979); *Church News* (Hob), 21 Oct 1921; *Mercury*, 16 Sept 1921; J. Hebblethwaite newspaper cuttings file (ML); Records, Education Dept (Tas), ED2/13/1437 (TA).   HILARY WEBSTER

HEDLEY, CHARLES (1862-1926), naturalist, was born on 27 February 1862 at Masham, Yorkshire, England, son of Canon Thomas Hedley, vicar of Masham and fellow of Trinity College, Cambridge, and his wife Mary, née Bush. Briefly at Eastbourne College, he was educated mainly in France. From boyhood he collected shells and was greatly influenced by a French work on molluscan anatomy.

A chronic asthmatic, Hedley in 1881 went to New Zealand; in September 1882 he crossed to Queensland. Enjoying a 'liberal allowance from his father', he sampled outback life and tried an oyster lease at Moreton Bay and fruit-growing at Boyne Island,

Port Curtis. An accident to his left arm rendered him unfit for manual work, so he went to Brisbane in 1888 and worked voluntarily for the Queensland Museum; in January 1889 he joined its staff and in May was elected a fellow of the Linnean Society of London. Early in 1890, at the invitation of Sir William MacGregor [q.v.5], Hedley collected extensively in Papua. In April 1891 he became a scientific assistant at the Australian Museum, Sydney, in 1896 conchologist and in 1908 assistant curator. He augmented the museum's collections, gave many older scientific books to its library and, to cope with the increasing number of specimens, paid assistants and illustrators. He was active in local scientific circles and president of the Linnean (1909-11), Royal (1914), Field Naturalists' and (Royal) Zoological societies of New South Wales.

Typical of self-taught nineteenth-century naturalists, Hedley wrote confidently on botany, ethnology and general natural history, as well as conchology. His many papers on molluscs established him as the foremost Australasian conchologist of his time. Scornful of the deficiencies of the earlier 'London School', he set a high standard of taxonomic work. Although mainly concerned with Australian fauna, he described the collections of molluscs made by the Shackleton (1907-09) and first Australasian (1911-14) expeditions to Antarctica. He also wrote on zoogeography, notably on the ancient relations of Antarctica to Australia and New Zealand. Hedley had accompanied the Royal Society of London's expedition to Funafuti Atoll in the Ellice Islands in 1896 and maintained a lifelong interest in coral reefs. He collaborated with Professor W. A. Haswell and Sir Joseph Verco [qq.v.] in investigating the continental shelf and co-operated with the Commonwealth Advisory Council of Science and Industry.

Early in 1919 disagreements over a superannuation scheme divided the museum staff, brought Hedley into open conflict with R. Etheridge [q.v.8] and involved F. A. Coghlan, auditor-general and museum trustee. After Etheridge's death in January 1920, Hedley became acting director but, despite the support of Haswell and Sir Edgeworth David [q.v.8], Coghlan ensured that he was passed over as director. Hedley was given the nominal position of principal keeper of the collections in 1921. He resigned in March 1924 and became scientific director of the Great Barrier Reef Committee.

Striking in appearance, Hedley was tall and lean with, in later life, a neatly trimmed grey beard and moustache. He was an intrepid traveller, genial colleague and an indefatigable worker. In Hobart on 19 January

1898 he had married Harriott Georgina Echlin. Survived by her and an adopted daughter, Hedley died of heart disease at his home at Mosman, Sydney, on 14 September 1926. He was cremated with Anglican rites and his ashes scattered at sea, off the Great Barrier Reef. His estate was valued for probate at £16 852. Hedley's work was recognized by the award of the David Syme [q.v.6] research prize of the University of Melbourne in 1916 and the (W.B.) Clarke [q.v.3] memorial medal of the Royal Society of New South Wales. He was a fellow of the Malacological Society of London and an honorary member of the New Zealand Institute and of many other societies.

J. C. Verco, *Combing the southern seas* (Adel, 1935); E. Frankel, *Bibliography of the Great Barrier Reef province* (Melb, 1978); R. Strahan et al (eds), *Rare and curious specimens* (Syd, 1979); Linnean Soc NSW, *Procs*, 61, 1936, and for publications; T. Iredale, 'Charles Hedley's papers indexed', *Procs*, Roy Zoological Soc NSW, 1956-57; Hedley papers (Aust Museum, Syd); information from Dr W. F. Ponder, Syd.   DENIS FAIRFAX

HEINICKE, AUGUST MORITZ HERMANN (1863-1949), musician, was born on 21 July 1863 at Dresden, Saxony, son of August Moritz Hermann Heinicke, brush manufacturer, and his wife, amateur musicians. From 10 Heinicke studied at the Royal Conservatorium of Music, Dresden; among his teachers was the violin virtuoso, Eduard Rappoldi. At 16 Heinicke was conducting three large male-voice choirs. A period of travelling with orchestras, mainly in Europe, followed; he was usually first violin or assistant conductor. In 1890 he was appointed violin teacher at the Adelaide College of Music; contracts had been signed in Berlin. He was met in Adelaide on 12 June by college founders Gotthold Reimann and Cecil Sharp [qq.v.] who recognized him by his long hair, 'surely the best characteristic by which to recognise a German musician'. Soon he was acclaimed as Adelaide's premier violinist and violin teacher: Daisy Kennedy and William Cade were among his pupils.

When the Elder [q.v.4] Conservatorium of Music opened at the University of Adelaide in 1898, the college closed and Heinicke became a senior teacher there. His other major impact in the 1890s was as a conductor. In 1893 Charles Cawthorne's [q.v.7] Adelaide Orchestra had become Heinicke's Grand Orchestra, with forty-five players; it soon became the most popular of the local musical groups. Heinicke planned to provide popular programmes, then to cultivate the taste of players and audience for orchestral music. In 1898 his group was known as the Conservatorium Grand Orchestra, including students and amateurs, but university regulations prevented his continuing as conductor when it became the Adelaide Grand Orchestra. Heinicke continued to conduct a depleted conservatorium orchestra until 1910. Next year he reformed his Grand Orchestra which survived until 1914.

In December 1890 Heinicke had publicly proposed a United German Gentlemen's Singing Society; the thought obsessed him. 158 people responded, many from the Adelaide Liedertafel and other defunct German choirs: sixty-four men formed the new Adelaide Liedertafel which Heinicke conducted successfully until World War I began. 1891 saw, for one year, the revival of the Adelaide String Quartet Club to which Heinicke belonged; he also played in several other ensembles.

On 12 September 1914, with strong anti-German feelings affecting Adelaide, nine university students, who felt that Heinicke 'had attempted to affront British sentiment at a public concert', assaulted him and painted the Union Jack on his bald head. Heinicke accepted their apology and declined to have them punished. He resigned from the conservatorium on 29 April 1916. He had married Minna Eugene Gebhardt, an amateur singer, at St Peter's Church, Glenelg, on 26 May 1908; they had two sons. Until the 1914 incident the family had enjoyed adulation and acceptance in Adelaide; now they left their grand Medindie home for a Plympton poultry farm. Heinicke taught privately until 1933.

In 1925-29 he had a city business—Heinicke's Pianos. In 1931 he formed his last orchestra, the Adelaide Philharmonic, arranging three concerts in the Exhibition Hall and mainly using unemployed musicians; but they failed financially.

Early pictures of Heinicke show him as debonair, confident, with a jauntily twisted moustache. Loved by his family and students, he was a perfectionist with his pupils and often impatient. He had a sense of humour, but 'professionally, took himself a bit seriously'. In 1897-98, 1910 and 1920 he had revisited Germany and Europe. When older he played chess at Kindermann's Café in Adelaide. He died intestate on 11 July 1949 and was cremated; there were no obituaries.

Music (Adel), 1898; M. J. Krips, 'History of music in South Australia before 1900', MS memoirs of Heinicke (B.A. Hons thesis, Univ Adel, 1973); Univ Adel, Staff records; information from K. H. Heinicke, Clapham, and James Glennon, Lockleys, SA.   JOYCE GIBBERD

HENDERSON, GEORGE COCKBURN (1870-1944), historian, was born on 1 May 1870 near Newcastle, New South Wales, eighth of nine children of Richard Henderson, an English coalminer who was a Methodist and illiterate, and his wife Ann, née Robinson. Henderson was educated at Hamilton Public School and Fort Street Model School, Sydney. He became a pupil-teacher and in 1889 went to the Fort Street Training School and next year to the University of Sydney (B.A., 1893; M.A., 1901). In his final year he won the University medal, (Sir) Francis Anderson's [q.v.7] prize and the Frazer [q.v.4] scholarship; he was markedly influenced by Professors Anderson, G. A. Wood and (Sir) Mungo MacCallum [qq.v.]. He resumed schoolteaching and joined the university's extension lecture staff. Next year the university awarded him the James King [q.v.2] of Irrawang travelling scholarship; he studied history and philosophy at Balliol College, Oxford (B.A., 1898). Henderson enjoyed Oxford life and worked with an East London settlement conducted by Mansfield College. His final second class honours were unexpectedly disappointing.

On 5 January 1899 at Leicester, Henderson married May Gertrude Sturge, a Quaker writer, and went with her to Sydney as acting professor of history and, next year, of philosophy. In September they returned to England and he resumed extension work. In 1901 in Italy he examined intensively the life of St Francis of Assisi. Next year the University of Adelaide appointed Henderson to the chair of modern history and English language and he began lectures in June. His wife stayed behind; in 1911 they were divorced. Henderson's domestic life blended boarding-houses with the Adelaide Club and he had many friends. However, he experienced periods of acute mental depression.

He taught an English course based on Shakespeare, especially *Hamlet*, Browning, and T. R. Lounsbury's *History of the English language*. Students who split infinitives were sternly treated. He centred his modern European lectures on St Francis and his English constitutional lectures on Cromwell; Burke was used for eighteenth-century American and English affairs. Henderson's innovative 1907 syllabus included Imperial and colonial history; that year he published *Sir George Grey, pioneer of Empire in southern lands*. Its research had shown him the need for collections of local historical records, so he arranged through Thomas Gill [q.v.] the purchase by the local branch of the Royal Geographical Society of Australasia of S. W. Silver's valuable York Gate library. In 1909 he lectured on early South Australian history and also persuaded the Murray [q.v.] family to establish a memorial scholarship for George Tinline [q.v.6], the holders to examine the State's history from original records.

Henderson believed that Australian universities should foster interest in Australian history, and undertake a 'systematic and scientific' history of the British Empire. In 1914 he spent a year's leave overseas and, as a member of the Public Library, Museum and Art Gallery board, reported on European archives and record offices; the outcome was the opening in 1920 of the South Australian archives department, the first in Australia.

Through Henderson's interest in continuing adult education, country centres were set up. His lectures were fervently evangical: 'His voice rings out at once as rich and powerful and under splendid control ...' Though no proseletyzer, he was convinced of the value of his literary, historical and philosophical views; these advocated a high moral idealism, opposed materialism, and stressed Nature's beauty and bounty. 'His look of cold, Red Indian stoicism' seemed forbidding to some students; others valued his idealism that made them aware of inner resources.

Though not formally religious, Henderson stressed Christian ideals; similarly, he admitted socialism's claims, but disapproved of its methods. While avoiding politics, he criticized the low standard of schoolteachers and their poor conditions. He had declined the government's 1906 offer of the post of director of education. He also raised funds for (Sir) Douglas Mawson's [q.v.] 1911 Antarctic expedition. He supported conscription in 1916-17 and the later formation of an Australian Imperial Association; some of his World War I lectures were published by G. Hassell [q.v.] to aid relief and memorial funds.

In 1922 Henderson's enormous teaching load was relieved by the appointment of extra staff, but his health remained precarious. Despair filled him every morning and he endured severe insomnia. On 27 October he married in Adelaide Dr Annie Heloise Abel, an American historian, but his mental state worsened. In June 1923 he was hospitalized; his wife returned home and the marriage was later dissolved. Henderson resigned and was made emeritus professor in 1924.

He returned to New South Wales and soon rediscovered the soothing effect of historical enquiry. In his youth he had written: 'to read order into chaos—this is the secret of happiness and the source of content'. Encouraged by old friends W. H. Ifould [q.v.] and Robert Hawkes, he took up new research on Fiji. He worked in the Mitchell

Library and in Europe and made four difficult sea journeys in the tracks of the
eighteenth-century European explorers to
Fiji. He published *Fiji and the Fijians,
1835-1856* (1931), *The journal of Thomas
Williams, missionary in Fiji, 1840-1853*
(1931), *The discoverers of the Fiji islands . . .*
(1933), as well as documents on Fiji's constitution and politics. He also lectured in history at the University of Sydney and as research professor in 1937-44 completed 'The
history of government in Fiji'; it remains unpublished. Although some of his work has
been violently attacked, he was a notable
pioneer in the field of Pacific history.

Though he was tended lovingly by nieces
and nephews on his small property at Dora
Creek near Port Macquarie, Henderson's
last years were depressed. He struggled
against this, but he felt that 'his brain was
on fire'. He committed suicide in his garden
on 9 April 1944 and was buried in Sandgate
Methodist cemetery. He had written of Fletcher Christian's death, 'It was probably a release: better dead than live on in a state of
undying unrest'. There were no children
and the residue of his estate of £14 919 went
to the University of Sydney to found the
G. C. Henderson research scholarship for
work on the South Pacific islands. He is commemorated in the history department of the
University of Adelaide by the Henderson
room (which includes part of his library) and
the Henderson Jubilee Fund — History.

M. R. Casson, *George Cockburn Henderson*
(Adel, 1964); D. A. Scarr, *I, the very bayonet* (Canb,
1973); *PP* (SA), 1915 (46); *Univ Adel Gazette*, Mar
1960, p 1; *South Australiana*, 6 (1967) no 1, p 3;
E. Kwan, Making good Australians: the work of
three South Australian educators (MA, Univ Adel,
1981); Henderson papers (PRG 6, SAA); Casson
papers (PRG 28, SAA).   G. L. FISCHER

HENDERSON, ISABELLA THOMSON
(1862-1940), educationist, was born on 10
May 1862 at Ballarat, Victoria, sixth child
of Presbyterian clergyman William Henderson [q.v.4] and his wife Isabella, née Thomson. Isabel (as she was known) was educated
at the then co-educational Ballarat College
and passed the University of Melbourne matriculation examination in 1878. Although
she 'wished passionately to be a surgeon',
her father's death in 1884 made this financially impossible and she followed the traditional female path into teaching. She
trained for one year as a pupil-teacher under
Andrew Harper [q.v.] at Presbyterian
Ladies' College in 1879, and taught from
1882 to 1886 at Clarendon Ladies' College,
Ballarat, then until 1891 at Tintern Ladies'
College, Hawthorn.

Possibly as a result of retrenchments at
Tintern during the depression, in 1891
Isabel Henderson and Adelaide Garton
opened a girls' school, Kalymna, in Acland
Street, St Kilda. The venture prospered and
they incorporated Kalymna with the long-
established school, Oberwyl, in nearby Burnett Street, purchasing it in 1898. By 1906
Oberwyl was one of the largest private girls'
schools in Victoria. It had an enrolment of
100 from kindergarten to matriculation, including eighteen boarders, a permanent
staff of thirteen and a curriculum including
Latin, Greek and mathematics, as well as the
usual subjects for girls.

In 1910 Miss Henderson ended her partnership with Miss Garton at Oberwyl in
order to purchase Faireleight, a private
girls' school in Alma Road, East St Kilda.
This school she renamed Clyde and again
built up a flourishing institution. In 1919 her
quest for excellence in the education of girls
led her to transfer Clyde to the rural beauty
of Woodend where she bought Braemar
House and converted it into a boarding-
school for some eighty pupils. In 1921, responding to pressures which were ending
private ownership in education, she negotiated the reconstitution of her school as a corporate institution under Clyde Girls' Grammar School Ltd (later Clyde School). She
retired as principal in 1924. The school
amalgamated with Geelong Church of
England Grammar School in 1976.

Isabel Henderson's career signals the
emergence of women educators into the
arena of public policy in the early 1900s,
when the theory and practice of secondary
education were being reshaped. She was a
key member of influential educational
bodies, such as the Incorporated Association of Secondary Teachers of Victoria, the
Council of Public Education, the University
of Melbourne Schools Board which controlled public examinations and hence
school curricula, the Headmistresses' Association and the Free Kindergarten Union
of Victoria. Working through these bodies
she defended the rights of independent
schools, especially in the areas of teacher
training and curriculum development.
Towards the end of her career she enthusiastically embraced the newly revived notion
of education for woman's 'true' vocation—
that of wife and mother. She led the campaign which saw domestic science become
a subject for the Intermediate and Leaving
examinations in 1917.

Tall and serene-faced, Isabel Henderson
never married, and her school was her
home. Her friend and colleague Olga Hay
left a sympathetic account of her as a wise,
warm and honest woman. For many years
she suffered from diabetes, which she con-

trolled by strict diet. She retired to England and died at South Milton, near Kingsbridge, Devon, on 29 November 1940. Her portrait by W. B. McInnes [q.v.] is at Geelong Grammar School.

O. J. Hay, *The chronicles of Clyde* (Melb, 1966); Clyde School papers (held at Geelong C of E Grammar School, Corio, Vic); Incorporated Assn of Secondary Teachers of Vic, Minutes and papers (Univ Melb Archives).   MARJORIE R. THEOBALD

HENDERSON, JESSIE ISABEL (1866-1951), social welfare worker, was born on 2 October 1866 in Hobart Town, fourth daughter of Charles Dodwell, shipping merchant, and his wife Martha, née Marshall. After the collapse of his business in the late 1880s, Dodwell moved to Melbourne where he became a successful land agent. Jessie was educated at a girls' academy in Hobart and briefly in the late 1880s worked as a governess in New South Wales. On 24 February 1891 at St Columb's Church of England, Hawthorn, Melbourne, she married 38-year-old George Gabriel Henderson (d. 1937), auctioneer and estate and financial agent.

Shortly after her marriage Jessie Henderson joined the Hawthorn Ladies' Benevolent Society. But it was not until 1912, when her youngest child was 3, that she joined the committee of the Melbourne District Nursing Society (Royal District Nursing Service). She was an eager campaigner for the establishment of the society's after-care home in Victoria Parade, Collingwood, opened in November 1926. As president in 1923-47 she saw the formation of the society's first auxiliary in 1927, its first ante-natal clinic in 1930 and the opening of a new wing to the after-care home in 1932. Possibly her most controversial action was her support of the Women's Welfare Clinic for birth control, opened in 1934 under the aegis of the society. She argued that it was necessary to aid women for whom child-bearing had become dangerous.

In 1923 Mrs Henderson became a member of the new Charities Board and for over twenty years worked for the integration and extension of Victoria's semi-voluntary charitable agencies and institutions. She attended almost every meeting of the board, and also served as member and later chairman of its metropolitan standing committee.

Jessie Henderson was on the executive of the National Council of Women of Victoria for over twenty years and was president in 1921-23. In her presidential address of 1922 she spoke of the difficulties faced by women attempting to obtain positions of power in social welfare work, and advocated equal pay for equal work. During the Depression she worked closely with Muriel Heagney [q.v.]. The success of their 'Girls' Week' in August 1930, which raised over £5000 for unemployed girls, inspired them to organize the Unemployed Girls' Relief Movement which provided, until May 1932, practical assistance for young women in suburban and some provincial centres. Of all her work this effort gave her the greatest satisfaction.

In 1915 Mrs Henderson was a founding member of the Housewives' Association of Victoria. She was on the committee set up to establish and select personnel for a trained medical social workers' course at the (Royal) Melbourne Hospital. She found time also to serve on the council of St Mark's Church of England Girls' Grammar School, Camberwell. During World War I she was fully occupied in relief work among families in distress and in the pro-conscription campaign; in World War II she chaired a large branch of the Australian Comforts Fund. Through pressure of her many positions in 1927 she had to decline the offer of appointment as one of Victoria's first female justices of the peace. She was appointed C.B.E. in 1936.

Mrs Henderson was a fine representative of the ideal of voluntary social service at a time when professionals were gradually taking over the administration of welfare agencies. Her extraordinary memory enabled her apparently never to use a notebook; even the smallest details did not escape her. Her magnificent constitution failed her only when she suffered a nervous breakdown after the deaths of her two sons in quick succession at Gallipoli, and at the end of her life. She died at her home in Harcourt Street, Hawthorn, on 11 January 1951, and was buried in Boroondara cemetery. Of her six children, the eldest, Kenneth Thorne (1891-1971) became director of religious broadcasting for the Australian Broadcasting Commission and was author of several books. Her younger daughter was one of Victoria's first almoners.

M. Heagney, *Are women taking men's jobs?* (Melb, 1935); H. E. Gillan, *A brief history of the National Council of Women of Victoria 1902-1945* (Melb, 1945); N. Rosenthal, *People, not cases* (Melb, 1974); family information from Mrs M. J. Sampson, Glen Iris, Melb.   RICHARD TREMBATH

HENDERSON, JOHN BROWNLIE (1869-1950), analytical chemist, was born on 29 April 1869 at Barrhead, near Glasgow, Scotland, son of Robert Henderson, cashier, and his wife Jane, née Kinloch. After primary education at board schools, he attended

Allan Glen's Technical School and in 1887-88 Anderson's University, Glasgow, now the University of Strathclyde. He became research assistant to Professor William Dittmar, particularly in a complex investigation of the gravimetric composition of water which won the Graham gold medal for research.

Following his parents to Queensland in 1891, Henderson became science master at Brisbane Grammar School and in 1893 government analyst. He returned to Britain in 1899 and married Jean Susan McKeown at Leenane, Connemara, Ireland; they had four sons. As analyst Henderson undertook chemical work for all State departments except the Department of Agriculture, and eventually for Federal departments in Brisbane. With J. C. Brunnich [q.v.7], his agricultural counterpart, he had a standing demarcation dispute. In a laboratory containing much equipment designed by him, Henderson and his staff undertook a constant flow of routine tasks, punctuated by such high points as the testing of the first significant Australian oil discovered at Roma. Something of an egotist, he spoke always of 'my laboratory'.

Asked to draft the Explosives Act of 1906, he became chief inspector under the Act in 1907 and supervised the creation of magazines all over Queensland; an explosives area at Narangba was named after him in 1951. During World War I he was a member of the State Munitions Committee which arranged the dispatch of 600 workers to Britain and chaired the committee which controlled all explosives in the State.

An enthusiast for education, Henderson was active both in the Sydney University Extension Committee and the movement which finally secured a university for Brisbane. In the first of three terms as president of the Royal Society of Queensland he devoted his presidential address to a review of Queensland education and a plea for a university. Nominated to the first university senate, he resigned only on retirement in 1936. Henderson chaired the chemistry section of the 1904 meeting at Dunedin of the Australasian Association for the Advancement of Science; in 1917 he was a founder (fellow 1918) of the (Royal) Australian Chemical Institute and was its first Queensland president. Appointed to the State committee of the Advisory Council for Science and Industry in 1916, he acted in 1917 for a chairman on war service and joined *ex officio* the national executive committee. He chaired the provisional State Advisory Board of the Institute of Science and Industry from March 1921 and became a member of the State committee of the Council for Scientific and Industrial Research in Nov-

ember 1928, resigning in 1949 when it was reconstituted. In 1937-42 he helped his son to develop a prickly-pear selection at Palardo.

Henderson was an executive member of the Queensland branch of the Australian Red Cross Society in 1914-18. Later, as an officer of the Boy Scouts' Association, he acted as providore for a world jamboree in Brisbane. Tall and thin with strong cheekbones and a 'handlebar' moustache, Henderson was an excellent lecturer despite a tendency to verbosity and over-emphasis of sibilants. He was scientifically cautious when asked for forensic evidence: policemen called him 'the silent witness' because he refused to venture opinions and stuck to facts. He died at Annerley on 19 October 1950 and was cremated with Presbyterian forms.

G. Currie and J. Graham, *The origins of CSIRO* (Melb, 1966); Advisory Council of Science and Industry, *and* Institute of Science and Industry, *and* CSIR, *Annual Report*, 1916-29, and Qld State Cttee, CSIR, Minutes (CSIRO Archives, Canb); personal papers held by I. Henderson, Brisb; information from S. B. Watkins, Toowong, Qld.

H. J. GIBBNEY

HENDERSON, KINGSLEY ANKETELL (1883-1942), architect, was born on 15 December 1883 at Brighton, Melbourne, son of ANKETELL MATTHEW HENDERSON (1853-1922), architect, and his wife Mary Louisa, née Andrew, from England. A. M. Henderson was born on 3 March 1853 at Cork, Ireland, son of an Independent clergyman, and came to Victoria at the age of 10 with his family. After education at Scotch College, Melbourne, he completed the University of Melbourne's engineering certificate course (1872) while articled to Reed [q.v.6] & Barnes. The partnership of Reed, Henderson & Smart was formed in 1883 and lasted until 1890, during which time Henderson was responsible for work for the Bank of Australasia and for the university. He retained the bank work when he set up on his own, practising in 1890-1906 as Anketell Henderson, architect, licensed surveyor and sanitary engineer, at 352 Collins Street. In 1890 he was appointed co-examiner in architecture for the university's engineering course and in 1891-1903 and 1905-16 was lecturer in architecture; he continued in an honorary capacity for a few years.

In 1897, 1910 and 1913 he was president of the Royal Victorian Institute of Architects. As lecturer in architecture for almost thirty years he was a major influence on students and staff alike both in matters of practice and design theory. His preference for the classical styles was well known, as was his insistence on the practical use of learning. The R.V.I.A.'s eventual support of the teaching of architecture at the university was achieved mainly by his endeavour. A diabetic, he died on 15 November 1922, survived by his wife, whom he had married on 8 January 1880, two sons and two daughters.

Kingsley Anketell Henderson was educated at Cumloden, East St Kilda. He studied architecture at the university and the Melbourne Technical College while articled to his father from 1901. When he joined his father as a partner in 1906 the firm became known as Anketell and K. Henderson. In 1913 he visited the United States of America. In 1920-24 the partnership included R. H. Alsop [q.v.7] and M. W. Martin. The firm won several competitions during the 1920s and in 1931 was awarded the R.V.I.A. Victorian Street Architecture medal for Lyric House, Collins Street, and in 1935 for Shell Corner, William Street. The work of the practice was carried out in all States of Australia and in New Zealand and its clients included notables such as Essington Lewis [q.v.], (Sir) Robert Menzies and (Dame) Enid Lyons, banks and insurance companies, hospitals and universities.

Kingsley Henderson was largely responsible for the success of the practice after 1922. He placed great emphasis on the functional and commercial aspect of city office planning, being especially adept at achieving the maximum natural light and space to let. He gave a paper on the subject to a meeting of the R.V.I.A. in November 1928. Another paper to the institute, in August 1930, was on 'Supervision and the relationship of contracting parties' and after a trip to England, Europe and America in 1935-36 inspecting hospitals, he spoke on hospital design.

Henderson's understanding of the functional requirements of commercial office development undoubtedly put the practice at the forefront of the profession in this type of work. He made a major contribution to the architecture of Melbourne, particularly in Collins Street which at one time boasted seven A. & K. Henderson buildings. In most cases, however, the design of the façades of the buildings is attributable to other members of the firm such as John Freeman and R. Jack Wilson. These façades were representative of the full range of architectural stylistic expression employed by Melbourne's architects generally over the period of the practice, beginning with the classical revival of the early banks, particularly the National Bank head office in Collins Street, and encompassing variations of 'art modern', 'neo-Gothic' and 'vertical

modern' before settling for the restrained modernistic of the Trustees, Executors & Agency Co. building in Queen Street.

Henderson was a fellow of both the Royal Australian Institute of Architects and the Royal Institute of British Architects. In 1921-24 he was president and in 1934-35 vice-president of the council of the R.V.I.A.; he was president of the federal council of the institute in 1924-25 and 1930-31 and in 1937 of the Architects' Registration Board. In 1927-30 he served on the Committee of Public Taste, Federal Capital Commission. He was appointed C.M.G. in 1938.

Well known as a businessman, Henderson was a director of companies including Were's, National Reliance and Capel Court (Aust) Ltd investment trusts, Chevron Ltd, Eagle Star Insurance Co. (Australian board) and the Argus and Australasian Ltd, of which he was chairman in 1940. From 1917 to 1922 he was a member of the Malvern City Council. Early in 1931, with S. Ricketson, Sir John Higgins [q.v.], (Sir) Robert Menzies and others, he had much to do with persuading J. A. Lyons [q.v.] to leave the Labor Party and accept leadership of the non-Labor forces. After working in the All for Australia League, in May Henderson became chairman of the central council of the United Australia Party in Victoria; he resigned in November. Lyons became a close friend.

Henderson was a member of the Savage, Melbourne and Athenaeum clubs and a founder of the Toc H boys' home. At Christ Church, South Yarra, on 10 December 1909 he had married Ruve Cutts Poolman who survived him on his sudden death at Portsea on 6 April 1942; he was buried in St Kilda cemetery. They had no children. His estate was valued for probate at £72 564. The practice was carried on by R. Cedric Staughton as principal with associates W. H. Lacey and L. C. Pillar until the early 1960s.

E. Lyons, *So we take comfort* (Lond, 1965); *Labour Hist*, 1970, no 17, p 44; Roy Vic Inst of Architects, *J*, Sept 1925, Nov 1928, Sept 1930, Sept 1931, Jan 1932, July 1933, Nov 1935, May, June, July, Aug, Sept 1936, Sept 1937; *Building* (Syd), Jan 1928, Jan, Aug 1929, Jan, Mar 1932; *Aust Home Beautiful*, Aug, Oct 1929, Aug 1930; A. & K. Henderson papers (LaTL).

SUSAN M. BALDERSTONE

HENEY, THOMAS WILLIAM (1862-1928), journalist, poet and novelist, was born on 3 November 1862 in Sydney, son of Thomas William Heney, printer, and his wife Sarah Elizabeth, née Carruthers. He was educated at Cooma and intended for the Catholic priesthood. His father, a proprietor of the *Manaro Mercury*, was a heavy drinker, whose death in 1875 left Heney in sole support of his mother; his commitment to hard work, sobriety and his mother's Anglicanism, and his dislike of Catholicism, were to be lifelong.

In 1878 he became junior assistant reader with the *Sydney Morning Herald*, and in 1884 a reporter for the *Daily Telegraph*. Fearing incipient tuberculosis, he moved in 1886 to Wilcannia, edited the *Western Grazier* for three years and contributed to the *Sydney Quarterly Magazine*. The pastoral outback is the setting for his novels and some verse. After a stay in Melbourne, he worked for the *Echo*, Sydney. He rejoined the *Herald* in 1893 as literary reviewer, essayist and later parliamentary reporter and political leader-writer. On 10 August 1898 he married Amy Florence, eldest daughter of Henry Gullett [q.v.], whom he succeeded as associate-editor next year. Dr Lucy Gullett [q.v.] was Amy's sister. In 1903 Heney was the first native-born Australian to become editor of the *Herald*.

He consolidated the paper's pragmatic conservative traditions and its reputation as a major journal, maintaining its non-sectarian approach and its support of free trade. During his editorship the paper eventually outsold its competitor, the *Daily Telegraph*. In World War I Heney believed that out of loyalty and self-interest Australia would follow Britain. Editorials urged an energetic home effort and direct income taxation for war finance. Although he agreed with press censorship, he argued that during the conscription referenda, in which the *Herald* supported the government, ignorant censors created suspicion of political censorship.

In June 1918 Heney was officially invited to join a press delegation to England and the war front. The management arranged for his replacement by (Sir) James O. Fairfax [q.v.8], a proprietor, but after protest Heney (foundation president of the Institute of Journalists of New South Wales in 1913-20) was also included. After a tense visit, and the proprietors' veto of publication elsewhere of his observations, Heney resigned in September. He then freelanced, mainly for the Melbourne *Argus*, edited the Brisbane *Telegraph* in 1920-23, and the Sydney *Daily Telegraph* in 1924-25.

Heney's descriptive and meditative verse (*Fortunate days*, Sydney, 1886; *In Middle Harbour*, London, 1890) is carefully crafted, distinctive, at times Whitmanesque in form, but lacks sharp poetic edge. The novels, *The girl at Birrell's* (London, 1896) and 'A station courtship', serialized in the Melbourne *Leader* in 1898-99, are authentically detailed romances. His criticism is precise, perceptive and antagonistic to the view that 'rub-

bish is to be consecrated, provided it be . . . Australian'. He denied that he was indifferent to needy writers and Australian writing; but he deprecated those Bohemian *Bulletin* poets who would 'haunt my office late on Friday night for aid'. Associated with several literary societies, he befriended such young artists as Florence Rodway and Ellis Rowan and sheltered Elioth Gruner [qq.v.], a victim of xenophobia, at his Moss Vale home. He cultivated native plants in his gardens and collected Australian semi-precious stones.

Heney died of heart disease at Springwood on 19 August 1928 and was buried in the Anglican cemetery. He was survived by his wife, two daughters, Helen (a novelist) and Lucy, and son John, who served with the Coldstream Guards in World War I. He left incomplete a volume on domestic policy for C. E. W. Bean's [q.v.7] official war history; it was rewritten by (Sir) Ernest Scott [q.v.] with acknowledgments.

J. Fairfax Ltd, *Century of journalism* (Syd, 1931); E. Scott, *Australia during the war* (Syd, 1936); G. Souter, *Company of Heralds* (Melb, 1981); T. Heney, Drafts and notes for his proposed war history (AWM); H. Heney, Notes on the Heney family (ML).   KEN STEWART

HENLEY, FRANK LE LEU (1888-1941), soldier, secretary and sales manager, was born on 7 December 1888 at Dandenong, Victoria, first child of James Robert Henley, bricklayer and later contractor, and his wife Emma, née Le Leu; both were born in South Australia. Soon afterwards, James and Emma Henley returned to Adelaide where Frank attended Pulteney Street School. He was working as a clerk when he married Elizabeth Elder Wisdom at St Paul's Church, Port Adelaide, on 16 January 1908.

Henley's military career began in December 1911 when he was commissioned as a second lieutenant in the Australian Army Service Corps (militia). When war broke out in 1914 he joined the Australian Imperial Force on 20 August as a lieutenant and was attached to the 4th Company, 1st Divisional Train. Promotion for Henley was rapid and he left for Egypt in October as a captain. By May 1915 he was serving at Gallipoli and in October was promoted major and appointed senior supply officer, 1st Division. By that time he had been mentioned in dispatches and in January 1917 received the Distinguished Service Order for his exemplary performance as senior supply officer. Throughout his tenure there were practically no complaints from unit commanders regarding logistical support and at no time were troops forced to rely on short rations.

Henley was present at the evacuation of Gallipoli and before being sent to France in March 1916 spent three months in Egypt. He served in France and Belgium with the 1st Divisional Train until January 1917 when he briefly took charge of the 4th Divisional Train. From 24 March 1917 until the end of the war he commanded the 3rd Divisional Train in the rank of lieut-colonel and was mentioned in dispatches four times in 1917-18 and appointed O.B.E. in the New Year honours of 1919. He returned to Australia in November 1918 and his appointment with the A.I.F. ended next March.

Henley rejoined the Australian Military Forces (militia) as a captain in the A.A.S.C. in 1919. After various appointments in South Australia he was awarded the Volunteer Officers' Decoration in 1928 and given command of the 4th Divisional Australian Army Service Corps as a lieut-colonel. He relinquished this position in 1939 after four extensions and joined the unattached list. In civilian life he worked in the 1920s as a secretary for W. C. Harrison & Co., flour millers and wheat merchants of Port Adelaide, and by 1931 had settled in Melbourne as a sales manager.

On the outbreak of World War II he was sent to Hobart as assistant director of supply and transport, 6th Division, although his conspicuous ability soon led to his recall to Melbourne as A.D.S.T. for the 3rd Military District. His final appointment was deputy director of supply and transport, Southern Command, in July 1941 with the rank of colonel. Survived by his wife, a son and a daughter, he died of septicaemia in Heidelberg Military Hospital, Melbourne, on 25 December 1941 and was cremated. His estate was sworn for probate at £3846.

London Gazette, 11 July, 29 Dec 1916, 2 Jan, 1 June, 25 Dec 1917, 31 Dec 1918, 1 Jan 1919; *SMH*, 29 Dec 1941; records (AWM).   CRIS ANSTEY

HENLEY, SIR THOMAS (1860-1935), politician and building contractor, was born on 4 February 1860 at Wootton Bassett, Wiltshire, England, son of George Henley, agricultural labourer, and his wife Margaret, née Seagle. His mother was illiterate and, after National schooling only, Thomas worked as a farm-hand and for ten years 'carried the hod'. He migrated to Sydney about 1884 and was a plasterer when he married Charlotte Smith in Balmain Congregational Church on 2 July 1886.

Henley bought land at Balmain, Petersham, Five Dock and Drummoyne, building on some blocks and subdividing others for sale at £10 deposit, 6 per cent interest and repayment over five years. During the de-pressed 1890s he continued to buy, especially at Drummoyne, where he built Tudor House for himself. In 1898-1905 he owned the Drummoyne, West Balmain and Leichhardt Steam Ferry Co., running three ferries. As alderman for Drummoyne in 1898-1934 and four times mayor, and as a member of the Metropolitan Board of Water Supply and Sewerage in 1902-33, Henley saw the tram-line extended to Drummoyne in 1902, its sewerage planned in 1903 and reticulation sewers laid by 1910, electricity supply introduced in 1910 and a beginning to sealing roads in 1916. As the solution to municipal indebtedness, he secured the amalgamation in 1902 of Five Dock and Drummoyne and the sale of municipal property. While an alderman for Lang Ward on the Sydney Municipal Council in 1902-06 Henley sought extended licensing powers for the council as a measure of additional revenue. He campaigned to have the abattoirs moved to Homebush, away from where he owned property.

Twice defeated for Ryde, Henley was elected in 1904 to the Legislative Assembly as a Liberal and Reform candidate for Burwood which he represented until 1935 (Ryde, 1920-27). He developed an aggressive parliamentary style, heckling Labor about caucus control, making provocative reference to Catholics, and affirming his own success and the merits of hard work. Opponents called him the 'great "I am"'. At his own expense he was in Europe in 1908 as commissioner for the Franco-British Exhibition. Litigious, he won his case against enemies who alleged he treated his employees unfairly. In 1913-14, with Sir William McMillan [q.v.] and (Sir) Arthur Cocks [q.v.8], he incurred £3500 costs (later paid by public subscription) in a case that went to the Privy Council challenging the Labor government's plans to convert Government House to other use.

In 1915 Henley volunteered to go to Egypt as a commissioner for the Citizens' War Chest Fund. Organizing the distribution of comforts from Alexandria, Marseilles and Le Havre, France, and London, Henley personally accompanied the goods. He was gazetted lieut-colonel to overcome objections to civilians entering the battle zone and was appointed C.B.E. and K.B.E. in 1920. A son had died in France in 1916.

Although Henley's demand in 1920 for an investigation into convents recalled his earlier sectarianism, his old fire had gone. He served as minister for public works and for railways and housing under Sir George Fuller's [q.v.8] seven-hour ministry (21 December 1921) and from April to June 1922, when he resigned because of ill health. Next year he was studying Fascism and in 1924 promoting the development of Canberra. He became a director of W. R. Carpenter [q.v.7] & Co. (1926) and the North Shore Gas Co. Ltd (1928). For thirty years he had been an adroit exploiter of press publicity and self-published pamphlets. His travels to the Pacific Islands led to publication of *A Pacific cruise* (1930) and an acrimonious exchange with Sir Joseph Carruthers [q.v.7] who criticized his account of the Samoan rebellion: Henley, he said, was 'qualifying for Callan Park'. Short, square-jawed and pugnacious, Henley had become increasingly irascible and been involved in more lawsuits. Nevertheless the *Bulletin* claimed 'everyone liked and respected him': he was always 'Tom' to his workers.

On 14 May 1935 Henley fell from a Manly ferry and was drowned. The man who tried to rescue him reported seeing a phial floating nearby and there were rumours of suicide. The coroner found no suspicious circumstances but a record of ill health: he had recently stood down from all public offices. He was buried in Field of Mars cemetery with Presbyterian forms, survived by his wife, two daughters and a son Herbert, grazier and member of the Legislative Council in 1937-64. Henley had been a Sunday school superintendent and left money from his estate, valued for probate at £139 037, to the Congregational and Presbyterian churches, the Salvation Army and Sydney City Mission. He had been presented by his constituents in 1929 with his portrait by Norman Carter [q.v.7].

S. H. Bowden (ed), *The history of the Australian Comforts Fund . . . 1914-19* (Syd, 1922); S. N. Hogg, *Balmain past and present* (Syd, 1924); J. Jervis, *The story of Drummoyne* (Parramatta, 1941); *SMH*, 14 June 1916, 15 May, 6 June 1935; *Fighting Line*, 26 Feb 1920; *Bulletin*, 22 May 1935; Carruthers papers (ML).   HEATHER RADI

HENN, PERCY UMFREVILLE (1865-1955), clergyman and headmaster, was born on 21 January 1865 in Manchester, England, tenth child of Rev. John Henn and his wife Catherine, née Holcroft. Educated at Christ's Hospital, London, and with a scholarship at Worcester College, Oxford (B.A., 1887; M.A., 1890), he then considered taking holy orders but first became assistant master at Hurstpierpoint, one of the 'Woodard Schools'. Here, through his admiration of Rev. Nathaniel Woodard's work, Henn became enthusiastic about education within the Church. Ordained priest in 1891, he was appointed chaplain at Hurstpierpoint in 1892.

Henn's teaching talent was first recognized in 1895 when he became a very suc-cessful founding headmaster of Worksop College. After he resigned in 1899 because of differences with a new superior, the governing chapter of the school testified to the 'bravery and self-reliance' which had been the hallmark of his work.

Seeking a change, Henn arrived in Perth in January 1900 as a missionary. After a brief stay at Kalgoorlie, he moved to Geraldton as rector. There, on 3 April 1902, he married Jean Elliott; they had two sons and two daughters. Rector of Northam in 1902-05, he returned to England at the conclusion of his missionary term. After this he used his knowledge of the colonial Church as organizing secretary of the Society for the Propagation of the Gospel in the dioceses of Canterbury and Rochester.

In 1909 Henn returned to Perth at the invitation of Bishop Riley [q.v.] to become headmaster of Guildford Grammar School, recently bought by the Church. His task was to oversee the first major attempt by the Church of England in Western Australia to provide secondary education since its loss of control of Bishop Hale's [q.v.4] school in 1873. He sought both to build up Guildford Grammar and to develop Church education generally in the State. The Council for Church Schools, for the creation of which he was largely responsible, had oversight and management of Church of England schools in 1917-50. He worked closely with (Sir) Walter Tapper, the English architect, to design worthy buildings for Guildford but was frustrated by financial considerations. He nevertheless saw Guildford develop into one of the State's leading schools and secured its noble Gothic chapel through the gift of Cecil Oliverson. Henn became a canon of St George's Cathedral in 1921.

He retired as headmaster of Guildford and returned to England in 1925. He came back to Perth again in 1931 at the invitation of Archbishop Le Fanu [q.v.] to become founding warden of St George's College within the University of Western Australia. Henn retired permanently to Perth in 1933 and continued to take an active interest in Church affairs, especially education, until his death on 25 February 1955; his ashes lie in Guildford Chapel. His estate, valued for probate at £41 483, provided bequests for Christ's Hospital and Worcester College and a sum of £6000 for Guildford Grammar School, primarily to remove any burden of debt. The remainder of his estate was left for the benefit of his family. His *An autobiographical retrospect* was published privately in 1977.

F. Alexander (ed), *Four bishops and their see* (Perth, 1957); W. E. Henn, *A life so rich* (priv print, Perth, 1982); J. A. Cardell-Oliver, 'Percy Umfreville Henn: visionary headmaster', in L. Fletcher,

Pioneers in Western Australian education (Perth, 1982); *West Australian*, 26 Feb 1953; Henn scrapbook, PR 8435 (Battye Lib, Perth), and Henn papers (held by the Venerable W. E. Henn, Darlington, and Dr G. Henn, Floreat Park, Perth).

JOHN CARDELL-OLIVER

HENNESSY, ARTHUR STEPHEN (1876-1959), football coach, was born on 24 September 1876 at Elizabeth Street, Sydney, sixth son of John Polding Hennessy, stonemason, and his Scottish wife Mary, née McGill. Arthur was a labourer living at Surry Hills when, on 25 November 1899, he married Emily Jane Hensley at Christ Church of St Laurence, Sydney.

In 1895 Hennessy had played Rugby Union football in the three-quarter line for the Boys' Brigade. Next year he played for Bayview and in 1897 was a South Sydney junior. A regular Souths first-grade forward, he represented New South Wales against New Zealand in 1901, and against Queensland in 1904, having toured New Zealand in 1902. He became honorary coach of The King's School in 1905.

A founder of Australian Rugby League, Hennessy was a selector for and captained the team of pioneers in Sydney on 17 and 21 August 1907 against New Zealand Rugby Union professionals. Expelled with his colleagues from the amateur code, Hennessy convened the meeting which founded South Sydney District Rugby League Club and was one of its first delegates to the New South Wales Rugby Football League. In 1908 he captained New South Wales against Queensland and a Maori team, and led Souths to victory in the inaugural Sydney grade competition. A hooker, weighing 12 st. 6 lb. (79 kg), he was 5 ft. 8 ins. (173 cm) tall. He toured Britain with the first Kangaroos in 1908-09 but, twice sustaining a broken jaw, did not play in a Test. In 1909 he played for the Kangaroos versus the rest and against New Zealand, then coached the Wallaby team which defected to the league. In 1910-11 he again played for Souths.

Hennessy had quickly absorbed the principles of the new code and became a sought-after coach; in 1911 he trained the Wyalong team. As coach of the 1913 tour of New Zealand he imposed a steak-only diet for lunch on match days. Hennessy strongly advocated the no kick principle, emphasizing the importance of ball possession to score tries. This came to be the mark of South Sydney's football, influenced by Hennessy as trainer in 1912, coach and trainer in 1913 and second-grade coach in 1916. With straight running and backing up the no kick policy produced fast, open football and for Souths ('Rabbitohs') a remarkable winning record.

During the 1920s Hennessy was football and boxing coach at Waverley College. He was non-playing coach of the 1929-30 Kangaroo tour of Britain, the first and only such appointment until Clive Churchill's in 1969. Hennessy prohibited kicking and the Australians were narrowly defeated. He coached country versus city in 1942-44, and Souths' firsts in 1946; about then he published a coaching manual, *Winning Rugby moves*.

A 'crack masseur', Hennessy also trained boxer Sid Godfrey [q.v.]. Connected with racing, possibly a bookmaker's clerk, he invested in the Maroubra Speedway and in mini-golf, and partly owned the Amusu cinema, Maroubra, living in a cottage opposite the theatre. Survived by his wife, Hennessy died on 19 September 1959 and was buried with Anglican rites in Botany cemetery. His estate was sworn for probate at £4703.

Sydney Mail, 22 Mar 1902, 30 May 1906; *T&CJ*, 22 July 1908; *Daily Telegraph* (Syd), 31 Aug 1909; *Referee*, 2 May 1910, 9 May 1917, 23 Jan 1924; *Sun* (Syd), 26 May 1911, 4 July 1913; *Rugby League News*, 28 May 1921, Oct 1959; *SMH*, 22 June 1942, 10 June 1944, 21 Sept 1959; *Telegraph* (Brisb), 2 Apr 1949; information from Messrs T. Brock, Maroubra, A. Clift, Mascot, S. Carey, Kensington, and G. Treweeke, Kogarah, NSW.

CHRIS CUNNEEN

HENNESSY, SIR DAVID VALENTINE (1858-1923), lord mayor and philanthropist, was born on 15 June 1858 in Melbourne, son of James Hennessy and his wife Margaret, née Power, both from Waterford, Ireland. He was educated at the Model High School and Fitzroy College. At 15 David joined his father's bakery business, which was based at Fitzroy, but later moved to Sydney Road, Brunswick; by the early 1880s he was in charge. On 23 February 1881, at St Patrick's Cathedral, he married 20-year-old Lizzie Walsh (d. 1889). He was a founding member of the Brunswick branch of the Australian Natives' Association in 1885 and later president. By 1889 successful speculations enabled him to retire from active commerce and in 1891 he toured the world.

Apart from maintaining speculative interests, notably in mining ventures in Victoria, Queensland and Tasmania, 'D.V.' Hennessy devoted the rest of his life to his chosen form of public service. In 1891 he became a justice of the peace and next year entered the Brunswick Town Council, becoming mayor in 1894. He helped to raise large sums of money for the relief of victims of the depression and bank failures. He joined the (Royal) Melbourne Hospital committee, and in 1895 entered the Melbourne City Council. On 17 February 1896 at St Patrick's Cathedral he married Mary (Minnie) Quinlan Daly. Meanwhile he sought a career in politics, but his bids for the Legislative Assembly seats of Melbourne West in 1892 and East Bourke Boroughs in 1894 and 1897 resulted in defeat and mortification. He won Carlton South in 1900 and 1902 but lost to Labor, of which he was an uncompromising foe, in 1904 and 1907.

Hennessy then devoted his time to the city council. Dust prevention and sanitary matters were an interest, and as a result of his efforts rubbish baskets were installed on street corners. He was also an advocate of an underground railway. In 1912 he was elected lord mayor, remaining so for a record successive five terms. During World War I he distinguished himself as a 'super patriot', appearing regularly on recruiting platforms, assisted ably by his wife, a talented linguist and musician and a capable hostess. In early August 1914 she established the Lady Mayoress's Patriotic League, later known as the Comforts Fund. For her work she was appointed C.B.E. and honoured by the governments of France and Belgium. For nine years she was president of the Alliance Française of Victoria. As fund-raisers the Hennessys were a formidable team. The Lord Mayor's Patriotic Fund alone raised more than £250 000, and the total figure contributed for patriotic purposes by organizations in which they were active exceeded £1 million. Hennessy was knighted in 1915.

After relinquishing the mayoralty in 1917 Hennessy remained active in council affairs, becoming a member of the new Tramways Trust in 1918. He died suddenly of bronchial pneumonia on 16 June 1923 at his Toorak home, and was buried in Melbourne general cemetery. He was survived by his wife and three daughters, one of whom married (Sir) Bernard Heinze, and by a son of his first marriage. Hennessy's estate was sworn for probate at £45 636.

He was an astute and energetic businessman who brought to public life a commitment normally only exhibited in the world of private gain. What he lacked in ability as a politician he more than made up for by zeal, circumspect political attitudes, and a philanthropic spirit.

J. Smith (ed), *Cyclopedia of Victoria*, 1 (Melb, 1903); *Scientific Australian*, 20 June 1913; Labour Hist, Melb, *Recorder*, Dec 1976, Feb 1977; *Who's Who in the World of Women*, Vic, 1930; *Punch* (Melb), 17 Oct 1912; *Argus*, 18 June 1923; Lord Mayors of Melbourne (bibliog file, LATL).

DAVID DUNSTAN

HENNESSY, JOHN FRANCIS (1853-1924), architect, was born on 21 April 1853 probably in Ireland, son of Bryan Joseph Hennessy, outfitters' manager from Cork, and his wife Ellen, née Swiney. By 1855 his parents had moved to Leeds, Yorkshire, where he grew up. After passing the Oxford senior local examination in 1868, he was articled to William Perkin & Son, architects and surveyors of Leeds. On completing his apprenticeship in 1875 he was awarded the Ashpitel prize of the Royal Institute of British Architects and a silver medal for measured drawings. While attending the architectural schools of the Royal Academy of Arts, London, he gained practical experience with Basil Champneys and Charles Eastlake, and the noted Gothic Revival architect William Burges.

After six months study in Spain, Hennessy worked in leading architectural offices in New York and Boston, United States of America, and spent two years in Los Angeles as junior partner in Kysor & Hennessy. Believing that Australia offered more opportunity, he arrived in Sydney in October 1880. Next year he became a draughtsman under the city architect. His ability was soon recognized and, appointed assistant city architect, he designed the Frazer [q.v.4] fountain in Hyde Park (1881) and the Centennial Hall extension of Sydney Town Hall (1883). He resigned in 1884 but in 1887 became consulting architect for the completion of the Centennial Hall. In 1884-88 he was instructor in architecture at Sydney Technical College. On 25 February 1884 in Sydney he had married Matilda Silk (d. 1898) of Delegate.

Hennessy's geniality earned him many friends including Joseph I. Sheerin who became his partner in 1884. Both were devout Catholics, active in Church charities, and friends of Archbishop (Cardinal) Moran [q.v.]. Their designs, a blend of neo-Gothic and Romanesque styles, for St Patrick's College, Manly, and the near-by episcopal residence were awarded a medal at the 1886 Colonial and Indian Exhibition in London.

Sheerin & Hennessy designed many other Catholic buildings in Sydney and New South Wales country areas, including St Joseph's College, Hunters Hill (1884-94), St Vincent's College, Potts Point (1886), and the Cathedral of St Mary and St Joseph, Armidale (1910-11), with its dominating turreted tower and needle spire in polychrome brick. Among their numerous commercial premises were Hordern Bros' drapery store (1886) and Tattersall's Club (1892) in Pitt Street and ten stores for (Sir) John See [q.v.]. Many large suburban residences were built to their plans. In 1912 Sheerin left the firm and Hennessy's son, Jack, joined it. They were responsible for completing W. W. Wardell's [q.v.6] plans for St Mary's Cathedral, Sydney, for which they designed the crypt. With Sir John Sulman [q.v.], Hennessy designed the model garden suburb of Daceyville in 1912. He retired in 1923.

For almost forty years Hennessy lived at Burwood and designed the council chambers (1887). An alderman on the local council from 1890 to 1895, he was mayor in 1892-93. During his presidency of the Institute of Architects of New South Wales in 1911-12 the registration of architects was achieved. He helped to establish the chair of architecture at the University of Sydney and to secure the recognition of public competition for public buildings.

An important figure in the development of church architecture in Australia, Hennessy was appointed knight of the Order of St Sylvester by Pope Benedict XV in 1920. He designed a wide variety of buildings, enabling him to experiment with a spectrum of architectural styles and building materials. Despite an eclectic but controlled approach to stylistic representation, examples of decorative details executed in two-tone brickwork bear witness to his virtuosity as a skilled and sensitive designer. He died of heart disease at his Burwood home on 1 November 1924 and was buried in the Catholic section of Rookwood cemetery, close to the sandstone mortuary chapel he had designed in 1886. His estate was valued for probate at £16 672. He was survived by three daughters and his son who carried on the firm Hennessy, Hennessy & Co.

E. Digby (ed), *Australian men of mark*, 2 (Syd, 1889); *SMH*, 4 Nov 1924; R. I. Howard, Sheerin and Hennessy—architects (B.Arch. thesis, Univ NSW, in preparation); Hennessy scrapbook (held by Mrs E. F. Doyle, Gresford, NSW).

ROD HOWARD

HENRY, ALICE (1857-1943), journalist and woman's rights advocate, was born on 21 March 1857 at Richmond, Melbourne, daughter of Charles Ferguson Henry, accountant, and his wife Margaret, née Walker, seamstress. Her parents, both Scottish-born, had met on the voyage out from Glasgow and married in Melbourne in 1853. Her brother Alfred was born in 1859. At one stage Charles Henry tried farming a selection of land in Gippsland. Here Alice received her first lessons from her mother. Remembering these as years of freedom and activity, she never lost her love of the bush. Back in Melbourne she attended several schools, matriculating with credit from Richard Hale Budd's [q.v.3] Educational Institute for Ladies in 1874.

Her father's discussions of the protective tariff introduced her to politics. She later attributed her passionate commitment to justice, democracy, and woman's rights to her Scots ancestry, the equal treatment she and her brother received from her parents and Budd's advanced educational ideas. Denied access to a university education, yet accepting the need to support herself, Henry tried teaching but following a serious illness turned to journalism. Her first article appeared in 1884. For twenty years she wrote for the *Argus*, the *Australasian*, and occasionally other newspapers and overseas journals, under her own name or a pseudonymn, 'A.L.F.', 'Wyuna', or 'Pomona'.

Her journalism publicized progressive causes: juvenile courts, women's hospitals, proportional representation, epileptic colonies, care for handicapped and dependent children, and labour reform. She became a close friend and working associate of leading reformers Catherine Helen Spence [q.v.6], Henry Bournes Higgins [q.v.] and his sister Ina, Bernard O'Dowd [q.v.], and Vida Goldstein [q.v.] and her family. She was active in women's clubs and the woman suffrage campaign, and gained a reputation as a courageous public speaker in support of social change. For a time she also ran a business, from a city office, as a town shopper for country women and employment agency for domestic servants.

In 1905, aged 48, she left for England sponsored by the Charity Organisation Society of Melbourne. There she heard George Bernard Shaw speak, observed the militant suffragists, and toured Scotland. In December she sailed for New York where American interest in Australian progressivism ensured her a ready audience. Her Fabian socialism fitted neatly with the philosophy of labour reform espoused by the new school of political economists, and her knowledge of Australian labour legislation and woman suffrage attracted the attention of the prominent reformer Margaret Dreier Robins. She invited Henry to work for the National Women's Trade Union League of America in Chicago where, as lecturer, as field-worker organizing new branches, and as journalist, she became a key figure in the campaign for woman suffrage, union organization, vocational education, and labour legislation. Her bearing was dignified and when she spoke it was with vigour and conviction. American audiences were 'in awe of her English accent, snowy head and great knowledge'. Despite some eccentricities in her dress, newspaper reports testified to her persuasiveness on the podium.

She wrote two books, *The trade union*

woman (1915) and *Women and the labor movement* (1923); in 1920-22 directed the league's educational department; and, with the assistance of her close friend Miles Franklin [q.v.8], for eight years edited the league's official journal, initially the women's page of the *Union Labor Advocate* (1908-10), then a separate publication, *Life and Labor* (1911-15). In 1924 the league executive sent her to England, Europe, and Australia; she arrived in Melbourne in February 1925, intending to stay for two months but remained for twelve. On her return to America in March 1926 she retired from active work, moving to Santa Barbara, California, in 1928. There, in 1929, her last significant article, on Henry Handel Richardson [q.v.], was published in the *Bookman*.

In 1923 Alice Henry had become an American citizen. Suffering financial hardship during the Depression, and wishing to be with her brother, she reluctantly returned to Australia in 1933. Although she was welcomed as a notable and successful Australian woman, settling back into Melbourne was slow and painful. She attempted to continue her old activities: she joined the Playgrounds' Association and the press, arts and letters committee of the National Council of Women of Victoria; she gave radio talks on prohibition and modern poetry; she assisted C. Hartley Grattan in his tour of 1936-38; and in 1937 she compiled a bibliography of Australian women writers. But she missed her American life. Then, in 1937, her brother was lost at sea, and her health began to deteriorate. In 1938 she gave up her American citizenship, and in 1939 she resigned from her committee work. A year later she entered a nursing home. She died in hospital at Malvern on 14 February 1943 and was cremated.

Memoirs of Alice Henry, N. Palmer ed (Melb, 1944); National Women's Trade Union League of America, *Union Labor Advocate*, 1908-10, and *Life and Labor*, 1911-15, and *Life and Labor Bulletin*, Apr 1943, and records (Lib Congress, Washington); National Council of Women, Records (Melb); Papers, Henry, *and* Palmer (NL), *and* Franklin (ML), *and* Spence (SAA, and ML).

DIANE KIRKBY

HENRY, HENRY GOYA (1901-1974), aviator and shipmaster, was born on 17 June 1901 at Grafton, New South Wales, third son of Thomas James Henry, medical practitioner, and his wife Emily, née Stephen, a great-granddaughter of John Stephen [q.v.2]. Known as Goya, Henry was educated at Grafton High School. He made one voyage in a sailing ship; hoping to transfer later to medicine, he studied science at the University of Sydney in 1922-23. At St Matthew's Church, Windsor, on 11 April 1925 he married Marjory Alison Pursehouse, schoolteacher. He worked as a clerk.

Qualifying for a private flying licence on 28 January 1928, Henry was issued with a commercial licence on 6 June 1929, which he used principally in a barnstorming venture. On 6 July 1930, flying a Junkers Junior monoplane, he was caught in bad weather and crashed at Manly, killing his passenger and losing much of one leg. With a successful artificial leg, he eventually regained his commercial licence in 1932 and was employed by Air Taxi Ltd. About 1934 he bought a Genairco biplane, decorated it with a 'Jolly Roger' and used it for joy-rides.

In September 1934 Henry's licence was suspended for a fortnight for breaches of the air navigation regulations. Considering the sentence unjust, he defied the order: his licence was suspended indefinitely and he was prosecuted. Henry's brother Alfred Stephen, a solicitor, launched proceedings in the High Court of Australia in October 1934 for an order *nisi*. While judgment was pending Henry was charged with further offences, his licence was suspended again and he was forbidden to enter any aerodrome. The Henry brothers appealed again to the High Court for an injunction. In 1936 the High Court ruled in respect of the action of October 1934 that the Commonwealth had a right to regulate flights but only in conformity with international conventions on the subject; the court considered that the regulations in dispute did not accord with those conventions. The parties then agreed out of court that on the payment of damages by the Commonwealth, the injunction application would be struck out. Charged by a flight controller at Mascot during the ensuing temporary confusion with flying below the prescribed height, Henry appealed, this time unsuccessfully to the High Court.

After a verdict against him in the District Court, arising from a collision while taking off from Mascot, Henry was bankrupted in October 1938 and was not discharged until September 1940. Debarred by his artificial leg from the Royal Australian Air Force at the start of World War II, he joined the small ships unit of the United States Army in 1943 and sailed a small work boat around New Guinea. After the war he worked for the Papua-New Guinea division of the Directorate of Shipping as mate on the *Kelanoa* plying between Rabaul and Kavieng, and as master of the *Matoko* in 1950-51. When the shipping service was taken over by the administration of Papua-New Guinea, he became master of the *Thetis* sailing up and down the Sepik River. He retired about 1963 and returned to Sydney; although his flying licence had lapsed he tried to revive contact with aviation. He died childless at Manly of arteriosclerosis on 14 July 1974 and was cremated.

Short, fair, straight-backed and nimble in spite of his disability, Henry became a New Guinea character. He had collected and sold snakes for many years, thereby reinforcing his reputation as a daredevil. In later years he suffered from some alcoholic excess.

Pacific Islands Mthly, Sept 1966, p 130; *Aircraft* (Melb), Dec 1936, p 8, 1 Apr 1937, p 17; *Cwlth Law Reports*, 1955, p 608, 695, 1961, p 634; *Aust Flying*, Sept 1974; *SMH*, 7 July 1930, 11 Nov 1936, 17, 18 Sept 1940, 21 July 1974; *Smith's Weekly* (Syd), 21 Nov 1936; Bankruptcy file 249/1938, Federal Court of Aust (NSWA); Service record, National Personnel Records Center, St Louis, Mo, USA; A518 DB112/5, A432 34/1802, MP274/6 FL3918 (AAO, Canb).   H. J. GIBBNEY

HENRY, JOHN (1834-1912), politician and merchant, was born on 1 September 1834 at Lerwick, Shetland Islands, Scotland, third of the seven sons of John Henderson Henry, merchant, and his wife Christina, née Henderson. Educated at Lerwick and the Normal School, Edinburgh, John worked for an Edinburgh grocer before migrating to Melbourne with his father and brothers William, George and Charles in May 1854. His father became a storekeeper at Forest Creek, but died in Sydney in 1856. John remained in Victoria. After a year on the Castlemaine gold diggings, he tried storekeeping at Chewton and Ararat before returning to Castlemaine as a traveller for Blythe Bros; in 1861 he bought out his employers and with William opened the wholesale and retail establishment J. & W. Henry. On 7 July 1862 at Campbell's Creek, near Castlemaine, he married Annie Gravely with Congregational forms. Business prospered, a store was opened at Malmsbury, and in 1868 John moved to Melbourne to take charge of a third branch.

In 1872 he settled at Don, Tasmania, after buying into the local merchant firm Cummings & Co., renamed, initially, Cummings, Henry & Co., and in 1880 when Edwin Cummings retired the River Don Trading Co. Ltd. About 1890 the company's headquarters were moved to West Devonport; Henry, as managing director, followed in 1893 and branches were subsequently established at Ulverstone, Zeehan, Burnie, Wynyard, Penguin and Sheffield. In 1898 the company reverted to a partnership between John and Annie Henry, William Shaw and James York, but new articles of association were drawn up in 1910.

Henry began his public career in the 1870s as a member of the Forth Road Trust and as warden (master warden in 1880-86) of the Mersey Marine Board. He was member of the Devonport Town Board in 1890 and a justice of the peace from 1895. He held the House of Assembly seat of Devon East (Devonport from 1897) in 1891-98 and was treasurer in the Dobson [q.v.8] ministry of 1892-94. In 1901-02 he represented Mersey in the Legislative Council. An ardent Federalist, Henry was a Tasmanian delegate and member of the finance committee at the 1897 Australasian Federal Convention where he opposed, against his fellow Tasmanians, financial powers for the Senate.

Patron or president of the great majority of local institutions, a director of the 1885 Mt Lyell Prospecting Association and a successful land speculator, 'the uncrowned king of Devonport' built for the town the Gentlemen's Club and the Federal Gymnasium and in 1896 attended the London conference of Empire Chambers of Commerce. He was a seasoned yachtsman, though the *Norma* and *Tasma* gave way in 1906 to the steam launch *Brynhild*. Remarked as a man of strong determination, and well-read in Scottish literature, Henry was appointed C.M.G. in 1907. He died on 14 September 1912 at Devonport, survived by his wife, three sons and three daughters. His estate was valued for probate at £4807.

John Henry's brother James Henderson (1830-1908) migrated to Castlemaine with his mother, three sisters and brother Frederick in 1857. A contributor to *Blackwood's Magazine*, James spent about twelve years in Queensland after the early death of his wife and two of his children. He then moved to Don as accountant to John's firm. He died at Evandale on 7 February 1908. The eldest brother, Robert (1828-1896), mariner, came to Castlemaine in 1864. For two years he operated a store, Henry & Brooks, at Malmsbury, before resuming a seafaring career. In the mid-1870s he began trading with various vessels from the River Don, but eventually he, too, entered John's office. Later he had charge of the sawmills and bonemills at Don where he died on 24 March 1896.

The youngest brother, FREDERICK ORMISTON (1846?-1916), merchant, was born in Edinburgh and educated there and after 1857 in Victoria. On leaving school he managed the Malmsbury branch of J. & W. Henry until about 1868 when he departed to seek opportunities in Fiji and New Zealand. Visiting Tasmania in 1880 he was drawn to the west coast by the tin-mining boom at Heemskirk. He recognized Strahan as the only accessible coastal outlet for the area and opened a store there with Percy Fowler, later proprietor of the *Zeehan*

nd Dundas Herald. Business slumped with
he decline in tin-mining but revived with
he discovery of gold at Lynch's Creek and
»f the Iron Blow at Mt Lyell in 1883. That
»ear Henry built commodious premises for
torekeeping and gold and timber-buying at
trategically placed Long Bay; he later es-
.ablished similar businesses at Queenstown,
3ormanston and Kelly Basin and was a part-
1er in (A.F.) Stenhouse & Co. at Devonport
.nd Ulverstone. His shop signs proclaimed
1im 'Pioneer Storekeeper and Universal
'rovider'.

In 1891 Henry was a leader in the public
»utcry against the A. W. Lawder bill which
.ought to give a private syndicate the right
»f deepening Macquarie Harbour bar and
.harging traffic tolls. An original member
»f the Strahan Marine Board, Chamber of
3ommerce and the Mt Lyell Tourist Associ-
.tion, he was the largest shareholder in the
√1t Lyell Prospecting Association and even-
ually became wealthy. But this 'corpulent,
ong-bearded, frock-coated little man who
oved his pinch of snuff' admitted to unful-
illed aspirations to statesmanship. He was
lefeated for Lyell in the House of Assembly
n 1900. He died at Strahan on 8 January
.916 and was buried in the local cemetery.
)n 16 April 1887 at Don he had married
√1ary Ann Lewis with Presbyterian forms.
1e was survived by their two sons and two
.aughters and left an estate valued for pro-
»ate at £15 617.

Cyclopedia of Tasmania, 1 (Hob, 1900);
 .. Whitham, *The book of Mt Lyell and the Gordon*
Hob, 1917); G. Blainey, *The peaks of Lyell* (Melb,
954); J. A. La Nauze, *The making of the Australian
 :onstitution* (Melb, 1972); *North-West Post*, 26 Mar
896; *Mercury*, 16, 17 Sept 1912; *Zeehan and Dun-
!as Herald*, 10 Jan 1916; notes by C. Ramsay, *and*
 .. R. Von Stieglitz (held by *ADB*).

ANN G. SMITH

HENTZE, MARGARET EDITH (1909-
.947), historian, was born on 15 July 1909
n Melbourne, only daughter of Frederick
'erdinand Hentze, Belgian wool-buyer, and
1is wife Edith May, daughter of Sir Graham
3erry [q.v.3]. After elementary education in
√1elbourne Margot went in 1919 with her
»arents to Basle, Switzerland, where she had
»rivate tuition. On their return to Australia
n 1923 her parents acquired the house at
<illara, Sydney, which remained her home.
3he attended Presbyterian Ladies' College,
'ymble, where she was dux in 1926. Not elig-
ble to enter the University of Sydney with-
»ut a matriculation pass in mathematics,
she overcame this obstacle in 1929 and en-
 -olled in the faculty of arts next year.

Outstanding among the undergraduates
»f her generation, Margot Hentze graduated

B.A. in 1933 with first class honours in English, history and philosophy and University
medals for English and history. Awarded
the (John) Frazer [q.v.4] scholarship in 1933
and appointed assistant lecturer in history
in 1934, she worked on labour problems in
the Pacific and graduated M.A. with first
class honours and the University medal in
1935. She contributed a chapter on Asian immigration to *Australia and the Far East*
(1935), sponsored by the Australian Institute of International Affairs.

The award of a travelling scholarship in
1935 gave her the opportunity to work in
European history. On a visit to Italy she foresaw the likelihood of official censorship of
research in an Italian university and turned
to the London School of Economics and Political Science, where Professor Harold Laski
agreed to supervise a thesis on Italian politics between 1871 and 1922. She was
awarded a Ph.D. by the University of London in 1938. Next year *Pre-Fascist Italy: the
rise and fall of the parliamentary régime*, a
revised version of her thesis, was published.
It was a work of mature and sensitive scholarship, a pioneer study of Italian political
life in the half-century before Mussolini. Attendance as an Australian delegate at the
conferences of the International Institute of
Intellectual Co-operation in Paris and
Prague in 1937 and 1938 brought new influences through meetings with leading
European scholars, especially Salvador de
Madariaga, with whom she continued to cor-
respond. In August 1938 Margot Hentze returned to the University of Sydney as a lecturer in history, the second woman appointed to the permanent staff of the faculty of
arts. Sensitive and intense, she found her
lectures in European history both demanding and sometimes unrewarding, especially
as the strains and tensions of imminent war
in Europe mounted. In July 1939 she resigned, intending to go at once to Switzerland. War prevented this, but she left the
university in December. Trying to reach
Europe in a neutral ship she was turned back
at Aden when France fell. For several years
in Australia she undertook research on Australia's political and economic relationships
in the South-west Pacific for the Department of Post-War Reconstruction.

An early recruit to the United Nations
Relief and Rehabilitation Administration,
Margot Hentze was sent to London early in
1946 to work on the economic aspects of rehabilitation problems in Europe. On service
in Europe, she died suddenly of pneumonia
on 21 June 1947 at Antwerp, Belgium, where
she was buried.

Union Recorder, 3 July 1947; staff records of
Registrar's Office (Univ Syd Archives).

MARJORIE JACOBS

HERBERT, CHARLES EDWARD (1860-1929), politician, judge and administrator, was born on 12 June 1860 at Strathalbyn, South Australia, eldest son of Lloyd Herbert, surgeon, and his second wife Mary Ann, née Montgomery. Educated at the Collegiate School of St Peter, Adelaide, Herbert was articled to his uncle, Henry Hay Mildred, in 1877 and in 1883 was admitted as practitioner to the Supreme Court of South Australia. He went to Palmerston (Darwin) in October as the only lawyer in the Northern Territory, but joined J. J. Beare's practice at Moonta, South Australia, next year. On 15 August 1885 in Adelaide Herbert married Anna Emilia Augusta, daughter of M. R. Schomburgk [q.v.6]. He practised in Sydney from 1889 before returning to Darwin in 1896.

At a by-election on 20 October 1900 Herbert was elected to the South Australian House of Assembly as a Conservative for the Northern Territory; he was re-elected in 1902. In 1905 he was appointed Northern Territory government resident, succeeding C. J. Dashwood [q.v.8], of whom he had been highly critical. From September 1906 until the following March Herbert served on the Commonwealth royal commission on the Territory of Papua. During his investigations he walked from Buna across the Owen Stanley Range to Port Moresby. His 1906 annual report on the Northern Territory emphasized the need for increased European settlement; next year he pleaded for legislation for the 'removal of aborigines from the Territory into other States'.

In 1910 Herbert was appointed deputy chief judicial officer for the Territory of Papua. As the second judge of the Port Moresby Central Court, under the lieutenant-governor and chief judicial officer (Sir) Hubert Murray [q.v.], he heard cases referred from the resident magistrates' courts. An *ex officio* member of the Legislative and Executive councils he was also responsible for drafting ordinances. For eighteen years Herbert backed Murray, sometimes in controversial decisions. In 1926 he supported Murray's White Women's Protection Ordinance which carried the death penalty for rape of a European woman or girl, although he opposed the same penalty being inflicted for attempted rape. At least twice Herbert held concurrent judicial appointments in separate Australian territories: late in 1918 he heard criminal matters in Darwin arising from the attempt to depose the administrator J. A. Gilruth [q.v.] and in May to October 1921 he was an acting judge of the Northern Territory.

A reclassification of the Papuan public service in 1926 removed Herbert from its ranks with the title of judge, thus severing the conflict of interests between the judicial and administrative areas of governmen that had dogged him throughout his official career. The effects of his long tropical service now began to show: he was physically unable to attempt the long walk to conduc a hearing in the hinterland during Murray' absence. In 1928 he accepted the post of administrator of Norfolk Island in preferenc to the more highly paid position of judge o North and Central Australia. He died o pneumonia on 21 January 1929 on Norfol Island, where he was buried. He was sur vived by his wife, two sons—the owners o Koolpinyah station in the Northern Terri tory—and a daughter. His eldest son ha been killed in action in Belgium in 1917. A active Anglican, Herbert had supported th building of St John's Church in Port Mor esby; in 1932 a sanctuary lamp in tha church was dedicated to his memory.

R. T. Gore, *Justice versus sorcery* (Brisb, 1965) I. Stuart, *Port Moresby, yesterday and today* (Syd 1970); A. Inglis, *Not a white woman safe* (Canb 1974); Northern Territory, *Annual Report*, 1906 08; Territory of Papua, *Annual Report*, 1925-26 1927-28; *NT Times*, 13 Oct, 3 Nov 1883, 31 Jul 1896, 21 May 1921; *Observer* (Adel), 4 Feb 1905 *Chronicle* (Adel), 26 Jan 1929; CRS A52 07/4458 A56, A518 624/35 (AAO); Davies cuttings (SAA).

PETER ELDER

HERBERT, HAROLD BROCKLEBANK (1891-1945), artist, was born on 16 Septem ber 1891 at Ballarat, Victoria, son of locally born George Herbert, organist and music teacher, and his wife Jane Brocklebank, née Coward, from Lancashire, England. He at tended Ballarat College and studied archi tecture and applied design at the Technica School of Design attached to the Fine Art Gallery. He later transferred with the schoo to the Ballarat School of Mines. Herbert's talents were early recognized by P. M Carew-Smyth [q.v.7], art inspector with the Victorian Education Department, and he moved to Melbourne in 1912 to become Carew-Smyth's assistant. Three years later he became art master at his old school but abandoned teaching in 1919.

Herbert exhibited first in 1915 at the Cen treway Gallery in Melbourne with four fel low Ballarat students. At this time he also worked as a designer of jewellery and craft work, but he was already noted for his skill in the demanding techniques of water colour wash. He participated in exhibitions with M. J. McNally [q.v.] and began painting and sketching tours with like-minded friends such as McNally, Penleigh Boyd [q.v.7], G. C. Benson and Charles Wheeler [q.v.]. He corresponded with and twice visited Hans Heysen [q.v.] for instruction.

In 1922-23 Herbert travelled for eighteen months in England, France, Spain and Morocco. On his return his first major exhibition in Melbourne was a huge success with every work being sold. The appeal of his skilled naturalism combined with the art boom of the 1920s brought him great status and financial reward. He was an esteemed member of the principal art societies and had work acquired by every public collection. Beyond art, his easy companionability won influential friends; he was especially popular in the Savage Club. From 1926 until his death he was a member of the Commonwealth Art Advisory Board. At Surry Hills, Sydney, on 19 October 1928 he married a divorcee Doris Mary Donaghy, née Rodda; she divorced him in 1934 for desertion. He married Dorothea Agnes O'Leary at Fitzroy, Melbourne, on 9 October 1935.

Stories abound of Herbert's pranks, biting repartee, and prodigal taste for the good life. That life was maintained by regular exhibitions in the 1920s and 1930s, as well as by art criticism for the *Argus* and *Australasian* and continued commercial illustration and poster design.

Herbert's career corresponded with the rise and decline of a strong school of watercolour painting in Australia. Herbert, however, eschewed the romantic directions of Penleigh Boyd, J. J. Hilder [q.v.] and Blamire Young [q.v.] in favour of an imitative naturalism that followed the British tradition of Tom Collier. This emphasized a view of art as a craft with the artist working wholly in the open air, drawing direct inspiration from picturesque aspects of the natural scene. To this end he travelled to Tumut and the Snowy Mountains in New South Wales and the Kiewa Valley in north-eastern Victoria where his trout-fishing skills were as renowned as his speed and ambidextrous abilities with a brush. His work was little troubled by introspection, just as his writings reveal a deep distrust of intellectualism. Such was his disregard of art history that when abroad he ignored completely the great collections of Europe. Not surprisingly, in later life he was an intemperate opponent of a developing Australian modernism.

Herbert's friendship with Lieut-General Sir Thomas Blamey resulted in his appointment early in 1941 as an official war artist. He resigned after six months in the Middle East and until 1944 was an accredited war correspondent for the *Australasian*. Inevitably, for a man who claimed to breakfast on whisky and milk, the demands of military life contributed to the collapse of his health and he died in Melbourne of cirrhosis of the liver on 11 February 1945. Herbert was cremated: he had left a cheque and a request that members of the Savage Club drink to his memory at his expense. His wife survived him; there were no children.

D. M. Dow, *Melbourne Savages* (Melb, 1947); R. Haese, *Rebels and precursors in Australian art 1930-1950* (Melb, 1981); *Art in Aust*, Sept 1928; *Age*, 3 Oct 1959.   RICHARD HAESE

HERITAGE, FRANCIS BEDE (1877-1934), soldier, was born on 21 September 1877 at River Don, Tasmania, eldest of the seven sons and two daughters of George Thomas Henry Heritage, teacher and later inspector of schools, and his wife Eleanor Boyce, née Hadfield. He was educated at Longford State School and Launceston Church Grammar School.

Heritage was commissioned lieutenant in the Tasmanian Infantry Regiment (militia) on 26 January 1897 and promoted captain in June 1899. During the South African War he served as a lieutenant with the 1st Tasmanian (Mounted Infantry) Contingent from October 1899 to December 1900. After discharge he joined the Administrative and Instructional Staff (permanent forces) of the Australian Army and was gazetted captain in 1901. His service in Tasmania in 1901-07 was marked by keen specialization in musketry and small-arms training and in 1907-08 he was sent to England for advanced instruction at the School of Musketry, Hythe.

In November 1908, after returning home, he was transferred to New South Wales and was promoted major in July 1909. In September 1911 he was appointed commandant and chief instructor of the school of musketry at Randwick, where his work contributed greatly to the army's high standard of training in small arms. When World War I began he was appointed brigade major of the Australian Naval and Military Expeditionary Force which embarked from Sydney in August 1914 to seize German colonies in the Pacific. After the occupation of German New Guinea he commanded the expeditions which occupied New Ireland and the Admiralty and Western Islands, and from October 1914 to March 1915 was deputy administrator of German New Guinea. He returned to Australia in mid-1915 and on 16 October, at St Patrick's Cathedral, Melbourne, married Rita Austen Hill; they had no children.

Promoted lieut-colonel next December, Heritage served throughout 1916 as director of military training at Army Headquarters, Melbourne. He was appointed to the Australian Imperial Force in the same rank in

December and saw active service in France as a general staff officer with the 2nd Division at Bullecourt and the 4th Division at Messines. From September 1917 he commanded the Anzac and the Australian Corps Schools but in February 1918 was evacuated with rheumatic fever; he was invalided home and demobilized in August. For distinguished service in France he was awarded the Croix de Guerre. Three of his brothers served in the A.I.F. (Captain Keith Heritage, M.C., who was killed in action at Pozières, Lieutenant Austin Heritage, M.C., and Private Robert Heritage) and a fourth (Corporal Stanley Heritage) with the Canadian Expeditionary Force.

On resuming duty with the Australian Military Forces in August 1918 Heritage served as director of personnel at Army Headquarters; in 1919 he was commandant in Western Australia and in January 1920 was promoted colonel. Next month he was reappointed commandant of the school of musketry, Randwick, and, after service on the staff of the Prince of Wales during his visit, was appointed M.V.O. In August 1922 he became commandant of the Royal Military College, Duntroon, Australian Federal Territory. This posting coincided with a period of stress in the defence services because of drastic economies and post-war revulsion against military training. By his tact, administrative expertise and strong personal qualities Heritage was able to prevent disbandment of the college and he maintained its prestige over a difficult period until 1929 when he was transferred to Sydney to command the 2nd Military District; his outstanding service to the college had been recognized by the appointment of C.B.E. in 1924.

When, in 1931, the Royal Military College, in reduced form, was moved to Sydney and placed under his command Heritage, then a brigadier, again maintained its quality under most unfavourable conditions. In January 1933 he was posted to Army Headquarters as quartermaster general and third member of the Military Board. He was operated on for acute appendicitis and on 9 July 1934 died of peritonitis in a Melbourne private hospital. He was buried with military honours in Melbourne general cemetery after a service at the Church of the Sacred Heart, Carlton. His wife survived him. Heritage's main contributions to the Australian Army were the standard of rifle and small-arms training he achieved before and during World War I and his sensitive leadership as commandant of the Royal Military College in 1922-29. When he died his promotion was imminent and he was expected on the retirement of Major General Sir Julius Bruche [q.v.7]

to be appointed chief of the General Staff.

Aust Defence Dept, *Official records of the Australian military contingents to the war in South Africa*, P. L. Murray, ed (Melb, 1911); S. S. Mackenzie, *The Australians at Rabaul* (Syd, 1927); J. E. Lee, *Duntroon* (Canb, 1952); *London Gazette*, 20 Sept 1919; *Reveille* (Syd), Jan 1933; *SMH*, 12 Jan 1917, 26 Feb 1919, 20 Aug 1920, 8, 10 July 1922, 3 June 1924, 20 Nov 1929, 26 Nov 1931, 13 Dec 1932, 10, 11, 14 July 1934; *Mercury*, 9 Oct 1931; *Argus*, 10 July 1934; *Weekly Courier* (Launc), 12 July 1934; Records (TA), *and* Church Grammar School, Launceston, Tas, *and* AWM (Canb).

C. H. FINLAY

HERMAN, HYMAN (1875-1962), geologist and engineer, was born on 16 August 1875 at Sandhurst (Bendigo), fifth of twelve children of Solomon Herman from Konin, Russia (Poland), and his wife Elizabeth, née Oxlake, from London. Solomon had come to Australia in 1864 when his father was appointed minister at Ballarat synagogue. A businessman and land agent, Solomon was a leader of the Jewish congregation in Bendigo and after 1894 in Perth.

Hyman Herman grew up amid the Bendigo mining revival; he later claimed that his first interest in geology arose from his boyhood adventures in the abandoned tunnel that ran under his school. He had a brilliant educational career, helped by scholarships at Gravel Hill (Camp Hill) State School, Sandhurst Corporate High School, and a final year at Scotch College, Melbourne, in 1890. He was to return to his home environment when as part of his D.Sc. (Melbourne, 1924) he submitted 'The Structure of the Bendigo goldfields', a thesis which Professor Sir Edgeworth David [q.v.8] reported to be a masterpiece of detailed analysis.

In 1891 Herman began a four-year engineering course at the University of Melbourne, specializing in mining and metallurgy (B.C.E., 1896). He quickly attracted attention, not only for his continuing scholastic excellence, but as the leader of a successful student protest against the quality of instruction. Herman wanted to become a mining engineer, but on completing his course he felt the need for practical experience in geology and so in 1895 joined the Geological Survey of the Victorian Department of Mines and Water Supply. His rise was spectacular. He was nominated as Victoria's mining representative in Britain, but Premier Turner [q.v.] considered he was too young: Herman was 23. He became acting director of the Geological Survey in 1900 and through its efforts and his own work on the Walhalla goldfields helped to reduce the mining industry's scepticism about the survey's value. His reputation was acknowledged, yet he confounded his admirers when, at 29, he refused the directorship of the Geological Survey. Instead he became assistant manager with the Mt Bischoff Tin Mining Co. at Waratah, Tasmania. The once rich mine was in decline. Herman rejuvenated it in his four years stay.

In 1907 he started his own practice in Queen Street, Melbourne, and for the next five years he worked across the Australian mining panorama of tin, gold, coal and copper. He was sought after as a company director, consultant manager and regular writer for the *Australian Mining Standard*. He established a reputation for versatility in practice, prudence in counsel and a nose for snide sampling. He became convinced that gold-mining could never be re-established as the staple of Victoria's economic growth, and perhaps with this in mind he accepted the position of director of the Geological Survey in 1912. For the next thirty years he became Victoria's leading crusader for the exploitation of her vast brown coal lands. He first persuaded the government to investigate the industrial potential of brown coal, arguing that there should be no further alienation of coal lands, and thereby thwarting German-British and Collins House commercial interests represented by W. L. Baillieu [q.v.7]. He also secured additional funds for a major boring policy carried out by William Baragwanath [q.v.7] and an experimental brown coal furnace and chemical retort.

Herman's belief in brown coal was not original, but a legacy from earlier Mines Department geologists. His distinctive contribution was in his professional advocacy and his use of the economic situation during the war years. Imported New South Wales black coal was now tenuous in supply and exorbitant in price; the growing demand for electrical power meant that Victoria's future rate of industrialization rested precariously on the need for a cheap, reliable source of energy. Against daunting opponents, Herman brought public opinion behind his cause by manoeuvring an industrial development lobby, the Victorian Institute of New Industries, to press for an inquiry into brown coal use as an energy source. In 1917 he became chairman of a State advisory committee on coal and electricity, which included H. R. Harper and W. Stone [qq.v.]. Their report became the blue-print for the future power and brown coal industry in Victoria. It envisaged three major operations: open-cut mining in the La Trobe valley; the establishment of a large power-station and briquetting factories (at what was to become Yallourn) and State-wide distribution of electricity. Herman expected to become the chairman of the newly created State Electricity Commission. But he was overlooked in 1919, and again in 1931. Instead he had to be content with the honour of becoming its first engineer in charge of brown coal research and briquetting (1920).

Until his retirement in 1940 Herman searched for new and efficient ways to use brown coal. He helped in the power-station boiler modifications that were necessary because of one of his few serious errors, when he and others had assumed that all the La Trobe valley brown coalfields had a moisture content of about 45 per cent whereas the new seams at Yallourn were found to have over 60 per cent. He was also able to make the briquetting industry profitable by introducing a high pressure steam system for drying the wet coal. Herman made several visits to Germany and the Soviet Union, the main sources of brown coal chemical engineering, and demonstrated that Victorian brown coal was technically suitable for carbonization, pulverized traction fuel and the production of town gas. He also encouraged work in hydrogenation (oil from coal) and initiated investigation of brown coal for this purpose.

Herman advised the South Australian government on brown coal-mining (1926), prepared the survey of coal resources for the Australian Power Survey (1928), and was Australia's representative to the World Power Conference in Washington (1936). He was also the royal commissioner into the Western Australian coal industry (1931 and 1933), again displaying his flair in exposing mining scandals.

After retirement Herman remained consultant engineer to the S.E.C. for another fifteen years. His most important task was to convene an inquiry (1943) into the means of securing Victoria's total independence from black coal imports, which recommended the expansion of power generation and briquetting facilities at Yallourn, hydro power in northern Victoria and the manufacture of town gas from brown coal. All were implemented by post-war governments, so that he lived to see the fulfilment of his dream. He documented much of its application in Victoria and overseas in his comprehensive book *Brown coal* (Melbourne, 1952), which contains a bibliography of his papers on Victoria's coal resources.

On 2 April 1902 at St Kilda Town Hall with Presbyterian forms, Herman had married Florence Leslie Ramsay Salmon. Predeceased by his wife and one of his three daughters, he died on 7 June 1962 and was cremated.

Herman described his recreations in *Who's who* as 'many mild ones, not a slave to any'. He had been an accomplished amateur Shakespearian actor, a poet ('H2') and horseman; he remained an avid reader, geologist, engineer, company director and mining raconteur. Although regarded as modest, he felt few men to be superior to him (one was Sir John Monash [q.v.]). He was a leader in all avenues of professional life, whether as sectional president of the Public Service Association, or the Chamber of Mines, or the S.E.C.'s Social League. He enjoyed banter that he had imprinted 'HH' on household briquettes for personal edification or that he was indeed the 'father of Yallourn'. As an employer he insisted on thoroughness in investigation, attention to detail and clarity in reporting. He followed all the S.E.C.'s activities with schoolboy enthusiasm. He was the only person in the S.E.C., according to the royal commissioner into its affairs (1926), who had sufficient breadth of mind and technical ability to understand the entire operation.

Herman received no civic honours. However, the S.E.C. has renamed its research station at Richmond the Herman Research Laboratories, in which there is a bronze commemorative plaque. He was also honoured by the Australasian Institute of Mining and Metallurgy, of which he was a councillor for a record sixty-four years, with the institute medal. Yet his greatest honour was to witness the mining and engineering triumphs in the La Trobe valley. 'Brown coal in Victoria', he once stated, 'has been waiting like a huge fortune in Chancery for the rightful heir to its riches and benefits'. Herman had foreseen its potential, and more than any other person harnessed that fortune.

C. Edwards, *Brown power* (Melb, 1969); *SEC Mag*, Sept 1952, p 12; A'sian Inst of Mining and Metallurgy, *Procs*, 113 (1939), 203 (1962); A. D. Spaull, 'The rise of the Victorian briquette industry 1895-1935', *Aust Economic Hist Review*, Mar 1969, *and* The origins and rise of the Victorian brown coal industry, 1835-1935 (M.Com, Univ Melb, 1967); *Punch* (Melb), 23 Aug 1917; Herman papers, 1896-1960 (SEC Archives, Melb); information from Mr G. E. Baragwanath, Herman Research Laboratories, Richmond, Melb.

ANDREW SPAULL

HERON, ALEXANDER ROBERT (1888-1949), soldier and pharmacist, was born on 25 December 1888 at Charters Towers, Queensland, son of Scottish-born Alexander Barbour Heron, pharmacist, and his English wife Susie Henrietta, née Holland. The family moved to Bowen in 1890 and he was educated at Bowen State School and Brisbane Grammar School, afterwards working on the family property, Allensleigh, and being apprenticed to his father as a chemist. In 1908 he joined the 15th Light Horse Regiment (renamed the 27th L.H.R. in 1912) as a private, was commissioned in February 1912 and promoted captain in September 1915. He had married Margaret Bolger at Bowen with Presbyterian forms on 29 August 1912.

On 16 February 1916 Heron enlisted in the Australian Imperial Force and was posted to the 42nd Battalion as a captain on 1 April. His unit joined the 3rd Australian Division in England then moved to the Belgian front in December as part of II Anzac Corps. Early in 1917 it served at Armentières and Ploegsteert Wood and on 6 June moved forward for the battle of Messines. Heron, who had been promoted major on 22 February, was awarded the Distinguished Service Order for leading his company 'to the relief of a battalion through extremely heavy shell fire, with great success and few casualties'. Despite a heavy barrage he sent back information to battalion headquarters. The citation praised his 'skill and devotion' which had 'contributed largely to the successful holding of our line' and concluded: 'throughout the whole period in the trenches his work has been consistently thorough'.

On 6 July Heron, as a lieut-colonel, was given command of the 41st Battalion whose entire staff had been lost in a mortar-attack. His command continued through the 3rd battle of Ypres and on 4 October the 41st was among the battalions which spearheaded the attack on the strategically important Broodseinde Ridge; it also participated in the unsuccessful assault on Passchendaele. During the winter the battalion served at Bois Grenier and Le Bizet until the German counter-attack began in March 1918. It then moved up to the front to play its part in halting the German advance at Villers-Bretonneux and Dernancourt and on 4 July was used in the attack on Hamel. When the great Allied offensive began on 8 August the 41st under Heron captured two enemy batteries and in September took part in attacks on the Hindenburg outpost line and in the final breach of the line itself. For his services throughout the Somme operations and for the 'marked ability and determination with which he led his command in the final attack on the Hindenburg Line' Heron was appointed C.M.G. During the last battle of the Somme he had held temporary command of the 11th Brigade four times. He was also mentioned in dispatches four times in 1917-19.

At the end of the war Heron was posted to London to assist with demobilization and repatriation. He embarked for Australia in October 1919 and next February returned o Bowen where he completed his apprenticeship and managed his father's pharmacy until World War II. He had been placed on the reserve of officers, Australian Military Forces, as a lieut-colonel in 1927, was recalled in 1939 and in 1942 commanded the 1st Australian Garrison Battalion and the 29th and 5th Australian Infantry Training Battalions. In 1944 he retired with the honorary rank of colonel. In the inter-war years he had played an active role in Bowen affairs and was president of the Royal Society of St George, the Kennedy Hospital Board, the cycling club and the local branch of the Returned Sailors' and Soldiers' Imperial League of Australia. A keen Freemason, he was an office-bearer in the Kennedy Lodge and compiled its history. In all his activities he showed the thoroughness, determination and great energy which had characterized his military career. He died suddenly in Brisbane on 22 October 1949, survived by his wife, two daughters and a son. His elder son, Lieutenant Robert Heron, had been killed in action in 1942. Colonel Heron was cremated with military honours after a Presbyterian service.

C. E. W. Bean, *The A.I.F. in France*, 1917-18 (Syd, 1933, 1936, 1942); *Bowen Independent*, 24 Oct 1949; A. R. Heron file, War Records Section (AWM); information from Mrs I. Tippetts, West Bundaberg, Qld.   DIANE MENGHETTI

HERRING, SYDNEY CHARLES EDGAR (1881-1951), soldier and estate agent, was born on 8 October 1881 at Gladesville, Sydney, second of nine children of English-born Gerard Edgar Herring, under secretary for lands, and his Australian wife Caroline Estella, née De Lange. After a private school education he became a clerk and later a land and estate agent. He was commissioned as a second lieutenant in the 1st Australian Infantry Regiment (militia) in 1904, was promoted lieutenant in 1906 and on the introduction of universal military training in 1911 was appointed an area officer at Drummoyne. On 17 August 1910, at North Sydney, he married Florence Elizabeth Murray-Prior with Anglican rites.

When World War I broke out Herring enlisted in the Australian Imperial Force on 9 October 1914 as captain commanding 'D' Company, 13th Battalion, and embarked in December. In Egypt in February 1915, he was promoted major. His battalion landed at Anzac Cove on the night of 25 April and moved into Monash Valley; next day his company was ordered to clear the enemy from Russell's Top and close a dangerous gap. After climbing the steep slopes under desultory fire his men met with fierce Turkish resistance on the summit and, with nothing but low scrub for cover, were soon driven back; the men to the left and right of Herring were killed and he withdrew his line under heavy fire. Though slightly wounded on 28 April he served continuously until the evacuation from Gallipoli and was temporary commander of his battalion from 27 June and commander from 26 August; he fought mainly at Pope's Hill and Quinn's Post and was also in the attack on Hill 60. For distinguished leadership on Gallipoli he was awarded the French Légion d'honneur and was mentioned in dispatches.

On 21 February 1916 Herring was transferred to command the new 45th Battalion, the nucleus of which had been formed in Egypt from two companies of the 13th Battalion. He was promoted lieut-colonel on 12 March and early in June reached France where his unit went into the line at Fleurbaix, moved to the Somme in July and, in August, during the battle of Pozières, suffered high casualties in one of the most severe and continuous bombardments of the war. He commanded the 45th at Wytschaete, Belgium, and throughout the winter of 1916-17 on the Somme. In the New Year honours for 1917 he was awarded the Distinguished Service Order for 'consistent, thorough and good work in raising and training his battalion and subsequently commanding it with conspicuous success in action near Fleurbaix and Pozières'. That year he fought at Gueudecourt and Bullecourt and, in the battle of Messines on 7-11 June, his battalion captured one of its two objectives near Owl Trench but could not dislodge the Germans from the other, the advance being held up by two concrete blockhouses. Herring's weary troops made four assaults on these but failed to take them; the battalion lost over 500 men in four days. In October, because of his long frontline experience, Herring was posted to England to command the A.I.F.'s 3rd Training Battalion. He resumed command of the 45th Battalion in May 1918 and next month was promoted colonel and temporary brigadier general and appointed to command the 13th Brigade; this was to play a major role in the battle of 8 August, the advance along the Somme and the penetration of the Hindenburg line. For outstanding leadership he was appointed C.M.G. and awarded the French Croix de Guerre; in 1917-19 he was mentioned in dispatches four times.

Herring's A.I.F. appointment ended in August 1919 and he resumed work as a land and estate agent. In 1921 he was New South Wales treasurer of the Returned Sailors' and Soldiers' Imperial League of Australia. At the massive 'loyalist' demonstration on

8 May in the Sydney Domain he railed against 'red-raggers' and 'disloyalists'. He became a councillor of the Royal Empire Society, vice-president of the Millions Club and in 1924 stood unsuccessfully as Nationalist candidate for the Senate. He was for some years secretary of the New South Wales Golf Club. He was placed on the retired list, Australian Military Forces, in 1946, with the honorary rank of brigadier; for many years his tall, lean figure had led the 4th Division, A.I.F., in Sydney's Anzac Day marches.

Survived by his wife and daughter, Herring died of heart disease on 27 May 1951 at his Killara home and was cremated with military honours after an Anglican service. His estate was sworn for probate at £29 482.

C. E. W. Bean, *The story of Anzac* (Syd, 1921, 1924), and *The A.I.F. in France*, 1916-18 (Syd, 1929, 1933, 1937, 1942); J. E. Lee, *The chronicle of the 45th Battalion*, A.I.F. (Syd, 1924, 1927); T. A. White, *The fighting Thirteenth* (Syd, 1924); *Reveille* (Syd), Sept 1951; *The Fighting Line*, 26 Feb 1920; *SMH*, 1 Jan 1917, 7 Apr 1920, 9 May 1921, 28 Oct 1924, 30 July, 5 Oct 1940, 29 May 1951; S. C. E. Herring file, War Records Section (AWM).

ANNA KATZMANN

HERROD, ERNEST EDWARD (1885-1966), soldier, draper and agriculturist, was born on 21 June 1885 at Redfern, Sydney, son of Edward Herrod, French polisher and cabinet-maker, and his wife Alice Maud Mary, née Moore, both of whom were born in New South Wales. Educated at Redfern Superior Public School and Sydney Boys' High School, he became a draper and later a warehouseman.

Herrod began his military career in the militia in the 1st Australian Light Horse Regiment, joining as a trooper in 1905; he was promoted corporal in 1909 and sergeant in 1911. In 1913 he transferred to the 25th Signal Company, Australian Engineers, as a lieutenant and on 17 August 1914 enlisted as a second lieutenant in the 2nd Battalion, Australian Imperial Force. On 29 August at St Patrick's Catholic Church, Parramatta, he married Kathleen Elizabeth Regan, a milliner. He landed at Gallipoli on 25 April 1915 as the battalion signals officer and was promoted lieutenant that day. He served at Lone Pine and was appointed officer commanding 'A' Company in August and promoted captain in September. From May to August he worked as a signaller, an intelligence officer and the battalion's assistant adjutant. He was evacuated sick from Anzac, suffering from jaundice and colitis, on 8 December and rejoined his unit in Egypt on 6 March 1916.

Herrod embarked for the Western Fron two weeks later and was to take part in al the 2nd Battalion's major operations in France and Belgium up to May 1917. In the battle of Pozières in July 1916 he was respon sible for the capture of the German concrete stronghold and observation post, known by the Australians as 'Gibraltar'. Next month while still commanding 'A' Company, he fought at Mouquet Farm on the Somme where the 2nd Battalion spent the winter o 1916-17. He was promoted major in Octobe 1916 and in 1917 took part in the capture of Hermies and the battle of Bullecourt.

On 10 May 1917 Herrod was appointed to command the 7th Battalion as a temporary lieut-colonel. His rank was confirmed in Au gust and he commanded this battalion fo the rest of the war, seeing action in some of the worst fighting in which Australian were involved. In September-October the 7th fought in the 3rd battle of Ypres, a Polygon Wood and Broodseinde, and it wa the first battalion to move into position in front of Hazebrouck, initially taking ove the whole of the 1st Division's front before the battle of the Lys. After operations a Strazeele in June Herrod took part in the bat tle of Amiens at Lihons, St Martin's Woo and Herleville in August. At Bellicourt on the Hindenburg line he was attached to the Australian mission appointed as advisers to the American Army. He described the period from April to October 1918 as one o particular interest because he was able to observe 'the process of stopping the enemy' vigorous offensive, gradually turning tha offensive into defence, then to a retreat and finally to a rout'.

Known by his men as 'Dad' and constantly concerned for their welfare, Herrod wa cool and resourceful in battle. An exemplary battalion commander, he was appointed C.M.G. and awarded the Distinguished Ser vice Order for his work in France and Bel gium and was mentioned in dispatches four times; he also received the Serbian Orde of the White Eagle. After demobilization h resumed service in the citizen forces and in 1921-26 commanded the 45th Battalion; in 1926 he was awarded the Volunteer Offi cers' Decoration. In civilian life he achieved prominence in various agricultural pur suits, including fruit-growing and poultry farming. In 1931 he was elected to the Roya Agricultural Society council and in 1945 be came a vice-president. He was also for a tim the general secretary of the Fruitgrowers Association of New South Wales. During World War II he held several A.I.F. staf appointments in Australia; he was placed o the retired list, Australian Military Forces as an honorary colonel in 1947. Survived b his wife, two sons and two daughters, he die on 7 June 1966 at Quaker's Hill, New South Wales, and was cremated.

C. E. W. Bean, *The A.I.F. in France*, 1916-18 (Syd, 1929, 1933, 1937, 1942); A. Dean and E. W. Gutteridge, *The Seventh Battalion A.I.F.* (Melb, 1933); F. W. Taylor and T. A. Cusack, *Nulli secundus: a history of the 2nd Battalion A.I.F., 1914-19* (Syd, 1942); *London Gazette*, 2 Jan, 13 Feb, 25, 28 Dec 1917, 28 May, 31 Dec 1918, 1 Jan 1919; *T&CJ*, 15 Jan 1919; *Reveille* (Syd), Mar, June 1930, Feb, Mar 1931, Dec 1932, Sept 1934; E. E. Herrod file. (AWM).   R. E. COWLEY

HERVEY, GRANT (MADISON) (1880-1933), versifier and swindler, was born George Henry Cochrane on 30 November 1880 at Casterton, Victoria, son of Robert Cochrane, contractor and storekeeper, and his wife Alice Jane, née Gill. Hervey described one of his grandfathers as a noble convict, 'most unjustly used'. As a youth Hervey worked as a blacksmith with a local coachbuilder, then in a Melbourne foundry. He contributed thundering verse to the *Bulletin* and from about 1900 was a journalist in Sydney, Melbourne and Perth and on the Western Australian goldfields. In 1902 in Sydney he tried to start a literary periodical. Wallace Nelson [q.v.] wrote of him in 1904: 'He turned out poetry by the square yard with mechanical regularity. When he had done a fair morning's work he used to put his coat on and go and have a drink'. In 1913 Hervey issued *Australians yet, and other verses*, 'ballads of Manhood, Work, Good Cheer, Mateship, Masculine Vigour and Nationalism' dedicated to James Edmond [q.v.8].

In November 1905 when an enraged actor saw his wife strolling arm in arm with Hervey in Bourke Street, Melbourne, he assaulted him, whereupon Hervey shot at him; he was acquitted of attempted murder. In 1911 he was engaged by the People's Party to lecture in western Victoria against the Federal Labor government's referendum proposals. John Norton [q.v.] of *Truth* occasionally employed him and in December 1914 Hervey offered to provide Norton, for payment, with intimate evidence against his wife. Charged with forgery and uttering the following month, he was sentenced to four years hard labour; he claimed that Norton had 'fixed' the jury. In 1919 he wrote an open letter to Premier Holman [q.v.], condemning prison conditions, quoting Montesquieu and Treitschke.

In the Mildura district, Victoria, in mid-1919 'Madison Harvey', posing as an American, presented a 'Greater Mildura' scheme for a new State for which he sought financial backing. On 2 August a crowd of 2000 listened to him spellbound until C. J. De Garis [q.v.8] dramatically revealed Hervey's criminal record. Hervey became editor of the *Mildura and Merbein Sun* in January 1921 in order to attack De Garis but in October vigilantes tarred and feathered him, and ran him out of town. At the subsequent hearings the judge, though he convicted Hervey's assailants, referred to Hervey's 'foul and filthy' journalism and branded his character as 'despicable'. Hervey's reception at Orange in March was also violent. Speaking on prohibition for the New South Wales Alliance he so incensed friends of the publicans that he needed police protection.

In December 1923 in Sydney Hervey received two years gaol for forging and uttering. In 1929 he was joint editor of *Beckett's Budget*, a short-lived journal of sensation and salacity. Sentenced to two years in April 1931 for 'another forged-telegram swindle', he became librarian at Bathurst gaol and wrote a novel, *An Eden of the good* (London, 1934). Nettie Palmer [q.v.] described him in 1933 as 'a bulky giant with a large reddish beard, . . . a caricature of those expansive young men of the nineties . . . patriotic and Utopian'.

Hervey died on 6 November 1933 in Melbourne, and was buried in Springvale cemetery. On 21 October 1918 at South Melbourne he had married a widow Annie Crowe, née Jeffreys. On 19 November 1920 in Sydney he married, probably bigamously, Florence Emily Lockwood. No children were recorded. 'Undoubtedly Hervey has a mental kink', the *Australian Worker* commented in 1923, 'and is more to be pitied than blamed'.

N. Palmer, *Fourteen years* (Melb, 1948); M. Cannon, *That damned democrat* (Melb, 1981); *Cavalcade*, 5 Jan 1947; *People* (Syd), 9 May 1951; *Aust Worker*, 26 Mar 1904, 26 Dec 1923, 22 Nov 1933; *Australasian*, 11, 18 Nov 1905; *Argus*, 1 Aug 1919, 26 Oct, 23, 24, 26 Nov, 14, 16 Dec 1921; *Sun* (Syd), 15 Mar 1921; *Bulletin*, 15 Apr 1931; E. J. Brady papers (MS 914, ML).   GEOFFREY SERLE

HERZ, MAX MARKUS (1876-1948), orthopaedic surgeon, was born on 17 February 1876 at Bochum, Westphalia, Germany, son of Jewish parents Hermann Herz, lacemaker, and his wife Anna, née Blumlein. He was educated at Barmen gymnasium and studied medicine at the University of Munich, while doing his compulsory military service; he graduated in 1898 with the distinction of *magna cum laude* and received the state examination certificate, Munich, in 1899. He worked at the Schanz orthopaedic clinic at Dresden and in Vienna studied under Professor Adolf Lorenz, famous for his treatment of club-feet. While assisting Professor Albert Hoffa in Berlin in 1902, Herz was asked by a patient to visit New Zealand.

Passing through Melbourne in 1903, he was invited to demonstrate Lorenz's techniques at the Hospital for Sick Children. At Ashburton and Christchurch, New Zealand, he attracted much publicity and many patients. On 28 February 1905 at Christchurch he married an Australian, Jane Ethel Cohen, cousin of A. W. Hyman [q.v.]. Next year Herz moved to Auckland and practised as an orthopaedic surgeon. His successful work was widely publicized, generating some resentment among more conservative practitioners. In 1908 he published *New Zealand* (Berlin), an account of the dominion's flora, fauna and people; it was eventually translated into fourteen languages and an English edition appeared in 1912. It received a mixed reception from the press: some New Zealanders were offended at his comments on their lack of culture and humour.

After visiting Germany, Herz in 1910 settled in Sydney where he practised at Macquarie Street and joined the New South Wales branch of the British Medical Association. He contributed to medical journals and was Sydney correspondent for the *Berliner Tageblatt*. He became honorary surgeon for the State Children Relief Board and, in 1911-12, the outpatients' department of St Vincent's Hospital.

On the outbreak of World War I in August 1914 Herz was naturalized, but the B.M.A. expelled him. In July 1915, less than a month after the birth of his only child, he was interned as an enemy alien at Holsworthy, near Liverpool, and from 1916 at Trial Bay, despite his offer of his medical skills to the Commonwealth government. His request in 1916 to be repatriated to Germany as a member of the German Army Medical Corps was refused. When the war ended he was denaturalized and his deportation recommended, but after insistent requests from patients and others, the prime minister W. M. Hughes [q.v.] intervened and he was released in April 1920. The federal committee of the B.M.A. continued to urge the government to deport him.

Avoided by other doctors and unwelcome at public hospitals, in 1921 Herz opened his own private hospital, the Odin (later Bona Dea), at Rushcutters Bay. He worked quietly alone, successfully treating many crippled Australians, often without charge. Many of his medical contemporaries considered him too radical and too anxious to operate, especially on patients with poliomyelitis. In defence he often appeared stiff-necked and brusque but was at all times outspoken. Most patients, staff and friends found him good-humoured, witty and compassionate. His greatest rapport was with children. Short and balding, with brown eyes, he wore thick glasses. Keenly interested in the arts and music, he entertained many visiting musicians at his Darling Point home; he always had a dog – usually an Irish setter.

Survived by his wife and daughter, Herz died of hypertensive heart disease on 17 December 1948 and was cremated with Anglican rites. His estate was valued for probate at £11 004. Through bigotry, much of his knowledge and his operating technique died with him. In 1980 Dr William J. Cumming, in a paper delivered to the Australian Orthopaedic Association, acknowledged Herz as the first fully trained orthopaedic surgeon to practise in Australia and New Zealand.

J. Clarke, *Dr. Max Herz, surgeon extraordinary* (Syd, 1976); *PD* (Cwlth), 30 Apr, 14 Sept 1920; *MJA*, Dec 1919; *Chirurg* (Berlin), 1 Jan 1929; *Argus*, 17 Apr 1903; *Canterbury Times* (Christchurch, NZ), 19 Aug, 16 Sept, 9 Dec 1903, 10 July 1904; *Auckland Star* (NZ), 14 July 1906; *NZ Herald*, 8 Aug 1906; *Daily Telegraph* (Syd), 3 Feb 1912; *Smith's Weekly* (Syd), 9 Mar, 23 Nov 1929, 29 Aug 1936; Naturalization file, A1 36/2296, *and* PM's Dept CRS, A457, item 406/3, *and* defence file MP 367, C 567/3/2913, 3695 and 4611 (AAO); family papers held by T. Hearst, Darling Point, Syd; information from Dr Hugh Barry, Syd.

JOAN CLARKE

HEWLETT, HERBERT MAUNSELL (1872-1957), radiologist, was born on 13 October 1872 at Fitzroy, Melbourne, younger son of Dr Thomas Hewlett from Berkshire, England, and his Irish-born wife Louisa Jane, née Blackham. Thomas Hewlett had come to Melbourne in 1862 after service in India as an army surgeon and established a large general practice in Nicholson Street, Fitzroy.

Herbert was educated at Alexander Sutherland's [q.v.6] Carlton College. After three years of a medical course at the University of Melbourne he completed his degree at the Edinburgh Medical School, graduating with distinctions in all subjects of the final year (M.R.C.P., 1896). He was greatly influenced by his teachers at Edinburgh, particularly the noted paediatrician Dr John Thomson. Hewlett had been keenly interested in reports of Röntgen's discovery of X-rays in November 1895 and closely followed developments in the field.

Hewlett returned to Melbourne in 1896

and joined his father's practice. Late that year he was appointed to the honorary staff of the Children's Hospital. There, because of long-standing interest in electricity and photography he was invited to instal X-ray equipment costing some £25, and thus in 1897 established the first radiology department in a Melbourne public hospital. He served the Children's Hospital for thirty-eight years. For the first fifteen years his duties combined those of honorary physician, surgeon and radiologist. In 1912 he was appointed skiagraphist, from then on confining his interests to radiology. He was also appointed skiagraphist at St Vincent's Hospital from 1911 until 1934.

Hewlett had X-ray equipment at Fitzroy in 1902, and in 1912 established his radiological practice in Collins Street. For some years early in his career he combined superficial therapy with radio-diagnosis. He was a member of the Melbourne Radiological Clinic from 1930 to 1952. He contributed little to the literature, but was regarded as an extremely good radiologist, whose reports based on clinical observation, good knowledge of anatomy and pathology, and sound radiological interpretations were models of their kind. He adopted with enthusiasm advances in technique and equipment. With Dr J. F. Wilkinson [q.v.] he pioneered in Melbourne the radiological investigation of the gastro-intestinal tract.

Hewlett was honoured as a pioneer radiologist by the Antoine Béclère Centre in Paris. He was vice-president of the Australian and New Zealand Association of Radiologists, fellow of the Royal Australasian College of Radiologists, and honorary fellow of the Faculty of Radiologists, London.

On 23 August 1899 at Christ Church, St Kilda, he had married Caroline Ada Louise (Dollie) Lincoln, and for many years they lived in Melbourne Mansions above his professional rooms. 'Herbie' Hewlett's immaculately dressed and spruce figure was a familiar sight at the Athenaeum Club where he was a member from 1896. He loved racing, played much golf and was a first-class shot. His only child Nancy often accompanied him on his annual fishing excursions to the Tasmanian lakes.

Although, like many workers in the field, Hewlett suffered from the effects of X-ray dermatitis to both hands, he was in active practice until 1953. He died at his Collins Street home of cerebro-vascular disease on 26 July 1957, and was cremated. He was survived by his wife and daughter.

J. Smith (ed), *Cyclopedia of Victoria*, 1 (Melb, 1903); *VHM*, 33 (Aug 1962), no 1, p 263; *MJA*, 14 Sept 1957; Hewlett papers (Brownless Lib, Univ Melb).   MALCOLM MCKEOWN

HEYDON, CHARLES GILBERT (1845-1932) and LOUIS FRANCIS (1848-1918), lawyers and politicians, were born on 25 August 1845 and on 23 April 1848 in Sydney, sons of English parents Jabez King Heydon [q.v.1], a recently converted Catholic printer and publisher, and his wife Sophia, née Hayes. Charles's godfather was Archbishop Polding [q.v.2]. Both boys were educated at St Mary's school, Sydney, Charles going on to Rev. Thomas Aitken's school at Ryde and Louis to Sydney Grammar School.

In 1860 Charles joined the Commercial Banking Co. of Sydney and became a branch manager. In his late twenties he resigned to prepare for the Bar and supplemented his income by journalism. After reading in the chambers of Gatward Coleridge Davis he was admitted to the Bar on 25 September 1875. His early work was largely in the country, but he later built up a robust commercial and common law practice in Sydney. He took silk in 1896. At the Villa Maria chapel, Hunters Hill, on 8 September 1880 he married Miriam Josepha (d. 1896), daughter of T. C. Makinson [q.v.2].

Heydon twice unsuccessfully contested Legislative Assembly seats. After the resignation of (Sir) Edmund Barton [q.v.7], he accepted the attorney-generalship in the Dibbs [q.v.4] ministry and was appointed to the Legislative Council on 15 December 1893. He remained in the council until 1900, except for a few months in 1898.

In 1896 Heydon had volunteered as sole royal commissioner to consolidate the statute law of New South Wales, a prodigious task that had earlier defied the exertions of several royal commissions. He reviewed nearly 1400 Acts, proposing the repeal of those that were obsolete, and the simplification of, and consolidation of amendments to the remainder. He had the assistance of draftsmen, but was not paid for his efforts that were said to distinguish him as 'the most inveterate worker that ever wore a wig'. He completed the project in 1902 while conducting his practice and acting at times as a Supreme Court judge, and notwithstanding his appointment as a judge of the District Court on 1 March 1900. He sat in the Northern District but, disliking cold weather, organized winter sittings in Sydney.

Heydon became president of the Court of Arbitration in July 1905, the judge of the Industrial Court from 1909 and president of the State Board of Trade in 1918. In 1905, in the Sawmillers' case, he cautiously outlined a consistent basis for a minimum wage to enable 'every worker however humble . . . to lead a human life, to marry and bring up a family and maintain them and himself with at any rate some small degree of comfort'. However his 'living wage' was governed by the degree of prosperity in the industry involved. He was an ardent patriot and in World War I accused striking coal-lumpers of 'fighting against the Empire and for the Germans' and later similarly castigated striking coalminers. By 1918, as wages failed to rise with inflation and fell below those in other States, he was responsible for much of the frustration and disillusionment in New South Wales, despite Governor Davidson's [q.v.8] comment, when unsuccessfully recommending him for a knighthood, that he 'possessed the entire confidence of both employer and employee'.

A prominent Catholic layman and a fellow of St John's College, University of Sydney, Heydon in a long letter to the *Sydney Morning Herald* on 19 November 1917 attacked Archbishop Mannix's [q.v.] anticonscription stand and claimed that for 'a Catholic Archbishop to lead his flock along the paths of sedition is to disobey the clearest teachings of the Catholic Church'. Next year he became a vice-president of the 'King's Men', who aimed at promoting loyalty to 'our country and the Empire'.

Obliged by the Judges Retirement Act, 1918, to stand down from the Bench, Heydon abhorred the enforced idleness: 'it was not my doing and I never consented'. He was a member of the Australian Club. In his youth he had been joint honorary secretary of the New South Wales Chess Association and later was a vice-president of the Sydney Amateur Orchestral Society and the Royal Philharmonic Society of Sydney. On 8 November 1909 at Mosman he had married a 28-year-old art student Sybil Russell.

Heydon died at his home at Potts Point on 6 March 1932 and was buried in the Field of Mars cemetery. He was survived by his second wife and by his son George who served with the Australian Army Medical Corps and won the Military Cross.

Louis was articled to E. G. Ellis in 1868 and was admitted a solicitor on 20 December 1873; he practised at Bathurst until 1881, when he returned to Sydney. On 15 August at Lithgow he married Mary Josephine Gell. A single-minded Protectionist, Heydon was elected to the Legislative Assembly for Yass Plains in 1882 and, with the support of the Catholic vote and local free selectors' association, represented the seat until he resigned in November 1886. With E. W. O'Sullivan [q.v.] he was a founder, and later president, of the Land and Industrial Alliance of New South Wales, which aimed at uniting workingmen, farmers and selectors. In December 1885 he became minister of justice in Sir John Robertson's [q.v.6] last ministry, but resigned on 4 February next year when

the government suggested a property tax of a halfpenny in the pound: the government fell three weeks later. Nominated to the Legislative Council in February 1889, he bitterly opposed Federation and Sir Alfred Stephen's [q.v.6] divorce bills. He withdrew from political activity after Fusion in 1909 but later supported the National Party.

In 1901 the Incorporated Law Institute reported Heydon to the Supreme Court for misconduct. Retained in an administration suit (*Moss* v. *Moss*) by the plaintiffs, he had also been asked to act for five defendants. Having declined, he arranged for their representation by solicitors who agreed to pay him a percentage of the costs they received. The agreement, although a long-standing practice among some solicitors, was unethical and was condemned by Chief Justice Darley [q.v.4] as 'vicious' and 'wholly indefensible'. He was heavily fined and penalized in costs and his professional standing suffered.

Heydon was president of St Joseph's Investment and Building Society from 1892 and the Society of St Vincent de Paul in Australia from 1897, a director of the Mutual Life Association of Australasia and a committee-member of the United Charities Fund. He served on the State Children Relief Board in 1892-1918. Associated with the Sydney Mechanics' School of Arts debating club in his youth, he was later a member of the Shakespeare Society of New South Wales.

Heydon died suddenly at his home at Hunters Hill on 17 May 1918 and was buried in the Field of Mars cemetery. His son and daughter survived him.

W. Blacket, *May it please Your Honour* (Syd, 1927); B. E. Mansfield, *Australian democrat; the career of Edward William O'Sullivan, 1846-1910* (Syd, 1965); J. M. Bennett (ed), *A history of the New South Wales Bar* (Syd, 1969); H. T. E. Holt, *A court rises* (Syd, 1976); *V&P* (LA NSW), 1902, 2, p 39; A. W. Martin, 'Electoral contests in Yass and Queanbeyan in the "seventies" and "eighties"', *JRAHS*, 43 (1957), pt 3, p 126; *Industrial Arbitration Report* (NSW), 4, 1905, p 308-9; *Sydney Mail*, 10 Feb 1904; *SMH*, 19, 21 Nov 1917, 18 May, 25 Sept, 21 Dec 1918, 7, 8 Mar 1932; I. Grant, Employers, unions and arbitration, New South Wales, 1918-1929 (Ph.D. thesis, Univ Syd, 1979); CO 448/18.
                                                J. M. BENNETT
                                                MARTHA RUTLEDGE

HEYER, JOHANNES (1872-1945), clergyman, was born on 29 April 1872 at Germantown (Grovedale) near Geelong, Victoria, son of Georg Heyer, pastor of St Paul's Lutheran Church, Germantown, for fifty-two years, and his wife Clara Elisabeth, née Kummer, who had both migrated from

Alsace-Lorraine, France, in 1868. An outstanding scholar, Heyer was awarded an Education Department exhibition while at Flinders School, and was dux of Geelong College in 1887. In 1889 he won a scholarship to Ormond College, University of Melbourne, where he specialized in modern languages (B.A., 1892; M.A., 1894). He studied theology at Ormond in 1893-96 and then in Edinburgh and Leipzig. At St Giles Cathedral, Edinburgh, he found his ideals for worship given clearest expression.

In 1897 Heyer was an Australian representative at the first international conference of the Student Christian Movement at Northfield, United States of America. Returning to Australia, he was licensed to preach the Gospel by the Presbytery of Geelong in December, and worked in association with the minister of Scots Church, Melbourne, for the next three years. He was ordained as a minister of the Presbyterian Church and inducted into the parish of Yarra Glen and Healesville in 1900; he was subsequently closely involved in the establishment of Healesville College.

In 1904 Heyer was called to be minister of St John's Presbyterian Church, Hobart, was inducted on 5 August and remained associated with this church for the rest of his life. Besides parish work, he became increasingly busy with the administration of the presbytery and the assembly, and in particular with the Foreign Missions Committee. (His sister Clara had married the Presbyterian missionary, F. H. L. Paton [q.v.] in 1896.) Heyer retired in May 1923, although after this date he was several times interim minister at St John's.

An outstanding personality of the Presbyterian Church in Tasmania, Heyer was scholar, theologian, historian, poet, organist and composer. Besides writing poems and hymns, he composed hymn-tunes and music for the *Te Deum*. He published a booklet, *The Lord's Prayer, its implications and confessional value* (undated), and also wrote local church histories. Of greatest and lasting importance is his comprehensive book on the history of Presbyterianism in Tasmania, *The Presbyterian pioneers of Van Diemen's Land*, published in 1935 to commemorate the centenary of the establishment of the Presbytery of Van Diemen's Land. He was a strong supporter of the Children's Aid Society and was secretary of the Hobart branch of the Royal Society for the Prevention of Cruelty to Animals. During World War I he withstood unjustified accusations of pro-German sympathies.

Heyer collapsed and died at the wheel of his car in Hobart on 18 October 1945 and was buried in Cornelian Bay cemetery. His wife, Amy Florence Isabel, née McGregor, whom he had married at Karelah, Sandy Bay, on 6 June 1905, had died the previous year; they had no children.

St John's Presbyterian Church, Hob, *Centenarian*, 1940; *Tas Presbyterian*, Dec 1945; *Investigator*, Sept 1971, Dec 1977, Sept 1979; *Mercury*, 19 Oct 1945; Rev J. Heyer papers, *and* historical material of Presbyterian Church, Tas (SLT); information from Mr P. L. Brown, Newtown, Geelong.

CHRIS MOSTERT

HEYSEN, SIR WILHELM ERNST HANS FRANZ (1877-1968), artist, was born on 8 October 1877 in Hamburg, Germany, sixth child of Louis Heinrich Wilhelm Heysen and his wife Maria Elisabeth Henriette, née Eberhard. Louis migrated to South Australia in 1883 and his wife followed with the five surviving children next year.

From 1885 Hans attended the East Adelaide Model and four other schools in Adelaide, acquiring a bilingual education and giving early indications of artistic skill. His father moved from one unsuccessful enterprise to another until he established himself as a produce merchant. Heysen left school in 1892, working first in a hardware store and then on one of his father's produce carts. At 14 he bought his first paints: 'I saw a drainpipe with stalks and reeds ... It seemed to me beautiful so I painted it', he later said.

His growing interest in painting and drawing led to enrolment in James Ashton's [q.v.7] Norwood Art School. He quickly achieved distinction. At 16 he was painting so well that Ashton bought his water-colour 'The Wet Road'. It eventually found its way into the Art Gallery of South Australia.

During the ensuing five years his work was exhibited regularly in Adelaide. From an early age he developed a deep love of the Adelaide Hills, tramping about with his paintbox and stool whenever he could. One of his favourite spots was the Onkaparinga Valley near the villages of Hahndorf and Grunthal, and many of his early pictures came from this area.

He was fortunate in his patrons. Robert Barr Smith [q.v.6] paid the fees for twelve months at the school of design at the Art Gallery of South Australia under Harry P. Gill [q.v.] and in 1899 four prominent businessmen offered Heysen an astonishing legal contract in which they agreed to advance £400 to finance his studies in Europe in return for the right to recoup their outlay by selling whatever he might paint while abroad. Heysen accepted the offer eagerly.

For four years he worked hard in Europe—first in Paris at the Académie Julian and Callarossi's Academy under various masters including Jean Paul Laurens and Benjamin Constant and at the Académie des Beaux Arts and later in Italy. There were also summer painting excursions to Holland and Scotland, and a hasty visit to Germany. He returned to Adelaide in 1903. He later reported that the impact of Australian light as he sailed up St Vincent's Gulf was like a slap in the face, profoundly affecting his attitude and vision. Almost at once he turned his back on Europe and concentrated on Australian landscape.

Soon Heysen was attracted by one of his pupils, Selma Bartels. They were married quietly on 15 December 1904 in the Bartels' bluestone house on Hurtle Square.

Heysen continued to earn his living by teaching and painting. He sold pictures to the State galleries in Sydney, Melbourne and Adelaide and to private buyers, but his one-man shows in Adelaide were failures and he still had to teach to eke out an income. Finally some of his friends, particularly E. Phillips Fox [q.v.8], arranged a one-man exhibition in Melbourne. It was opened by Prime Minister Alfred Deakin [q.v.8] on 8 August 1908 and was a phenomenal success. Encouraged by his wife, Heysen decided to give up teaching and rent a cottage in the hills. On 11 November he left Adelaide forever.

The success of the Melbourne exhibition brought commissions from prominent patrons such as (Dame) Nellie Melba [q.v.] and Victoria's governor. There was also increasing publicity and appreciation from critics and collectors such as (Sir) Lionel Lindsay and (Sir) Baldwin Spencer [qq.v.]. A second Melbourne exhibition in 1912 enabled him to buy The Cedars, set in thirty-six acres (15 ha) of the Hahndorf countryside. He lived there for the rest of his life, recording the essence of the landscape and the labours of the German farmers in the fields.

From now on Heysen was envied for the peace and freedom of his country life. His newly built studio, standing among trees on the slope above the house, was idyllic in its setting, and a large family of growing children made for a busy, happy household which the passions of World War I did not entirely cloud.

Heysen was fortunate in being able to mount a third successful Melbourne exhibition before the war intensified. It was opened by Melba on 4 March 1915 and sales were again outstanding. Seven weeks later came Gallipoli, and Heysen and his family, along with other German-born citizens, were soon being subjected to suspicion and insult. Ironically he was a quiet, gentle man who loved Australia and who was deeply opposed to war and violence. In 1918 he wrote

to Elioth Gruner [q.v.] of the war's 'constant prey on one's mind'.

After the war Heysen's exhibitions took up where they had left off. Show after show was phenomenally successful. This, together with frequent press notices, articles by Lionel Lindsay, and publications with fine colour reproductions by Ure Smith [q.v.], made Heysen's name a household word. Although gum-trees and pastoral landscapes were still his favourite subjects, he now also painted large numbers of still life studies.

In 1926 he went to the Flinders Ranges for the first time and later made many visits which produced a torrent of sketches and water-colours, chiefly from the Aroona and Arkaba areas. Some of these were completed on site but most were brought back to be worked on in the studio. Heysen, now 50, was physically vigorous and welcomed long hard days in the field. His artistic output was enormous.

In 1934 he went to Europe and on his return settled down as a kind of elder statesman in the world of Australian art. He assisted aspiring young artists unstintingly and gave long service as a board-member of the National Gallery of South Australia. He continued to sketch and paint, holding periodic exhibitions and contributing generously to appeals and group shows. This was particularly so during World War II which passed with much less bitterness than the first, even though soldiers were billeted at The Cedars for a time.

Heysen was a small, thin, unostentatious man whose blue-grey eyes peered through horn-rimmed spectacles. In old age he was almost bald and usually dressed in polo-necked sweater, knickerbockers and socks to the knee. He worked on steadily, ultimately leaving a vast legacy of thousands of sketches and charcoal drawings to the State gallery. His wife died in 1962 at 83, and he himself died in the Mount Barker Soldiers' Memorial Hospital on 2 July 1968 at 90. Both were buried in Hahndorf cemetery. Heysen's estate was sworn for probate at $195 882. There were five daughters, three sons and one adopted daughter in the family: Nora (b. 1911) showed artistic talent from childhood and made her own reputation, winning the Archibald Prize in 1938.

Heysen holds a distinctive place in the history of Australian landscape art. He won the Wynne prize nine times between 1904 and 1932, the Crouch [q.v.8] prize in 1931, and the Maude Vizard-Wholohan prize in 1957. He was knighted in 1959.

Technically he was an outstanding draughtsman. His control over line was superb. According to Lionel Lindsay he drew as painstakingly as Dürer in his respect for organic form. Although his response to nature was personal and lyrical, his approach to recording and interpreting it was analytical. The whole nation came to see the gum-tree as he saw it. In 1939 he had said: 'In all its stages the gum tree is extremely beautiful—first for being a tiny sucker with broad leaves, shooting up like a fountain answering to the slightest breeze—at middle age it becomes more sturdy, more closely knit and bulky, yet never losing grace in the movement of its limbs and the sweep of its foliage'. He was a fine water-colourist, etcher and painter in oils, and he sketched magnificently in charcoal and crayon. He was fascinated by the effects of light on land and sky, and on the apparent weight or weightlessness of natural objects under changing conditions of light, shadow, mist or sunshine.

In spite of his achievements Heysen's vision was limited. His art tended to remain static, to lack variety and experiment. From a twentieth-century standpoint he was unsophisticated and unscholarly. The sweeping changes that wrenched the world of art and the accompanying turmoil of theory and thought tended to pass him by. There was a sameness of treatment, a staleness of subject-matter, which was compounded in the public mind by scores of imitators who lacked his skill in composition or draughtsmanship. Nevertheless his honesty and integrity are acknowledged and his real achievements remain.

Heysen was a conservationist far ahead of his time. He fought to preserve the flora of the Adelaide Hills—particularly the great red gums and white gums—and repeatedly warned of the dangers of destroying the natural environment. He also recorded the human activities of the region in great detail. In this he has been compared with the Barbizon painters of France for his deep understanding of simple labour in the fields. No other Australian artist has preserved a regional way of life so fully and faithfully. He was not a religious man, but he had a pantheistic reverence for Nature.

Heysen's association with Hahndorf was lifelong and artistically productive. J. S. MacDonald [q.v.] summed it up by saying that the drawings were 'packed with a sort of Virgilian wisdom, the simpler and higher awareness of the meaning of the soil and all its progeny and products: halcyon days, foul weather, thunder, and rain-laden clouds, and winds made visible'.

C. M. Thiele, *Heysen of Hahndorf* (Adel, 1968); Heysen papers (NL); I. North (ed), *Hans Heysen centenary retrospective 1877-1977* (Adel, 1977), and *Heysen* (Adel, 1979).

COLIN THIELE

HICKEY, SIMON (1878-1958), leather goods manufacturer and politician, was born on 6 June 1878 at Botobolar, New South Wales, son of Patrick Hickey, farmer, of Ireland, and his wife Mary, née Swift, native born. Educated at public schools near Mudgee, in 1890 Hickey moved with his family to Auburn, Sydney, and continued at the local public school. At first he helped his father as a drayman, then worked as a bartender and a shearer; in 1893 he was apprenticed to a saddler at Mudgee. In 1903 in Sydney he worked for John Brush & Co., saddlers. He started his own leather firm at Redfern in 1908, Simon Hickey Industries Ltd.

Hickey had joined the Australian Natives' Association in the mid-1890s. His disadvantaged upbringing inclined him to the Labor Party and he became a member about 1900; by 1906 he was president of the South Sydney branch. At Our Lady of Mount Carmel Church, Waterloo, on 25 February 1911, he married Hilda Ellen, daughter of J. R. Dacey [q.v.8]; on the latter's death next year Hickey succeeded him in the State seat of Alexandria. He was then improving his financial position and was part of the general movement of Catholics to Labor after Cardinal Moran [q.v.] had favourably compared Australian to Continental socialism in 1905. Labor formed a government in 1910 under J. S. T. McGowen [q.v.], and of its forty-six parliamentarians seventeen were Catholics.

Made a justice of the peace in 1912, Hickey was ambitious politically and in 1912-15 was secretary of the parliamentary Labor Party; but he also looked after his business, and did not form a power base in the party. He was an anti-conscriptionist in World War I, but before the 1917 general election, with J. Storey [q.v.], he urged the central executive to re-admit the pro-conscriptionists who had been expelled the previous year. He made a notably wrong prediction that once the war was over the Labor Party would quickly return to its pre-1916 position. With several other parliamentarians, he was worried by the radicalism of the trade unionists who controlled the party executive, and found it impossible to adjust to the tortuous factionalism that prevailed in the 1920s. He was chairman of the Public Works Committee in 1920-21, and in the exchange of ministries by J. Dooley and Sir George Fuller [qq.v.8] in December 1921, Hickey was Speaker for eight days. He lost his seat next year, but was a member of the Legislative Council in 1925-34.

Hickey's business prospered and in 1923 he opened the first silk-weaving mill in Australia; but it failed. He held enlightened views on the employment of youths and suggested that apprenticeship rules be altered to help obviate dead-end jobs. In the 1920s and 1930s he gave several lectures, those on politics revealing his late cynicism about party discipline. In 1931 J. T. Lang [q.v.] removed him from the Milk Board. The same year his friend R. D. Meagher [q.v.] died and Hickey eulogized him in terms that Meagher would have approved: 'to him a primrose by a river bank was a fadeless immortelle'. Abstemious, 'swarthy and rotund', Hickey was well stocked with bush lore; he wrote many paragraphs for the *Bulletin*, and in 1951 published a book of reminiscences, *Travelled roads*, enlivened by his joviality.

Hickey died on 18 May 1958 at his home at Bellevue Hill, and was buried in the Catholic section of Botany cemetery, survived by his wife, a daughter and two sons. His estate was sworn for probate at £11 806.

P. Ford, *Cardinal Moran and the A.L.P.* (Melb, 1966); *Bulletin*, 24 June 1931, 4 June 1958; *SMH*, 8 Mar 1917, 14 Dec 1921, 24 Aug 1922, 15 Mar 1923, 22 Dec 1925, 18 Sept, 29 Dec 1931.

BEDE NAIRN

HICKSON, ROBERT NEWBURGH (1884-1963), architect, was born on 2 May 1884 at Newcastle, New South Wales, fifth son and seventh child of Irish parents Robert Rowan Pendon Hickson, civil engineer, and his wife Sophia, née Haire. Educated at Sydney Church of England Grammar School (Shore) in 1897-1902, he was senior prefect and captain of the cricket and Rugby teams in 1901. He worked for Dalgety & Co. Ltd but was soon articled to Joseland [q.v.] & Vernon, architects. In 1903-07 he played cricket for New South Wales, mainly as an opening batsman when Victor Trumper [q.v.] was unavailable.

Going to Armidale in 1907, Hickson established a successful practice as a competent designer of domestic and public buildings. He became regional architect for the Rural Bank of New South Wales and for the Anglican diocese of Armidale, and was responsible for extensions to The Armidale School and New England Girls' School.

A popular captain of the New England XI for some years, Hickson also played Rugby Union, baseball, golf and bowls. Renowned for good works and civic service, he was a member of the Armidale and New England Hospital board for fifty years and was associated with St Peter's Cathedral council, the Armidale Diocesan Synod, Boy Scouts' Association and Technical College, the Armidale District Handicapped Children's Centre, the New England National Park trust, and the literary, musical and operatic

societies. He was a director of all thirteen co-operative building societies represented in the city and of the Armidale Newspaper Co. Ltd, and was a trustee of the showground and racecourse. This large and affable, if sometimes temperamental, man was a familiar sight in his small car.

In the 1920s Hickson was involved with (Sir) Michael Bruxner and D. H. Drummond [qq.v.7, 8] in the foundation of the Country Party and remained interested in the party, often as campaign director, and in the New England New State Movement. He was an alderman on Armidale Municipal Council in 1925-28.

On 31 December 1912 at St Peter's Cathedral, Hickson had married ELLA VIOLET BELL (1879-1955). She was born on 29 January 1879 at Young, daughter of Sydney Bell, bank manager, and his wife Esther, née Miller. She had trained as a nurse at Royal Prince Alfred Hospital and was matron of Armidale and New England Hospital in 1908-12.

Involved in the foundation of the local branch of the Red Cross Society in 1914, Ella Hickson commanded the Voluntary Aid Detachment associated with the 33rd Battalion, which soon camped at the showground. She ably supported the Country Women's Association of New South Wales, was treasurer of the Armidale Ladies' Relief Society and was a founder of the women's auxiliary of the local hospital. With her husband she worked to establish Homes for the Aged and two church hostels for children attending Armidale High School. Crisp and efficient, Mrs Hickson had a 'gentle, kindly personality'. She was appointed M.B.E. in 1941. She died, childless, on 29 October 1955.

Hickson died at his home at Armidale on 21 June 1963 and, like his wife, was cremated with Anglican rites. His estate was valued for probate at £22 713.

Armidale Express, 31 Oct, 2, 4 Nov 1955, 21, 24 June 1963; *Northern Daily Leader*, 22 June 1963; personal information.

L. A. GILBERT

HIDES, JACK GORDON (1906-1938), public servant and explorer, was born on 24 June 1906 in Port Moresby, Papua, second of the seven children of Horace Herbert Hides, head gaoler of Port Moresby Gaol, and his wife Helena Marie, née Shanahan. His limited formal education came from the Port Moresby European School (1911-17), Einasleigh State School, Queensland (1917), private tuition (1918-19) and Maleny State School, Queensland (1920). He was a Roman

Catholic, a fine swimmer, a sprint runner and an amateur boxer.

In July 1925 Hides joined the Papuan Public Service as a cadet clerk and in May 1926 transferred to the magisterial branch of the Government Secretary's Department as a cadet patrol officer. Appointed patrol officer in February 1928, he became assistant resident magistrate, 2nd grade, in February 1934, serving in succession at Kambisi Police Camp, Cape Nelson, Kairuku, Kerema, Kikori, Daru, Buna Bay, Mondo Police Camp and Misima. He first demonstrated outstanding qualities of leadership and bushcraft on a series of patrols from Kerema in 1930-31 into the partially unexplored Kukukuku country. Later murder patrols from Daru, Kikori and Mondo extended his experience.

In 1935 Hides was personally chosen by Lieut-Governor Sir Hubert Murray [q.v.] to lead an expedition into the last large unexplored region of Papua, between the Strickland and Purari rivers. Patrol Officer Louis James O'Malley was his second-in-command. The patrol left Daru by water on 1 January 1935, ascended the Strickland to the Rentoul River junction, then followed the Rentoul to the limit of canoe travel. With ten police under Sergeant Orai and twenty-eight carriers, Hides and O'Malley then entered unknown country, crossing the great Papuan Plateau and the limestone barrier of the Central Range into the Tari basin. After a violent conflict with the wig-wearing Huri tribesmen, they passed on to the heavily populated Waga and Nembi River valleys. Attacked by bowmen, they went on to the Erave River and thence through the Samberigi valley to Kikori on 17 June. The patrol fought at least nine skirmishes and shot dead at least thirty-two tribesmen. One carrier and a police constable died from exposure and exhaustion. It was the last major exploratory expedition in Papua-New Guinea to be carried out without radio or aerial support. It completed the work of the Leahy [q.v.] brothers, J. L. Taylor and administration officers in the highland districts of the Mandated Territory of New Guinea and proved that the dense populations found there extended into Papua.

Handsome, a fluent speaker and the epitome of the dashing explorer, Hides was the centre of intense publicity when he arrived in Sydney in August. He was widely criticized for the bloodshed, particularly after Ivan Champion and C. J. Adamson successfully completed their Bamu-Purari patrol in 1936 through the same general region without firing a shot. Sir Hubert Murray, however, praised both leaders, calling the Strickland–Purari patrol 'the most difficult and dangerous' ever carried out in Papua.

During the course of the patrol, Hides discovered traces of what he thought was gold in the upper reaches of the Strickland, and in July 1936 he resigned from the Papuan service. Backed by a Sydney company, Investors Ltd, he led a private prospecting expedition up the Strickland River in February 1937. His companion David Lyall became seriously ill with a stomach ulcer when the party was in sight of its goal. Forced to retreat to the coast with the dying Lyall, Hides lost five carriers from beri-beri in the Strickland Gorge and Lyall died at Daru on 16 September. Depressed and suffering from the effects of the journey, Hides returned to Sydney. He died of pneumonia on 19 June 1938 and was buried in Northern Suburbs cemetery. At Liverpool, New South Wales, on 20 September 1932, he had married Margeurite Montebell Priestley; they had two children.

Though daring and courageous, Hides was sometimes rashly over-confident. The loss of men during several of his journeys might have been avoided by better planning and more caution. He wrote four successful books based on his experiences: *Through wildest Papua, Papuan wonderland, Savages in serge* and *Beyond the Kubea*, the last published posthumously. *Papuan wonderland* and *Beyond the Kubea* were reissued in 1973.

L. Lett, *Knights errant of Papua* (Lond, 1935); G. Souter, *New Guinea* (Syd, 1968); J. P. Sinclair, *The outside man* (Melb, 1969); Cwlth record series, G91, 97, 148, 212, 302, 346, 383, 559, AS 13/26/1, 3, 57, A 518, C 251/3/1, 852/4/100 (AAO).

JAMES SINCLAIR

HIGGINS, ERNEST HENRY (1871-1945), TASMAN GEORGE (1888-1953) and ARTHUR EMBERY (1891-1963), film cameramen, were born on 9 October 1871, 8 April 1888 and 25 October 1891 in Hobart, sons of Henry Higgins, butcher, and his wife Ann Maria, née Hooper. They were educated locally. Their father was one of the first to illuminate his shop by electricity. About 1900 Ernest rigged up a projector on the shop's balcony with a screen on a building across the street.

By 1903 Ernest was a bioscope operator at a Hobart theatre. Next year be bought a 'movie' camera and began to take and exhibit films of Hobart and its environs. Later that year he moved to Sydney and soon became an integral part of Cozens Spencer's [q.v.] production team. He filmed newsreels, travelogues and the Burns-Johnson fight in 1908, and made an industrial film, *The history of a loaf*. In 1910 he made his first feature film, *The life and ad-*

ventures of John Vane; several more bush-ranger films, including *Captain Starlight*, followed. In 1912 he flew eighteen times with the aviator W. E. Hart [q.v.] and made three documentaries.

Arthur had started work in an architect's office, but joined Ernest in Sydney in 1908 and was taken on by Spencer. In 1912 he made some documentaries for the Western Australian government. From 1911 Ernest and Arthur were closely associated with Raymond Longford [q.v.]. Arthur was barely 20 when he shot Longford's first film, *The fatal wedding*. Tasman, who worked as a clerk in Hobart, had joined them by 1912, when he helped Arthur to film Longford's *The tide of death*. Next year all three were cameramen for Longford's racist outburst, *Australia calls*, in which Sydney was bombed by invading Asians. In this period they 'had to devise all the trick effects; process and edit their own films, and—most difficult job of all—do all the photography by daylight'. To film interior scenes they removed part of the studio roof.

After Spencer's Pictures Ltd merged with Australasian Films Ltd in 1913, Ernest, Tasman and Arthur founded Higgins Bros, cinematographers. They made documentaries and compilation films such as *Australia's response to the Empire's call* (1914), and one feature film, *A long, long way to Tipperary* (1914), but were discouraged by their failure to get fair payment from Australasian Films. From January 1917 Ernest was sole proprietor of Higgins Bros. At the Methodist church, Lindfield, he married Elsie May Dickson on 24 April 1919. He made his last feature film in 1922 but continued to work in the industry, as Higgins Bros, until his death. Survived by his wife and son, he died at his Darling Point home on 28 November 1945 and was cremated.

Tasman had married Gladys Mary Walker at St Mary's Church of England, Waverley, on 4 September 1915. In the 1920s and 1930s he made about one feature film a year for different directors: these included Louise Lovely's [q.v.] *Jewelled nights* (1925) and *When the Kellys rode* (1934). He also worked on newsreels and became known for the high quality of his outdoor photography. In 1932 he spent three months with Charles Chauvel [q.v.7] on Pitcairn Island to film *In the wake of the Bounty*. Shooting from whaleboats was perilous and 'one scene was shot in a cave ... accessible only by ropes'. He was cameraman for other Chauvel films, including the cavalry scenes in *Forty thousand horsemen* (1940). His last feature film was made in 1941. He died in a Parramatta mental hospital on 4 June 1953 and was cremated. His wife, daughter and three sons survived him.

After leaving Higgins Bros, Arthur worked closely with Longford & Lottie Lyell [q.v.]. He made Longford's best-known films, *The sentimental bloke* (1919) and *On our selection* (1920); the latter included the bush-fire scene that was perhaps his most famous piece of photography. In 1928 he set up Arthur Higgins Productions and made a racing film, *Odds on*, and in 1930, with Tasman as cameraman, the visually spectacular *Fellers*. Set in Palestine, desert scenes were shot in sandhills near Sydney. The last reel was synchronized with a few minutes of dialogue. In May *Fellers* won the third (and only) prize in the Commonwealth film competition. After visiting the United States of America, from 1931 Arthur made features and a series of documentaries, *Cities of the Empire*, for F. W. Thring's [q.v.] Efftee Film Productions in Melbourne, and two films for Pat Hanna [q.v.]. He joined Cinesound Productions in 1936 but continued to make feature films for different directors until 1946.

Noted for his poetic outdoor photography, especially in Longford's *The woman suffers* (1918), *The Blue Mountains mystery* (1921) and *The bushwhackers* (1925), Arthur was also skilled at trick photography. He was the most experimental of the brothers, he developed his own colour process and about 1937 established a production company, Solarchrome Colour Processing Co., to produce screen advertisements, documentaries, and industrial shorts. For eight years he filmed races at all Sydney courses and was a familiar figure at 'the turn' at Randwick. Arthur had married Sheila Elizabeth Smith on 27 June 1917 at Moonee Ponds, Melbourne; they were childless. He died at his home at Potts Point on 22 September 1963 and was cremated with Methodist forms.

The quality of the Higgins brothers' cinematography was acclaimed by their contemporaries and can still be recognized in the few prints that survive. While the subject matter of these early films was often limited and repetitive, their photography equalled the standards that prevailed overseas, their documentaries recorded significant aspects of Australian social, cultural and economic history.

C. E. Chauvel, *In the wake of the 'Bounty'* ... (Syd, 1933?); J. Cato, *The story of the camera in Australia* (Melb, 1955); E. Reade, *History and heartburn* (Syd, 1979); A. Pike and R. F. Cooper, *Australian film 1900-1977* (Melb, 1980); *Theatre Mag* (Melb, Syd), 1 Mar 1915; *Register* (Adel), 25 Mar 1918; *SMH*, 6 May 1962, 24 Sept 1963; R. F. Cooper, 'And the villain still pursued her'. Origins of film in Australia, 1896-1913 (MA thesis, ANU, 1971); Higgins file (Film Archives, NL); information from M. J. Wasson, Armidale, NSW.

GRAEME OSBORNE
MARTHA RUTLEDGE

HIGGINS, HENRY BOURNES (1851-1929), politician and judge, was born on 30 June 1851 at Newtownards, Down, Ireland, second son of Rev. John Higgins and his wife Anne, née Bournes. John Higgins, brought up in the Church of Ireland and destined for a safe career in a bank, displeased his father by entering the Wesleyan ministry. He and Anne Higgins were devoted parents to their six sons and two daughters, who grew up in an atmosphere of evangelical piety and genteel frugality. Henry, deemed to be a 'delicate' child and inhibited by a bad stammer, was particularly dependent on his proud and ambitious mother. At 10 he was sent to St Stephen's Green (the Wesleyan Connexional School), Dublin, an austere institution which nevertheless provided the rudiments of a classical education. Ill health led to his withdrawal at 14, but he was able briefly to resume his studies at a local school at Newry. After lowly jobs in a drapery warehouse in Belfast and a merchant tailor's shop at Clonmel, Henry gained more congenial employment as a clerk in a furniture warehouse in Dublin. In 1869 the death from consumption of his elder brother James confirmed John and Anne Higgins in their resolve to migrate. A doctor recommended Victoria for its healthy climate.

The family arrived in Melbourne on 12 February 1870. Henry gained his common schools teacher's certificate and also matriculated. Working his way through the University of Melbourne (LL.B., 1874; M.A., 1876), he taught at various schools and undertook private tutoring, his pupils including sons of Andrew Chirnside and David Syme [qq.v.3,6]. Higgins had an outstanding record at university in languages, logic, history, political economy and in Shakespeare, being several times exhibitioner. But he committed himself to law, reasoning that it would force him to cure his stammer in order to speak in court, though when he went to the Victorian Bar in 1876 he chose equity because it would not require him to address juries.

His years at university introduced him to the great intellectual issues of the day and acclimatized him to colonial society. He was much influenced by the teaching of W. E. Hearn [q.v.4] in political economy and history; in particular, chapter 16 of Grote's *History of Greece*, in which the author analysed the decline of 'Grecian Mythes' as religious truth, shook his spiritual world 'like an earthquake'. Disturbed by the Christian concept of hell, Higgins committed his anguished doubts to a diary in cipher, and shed the simple Wesleyanism of his father. Though he came close to agnosticism, he seems to have retained some sort of religious faith; years later G. V. Portus [q.v.] said that he had never met anyone 'so aloof from religion in any sense of creed, whose life lay so deep in the things of the spirit'. Higgins was a foundation member of the debating society which C. H. Pearson [q.v.5] inspired. His closest friends were Alfred Deakin, Alexander Sutherland and Richard Hodgson [qq.v.8,6,4]: Catherine Deakin was to recall them as 'a brilliant quartet'.

Higgins began to prosper at the equity Bar. In 1883 he bought land on Glenferrie Road, Malvern, on which he built the mansion Doona. In 1887 when he succeeded (Sir) T. à Beckett [q.v.3] as leader of the equity Bar, he was expecting to earn about £5000 a year. He did not take silk until 1903. Higgins's success was central to the family's fortunes, and enabled his younger brothers also to enter the professions, John becoming an accountant, George a civil engineer (and later associate professor at the university) and Samuel a doctor. His sister Anna was among the first women to enter the university; Ina studied at the Burnley Horticultural College and practised as a landscape gardener.

On 19 December 1885 Higgins married Mary Alice, daughter of Dr George Morrison [q.v.5] and sister of George Ernest 'Chinese' Morrison [q.v.]. Mary Alice was a tall, imposing young woman described by Higgins's niece Nettie Palmer [q.v.] as possessing 'a prominent sense of duty combined with a sense of humour nourished by a household of brothers'. After the wedding they went on a world tour. In 1887 Mary Alice gave birth to their only child Mervyn Bournes. He was educated at Melbourne Church of England Grammar School, Ormond College, University of Melbourne, and Balliol College, Oxford, where he achieved more success as a rower than as a scholar. When in 1903 Higgins acquired Heronswood at Dromana, which had been built by his old teacher Hearn and later owned by his friend Sutherland, it was largely with Mervyn's enjoyment in mind.

Once his success at the Bar was established, Higgins turned to public affairs. Perhaps his first appearance on a public platform was in 1883 when John and William Redmond [qq.v.6] visited the colonies to rally support for Irish Home Rule. The Redmonds met a hostile and sectarian reception but the fear of Higgins and his colleague (Sir) Frank Gavan Duffy [q.v.8] that they were jeopardizing their careers by appearing on the Redmonds' platform (solicitors, according to Higgins, were 'usually bitter reactionaries') proved groundless. In 1887 Higgins was prominent in a protest against the Irish coercion bill, and throughout his political career he was dedicated to the Irish cause, culminating in 1905 in his moving a resolution in the Commonwealth parliament which urged Britain to grant Home Rule.

The fact that Higgins entered politics just as Victoria's prosperity evaporated had a marked influence on the development of his outlook. In 1892 he stood unsuccessfully for Geelong. He ran again in September 1894 and was elected as a general supporter of (Sir) George Turner [q.v.] whose government was committed to balancing the budget, while making some gestures toward social reform. Like his mentors Hearn and Pearson, Higgins had grown up in the tradition of free-trade liberalism, but recognized that to oppose protection in Victoria was, particularly for a liberal, political folly. Although not a single taxer he had been influenced by Henry George [q.v.4] and was an ardent supporter of the tax on the unimproved value of land, which Turner made a desultory attempt to introduce; and Higgins voted for the income tax as a financial necessity rather than as intrinsically just. In the 1890s his analysis of 'the social problem' led him to assert the need for a more positive state role in the economy. Consequently he supported the Factories and Shops Act, passed in 1896, providing for the trial introduction of a general minimum wage in some of the trades worst hit by the depression. The Act paved the way for the wages board system and stimulated Higgins's interest in industrial relations. In 1897-99 he was chairman of a royal commission on legal procedure.

In 1897, after an energetic campaign, Higgins was elected on the *Age* ticket as one of Victoria's ten delegates to the Australasian Federal Convention of 1897-99 which framed the Commonwealth Constitution. The great majority of delegates tended to assume that only a Federation along American lines was feasible. But to Higgins Federation was 'a mere word' and 'a mere question of a mode of government'. Although he was hardly a unificationist, he believed that Federation was 'unification for certain purposes', and once these purposes had been defined he saw no justification for the Senate being a States' House; he was one of the few delegates who opposed the equal representation of the States in the Upper House. His concern lest a written constitution became 'a dead, lifeless thing which no arts of persuasion can reach' led him to urge the need for flexibility, with a practicable means of amendment. Although some of his convention colleagues were quick to dismiss Higgins as a constitutional eccentric, his role in the proceedings was recognized as significant and often constructive. At the Melbourne session he finally carried, with C. C. Kingston's [q.v.]

help, the conciliation and arbitration amendment; while both would have preferred a much wider power for 'the prevention and settlement of industrial disputes', they realized that only a provision covering interstate disputes would win acceptance. His other major contribution reflected his concern for personal rights. When P. M. Glynn [q.v.] succeeded in introducing 'Almighty God' into the preamble, Higgins carried an amendment, which became section 116, preventing the Commonwealth from making any law prohibiting the establishment of, or free exercise of any religion, or the imposition of any religious observance or test.

During the convention it was by no means clear that Higgins would emerge as an opponent of the Constitution; indeed, even during the last Melbourne session he was still urging moderation on some of his colleagues. Only when the convention rose did he confess his opposition to Deakin, who persuaded him to reflect further. This delay may have been significant, because the lack of focus for opposition in Victoria helped to persuade the waverers, among whom were the *Age* and Premier Turner, that victory for the Federalists was certain. When Higgins did speak out he found only scattered and ill-organized allies, the most notable of which was the Trades Hall Council. In Victoria Higgins conducted a lively if fatalistic campaign, but his help was much sought after in New South Wales where opponents of the Federal enabling bill were anxious to refute the charge of provincialism. Even in final defeat Higgins feared that Australia had been saddled with a rigid and repressive Constitution. He was one of only two convention delegates to oppose the bill.

Higgins's lonely dissent over Federation made him a controversial figure in Victoria, a reputation which he soon compounded by being one of the small minority to oppose the dispatch of a contingent to the South African War in 1899. He was shocked that people could 'go into war with a light heart, and without inquiring closely into the justice of it', and objected that Imperial sentiment was being exploited to excuse the colony from making its own assessment. Higgins further isolated himself from many of his liberal friends by defecting from Turner and assisting in the defeat of his government. It was widely expected that he would be attorney-general in the ministry formed by A. McLean [q.v.] in 1899, but the new premier shrank from an appointment which would have alienated many of his supporters. Two months later Higgins launched a motion of no confidence against the McLean government, but suffered parliamentary humiliation when he was deserted at the last moment by the Liberals. Thus when Higgins faced his Geelong electors in 1900 he no longer seemed the cautious progressive they had re-elected in 1897, but was easily depicted as a perverse and wayward radical. At a memorable campaign meeting he was asked why he had opposed the South African contingent, and promptly responded, 'Because I regarded the war as unnecessary and unjust'. Members of the audience immediately produced Union Jacks and the ensuing patriotic demonstration broke up the meeting. Higgins's other heresies—his anti-Federalism, secularism, support for Home Rule, even his lack of enthusiasm for protection—were all quoted against him, and he suffered a decisive though not overwhelming defeat.

Though his career in Victorian politics ended in notoriety, many in the labour movement now looked to him for leadership in preference to W. A. Trenwith [q.v.], who had supported the Constitution. In the first Federal elections Higgins stood for North Melbourne, a predominantly working-class constituency. He pledged himself to the Labor platform, though declining to join the party which nevertheless gave him tacit support. Although a Deakinite, on issues such as conciliation and arbitration, defence and White Australia Higgins was in broad agreement with the Labor party. In 1904, in what he called 'the most good-humoured crisis I have ever known', he was one of the radicals who helped bring down Deakin's government, when it shrank from bringing State railway workers within the ambit of the arbitration legislation. Labor suddenly found itself in office, and Prime Minister J. C. Watson [q.v.] invited Higgins to be attorney-general. Feeling, as he put it to Deakin, that 'the poor fellows need encouragement', Higgins accepted, but maintained a low profile during the government's few months of office. He was angered, however, by the tactics used to eject the government: 'we came into office without cadging', he said, 'and we shall go out without cringing'.

Perhaps alone among the parliamentary 'friends of labour', Higgins defended Labor's caucus system and the party pledge, arguing that 'if they had not compelled their elected candidates to sign it, they would have had a number of false friends'. He also warned the party 'never to allow itself to be incorporated with any other party' at a time when radical protectionists, led by (Sir) W. J. Lyne and (Sir) Isaac Isaacs [qq.v.], were attempting to negotiate an alliance. When asked why he did not join the Labor Party himself, Higgins was evasive, but implied that he did not attach to 'ultimate theories', by which he presumably meant

socialism, the importance which Labor did. Yet Labor was hardly a socialist party, and Higgins himself was a persistent critic of the 'bourgeois principle', his political convictions reflecting an analysis of social class with at least a flavour of Marx; but perhaps his very sensitivity to class divisions helps explain his reluctance to enter the mainstream of the labour movement. Certainly, the high valuation he placed on individual conscience would have made it difficult for him to accept the constraints of caucus.

By 1906 the Labor Party in Victoria was unwilling to continue granting electoral immunity to the radical protectionists. In North Melbourne the party was deeply divided over whether Higgins should be opposed, and an agonizing decision was only avoided by the news of his appointment in October as a justice of the High Court of Australia. Higgins was appointed one day after Attorney-General Isaacs, who thus gained seniority. The new judges, whose appointments were generally well received, joined a bench composed of three other founding fathers, Sir Samuel Griffith [q.v.], Sir Edmund Barton [q.v.7] and R. E. O'Connor [q.v.]; it was also understood that Higgins would, after a year's interval, replace O'Connor as president of the Commonwealth Court of Conciliation and Arbitration, in which capacity Higgins was to achieve his greatest fame. In his first case late in 1907 he had to decide whether manufacturer H. V. McKay [q.v.] was paying the 'fair and reasonable' wages to his employees required by the New Protection legislation. Wages boards and State arbitration courts had already made pronouncements about what constituted a fair minimum wage, but in his celebrated Harvester judgment Higgins seized the initiative in spelling out the rights of the worker 'as a human being in a civilized community', entitled to marry and raise a family. Having calculated a family budget for a household of 'about five persons', he settled on seven shillings a day as the minimum wage for an unskilled labourer. Although the New Protection legislation was later declared unconstitutional by the High Court—Higgins and Isaacs dissenting—Higgins continued to apply the Harvester wage as a sacrosanct minimum. In 1909 he earned the wrath of the Broken Hill Proprietary Co. Ltd when he refused to reduce the minimum in the face of the company's threat to close its mine. As the Harvester minimum was considerably higher than that allowed by most State tribunals, trade unions sought to bring their disputes within the jurisdiction of the Commonwealth court. Even the militant Tom Mann [q.v.], a critic of the arbitration system, conceded that Higgins was 'sympathetic and fair-minded'. On the other hand, to Higgins's distress, employer organizations vilified the court and its president.

In 1914, feeling the stress of work, Higgins took leave of absence from his duties and travelled with Mary Alice to England; there he followed the drama of the outbreak of war with intense interest. He saw no alternative to fighting Germany, and was at first heartened by the unanimity of feeling not only in England, but in Ireland too. He was soon to become disillusioned with the rise of jingoism, and increasingly concerned with the rights of minorities. Their son Mervyn enlisted while they were in Europe; 'brave to the point of fearlessness', he survived Gallipoli, but was killed at Magdhaba, Egypt, in 1916. Mother and father were desolate. 'My grief has condemned me to hard labour for the rest of my life', Higgins wrote.

The war also destroyed the social optimism which had conditioned the growth of wage regulation. Inflation, the conscription referenda and the apostasy of Labor Prime Minister W. M. Hughes [q.v.] combined to cause discontent in the trade unions, while employers blamed much of the unrest in the unions on what they deemed the false expectations created by arbitration itself. The Arbitration Court had already been frustrated by decisions of the High Court which created, according to Higgins, 'a Serbonian bog of technicalities'; now it also had to contend with the unpredictable policy of Hughes, who at times urged the court to discipline labour, while at other times he made hasty and irregular settlements with striking unions. From the bench Higgins publicly berated Hughes, who he believed was undermining the arbitration system: in 1920 he gave notice of his resignation as president in protest against the government's legislation providing for special tribunals. Much of the trade union movement, particularly the Australian Workers' Union and the craft unions, rallied to his support, so that when he left the court he was still, for many, 'a friend of labour'. In 1922 he published his apologia, *A new province for law and order*, which earned him a D.Litt. from the University of Melbourne. The province survived, and Higgins is entitled to be regarded as its greatest explorer.

He remained on the High Court bench until his death in 1929. Through his arbitration years he had joined the other justices in hearing constitutional cases. Although Higgins and Isaacs were both individualists, they united in resisting the narrow federalism of Griffith, Barton and O'Connor. As the personnel of the court changed, Higgins found himself in the majority, and the 1920 Engineers' case marked the new, broader interpretation of Commonwealth power. This shift disguised the fact that Higgins had been consistent in his sympathetic interpretation of legislation, whether Commonwealth or State; he considered the court should be reluctant to pronounce either invalid. Throughout his judicial career he pursued his own distinctive path as a jurist, making his own judgments and hardly ever 'concurring' with his brothers.

Higgins maintained a broad range of cultural interests. He served on the Council of the University of Melbourne in 1887-1923, supporting the admission of female graduates to all privileges and advocating a university extension system. He was privately generous in financial support of students and in 1904 donated £1000 for a poetry scholarship. Poetry was his particular love, and Browning his favourite poet. As early as 1885 he lectured to the Melbourne University Union on 'The Muses in Australia', and he was quick to recognize the contribution of the *Bulletin* to Australian literature. Deakin acknowledged him as 'one of the parents; if not the chief parent' of the Commonwealth Literary Fund. His strong ties with his niece Nettie Palmer helped to sustain these Australian cultural interests. Nevertheless his interest in Ireland and Irish culture did not decline. After consulting the Irish poet 'A.E.' (George Russell) he made a £20 000 bequest to the Royal Irish Academy which was surprising to friends and family alike.

Always conscious of his childhood 'delicacy' Higgins was in adult years devoted to health and fitness. As a young man he took up a selection in Gippsland to savour something of the pioneering experience. In his early days at Doona he used to ride to St Kilda for a swim before breakfast; he was well known as a rigorous walker, and was a member of the Wallaby Club. He enjoyed conversation and debate, and the shy Irish youth became an 'eminently clubbable' man of affairs. Although critics sometimes thought him self-righteous, his friends generally did not. He delighted in the company of children, many of whom remembered him with affection. In his mature years he presented a deceptively stern image, with his balding pate, serious moustache and direct gaze. Very erect in carriage and rather formal in manner, he was a capable public speaker and lecturer, whose speech still bore the trace of a stammer, and who consequently eschewed oratorical flourishes.

On 13 January 1929 at Heronswood, Higgins went for his regular morning walk to Arthur's Seat, after which he relaxed on the porch with his books. Early in the evening he collapsed and died. The conservative

Argus described him as a 'jurist and states-man', while the Trades Hall flew the Australian flag at half mast. He was buried in Dromana cemetery, with Anglican rites, under the Celtic cross which he had built to commemorate his son. He was survived by Mary Alice, and his estate was valued for probate in Victoria at £69 187.

National A'sian Convention, Syd, *Official record of the proceedings and debates* (Syd, 1891); A'sian Federal Convention, *Official report of debates* (Adel, 1897); N. Palmer, *Henry Bournes Higgins* (Lond, 1931); G. V. Portus, *Happy highways* (Melb, 1953); *PD* (Vic), 1899-1900, p 1777; *PD* (Cwlth), 1904, pp 1224, 4185, 4794, 1906, p 5463; *Cwlth Arbitration Reports*, 1907-8, p 2; *Argus*, 11, 18 Feb 1890, 21 Feb 1917, 14 Jan 1929; *Age*, 30 Aug 1904; C. G. W. Osborne, Tom Mann: his Australasian experience, 1902-1910 (Ph.D. thesis, ANU, 1972); P. Coward, Henry Bournes Higgins and the Australian Constitution (LL.M. thesis, ANU, 1975); P. Grant, Henry Bournes Higgins, Victorian Liberal, 1851-1901 (M.A. thesis, Univ Melb, 1975); Deakin, *and* Higgins, *and* Palmer papers (NL).

JOHN RICKARD

HIGGINS, SIR JOHN MICHAEL (1862-1937), metallurgist, government adviser and company director, was born on 9 December 1862 at Eureka Reef, Castlemaine, Victoria, son of Cornish parents Enedor Stephens Higgins, miner, and his wife Elizabeth Jane, née Stephens. Educated at Rae's School, Sandhurst, and Bendigo High School, at 14 he was indentured to a local pharmacist. After graduating in chemistry and metallurgy at the Bendigo School of Mines he ran his own chemist shop and reputedly studied surgery before becoming an analyst with a New South Wales mine. On 14 November 1889 at Christ Church, North Adelaide, he married Frances Anna Macgraith, a talented musician.

Next year, on the invitation of C. W. Chapman, once fellow-student at the school of mines and now a Melbourne director of the newly formed Australian Smelting Co., Higgins became metallurgical chemist at the Dry Creek Railway Station, Adelaide, reduction works. Within a few years he was manager and when the works closed about 1900 part-owner with Chapman of the company. He settled in Melbourne as a metals consultant and with Chapman, as Chapman, Higgins & Co., acquired pastoral holdings in New South Wales and Queensland. When Higgins retired from the partnership he retained an interest in wool technology. Before the outbreak of World War I travel in Asia and Europe also sharpened his concern with metallurgical issues.

Nevertheless he was reluctant to accept W. M. Hughes's [q.v.] offer of a position as independent metallurgical adviser to the Federal government; he believed that the 1914 War Precautions Act was worded specifically to requisition his services. Asked to submit proposals which would establish Commonwealth control over the treatment, refining and sale of Australian metals in order to preserve their use for the allies and negate enemy access via neutral countries, Higgins on 6 September 1915 established the Australian Metals Exchange. The following year he helped to found and became government nominee on the Zinc Producers' and Copper Producers' associations. He also acted as company adviser to the Federal Treasury, a sensitive area which brought his work under public scrutiny. On 28 November 1918 he was accused in parliament of secret, autocratic power over government policy on the embargo on sale of scrap metals overseas, particularly to Japan. There were hints of collusion with Colonel W. J. N. Oldershaw [q.v.], another government adviser and chairman of directors of a Melbourne de-tinning factory. Higgins's name was cleared after he proposed that a judicial enquiry be conducted into his honorary position.

His 'herculean labours' in the complex metals field led to his appointment in November 1916 as chairman of and government nominee to the Central Wool Committee, founded that year on the same principles as the metals exchange. Essential to the committee's success was the chairman's ability to elicit co-operation from leaders in the industry. In 1918 Higgins's service to the nation was acknowledged by appointment as K.C.M.G. and next year W. A. Watt [q.v.], treasurer and acting prime minister, paid tribute to him as one who had 'laboured himself almost to a standstill for over four years in patriotic service'.

In January 1921 Sir John was founder and chairman of directors of the British Australian Wool Realisation Association Pty Ltd, the largest public company in Australia, established to safeguard the national wool trade and, in association with a temporary London directorate, to realize the wool carried over from the war period. By May 1924 the surplus had been cleared, with a profit of £6 million. Higgins's company addresses insisted on high standards from producers and sellers. Standardization of documents and classification and cataloguing of wool became accepted procedures in wool-marketing, as did double-dumping in transport. After the liquidation of B.A.W.R.A. in 1926 Higgins was trustee for the Wool Selling Brokers' Commission Trust until the final clearance of B.A.W.R.A. wool in 1932.

In his published address to the Empire

Wool Conference (Melbourne, 1931), *The stabilisation or equalisation or the insurance of wool values*, Higgins outlined a scheme for an Empire wool-marketing collective. It attracted favourable interest overseas but was rejected by Australian wool-brokers and graziers who feared government monopoly. Aggrieved growers and brokers had unsuccessfully demanded a parliamentary enquiry into the exclusive distribution of profits to shareholders on B.A.W.R.A.'s liquidation; they viewed Higgins and the 'aristo-plutocrat squattocracy' of B.A.W.R.A. as a dictatorship which had destroyed Australia's subsidiary wool industries and created large-scale unemployment. Higgins believed he was working to offset economic recession. Early in 1931 he was prominent in the plot to capture J. A. Lyons [q.v.] from the Labor Party in order to lead the United Australia Party.

A member of the Victorian committee of the Commonwealth Institute of Science and Industry and vice-chairman of the Metropolitan Gas Co., Higgins was also a Victorian director of the Bank of New Zealand. A chevalier of the French Legion of Honour, he was appointed G.C.M.G. in 1934. He was short and dark with a trim beard and dressed carefully 'like the youngest clerk'. Detractors stressed his ambition. An indefatigable worker of retiring disposition, he avoided public exposure; when he was forced to comment publicly his statements were informative and carefully worded. The 'absolutely Perfect Official', he was seen to inspect the arrangement of chairs before board meetings. This careful façade, however, hid a man of unusual generosity. As chairman of B.A.W.R.A. he worked initially at half the salary of his English counterpart. Although a buyer of books and *objets d'art*, when his salary was doubled he donated the extra £5000 a year to charitable and educational institutions. His commission on the Wool Selling Brokers' Commission trust was similarly given away. He was a member of the Melbourne (president, 1933) and Adelaide clubs and enjoyed recreational walking.

Higgins died, childless, on 6 October 1937 at Toorak, Melbourne, and was buried in Box Hill cemetery; his wife had died on 10 August 1932. His estate was sworn for probate at £157 476 in four States. The University of Melbourne promotes agriculture and veterinary science through the J. M. Higgins Research Foundation and the annual J. M. Higgins exhibition; the Royal Melbourne Institute of Technology's chemistry laboratory is named after Sir John and Lady Higgins.

E. Scott, *Australia during the war* (Syd, 1936); W. S. Robinson, *If I remember rightly*, G. Blainey ed (Melb, 1967); R. Cooksey (ed), 'The great Depression in Australia', *Labour Hist*, 1970, no 17; L. F. Fitzhardinge, *The little digger* (Syd, 1979); *PD* (Cwlth), 1914-17, p 2124, 1918, pp 8458, 8654, 1919, p 10360; *PP* (Cwlth), 1917-19, 5, p 5; *Aust Industrial and Mining Standard*, 6 June 1918, p 567; *Economic Record*, Feb 1928, p 51; Univ Melb, *Calendar*, 1942, pp 558, 565; *Punch* (Melb), 20 June 1918, 16 July 1925; *Australasian*, 22 Jan 1921, 28 Oct 1922; *Argus*, 29, 30 Jan 1924, 7 Oct 1937; *Labor Daily*, 8, 22 Apr 1930; *SMH*, 19 Mar, 2 Apr, 10 Aug 1932, 1 Jan, 15 Dec 1937; F. W. Eggleston, Confidential notes (Menzies Lib, ANU); Attorney-General's Dept, A 432 29/2061 *and* Prime Minister's Dept, AM 500/11 (AAO).

HELGA M. GRIFFIN

HIGGINS, JOSEPH (1838?-1915), Roman Catholic bishop, was born at Moyvore, Westmeath, Ireland. His home environment with its 'more than ordinary comfort and refinement' nurtured an appreciation of the fine arts. From St Finian's Seminary, Navan, he proceeded to St Patrick's College, Maynooth, where a fellow-student was Thomas Carr [q.v.7] who became a lifelong friend. Higgins distinguished himself particularly in theology and ecclesiastical history. Ordained priest at Maynooth in 1863, he returned to the diocese of Meath, serving as a curate at Tullamore for four years. From 1867 he was president of St Finian's Diocesan Seminary, Navan, until in 1884 he became parish priest of Castletown Delvin, where the parochial church he erected and embellished with stained glass established his reputation for high standards in ecclesiastical architecture.

On Cardinal Moran's [q.v.] recommendation, the Holy See appointed Higgins auxiliary bishop of Sydney. On 31 March 1889 he was consecrated titular bishop of Antifelle and a few months later arrived in Sydney, taking charge of St Benedict's Church which he tastefully renovated. For ten years he carried out his episcopal visitation of parishes with characteristic thoroughness and efficiency.

In 1899 he was appointed bishop of Rockhampton to succeed Bishop Cani [q.v.3]. His new diocese was extensive, and Higgins often endured long journeys on horseback. Scarcity of priests was his great difficulty, but by 1905 he had increased the number of clergy from sixteen to twenty-four, six new parishes had been formed and nineteen churches erected. He built ten primary and secondary schools, introducing eight religious communities of women and two of men to assist in the work of Catholic education. On his arrival at Rockhampton he found St Joseph's Cathedral unfinished but collected sufficient funds to erect a temporary back wall, calling the cathedral 'as completed as the present generation can hope o see it'. However, he managed to ornament t with beautiful stained glass in all the aisle windows, and with stations of the Cross which he considered the best he had seen n Australia.

For the sake of his health, Higgins was translated to the see of Ballarat in 1905 and was enthroned as bishop on 7 June. In spite of impaired health he extended the facilities already provided by his predecessor, Bishop ames Moore [q.v.5]. By 1914 the 25 parishes of 1905 had increased to 35, the 62 clergy o 77. There were 9 new presbyteries, 30 more schools and 10 new convents. He introduced the Presentation Sisters to Inglewood, the Josephites to Dunolly and the Good Samaritan Sisters to Koroit and Port Fairy. He carried out extensive improvements to St Patrick's Cathedral, Nazareth House was enlarged, St Joseph's Home at Ballarat established, and St John of God Hospital was opened. He gave generously to such diocesan undertakings as well as to other philanthropic causes.

Distinguished in appearance, courteous in manner, Higgins was praised by those outside his Church for his broadmindedness and helpful participation in civic movements. As a preacher and public speaker he was earnest and eloquent, with a purity of diction and an impressive style. His life as a priest was marked by a simple piety and strict observance of religious duties, his episcopal life by a fervent zeal. As ruler of a diocese he was mild and lenient, avoiding public controversy wherever possible.

Bishop Higgins died of heart failure on 16 September 1915 and was buried in the vault of St Patrick's Cathedral, Ballarat.

P. F. Moran, *History of the Catholic Church in Australasia* (Syd, 1895); M. M. McCallum, *Ballarat and district citizens and sports at home and abroad* (Ballarat, 1916); *Light*, June 1971, p 25; *Footprints*, 2, no 7, July 1975, p 4; *T&CJ*, 11 Aug 1894, 22 Sept 1915; *Advocate* (Melb), 27 May, 10 June 1905, 18, 25 Sept, 11 Dec 1915; *Argus*, 17, 22 Sept 1915; *Australasian*, 25 Sept 1915; J. Higgins–Bishop of Christchurch, 25 April 1905 (MDHC Archives).

FRANCES O'KANE HALE

HIGGS, WILLIAM GUY (1862-1951), printer and politician, was born on 18 January 1862 at Wingham, New South Wales, son of William Guy Higgs, Cornish storekeeper, and his Irish wife Elizabeth, née Gregg. In 1869 the family moved to Parramatta and in 1872 to Orange. Higgs was educated at public schools, but when his Anglican parents settled near a convent school, he attended it, waiting outside while others took religious instruction. At 13 he left school and was apprenticed to the *Western Advocate* at Orange.

Higgs arrived in Sydney as a journeyman printer of 20, worked briefly for the commercial printers, John Sands [q.v.6] & Co., and for the *Daily Telegraph*, then settled in the composing room of the *Sydney Morning Herald* for four years. He joined the New South Wales Typographical Association on 18 March 1882, was elected to the board on 24 July 1886 and on 31 August became its full-time paid secretary. Described as 'a burly well-looking man with a beaming black eye and a nobby head of hair of the same colour', Higgs had inherited from his Celtic forbears a strong religious streak. His Anglican upbringing did little to satisfy it but unionism did. He rapidly became an enthusiastic activist and was said to have coined the expression 'Socialism in our time'. On 18 April 1889 at St Paul's Church of England, Redfern, he married Mary Ann Knight: they had three children.

The following July Higgs resigned as secretary of the union and, with a fellow unionist S. D. Townsend, established the job printing firm Higgs & Townsend in Oxford Street. For three months they published the *Trades and Labour Advocate*, and supported moves on the Trades and Labor Council to found a Labor Party. Higgs was chairman of the first annual conference of the Labor Electoral League in January 1892. In February, having failed the previous year to enter the Legislative Assembly as Labor candidate for South Sydney, he accepted the editorial chair of the *Australian Workman* vacated by 'Dr Oswald Keatinge' [q.v.3, J. J. Crouch]. Twelve months later, disgusted by faction fighting, he resigned and returned to printing on the *Evening News*. Then, in August 1893 when Ernest Blackwell resigned as editor of the *Queensland Worker*, Higgs, who had sworn never again to be a Labor editor, accepted the position. Presented with an illuminated address in Sydney at a public dinner presided over by George Black [q.v.7], he reached Brisbane in mid-August and signed his first leader on 2 September. He later described his term as 'a daily dish of sorrow'. Probably his most useful work for the party in this period was his sustained, intelligent attack on the curious affairs of the Queensland National Bank. He admitted himself that he had not given entire satisfaction—some thought his policy too extreme but he succeeded in enlarging the paper and making it a powerful voice.

Higgs had not lost his political ambitions: in 1895-96 he was a member of the Labor Party's central political executive and in February 1899 he was elected for the North Ward to the Brisbane City Council. Later that year he and Frank McDonnell [q.v.] convincingly won Fortitude Valley in the Legislative Assembly. In March 1901 he became one of the first Queensland senators in the Commonwealth parliament. With a mind described as 'disciplined rather than vivid and original', a reputation as an agitator and conspirator, a voice like 'distilled sorrow' and gifts of cross-examination and dead pan humour, Higgs was an immediate asset to the party and felt at home in its idealistic atmosphere; he became chairman of committees and member of the royal commission on the tariff in 1904. Defeated in 1906 by a State-rights reaction in Queensland, he was temporarily lost but found a living by establishing William Guy Higgs & Co., auctioneers, in Pitt Street, Sydney. In December 1907 he was appointed to represent the Queensland government in securing settlers for Queensland. When the original agreement proved too loose he was appointed director of the Sydney branch of the Queensland Intelligence and Tourist Bureau at £150 a year.

Elected to the House of Representatives for Capricornia in April 1910, Higgs became one of the more respected figures in the party hierarchy. He was among the parliamentary delegation to the coronation of George V and when W. M. Hughes [q.v.] constructed his first cabinet in 1915 Higgs, who two years earlier had challenged Andrew Fisher [q.v.8] for the leadership, was elected by caucus and appointed treasurer. In October 1916 he resigned his portfolio together with the anti-conscription group. When the smoke of conflict died, Higgs found that many old friends had left the party and the rump contained an uncomfortably high proportion of radicals. Once a firebrand himself, he had begun to turn again to religion, taking up Christian Science. Deputy leader from June 1918, he revolted from Labor at last over Hughes's renewed attempts in 1919 to increase Commonwealth powers over industry and commerce. Believing that the proposals were still sound, Higgs urged a 'Yes' vote; the Queensland Central Executive advocated 'No'. At the declaration of the poll in Rockhampton for the general election of December 1919, he denounced the domination of the central executive and declared that, were he able, he would abolish the cast-iron pledge. People, he said, would not be educated to some planks of the party platform for 100 years. He urged coalition with the Country Party. Assailed violently from all over Australia, he was expelled from the party on 15 January 1920. He joined the National Party in September and was defeated as a Nationalist candidate at the 1922 general election.

After his defeat Higgs retired to his home at Kew, Melbourne, and became a Christian Science practitioner. In 1929 he chaired a royal commission on the effect of Feder-

ation on the finances of Western Australi. but gradually sank into obscurity. Seekin; a cause, he came across evidence of ma treatment of mental patients, became an ac tive president of the Society for the Welfar of Mental Patients in 1929, and publishe a *Plea for better treatment of the mentally a flicted* (1931). During World War II he un successfully peddled a scheme for securin; peace by gaining the adherence of German to the Atlantic Charter. He died, a widower at Kew on 11 June 1951 and was cremated His estate was valued for probate at £14 683

J. Hagan, *Printers and politics 1850-1950* (Canb 1966); *V&P* (LA Qld), 1895, 1, p 595, 727; *PL* (Cwlth), 1910, 39, p 6216; *Worker* (Brisb), 26 Aug 1893, 18 Mar, 8, 15 Apr 1899, 2 Mar 1901, 8, 2. Jan 1920; *Street*, 5 Mar 1898; *Punch* (Melb), 6 Ap 1905, 13 Oct 1910, 4 June 1914; *Aust Worker*, 2. Nov 1932, 20 June 1951; NSW Typographica Assn, Minutes (ANU Archives); Industrial Work ers of the World, Correspondence, MS 3516, *and* Boote papers, MS 2070 (NL); Philp papers (Oxley Lib); PRE/A271/347 (QA).

H. J. GIBBNEY

HILDER, JESSE JEWHURST (1881 1916), artist, was born on 23 July 1881 at Too woomba, Queensland, fourth son and eighth child of Henry Hilder, a Sussex-born engine driver, and his Indian-born wife Elizabeth née Hall. His father had reached Queens land with his family in the *Gauntlet* in 1875 all were musical. Jesse attended the Too woomba North State School until in 1890 the family moved to Brisbane, when he went to Fortitude Valley State School and to Brisbane Grammar School on a three-year scholarship. He had already developed a keen interest in drawing and painting, encouraged by the architect T. H. Addison and artist Walter Jenner [q.v.].

In 1898 Hilder entered the Brisbane branch of the Bank of New South Wales; he was transferred to Goulburn, New South Wales, in February 1901 and to Bega in June 1902. A shy lad, he found at Bega a congenial circle of friends, and made his first sales; here the first signs of his pulmonary illness appeared.

Transferred to the Waverley branch in April 1904, Hilder contacted Dr Moffit who encouraged him in the use of colour. He began to frequent the National Art Gallery of New South Wales, particularly admiring the work of Streeton, Sydney Long [qq.v.] and J. W. Tristram. At Waverley he met Fred Leist [q.v.] who advised him to show some of his water-colours to Julian Ashton [q.v.7], who was impressed. Hilder began to study at Ashton's late afternoon classes, giving the name of 'Joyce' for fear that the bank would disapprove of his artistic interests; similarly, he signed as 'Anthony Hood' on some of his paintings about 1905. Through Ashton's Hilder made a few friends who eventually helped to establish his reputation: Sydney Ure Smith, Bertram Stevens [qq.v.] and Harry Julius. However Hilder was proud and touchy; his friendships were troubled by his extreme sensitivity.

In March 1906 he moved to head office at Sydney, then to the William Street branch; he became very ill, learning for the first time of his tuberculosis. The remainder of Hilder's life was a search for a dry, congenial climate. He first exhibited at the Society of Artists, Sydney, in 1907 where his work made quite a sensation; Streeton hailed him as a genius. Illness dogged Hilder and, on leave, he stayed for a time with a school teacher named McCoy, of Dumaresq, near Armidale. He slept in a tent and spent much of the day in the open, reading, walking, sketching. He quarrelled with McCoy, then entered the Queen Victoria Home for Consumptives at Wentworth Falls. Somewhat restored to health, he was transferred to Young, and sent fourteen water-colours to the Society of Artists' exhibition (1908). All were sold.

In Sydney on 28 April 1909 he married Phyllis Meadmore. Encouraged by her, and with nine months salary, he began life as a full-time professional artist. They rented a house at Lawson in the Blue Mountains, but in September moved to Parramatta, where their first son was born. The 1909 Society of Artists' exhibition brought disappointment: only five paintings sold. The prospect was desperate, but a Sydney dealer A. W. Albers took charge of his unsold paintings and by the end of the year sales totalled £200. Hilder bought himself a pony and trap to extend his range of sketching sites. From mid-1911 his work began to sell steadily and increase in value. The family moved to Ryde, where they lived until July 1912, then to Inglewood, near Hornsby. Between increasing bouts of illness Hilder continued to paint and made many sketching trips: to Valley Heights (1911), Berowra and Lake Macquarie (1913), and Dora Creek (1915). In the previous year W. H. Gill arranged an exhibition for Hilder in Melbourne. He died of pulmonary tuberculosis at Inglewood on 10 April 1916 and was buried in the Anglican section of Rookwood cemetery. He was survived by his wife and two sons.

Hilder's work is small in scale but deep in feeling. It may be compared with the poems of his contemporary John Shaw Neilson [q.v.] in its purity and transparence. He gave to the subjects and themes of the public art of the Heidelberg School its purest, most subjective and most lyrical expression; his work is haunted by a pathos that, even in bright sunlight, covers all things seen and experienced, with a tremulous vision of mortality. In 1916 Ure Smith published a tribute, *J.J. Hilder watercolourist*, his first success in colour printing; the proceeds were given to Mrs Hilder.

S. Ure Smith and B. Stevens (ed), *The art of J. J. Hilder* (Syd, 1918); B. Hilder (ed), *The heritage of J. J. Hilder* (Syd, 1966); Qld Art Gallery, *Jesse Jewhurst Hilder: anniversary exhibition* (Brisb, 1966).
BERNARD SMITH

HILL, ALFRED FRANCIS (1870-1960), musician, was born on 16 December 1870 at Richmond, Melbourne, sixth son of Charles Hill, hatter, and his wife Eliza Ann, née Hulbert, both born at Bristol, England. In 1872 the family moved to Auckland, New Zealand, and from 1875 lived in Wellington, where Alfred attended Thorndon School. His father, a talented amateur violist, encouraged his children's musical abilities—at 9 Alfred played the cornet in Martin Simonsen's opera company, and toured New Zealand as first violin with Charles Harding's Grand Opera Company in 1884. With his elder brother John he studied in 1887-91 at the Royal Conservatorium of Music, Leipzig, Germany, under Gustav Schreck, Hans Sitt and Oscar Paul. He won the Helbig prize and played the violin with the Gewandhaus Orchestra under such conductors as Brahms, Grieg, Tchaikovsky and Max Bruch. While Hill was a student his *Scotch sonata* and other works were published in Europe.

Returning to Wellington, Hill was active as a violin pedagogue, recitalist, chamber music performer, but principally as conductor of choirs and orchestras, including the Wellington Orchestral Society. His Maori cantata *Hinemoa*, with words by Arthur Adams [q.v.7], was performed at the Wellington Industrial Exhibition in 1896. He toured New Zealand with the Belgian violinist Ovide Musin and in March 1897 they opened in Sydney. Stranded there, Hill began teaching; he conducted the Sydney Liedertafel (in 1898-1902) and the Great Synagogue choir and played in Henri Staell's quartet. At St George's Anglican Church, Paddington, he had married a New Zealander Sarah Brownhill Booth on 6 October 1897; they gave their children the Wagnerian names Isolde, Tristan and Elsa.

On 1 January 1901 Hill conducted the Commonwealth Celebrations choir of 11 000 voices with ten brass bands. Next year he returned to New Zealand to write an opera, *Tapu, or a tale of a Maori pah*, which featured a visiting Australian politician modelled on (Sir) George Reid [q.v.], first staged in Wellington on 17 February 1903. In August Hill was back in Sydney conducting for J. C. Williamson [q.v.6], whose Royal Comic Opera Company performed *Tapu* next year in Sydney, Brisbane and Melbourne. At the end of 1904 he became conductor of the Auckland Orchestral Society and the Auckland Liedertafel, and meanwhile wrote another opera, *A Moorish maid, or queen of the Riffs*, performed in Sydney in 1906 with Hill as musical director.

In July Hill was invited to recruit and direct a professional orchestra for the New Zealand International Exhibition of Arts and Crafts at Christchurch; he also composed an ode for the opening. In 1907 the orchestra toured New Zealand before being disbanded. Serious illness prevented him from going to London in 1909 to produce *A Moorish maid* there. Williamson engaged him as deputy to Hazon [q.v.] for the Australasian tour of *Madam Butterfly* in 1910. Settling in Sydney in 1911, Hill became principal of the Austral Orchestral College and played the viola in Cyril Monk's [q.v.] Austral String Quartet (which lasted until 1917), and also conducted the Sydney Amateur Orchestral Society in 1912-14.

In the first phase of his creativity Hill wrote mainly for the theatre, including the comic operas *The whipping boy* (1893) and *Lady Dolly* (1900). With Fritz Hart [q.v.] he tried to create an Australian operatic tradition and founded the short-lived Australian Opera League (1913-14), which in 1914 presented in Sydney and Melbourne Hill's *Giovanni* and Hart's *Pierrette*, although neither was on an Australian theme. In 1913 Hill was a founder of the Sydney Repertory Theatre Society (for which he wrote three one-act plays under a Maori pseudonym, 'Arapeta Hia', in 1914) and was a foundation council-member (later president) of the Musical Association of New South Wales. With David Souter [q.v.] as librettist, he wrote *The rajah of Shivapore* (performed in 1917), *Auster* (staged in 1922) and in 1923 set to music Hugh McCrae's [q.v.] poem *The ship of heaven* (staged in 1933). Unfortunately the librettos for his operas never reached the standard of his music.

Hill's instinctive love of Maori music and legends inspired some of his most notable works—the cantata, *Hinemoa*; the operas, *Tapu* and *Teora* (1913); the *Maori symphony* (1896); and many songs including 'Waiata Poi' (made famous by Peter Dawson and Ada Crossley [qq.v.8] among others). He recorded Maori music and for many years tried to found an institute of Maori studies at Rotorua and worked for a New Zealand conservatorium of music. Meanwhile in 1913 Hill had been appointed to the advisory committee for the establishment of the New South Wales State Conservatorium of Music, and on 18 January 1916 became first professor of theory and composition—over the years his distinguished pupils included Roy Agnew, F. M. and Bryce Carter [qq.v.7] Monk and John Antill. The early years at the conservatorium under Henri Verbrugghen [q.v.] were inspiring. In 1916-25 Hill was conductor for the Royal Sydney Apollo Club and was deputy conductor of the New South Wales State Orchestra in 1919-22. From 1924 he played in the new conservatorium quartet.

In May 1921 Hill had divorced his wife and on 1 October, at Mosman Registry Office, married one of his ex-students Mirrie Irma Solomon, a musician and composer teaching at the conservatorium; they lived at Mosman. Hill visited the United States of America and Britain in 1926, seeking publishers. He also conducted his own works for the Minneapolis Symphony Orchestra, now under Verbrugghen, and for Sir Dan Godfrey's Bournemouth Municipal Orchestra in England.

Between 1924 and 1938 Hill concentrated upon creating string quartets and concertos for piano, violin, viola, French horn and trumpet. He was a much practised chamber musician and his part-writing is characterized by its idiomatic assurance and easy execution. His best-known concert work is the *Viola concerto* (1940): the soloist is offered an exceptionally graceful part, emphasizing both the lyrical and virtuoso personality of the instrument.

According to Roland Foster [q.v.8] Hill was 'a temperamental virile musician who would have fitted perfectly into the scheme of Alfred de Musset's 'La Vie Bohême' and been thoroughly in his element at the London Savage Club'. A forceful and outspoken member of the conservatorium staff, Hill was passed over twice in the appointment of a director. He resigned at the end of 1934 because of differences with the new director Edgar Bainton [q.v.7]. In 1935 he opened the Alfred Hill Academy of Music, but it closed in January 1937. In the early 1930s he had conducted the Sydney Professional Symphony Orchestra; he was sometime president of the Sydney centre of the British (and International) Music Society and in 1940 first president of the New South Wales Guild of Composers.

Devoting all his time to composing from 1937, Hill revised earlier chamber music pieces to create twelve symphonies. Bubbling with energy in his old age, he was 'a short, alert man with a backswept thatch of iron hair and brown eyes'. He now clipped his once-swaggering waxed moustache. His works were better known overseas than in

Australia, but in February 1946 Henry Krips conducted the Sydney Symphony Orchestra in an entire programme of Hill's works including the *Life symphony* (1941). Neville Cardus commented that Hill was 'still the most substantial and comprehensively cultivated of Australia's composers'. In September 1953 he was guest conductor for the first performance of his *Australia symphony in B minor* by the Sydney Symphony Orchestra. He was appointed O.B.E. in 1953 and C.M.G. in 1960.

Hill died in hospital in Sydney on 30 October 1960 and was cremated. He was survived by his second wife and by a son and two daughters of his first marriage. His daughter Isolde was well known as a singer. Hill was equipped with such an assured technical facility that his speed of composition would have frequently defied rigorous self-criticism—his *oeuvres* totalled more than 500. He adopted the conservative and professional stance of Leipzig romanticism, thereafter adapting Celtic, Maori and even Aboriginal musical folk-lore to meet its traditions and requirements. His major works bespeak the influence of his teachers, in particular the violin and viola concertos which recall works for the same medium by Hans Sitt. His string quartets in form and execution reveal a strong stylistic kinship to central and northern European mainstream works in the genre by Mendelssohn, Schumann, Gade, Gernsheim, Brahms and Dvořák. His music thus established new standards in technical accomplishment and professionalism and he can be regarded as an innovator of the existing Victorian tradition. This marked an historically significant advance in Australian musical composition at the start of the twentieth century.

Syd Amateur Orchestral Soc, *Prospectus* (Syd, 1913); A. D. McCredie, *Musical composition in Australia* and *Catalogue of 46 Australian composers and selected works* (Canb, 1969); A. D. McCredie, 'Alfred Hill (1870-1960)' in F. Callaway and D. Tunley (eds), *Australian composition in the twentieth century* (Melb, 1978); J. M. Thomson, *A distant music: the life and times of Alfred Hill* (Auckland, 1980); *Aust Musical News*, 1 May 1931; *People* (Syd), 30 Aug 1950; A. D. McCredie, 'Alfred Hill (1870-1960): some backgrounds and perspectives for an historical edition miscellanea musicologica', *Adelaide Studies in Musicology*, 3 (1968); *SMH*, 18 Dec 1925, 9 Oct 1933, 16 Dec 1950, 12 Dec 1959, 31 Oct 1960; A.B.C. Archives (Syd); A. Hill papers (ML) *and* (NSW State Conservatorium of Music); Hill family papers (Alexander Turnbull Lib, Well).   ANDREW D. McCREDIE

HILL, CLEMENT (1877-1945), cricketer, was born on 18 March 1877 in Adelaide, South Australia, third son in a family of six-teen children of Henry John Hill [q.v.4] and his wife Rebecca Eliza, née Saunders. His father and six of his brothers played cricket for South Australia and a sister played in an Adelaide ladies' team. Clem played football (for South Adelaide and the State), tennis, golf and bowls, but his fame in cricket eclipsed all else. A. G. Moyes assessed him as 'one of Australia's four greatest batsmen' with Victor Trumper, Charles Macartney [qq.v.] and Don Bradman: 'a superb player, the finest left-hander ever ... shortish, thickset, powerful ... swift on his feet, a master of attack and of defence'.

Educated at Prince Alfred College, Hill played his first intercollegiate match at 13, 'keeping wicket and batting at number ten'. He scored 360 retired in the annual match against The Collegiate School of St Peter in 1893—a schoolboy record which bettered Joe Darling's [q.v.8] and which still stands. At 17 he was named in the South Australian team and scored 155 against the Englishmen. He was included in the Australian side to tour England in 1896 and remained a regular selection in the national team until 1912.

During his first-class career Hill scored 17 216 runs at an average of 43.47 and made 45 centuries and many nineties. He played 49 Tests for Australia (3412 runs at an average of 39.21), captaining the team in the 1910-11 and 1911-12 series. His best innings was probably in the fourth Test of the 1897-98 series: Australia was 6 for 58 when Hill and Hugh Trumble [q.v.] made an unbeaten seventh wicket partnership of 165 to win the match. Hill was also a brilliant fieldsman and in the Old Trafford Test of 1902 took what many cricket historians consider to be the finest catch ever.

Although reputed to be 'of a jolly disposition', during the 1911-12 series he was involved in a 'punch-up' with fellow selector Peter McAlister over the selection of players and the right of the newly formed Australian Board of Control for International Cricket Matches to appoint a manager, six senior players having unsuccessfully demanded a manager elected from and by the players. Hill blackened McAlister's eye at the widely publicized selectors' meeting and the six— Hill, Warwick Armstrong [q.v.7], Trumper, Albert Cotter [q.v.8], Vernon Ransford [q.v.] and Hanson Carter— declined to tour with the team to England. For Hill it was virtually the end of a splendid career: after the war he played again, briefly, for South Australia.

Hill had served an engineering apprenticeship in the government workshops at Islington but on retirement he became a stipendiary steward to the South Australian Jockey Club and later a handicapper. In 1937 he moved to Melbourne as handicapper to the Victoria Amateur Turf Club. He resigned in 1943 because of ill health and became a handicapper for the Geelong Racing Club. He died of heart disease on 5 September 1945 in Melbourne. His wife Florence Mary Clewer, née Hart, whom he had married on 17 January 1905 at Launceston, Tasmania, had died in 1938 and a son had died in infancy. Two daughters survived him. He was buried in North Road cemetery, Adelaide.

A. G. Moyes, *Australian cricket* (Syd, 1959); S. Downer, *100 not out* (Adel, 1972); C. Martin-Jenkins, *The complete who's who of Test cricketers* (Adel, 1980); *Parade*, Mar 1960; *T&CJ*, 29 Jan 1908; *Advertiser* (Adel), 6 Sept 1945; *Daily Mirror*, 8 Sept 1978.   JOHN A. DALY

HILL, JAMES PETER (1873-1954), embryologist, was born on 21 February 1873 at Kennoway, Fifeshire, Scotland, younger son of John Hill, a prominent farmer and cattle breeder, and his wife Catherine Campbell, née McInroy. Educated at the Kennoway village school and in Edinburgh at the Royal High School and Heriot-Watt College, in 1889 he entered the University of Edinburgh (B.Sc., 1898; D.Sc., 1903). In 1891-92 he studied at the Royal College of Science, London, under G. B. Howes, who recommended him as a demonstrator to Professor W. A. Haswell [q.v.] at the University of Sydney. With his degree incomplete, Hill sailed for Sydney in August 1892. In Sydney he was stimulated by such part-time lecturers in the medical school as (Sir) Alexander MacCormick and (Sir) Charles Martin [qq.v.] and especially by Professor J. T. Wilson [q.v.], with whom he lived for about five years.

Elected a fellow of the Linnean Society of London in 1895, Hill visited Edinburgh in 1897-98 where he graduated in 1898 and received scholarships and grants which assisted his work on monotremes in Sydney. On a brief visit to London he married Marjorie Marshall Forrester (d. 1953) at Finchley on 6 January 1900; they returned to Sydney and in 1904 he became lecturer in embryology. In 1906 he was awarded the Mueller [q.v.5] medal of the Australasian Association for the Advancement of Science. That year he was appointed to the Jodrell chair of zoology and anatomy at University College, London. Here he did more than his fair share of teaching, but was rewarded by the enthusiasm he generated in his students. (Sir) Grafton Elliot Smith [q.v.], head of the department of anatomy, arranged for Rockefeller money to endow a personal chair of embryology and his-

tology for Hill, to which he was appointed in 1921. Although it was intended as a research position, Hill continued to teach, especially research students. He retired in 1938 but continued to work in the department of anatomy and at home until 1954. Elected in 1913 to the Royal Society, London, he had served on its council in 1925-27 and was its Darwin medallist in 1940. He also received honorary doctorates of science from Trinity College, Dublin (1925) and the Queen's University of Belfast (1938); he was a fellow of the Zoological Society of London, and an honorary member of many societies including the Royal and Linnean societies of New South Wales.

While in Australia Hill had published nineteen articles. His interest in monotremes and marsupials dates from a paper, with Martin, on a platypus embryo, published in 1895 in the *Proceedings* of the local Linnean Society. His interest was continued in eight other Sydney publications and eighteen in London, the last appearing posthumously in 1955. Some of his papers were short, but others were major works, such as his article with T. T. Flynn [q.v.8] on 'The Development of the Monotremata. IV.' in the *Transactions* of the Zoological Society, London, in 1939. Hill's other embryological work was on the development of eutherian mammals, especially primates. One of his peers, G. R. de Beer, claimed that Hill had 'laid the foundations of our knowledge of the development of the Monotremes and Marsupials . . . which constitutes a contribution to science of permanent and inestimable value'. Although noted for his detailed and accurate descriptions, he was diffident in contributing to public discussion. He enjoyed the camaraderie of marsupial collecting trips in Australia and Brazil. At home he was a keen golfer.

Hill died at his home at Finchley, London, on 24 May 1954 and was survived by two daughters; his only son died in Sarawak in 1935. Hill's estate in New South Wales was valued for probate at £6293, and in England £24 152.

Obituary Notices of Fellows of the Roy Soc, 2 (Jan, 1938), no 6, p 323, 6 (Nov, 1949), no 18, p 643; *Journal of Anatomy* (Lond), 82 (1948), pp 3, 5; *Biographical Memoirs of Fellows of Roy Soc*, 1 (1955), p 101, and for publications.   K. W. CLELAND

HILL, KATE (1859-1933), nurse, was born on 7 May 1859 at Walsall, Staffordshire, England, daughter of Joseph Hill, journeyman, and his wife Mary, née Evans. Orphaned early, she lived with her sister

Emily Louisa and her brother-in-law Joseph William Coudrey, foundry-owner of Walsall. Kate was influenced by the work of Dorothy Wyndlow Pattison, Sister Dora of an Anglican nursing community, especially by her cool care of injured miners. In 1879, following a slump in the pig-iron industries, the Coudreys and Kate migrated to Adelaide with their friend Alice Tibbitts.

In 1883 Kate Hill was admitted as a probationer to the Adelaide Children's Hospital where her promotion was rapid. Nurses were claiming that training was farcical and in 1885 control of the hospital was taken over by a house surgeon. Hill became head nurse in 1887. Two years later she left for fifteen months to be head nurse at the Private Hospital, Wakefield Street, owned by Alice Tibbitts. On her return to the Children's Hospital in 1891 Hill became superintendent of nurses (the first trained nurse appointed as matron since 1885). Her span embraced 'The halcyon years', 1893-99, of the hospital: it saw advances in medicine, the gift of a new wing by John Howard Angas [q.v.3], and the beginning of the upper classes' meticulously organized fundraising activities. Hill was devoted to her staff, showing 'zeal, fidelity, diligence and kindness' and an 'ability to educate and command without alienating the sympathies of her subordinates'.

She resigned in 1902 to become a partner, and soon owner, of Tibbitts's hospital: to own a private hospital was highly regarded. This hospital had been the first private training school in the State; Hill continued the same thorough nursing, attending most operations and supervising patients' aftercare. In 1905 Dr A. A. Lendon and Dr T. G. Wilson, with Hill as honorary secretary, founded a State branch of the Australian Trained Nurses' Association. She remained on the committee until 1918.

Hill sold her hospital to Sophy Laurence in 1913 and retired, but she remained a life member of the Children's Hospital's board of management. From 1915 she was a council-member of the District Trained Nursing Society and became an honorary life member in 1929.

Kate Hill had a strong face which inspired confidence; a quietly spoken woman who collected beautiful furniture, she tried to learn something new each day. She visited England in 1914 and 1924. A leader in her family, she trained several nieces at her hospital; they inherited most of her estate, valued for probate at £18 742. She was an active Baptist. On 2 February 1933 she died at Woodside of respiratory disease and was buried in Mitcham cemetery. The Kate Hill honour board was established by the Adelaide Children's Hospital Nurses' Association in 1939; on it is inscribed the name of each year's outstanding student.

SA Trained Nurses' Centenary Cttee, *Nursing in South Australia* . . . (Adel, 1939); M. Barbalet, *The Adelaide Children's Hospital, 1876-1976* (Adel, 1975); *A'sian Nurses' J*, 15 Apr 1933; *Chronicle* (Adel), 16 Feb 1933; J. W. Coudrey, Diary (D5516 (L), SAA).   JOYCE GIBBERD

HILL, LIONEL LAUGHTON (1881-1963), premier, was born on 14 May 1881 at Victoria Square, Adelaide, son of Thomas Henry Hill, farmer, and his wife Gertrude, née Hurst. He was educated until 12 at Maitland and at Adelaide public schools. 'Slogger' Hill played league football, representing the State, and also excelled at other sports. He worked first at a city chaff merchant's and then at the government's railway workshops. In 1901-14 Hill was secretary-treasurer of the Boilermakers' Assistants' Union; he attended business college at night to equip himself for whitecollar work, and became secretary of the State branch of the Australian Tramway Employees' Association in 1910-24 and the union's federal president in 1912-24. On 18 April 1908 he had married Elma Evelyn Attrill, a dressmaker, in Holy Trinity Church.

In 1915 Hill entered the House of Assembly as the Labor member for East Torrens. Next year he became president of the Anti-Conscription Council. In 1917 he resigned his seat to contest unsuccessfully the Senate election, but next year won the State seat of Port Pirie. He was president of the party's State branch in 1917-18. Although a slow thinker and unimpressive orator, with the election of a Labor government in 1924 Hill became commissioner of public works, and minister of education and industry in John Gunn's [q.v.] ministry. When Gunn resigned in August 1926 Hill became premier, treasurer and minister of education. Little important legislation was passed. Next April the Liberals regained office under (Sir) Richard Butler [q.v.7].

In April 1930 Hill led Labor in a runaway electoral victory and became premier and treasurer again. Butler considered his defeat no bad thing. The Depression had already deepened dramatically and the government was in a parlous financial situation. Repayment of interest on overseas borrowings of the 1920s for public works absorbed nearly half the State's 1930-31 income. In such a situation Hill endorsed the deflationary economic approach of the visiting Bank of England adviser, Sir Otto Niemeyer. The subsequent Premiers' Plan of June 1931 involved reductions in government spending, public works and wages, and was opposed by most of the labour movement.

Hill was seen as having little grasp of economics. He was guided by leading Adelaide businessmen and Governor Sir Alexander Hore-Ruthven [q.v. Gowrie] rather than by party advisers. (Sir) Lloyd Dumas, editor of the *Advertiser*, (Sir) Walter Young [q.v.] and other businessmen accompanied him to the premiers' conferences of 1930 and 1931. Hill's alliance with Dumas dismayed the Labor Party.

Within six months of being elected the government was at loggerheads with the Trades and Labor Council and the party. Before the election Hill had promised 'Work for the Workless; Land for the Landless and Equitable Taxation for all', but now he seemed to many supporters to have little commitment to Labor principles.

The government staggered from crisis to crisis. Long-running unrest between the shipping companies and the Waterside Workers' Federation had resulted in 1929 in the introduction of volunteer labour backed by a citizens' militia. The Trades Hall urged Hill to remove the 'scabs'. Instead, in September 1930, he passed a Public Safety Preservation Act which gave the police extraordinary powers. On the advice of the commissioner of police, Brigadier Leane [q.v.], Hill stated that the purpose was to 'smash Communism'.

Unemployment was rising, eventually to 35 per cent in 1932. The government had established the Unemployment Relief Council but the relief was meagre and administered as humiliating food ration tickets. Then, as a further economy, beef was removed from the rations and replaced by inferior mutton. This led to the largest demonstration of the Depression in Adelaide. The 'Beef Riot' of 9 January 1931 was a watershed in the deterioration of relations between the government and the unemployed, who marched to the Treasury to protest. Hill's refusal to see them ignited a battle between police and demonstrators.

As early as 10 July 1930 the A.L.P. State Council had carried a motion viewing with grave concern Hill's economic policy. Eventually in August 1931 it expelled him and his cabinet from the party for supporting the Premiers' Plan. Hill remained premier and leader of an unofficial Parliamentary Labor Party minority government, supported by the Opposition.

Hill and others attempted to form a 'national' government, a move endorsed by some Adelaide businessmen and by the national backers of the United Australia Party, who favoured having a former Labor premier leading a conservative coalition. Others within the two parties were scepti-

cal: some of Hill's colleagues disliked associating with the Opposition, thereby removing any chance of returning to the A.L.P The Liberal leaders, while ostensibly considering an alliance, despised Hill and believed they would win the following electior with or without him.

The unofficial agreement between Hil and the newly formed Liberal and Country League, reached in August 1932, collapsec and the L.C.L. planned to run for the coming election alone. Meanwhile the governmen continued ineffectually. Hill was unable to arrange his pre-selection in Port Pirie, ther Burra, then East Torrens, and also quar relled with cabinet. So, on 8 February 1933 with his 'bullocking way of pushing through difficulties', he arranged to be appointec agent-general in London. He forced excep tionally generous financial terms upon cabi net, resigned the premiership on 13 Febru ary and departed for London. R. S. Richard [q.v.] briefly succeeded him as premier.

In April the P.L.P. and A.L.P. fared badly in the election: Butler's return as premier began thirty-two years of L.C.L. govern ment. On 10 April the auditor-general founc that £1077 paid to Hill was 'not legally justi fied' and in the crown solicitor's opinion it was the government's 'constitutional duty to recover it. The scandal exercised parlia ment until October: Hill repaid the money Then complaints about his administratior of the London office began. Hill was askec to resign and did so in August 1934, receiv ing £4300 compensation.

In 1935 Hill returned home, keen to re enter politics for the L.C.L. In 1936-44 having been appointed by the Lyons [q.v. government, he chaired in Sydney the Aus tralian Capital Territory's Industrial Boarc at £552 a year. He subsequently conductec a business in Sydney until 1958 when he re turned to Adelaide. In 1961 he was electec to the Kensington and Norwood council. Hil died on 19 March 1963, survived by his wife daughter and son, and was buried in West Terrace cemetery. His estate was sworn foi probate at £1785.

L. Dumas, *The story of a full life* (Melb, 1969) C. R. Broomhill, *Unemployed workers: a social his tory of the great Depression in Adelaide* (Brisb 1978); *PD* (SA), 1933, 1934; *To-day* (Melb), 1 Dec 1932; *Univ Studies in History*, 4 (1963-64), no 2 *Labour Hist*, 1970, no 17 *and* 1976, no 31; *Advertiser* (Adel), 29 Mar 1915, 13 Sept 1917, 19, 24 Aug 1926 10 May 1933, 20 Mar 1963; *Herald* (Melb), 25 Jar 1918, 8 Sept 1930, 15 Dec 1932; *News* (Adel), 7 Apr 1924; *SMH*, 14 Sept 1929, 23 Jan 1935; *Mail* (Adel) 25 Jan 1958; R. Pettman, Factionalism in the A.L.P.: a South Australian case study, 1930-33 (B.A. Hons thesis, Univ Adel, 1967); S. R. Whit ford, An autobiography (SAA).

RAY BROOMHILL

HILL, THOMAS (1867-1944), engineer, was born on 6 June 1867 at Wednesbury, Staffordshire, England, son of James Hill, bricklayer, and his wife Hannah, née Hawkins. Educated at the Grammar School, Walsall, he went to the United States of America at 16 before migrating to Victoria in February 1886. He became a cadet with Thomas Fender, district surveyor at Geelong, then worked at Collingwood and in the Croajingalong district. From about 1890 he was employed by the Department of Victorian Water Supply. He obtained a surveyor's certificate in 1894. In January 1896 he joined the Melbourne and Metropolitan Board of Works as a draughtsman; he was promoted to surveyor's assistant next year and engineering assistant in 1898. On 15 April 1897 at Albert Park he married Annie Mabel Thompson with Anglican rites.

In 1902 Hill joined the newly formed Commonwealth Department of Home Affairs as a draughtsman in the public works branch, Victoria. Quickly promoted, he became works director for Victoria in 1908 and in 1914 engineer in the central administration. His activities extended to the projected Federal capital at Canberra—a site of which he personally disapproved, preferring Albury. He was on the board which reported on the 'premiated' designs for the city and was concerned with the earliest engineering works, including the Cotter dam which he later claimed to have designed. Although closely questioned in 1916 and 1917 by the commission investigating Burley Griffin's [q.v.] complaints of obstruction in the implementation of his plan for Canberra, Hill himself was not criticized. He became chief engineer of the department (now Works and Railways) in 1923 and visited the United States and England in 1927 to report on road construction and maintenance before the Federal Aid Roads Act (1931) was framed. In 1929 he was made director-general of works in Canberra. He returned to his family in Melbourne in September 1931 for furlough before his official retirement in June 1932.

From February 1918 Hill was deputy commissioner under the River Murray Waters Act (1915). An excellent chairman, he presided over meetings which approved the Hume and Lake Victoria reservoirs and the locks and weirs which made 600 miles (966 km) of the River Murray navigable, as well as the Euston, Torrumbarry and Yarrawonga weirs, and the important barrages at the Murray mouth. His last concern was the project to enlarge the Hume reservoir to two million acre feet (2 467 000 megalitres), and on his deathbed he tried to ensure that his successor should be someone not opposed to the scheme.

Hill was a member from 1896 and a past president of the Victorian Institute of Surveyors and a life member of the Victorian Institute of Engineers, having joined in 1897 and held the presidency in 1925-26. His membership of the Victorian branch of the Institute of Municipal Engineers entitled him in 1926 to associate membership of the Institution of Engineers, Australia; he became a member in 1930. He was appointed O.B.E. in 1928. A sound administrator, Hill is remembered as being friendly but discreet, tall, well built and strong even in his declining years, with a good head for whisky. He died on 12 May 1944 in Melbourne, and was cremated. His wife had died the previous year; his three sons survived him.

State Rivers and Water Supply Com, *Pioneers of Victorian irrigation*, J. N. Churchyard comp (Melb, 1958); Reports, River Murray Commission, *PP* (Cwlth, *and* Vic), 1917-18 to 1944-45; *Argus*, 12 Aug 1927, 5 Sept 1931, 15 May 1944; *Age*, 15 May 1944; family information; information from Sir L. R. East, Mt Waverley, Melb.

RONALD McNICOLL

HILL, WILLIAM CALDWELL (1866-1939), farmer and politician, was born on 14 April 1866 at Burnt Creek, near Dunolly, Victoria, son of English parents John Hill and his wife Sarah, née Baker. When the Dunolly flour-mill, established by John Hill and his elder brother Joseph, was burnt down the Hills moved to pioneer a forest selection at Stradbroke, Gippsland, where William attended part-time school. At 21 he joined the clerical division of the Victorian Railways. His mother, who could not read or write, had impressed the value of education upon her family and while serving as stationmaster at Elphinstone he walked four miles to Castlemaine three times a week to attend evening classes. On 23 March 1892 at a Wesleyan ceremony at Chewton he married Lucy Isabella, daughter of Edward Shields, a tannery-owner who had been mayor of Chewton Borough. On Shields's death Hill left his position as assistant stationmaster at Ascot Vale to manage the Chewton tannery. A keen Rechabite, he was also secretary of the Castlemaine Rifle Clubs' Union and was on the Chewton Borough Council in 1900-06.

In 1906 the Closer Settlement Board purchased David Mitchell's [q.v.5] Colbinabbin estate for subdivision for wheat and sheep-farming. Hill and his wife selected blocks in 1908. A large, strong, rather stern and austere yet affectionate man who demanded high standards of himself and his family, William not only farmed successfully but worked to improve the lot of settlers; he was secretary of the Colbinabbin Progress Association and supported the Church of England on the settlement.

In 1915, suspecting that wheat-merchants were conniving with the government to decrease the price paid to farmers for wheat pooled to alleviate wartime shipping problems, angry settlers formed a Wheat Pool Vigilance Committee and elected Hill secretary. In 1916-19 Hill was founding president of the Victorian Farmers' Union, pledged to send farmers to Federal and State parliaments. He was also a delegate to the Australian Farmers' Federal Organization formed in 1916, a growers' representative on the Australian Wheat Board (1919), a member of the advisory council of the Victorian Wheat Commission and chairman of directors of the Farmers' Advocate Newspaper Co. During this period he led a movement to supply cheaper superphosphate to farmers: in 1919, as chairman of directors of the Phosphate Co-operative Co. of Australia Ltd, an office he held until his death, he defied proprietary companies and established a fertilizer works on the Geelong waterfront. An often-quoted example of farmer co-operation, the works producing Pivot fertilizers developed into reputedly the largest in the Southern hemisphere. Faith in voluntary farmer co-operation and an encyclopaedic yet practical knowledge of the wheat industry enabled Hill to launch the Victorian Wheat-Growers' Corporation Ltd in 1921; he was first chairman and a director until his death.

Hill entered Federal parliament in September 1919 after winning the Echuca by-election as a V.F.U. candidate. He was active in the founding of the Country Party in 1920. In parliament he took a typical middle-of-the-road Country Party stance: he refused to co-operate with the Hughes [q.v.] government, but accepted the portfolio of works and railways when P. G. Stewart [q.v.] resigned as a protest against the electoral pact with the Bruce [q.v.7] government in August 1924. Both his national vision and his impatience to get things done for country people are reflected in his four major ministerial achievements: the standardization of the railway gauges by construction of the line from Kyogle, New South Wales, to South Brisbane; the construction of the rail line from Oodnadatta, South Australia, to Alice Springs in pursuit of the dream of a north-south transcontinental line; the introduction of a Federal aid road scheme to subsidize States for highway construction; and the building of the Hume Weir, which he pursued as president of the River Murray Water Commission.

By 1928 signs of depression made development schemes unpopular; Hill was dropped from cabinet in favour of W. G. Gibson [q.v.8]. Next year he left work on the farm to his sons and moved to Ivanhoe, Melbourne. He retired from parliament in 1934, refusing to sign a pledge to vote according to the will of the Victorian Country Party, which he now considered unacceptably radical. (Sir) John McEwen, a future leader of the Federal Country Party, filled his place as member for Echuca.

Hill died at Nar Nar Goon on 15 November 1939 and was buried in Heidelberg cemetery. He was survived by his wife Bella—the cheerful, capable manager of family and farm over many long parliamentary sessions—and by six children, five of whom remained on the land. His estate was valued for probate at £21 646.

U. R. Ellis, *A history of the Australian Country Party* (Melb, 1963); B. D. Graham, *The formation of the Australian Country Parties* (Canb, 1966); *PD* (Cwlth), 1926, p 479, 1939, pp 1162, 1285; *Farmers Advocate*, 26 Nov 1919; L. G. Lomas, The Western District farmer 1914-27 (Ph.D. thesis, Monash Univ, 1979); information from R. Hill, Bendigo, and C. B. Hill, Colbinabbin, Vic.   L. LOMAS

HILL, WILLIAM DUGUID (1858-1921), festival administrator, was born on 7 January 1858 at Magpie, near Ballarat, Victoria, fourth surviving child of Archibald Hill, baker and riding teacher, and his wife Robine, née Somerville; both parents were Scottish. Hill left Redan State School at an early age. By 1883 he had formed the auctioneering firm of Wicks & Hill; subsequent partnerships were Hill & Paine, Hill & Grose and Hill & Blackman. At St Andrew's Presbyterian Manse, Ballarat, on 13 November 1895, he married Katherine Elizabeth Bloore, daughter of a chemist.

In 1879, while a student at the Central State Night School, Hill and eight others held a meeting at his mother's hotel in South Street, to form the Young Men's General Debating Society, with the intention of 'refining the manners, cultivating the mind and stimulating the intellect' into fitness for community service. Hill was president, then secretary and held this position, which in 1890 became salaried, until his death. As a founder and secretary of the Mutual Improvement Associations' Union in 1882, he first introduced debating contests. Their success and Hill's belief in the educative value of competition led to their continuation by the debating society after the union's collapse in 1889.

By then the South Street Literary and Debating Society, as it was now popularly called, had its own hall seating one thousand. This housed the contests whose expanded programme reflected Hill's interest in music, already evident through his secretaryship of the Liedertafel. By 1891 literary, elocutionary and musical items made up the programme and six years later the first choral items were included. In 1902 Hill brought out from England an eminent musician as adjudicator. By 1906, with the exalted title of Grand National Eisteddfod of Australasia, the annual contests lasted a month and were attracting 2250 entries. Their success can be attributed to the secretary's promotional skills. Public support for South Street, however, was not unanimous: one citizen described it as 'pure theatrical commercialism'. Hill sometimes complained of the widespread indifference to that which made Ballarat 'the Athens of Australia'.

Hill belonged to many civic and charitable organizations. Emphasizing the city's potential as an agricultural and manufacturing centre, he was prominent in the Forward Ballarat movement, was a councillor of the mining and agricultural schools, secretary of the agricultural and pastoral society and founder of Manufacturers' Day and the tourist bureau. From 1905 to 1921 he was councillor for the South Ward of Ballarat City. Elected mayor in 1909, 1916 and 1920, he was the first mayor of Greater Ballarat after the amalgamation of city and town in 1921.

Proud of his Scottish origins, Hill was active in the Caledonian Society and often sported a kilt. He was secretary of St Andrew's Kirk and found time to assist the orphanage, the benevolent asylum and the Red Cross. As recognition for his services to the city, in 1906 James Oddie [q.v.5] commissioned Thomas Price to paint Hill's portrait for the Ballarat Fine Art Gallery. Survived by his wife and two daughters, Hill died on 14 November 1921 and was buried in the new cemetery, Ballarat. Small, with great charm, he was a devoted family man. His favourite activities were gardening and reading: 'I like to read about great men with big ideas . . . Warren Hastings has been my ideal'.

L. A. Blackman, 'A history of the Royal South Street Society of Ballarat', *VHM*, 37 (1966); *Ballarat Courier*, 15 Jan 1908, 15 Nov 1921; *Table Talk*, 16 June 1921.　　　　KIMBERLEY WEBBER

HILLARY, MICHAEL JAMES (1886-1976), public servant and soldier, was born on 20 February 1886 at Carrieton, South Australia, son of Thomas Hillary, farmer, and his wife Annie, née Strickland. Michael was educated at Newman College, Adelaide, then studied at the University of Adelaide in 1912-14. In 1909 he joined the Commonwealth Treasury as a clerk. He was a member (later fellow) of the Australian Society of Accountants.

Hillary was commissioned lieutenant (provisional) in the 77th Infantry Battalion, Australian Military Forces, on 1 March 1916. In August he enlisted in the Australian Imperial Force as a second lieutenant and embarked from Melbourne on 22 August with the 4th Reinforcements for the 1st Australian Wireless Signal Squadron. Promoted lieutenant in October, he disembarked at Basra on the Persian Gulf and served in Mesopotamia until October 1918 with the small Australian and New Zealand contingent sent to assist British and Indian units in protecting Anglo-Persian oil supplies. In January 1918 Hillary was promoted temporary captain (confirmed in July). Maintaining the communication links was very arduous because of the bulkiness of the radio equipment and the inhospitable terrain and climate. In February Hillary was granted four months leave to Australia. He rejoined his unit in September and returned to Australia in April 1919. He had been mentioned in dispatches in August 1917 and June 1919, was awarded the Distinguished Service Order in September 1917, and was appointed O.B.E. in June 1919 shortly before his demobilization. In 1921-23 Hillary commanded the 3rd Divisional Signals, A.M.F., retiring with the rank of major.

Back in civilian life he returned to the Treasury, serving as secretary to the War Gratuities Board, then with the war pensions branch of the Repatriation Department. In 1921-22 he was private secretary to Prime Minister W. M. Hughes [q.v.]. He was then transferred to Australia House, London, to collect information for the Australian royal commission on national health and unemployment insurance. In 1925 he joined the Sudan Civil Service as assistant director of accounts. He rose to be auditor-general from 1933 before returning in 1938 to London as head of the administrative division within the Coal Commission and in 1947-54 deputy registrar of the National Coal Board. He settled in London and was honorary secretary of the Sudan Government British Pensioners' Association until 1973.

Hillary had married Edwyna Mary Hope on 16 August 1916 at St Kilda, Melbourne, with Catholic rites. Their only son Richard, author of *The last enemy*, was killed in action with the Royal Air Force in 1943. After his wife's death in 1966 Hillary married Christine Mary Bladon in London on 7 March 1974. He died on 23 October 1976 at

Middlesex Hospital, London, and was buried in East London cemetery.

C. E. W. Bean, *The A.I.F. in France*, 1918 (Syd, 1937); *The Times*, 25, 27 Oct 1976; J H. Thyer, Royal Australian Corps of Signals: Corps history 1906-1918 (1974, AWM); correspondence with family.   KEVIN J. FEWSTER

HILLS, JOHN FRANCIS (1867-1948), teacher and anti-conscriptionist, was born on 15 October 1867 at Great Tey near Kelvedon, Essex, England, son of John Harrison Hills, farmer, and his wife Lucy, née Barritt. He attended the Society of Friends' school at Bootham, York, in 1882-84 and then taught there. From 1884 he was an external student of the University of London (B.A., 1893). Hills was teaching at the Battersea Polytechnic in London in 1898 when he was appointed to The Friends' School, Hobart. He had been recommended as very capable and willing and for his love of games and natural history; he was a firm disciplinarian. This quality, together with his views on the nature and purpose of education, caused disagreements with the headmaster Samuel Clemes [q.v.8]. Hills undertook further study at the University of Tasmania (M.A., 1908).

On 21 June 1900 at the Friends' Meeting House, Hobart, Hills married Alice Mitchell, a science graduate who also taught at the school. Following her appointment as lady inspector of state schools and teacher of domestic economy in Adelaide, they left Hobart in October. They established a private school at Semaphore in 1903, which became known as Largs Bay College. In 1915 Hills became assistant master at Woodville High School while his wife ran their school, called Holdfast Bay College in 1917-36. From 1919 until 1932 he taught at Unley and Norwood High schools. A quiet man, he was tall and angular. He felt intensely about social matters and spoke of them with such fervour and emotion that he trembled and stammered.

Hills was a devoted member of the Adelaide monthly meeting of the Society of Friends and shared their opposition to military training and participation in war. In 1909 the Commonwealth Defence Act had been amended to provide for compulsory drills for boys and a period of military training for youths between 18 and 20. Those whose religion forbade them to undertake military duties were to be allotted, as far as possible, non-combatant tasks. In 1912 Hills and a visiting English Friend, J. P. Fletcher, founded the Australian Freedom League to campaign against compulsory military training. The league quickly extended to other States and at one time claimed 50 000 members. Hills spoke often at public meetings and even paraded in a sandwich board at Victoria Park racecourse. The league was disbanded soon after the outbreak of World War I in 1914. Hills was a delegate to the first interstate conference of the Australian Peace Alliance in Melbourne in 1916.

Of his many pamphlets the most powerful probably was *Child conscription: our country's shame* (1912) which not only condemned military training but, implicitly, war itself. These themes were reiterated in the small book Hills and Fletcher wrote in 1915, *Conscription under camouflage*, which was not published until 1919.

Predeceased by his wife in 1945, Hills died in Parkside Mental Hospital on 6 September 1948. They had no children.

L. C. Jauncey, *The story of conscription in Australia* (Melb, 1968); J. Barrett, *Falling in* (Syd, 1979); W. N. Oats, *The rose and the waratah* (Hob, 1979); *School Echoes*, 25 Oct 1900; *Norwood District High School Mag*, Oct 1933; *Advertiser* (Adel), 22 Oct 1912, 27 Sept 1948; M. T. Shepherd, Compulsory military training: the South Australian debate (M.A. thesis, Univ Adel, 1976); Friends High School Cttee, Report F4/1, 4/5 *and* Minutes, 18 Aug 1898, 13 Aug, 12 Nov, 10 Dec 1900 (Univ Tas Archives); information from Mrs Ruth Beckwick, Blackwood, SA.   J. M. MAIN

HINCHCLIFFE, ALBERT (1860-1935), printer and trade union and Labor administrator, was born on 14 February 1860 at Ashton-under-Lyne, Lancashire, England, son of Ezra Hinchcliffe, cotton warehouse worker, and his wife Alice, née Garside. When his father died in 1866 after migration to Brisbane in 1864, Albert and his mother settled at Toowoomba. He received a brief, intermittent education at the Toowoomba State School and worked on Clifton station before he was 8.

Employed at a Stanthorpe tin mine, he is said to have refused to share a room with a 'Chinaman' and left. A butcher for six months, he was apprenticed in 1872 to a compositor on the *Darling Downs Gazette* where, despite his industrial agitation, he became foreman. After following his trade in England in 1881-82, he married Mary Ann Beer at Toowoomba on 31 July 1883; they had one son. He then settled in Brisbane as a printer on the *Courier* and moved after 1885 to the *Telegraph*. He was a teetotaller and became a Christian Scientist.

Hinchcliffe helped to reconstitute the

Queensland Typographical Association in 1884 and became secretary. When the union affiliated with the Brisbane Trades and Labor Council in 1886, he became its delegate. By 1899 his union was the most inclusive printers' organization in Australia, admitting all workers in the trade. In 1887 he became secretary of the T.L.C., using it to campaign for a federation of all trade unions and for the direct parliamentary representation of the labour movement.

Hinchcliffe believed that reason and goodwill could create an equitable Australian society, though non-Europeans would have to be excluded. When in the 1888 general election he stood for the Brisbane seat of Toombul with T.L.C. endorsement, he was immediately dismissed by the *Telegraph*. Earlier in 1888 he had acted as secretary to the Fifth Intercolonial Trade Union Congress in Brisbane which delegated to the T.L.C. the task of planning a federation of labour. After steering the typographical association through a disastrous strike in 1889 over non-union labour, and enhancing his own reputation, he became more enthusiastic about the scheme. Appointed full-time paid secretary of his union, he engineered the dissolution of the Brisbane T.L.C. and its replacement on 12 June 1889 by the Australian Labor Federation which dominated the Queensland labour movement for the next twenty-three years with Hinchcliffe as secretary from early 1890. When he became secretary in August 1889 of the widely supported London Dock Strike Fund Committee, the reputation of the A.L.F. grew. Following the creation in December 1889 of the monthly newspaper, the *Worker*, Hinchcliffe became treasurer on an elected board of trustees and subsequently manager, a position carrying both salary and influence. The paper appeared first at the eight-hour procession in March 1890.

Hinchcliffe, with the help of W. G. Spence [q.v.6], won the legendary Jondaryan victory in May: wool shorn on the station by 'scab' labour was declared 'black' by maritime workers and the squatters conceded the closed shop. The euphoria of Jondaryan was followed, as the economy deteriorated, by the sharp reversals of the maritime and pastoral strikes. While Utopians such as William Lane [q.v.] and Gilbert Casey [q.v.7] built visions of general strikes and a socialist paradise, Hinchcliffe counselled caution, a realistic appraisal of the opposition, tighter organization and a renewed emphasis on parliament. The survival of central Labor organization in Queensland during the bleak 1890s owed much to him.

When a convention of August 1892 established the Labor Party in Queensland,

Hinchcliffe became secretary of its executive council and in July 1895 of its successor, the central political executive; he held office until 1910. His role as a pivot between political and industrial Labor was obvious in his parliamentary notes for the *Worker*; his technical skill and business acumen helped the paper to survive the hard times of the 1890s. Typically, he reversed the original ban on advertising in the paper and sold space to ensure survival. By the end of the century the *Worker* was both the voice of Labor and a profitable commercial printery. Determined to keep the party straight, he used the *Worker* to denounce parliamentary 'wobblers', particularly Thomas Glassey [q.v.] who tended to ignore the A.L.F. Hinchcliffe himself failed as a candidate in 1893 and again in 1900 when he opposed the defecting Glassey at Bundaberg. Appointed by the Morgan-Kidston [qq.v.] coalition, he was a member of the Legislative Council in 1904-22 but spoke rarely. When the party was gravely weakened after Kidston's 1907 defection, he sharpened his attacks on 'practical politicians' who saw the party as a seat-capturing machine.

Hinchcliffe could work well with men of diverse backgrounds and outlooks. He represented the Q.T.A. on a royal commission of 1894 into the Government Printing Office, and was secretary in 1911-12 of a Commonwealth royal commission into the sugar industry. A councillor of the Brisbane Technical College, he served in 1916-17 on the Senate of the University of Queensland.

The failure of the 1912 strike and the preference of the powerful Amalgamated Workers' Association for amalgamation rather than federation of unions signalled the end of Hinchcliffe's cherished dreams for the A.L.F. and virtually closed his Queensland career. His wife died in 1911 and on 3 March 1913 he married in Sydney Frances May Hickman, who wrote for the Sydney *Worker* under the pseudonym 'May Day'. They had one son. After visiting England in 1915 Hinchcliffe settled in Sydney in 1917 as business manager of the *Australian Worker*, edited by his friend H. E. Boote [q.v.7]. Hinchcliffe retired in 1925 and died in Sydney on 4 January 1935. He was cremated with Christian Science forms.

D. J. Murphy et al (eds), *Prelude to power* (Brisb, 1970); D. J. Murphy (ed), *Labor in politics* (Brisb, 1975); *PD* (Qld), 1906, p 1890, 1915, p 28; *Boomerang* (Brisb), 10 Apr 1888; *Queenslander*, 19 Mar 1898; *Worker* (Brisb), 30 Mar 1907, 7 Nov 1912, 12 Mar 1925; *Daily Standard*, 13 Mar 1925; R. J. Sullivan, Early labour in Queensland with special reference to Albert Hinchcliffe (M.A. qual thesis, Univ Qld, 1969), *and* The A.L.F. in Queensland 1889-1914 (M.A. thesis, Univ Qld, 1973).

RODNEY SULLIVAN

HINDER, ELEANOR MARY (1893-1963), welfare officer and international public servant, was born on 19 January 1893 at East Maitland, New South Wales, third daughter of Australian-born parents Robert John Hinder, headmaster, and his wife Sarah Florence, née Mills. Educated at Maitland West Girls' High School, Teachers' College and the University of Sydney (B.Sc., 1914), she taught biology at North Sydney Girls' High School and gave extension tutorials at the university, where her uncles Henry Hinder and A. E. Mills [q.v.] filled chairs in surgery and medicine. She held office in the Student Christian Movement, the Sydney University Women Graduates' Association and the Workers' Education Association Club.

In 1919 Hinder became welfare superintendent at Farmer [q.v.4] & Co. Ltd's department store, one of the first such appointments by an Australian firm. She monitored training and placements and women employees' health, formed a social club and encouraged participation in healthy recreation. With Jean Stevenson of the Young Women's Christian Association, Hinder helped to found the City Girls Amateur Sports Association. Her aim was to promote loyalty of employees to the firm.

Through her Y.W.C.A. connexions her work became known internationally. When Farmer's financed an overseas study tour for her in 1923-24, Eleanor Hinder went first to Shanghai, China, which recently had experienced serious industrial troubles, on the personal invitation of the international industrial secretary of the Y.W.C.A., Mary Dingman, who thought her 'the most intelligent and ablest young woman met in Australia'. Hinder went on to the International Labour Organization, Geneva, and the International Federation of University Women's congress at Oslo. In 1926 she returned to Shanghai to work for the National Y.W.C.A. of China. Because of the extraterritorial rights of Europeans under the unequal treaties, China's labour laws could not be enforced in Shanghai where the British-dominated municipal council resisted regulation of labour. Hinder became a publicist for regulation. She met A. Viola Smith, the American assistant trade commissioner, and they became intimate friends for life.

In 1928 Miss Hinder attended the first Pan Pacific Women's Conference in Honolulu. On a visit home she lectured on China. In 1929 she was an Australian delegate to the third conference of the Institute of Pacific Relations at Kyoto, Japan, then resumed her work with the Y.W.C.A. in Shanghai. After visiting the United States of America and Europe in 1932, where she studied in England at the Home Office's industrial safety museum and with the I.L.O., she was appointed chief of Shanghai municipality's new (social and) industrial division. The council's continued refusal of China's labour laws left Hinder without power to control working conditions except by disseminating information about industrial health and safety and by providing training for workers. She was within a few blocks of Japanese bombs in 1937 and, as the war extended, the care of orphans became an important part of the work of her division. In August 1942 she was repatriated to London and joined the Foreign Office, and in December was sent to Montreal, Canada, to work for the I.L.O.

In 1944-48 Hinder was British representative on the Far Eastern sub-committee of the United Nations Relief and Rehabilitation Association's technical committee. Appointed O.B.E. in 1950, she was British representative on the United Nations' Economic Commission for Asia and the Far East until 1951, when she resigned from the Foreign Office to become chief of the project planning division of the Technical Assistance Administration of the United Nations, for Asia and the Far East. In 1953 she became chief of operations. Hinder retired in 1956; failing to come within the United States immigration quota, she and her friend Viola Smith came to Sydney to live.

Hinder took occasional assignments for the United Nations: en route to New York she died at San Francisco on 10 April 1963 of coronary occlusion. Her ashes were brought back for a memorial service at Wesley College, University of Sydney. Her collection of Chinese ceramics was displayed at the university and East Sydney Technical College before a selection was made for the Art Gallery of New South Wales. Eleanor had drafted sections of an autobiography before her death. In 1976 Viola Smith bequeathed an award for a biography of her friend to be written.

F. Wheelhouse, *Eleanor Mary Hinder, an Australian woman's social welfare work in China between the wars* (Syd, 1978); *SMH*, 15 Apr 1963; Hinder papers (uncat MSS 770, ML).

MEREDITH FOLEY
HEATHER RADI

HINDLEY, WILLIAM GEORGE (1853-1936), clergyman, was born on 16 March 1853 at East Retford, Nottinghamshire, England, son of John Hindley, shoemaker and later merchant, and his wife Catharine, née Hall. After a private-school education at Sheffield he began a commercial career, but in 1878 he responded to an appeal by Bishop Moorhouse [q.v.5] for Englishmen to offer themselves for service in the Victorian bush. With his wife Sarah Jane, née Johnson, whom he had married at Sheffield on 30 March 1875, Hindley sailed for Melbourne in the *Cuzco*; the ship broke its shaft in the Great Australian Bight and only reached Portland with the aid of a rigged sail. After a week of elementary theology at Bishops-court in Melbourne, Hindley went as a stipendiary lay reader to the remote mining town of Omeo in Gippsland. He held services in the Rechabite Hall, visited the gold-miners and prepared himself for ordination by further study. A year later his wife and two young children joined him.

In 1880 Hindley was made deacon by Moorhouse and sent to Milawa, where he substantially reduced the debt on the church. In 1882 he was ordained priest and appointed to the charge of St John's, Bairns-dale. During his four years there a new church was built and Hindley ministered to a parish extending over 10 000 square miles (25 900 km²) of eastern Victoria with the aid of three lay readers.

Hindley was appointed vicar of St Michael's, North Carlton, in 1886 but re-signed two years later to become organizing secretary of the Bishop of Melbourne's Fund at the request of Bishop Goe [q.v.]. He assisted at Holy Trinity, East Melbourne, taking charge of the parish in 1892. Hindley was already demonstrating a capacity for financial management, but the coincidence of his work as secretary of the fund with the building boom in Melbourne gave him a solid, cautious approach to church finances in later years.

In 1895 he succeeded G. O. Vance [q.v.6] as vicar of Holy Trinity, Kew; five years later he was appointed a canon of St Paul's Cathedral and in 1902 became archdeacon of Melbourne. He resigned the charge of Kew in 1904 in order to devote his time more fully to the archdeacon's duties, but in 1910 he became incumbent of St James Old Cathedral. Archbishop Lowther Clarke [q.v.8] had appointed him vicar-general and chaplain to the archbishop of Melbourne in 1908. He administered the diocese from the resignation of Lowther Clarke in 1920 to the enthronement of Harrington Clare Lees [q.v.] as archbishop in 1921.

One of the most influential figures in the history of the diocese, Hindley was chiefly responsible for the legislation which subdivided the Melbourne diocese in 1903 and created the dioceses of Bendigo, Gippsland and Wangaratta, and for the establishment of the Clergy Provident Fund in 1917. He was also a guiding hand in founding a number of Church of England schools. He was

co-editor and later chief-of-staff of the *Church of England Messenger* from 1899 to 1918. Affable in manner, he had a quiet sense of humour, and his epigrammatic sayings punctuated his speeches and sermons. His chief ability lay in his capacity to sum up men and policies accurately and he had the acumen to put policies into practice. In 1927 he resigned to live at Mount Eliza. His wife died in 1932. Hindley died on 18 May 1936 and was buried in Boroondara cemetery, Kew. Of their ten children, five daughters and a son survived him. A portrait by W. B. McInnes [q.v.] is in the chapter house of St Paul's Cathedral, Melbourne.

A. E. Clark, *The Church of our fathers* (Melb, 1947); *Church of England Messenger* (Vic), 22 May 1936; *Weekly Times* (Melb), 13 Oct 1900, 1 Dec 1906; *Table Talk*, 4 Oct 1895, 19 Apr 1928; *Argus*, 19 May 1936.   A. DE Q. ROBIN

HINKLER, HERBERT JOHN LOUIS (1892-1933), aviator, was born on 8 December 1892 at Bundaberg, Queensland, son of John William Hinkler, German-born stockman, and his wife Frances Atkins, née Bonney. Educated at North Bundaberg State School in 1898-1906, he found work with a photographer at Gympie and soon became interested in aviation. He worked in sugar-mills and the foundry at Bundaberg; then briefly visited Brisbane seeking other aviation enthusiasts. There he joined the Queensland Aero Club of 1910 and the Aerial League of Australia. Learning mechanics by correspondence in 1911, he built two gliders in 1911-12; the second design was based on his own observation and analysis, including photographs, of ibises in flight. An application to join the new aviation section of the Australian army was rejected. When the American airman Arthur Burr Stone brought his Bleriot monoplane to Bundaberg in 1912, Hinkler became his mechanic on a tour of southern Australia and New Zealand. Coping with the numerous mishaps to Stone's plane confirmed Hinkler's grasp of construction fundamentals.

Hinkler sailed for England at the end of 1913 and found work in the Sopwith aircraft factory. On 7 September 1914 he enlisted in the Royal Naval Air Service. After training at the Central Flying School, Upavon, he was posted to Newcastle-upon-Tyne and, early in 1915, to Whitley Bay, Northumberland. An excellent rifle-shot, he was chosen as the commanding officer's observer and by the end of 1915 was a petty officer.

Having invented an improved dual-control system which enabled the gunner to relieve a disabled pilot, Hinkler completed an aerial gunlayer's course in 1916 and was posted to No. 3 Wing, R.N.A.S., escorting bombers in Sopwith '1½ Strutters' from Luxeuil and Ochey near Nancy, France. When the wing was disbanded in June 1917 the crews went to other units and for several months Hinkler flew on night raids in Handley-Page bombers. Flying in D.H.4s on day bombings for No. 5 Squadron, R.N.A.S., Canadian pilot Charles B. Sproatt gave him his first chance to fly a plane. Awarded the Distinguished Service Medal, he was promoted to warrant rank and recommended for a commission and pilot training. As a gunner, Hinkler privately claimed destruction of six enemy planes. On 30 December he began training at the Royal Naval College, Greenwich, moving later to Eastbourne and to No. 2 Fighting School at Marske, Yorkshire. After graduation in July 1918 he was posted to No. 28 Squadron, Royal Air Force, stationed in Italy. There he was repelled by one of his duties, the work of 'ground strafing' Austrian troops.

Failing in his application to fly a Sopwith Dove in the 1919 air race to Australia, Hinkler undertook rehabilitation training with A. V. Roe & Co. at Hamble, near Southampton. He bought a 35-horsepower Avro Baby and, on 31 May 1920, flew from Croydon to Turin, Italy, over the Alps in 9½ hours. Because of mechanical problems he abandoned the idea of flying on to Australia when he reached Rome; the flight won him the Britannia Trophy. Shipping the plane to Australia in 1921, he made a series of flights including one from Sydney to Bundaberg, non-stop. After an emergency landing due to bad weather on the return flight, strong winds overturned the plane.

Hinkler returned to England via Canada and until 1926 was chief test pilot for the Avro company at Hamble. In December 1922 he tested the Avro Aldershot, the first plane powered by a 1000-horsepower engine. He won the light aircraft trials at Lympne in 1923 in a monoplane motor-glider and in 1924 the Grosvenor Challenge Cup. In 1925 he was reserve pilot for the British Schneider Trophy team at Baltimore, United States of America, and in 1927 he flew his Avro Avian G-EBOV non-stop from London to Riga, Latvia, receiving a Latvian decoration. He also tested autogiros for the Spanish designer, Juan de La Cierva, in 1927 and, to secure funds for a flight to Australia, made an unsuccessful attempt with R. McIntosh on the London to India air record.

In February 1928 Hinkler made the first solo flight to Australia in G-EBOV and won fame; he took slightly over fifteen days. Hinkler's flight proved an unexpected financial success when the Australian gov-

ernment gave him £2000. He was made an honorary squadron leader in the Royal Australian Air Force Reserve and was awarded the Air Force Cross.

Returning to England by sea in October, he began building an amphibian aircraft of his own design called the 'Ibis'. On 11 January 1930 he and an Avro engineer, Rowland Bound, registered the Ibis Aircraft Co. The prototype, G-AAIS, was successfully flown but the potential market vanished in the Depression. Hinkler went to Canada in September 1930 to survey American prospects and in April 1931 he acquired a Puss Moth, CF-APK, which later the same year he flew from Canada to New York, then via the West Indies, Venezuela, Guiana, Brazil and the south Atlantic to Great Britain. Informed people declared him Britain's leading aviator. He was awarded the Segrave trophy, the Britannia challenge trophy, the gold medal of the Royal Aero Club and the Johnston memorial air navigation trophy. For the flights in 1920 and 1928 he had already won two Britannia trophies and the gold medal of the Fédération Aéronautique Internationale.

Failing to secure aerial employment in Britain, Hinkler returned to America early in 1932 contemplating a global circumnavigation by light plane. He went back to England and prepared for another flight to Australia, intending later to cross the Pacific to Canada. He began the flight from Heathrow on 7 January 1933 in his Puss Moth and disappeared. The crashed plane and Hinkler's body were found on the northern slopes of Pratomagno in the Apennines between Florence and Arezzo, Italy, on 27 April. He had survived the crash and died outside the wreckage. On Mussolini's orders he was buried in Florence with full military honours.

An Italian enquiry was held into Hinkler's death; a separate enquiry by an air force officer sought to establish the causes of the crash. His finding that the crash was caused by the loss of a wing in flight was contradicted by eye-witnesses who found the wing against the tree which had knocked it from the plane. Independent investigation establishes that Hinkler attempted an emergency landing after the loss of a propeller blade in flight.

His closest associates described Hinkler as a man without fear, an ideal aerial companion, a man without pretensions who achieved without fuss, and a flying genius. He was 5ft. 4ins. (163 cm) tall. The prominent Queensland flyer Maud Rose Bonney, who married his cousin, is said to have been inspired by a flight with him. Enrolled for school in 1898 as Bertie Hinkler, he remained Bert Hinkler for the rest of his life.

On 21 May 1932 in Connecticut, U.S.A., he married Katherine Rome; they had no children. His name is commemorated by parks and streets in Queensland and elsewhere and in an occasional air race centred in Queensland. A monument stands on Pratomagno. Two of his aircraft are displayed in the Queensland Museum.

H. A. Jones, *The war in the air* (Oxford, 1922); J. A. Mollison (ed), *The book of famous flyers* (Lond, 1934); R. D. Mackenzie, *Solo: the Bert Hinkler story* (Brisb, 1963); *British A'sian*, 23 Sept 1915; *Aircraft* (Melb), 20 May 1921; *Sea, Land, and Air*, July 1920, Apr, May 1921; *Flight* (Lond), 11 Dec 1931, 1 Jan, 15 Dec 1932, 16 Feb 1933; *Aeroplane*, 1 Feb 1933; *Aust Flying*, Feb 1974; *Australasian*, 31 July 1920, 16, 23 Apr 1921; *Queenslander*, 9 Oct 1920, 1 Mar 1928, 17 Jan 1929, 7 May 1931, 30 Apr, 28 May 1936; *Brisbane Courier*, 3 Mar 1928; *Courier Mail*, 8 Feb 1934; A 458.AB, AC, BS., CF 314/4 (AAO, Canb); Hinkler papers (NL), (Oxley Lib).

E. P. WIXTED

HINTON, HOWARD (1867-1948), company director and patron of art, was born on 10 November 1867 at Croydon, Surrey, England, second son of Thomas Alexander Hinton, commission agent, and his wife Mary, née Howard. He attended Whitgift Grammar School, Croydon, leaving from fifth form in 1883. In his school holidays Hinton had visited the great art galleries of Europe. At every opportunity he attended art classes, but acute myopia frustrated his wish to become an artist.

Hinton arrived in Sydney in the *Loch Torridon* in 1892. Through Dangar, Gedye & Co., the ship's agents, he obtained a position as junior clerk with W. and A. McArthur [q.v.5] Ltd. He travelled widely—in 1894 and 1898 visiting New Zealand; on the second trip he met Charles Goldie, the New Zealand artist, and stayed with him before going on to Rarotonga and Tahiti. When the Russo-Japanese War broke out in 1904 Hinton took the company steamer *Macquarie* with a cargo of wheat, oats and coal to Yokohama, Japan. After two adventure-packed years he sold the ship to the Japanese, and returned to Sydney. When his company became the McArthur Shipping & Agency Co. Ltd. in 1908, Hinton remained, becoming a director in 1916. His poor eyesight prevented his serving in World War I, despite two attempts to enlist. This was a matter of great concern to him as he was a patriotic loyalist, who gave freely of his money during the war and in World War II. His generosity was usually anonymous.

On first reaching Sydney, Hinton had probably lived with artist friends in the many camps which dotted the harbour. It was here that he met Livingstone Hopkins, Julian Ashton [qq.v.4,7], Tom Roberts and Arthur Streeton [qq.v.], and began buying their paintings. Some time after 1900 he moved to Hazelhurst, Cremorne, where he lived for the rest of his life. He made his first gift (a collection of Phil May [q.v.5] sketches) to the National Art Gallery of New South Wales in 1914. By 1948 he had given 122 pictures, including important works by E. Phillips Fox [q.v.8], G. W. Lambert and E. Gruner [qq.v.], Roberts and Streeton. He was a trustee of the gallery in 1919-48. For his many benefactions, the trustees commissioned his portrait by Lambert in 1927. In 1932 the Society of Artists, Sydney, presented him with its gold medal for services to art and in 1935 he was appointed O.B.E.

Hinton retired in 1928 and visited England, returning to Australia in 1931. While abroad, possibly because the Art Gallery refused several of his gifts, he conceived the idea of endowing the Teachers' College, Armidale, with an art collection—S. H. Smith [q.v.], director of education, co-operated with him. The first picture 'The Lock Gates' by Sir Adrian Stokes, R.A., arrived in 1929. He gave over 1000 works to the college and an art library of some 700 volumes. He hoped to illustrate the development of Australian art from 1880, and the collection is widely recognized as a priceless anthology of the artistic impulse in nineteenth and early twentieth-century Australia. Norman Lindsay [q.v.] described it as the only complete collection of Australian art in the country, but as Hinton had no patience with modern art, this is largely unrepresented.

A shy, almost reclusive man, he was diffident in manner and hesitant in speech, and never married. Little known except to a close circle of friends, which included many artists, F. Du Boise, R. H. Goddard and the Sabiel and McGlew families, he was described as the true English gentleman, dignified yet brimming with fun. Lindsay acknowledged his personal debt to Hinton, describing 'a certain emanation of spirit from him that I can define only by the bedraggled label of faith'. As well as loving art and music, Hinton delighted in writing poetry and enjoyed surfing, philately and meeting friends at the Millions Club.

Arthur Streeton and Norman Lindsay placed him with Alfred Felton, David Scott Mitchell [qq.v.4,5] and Sir Baldwin Spencer [q.v.] as one of the great benefactors of the arts in Australia. Hinton died at Cremorne on 23 January 1948 and was cremated with Anglican rites, after a service at St James's

Church, King Street, where he had worshipped.

His portrait by Norman Carter [q.v.7] and a bust by Rayner Hoff [q.v.] are held by the Armidale College of Advanced Education.

C. B. Newling et al, *A memorial volume to Howard Hinton, patron of art* (Syd, 1951); Trustees of the Art Gallery of NSW, Minutes; Armidale College of Advanced Education, NSW, Archives; H. Hinton papers (ML).   E. S. ELPHICK

HIRSCH, MAXIMILIAN (1852?-1909), economist and political activist, was born in Prussia into a well-known Cologne family. He was educated at Cologne Gymnasium and the Humboldt University of Berlin before becoming a commercial traveller in 1872, representing British manufacturers in Europe, North Africa and western Asia; he attended the exhibitions at Sydney in 1879 and Melbourne in 1880. After a lengthy stay in Germany he spent three years as a coffee planter in Ceylon where he achieved his first and proudest success as an agitator and reformer: the abolition of the rice tax.

Hirsch returned to Melbourne in February 1890 and for the next decade was prominent as Victoria's chief spokesman for land values taxation and as a leading light in the colony's free-trade movement: he became president of the Single Tax Society, reorganized under that name after Henry George's [q.v.4] visit in April 1890, and at the inaugural meeting of the Free Trade Democratic Association in May he was elected treasurer.

Backed by the *Argus*, Hirsch quickly became a leader in the anti-tariff party. George's visit had served to point out that there was no ideological conflict between supporting abolition of all taxes except a tax on land values, and supporting free trade. In Victoria the Free Trade Democratic Association was an uneasy alliance between radical single taxers and politically conservative land-owning merchants and squatters. While it restricted its activities to promoting free trade and preparing for the August 1894 elections this alliance held; but Hirsch's decision to insert a single-tax plank into the platform at this time split the organization, and R. Murray Smith [q.v.6] led the conservatives into the Free Trade League of Victoria in December 1894.

Hirsch lectured and debated up to five times a week at indoor and outdoor city venues and claimed to have visited almost every town in Victoria. As well, he produced many pamphlets and books on statistical, economic and political themes, the most important being *Democracy vs socialism* (London, 1901; 3rd ed., 1940). He also belonged to the 1898 Rating Reform League which collected evidence for the royal commission into local government in 1899. He supported Federation and was in 1894 vice-president of the Australasian Federation League. He was an honorary member of the British Cobden Club and distributed its pamphlets through the Single Tax League. He visited England in 1905 as guest speaker at the London Free Trade Congress and had for some time been the Victorian correspondent for the British Board of Trade.

As a reformer Hirsch was keenly interested in the conditions of workers. He was secretary to the Victorian board of inquiry on unemployment in 1900 and wrote many articles in the *Beacon* and elsewhere criticizing labour conditions. Although an opponent of trade unions he was rumoured to belong to the Knights of Labor and certainly spoke regularly to their Newport Railway Workshop branch. He was a keen supporter of women's causes, notably female suffrage and the Queen Victoria Hospital.

Hirsch first stood for the Victorian Legislative Assembly in 1893 for Benalla but was disqualified when found to have been naturalized only in May 1892. His bid for Mandurang in 1897 was unsuccessful but in 1902 he won the seat. A frequent speaker in the House, he joined in debates on rural matters but spoke best on subjects such as income taxation and tariff proposals. He resigned in November 1903 to contest the Federal seat of Wimmera but was defeated.

In 1891 Hirsch was declared by the *Bankers' Magazine of Australasia* to be too earnest to be popular, but the article paid tribute to his impressive personality and great intelligence; other observers found him less sombre. He was remembered from a few years earlier as 'a giddy youth, chiefly remarkable for the ease with which he executed the "military valse" ', and Beatrice Webb, who met him over dinner in later days, found him 'a courtly and attractive German Jew . . . and complete individualist'.

Hirsch was totally consumed by his beliefs. He gave up his business interests for full-time activism in 1892, supporting himself by lecturing, freelance journalism and donations from friends. He lived in rented rooms and never married. His health began to fail as early as 1895 and by 1906 he had had several breakdowns.

After Federation and consequent interstate free trade Hirsch had returned to commerce, taking up an interest in the Oriental Timber Corporation Co. Pty Ltd. In October 1908 he sailed for Siberia to conduct company negotiations with the Russian government. He died suddenly in Vladivostok on 4 March 1909.

B. Webb, *The Webbs' Australian diary, 1898,* A. G. Austin ed (Melb, 1965); *Bankers' Mag of A'sia,* 12 July 1895; *Beacon* (Melb), Sept 1897; *Argus,* 13 June 1892, 5, 10, 28 Oct 1893, 5 Mar 1909; *Australasian,* 23 Dec 1905; A. Worrall, The new crusade: the origins, activities and influence of the Australian Single Tax leagues, 1889-1895 (M.A. thesis, Univ Melb, 1978).   AIRLIE WORRALL

HIRSCHFELD, EUGEN (1866-1946), medical practitioner, was born on 22 January 1866 at Militsch (Milicz), Silesia, Prussia, son of Julius Hirschfeld, banker, and his wife Joanna, née Lvervey. He studied medicine, passing his *testamur physicum* at Wurzburg, and graduated from Strasburg University in 1887. He took his Staats Examination in 1888 and graduated M.D. in 1889 for research on eye pigmentation.

Hirschfeld arrived in Brisbane in July 1890 and was registered for practice on 7 August. Deeply involved in the medical and scientific world of Brisbane, he became honorary bacteriologist to the Brisbane Hospital and, influenced by the work of Koch, specialized in tuberculosis. He investigated the clinical features of dengue fever in southern Queensland and in 1895, as vice-president, read to the Royal Society of Queensland a pioneering paper on the medical and economic necessity for compulsory inspection of meat. His ideal was to stamp out tuberculosis 'in man and beast'. Naturalized in May 1893, he married Annie Sarah Eliza Saddler at Kew, Melbourne, on 21 April 1897.

A leader of the German community in Queensland, Hirschfeld enrolled himself at the consulate as a German citizen to comply with German regulations and in the belief that dual nationality was possible. In 1906 he was appointed Imperial German Consul in Brisbane and, after consulting Governor Sir William MacGregor [q.v.5], later founded a society for the propagation of German language and culture. Admitted M.D. *ad eund* by the University of Queensland in 1911, he became a founding senator of the university and in 1912 represented it at a congress in London of British universities. While overseas he investigated tuberculosis and cancer hospitals for the government as a member of the Queensland Medical Board. In July-November 1914 he was a member of the Legislative Council.

Hirschfeld lived and practised quietly through 1915 but in February 1916 was interned at Enoggera and transferred a week later to Liverpool, New South Wales. Released in August 1917 on account of ill health, he was taken again soon afterwards on the alleged ground that he had falsified medical evidence to secure his release. Following a magisterial investigation and a review by Sir Robert Garran [q.v.8] in June 1920, he was deported. He stayed briefly in Germany and Holland, then went to the United States of America and practised until 1926 at Allantown, Pennsylvania. He was finally permitted to return in 1927, partly because of representations from Sir John Monash [q.v.].

After practising for a time in Wickham Terrace, Hirschfeld purchased station properties at Inglewood and at Yelarbon on the Darling Downs. Applying systematic botanical method, he carried out and published research into pasture improvement, with particular reference to the development of brigalow and belah country because of its drought-resisting capacity. He also investigated the range and potential of Australian native vegetables, especially in relation to Aboriginal nutrition. He died at Bybera, his Yelarbon property, on 18 June 1946 and was buried there. His wife had predeceased him. He was survived by a daughter and three sons, two of whom pursued distinguished medical and academic careers in Queensland.

Hirschfeld was a man of colourful personality, of exceptional gifts and strength of character, who adorned the medical and scientific professions in Queensland.

G. Serle, *John Monash: a biography* (Melb, 1982); *Qld Agr J,* Aug 1946; Monash papers (NL); A 456 W8/4/129, 163 (AAO, Canb), *and* BP 242/1 Q23532, BP 4/1 66/4/891 (AAO, Brisb).
                                        C. A. C. LEGGETT

HIRST, GODFREY (1857-1917), woollen manufacturer, was born on 6 January 1857 at Royd Edge, Meltham, near Huddersfield, Yorkshire, England, son of Charles Hirst, spinner, and his wife Minerva, née Holmes.

Trained as a weaver in a family business, Hirst arrived in Victoria for the sake of his health in 1885. Initially an insurance agent in the Western District, he soon joined the ailing Victorian Woollen & Cloth Manufacturing Co. in Geelong, only to disagree with its management over the best means of competing with imports. Believing that there was a living to be made from quality products, Hirst decided to go into business for himself. Renting a shed in Fyans Street, he built his own loom and, using yarn supplied by his former employers and the Albion mill, began manufacturing flannels in 1888. Doing well despite the pall hanging over the industry as a whole, he moved to larger premises in 1889 and, in partnership with

Charles Shannon, a woolbroker, and Charles Smith, a fellmonger, bought the defunct Barwon woollen factory in July 1890. Renamed the Excelsior Number One mill, the old factory prospered and, with Hirst in personal charge of its raw materials and sales, employed about one hundred people by February 1895. In 1899 the adjoining Victorian factory was added to the proprietary and refurbished as the Excelsior Number Two mill. Advantaged by interstate free trade after Federation and government contracts during World War I, the firm's pay-roll increased to more than 300 in 1917. The company then manufactured blankets, rugs, tweeds, and worsteds as well as flannels. After the death of Charles Smith in 1908, the business was incorporated as Godfrey Hirst & Co. Pty Ltd in October 1909.

In 1911 and again after the Number One mill was destroyed by fire in March 1912 Hirst returned to England in search of the latest machinery. In Geelong he supported the Gordon Technical College as a centre of textile education and was its president in 1913-16. His principal avocations were the Belmont and Corio clubs, music and bowls. A self-taught musician, he was organist at St George's Presbyterian Church from 1889 and a vice-president of the Geelong Musical Society. He also sponsored the Excelsior Mills choir and was active in the musical life of the Belmont Methodist Church. A man of strong principles and high expectations but reserved and lacking the common touch, he once stood unsuccessfully for the South Barwon Shire Council. He became a justice of the peace in 1908.

Hirst died after several years of failing health at his home, Royd Grange, Belmont, on 15 February 1917 and was buried in the Methodist section of Geelong Eastern cemetery. He was survived by his wife Sarah, née Carter, whom he had married at Huddersfield on 22 July 1876, three sons and two daughters. His estate was valued for probate at £65 999.

Hirst's example contributed to a revival of the woollen industry in Geelong during the 1910s and 1920s. The Excelsior mills were taken over in 1966 but continued to operate as Godfrey Hirst & Co. Pty Ltd, carpet manufacturers.

I. Southall, *The weaver from Meltham* (Melb, 1950); *Geelong Advertiser*, 16 Feb 1917, 28 May 1957; Hirst papers (ANU Archives).

GRAEME COPE

HITCHCOCK, HOWARD (1866-1932), businessman and civic leader, was born on 31 March 1866 at Geelong, Victoria, son of George Mitchelmore Hitchcock [q.v.4] and his wife Annie, née Lowe. He was educated at Flinders State School and private schools before beginning at 18 as an assistant in the family firm of Bright & Hitchcocks, drapers. Five years later he became a junior partner; on his father's death in 1912 he took over as managing director. In 1926 he sold the business to five of his employees.

Hitchcock was prominent in the Yarra Street Wesleyan Church, serving for over twenty-five years as organist and over ten years as secretary and superintendent. He was also a member of the church tennis and cricket teams. These activities formed his main interests until 1915 when, after successfully campaigning to prevent the Geelong City Council from moving its headquarters to the recently vacated Geelong Church of England Grammar School buildings, he was prevailed upon to stand for council. Elected as representative for Bellarine Ward, within two years he was chosen as mayor and served a record consecutive five years in that office in 1917-22. He became an alderman in 1920, and was appointed O.B.E. that year and C.M.G. two years later.

During his mayoralty Hitchcock accepted all invitations, attending three or four functions in an evening, and travelled 80 000 miles (130 000 km) in his own car. His slogan was 'civic improvement and beautification' which he put into practice in development schemes for Johnstone's Park and the Eastern Beach. He firmly believed that those who had made their fortune in the town should be prepared to plough it back into its development, and he established a Junior Civic Association to instil his 'new civic ideal' into the minds of the young. He never ceased to push the merits of Geelong, extending to visitors lavish, though teetotal, hospitality out of his own pocket.

Hitchcock was active in fund-raising activities during and just after the war. He helped to obtain £1.5 million for war loans and £132 000 for various war and peace funds, including the Kitchener Memorial Hospital. His own donations often reached four figures. While mayor Hitchcock was also active president or chairman for thirty-one public bodies, vice-president of five, trustee of ten, secretary of four, treasurer of four and committee-member of seven.

Hitchcock's interests turned outside Geelong when he espoused William Calder's [q.v.7] proposal for the establishment of the Great Ocean Road as a memorial to the soldiers of the Western District. He became president of the Great Ocean Road Trust in 1918; he gave nearly £3000 to its appeal and it was his enthusiasm and energy as much as anything that kept the project afloat. He died before he was able to open the com pleted road in 1932; in tribute, his car was driven behind the governor's in the procession along the road on opening day.

In 1923 Hitchcock embarked on his third trip abroad and was absent for nearly three years. On his return he was met by a cavalcade of cars at the outskirts of the town and escorted to a huge civic reception. In June 1925, in his absence, he had been elected member for South-Western Province in the Legislative Council. In 1931 he resigned all public positions because of ill health. He died of heart disease on 22 August 1932, survived by his wife Charlotte Louisa Turnbull, née Royce, whom he had married on 16 April 1890; they had no children. He was buried in Eastern cemetery after a service at the Yarra Street Wesleyan Church. His estate was valued for probate at £71 276.

Geelong Advertiser, 8 May 1912, 23, 25 Aug 1932; *Age*, and *Argus*, 23 Aug 1932; Howard Hitchcock's mayoral scrapbook (Geelong Historical Records Centre).   IAN WYND

HOAD, SIR JOHN CHARLES (1856-1911), soldier, was born on 25 January 1856 at Goulburn, New South Wales, son of George Hoad, labourer and later baker, and his wife Catherine, née Kearney. Nothing is known of Hoad's boyhood or education, but it is believed that at 6 he was orphaned and brought up by relations in the Wangaratta district of Victoria.

On 1 January 1878 he entered the Victorian Education Department and was appointed head teacher at Gooramadda State School; in September he became an assistant at Wangaratta School and in April 1881 head teacher at Wangaratta North. Interested in sport, Hoad proved himself a keen horseman and good cricketer, footballer and athlete. His last teaching appointment was at Brighton Road, St Kilda, school.

On 5 December 1884 Hoad became a militia lieutenant in the 1st Battalion, Victorian Rifles. He resigned from the Education Department and joined the permanent staff of the Victorian Military Forces on 11 February 1886. Posted first to the Cadet Corps, on 4 June he became adjutant of the Victorian Mounted Rifles commanded by Lieut-Colonel Tom Price [q.v.]. A captain since March 1887, Hoad was promoted major in April 1889.

In October Hoad left Melbourne for England where he underwent training courses in signalling, military engineering and musketry. He returned to Melbourne in March 1891 and in January 1892 was appointed second-in-command of the Victorian Mounted Rifles. He pushed ahead in the service and consolidated his position. In March 1895 he was promoted lieut-colonel and appointed assistant adjutant general at Victorian Headquarters—a post which had hitherto been reserved for a British Army officer.

In England again in 1897, Hoad attended Queen Victoria's diamond jubilee celebrations in London and served on the personal staff of Lord Roberts and the duke of Connaught. He returned to Melbourne in October. On 28 April 1899 he attained the rank of colonel.

During the South African War Hoad served as a special service officer, and on arrival at Cape Town on 26 November 1899 was given command of the 1st Australian Regiment, the first force composed of troops from Victoria, South Australia, Western Australia and Tasmania. The regiment moved to the Orange River on 1 December and joined the Kimberley Relief Force. At Bloemfontein in April 1900 when the regiment was absorbed into the 1st Mounted Infantry Brigade, Hoad became assistant adjutant general to the brigade under Major General Sir Edward Hutton [q.v.]. In July Hoad was evacuated to hospital in Cape Town and from there was invalided to Australia, arriving in Melbourne on 26 August. For his services he was appointed C.M.G., awarded the Queen's Medal and mentioned in dispatches. He was aide-de-camp to the governor-general from August 1902 to October 1906.

During Hutton's period in command of Australia's military forces after Federation, Hoad was his principal staff officer with the title of deputy adjutant general and chief staff officer. From November 1903 to January 1904 he temporarily commanded the 6th Military District (Tasmania). Early in 1904 relations between himself and Hutton became strained because, against Hutton's advice, the Deakin [q.v.] government sent Hoad for attachment to the Japanese Army, as an observer, in the Russo-Japanese war in Manchuria. For his services he received the Japanese Order of the Rising Sun, 3rd class, and the Japanese War Medal.

When the Military Board was set up in January 1905 Hoad became its principal military member with the title of deputy adjutant general. In September 1906 he was appointed, temporarily, inspector general with the temporary rank of brigadier general. In January 1907 he was promoted major general and confirmed as inspector general.

In 1908 Hoad was sent to England to discuss the creation of an Imperial General Staff at the War Office, London, and to take part in the autumn manoeuvres of the British Army. Hoad was an ambitious officer and adept at cultivating friends in high places. During his absence in London Bridges's appointment as first chief of the Australian General Staff in January 1909 did little to improve their long-standing antipathy.

On Hoad's return in May (Sir) George Pearce [q.v.], minister for defence, recommended that Hoad's recommendations for an Australian section of the Imperial General Staff be accepted and that Hoad be appointed chief of the Australian General Staff vice Bridges who was posted to the Imperial General Staff, London. On the creation of the Imperial General Staff Hoad, though not a staff college graduate, became concurrently, on 1 July 1909, chief of the Australian section of the staff.

On 21 December 1909 Hoad met Field Marshal Lord Kitchener at Darwin and accompanied him on his exhaustive tour of inspection of Australia's land defences which was completed in Melbourne on 12 February 1910. Later, while immersed in the planning for introduction of Australia's universal training scheme, his health deteriorated and he went on sick leave on 1 June 1911. On the occasion of the coronation of King George V on 22 June Hoad was appointed K.C.M.G. He was unable to attend the official opening of the Royal Military College, Duntroon, in June and died in Melbourne of heart disorder on 6 October 1911. He was buried with military honours in St Kilda cemetery.

By ambition, industry and sustained work at high pressure Hoad held the two highest posts open to an officer of his time in Australia's military forces. He had spent most of his official life as a staff officer as few opportunities existed in his time for a regular officer to gain command experience. Despite a 'spare military figure' Hoad was 'full of suppressed energy', and his manner was quiet, tactful and unpretentious. He was a good listener; he spoke little but at the appropriate time had 'a ready flow of speech'.

Hoad had married a widow, Sarah Denniston Sennetts, née Brown, at Wangaratta Post Office, with Wesleyan forms on 22 December 1881. They had a daughter, who died as a child, and two sons.

Their younger son OSWALD VICK (1888-1963), was born on 30 July 1888 at South Melbourne and educated at Melbourne Church of England Grammar School. He was commissioned in the militia in February 1907 and in May 1909 became an honorary aide-de-camp to his father. In 1910 he transferred to the staff of the permanent military forces.

In 1913-15 he was an exchange officer with the Canadian Army. After staff postings in Victoria and Tasmania he was seconded to the Australian Imperial Force as a captain and in 1917-18 saw active service on the Western Front with the 21st and 22nd Battalions. He was wounded in action on 5 October 1918 and invalided to Australia in May 1919.

Resuming duty with the permanent forces in June 1919, Hoad was promoted major in November and in October 1920 became one of the original officers of the newly formed Australian Staff Corps. From February 1921 to July 1922 he was director of drill at the Royal Military College, Duntroon. During World War II Hoad occupied staff positions in Australia; he was promoted temporary brigadier in 1942 and retired in March 1946. He died at Southport, Queensland, on 12 September 1963. On 10 June 1913 at St Peter's Church, Melbourne, he had married Sheila Mairi McDonald; there was one son of the marriage.

R. A. Preston, *Canada and 'Imperial defense'* (Durham, NC, 1967); C. D. Coulthard-Clark, *A heritage of spirit* (Melb, 1979); W. Perry, 'The military life of Major-General Sir John Charles Hoad', *VHM*, 29 (1959), no 3; *Lithgow Mercury*, 18 Oct 1907; *Punch* (Melb), 30 Dec 1909; *Age*, 19 Jan 1912.

WARREN PERRY

HOADLEY, ABEL (1844-1918), manufacturer, was born on 10 September 1844 at Willingdon, Sussex, England, only son of Peter Hoadley, blacksmith, and his second wife Elizabeth Ann, née Wheeler. Abel was apprenticed to a draper and grocer, but his health failed and he migrated to Melbourne in 1865. His first employment may have been with the nurseryman George Brunning [q.v.3]. On 14 November 1868 at Fitzroy, with United Presbyterian Church forms, he married Susannah Ann Barrett; they had fourteen children.

By the early 1880s the Hoadleys were established as orchardists at Burwood. According to family legend, jam was first made from windfallen fruit in a copper under a chestnut tree, and the children sold it in the district after school. About 1889 Hoadley opened a small factory in South Melbourne trading as A. Hoadley & Co. under the trade mark of the rising sun. The business expanded rapidly and five-storey premises the Rising Sun Preserving Works, were built in 1895: jams, jellies, preserved fruits candied peels, sauces and confectionery were made by a workforce as large as 200 Late in 1901 there were four preserving factories, and a large confectionery works near Princes Bridge, Hoadley having acquired the old-established firm of Dillon, Burrows & Co. He had extended his products to vinegar, cocoa and chocolate. 800 were em ployed at the height of the season, and in the early 1900s Hoadley was by far the largest Victorian customer of the Colonial Sugar Refining Co.

Hoadley adopted a paternal attitude to his workers. The premises were praised for their cleanliness, airiness and well-equipped dining rooms. He supported wages boards, but after Federation the intensely competitive nature of business made him favour industry rather than occupational boards, and a State-wide and ultimately uniform Federal system. As a devout and active Methodist, he supported the establishment of the Central Mission in 1893, was its treasurer in 1895-1906, and an executive member thereafter. He was remembered as a prudent, independent committee-man, 'conservative without being retrogressive'. In 1903 when the mission decided to extend its boy rescue work by establishing a country home, Hoadley offered his 38-acre (15 ha) Burwood orchard for £1000, some £500 less than the market price; with another property purchased on similar terms it became the nucleus of the Boys' Training Farm at Tally Ho.

In 1910 the jam business was sold to Henry Jones [q.v.] Co-operative Ltd. When Hoadley retired from business in 1913 Hoadley's Chocolates Ltd was formed. He died of cancer on 12 May 1918 at his home, Bella Vista, Kew, leaving an estate valued for probate at £58 946, and was survived by his wife, four daughters and four sons. All these sons were involved in the business, Charles [q.v.] in a minor way as chairman of directors in the 1940s and Peter as purchasing officer. Walter was managing director at his father's death, but by the 1930s the firm was on the verge of bankruptcy. Albert re-established Hoadley's, largely by imaginative marketing of candy bars, notably the Violet Crumble, named by Mrs Abel Hoadley after her favourite flower. Albert's son Gordon presided over the company during a series of mergers in the post-war period, the last being that with the English firm as Rowntree Hoadley Ltd in 1972.

A. J. Derrick, *The story of the Central Mission* (Melb, 1918); *PP* (LA Vic), 1902-03, 2 (31); *Leader* (Melb), 6 June 1896; *Weekly Times* (Melb), 28 Sept 1901; *Spectator*, 15 May, 26 June 1918; Colonial Sugar Refining Co. Records (ANU Archives); information from G. Hoadley, Toorak, Melb.

JOHN LACK

HOADLEY, CHARLES ARCHIBALD BROOKES (1887-1947), explorer, educationist and scout leader, was born on 1 March 1887 at Burwood, Victoria, tenth of fourteen children of Abel Hoadley [q.v.], and his wife Susannah Ann, née Barrett. He was educated at Toorak Grammar School and from 1900 at Wesley College. By 1911 he had completed degrees in mining engineering and science at the University of Melbourne, and two years employment followed with Broken Hill Proprietary Co. Ltd at Port Pirie, South Australia.

Late in 1912 he joined the Australasian Antarctic Exploration Expedition led by (Sir) Douglas Mawson [q.v.], spending a year as geologist to the western base party which covered more than 800 miles (1290 km) in Queen Mary Land. Hoadley was one of the group which undertook a 300-mile (483 km) trip into Kaiser Wilhelm II Land. He examined Haswell Island and Gaussberg, collected specimens, and later praised the geological work of Drygalski, leader of the German Antarctic Expedition (1901-03). Hoadley did not return to the Antarctic, but in 1916 he offered his services to the Ross Sea landing party, projected as part of the *Aurora* relief expedition to rescue (Sir) Ernest Shackleton's men.

Upon his return to Australia in 1913 Hoadley took his M.Sc. and was awarded the Caroline Kay scholarship in geology. In 1914 he had a government research scholarship to undertake the analysis of rocks gathered in the Antarctic, but shortly he was appointed senior lecturer at the Ballarat School of Mines and Industry. January 1916 saw his appointment as the first principal of Footscray Technical School. Hoadley instructed in geology, metallurgy, science and surveying, kept abreast of developments in industry by engaging (1921-22) with a local engineering firm, and practised leather craft and metal-work in his spare time. He proselytized for technical education among district parents in press articles and public addresses. Footscray became the largest diploma teaching school in the State system.

In 1921 he joined the Boy Scout Association and became scoutmaster of the reformed 1st Footscray troop. While investigating technical education in the United States of America and Europe in 1924, he completed a course at Gilwell, England, and in 1925 he helped to organize the earliest Gilwell courses in Australia. Appointed commissioner for scouter training, he was active in the creation and development of Gilwell Park at Gembrook, Victoria. As chief commissioner of Victoria in 1928-37 he reorganized the district and county workings of the association and was credited with infusing a new spirit and purpose into scouting. On 21 May 1932 at Holy Trinity, Kew, Hoadley married Rita Cadle McComb, a nurse. Marriage and ill health curtailed his scouting activities in the 1930s but he was warden of Gilwell Park from 1937, chairman of the

State executive committee from 1944, and president of the federal council of the Boy Scouts' Association from 1946.

In 1929 he visited England as commissioner in charge of the Australian jamboree contingent, and attended for the Education Department a world conference on adult education at Cambridge. Hoadley returned much impressed by the community leadership displayed by men of influence in English towns. A Freemason from 1915, he became foundation deputy worshipful master of the Baden-Powell Lodge in 1930, and a member of Melbourne Rotary in 1932. He was also an active member of local societies and the Church of England.

At the time of his death from coronary thrombosis at his Footscray home on 27 February 1947 Hoadley was the suburb's most respected figure, widely revered for his warm friendship, inspiring leadership and outstanding community service. His ashes were interred beneath the altar in the chapel at Gilwell Park. His wife and their two sons survived him. He is commemorated by the Hoadley Memorial Lodge (1951), a memorial hall at Gilwell Park (1955), a bust erected by the Footscray Rotary Club, and the physical education centre at the Footscray Institute of Technology. He was awarded the King's Polar Medal (1915) and the Order of the Silver Wolf (1931) and was appointed C.B.E. (1936). Cape Hoadley in Antarctica is named after him.

The story of Gilwell in Victoria (Melb, 1963); A'sian Antarctic Expedition, 1911-1914, under the leadership of Sir D. Mawson, Scientific Reports, series A, 1, 1916; Vic Scout, 15 Mar 1947, 16 Aug 1948; Independent (Footscray), 22 Jan 1916; Footscray Advertiser, 15 Mar 1947, 16 Aug 1948; Argus, 25 Sept 1928, 17 Jan 1930, 14 July 1937; Herald (Melb), 27 Sept 1947; Records, Masonic Centre, East Melb, and Mawson Inst for Antarctic Research, Univ Adel; Univ Melb Archives.

JOHN LACK

HOARE, BENJAMIN (1842-1932), journalist, was born on 22 July 1842 at Tyler's Hill, Buckinghamshire, England, eldest child of Richard Hoare, bricklayer, and his Catholic wife, Mary Ann, née Bluff. In 1855 the family arrived as assisted immigrants at Portland, Victoria, where they rented a small farm. Educated in English parish schools (one Anglican, one Catholic), Hoare received further instruction privately in Australia. He adopted the Catholic faith and at 15 joined the Portland Chronicle.

After moving to the Hamilton Spectator in 1861, he left in 1865 for Adelaide where he worked as a printer on the Advertiser. In 1869 he published two poetic works, The Maori and Figures of fancy, and achieved his first editorship with the Gawler Bunyip. He returned to Victoria and in October 1871 joined a co-operative to establish the Geelong Evening Times with Horatio Rowcroft as editor and manager. However, cooperative membership fell away, leaving an increasing burden of work to Hoare, and when Rowcroft also left Hoare formed a partnership with William Bell and Mrs Ann Knight, whose daughter Maria he married on 24 October 1877 at Geelong with Catholic rites. The partners expanded the Times, converting it to a morning daily with Hoare as editor, and founding the Evening Star, edited by Bell in 1879. Hoare also founded and edited the Colac Reformer.

His policy avowedly 'constitutional', Hoare opposed (Sir) Graham Berry [q.v.3] in his quarrel with the Legislative Council in spirited and partisan style, attacking both Berry and David Syme [q.v.6] as 'this pair of traitors to the commonweal'. His reply to criticism of Bell in the Geelong Advertiser, recognized as Hoare's by its liberal quotation from Shakespeare (he was a keen amateur Shakespearean actor), brought a libel suit upon both from which they escaped in February 1886 with a farthing's damages. In April James Bell replaced his father as Hoare's partner but disputes soon arose over money and control of staff, and legal hearings dragged on until 1890.

Hoare joined the editorial staff of the Daily Telegraph in 1886 and moved to Melbourne in February 1888. In 1890 he became leader-writer on the Age. Always sympathetic to the 'unlock the lands' movement, having queued as a 'poor pressman' in Hamilton to obtain his father's selection, by the 1860s he had changed from a free trader to a protectionist; he eventually came to support Berry's land tax and attempt to reform the Upper House: all requisites for an enduring association with David Syme. The Age's policies and quarrels were henceforth to be his own, on secular matters at least, his leaders being sometimes marked by 'brutal force'. In the late 1890s he served as secretary of the Protectionists' Association and in 1904 celebrated protection (and Syme) in his book Preferential trade. After World War I he wrote pamphlets for the Progressive and Economic Association, condemning Bolshevism and the One Big Union. He had retired from the Age in May 1914 but continued writing weekly articles until January 1921.

In Geelong Hoare had supported state aid for Catholic schools and in Melbourne quickly became prominent in church affairs as first vice-president of the Catholic Young Men's Federation. He helped to found and edit the Catholic Magazine (later Austral Light) and wrote articles for these and church newspapers, also pamphlets for the Australian Catholic Truth Society. In 1909 he received the Cross 'Pro Ecclesia et Pontifice' for services to Catholic literature and for federating the Young Men's societies. In 1911 he moved the establishment of an Australian Catholic Federation in Victoria and was elected to its provisional committee and later to its council. When, during the federation's campaign against impure literature, he attacked John Norton's [q.v.] *Truth* Hoare faced another libel suit. This and his counter-suit, both seeking £5000 damages, extended over 1913-14 before a private settlement, favourable to Hoare, was reached.

Hoare had worked for his Church in close consultation with Archbishop Carr [q.v.7]; in 1916, however, he found himself in profound disagreement with Carr's coadjutor Dr Mannix [q.v.], then publicly opposing conscription. His denunciation of Mannix in the *Age* in February 1917 both ended his association with the Australian Catholic Federation and caused his dismissal from the executive of the Australian Catholic Truth Society. Unrepentant, Hoare expounded his pro-British views in *War things that matter* (1918).

In old age Hoare stood aside from controversy, in 1927 producing the *Jubilee history of the Melbourne Harbor Trust* and his reminiscences, *Looking back gaily*. Colleagues attested to his good nature, courtesy, and alertness. Maria Hoare had died in February 1901. On 9 April 1902 at St Patrick's Cathedral, Melbourne, he married Emilie Tuite who also predeceased him. Hoare died on 9 February 1932 at East Melbourne, survived by five of the nine children of his first wife, beside whom he was buried in Eastern cemetery, Geelong.

W. R. Brownhill, *The history of Geelong and Corio Bay* (Melb, 1955); I. Hebb, *The history of Colac and district* (Melb, 1970); *Catholic Press*, 8 Sept 1900, 17 June 1909; *Colac Reformer*, 27 July 1878, 19 Nov 1879; *Age*, 16 Feb 1917, 10 Feb 1932; C. E. Close, The organisation of the Catholic laity in Victoria 1911-1930 (M.A. thesis, Univ Melb, 1972); Vic Supreme Court records, 1885-90, 1913-14 (PRO, Vic); Archer papers (Univ Melb Archives), Higgins and Deakin papers (NL), Mackinnon and Syme papers (LaTL).   CECILY CLOSE

HOBBS, SIR JOSEPH JOHN TALBOT (1864-1938), architect and soldier, was born on 24 August 1864 in London, son of Joseph Hobbs, a journeyman joiner who became a clerk of works, and his wife Frances Ann, née Wilson. He was educated at St Mary's Church School, Merton, Surrey. He worked as architectural draftsman to a builder, John

Hurst, with whom he migrated to Perth in 1887. There he began work as a carpenter but soon set up practice as an architect. On 24 April 1890 he married Hurst's daughter, Edith Ann, at St George's Anglican Cathedral; they had three sons and four daughters. Talbot Hobbs became a leader in the small band of Perth architects. He was first treasurer of the newly formed West Australian Institute of Architects in 1896 (president, 1909-11) and prospered in the 1890s. His success in the competition for the design of the Weld Club in 1891 began a series of commissions for important buildings, both public and private, in Perth and Fremantle. In 1905 he set up the firm Hobbs, Smith & Forbes in which he was the senior partner.

His small stature and seeming frailness belied the energy and range of activities which distinguished Hobbs throughout his life. He was a keen sportsman, interested in fencing, gymnastics, rowing, sailing and boxing. A devout Christian, he was deeply involved in the affairs of the Anglican Church, serving in synod and on various councils and as architect to the diocese of Perth. Above all he was devoted to soldiering which became virtually a second career parallel to architecture. Beginning with service in the 1st Cinque Ports Artillery Volunteers in 1883, he joined the Volunteer Field Artillery in Perth in 1887 and was commissioned in 1889. In 1903 he commanded the 1st (Western Australian) Field Battery, Australian Field Artillery, by 1908 as lieutcolonel the Western Australian Mixed Brigade, and in 1913 the 22nd Infantry Brigade in the rank of colonel. He studied to prepare himself for war, attending gunnery courses in England in 1902 and 1906 and the department of military science course, University of Sydney, in 1909. He was attached to the British Army for training in 1897 and 1913. Most of this was at his own expense. He was also staff officer for army engineering services in 1906-12 and aide-de-camp to the governor-general in 1908-17. He supported the introduction of compulsory training and was a leader in the development of service rifle-shooting. His devotion to the army made lasting impressions typified in a letter from a Gallipoli veteran in 1934: 'He gave his Youth, Leasure [sic] and Purse to perfect himself and us'.

On the outbreak of war in 1914 Hobbs was given command of the artillery of the 1st Division, Australian Imperial Force. During the first few weeks on Gallipoli in 1915 he clashed with his commander, Major General (Sir) W. T. Bridges [q.v.7], over the employment of his guns. Bridges insisted that they be dragged up the steep ridges and emplaced in the front line although their fire was ineffective. However, by June Hobbs and the other artillery commanders had organized a workable deployment of all batteries so that the Anzac front was covered. He commanded the 1st Division temporarily in October but despite his protests was evacuated from Gallipoli on 9 November suffering from dysentery. He was appointed C.B. at this time.

After the expansion of the A.I.F. in March 1916 Hobbs went to France with the increased 1st Divisional Artillery which he commanded successfully throughout the heavy fighting for Pozières and Mouquet Farm. He was acting commander of the 1st Anzac Corps Artillery from October until December when he was given command of the 5th Division. His promotion to major general followed on 1 January 1917. For two years Hobbs 'commanded a division with great distinction, made fewer mistakes than most, and earned the undying affection of 20 000 men', according to Major General Sir Brudenell White [q.v.] who had special opportunities for observing him. Lieut-General Sir John Monash [q.v.] considered he 'succeeded fully as the Commander of a Division, by his sound common sense, and his sane attitude towards every problem'. Hobbs was known for his justice and integrity and quickly won the affection and loyalty of his staff. He created harmony throughout his division which became 'the ruling passion of his life'. Looking back to 1917-18 in 1938, he declared those years to have been the most momentous and wonderful of all.

When his division was in the line he was frequently with his brigadiers, one of whom was the redoubtable H. E. Elliott [q.v.8]. During the advance to the Hindenburg line in March 1917 Elliott ordered an attack in flagrant disobedience of Hobbs's orders, the latter stopped the operation and drove immediately to Elliott's headquarters. Had word of this affair reached the corps commander, Lieut-General Sir William Birdwood [q.v.7], Elliott could hardly have escaped dismissal. Hobbs would also speak bluntly to his superiors; on at least three occasions he protested against the employment of his division when he knew that it was in dire need of rest. He so impressed Birdwood on this point in May 1917, before the 2nd battle of Bullecourt, that his representations were passed on to General Headquarters with the result that all the Australian divisions were withdrawn to rest as they came out of that battle. He played a notable part in the heavy fighting of 3rd Ypres, especially in September at Polygon Wood, where his determination helped to turn an adverse situation into a remarkable victory. He was appointed K.C.B. in December.

In April 1918 Hobbs was largely responsible for the recapture of Villers-Bretonneux. His diary for 27 April claims: 'I really planned it—but I feel I should never get the credit of it'. In the quieter period following this feat he was concerned with the development of a steel casemate for machine-guns in the trenches. It was his own invention and its manufacture was ordered by (Sir) Winston Churchill, the British minister for munitions. The early deliveries of the casemate in France coincided with the great allied offensives so that it was never used in battle. During the controversy over the command of the A.I.F. Hobbs made clear to Prime Minister W. M. Hughes [q.v.] and others his support for Birdwood's retention of the position. He was one of the three generals considered by Birdwood for command of the Australian Corps. In the offensive battles opening on 8 August 1918 he won further laurels especially in the capture of Péronne on 2 September and the piercing of the Hindenburg line at Bellicourt. He temporarily commanded the Australian Corps when it was withdrawn to rest in October and succeeded Monash in command on 28 November 1918 as acting lieut-general. Appointed K.C.M.G. in January 1919, he was also awarded the Serbian Order of the White Eagle (1917), the French Croix de Guerre (twice) and was mentioned in dispatches eight times. His son, John Mervyn, a gunner on Gallipoli, was commissioned in 1915, won the Military Cross in France and served after the war in the Indian Army where he was awarded a Bar to the M.C. and became a brigadier. Hobbs's brother, Lieut-Colonel Howard Frederick Hobbs, joined the British Army in 1914 and won the Distinguished Service Order and the Military Cross.

Even before he relinquished command of the Australian Corps in May 1919 Hobbs became deeply involved in the erection of memorials to the Australian divisions, having been appointed to select sites, prepare designs and arrange for construction. Four of the five designs were his. He chose Polygon Wood for the memorial to the 5th Division and Villers-Bretonneux for the Australian national memorial. On returning to Perth in October he told an interviewer that he would 'try to become a good citizen again' and that 'for the rest of my life I shall be at the service of the men who did so very much to win this war, the Australian soldiers'. He had hardly resumed civilian life when, in February 1920, he was called to Melbourne as one of a committee of six generals advising the government on the organization, size and equipment of the army. In 1921 he was made commander of the 5th Division and the 13th Mixed Brigade, Australian Military Forces, appointments which he held until retirement from the army in 1927. From 1922 he was military representative on the faculty of engineering, University of Western Australia, which had conferred on him the honorary degree of LL.D. on his return from the war.

Hobbs was busy with his profession; the architect now vied with the soldier but the two were united when he was chosen to design the Western Australian War Memorial which was dedicated in 1929. Athol, his younger son, who had resigned from the Indian Army in 1923, had by then joined his firm. Hobbs was on the Western Australian Board of Architects and was a fellow of the Western Australian, Victorian and British institutes. His success in war had made him an important public figure whose help was continually sought by government, ex-service and private bodies. He was chairman of a committee organizing the visit of the prince of Wales to Western Australia in 1920, Western Australian commissioner at the Empire Exhibition at Wembley in 1924, and a delegate to the League of Nations Assembly in 1933. At various times he was chief scout of Western Australia, State president of Toc H, a patron of Legacy, warden of the Western Australian War Memorial, and a director of three companies. Above all he devoted himself to the welfare of returned soldiers to whom he was, in the words of one of them, 'our loved commander of the 5th Divvy'.

In April 1938 Hobbs left for France with his wife and daughter to attend the unveiling of the Australian war memorial at Villers-Bretonneux, the competition for which he had adjudicated. He suffered a heart attack at sea and died on 21 April. His body was brought back from Colombo to Perth for burial with state and military honours on 14 May after a service at St George's Cathedral. He was survived by his wife and children. His estate was valued for probate at £31 137. A memorial to Hobbs was unveiled in 1940 on the Esplanade in Perth. Portraits by James Quinn, Frederick Leist [qq.v.] and Albert Fullwood [q.v.8] are in the Australian War Memorial, Canberra, and by Ernest Buckmaster in the West Australian Army Museum, North Perth.

J. S. Battye (ed), *Cyclopedia of Western Australia*, 1 (Adel, 1912); A. D. Ellis, *The story of the Fifth Australian Division* (Lond, 1920?); J. Monash, *The Australian victories in France in 1918* (Lond, 1920); C. E. W. Bean, *The story of Anzac* (Syd, 1921, 1924), and *The A.I.F. in France*, 1916-18 (Syd, 1929, 1933, 1937, 1942); J. M. Freeland, *The making of a profession* (Syd, 1971); L. Hunt (ed), *Westralian portraits* (Perth, 1979); *Reveille* (Syd), Jan 1935, June 1938; *West Australian*, 11 Oct, 9 Nov 1901, 4 Jan 1918, 31 Oct 1919, 22, 23 Apr 1938; *SMH*, 24 Apr 1919, 23, 28 Apr, 16 May 1938; *Daily News* (Perth), 22 Apr 1938; *Argus*, 14 May 1938; J. J. T. Hobbs papers and copies of his diaries (AWM).

A. J. HILL

HOBLER, GEORGE ALEXANDER (1864-1935), railway engineer and administrator, was born on 18 January 1864 at Coorada, Upper Dawson district, Queensland, third child of English-born Francis Helvetius Hobler, squatter, and his Scottish wife Jessie Ann, née Learmonth, and grandson of George Hobler [q.v.1]. After a state school education Hobler entered the Queensland Railways in January 1879 as a civil engineering cadet. In 1885 he was promoted from junior draughtsman to second-class assistant surveyor and in 1888 became assistant engineer on the Cairns line. He married Antoinette Gertrude van Heucklelum at St John's Church of England, Cairns, on 16 December 1890.

In 1892 Hobler was engaged to prepare the evidence for the Queensland government in the John Robb [q.v.6] case. After the Supreme Court verdict of mid-1893 against Robb, who had claimed over £250 000 additional payment as contractor on the difficult second section (Redlynch to Myola) of the Cairns-Herberton railway, Hobler was promoted to district engineer. He was given charge of the construction of the mountain section of the line as far as Mareeba, and was subsequently appointed by the London trustees of the Chillagoe Railway and Mines Co. Ltd to supervise the continuation of the line to Chillagoe. He also supervised the building of the Chillagoe smelters (completed in 1901) and a wharf at Cairns. In 1909 he became inspecting engineer and in 1911 constructing engineer for lines throughout the State, including those built by local authorities under special Acts of parliament.

On 31 August 1912 Hobler joined the newly formed Commonwealth Railways in Melbourne as deputy-engineer-in-chief under Henry Deane [q.v.8] for the construction of the transcontinental railway. Under an administrative rearrangement in April 1914 he was given charge of the civil engineering branch and in February 1918 he was appointed engineer (later chief engineer) of the way and works branch, Port Augusta, South Australia. Throughout World War I he held the appointment of honorary lieut-colonel, Railway Staff Corps.

Hobler was regarded as an expert on northern Australia. In November 1914 he travelled from Pine Creek to Bitter Springs (Mataranka), Northern Territory, along the proposed extension of the Pine Creek–Katherine River railway and next year reported to the Standing Committee on Public

Works. In May–June 1920 he represented the Federal government on an expedition to the North-West and Kimberley district of Western Australia, organized by the Western Australian government and the North Australian Railway and Development League, to report on the country from Meekatharra to Wyndham. Hobler concluded that 'with proper development the country could carry a great population, and support numbers of wealth producing industries'; he advocated construction of a railway from Meekatharra across the desert to Newcastle Waters, Northern Territory, with branch lines to Wyndham, Derby, Port Hedland and Carnarvon. His exploring earned him a fellowship of the Royal Geographical Society (London).

Hobler retired from the Commonwealth Railways in 1926 when he joined the advisory North Australian Commission in Darwin. When the commission disbanded in 1931, Hobler moved to Mosman, Sydney, whence he travelled the world as an observer of railway systems. He died at Mosman on 6 October 1935 and was cremated; his ashes were scattered from an aircraft over Darwin. He was survived by his wife and two daughters; his son, Cyril, had been killed in the battle of the Somme in 1916.

PP (Cwlth), 1914-17, 4 (323, 344), 1920-21, 5 (58); *Capricornian*, 6 Nov 1926; *SMH*, 8 Oct 1935; Hobler papers (MSS 1861 ML); personal information.

A. E. CREELMAN

HOCKING, SIDNEY EDWIN (1859-1935), newspaper proprietor, was born on 24 December 1859 at Nairne, South Australia, son of Nicholas Hocking, blacksmith, and his wife Sarah, née Shore. Educated at Prince Alfred College, he joined the Adelaide *Advertiser* in 1874 as a general reporter and became the paper's mining writer at the Teetulpa goldfield, Baker's Creek and Hillgrove. In 1889 he went to the new mining field at Broken Hill, New South Wales, as representative for a syndicate of evening papers in Melbourne and Sydney. Leaving Broken Hill in 1893, he arrived at Coolgardie, Western Australia, next year and sent articles to the Adelaide *Advertiser* and *Register*, the Melbourne *Age* and *Argus* and the *West Australian*. With James Mac-Callum Smith [q.v.], and later joined by his brother Percy, he floated a company to publish the weekly *Goldfields Courier*, which he edited, and the daily *Golden Age*. He also ran a stationer's and newsagent's business and speculated in town lots.

When the new Kalgoorlie goldfield began to drain the life from Coolgardie, Hocking inspected the fabulous 'Golden Mile' and decided that its future was assured. He and his partners sold the Coolgardie company and in August 1895 Hocking bought the weekly *Kalgoorlie Western Argus*, founded by Mott [q.v.] Bros., the previous November. After buying an up-to-date plant, Hocking also launched the daily *Kalgoorlie Miner*. He temporarily employed (Sir) Hal Colebatch [q.v.8] as editor and, in Adelaide, recruited (Sir) John Kirwan [q.v.]. In 1896 he launched Hocking & Co. Ltd with himself, Percy, another brother Ernest, Kirwan and their printer W. W. Willcock as shareholders. Hocking became mining editor, leaving the business management of the two papers and an associated stationery and job-printing house to Percy and the editorial management to Kirwan. When Percy died in 1900 Hocking took over the commercial side and Kirwan, when he became too deeply involved in politics, was replaced by Edward Hamilton Irving who managed the paper until his death in 1929.

Hocking shared a house with his sister Emma until his marriage on 15 August 1900 to 21-year-old Effie Fenn; they had eight children. For many years chairman of the Kalgoorlie Racing Club and president of the Kalgoorlie Chamber of Commerce, he was also almost permanent president of the Fresh Air League, which sent goldfields children for seaside holidays. He was an enthusiastic gardener, who is said to have planted the first of Kalgoorlie's many peppercorn trees, and in his later years he enjoyed golf. His reputation as a good boss was valuable in a town like Kalgoorlie, dominated by the democratic ethos; the accepted legend that he had never sacked a man was not true, but he was certainly remarkably lenient. In 1895, and from 1907, he served on the Kalgoorlie Municipal Council and was mayor in 1909-10. Modest and intensely domestic, however, he generally shunned the limelight. He left Kalgoorlie rarely and was only twice overseas, first in 1899, when he purchased modern newspaper plant, and in 1930 when he was a delegate to the Imperial Press Conference in London. In an endeavour to keep his newspapers unbiased he avoided political involvement.

Hocking died on 29 January 1935 during a heat wave and was buried in Kalgoorlie cemetery. His estate, valued for probate at £54 769 in Western Australia and Victoria was left to his family, all of whom survived him. Three of his sons became directors of Hocking & Co. Ltd.

J. S. Battye (ed), *Cyclopedia of Western Australia* 1 (Adel, 1912); J. Kirwan, *My life's adventure* (Lond 1936); *Critic*, (Adel), 11 June 1898; *WA Law Reports*, 1909; *Kalgoorlie Western Argus*, 15 Mar 1900 *Kalgoorlie Miner*, 29 Jan 1935, 14 Sept 1945; J. Kirwan papers (Battye Lib).   H. J. GIBBNEY

HODEL, JOSEPH (1850-1943), business-man, was born on 9 October 1850 at St Helier, Jersey, Channel Islands, son of François Charles Hodel, carpenter, and his wife Anne, née Fauvel. Arriving in Brisbane in March 1863 with their ten children, his parents went to Robert Towns's [q.v.6] Townsvale plantation.

At 18, while a labourer at Undallagh, Hodel married Johanna, née Hickey, a widowed 28-year-old Irish servant. Arriving in Townsville in 1870, he opened a bakery, then in 1875 built and ran the North Star hotel. In Brisbane on 26 October 1877 he married his Scottish-born second wife, Alice Mary Coutts. Next year he bought the New-market hotel and added livery stables. This led him into pastoral activities at Oaklands, Cluden. One of the original members of the Townsville Pastoral Association, by 1886 he was judging horses at the Townsville show and winning prizes for his own stock. He ac-quired more land at Clevedon, south of Townsville, in the late 1880s.

In 1888-1916 Hodel served on the Thurin-gowa Divisional Board and was chairman for eighteen years. He joined the Townsville City Council in 1895 and was mayor in 1910. He played a major role in the construction and operation of the tramway which linked Ayr to the railway at Stuart's Creek and facilitated the marketing of Burdekin dis-trict sugar. As a foundation member of the Townsville Harbour Board he was involved in development of the harbour but, although chairman of the board for seven of his twenty-five years service, his re-election de-pended sometimes on his own casting vote. His concurrent offices as president of the Ayr Tramway Board and chairman of the Thuringowa Divisional Board earned him the reputation of being power hungry. An unsuccessful opponent once accused him of wanting to be 'lord of the land and admiral of the seas'. Selfless and progressive, Hodel demonstrated his independent spirit on the harbour board by frequently being in a dis-senting minority. In 1916, as one of those opposing the Mt Elliott Ltd proposal to build a copper refinery at Townsville, he called for a health commission report on the likely effect of the fumes on public health.

Retiring from active business before he was 40, Hodel worked for the hospital and orphanage committees, the Townsville Turf Club, Show Association, Waterworks Board and Chamber of Commerce, and was in regular demand as an adviser on new busi-ness ventures. He was a member of the Legislative Council in 1914-22. Although other members of his family were involved with North Queensland newspapers and Joseph had once financed his brothers in management of the *Northern Standard*, he himself did not enter the newspaper world until 1908 when he bought shares in the Townsville Newspaper Co. Ltd. From 9 March 1914 to his death he was chairman of its successor, the North Queensland Newspaper Co. Ltd.

Hodel died at Townsville on 4 September 1943 and was buried in the local cemetery. His estate, valued for probate at £63 058, was left to his family. He had married Sarah Ann Waldie on 24 March 1891. A son of that marriage survived him together with two sons of his first and a son and daughter of his second marriage.

A. Donnelly (ed), *The port of Townsville* (Towns-ville, 1959); J. Manion, *Paper power in North Queensland* (Townsville, 1982); *Townsville Her-ald*, 10 July 1886; *North Qld Herald*, 18 Mar 1896, 14 Apr 1908; *Townsville Daily Bulletin*, 3 July 1914, undated cutting Sept 1943; *North Qld Register*, undated cutting Feb 1916; *Pugh's Almanac*, 1875, 1876, 1877, 1878; North Qld Newspaper Co. Ltd, Minute-books, 1911-43, *and* annual return of shareholders (QA); correspondence on sale of Ayr tramway (Nth Qld Newspaper Co. Ltd Archives, Townsville).

JIM MANION

HODGE, CHARLES REYNOLDS (1857-1946), university administrator, was born on 20 September 1857 at Geelong, Victoria, eld-est son of Cornish parents Rev. Charles Hodge, Bible Christian minister, and his wife Martha, née Reynolds. In 1861 the fam-ily moved to South Australia where Charles senior joined the Congregational ministry. Hodge was educated at Encounter Bay Public School and Rev. James Hotham's pri-vate school, Port Elliott. On 24 March 1880 at Kent Town he married Emily Annie Daws. A decade of commercial employ-ment, including work as a draper, preceded his appointment in August 1884 as clerk to the registrar of the University of Adelaide. During the absence of J. W. Tyas [q.v.6] he acted as registrar briefly in 1889 and in 1891-92 with such competence that when the registrarship became vacant in Febru-ary 1892 the council appointed him to the position without competition.

When Hodge became a university clerk in 1884 the law course was in its second year, arrangements were nearing completion for degree courses in medicine and music to begin in 1885, the staff totalled 10 and the students 152. In 1923, Hodge's last year as registrar, the total staff was 119 and the student body 2010. Additions to the aca-demic work of the university during his registrarship included engineering, com-merce and dentistry and the opening of the Elder [q.v.4] Conservatorium of Music; ac-tive discussions were proceeding for the opening of the Waite [q.v.] Agricultural Research Institute. Hodge published a guide to the university in 1899. In his commemoration address on 12 December 1923, when Hodge was on pre-retirement leave, the chancellor Sir George Murray [q.v.] referred to him as 'an able, trustworthy and loyal officer' who held his colleagues' 'admiration, gratitude and affection'. A former student (Sir) Walter Crocker later wrote approvingly of him as 'a good registrar'. However, Hodge's ability was not that of the innovator and it was his successor F. W. Eardley who made several noteworthy administrative advances.

Hodge was an executive member of the South Australian Literary Societies' Union in 1888-1901 and winner of prizes for humorous elocution (1885) and a novelette (1890). He was an active member of the Shakespeare Society and the Australian Natives' Association and reputedly the author of a number of ephemeral short stories published in the daily press under the name 'U-no'. In 1900 he published an undistinguished novel *'That Codicil': an Australian story of treachery and triumph* as a revised version of his *Express* serial 'Olive Temple'.

Hodge was a deacon of the Rose Park Congregational Church for thirteen years, an executive member of the Congregational Union for five years, a delegate to the assembly of the Congregational Union of Australia and New Zealand in 1913, and secretary of the committee organizing the denomination's centenary celebrations in South Australia in 1939. He was also a justice of the peace.

On retirement Hodge moved to Victor Harbor and for the next seven years devoted himself to compiling a history of Encounter Bay. He published several historical sketches and in 1932 *Encounter Bay: miniature Naples of Australia*. He died at Victor Harbor on 27 April 1946. His wife had died in 1935 and he was survived by six of his seven daughters.

J. J. Pascoe (ed), *History of Adelaide and vicinity* (Adel, 1901); P. Depasquale, *A critical history of South Australian literature, 1836-1930 with subjectively annotated bibliographies* (Adel, 1978); *JHSSA*, no 3 (1977); *Register* (Adel), 13 Dec 1923, 4 Mar 1924; *Advertiser* (Adel), 29 Apr 1946; SA Literary Societies' Union records (SAA); Congregational Union of SA records (SAA, and Rev. J. Cameron, Findon, SA); records (Univ Adel).

V. A. EDGELOE

HODGES, SIR HENRY EDWARD AGINCOURT (1844-1919), judge, was born on 14 October 1844 in Liverpool, England, fifth child of Henry Hodges and his wife Eliza, née Van Wyck. The father, formerly a ship's captain, brought his family to Australia in 1854 and went to the Bendigo goldfields, where he took up teaching. After early education in the Bendigo district Hodges entered Melbourne Church of England Grammar School in 1863 where he spent two years and played in the first XI. In 1865 he enrolled at the University of Melbourne to study arts and law but completed only the arts course, having been delayed for one year by his rustication for assisting a fellow student in an examination; he graduated B.A. in April 1870. He then acted as private tutor to the families of J. G. Francis and Sir William Stawell [qq.v.4,6] and, although he had originally intended to enter the Anglican ministry, resumed study of the law. In 1873 he became a member of Trinity College in the University of Melbourne and on 9 December was called to the Bar. He read as a pupil in the chambers of (Sir) Hartley Williams [q.v.6] and at a time when there was much legal business in the colony quickly established a substantial practice. He showed marked ability and became a strong advocate.

Hodges was appointed an acting judge of the Supreme Court of Victoria on 12 February 1889 during the absence on leave of Mr Justice Webb [q.v.6]. His appointment, made permanent on 20 January 1890 on the death of Mr Justice Kerferd [q.v.5], was well received. He became a strong judge, clear and definite in his opinions. His judgments were severely logical. A rapid worker, he took notes of evidence in shorthand, a practice not common among judges. He could sit for long hours without showing fatigue. Yet he did not escape criticism from the Bar. His temper could be violent and he had little sense of humour. He had developed a sharpness of manner, sometimes extending to biting sarcasm, which on occasion made the presentation of argument difficult, and he was quick to resent whatever he perceived as impertinence. In spite of his demeanour, he was often emotional and this quality, whilst it led to humane sentences in criminal cases, also led to unwarranted outbursts in court. He was apt to react most strongly against any witness who was thought to have departed from the truth.

In 1913 the committee of the Bar on the motion of (Sir) H. E. Starke and W. J. Schutt [qq.v.] passed a resolution deploring the violent discourtesy of Hodges towards litigants, witnesses and members of the legal profession and recording the opinion that his conduct was most detrimental to the administration of justice. A copy of the resolution was forwarded to Hodges and thereafter there were no more formal complaints. The same qualities however led to his being conspicuously fair when presiding over a criminal trial: his responsibilities bore heavily upon him. In 1892 he presided over the trial of the notorious murderer F. B. Deeming [q.v.8].

In 1901 whilst on a visit to England Hodges represented the Commonwealth government at a conference in London on the establishment of an Imperial Court of Federal Appeal. He advanced the view that there should be only one court of final appeal which should have vested in it the jurisdiction of the House of Lords and of the Privy Council.

A staunch Anglican and a very religious man, he was chancellor of the diocese of Melbourne from 1889 until 1909 and made many earnest and fearless addresses to synod. *Virtute officii* he was a member of the Council of Melbourne Grammar for the same period. Hodges became first president of the Old Melburnians' society in 1895 and made many brilliant speeches at its gatherings. He chaired and addressed the first Pleasant Sunday Afternoon in Wesley Church, Melbourne, in 1893. At all times he spoke deliberately, earnestly and incisively. He was knighted in June 1918 and was a member of the Melbourne Club.

Hodges married on 8 January 1879 at Chalmers Presbyterian Church, East Melbourne, Margaret, sister of William Knox [q.v.]. They had two sons, one of whom died on active service in World War I, and two daughters who married and lived in England. His first wife died in 1908 and he married on 27 November 1909 Alice Belinda, widow of Robert Chirnside of Caramballac and daughter of Joseph Ware.

Hodges lived in a substantial mansion, Homeden, Lansell Road, Toorak. He was a keen gardener and played a little tennis. He also had a country house, Dreamthorpe, Macedon, and was a popular and respected figure in that district. He died at Dreamthorpe on 8 August 1919 after a short illness and was buried in Boroondara cemetery after a service at St Paul's Cathedral.

J. L. Forde, *The story of the Bar of Victoria* (Melb, 1913); Melb C of E Grammar School, *Liber Melburniensis* (Melb, 1914); P. A. Jacobs, *Judges of yesterday* (Melb, 1924), and *A lawyer tells* (Melb, 1949); M. B. Brookes, *Riders of time* (Melb, 1967); J. S. O'Sullivan, *A most unique ruffian* (Melb, 1968); A. Dean, *A multitude of counsellors* (Melb, 1968); J. A. Grant (ed), *Perspective of a century* (Melb, 1972); *Aust Law Times*, 19 Apr 1902; *Punch* (Melb), 24 Sept 1903; *Argus*, 9 Aug 1919.

J. McI. YOUNG

HODGSON, WILLIAM ROY (1892-1958), soldier and public servant, was born on 22 May 1892 at Kingston, Victoria, son of Robert Hodgson, schoolmaster, and his wife Margaret, née Willson. He was educated at the School of Mines, Ballarat, and, as a member of the original class of 1911, at the Royal Military College, Duntroon, Australian Capital Territory. Graduating in 1914, he was posted to the Administrative and Instructional Staff, Australian Military Forces, on 15 August and three days later was appointed to the Australian Imperial Force. He embarked for Egypt in October as lieutenant in the 5th Battery, 2nd Field Artillery Brigade.

Ater the landing on Gallipoli on 25 April 1915 Hodgson was detailed as forward observing officer for his battery; his commanding officer subsequently praised his 'great gallantry' in a position of 'great risk and responsibility'. On the third day, however, Hodgson was wounded in the hip joint by a Turkish sniper. Reported dead, he was able to read his own obituary, while he lived to survive numerous operations in Egypt and England which left him with one leg considerably shorter than the other, necessitating the use of a walking-stick. Mentioned in dispatches and awarded the Croix de Guerre avec palme in 1916, he was invalided back to Australia next year. Undeterred by his physical disability which denied him the active service career in which he would undoubtedly have made his mark, Hodgson remained an army man at heart, with a quick mind and a bold spirit. He was attached to the A.M.F. General Staff, Army Headquarters, in Melbourne in 1918 and, after serving in the training and administrative sections, became head of military intelligence in 1925. He was promoted major on 1 January 1926. He resigned from the permanent military forces in 1934, being placed on the unattached list with the honorary rank of lieut-colonel, although he continued his involvement with military intelligence until 1936.

In his spare time Hodgson had acquired accountancy qualifications and studied law at the University of Melbourne, graduating LL.B. in 1929. That year he was seconded for six months to the Development and Migration Commission. In 1932 he applied for the position of Australian political liaison officer, London, but, although given strong supporting testimonials by General Sir Harry Chauvel [q.v.7] and Major General (Sir) T. A. Blamey, was unsuccessful. In 1934 he became assistant secretary supervising that branch of the Prime Minister's Department which dealt with external affairs; next year he was made secretary of external affairs as a separate department. As adviser on foreign affairs he attended the 1937 Imperial Conference in London. By the time of his resignation as head of the department in 1945 he had contributed substantially to the development of a professional diplomatic service.

In 1945-57 Hodgson served overseas as Australian head of mission, carrying out a wide variety of functions at international conferences and on international commissions. Acting Australian high commissioner in Canada in 1945, he was appointed minister (later ambassador) to France the same year. He was involved in the formative stages of the United Nations Organization and was Australian delegate to the first General Assembly, held in London in 1945-46, and Australian representative on the Security Council and the Human Rights Commission. He was also an Australian delegate to the Paris Peace Conference in 1946. In 1949 he was sent to Tokyo as British Commonwealth representative on the Allied Council for Japan, and, in 1952, to South Africa as Australian high commissioner. Appointed O.B.E. in 1934 and C.M.G. in 1951, he retired from the diplomatic service in 1957.

Always something of a martinet, Hodgson, known to his friends as 'Hoddy', was not cut out temperamentally for the life of a diplomat. His direct, blunt and rather aggressive style was apt to give offence, as shown in the degree of resentment aroused in Dutch circles when during a 1948 Security Council session he described the terms of the 'ultimatum' which preceded the second Dutch 'police action' in Indonesia as 'even worse than what Hitler did to the Netherlands in 1940'. A voracious reader, Hodgson was a connoisseur of old silver and Chinese porcelain and took a keen interest in most forms of sport. He had married Muriel Daisy McDowell on 18 October 1919 at Christ Church, South Yarra, Melbourne; her death in Paris in 1946 left him a somewhat lonely and less secure man. But the courage and determination which had marked his career never left him. He died of cancer on 24 January 1958 in Sydney and was cremated. A son and a daughter survived him.

P. Hasluck, *Diplomatic witness* (Melb, 1980); UN Security Council, *Official Records*, no 133, 390th, 391st Meeting (Paris), 23 Dec 1948; *Stand-To* (Canb), May-June 1954, p 15; *SMH*, 3 Feb 1945, 24, 31 Dec 1948, 25 Jan 1958; Hodgson papers (held by Mr R. Hodgson, Red Hill, Canb).

ALAN WATT

HOFF, GEORGE RAYNER (1894-1937), sculptor and teacher, was born on 27 November 1894 at Braddan, Isle of Man, son of George Hoff, bricklayer, and his wife Elizabeth Amy, née Coole. Early training came from his father, who restored ancient buildings and was a capable woodcarver and stonemason. After the family had moved to Nottingham, Rayner worked in a mason's yard after school and entered an architect's office at 14. From 1910 he studied drawing and design at Nottingham School of Art.

Enlisting for active service in World War I in 1915, Hoff served in France in 1916. Next year he was transferred to a topographical survey unit and made maps from aerial photographs until the end of the war. Returning to Nottingham, he married Annis Mary Briggs on 30 June 1920 at Sutton in Ashfield.

In 1919 Hoff had begun studies at the Royal College of Art, London, under the professor of sculpture, Francis Derwent Wood, R.A. He exhibited two sculptures at the Royal Academy Summer Exhibition in 1920 and one in 1922. Winning the Prix de Rome scholarship in 1921 he visited Italy next year. In 1923 he was awarded the Royal Society of British Sculptors' diploma. After meeting the Australian architect Hardy Wilson [q.v.] at Naples, and discussions with Derwent Wood in London, he accepted appointment as teacher of drawing, modelling and sculpture at East Sydney Technical College in May 1923 and reached Sydney in August.

A short, dark and physically powerful man, Hoff possessed a mature outlook and a strong commitment to his art. At the college he energetically reorganized the courses and was a vigorous administrator. He created a lively school of sculpture that attracted a group of notable students and in 1931 he was placed in charge of the entire art department. In the same year he edited and produced *The art of Eileen McGrath*, a book on his first successful diploma student, and concentrated on raising the profile of the 'National Art School' by astute publicity.

Joining the Society of Artists, Sydney, in 1924 Hoff served on its executive and became a force for liberal ideals combined with stylistic moderation in art. His friendship with Norman Lindsay [q.v.] and Hardy Wilson influenced the ideas underlying his work and his sources of inspiration were broad. Greco-Roman, European Renaissance, Assyrian, Oriental and Art Deco features can be noted in a stylistically diverse and eclectic output.

The medal for the Society of Artists was created by Hoff in 1924. Later he produced, among others, the Sir Peter Nichol Russell [q.v.6] memorial medal for the Institution of Engineers, Australia (1927), the Sir John Sulman [q.v.] medal for the Institute of Architects of New South Wales (1932) and the contentious Victorian centenary medallion (1934). He showed sculpture regularly with the Society of Artists, the Victorian Artists' Society and the Australian Sculptors' Society. He entered various official and prize exhibitions, and was awarded the Wynne prize in 1927. In 1937 he exhibited with, and became a foundation council-member of, the short-lived Australian Academy of Art.

The most significant visible contribution that Hoff made was his large-scale sculpture for various buildings and public memorials: he produced the large reliefs of the war memorial at Dubbo, New South Wales, in 1925, the figures for the National War Memorial, Adelaide, in 1927-31 and the more numerous and controversial sculptures for the Anzac Memorial, Sydney (made with the aid of students and assistants) in 1930-34. Hoff was also responsible for fine decorative reliefs for the now demolished Liberty Theatre (1934) and Hotel Australia (1934-35). After winning the competition he had begun work on the King George V Memorial, Canberra, in 1936, which was completed posthumously by John Moorfield.

Rayner Hoff's last years took a tragic turn. He was embroiled in controversy with the Catholic Archbishop Kelly [q.v.], the Master Builders' Association of New South Wales and the local chapter of the Royal Australian Institute of Architects over the morality of the form and symbolism of the Anzac Memorial Group 'Sacrifice', 'Crucifixion of Civilisation' and 'Victory' in 1932. He was also attacked for his design for the Victorian centenary medal in 1934. His consumption of alcohol became excessive, his health deteriorated and his marriage fell apart. After being dumped by a wave while surfing, Hoff died of pancreatitis on 19 November 1937 at Waverley and was cremated with Anglican rites. He was survived by his wife and two daughters. A memorial retrospective exhibition of his sculpture and drawings was held at the David Jones' [q.v.2] Art Gallery, Sydney, in 1938. Examples of his sculpture are held by the major Australian galleries.

Rayner Hoff stands as the outstanding public sculptor in Sydney between the wars. Given the demands of his administrative and educational duties, his contribution to Australian art was considerable. While not an artistic innovator himself, he did much to help to build an attitude of liberal tolerance for the younger artists of the time.

W. L. Beauchamp et al, *Sculpture of Rayner Hoff* (Syd, 1934); G. Sturgeon, *The development of Australian sculpture 1788-1975* (Lond, 1978); K. Scarlett, *Australian sculptors* (Melb, 1980); *Art in Aust*, Oct 1932; *SMH*, 20 Nov 1937.

NOEL S. HUTCHISON

HOGAN, EDMUND JOHN (1883-1964), farmer and premier, was born on 12 December 1883 at Wallace, Victoria, second son of Jeremiah Hogan, Irish immigrant and farmer, and his Melbourne-born wife Bridget, née Burke. Edmund was educated primarily at the Springbank Catholic School; in 1898 when the Hogans moved to Bunding, Edmund attended the state school there but remained only two weeks because of a difference of opinion with the teacher. (It was said of Hogan in adulthood that he resented criticism.) Although his education was often interrupted and he left school to drive a team of horses, he compensated by voracious reading.

Hogan's various jobs included road-making, timber-cutting, farm-labouring and rabbiting in addition to farm chores at home. In 1903 he began cutting timber at Walhalla for the Long Tunnel Gold Mine and in 1905 he left for Western Australia where he worked on the Kurramia timber-lines supplying the Westralia Timber & Firewood Co. with wood for Kalgoorlie. Conditions on the timber-lines were appalling and after Hogan advanced from cutter to check-weigher at the company offices he became involved in the formation of the Kurramia Firewood Workers' Union. As secretary he was prominent in industrial negotiations in the strikes of 1908 and 1911. He did much to encourage the timber-workers, many of whom were Italian and Austrian, to join the union, visiting camps and conducting Sunday afternoon lessons for unionists. In 1911 he became secretary of the Kurrawang Firewood Workers' Union. For several years he was also a champion caber-tosser, weight-putter and hammer-thrower in the goldfields district.

Hogan was vice-president then president of the goldfields Social Democratic Federation in 1910-11 and was the Social Democratic delegate to the Australian Labor Federation. He used his association with these groups to school himself in political organization and public speaking. He was at one time nominated for Labor preselection at Kalgoorlie but lost the ballot. In 1912 he contracted typhoid fever and pneumonia and after a long battle to regain health he left the goldfields for convalescence in Victoria. During this visit home the local State electorate of Warrenheip came up for by-election and in 1913 Hogan won the seat for Labor on a narrow margin of preference from three Liberal candidates; he held Warrenheip (Warrenheip and Grenville from 1927) for the next thirty years and became a farmer at Ballan.

Ned Hogan was a hard-working politician and a frequent and lengthy speaker both inside and outside the House. A very tall, athletically built man with piercing blue eyes and in later years a shock of grey hair, he was forthright and effective. An avowed pacifist, he was active in the anti-conscription campaigns around the Ballarat area in 1916-17. At the 1922 conference he was elected president of the Victorian branch of the Labor Party. In 1924 he was minister of railways, agriculture and markets as well as vice-president of the Board of Land and Works in the short-lived Prendergast [q.v.] Labor government. In 1926 he became leader of the Labor Party in Victoria and next year, when the Allan [q.v.7]–Peacock [q.v.] administration resigned after the election in April, Hogan was commissioned to form a government.

He came into office on 20 May, holding 28 of 65 seats in the assembly, but supported by Albert Dunstan [q.v.8] and the Country Progressive Party. He was known as a (John) 'Wren [q.v.] man', and allegedly consulted Wren before finalizing his ministry. As well as premier Hogan was treasurer and minister of markets and did much during his six months term to initiate new policy and legislation, especially in rural matters. Sir Frederick Eggleston said of him that with the economic decline he 'had to shed the revolutionary and become an Irish peasant'. He supported a compulsory wheat pool and arranged for a growers' ballot in May 1928; the proposal was narrowly defeated. He represented Victoria at the 1927 Premiers' Conference in Sydney which agreed to new financial arrangements between the Commonwealth and State governments and the establishment of the Loan Council. In November 1928 his government, having lost the support of the Country Progressive Party by the introduction of a redistribution bill, was defeated on its handling of the Melbourne waterside workers' strike. However, the McPherson [q.v.] ministry collapsed in October 1929 and at the subsequent election Labor won thirty seats. Hogan carried a no confidence motion and formed a government on 12 December.

His second government, supported again by the Country Progressive Party and after September 1930 by the reunited Country Party, spanned most of the worst years of the Depression. At the Premiers' Conference of May–June 1931 in Melbourne, Hogan, who had already reduced public service salaries, agreed to the Premiers' Plan; its implementation in Victoria reduced government expenditure by 29 per cent. Hogan was always at odds with the industrial section of the party, particularly with the militant Australian Railways Union, and from mid-1930 he had been continually criticized by the Trades Hall Council and the party's central executive for his refusal to give personal assurances that he would not support any plan to reduce wages and welfare payments. The strains on him resulted in periods of nervous illness and collapse and in March 1932 he voyaged to England to recuperate. On 6 April T. Tunnecliffe [q.v.], as acting-premier, refused to pledge the government's continuing adherence to the Premiers' Plan and on 13 April the government fell on a vote of no confidence.

In the election of 14 May Labor suffered a crushing defeat. Hogan cabled his resignation as premier from London on 16 May; unendorsed by the Labor Party, he had retained his own seat by standing as a Premiers' Plan Labor candidate. During Hogan's absence Tunnecliffe agreed to comply with central executive demands to take action against members who contravened the resolution to reject the Premiers' Plan and in July Hogan, with J. P. Jones, E. L. Kiernan, H. R. Williams [qq.v.] and E. E. Bond, was excluded from the Victorian branch of the A.L.P.

Having declined to remain in London as Victorian agent-general, Hogan returned home in October. In December he issued a Supreme Court writ against the central executive over his expulsion. He lost in what was a long and bitter case which left him totally alienated from the Labor Party. The final judgment, handed down by the High Court of Australia in August 1934, set a precedent of fundamental importance to Australian party politics when it made clear that grievances against executive decisions within a political party were not the province of the courts.

Hogan remained an Independent Labor member until 1935 when he joined the Country Party under Dunstan. He was minister of agriculture and mines and vice-president of the Board of Land and Works from April in the Dunstan government which, supported by Labor lasted until September 1943. Defeated at the elections, Hogan amid much controversy was appointed chairman of the Soil Conservation Board in 1945 by the Dunstan–Hollway coalition and held this position until 1953.

Hogan was a deeply religious man and a practising Catholic throughout his life. In retirement he wrote *What's wrong with Australia?* (1953) and three pamphlets dealing with the menace of communism. He also worked for government funding of church schools. Hogan died on 23 August 1964 at St Vincent's Hospital, Melbourne, and was buried in the new Cheltenham cemetery. His family refused the offer of a state funeral. He was survived by his wife Molly Magdelene, née Conroy, whom he had married on 14 February 1917 at St Brigid's Catholic Church, Ballan, and by two sons. Their third son had been killed while serving with the Royal Australian Air Force in Rhodesia in 1942.

M. M. McCallum, *Ballarat and district citizens and sports at home and abroad* (Ballarat, 1916); B. D. Graham, *The formation of the Australian Country Parties* (Canb, 1966); L. J. Louis, *Trade unions and the Depression* (Canb, 1968); J. Robertson, *J. H. Scullin* (Perth, 1974); L. Ross, *John Curtin* (Melb, 1977); K. White, *John Cain & Victorian Labor 1917-1957* (Syd, 1982); *SMH*, 25 Apr 1932; *Argus*, 4 Aug 1934; *Age*, 25 Aug 1964; Memoir of Honorable E. J. Hogan, 1884-1964 (Parliamentary Library, Melb).   PAM JONAS

HOGAN, PERCIVAL JAMES NELSON (1883-1949), naval engineer, was born on 22 December 1883 in Hobart, son of James Hogan, builder, and his wife Rebecca Rachael, née Burt. He was educated at The Friends' School, Hobart, and attended the University of Tasmania before training as an engineer with the Tasmanian government. He then worked in Scotland with Denny & Co. of Dumbarton and Fairfield Shipbuilding Co. of Govan, and with the Peninsular and Oriental Steam Navigation Co.

In 1909, while in Britain, Hogan joined Australia's Commonwealth Naval Forces, as one of a team supervising the construction of the C.N.F.'s first torpedo-boat destroyers, H.M.A.S. *Parramatta* and H.M.A.S. *Yarra*; his initial rank was acting engineer sub-lieutenant but by December 1910 he was an engineer lieutenant. With the destroyers completed he returned to Australia in 1910 to serve as engineer officer in *Parramatta* until 1913. That year, on 3 November, he was transferred to H.M.A.S. *Pioneer*, a 3rd class protected cruiser which the British government had presented to the Royal Australian Navy as a sea-going training ship for naval reservists. On 26 November he married Cissie Laura Crisp at Melville Street Methodist Church, Hobart; they had a son and a daughter.

Hogan's service in *Pioneer* was wide-ranging. In World War I his ship was posted to East Africa in 1915 during the campaign against the German colonies. He was appointed acting engineer lieut-commander early in 1915, joined the cruiser H.M.S. *Encounter* in April 1918 and was confirmed in rank in December; he was promoted engineer commander in July 1919. Transferred to H.M.A.S. *Brisbane* in the same rank in September, he remained in this ship until 1921 when he returned to Britain for advanced engineering courses. He was then appointed to H.M.A.S. *Melbourne* in January 1923 as fleet engineer officer; in October he went to Flinders Naval Depot, Victoria, as engineer commander. By January 1926 he was back at sea as squadron engineer officer in H.M.A.S. *Sydney*. His next appointment was to Britain to 'stand by' the new cruiser *Australia*, then being built at Clydebank, Scotland, and after serving as her squadron engineer officer from May to December 1928 he became engineer manager at H.M.A. Naval Dockyard, Garden Island, Sydney. His term at Garden Island was dogged by financial cut-backs during the Depression as the R.A.N. was gradually scaled down to four ships and work at the dockyard was reduced.

In 1933 Hogan retired from the R.A.N. as an engineer commander but remained active as a consulting engineer and director of several companies. During World War II he was recalled for naval service as engineer officer, H.M.A.S. *Penguin*, the base ship for Garden Island. Diabetes and hypertension forced his retirement in 1944. Survived by his wife and daughter, he died on 26 February 1949 at Concord, Sydney, and was cremated with Methodist forms. Though not the easiest man to get on with, Percy Hogan commanded wide respect as a practical engineer and administrator. He was one of the first engineer officers of the R.A.N.

H. J. Feakes, *White ensign—Southern Cross* (Syd, 1951); *SMH*, 28 Feb 1949; records, United Service Institution, NSW.   HARRY ADLAM

HOGUE, JAMES ALEXANDER (1846-1920), journalist and politician, was born on 2 September 1846 at Clarence Town, New South Wales, son of Fitzarthur Hogue (d. 1878), a Scottish-born innkeeper and later a miller and farmer, and his wife Elizabeth, née Mackay. Educated at local schools and Newcastle Grammar School, Jimmy was briefly a pupil-teacher. He trained as a compositor with the *Newcastle Chronicle* and in 1873 joined the literary staff of the *Maitland Mercury*.

Two years later Hogue moved to Sydney to become parliamentary reporter for the *Empire*, *Evening News* and *Australian Town and Country Journal*. In 1880 he became a sub-editor on the *Evening News* and was its editor in 1884-95; to some extent he made it a working man's paper. The governor, Lord Carrington [q.v.3], remarked in 1889 that Hogue was 'a most remarkably quick, clever, intelligent man with a great knowledge of Australia: and an extraordinary grasp of what is really going on in the political & social world'.

The *Evening News* on 26 January 1894 accused members of parliament of drunkenness and gambling in the parliamentary refreshment rooms. Hogue was summoned to the Bar of the Legislative Assembly on a charge of contempt and reprimanded. Instead of apologizing, he refused to name the writer of the offending article and vigorously 'took exception to the judicial position which the Assembly had taken up'. After nearly seven hours the House, on finding it had no power to imprison him for contempt, dismissed him 'as quickly as possible, lest worse befell'.

Standing as a free trader, Hogue was elected to the Legislative Assembly for Glebe in July that year; he held the seat until 1910. He resigned as editor in 1895 but continued to contribute to the *Evening News* until he served as minister of public instruction and for labour and industry under his old friend (Sir) George Reid [q.v.] in 1898-99. As colonial secretary in the Carruthers [q.v.7] ministry in 1904-07, he introduced little legislation, but made important changes to the administration of hospitals and charities. He held his former portfolios from May 1907. When (Sir) Charles Gregory Wade [q.v.] took over in October, Hogue continued as minister of public instruction in 1907-10 and for labour and industry from January 1908. As minister, he took a 'keen and judicious' interest in the Public Library of New South Wales and watched over the construction of the Mitchell [q.v.5] Library.

A firm supporter of Federation, Hogue was president of the New South Wales branch of the Australian Natives' Association in 1904-05. From 1901 he had succeeded Andrew Garran [q.v.4] as author of the weekly column 'Sydney Topics' in the *Australasian*. He was a director of the Yorkshire Fire and Life Insurance Co. from 1904 and a trustee of the (Royal) National Park from 1906.

A good cricketer, rifle-shot and athlete in his youth, Hogue was a vice-president of the New South Wales Rowing Association for many years, and was State bowls champion in 1900-01 and pairs winner in 1902-03. Widely read and a student of English, he was a member of the (Royal) Australian Historical Society and also a good flautist. Known as 'Dismal Jimmy', perhaps because, according to Sir Joseph Carruthers, he was 'always cheerful', he had a high-domed forehead, large slightly hooded eyes and a trim beard and moustache.

At Clarence Town Presbyterian Church, Hogue had married Jessie Robards (d. 1932) on 17 April 1878. Accompanied by her husband, she was reported to be the first woman to ride the summit of Mt Kosciusko. Three of their sons saw active service in World War I, including Oliver [q.v.], who died in London in 1919. Their daughter Amy had

died in 1918. James Hogue died at his home at Mosman on 2 August 1920 and was buried in the Presbyterian section of Waverley cemetery. He was survived by his wife, five sons and three daughters. To Carruthers, he was 'my dear old friend and colleague', always 'incorruptible, steadfast and loyal'. Reid recalled that Hogue was 'one of the best editors of a leading daily newspaper' that he had known.

G. H. Reid, *My reminiscences* (Lond, 1917); *PD* (LA NSW), 1894, p 339; *V&P* (LA NSW), 1894, 1, p 34; *SMH*, 1 Feb 1894, 3 Aug 1920, 23 July 1932; *Bulletin*, 10 Feb 1894; *Evening News* (Syd), 26 Jan 1894; *T&CJ*, 24 July 1907; *Australasian*, 14 Aug 1920; *Fighting Line*, 26 Aug 1920; J. A. Hogue papers (ML); newspaper cuttings (held by Mr O. Hogue, Canb).   MARTHA RUTLEDGE

HOGUE, OLIVER ('Trooper Bluegum') (1880-1919), journalist and soldier, was born on 29 April 1880 in Sydney, second son of native-born parents James Alexander Hogue [q.v.] and his wife Jessie, née Robards. The family comprised six boys and four girls.

Oliver was educated at Forest Lodge Public School, Sydney. Tall, active and wiry, an all-round athlete and a skilled horseman and rifle-shot, he considered himself a 'bushman'. After leaving school he cycled thousands of miles, exploring most of Australia's eastern and northern coast, and worked as a commercial traveller before joining the *Sydney Morning Herald* in 1907.

He enlisted in the Australian Imperial Force in September 1914 as a trooper with the 6th Light Horse Regiment. Commissioned second lieutenant in November, he sailed for Egypt with the 2nd L.H. Brigade in the *Suevic* in December.

Hogue served on Gallipoli with the Light Horse (dismounted) for five months, then was invalided to England with enteric fever. In May 1915 he was promoted lieutenant and appointed orderly officer to Colonel (Sir) Granville Ryrie [q.v.], the brigade commander. Charles Bean [q.v.7] observed: 'Day after day the Brigadier ... tramped round the front line with his enthusiastic and devoted orderly officer, Oliver Hogue'. In letters to his family and to the *Sydney Morning Herald* from Gallipoli, he was always cheerful, enjoying 'a scrap'. Insisting on fair reporting, he denied incorrect reports of mutilations by the Turks. His letters and articles present a well-perceived picture of events and good understanding of the soldiers. In a letter to his father he remarked: 'I might be rather angry with Captain Bean first because he beat me to the post for the big job, and second because he seems to have ignored our Brigade all along, but I find him so absolutely straight and sincere and honest that I like him immensely and always have'.

As 'Trooper Bluegum' he wrote articles for the *Herald* subsequently collected in the books *Love letters of an Anzac* (London, 1916) and *Trooper Bluegum at the Dardanelles* (London, 1916). Sometimes representing war as almost a sport, he took pride in seeing 'the way our young Australians played the game of war'.

Hogue returned from hospital in England to the 6th L.H. in Sinai and fought in the decisive battle of Romani. Transferred to the Imperial Camel Corps on 1 November 1916, he was promoted captain on 3 July 1917. He fought with the Camel Corps at Magdhaba, Rafa, Gaza, Tel el Khuweilfe, Musallabeh, and was with them in the first trans-Jordan raid to Amman. In 1917 Hogue led the 'Pilgrim's Patrol' of fifty Cameliers and two machine-guns into the Sinai desert to Jebel Mousa, to collect Turkish rifles from the thousands of Bedouins in the desert.

After the summer of 1918, spent in the Jordan Valley, camels were no longer required. The Cameliers were given horses and swords and converted into cavalry. Hogue, promoted major on 1 July 1918, was now in Brigadier General George Macarthur-Onslow's [q.v.] 5th L.H. Brigade, commanding a squadron of the 14th L.H. Regiment. At the taking of Damascus by the Desert Mounted Corps in September 1918, the 5th Brigade stopped the Turkish Army escaping through the Barada Gorge. (Sir) Henry Gullett [q.v.] wrote: 'A handful of Australians of the 14th Light Horse Regiment under Major Oliver Hogue occupied a house at the entrance of the gorge, and poured galling fire at a few yards' range into the now distracted Turks'.

Oliver Hogue went through the whole campaign of the Desert Mounted Corps, but died of influenza at the 3rd London General Hospital on 3 March 1919. He was buried in the Australian military section of Brookwood cemetery. He was unmarried. His twin sister Amy had died the previous year.

As well as the articles sent to Australia, and some in English magazines, Hogue wrote a third book, *The Cameliers* (London, 1919), also some verse. His contributions to *Australia in Palestine* (Sydney, 1919), edited by H. S. Gullett and C. Barrett, were two poems and an essay on the Camel Brigade.

Hogue's verse was not, according to Bertram Stevens [q.v.], poetry 'in the serious sense of that word'. His first two books, Stevens wrote, 'contain the impressions of a

buoyant and generous soul—a healthy athlete enjoying life thoroughly, and regarding danger as absolutely necessary to give it zest'. His letters 'conveyed a good deal of the happy-go-lucky spirit of the Australians, their indifference to danger, and laughter when in difficulties or in pain'.

H. S. Gullett, *The A.I.F. in Sinai and Palestine* (Syd, 1935); C. E. W. Bean, *The story of Anzac*, 2 (1924); J. R. Hall, *The desert hath pearls* (Melb, 1975); G. F. and E. M. Langley, *Sand, sweat and camels* (Kilmore, Vic, 1976); *Kia Ora Cooee*, Apr, May, Dec 1918; *Aussie*, 15 Sept 1920; *SMH*, 12 Mar 1919; Hogue letters (AWM).

ELYNE MITCHELL

HOLDEN, ALBERT THOMAS (1866-1935), Methodist minister, was born on 21 August 1866 at Geelong, Victoria, eldest child of Thomas Holden, produce merchant at Wallace, and his wife Mary née Hague. His younger brother was George Frederick Holden [q.v.].

Holden matriculated from Geelong College in 1882, taught in 1883-84 at Prospect House Academy, Kyneton, where he came under the influence of Rev. Charles Lancaster, and became a Methodist lay preacher. In 1885 he entered Ormond College, University of Melbourne, to study law, graduating B.A. in 1888. He played football and was a member of the first Ormond eight-oar crew.

After entering the Methodist ministry in 1887 Holden served as probationer at Camberwell in 1888, working at Burwood with railway construction workers and then with miners while at the Omeo Home Mission (1890-91). He toured Europe and the Middle East with Rev. E. S. Bickford during 1892. On 29 March 1893 at Omeo he married Martha Mesley, daughter of a mining manager; both Holden and his wife were expert in equestrian skills. After his marriage Holden was appointed to Port Cygnet, Tasmania (1893-95), Dunkeld and Penshurst (1896-98), Hawthorn (1899-1901) and Elsternwick (1902-03).

From 1898 Holden was an army chaplain and in 1900 he accompanied the Victorian Fourth Contingent (Imperial Bushmen) to the South African War. He became Methodist chaplain general in 1913, serving with the Australian Imperial Force between 1916 and 1919, when he was appointed C.B.E. He was generally known as Major, later Colonel Holden. His second son was killed in France in 1917.

On Bickford's death in 1904 Holden had become secretary of Methodist Home Missions, and in 1925 established the Home Missionaries' Training College. In 1915-16 he was elected president of the Methodist Conference of Victoria and Tasmania. As founder in 1926, and director until his death, of the Federal Methodist Inland Mission, he travelled throughout Australia. He was general superintendent of the Methodist Church of Australasia from 1929 to 1932, then president-general. A strong advocate of Australian church union, Holden attended, as opening speaker, the meeting in the Albert Hall, London, in 1932 which brought about Methodist Union. He received the Freedom of the City of London in that year, and the University of Toronto conferred on him an honorary doctorate of divinity in 1934.

Holden had become a Freemason at Hamilton in 1898 and held many offices both in Australia and England, including grand master of the Grand Lodge of Freemasons of Victoria in 1912-14, grand chaplain in 1908-19, and past grand master in 1935. The Holden Lodge was named after him. In 1911 he was awarded the certificate of the Royal Humane Society of Australasia for saving a person from drowning at Sorrento. He was a member of the Naval and Military and the Masonic clubs, Melbourne.

Holden was an outstanding Church leader. Reserved rather than rhetorical in speech, he had a mind 'swift and accurate in analysis and a delicately balanced judgment'. (Sir) Irving Benson said that he was 'one of the greatest personalities that God has given to Methodism, and indeed to Australia'. He died of cancer on 20 August 1935, two months after the death of his wife, and was buried in Boroondara cemetery after a service at Wesley Church, Melbourne. His two daughters and one of his three sons survived him.

C. A. Grant, *500 Victorians* (Melb, 1934); C. I. Benson (ed), *A century of Victorian Methodism* (Melb, 1935); W. E. Jennings, *M. W. Bro. Dr. A. T. Holden P. G. M. churchman and Freemason* (Melb, 1948); *Craftsman* (Syd), Aug 1935; *Herald* (Melb), 9, 22 Mar 1929, 6 Nov 1931, 22, 23 Sept, 24, 26 Nov, 31 Dec 1932, 7 Jan, 26 May 1933, 1 Mar, 10, 27 Apr 1934, 16 Apr, 6 May, 21 Aug 1935; *Sun-News Pictorial*, 25 May 1929, 5 Oct 1932, 3 Jan 1933; *Argus*, 22 June 1932, 21 Aug 1935; *Age*, 23 Sept 1932, 17 Aug 1933, 21 Aug 1935; *Spectator* (Melb), 28 Aug 1935.   IAN F. McLAREN

HOLDEN, FRANCES GILLAM (1843-1924), nurse, was born on 9 February 1843 at Ella-long, Brisbane Water, New South Wales, eldest daughter of Alfred Holden, police magistrate, and his wife Jane, née Osborne, and niece of G. K. Holden [q.v.4]. For several years the family lived at Newport and in 1849 moved to Penshurst on the Pat-

erson River. With her brothers and sisters, Fanny, as she was known, was educated at home by tutors and encouraged by her father to read avidly. She was a governess for many years. Aged 31, despite an inherited delicate constitution, she took up nursing, with her younger sisters Laura, Rosamund and Edith. On 10 June 1874 Frances and Rosamund entered Sydney Infirmary and Dispensary to train under Lucy Osburn [q.v.5]. Frances, forthright and indomitable, did not get on with her superior. On 3 March 1875, having worked in men's and accidents wards she was dismissed as incompetent.

After nursing privately for a few months, in January 1876 Frances Holden went to Hobart General Hospital with her sisters Laura and Rosamund to assist the new lady superintendent, Florence Abbott, to reconstruct the administration. In December a royal commission upheld their complaints against conditions and the management. Next year Frances contracted typhoid and went to Melbourne. Rosamund returned to Sydney about 1879 to nurse at the new Hospital for Sick Children, Glebe, that their cousin J. B. Watt [q.v.6] had helped to found. In September 1880 Frances was appointed lady superintendent.

Although the hospital made excellent progress under her skilled supervision, Frances Holden deplored the lack of a resident medical officer and the manner in which visiting physicians and surgeons discharged their duties. The dispute began in 1884 when the honorary medical staff resigned, and finally erupted in 1887 in a bitter public debate in the press. When she claimed that a child had died through negligence, a government inquiry was held. Although ill again with typhoid, she welcomed the investigation and prepared her case. Despite testimonials from colleagues, ex-patients and friends, including Dr Andrew Ross [q.v.6] she failed to prove her charges and was dismissed in October 1887; several of the staff went with her.

From the early 1870s Miss Holden had contributed verse and articles to journals and newspapers, sometimes under the pseudonyms, 'Australienne' and 'Lyra Australia'. Some of her most acclaimed works were written during the controversial years she was lady superintendent. Her treatise, *Trained nursing*, was published in 1882, and in 1884 *The travels of Red-jacket and White-cap; or, a history of the circulation of the blood*, an instructive booklet, written 'in à la Bunyan or allegorical style'; Dr Ross wrote the preface and recommended it as a textbook in schools. In 1887 she published a small collection of verse and prose, *Her father's darling, and other child pictures* with an introduction by Rev. William Woolls [q.v.6]. She lectured and wrote on nursing, physiology, hygiene and hospital reform and advocated higher education for women. Her experience of typhoid, both as a sufferer and as a nurse, prompted several articles on its treatment.

In support of women's rights and social reform she founded the Dawn Club in 1888 with Louisa Lawson [q.v.] and other women; she became its vice-president, composed its manifesto, and contributed irregularly to its journal, *Dawn*. In the 1880s and 1890s she contributed to the *Sydney Mail, Humanity and Health*, a New York journal, to the *Sydney Quarterly Magazine*, and to journals of Sydney and Melbourne universities.

In 1902 the editors of *Dawn* lost contact with Frances Holden: in the latter half of the year her father, brother and a sister died. During World War I, although an invalid, she worked for the soldiers, for the Red Cross Society and kindergartens. On 21 August 1924 she died at Burwood and was buried in the Church of England section of Rookwood cemetery. Her devotion to her calling and her ardent desire to make it better for all aspirants was expressed with evangelical fervour in all her work, both written and practical. The keynote of her papers on hospital reform was always the quality of the nurses: 'to reform the nursing staff is to reform the hospital'.

P. L. Hipsley, *The early history of the Royal Alexandra Hospital for Children, Sydney, 1880 to 1905* (Syd, 1952); A. Downie, *Our first hundred years: the history of nursing at the Royal Hobart Hospital* (Hob, 1975); *T&CJ*, 3 Sept 1887; *SMH*, 28 Aug 1924; Roy Alexandra Hospital Archives; Syd Hospital Archives.   B. E. BRIGGS

HOLDEN, GEORGE FREDERICK (1868-1934), businessman, politician and administrator, was born on 26 May 1868 at Geelong, Victoria, second son of Thomas Holden, produce merchant, who had arrived at Geelong from the Sydney area as a child in 1847, and his wife Mary, née Hague, daughter of an early exporter of wool in Melbourne. George was educated at Geelong State School and at 13 began work in the office of his uncle's firm, George Hague & Co., woolbrokers, Geelong. In 1886, after four years experience there, he was sent to manage the produce store his father had bought two years earlier at Wallace, near Ballarat. He purchased the business in 1897. On 6 June 1889 at the Wesleyan parsonage, Lydiard Street, Ballarat, he had married Minnie Elizabeth Ireson. His sister Millie married (Sir) Alexander Peacock [q.v.].

In 1896 Holden was elected to the Buninyong Shire Council and remained a councillor until 1904, serving as president in 1898. In 1900 at the age of 31 he was elected for Warrenheip in the Legislative Assembly, continuing as member until his resignation in 1913. His friend E. J. Hogan [q.v.] succeeded him. Holden was described as quiet but influential in the House.

In 1902 he bought St Helen's, a mansion on Corio Bay, and became involved in Geelong affairs. He worked closely with Premier (Sir) Thomas Bent [q.v.3] in drawing up the bill to establish the Geelong Harbor Trust and in December 1905 was appointed its first chairman. The decision was 'a popular one to the whole Western district', as the establishment of the trust was regarded as proof of the government's good intentions about decentralization.

As well as carrying out the normal functions of a harbour authority, Holden also set about attracting industry to Geelong, and established a freezing works and an experimental farm. These ventures brought him into conflict with some of his fellow townsmen, resulting in charges of mismanagement and nepotism. A royal commission exonerated him of all charges in 1912.

Next year, when the Melbourne Harbor Trust was reorganized, Holden was appointed chairman, superseding the previous elected chairman, W. T. Appleton [q.v.7]. There was criticism on the grounds that his record was mediocre, the appointment was political, and he was not a Melbourne man. Over the next twenty years, however, his critics came to acknowledge his achievements as, under his direction, the facilities of the port of Melbourne were steadily improved, charges were lowered, revenue increased, and a new headquarters for the trust was built. Domineering and uncompromising, overcautious at times, Holden nevertheless showed great organizing ability both in Geelong and Melbourne, playing an important role in establishing their port authorities.

Holden died suddenly at his home in South Yarra on 15 August 1934, survived by one son, F. C. T. Holden, member of the Legislative Assembly for Grant, and two daughters. He was buried in Eastern cemetery, Geelong, after a service in the Ashby Methodist Church.

J. Smith (ed), *Cyclopedia of Victoria*, 1 (Melb, 1903); B. Hoare, *Jubilee history of the Melbourne Harbor Trust* (Melb, 1927); T. Brentnall, *My memories* (Melb, 1938); O. Ruhen, *Port of Melbourne, 1835-1976* (Syd, 1976); *Geelong Advertiser*, 10 July, 17 Nov, 19, 23 Dec 1905, 26 Sept, 12 Oct, 17, 29, 30 Nov, 6 Dec 1911, 11, 13, 14, 23 Jan 1913, 16 Aug 1934; *Argus*, 11, 13, 14 Jan 1913, 16 Aug 1934; *Age*, 16 Aug 1934.

IAN WYND

HOLDEN, HENRY JAMES (1859-1926), saddler, carriage-trimmer and motor-body manufacturer, and SIR EDWARD WHEEWALL (1885-1947), motor-body manufacturer, were father and son. Henry was born on 18 July 1859 at Kensington, Adelaide, eldest of nine children of James Alexander Holden (1835-1887) and his wife Mary Elizabeth, née Phillips. After falling out with his stepmother J. A. Holden had in 1854 left his late father's flourishing leather business at Walsall, Staffordshire, England, for the United States of America. Attracted then to Australia by the goldfields, he settled in Adelaide where he began a leather and saddlery business, by 1883 a considerable establishment in the colony. He was a staunch Baptist, chairman of the Chamber of Commerce and active in the foundation of the Chamber of Manufactures. His son Henry was educated at Thomas Caterer's School, Norwood, and the Hahndorf Academy. At 19 he was sent to England to consolidate family business links. With both father and business ailing, he returned to the Adelaide leather trade. On 7 April 1881 at the Norwood Baptist Church he married Mary Ann Dixon Wheewall, daughter of an Alberton grocer. After gaining experience in several departments he became a partner in 1883; two years later H. A. Frost, a carriage-builder, joined the partnership. On James's death in 1887, Henry became head of the troubled firm which weathered further financial crises that year and in 1893.

During the South African War Henry captured large government saddlery contracts in the teeth of interstate competition. Mechanically ingenious, he set up rows of machinery in a rented shed, personally trained the workforce, and developed large-scale, low-cost production methods. When Frost died in 1909 Holden bought his interest and extended the firm's activities to include motor-body trimming: it produced hoods, upholstery and carriage hardware, and painted bodies for steam and petrol cars. Batches of motor-cycle sidecars were also manufactured.

World War I presented further opportunities in the leather-manufacturing market; but more important were the economic consequences of the 1917 government embargo on the import of completed car-bodies. Holden, having built two car-bodies in the previous year, joined forces with Dodge distributor S. A. Cheney [q.v.7] to build a standardized body for imported chassis at a highly competitive price. This prototype, designed by Edward Holden, was an instant success with distributors. Henry swiftly acquired the Adelaide premises of another carriage and body-builder F. T. Hack & Co., and began production. With a

loan of £50 000 from the Bank of Adelaide, arranged by local financier Charles Irwin, and Edward as managing director, Holden's Motor Body Builders Ltd was floated late in 1917. Shareholders subscribed £35 000. Initially mass production techniques at the King William Street premises were static: the moving assembly line came later. Holden exercised rigorous quality control; he sought to establish direct command over raw material supplies, and negotiated labour agreements in 1918 to minimize production disturbances. After the war Holden pressed the Federal government to maintain high protection: in the 1920s the tariff on imported motor-bodies was 100 per cent.

By 1923 Holden's employed over a thousand men and produced 240 car-bodies per week (for numerous makes of imported chassis), more than half the national output. Rapidly expanding demand required innovative production methods, and repeated restructuring of the firm's finances to provide capital. In April the company expanded its plant to a 22-acre (9 ha) site at Woodville; production rose from 6661 bodies in 1922 to 22 060 in 1924. Increasingly under Edward's leadership, the Woodville development incorporated the latest technology, including automated production lines, and became the largest plant of its type outside North America. Holden had undertaken expansion in South Australia notwithstanding its relative remoteness from its major markets in the eastern States, because of cheap transport facilities, favourable labour supply, and his feeling of local patriotism. Approached by General Motors Export Co., the American-owned firm to which it was already supplying car-bodies, Holden's agreed to devote the Woodville plant exclusively to production for General Motors, on a system of cost-plus pricing, with General Motors supplying designs and technical help. Thus Holden's and General Motors became highly interdependent, with General Motors taking about 60 per cent of Holden's output throughout the 1920s. This symbiosis led eventually to control of the firm by General Motors.

H. J. Holden, a self-made entrepreneur, enjoyed a close patriarchal relation with his workforce. He fostered generous social welfare arrangements and good labour relations, using a factory consultative council. His passion for quality caused him to slash poor work under the noses of his workers; but he reputedly knew each personally and was remembered as a generous employer. He was not fully attuned to the scale and style of the new methods, and increasing tension marked his dealings with his innovative son.

As well as being the State's leading industrialist, Henry Holden contributed substantially to civic life. He was mayor of Kensington and Norwood for eight years, a member of the Norwood School Board, and as a foundation member of the Municipal Tramways Trust initiated moves for electrification of the system. President of the Municipal Councils Association in 1903 and later vice-president, he acted as chief magistrate in the eastern suburbs and was chairman of a committee formed to draft a bill for town planning. He was president of the Baptist Union for twenty-one years, a deacon for twenty-five and a Sunday-school superintendent. In 1904 he established the Norwood Cottage Homes for the aged poor. He was president of the Young Men's Christian Association and official visitor to the Parkside Asylum. When visiting England in 1911 he was commissioned to investigate management of hospitals for the mentally defective. A diabetic, in his last years Holden appeared infrequently at board meetings. He died at Norwood on 6 March 1926, survived by his wife, three daughters and two sons.

Edward Holden was born on 14 August 1885 at College Town. Educated at Prince Alfred College and the University of Adelaide (B.Sc., 1905), on graduation he joined the family firm (still trading as Holden & Frost Ltd). He was influential in Holden's expansion into motor-body building, and its use of highly automated mass production technology. Widely travelled, and much influenced by American methods, he introduced to the business new standards of scientific management, cost accounting and production control. A strong advocate of piecework, he achieved a rapid improvement of labour productivity at Woodville, though the new processes apparently diminished goodwill among the workforce. In close association with General Motors, Holden's established a dominant market position throughout mainland Australia. Output rose spectacularly: 36 171 motor-bodies were produced in 1926 and 46 981 in 1927, with a downturn to 33 785 in 1928. In 1929 the company employed 3400 workers and was the biggest body-builder in the Empire; but that year it suffered a double crisis with a further decline in orders and the death of Holden's younger brother William Arthur (1899-1929), a director and production manager at Woodville.

In August 1929 General Motors revised its order levels downwards, and Ford suspended expected orders. In September Holden informed the annual general meeting that the business remained 'inherently sound', but in October the plant closed temporarily for lack of continuous work, and Ford announced it would be placing no further orders. To utilize slack capacity Holden's diversified to the production of golf-club heads, steel filing cabinets, and wooden packing-cases for fruit. Merger with three other Australian motor-body manufacturers was considered, but rejected, and in January 1930 Holden set out for the United States of America to discuss amalgamation with General Motors. That year the entire plant was closed for weeks on end and mass production methods became inappropriate as output collapsed to just over 9000 bodies. (Output for 1931 totalled only 1630 bodies.) Holden's major competitors had effectively ceased business and a similar fate appeared to confront Holden's, although it remained solvent: its continued existence depended on orders from General Motors, which then constituted three-quarters of Holden's remaining demand. In February 1931, after withdrawing an all-cash offer, General Motors offered £1 116 000 for Holden's—£550 000 in cash, and the remainder in non-convertible cumulative preference shares in the proposed new company. No ordinary shares were to be held by the former Holden's shareholders. After disorderly debate among shareholders, the offer, recommended by the directors, was accepted: although the price paid was below the balance-sheet value of £1 410 666, it exceeded the market value of the shares by about half a million pounds. The issue of preference shares reduced the cash burden of the merger for General Motors, and also gave it complete control while maintaining an Australian character in name, ownership and management.

Holden became chairman of General Motors-Holden's Ltd, and was appointed joint managing director in August 1931 and later sole managing director in a reconstituted administration. However, with the arrival of (Sir) L. J. Hartnett in March 1934 from General Motors' English subsidiary, Vauxhall Motors, Holden was supplanted as managing director, although he remained chairman through the period of economic recovery when new plant and central administration were established in Melbourne. Bitter and disappointed at his displacement, he turned to other business activities and parliamentary service. As the company became involved in the munitions programme for World War II his contribution to the company declined further. He became honorary controller-general of army canteens in 1939-45 and visited troops in the Middle East. In 1942 the canteen administration ran into controversy over contracts and Holden was called upon to defend his policies. He remained chairman of directors of General Motors-Holden's until, in ill health, he resigned in January 1947.

Holden had been prominent in many

South Australian enterprises in the previous twenty years. He was chairman of directors of the South Australian Brush Co. and Australian Cotton Textile Industries as well as director of the Bank of Adelaide and several other companies. As foundation director and first chairman of the South Australian Industries Assistance Corporation he did much to entice foreign enterprise to the State. He was president of the South Australian Chamber of Commerce and the Chamber of Manufactures, and of the Associated Chambers of Manufactures of Australia. He was a councillor and alderman of the Adelaide City Council, president of the National Safety Council and a member of the Council for Scientific and Industrial Research. His conspicuous absence from the membership of the Adelaide Club has been attributed to blackballing in his early days by two doctors. In 1925-31 he was a member of the Council of the University of Adelaide; he helped to finance, and accompanied, a university expedition to Central Australia to study the Aboriginals in 1927; and in 1943 he donated £5000 towards the establishment of a chair of electrical and mechanical engineering. He was knighted in 1945.

Holden served as a Liberal in the Legislative Council in 1935-47 and, though not loquacious, was a consistent spokesman for industry and a strong advocate of technical education. He supported governmental efforts to attract industry to the State in the 1930s, especially by reducing wharfage costs, and by developing the South Australian Housing Trust in order to depress living costs and thereby preserve the low labour cost advantage. He supported the auditor-general J. W. Wainwright [q.v.] in a sustained campaign to preserve and expand South Australian industry, and later helped to gain wartime contracts for the State. He approved of government initiatives to foster small business but, increasingly, he emphasized the dangers of 'socialistic' legislation and price and investment controls. In 1947 he refused to vote for the government takeover of the Adelaide Electric Supply Co., despite pressure from Premier Thomas Playford.

Holden died in North Adelaide of cerebrovascular disease on 17 June 1947, survived by his wife Hilda May, née Lavis, whom he had married in Adelaide on 18 March 1908, and by a son and two daughters.

The Holden family made a signal contribution to the development of Australian manufacturing and to the shaping of the South Australian economy. Through their outstanding managerial abilities they demonstrated that large-scale, mass production methods could be adapted to Australian industry despite the disadvantages of remoteness and a small local market. Their name is commemorated on hundreds of thousands of Australian motor vehicles.

H. T. Burgess (ed), *Cyclopedia of South Australia*, 1 (Adel, 1907); L. J. Hartnett, *Big wheels and little wheels* (Melb, 1964); S. A. Cheney, *From horse to horsepower* (Adel, 1965); J. Miles, *A richness of people* (Adel, 1969); N. Buttfield, *So great a change* (Syd, 1979); *PP* (SA) 1926 (57), 1927 (59); *Aust J of Politics and Hist*, May 1962; *VHM*, 38 (1967); *Register* (Adel), 8 Mar 1926; *Advertiser* (Adel), 8 Mar 1926, 28 Jan 1928, 18 June 1947; *Daily Mirror* (Syd), 26 Feb 1973; P. L. Swan, General Motors-Holden's and the Australian automobile industry in economic perspective (Ph.D. thesis, Monash Univ, 1972); R. W. Keeley, Politics and the motor industry in South Australia from depression to war (B.A. Hons thesis, Flinders Univ, 1979); J. Sutterby, Workers and the rise of mass production: Holden's in the 1920s and the 1930s (B.A. Hons thesis, Flinders Univ, 1981); Holden family papers (NL—copies in SAA); papers held by *and* information from Dame Nancy Buttfield, Adel; information from General Motors-Holden's, Melb.

JOAN HANCOCK
ERIC RICHARDS

HOLDEN, LESLIE HUBERT (1895-1932), aviator, was born on 6 March 1895 in Adelaide, son of Hubert William Holden, commercial traveller, and his wife Annie Maria, née Turner. In 1905 the family moved to Sydney where Holden's father became a partner in the Australian branch of the Nestlé Swiss Milk Co. Holden attended Sydney Church of England Grammar School (Shore) in 1909-11 before becoming a salesman with Nestlés. He showed an early aptitude for things mechanical.

In May 1915 Holden enlisted in the Australian Imperial Force and went to Egypt as a motor driver, though he quickly became interested in flying. A friend remembered how 'we used to lie on the sand at Heliopolis and watch the old Maurice Farmans go lumbering overhead at a scorching 55 miles an hour'. In December 1916, now in France, he was one of the first batch of 200 volunteers to train in England for the Australian Flying Corps. His mechanical sense and his calm but adventurous nature made him a natural pilot and he quickly won his wings as a lieutenant. Flying a D.H.5 in No. 2 Squadron, A.F.C., Holden saw the first Australian air action of the war over St Quentin on 2 October 1917. Throughout the battle of Cambrai in November he participated in the hazardous task of strafing the enemy front line from a height of only fifty feet (15 m). His ability to return alive in wrecked machines riddled with bullet holes earned him the nicknames of 'the homing pigeon' and

'Lucky Les'; Three of his machines were 'written off' under him. Perhaps his closest encounter was when the famous von Richthofen fired at him from below and the bullets ripped up through the floor and tore his leggings. He nursed his badly damaged machine home, losing a wing on impact.

Holden was awarded the Military Cross in February 1918 and was promoted captain in March. In May, after having shot down at least five enemy aircraft, he returned to Britain as an instructor. His teaching work earned him the Air Force Cross before he returned to Australia in June 1919. After demobilization he became Sydney manager of Holden's Motor Body Builders, the Adelaide company formed by his uncle H. J. Holden, with his son (Sir) Edward W. Holden [qq.v.], but he yearned for a career in aviation. In 1928, with financial support from friends, he bought a D.H.61 biplane which he named *Canberra* and operated charter flights from Mascot, Sydney.

In April 1929 Holden was engaged by the Sydney Citizens' Relief Committee to fly to north-western Australia in search of (Sir) Charles Kingsford Smith and Charles Ulm [qq.v.] who had disappeared while flying to England. After twelve days Holden found them on a mud-flat on the Glenelg River near the Kimberleys and returned a hero, but when newspapers accused Kingsford Smith and Ulm of a publicity stunt, the Sydney committee refused to cover Holden's expenses.

In September 1931 Holden made what was probably the first flight from Sydney to New Guinea, and began a successful airfreight business there. He returned to Sydney next year to purchase extra aircraft and formed Holden Air Transport. On 18 September 1932, while travelling as a passenger in a New England Airways Puss Moth from Sydney to Brisbane, he died instantly when the plane crashed near Byron Bay.

Les Holden was a courageous but modest man with a sunny temperament and whimsical humour. He had married Kathleen Packman at St Mark's Anglican Church, Darling Point, Sydney, on 3 June 1924 and was survived by his wife and three daughters. There is a memorial window in the Sydney Church of England Grammar School chapel.

F. M. Cutlack, *The Australian Flying Corps . . . 1914-18* (Syd, 1923); C. E. Kingsford Smith, *My flying life* (Lond, 1937); N. Buttfield, *So great a change* (Syd, 1979); *London Gazette*, 1 Feb 1918, 3 June 1919; *Aircraft* (Melb), Oct 1932; *SMH*, 29 Apr, 18 May, 11, 12, 13 June, 8 Oct 1929, 23 Sept, 13, 29 Oct 1932, 27 Apr 1933, 29 Dec 1934; *Chronicle* (Adel), 22 Sept 1932; Records, Sydney Church of England Grammar School; Holden papers, held by Mrs J. Furber, Double Bay, NSW; information from Mrs J. Furber, *and* Dame Nancy Buttfield, Adelaide, SA, *and* Mrs W. Graham, Gordon, NSW.

CARL BRIDGE

HOLDER, SIR FREDERICK WILLIAM (1850-1909), parliamentarian and journalist, was born on 12 May 1850 at Happy Valley, near Adelaide, eldest son of James Morecott Holder, a freeman of the City of London, who had migrated to South Australia shortly after his marriage on 9 September 1848 to Martha Breakspear Roby, daughter of a London tailor. James Holder became a schoolteacher at Happy Valley and, about 1870, stationmaster at Freeling. Frederick was educated initially by his father, later at state schools, then at the Collegiate School of St Peter, Adelaide. He also became a teacher, first at Prince Alfred College, then at Freeling. In August 1875 he was made headmaster of the Kooringa Public School at Burra Burra.

In 1877 Holder, whose school was superseded by a new Model School, became manager of a Burra store, town clerk and first managing editor of the newly established *Burra Record*, of which he was later proprietor. He had already been active in the Burra Parliamentary Club and in the *Record* developed ideas on government at both the colonial and local level. He was elected to the Burra Corporation and as mayor in 1885 and 1886 was largely responsible for a waterworks scheme and bridge construction. He served as captain in the South Australian Volunteer Force and on the council of the South Australian School of Mines and Industries.

On 29 March 1877, at Burra, Holder married Julia Maria, daughter of John Riccardo Stephens, a Cornishman, homeopathic doctor, farmer, teacher and shopkeeper, who had studied for the Methodist ministry. Julia Holder eventually became Australian president of the Woman's Christian Temperance Union. Holder shared her Wesleyan convictions and as a lay preacher regularly conducted services on Sundays in Adelaide and country churches. He was also active in the administration of the Church and in seeking unity of the different Methodist denominations. He supported his wife's campaigns for temperance and against gambling, but he had a keen sense of fun and made a happy home life for his four sons and four daughters.

In 1887 Holder was elected senior member for Burra in the South Australian House of Assembly. He described himself as a free trader opposed to selling Crown lands in order to remove the deficit and was against a property tax. He favoured increase of the land tax, reduction of income tax and customs duties, and payment of members. He opposed the totalizator and agreed with the Chaffey [q.v.7] irrigation scheme. In his first arduous session Holder was a member of the commission on the land laws, the select committee on the *Star of Greece* shipwreck disaster, and chairman of the Barrier trade select committee. On 27 June 1889 he became treasurer in the Cockburn [q.v.8] ministry which introduced succession duties and a progressive tax on unimproved land values. Next year he was chairman of a select committee, later converted into a royal commission, which advocated the adoption of intercolonial free trade on the basis of a uniform tariff. He was also a member of the commission on European mails.

After the fall of the Cockburn ministry in August 1890, and particularly as leader of the Opposition and member of the pastoral lands commission in 1891, Holder travelled extensively in the colony and wrote a series of articles on the pastoral industry for the *South Australian Register* urging caution in subdivision of pastoral properties, steady improvement of water resources and more rabbit-proof fencing. On 17 June 1892 he defeated Thomas Playford [q.v.] in the House on a motion of confidence and became premier and treasurer. But it was a time of great financial difficulty and the ministry fell on 15 October.

After the Liberal win in the election of 1893, Holder, though still leader of the Opposition, made way for Charles Kingston [q.v.] to become premier; he himself became commissioner of public works and, from April 1894, treasurer and minister in charge of the Northern Territory. The State Bank of South Australia was established during Holder's treasurership and he produced a balanced budget, despite successive years of drought and depression. As minister controlling the Northern Territory, and as a commissioner to report on the best means of promoting settlement, he made an extensive journey by train and camel in 1895 beyond the MacDonnell Ranges.

On 28 November 1899 the Kingston government was defeated and, when V. L. Solomon [q.v.] was unable to form a ministry, Holder again became premier and treasurer, and also minister of industry, positions which he retained until he moved to the Federal parliament in May 1901. The second Holder government established libraries in country towns and introduced standard time throughout South Australia. It also ensured completion of the Bundaleer and Barossa water schemes.

Though not in favour of Federation 'at all hazards and at any price' Holder was a 'warm Federalist' who saw the free ex-change of goods as the first step towards a united Australia. He was elected to the 1897 Federal convention second only to Kingston, and by the close of the convention was in the first rank of influence, particularly on financial matters. He presented the Adelaide draft for a Federal constitution to the South Australian parliament on 6 July 1897 and when the bill, after revision in Sydney and Melbourne, was submitted to the electors, its acceptance by a preponderating vote in South Australia was largely due to Holder's influence and advocacy. Having, with other premiers, refused to serve in a Federal ministry under Sir William Lyne [q.v.], he hoped to be treasurer in Barton's [q.v.7] cabinet. But an invitation failed to reach him and Barton asked Kingston to be his South Australian colleague. Holder was bitterly disappointed. However, in the election of 30 March 1901 conducted in South Australia as a single constituency, he was elected to the House of Representatives. He stood fourth to Kingston, Bonython [q.v.7] and Glynn [q.v.] in the total poll but received the largest number of votes in the twenty-one country districts.

On 9 May, when parliament was inaugurated in Melbourne, Holder was elected first Speaker of the House of Representatives. Working with Sir Richard Chaffey Baker [q.v.7], first president of the Senate, he had the responsibility of adapting the forms and practices of Westminster and of the colonial legislatures to the needs of the new parliament. He carried out this role with skill and dedication, earning the respect and affection of members of all parties. He was appointed K.C.M.G. in 1902. Standing as an Independent, Holder was returned to parliament for Wakefield in 1903 and 1906. He was re-elected Speaker without contest after each election and kept aloof from party politics, though he once admitted to 'an almost overwhelming desire to step out of the Chair and tear off the gag'. He gave particular care to his administrative duties as Speaker, especially as chairman of the Joint Library Committee. His report of 1903 was, in fact, a blueprint for the eventual National Library of Australia.

Never a very robust man, Holder showed a disregard for his health and for the advice of doctors and friends. In 1899, when the mules pulling his vehicle on a country trip bolted and he seriously injured his hip, he refused to seek medical advice. The campaign for Federation, the establishment of the new parliament and the vigorous interplay of the parties all took their toll. About 6 a.m. on 23 July 1909, when the House was in committee after a stormy all-night sitting, Holder, who had confided to friends his distress at the bitter feeling between the parties, was heard to say: 'Dreadful! Dreadful!' and fell insensible to the floor of the House. He died that afternoon from cerebral haemorrhage without recovering consciousness. The town hall bells in Adelaide were tolled when the news was received. After a memorial service in the House his body was taken by train to Adelaide for a state funeral and burial in West Terrace cemetery. He was survived by his wife and their eight children.

Holder made a notable contribution to the development of Burra and of South Australia, particularly as a political leader. He marshalled his arguments well and spoke fluently and with fervour. (Sir) William Sowden [q.v.] described him as 'one of the smartest administrators ever known in Australian politics'. Alfred Deakin [q.v.8] paid high tribute to his contribution to the attainment of Federation and there has been no dissent from his statement that Holder 'presided over the House of Representatives with conspicuous ability, firmness and impartiality'. Several of Holder's articles were reprinted in 1892 under the title *Our pastoral industry*, and a small book of his sermons, *Condensed sermons by a layman*, was published in Adelaide in 1922. There are portraits by George A. J. Webb in the South Australian House of Assembly and in the House of Representatives in Canberra. Another portrait, by Holder's daughter Rhoda, is held by the National Library. His name is commemorated by a Canberra suburb.

J. J. Pascoe (ed), *History of Adelaide and vicinity* (Adel, 1901); A. Deakin, *The Federal story*, H. Brookes ed (Melb, 1944); J. Reynolds, *Edmund Barton* (Syd, 1948); J. A. La Nauze, *The Hopetoun blunder* (Melb, 1957); G. D. Combe, *Responsible government in South Australia* (Adel, 1957); J. A. La Nauze, *The making of the Australian Constitution* (Melb, 1972); *Sydney Mail*, 28 June 1909; *T&CJ*, 4 Aug 1909; *Christian Advocate*, 14 Oct 1909; *Brisbane Courier*, 8 Nov 1930; Holder papers (NL, and AAO).   RALPH HARRY

HOLDSWORTH, ALBERT ARMYTAGE (1875-1932), businessman and soldier, was born on 4 November 1875 at Ascot, Victoria, ninth child of John Holdsworth, druggist, and his wife Cate Lancashire, née Vick, both English-born. Nothing is known of his early life and education. He was commissioned lieutenant in the Victorian Volunteer Cadet Corps in 1895 and in 1896 was appointed to the 2nd Battalion (militia).

In January 1900 Holdsworth embarked for active service in South Africa as a lieutenant with the 2nd Victorian (Mounted Rifles) Contingent. He took part in operations in Cape Colony, Orange River Colony and Transvaal, during which he was attached to the British Army Service Corps for twelve months. He was invalided to Australia via England in 1901, arriving in October, and on 4 December married Elizabeth Wellwood (d. 1904) at St Martin's Anglican Church, Hawksburn, Melbourne. While working as an estate agent he resumed duty with the militia, first with the 2nd Battalion and later with the 6th Australian Infantry Regiment, but in July 1903 transferred to the Australian Army Service Corps and was promoted captain. In 1908 he joined the Australian Intelligence Corps and was promoted major in December 1911. He was an enthusiastic citizen soldier and in 1911-12 contributed five articles—mainly on the military application of motorization—to the *Commonwealth Military Journal*. In August 1913 he returned to the A.A.S.C. Holdsworth was also active in civic affairs, gaining election to the Prahran City Council in 1909. He served until 1912, by which time he had pioneered all-night bus services between Prahran and the city. On 9 June 1910 at St Martin's, Hawksburn, he married Annie Allen.

On the outbreak of World War I Holdsworth was temporarily attached for duty at Army Headquarters but on 21 August 1914 he was appointed as a major to command the headquarters company of the supply train of 1st Division, Australian Imperial Force. In Egypt in November 1915 the 1st Divisional Train took part in the Sollum expedition against the Senussi as part of Major General Sir A. Wallace's Western Frontier Force. Holdsworth was in command when the train was ordered to move on 17 November but three days later was appointed assistant director of supply and transport on Wallace's staff at Matruh. For his work during the campaign he was awarded the Distinguished Service Order and was later mentioned in dispatches for his services both in Egypt and France. He also received the Volunteer Officers' Decoration in 1916. Transferred to command the 4th Divisional Train in March 1916 with the rank of lieutcolonel, he remained with his unit in France and Belgium for almost the rest of the war. He returned to Australia in September 1918, his A.I.F. appointment ended in January 1919 and he was placed on the retired list of the Australian Military Forces with the honorary rank of colonel in February 1924.

After the war he resumed business as a real estate agent in Prahran, and became chairman of directors of Taxation Services of Australia Ltd and bondholders' trustee of Colonial Tobacco Growers Pty Ltd. He was again elected to the Prahran Council in 1920 and served a term as mayor in 1925-26; the council's purchase in 1921 of part of the Como estate as a public park was due largely to his representations.

Holdsworth died from a heart condition in a private hospital at Prahran on 9 October 1932 and was cremated. He was survived by his second wife and their son and daughter as well as a son by his first marriage; his eldest son had predeceased him.

Aust Defence Dept, *Official records of the Australian military contingents to the war in South Africa*, P. L. Murray ed (Melb, 1911); J. B. Cooper, *The history of Prahran* (Melb, 1912); C. E. W. Bean, *The A.I.F. in France*, 1916 (Syd, 1929); C. D. Coulthard-Clark, *The citizen general staff* (Canb, 1976); *London Gazette*, 2, 20 June 1916; *Argus*, 10, 12 Oct 1932; *Herald* (Melb), 10 Oct 1932; records (AWM).
C. D. COULTHARD-CLARK

HOLLAND, HENRY EDMUND (1868-1933), Labor leader, was born on 10 June 1868 at Gininderra, New South Wales, younger son of native-born parents Edward Holland, farmer, and his wife Mary, née Chaplin. He received elementary schooling until he was 10, then worked on a farm until he was apprenticed at 14 as a compositor to the *Queanbeyan Times*. After he had served his time, in 1887 Holland left Queanbeyan to find work in Sydney. On 6 October 1888 at the Palmer Street manse he married Annie McLachlan, whom he had met at a Salvation Army meeting. In 1890 he became unemployed, and after two years of privation he left the Salvation Army and joined the Australian Socialist League in Sydney in 1892.

Henceforth Holland actively espoused a radical and militant socialism as a journalist and public speaker, becoming increasingly critical of the new Labor Party, which he regarded as insufficiently revolutionary: he finally broke with it in 1898. He found erratic work on the *Australian Workman* in 1893 and in October next year he and a friend Tom Batho launched the *Socialist* as a voice for the left-wing militants and unemployed. In 1896, after a conviction for libel in which he was unable to pay the fine, Holland was gaoled for three months. At the end of that year he transferred his newspaper to Newcastle, calling it *Socialist Journal of the Northern People*, and in 1898 he secured its amalgamation, under his editorship, with a Sydney paper, as the *People and Collectivist*. In 1900 this paper moved to Sydney, still under Holland, as the *People*.

Standing for the Socialist Labor Party in 1901, Holland was defeated for the Senate and for the State seat of Lang. That year he also organized the Tailoresses' Union of

New South Wales, leading them into a bitter strike in November. But in 1902 he withdrew from organized socialism to edit the *Grenfell Vedette* owned by his friend W. A. Holman [q.v.]. He soon tired of Grenfell and in 1905 returned to Queanbeyan to edit the unsuccessful *Queanbeyan Leader*. In February 1907 he left for Sydney to launch a new militant socialist publication, the *International Socialist Review for Australasia*. This coincided with a vigorous resurgence within the socialist movement and an increase in industrial disturbances. Holland again entered a State election campaign in 1907 and was defeated for Darling Harbour. In 1909 he became involved in the Broken Hill strike and was convicted of sedition, serving five months of a two-year sentence. As a Revolutionary Socialist, he was defeated for West Sydney in the 1910 Federal elections by W. M. Hughes [q.v.]. General physical breakdown and a knee injury forced him into hospital in 1911.

Next year Holland was asked to make a lecture tour of New Zealand. He arrived during the Waihi gold-quartz miners' dispute, in which a striker was killed; he collaborated in writing the history of these events. He accepted the editorship, in Wellington, of the *Maoriland Worker*, the New Zealand labour weekly, and became involved in the massive 1913 strike agitation. Imprisoned for seditious language, Holland served three months of a twelve-month sentence. Defeated as a Socialist Democratic Party candidate in 1914, he was prominent in the formation of the New Zealand Labour Party in 1916 and in 1918 was elected to the House of Representatives for Grey. Next year he became chairman of the Parliamentary Labour Party, a position he held until his death in 1933, despite occasional criticism and challenges. The growth in Labour's support made him leader of the Opposition in 1925 but Labour did not gain power until the election of 1935.

Holland was a socialist of extraordinary and selfless dedication and character. Self-educated and sensitive, he was a voracious reader and prolific writer: in addition to his constant journalism and public speaking, he wrote thirty-six pamphlets, mainly on labour issues, but also on subjects such as Samoa, China, Ireland and Mussolini and a volume of sentimental verse, *Red roses on the highways* (Sydney, 1924). His commitment to doctrinaire socialism was passionate and total, though it mellowed somewhat under the pressure of political practicalities. He worked incessantly and this, combined with deep conviction and a forceful personality, made him a formidable political advocate and adversary. Both rigid and humane, Holland contained powerful contradictions.

While his colleagues sometimes regarded his socialism as an electoral liability, his unceasing drive and sheer force of will did much to take the New Zealand Labour Party from obscurity to the verge of office.

While attending the funeral of a Maori 'king', Holland died suddenly of a heart attack on 8 October 1933 at Huntly, New Zealand, and was buried in Wellington cemetery: the New Zealand Labour Party erected a memorial over his grave. After leaving the Salvation Army he had no religious denomination, but he held strong moral views. He was survived by five sons and two daughters.

P. J. O'Farrell, *Harry Holland, militant socialist* (Canb, 1964), and for bibliog; Holland papers (ANU Archives, *and* NL).   PATRICK O'FARRELL

HOLLIS, ROBERT (1851-1937), engine driver, trade union leader and politician, was born on 14 January 1851 at Field Head, Belper, Derbyshire, England, son of Robert Hollis, an illiterate labourer, and his wife Mary Ann, née Wragg. At 13 he joined the Midland Railway Co. and reached engine driver grade in 1878. On 30 March 1875 at Ripley he married Alice Turton. Hollis was active in such political and social movements of his day as the Liberal Party, consumer co-operatives, building societies and railway provident, friendly and benevolent associations. Although he served on the executive committee of the Amalgamated Society of Railway Servants in 1877-79, he was disappointed by its conservatism. Correctly sensing major industrial conflict in the Midland Railway Co., Hollis left for New South Wales in 1884 and joined the Department of Railways in January 1885 as a fireman.

His abilities soon came to the attention of his fellow enginemen, and in December 1886 Hollis became general secretary of the New South Wales Engine Drivers', Firemen's and Cleaners' Association (founded in 1884); he resigned in October 1910. His experience in England had convinced him that railwaymen's best interests were served by sectional unions. Thus he opposed the efforts of William F. Schey [q.v.] in 1886-87 to organize all railway employees in a single union. The depression of the 1890s and the merciless anti-unionism of the chief commissioner E. M. G. Eddy [q.v.8] suppressed mass unionism in the railways for a decade and led to a confrontation with the enginemen which brought about Hollis's resignation from the railways in 1893.

He had turned increasingly to politics as a medium for restoring the industrial gains made in the late 1880s. In 1891 Hollis was prominent in organizing the first Labor League at Newtown, Sydney. After several attempts he won the State set of Newtown-Erskine, an inner suburban working-class electorate, for Labor in 1901. Nevertheless, he continued with his union work in the railways. He was the prime mover in the formation of the Federated Railway Locomotive Enginemen's Association of Australasia in 1900 and served as its secretary until 1913. As an ex-railwayman and member for an electorate with a high proportion of railwaymen, he often spoke in parliament on aspects of railway administration and the protection and improvement of its workers.

In early 1914 Hollis was sufficiently well off to visit England via the United States of America. On his return he continued as before, but as World War I progressed he was increasingly unable to come to terms with its adverse effects on the living standards of working people and the growth of anti-war sentiment. In 1916 he supported conscription in defiance of his electorate. In the ensuing upheaval he and many of the other British-born first generation founders of the State labour movement were expelled from the Political Labor League in November 1916. In the March 1917 election, Hollis, standing as a Nationalist, was defeated.

Thereafter, he devoted himself to benevolent work—most importantly, as a director of Royal Prince Alfred Hospital in 1913-33. He died in the Masonic Hospital, Ashfield, on 25 May 1937 and was buried in Rookwood cemetery. A member of the Church of England and a prominent Freemason, Hollis was survived by three of his five sons.

Daily Telegraph (Syd), 10 July 1888, 10 July 1901; *Aust Workman*, 26 May 1894; J. C. Docherty, The rise of railway unionism: a study of New South Wales and Victoria, c. 1880-1905 (MA thesis, ANU, 1973); D. H. Coward, The impact of war on New South Wales: some aspects of social and political history, 1914-1917 (Ph.D. thesis, ANU, 1974); Aust Federated Union of Locomotive Enginemen, NSW Division, Records (ANU Archives).

J. C. DOCHERTY

HOLMAN, ADA AUGUSTA (1869-1949), journalist, was born on 3 October 1869 at Ballarat, Victoria, eldest surviving child of Ebenezer Kidgell, English-born journalist and his Irish wife Agnes, née Martin. No record survives of her schooling which may have been disrupted by her father's erratic career: he worked on the *Clunes Guardian*, the *Hawthorn and Boroondara Standard* and in 1895-1902 as sub-editor, *Sunday Times*, Sydney. He died in March 1902, leaving his family in straitened circumstances. Ada later recalled her many years 'doing nothing but work'.

Well informed on literature and current politics, she was active in debating societies, winning the essay and the short story prizes of the New South Wales Literary and Debating Societies Union. By 1896 Ada Kidgell was placing short stories, reviews and political and literary items, using her own name, 'Marcus Malcolm' and 'Nardoo'. As 'Myee' she sent 'Our Sydney letter' to Melbourne *Punch*. She frequently contributed to the *Sydney Mail, Sydney Morning Herald* and the *Freeman's Journal*. She edited and wrote most of the copy for the *Co-operator*, a trade journal for rural producers.

In Sydney on 22 January 1901 Ada Kidgell married W. A. Holman [q.v.] with Australian Church forms; their only child was born in 1903. Her political views were already formed: she was republican and a critic of the Constitution, of the South African War and of inequality, whether related to class or sex. She continued journalism after marriage, sometimes ghosting items which appeared under her husband's name. The Labor Party benefited from her ability to place items sympathetic to its programme in the non-Labor press. With her husband in State cabinet from 1910, she was more restricted: her short stories continued to appear but little else. The *Daily Telegraph* accepted articles from an overseas trip, later published as *My wander year* (1912); as 'Literoctopus' in 1914 she wrote sporting and dramatic news for *Society*. Her *Little Miss Anzac* (London) appeared in 1917 and *Sport of the gods* (Melbourne) in 1921. Two other novels, 'Eve in the desert' (1934) and 'Good courage' (1936), were serialized in the *Sydney Morning Herald*.

Ada Holman resented both the limitations to her own work consequent on being married to a prominent politician, and the demands on women to fill one role only, that of wife and mother. Women would be free, she wrote to Dowell O'Reilly [q.v.], when motherhood affected woman's life 'only to the same degree as parenthood does a man'. She believed in woman's right to decide whether or not to have children. A recurring theme to her stories was tension in marriage as when a wife's interests were suppressed or ignored, or a woman married unwillingly from economic necessity or family pressure. Her famous reply to the *Sunday Express* question, 'How to handle a husband', was not to be a doormat. Her feminism was ahead of its times in criticism of sex roles and sexist language: she castigated publicly the Labor delegate who used 'old woman' as a term of contempt.

Ada Holman was devoted to her daughter Portia. She began writing children's plays for performance at the school Portia attended. In 1923 she took her to England for tertiary education. In 1925 she wrote begging William to abandon his intention of entering English politics: 'People not in the swim have no life at all'. When she left next year her adored daughter remained in England. In Australia Ada continued to make a useful contribution to family income by writing and, from 1927, by radio talks. A second children's story *Elka Reva-Ree* appeared in 1928. In Europe again in 1930 and 1933, she denounced Nazi anti-Semitism in her reporting for the *Herald*.

In impecunious circumstances after William died in 1934, she was helped a little by the award in 1938 of a Commonwealth Literary Fund pension of £1 a week. Shortly before her death she was complaining of delay in publication of her *Memoirs of a premier's wife* (1947), the disappointingly anecdotal memoir of meetings with famous persons. In a fragment of a play similarly entitled, the wife has bitter words: 'The leader of the state has no time for his wife and children'. Ada Holman died on 3 April 1949 and was cremated with Anglican rites. The *Bulletin* remembered her for having 'an amused and amusing chuckle for life generally'. That would have made her chuckle again.

A. A. Holman, and W. A. Holman, and Miles Franklin, and D. P. O'Reilly papers (ML).

HEATHER RADI

HOLMAN, MARY ALICE ('MAY') (1893-1939), politician, was born on 18 July 1893 at Broken Hill, New South Wales, first of nine children of John Barkell Holman, miner, and his wife Katherine Mary, née Row. That year her father moved to the Murchison goldfields in Western Australia, the family following in 1896. May was educated at convents in Dongara and Perth. She was a gifted musician, gaining licentiates in singing and pianoforte, and she organized choirs and performed in concerts, plays, balls and fêtes with flair and enthusiasm; she had her own band, 'The Entertainers'. Her first jobs were in 1911 as a typist at the Trades Hall, as a pianist at cinemas, in a pierrot show and from 1914 on the *Westralian Worker*. On 9 May 1914 she married Peter Joseph ('Joe') Gardiner, a Labor member of the State parliament, in the District Registrar's Office, Perth; they were divorced in 1920, having never lived together.

Holman's mother was active in Labor women's organizations and her father was a Labor member of the Legislative Assembly in 1901-21 and 1923-25. He was secretary of the State branch of the Australian

Timber Workers' Union almost continuously from 1908 to 1925. May had grown up in an atmosphere where men and women are credited with existing on the same intellectual plane' and with great family and Labor loyalty. From 1918 she assisted her father at the Timber Workers' Union in clerical and book-keeping work and arbitration, spending nine months in the Victorian Arbitration Court. She knew much about timber families' lives and, after J. B. Holman's death in 1925, was briefly acting secretary of the union and won pre-selection for his blue-ribbon seat of Forrest, a predominantly timber electorate.

She won the by-election, thereby becoming the first Labor woman parliamentarian in Australia, and retained the seat through four following elections. A woman friend noted that, although 'a good looker and well dressed', May Holman was 'never assertive or spectacular, she was a woman of the people'. She saw herself primarily as the representative of the families' interests, in the small forest settlements of her electorate. She spoke effectively in the House of their lack of medical care, decent housing and schooling, and their dangerous work. The Timber Industries Regulation Act, 1926, was largely her work. Holman visited the camps regularly, at first in timber trains, perched on the 'cow catcher', and later in her own 'Tin Lizzie'. She had excellent rapport with the workers, a good grasp of industrial problems, and could discuss women's affairs with the housewives.

From 1933 Holman was secretary to the Parliamentary Labor Party. She was involved with the Labor Women's Organization, having been minute secretary at its first State conference in 1912. She was a long-time president of Perth Labor Women; president, then secretary of the Labor Women's Central Executive from its foundation in 1927; and president, from its inception in 1929, of the Labor Women's Interstate Executive. She established country women's branches and in 1935 made a successful interstate tour for the Labor Women's organizations. On the nomination of the Women's Service Guilds and the women's executive of the State branch of the Labor Party, she had been a substitute delegate to the League of Nations Assembly at Geneva in 1930. She was ill while overseas; her health was always poor, she suffered from asthma and a weak heart. Particularly after the 1930 trip, Holman spoke out in favour of equal citizenship rights for women.

In 1937, in evidence to the royal commission on youth employment, she described her work as convener of a party committee dealing with youth employment problems. She supported raising the school leaving age to 16, child endowment, equal pay for men and women, and improving training and working conditions of female domestic servants. In 1938, at her instigation, a royal commission to inquire into sanitation, slum clearance and health and housing regulations in Perth was set up; Holman was a member. She also attended the British Commonwealth Relations Conference in New South Wales.

Holman was not a radical and belonged to the mainstream of the moderate Western Australian Labor movement: she came to oppose non-British migration and she supported an isolationist foreign policy. She dedicated her life to the reform of society as it existed. When she died on 20 March 1939, following a car accident, on the day of her re-election to the Forrest seat, she was widely mourned. At the requiem Mass at St Mary's Cathedral, Perth, her pall was accompanied by a guard of honour of eight women representing Labor organizations. She was buried in Karrakatta cemetery. Her brother E. J. F. Holman was elected in her place and held the seat till 1947.

D. Popham (ed), *Reflections* (Perth, 1979); *PD* (WA), 1925, p 10, 1926, p 1469; *V&P* (WA), 1938, 1, (4); *Aust Women's Weekly*, 8 Apr 1939; *Labour Hist*, 1981, no 41, p 110; *Herald* (Melb), 10 June 1927, 13 June 1930; *Observer* (Adel), 4 Aug 1928; *SMH*, 28 Apr, 20 July 1928; 12 Apr 1930, 3 Sept 1938; *Mail* (Adel), 2 Mar 1929; *Daily News* (Perth), 15 Dec 1930, 22 Mar 1939; *Westralian Worker*, 31 Mar 1939; R. Joyce, Feminism: the ideology, application, successes and failures in the Labor women's organizations 1905-1917 (B.A. Hons, Univ WA, 1977); MS 842/6, no 11 (NL); ALP, State Executive file 1688A/340.454, 378, 474, 486, and minutes 1573A, vol 5, 6, *and* Labor Women's Central Executive, Minutes, 2011A/2, *and* Souvenir of May Holman's 10th anniversary, 1935, PR 5652/2, *and* Holman family papers 1744A (Battye Lib); information from Miss M. Holmes, North Perth.

MARGARET BROWN

HOLMAN, RICHARD CHARLES FREDERICK (1861-1933), soldier, was born on 26 September 1861 at Broadway, Dorsetshire, England, son of Frederick Holman, pharmacist, and his wife Louisa Thomson, née Puckett. Educated at King's College, London, he enlisted in the ranks of the British Army and served with the 1st Mounted Rifles in the Bechuanaland Expedition of 1884-85. He came to Australia soon afterwards and served with the New South Wales Police Force in 1886-88. On 23 June 1890 Holman was granted warrant rank in the New South Wales Permanent Mounted Infantry. In 1897 he spent several months in the United Kingdom on attachment to the 4th

Dragoon Guards and the 1st Battalion, Scots Guards. He also attended Queen Victoria's Diamond Jubilee celebrations as a member of the New South Wales military detachment.

Holman served with distinction in the South African War. On 3 November 1899 he embarked as regimental sergeant major with the 1st New South Wales Mounted Rifles. He took part in Lord Roberts's great drive into the Boer republics in February-June 1900, and then in other operations in western Transvaal before leaving for home with his unit in December 1900. For his gallantry in the field, he was mentioned in dispatches and awarded the Distinguished Conduct Medal. After only two months in Australia he embarked again for the front as lieutenant and adjutant with the 2nd New South Wales Mounted Rifles. He arrived in Cape Town in April 1901 and his unit spent the remaining thirteen months of the war in sporadic operations against Boer guerrilla forces. His military efficiency during this period earned him promotion to captain and award of the Distinguished Service Order.

After returning from South Africa, Holman reverted to his pre-war rank of warrant officer and served as such with the Commonwealth Military Forces until he was commissioned as lieutenant, Adminstrative and Instructional Staff, on 1 January 1905. He was promoted captain on 26 September 1906 and major on 1 October 1911. He visited Canada as an exchange officer in 1912-13. Holman was brigade major with the 3rd Light Horse Brigade from December 1913 to September 1916 when he relinquished the post to take command of the Liverpool Concentration Camp, New South Wales, with the rank of lieut-colonel. Liverpool was the main internment centre in Australia for enemy aliens, and internees numbered over 5000 when Holman assumed a command which he carried out with competence and compassion until his retirement on 4 February 1920 with the honorary rank of colonel.

Holman had married Harriette Blanche Mills at St Mary's Anglican Church, Balmain, Sydney, on 10 December 1890. They had three daughters and a son Richard Dudley, who served with the Australian Imperial Force at Gallipoli and in France as a commissioned officer and was twice wounded. Survived by his wife and children, Holman died of cancer on 13 December 1933 at Ingleburn, and was buried in the Anglican section of Denham Court cemetery, Ingleburn.

Aust Defence Dept, *Official records of the Australian military contingents to the war in South Africa*, P. L. Murray ed (Melb, 1911); E. Scott, *Australia during the war* (Syd, 1936); L. M. Field, *The forgotten war* (Melb, 1979); *London Gazette*, 27 Sept 1901, 29 July, 31 Oct 1902; *SMH*, 16 Dec 1933.

L. M. FIELD

HOLMAN, WILLIAM ARTHUR (1871-1934), cabinetmaker, politician and barrister, was born on 4 August 1871 at Pancras, London, son of William Holman and his wife Martha Mary, née Bingley, both actors. He went to an Anglican school in London, winning many prizes, and was apprenticed as a cabinetmaker at the Cleveland Works. Motivated and encouraged by his parents Holman attended night classes and literary societies; he developed a fine speaking voice and became an insatiable reader. In 1916, when premier of New South Wales, in welcoming Sir Rider Haggard to Sydney, he recalled his purchase in London 'for a few coppers' of 'a tattered copy of . . . *She* . . . an introduction to a new world'. He was also enthusiastic about radical, socialist, economic and philosophical literature. He never lost his love for books.

Tall, wiry, graceful and handsome, with dark curly hair, Holman was conscious of his talents, but not his appearance. His wide cultural interests included music; and he mastered the French language and honoured French wines—a confirmed Francophile. He was emotional, gregarious and compassionate, though his patience had its limits. Most liked him, but some claimed to detect that his fastidiousness often changed to disdain; others noted petulance under pressure. H. V. Evatt said he was shy; that is debatable, though there was no doubt about his charismatic charm. He became Australia's best all-round orator, mellifluous, logical, convincing.

With his father, mother and brother Charles, Holman arrived in Melbourne in September 1888 on the *Cuzco*. A fire cut short his parents' theatrical engagement and next year the family settled in Sydney, where he worked at his trade. By 1890 he was frequenting the Sydney Mechanics' School of Arts reading room, where 'schemes for the redemption of society' were formulated. With W. M. Hughes [q.v.] he led the Ethical Society, an impoverished students' group, soon joined by (Sir) George Beeby [q.v.7]; they studied the works of Herbert Spencer, Karl Marx, John Stuart Mill and Boehm-Bawerk. Holman's father set up as an actors' coach and elocution teacher, and their home attracted many young radicals, including D. R. Hall [q.v.]. In 1890 Holman belonged to the Australian Socialist and the Sydney Single Tax leagues.

He joined the Labor Electoral League (Labor Party) in 1891, although he had taken no part in its foundation by the Trades and Labor Council in 1890-91. Trade unions never quite harmonized with Holman's style or ambitions; but he was secretary of the Railways and Tramways Employees' Union in 1893 and represented it briefly on the T.L.C.; he organized intermittently for the Australian Workers' Union in 1896-98. He responded to the zestful reforming appeal of the new party by throwing himself into its early activity; by 1892 he represented Leichhardt on the central executive. The theoretical socialist aspect of Labor appealed to him: in 1893 he enlarged the appeal of the party and his own reputation for precocious intellectualism by a series of notable public lectures on Marx, Henry George [q.v.4] and Boehm-Bawerk.

He also revealed a flair for grass-roots organizing. The president, J. C. Watson [q.v.], welcomed his zeal and gifts, and Holman became one of the executive's chief spokesmen, useful in Watson's efforts to apply the trade unions' principle of solidarity to the parliamentary Labor Party, which consisted of thirty-five members in 1891, but which had split that year and in 1892. At a unity conference in November 1893 Holman proposed that the executive's pledge for parliamentarians be accepted and it became the basis of a successful motion, helping to unite the party for the 1894 and future elections. His own parliamentary aspirations were frustrated at Leichhardt in 1894.

Although he was poor for most of the 1890s, Holman spent much time in proselytizing. In 1894 he was involved with Beeby in a publication at Hillgrove in the northwest; the same year with Hughes and others he produced the *New Order*, which occasionally featured irreverent comments on trade unions and their leaders, including W. G. Spence [q.v.6], the shearers' (A.W.U.) president. The most ambitious, and disastrous, project was the *Daily Post* which ran from January to April 1895. In November Holman was charged, with other directors, with conspiracy to defraud a creditor. Mercurial optimism and enthusiasm and lack of business experience, rather than dishonesty, had produced the crisis, but a miscarriage of justice saw him sentenced to two years in March 1896. The conviction was quashed in May, but his imprisonment was wounding and salutary. T. Routley, secretary of the party executive, had organized his appeal; Holman claimed later that Watson and Hughes did not help him.

Holman also believed in improvement through parliament. He became aware by 1895 that Labor's support was greater in the country than in the city. He was attracted, too, by the romantic aura of 'the bush'. That year he ran for Grenfell; his loss did not dis-

pel his fervour, especially as the electorate was in a picturesque region combining agriculture and sheep with gold-mining and an exciting bushranging past. He gradually improved his connexions there, becoming widely known for his bicycle tours. In 1898 he managed to buy the *Grenfell Vedette*.

He remained in the centre of Labor activity in Sydney and attended the 1897 conference, arguing that socialism was all right as a basic party principle, but had no place on the fighting platform. He was elected to the executive and selected to run as one of Labor's ten candidates for the Australasian Federal Convention. Labor supported Federation and he was a leader of the party's efforts to liberalize the draft constitution. None of the Laborites was elected. Holman's analysis of the causes of the defeat emphasized the need for modern electioneering tactics, including house-to-house canvassing; 'their platform', he said, 'was advanced enough to serve for the next twenty years'. He was becoming restless at the parliamentary party's support of the Reid [q.v.] government, realizing that the premier's radical liberalism was fading under pressure from the Legislative Council and his increasing concentration on Federation.

At the July 1898 elections Holman won Grenfell and quickly became a force in parliament, emphasizing Reid's 'inertia' and the need for reforms to help country as well as city people. But in 1898-99 New South Wales politics was dominated by the approaching culmination of Federation, and his patience was tested. Influenced by J. S. T. McGowen [q.v.] and Watson, the Labor Party agreed to back Reid's parliamentary plans to have the final draft constitution submitted to a referendum in 1899. With Hughes, Holman claimed that the draft was still too undemocratic, and at the March 1899 conference they tried to have Labor's support for the referendum withdrawn; but Watson pointed out the primacy of the principle to the party and overcame them, much to Holman's annoyance. Federation was becoming boring to him and he was keen to get on with reforming New South Wales. With the party, he campaigned strongly in June against the constitution 'bill' but the referendum was carried.

Criticism of Reid widened in the Labor caucus, with Holman, Hughes, A. Edden and J. R. Dacey [qq.v.8] threatening to resign their seats unless the party abandoned him. It climaxed in August-September 1899 in an agreement with (Sir) William Lyne [q.v.], leader of the Opposition, for legislation on old-age pensions and early closing of shops. In a complex censure motion Labor withdrew its support from Reid and he was defeated.

The Lyne government was immediately confronted with the problem of sending a contingent to the South African War. In the debate Holman acknowledged his loyalty to the British Empire, but claimed that at stake was the interest of 'a little gang of swindling speculators on the Rand'; his courageous and eloquent speech aroused the jingoism of most members and provoked wild interjections. He became increasingly agitated and, when baited by (Sir) Edmund Barton [q.v.7], blurted out, 'I believe from the bottom of my heart that this is the most iniquitous, most immoral war ever waged with any race. I hope that England may be defeated'. Parliament, including most of Holman's confrères, was shocked. But his view, when shed of its hyperbole, had much support in the party, notably from A. Griffith [q.v.], and represented a significant minority opinion in the community, though it held great electoral risks. Above all, it revealed Holman's own repugnance for 'capitalistic militarism'. As a member of the Anti-War League he campaigned against the war in 1901-02.

By 1900 the Labor Party had become an integral part of the New South Wales political system. At the 1901 election it increased its seats from 20 to 24 in a House of 125. It offered rewarding careers to ambitious members, but made great demands on them. Holman had quickly perceived the links between politics and law, and realized that the party needed legal men: Hughes, Beeby, Hall and J. D. Fitzgerald [q.v.8] reacted similarly. In 1900 Holman became a part-time student at law and next year matriculated for the University of London; in 1903 he passed the intermediate examination of its faculty of laws. On 31 July, after a futile objection by a barrister over the *Daily Post* affair, he was admitted to the Bar.

Holman's deep intellectual and emotional commitment was to the development of the party in New South Wales, and to the improvement of that State. These goals, with his distrust of the Constitution, led him to disregard Federal politics. But he was far from a crude 'States-righter'. Moreover, he believed that the States had more important 'national' powers than the Commonwealth and would be the more dynamic arena. In 1901 he decided to remain in local politics. Watson and Hughes won Federal seats. McGowen remained the New South Wales Labor Party's leader, but Holman was determined to improve his position in it. On 22 January, at the Oddfellows' Temple, Sydney, with the rites of the Australian Church, he married Ada Augusta Kidgell [q.v., A. A. Holman], a Victorian journalist.

In 1901-10 Holman emerged as the party's most successful propagandist, and earned a State-wide reputation as a brilliant and popular politician. Yet he found time to practise at the Bar. Mostly his work was on the recent industrial legislation of the State and Federal parliaments, but it included some constitutional and criminal cases. By 1910 he had achieved success, but little remuneration, as trade unions were not good payers. He was frustrated by the judiciary's reactionary approach to the new field of industrial law; and the High Court's narrow interpretations reinforced his doubts about the general role of the Commonwealth.

He retained Grenfell at the 1901 election despite being labelled 'pro-Boer' and 'pro Catholic': he supported Home Rule for Ireland, and was even handed towards all religions. Holman's seat was abolished in the 1904 redistribution, but his win in nearby Cootamundra showed how he had regulated his radicalism to the cautious tempo of country conditions; it also reflected the advance of the Labor Party which won twenty five out of ninety seats. The party had adjusted well to the new demands of the Federation era. But it now had to prepare to move from its role as a 'third party' seeking 'concessions in return for support', to a new function as the parliamentary Opposition. It needed improved leadership, both in and out of parliament. McGowen was not able to provide it, but from 1904 Holman substituted for him.

In 1905 he became deputy leader and at the annual conference spoke strongly of the need to win more country and suburban seats. He linked this aim with the electoral dangers of the party's current socialist objective, and had it replaced with an evolutionary goal which emphasized state acquisition of monopolies and 'the extension of the industrial and economic functions of the State and municipality'. This policy suited most Labor members, but it tended to alienate many radicals, including some unionists. Holman had grown farther away from the unions even as they increased in numbers and prominence as a result of industrial legislation. They remained a powerful and complex element in the party.

He was the obvious Laborite to challenge Reid who in 1905 campaigned to check the party by emphasizing its 'dangerous socialistic base'. Reid, now an ex-prime minister and portlier than ever, was past his best but still formidable and a favourite of Sydney. Their debate took place in the Centenary Hall on 2 and 3 April 1906, on 'The Principles of Socialism as Defined in the Objective of the Platform of the Labour Party'. Seconded by Hall, Holman prepared for the event like a prize-fighter; nervous at the start, he soon sparkled. Reid played it by ear and was cramped by the ban on interjections; but shafts of his great wit and repartee hit home sufficiently to help make the contest a feast for capacity audiences. The splendid occasion generated nation-wide publicity. No vote was taken but Holman had excelled, and boosted Labor significantly. He claimed that the interest in the debate showed that 'Australian intelligence, debauched (lately) by a muddle-headed Imperialism, is recovering its firm and healthy tone'.

In parliament his prowess was recognized by the premier (Sir) Joseph Carruthers [q.v.7] and other opponents. In June 1906 the report of the royal commission into the administration of the Department of Lands made charges of corruption against W. P. Crick [q.v.8], an ex-minister of lands, and referred to Carruthers. Holman was Labor's chief speaker on the report and the government tried to silence him. Their tactics coincided with the dubious plans of John Norton [q.v.], a notorious ex-associate of Crick, who blamed Holman for an article in the *Worker* which denounced Norton's failure to mention the land scandals in his newspaper, *Truth*. Norton raked up the *Daily Post* case, accused Holman of venality and, in a fine frenzy, proposed that each should resign his seat and contest Cootamundra. Holman effectively disposed of the charges, and quixotically accepted the challenge. Norton scuttled out of the fight, but a strong candidate ran against Holman, who won.

Labor Party hopes at the 1907 general election were shaken when Carruthers astutely raised the question of States-rights over customs charges on wire netting imported by his government. In the confusion the land scandals and Labor's reform policy were obscured. Nevertheless the party increased its seats to thirty-two. Holman was inspired to systematize and intensify his political organizing, especially in the country. His bicycle, which he also used in the city, was again a chief means of transport. He was on the State executive in 1906-12 and had the necessary help of many capable men and women. But more than any other person he was responsible for the powerful growth of the Labor Party in New South Wales, to make it the most important branch in the Commonwealth. His work greatly assisted the development of the federal party, and he was present at the 1908 Interstate (federal) Conference, which decided to seek only limited extra powers for the Commonwealth parliament.

Holman's misgivings about trade unions were hardened by an upsurge in strikes in 1908-09, partly related to deficiencies in the State and Federal arbitration systems. Overseas ideas brought in by the Industrial Workers of the World and Tom Mann [q.v.] were also influential. Holman perceived the possible dangers of these militant trends to the well-being of the Labor Party and determined to blunt them. But his intervention in the tramways strike was ineffective and rekindled the A.W.U.'s hostility. Nevertheless, although he stressed moderation and adherence to the law, he supported the strikers and strongly opposed the coercive policy of the new premier (Sir) Charles Wade [q.v.]. Only a few unions were antagonistic to Holman but his attitude was likely to provoke more, as he believed that 'Comprehensive ideas for the advancement of Labor . . . can only be evolved by minds who have had a training in politics and national policies'.

In April 1910 the Federal Labor Party won the Commonwealth general election: Holman had been the most effective and assiduous worker in the campaign in New South Wales. In the State he continued his potent criticism of Wade who was proving an inept premier. The rewards of his parliamentary and electoral leadership, and of the devoted and experienced backing of all Labor Party members, were gained when the party won forty-six seats in the October election. McGowen formed a ministry with Holman as attorney-general and minister of justice. But they had a majority of only two.

Holman now found that, in effect, he had to lead a government. It had a capable and energetic cabinet, including Beeby, Griffith, F. Flowers [q.v.8] and A. C. Carmichael [q.v.7], aware of their talents. Some friction arose, testing Holman's patience and skill, and increasing the great pressure on him. Hints of temperamental and health weaknesses appeared; his non-Labor enemies increased in number and sound. The structure of the party responded jerkily to the new prestige of the Commonwealth parliamentarians, now driven by the aggressive ambition of Hughes, who saw Holman as an obstacle to his hopes to make the federal branch supreme. Hughes's relentless craftiness contrasted with Holman's subtle flair. Their combat put him under further stress.

The issue was joined in 1911 on the question of constitutional amendments to give extra powers over industry, trade and commerce to the Commonwealth. The proposals went well beyond the decisions of the 1908 federal conference. Powerful support was given them by the A.W.U. and, despite Holman's opposition, the 1911 State conference directed a 'Yes' vote at the April referendum. His arguments against the amendments were restricted by conference's decision, and by the complexity of the issues in relation to current State and Federal needs, and to the structure of a party based on the States but with a strong and growing Federal component. But he wrote cogently, if anonymously, and organized skilfully, keenly conscious that at last he was in a position to realize some of his dreams for the betterment of the working-class of his State—already he and Beeby were planning comprehensive industrial legislation changes. Moreover, he feared the use of the new powers by non-Labor governments and the dangers of centralized authority, and he showed that, at the time, the idea of 'national' was not limited to the Commonwealth.

But Holman went close to breaching official Labor solidarity and the referendum was lost. Intellectually, he had the better of Hughes in the uncomfortable circumstances of the campaign, and some of his points remain relevant to a consideration of the problems of a Federal system. However, the tide of events and opinion was moving against him, and in the long run his views did not prevail. H. Lamond [q.v.], editor of the A.W.U.'s *Worker*, now became his bitter critic.

Acting premier in McGowen's absence at King George V's coronation, Holman found his parliamentary skill tested when W. F. Dunn [q.v.8] and H. E. Horne, country Labor members, resigned on 26 July 1911 during a censure motion: they opposed a party decision to withdraw the right of Crown land lessees to convert to freehold. With the defeat of the government imminent Holman tendered its resignation; the acting governor had to refuse Wade's request for an advance approval of a dissolution if he were commissioned and later defeated in the House; whereupon Holman was recommissioned and granted a prorogation until after the by-elections in August. One seat was regained, leaving the assembly equally divided. The Labor Speaker had resigned and Holman, with Griffith's help, persuaded H. Willis [q.v.], a Liberal, to replace him. Public sympathy was with Holman and his tactics were received with amused appreciation. Coincidentally during the excitement, a special Labor conference was held, at which Hughes planned to have Holman, Beeby and others censured for their ambiguous work in the April referendum: but Holman foiled him again.

McGowen's return made little difference to Holman's work-load. He either prepared or encouraged a flow of reforming legislation. The cabinet responded well, with Beeby's Industrial Arbitration Act and Carmichael's Bursary Endowment Act landmarks of 1912. He backed Griffith's successful negotiations with the Broken Hill Proprietary Co. Ltd to establish a steel works at Newcastle, though the Labor platform provided for state ownership. But they rescued a city, even as party criticism flared

up. He also encouraged Griffith's energetic railway extension policy and above all his determination to establish state enterprises in several fields. Those and other successes consolidated Labor's role as the efficient and positive element in State development helping to lay the foundations of the widely held belief that New South Wales became 'a Labor State'. On the other hand the Opposition, which had regarded its rule as part of the natural order, was losing dignity and credibility.

Holman was now a parliamentary, ever a national personality and his stature posed problems for his role as a leader of a mass democratic party. The Legislative Council was proving a stumbling block: even with 12 appointments in 1911-12, Labor had only 13 members out of 70. Inevitably there were delays and failures in effecting the government's industrial programme. Holman resented rank and file and executive criticism, especially as he regarded much of it as provoked by Hughes and the A.W.U. But he had many supporters outside parliament and was not above factional intrigue. In parliament, despite the government's overall achievements, party troubles were aggravated. The anomalous position of McGowen as premier created confusion, leading to independent action by ministers. Holman tried to ease his problems in 1912 by appointing Hall to the Legislative Council to relieve himself of the justice ministry. The cabinet's difficulties were accentuated by the temperament of Carmichael, the resignation of N. R. W. Nielsen [q.v.] in 1911 and the deaths of D. Macdonell [q.v.], 1911, and Dacey, 1912. Holman's attempts to ease McGowen out were unsuccessful.

By the end of 1912 Holman was sick soured and dispirited. In August his wife and daughter had gone to England, and in December he asked to be made agent general in London. Before a decision could be reached another emergency arose when Beeby resigned his seat and portfolio; it had been rumoured that he had tried to persuade Holman to join a new 'Centre Party'. Holman withdrew his application and was reconciled to staying in Sydney as he lacked money for the trip. But out of the blue his new friend H. D. McIntosh [q.v.] made him a loan, and he spent four months in England returning on 6 June 1913 apparently recuperated.

In his absence McGowen proved his ineptitude and on 30 June Holman became premier, although several influential party members, including Watson, opposed it; he remained attorney-general until 1914. In May 1913 the Federal Labor government had lost the election and Hughes's redrafted constitutional amendments had been de feated. Conservative forces feared a renewed State Labor Party under Holman and attacked the government at its most obvious progressive point—Griffith's administration of public works—hoping to defeat it at the forthcoming election. But with the premier's help Griffith defended his probity vigorously and successfully. Holman revived his great resources for the October campaign, inspiring the party with a fresh sense of purpose and enthusiasm; he turned to his advantage an attempt by Fr M. O'Reilly [q.v.] to introduce sectarian issues. Labor won 50 seats to the Opposition's 40. Holman was euphoric, but his vision of his importance to the party no longer corresponded with reality.

In 1913 Holman was the outstanding Labor man in Australia. But his success had changed him and, while he retained much of his youthful figure and looks, his health had deteriorated and he was tired. He was also treasurer in 1914-18, acquiring more power and suffering more strain. Parliamentary achievement and ministerial status had eroded his recognition of the significance of the contribution of very many politicians and ordinary members to the strength of the party. An element of vanity, hitherto kept in check by his sense of humour and enthusiasm, now obtruded to blunt his sensibility. He thought that his stature and his responsibilities to State and Crown had given him the right not only to the respect but also the subservience of the Labor caucus and conference. He was oblivious to new radical forces influencing the trade unions and often contemptuous of the new ideas of Labor parliamentarians, notably R. D. Meagher [q.v.]. His wife, a strong character, encouraged him. He had acquired many elevated non-Labor acquaintances; from McIntosh he received a raffish and beguiling friendship—later, he saw him more clearly as an 'adventurer'. Once a liberal Spartan, Holman was now an Epicurean.

The 1914 conference, knowing that he had promised to make McIntosh a member of the Legislative Council, decided that the executive should approve all nominees. Caucus also wanted to ratify them. Holman scorned the rulings; it was the ministry's prerogative, he said. Despite party pressure he asked for no appointments, even though the council continued to reject and mutilate legislation, especially industrial measures. World War I affected him profoundly. Its massive scale put it apart from the South African War, and he now had a deeper appreciation of the British Empire and a keen perception of the sufferings of France. His new-found sense of responsibility forced him to concentrate on the demands of war—

excessively, as defence was a Federal task. His reforming zeal ebbed further and he was not sufficiently responsive to the decline in workers' standards of living. The 1915 conference rebuked him for his failure to put Laborites into the Legislative Council and wanted renewed attempts to implement the platform. He responded by revitalizing his own rank and file support: Fitzgerald was party president in 1915-16. But it was not enough.

The gap between Holman and the labour movement widened over conscription for overseas war service. The A.W.U. and most other trade unions strongly opposed it; they gradually gained backing from local party branches; more caucus members became disaffected, especially after the 1916 Easter rebellion in Dublin. Holman's attitude to the war hardened as casualties soared; he began to see conscription as a possible necessity. Early in 1916 his health again troubled him and be began surfing, increased his fencing sessions and took up hill-climbing. The annual conference met in April with the trade union, notably A.W.U., opposition organized as 'the industrialists'. A censure motion on the government provoked another Holman manoeuvre which somehow lacked the glitter of earlier stratagems: the ministers quickly resigned to caucus, and an unwilling John Storey [q.v.] was elected leader; he convinced conference of the electoral dangers confronting him; and a compromise brought Holman back with a promise to submit the question of the abolition of the Legislative Council to a referendum at the impending elections. Conference decided that the Labor Party should oppose conscription and thus confirmed a powerful conviction of the whole movement.

Late in August Hughes, now prime minister, announced that conscription would be introduced subject to a referendum in October. The State Labor executive ruled that any parliamentarian who supported it would have his seat endorsement withdrawn. Holman campaigned strongly for 'Yes' and, when the referendum was lost, he judged that his own best interests and the nation's would be served by inviting the Opposition to coalesce with him in the formation of a National party and ministry. The decision was precipitated by the war, but was inherent in Holman's personal dilemma and official actions after his accession to the premiership, when his life changed direction and the Labor Party organization became a hindrance to him.

With seventeen other Labor members of the assembly he was expelled in November. Following devious negotiations, aided by McIntosh and P. T. Taylor [q.v.], he formed a new cabinet, including Hall, Fitzgerald,

W. C. Ashford and W. C. Grahame [q.v.] from the old ministry: Wade became agent-general, and Beeby was brought back. A new law extended parliament for an extra three to four years. Holman soon perceived that the Labor Party was in disarray after the convulsive split. He persuaded his new colleagues that much of Labor's legislative and administrative reforms should be retained and built on; but he stressed that 'Parliamentary government [should be] free from dictation'. Thus armed, he cleverly called an election for March 1917. He stressed the need to win the war and gained 50 seats. He and others had proclaimed that the Labor Party was not only unpatriotic but also obsolete: but it won 33 seats.

In May Holman went to England, arranging that his twenty-three appointments to the Legislative Council, including McIntosh and Taylor, should be announced after his departure. He was welcomed and flattered overseas. On an inspection of the Australians at the front in France he was injured and shocked when a shell exploded near the group, killing Major General W. Holmes [q.v.]. He returned through the United States of America and arrived back in November, in time to take a half-hearted part in the second conscription referendum next month. Berating Hughes for his deviousness, he even proposed that F. Tudor [q.v.], the Federal Labor leader, should become prime minister. But Hughes was now beyond his criticism.

Holman's control of the ministry was lax and he achieved little in parliament. In 1918 he attempted to stop the rot by shedding his treasury post. From 1917 allegations had spread of weak government, sometimes involving possible corruption: doubtful relations with 'coal baron' J. Brown [q.v.7], and the indiscretions of Grahame in negotiating a grain elevator contract, were followed in 1919 with Beeby's resignation from cabinet making four charges of maladministration. Two royal commissions into one of the complaints, concerning a wheat contract with G. Georgeson without public tenders, did not clear the air. The press, with some scores to settle, harried Holman relentlessly. A consolation was the praise of General Pau, on a French mission to Australia, 'We have found in you . . . a faithful and sincere friend of France'; he was appointed to the Légion d'honneur. He was also made a commander of the Belgian Order of the Crown.

Holman's style, leavened with a residual radicalism, brought about much demoralization in non-Labor forces, and hastened the process, begun by Beeby, of separating country from city conservatives. The Nationalists were emerging as an urban pressure group with some questionable con-nexions. Holman's attempted solution to his problems facilitated the new political directions: with the help of McIntosh and Taylor he contacted city magnates and obtained monetary and moral backing, but it did not prevent his electoral decline. At the 1920 election he campaigned as skilfully as ever, using an aeroplane and surviving a minor crash; he expatiated on the new 'Bolshevik menace of the Labor Party, but it won. Holman lost his seat. The year before, T. J. Ley [q.v.], a grubby and sinister ex-Nationalist, gibed, 'he clings to office like the proverbial leech'.

Holman became a K.C. in June; he was appointed knight commander of the Finnish Order of the White Rose in August. He returned to the Bar and in the 1920s, despite recurring ill heath, revealed again his great capacity for hard work, his learning and intellectual versatility, by attaining a leading position in a competitive profession. He delivered the Macrossan [q.v.5] lectures in Brisbane in 1928. Politics still fascinated him, and he was president in 1917-20 and vice-president of the New South Wales National Association in 1920-29 and 1931-32. But he was not trusted by the powerful men who ran the party machine or by the wealthy interests that financed it. However, he helped the Fuller [q.v.8] government in the 1925 elections, and (Sir) Thomas Bavin [q.v.7] prevailed on him to be director for the successful 1927 campaign. He failed narrowly next year to win pre-selection for the Federal electorate of Martin after a party official had organized against him, but he was the party's candidate in 1931, and won. Age and health were against him and he made little impact on the Commonwealth parliament.

Holman's honesty was impregnable, but one of the intriguing aspects of his life was his attitude to money. He had small regard for it and never accumulated much, although in 1898-1910 he received a parliamentary salary (£300) plus professional fees, and in 1910-20 his income as a minister and premier ranged from £1500 to £2000. For the times those were not insubstantial remunerations. In the 1920s his receipts were somewhat discontinuous, but seem to have been adequate, and he had been given a gratuity by some of his supporters. Yet he often complained about being short of money. In the end his association with McIntosh was costly, for he invested in his *Sunday Times* and apparently lost at least part of savings of £4000: at McIntosh's bankruptcy proceedings in 1932 he said that he had put aside that sum between 1910 and 1920. After his death his intestate estate was valued at £4385, and the *Worker* commented, kindly for it, that it 'was much more than it was generally thought he possessed'. But it was an insignificant amount for a life of achievement and of intense physical and intellectual effort, mostly expended for others.

On 4 September 1933 Griffith, who had recently been readmitted to the Labor Party (federal branch), and Holman had reason to write to the *Sydney Morning Herald*, defending on economic and social grounds the remaining state industries established by Labor in 1910-16: they sought a 'full public inquiry . . . before any final step be taken for their abandonment or disposal'. Next year on 5 June Holman died of heart disease at his home at Gordon and was cremated after a state funeral from St James Anglican Church: the pallbearers included Watson, Hughes, Hall and Griffith. He was survived by his wife and daughter.

Socialism as defined in the Australian Labor Party's objective and platform. Official report of a public debate . . . (Syd, 1906); H. V. Evatt, *Australian Labour leader* . . . *W. A. Holman* (Syd, 1942); V. G. Childe, *How Labour governs*, 2nd edn, F. B. Smith ed (Melb, 1964); L. F. Fitzhardinge, *William Morris Hughes*, 1 (Syd, 1964); P. Ford, *Cardinal Moran and the A.L.P.* (Melb, 1966); B. Nairn, *Civilising capitalism* (Canb, 1973); *V&P* (LA NSW), 1892-93, 2, p 1233; *PD* (NSW), 1899, p 100, 102, 1460, 3520; *Labour History*, 1970, no 18; *Daily Telegraph* (Syd), 4 July 1894; *Catholic Press*, 18 Jan 1902, 21 Jan 1902, 5 Apr 1906; *Punch* (Melb), 23 Feb 1911, 23 Feb 1916; *Freeman's J* (Syd), 27 Apr 1916, 8 Feb 1917, 14 Aug 1919; *SMH*, 27 Apr, 5 Sept, 7 Nov 1916, 8 Oct 1918, 20 Feb 1920, 6 June 1934; *Sun* (Syd), 10 Mar 1918; *Brisbane Courier*, 11 Apr 1928; *Argus* (Melb), 9 June 1934; Holman and Ada Holman papers (ML).   BEDE NAIRN

HOLME, ERNEST RUDOLPH (1871-1952), professor of English, was born on 18 March 1871 at Footscray, Melbourne, third son of Rev. Thomas Holme, Anglican clergyman and native of Manchester, England, and his Queensland-born wife Martha Louisa Maria, née Zillman; J. B. Holme [q.v.] was a brother. Their father became incumbent of All Souls Church, Leichhardt, Sydney, in 1882 and Ernest was educated at The King's School, Parramatta, and at the University of Sydney (B.A., 1891; M.A., 1909); he graduated with first-class honours in Latin and English. In 1891-94 he was an assistant master at Sydney Church of England Grammar School (Shore) and in 1894 was appointed lecturer in English (and also taught French and German) at the university under Professor (Sir) Mungo MacCallum [q.v.].

On leave in 1905, Holme studied at the universities of Paris and Berlin. In Berlin he was stimulated by German research on early Germanic languages and literature and also studied phonetics at the famous Tilly Institute. These experiences helped him to develop his style of teaching in his special area—English language and early English literature. Next year his report to the university senate on *Aspects of commercial education in Europe* was published. In 1908 Holme was appointed associate professor and continued to teach modern languages. With Emile Saillens he published *First principles of French pronunciation* (1909) which applied phonetics to the direct teaching of modern languages.

Interested in the physical and social welfare of students, Holme originated the plans for a reconstituted university union in 1912, providing it with its own building, gardens and lawns; he was president of the Sydney University Union in 1912-13. He tried to make evening students feel a valued part of the university and was 'almost perpetual' patron of their association.

On the outbreak of World War I in August 1914 Holme was appointed interpreter on the censorship staff, and was in charge of censoring foreign mail. In 1918 he helped to organize reinforcements for the Australian Imperial Force raised by the Sydney University Undergraduates' Association. In August he was appointed honorary captain in the A.I.F.'s education service, embarking for London after the Armistice. In February 1919 he became assistant director of education (university studies) under Bishop Long [q.v.], and superintended the entry of Australian servicemen, waiting for demobilization, into British and French universities. He returned to Sydney in February 1920 through the United States of America and wrote a discursive survey, *The American university* (1920).

Upon MacCallum's retirement, chairs were created in English literature and language; Holme was appointed to the new McCaughey [q.v.5] chair of English language in July 1920. He specialized in the study of the history and development of language to current usage and pronunciation, and particularly observed and recorded Australian speech. Anglo-Saxon and middle literature were prominent in his courses while he continued to contribute to modern literature studies. 'Many were imbued by Professor Holme with a life-long feeling for *Beowulf*, for Chaucer, for Dryden and certain eighteenth century writers'.

Dean of the faculty of arts and a fellow of the senate in 1921-25, Holme contributed to the expansion of the range of faculties and was prominent in the group of academics and administrators who shaped the course the university was to pursue for the next twenty years. In a sense he was a university man first and a teacher of English second. A strongly conservative force in the formation of policies and attitudes, he disapproved of radical tendencies in the 1930s, while remaining a stern upholder of the university's autonomy. An ardent patriot, he was a driving force behind the development of the university's war memorials—the bronze honour rolls in the main entrance of the quadrangle unveiled in 1931; the university's *Book of remembrance* (1939); and the War Memorial Carillon. In 1926 he toured Britain and Europe observing carillons and in 1927-28 he was director of the university's seventy-fifth anniversary appeal which raised £300 000. Known as 'Sonny', he was also secretary of the University Extension Board, a director of the University Club and a founder in 1923 and later president of the (Australian) English Association. He believed in the value of independent religious education and was a council-member of Shore and later of the Sydney Church of England Girls' Grammar School. In 1951 he published *Shore*, a history of its first headmastership.

Holme had been appointed O.B.E. in 1920 and commander of the Belgian Order of Leopold II in 1935. He retired from his chair in 1941 and, unmarried, lived with his sister Ada at Neutral Bay. He retained a keen interest in the affairs of his beloved university, which awarded him an honorary D.Litt. in 1952. He died in hospital on 20 November the same year and was cremated with Anglican rites.

Southerly, 3 (1954), p 154; *SMH*, 7, 10 July, 16 Oct 1920, 17 Mar 1921, 22 July 1935, 30 Aug, 21 Nov 1952; J. Le Gay Brereton papers (ML); information from Prof. K. J. Cable, Univ. Syd.

A. G. MITCHELL

HOLME, JOHN BARTON (1872-1929), public servant and barrister, was born on 24 August 1872 at Footscray, Melbourne, fourth son and fifth child of Rev. Thomas Holme, an Anglican clergyman from Manchester, England, and his Queensland-born first wife Martha Louisa Maria, née Zillman; an older brother was Ernest Rudolph [q.v.]. His father became rector of All Souls, Leichhardt, Sydney, in 1882; John was educated at The King's School, Parramatta, and the University of Sydney (B.A., 1893; LL.B., 1895). After admission as a solicitor on 30 May 1896, he practised at West Wyalong until 1898, and in 1901-02 and 1907-09 at Aberdeen, where he had a model dairy farm. In between he worked in Sydney—he was chief clerk of the Industrial Arbitration

Office in 1903-04 and in private practice with G. S. Beeby [q.v.7] in 1905-07.

Interested in industrial arbitration and working conditions, Holme joined the Department of Labour and Industry as investigation and statistical officer in May 1911 and helped the minister, Beeby, to draft the Industrial Arbitration Act of 1912. He was successively appointed industrial registrar and permanent head of the department, which had been reorganized; in July 1912, he started the *New South Wales Industrial Gazette*. Following an alteration in the status of the permanent head, he was appointed the first under secretary of the department on 10 February 1914. On 18 February next year he was admitted to the Bar. In 1912-26 Holme was also special commissioner and in the event of an imminent lock-out or strike he would arrange conferences to endeavour to resolve the problem; his most notable activity related to the great transport crisis in New South Wales in 1917.

Holme's appointment in 1918 as deputy president of the newly constituted New South Wales Board of Trade was singularly appropriate for a man at ease in any company, with a wide range of interests including dairy and sheep-farming, the growing of agricultural crops, the law, English literature, industrial history and modern conditions in overseas countries. His time with the board was perhaps the most productive period of his life and the reports with which he was identified exemplify his creative thinking and his attention to research and the study of evidence: in addition to the cost of living inquiries, his reports included *Miners' phthisis* (1918-19), which led to the technical commission of inquiry chaired by Professor H. Chapman [q.v.7] in 1919-20, *Apprenticeship in industries* (1920), *White lead as used in the painting industry* (1921), which stopped local agitation for the prohibition of the use of that mixture, and *Conditions of production and distribution of milk* (1923). In 1918-19 he had also chaired the royal commission into Sydney Ferries Ltd. After the board's abolition in 1926 Holme was asked to undertake special investigations (such as the transport services between Sydney and Jenolan Caves) and functioned as inter-departmental commissioner.

In 1929 Holme visited the Mayo Clinic, Rochester, Minnesota, United States of America, for treatment for a cerebral tumour but, soon after his return, he died on Christmas Day at Woollahra and was buried in the Church of England section of South Head cemetery. He was survived by his wife Lilian Florence, née Bakewell, whom he had married at St Philip's Church, Church Hill, Sydney, on 10 November 1913, and by one son and two daughters; his son

John Leicester became a pathologist. Holme's estate was valued for probate at £8616.

SMH, 27 Dec 1929; Domestic meetings of NSW Bd of Trade, Minutes, 28 May-31 Dec 1919, 2/5772, *and* Inquiry into the cost of living and conditions for the rural industries, female adult workers and general costs of living as from 1918-25, 2/5773-5801 (NSWA); information from Mr J. L. Holme, Nedlands, Perth.   JACK WATSON

HOLMES, MARION LOUISA (1856-1921) and MARION PHOEBE (1880-1966), workers for charity, were mother and daughter. Marion Louisa was born on 24 May 1856 at Kooringa, South Australia, daughter of Joseph Charles Genders, wine and spirit merchant, and his wife Albina Louisa, née Perry. On 5 December 1878, at Holy Trinity Church, Adelaide, she married Henry Diggens Holmes (1846-1931), a banker. Both were devout Anglicans. Marion Phoebe, their elder daughter, was born in Adelaide on 29 September 1880. Mrs Holmes suffered many childbirth difficulties resulting in miscarriages and three stillborn children. Albina Emma (Emmie) was born in 1883 and Henry William (Willy) in 1889; he was mentally retarded. The family moved to Perth in 1890 when Henry, a stern and conservative financier, became general manager of the Western Australian Bank.

Next year Marion and Henry founded a branch of the Ministering Children's League, a British organization 'for children of the educated and wealthier classes—to train them in habits of unselfishness and thoughtfulness for . . . their poorer brothers and sisters'. Phoebe, Emmie, and seventy-one others, joined. They raised sufficient money to build a large adults' convalescent home (opened 1897) at Cottesloe Beach. Marion was secretary till 1914, vice-president in 1897-1913 and president in 1913-21. Henry was treasurer and trustee.

Marion Holmes was a leader in a circle of influential ladies working for welfare reforms for women and children that included Edith Cowan [q.v.8], Lady Onslow, (Lady) Gwenyfred James, Janetta Griffiths-Foulkes and Dr Roberta Jull [q.v.], Phoebe's close friend. In the 1890s the group petitioned the government for female suffrage and later established several reformist organizations. Their favourite meeting-place was Banksia, the Holmes family home at Cottesloe Beach. Marion Holmes was in 1894 a founder and active leader of the Karrakatta Club for women, an intellectual discussion group; she helped to found the Women's Service Guilds and was on the first executive of the Western Australian National Council of Women; she and Henry also supported the Children's Protection Society of Western Australia. Noted for her 'philanthropic zeal' and 'lovable nature', Marion died of Bright's disease on 3 August 1921 and was buried in the Anglican section of Karrakatta cemetery.

Phoebe was educated with her sister at Miss Amy Best's [q.v.3] High School for Girls, Perth. They remained unmarried and devoted their lives to good causes and caring for their brother. Emmie supported the Ministering Children's League and the Girls' Friendly Society. Phoebe, more forceful, even autocratic, was active in the Karrakatta Club from 1897. As her mother faded, Phoebe took a more prominent role in the league; she was secretary in 1914-21. In 1957 it disbanded and gave the remaining funds to the Slow Learning Group of Western Australia. After her father's death in 1931, she was trustee and president of the convalescent home; the government bought it in 1963. Phoebe bequeathed most of her estate of £46 218 for the building of a home for the frail aged at Trigg, the Meath Ministering League Anglican Homes (Inc.). It accommodates seventy people.

As president of the Western Australian National Council of Women from 1925, Phoebe Holmes advocated the inclusion of women on juries, anti-gambling legislation, the establishment of a university chair of obstetrics, and community care for the mentally handicapped. She worked for years for the Young Women's Christian Association, as president in 1936, member of the national executive in 1939, and president in 1966. She also belonged to the University of Western Australia Women's College Fund Committee and the League of Nations Union.

On 6 September 1966 Phoebe Holmes died at her home at West Perth where she had lived with her sister and brother, both of whom predeceased her. Her ashes are buried in Karrakatta cemetery, Perth.

J. G. Wilson (ed), *Western Australia's centenary, 1829-1929* (Perth, 1929); R. M. James, *The Meath story* (Perth, 1982); Ministering Children's League records, *and* Holmes papers (Battye Lib).
          JUNE OGILVIE

HOLMES, WILLIAM (1862-1917), soldier and civil servant, was born on 12 September 1862 in Sydney, son of Captain William Holmes, chief clerk at Headquarters, New South Wales Military Forces, who had come to Australia in 1845 as a private in the 11th Foot, and his Tasmanian-born wife Jane, daughter of Patrick Hackett, also from the

11th Foot. Young William lived in Victoria Barracks until his marriage and was educated at Paddington Public School and later at night school. Though he had always wanted to become a soldier his father considered that the New South Wales Public Service offered greater opportunities. After working at the Sydney Mint he joined the accounts branch of the Department of Public Works as a clerk on 24 June 1878. On 24 August 1887, at St Mathias Anglican Church, Paddington, he married Susan Ellen Green whose family also lived in Victoria Barracks. They had a son and a daughter.

On 20 April 1888 Holmes was appointed chief clerk and paymaster of the newly formed Metropolitan Board of Water Supply and Sewerage, Sydney. In 1895 he was promoted secretary and chief clerk, being the second person to hold the secretaryship which he retained until his death. During his term as chief executive of the board the Cataract, Cordeaux and Avon dams were built to provide water for the city. According to family tradition Holmes maintained that the board had built these dams in the wrong places and that the correct area would have been Warrangamba, where the large dam was later built. His administrative ability when so young and his leadership of the board during a period of great expansion were a remarkable achievement.

With his military background it was natural that Holmes should become a citizen soldier. He joined the 1st Infantry Regiment, New South Wales Military Forces, as a bugler at the age of 10 and served in almost every rank in the regiment until he commanded it in 1903. He was commissioned second lieutenant in 1886 and promoted lieutenant in 1890, captain in 1894 and major in 1900. For eighteen months, between his non-commissioned and commissioned service, he served in a company of submarine miners whose task was to mine Sydney Harbour in the event of enemy sea attack. In October 1899 Holmes volunteered for active service in the South African War with the New South Wales Infantry Contingent; although a captain at the time, he accepted a lieutenancy in order to serve. On arrival in South Africa the unit was issued with horses and joined the Australian (Mounted Infantry) Regiment. Holmes was promoted captain commanding 'E' Squadron, 1st New South Wales Mounted Rifles, the new title of his original contingent. He saw action at Colesberg, Pretoria and Diamond Hill, and Australian newspapers praised his daring and courage; he was awarded the Distinguished Service Order, mentioned in dispatches and promoted brevet lieut-colonel. Wounded at Diamond Hill in June 1900, he was invalided home in

August and led the returned soldiers in the Federation procession in Sydney in January 1901. He had returned from South Africa with 'a record of good service, and a reputation for personal bravery, ability and capacity for command'.

Holmes resumed work as secretary of the M.B.W.S. & S. but continued his voluntary military service, first as lieut-colonel commanding the 1st Australian Infantry Regiment in 1902-11 and as colonel commanding the 6th Infantry Brigade from August 1912. After the beginning of compulsory military training in 1910 he became well known for his conduct of rifle-shooting competitions and for his introduction of the first fire and movement competitions (under the title of The Governor's Cup) in the Australian Army. When war was declared in 1914 he was chosen to command the Australian Naval and Military Expeditionary Force. Commenting later on his appointment, S. S. Mackenzie, [q.v.] author of *The Australians at Rabaul* (Sydney, 1927), wrote that he had 'a keen, practical brain, a quick grasp of essentials, a knowledge of men, and a capacity for organisation and administration'. The A.N. & M.E.F., consisting of 500 Royal Australian Naval reservists and a battalion of infantry and ancillary troops, was specially raised in the first week of the war. A volunteer force, it was recruited, equipped, trained and embarked within ten days to leave on H.M.A.S. *Berrima* on 19 August for a destination which was not revealed to Holmes until the convoy was off the Queensland coast. He then received a wireless message ordering him to 'seize all German Wireless Telegraph Stations in the Pacific and to occupy German Territory as soon as possible, hoist the British flag, and make suitable arrangements for temporary administration, but to make no formal proclamation of annexation', as Holmes wrote in his dispatch of 26 December.

After capturing Rabaul, German New Guinea, on 12 September 1914 Holmes accepted the governor's surrender of all German possessions in the Pacific except Kiaochao in China and Samoa (which a New Zealand force had already taken). In Australia some provisions of the terms of surrender were criticized, but the instructions given to Holmes specified that he was only to occupy the territory, not to annex it. This was not fully understood at the time and his claim that he had acted in strict accordance with international law was later conceded. That he had other views, however, is borne out by his blunt statement that his objective was to maintain military occupation until the end of the war and that 'the islands would be retained as valuable British possessions for colonizing territories'.

In January 1915 Holmes handed over the administration of German New Guinea to Colonel (Sir) Samuel Pethebridge [q.v.] and returned to Sydney, having asked for an appointment for active service with the Australian Imperial Force. His A.N. & M.E.F. appointment ended on 6 February 1915 and on 16 March he was given command of the 5th Brigade, with the rank of brigadier general. The brigade left Australia in May and landed at Gallipoli in August. Holmes commanded the Russell's Top-Monash Valley area during the holding action from September. At the evacuation in December he was temporarily in command of the 2nd Division, and the troops under his command were among the last off Anzac.

After the evacuation he resumed command of the 5th Brigade, took it to France in April 1916 and commanded it in all its fighting, notably in the battles of Pozières and Flers, until January 1917 when he was promoted major general and commander of the 4th Division. He was the third citizen-soldier after Sir J. W. McCay and Sir John Monash [qq.v.], to be given a divisional command. He remained the general officer commanding the division, through the battles of 1st Bullecourt and Messines, until he was mortally wounded by a chance shell on 2 July while escorting the premier of New South Wales, W. A. Holman [q.v.], to survey the Messines battlefield. He died on the way to a field hospital and was buried in Les Trois Arbres British cemetery near Armentières. He had been appointed C.M.G., awarded the Russian Order of St Anne and been mentioned in dispatches four times. He was survived by his son, Captain Basil Holmes, later a colonel in the Indian Army, and by his daughter. His wife had predeceased him in 1912.

Writing to Australian newspapers from France in 1917 C. E. W. Bean [q.v.7] commented: 'There is naturally a tendency to wonder how far citizen soldiers, who have been more or less complete amateurs until the war plunged them into soldiering as by far the most important business in their lives, could be suitable for high commands . . . None will grudge it to General Holmes that he was, of all others, the Australian who first showed that it could be done with complete success'. He was 'an experienced administrator who possessed fine moral qualities, transparent sincerity, energy and great courage, and was one of Australia's most eminent citizen soldiers'. In appearance Holmes was, according to a Melbourne *Punch* article of February 1915, 'a dapper man, well-groomed, well-tailored, well-manicured . . . His speech is accurately faultless. His manner is masterful but courteous. In everything he is meticulously cor-rect. His moustache is symbolical of him. It is one of these faultless moustaches exactly suited to his face, beautifully curled, glossy, accurate . . . Neatness and precision are the keynotes of his character'. His portrait, by Norman Carter [q.v.7] is in the Australian War Memorial.

Aust Defence Dept, *Official records of the Australian military contingents to the war in South Africa*, P. L. Murray ed (Melb, 1911); C. E. W. Bean, *The story of Anzac* (Syd, 1921, 1924), and *The A.I.F. in France*, 1916-1917 (Syd, 1929, 1933); P. Ryan (ed), *Encyclopaedia of Papua and New Guinea*, 1 (Melb, 1972); *London Gazette*, 16 Apr 1901, 2 June, 11 July 1916, 2 Jan, 13 Feb, 1 June, 15 Dec 1917; *Punch* (Melb), 4 Feb 1915; *SMH*, 30 Nov 1915, 3 June, 14 July, 23 Nov 1916, 16 Feb, 26 May, 5, 10 July, 3 Aug, 2 Nov 1917, 4 Apr 1918; *TCJ*, 11 July 1917; *Rabaul Record*, 1 Aug 1917; Holmes collection (AWM); family papers (held by author, Syd C of E Grammar School, Nth Syd).

B. H. Travers

HOLMES à COURT, ALAN WORSLEY (1887-1957), physician, was born on 19 June 1887 in Brisbane, second surviving son of the Honourable Charles George Holmes à Court (fourth son of the 2nd Baron Heytesbury), parliamentary officer, and the second of his four wives Mary West, née Howe. He was educated at Brisbane Grammar School and St Andrew's College, University of Sydney (M.B., 1910; Ch.M., 1911; M.D., 1920), where early studies ran a poor second to his rowing. In 1911-12 he was a resident and later a registrar at Sydney Hospital. In 1913 he began general practice at Manly and on 3 June married a Sydney Hospital nurse Eileen Rouse.

In 1916-17 Holmes à Court served as a captain with the Australian Army Medical Corps in the hospital ship, *Karoola*. He was then posted to the 2nd Australian General Hospital in France, and promoted major on 28 January 1918. In May he transferred to the 4th Australian Field Ambulance and trained forward resuscitation teams whereby severely wounded patients were revived, emergency surgery performed earlier, and many lives were saved. He was mentioned in dispatches in December 1918 and awarded the French *Médaille des Epidémies* in January 1919. He qualified M.R.C.P. in London and returned to Australia in August. He was admitted F.R.C.P. in 1930 and remained in the army reserve until 1943.

Holmes à Court returned briefly to his Manly practice. For six months in 1920 he was assistant editor of the *Medical Journal of Australia* and by 1921 was a consultant physician at Macquarie Street, Sydney. He was a council-member of the New South

Wales branch of the British Medical Association (1925-29 and 1931-35) and president in 1933-34. He was a member of the New South Wales Medical Board (1932-38), honorary physician at the Coast (Prince Henry) Hospital (1920-32) and at the Royal Hospital for Women (1935-46).

At Sydney Hospital he was honorary assistant physician from 1914, physician (1923-47) and finally consulting physician. He helped pioneer blood-transfusion techniques and was the hospital's first tutor in anaesthetics in 1920-21, but waited until 1931 for appointment as lecturer in clinical medicine. On retiring he expressed regret at leaving the clinical school and distaste for hospital politicking, yet his desire for 'peace and harmony' at all costs and his unwillingness to vent open disapproval of anyone or anything often confused those who did not know him well.

To his patients and students Holmes à Court was charming if somewhat austere, always immaculately dressed, learned and kind. To nervous examinees of the Royal Australasian College of Physicians he was 'smiling death'. He had represented the earlier Association of Physicians of Australasia in negotiations leading to the foundation of the college in 1938. As censor from 1938 and censor-in-chief in 1945-50, he was one of its most influential servants—continuously a member of its council and senior standing committees, president in 1950-52 and first chairman of the editorial committee for its journal, *Australasian Annals of Medicine*. His remarkable memory, reputation as a fine clinician and teacher, and the demands of professional office, combined to put him on the lecturing platform and to publish numerous articles in the *Medical Journal of Australia* that had practical teaching value but displayed little investigative patience or originality.

Holmes à Court had a retiring disposition and was uninterested in material advancement. In his younger days he had flirted briefly with the New Guard and with Freemasonry. He was a member of the Union and Royal Sydney Golf clubs and his preferred relaxation was with his family, to whom he was the mildest of men, or sailing his yacht *Brilliant*, fly-fishing, or swimming. He loved Nature and had a special affinity with his dogs who were inconsolable for weeks as he grieved for his son Brian, a Royal Australian Air Force pilot killed whilst training in 1943.

Holmes à Court was well built, moderately tall, blue eyed, thin lipped, high domed and, in maturity, almost completely bald. The posthumous portrait painted by William Dargie and presented to the R.A.C.P. in 1959 is a convincing likeness. A director of the Colonial Mutual Life Assurance Society Ltd since 1942, he collapsed on 16 April 1957 at a board meeting and died of coronary vascular disease soon after admission to Sydney Hospital. He was cremated after a large funeral at St Mark's Anglican Church, Darling Point, attended by the governor Sir John Northcott, to whom he had been medical adviser. He was survived by his wife (d. 1971), daughter and son.

G. E. Hall and A. Cousins (eds), *Book of remembrance of the University of Sydney . . . 1914-18* (Syd, 1939); A. G. Butler (ed), *Official history of the Australian Army Medical Services . . . 1914-18* (Canb, 1940); Faculty of Medicine, Univ Syd, *Senior Year Book*, 1925-46; *MJA*, 27 July 1957; Syd Hospital Bd and House Cttee, Minutes, 1910-47; NSW Medical Bd, Minutes (NSWA, 7/5153); Benevolent Soc of NSW, Annual Report, 1957; information from Aust Medical Assn (NSW branch), Colonial Mutual Life Assurance Soc Ltd, Mr and Mrs P. Holmes à Court and Miss D. Roseby, Syd.

ANN M. MITCHELL

HOLT, MICHAEL (1879-1951), racehorse trainer, was born on 14 November 1879 at Berwick, Victoria, youngest child of Michael Holt, a Melbourne-born labourer, and his wife Mary, née Corkery, from Cork, Ireland. Young Michael attended the local state school, sang in the Catholic church choir and learned to ride. After a postal-delivery job, he obtained a jockey's licence in 1898 and rode at Sandown, then received his Victoria Racing Club trainer's licence in 1902 and moved to Epsom in 1908, having his first metropolitan victory in 1911.

In the seventeen seasons from 1918-19 to 1934-35 he headed the Victorian Trainers' Premiership on thirteen occasions, came second on three and third once. His horses won all the important cups in Melbourne and Sydney, practically every major handicap and weight-for-age race in the V.R.C. and Australian Jockey Club calendars, as well as many events on country courses. In a career lasting until 1948 'the wizard of Mordialloc' trained some one thousand winners, earned an estimated £500 000 stake-money for his clients and was dubbed 'the most famous of all Australian racehorse trainers'.

Craft underlay his sensational successes. Holt could sound out horses with his eyes and hands, and had a sensibility toward their idiosyncrasies; he trained them lightly, fed them scientifically and kept them close to racing trim so as to bring them to peak condition quickly and sustain their fitness; and he also placed them astutely. Moreover, he employed competent stable-foremen, chose the best jockeys, including Frank Dempsey and Billy Duncan, and attracted patrons with outstanding thoroughbreds: Eurythmic won ten races on end in 1920, including the Caulfield Cup; Heroic scored in the 1926 Newmarket and W. S. Cox Plate and became a top sire; in 1933 Hall Mark triumphed in the A.J.C. Sires' Produce and the Underwood Stakes, the A.J.C. and Victoria Derbys, and the Melbourne Cup (as a three-year-old), while two years later he won the Doncaster carrying 9 st. 8 lb. (61 kg); in 1938 Nuffield completed the coveted treble of A.J.C. Derby, Caulfield Guineas and Victoria Derby. Believing that 'any price about a winner is a good price', Holt appreciated his betting coups by investment in suburban land, stocks and shares.

Bald, ruddy, chubby and dapper, he remained a bachelor and lived modestly and clannishly with his spinster sisters, Madge and Kitty, at Lethe, an eight-roomed spic-and-span weatherboard dwelling with a corrugated-iron roof and L-shaped verandah in Francis Street, Mordialloc. In preference to his Christian name, he answered to John, Jack and Jackson. His wardrobe and 1938 Packard limousine were among his few indulgences, while he enjoyed poker, billiards and golf. Insisting on order, a regular communicant, paterfamilias to his apprentices and strappers, and generous to children, the elderly and his Church, Holt retained his brusquerie, guile and wryness as shields against would-be imposers in a tough milieu.

Invalided after a heart attack in 1948, 'Jack' Holt died of coronary occulusion on 10 June 1951 at Mercy Hospital, East Melbourne, and, after a requiem Mass, was interred in his family's grave at Berwick cemetery. His estate was proved at £228 815, of which he bequeathed about £200 000 to St Vincent's Hospital for the establishment of its School of Medical Research.

M. Cavanough, *The wizard of Mordialloc* (Melb, 1962); *Age*, 8 Jan 1933, 11 June 1951, 24 Apr 1958; *Argus*, 7, 8 Nov 1933, 11, 12 June 1951; *Sun-News Pictorial*, 7-9 Nov 1933, 11, 14 June 1951, 24 Apr 1958; information from Mr R. Bould, Mordialloc, Vic.   JOHN RITCHIE

HOLTZE, MAURICE WILLIAM (1840-1923), botanist, was born at Hanover (Germany) on 8 July 1840, son of C. Holtze, chief inspector of orphan houses. Educated at the Academy of Hildesheim and Osnabrück Gymnasium, Holtze was apprenticed to Th. Brown & Sons, Nurserymen and Landscape Gardeners of Hanover. He worked for four years at the Royal Gardens in Hanover while studying botany under Professor Johannes Leunis. In 1862 Holtze migrated to Russia where he spent two years at the Imperial Gardens, St Petersburg, and married on 23 April 1867 Evlampia Misinzoff.

In 1872, after returning to Germany, they migrated to Australia, landing at Melbourne but travelling to the new settlement of Palmerston near Port Darwin. In 1878-91 he was government gardener of the Palmerston Botanic Gardens. They had been used chiefly to supply government officials with fruit and vegetables but Holtze declared that the raising of cabbage heads was not the greatest ambition of the true botanist and suggested changes of function and site. With his eldest son Nicholas (d. 1913) he pioneered tropical agriculture in the Northern Territory. They tested the suitability of a range of crops including rubber, rice, peanuts, tobacco, sugar, coffee, indigo and maize, and urged 'the introduction of cheap coloured labour, the passing of more attractive land legislation, and ... Government assistance to settlers'. After touring Asian botanical gardens in Hong Kong, Canton, Saigon, Singapore and Batavia in 1887, the 'far-seeing' Holtze reflected that cheap labour could make 'the Northern Territory ... the great rice field for the Australian colonies'.

He had a profound experience of local native tropical vegetation and sent many plants to Sir Ferdinand Mueller [q.v.5] for identification. In 1892 Holtze published an account of his exploration of Melville Island and a list of introduced plants in the Territory in the Royal Society of South Australia's *Transactions*. Next year the Australasian Association for the Advancement of Science published his 'A plea for a rational popular nomenclature for Australian plants'. Holtze spoke most European languages and read Latin and Greek. At Palmerston his geniality and his wife's hospitality made their home a centre of culture and sociability.

In 1891 Nicholas Holtze became curator of the Darwin Botanical Gardens when his father was appointed director and secretary of the Adelaide Botanic Garden. In Adelaide Maurice Holtze removed unsightly old trees and replanted with acacias and eucalypts. Lakes and canals were refurbished and the collection of water-lilies and lotuses became world famous. He was the first director to open the garden to the public and delighted in the response. He reputedly added 5000 specimens to the herbarium and over 1000 to the museum of economic botany. The following species, named by Mueller, recall him: *Clerodendron holtzei, Sida holtzei, Habenaria holtzei* and *Polyalthia holtzeana*.

In 1899 he established a branch, the Mylor Typical Orchard, in the Mount Lofty Range where growers could sample and obtain grafts and buds of 1500 varieties of apples, and 1100 varieties of pears. In 1913 Holtze was appointed I.S.O.; he was a fellow of the Linnean Society of London and of the Royal Geographical Society of Australasia. He retired in 1917.

A placid, tolerant, generous man, Holtze died at his daughter's home at American River, Kangaroo Island, on 12 October 1923, survived by his wife, two sons and a daughter.

H. T. Burgess (ed), *Cyclopedia of South Australia*, 1 (Adel, 1907); M. Lamshed, *A centenary history of the Adelaide Botanic Garden, 1855-1955* (Adel, 1955); Roy Soc NSW, *J*, 24 (1890); *Australian Territories*, 1 (1960), 2 (1961); *Observer* (Adel), 9 May 1891; *Mail* (Adel), 14 June 1913; *Register* (Adel), 15 Oct 1923; items 111/A1, 112/A1, 1047/152 (SAA).

DARRELL N. KRAEHENBUEHL

HOLYMAN, THOMAS HENRY (1856-1933), WILLIAM (1858-1921) and JAMES (1862-1944), master mariners and shipowners, were sons of William Holyman [q.v.4] and his wife Mary Ann, née Sayer. All three were born at Torquay (East Devonport), Tasmania, as was their sister, Susannah (1860-1928), who contributed to the success of the family by marrying a shipbuilder Harry Wood in 1882. The young Holymans absorbed the waterfront life of the Mersey River, its salty jargon and their father's seafaring tales. Each attended a small school run by a retired sea-captain, James Cartledge, who had sold the ketch *Cousins* to William Holyman senior in 1861. In time the sons handled cargoes alongside their father, learning the language of barter and business and discovering where to look for trade and how to approach it.

Thomas Henry, born on 24 October 1856, joined his father in 1868 on *Cousins*. He was an independent, venturesome boy and after three years he left to serve on the brigantine *Emma Jane*. A year later he was aboard the schooner *Leslie* but, satisfied by nothing short of deep-sea sailing, he joined the brig *Assyrian* as third mate and sailed to England around Cape Horn. From England he joined vessels carrying freight into Baltic ports and other centres of British trade; he gained his second mate's papers, being the only member of his family to secure a foreign-going master's certificate. Thomas returned to Tasmania in 1878 on the barque *Westbury*. In maturity he was a large, forthright man, barrel-chested and spade-bearded, who fluently demonstrated his command of the loud language of a seafarer—he was known to everyone as 'Roaring Tom'. His ill-fortune in losing several

ships during a career of over sixty years was due to impulsiveness: over-confidence induced him to accept risks with both sail and steam and, in later life, to speculate foolishly in Tasmanian mining shares.

In 1890 Thomas again left the family business to work on vessels trading between Melbourne, Launceston and Beauty Point. But he returned in 1902 and, until his retirement in 1929, commanded many ships of the Holyman fleet. In December 1911 his steamer *Toroa* carried stores and equipment from Hobart to Macquarie Island for (Sir) Douglas Mawson [q.v.]. His first wife Grace Victoria, née Young, whom he had married about 1883, died in 1885; on 22 April 1889 at the Anglican Church of Holy Trinity, Beaconsfield, he married Helena Josephine Wyett; he had no children. A Freemason, Holyman died on 13 May 1933 at St Margaret's Hospital, Launceston, survived by his wife, and, like his brothers, was buried in Carr Villa cemetery.

William was born on 23 July 1858. More settled than the vehement Tom, he saw his future in the family ships and from that commitment he never wavered. For six years he learned the ropes; then the purchase in 1877 of the ketch *Catherine* made it possible for him to take over *Colleen Bawn*, a converted schooner bought in 1874 and destined to be the 'mother' of the Holyman fleet. William married Honora Ballard on 1 January 1878 at Launceston according to the forms of the Independent Church, and his first voyage as master was also his honeymoon.

There followed years of growth and consolidation: the flag of the Holyman White Star Line became well established, Holyman senior retired from the sea in 1886 to manage the business ashore, sailing ships were gradually replaced by steamers, and in 1899 the head office was moved from East Devonport to Launceston. In 1901, on his father's complete retirement, young William took over the management. It was a time of intense competition between Holymans, the Union Steam Ship Co. of New Zealand Ltd and Huddart [q.v.4] Parker & Co. Ltd, leading, over the ensuing forty years, to the registration of Wm Holyman & Sons Ltd, Holymans Pty Ltd, Holyman Bros Pty Ltd, James Holyman Pty Ltd, and other proprietary companies.

William Holyman junior died on 29 September 1921 of coronary vascular disease, two years after his father, at his home in Launceston. He was survived by his wife (d. 1932) who, having devoted much time to charitable work, was appointed M.B.E. after World War I, and by four of their six sons and five of their seven daughters. His daughter Love, who had 'embraced the Roman Catholic religion', was excluded from his will which divided among the family an estate valued for probate at almost £60 000.

James, born on 8 September 1862, succeeded William as head of the business. Under his management there was growth and by 1931 nine steamers were plying the waters between Tasmanian ports, Bass Strait islands, Melbourne and Adelaide. As a young boy, James had followed his brothers by sailing with his father. In 1881 when the ketch *Pauline* was added to the fleet under the control of young William, James took over *Colleen Bawn*. Next year, when Thomas was allotted the *Albion*, four ships were commanded by four Holymans.

In 1907 the Holymans began acquiring Bass Strait island grazing properties, first Waterhouse Island, then Twenty Day Island (called Ninth Island on Admiralty maps), followed by Robbins and adjacent Walker Island in 1916. The company King Island Steamers was formed in 1910. For several years James, whose life-long eccentricity was punctiliously to wear a formal, high, starched collar held by gold studs front and back, but to refuse to wear a tie, managed Robbins Island with sheep, cattle, pigs and a small cheese and butter factory; the property, sold in 1957, supported several families and a Holyman-sponsored Education Department school of twelve to fourteen pupils. Trefoil Island was bought in 1926 and sold in 1948. In 1932, with two of William's sons, Victor and (Sir) Ivan (1896-1957), James founded the airline which became Australian National Airways Pty Ltd, later to be absorbed into Ansett Transport Industries Ltd.

James died at Launceston on 7 April 1944, leaving an estate valued for probate at £22 671. His first wife Amelia, née Lewis, whom he had married at Launceston on 17 July 1884 and by whom he had five children, died from the effects of childbirth on 17 July 1894. He married Mary Isobel, née Cameron (d. 1970), on 31 December 1895; they had seven children.

M. Hodges, *Veil of time* (Melb, 1945); C. Ramsay, *With the pioneers* (Hob, 1979); R. A. Ferrall, *Notable Tasmanians* (Launc, 1980); J. M. Millar, *The start of a saga* (Launc, 1973); *Examiner* (Launc), 30 Sept 1921, 15 May 1933, 10 Apr 1944; S. Barnes, From sea to air, a history of the Holyman family 1854-1957 (Tas CAE Lib, Launc); C. Ramsay, Footsteps in the sea, the Holyman story (Melb Univ Archives).　　　　　　ALAN WARDEN

HOMBURG, ROBERT (1848-1912), politician and judge, and HERMANN ROBERT (1874-1964), lawyer and politician, were father and son. Robert was born on 10 March 1848 at Brunswick, Saxony, son of Wilhelm

Homburg (d. 1860), grain merchant, and his wife Caroline Magdalene Pauline, née Schumacher. In 1853 Wilhelm left for the Victorian goldfields and his wife and children followed twelve months later. In 1856 the family went to Tanunda, South Australia, where Robert attended the English-German Educational Institution of Leschen and Niehuus; later he worked for Dr Koehnke, a local land agent. In 1867 he was articled to (Sir) James Boucaut [q.v.3]. Next year he moved to the Tanunda branch of (Sir) John Downer's [q.v.8] legal firm, and in 1874 he was admitted to the Bar.

On 30 April 1873 Robert married Emilie Peters at Angaston. After her death from tuberculosis he married, on 16 October 1882 in Adelaide, Johanne Elisabeth Fischer. From 1880 he was president of the German Club, which was patronized by relatively wealthy conservative German-Australians who wished to keep German culture alive. He was naturalized in 1883.

In 1884 Homburg was elected to the House of Assembly for Gumeracha, a seat with a strong German-Australian element, which he retained until 1902. He then transferred to Murray and retired in 1905. He was attorney-general in 1890-92 in the Playford [q.v.] ministry, in 1892-93 in the Downer ministry, and in 1904-05 in the Jenkins [q.v.] ministry when he was also minister of education. He was a good speaker in the House; his views shifted gradually to the right as he shook off the mild radicalism of his youth.

In 1905 Homburg was appointed a justice of the Supreme Court; this aroused much criticism in the legal profession as a political move, both his experience at the Bar and legal expertise being questioned. Some sources suggest that his national origin was the unspoken objection. However he proved his critics wrong and gained respect by bringing to the bench the incorruptible integrity, impartiality and compassion that had marked him as a politician. He was the first non-British migrant to be appointed to such a position in Australia.

Homburg's home life was cited as a model, for it was filled with love, music, literature and art and, although he was not a strict Lutheran, he enjoyed the full confidence of the Lutheran pastors. He was one of the first men in Australia to bridge successfully the gap in public life between British and non-British cultures. He died on 23 March 1912 at Medindie, South Australia, survived by four sons and four daughters: three children by his first wife and five by his second. The family declined a state funeral and he was buried in North Road cemetery.

Robert's eldest son Hermann Robert was born on 17 March 1874 at Norwood. Educated at Prince Alfred College and the University of Adelaide, he received his final certificate in law and was admitted to the Bar in 1897. He entered his father's legal firm, Homburg & Melrose, and on 29 November married Emma Lydia Louisa Herring in an Anglican ceremony, although he was a freethinker. In 1906-15 and 1927-30 he was a non-Labor member for Murray in the House of Assembly and from 1933 to 1941 was a member of the Legislative Council (Central No. 2). He was attorney-general under Peake [q.v.] in 1909-10 and minister for industry as well in 1912-15, and attorney-general and minister for industry in 1927-30 in the R. L. Butler [q.v.7] ministry.

Hermann Homburg was a tall impressive-looking man of powerful personality, 'an intellectual' and 'a man of culture', being widely read in both English and German. His fluent German was accent-free and he increased his knowledge of German literature by trying to read, and commit to memory, one passage a day going to work in the tram-car. He did not suffer fools gladly and his patriarchal manner annoyed those who politically or personally crossed him. As attorney-general he added to the reputation for integrity laid down by his father; he was also an extremely efficient and capable minister. He employed a quick turn of phrase against political opponents and hecklers at meetings.

Such men polarize feelings towards them and it was Homburg's misfortune that Australia was at war twice with Germany during his life. In 1914 while he was attorney-general, his government office in Adelaide was raided by soldiers with fixed bayonets while he was there. Next January he resigned his portfolio, to avoid embarrassing the government in the forthcoming election. His resignation, which had been offered earlier, was now regretfully accepted by Peake. Homburg wrote of the 'campaign of lies and calumnies against me . . . because I am not of British lineage'.

Defeated at the election in April, he was as much a victim of the swing to Labor as to any disadvantage of ancestry. He unsuccessfully contested Murray again in 1924, won it in 1927, and lost it in 1930. Between the wars he was a leader of Adelaide's secular German community. His home continued the inherited traditions of German culture: indeed, some said that he became even more German after World War I. Certainly his war experiences destroyed his ability to straddle naturally German-Australian culture. The German way became something ideological; it was no longer unselfconscious. Homburg was bitter that sixty-seven German place-names, a constant reminder of the German contri-

bution to South Australia, had been changed in 1918.

With Hitler's rise he was perhaps naive in failing to appreciate the use made of culture by the Nazis for political purposes. His voluble support for German ways was tactless. Certainly the authorities suspected him by the time war was declared in 1939, even if he himself was able to see clearly the difference between culture and politics: 'Because you prefer to run your home a certain way, teach your children a particular set of moral values, and cultivate a love of German literature and music, does not mean you are disloyal to the country you have adopted as your own. Rather the fact that you can do these things in political peace and without economic hardship kindles within you a desire to protect and foster the society in which you live'.

At this time Homburg was in parliament but not in office. His home and private office were searched and he was interned on 25 November 1940 but released after appeal on 21 December, under open conditional arrest, one condition being that he moved interstate. In January 1941 he was taken to Melbourne and in February moved to Ballarat whereupon he retired from parliament and did not recontest his seat. On 18 December 1942 he was allowed to return to Adelaide, reporting to the police three times a week for the next eighteen months. None of the evidence presented against Homburg was more than circumstantial, unsubstantiated or inconsequential. The judges at his appeal stated, 'it is obvious that one or more of the persons reporting [unanimously] may have a grudge against the objector Homburg and under pledge of secrecy be willing to lie to cause him distress and trouble'. The War Precautions Act that allowed accusation without proof permitted many an old score to be settled. He recorded his experiences in both wars in *South Australian Lutherans and war-time rumours* (Adelaide 1947).

Homburg continued to practise as a solicitor until the day before his death on 12 December 1964 at Dulwich. Survived by one son and two daughters, he was buried at Centennial Park cemetery.

Robert Homburg's second son, also Robert (1875-1948), a lawyer and politician, was a member of the House of Assembly for Burra Burra from 1912 to 1915 when he also resigned in the face of 'gross slanders' about his loyalty.

Quiz (Adel), 24 Feb 1905; *Register* (Adel), 25 Apr 1890, 25 Mar 1912; *Australische Zeitung*, 27 Mar 1912; *Advertiser* (Adel), 23 Oct 1948, 14 Dec 1964; Way letters 1905, PRG 30/5/9 (SAA); CRS A367 item CE 5376 (AAO); information from M. Gerth, Rose Park, SA.   IAN HARMSTORF

HONE, FRANK SANDLAND (1871-1951), medical practitioner, was born on 7 January 1871 at Mount Gambier, South Australia, son of Nathaniel Johnson Hone, Baptist clergyman, and his wife Emily, née Sandland. He was educated at Prince Alfred College, where he gained a university exhibition, and at the University of Adelaide (B.A., 1889; M.B., B.S., 1894). In 1895 he began medical practice at Morphett Vale, transferred to a suburban general practice at Semaphore in 1903, and began consultant work as a North Terrace physician in 1919.

Hone's practice was not very lucrative, being conducted initially among the less affluent and later in competition with his medico-political and muscular Christian interests, work for child welfare and efforts to establish an anti-cancer committee. He was prominent in the Student Christian Movement at the university and in the Baptist Union of South Australia, being president in 1935 and at other times chairman of the Home Mission and of the Baptist Brotherhood, which failed to respond to his energy.

Hone was president of the South Australian branch of the British Medical Association in 1911 and a founding director of the Australasian Medical Publishing Co. Ltd, which published the *Medical Journal of Australia*, from 1914. He emphasized that the chief pursuits of professional bodies should be scientific inquiry and the advancement of public health, not political power; half a century before it happened he warned of the eventual alienation of public sympathy from a self-interested profession. He also recognized that effective medicine must deal with social and preventive questions as well as individual curative ones, and saw no inconsistency in associating himself and his profession with government in policy-making and administration. Hone supported Thomas Borthwick [q.v.7] in the effort to give Adelaide an effective public health administration, was chief quarantine officer for South Australia from 1915 to 1930, did yeoman service at the quarantine station during the epidemic of Spanish influenza of 1918-19 and became a councilmember of the Commonwealth School of Public Health and Tropical Medicine established in Sydney in 1930.

He was appointed a member of the Commonwealth royal commission on national health in 1925. The links between clinical and preventive medicine and between government and medical practitioners were articulated in the *Report* in 1926 which proposed a network of local, district, regional and State facilities and clinicians to provide services directed towards an improvement of maternal, infant and occupational health.

According to J. H. L. Cumpston [q.v.8], whose praise Hone earned without sharing Cumpston's more doctrinaire views, Hone was 'the spirit of enterprise' in the commission. The commission's vision of a national health service did not prevail against the advocates of a government-guaranteed private medical service. In 1948, when medical politics was degenerating into a fight about medical economics, Hone said that 'those of us who have for years fought for the value of prevention rather than of remedial measures as the keynote to modern medical ideas cannot but oppose proposals to substitute medical benefits for preventive benefits'.

In 1921 Hone was appointed lecturer in preventive medicine in the University of Adelaide. He taught a generation of medical students who regarded him affectionately and who made him president, for a time, of their society. A student when Australian medical schools were staffed by men like (Sir) Harry Allen [q.v.7], (Sir) Edward Stirling [q.v.6], (Sir) Anderson Stuart and (Sir) Joseph Verco [qq.v.], who were young enough to have acquired in Britain and Europe the ascendant experimentalists' interest in specific causation of disease, Hone had learned to emphasize the proper understanding of aetiology as the basis for prevention and added to this an earlier nineteenth-century interest in the social significance of disease. The product was a spirit of purposeful observation which is evident in a number of his papers, including his studies on the vector of typhus fever, which Sir Macfarlane Burnet has ranked with Maxcy's study. Hone transmitted the traditions of careful description and social concern to students and colleagues, most notably in C. C. Jungfer's study of *Child health in a rural community* (1944).

A keen sportsman, Hone excelled at cricket and tennis; he won the South Australian men's doubles lawn tennis championship in 1891, served on the University Sports Association for nearly thirty years and was chairman of the South Australian Amateur Football League, 1927-33. He was also active in the Red Cross Society and Crippled Children's Association. A member of the university council for twenty-nine years, he was appointed C.M.G. in 1941.

Hone died at an Adelaide private hospital on 9 May 1951 and was buried in West Terrace cemetery. He was survived by his wife Lucy, née Henderson, whom he had married on 6 May 1896 at the Flinders Street Baptist church, Adelaide, and by four sons and two daughters. Tributes in the *Medical Journal of Australia* reflected accurately a physician who had combined scientific intelligence with humanity and social purpose. Two of his sons became medical practitioners and (Sir) Brian William (1907-1978) was a distinguished educationist.

MJA, 22 June 1951; *Adel Medical Students' Soc, Review*, May 1949; papers held by author (Faculty of Medicine, Univ Adel).   NEVILLE HICKS

HOOD, SIR ALEXANDER JARVIE (1860-1934), physician, was born on 21 October 1860 at Tarbolton, Ayrshire, Scotland, seventh of nine surviving children of William Hood, manager of Robert Wotherspoon & Co., confectioners, and his wife Mary, née Jarvie. Educated at the High School and the University of Glasgow (M.B., Ch.M., 1882), he was resident medical officer at Glasgow Western Infirmary in 1882-83. In 1884 he followed two uncles to Australia.

Registering on 16 June 1884, Hood took the advice of Samuel Macnaughton and began practice at Rockymouth (Maclean) on the Clarence River. He served gratuitously as medical officer of the Lower Clarence Hospital from 1887, and next year was appointed government medical officer for the district. Overwork and ill health led him to move to Sydney in 1889, where he succeeded to the practice of Henry William Jackson.

Jarvie Hood joined the New South Wales branch of the British Medical Association in 1887 and contributed papers to several of the earlier Australasian Medical congresses. In 1889-1934 he was chief medical officer to the City Mutual Life Assurance Society Ltd, becoming a director in 1916. He was consultant to a succession of New South Wales governors from 1893; honorary medical officer to Sydney Hospital (surgeon 1890, resigned; assistant physician 1893, physician 1895, consulting physician 1920), joint honorary secretary of the New South Wales Medical Union in 1894-1921; official visitor to Gladesville and Callan Park hospitals for the insane (1903-28); first medical adviser to the Commonwealth Bank of Australia (1912-34); and vice-president of the Highland Society of New South Wales (1911-34). Commissioned captain in the Army Medical Corps in 1890 and promoted major in 1900, Hood was with the New South Wales Scottish Rifles in 1904-09, and on the unattached list from 1909. As temporary lieut-colonel he was senior consultant physician at the Military Hospital, Randwick, from July 1915. For his honorary war service he was knighted in 1921 and known as Sir Jarvie. He was adviser to and, in 1920-34, council-member of the War Memorial Hospital, Waverley, established by the Methodist Church.

Interested in the education and encouragement of youth, from 1904 he gave an annual prize for the best first-year medical student at St Andrew's College, University of Sydney, and was a member of its council (1907-34). He was council-member of the Presbyterian Ladies' colleges at Croydon and Pymble for twenty years and furnished the new hospital for the latter in 1926. He avoided committee-room politics and his attendance at all meetings declined in the mid-1920s.

Hood's medical reputation was as a diagnostic physician. Short of stature, with winning manners, he was immensely popular with his patients. His punctuality and attention to detail also endeared him to hospital residents and nurses.

Always generous to his family, Hood had brought two unmarried sisters out from Scotland in the early 1890s; the younger, Margaret, became his housekeeper and devoted guardian. He died at his home, St Mungo, Potts Point, on 8 May 1934, and was cremated after a funeral service conducted there by the Presbyterian Rev. Samuel Angus [q.v.7]. Despite his large practice, Hood did not make his money from his profession but from investing wisely on the advice of his many influential friends. After providing for Margaret Hood, he left the residue of his estate, proved for probate at £186 325, in trust to his four married sisters or their children.

Roy Com on lunacy law and administration, *PP* (NSW), 1923, 1, p 651; *A'sian Medical Gazette*, Mar 1887; *Scottish A'sian*, May 1911, Jan 1921; *MJA*, 7 July 1934; *Clarence and Richmond Examiner*, 15 July 1884, 10 Aug, 14 Sept 1889, 29 Dec 1894; *SMH*, 9 May 1934; information from Mrs Muriel Bucknell and Miss Mary Fenwick of Sydney.
        ANN M. MITCHELL

HOOD, SIR JOSEPH HENRY (1846-1922), judge, was born on 1 June 1846 in Melbourne, son of John Hood, Irish-born chemist and member of parliament, and his wife Jane, née Plummer. Educated at Scotch College in 1859-63, he was dux in mathematics and equal dux of the school in his final year. He enrolled at the University of Melbourne in 1864 where he studied both arts and law (B.A., LL.B., 1868; M.A., 1874), consistently gaining second-class honours. He was called to the Bar on 9 December 1868 and quickly established a large practice in the County Court. It was said that there were few cases of any note in that court in which he did not appear on one side and (Sir) Frank Gavan Duffy [q.v.8] on the other. In due course he obtained a practice on the common law side of the Supreme Court. In 1882 he was one of the first barristers to take chambers in Selborne Chambers.

Hood was appointed an acting judge of the Supreme Court of Victoria on 1 February 1890 during the absence on leave of Mr Justice (Sir Edward) Holroyd [q.v.4]. He was the first barrister born and educated in Melbourne to reach the bench. On the death of Mr Justice Webb [q.v.6] in October 1891, his appointment was made permanent. Thereafter he sat continuously in the court, save for a holiday in England in 1905, until April 1916 when his health broke down. An able and sound lawyer, he was a very rapid worker, earning, it is said, the sobriquet of the 'lightning judge'. In spite of Frank Gavan Duffy's comment 'But less fast were more fair' in his poem 'A Dream of Fair Judges', Hood seems at all times to have been very careful and conspicuously fair. Clearness of mind and close analytical reasoning marked his judgments. He was fearless, independent and outspoken. When at the Bar, Hood often took technical objections but as a judge he deprecated them. When counsel urged a technical objection before him his response was 'How are you hurt?' He had a robust common sense and was a strong and popular judge. He insisted on decorum in his court but was not without a sense of humour and enjoyed telling an anecdote against himself.

Some time after the breakdown in his health he resumed his place on the bench. On 3 June 1920 he was knighted. He resigned on 31 December 1921 on the ground of ill health, having been on leave for twelve months. He died at his home in Alexandra Street, East St Kilda, on 28 January 1922 and was buried in Melbourne general cemetery.

As a young man Hood was keenly interested in sport. He played in the first XI at Scotch College and subsequently became a notable oarsman. He rowed first with the Melbourne university crew but later joined the Richmond Club. For some time he contributed the rowing notes to the *Australasian*. He retired from rowing in 1873. He had no significant hobbies but was a wide reader and a regular visitor to the library of the Melbourne Athenaeum. He was an examiner in the law faculty of the University of Melbourne in 1880-81, 1884 and 1887 and was a member of the university council from 1891 until his death.

On 8 November 1869 at St John's Church, Melbourne, Hood had married Georgina McKee. She survived him with four daughters and two sons.

J. L. Forde, *The story of the Bar of Victoria* (Melb, 1913); P. A. Jacobs, *Judges of yesterday* (Melb, 1924); A. Dean, *A multitude of counsellors* (Melb, 1968); *Argus*, 5 Feb 1890, 3 June 1920, 30 Jan 1922.

J. McI. YOUNG

HOOD, ROBERT (1821-1891) and **ROBERT ALEXANDER DAVID** (1863-1934), pastoralists and sheep-breeders, were father and son. Hood senior was born on 12 February 1821 at Longformacus, Berwickshire, Scotland, sixth son of William Hood, farmer, and his wife Martha, née Bertram. Robert's first wife Margaret, née Weatherly, whom he married at Cockburnspath on 22 June 1843, died in 1849. In 1854, with his daughter and two sons, Hood migrated to Victoria where he bought Bolac Plains from Robert Anderson and in 1856 Merrang, West Hexham, from the executors of Adolphus Sceales. On 30 December at Merrang he married Sceales's Scottish widow Jane, née Paton. Robert Alexander David, born at Merrang on 8 August 1863, was their only surviving son.

First cattle, and then merinos had been tried at Merrang. The cold, wet climate and the rich river flats did not suit the latter; but after Thomas Austin [q.v.1] had shown at Barwon Park in the 1860s that the Lincoln breed could flourish in similar terrain, Hood formed a flock in 1872-73, importing two rams and ewes from Marshall and Kirkham in Lincolnshire, and buying part of the Barwon Park stud (built up from the same flocks) on its dispersal. In 1880 he bought part of the Langi Kal Kal flock, which shared the same bloodlines. Hood's breeding policy paid off: at shows his flock was 'almost invincible' from 1874 and buyers sought his stud rams.

A founder of the Long-woolled Sheep Association and president of the Hexham Show from 1873, Hood was elected one of the first vice-presidents of the Australian Sheepbreeders' Association in 1877. Like many breeders, he was also an acclimatizer, and attempted to propagate trout in the Hopkins River. Hood served on the Warrnambool Shire Council in 1874-83 (president, 1876) and was chairman of the reorganized, but unsuccessful, Warrnambool Woollen Mill Co. Ltd.

In the mid-1880s Hood leased Merrang to the younger Robert. Educated at Geelong Church of England Grammar School (where he won triple colours), Robert gained experience on the Queensland property Burenda, managed by his elder half-brother William. After his father died, at Warrnambool on 30 October 1891, Robert bought Merrang from the family trustees. Continuing his father's breeding policies, he introduced rams from the same Lincolnshire studs and their daughter flocks in Victoria. In the 1920s he began a Polwarth stud based on Barunah Plains ewes, Lincoln rams and their progeny mated with Barunah Plains stud merino rams.

Hood bred racehorses and polo ponies.

President of the Western District Racing Association from 1924, he was a long-serving committee member and office-bearer of the Warrnambool Racing and Amateur Turf clubs. He captained the Cara-mut polo team and the Victorian team which toured and beat New Zealand in 1901 and represented the State in other seasons; he played his last competitive game when 63. A member of the Mortlake Shire Council for thirty-four years, Hood was three times president.

Hood died at Hexham of cerebro-vascular disease on 10 April 1934 and was buried in the local cemetery. He had married Edith Mary, daughter of Robert Calvert of Yan-Yan-Gurt, on 18 July 1906 at St George's Presbyterian Church, Geelong; she died in 1907. On 24 June 1909 at the South Yarra Presbyterian Church he married Georgina Martha McCall Anderson, sister-in-law of (Viscount) S. M. Bruce [q.v.7]. She survived him with their son and three daughters. Hood's estate was valued for probate at £68 657.

J. B. Burke, *A genealogical and heraldic history of the colonial gentry* (Lond, 1891); G. A. Brown, *Sheep breeding in Australia* (Melb, 1890); Pastoral Review Pty Ltd, *The pastoral homes of Australia—Victoria* (Melb, 1910 *and* 1931); R. A. D. Hood et al, *A brief history of the Shire of Mortlake* (Mortlake, 1967); R. Osburne, *The history of Warrnambool* (Warrnambool, 1980); *Pastoral Review*, 16 Nov 1891, 16 Oct 1929, 16 Apr 1934; *Flock Book for British Breeds of Sheep in Australia*, 1 (1898).

P. H. DE SERVILLE

HOOLAN, JOHN (1842-1911), newspaper-owner and politician, was born in Tipperary, Ireland, son of James Hoolan and his wife Margaret, née Kennedy. Trained as a carpenter and married in Ireland to Ellen Lawlor about 1868, he probably brought his family to New South Wales about 1878. He worked briefly around Bathurst, then went to Queensland about 1880 and was first registered on the electoral roll for Charters Towers in November 1883. In October 1886 he was chairman of the Black Jack Deep Block Gold Mining Co. Ltd.

In 1887 Hoolan moved to Croydon to establish the *Mining News* and the *Mundic Miner* at Georgetown. The latter paper, which became his main mouthpiece, was soon notorious for its pungent prose. Hoolan himself acquired the nickname 'Plumper' because of his advocacy of 'whole hog' principles. Failing as a radical candidate for Burke in 1888, he entered parliament after a by-election in August 1890 and, because of his appalling flow of adjectives which 'paralysed' the House, he was known as 'the Wild Man'. As there was still no Labor Party, he joined forces with Thomas Glassey [q.v.] as a defiant minority. When the two arrived at Gympie on the same train as the governor and cabinet, however, the crowd welcomed them and ignored the official party. Both he and Glassey were elected to the executive which the Labor Party convention of August 1892 created. After his electorate was divided in 1893, Hoolan was returned unopposed but, although fifteen Labor members were elected, Glassey was defeated. Hoolan was chosen as leader. When Glassey sought to return to politics in 1894, Hoolan resigned his seat; Glassey won it easily in the by-election and Hoolan regained it when Glassey moved on to represent Bundaberg in March 1896.

Like Glassey, Hoolan became increasingly restive in the strengthening Labor machine. He refused to sign the pledge in 1896 and stood as a Labor independent, but was not opposed by a Labor candidate. About this time he acquired a small grazing property. He now openly branded the theory of 'Socialism in our time' as 'impracticable' and as 'hanging a millstone around the neck of the Labor Party'. In the debates on the Queensland National Bank Ltd (agreement) bill of 1896, the rift became obvious and he voted against the party on the Mareeba to Chillagoe railway bill of 1897. His activities as an emissary of Glassey in a bid to secure control of the *Worker* were investigated by a special party conference of 1897; he refused to appear. Having left the Labor Party, he abandoned Burke in 1899 and challenged Thomas Givens [q.v.] at Cairns on behalf of a Glassey faction, but was defeated. After failing in an attempt on the Senate in 1901, he abandoned politics permanently.

Able but unorthodox, Hoolan generated a host of anecdotes. When Charles McDonald [q.v.] was suspended in 1894 and ordered to retire from the House, Hoolan held him down by force and encouraged him to defy the Speaker. His own suspension followed. At one of his last parliamentary appearances, he was suspended again for defying the Speaker. 'Mr Hoolan thereupon proceeded to the table and, filling a glass with water said, "Here's luck all round". The honourable member then left the chamber, raising his coat tails as he retired.'

In Hoolan's declining years he worked sometimes as a journalist and sometimes at his trade as a carpenter. He settled in Brisbane and died there in the Diamantina Hospital of a rodent ulcer on 15 June 1911. He was buried in Toowong cemetery. His wife, a son and a daughter survived him.

C. A. Bernays, *Queensland politics during sixty years* (Brisb, 1919); R. Gollan, *Radical and working class politics* (Melb, 1960); G. C. Bolton, *A thousand miles away* (Brisb, 1963); W. J. H. Harris, *First steps* (Canberra, 1966); *Worker* (Brisb), 25 July 1891, 23 June 1894, 9 June 1897, 7 July 1900, 12 Dec 1903; *Boomerang* (Brisb), 26 May 1888; *Brisbane Courier*, 2 Mar 1901; cutting book, 1893 elections (Oxley Lib, Brisb).   W. J. H. HARRIS

HOOPER, RICHARD (1846-1909), miner, trade unionist and politician, was born on 4 May 1846 at Wheal Hope, Cornwall, England, son of Francis Hooper, farmer, and his wife Matilda, née Boundy. The family migrated to South Australia in 1858 and settled at Burra Burra. In 1860 they moved to Kadina and two years later to Moonta. Hooper worked as a miner from 1859 until his election to parliament at the Wallaroo by-election on 23 May 1891 with an absolute majority over four opponents.

Hooper was the first Labor member of the South Australian House of Assembly, but was not a member of the newly formed United Labor Party. His electoral success followed his trade union work at Moonta where the copper industry had been in jeopardy since the 1870s. In 1889 when the Moonta Miners' Association re-formed to become a branch of the Amalgamated Miners' Association, Hooper was made president. Next year he was also first president of the Colonial District A.M.A. He contested the 1891 by-election as the A.M.A. candidate and was re-elected as an Independent Labor member in 1893, 1896 and 1899; although he attended caucus meetings he never joined the United Labor Party.

A small, sprucely dressed man sporting a trimmed billy-goat beard, he was an active and popular local politician who gained for his electorate a water-reticulation scheme, a railway connexion to Adelaide and a horse-tram service between Moonta and its outlying townships; these gains surpassed anything Wallaroo had previously obtained. On wider issues Hooper supported the development and regulation of mining and the establishment of a board of conciliation; he opposed Federation and free trade.

Hooper's union support eventually dwindled because, it is said, the miners detected a cultivated affectation in his speech. His new accent was certainly not developed in the assembly itself since 'Dicky Hooper, the silent member' made only one speech in the House during his decade as a politician. In 1902 the Wallaroo electorate was given an extra member and the boundaries were redrawn to include an agricultural area south of Moonta. The A.M.A. pledged support for John Verran [q.v.] and Hooper failed in his bid to gain the farmers' vote.

Bereft of income Hooper moved to Perth where he worked as a night-watchman and where he died in poverty of cancer on 24 July 1909. His first wife Eliza Jane, née Williams, whom he married on 8 June 1866 at Moonta, had died in childbirth in 1867. He was survived by his second wife Josephine, née Lean, whom he married at Moonta on 12 April 1870, and by their five daughters and three sons. An area of scrub in the Murray Mallee, the Hundred of Hooper, was named after him. Many agreed with the official who lamented after Hooper's death: 'We should have found Dicky Hooper a job. He would have earned his salary'.

O. Pryor, *Australia's little Cornwall* (Adel, 1962); J. B. Hirst, *Adelaide and the country, 1870-1917* (Melb, 1973); *Pictorial Aust*, May 1891; *Observer* (Adel), 29 Aug 1891, 10 June 1893, 31 July 1909; L. L. Kiek, The history of the South Australian labour unions (M.A. thesis, Univ Adel, 1948).

                                                              RON SLEE

HOOVER, HERBERT CLARK (1874-1964), mining engineer, humanitarian, and American statesman, was born on 10 August 1874 at West Branch, Iowa, United States of America, second son of Jesse Clark Hoover, blacksmith and farm implements dealer, and his wife Hulda Randall, née Minthorn. Hoover's forebears were Quakers. His father died in 1880, and his mother in 1884; for the next seven years Hoover was raised by relatives in Iowa and Oregon. In 1891 he entered Stanford University in California. Upon graduating in 1895 (B.A., geology), he worked for about two years in various mining-related jobs in California and the south-west. In 1897 the British mining-engineering firm of Bewick, Moreing & Co. invited him to undertake mine examination and exploration work on the Western Australian goldfields. In mid-May of that year he went to Coolgardie.

Hoover's principal duties at first were those of an expert 'inspecting engineer', evaluating mines and prospects in the 'bush' far to the north of Coolgardie and Kalgoorlie. On an early trip he visited the remote, little-developed gold mine, the Sons of Gwalia, near Leonora. Convinced that it was a mine of promise, he urged his principals in London to secure an option. Late in 1897 he methodically examined the mine, recommended purchase, and outlined a programme of development. Primarily on the basis of his work, his backers bought the property and floated the Sons of Gwalia Ltd in London in early 1898. From May to November Hoover was the Sons of Gwalia's superintendent and initiated its transformation into a spectacular mining success.

By the time Hoover left Western Australia in December 1898, he was one of the ablest and best-known mining engineers in the colony. Blunt and laconic, he had a phenomenal memory, prodigious capacity for work, and high ambition. An ardent exponent of American mining methods, he helped to establish single-hand drilling, disciplined management, and high standards of efficiency in the aftermath of a boom.

On 10 February 1899, in California, Hoover married Lou Henry, an Iowa-born banker's daughter who was also a geologist; they had met in college. They had two sons: Herbert Charles (1903-1969) and Allan Henry (b. 1907).

Late in 1901 after nearly two years as a mining engineer in China, Hoover became a partner in Bewick, Moreing & Co. He inaugurated a crusade for improved management and cost reduction in their mines in Western Australia. In 1902, 1903, 1905 and 1907, he visited Australia for long periods, inspecting, reorganizing and rationalizing. By the time he retired from Bewick, Moreing and Co. in 1908, it had surged to pre-eminence in Western Australia; but its success and drive provoked controversy on the goldfields, including allegations of monopoly and of favouritism toward immigrant Italian labour. However, with Bewick, Moreing mines in the lead, Western Australian gold-mining in these years underwent a transition from the speculative excesses of the 'roaring nineties' to a new era of scientific, cost-efficient low-grade production. As much as any other man, Hoover was responsible for this transformation.

After 1908 the focus of his mining engineering career shifted, but he did not abandon interest in Australia. In 1905, with W. L. Baillieu [q.v.7] and others, he had founded the Zinc Corporation (later Rio-Tinto-Zinc Corp Ltd) at Broken Hill and influenced its operations for several years. In collaboration with F. A. Govett, a London stockbroker, Hoover engineered several important mergers and flotations, including the creation of Lake View and Star Ltd, in 1910. By 1914 Hoover was a mining engineer, administrator, and financier of international repute. He was also the author of a standard mining textbook and, with his wife, the acclaimed translator into English of the Latin mining classic *De re metallica*.

The rest of Hoover's succession of careers is better known, notably his direction of gigantic humanitarian food relief projects

in Europe during and after World War I and his tenure as president of the United States (1929-33). He was a prolific author, writing three volumes of *Memoirs*, two books of political philosophy, and hundreds of articles and addresses. He almost certainly, however, did not write something often attributed to him in Australia: a love poem to a barmaid at Kalgoorlie.

Hoover died in New York City on 20 October 1964 and was buried in his native West Branch, Iowa, alongside his wife, who had died in 1944.

K. Tracey, *Herbert Hoover—a bibliography of his writings and addresses* (Stanford, California, 1977); G. H. Nash, *The life of Herbert Hoover*, 1 (NY, 1983); Hoover mining reports, 1897-98 (WA Dept of Mines, Perth); Sons of Gwalia records (Battye Lib, Perth); Hoover papers (Herbert Hoover Presidential Lib, West Branch, Iowa, *and* Hoover Inst on War, Revolution and Peace, Stanford Univ, California); W. S. Robinson papers (Univ Melb Archives).   GEORGE H. NASH

HOPETOUN, JOHN ADRIAN LOUIS HOPE, 7th EARL (1860-1908), governor-general, later 1st Marquess of Linlithgow, was born on 25 September 1860 at Hopetoun House, South Queensferry, Scotland, eldest son of John Alexander Hope, sixth earl, and his wife Ethelred Anne Birch, née Reynardson. After education at Eton, where he rowed and debated a little, he went to the Royal Military College, Sandhurst, passing in 1879. The affairs of his family estate, over 42 500 acres (17 200 ha) on both sides of the Firth of Forth, to which he had succeeded at 13, and probably his poor health, prevented his entering the army.

In 1883 Hopetoun was appointed Conservative whip in the House of Lords. He became a lord-in-waiting to Queen Victoria in 1885 and in 1887-89 represented the Queen as lord high commissioner to the general assembly of the Church of Scotland. On 18 October 1886 at All Saints' Church, Knightsbridge, he had married a childhood friend Hersey Alice Eveleigh-de-Moleyns, daughter of the 4th Baron Ventry.

In 1889 Hopetoun was appointed governor of Victoria and G.C.M.G., arriving in Melbourne in sumptuous style in November. During a time of depression and ministerial instability, Hopetoun entertained extravagantly and handled the political situation ably. Notwithstanding poor health and colonial astonishment at his habit of wearing hair-powder, his youthful enthusiasm for routine duties and his fondness for informal horseback tours won him many friends, even in Sydney. But Lady Hopetoun was criticized for her haughty manner. His governorship coincided with important years of the Federation movement of which he was a fervent supporter. After an extension of his term he left Melbourne in March 1895.

In 1895-98 Hopetoun was paymaster-general in Salisbury's government. In 1898, having declined the governor-generalship of Canada, he became lord chamberlain. On 13 July 1900 it was announced that the Queen had approved his appointment as first governor-general of the Commonwealth of Australia. He was made Knight of the Thistle and G.C.V.O.

After a disastrous journey via India, where he caught typhoid fever and Lady Hopetoun malaria, Hopetoun arrived in Sydney on 15 December 1900. Ill and poorly advised, he invited the New South Wales premier (Sir) William Lyne [q.v.] to form the first Australian ministry—a choice subsequently known as 'the Hopetoun blunder'. Upon Lyne's failure (Sir) Edmund Barton [q.v.7] was commissioned. The governor-general took the oaths of office at the inauguration ceremony on 1 January 1901, and then swore in Barton's ministry.

Hopetoun's term was brief but beset with difficulties. His relationship with State governors was strained by a controversy over his attempt in February to obtain copies of all their correspondence with the British government. In May-July he supervised successfully the tour of the duke of Cornwall and York (later King George V). A speech Hopetoun made in January 1902 to the Australian Natives' Association on the delay in sending an Australian contingent to the South African War earned him a gentle rebuke from (Sir) George Reid [q.v.], leader of the Opposition. In May Hopetoun was humiliated when parliament refused to agree to Barton's proposal that the governor-general's salary of £10 000 be augmented by an allowance of £8000. He had already spent considerably out of his private income, and he asked the secretary of state, Joseph Chamberlain, to recall him. On 17 July Hopetoun sailed from Brisbane for England. He was created Marquess of Linlithgow in October.

Slightly built, with what the *Bulletin* described as a 'willowy stoop and a cat like, Lord Chamberlain's tread', he was usually clean shaven, but sometimes grew a moustache. Sir George Clarke [q.v.8] regarded him as 'charming but not at all clever'. Hunting was his one hobby; a fearless rider, 'Probably he had more of his bones broken in the hunting-field than any man of his time in England'. Secretary of state for Scotland during the last months of Balfour's ministry in 1905, Linlithgow was already seriously ill. He died of pernicious anaemia while wintering at Pau in France on 29 February 1908. He was survived by his wife, a daughter and two sons, the elder of whom, the second marquess, in 1935 declined the governor-generalship of Australia, and was viceroy of India in 1936-43. Hopetoun's portrait, by James Quinn [q.v.], is in Parliament House, Canberra, and another by Robert Brough is in Hopetoun House. A statue by Bernie Rhind was erected in Melbourne in 1911.

J. A. La Nauze, *The Hopetoun blunder* (Melb, 1957); D. I. Wright, *Shadow of dispute* (Canb, 1970); *Bulletin*, 14 June 1890, 2 July 1892, 16 Nov 1901; *Argus* (Melb), and *The Times*, 2 Mar 1908; C. Cunneen, The role of governor-general in Australia 1901-1927 (Ph.D. thesis, ANU, 1973); Hopetoun House MSS, M936, 937, 1154-56 (AJCP, NL).

CHRIS CUNNEEN

HOPKINS, FELICIA (1841-1933), social worker, was born on 4 January 1841 at Bocking, Essex, England, daughter of Lister Smith, who was an 'upper class artisan' (her own description) employed in Courtauld's knitting mills, and his wife Deborah, née Hayward, who had conducted a ladies' school at Braintree. Both parents were members of the Society of Friends and held radical political views, supporting Chartism and the rights of women. After education at a Quaker boarding-school at Croydon, Felicia worked as a governess.

In 1861-62 she and four brothers and sisters joined their friends the Hopkins family, also Quakers, in migrating to Queensland. Felicia reached Brisbane in the *Wansfell* in 1862. On 18 December 1865 she married the 21-year-old Francis Hopkins. He found employment in Brisbane and Rockhampton newspaper offices, then worked as a schoolteacher at Pink Lily Lagoon near Rockhampton in 1872-73; Felicia taught needlework to the girls. In 1874 he established a bookselling and stationery business at Rockhampton. While he returned to teaching in 1874-76, Felicia presumably managed the shop and, after he died in 1913, she kept up the business until 1924. They had five children.

Mrs Hopkins first became involved with the Young Women's Christian Association in 1888. This interdenominational religious society, then concerned mainly with the welfare of single working girls, had been founded in England in 1855 and was launched in Australia at Geelong, Victoria, in 1872. In 1888 six branches were established in Queensland but, of these, only the Rockhampton branch, of which Felicia Hopkins was secretary for twenty-four years, survived for more than a year or two. Their main work was to meet and protect young women on migrant ships and to organize lectures, classes and social evenings for working girls. Felicia Hopkins's personal concern for the girls went further. She is known to have taken unmarried pregnant girls into her own home until their future could be settled. In a new effort to expand the Y.W.C.A. in 1899, the Brisbane branch was re-formed and Felicia Hopkins undertook an extended tour of Queensland, setting up new branches at Townsville, Clermont, Barcaldine and Longreach and finding referees for girls new to the town in four other centres.

The Y.W.C.A. was not the sole public interest of Mrs Hopkins. A keen member of the Society of Friends, she was Rockhampton correspondent for the London connexion and had helped to establish a Rockhampton meeting-house by 1880. She was also a member of the Benevolent Society from 1867-68; she and her husband were interested in the welfare of orphans and in the late 1860s founded their own children's home where orphans could be boarded. The couple were active in the political Central Separation Movement. They also promoted temperance—her enthusiasm for this cause is vividly remembered by those who knew this tiny, active woman. She died on 15 July 1933 and was buried in North Rockhampton cemetery with Methodist forms. Two daughters survived her.

L. McDonald, *Rockhampton* (Brisb, 1981); papers and press cuttings held by Mr L. Hopkins, O'Connor, ACT, Mrs W. Morgan, Bowenville, Qld and Mrs E. Jordan, Lambton, NSW.

ELLEN JORDAN

HORDER, HAROLD NORMAN (1894-1978), footballer, was born on 23 February 1894 at Surry Hills, Sydney, fourth surviving son of Charles Horder, machinist and sometime professional runner, and his wife Ellen, née McBride, both native born. Harold went to Albion Street Superior Public School, leaving in 1907 to join the Government Printing Office, where he worked for over ten years.

Following his brother Clarence, later also a representative footballer, into South Sydney Kinkora junior Rugby League team, Horder represented Souths in the under-21 President's Cup in 1911 and also in 1912, when in his first-grade debut for the 'Rabbitohs' he scored a sensational, length of the field try. In September the *Referee* reported the meteoric rise of the young inside centre—more orthodox than Messenger [q.v.], resembling 'in his dodging and swerving runs' A. S. Spragg [q.v.]. A 'finely built,

well-balanced athlete', Horder weighed 9 st 7 lb. (60 kg); later his playing weight was about 10 st. 9 lb. (67 kg) when he was normally a winger.

He toured New Zealand with New South Wales in 1913. Horder contributed to Souths winning the premiership in 1914 and 1918. During the war he served with the naval reserve. In 1913-24 he represented his State against England five times, Queensland seven times and New Zealand five times. First picked for Australia in June 1914 against Wagstaffe's touring English side, he did not shine. But in 1920 he played in all tests against England, and went to Britain with the third Kangaroos in 1921-22, again playing in all tests; with 35 tries and 11 goals (127 points) he was leading scorer on the tour.

By 1919 Horder was a steward at the New South Wales Leagues Club. He also worked as a labourer and a plasterer's assistant. In 1920 he left Souths, joining North Sydney at a retainer of 30s. per week. With Ceci Blinkhorn and Duncan Thompson [q.v.] he was responsible for the 'Shoremen' winning the premiership in 1921 (with Horder as captain) and 1922 (when he was vice-captain); up to 1982 Norths have never repeated this success. He returned to Souths in 1924 and played in two tests against England. In November, promised a job as a traveller for the Perdriau [q.v.] rubber company, he moved to Brisbane, where he was captain-coach of Coorparoo Club in 1925-27. He represented Queensland against New Zealand in 1925 and continued playing club football until he injured his knee in 1926. In 1928-30 he was a referee.

A motor-vehicle salesman in Sydney from 1935, Horder returned to Brisbane in 1937 and was a salesman with Moreton Rubber Works, then with Hirmac Remoulds. For about ten years he was a clerk with Brown's Transport, retiring in 1960. He was a keen bowler with East Brisbane and Coorparoo clubs. He had married Ruby Anne Clay (d. 1975), a book-sewer, at St Pius Catholic Church, Enmore, Sydney, on 8 January 1916. Survived by his son, he died at South Brisbane on 21 August 1978 and was cremated.

Although not a robust defender, Horder was one of the greatest attacking wingers of the code, and a good goal-kicker. He rarely used the short kick. His speed off the mark, side-step off either foot and hare-like swerves left worthy opponents flabbergasted and 'gave the League game a splash of the spectacular'; he was a main reason for it consolidating its appeal as the top winter game in Sydney by the 1920s. A show man, after scoring a try Horder would 'trot back jauntily, like a peacock with feather preened'. The mob loved it; they called him the 'wonder winger'.

'Redcap', *Qld Rugby League Annual*, 1927; *Rugby League Annual* (NSW), 1928; *Referee*, 18 Sept 1912; *Brisbane Telegraph*, 27 Mar, 2, 9, 16, 23, 30 Apr, 7, 14, 21, 28 May, 4, 11, 19, 26 June 1949; *SMH*, 23 Aug 1978; information from Mr T. Goodman, Potts Point, Syd, *and* Mr N. W. Horder, Chermside, Brisb.   CHRIS CUNNEEN

HORDERN, SIR SAMUEL (1876-1956), merchant and stockbreeder, and ANTHONY (1889-1970), grazier and stockbreeder, were born on 24 September 1876 and on 21 February 1889 at Retford Hall, Darling Point, Sydney, eldest and third sons of native-born parents Samuel Hordern [q.v.4] and his wife Jane Maria, née Booth. Educated at Sydney Grammar School and Bath College, England, Samuel returned to Sydney in 1895 to work in the family's department store, Anthony Hordern [q.v.4] & Sons.

On his father's death in 1909, Hordern was fully trained to assume control of the remarkable Italianate Palace Emporium, opened in 1906 as universal providers. 'The Empo', run with imagination and enterprise, employed some 4000 people and dealt in 'everything from a needle to an anchor', mostly manufactured in the firm's Sydney factories or imported by its own agents abroad. Their familiar household catalogue was known as the 'Bush Bible'. In accordance with his father's will the firm was sold to a private company in 1912; Hordern became governing director. With inherited wealth, particularly from the sales in 1918 of his father's city and suburban properties, he perhaps lacked the trading flair that called for ruthlessness to keep control of the vast emporium and abreast of modern merchandising. He retired from the company in 1926 when it was sold to public investors.

A council-member and honorary treasurer of the Sydney Chamber of Commerce, Hordern attended congresses of the Chambers of Commerce of the British Empire in London in 1912 and 1924. He was president of the Master Retailers' Association, a vice-president of the Employers' Federation of New South Wales, chairman of the Australian Mutual Provident Society in 1932-47, and a director of the Royal Insurance Co. Ltd, the Commonwealth Bank of Australia, and Perpetual Trustee Co. He contributed generously, as did Anthony, to the purchase in 1918 of Cranbrook, Bellevue Hill, for a Church of England boys' school

and to the establishment in 1926 of Kambala, Rose Bay, for a Church girls' school. He was a director of Royal Prince Alfred Hospital in 1913-39 and chairman in 1933-34.

As president of the Royal Agricultural Society of New South Wales in 1915-41, Hordern was largely responsible for the growth of the Royal Easter Show from a small fair to one of the world's greatest agricultural shows. Despite the annual protests of Archbishop Wright [q.v.], he kept the show open on Good Friday.

At Retford Park, Bowral, Hordern vigorously pursued the improvement of his stock. He imported Jersey and Ayrshire stud cattle, Clydesdales, thoroughbred mares, hackneys, hunters and Welsh ponies, and exhibited them at the Easter Show. He also bred deer-hounds and Scotch and fox-terriers. His love of horses extended to the turf: he was a committee-member of the Australian Jockey Club in 1917-44. With Artilleryman (in partnership) he won the 1919 Melbourne Cup and A.J.C. Derby, and the Victoria Racing Club St Leger in 1920; next year his Violincello won the Caulfield Cup. Like his father, he also bred and raced homing pigeons. He visited England and Europe every few years following his stockbreeding and racing interests and gathering ideas for the R.A.S. For the first exhibition in 1927 of the New South Wales Applied Art Trust, Hordern presented a collection of Damascene ware.

At St Jude's Anglican Church, Randwick, on 4 March 1900, he had married Charlotte Isabel Annie (d. 1952), daughter of (Sir) John See [q.v.]. They lived at Strathfield and later bought Mount Adelaide at Darling Point, which was demolished to build Babworth House in 1912; designed by Morrow and De Peutron, it was considered the finest Art Nouveau house in Sydney. Hordern belonged to the Union, Australian, Warrigal and New South Wales clubs, played golf at Concord and Royal Sydney Golf clubs and sailed with the Royal Sydney Yacht Squadron and Royal Prince Alfred Yacht Club. He was an early member of the (Royal) Automobile Club and president in 1910-12 and 1914-30.

From a public viewpoint Hordern was a spectacular and versatile character with a zest for living. Tall, robust, good-looking and well-dressed, he was described as 'the last of the elegant Edwardians'. To one he could converse on silks and satins, to another on butter-fat, on both with the knowledge of a connoisseur. He was knighted in 1919 and appointed K.B.E. in 1938. Lady Hordern avoided the limelight and devoted herself to charitable works and her gardens at Retford Park and Babworth House. She was a foundation trustee in 1938 of Morton National Park where the Lady Hordern Falls honour her interest.

In 1946 Hordern injured his hip and became a semi-invalid; social changes annoyed him. He was a diabetic and an early user of insulin. On 3 June 1956 he died at Babworth House and was cremated after a service at St Mark's, Darling Point. His estate was valued for probate at £279 615. He was survived by his son Samuel (1909-1960) and by two daughters.

Anthony was educated at St Mark's Crescent Grammar School and in England at Hitchin Grammar School, Hertfordshire, and Worcester College, Oxford, in 1907-08. After returning to Sydney he worked in Anthony Hordern's and its offices in London and New York; he sold his interest in the store in 1924. He had married Viola Sydney (d. 1929), daughter of Brigadier General Edmund Bingham, R.E., on 27 February 1911 at St Paul's Cathedral, Melbourne. In 1915 he sailed for Egypt to assist the Australian Red Cross commissioner (Sir) Adrian Knox [q.v.]. Granted the relative honorary rank of major in March 1917, he went on to France. Appointed C.B.E. in 1918 he returned to Australia in December next year. He was again a Red Cross commissioner in World War II.

In 1910 Hordern had bought rich land at Bowral where he built Milton Park, created a model farm with Shorthorn, Guernsey and later polled Hereford cattle and Romney Marsh sheep, and established a now famous garden. He leased Wilton Park near Picton (1909-27) where he continued the breeding of horses (established for Anthony Hordern's delivery carts) with thoroughbreds, Clydesdales and Welsh ponies with the notable stallion Greylight. He took a brief interest in racing but gave up after he was criticized for running two horses in the 1921 Moonee Valley Cup. He imported and bred a variety of dogs, particularly gun dogs. Hordern owned Bywong at Gundaroo (1915-23) where he established a stud flock of Lincoln sheep which he presented to the State government, and Mungadal at Hay (1923-63) where he improved the merino flock established by C. W. Simson in 1865 with Boonooke merinos from O. R. Falkiner [q.v.8]. He later owned Wingadal at Bowna and Ulladulla at Holbrook. At all his properties he made many improvements and used his wealth to import the best stock; however it was not only his patronage that ensured their success but rigorous culling to achieve his ideal animal.

A council-member of the New South Wales Sheepbreeders' Association for nearly fifty years, Hordern was president in 1931-37 and 1954-57. He promoted interest in showing in pens of five to obtain a higher overall standard and won the Stonehaven [q.v.] Cup (for pens of five) at the Sydney Sheep Show in 1950-52 and 1956. He was also foundation chairman of the Guernsey Cattle Society of Australia and foundation president in 1931 of the Australian Pony Stud Book Society. A vice-president of the R.A.S. in 1933-58, and councillor for forty-four years, he chaired its cattle committee from 1938. He helped his brother Samuel to build up the show and, a regular exhibitor, won many major prizes with his horses and cattle. At Milton Park he bred Mandarin ducks, native and exotic finches and parrots and produced colours in budgerigars and canaries never before seen.

In his youth, Hordern was a keen polo-player with his own team, the Wanderers, and provided mounts for the Ashton brothers for their first overseas tour; later he was president of the New South Wales Polo Association. He enjoyed racing speed-boats, winning in 1912-13 the Australian speedboat championships with his *Kangaroo*, and later big-game fishing; his craft *Seeka* served with the Australian navy in World War II. He belonged to the Union, Australian, New South Wales and Royal Automobile clubs.

At All Saints' Church, Woollahra, on 3 March 1932 Hordern had married Ursula Mary Bullmore (d. 1961). She was fashion editor of the *Australian Women's Weekly* in 1946-57 and influenced noteworthy changes to the Milton Park landscape. In the 1950s they built a round house, designed by Guilford Bell, at Point Piper. Hordern died at his apartment at Point Piper on 18 April 1970 and was cremated with Anglican rites. He was survived by a son and one of the two daughters of his first marriage and by two daughters of the second. His estate was valued for probate at $985 048.

Affectionate and generous, he hated publicity. His eye for animals, which he loved, his skill in their breeding and unfailing vision for future trends were his greatest strength.

Pastoral Review Pty Ltd, *The pastoral homes of Australia—NSW* (Melb, 1910); T. J. Redmond, *History of Anthony Hordern and Sons . . . 1823-1932* (Syd, 1938); G. N. Griffiths, *Some houses and people of New South Wales* (Syd, 1949); NSW Sheepbreeders' Assn, *The Australian merino* (Syd, 1955); H. Tanner, *The great gardens of Australia* (Melb, 1976); M. H. Ellis, *The Beef Shorthorn in Australia* (Syd, 1932); Roy Agr Soc (NSW), *R.A.S. Annual*, 1911, 1912, 1914, 1915, 1919; *Lone Hand*, 1 Mar 1919; Welsh Pony & Cob Society (Aust), *Journal*, 1981; *Evening News* (Syd), 14 Aug 1909; *SMH*, 8 Apr 1912, 25 May 1918, 1 Jan, 25 Dec 1919, 25 Feb, 10 Mar 1920, 24 Feb 1923, 4 July 1924, 21 Apr 1926, 11 Mar 1927, 3 Sept 1930, 10 July 1931, 22, 23, 25 Mar 1937, 8 Jan, 9 June 1938, 21 Sept 1940, 4 Nov 1941, 4 Feb 1944, 2 Apr 1950, 30 May

1952; *Punch* (Melb), 2 July 1925; *Daily Telegraph* (Syd), 24 Mar, 4 June 1956, 5 Mar 1960; *Sun Herald* and *Sunday Telegraph* (Syd), 19 Apr 1970.

CAROLINE SIMPSON

HORE-RUTHVEN, ALEXANDER GORE ARKRIGHT; *see* GOWRIE

HORGAN, JOHN (1834-1907), lawyer, was born on 16 July 1834 at Macroom, Cork, Ireland, son of John Horgan, shopkeeper, and his wife Elizabeth, née Murphy. Educated at Macroom and Cork, he was articled in 1856 to a solicitor and practised from 1861, becoming honorary secretary of the Cork law society. An ardent Home Ruler, he was political agent for Joseph Ronayne, the parliamentarian.

With his wife Mary, née Horan, whom he had married on 9 March 1859, and eight children, Horgan migrated to Sydney in 1875. Admitted to practice on 25 March 1876, he spent two years at West Maitland and moved to Wagga Wagga in 1879. Following the loss of a libel suit launched by him over criticism of his fees, he was bankrupted early in 1880. Soon after his 19-year-old son died in February 1881, Horgan moved to Perth.

He rapidly won a reputation there as a working-class champion, acting often for minimal fees. Active in the Perth Working Men's Club, then an important forum for those with grievances, he campaigned energetically for repeal of the draconian Master and Servant Act. In June 1886 Horgan with R. S. Haynes and J. McF. Lapsley [qq.v.] formed the colony's first Eight Hours Association. At a by-election for the Legislative Council seat of Perth, he finished second in a three-way contest. His good showing alarmed many because he had campaigned on a radical programme which included the immediate introduction of responsible government, payment of members, manhood suffrage, a land tax, triennial parliaments and a single-chamber legislature. Still more alarming was his acrimonious criticism of the government and its supporters. He described the Weld Club as a 'pot house', the important families as 'the six hungry families', hungry for land and wealth, and Bishop Salvado [q.v.2] as the colony's largest land-grabber and squatter. This sort of platform demagoguery, new to Western Australia, led to a successful suit for libel by police magistrate G. W. Leake [q.v.5], with a £500 fine and costs.

In May 1888 after an economic recession leading to the suspension of major public works, and a wave of immigration caused by the Kimberley gold rush and private railway construction, Horgan capitalized on a series of controversial political incidents (including the sacking and subsequent reinstatement of the popular chief justice (Sir) Alexander Onslow [q.v.5]) and captured the blue-ribbon Legislative Council seat of Perth from the Anglican lawyer-pastoralist Septimus Burt [q.v.7]. His three-vote victory led Governor Broome [q.v.3] to advise the Imperial government to be cautious about granting self-government to the colony. Horgan, he wrote, belongs to 'the extreme radical party' and 'deals considerably in personal abuse'.

Horgan's victory caused town and country conservatives to mobilize fully for the 1889 election. Radicals (including Horgan) and liberals were defeated everywhere and the constitution bill was eventually drafted by conservatives determined to prevent men like Horgan from entering parliament. In private practice until his death, he was briefly in partnership with Richard Pennefather, then in 1890-96 with Frederick Moorhead and finally with Michael Lavan. The partnerships usually foundered on the rock of Horgan's ungovernable temper. Subsequently he practised alone.

After the death of his wife in 1889, Horgan married Mary Ann Coffey on 7 February 1891 in the Catholic Cathedral, Perth. He revisited Ireland in 1897 and was for a time solicitor to Bishop Gibney [q.v.8]. Horgan died on 8 July 1907, survived by his wife and eight of the twelve children of his first marriage. He died in debt and was buried in East Perth cemetery.

C. T. Stannage, *The people of Perth* (Perth, 1979); *WA Bulletin*, May-June 1888; *Western Mail* (Perth), 13 July 1907; *Magistrate* (Perth), 14 Sept 1930.

TOM STANNAGE

HORN, WILLIAM AUSTIN (1841-1922), mining magnate, pastoralist and politician, was born on 26 February 1841 at Menaroo, New South Wales, eldest son of Edward Kirk Horn, storekeeper, and his wife Emily, née Austin. They moved to South Australia in 1852 where Horn entered the Collegiate School of St Peter. Afterwards he worked on (Sir) Walter Hughes's [q.v.4] property at Wallaroo and while he was there a shepherd, Patrick Ryan, found copper ore. Hughes learned from Ryan the exact location, then contacted Horn, who had started on a trip, asking him to return. A rival syndicate had left for Adelaide seventeen hours before to lodge a claim; Hughes told Horn to try to reach Adelaide before 10 a.m. the next day to forestall them. After a marathon ride of

164 miles (264 km) in twenty-two hours, Horn reached the lands office but found the rival syndicate there. When the clerk opened the office he recognized Horn and processed his claim first. The other syndicate also lodged a claim and the matter was investigated by a select committee which reported against Hughes but left it to be settled in court. Hughes settled out of court, paying thousands of pounds for one of the richest mines in Australia; Horn became a shareholder.

In 1863 he bought the station Maryvale between Streaky and Venus bays, and 15 000 sheep, with (Sir) John Morphett [q.v.2] and W. Mair. Several disastrous seasons put the property heavily in debt and financial backing was withdrawn. Horn went to his bank but refused their terms. He poured more money into the venture until at last the tide turned; his perseverance in adversity became proverbial. While at Maryvale he made many trips buying land in South Australia and New South Wales; two of his stations, Poolommaca and Mundi, bordered on the still undiscovered Broken Hill.

In 1872-74 Horn visited England to raise money for a mining venture, and matriculated at Worcester College, Oxford. Though he never took a degree he continued to read the classics. In 1878 he travelled in New Zealand and on 24 September next year in St Andrews Church, Walkerville, Adelaide, married Penelope Elizabeth Belt; they had two daughters and six sons.

Horn's capital developed the Mutooroo copper mines and he helped to form the Octagon Syndicate to explore and prospect Western Australian mining areas. In New South Wales, when discoveries of silver were made east of Umberumberka in the Barrier Ranges, the town of Silverton sprang up in 1882 and Horn was a director of the Silverton mine. He and others built the Silverton Tramway, on the same gauge as the South Australian Railways, hoping that they would eventually be connected. Next year when Broken Hill was discovered he became a shareholder in the Broken Hill Proprietary Co.

Horn believed that the men best fitted for politics were those 'with a stake in the country and leisure to attend to its interests'. He entered the South Australian House of Assembly for Flinders in 1887. He favoured selling land on deferred payments. For public works he advocated that interest be paid on unpaid instalments and this money be added to general revenue; he supported the importation of coloured labour into the Northern Territory and opposed payment of members and further taxation. His caustic sarcasm enlivened parliamentary debates.

After one series of bad seasons farmers unsuccessfully petitioned the government for a wheat subsidy. Horn had supported the petition and he was said to have lent seed wheat to every farmer in his constituency. All repaid him except one man who was unable to do so; Horn bought his holding and returned it to the farmer as a gift. He retired from politics in 1893.

He donated three statues to Adelaide: 'Venus of Canova' on North Terrace; the Farnese 'Hercules' in Pennington Garden West; and 'The Athlete' in Angas Gardens. In 1890 he had given the National Gallery of South Australia the famous Heinrich Heuzenroeder collection of coins, comprising 11 000 specimens, some of which were Roman.

In 1894 he organized and equipped the Horn Scientific Expedition to Central Australia which hoped to find evidence of older forms of life in the MacDonnell Ranges. Horn accompanied the party as far as Idracowra on the Finke River; it was led by explorer and surveyor C. A. Winnecke and included Professor (Sir) Baldwin Spencer [q.v.], and Horn's brother-in-law F. W. Belt. They reached Larapinta Land and Spencer edited, and published in 1896, a four-volume report detailing their geological, biological, botanical and ethnological discoveries.

Horn was a director of the Kuala Selangor Rubber Co. Ltd and for nearly fifty years helped to develop parts of Papua, the Malay States, India and Ceylon (Sri Lanka). In 1896 he relinquished all his official positions in Adelaide and from 1898 lived at Wimbledon Park House in England, returning briefly to Adelaide in 1901 and in 1907 to sell his Walkerville house, Holmwood. He held that an Australian was simply an Englishman born in the sun.

Horn published two books, *Bush echoes* (1901), verse of the stockwhip-and-saddle-school, and *Notes by a nomad* (1906). He was a keen woodcarver and his self-portrait etched in a rock remains in the garden of his old summer home, Wairoa, at Mount Lofty. The house was used in the 1975 film *Picnic at Hanging Rock*. In England Horn was a director of the London board of the Bank of Adelaide and other companies. He donated £1000 to (Sir) Douglas Mawson's [q.v.] Australasian Antarctic Expedition of 1911-14 and contributed to various World War I causes. Although a prominent capitalist, he had supported the London dock strikers. He refused a knighthood, as he objected to 'titular distinction being made a matter of diplomacy, personal influence and barter' but one of his sons said that he would only have accepted a hereditary title.

Horn was both shy and aggressive. He did not suffer fools gladly but was able, humane and cultured, 'one of the most generous public men' in South Australian history. He died on 23 December 1922 in London and his estate, sworn for probate in England and Australia at over £200 000, was left to his family.

J. J. Pascoe (ed), *History of Adelaide and vicinity* (Adel, 1901); W. B. Spencer and F. J. Gillen, *Across Australia* (Lond, 1912); J. M. Brown, *'The Almonds' of Walkerville* (Adel, 1970); *Quiz* (Adel), 1 Aug, 14 Nov 1890, 23 July 1892; *Critic* (Adel), 23 Nov 1901; *Observer* (Adel), 21 Sept 1889; *Advertiser* (Adel), 3 May 1894; *Register* (Adel), 19 Apr 1919, 27 Dec 1922; *The Times*, 28 Dec 1922; *Sunday Telegraph* (Syd), 5 Nov 1961.

JUDITH M. BROWN

HORNIMAN, VICARY (1863-1929), civil servant and sportsman, was born on 28 November 1863 at Victoria Street, Sydney, fourth surviving son and twelfth child of Robert John Horniman from Devon, England, and his Scottish wife Catherine, née McLachlan. His father taught at Rev. J. D. Lang's [q.v.2] Australian College, then started his own school where Vicary was educated. Horniman entered the Treasury on 23 January 1882 as a clerk, rising to the positions of assistant paymaster in November 1915 and paymaster on 1 July 1923, but was temporarily transferred to the Resumed Properties Department, of which he became manager in December 1924. He retired in 1927.

Commissioned in the 1st Infantry Regiment of New South Wales in January 1890, Horniman was promoted captain in 1898. His militia service ended when the regiment passed to Commonwealth control in 1901, but he continued to parade a military-looking moustache. A keen sportsman, Horniman rowed regularly till late in life, although he never represented his colony or country. He was a foundation member of the North Shore Rowing Club (1879) and its honorary secretary or captain for forty-three years, and an early member of the Manly Life Saving Club (1911). However, his major contribution was in administration—he was a committee-man, starter, judge and umpire of the New South Wales Rowing Association for over a decade and its chairman in 1917-18; he was also vice-president of the New South Wales Rugby Union in 1924-27.

A strong belief in amateurism guided Horniman's involvement. For twenty-seven years he was an active honorary director of the New South Wales Sports Club Ltd, formed in 1896 to support amateur sporting clubs with a central location for meetings, the promotion of 'honourable practice' in sport and the repression of 'malpractice'. The club was the patron of State boxing and wrestling championships and Horniman himself managed a team which toured New Zealand in 1911.

In 1912 Horniman was appointed manager of the twenty-six-member Australasian Olympic team to Stockholm. All but one of the athletes earned diplomas of merit; Fanny Durack [q.v.8] and the men's free-style relay team won gold medals. In July, before the Olympics, the Australian Eight had won the Grand Challenge Cup rowed at Henley-on-Thames, England, defeating the English club, Leander. However at Stockholm Leander turned the tables on the Australians. Predictably, Horniman rebuked the irate Australian coach for his 'ungentlemanly' outburst when he complained about the course and the winning crew. Yet Horniman was enough of a nationalist to reject any suggestion that Australian Olympic athletes should be absorbed into an Empire team. He remained interested in Olympic affairs and attended the 1928 Amsterdam games as an official.

At St Thomas' Anglican Church, North Sydney, on 20 November 1894, Horniman had married Mary Cosgrove. Survived by their son, he died at his home at Manly on 5 September 1929. He was buried with Anglican rites in Manly cemetery.

NSW Sports Clubs, *Fiftieth anniversary, 1896-1946* (Syd, 1946); R. G. Harris, *Heroes of the surf* (Syd, 1961); *Rugby Annual*, 1925, 1930; Nth Shore Hist Soc, *J*, Feb 1979, p 2; *SMH*, 8 July, 24 Sept, 10, 30 Oct 1912, 6, 7 Sept 1929; *Referee*, 11 Sept 1929; NSW Sports Clubs, Annual Report, 1900-09, and NSW Rowing Assn, Annual Report, 1907-31.

RICHARD BROOME
CECIL J. BROOME

HORNUNG, ERNEST WILLIAM (1866-1921), writer, was born on 7 June 1866 at Middlesbrough, Yorkshire, youngest of eight children of Hungarian-born John Peter Hornung, iron and coal merchant, and his wife Harriet, née Armstrong. Throughout his life he was known to family and friends as 'Willie'; he was an asthmatic. In December 1883, before he had reached the upper sixth, Hornung left Uppingham School and arrived in Sydney next year. He became tutor to the large family of Cecil Joseph Parsons, owner of Mossgiel station in the Riverina and brother-in-law of Thomas Russell [q.v.6]. Opportunity to travel in Victoria probably followed.

Hornung returned to England in February 1886 when his father's business and health were both in jeopardy. He worked as a journalist and began writing stories and novels, several with Australian settings. On 27 September 1893 in London, with Catholic rites, he married Constance Aimée Monica, sister of his friend (Sir) Arthur Conan Doyle.

Like Doyle, Hornung is best known as a crime writer, the creator of Raffles 'the amateur cracksman'. But by no means all of his many stories have criminal plots. His short period in Australia apparently had a crucial influence on his work not only by supplying him with raw material but by developing the attitudes which direct his most incisive writing. His earliest novels employ the Australian experience as a lens to examine British society for flaws. In *A bride from the bush* (1890) and *Tiny Luttrell* (1893) Australian women travel to England and their direct vigour soon exposes the hypocrisy of British society. *The unbidden guest* (1894) shows that a lower-class immigrant actress who impersonates an English lady visiting Australia has more 'civility' and 'kindness' than the real article. Hornung's other Australian-based novels lack this sharp treatment of British social life. They are usually bush melodramas with thoughtful moments, such as *The boss of Taroomba* (1894) or *The belle of Toorak* (1900). *The rogue's march* (1896) is a historical romance about convict days with a clear view of cruelty and corruption.

Hornung apparently moved towards the social satire of Raffles through an Australian character Stingaree, who appears in *Irralie's bushranger* (1896) and in short stories (*Stingaree*, 1905). A gentleman as well as a thief, Stingaree casts doubt on conventional responses to both figures. Raffles, who began his criminal career when visiting Victoria with a touring English cricket team, is himself well bred—Eton, Oxford and the Marylebone Cricket Club. Being penniless he turns to crime, made easy by his athletic daring and his social connexions. He and Bunny (his former fag, now a hack writer and not unlike Hornung the journalist) are a deliberate reversal of Holmes and Watson, but the lasting success of the stories shows they are more than a family joke. Raffles ironically demonstrates that gentlemanliness may have nothing at all to do with moral or even economic substance.

In spite of his cool treatment of English society, Hornung remained a respectable literary and sporting gentleman. Raffles too fell into line and did the decent thing by being killed for Queen and country in the South African War. Hornung arranged ambulance services in World War I; after the death of his son at Ypres he took up work in France with the Young Men's Christian Association and wrote some grief-stricken prose and poetry. Ill health, which had orig-

inally led to his Australian visit, returned after the war and he died at St Jean de Luz, France, on 22 March 1921. His obituarists emphasized his kindness and generosity: Doyle later recalled him as 'a Dr Johnson without the learning but with a finer wit'.

A. C. Doyle, *Memories and adventures* (Lond, 1924); S. J. Kunitz and H. Haycraft, *Twentieth century authors 1600-1900* (NY, 1942); J. D. Carr, *Life of Arthur Conan Doyle* (Lond, 1949); P. W. Friedrich, *Australia in western imaginative prose writings, 1600-1960* (Chapel Hill, US, 1976); B. M. Collin, *J. P. Hornung; a family portrait* (Orpington, Eng, 1971); *Australasian*, 2 July 1921; *The Times*, 24 Mar 1921.   STEPHEN KNIGHT

HORSFALL, ALFRED HERBERT (1871-1944), military surgeon, was born on 29 January 1871 at Fitzroy, Melbourne, third son of Yorkshire-born Jonas Horsfall, head teacher at the United Methodist Common School, Fitzroy, and his wife Emily, née Nichols, from Tasmania. He attended Scotch College and the University of Melbourne (M.B., B.S., 1893), then, after a posting as resident surgeon at the (Royal) Melbourne Hospital, moved to Newcastle, New South Wales, where he was a medical practitioner and medical superintendent at Newcastle Hospital. He contributed to local public affairs, becoming an alderman and president of the Newcastle Scientific Society.

In January 1900 Horsfall was commissioned lieutenant in the 2nd New South Wales Army Medical Corps Contingent which had been speedily raised for service in the South African War. Arriving at East London late in February, the unit was soon in action, Horsfall being the first to come under fire when he rode to the assistance of a wounded policeman. During his twelve-month tour he was in operations in the Orange Free State, the Transvaal and the Orange River Colony. He was also attached briefly to the 1st Battalion, Cameron Highlanders, as medical officer, and for his service in South Africa was mentioned in dispatches and awarded the Distinguished Service Order. On returning home he resumed practice at Newcastle and on 21 April 1903, at All Souls Anglican Church, Leichhardt, Sydney, married Gertrude Emily Stokes.

Horsfall served with the Australian Army Medical Corps in the Newcastle district until his resignation in the rank of major in 1914. During World War I he enlisted in the British Army (Territorials). In October 1915 he was appointed a major in the Royal Army

Medical Corps and worked at Salonika, Greece, until February 1916. He became officer-in-charge of sanitation in the Suez Canal zone and until January 1917 was also a surgeon specialist at Alexandria, Egypt. He was invalided to England from January to August 1917, then served as a surgeon specialist with casualty clearing stations in Palestine until he was again evacuated with illness. From March to October 1918 he was officer-in-charge of the surgical division, 82nd General Hospital, Salonika.

After the war Horsfall settled in England, living at various times in Kent, Nottingham and London, but for the rest of his life he travelled widely, studying anthropology, ethnology and politico-economic conditions. He had a deep attachment to the British Empire and gave lectures and wrote pamphlets stressing the British character of the Dominions and promoting migration within the Empire. In 1923-26 he visited Australia, advocating migration and closer settlement. He became a lecturer for the Social and Political Education League and a member of the Royal Institute of International Affairs. Survived by his wife, son and daughter, he died on 26 November 1944 in London.

J. C. Redpath et al, *Story of South Africa* (Syd, 1902); Aust Defence Dept, *Official records of the Australian military contingents to the war in South Africa*, P. L. Murray ed (Melb, 1911); Univ Melb, *Record of active service* (Melb, 1926); *London Gazette*, 27 Sept 1901.   ANTHONY D. WHITE

HOSKINS, CHARLES HENRY (1851-1926), and SIR CECIL HAROLD (1889-1971), iron and steel manufacturers, were father and son. Charles was born on 26 April 1851 in the City of London, third son of John Hoskins, gunsmith, and his wife Wilmot Eliza, née Thompson. He reached Melbourne with his family in the *Barrackpore* in February 1853, and went to school there. After his father's death the family moved to Smythesdale, near Ballarat. Hoskins began work as a mail boy, tried his luck on the goldfields and worked as an assistant in Connelly's ironmongery store at Sandhurst (Bendigo).

In 1876 Hoskins joined his brother George (1847-1926) in Sydney in a small engineering workshop at Hay Street, Ultimo, which became G. & C. Hoskins Ltd in 1903. Despite their lack of capital, they gradually became known as skilled and ingenious craftsmen: one of their inventions, a 'Potato Thrower', was modified for a troupe of actors to use in a sensational acrobatic display.

Through hard physical work the brothers began to prosper mildly. Charles took over financing and management of the business, leaving George to supervise the workshops. On 22 December 1881, with Congregational forms, Charles married Emily Wallis (d. 1928), who had been brought up as a Quaker. About 1889 the firm moved to larger premises in Darling (Wattle) Street and established a foundry, pipe-works and boiler shop. They achieved a breakthrough when they secured the contract to lay and join the six-foot (183 cm) main for the Sydney water-supply. In the 1890s they opened a branch in Melbourne to make steel pipes and in 1898, after negotiations, the Hoskins and Mephan Ferguson [q.v.4] shared the contract to manufacture (in Western Australia) and lay 350 miles (563 km) of pipes for the Perth to Coolgardie water-supply, designed by C. Y. O'Connor [q.v.].

From the early 1880s Charles Hoskins was anxious about the small size of the Australian market and his own dependence on imported raw materials. A convinced protectionist, he helped to found the New South Wales Chamber of Manufactures in 1885 and to reconstitute it in 1895, when he became president. He regarded the protectionist and manufacturing causes as inseparable, served on the committee of the Protection Union of New South Wales and was closely associated with (Sir) George Dibbs [q.v.4] in the National Protection Association. No friend of trade unions, Hoskins firmly believed in freedom of contract and opposed a minimum wage. He was a leader in the Iron Trades Employers' Association of New South Wales and was prominent in the foundation of the Employers' Federation of New South Wales in 1903.

Although in 1899 the Hoskins refused William Sandford's [q.v.] offer to sell his Esbank ironworks at Lithgow, Charles remained one of Sandford's closest friends, his largest customer and one of the few outside shareholders in William Sandford Ltd. After government efforts to save that firm in December 1907 failed, largely because of Labor pressure for nationalization and foreclosure by the Commercial Banking Co. of Sydney, Charles Hoskins was asked by the secretary for public works, C. A. Lee [q.v.], to take over the ironworks. G. & C. Hoskins accepted the offer, taking over Sandford's overdraft of £138 000, paying £14 000 to shareholders in the form of 4 per cent bonds and paying £50 000 to Sandford himself. They had acquired a blast furnace, iron and steel works, colliery, iron leaseholds at Cadia and Carcoar, stocks of raw materials, some 400 acres (162 ha) of freehold town estate at Lithgow, Eskroy Park at Bowenfels, and a seven-year government contract.

George henceforth confined his interests to the Sydney business and Charles undertook the development of the iron and steel industry. Early in January 1908 he moved with his family to Lithgow. He soon found that enterprise and business ability were not enough. The plant was badly located; technological difficulties raised costs; facilities for manufacturing steel rails and structured steel were lacking; and there were other bottle-necks. By 1909, after building a new steel-furnace, a rolling-mill and a bar-mill, he realized his geographical difficulties were probably insurmountable; moreover he lacked knowledge of metallurgy and practical experience of advances in iron and steel production.

An imperious, impatient entrepreneur, Hoskins was confronted with immediate strikes when he tried to change from the contract to day-labour system of wages and the plant was closed on 10 July 1908. The company was found guilty by the Industrial Court of deliberately engineering a lock-out and fined £50 and costs; Hoskins himself was fined £10 and costs. The establishment of the Iron Trades (Lithgow) Wages Board did not improve the situation. In 1911 hostility increased when Hoskins dismissed a miners' union delegate and inflamed the ensuing strike by importing blackleg labour from Sydney. On 29 August there was a riot at the plant. The strike dragged on for nine months until April 1912, then ended in a compromise.

Even with large-scale government aid in the form of reduced freights and generous contracts for steel rails (especially for the Transcontinental Railway), Hoskins had a struggle but made many improvements such as installing electric lighting, an overhead crane and a pig-iron-breaking machine. Despite increasing competition from the Broken Hill Pty Co. Ltd's new steelworks at Newcastle, Hoskins's Lithgow works flourished during World War I: demand exceeded supply and he was called upon to manufacture many special steels that could no longer be imported, such as those required by the Commonwealth Small Arms Factory at Lithgow, spring steel, and hollow drill steel for Professor (Sir) Edgeworth David [q.v.8] to take to France; in 1915 he built a ferro-manganese furnace to aid munitions production.

In 1919 Charles bought out his brother George and the name of the company was changed in July next year to Hoskins Iron and Steel Co. Ltd. In the early 1920s the company fell steadily behind B.H.P. in technological sophistication and productivity and was crippled by freight charges. Charles retired as managing director in 1924.

In 1912 he had moved to Cadia Park, Law-son, in the Blue Mountains, where he and his wife made a beautiful garden and kept koalas, wallabies and birds. Bearded in his youth, with crisp wavy hair, he continued to sport a clipped moustache. Infatuated with cars, he owned seven in seven years, starting in 1904. Saddened by the deaths of two grown-up daughters, and of his eldest son in 1916 in an explosion at the works, he gave the land and built, for £50 000, a parish hall and the Hoskins Memorial Church (Presbyterian) at Lithgow which he did not live to see completed in 1928. Survived by his wife, two sons and three daughters, he died at his home at Elizabeth Bay, Sydney, on 14 February 1926 and was buried in the Congregational section of Rookwood cemetery. His estate was valued for probate at £12 108. He had formed a private family company, C. H. Hoskins Co. Ltd, in 1904 to look after the financial interests of his family; Kembla Building (since demolished) in Margaret Street, Sydney, was built by this company in 1924.

His second son Cecil Harold was born on 11 November 1889 at Petersham, Sydney, and was educated at King's College, Goulburn, and Newington College, Sydney. He worked for Briscoe & Co. Ltd, ironmongers of Sydney, and joined the family firm at Lithgow in 1908, becoming a director in 1912. At Burwood he married Dorothy Gwynne, daughter of Thomas Loveridge, on 1 November 1913.

In 1925 Hoskins became chairman and with his brother Arthur Sidney (1872-1959) joint managing director of the family enterprises. His father had already begun to plan to move from Lithgow and to build integrated steelworks at Port Kembla where he had acquired 400 acres (162 ha) in 1924. After complex negotiations in 1927 the State government agreed conditionally to build a railway connecting Port Kembla with the main southern line at Moss Vale, and construction of a blast-furnace and deep-water wharf began. That year Hoskins went overseas seeking technical information and new plant; he acquired the rights to manufacture and sell de Laval centrifugally spun pipes. Most of the new plant was erected to the latest American or German designs. To finance the operations, in 1928 Hoskins formed a new company, Australian Iron and Steel Ltd with Baldwins Ltd of England, Dorman Long & Co. and Howard Smith [q.v.6] Ltd; he became chairman and joint managing director of the new company. Hard-hit by the Depression, A.I. & S. was sued by the government for breach of contract in 1932 and had to pay £25 000. In 1935 A.I. & S. became a subsidiary of B.H.P., which exchanged 750 000 £1 shares for the company. Hoskins remained general manager of A.I. & S. until 1950 and a director until 1959.

Hoskins had moved to Sydney in 1924 and became a local director of the Royal Insurance Co. Ltd, a director of the United Insurance Co. Ltd and chairman of Southern Portland Cement Ltd in 1928-57. In 1929 he joined the board of the Australian Mutual Provident Society Ltd and was chairman in 1947-60. He was a strong protectionist and a council-member of the Chamber of Manufactures of New South Wales in 1925-46 and an executive member of the All for Australia League. Closely linked with the United Australia Party, he was a good friend of (Sir) Robert Menzies. He was also chairman of the Institute of Public Affairs (New South Wales). He was knighted in 1960.

From 1937 the Hoskins family lived at Invergowrie, at Exeter in the southern highlands. Here they created a famous garden and during World War II accommodated many allied servicemen and women on recreation or sick leave; here too he could enjoy his recreations of farming and motoring. In 1949 they moved to Cardona at Moss Vale; he remained a member of the Australian and Union clubs, Sydney. Active in scouting from the 1920s, he was foundation president of the South Coast and Tablelands area of the Boy Scouts' Association in 1946-66. In his retirement he wrote *The Hoskins saga* (1969). Survived by his wife, four sons and two daughters, he died at Moss Vale on 8 March 1971 and was cremated with Anglican rites. His estate was valued for probate at $133 697.

His brother Arthur Sidney was joint managing director of Hoskins Iron and Steel and supervised the construction of the Port Kembla steelworks. He remained a director of A.I. & S. and manager at Port Kembla. He had married another daughter of Thomas Loveridge, Helen Madoline, in 1917; they had three sons and four daughters.

'Mr Cecil', of medium height and sturdy build, was reserved in manner and very much the senior partner. 'Mr Sid' lacked his brother's quick mind but was more approachable. Their basic knowledge and experience 'from the floor up' had been gained in their father's works among family and long-serving employees. Limited technical expertise was their main handicap and the Depression their downfall.

H. Hughes, *The Australian iron and steel industry, 1848-1962* (Melb, 1964); C. R. Hall, *The manufacturers* (Syd, 1971); *Industrial Aust and Mining Standard*, 18 Feb 1926; *ANA*, 7 Apr, 7 June 1926; *SMH*, 15 Feb 1926, 17 Nov 1928, 11 Jan 1958, 10 May 1969, 9 Mar 1971; information from Mrs N. Phillips, Canb.　　　　　GEORGE PARSONS

HOUGHTON, SYDNEY ROBERT (1893-1951), soldier and civil servant, was born on 22 March 1893 at Perth, Tasmania, fourth of seven children of Edgar Houghton, commission agent, and his wife Kate Charlotte, née Molloy. Educated at Glen Dhu State School, Launceston, he joined the telegraph branch of the Postmaster-General's Department at Launceston in 1907, transferring to Hobart in 1911.

After enlisting in the 12th Australian Infantry Regiment (militia) in 1907, Houghton joined the Australian Signals Corps in 1911 and in August 1913 was commissioned as a second lieutenant with the Australian Engineers, Hobart Signals Unit. On 28 August 1914 he was appointed to the Australian Imperial Force as a second lieutenant and signals officer in the 12th Battalion and in October embarked for active service. He was promoted lieutenant in February 1915. After a training period in Egypt the 12th took part in the Gallipoli landing on 25 April and was immediately involved in heavy fighting. Realizing the impossibility of establishing visual signalling stations, Houghton used his section as runners. His unit fought in the Turkish attack on 19 May, at Tasmania Post and Lone Pine; after the evacuation in December he returned to Egypt and from February 1916 spent six months on sick leave, rejoining his unit at Pozières, France, in August. He was promoted captain next month.

In 1917, after operations at Ligny-Thilloy, Houghton was awarded the Military Cross for 'conspicuous daring and initiative under fire in attack at Ligny 27 February 1917 and obtaining valuable information'. While serving at Dernancourt in March he suffered further illness and in May was wounded at Ecoust-St Mein. He was in hospital through illness again in January 1918 during operations at Wulverghem, returned to his unit in March and did temporary duty as signals officer with the 9th Battalion near the Ypres–Comines Canal, returning as second-in-command of 'D' Company, 12th Battalion, in April. After another period in hospital he was wounded again on 18 September during an attack on the Hindenburg line east of Jeancourt. That day he won the Distinguished Service Order. His company 'had to advance over 2500 yards before attaining their objective. His gallant and able leadership resulted in a rapid and successful capture of each point of resistance by successive operations'. Mentioned in dispatches in July 1919, he returned to Australia that month and was demobilized in October. He retained his military interests and commanded the 12th Mixed Brigade Signals, Australian Military Forces, in 1925-33. He was placed on the reserve of officers in 1938, having been an honorary major since 1929.

Houghton had returned to the Post Office as a telegraphist until 1922 after which he worked in the Department of Taxation as inspector of entertainments until ill health forced his retirement in 1936. He was a very reserved man, largely confining his interests to the Hobart Signals Unit which later named a training ground, near Apsley, Camp Houghton in his honour. On 23 October 1919 he had married Eleanor Isabel Caulfield at St George's Anglican Church, Battery Point. They had no children. Houghton died in Hobart on 5 February 1951 and was buried in Cornelian Bay cemetery. His wife survived him.

L. Broinowski (ed), *Tasmania's war record 1914-1918* (Hob, 1921); L. M. Newton, *The story of the twelfth* (Hob, 1925); *Cyclopedia of Tasmania* (Hob, 1931); C. E. W. Bean, *The A.I.F. in France*, 1918 (Syd, 1942); *London Gazette*, 24 Apr 1917, 2 Apr, 11 July 1919; *Mercury*, 8 Feb 1951; CRSP 110 *and* CA 1635 (AAO, Hob); information from Mrs M. L. Houghton, Taroona, and Col. J. H. Hall, Kingston Beach, Tas.   MARGARET GLOVER

HOUGHTON, THOMAS JOHN (1862?-1933), printer, politician and journalist, was born probably at Manchester, England. He arrived in New South Wales about 1866 and was orphaned a few years later. In July 1875 he was apprenticed as a printer for six years to J. D. Gray and James McNaughton of the *Clarence and Richmond Examiner*, Grafton. He then entered the Government Printing Office, Sydney, serving there for nine years on the Hansard staff. He established the office's dramatic and musical society and soon joined the New South Wales Typographical Association, becoming a collector and in 1888 its delegate to the Trades and Labor Council. On 31 December 1884 at Grafton he had married Catherine Susanna Kritsch with Anglican rites.

By September 1889 Houghton (pronounced Howton) was part-time secretary of the T.L.C. at £30 a year. That month he arranged 'a monster demonstration' in the Sydney Domain on behalf of the London dock strikers, ensuring maximum publicity and successful fund-raising by arranging speakers such as Cardinal Moran and John Norton [qq.v.]. Next month he resigned because of the 'enormous increase in duties and failing health', but was persuaded to remain 'with assistance' and in December became the T.L.C.'s first full-time general secretary.

In August 1890 Houghton served on the Labor Defence Council which controlled the maritime strike in New South Wales. He and Frank Cotton [q.v.8] were on the sub-committee which, in February 1891, drafted a scheme of government for what became the Labor Electoral League. He was an important progenitor of the Labor Party in New South Wales.

Houghton had been appointed in November 1890 to the royal commission on strikes, which reported in May 1891. In June he won the Legislative Assembly seat of Glebe and became secretary of the Labor caucus. The party decided not to choose a leader, but he was elected to a committee of advice of five. An eager protectionist, he moved in the House for a plebiscite on the fiscal issue, and losing touch with his power-base, sided with (Sir) Joseph Cook [q.v.8] and other Labor parliamentarians in their battle with conference over solidarity. After a unity conference of 1894 he agreed to sign the T.L.C.'s pledge, but it was too late and, at J. C. Watson's [q.v.] insistence, the council's executive withdrew its support from Houghton. He lost as a Protectionist Labor candidate for Glebe in 1894, as an Independent in 1895 for Sydney-Pyrmont and as a free trader in 1898 for Robertson. In 1894-97 T. J. Houghton & Co., letterpress and lithographic printers, were proprietors of the *Australian Workman*. He had resigned as the Typographical Association delegate to the T.L.C. in September 1893. Houghton was active in the campaign for Federation, then went to Tasmania, returning in 1904 to Sydney.

His later career is obscure: he worked as a journalist from about 1907, and after 1912 was associated with *Commerce* and the *Australian Manufacturers' Journal*. In the 1920s he was a traveller and in 1930 a publicity agent. Survived by two sons and a daughter, he died at Artarmon on 30 August 1933 and was cremated with Anglican rites.

B. Nairn, *Civilising capitalism* (Canb, 1973); *Worker* (Syd), 2 Sept 1923; *SMH*, 2 Sept 1933.
CHRIS CUNNEEN

HOWARD, AMOS WILLIAM (1848-1930), nurseryman and pasture improvement pioneer, was born on 31 May 1848 at Silk Mills, Watford, Hertfordshire, England, son of William Howard, gardener, and his wife Ann, née Hester. On 23 July 1871 at the Wesleyan Chapel, Tendring, Essex, he married Eliza Rowe. Arriving in South Australia in 1876, Howard established a nursery in the Adelaide hills between Nairne and Littlehampton. He became clerk of the local district council, but resigned to contest a council seat which he won and held for ten years. About 1880 he joined the Glen Osmond chapter of the Oddfellows' Lodge.

In 1889, intending to purchase a cow, Howard visited Michael Daley's property adjoining the Mount Barker Springs and Nairne roads. As Daley was away, Howard 'strolled along one of the valleys . . . to fill in time until the owner returned' and was attracted by the growth of a kind of clover. It was later identified as subterranean clover, *Trifolium subterraneum* Linn., a widely variable species probably inadvertently introduced to Australia from Britain or Europe fifty or sixty years earlier, and known in the Adelaide hills since about 1880. Sir Ferdinand Mueller [q.v.5] recorded the plant as naturalized in Victoria by 1887, and it was reported from the Riverina as 'a vigorous grower' in 1896 when J. H. Maiden [q.v.] made his guarded comment: 'I know nothing against its character, except a certain aggressiveness . . . It is not an introduction which need render us uncomfortable'.

On 3 February 1906 Howard began his correspondence with the Adelaide *Advertiser*, enthusiastically extolling the virtues of the plant for improving pastures. Overcoming technical problems, he harvested the seed and offered samples to the South Australian Agriculture Bureau. By January 1907 he was able to sell 30 lb. (13.6 kg) to E. & W. Hackett, Adelaide nurserymen. Further experience with the clover prompted Howard to write to the press in 1907-09 vigorously promoting its use. By this time he and his sons were selling up to a ton (tonne) of seed annually.

State agriculture authorities made experimental sowings of the clover before 1920 and tentative recommendations concerning its use, but when superphosphate was advocated for pastures as well as for crops clover sowings responded remarkably, and the formula of 'sub and super' was widely followed. In 1923 the importation of a clover huller from the United States of America by Howard's son Cecil lifted annual seed production to over eight tons and in 1930 it was claimed that annual production of clover seed was responsible for about £50 000 coming into the Mount Barker district. By 1961 some 20 million acres (8.1 million ha) of southern Australia had been sown with subterranean clover, notwithstanding the discovery that some strains had oestrogenic properties injurious to sheep. The clover not only improved pastures but upgraded soil fertility through its nitrogen-fixing qualities.

Howard died at Beau Vale, Blakiston, on 2 March 1930, predeceased by his wife, a son and a daughter; he was buried in Blakiston cemetery, survived by three daughters and seven sons. A memorial to Howard's work on 'the most important pasture plant in Australia' was unveiled on 3 October 1963 on the Mount Barker road near the sites of his original observations and of his home. An appeal launched at the ceremony by the Australian Institute of Agricultural Science led to the establishment of the Howard memorial research fellowship in 1967. Two of the several cultivars of subterranean clover are named 'Howard' and 'Mt Barker'. A portrait is in the South Australian Archives.

D. E. Symon, *A bibliography of subterranean clover together with a descriptive introduction* (Berkshire, 1961); R. M. Moore (ed), *Australian grasslands* (Canb, 1970); M. Williams, *The making of the South Australian landscape* (Lond, 1974); Aust Inst of Agr Science, *J*, 30 (1964); *J of Agr* (SA), Nov 1936, Jan 1964; *Advertiser* (Adel), 6 Mar 1930.

L. A. GILBERT

HOWARD, ARTHUR CLIFFORD (1893-1971), inventor, was born on 4 April 1893 at Crookwell, New South Wales, eldest son of John Howard, farmer, and his first wife Mary Ellen, née Smith. After attending schools at Crookwell and Moss Vale, he studied engineering through a correspondence course while an apprentice at Moss Vale.

Encouraged by his father, who had brought the first steam tractor to Gilgandra where he had taken up a property, Howard began in 1912 experiments in rotary tillage which culminated in his invention of the rotary hoe. Using various pieces from farm machinery, he rigged a drive from the tractor engine to the shaft of a one-way notched disc cultivator. He found that the ground could be tilled without the soil-packing that occurred with normal ploughing. But the fast-spinning discs threw the soil sideways until he developed an L-shaped blade mounted on widely spaced flanges fixed to a small-diameter rotor.

Howard, with a fellow apprentice, Everard McCleary (d. 1918), established a company to manufacture rotary hoe cultivators, but soon found that there was little demand for their small model. Work on a larger model was interrupted by World War I. Unfit for active service, Howard went to England under a scheme initiated by (Sir) Henry Barraclough [q.v.7] to work on munitions and aircraft engines.

Unable to interest English agricultural implement firms in his ideas, Howard returned to Moss Vale in 1919. Next year he tested and patented his rotary hoe cultivator. It consisted of a main frame carrying an internal combustion engine and a subsidiary frame carrying five rotary hoe cultivators.

In March 1922 Howard formed a syndicate, Austral Auto Cultivators Pty Ltd. The firm moved to Northmead, Sydney, in 1927. He continued to develop his ideas, building models to suit particular terrains and types

of farming, a rotavator to fit a Fordson tractor and several types of hand-controlled
machines. His DH22 tractor, designed in
1927 to work with rotary hoes, initiated the
first large-scale production of tractors in
Australia.

Despite reduced sales during the Depression, Howard raised new capital for the
company, now known as Howard Auto Cultivators. Finding it difficult to meet overseas demand stimulated by a successful export drive, he arranged a ten-year licence
with an English firm to make his machines
for markets outside Australia. In 1937 unauthorized design alterations took Howard
to England where the licence was terminated. He returned briefly to Australia to resign his position of managing director at
Howard Auto Cultivators and in July 1938
formed an English company, Rotary Hoes
Ltd, which established branches in the
United States of America, South Africa,
Germany, France, Italy, Spain, Australia
and New Zealand. It later became a holding
company for a wholly owned subsidiary,
Howard Rotavator Co. Ltd, to which it transferred the manufacture and distribution of
rotavators, manure spreaders, trench diggers and soil stabilization machinery. The
company received the Queen's award to
industry in 1966.

Howard had married Daisy May Hayes at
the Methodist Church, Moss Vale, on 19 September 1925. After moving to England, they
lived at Upminster, Essex. A determined,
quiet but outgoing man, devoted to his family, Howard was a practical engineer who
combined business acumen with vision and
outstanding inventive ability. As well as
being managing director of Rotary Hoes Ltd
until 1970, he was a director of G.D.H. Ltd,
Harleston Industries Ltd, Howard (Forge &
Foundry) Ltd and Howard Rotavator Co.
Ltd. In 1970 he was appointed C.B.E. He died
on 4 January 1971 at Harold Wood Hospital,
Essex, leaving an estate in England valued
for probate at £111 476. He was survived by
his wife, two daughters and a son, who became managing director of Howard Rotavator Pty Ltd in Australia.

F. Wheelhouse, *Digging stick to rotary hoe* (Melb,
1966); L. W. Port, *Australian inventors* (Syd, 1978);
Power Farming and Better Farming Digest, Feb
1971; *The Times* (Lond), 5 Jan 1971; biog file (NL);
Aust patent and patent application record
18,137/20 (Patents Office, Canb); information
from Mr John Howard, Northmead, Sydney.

DIANE LANGMORE

HOWARD, HENRY (1859-1933), Methodist minister, was born on 21 January 1859
in Melbourne, son of Henry Howard, accountant, and his wife Mary Ann, née

Graham. Little is known of his childhood but
in later sermons Howard sometimes re-
ferred to the penurious circumstances of his
early years. At 17 he underwent a religious
conversion through the preaching of a
leading Wesleyan minister, Dr Joseph Dare.
He became a local preacher and four years
later was accepted as a candidate for the
Wesleyan ministry. After a year at Wesley
College, Melbourne, under the Irish
Methodist scholar, Dr James Swanton
Waugh [q.v.6], he was appointed in 1881 to
Warragul. This was followed by terms in the
Wesleyan circuits of Hotham, Merino,
Prahran, Warragul (a second time), Haw-
thorn and Ballarat. In this twenty-year
period Howard became 'a preacher of great
acceptance and power'. On 4 April 1885 at
Carlton Howard married Sarah Jane
Reynolds (d. 1918).

In 1902 he was transferred to the South
Australia Conference of the Methodist
Church and was appointed to the Pirie
Street Church in Adelaide, the 'cathedral'
church of South Australian Methodism.
Under Howard's ministry it drew each Sunday evening a congregation of over one
thousand, including many of the State's
leading citizens. Tall and bearded with an
organ-like voice he often spoke at civic and
community gatherings. In 1913 he was
president of the Methodist Conference in
South Australia.

During World War I Howard campaigned
strongly for the allied cause, speaking at recruiting and conscription rallies in South
Australia and Victoria. His eloquent identification of the battles in France with the
battle of God proved disturbing to later in-
terpreters of the church's role in society.

After nineteen years at Pirie Street
Howard was granted 'permission to rest' by
the South Australia conference in 1921.
Visiting England where his son Stanford
was a Rhodes Scholar, he was soon invited
to preach in London's largest Methodist
churches. Eventually he became minister of
the Hampstead Wesleyan Church while still
retaining membership in the South Australia conference.

In 1926 Howard was invited to become co-
pastor of the famous Fifth Avenue Presbyterian Church in New York City. He was to
be the preacher while his colleague would
attend to matters of administration. Howard
resigned from the Methodist ministry and
joined the Presbyterian Church. His pulpit
work became as highly acclaimed in the
United States of America as it had been in
Australia and Britain. He was awarded two
honorary degrees, a D.Litt. by South-
western University (Memphis) in 1928 and
a D.D. by New York University in 1930.

Howard visited Australia in 1931 to celebrate his ministerial jubilee. He preached in leading churches in Melbourne and Adelaide and in his first circuit, Warragul.

In 1933 a few months before his projected retirement from Fifth Avenue, Howard became ill with cancer of the throat. He sailed for England, where three of his children were living, and died on 29 June 1933, two days after his arrival. He was buried at Hendon Park cemetery in London. Three of his four sons and a daughter survived him.

Howard published thirteen books, mainly collections of sermons, between 1907 and 1933, some in England and some in America. The best-known volumes, widely read by ministers, were *The raiment of the soul, The conning-tower of the soul, The Shepherd Psalm* and *The Church which is His body.*

Howard was unquestionably one of the greatest preachers in the history of Australian Protestantism. Without any elaborate promotional organization he was able over more than thirty years to attract and maintain capacity congregations. As an orator he excelled in the use of poetry, vivid metaphors and illustrations drawn from a wide range of contemporary literature. He was an expository preacher, standing in the dominant liberal Protestant tradition of his time and accepting readily the literary-historical analysis of the Bible.

W. Hunt (ed), *Methodist ministerial index for Australasia* (Melb, 1914); H. Copeland, *The path of progress* (Warragul, Vic, 1934); Methodist Church (Vic and Tas), *Minutes of the annual conference*, 1902; *Aust Christian Cwlth*, 8 Oct 1915; *New York Times*, 11 June 1930, 30 June, 1, 2, 4 July 1933; *SMH*, 11 Oct 1924, 6, 9 July 1931; *Argus*, 1, 3, 10 July 1933; Church and newspaper references supplied by Miss E. A. Kraeger, official historian, Fifth Avenue Presbyterian Church, New York City.   ARNOLD D. HUNT

HOWCHIN, WALTER (1845-1937), geologist and clergyman, was born on 12 January 1845 at Lakenham, Norwich, Norfolk, England, one of eleven children of Rev. Richard Howchin, Primitive Methodist minister, and his wife Mary Ann Ward, née Goose. He left the Academy, King's Lynn, at 12 to become a junior clerk in London; then, joining his father at Great Yarmouth, he was apprenticed in the printing trade. In his spare time he studied for the ministry and was admitted to the Primitive Methodist Society at King's Lynn in 1860; he was called to his first circuit at Shotley Bridge, Durham, on 16 October 1864. On 25 August 1869 at the Primitive Methodist Chapel, Howsham, Lincolnshire, he married Esther Gibbons; they had one son and two daughters.

During his ministry in Northumberland, Howchin became interested in geology and, through his association with H. B. Brady, in the study of foraminifera. His first papers, published in church journals in 1874-75 were on scientific deep-sea dredging. In 1876 he collaborated with Brady in a monograph on Carboniferous and Permian foraminifera and on 6 November 1878 he was admitted a fellow of the Geological Society of London.

At this time Howchin developed lung disease, probably tuberculosis, and was forced to retire from the ministry. On medical advice he migrated to Australia with his family on 27 August 1881 and settled in Adelaide. His health restored, he was elected to the Royal Society of South Australia in 1883, beginning an association of fifty-three years: he was editor for most of the time until 1933, president in 1894-96 and published seventy-seven, mostly geological, papers in the *Transactions*, the first in 1884, on South Australian Cretaceous foraminifera.

Although he remained an ordained minister of the Methodist Church and occasionally took the pulpit as a supernumerary, Howchin never held a circuit in South Australia. Within the Church, at a time of controversy following the publication of Darwin's works, he was regarded both as a man of science and as a humble Christian engaged in the reconciliation of science and religion. He enlisted the help of friends among the clergy to collect and record material and demonstrated the use of the microscope to students.

In his early years in Adelaide Howchin worked as a journalist and in 1886-1901 as secretary of the Adelaide Children's Hospital. In 1901-23 he was a governor of the Public Library, Museum and Art Gallery and was subsequently honorary palaeontologist to the museum. He was lecturer in mineralogy at the Adelaide School of Mines in 1899-1904 and, following the death of Professor Ralph Tate [q.v.6], he was appointed lecturer in geology and palaeontology at the University of Adelaide in 1902; in 1918 he was designated honorary professor. On retirement in 1920, when he retained the title of professor, he continued his extremely productive work in geology. Short with a white beard, in old age he still searched vigorously in the field for specimens. From 1894 he was closely associated with (Sir) Edgeworth David [q.v.8].

With the exception of Tate's pioneering work on the Tertiary Period, Howchin laid the foundation of South Australian stratigraphy. His great contributions were first, tracing the extent of and describing the two great glaciations affecting South Australia, the oldest in the Precambrian (which Howchin believed to be Cambrian) and the other in the Permo-Carboniferous; and second, the clear definition of the stratigraphic sequence in the Adelaide geosyncline. His book *The geology of South Australia* (1918) remained a student text for forty years. In 1925-30 he contributed to the series of handbooks on the flora and fauna of South Australia *The building of Australia and the succession of life, with special reference to South Australia*. A list of his scientific works was published in the *Transactions* of the Royal Society of South Australia in 1933.

In 1914 the Geological Society of London awarded Howchin a moiety of the Lyell fund and in 1934 the Lyell medal. He was awarded the (W. B.) Clarke [q.v.3] medal by the Royal Society of New South Wales in 1907 and the Ferdinand von Mueller [q.v.5] medal by the Australasian Association for the Advancement of Science in 1913; he was also the first recipient of the Royal Society of South Australia's Sir Joseph Verco [q.v.] medal in 1929. Several fossils were named after him.

Howchin died in Adelaide on 27 November 1937. Survived by his two daughters, he was buried in Mitcham cemetery with his wife who had died in 1924. The Methodist Church, the Royal Society of South Australia and the University of Adelaide were among his beneficiaries as was the South Australian Museum which received his collection of foraminifera and literature relating to this group of animals.

Roy Soc SA, *Trans*, 61 (1937); Geological Soc of Lond, *Procs*, 94 (1938); *Aust Christian Cwlth*, 50, no 1 (1937); *Advertiser* (Adel), 29 Nov 1937.

N. H. LUDBROOK

HOWE, JAMES HENDERSON (1839-1920), farmer and politician, was born on 4 March 1839 at Forfar, Angus, Scotland, son of James H. Howe and his wife Elizabeth, née Inverwick. He was educated at Mr Burns's School, Forfar, and at 13 apprenticed to a merchant. He was a good horseman. At 17 he migrated to South Australia and, joining the mounted police, was stationed at numerous country centres; his colleagues included (Sir) Jenkin Coles [q.v.8] and Adam Lindsay Gordon [q.v.4].

On 2 June 1864 at Angaston he married Harriette Keynes. About the same time he settled at Gawler where he became a publican and member of the Gawler Municipal Council, and worked to promote the eight-hour day system. In 1876 Howe joined an extensive move into the mid-northern grain and sheep lands, and opened up a property,

Mambray Park in the Baroota district, where he bred Clydesdale horses. He helped to form the Farmers' Mutual Association, ostensibly a non-political body, but one which quickly began to sponsor its own parliamentary candidates. In 1881 he successfully stood as F.M.A. candidate for Stanley in the House of Assembly. With his practical knowledge of country business, farming and grazing, he was an effective representative of farming interests. In 1884, when his electoral district was divided, he won the northern seat of Gladstone, retaining it until 1896 when he was defeated by a Labor man.

Howe was a member of the 1883-84 royal commission on railways and was a cabinet minister four times: as commissioner of crown lands and immigration (1885-87) under Downer [q.v.8], of public works (1889-90) under Cockburn [q.v.8], of crown lands and immigration (May-July 1890) under Cockburn again, and of crown lands (1892-93) under Downer again. A capable administrator with a genial disposition, he quickly won repute for hard work and reliability. He was conservative on most matters, but had a genuine concern for the plight of the poor. In industrial relations he stressed the role of education in bridging the gap between labour and capital.

The part Howe played as a delegate to the 1897-98 Australasian Federal Convention ensured his inclusion among the fathers of the Australian Constitution. The 1891 convention had not included old age and invalid pensions in the Federal powers, and Howe twice raised the issue at the 1898 session in Melbourne. He based his uncharacteristically eloquent case on the humanism of Charles Booth, Joseph Chamberlain and John Morley and the experiences of the Bismarckian Empire. Although Australians on the whole, he argued, were a thrifty people, many had seen their life-savings disappear during the recent depression and consequently faced pauperism in old age. His persuasive argument that because Australia's population was migratory the matter could not properly be left to the individual States helped to reverse a negative vote and bring about a sweeping victory.

Howe was elected to the Legislative Council in 1897 and retired as 'father of the house' in 1918. A tall and heavy man, he enjoyed robust health until his death at St Peters on 5 February 1920. Predeceased by his wife, he was survived by two sons and four daughters.

A'sian Federal Convention . . . Melb . . . 1898, *Official record of the debates* (Melb, 1898); E. H. Coombe (ed), *History of Gawler 1837 to 1908* (Adel, 1910); A. Deakin, *The Federal story*, H. Brookes ed (Melb, 1944); J. A. La Nauze, *The making of the Australian Constitution* (Melb, 1972); R. Norris,

The emergent Commonwealth (Melb, 1975); *Observer* (Adel), 14 Feb 1920, 27 July 1889; *Aust Worker*, 27 Feb 1920; *Advertiser*, 6 Feb 1920.

ROB VAN DEN HOORN

HOWE, JOHN ROBERT (1861?-1920), shearer and publican, was born probably on 26 July 1861 at Killarney near Warwick, Queensland, son of John Howe, circus acrobat turned stockman, and his wife Louisa, née Stokes, who had come to Queensland as a companion to the wife of Patrick Leslie [q.v.2]. Howe probably began shearing in the late 1870s and after a season in New Zealand settled at Blackall. At the Roman Catholic church there on 24 April 1890 he married Margaret Alexandra Victoria Short.

Howe first achieved more than local fame in 1892, when he shore 237 sheep by machine in one day at Barcaldine Downs station early in October, and on the 10th shore 321 weaners with the blades at Alice Downs. In the previous week he had shorn 1437 sheep in 44 hours. An old shearing mate told how other shearers attempted to slow him down by tickling him and jumping on his back, but his feats were recognized by two gold medals, offered for shearing records by Coleman & Sons, eucalyptus manufacturers of Cootamundra, and by the presentation in January 1893 of an inscribed shearing machine from the Wolseley [q.v.6] Shearing Machine Co.

Howe was an enthusiastic member of the Queensland Shearers' Union and prominent on its committee. In 1900 he abandoned shearing and bought the Universal Hotel at Blackall. He moved to the Barcoo Hotel in 1902 but repurchased the Universal in 1907 and retained it until 1919. He remained a loyal member of the Australian Labor Party and, as president of the Blackall Workers' Political Organisation in 1909, took the lead in arranging for T. J. Ryan [q.v.] to stand for election to the Legislative Assembly. Late in life he bought Sumnervale and Shamrock Park, pastoral properties near Blackall. When he moved to Sumnervale in 1919 he was given the biggest send-off in the town's history. However his health was already broken and he died aged 58 at Blackall on 21 July 1920. His wife, six sons and two daughters survived him. He was buried in the local cemetery.

An 'extraordinary physical specimen', Howe weighed 18 stone (114 kg), with a 50 ins. (127 cm) chest, 27½ ins. (70 cm) thigh, 17 ins. (43 cm) biceps and a hand the size of a small tennis racket. He is reputed to have run 100 yards in eleven seconds in his socks and to have been well above average in field events. He is also known to have taken prizes for Irish dancing. He became a legend long before he died and the flannel shirt worn by shearers is still widely known as a 'Jacky Howe'.

P. J. Brixey, *Jackie Howe: Australia's all time champion blade shearer* (Warwick, Qld, 1982); *Brisbane Courier*, 13 Oct 1892; *Pastoral Review*, 15 Oct 1892, 15 Nov 1894; *Catholic Advocate*, 13 Apr 1916; *Worker* (Brisb), 5 Aug 1920; information from H. J. Howe, Blackall.

H. J. GIBBNEY

HOWELL, CEDRIC ERNEST (1896-1919), airman and draftsman, was born on 17 June 1896 in Adelaide, son of Ernest Howell, accountant, and his wife Ida Caroline, née Hasch. He attended Melbourne Church of England Grammar School in 1909-13, became a draftsman, and was a second lieutenant in the 49th (Prahran) Cadet Battalion by 1914. He enlisted as a private in the Australian Imperial Force on 1 January 1916 and embarked in March with the 16th Reinforcements for the 14th Battalion. He became an acting sergeant before joining the 46th Battalion with which he served briefly in France.

On 11 November 1916 Howell transferred to the Royal Flying Corps and joined No. 1 Royal Flying Officers' Cadet Battalion, Durham, England. Commissioned as a second lieutenant, R.F.C., on 17 March 1917, he was posted to No. 17 Reserve Squadron on 30 April. On 25 July he was promoted flying officer and was attached to the Central Flying School. He married Cicely Elizabeth Hallam Kilby at St Stephen's Anglican Church, Bush Hill Park, London, on 12 September and next month was posted to No.45 Squadron in Italy. With the creation of the Royal Air Force on 1 April 1918 he held the rank of lieutenant, R.A.F. On 1 June he was promoted temporary captain and examining officer with No.28 Squadron.

During his service in Italy between October 1917 and August 1918, Howell displayed extraordinary bravery and skill. One of his tasks was to destroy enemy transport crossing the Alps. In August 1918 he was awarded the Distinguished Flying Cross: while leading a patrol of three machines he 'attacked nine enemy aeroplanes, destroying six and driving down one out of control; he himself accounted for two of these'. The citation described him as 'a fine fighting officer; skilful and determined'. Next month his Military Cross was gazetted. He had 'bombed an electrical power-house with great skill, obtaining three direct hits from 100 feet (30.5m). With two other machines he carried out a most dashing attack on a formation of twelve enemy aeroplanes. Although badly hampered by frequent jams in both of his machine guns, he destroyed three and drove one down out of control'. This award was followed by the Distinguished Service Order in November, the citation stating:

This officer recently attacked, in company with one other machine, an enemy formation of fifteen aeroplanes and succeeded in destroying four of them and bringing down one out of control. Two days after he destroyed another enemy machine, which fell in our lines, and on the following day he led three machines against sixteen enemy scouts, destroying two of them. Captain Howell is a very gallant and determined fighter who takes no account of the enemy's superior numbers in his battles.

Howell's service record included an A1 grade from the advanced precision flying school at Gosport, confirmation of nineteen enemy planes destroyed, with other possible kills, and three gallantry awards. These ensure his recognition as a true 'ace' of World War I. He was demobilized on 31 July 1919 and on 15 August was nominated by Martinsyde Ltd of Woking, England, as pilot of their Martinsyde A1 aircraft in the England–Australia air race for which a prize of £10 000 had been offered by the Australian government. He was to be accompanied by Lieutenant George Henry Fraser, a qualified navigator and engineer.

Howell and Fraser took off from Hounslow aerodrome on 4 December 1919 with a minimum of fuss. They were dogged by bad weather and landed at Dijon, France. Next day they reached Pisa, Italy, where they fitted a new tail skid to the aircraft and on 6 December reached Naples. At noon on 10 December they left Taranto for Athens. At 8 p.m. the plane was reported flying over St George's Bay, Corfu, in semi-darkness and shortly afterwards it fell into the sea. Howell's body was washed ashore several days later and some effects, including the log, were recovered from the aircraft. Attempts to tow the plane to shore were unsuccessful.

Many conflicting reports were given concerning the loss of the aircraft and crew. It was later proven that the A1 had been fully fuelled at Taranto; the details of what happened will never be established. Howell's remains were returned to Australia and on 22 April 1920 he was buried with full military honours in Heidelberg cemetery, Victoria. His wife survived him.

Melb C. of E. Grammar School, *Liber Melburniensis* (Melb, 1937); *Flight* (Lond), 6 Nov, 11, 18 Dec 1919; *Aeroplane*, 17 Dec 1919; *Sea, Land, and Air*, May 1920; *SMH*, 18 Aug, 22 Sept, 9, 10, 16, 17, 18, 20, 27, 29 Dec 1919, 8 Jan, 23 Feb, 23 Apr 1920; CRS A 457, item G506/4 *and* CRS A2, item 20/2254 (AAO).

T. H. COOKE

HOWELL, GEORGE JULIAN (1893-1964), soldier, builder and newspaper representative, was born on 19 November 1893 at Enfield, Sydney, fourth son of Francis John Howell, a carpenter from Brighton, England, and his Sydney-born wife Martha, née Sweeny. He was educated at Croydon Park and Burwood public schools, served an apprenticeship in bricklaying and was working as a builder when he enlisted as a private in the Australian Imperial Force on 3 June 1915. He sailed for Egypt on 14 July with the 7th Reinforcements for the 1st Battalion, joined his unit at Gallipoli on 1 November and served there until the evacuation.

Howell accompanied his battalion to France in March 1916, was wounded in the battle of Pozières in July and evacuated to England. Before returning to the front he attended a training school and was promoted corporal on 6 February 1917. For 'courage and devotion to duty while leading a rifle bombing section' during the capture of Demicourt in April, he was awarded the Military Medal. On 6 May, near Bullecourt, where the 1st Battalion experienced some of its heaviest fighting, he won the Victoria Cross. Realizing that a large party of Germans threatened to outflank his battalion, he climbed onto the parapet and despite heavy bomb attacks and rifle-fire proceeded to bomb the enemy back along the trench. Lieutenant T. J. Richards supported him with a Lewis-gun, following him along the trench and firing bursts. When he ran out of bombs Howell continued his assault by jabbing down at the Germans with his bayonet until, severely wounded, he fell into the trench. His citation stated that the 'prompt and gallant conduct of this non-commissioned officer in the face of superior numbers was witnessed by the whole battalion and greatly inspired them in the subsequent successful counter-attack'. After a fierce, close fight his unit regained all the ground taken by the enemy. Howell had received multiple injuries; even before leaving his own trench he had machine-gun wounds in both legs and when he was brought in hours later he had over twenty wounds. He was hospitalized in England before returning to Australia in November and was demobilized on 5 June 1918.

'Snowy' Howell came from a fighting family. His father and two brothers, one of whom was killed in action, served in France with the A.I.F. On 1 March 1919 he married a nurse, Sadie Lillian Yates, at St Stephen's Presbyterian Church, Sydney. They settled at Coogee and Howell worked on the advertising staffs of Smith's Newspapers Ltd and later the Bulletin Newspaper Co. Pty Ltd. By 1933 he was New South Wales representative for the *Standard*, Brisbane, and the *Queensland Worker*. In World War II he served with the 2nd A.I.F. as a staff sergeant with Eastern Command, New South Wales, but found this work 'too unexciting' so in August 1944 joined the United States Army Sea Transport Service and took part in the landing at Leyte during the invasion of the Philippines. In December 1953 he retired to Perth to join his married daughter and later lived at Gunyidi, Western Australia. Survived by one daughter, he died on 23 December 1964 in the Repatriation General Hospital, Hollywood, and was cremated with military honours after an Anglican service.

C. E. W. Bean, *The A.I.F. in France, 1916-18* (Syd, 1929, 1933, 1937, 1942); L. Wigmore (ed), *They dared mightily* (Canb, 1963); B. V. Stacy, F. J. Kingdom and H. V. Chedgey, *The history of the First Battalion, AIF (1914-1919)* (Syd, 1931); *London Gazette*, 25 May, 26 June 1917; *Newspaper News*, 1 Dec 1933; *Reveille* (Syd), Mar 1965; *SMH*, 28, 29 June 1917, 3 Mar 1919, 26 Dec 1964; *Sydney Mail*, 4 July 1917, 9 Jan 1918; *West Australian*, 25 Dec 1964.   W. H. CONNELL

HOWELL-PRICE, JOHN (1886-1937), naval officer, FREDERICK PHILLIMORE (1888-1978), OWEN GLENDOWER (1890-1916), PHILIP LLEWELLYN (1894-1917) and RICHMOND GORDON (1896-1917), soldiers, were sons of Rev. John Howell Price, for many years vicar of St Silas's Anglican Church, Waterloo, Sydney, and his wife Isabel Virginia, née Winchcombe, sister of F. E. Winchcombe [q.v.]. He was born in Wales and she in Victoria. The five sons were registered at birth as Price, not Howell-Price.

Their second son John was born on 16 September 1886 at St Alban's Parsonage, Five Dock, Sydney, and after running away to sea at 14 served an apprenticeship as a merchant-navy officer in clippers before obtaining a master mariner's certificate. He joined the Royal Naval Reserve as a temporary sub-lieutenant on 24 March 1915 and was serving as an acting lieutenant in the armed merchant cruiser H.M.S. *Alcantara* when she met the German raider S.M.S. *Greif* in the North Sea on 29 February 1916. After a fierce fight both ships were sunk, the survivors nearly freezing to death in open boats before they were rescued. For his part in the engagement John was awarded the Distinguished Service Cross. He later transferred to submarine service and was promoted temporary lieutenant, R.N.R., on 24 July 1917. He was second-in-command and navigator of the old British submarine *C3* which, filled with explosives, was blown up at Zeebrugge, Belgium, on the night of 22-23 April 1918. The commander of the submarine was awarded the Victoria Cross and John Howell-Price the Distinguished Service Order. After the war he transferred to the Royal Australian Navy in the same rank and returned to Australia in command of the submarine *J3*; he served with the R.A.N. until 1921 when he rejoined the merchant navy as a master with the Federal Steam Navigation Co. Ltd, making several trips to Australia. He married Margaret Williams of Liverpool, England; they had one daughter. He died of hypertensive cerebro-vascular disease on 13 November 1937 at Liverpool.

Frederick was born on 11 June 1888 at Kiama, New South Wales, and was educated at Windsor Grammar School. He was employed as a bank clerk with the Commercial Banking Co. of Sydney until 17 September 1914 when he enlisted in the Australian Imperial Force as a driver in the 6th Company, Australian Army Service Corps. On 16 December he was promoted second lieutenant and five days later sailed from Sydney with the 2nd Light Horse Divisional Train. He served at Gallipoli from September to December 1915, was promoted lieutenant in November, and on 23 March 1916, after his company had been disbanded, was appointed adjutant of the Anzac Mounted Divisional Train in Egypt. In July he was promoted captain, A.A.S.C., and appointed supply officer to the 2nd Light Horse Brigade. He was later supply officer of the 4th Light Horse Brigade, senior supply officer of the Australian Mounted Division, deputy assistant director of supply and transport to the Desert Mounted Corps, acting commander of the Anzac Mounted Divisional Train and acting assistant director of supply and transport in the Mounted Corps. He served during the Romani, Beersheba, Jericho Valley and Syrian operations, was promoted major on 1 November 1917, awarded the D.S.O. and twice mentioned in dispatches. In 1919 he rejoined the Commercial Banking Co. for a few months, then became an accountant with a rubber company in Sumatra. He retired in 1941 and returned to Australia. During World War II he undertook war-work for the division of import procurement, Department of Trade and Customs, and in 1946-68 was accountant for the Metropolitan Burial & Cremation Society in Sydney. He had married Mabel Constance Beer on 24 July 1919 at St Jude's Anglican Church, Randwick; they had two sons and a daughter. He died on 22 April 1978 and was cremated with Anglican rites.

Owen was born on 23 February 1890 at Kiama and was educated at Windsor Grammar School and Kogarah High School. A bank clerk before beginning training in agriculture at the Government Experiment

Farm at Nyngan, he served for a period in the citizen forces and on 27 August 1914 was commissioned second lieutenant in the 3rd Battalion, A.I.F. The battalion left Sydney in October and arrived in Egypt in December. During this time he was appointed assistant adjutant and when the adjutant was killed on the first day of the Gallipoli landing he succeeded him. He was promoted captain on 4 August 1915. During the fighting at Lone Pine he won the Military Cross and was also mentioned in dispatches. Casualties were heavy and on 5 September he was promoted temporary major and assumed temporary command of the battalion. He was wounded on 9 September but remained on duty. Having revealed his ability as a fine trainer and organizer, Owen was confirmed in rank on 1 December. For a short period in Egypt after the evacuation he was temporarily superseded in command.

The 3rd Battalion arrived in France on 28 March 1916 and Owen was promoted lieutcolonel on 12 May. In July and August the battalion fought bloody battles at Pozières and Mouquet Farm during which time Howell-Price set a magnificent example of courage, always visiting the most forward positions. For his leadership he was awarded the D.S.O. and mentioned in dispatches again. On 3 November 1916, near Flers, he was shot in the head and he died next day. His last words were 'Give my love to the battalion'. He was buried at Ancre-side Wood, and a commemorative service was held at Flesselles attended by the whole unit. Probably because of his youth, Owen Howell-Price took his responsibilities too seriously to be popular with his officers and men, but underlying his sternness and austerity was a deep and single-minded loyalty to his unit.

Philip was born on 11 September 1894 at Mount Wilson and educated at Kogarah High School. He was a bank clerk and had served as a citizen soldier before enlisting in the 1st Battalion, A.I.F., as a private on 14 September 1914. He was commissioned second lieutenant four days later and embarked for Egypt on 18 October. The battalion landed at Gallipoli on 25 August 1915 and Philip was promoted lieutenant next day. He was mentioned in dispatches for work in the battle of Lone Pine, during which he was severely wounded. Returning after three months in hospital, he was one of the last to evacuate Gallipoli. He was promoted captain on 28 January 1916 and was awarded the D.S.O. for leading a raiding party near Armentières, France, on 27 June. He fought on the Somme in July, at Flers in November and was wounded at Bullecourt in March 1917. General Sir William Birdwood [q.v.7] soon had him appointed to the staff of the 1st Anzac Division; he was

promoted major on 7 June 1917 and attached to the staff of the 2nd Brigade. That month he was awarded the Military Cross. On hearing that his old battalion was going into action he begged to be sent back to it and on 4 October was killed in an artillery barrage at Broodseinde. His body was never recovered.

Richmond was born on 18 July 1896 at Richmond and educated at Fort Street Public School, Sydney. A bank clerk before enlisting in the A.I.F. in December 1915, he served as a trooper and a corporal in light horse units in the Middle East and was commissioned second lieutenant in the 1st Battalion on 31 December 1916. On 4 May 1917 he was wounded at Bullecourt, France, and died later that day. Three days later it was announced that he had been awarded the Military Cross.

The eldest of the family, David Clayton Winchcombe Howell-Price (b. 1881), served in the South African War, and in Australia on the Army's Administrative and Instructional Staff in World War I.

C. E. W. Bean *The Story of Anzac* (Syd, 1921, 1924), and *The A.I.F. in France*, 1916-18 (Syd, 1929, 1933, 1937, 1942); B. V. Stacey et al, *The history of the 1st Battalion, A.I.F. (1914-19)* (Syd, 1931); E. Wren, *Randwick to Hargicourt, history of the 3rd Battalion, A.I.F.* (Syd, 1935); *Reveille* (Syd), Dec 1930, Nov 1932, Dec 1937; *Sun* (Syd), 30 July 1916; *News* (Perth), 27 May 1919; *Register* (Adel), 12 Oct 1924; *SMH*, 25 Jan, 3 May 1930; Howell-Price papers, files 58/9-14 and 12/11/49, *and* war diaries, 1st and 3rd Battalions, AIF (AWM); information from Mr O. Price, and Dr J. Howell-Price, Singapore, Dr E. J. Milverton, Woolwich, NSW, and Mrs K. Morrow, Strathfield, NSW.

D. M. HORNER

HOWIE, SIR ARCHIBALD (1879-1943), building contractor and politician, was born on 12 May 1879 at Glasgow, Scotland, son of Archibald Howie, mason, and his wife Janet, née Ferguson. He and his mother reached Sydney in the *Clyde* on 23 June 1881, joining his father, who established a building business. Archibald junior was educated at Fort Street Public and Sydney Boys' High schools and at 16 joined his father's business. The company, Howie, Moffat & Co. Ltd by 1918, won many prestigious and lucrative contracts.

At St Philip's Anglican Church, Church Hill, Howie married Emily Clara Manuelle on 14 September 1912. Like many leading businessmen, he stayed at his post during the war. On the death of his father in 1923 he became chairman of the company. In the 1920s he was a director of the Port Jackson & Manly Steam Ship Co. (chairman from 1931) and of the Manly Gas Co. Ltd (chairman of the North Shore Gas Co. Ltd from 1937, after the firms' merger) and a director of numerous companies connected with the building industry. In 1927 he was elected president of the Master Builders' Association of New South Wales and next year attacked compulsory arbitration because it was 'inefficient'.

An influential member of the consultative council of the United Australia Party, Howie was elected to the reconstituted Legislative Council in December 1933 and represented Macquarie Ward on the Sydney Municipal Council in 1934-41. He served as lord mayor in 1936 and 1937. Elected as the Citizens Reform Association candidate on a programme of economy, he refused an increase in the mayoral allowance in 1937. As chairman of the State government's Housing Improvements Board in 1936-41, he was charged with the responsibilities of fostering home-ownership and slum demolition and rehabilitation; he achieved a small amount of the latter at Erskineville.

A council-member of the Sydney Chamber of Commerce, he was president for two terms in 1938-40. Knighted in 1939, he was appointed chairman of the Advisory Panel for Defence Works that year and in 1939-42 served on the Senate of the University of Sydney. He was a council-member of the Highland Society of New South Wales, a trustee of the Sydney Cricket Ground and a member of the New South Wales Club and the Royal Sydney Yacht Squadron.

From about 1930 Howie had bred stud Jersey cattle and Shetland ponies at his Navua stud, near Richmond, and won championships for his bulls at the Royal Easter Show. He was president of the New South Wales branch and of the federal council (1938-43) of the Australian Jersey Herd Society and was president of the Royal Agricultural Society of New South Wales in 1941-43. Clean-shaven, his distinctive bushy eyebrows remained black after his hair had greyed.

On 26 October 1943 Howie died of heart disease at his home at Hunters Hill and was buried in the Presbyterian section of South Head cemetery. He was survived by his wife, son and daughter. His estate was valued for probate at £61 306. The Royal Agricultural Society holds his portrait painted posthumously by H. A. Hanke.

PD (NSW), 1943, p 748; SMH, 27 June 1923, 18 Feb 1927, 6 June 1928, 26 Dec 1936, 26 Jan 1937, 27 Oct 1943.
                                          PETER SPEARRITT
                                          KATHERINE VASEY

HOWIE, LAURENCE HOTHAM (1876-1963), artist and teacher, was born on 22 August 1876 at Norwood, Adelaide, eldest of five children of George Cullen Howie, merchant, and his wife Clara Jane, née Hotham, both Scottish migrants. G. C. Howie died in 1883 and in 1885 his widow took the children to live with her father Rev. John Hotham, a Congregational minister at Port Elliot where she conducted a small private school.

Howie was educated locally before spending 1891 at Prince Alfred College, Adelaide; he studied art under James Ashton [q.v.7]. Next year he enrolled at the School of Design and soon became an assistant teacher there. He qualified as an art teacher, completed the certificates of the Royal College of Art, South Kensington, London, and studied wood-carving and china-painting in Melbourne. Howie read Ruskin and Pater and admired Turner, Corot, Whistler and the Impressionists. His greatest gifts were in design. From about 1905 he supported the movement to Australianize design, using native floral motifs; his 1910 waratah vase, a *tour de force*, is in the Sydney Museum of Applied Arts and Sciences. After 1909 the School of Design became the Adelaide School of Arts and Crafts, under H. P. Gill's [q.v.] directorship, and Howie was his chief assistant. He enlisted in the Australian Imperial Force on 28 August 1915 in the army engineers.

He embarked in January 1916 and from March served with the 13th Field Company in North Africa and on the Western Front until December 1918. He continued painting and sketching and was appointed an official war artist after hostilities ended. He worked with the A.I.F. War Records Section in London under the sculptor C. Web Gilbert [q.v.] and in 1919 returned to France to make studies which were later used to construct dioramas at the Australian War Memorial, Canberra. In 1920 the war memorial acquired two pen-drawings, a sketch-book and twelve water-colours from his visits to the battlefields.

On 17 July 1919 at St Saviour's Church, Alexandra Park, London, Howie had married Janet Johnstone Isabella Davidson, an Adelaide infant mistress. Next year they went home and in July Howie became principal of the School of Arts and Crafts. His term as principal was not marked by radical developments. He faced serious problems for much of this period: the school's very existence was threatened in the Depression of the 1930s, but Howie's conservative, kindly management maintained a stable learning environment.

He was president of the (Royal) South Australian Society of Arts in 1927-32 and 1935-37 and exhibited regularly with the society, whose seascape prize he won in 1928. He also contributed to exhibitions interstate and in New Zealand. Although unadventurous in his taste and policies, he did not join the extreme reactionary movement in Australian art at that time.

Howie retired as principal in 1941. He continued painting and woodcraft; an enthusiastic yachtsman, he frequently painted peaceful sea scenes. His pulpits adorn many Adelaide churches. Survived by his two daughters, he died on 18 October 1963 and was buried in Mitcham Anglican cemetery. In 1978 a memorial exhibition of his work was held at the South Australian School of Art.

D. S. Dolan, *L. H. Howie* (exhibition cat, Adel, 1978); *Ormolu*, 1 (1979), no 1; information from Miss M. H. Howie, Parkside, SA.

DAVID DOLAN

HOWITT, WILLIAM (1846?-1928), woodcarver, was born at Manchester, England, elder son of William Howitt, engineer, and his Spanish wife Betsy, née Brahma. He was educated in Nottingham, Liverpool and London and from 1866 worked at decorating ships' interiors and repairing ecclesiastical fittings and ornaments. In 1869 he married Isabella Patrick at Glasgow, Scotland.

In 1888 they migrated to Melbourne. Howitt was commissioned in 1896 to carve the furnishings for St Paul's Cathedral, notably the pulpit and the bishop's throne. About 1899 he moved to Perth where he taught wood-carving at Perth Technical School until 1906; James Linton [q.v.] was a colleague. Howitt became well known in the West for his carved wooden plaques, some of which were displayed by the Western Australian government at international exhibitions. He discovered jarrah as an art medium and among the most celebrated of his jarrah reliefs were 'Marguerite Leaving the Church' for the Paris exhibition (1900), and 'Dante and Beatrice' for the Panama-Pacific Exhibition at San Francisco (1915). His sectional model of the Great Boulder Pty Mine had been presented to the princess of Wales in 1904. Howitt also sculpted in marble and clay.

Furniture hand made from native woods was another of his specialities. A carved jarrah dining suite, comprising sideboard, table, six chairs, and a side-table, which was shown at the Western Australian Exhibition in 1906, is said to have represented six years of work. An inlaid octagonal table made of she-oak, jarrah and native pine, incorporating a Maltese cross with a black swan in the middle, remained on display in 1982 at the museum of the Western Australian Forests Department. Occasionally Howitt also exercised his original craft of ecclesiastical furniture-making, a good example of his later work being the pulpit of Christ Church, Claremont.

Although his effects were sometimes florid through excess of design, Howitt's work had a practical as well as an artistic dimension in that he was expert in the qualities and use of a wide range of native timbers and an effective propagandist for their value. He worked in karri, red gum, wandoo, she-oak, York gum, blackbutt, jam, banksia, salmon gum, tuart, sandalwood, morrell and pine. The 1908 display of his furniture in London at the Franco-British Exhibition of Science, Arts and Industries led to immediate orders for jarrah furniture.

Howitt died at Subiaco on 19 June 1928, survived by two sons and two daughters, and was buried in the Presbyterian section of Karrakatta cemetery. For a time his reputation faded, but recent enthusiasm for hand made furniture and native wood has led to a well-merited revival of interest.

Railways Select C'ttee report, no 2, *PP* (LA Vic), 1896, 2, p 118; *Art in Australia*, 26 Dec 1928; *West Australian*, 9 May 1917, 23 June, 5 July 1928; information from Mr K. Legge, Applecross, and papers in the possession of Mr G. C. Miller, Claremont, Perth.

B. K. DE GARIS

HOWSE, SIR NEVILLE REGINALD (1863-1930), surgeon, soldier and politician, was born on 26 October 1863 at Stogursey, Somerset, England, son of Alfred Howse, surgeon, and his wife Lucy Elizabeth, née Conroy. He was educated at Fullard's House School, Taunton, and studied medicine at London Hospital (M.R.C.S., L.R.C.P., 1886). Howse was a demonstrator in anatomy at the University of Durham when declining health caused him to migrate to New South Wales. Registered to practise on 11 December 1889 he set up at Newcastle but soon moved to Taree. In 1895 he visited England for postgraduate work in surgery, became F.R.C.S. in 1897, then bought a practice at Orange.

On 17 January 1900 he was commissioned lieutenant in the New South Wales Medical Corps and sailed with the 2nd Contingent for South Africa. While with a mounted infantry brigade in the Orange Free State during the action of Vredefort on 24 July, Howse 'went out under a heavy crossfire and picked up a wounded man and carried him to a place of shelter'. For this action he was awarded the Victoria Cross on 4 June 1901. Howse had been promoted captain in October 1900. Later he was captured by the

Boers but released as a non-combatant. After returning to Australia, he went back to South Africa as an honorary major in the Australian Army Medical Corps in February 1902, just as the war ended.

Howse became widely known in Orange for his skill as a surgeon and was twice mayor. On 31 January 1905 he married Evelyn Gertrude Northcote Pilcher at Bathurst. He remained a major in the A.A.M.C. Reserve and in August 1914 was appointed principal medical officer to the Australian Naval and Military Expeditionary Force to German New Guinea, with the rank of lieut-colonel. On his own initiative drugs and medical equipment (including a unique dental arrangement) suitable for a tropical campaign were obtained and the troops were protected against typhoid and smallpox. The brief action in New Britain was completed without a single case of serious illness up to 15 October as a result of his thoroughness. The ambitious Howse returned alone just in time to join the Australian Imperial Force and sail with the first convoy as staff officer to Surgeon General (Sir) W. C. D. Williams [q.v.], director of medical services. During the voyage he won the confidence of the commander of the A.I.F. Major General (Sir) W. T. Bridges [q.v.7] and the friendship of Colonel (Sir) Brudenell White [q.v.].

In December Howse was appointed assistant director of medical services, 1st Australian Division, with the rank of colonel. He was gravely perturbed by the inadequacy and confusion of the Imperial forces' medical plan for the Gallipoli landing and obtained improvements in the arrangements for the evacuation of Australian wounded. When the perilous situation of the 1st Division at the landing made his plans impossible Howse took personal charge of the evacuation of the wounded men crowding the beach under increasing shell-fire, 'giving and disregarding orders in a manner quite shocking but strangely productive of results. Shells and bullets he completely disregarded', wrote White. 'To the wounded he was gentleness itself'. By 3 a.m. on 26 April the beach was clear but Howse continued to superintend evacuation to the ships for two more days.

To Howse the medical service was no mere humane amenity for soldiers but a fundamental of fighting efficiency. So he strove to improve sanitation and food, to expedite the return of the wounded to units and, after Gallipoli, to combat venereal disease and to resist every attempt to lower the physical standard of the A.I.F. On Gallipoli he established the Anzac Medical Society which met regularly to disseminate knowledge among his officers. In July 1915 he was appointed

C.B. and in September was given command of the medical services, Australian and New Zealand Army Corps, as deputy director; from November he was director of medical services of the A.I.F. In this appointment, which he had been strongly urging, Howse could ensure the independence of the A.A.M.C. from the British medical authorities and give it the cohesion and leadership which it had lacked.

When the infantry divisions went to France in 1916 Howse set up his headquarters with A.I.F. administrative headquarters in London. He retained control of the A.A.M.C. in Egypt and Palestine, made frequent visits to the A.I.F. in France and reported each month to the director general of medical services in Melbourne. If he had much to learn about the vast, complex organism of the army at war, he revealed a capacity to learn and grow with the magnitude of his task. Mistakes were made but Howse never lost the confidence of the commander of the A.I.F., Lieut-General Sir William Birdwood [q.v.7], nor of Brudenell White. Among his achievements were recognition by the army of the need for direct access by the director of medical services to the general officer commanding the A.I.F., and his acceptance by the War Office as chief medical officer of the A.I.F. He established clear policies for the A.A.M.C. in line with those of the Royal Army Medical Corps and preserved the independence of his corps. When Major General (Sir) John Monash [q.v.] ordered A.A.M.C. officers on his headquarters to wear the 3rd Division colour patch instead of their own, Howse forced Monash to withdraw the order; he won the same battle against Major General (Sir) Talbot Hobbs [q.v.]. In January 1917 he was promoted major general and appointed K.C.B. Howse gave evidence before the Dardanelles Commission in 1917. The arrangements for the wounded at the landing he characterized as 'so inadequate that they amounted to criminal negligence' on the part of the Imperial authorities.

In the field, Howse had introduced surgical teams and had supported the work of Major A. W. Holmes à Court [q.v.] in developing resuscitation teams with each division. His reorganization of the field ambulances in two sections, rejected by the War Office in 1916, was readopted in the A.I.F. in September 1918. In October Howse went briefly to Australia to advise the minister of defence on A.I.F. affairs and on crippled returned soldiers. He returned to London in February 1919 to assist on the medical side of repatriation. He was mentioned in dispatches, and was appointed K.C.M.G. and knight of the Order of St John of Jerusalem in 1919.

Howse returned home in January 1920 but his resumption of private practice was short lived. He had been appointed chairman of a committee on the reorganization of the Army Medical Service which began work in 1921 but in July 1921 he was made D.G.M.S. as a regular major general stationed in Melbourne. From the day of his return he had spoken out in public on the achievement of the A.A.M.C. in maintaining the health of the A.I.F. and had insisted that the same must be done for all Australians in peacetime. As a regular officer could not campaign in public he resigned in November 1922 and was elected to the House of Representatives for the seat of Calare, which included Orange, as a member of the National Party. He was then reappointed D.G.M.S., on a part-time basis, until he entered the cabinet in 1925.

He was a member of the Australian delegation to the fourth assembly of the League of Nations in 1923 and commissioned by the government to inquire into the medical examination of migrants to Australia and into the Spahlinger treatment of tuberculosis. From January 1925 to April 1927 Howse was minister for defence and health and minister in charge of repatriation. He accompanied the prime minister, S. M. (Viscount) Bruce [q.v.7] to the Imperial Conference in 1926 but was taken ill and returned to Australia. He relinquished defence and health but remained in the cabinet as assistant minister without portfolio. Nevertheless he continued to administer repatriation and even acted as secretary to the cabinet. In February 1928 he again became minister for health and repatriation and also for home and territories. He was campaign manager for the 1929 election in which he lost his seat. In his brief parliamentary career he was recognized as champion of the returned servicemen and as a pioneer in public health. He spoke on the need for the Commonwealth to improve public health, on the treatment of cancer and venereal disease, maternity allowances and the welfare of returned servicemen. With the purchase of £100 000 worth of radium in 1928 Howse set up one of the world's first radium banks. The first conference of cancer organizations in Australia was inspired by him and he was responsible for the transfer of the Institute of Anatomy to Canberra. He helped to found the Federal Health Council in 1925 and the College of Surgeons of Australasia in 1928.

Howse went to England for medical treatment in 1930. He died of cancer on 19 September 1930 and was buried in Kensal Green cemetery, London, survived by his wife, two sons and three daughters.

Neville Howse was an Englishman who expressed the nascent Australian nationalism vigorously and directly. He was a pragmatist who nevertheless saw far ahead, a surgeon who had a flair for soldiering, an organizer who had deep insight into the essential relationship between the medical service and the force it served and who had the courage and persistence to establish policies not always understood by combatant officers. His confidence, good humour and diplomacy were matched by his shrewd appreciation of character. If his ambition carried him far, it was motivated by his recognition of human need in war and peace and sustained by confidence in his own capacity to help. His successes, in the words of another great D.G.M.S., Colonel R. M. Downes [q.v.8], 'made him one of the outstanding Australians of the Great War ... one of the most remarkable and self-sacrificing medical administrators any military force has ever known'.

Memorials to Howse are at the Orange sub-branch of the Returned Servicemen's League of Australia, in the Orange Base Hospital and in the Australian Institute of Anatomy. His portrait by James Quinn [q.v.] is in the Australian War Memorial and a painting of Howse winning the V.C., by William Dargie, is in the headquarters of the R.A.M.C., London.

Aust Defence Dept, *Official records of the Australian military contingents to the war in South Africa*, P. L. Murray ed (Melb, 1911); C. E. W. Bean, *The story of Anzac* (Syd, 1921, 1924); S. S. Mackenzie, *The Australians at Rabaul . . .* (Syd, 1927); A. G. Butler (ed) *Official history of the Australian Army Medical Services . . . 1914-18* (Melb, 1930, Canb, 1940, 1943); A. S. Walker, *Middle East and Far East* (Canb, 1953); C. E. W. Bean, *Two men I knew* (Syd, 1957); *MJA*, 31 January 1931-28 March 1931; Dardanelles Commission Evidence *and* Butler *and* Howse collections (AWM).

A. J. HILL

HUDD, SIR HERBERT SYDNEY (1881-1948), politician, was born on 25 February 1881 in Adelaide, son of William Hudd, confectioner, and his wife Mary Ann, née Haylett. Educated at Grote Street Public School, Adelaide, he left at 13 to work in his father's chocolate factory at Medindie. He later became a managing partner of W. Hudd & Sons. Hudd showed an early interest in debating and joined the Pirie Street Literary Society in 1903 as an enthusiastic secretary and organizer; he became vice-president of the South Australian Literary Societies' Union in 1909 and president in 1912-13, and was a member of the debating team which won an interstate contest in

1911. He extended his education by reading three nights a week in the public library.

In 1910 Hudd was defeated in an attempt to enter parliament as a Liberal Union candidate for Torrens, but he won the seat in 1912 and for three years was secretary of the Parliamentary Liberal Party. In 1915, following a redistribution, he stood unsuccessfully for Sturt. In September he enlisted in the Australian Imperial Force as quartermaster sergeant and served in France and Belgium in 1916-18 with the 43rd Battalion. In August 1916 he was commissioned second lieutenant and was promoted lieutenant next January; from November 1916 he acted as quartermaster and was awarded the Military Cross in June 1918 especially for 'his energy, organizing ability and constant devotion to duty' during operations east of Ypres in October 1917. Confirmed as quartermaster and promoted honorary captain in January 1918 he was next year commissioned by the South Australian government to inquire into town planning and country public house trusts in England. On 7 May 1919 at Kensington, London, he married a fellow South Australian, Mabel Law, daughter of Richard Smith [q.v.6]; in November they returned to Adelaide where Hudd was demobilized next February.

In June 1920 Hudd was elected to the House of Assembly for Alexandra at a by-election following the death of his friend the premier A. H. Peake [q.v.]. He held the seat until 1938 and from 1941 until his death. A senior member of the Liberal Union and the Liberal Party, he was again secretary of the parliamentary party and in 1927-30 government whip. In the Butler [q.v.7] government of 1933-38 he held the portfolios of public works, railways and marine which together accounted for the greater part of the State's budget. Appointed K.B.E. in 1937, he was regarded as one of the ablest debaters in public life in South Australia, although at least one contemporary was critical of his administrative ability.

Hudd was a member of the Council of the University of Adelaide (1921-24), the Adelaide Hospital Board (1912-15) and the Institutes' Association of South Australia and deputy chairman of the Institute of Medical and Veterinary Sciences. He belonged to the Commercial Travellers' Association and the Adelaide Club. He died of cardiac disease at Glenelg on 30 April 1948. Childless, he was survived by his wife and was buried in St Jude's cemetery, Brighton.

Literary Societies' J, 10 May 1908; *Observer* (Adel), 1 May 1920; *Mail* (Adel), 11 Nov 1922; *Advertiser* (Adel), 1 May 1948; R. F. I. Smith, The Butler government in South Australia, 1933-1938 (M.A. thesis, Univ Adel, 1964).

DEAN JAENSCH

HUGHES, AGNES EVA (1856?-1940), political organizer, was born probably in 1856 at South Yarra, Melbourne, daughter of Peter Snodgrass [q.v.2] and his wife Charlotte Agnes, née Cotton. She was educated at Miss Murphy's school, South Yarra. Her elder sister Janet [q.v.3] married Sir William Clarke [q.v.3] and a brother, Evelyn, became a canon in the Church of England.

On 1 October 1885 at All Saints Church, St Kilda, Eva married FREDERIC GODFREY HUGHES (1858-1944), son of Charles William Hughes, grazier, and his wife Ellen, née Man. The Hughes and Snodgrass families had been neighbours in the Seymour district. Frederic was born on 26 January 1858 at Windsor, Melbourne. His brothers were (Canon) Ernest Selwyn Hughes [q.v.] and Dr Wilfrid Kent Hughes. Educated at Melbourne Church of England Grammar School, he began as a clerk with a prominent Melbourne land valuer and agent, setting up on his own about 1884. He was a noted athlete, footballer and rower. A St Kilda councillor for twenty-three years, he was mayor in 1901-02 and 1911-12. He was best known as a citizen soldier, joining the field artillery in 1875 as a gunner. In 1889 he went to the Victorian Horse Artillery in the rank of captain, commanding the Rupertswood Battery until 1897, and was promoted major in 1891 and lieut-colonel in 1900. In 1903 he became commander of the 11th Australian Light Horse Regiment (Victorian Mounted Rifles) and in 1909 aide-de-camp to the governor-general.

On the outbreak of World War I Hughes commanded the 3rd Light Horse Brigade, Australian Imperial Force, and as temporary brigadier general served on Gallipoli. His men took part in the disastrous storming of the Turkish trenches at The Nek on 7 August 1915. Hughes was evacuated to Australia in March 1916 suffering from pneumonia and typhoid fever, and his A.I.F. appointment was terminated; he had been far too old for active service. He was re-appointed in July 1918 as brigadier general, retiring as major general in March 1920. After the war he concentrated on business, mining and pastoral interests, his directorships including Dunlop Rubber Pty Ltd and South Broken Hill Pty Ltd. In old age a gentle man who enjoyed gardening and picnics, he died at St Kilda on 23 August 1944, survived by two sons and two daughters. His estate was sworn for probate at £22 314.

Eva bore four children between 1886 and 1891 and devoted her time to their rearing but as they grew older she took to public life. In February-April 1904 she was one of six women who, in the conservative cause, established the Australian Women's

National League. She chaired the first general meeting on 14 April, when Janet Lady Clarke became president, and afterwards organized the St Kilda branch. In September 1909 she became State president and for the next thirteen years was identified with the league. Fellow officers acknowledged her enthusiasm and administrative ability; by 1914 she had built the A.W.N.L. from 120 branches to 420 with over 50 000 members, reputedly 'the largest body of organised women in Australia'. She kept the league firmly independent of other electoral organizations, particularly the city-based Deakinite Liberals led by Herbert and Ivy Brookes [qq.v.7].

After August 1914 Mrs Hughes encouraged league members in war-work. She herself joined the Australian League of Honour, the Lady Mayoress's Patriotic Fund and the Friendly Union of Soldiers' Wives and Mothers. The league branches raised over £21 000 for the War Loan Bond; they supplied tons of food, tobacco and rugs for the Young Men's Christian Association's 'Kitchener Memorial Huts', bought motor ambulances and even purchased a piano for the nurses. On 4 December 1916 Mrs Hughes formally presented to the minister for defence, (Sir) George Pearce [q.v.], a ward of thirty-six beds in Caulfield Military Hospital.

In State politics Eva Hughes inveighed against the liberalism of Peacock's [q.v.] administration, especially the intention to make 'dangerous alterations' to the country-city electoral ratio and to broaden the voting qualifications for the Legislative Council. At the Federal elections in September 1914 she worked strenuously for a Liberal victory. She keenly supported the government's recruitment campaign and used her influence as an A.W.N.L. delegate to exclude dissident representatives from the National Council of Women. In May 1916 the league gathered 22 000 signatures in support of conscription: Mrs Hughes was a strident advocate. She was appointed O.B.E. in 1918. She had always refused to approve parliamentary candidature of women, and in accepting presidential nomination for the league in September 1921 she suggested that women elect their own council to consider bills concerning the home, women and children.

Eva Hughes refused to extend her presidency of the A.W.N.L. after 1922. For her 'gracious but firm rule' and her 'unswerving integrity of principle', she was made life patroness and a life member of council; she also continued to act as the league's adviser. In her later years she worked for various welfare associations and was a vice-president of the Girls' Friendly Society. She died at her St Kilda home on 10 June 1940 and was buried in St Kilda cemetery.

C. E. W. Bean, *The story of Anzac*, 1, 2 (Syd, 1921, 1924); J. Rickard, *Class and politics* (Canb, 1976); *Argus*, 11 June 1940; *Age*, 11 June 1940, 24 Aug 1944; *Herald* (Melb), 23 Aug 1944; AWNL papers, MS 8313 (LaTL); Brookes papers (NL).

JUDY SMART

HUGHES, ERNEST SELWYN (1860-1942), Anglican clergyman, was born on 12 May 1860 at Cobram, Victoria, second son of Charles William Hughes, grazier, and his wife Ellen, née Man, both from England. His elder brother was Frederic Godfrey [q.v. A. E. Hughes]. Ernest was educated at All Saints Grammar School, St Kilda, and then at Melbourne Church of England Grammar School. He worked at the Royal Mint for seven years. His mother had chosen him of her three sons to become a priest, and under Bishop Moorhouse's [q.v.5] influence he decided to study for holy orders. He entered Trinity College at the University of Melbourne in 1883 and graduated B.A. in 1887. He was nominated as curate at St Mark's, Fitzroy, and began his ministry on 25 January 1888.

In May Hughes sailed for England. For part of his time there he worked with Father Wainwright at St Peter's, London Docks. After his return to Melbourne on 23 February 1889 he established the Mission of the Holy Redeemer at St Mark's, with enthusiastic support from Toorak ladies and the Fleur de Lys Club at Trinity College. A new building was opened by the governor of Victoria on 27 August 1891 and the mission was an outstanding success, attracting interest throughout Australia. When the vicar of St Mark's was translated to a new parish in August 1892, the parishioners petitioned unsuccessfully for the appointment of Hughes. The new vicar dismissed Hughes, partly because attendance at the church was much below attendance at mission services. Hughes was reinstated as a result of local pressures in May 1893 but then accepted a curacy at St Peter's, Eastern Hill, in 1894. The 'Big Curate', 6 ft. 3 ins. (191 cm) tall, began an association that lasted for thirty-two years. On the death of Canon Handfield [q.v.4] in 1900, he was nominated as vicar of St Peter's and inducted by the dean of Melbourne on 27 September. Hughes resigned on 24 May 1926 because of ill health.

His nomination was not a unanimous one because of his firm Anglo-Catholic allegiance. Like Handfield he was an Oxford Movement clerk rather than an Evangelical like Perry [q.v.5] and Goe [q.v.]. A rather tired Handfield had supported his dynamic curate in introducing the stations of the Cross. Hughes quickly became the leader of the Anglo-Catholic wing of the Church of England in Australia. Shortly after his appointment, he introduced the use of Eucharistic vestments and plain-song. Banners were carried in procession in the church and incense was used until the archbishop imposed a temporary ban. The Evangelical wing of the Church was hostile and 'no popery' agitations took place in 1906 and 1909. More liberal views led to the appointment of Hughes as canon of St Paul's Cathedral in 1911 and then as rural dean of Melbourne in 1912. Lesser attacks were made in 1916 and 1917, but most of the hostility had disappeared by the time the Cross of Sacrifice was unveiled by the governor-general in 1924. This European-style wayside Cross was a memorial to those who died in World War I.

Melbourne *Punch* in 1909 described Hughes as easily 'the most interesting figure in the Church of England in Victoria'. As vicar of St Peter's, building on his great experience of poverty in both the East End of London and Fitzroy, he maintained a deep interest in the work of missionary bodies in Melbourne. One of his great contributions to the Church was his ability to bring together the rich and the poor in a common worship. With his splendid speaking voice and great stature he was a dominant and appealing figure in the pulpit and on all church occasions, especially during his open-air street preaching at Fitzroy.

Hughes was an outstanding athlete. He stroked Trinity College crews and played football with St Kilda in 1890 in the days of its glory. He then transferred to Essendon, playing as an ordained priest in its four premiership sides in 1891-94. He was vice-president and president of the East Melbourne Cricket Club until 1920, the first president of the new Hawthorn-East Melbourne club until his death, and president of the Victorian Cricket Association in 1932. An active member of the Amateur Boxing Association, he became known as the 'Fighting Parson' after having with two blows ejected two youths from a church wedding celebration.

On 20 April 1904 at St Peter's he had married a widow, Isabell Janet Thomson, née Thomson. She died in 1933. Canon Hughes died at his Aspendale home on 16 June 1942. After a funeral service at St Paul's Cathedral he was cremated. He left no family.

St Peterite (Lillian Brocklebank), *Invictus Pax* (priv print, Melb, 1921); F. Howard, *Kent Hughes* (Melb, 1972); *Punch* (Melb), 15 Feb 1906, 14 Oct 1909, 28 May 1914; *Table Talk* (Melb), 3 Feb 1893.

NORMAN HARPER

HUGHES, FRANCIS AUGUSTUS (1874-1951), soldier and company executive, was born on 9 March 1874 in Brisbane, son of Alfred Hughes, grocer, and his wife Margaret, née Rock, both Sydney-born. He was educated at St Joseph's College, Brisbane, and was dux in his final year. Gus Hughes then joined the Castlemaine Brewery and Quinlan Gray & Co. Brisbane Ltd, eventually becoming an accountant. As a young man he was active in sculling and lacrosse.

By 1907 Hughes was convinced of the need for citizens to take an active part in defence. He joined the Australian Field Artillery, Australian Military Forces, was commissioned second lieutenant on 1 October 1907, and advanced to major in six years. In 1911-12 he was militia adjutant for eighteen months and commanded the 2nd Battery, 1st A.F.A., from February to August 1914. On 20 August he joined the Australian Imperial Force and, as major commanding the 7th Battery, 3rd Field Artillery Brigade, sailed for Egypt on 25 September. After intensive training there the battery embarked for Gallipoli.

Going ashore on the day after the landing, the 7th Battery was the first artillery moved forward to support the infantry who had been hard pressed for nearly thirty-six hours. The terrain was steeply broken and suitable positions for firing over the ridges could not be found. Under Hughes's direction three guns were dragged up the slopes to Bolton's Hill and were roughly dug in immediately behind the infantry forward positions. When the enemy attacked after dark the shrapnel from one gun was timed to burst just clear of the gun muzzle, the field-piece thus acting as a gigantic shotgun. C. E. W. Bean [q.v.7] recorded that 'it was a weapon which the Turks could not face, and the attack collapsed'. The fourth gun was brought into action next day and that night all guns repeated the point-blank defensive fire. On 5 May enemy artillery shelled Bolton's Hill and two of Hughes's guns, though entirely exposed, were turned against the hidden gun-line and continued firing until the shelling ceased. Similar enemy attacks were launched at intervals against sites now better prepared. All were repulsed. Apart from brief rest periods, the battery remained in action until the evacuation in December and except for a month in hospital Hughes continued in command.

When the 4th Division was formed in Egypt in March 1916 Hughes was appointed to command the 11th A.F.A. Brigade in the rank of lieut-colonel. From June 1916 he was in action with his brigade in France and Belgium near Merris, Ypres, Armentières, Fleurbaix, and the Somme. He was awarded the Distinguished Service Order for especially good leadership at Fleurbaix and in the Ypres salient and was mentioned in dispatches in January 1917. In February he was transferred to command the 5th Divisional Ammunition Column, had a period in command of the Artillery Training Depot in England and returned to the ammunition column in June. He had taken part in the first advance to the Hindenburg line which involved great difficulties in getting the ammunition forward. He relinquished command of the 5th D.A.C. on 15 February 1918.

In March Hughes left for Australia to attend to his father's estate. Released from active duty on 1 July, he married Winifred Ada Teasdale three days later at St Stephen's Cathedral, Brisbane. He resumed work at the brewery and in April 1920 was appointed company secretary, a post which included management of the company hotels. His interest in military service continued: in December 1919 he was appointed to command the 2nd Field Brigade, Royal Australian Artillery, and in 1927 the 5th Divisional Artillery, A.M.F., as colonel. He was transferred to the retired list in 1933.

In the brewery company, now known as Castlemaine Perkins Ltd, Hughes became a director in September 1939; in 1942 he retired as secretary. He died of cancer on 16 September 1951 in the Mater Misericordiae Private Hospital, Brisbane, and was buried in Toowong cemetery with Catholic rites. His wife and daughter survived him. For twenty-five years his military career had run parallel with his business life and he tended to think of himself as a professional army officer rather than a company executive. In dress uniform, even in his fifties, he had a lean, straight-shouldered, strong appearance. As a company executive he was forceful and decisive, working conscientiously and vigorously. He was generally regarded as fair-minded and popular, if authoritarian. His estate was sworn for probate at £22 541.

C. E. W. Bean, *The story of Anzac*, 1, 2 (Syd, 1921, 1924); *Notable Queenslanders* (Brisb, 1950); *London Gazette*, 29 Dec 1916, 2 Jan 1917; War diary *and* records, 5th Divisional Ammunition Column, AIF (AWM).   F. W. SPEED

HUGHES, FRED WILLIAM (1869-1950), pastoralist, industrialist, racehorse breeder and owner, was born on 12 September 1869 in Brisbane, third son of Henry Benjamin Hughes, butcher, and his wife Sarah, née McLaren, both Australian born. Beginning as a farmhand, he later worked for the Sydney firm Thomas Geddes & Co., wool-scourers of Harris Street. By 18 he was as-

sistant wool-valuer, graduating through wool sales to control the firm's scouring. Soon Hughes bought out Geddes and became sole proprietor of Buckland Mills, Waterloo. At St Philip's Anglican Church, Sydney, he married a widow Matilda Morris, née Hawthorne, on 7 September 1898; they were childless.

Enterprising qualities characterized Hughes's business career. Moving his plant to Botany in 1898, he analysed the whole process of wool treatment. A government bounty for wool-top production in 1907 led him to expand and to move into exports. By 1914 the Colonial Combing, Spinning and Weaving Co., which he operated in partnership with E. A. Coghlan, had an output of three million lb. (1.36 million kg) of tops. During World War I, despite the controls of the Central Wool Committee, Hughes doubled his plant and his output.

Meanwhile Hughes moved into other processes of the sheep industry—fellmongering, tanning, glue-manufacture and meat-processing with his company, Colonial Wholesale Meat Co. Ltd. He imported, and built, new machinery for spinning and weaving in his own mills, organizing production from the shearing shed to the spun products of his 'Sunbeam' and 'Sunglo' wools and worsted cloth. Botany remained the site of Hughes's industrial activity which, with 1000 employees, covered almost thirteen acres (5.3 ha). In 1908 Hughes drew his ventures together in one company, F. W. Hughes Ltd, of which he was managing director.

Tough and determined, Hughes had a relentless streak. He resisted the controls placed on his wool-top business during both wars and, becoming involved in long-drawn-out conflict and litigation with the Commonwealth government, threatened to close down. Charges were made, in public and in parliament, that he won concessions for his companies through political influence, such as by using the connexion of his friend, the former Labor leader J. C. Watson with the W. M. Hughes [qq.v.] wartime government. Hughes reacted strongly, asserting that no politician had any links with his companies. After the war Hughes visited Japan and tenaciously negotiated a large tops contract; he later exported to Canada, China, Mexico, Greece and England. Hughes advocated a strong economic nationalist line, consistent, of course, with his own commercial interests in seeking support and protection for the Australian wool industry and access to overseas markets.

Overall, Hughes's industrial relations with his employees appeared good: the Australian Textile Workers' Union supported his nationalist and protectionist stand. However he strongly opposed the granting of the 44-hour week and forecast bankruptcy and loss of jobs if there was no exemption for the industry.

In 1925 Hughes bought his first grazing property Welbondongah, near Moree. He soon acquired other properties near Wagga Wagga and Tumut for Merino sheep and Corriedale fat-lamb raising, and Kooba in the Riverina. By extensive irrigation he grew grain crops and lucerne and with improved pastures built up a huge flock of sheep, reputedly 600 000 by the end of World War II.

After the death of his wife in 1935, Hughes turned to horse-racing on doctor's advice. Doing nothing by halves, he entered the racing world with the same zest and drive he gave his business operations. Starting with the purchase of Highborn in 1937, he acquired a string of horses which were trained by J. W. McCurley, and at the same time began his thoroughbred stud at Kooba. Within ten years he had acquired some 300 racehorses and in his thirteen years of racing had 270 winners, some in partnership with his long-term associate Coghlan. Hughes's greatest successes were winning the Sydney Metropolitan twice, with Dashing Cavalier (1941) and Nightbeam (1944), and in his crowning year 1947 the Melbourne Cup with Hiraji.

At Kooba Hughes was the first Australian breeder to import a son of Hyperion in 1940. He also had Nizami, sire of Hiraji, and sixteen other stallions (ten imported). By 1950, as part of a long-range plan to produce a Derby winner, Hughes had acquired 300 brood mares. His career as a racehorse owner and breeder is legendary and the sums that he spent on buying, breeding and racing his horses will never be known. During World War II Hughes donated a percentage of his stake winnings to the Australian Red Cross Society.

A 'dapper little figure', Hughes was seldom seen in public except at the races and led a very private life. He died at his Edgecliff home on 18 August 1950 and was cremated. He left instructions that there was to be no public announcement. His horse Marconi raced and won at Rosehill the next Saturday, but only his near relations knew its owner was not alive. He left an estate valued for probate at £83 853: later J. B. Renshaw, the State Labor treasurer, claimed that Hughes had died a millionaire and when a company, F. W. Hughes Industries Ltd, was registered a year later with a nominal capital of £7½ million, an enquiry was set up into the estate.

A larger significance may be found in the career of F. W. Hughes, as it reflects something of the experience and mythology of Australia itself: the success of the common man transcending social origins, a vindication of the colonial belief that it's 'what you are' not 'who you are'; the transition from a rural-based to an urban industrial economy in twentieth century Australia—that he did this within the basic economic staple, riding on the sheep's back, makes it more interesting; and finally, personified in his own career, faith in the gospel of 'Australia Unlimited'.

C. R. Hall, *The manufacturers* (Syd, 1971); *Pastoral Review*, 6 Sept 1950; *Daily Telegraph* (Syd), 30 May 1947, 24 Oct 1951; *Age*, 3 Nov 1947; *Country Life*, 25 Aug 1950; S. Tweedie, Between depressions: Australian dilemmas in the search for Asian markets, 1893-1933 (M. Com. Hons thesis, Univ NSW, 1982); Records, Aust Jockey Club, and Aust Textile Workers' Union, NSW Division, and Chamber of Manufactures of NSW (Syd).

J. A. RYAN

HUGHES, GEOFFREY FORREST (1895-1951), solicitor and aviator, was born on 12 July 1895 at Darling Point, Sydney, second surviving son of Sydney-born parents Sir Thomas Hughes [q.v.], solicitor, and his wife Louisa, née Gilhooley. He was educated at St Ignatius' College, Riverview, and in 1914 began arts at the University of Sydney; in June he was commissioned in the 26th Infantry Regiment. A youthful interest in aeronautics led him to try unsuccessfully to join the Australian Flying Corps. In 1915 he was honorary aide-de-camp to the governor Sir Gerald Strickland [q.v.]

In March 1916 Hughes went to England and was commissioned in the Royal Flying Corps on 3 June and promoted flying officer on 28 July. He flew two tours of duty in France with No. 10 Squadron in 1916 and No. 62 in 1918, serving with training squadrons in England in 1917. Like his father and mother, he criticized widespread opposition in the Australian Catholic community to conscription. Writing to his parents in 1917 he claimed that priests who opposed the war were doing 'more harm to the cause of Catholicity in Australia, than the bitterest orangeman could ever do'. Promoted captain on 1 April 1918, he was twice mentioned in dispatches for showing 'great coolness and courage in action' and was awarded the Military Cross in May. After the final German offensive in France, he returned to a flying training unit and, on graduating, trained recruits for the Royal Air Force in 1918-19 and was awarded the Air Force Cross in June 1919.

Back in Australia Hughes returned to the University of Sydney (B.A., 1920; LL.B., 1923). He was admitted a solicitor on 10 May

1923 and joined the family firm, Hughes & Hughes. At Darlinghurst on 8 January that year he had married Margaret Eyre Sealy, née Vidal; they lived at Rose Bay. His first love remained flying: he was president of the (Royal) Aero Club of New South Wales in 1925-34 and persuaded the Commonwealth government to assist the aero club movement throughout Australia so that a steady stream of trained pilots would be available for civil and military purposes. In July 1940 he was granted a citizen commission in the Royal Australian Air Force as flying officer and, as a temporary wing commander, was appointed commanding officer of the flying school at Narrandera in 1941; he relinquished his commission, as acting group captain, in April 1943.

Hughes became a director of several public companies with which his father was linked, including the Australian Hotel Co. Ltd, the United Insurance Co. and the Commercial Banking Co. of Sydney, and was chairman of Tooheys [q.v.6] Ltd and Tooheys Standard Securities Ltd. He bitterly opposed the Chifley government's bank nationalization proposals in the late 1940s and refused a seat on the board of Qantas Empire Airways Ltd. He was a council-member of Sancta Sophia College, University of Sydney, a member of the Australian Club and Royal Sydney Golf Club, and a keen trout-fisherman.

Hughes died of pneumonia in Lewisham Hospital on 13 September 1951 and was buried in the Catholic section of Waverley cemetery. His estate was valued for probate at £29 492. He was survived by his wife, daughter and three sons: Thomas, a leading barrister, was Commonwealth attorney-general in 1969-71, and Robert has developed an international reputation as a provocative art critic. A portrait of Geoffrey Hughes by Florence Rodway [q.v.] is owned by the family.

Cyclopedia of N.S.W. (Syd, 1907); C. Cole, *Royal Air Force 1918* (Lond, 1968); *Sea, Land, and Air*, Nov 1919; *Aust Q*, Dec 1951; Lady Hughes, News-cutting book *and* Hughes family papers (ML).

PETER SPEARRITT

HUGHES, JOHN FRANCIS (1857-1912) and SIR THOMAS (1863-1930), solicitors and politicians, were born on 11 May 1857 and on 19 April 1863 in Sydney, eldest and third sons of Irish parents John Hughes, grocer and later grazier, and his wife Susan, née Sharkey. They were educated in England at Stonyhurst College, Lancashire, and matriculated for the University of London in 1876 and 1880. Returning to Sydney,

John was articled in 1878 to H. M. Makinson and was admitted as a solicitor on 1 March 1884. After touring Europe, Thomas returned to Sydney and in 1882 was articled to T. M. Slattery [q.v.] and admitted as a solicitor on 28 May 1887. From that year the brothers practised as Hughes & Hughes.

At St Mary's Cathedral, John married Mary Rose, daughter of James Charles Gilhooley, physician, on 2 July 1884 and Thomas married her younger sister Louisa on 19 October 1887.

On their father's death in 1880 the brothers inherited Lyndhurst Chambers and 26 Hunter Street in the city. John soon acquired other city property and became a director of the Australia Hotel Co. Ltd and chairman of Bannockburn Estate Ltd. A leading Catholic layman like his brother-in-law John Lane Mullins [q.v.], he was treasurer of St Vincent's Hospital in 1885-1912 and of St Mary's Cathedral building fund, a trustee of the Public Library of New South Wales in 1885-1912, president of the Prisoners' Aid Association, and a vice-president of the (Royal) Sydney Liedertafel. In 1903 the Pope appointed him knight commander of the Order of St Gregory.

In 1891-94 John Hughes represented Fitzroy Ward on the Sydney Municipal Council and in 1895 was nominated to the Legislative Council. He was vice-president of the Executive Council in 1898-99 and in 1904-10 in the Reid and Waddell [qq.v.] ministries, and minister of justice from July to September 1899. He served on the Parliamentary Standing Committee on Public Works in 1901-04 and was treasurer of the Federal Freetrade and Liberal Committee in 1901.

A biggish man with a crown of silvery-white hair above a cleanly moulded face, John Hughes cut a commanding figure in Sydney's legal, business and religious circles. He lived at Rockleigh Grange, North Sydney, which was later sold to the Catholic Church to house the apostolic delegate. A chronic asthmatic, he died unexpectedly on 18 December 1912 at North Sydney and was buried in Waverley cemetery. He was survived by his wife, two daughters and six sons, four of whom served overseas in World War I—one was killed in action. His estate was valued for probate at £34 114.

Thomas took little part in public affairs until he openly supported Federation in 1898 and next year became secretary to the government representative in the Legislative Council. In January he accompanied Reid, as his secretary, to the Federal Conference of Premiers in Melbourne which made concessions to New South Wales in the draft Constitution. Defeated for the State seat of Sydney-King in 1901, Hughes threw himself into municipal affairs. He represented

Bourke Ward on the Sydney Municipal Council in 1898-1912 and, an advocate of municipal reform, in 1898 had instituted a vigorous investigation into the city's finances, which resulted in the formation of a citizens' reform movement. With (Sir) James Graham [q.v.4], he helped to organize the Citizens' Vigilante Committee which co-operated with the government to control the first plague outbreak in 1900.

While Hughes held office as mayor in 1902, the title was changed to lord mayor. An imposing figure with dark hair, parted in the centre, and a waxed moustache, he again became lord mayor in 1903, 1907 and 1908. He was a member of the royal commissions on Sydney water supply (1902-03) and on the decline of the birth-rate (1903-04). With Sir Matthew Harris [q.v.], Hughes became an ardent campaigner for a unified 'Greater Sydney'. He favoured a centralized municipal body owning and controlling key public services and a programme of slum clearance and rehousing. By 1906 he had managed to extend the franchise to joint and individual occupants of business premises—a move designed to offset the working-class vote. In 1908-09 he presided over the royal commission for the improvement of the city of Sydney and its suburbs; its final report, a planning document of lasting importance, included recommendations on transport, beautification, town planning and social welfare.

In World War I, with his wife, Thomas Hughes was a foundation executive-member of the Universal Service League and a leading representative of a small group of upper-class Catholics who criticized the 'disloyal' anti-conscription attitudes of Dr Mannix [q.v.] and other Catholics. His sons Geoffrey [q.v.] and Roger, who was killed in action in 1916, fought in France.

Thomas was nominated to the Legislative Council in 1908 and knighted in 1915. His business interests soon outstripped those of his brother: he was chairman of Washington H. Soul [q.v.6], Pattison & Co. Ltd, S. Bennett [q.v.3] Ltd (publishers of the *Evening News*), Tooheys [q.v.6] Ltd and the Sydney boards of the London & Lancashire Fire Insurance Co. and National Mutual Life Association of Australasia Ltd, and was a director of the Commercial Banking Co. of Sydney and the Australia Hotel Co. Ltd. As chairman of Amalgamated Wireless (Australasia) Ltd, in the early 1920s he engaged in complex negotiations with the Commonwealth government to establish a direct commercial wireless service between Australia and Britain.

Hughes served as secretary of the first and third Catholic congresses in 1900 and 1909 and was appointed a knight commander of the papal Order of St Gregory in 1915. He was a member of the Australian Club and of the council of the Women's College, University of Sydney, and had been nominated to the Legislative Council in 1908. Suffering from chronic nephritis and arteriosclerosis, he died on 15 April 1930 in St Vincent's Hospital and was buried in Waverley cemetery after a service at St Canice's Church, Darlinghurst (he had donated the site and given £4000 for the establishment of this church). Two of his sisters were nuns in the Sacred Heart Order. His estate was valued for probate at £42 752.

He was survived by his wife and one of his three sons. Lady Hughes shared her husband's interest in municipal reform and supported many charitable causes; in 1914 she was a foundation member of the executive committee of the New South Wales division of the British Red Cross Society. Through the National Council of Women she advocated the registration of women for national service in World War I. She died in 1948.

Cyclopedia of N.S.W. (Syd, 1907); P. J. O'Farrell, *The Catholic Church and the community in Australia: a history* (Melb, 1977); N. Hicks, *'This sin and scandal'* (Canb, 1978); J. Roe (ed), *Twentieth century Sydney* (Syd, 1980); Syd Municipal Council, *Vade Mecum*, 1900-1912; *Lone Hand*, Dec 1908, Nov 1915; *T&CJ*, 5 June 1907, 2 Dec 1908; *SMH*, 19 Dec 1912, 16 Apr 1930; *Daily Telegraph* (Syd), 18 Aug 1915; *Freeman's J* (Syd), 26 Dec 1912, 24 Apr 1930; D. H. Coward, The impact of war on New South Wales (Ph.D thesis, ANU, 1974); Lady Hughes, Newscutting book *and* Hughes family papers (ML); information from T. E. F. and G. E. Hughes, Sydney, *and* Mrs C. M. Curtin, North Syd.

PETER SPEARRITT

HUGHES, WILLIAM MORRIS (1862-1952), prime minister, was born on 25 September 1862 at Pimlico, London, son of William Hughes, a carpenter from North Wales employed at the Houses of Parliament, and his wife Jane, née Morris. His father was Welsh speaking, a deacon of the Particular Baptist Church and a conservative in politics. His mother, a farmer's daughter from Llansantffraid, Montgomeryshire, who had been in service in London, was English speaking and Anglican. She was thirty-seven when she married, and William Morris was her only child. She died when he was seven and for the next five years Hughes lived with his father's sister at Llandudno, where he went to school, spending his holidays on the Morris farm. In 1874 he became a pupil-teacher at St Stephen's School, Westminster, where he had large classes of boys little younger than himself, but where he was well grounded in English history and literature. A lively youth, fonder of games than of lessons, he won a prize for French and caught the eye of the inspector, Matthew Arnold. He remained as an assistant after his five years apprenticeship, and joined a volunteer battalion of the Royal Fusiliers nearby.

Why Hughes decided to migrate is unknown. Long hours in ill-ventilated and overcrowded classrooms had probably affected his health, and his deafness may already have begun. In October 1884 he embarked for Queensland as an assisted migrant on the *Duke of Westminster*, reaching Brisbane on 8 December. For two years he led a roving life, taking various jobs and acquiring knowledge of the outback, as well as material for reminiscences that grew more colourful with time. Finally, as a galley-hand on a coastal boat, he arrived at Sydney. After a period of acute poverty he found a steady job as assistant to an ovenmaker and domestic stability in a boardinghouse near Moore Park. He married his landlady's daughter, Elizabeth Cutts, and in 1890 moved to Balmain where he opened a small mixed shop, took on odd jobs and mended umbrellas.

It was a time of ferment, not least in Balmain, where industry was encroaching on a mainly middle-class suburb. Hughes's shop sold political pamphlets, and the back room became a meeting-place for young reformers, among them W. A. Holman [q.v.] and (Sir) George Beeby [q.v.7]. The visit to Sydney that year of Henry George [q.v.4] stirred their imagination and Hughes made his political début as a street-corner speaker for the Balmain Single Tax League. In 1892 he joined the Socialist League and debating societies at Balmain and the Sydney School of Arts; he had probably already joined the Balmain Labor Electoral League.

He apparently took no part in the election of 1891 which brought the first Labor Party into parliament; next year it was split by older and shrewder politicians and lost the balance of power. Hughes and Holman followed J. C. Watson's [q.v.] lead to convert the Labor Electoral Leagues to 'solidarity' and to win new supporters. Hughes spent eight months organizing in the central west under the auspices of the Amalgamated Shearers' Union, returning to Sydney to win pre-selection for Lang for the 1894 election. His electioneering in the harbour-side city seat was enlivened by his and his friends' production of a weekly newspaper, the *New Order*; when he won by 105 votes he was drawn in triumph through the city in a dogcart, his supporters having first bought him a decent suit. In parliament he proved a shrewd tactician and effective speaker.

When (Sir) George Reid [q.v.] failed to deliver the legislation Labor wanted, in 1899 Hughes helped to replace him with (Sir) William Lyne [q.v.].

Hughes, a free trader, had opposed Federation on the terms proposed, but he turned at once to the Federal arena where he foresaw that the issues which interested him most—defence, immigration and industrial relations—would be dealt with. He won West Sydney, which included his State electorate, in 1901 and held it easily until 1916. In the first parliament, in which Labor backed the Protectionists under (Sir) Edmund Barton [q.v.7] against Reid's Free Trade Opposition, Hughes supported the Immigration Restriction Act; he feared that migrants of a lower standard of living would undermine wages, while a wide difference in cultural and political experience would thwart the development of a democratic society. On defence, he opposed the government's proposal for a small professional army backed by a *levée en masse*, advocating compulsory universal training on the Swiss model, a cause to which he returned until it was finally introduced by Alfred Deakin [q.v.8] in 1909.

Following the Deakin government of September 1903-April 1904 Labor briefly held office under Watson. Hughes, who had qualified for the Bar in November 1903, showed uncharacteristic modesty in refusing the post of attorney-general and took external affairs, with second rank to Watson. This was the first Labor government anywhere to last for more than a few days; it demonstrated that 'ordinary working men' could handle administration, and it gave the leaders practical experience. The government was defeated by the Reid-McLean [q.v.] coalition in August, but in July 1905 Deakin returned to power with the support of Labor, held office for three years, and carried out many of the policies common to both parties.

Politics was not Hughes's only activity. In 1899 he organized the Sydney wharf-labourers, whose union had been shattered by the early 1890s strikes. Sheltered from intimidation by his place in parliament, he was a match for the employers in negotiations. By the end of the year the union had 1300 members; Hughes remained secretary until 1916. With his toughness, his eloquence and his argumentative ability he became a kind of mascot to his members. He could win over the rowdiest meeting and any attempt to step out of line in his absence was quelled on his return. As a sideline, he organized the Trolley, Draymen and Carters' Union and became its president. He took advantage of the Federal parliament's location in Melbourne to organize the

Waterside Workers' Federation; the executive was recruited from the members of parliament for the various ports, and again Hughes was president. As chairman of the royal commission on navigation (1904-07) he became familiar with conditions on the ships as well as on the wharves, and made useful contacts with other maritime unions.

In 1907 Deakin appointed Hughes and Lyne to represent Australia at a shipping conference in London. Hughes's knowledge of the industry and his clear arguments impressed everyone, especially the chairman Lloyd George. This was his first return to England: he visited the Morris family in Wales and addressed a meeting of the National Service League chaired by Lord Roberts. A meeting of the Fabian Society led to a heated argument with Ramsay Mac-Donald over White Australia—Hughes found the Fabians unpractical, poor men to be in a strike with. He also noted the visit to England of the Japanese Prince Fushimi and, returning home through the United States of America and Canada, noted the trouble caused by Japanese migration to California and British Columbia. The trip launched Hughes into journalism. From October 1907 to October 1911 he contributed a widely read weekly column to the *Daily Telegraph*. The articles, some of which were published separately in 1910 as *The case for Labor*, sparkled with wit and humour, and ranged discursively over all Labor policies; they did much to disarm middle-class hostility and prepare the way for the party to win office.

At Hughes's insistence the Sydney wharflabourers were among the first to register with the New South Wales Arbitration Court in 1902, and they later registered with the Commonwealth commission. An exception to his general opposition to strikes came in 1908 when his clever, month-long orchestration of strikes and non-co-operation by wharflabourers, carters, seamen and the engineers and officers he was currently representing in the court, forced coastal shipowners to drop their opposition to the wharflabourers' award. Eighteen months later Hughes, as chairman of a congress of all the unions involved, attempted to apply similar tactics to a coal strike. This led to a bitter dispute with Peter Bowling [q.v.7], the leader of the coalminers, who broke away from the congress. The strike dragged on for some time, the miners gained nothing and Hughes, now a national figure, incurred the undying hostility of an extreme section of the labour movement.

The replacement of Watson by Fisher [q.v.8] as Labor leader in 1907 led to cooler relations with Deakin; next year Fisher ended the alliance and formed a short-lived government in which Hughes was attorney-general. The other parties regrouped in the Fusion which took office in 1909 under a somewhat reluctant Deakin, supported by (Sir) Joseph Cook [q.v.8]; the improbable arrangement occasioned some of Hughes's choicest invective. This marked the end of the 'three elevens'. At the 1910 election Labor won large majorities in both Houses. Hughes, again attorney-general, was Fisher's chief lieutenant.

At last Labor looked to be in a position to effect its policies, but already under Deakin reform had reached the constitutional limits as interpreted by the High Court of Australia. In 1911 and 1913 referendums to widen Commonwealth powers over trade and commerce, industrial relations, corporations and monopolies were defeated, while the judgments of the High Court in the Vend (1911) and Colonial Sugar Refinery (1912) cases defined the limits more sharply. Nonetheless the achievements of the government were considerable. It established the Commonwealth Bank and note issue, introduced a Federal land tax, took over the Northern Territory from South Australia and began work on the national capital at Canberra. The election of 1913 gave Cook a majority of one in the Lower House with a minority in the Senate. A double dissolution was followed by an election on 5 September 1914.

The campaign was interrupted by the outbreak of war. Both parties at once proclaimed their support for Britain. Hughes, carried away by emotion, tried hard to stop the election, but both Fisher and Cook rejected the idea and Hughes returned to the fight with refreshed enthusiasm. The result was a clear win for Labor, with thirty-one out of thirty-six seats in the Senate. This gave a mandate for the vigorous conduct of the war, but in view of the nature of the campaign, for nothing else. In the new cabinet Hughes, attorney-general, held a key position, becoming the most active and vocal of the ministry.

His attention was early drawn to the base metals industries, zinc, lead and copper, which were vital both for munitions and for the Australian economy. The metals were tied by long-term contracts to a small group of German firms which had monopolized the market and in the case of zinc the refining facilities. With the help of W. S. Robinson [q.v.] Hughes bullied or persuaded the producers to cancel their contracts. To keep the industries going and ensure that German interests were excluded after the war and control kept within the Empire, and as far as possible in Australia, Hughes set up the Australian Metals Exchange to control exports, with (Sir) John Higgins [q.v.] as government representative and chairman. Marketing associations of zinc and copper producers were formed, existing works for smelting lead and copper expanded, and arrangements made for the production of copper wire and cables. The Electrolytic Zinc Co. was established by W. L. Baillieu [q.v.7] with refining facilities in Tasmania. All this was done by private enterprise with government control and monetary guarantee. Sugar, wheat, wool and meat were similarly regulated, arrangements differing only in detail. The pattern was set by Hughes who, while relying on expert advice for each industry, was himself the only common factor.

When Fisher, his health undermined by the stress of war and growing party division, resigned as prime minister in October 1915 Hughes was unanimously chosen to succeed him. He had already devised a referendum to give the Commonwealth powers over commerce, monopolies and industrial relations and, as prime minister, he pressed on the campaign. But there was strong criticism and the proposals were disliked by many Labor men in the States, especially Holman in New South Wales and T. J. Ryan and E. G. Theodore [qq.v.] in Queensland. Hughes accepted a compromise at the Premiers' Conference in Melbourne in November whereby the powers were to be handed over for the duration of the war. In the event none of the States transferred the powers, which in 1916 were given to the government by the High Court in the case of *Farey* v. *Burvett*. There were charges of betrayal from the left wing of the party, which attributed to Hughes the 'blushless impudence of Iscariot'.

When he took office Hughes received from the governor-general, Sir Ronald Munro Ferguson [q.v.], information about the intentions of Japan in the Pacific which convinced him that discussions with the British government and the prime ministers of Canada and New Zealand were urgent. The Colonial Office was unenthusiastic, but Hughes interpreted a cool suggestion that he might come to London by himself as a special invitation. Just before leaving he found time to set up the Advisory Council of Science and Industry. Travelling by way of the Pacific he talked briefly with the New Zealand prime minister, W. M. Massey, and spent a crowded four days in Ottawa, where he was made a member of the Canadian privy council (cabinet), then a unique honour.

Hughes reached England on 7 March 1916. His public activity, in which he urged greater economic pressure on Germany and more co-operation with the dominions, was strenuous. Coming at a time of apparent stalemate these speeches (collected as *The day—and after* (1916)) were electrifying and widely reported. Some even thought Hughes might be the leader the country needed to replace Asquith. That this flamboyant rhetoric should have had such an effect now seems incredible, but at the time Hughes swept his hearers off their feet.

More important was the incessant round of interviews with politicians, generals and public servants by which he sought to know at first hand the men responsible for directing the war and to find out how to make Australia's voice heard. He renewed his acquaintance with Lloyd George, the bustling minister for munitions, in whom he found a kindred spirit; and he took part in two meetings of cabinet and two of the war committee, forming a low opinion of most of the ministers and especially of Asquith.

Hughes was also constantly engaged in difficult negotiations to sell Australian products and, even harder, to find ships to carry them. His support staff was negligible, but he received valuable help from Robinson in the negotiations on zinc and from (Sir) Keith Murdoch [q.v.] in public relations. Under the strain of overwork and the English winter he broke down at the end of March and was confined to bed for a fortnight, after which the hectic round was resumed.

In June he went as one of the British delegation to an allied conference in Paris to determine economic policies towards Germany, having with difficulty won from Asquith the right to speak independently on behalf of Australia. He agreed with the French that drastic restrictions should be imposed on German trade after the war. This was the first participation of Australia at an international conference and, as in the link forged by Hughes with the French, it was an important precedent for the eventual peace conference, on which Hughes's eyes were already fixed. While in France he visited the front, where Haig told him of the coming offensive on the Somme and where contact with the Australian troops deepened his devotion to them. Just before leaving for Paris, unable to get ships to lift the Australian wheat crop by any other means, he had secretly bought fifteen cargo vessels. On his return to England, at a lively meeting of the war committee he successfully defended the purchase against threatened requisition. The ships were the nucleus of the Commonwealth Shipping Line.

Hughes landed at Fremantle on 31 July. He found a country in which attitudes to conscription had polarized and he was forced to make a quick decision. Almost all his associates, including his defence minister (Sir) George Pearce [q.v.] pressed the need for conscription, and he was not fully aware of the strength of opposition within the trades unions and the Labor Party. He had returned half convinced of the need for compulsion and wholly determined to give the troops at the front whatever reinforcements they needed. Talks with the Foreign Office and the Japanese ambassador in London had confirmed his suspicion of the Japanese. Now mounting casualties on the Somme and falling enlistments decided him. Unable because of a hostile Senate to legislate for conscription, and believing that a majority of the people would support him if the issues were fully explained, he hit on the expedient of a referendum which, while having no legal force, would give him a mandate clear enough to override the Upper House. He opened the 'Yes' campaign on 18 September: voting was on 28 October. Increasingly aware of the opposition even within his cabinet, Hughes fought with growing desperation. On the eve of the ballot three ministers, provoked by an ill-judged regulation, resigned. The referendum was lost by a comparatively small majority of the total vote and in three States.

For his advocacy of conscription Hughes was expelled from the Labor Party. Long afterwards he said with some truth: 'I did not leave the Labor party. The party left me'. The Labor Party that emerged was indeed very different from that of the 1890s, and most of his older colleagues followed him out. He formed a cabinet from these, hoping to build around them a new party which would maintain the social radicalism and the Australian nationalism of the early party. He had misread the signs and was soon forced to merge with the Opposition in a National, or 'Win the War', Party. The Senate prevented endeavours to prolong the life of the parliament and, amid charges of attempted bribery and sharp practice, Hughes called an election for 5 May 1917. The new party won a sweeping victory in both Houses. Hughes, abandoning West Sydney, was returned with a large majority for the formerly Labor seat of Bendigo, Victoria. But his victory was a hollow one. Cut off from his political, social and even geographical roots, expelled by the party and the union which had been such a large part of his life, distrusted by his new supporters, he never, for all his public triumphs, regained the authority and confidence of his early days.

In the election campaign Hughes had promised not to reopen the conscription issue unless 'the tide of battle which flows strongly for the Allies turns against them'. In November 1917 this seemed to have happened and Hughes, under strong pressure, announced another referendum for 20 December. This time passions rose even higher, inflamed by mounting hysteria in Hughes and by the cold, Irish logic of Archbishop Daniel Mannix [q.v.]. There was a degree of violence unusual in Australian politics, which turned to farce when Hughes, after being struck by an egg on the railway station at Warwick, Queensland, promptly established a Commonwealth police force to combat disloyalty. The referendum was lost by a larger majority than before. Hughes had unwisely declared that he would not govern without conscription. He accordingly resigned, but the governor-general, unable to find anyone else who could command a majority, recommissioned him with the same cabinet as before.

The turmoil of local politics had prevented Hughes from attending the first session of the Imperial War Cabinet in 1917, so there was all the more reason why he should go to the meetings planned for 1918. On his way through America he met, and failed to impress, President Wilson, and in a widely reported speech in New York he called for a 'Monroe Doctrine' to exclude Japanese expansion from the Pacific. He reached London in June and the meetings, alternating with the Imperial War Conference sessions, lasted till August. Each of these bodies, the membership of which was the same, met on two days a week, the remaining time being occupied by meetings of the prime ministers and of committees. Hughes was active in both: in the cabinet he argued for greater use of tanks and aeroplanes to avoid the drain on manpower which he foresaw would place Britain at the economic mercy of the United States and he chaired a committee on reparations; in the War Committee, which dealt with intra-imperial questions, he pressed for the bypassing of the Colonial Office in communications between prime ministers. After the meetings Hughes stayed on in England, immersed in negotiations for the sale of 'copper, glycerine, tallow, butter, wheat, hides, leather, meat and rabbits'.

He was still in England when the armistice was signed in November. His first reaction was of furious protest that he had not been consulted and that Australia's vital interests had been compromised by the acceptance in the armistice of President Wilson's 'Fourteen Points'. Then, by calculated obstruction, he ensured that Australia would be represented at the peace conference not only within the British Empire delegation but in its own right.

At the peace conference which sat in Paris from January till June 1919 Hughes's irreverence and impish humour made him something of an *enfant terrible* to the more dignified delegates, especially Wilson, and the joy of lesser fry who delighted in circulating stories about him, some of them true. The aged French president Clemenceau and Lloyd George appreciated his audacious pugnacity and shared to some extent his dislike of Wilson. In the conference Hughes concentrated on three questions which he considered vital to Australia and likely to go against her by default. On reparations he had already taken a strong line in the Imperial War Cabinet. Now on the Reparations Commission he was primarily representing Britain, though Australian interests were also involved. The problem was whether Germany should be held liable for all the costs of the allies or, as Wilson insisted, only for material damage, in which case France and Belgium would get the lion's share, Britain little and Australia nothing. Hughes argued against John Foster Dulles that the criminal should pay all costs, Dulles that the acceptance of the 'Fourteen Points' in the armistice constituted a binding contract. Eventually a compromise suggested by Smuts of South Africa included pensions under the heading of damage, thus giving Australia a small and Britain a larger claim on reparations.

The other two questions concerned the Pacific, vital to Hughes, peripheral to all others except the Japanese. The first, fought out with Wilson before the Council of Ten, concerned German New Guinea. 'No annexations' was to Wilson a vital principle, enshrined in the 'Fourteen Points'; to Hughes full control of German New Guinea with power to exclude Japanese entry was essential to Australia's defence. Hughes, claiming to speak for '60,000 dead', held his ground even when Wilson threatened to leave the conference. Eventually Hughes gained the substance of his claim by the creation of a special class of mandate which permitted the subject territory to be administered as 'an integral portion' of the mandatary and under its laws.

On the remaining question Hughes had to work indirectly through the British Empire delegation and by private lobbying, and even by a threat to go outside the conference and arouse the American press. The Japanese wished to insert in the covenant of the League of Nations a guarantee of the 'equality of nations and of equal treatment of their nationals'. Hughes saw in this a threat to White Australia and rejected all wordings suggested, while the Japanese, though denying any intention to apply the formula to immigration, refused to exclude it explicitly. After many fruitless meetings between the parties, the Japanese put their amendment to the final meeting of the Commission on the Covenant. Wilson, known to favour the Japanese amendment, was in the chair. The British representative opposed it,

but it was clear that a majority would support it. The United States delegate E. M. House, passed a note to Wilson that if the amendment was carried 'it would surely raise the race issue throughout the world'. Wilson called a vote, and when twelve out of sixteen voted in favour, declared the amendment lost because the vote was not unanimous. Again Hughes had his way.

His conduct at the conference has often been criticized; his methods were certainly unorthodox, but they were probably the only ones that would have succeeded. (Sir) Ernest Scott [q.v.], the official historian, wrote: 'By characteristic methods he had gained single handed at least the points that were vital to his country's existence'.

'Billy' Hughes came home to a hero's welcome, but with the end of the war his political base had become insecure. Many of his ideas were still those of pre-war Labor and seemed 'socialistic' to his Nationalist colleagues. He encouraged the Commonwealth Shipping Line to compete with the private shipowners, and he brought the government further into commerce with joint ownerships of Amalgamated Wireless and Commonwealth Oil Refineries. This alienated businessmen as his desire to maintain orderly marketing of primary products alienated the farmers. He was very tired, and though still fertile in ideas he had no longer the drive to carry them through. In 1920 £25 000 was subscribed for him in recognition of his services to Australia and the Empire.

Only at the Imperial Conference in London in 1921 did Hughes's old form return. He prevented the termination of the Anglo-Japanese treaty sought by Canada, securing its retention until some better arrangement in which the United States would participate could be found. He prevented Smuts's proposals for a formal constitution for the British Commonwealth from even reaching the conference; instead he urged bold exploitation of aviation and wireless to make possible direct consultation. The conference closed in a confused flurry of proposals for a conference on Pacific security involving both the United States and Japan. From this came the Washington Treaty of 1922, which gave some, though not all, of the protection Hughes sought. His continued loyalty to the Imperial idea was later expressed in *The splendid adventure* (1929).

The election of 1922 gave the Country Party the balance of power, and when its leader (Sir) Earle Page [q.v.] refused to work with Hughes he was forced to give place to a coalition led by S. M. (Viscount) Bruce [q.v.7] with Page as deputy and treasurer. Hughes may have hoped for an early recall, but for any chance of this he had to lie low for a time. A friend arranged a lecture tour of America in 1924; the lectures were not a success, and in New York Hughes became seriously ill.

Back in Australia he returned to Sydney from Melbourne, where he had lived since 1917, buying a house at Lindfield but keeping his farm at Sassafras, Victoria. Hughes had already, in 1922, exchanged Bendigo for North Sydney as his electorate. For a time he kept his dislike of Bruce under control, but after the 1925 election his criticism of Bruce's handling of industrial relations and Page's extravagance became increasingly outspoken. With economic depression looming he held secret talks in 1929 with Theodore, and together they prepared a policy on lines similar to those being suggested by (Lord) Keynes in England. In August, when the government sought to abandon industrial arbitration to the States, Hughes, with a small group of Nationalist malcontents, organized its defeat by one vote. The result in doubt till the last, Hughes is said to have mounted guard over one waverer in the billiard-room to prevent him from being 'got at' during the dinner break. Bruce secured a dissolution and was soundly beaten, losing his own seat.

J. H. Scullin [q.v.] became prime minister with Theodore as treasurer. Hughes, expelled by the Nationalists, tried, as in 1916, to form a new party. At first he supported Scullin, but when the opposition of the Senate and the Commonwealth Bank, caucus faction and Scullin's timidity combined to paralyse the government and when Theodore was hounded out of office and replaced by Lyons he became progressively disillusioned. He vehemently attacked the mission of Sir Otto Niemeyer and was dismayed by the Premiers' Plan which resulted. In March 1931 he voted against the government on a no confidence motion by (Sir) John Latham [q.v.], along with Lyons who became prime minister in January 1932. Hughes, his own party in tatters, joined Lyons's United Australia Party which replaced the old National Party.

The fall of Bruce was the last time Hughes directly influenced political events, but he remained a force to be reckoned with. In 1932, as a delegate to the General Assembly of the League of Nations, his attention was drawn to the international situation in Europe and the Far East and for the next eight years he carried on a lone crusade on the need to prepare for war. In 1934 he became minister for health and repatriation and vice-president of the Executive Council. Because of his support of the George V Jubilee Fund he became known as 'minister for motherhood' and he linked this with defence in the slogan 'populate or perish'. In July,

under the auspices of the Defence of Australia League, he published *The price of peace*. Next year publication of an updated version, *Australia and war to-day*, in which he described economic sanctions as 'either an empty gesture, or war', coincided with a parliamentary debate on Abyssinia in which the government asserted the precise opposite; Hughes was forced to resign, but was soon restored to office. In 1937 he became minister for external affairs, though with no effective control of policy. His attacks on Hitler and Mussolini and especially on their colonial claims, to yield to which would, he said, be 'like giving a snack of sandwiches to a hungry tiger', and his new slogan 'what we have we shall hold', angered the German consul-general and embarrassed Lyons. Munich, which Lyons and Page hailed with satisfaction, left him dismayed and apprehensive.

In March 1939, when (Sir) Robert Menzies resigned from the ministry, Hughes became attorney-general and minister for industry. On 7 April Lyons died unexpectedly, and two weeks later Menzies became prime minister. Hughes retained his new portfolios (later exchanging industry for the navy) and was elected deputy leader. On the formation of a Labor government in October 1941 he was made leader of the United Australia Party and deputy leader of the Opposition. He remained a member of the War Advisory Council, and often found it easier to cooperate with the Labor prime minister, John Curtin, than with his own party. Deputy leader after Menzies returned to the leadership in 1943, he was in 1944 expelled from the party for rejoining the Advisory War Council after the party had left it.

With the war ended, Hughes joined the Liberal Party, formed by Menzies from the wreckage of the United Australia Party, and in 1949 moved from North Sydney to the new seat of Bradfield. At last he seemed to mellow, though there were still eruptions of the old fire and the old wit, evident in his reminiscences *Crusts and crusades* (1947) and *Politicians and potentates* (1950). At the time of his death he was preparing an attack on the government for its proposal to sell its share in Commonwealth Oil Refineries. On 25 September 1952 all parties joined to give him a dinner in honour of his eighty-eighth (actually his ninetieth) birthday. A few days later he caught a severe chill followed by pneumonia, and on 28 October he died at his Lindfield home. After a state funeral at St Andrew's Anglican Cathedral, he was buried in Northern Suburbs cemetery. His estate was valued at £70 886 in New South Wales and £45 759 in Victoria. Hughes's first wife died in 1906, leaving six children who all survived him. On 26 June

1911 at Christ Church, South Yarra, Melbourne, with Anglican rites, and without the knowledge of colleagues or press, he married Mary Ethel Campbell (D.B.E., 1922); their only daughter died in 1937. Dame Mary, by her social gifts, tact and management, gave Hughes the domestic background he had always lacked and provided precisely the feather-bedding that his restless activity and frail physique required.

Hughes was slightly built, 5 ft. 6 ins. (167 cm) tall, with a large head and long bony hands. In youth he had been handsome; in middle age his face became deeply lined and in old age a pronounced stoop and wizened frame gave him a gnome-like appearance. He suffered all his adult life from severe deafness, occasionally turned to good account, and from chronic dyspepsia. His voice was harsh and monotonous, but he trained himself to use it effectively—it was particularly suited to the satire at which he excelled. Like many whose health is precarious, he was a physical fitness fanatic. When young he enjoyed rowing and cricket; later his favourite exercise was horse-riding. He loved motoring, and his driving terrified passengers and other road-users alike. Lacking time for a honeymoon, he took his second wife for a drive after the wedding and overturned the car.

A controversial figure all his life, he remains so still. To some a great statesman and patriot, to others he was a renegade and mountebank. He aroused extremes of admiration or hatred, but never indifference. Abrasive and ruthless, he could also be charming and amusing. Often mean, he could sometimes be very generous. He would fly into violent rages, which would soon be forgotten. A gift to cartoonists, he became in old age a figure of fun to those who knew nothing of his prime. Flexible as to means, his broad objectives were remarkably consistent. These were 'to fight for the under-dog' and to defend the right of Australia to develop its own form of democratic society, combining the best of British traditions and institutions with the maximum of freedom and equality. His old opponent Lord Bruce said of him after his death: 'he had two qualities which are very rare and very important in a politician: he had imagination and he had courage'. With all his faults, his place in Australian history is secure, no less for his contribution to the early labour movement than for his achievements as a national wartime leader and on the world stage.

L. F. Fitzhardinge, *William Morris Hughes* 1-2 (Syd, 1964, 1979) and for bibliog; W. J. Hudson, *Billy Hughes in Paris* (Melb, 1978); M. Booker, *The great professional; a study of W. M. Hughes* (Syd, 1980).   L. F. FITZHARDINGE

HUIE, ALEXANDER GORDON (1869-1964), single taxer, was born on 16 October 1869 at Tayco, in the Riverina, New South Wales, son of Alexander Huie, Scottish farmer, sometime carrier and storekeeper, and his wife Mary Eliza, née Carige, born in British Grenada. The family were 'all temperance people'. In 1883 he moved to Lake Cargelligo where he worked as a carpenter. In 1889 he read Henry George's [q.v.4] *Progress and poverty* and was aroused by its message, but remoteness prevented his attending rallies when George visited Australia next year. Huie became correspondent for the *Hillston Spectator* and secretary of the local progress committee.

In 1894 he failed to win the seat of Lachlan, after 'travelling some 1600 miles (2575 km), mainly on one horse' preaching land-value taxation and free trade. He was to lose eleven more State, Federal and city council elections. In 1898 he moved to Sydney where he worked in the building trade, frequented parliament's public gallery, joined debating societies and continued writing for country newspapers. He became founding honorary secretary in September 1901 of the Sydney Single Tax League (Free Trade and Land Values League in 1913-29 and from 1943—Henry George League of New South Wales in 1929-43). In the 1904 and 1907 State elections he worked for (Sir) Joseph Carruthers' [q.v.7] Liberal and Reform Association.

Huie founded the *Standard*, organ of the single taxers, in December 1905. In 1908 members subscribed to open an office and pay him a small salary. Thenceforth, 'single-minded in outlook and strongly dedicated, determined and capable', he devoted himself full time to expounding Georgeism—writing, debating, organizing deputations and addressing meetings. In 1910-36 he made several country tours, from 1926 in a donated model T Ford. He resigned as editor and secretary of the league in December 1953.

An indefatigable writer of letters to most newspapers in the State—the *Sydney Morning Herald* published about 220 in 1916-62—Huie also contributed articles and editorials, sometimes using pseudonyms. His style was 'that of the late Victorian era', wrote the *Canberra Times*, 'but his popularity with editors was the direct result of his clarity of writing'. He regarded land-value rating for local government in New South Wales as 'chief among his achievements'. He also crusaded for proportional representation, claiming credit for Carruthers' 1906 Local Government Act and the 1918 Parliamentary Elections (Amendment) Act. But Huie's influence on these decisions is arguable.

At Ashfield on 1 October 1921 with Methodist forms, he had married a Maltese-born widow Annie Bertha Lark, née Bartlett (d. 1948); they lived at Ashfield. Handsome, tall with trim beard and moustache, Huie was a relentless rather than a good speaker. He was a regular spruiker in the Sydney Domain; in later years gaunt, solemn and often barely audible, he attracted few listeners. Huie died on 7 November 1964 while visiting Lake Cargelligo and was buried there with Presbyterian forms. His estate was sworn for probate at £6139. In 1983 the league he served continues as the Association for Good Government.

Jill Roe (ed) *Twentieth century Sydney* (Syd, 1980); *V&P* (LA NSW), 1897, 4, pp 633, 821; *Standard*, 15 Sept 1916, 15 Jan 1954, Nov, Dec 1964; *Good Government*, Mar 1966; Henry George League (Melb), *Progress*, Feb 1965; *SMH*, 10 Mar 1922, 5 Dec 1964; *Canberra Times*, 9 Dec 1964; A. G. Huie, scrap-books, *and* Single Tax League minute-books (ML); information from Dr D. L. Clark, Syd.   CHRIS CUNNEEN

HULL, ARTHUR FRANCIS BASSET (1862-1945), public servant and naturalist, was born on 10 October 1862 at O'Brien's Bridge, Hobart Town, son of Hugh Munro Hull, coroner and later clerk of the House of Assembly, and his wife Margaret Basset, née Tremlett. Educated at the High School, Hobart, he was lamed by infantile paralysis at 15 and had to wear a surgical boot and use a walking-stick for the rest of his life.

In 1883-89 Hull was a clerk in the registry of the Supreme Court. Secretary and treasurer of the Orpheus Club in the 1880s, he performed as a tenor and in plays; he worshipped and sang at St Andrew's Presbyterian Church. He also tried his hand at short stories and verse in *A strange experience* (1888). At the Congregational Church, New Town, he married Laura Blanche Nisbet on 29 April 1891; she bore a son and died in 1893.

Hull moved to Sydney and on 12 October 1892 became a clerk in the General Post Office. On 1 July 1900 he transferred to the Department of Public Works as secretary to the labour commissioners. Sued for breach of promise of marriage by Bertha Cligny de Boissac in March 1899, Hull had been unable to pay £500 damages and was forced into bankruptcy. At Annandale on 15 January 1902 he married a 53-year-old widow Caroline Ann Lloyd, née Baker. He was discharged from bankruptcy in March and later visited Britain and Europe. On his return he joined the Department of Mines as a clerk in January 1903; he retired in 1921.

A keen amateur scientist, Hull was active as secretary for many years and president of the Royal Zoological Society of New South Wales in 1917-19, 1928-29 and 1938-39. He was a member of the Taronga Zoological Park Trust from 1926. He was also president of the Royal Australasian Ornithologists' Union in 1919-20 and of the local Linnean Society in 1923-24 and published in their journals; he discovered the nest and eggs of the Gould Petrel *Pterodroma (Oestrelata) leucoptera* and in 1909 published an important work, 'Birds of Lord Howe and Norfolk Islands', in the *Proceedings* of the Linnean Society (vol. 34, 1909).

However Hull's greater interest was conchology, particularly loricates (Chitons). He pursued these around Australia, Santa Cruz and New Caledonia, becoming very agile over rocky terrain. With Tom Iredale [q.v.] he published a *Monograph of Australian loricates* (1927) and other articles with Charles Hedley [q.v.]. His name was commemorated in the genus *Bassethullia* and several species. He gave a duplicate set of his specimens to the Australian Museum, Sydney, where he was honorary ornithologist in 1917-45.

From his boyhood Hull collected stamps and was an honorary fellow of the (Royal) Philatelic Society, London, from 1887. He published *Stamps of Tasmania* (London, 1890), *The postage stamps . . . of New South Wales* (London, 1911) and *The postage stamps . . . of Queensland* (1930). He contributed many articles on stamps, envelopes, wrappers, postcards and coins to journals, and edited the *Australian Philatelist*. In his later years he collected and annotated revenue stamps. He received many philatelic honours.

Short in stature with brilliant, piercing brown eyes, Hull was 'silver-haired . . . dapper in his grey suit' and 'crisp in manner'. Somewhat autocratic when dealing with committees, he was always kind to anyone willing to learn. Visitors to his home at Queenscliff, Sydney, remember his dining-room as a veritable museum holding collections of stamps, coins, eggs, skins, shells and books. His wife had divorced him in 1912; at Manly on 3 December 1926 he married a 56-year-old divorcee Diana Farley, née Cater. Survived by his third wife and son of his first marriage, Hull died on 22 September 1945 and was cremated with Anglican rites. His portrait, painted by W. Hayward Veal in 1941, is held by the Royal Zoological Society of New South Wales.

H. M. Whittell, *The literature of Australian birds* (Perth, 1954); *Aust Stamp Mthly*, 15 (Dec 1944), p 755; Roy Zoological Soc NSW, *Procs*, Oct 1945-46, p 15; *Emu*, 45 (Apr 1946) pt 3, p 255; *SMH*, 18 Mar 1899, 1 Jan 1936, 26, 29 Sept 1945; G. Whitley collection (Aust Museum, Syd); Bankruptcy file 10/23251 (NSWA); family and personal information from Mrs N. T. S. Jones, Yenda, *and* Iredale family, Lindfield, NSW, who hold Hull scrap-book.

TESS KLOOT

HUME, WALTER REGINALD (1873-1943), inventor and entrepreneur, was born on 29 November 1873 at Fitzroy, Melbourne, second son of James Hill Hume, a professional phrenologist and mesmerist from Scotland, and his second wife Caroline, née Gill, from Bristol, England. As James Hume regularly moved round Victoria lecturing, Walter attended a large number of schools until his father died, and at 12 he had to find employment. For the next five years he worked at several trades, finally becoming a plasterer.

In the depression of the 1890s he joined forces with his brother Ernest (1869-1929), a carpenter, and in September 1892 they sought employment in the country. They tried a variety of construction, repair, and farming jobs before establishing a workshop at Malmsbury where they produced fencing droppers under the protection of their first patent. Their business flourished owing to extensive vermin fencing being constructed in South Australia and Walter moved to Adelaide about 1904 to establish a second factory. A major decline in pastoral capital formation forced the brothers to close their Malmsbury business in 1906 and to turn their energies to the manufacture in Adelaide of ornamental steel fencing. They continued in this business until early 1910 when they formed Humes' Patent Cement Iron Syndicate Ltd to develop Walter's revolutionary centrifugal process for the manufacture of concrete pipes. This important invention transformed not only Walter's own career, but also the nature of the pipe manufacturing industry world wide. A measure of his achievement with this and another eighty of his patented inventions is that his firm was the only one in Australia before World War II to pioneer a major new technology and to export it (under royalty agreements) throughout the world. As well, his inventions had an important impact upon the development of urban Australia by significantly reducing the cost of constructing essential water, sewerage and drainage facilities.

To begin production of concrete pipes using the newly developed centrifugal process, Hume Bros Cement Iron Co. Ltd was incorporated in Adelaide in April 1911. In this new company Walter (who was to be managing director) and Ernest each held one-third of the shares; the remaining third was subscribed by South Australian graziers and farmers. The firm grew slowly in its first decade. By 1920, however, Hume was determined to extend his operations throughout Australia, and a new company, Hume Pipe Co. (Aust.) Ltd, was incorporated in Melbourne in July of that year. Although Hume's ownership of the new company was reduced to only 14 per cent, he was able to maintain control, due to his forceful personality and his highly inventive and innovative mind. While the new board of directors included prominent men like Sir John Monash and Senator A. J. McLachlan [qq.v.], the key members of the managerial group who presided over the firm's remarkable inter-war growth were Walter Hume as managing director, L. J. (Lord) Clifford as director in charge of financial matters, and J. A. Cussen as secretary. Ernest resigned in 1923 to establish and direct the first commercial wireless transmitting station in Adelaide (5DN).

In the early 1920s the company established branches in all States, extending to New Zealand in 1922 and Singapore in 1923. The success of this rapid expansion of the concrete pipe business encouraged Hume to diversify production by establishing a new company, Hume Steel Ltd, in 1923 to manufacture steel pipes using his pioneering inventions in the new field of automatic electric-arc welding. Although economic conditions were far from favourable during the 1930s and early 1940s, Hume's companies continued to expand, so that by 1943 they controlled over sixty factories throughout Australasia.

Walter Hume married Alice Louisa Bourne, née Mudford (1884-1972), at Moonta, South Australia, on 23 November 1909, and they had five sons and four daughters. All the sons joined the business between 1929 and 1940, but left soon after Walter's death, and until 1960 traded successfully (as W. R. Hume Pty Ltd) in opposition to the parent company. What little leisure time Hume had was devoted to Freemasonry and recording his general observations of the world around him. He died from cancer on 21 July 1943 and was buried in the Presbyterian section of Springvale cemetery. His estate was valued for probate at £39 951. There are two portraits by William Dargie, one in the Melbourne offices of Humes Ltd and the other held by the family.

G. D. Snooks, 'Innovation and the growth of the firm: Hume enterprises, 1910-1940', *Aust Economic Hist Review*, March 1973, *and* Hume enterprises in Australia, 1910-1940 (Ph.D. thesis, ANU, 1971); personal and company papers (ANU Archives).   G. D. SNOOKS

HUME-COOK; *see* COOK, James Newton Haxton Hume-

HUNGERFORD, RICHARD COLIN CAMPBELL (1865-1931), contractor and trotting official, was born on 1 January 1865 at Dunedin, New Zealand, elder son of Thomas Walter Hungerford, contractor, and his wife Elizabeth Mary, née Delaney, both from Kildare, Ireland. He attended the Otago Boys' High School and then began working with his father. His extensive sporting interests included cricket, Rugby Union, athletics, trotting and racing. As the first secretary of the Greymouth Trotting Club, he uncovered several swindles and at the 1896-98 New Zealand trotting conferences was actively involved in framing the rules. He was also a committee-member of the Greymouth Jockey Club and represented it at the racing conference in 1894.

In August 1898 Hungerford moved to Sydney to join Hungerford & Sons, the family's contracting firm, and was the managing partner for harbour works at Cape Hawke. His love of horses led him to resign in October 1902 to become the first salaried secretary of the newly formed non-proprietary New South Wales Trotting Club.

From 1904 Hungerford edited the *Trotting Register* annually, and was involved in the production of the *Australian Stud Books for Trotters* which appeared from 1910. He was ruthless in tracking down 'ring-ins' and uncovering crooked practices at race meetings. He had dark wavy hair and a handlebar moustache; although a relatively short man, it was said that 'many a strapping horseman quaked in his presence such was his overbearing demeanour'. For many years he was handicapper, starter and timekeeper for the club's race meetings and was known to be scrupulously fair. Clubs outside Sydney benefited from his encouragement and willingness to act as stipendiary steward. He also travelled interstate to foster good relations with trotting bodies.

After difficult early years, the New South Wales Trotting Club raised trotting from a disorganized, disreputable and waning sport to a firmly established, popular one. Hungerford played a central role in this process. While his opponents accused him of being dictatorial, his overall achievements were widely recognized. At a public presentation, following his retirement because of ill health in October 1923, the formal address maintained that his slogan was 'Favours to all, privileges to none'.

For many years Hungerford was a member of the New South Wales Rugby Union council, a vice-president of the Sydney Bicycle and Motor Cycle Club and a judge at the pony and galloway meetings at Kensington and Rosebery. He was also an active Freemason and frequented the Commercial Travellers', Tattersall's and City Tattersall's clubs. In June 1908 he was appointed a justice of the peace.

At the Registry Office, Christchurch, New Zealand, Hungerford had married Florence Mary Eliza Lawes on 4 March 1897, but they separated later; Florence moved to Melbourne with their daughter. Hungerford died in Manly of myclocythaemia on 13 February 1931, and was buried in the Roman Catholic section of Randwick cemetery.

Cyclopedia of N.S.W. (Syd, 1907); M. J. Agnew, *Australia's trotting heritage* (Melb, 1977); G. Brown, *One hundred years of trotting 1877-1977* (Syd, 1981); *Aust Trotting Record*, 21 Nov 1923; *SMH*, 16 Feb 1931; *Sydney Sportsman*, 17 Feb 1931.
I. G. CARNELL

HUNT, ATLEE ARTHUR (1864-1935), lawyer and public servant, was born on 7 November 1864 at Baroonda station on the Fitzroy River, Queensland, son of Arthur Hunt, grazier and later a footwear manufacturer, from Middlesex, England, and his Adelaide-born wife Hannah, née Watson. He was educated at Balmain Public School and Sydney Grammar School. In 1879 he entered the New South Wales Lands Department as a junior clerk. He visited England in 1887, returned to Australia to study law, tutoring part time at Sydney Grammar School, and on 21 March 1892 was admitted to the New South Wales Bar. On 4 September 1897 he married Lilian Hunt, a second cousin.

In 1896, as junior counsel to A. Bruce Smith [q.v.], he defended the colonial government in the two-year McSharry railway arbitration case. When the New South Wales Federal Association was formed in 1898 Hunt became secretary and in 1899 general secretary of the Federal League of Australasia. With (Sir) Robert Garran [q.v.8] Hunt was part of that coterie which surrounded (Sir) Edmund Barton [q.v.7] and planned the Federation campaign. When Barton became prime minister in 1901 Hunt accompanied him as his private secretary, managed his electoral campaign, and was sometimes taken for the prime minister himself because of his impeccable clothes. The diaries he kept during 1902 and 1904 contain sharp observations of the political figures with whom he mingled.

In May 1901 Barton appointed Hunt secretary and permanent head of the Department of External Affairs (to which, until 1909, the Prime Minister's Office was also attached). When the Commonwealth took responsibility for British New Guinea, Hunt, frustrated by lack of information and distance, undertook an official visit. His report of 1905, published as a parliamentary paper, argued for the immediate passage of the Papua bill (frustrated since 1903); it was passed in 1906. Hunt proposed that priority be given to agriculture and the establishment of a career public service for the territory. Complaints of administrative inefficiency led, through his intervention, to the royal commission of 1906 whose findings resulted in the dismissal of the administration. The commission approved Hunt's recommendations on the compulsory acquisition of native land and on the encouragement of native industry that paved the way for individuals and companies to settle and develop the territory.

Australian influence in the South-West Pacific also grew notably under Hunt. He awarded Burns [q.v.7] Philp [q.v.] & Co. the mail services contract, influenced by their ownership of land in the New Hebrides at a time when he intended to promote the resettlement of soldiers returning from the South African War. Hunt also fought successfully for favourable conditions for British planters. When he attended the 1907 Imperial Conference with Deakin [q.v.8] Hunt corresponded informally with the Colonial Office over the New Hebrides question, but the Anglo-French Condominium proclaimed at Vila in 1907 was decided without reference to the Commonwealth government.

Hunt had a major influence in the drafting of the immigration restriction bill and was responsible for the discretionary passport system for students, merchants and travellers from India or Japan. The Pacific Islands Labourers' Act (1902), whose provisions he also influenced, paved the way for the repatriation of islanders after 1906 though Hunt, heeding the appeals of a Pacific Islanders' Association founded in 1906, moved to allow certain exemptions. To deal with the problem of large numbers of Chinese stowaways Hunt set up an ever-widening circle of vigilant informants and in 1908 recommended stiff fines on shipowners, adopted in an amendment to the Immigration Restriction Act.

The establishment of the Australian High Commission in London in 1910 brought Australia's dealings with the Imperial government within the ambit of Hunt's department. In 1910 he was appointed C.M.G. and in 1911 again attended an Imperial Conference. He was henceforth suspected, however, for his conspicuous political associations by Labor prime ministers who dissociated themselves from the Department of External Affairs. When Andrew Fisher [q.v.8] established an autonomous

Prime Minister's Department in 1913 and appointed Malcolm Shepherd [q.v.], a former subordinate of Hunt, permanent head, Hunt's department lost some of its prestige and status. In 1914 Hunt produced a report on Norfolk Island and in 1915 visited the Northern Territory whose proclamation in 1913 had added another significant responsibility to his department. On the rearrangement of departments in November 1916 Hunt became secretary and permanent head of the Department of Home and Territories. In 1918 he was appointed to a Federal committee to consider post-war problems connected with enemy aliens. He was a member of the royal commission appointed in 1919 which travelled to New Guinea and reported on the administration of the ex-German mandated territories.

In February 1921 Hunt was appointed the first public service arbitrator provided for by the Arbitration Public Service Act of 1920. Initially he made himself unpopular by stringent rulings on pay increases, on the grounds that the country could not sustain the costs. From 1923 when the Bruce [q.v.7]-Page [q.v.] ministry set up the Public Service Board under the chairmanship of Sir Brudenell White [q.v.] relations between the board and the arbitrator were increasingly strained by Hunt's independent decisions. The board openly criticized Hunt and recommended abolition of his position. Hunt's tenure was renewed when his term expired in March 1928, but a special amending Act for retirement at 65 reduced his occupancy to November 1929. It was suspected that the government might not even appoint a successor and the future of arbitration became a major issue in the October 1929 election, lost by the Bruce-Page government. The Scullin [q.v.] government confirmed Hunt's appointment temporarily and he retired on 31 May 1930.

Dapper, courteous and kind, Hunt left a reputation for initiative, political acumen and common sense. The *Federal Public Service Journal* gratefully testified that 'His judgments are a sheer delight to read'. Always judicial, he concerned himself with establishing guiding principles of permanent value. Hunt was chairman of the Charities Board of Victoria several times after 1925 and honorary treasurer of the Royal Humane Society of Australasia. He died on 19 September 1935 at Perth, and was buried in Karrakatta cemetery with Anglican rites. His wife, two sons and a daughter survived him.

Punch (Melb), 24 Jan 1907, 2 July 1908; *SMH*, 21 Sept 1935; H. M. Davies, The administrative career of Atlee Hunt, 1901-1910 (M.A. thesis, Univ Melb, 1969), and for bibliog.

HELEN M. DAVIES

HUNT, HENRY AMBROSE (1866-1946), meteorologist, was born on 7 February 1866 in London, son of Edwin Jackson Hunt, marine engineer, and his wife Annie, née Padley. After three years with his family in St Petersburg (Leningrad), where his father managed the Baltic Ironworks and designed engines for battleships, he returned to England and was educated at Dartford Grammar School, Kent, where he won a scholarship in mathematics.

Accompanying his father to Sydney in March 1884, he came under the influence of H. C. Russell [q.v.6], the government astronomer, and became a temporary clerk at the observatory. Rejected for the Sudan Contingent in 1885, he was appointed meteorological assistant in January 1886 at a salary of £145; in his spare time he trained as a mechanical draughtsman and studied applied mechanics. In 1890 he was promoted second meteorological assistant responsible for preparing the daily weather map and began valuable work for Russell's notable paper on the movement of anti-cyclones in the Southern Hemisphere. In 1894 he won the Ralph Abercromby prize for *An essay on southerly bursters* (Sydney, 1894) and next year again attracted favourable attention with *Types of Australian weather* (Sydney, 1895), a study of twenty different weather types undertaken at Abercromby's request. In January 1904 he was appointed acting meteorologist.

In November 1906 Hunt, a fellow of the Royal Meteorological Society, London, was appointed first Commonwealth meteorologist and head of the new Commonwealth Meteorological Bureau in Melbourne. He took up his position on 1 January 1907 and on 20-23 May presided over a conference in Melbourne designed to secure uniformity in meteorological methods throughout Australia. In 1910 he reported favourably on the climatic suitability of the Yass-Canberra site for the seat of government. Initially Hunt was mainly concerned with synoptic meteorology but upper air explorations were begun in 1913 when with Griffith Taylor [q.v.] and E. T. Quayle he published *The climate and weather of Australia* (Melbourne, 1913), the first Australian textbook on the subject. In September 1919 Hunt attended a conference of representatives of the meteorological services of the British Dominions in London. In his annual report for 1921-22 he detailed 'the direct monetary value derived from the activities of the Weather Bureau' and stressed the urgent need for more money and better facilities. In 1926 he contributed the article on meteorology and climate to the *Australian encyclopaedia*.

In October 1929 Hunt published 'A basis for seasonal forecasting in Australia'; his proposed four-year weather cycle was novel in that it considered the non-meteorological element—vegetation—in a relationship with temperature and rainfall. The 'heat pool' theory, Hunt's suggested mechanism for his cycle, postulated that droughts in central Australia induced the moisture-laden monsoons to swing further south and when the natural vegetation returned, the monsoon retreated setting the stage for another period of drought. Hunt retired in February 1931. His greatest achievement was to found and with limited money build up Australia's best-known scientific service to the stage where it could meet the increased demands of civil and military aviation and move into the new age of frontal analysis.

Somewhat reserved and mild-mannered, Hunt had few social recreations apart from chess. An expert handyman, he spent much of his spare time on carpentry and metalwork; he invented a 'rotating rain clock' and several mechanical devices including a pressure-cube anenometer which recorded simultaneously, at the bureau, wind pressure, velocity and direction.

Hunt died of myocarditis at his Elwood home on 7 February 1946 and was buried in Brighton cemetery. He had married on 11 December 1899 at St Paul's Church of England, Redfern, Sydney, Wilhelmina Eve Linden, who predeceased him. Two of their three daughters survived him.

A cartoon of Hunt by Will Dyson [q.v.8] appeared in *Table Talk*, 27 May 1926.

T. G. Taylor, *Australian meteorology* (Oxford, 1920); *Qld J of the Roy Meteorological Soc*, 55 (1929), no 232; *PP* (Cwlth), 1907-08, 2, p 879, 1203; *Punch* (Melb), 3 Aug 1911; *SMH*, 5 May, 2 June 1916, 17 Sept, 3 Oct 1919, 16 Jan 1920, 19 Apr 1929; *Argus*, 13 Oct 1923; *Sun* (Melb), 6 Feb 1931; *Herald* (Melb), 10 Jan, 6 Feb 1931, 8 Feb 1946.   G. P. WALSH

HUNT, JOHN CHARLES (1856-1930), grazier, orchardist and politician, and ALFRED EDGAR (1861-1930), pastoralist and politician, were born on 27 July 1856 and on 2 May 1861 at Dural, New South Wales, sons of native-born parents George Thomas Hunt, farmer, and his wife Elizabeth, née Williams. John was educated at Parramatta North Public School, and both brothers attended Newington College.

John returned to his father's property at Dural in 1873 and became a successful orchardist, growing citrus and summer stone-fruits. He married Annie Maria Golledge on 29 May 1879 at Parramatta. Although he lived at Parramatta after his father died in 1899, he was strongly attracted to the fertile area known as 'the hills' district in Hornsby Shire. He advocated extending the railway to Dural and in 1900, in evidence to the Parliamentary Standing Committee on Public Works, dealt graphically with the difficulties of transporting produce to the railway at Hornsby in horse-drawn vehicles. He was a member of the Carlingford-Dural Railway League.

In 1906 Hunt became a councillor of Hornsby Shire and its first president in 1907, the year in which he was also president of the Central Cumberland Agricultural and Horticultural Association (Castle Hill) and vice-president of the Fruitgrowers' Union of New South Wales. He easily won the State seat of Sherbrooke in 1907 as a Liberal, holding it until the redistribution of 1913, and then represented Camden until he retired in 1920. He retained his close interest in rural affairs as a shareholder in, and later a director of, the family pastoral firm of Hunt Brothers, owners of Burdenda and other pastoral stations on the Bogan River and orchards at Dural.

Positive and forthright, Hunt adhered to his Methodist principles, ready to assist the needy, and worthy causes. The delights of his later years were his motor car and listening to his crystal set.

John Hunt died at his home at Parramatta on 23 March 1930 and was buried in the Methodist section of Dural cemetery. Predeceased by a son killed on active service and by a daughter, he was survived by his wife, four sons and three daughters; and left an estate sworn for probate at £10 139. His wife was a noted needlewoman who won many prizes for her embroidery and gave long years to community work, including the Australian Red Cross Society.

Alfred went to the Bogan district in 1878 and selected land near Dandaloo. He worked hard to improve his holding and his financial position and on 24 December 1881 married Sarah Ruth, sister of C. B. Fletcher [q.v.8], at the Pitt Street Wesleyan Church, Sydney. He became a successful sheep-farmer and later owned Wyoming, near Nevertire, other pastoral properties and Orange Grove near Parramatta; he was never a partner in Hunt Brothers. His modest prosperity and the ability of his two elder sons to manage the properties enabled him actively to promote rural interests. A member from 1904 of the Farmers and Settlers' Association, he was president in 1914-16, treasurer in 1916-30 and a director of its newspaper, the *Land*. He was also president of the Graziers' Association of New South Wales in 1921-22, president of the Australian Farmers' Federal Organisation and a council-member of the Royal Agricultural Society of New South Wales.

During World War I, Alfred Hunt was a member of the State Wool Committee, supporting moves for practical marketing and equitable returns from primary products subject to wartime controls, and took a leading part in recruiting drives. In 1929 he was president of the New South Wales division of the New Settlers' League of Australia.

As chairman of the Progressive Party's central council, Hunt was influential in the formation of the party, advocating retention of its separate identity and establishment of its headquarters in Bligh Street, Sydney. He was nominated to the Legislative Council in 1916. Throughout his political career he strongly promoted rural interests. In 1918 he became one of the first directors of the McGarvie-Smith Institute, a state-owned venture for the manufacture and sale of anthrax vaccine. He deplored the costly depredations caused by blowflies and rabbits, and supported moves to establish a branch of the Pasteur Institute to investigate possible biological eradication of these pests. After a 1925 visit to England he stressed the need to improve dressing of meat for overseas markets.

A quiet but consistent supporter of the needy, Alfred was also a member of the New South Wales Conference of the Methodist Church of Australasia, and an originator of the Far West Children's Health Scheme. He had been 'ailing for some years' with nephritis and arteriosclerosis when he died at his home at Mosman on 16 August 1930 of coronary thrombosis; he was buried in the Methodist section of Northern Suburbs cemetery. Predeceased by two sons killed in action, he was survived by his wife, three sons and three daughters. His estate was sworn for probate at £32 028.

John and Alfred Hunt were typical of the hard core of influential Nonconformist pastoralists and businessmen; they faithfully served both urban and rural communities, and sought legislative improvements for primary producers.

V&P (LA NSW), 1900, p 1350; *PD* (LC NSW), 1930, p 6; *Daily Telegraph* (Syd), 12 Sept 1907, 18 Aug 1930; *SMH*, 11-15 July, 17 Nov 1916, 18 July 1918, 18, 19, 30 July, 7 Dec 1921, 21, 25 Jan, 11, 12 July 1922, 20 Mar, 18 July 1923, 16 Apr 1924, 27 Mar, 1 Apr, 31 Oct 1925, 6 Oct, 9 Nov 1927, 24 Mar, 18, 19 Aug 1930; *Queenslander*, 27 Mar, 18 Aug 1930; *Bulletin*, 20 Aug 1930; *Land* (Syd), 22 Aug 1930; family information.

NAN PHILLIPS

HUNT, PHILIP CHARLES HOLMES (1874-1941), gas engineer and company director, was born on 19 July 1874 at Aston, Warwickshire, England, eldest son of

Charles Hunt, gas engineer, and his wife Lucy Ann Miller, née Holmes. Hunt attended Malvern College and studied engineering and chemistry at Mason University College (Birmingham University). An associate of the Institute of Chemistry in 1896 and a fellow in 1920, he was among the first members of the Institution of Gas Engineers, London (founded 1902), and a member of the Institution of Civil Engineers from 1911.

Hunt started work as assistant to his father, then engineer at Birmingham Gas Works, and became superintendent of the Adderley Street Gas Works in 1899. In 1902 he was appointed assistant engineer to the Metropolitan Gas Co., Melbourne, and arrived in Victoria on 24 March 1903; he was promoted acting engineer in 1906 and engineer in 1907. Hunt gave excellent service to the company: he introduced slot meters, making gas available to Melbourne's working class, and after visiting Europe in 1910 to investigate new carbonising plant he recommended and supervised impressive construction and developmental projects, including in 1912 Australia's first vertical retort installation. His roles as principal witness before the Gas Enquiry Board (1912) and as advocate for the company in the Commonwealth Court of Conciliation and Arbitration were praised by the company chairman (Sir) John Grice [q.v.] when in 1914 Hunt resigned to go into business as a consulting engineer and to devote more time to his new appointments as chairman of the local board of the Colonial Gas Association Ltd and as a director of Mount Lyell Mining and Railway Co. Ltd. Highly esteemed by (Sir) John Monash [q.v.], he also received many letters of appreciation from company employees. (He replied to one, from union delegates at the Fitzroy works, with the keenest satisfaction that his efforts to 'weigh the scales evenly' had earned him their regard.) Hunt became a director of the Metropolitan Gas Co. in 1922 and was deputy chairman at the time of his death.

In 1922 Hunt was also appointed managing director of the local board of the Colonial Gas Association. As plans for expansion were hindered by English Treasury restrictions on raising capital and by taxation on dividends paid to shareholders in Australia, Hunt convinced British shareholders that great advantage lay in transferring head office to Melbourne. The transfer was effected from 1 January 1924, and with Hunt as chairman and managing director C.G.A. developed from a minor gas company to fifth largest in Australia, in terms of gas output, with numerous subsidiaries exploiting by-products from gasworks.

The acknowledged leader of the gas industry in Australia, Hunt acted as consultant to the Australian Gas Light Co., Sydney, the South Australian Gas Co., the Hobart Gas Co. and the Newcastle Gas and Coke Co. He was founder and first president of the Australian Gas Institute and chairman of the Gas Companies Association (later the National Gas Association, of which he was president). John Duggan, later manager of the C.G.A., described 'P.C.' as 'extremely farsighted ... an amazingly energetic and well-preserved man ... To the outsider he sometimes seemed austere and pompous; to employees he was kindly, considerate and loyal, and greatly respected and admired'.

In addition to his gas industry commitments, Hunt at the time of his death was chairman of the board of Johns and Waygood Ltd and of Mount Lyell and a director of a dozen companies. He was a keen movie photographer, tennis enthusiast and devoted family man. He collapsed and died when visiting the Commonwealth Bank Building, Sydney, on 6 May 1941 in connexion with his wartime appointment as Commonwealth director of substitute fuels. Survived by his wife Frances Annie, née Lugg whom he had married at Christ Church, South Yarra, on 16 April 1907, and by his two daughters, he was buried in Brighton cemetery. His estate was valued for probate at £44 264.

The Metropolitan Gas Company Jubilee book (Melb, 1928); *Fifty years of good public service* (Melb, 1938); G. Blainey, *One hundred years: Johns and Waygood Ltd, 1856-1956* (Melb, 1956), and *The peaks of Lyell* (Melb, 1967); *National Gas Bulletin*, 5 (Aug 1940), no 1, (May 1941), no 10; Colonial Gas Assn, *Service Messenger*, 66, June 1941, p 2; Hunt papers (Melb Univ Archives).

MERLE RICHMOND

HUNTER, JAMES AITCHISON JOHNSTON (1882-1968), accountant and politician, was born on 4 July 1882 at Springburn near Glasgow, Scotland, third of five sons of Samuel Fowler Hunter, master joiner, and his wife Margaret, née Stenhouse. In 1884 the family migrated to Brisbane where Hunter was educated. He joined the State public service as a clerk, working first in the Department of Public Instruction then in the audit office of the Queensland Railways. He qualified as an accountant. On 16 November 1908, at Ipswich, Hunter married Florence Phoebe Nason. His interest and involvement in rural politics arose from his marriage into the Nason clan, an extended family of pastoralists long established in the Surat district, and from his move in 1912 to Dalby where he set up as a public accountant.

Hunter threw himself wholeheartedly

into the work of creating a rural political organization in south-western Queensland. In 1919 he unsuccessfully contested the Federal seat of Maranoa (then held by the Australian Labor Party), won it at a by-election in 1921 and continued to hold it for the Country Party until his retirement in 1940. He was party whip and parliamentary secretary in 1924-34 and government whip in the House of Representatives in 1924-29. When the Country Party and the United Australia Party entered into a composite ministry in 1934, Hunter became a minister without portfolio in the Lyons [q.v.] government. From September 1935 to November 1937 he assisted the ministers for repatriation and the interior and also the minister for commerce for four months in 1937. From September 1936 he was minister in charge of war service homes. He was dropped from the ministry after the October 1937 election. He had also been a member of the joint committee of public accounts, 1923-25, and of the royal commission on national insurance, 1923-24.

Hunter had to rely largely on his own personal organization to conduct his election campaigns at considerable cost to his family life and business affairs. He and Alan J. Campbell were founders of the Queensland Country Party at Toowoomba in March 1936, which led to the final disintegration of the Country and Progressive National Party. Hunter loyally supported (Sir) Earle Page [q.v.] in his conflict with (Sir) Robert Menzies and in the leadership struggles within his own party in 1939. When (Sir) Arthur Fadden secretly negotiated the fusion of the parliamentary wings of the United Australia Party and the Country Party in Queensland into the Country Nationalist Party in April 1941, Hunter held aloof. He had been made a life member of his party in 1939 and continued to work tirelessly for the western division of the Country Party and for the creation of an independent Country Party in Queensland, not achieved until 1944-45.

In appearance and manner Hunter was quite unlike the stereotype rural politician of his era. He was quiet and unobtrusive, slight in stature and build, with a somewhat austere mien, further enhanced by the wearing of pince-nez spectacles. After his retirement from parliament, Hunter continued as director of a number of companies and maintained his interest in Country Party affairs, regularly attending the annual conferences. From May to December 1944 he acted as managing director of the Queensland Country Party. He was a fellow of the Commonwealth Institute of Accountants, the Institute of Cost Accountants and the Chartered Institute of Secretaries. An ardent

Freemason and a devout Presbyterian with two brothers in its ministry, Hunter spent his declining years in the Freemasons' Home, Sandgate. He died on 27 October 1968 and after a state funeral was buried in Toowong cemetery. His wife and two sons survived him.

A. J. Campbell, *Memoirs of the Country Party in Queensland, 1920-1974* (Brisb, nd); U. R. Ellis, *A history of the Australian Country Party* (Melb, 1963); E. C. G. Page, *Truant surgeon*, A. Mozley ed (Syd, 1963); C. W. Russell, *Country crisis* (Brisb, 1976); *Telegraph* (Brisb), 27 Oct 1968; *Courier Mail*, 28 Oct 1968; A. J. Campbell papers (John Oxley Lib, Brisb).   MARGARET BRIDSON CRIBB

HUNTER, JOHN IRVINE (1898-1924), professor of anatomy, was born on 24 January 1898 at Bendigo, Victoria, third son of Victorian-born parents Henry Hunter, furniture dealer, and his wife Isabella, née Hodgson. After an attack of pneumonia when he was 8, he was brought up at Albury, New South Wales, by an aunt and was educated at Albury Public School (1906-12). A bursary enabled him to attend Fort Street High School (1912-14). Awarded an exhibition and bursary, he entered the medical course at the University of Sydney in 1915. In each year of his undergraduate career he won awards, and in his two final years, all the prizes, despite having to support himself by coaching. He was prosector in anatomy (1916-17), in residence and medical tutor at Wesley College (1917-20) and demonstrator in anatomy in 1918-20. In July 1918 he had enlisted in the Australian Imperial Force but was not called up.

After graduating M.B. and Ch.M., with first-class honours and the University medal in 1920, Hunter was appointed almost immediately associate professor in anatomy. In August 1921 he was given leave of absence to study in Britain, the United States of America and Canada. On his return, from 1 March 1923, he occupied the Challis [q.v.3] chair of anatomy. In 1924 the university senate conferred upon him the degree of doctor of medicine with first-class honours, the university medal and the Ethel Talbot memorial prize. His thesis was on the forebrain of the kiwi.

Hunter was a prolific research worker and published twenty papers in medical and scientific journals. His earlier papers were chiefly on topics in embryology and neurology, but those of 1924 and 1925 were mostly concerned with the innervation of muscle. He considered that 'voluntary' or striated muscle fibres received nerve supply alternatively from cerebrospinal nerve fibres or from the fibres of the sympathetic nervous system, which is generally involved in the supply of glands and of the 'involuntary' or smooth muscle in the walls of viscera. He thought that a plastic tonus which had been noted in voluntary muscle could be explained by sympathetic innervation: this tonus might also be the basis of spastic paralysis appearing after strokes and other diseases of the central nervous system. In consequence, Hunter and his surgical colleague N. D. Royle made experimental and clinical attempts to treat spastic paralysis by sectioning sympathetic nerves.

Hunter's work on the dual innervation of muscle fibres was of much topical interest. In October 1924 he and Royle were invited by the American College of Surgeons to deliver the John B. Murphy oration in surgery in New York. From this engagement Hunter went to England to lecture at Cambridge and then in London. However, he fell ill on arrival in London and died of typhoid in University College Hospital on 10 December. He was survived by his wife, Hazel Annie, née McPherson, whom he had married at Summer Hill, Sydney, on 30 January 1924, and by a posthumous son born on 6 September 1925. He was an Anglican.

The hypothesis of double innervation of muscle, the most acclaimed part of Hunter's work, was disproved within five years of his death, and hope of his findings being applicable to the relief of spastic paralysis was subsequently abandoned. Nevertheless his research constituted a valid and highly stimulating contribution to an intricate dialectic concerning the innervation of muscle, in the context in which it was made. The nature of the plastic tonus in muscle, to which the work related, was not resolvable until the development of sophisticated electromyographic analysis in the 1950s.

The survival of the Hunter legend depended both on the quality of the work and on the calibre of the man. He was loved and even revered by his mentors, peers and students on account of a particularly joyous and unselfish nature, modesty and deep spirituality. His intellectual brilliance attracted much comment. (Sir) Grafton Elliot Smith [q.v.] said of him, 'Had he lived, he might have become the foremost man of science of the age'. In a letter to Sir Arthur Keith he wrote, 'Hunter was the biggest man I have ever met'. Two future medical knights and chancellors of the University of Sydney, (Sir) Charles Bickerton Blackburn [q.v.7] and (Sir) Charles McDonald, were among those who wrote of his genius and of the renown he brought to the Sydney Medical School.

Portraits by John Longstaff and W. B. McInnes [qq.v.] were painted after his death; both hang in the Anderson Stuart [q.v.] building of the University of Sydney. Bronze medallions, sculpted by Rayner Hoff [q.v.], are held at Wesley College, the university and Fort Street High School.

W. R. Dawson (ed), *Sir Grafton Elliot Smith* (Lond, 1938); *Lancet* (Lond), 1305 (1924); *Syd Univ Gazette*, Oct 1958, p 225; *Daily Telegraph* (Syd), 13 Dec 1924; *SMH*, 12, 13, 19 Dec 1924; *Aust Christian World*, 12 Nov 1926.   MICHAEL J. BLUNT

HUNTER, JOHN McEWAN (1863?-1940), businessman and politician, son of Daniel McEwan Hunter and his wife Jane, née Dampsey, was born on a Scottish migrant ship in Queensland waters. His parents had been enticed to migrate to Queensland by the speeches of the emigration agent Henry Jordan [q.v.4] who promised free grants of land in 'the future cotton field of England'. The family settled at Pittsworth on the Darling Downs. John later attended state primary schools at Redbank and Clifton.

Hunter was to exemplify the virtues of the Scottish migrant: hard work, thrift, ambition for financial success. Failing in an attempt to become an engineer, he entered the grocery trade as an employee of McLeish & Co., Toowoomba. In 1888, when he was western Queensland manager for the company, he opened his own business as a general merchant at Roma. Despite the depression and drought of the following decade, Hunter's influence in the west expanded. He opened three branch stores at Mitchell, Yuleba and Amby; he promoted the successful Roma Co-operative Milling Co. and became chairman of directors; and he was elected president of the Western Queensland Pastoral and Agricultural Society. By 1915 he was employing 100 people.

At Roma Hunter was prominent in the Masonic lodge, the Presbyterian Church and the School of Arts. In 1898 he was elected to the Roma Town Council at the top of the poll and became mayor in 1900. Because of his local standing Hunter was invited to nominate as the ministerial candidate for Maranoa in the 1899 Legislative Assembly elections but declined and allowed (Sir) Arthur Rutledge [q.v.] to run. The coalition of the Labor Party and a number of Liberals in 1903 brought a significant change in Queensland politics. In 1907 Hunter was one of several prominent people from rural areas who, though lacking trade union background, stood successfully as Labor candidates. His closest friend in politics was to be the barrister T. J. Ryan [q.v.], elected for Barcoo in 1909.

When the Ryan government was formed

in 1915 Hunter was made secretary for public lands. His two major contributions in that portfolio were the introduction of perpetual lease instead of freehold title and the provision of land for closer settlement and soldier settlement. However it was to be as Ryan's principal aide that Hunter left his mark. He managed the administration of the Chief Secretary's Department and deputized for Ryan as chairman of important public committees like the War Council. The state butchery and state stations which were to be controversial but successful during the war were administered by Hunter. They lost heavily under less efficient managers and were ultimately disposed of.

The close friendship between Hunter and Ryan survived the sectarian animosities of the two conscription referenda and the constant charges of Popish domination of the cabinet. When Ryan and his wife went to England in 1919 Hunter became guardian of their children and executor of Ryan's will.

Although elected by caucus to be agent-general in 1916, Hunter did not take up his post until 1919 because Ryan needed him. During 1918-19 he was minister without portfolio assisting the premier. His health was poor in England, he was unpopular with the trade union faction in caucus who disliked his non-union background, and he was personally disliked by E. G. Theodore [q.v.]. After Ryan's death, he was recalled in 1922.

Hunter returned to business and in 1935-40 was president of the Queensland United Chamber of Agricultural Societies and chairman of Queensland Country Traders. At Booroodabbin he played bowls and served the Presbyterian church as an elder. He died in Brisbane on 18 April 1940, leaving an estate valued for probate at £38 533 to his wife Ellen Guthrie, née Moffat, whom he had married at Toowoomba on 2 June 1890, and their only daughter. He was cremated after a state funeral.

D. J. Murphy, *T. J. Ryan* (Brisb, 1975); *Aust Jane's Annual*, 1919; *Queenslander*, 10 Mar 1900; *Courier Mail*, 20 Apr 1940; *Worker*, 23 Apr 1940.

D. J. MURPHY

HUNTINGFIELD, WILLIAM CHARLES ARCEDECKNE VANNECK, 5th BARON (1883-1969), governor, was born on 3 January 1883 at Lake Clarendon station, Gatton, Queensland, eldest son of William Arcedeckne Vanneck, grazier, from Suffolk, England, and his Queensland-born wife Mary, née Armstrong. Educated at The Downs School, Toowoomba, and in 1898-1900 at Wellington College, Berkshire, Vanneck joined the 13th Hussars, stationed in India, in 1906. On 21 December 1912 at St George's Church, London, he married Margaret Eleanor, daughter of Judge Ernest Crosby of New York. Invalided home to England from India in 1914, he spent the war years with a reserve regiment at Aldershot, Hampshire, resigning from the army in 1921 with the rank of captain.

In 1915 Vanneck succeeded his uncle as Baron Huntingfield, an Irish title. He was elected to the House of Commons in 1923 as Conservative member for the Eye Division, East Suffolk. Parliamentary private secretary to the under secretary of state for the Home Department (1926-27) and to the president of the Board of Trade (1927-28), Huntingfield did not stand at the 1929 election because of ill health.

Following the departure of Lord Somers [q.v.] in 1931, the vice-regal post had been left vacant in Victoria because of the Depression, the chief justice, Sir William Irvine [q.v.] having discharged the duties of lieut-governor. With the centenary of settlement approaching in 1934, the Argyle [q.v.7] ministry decided to secure a British governor who could afford to preside over the celebrations. The Labor Party preferred a native-born candidate, and even some United Australia Party and Country Party supporters considered the prospective appointment an untimely luxury. Loyalists were delighted. When Huntingfield's appointment was announced in December 1933, much was made of his Australian childhood: he was the first native-born State governor.

A good shot and sportsman, fluent in French and German, articulate, worldly and agreeable in personality, Huntingfield was a suitable choice for a State devastated by the Depression, perplexed by events in Europe and Asia and provincial in outlook. He arrived in Melbourne in May 1934 accompanied by his wife and younger children.

Centennial celebrations and the visit of the duke of Gloucester in October-December initially concealed disharmonies which surfaced in March 1935 with the fall of the Argyle ministry. Huntingfield's delay in commissioning the Country Party leader Albert Dunstan [q.v.8] to form a minority government was criticized by Labor. However Huntingfield and his wife carried out their duties with a disarming mixture of dignity and friendliness. Thomas Tunnecliffe [q.v.], an erstwhile critic, conceded Huntingfield would have made 'an excellent democratic politician'.

His interest in agricultural, industrial and technical matters was balanced by his wife's work for women and children. In the old vice-regal tradition, they made extensive tours of towns and shires. Lady Hunting-field's social work was later acknowledged by the establishment of a scholarship in her name at the University of Melbourne. As war threatened Huntingfield advocated national and Imperial unity, drew attention to freedoms taken for granted and involved himself in the Royal Australian Air Force. During the absence of Lord Gowrie [q.v.], he acted as governor-general for six months in 1938. At the expiry of his term in March 1939 Huntingfield returned to England having done much 'to promote affectionate good feeling in uniting England and Australia'. He was the last British peer to act as governor of the State.

Appointed governor of Southern Rhodesia in 1941, Huntingfield did not proceed because of ill health. His wife died in 1943 and on 24 May 1944 at St Faith's Chapel, Westminster Abbey, he married Muriel Mary Georgiana Newton, née Duke, widow of the 1st Baron Eltisley. She died in 1953. Huntingfield died on 20 November 1969 at Hove, Sussex, survived by two daughters and two sons, the elder of whom, Gerard Charles Arcedeckne, succeeded to the barony.

A. A. Calwell, *Be just and fear not* (Melb, 1972); *Argus*, 30, 31 May, 1, 3, 5 June, 12, 19, 27 July, 17 Nov 1933, 15, 29, 30 Mar, 1, 2 Apr 1935, 17 Mar 1938; *Herald* (Melb), 23 Jan 1934; *Age*, 15, 29, 30 Mar, 1, 2, Apr 1935; *The Times*, 9 Oct 1941, 6 Jan 1942, 21 Nov 1969; Biographical cuttings (NL).

P. H. DE SERVILLE

HURLEY, JAMES FRANCIS (1885-1962), adventurer, photographer and film maker, was born on 15 October 1885 at Glebe, Sydney, second son of Edward Harrison Hurley, Lancashire-born printer and trade union official, and his wife Margaret Agnes, née Bouffier, of French descent. At 13 Frank ran away from Glebe Public School and worked in the steel mill at Lithgow, returning home two years later. At night he studied at the local technical school and attended science lectures at the University of Sydney. He became interested in photography, buying his own Kodak box camera for 15 shillings. In 1905 he joined Harry Cave in a postcard business in Sydney and began to earn a reputation for the high technical quality of his work and for the extravagant risks he took to secure sensational images, such as a famous shot taken from the rails in front of an onrushing train. He also gave talks at photographic club meetings and in 1910 mounted the first exhibition of his work in Sydney.

In 1911 (Sir) Douglas Mawson [q.v.] invited Hurley to be official photographer on the Australasian Antarctic Expedition. From December 1911 to March 1913 Hurley worked enthusiastically under arduous conditions, taking both still photographs and movie film, and his high spirits made him a popular and valued member of the team. Back in Sydney he rapidly assembled his movie footage and successfully presented it to the public in August as *Home of the blizzard*. In November, after a brief filming trip to Java, Hurley joined another expedition to Antarctica to relieve the stranded Mawson.

Hurley's fame grew rapidly and he was commissioned by Francis Birtles [q.v.7] to film an expedition by car through northern Australia. In October 1914 he joined Sir Ernest Shackleton in yet another Antarctic expedition and produced his most famous still photographs—a series showing the ship *Endurance*, being gradually destroyed by pack-ice, and the heroic struggle for survival of Shackleton's men. He ended the adventure in November 1916 in London where he assembled the film and photographs, including colour plates. Early in 1917 he briefly visited South Georgia to secure additional scenes to complete his film, *In the grip of polar ice*.

In August Hurley joined the Australian Imperial Force as official photographer with the rank of honorary captain. Shocked by the carnage in France and Belgium, he showed his 'burning resentment' in such photographs as 'Morning at Passchendaele'. At the same time he found Ypres 'a weird and wonderful sight, with the destruction wildly beautiful'. He ran great risks to film exploding shells and clashed with C. E. W. Bean [q.v.7], the official historian, over his desire to merge several negatives into one impressive picture: to Bean such composite pictures were 'little short of fake'. Disgusted with army administration and irked by censorship, Hurley resigned, but was sent to the Middle East, smuggling out some coloured photographs. In Palestine he flew for the first time and had many adventures while photographing the Light Horse during the battle of Jericho. In Cairo he met a young opera-singer, Antoinette Rosalind Leighton, daughter of an Indian Army officer, and after a ten-day courtship, they were married on 11 April 1918. Later that year in Sydney, Hurley worked furiously to arrange exhibitions of his photographs and to give lecture tours with his films, to great public acclaim and commercial success. In December 1919 he was invited to join the pioneer aviator, (Sir) Ross Smith [q.v.], on the final leg of the historic flight from England to Australia. Hurley filmed Australia from the air—*The Ross Smith flight* was also highly popular.

Between December 1920 and January

1923 Hurley made two long and well-publicized filming expeditions to the Torres Strait Islands and to Papua, and attracted further attention by shipping two small planes to Port Moresby and flying them along the coast. Again, the Papuan films (especially *Pearls and savages* released in December 1921) were major commercial successes. He followed them up with a book of traveller's tales and photographs, also called *Pearls and savages*, as he was to do with several other of his films.

However, he clashed bitterly with (Sir) Hubert Murray [q.v.] and the Papuan administration over allegedly bad publicity that he was giving to the Territory through his sensational stories of head-hunters and unexplored jungle wilds, and more seriously over allegedly improper methods used to gather a large collection of artefacts for the Australian Museum, Sydney. In 1925 Hurley was refused entrance to Papua to make a fiction film for the Australian-born magnate of the British film industry, Sir Oswald Stoll: the film crew was forced to relocate the production in Dutch New Guinea; *Jungle woman* was released in May 1926, followed by *Hound of the deep*, made for Stoll on Thursday Island. After spending 1927 as pictorial editor for the *Sun* in Sydney, Hurley set off on an abortive attempt to fly from Australia to England, then in 1929 joined the British, Australian and New Zealand Antarctic Research Expedition again under Mawson's command. Two films—*Southward ho with Mawson* and *Siege of the south*—were both shown widely in Australia with accompanying lectures from Hurley in 1930-31. He was awarded the Polar Medal and two bars and in 1941 was appointed O.B.E.

The 1930s were no less busy for Hurley, but entailed a more settled life with his family at Vaucluse. He worked with the Cinesound studio as cameraman on four feature films, but his meticulous style did not adapt well to the high pressure of expensive studio productions, and Cinesound established him instead as the head of a special documentary unit, to produce films for government and private sponsors. In World War II, Hurley again served as official photographer with the A.I.F. in the Middle East, but the methods that had brought him fame in World War I now caused clashes with younger film makers like Damien Parer, who found him old-fashioned and eccentric. He remained in the Middle East until 1946 making documentary films for the British government, but they attracted little attention. After his return to Australia, he concentrated on still photography and published several books of photographs of Australian landscapes and city portraits.

Lecturing and journalism filled more of his time and he continued to travel frequently, although mainly within Australia. He died of myocardial infarction at his home on the Collaroy plateau on 16 January 1962 and was cremated. He was survived by his wife, son and three daughters.

Frank Hurley was always restless, a self-styled loner who braved danger in exotic areas to provide romance and adventure for armchair travellers. He retained the use of 'Captain', to help cultivate this image. For three decades he inspired Australian film makers and photographers and was the most powerful force to shape Australian documentary film before World War II.

F. Legg and T. Hurley, *Once more on my adventure* (Syd, 1966); L. Bickel, *In search of Frank Hurley* (Melb, 1980); A. Pike and R. Cooper, *Australian film 1900-1977* (Melb, 1980); R. Lansell and P. Beilby (eds), *The documentary film in Australia* (Melb, 1982); Cwlth of Aust, *Royal commission on the moving picture industry in Australia: Minutes of evidence* (Canb, 1928); Hurley diaries (NL).

A. F. PIKE

HURST, JOHN HERBERT (1869-1953), soldier and architect, was born on 26 December 1869 at Teddington, London, son of John Hurst, builder, and his wife Elizabeth, née Reader. Educated at the Queen Elizabeth Grammar School, Kingston-on-Thames, and the Protestant Grammar School, Shoreham, Sussex, he migrated to Western Australia in February 1887 with his family and joined his father as a builder and contractor in Perth. He later turned to architecture, although he does not seem to have gained formal qualifications, and worked with his brother-in-law, (Sir) J. Talbot Hobbs [q.v.].

In March 1887 Hurst enlisted in the Western Australian volunteer forces (field artillery) and was commissioned lieutenant on 24 May 1897. On 28 March 1894 at St George's Cathedral, Perth, he had married Emma Florence Rostron. Forsaking architecture and building, he 'went for a soldier' and was commissioned lieutenant in the permanent artillery on 20 February 1899. Promoted captain in January 1908, he went to England that year to attend the long gunnery staff course, returning to Australia in February 1910. After a period as instructor, Australian Garrison Artillery (militia) in Victoria, he was promoted major and served as chief instructor, School of Gunnery, Sydney, in 1911-13. He returned to Perth in 1913 and was commanding Fremantle coast defences when World War I broke out.

After the destruction of the German

Pacific Fleet at the Falkland Islands in December 1914 the threat of enemy attacks against Australian ports diminished and the permanent members of the Royal Australian Garrison Artillery were free to enlist in the Australian Imperial Force. From about 450 members of the R.A.G.A. the Australian Siege Brigade was formed on 21 May 1915. This was a little known but unique force. The men were regular soldiers, enlisting under A.I.F. conditions of service but their unit was officially part of the British Army and was known as the 36th Heavy Artillery Group, Royal Garrison Artillery. It consisted of headquarters and two batteries, the 54th and 55th. Hurst took command of the 55th Battery. Apart from a small transport unit, the siege brigade was to provide the first Australian troops in action in France, arriving early in March 1916. The unit served on the Somme in 1916, at Vimy Ridge (where they were the only Australians involved), at Passchendaele and Cambrai in 1917 and in Flanders in 1918. The brigade served in support of some seventeen allied formations during the war.

Hurst also commanded the 22nd Field Artillery Brigade in July-December 1916. He then commanded the 36th Heavy Artillery Group, R.G.A., until wounded in action on 23 September 1917. Next day he was promoted brevet lieut-colonel for 'specially meritorious service'. In October-December his unit was attached to the British XIX Corps and then to the Belgian Army. He retained command throughout 1918, serving with the Australian Corps in Flanders until April and with British and French Army Corps at Armentières, Meteren, Passchendaele and Warneton. In January 1919 he was transferred as a major and personnel staff officer to the 5th Australian Division during the A.I.F.'s final months in France. For his war service he was awarded the Distinguished Service Order, the Belgian Croix de Guerre and Ordre de la Couronne and was twice mentioned in dispatches. He returned to Australia in August 1919 and resumed duties as commander of the garrison artillery at Fremantle.

Hurst was appointed lieut-colonel, Australian Military Forces, and chief instructor at the School of Artillery, Sydney, from May 1921 until August 1922 when he was placed on the unattached list. He returned to architecture, being registered by the Board of Architects in Sydney in December 1922; he became 'a long time secretary and councillor of the Royal Australian Institute of Architects'. During World War II he undertook war-work with the departments of Defence Co-ordination and Labour and National Service.

Survived by his son and daughter, Hurst died on 7 July 1953 at his Vaucluse home and was cremated with Anglican rites.

J. M. Freeland, *The making of a profession* (Syd, 1971); *London Gazette*, 25 Dec 1917, 25 July 1918, 3 June, 11 July 1919; *Age*, 8 July 1953; B. M. Morris, The Australian Siege Brigade 1916-18 (held at School of Artillery, Syd); Records, Roy Aust Inst of Architects, NSW Chapter, Syd; J. H. Hurst file, war records section (AWM).   RICHMOND CUBIS

HUTCHENS, FRANCIS (1892-1965), pianist, teacher and composer, was born on 15 January 1892 at Leeston, near Christchurch, New Zealand, son of Cornish parents Richard Lavers Hutchens, and his wife Maria Siles, née Hoskins. His father had migrated to Christchurch in 1879 and, after failing at farming and bootmaking, settled at Hawera and taught the piano. Frank was educated at Hawera District High School and when only 12 played for Paderewski, who advised him to study abroad. In 1905 he entered the Royal Academy of Music, London, and studied under Tobias Matthay and Frederick Corder. Hutchens won the Sterndale Bennett and the Thalberg scholarships, and the Chappell gold medal for pianoforte playing. In 1908 he became the youngest sub-professor yet appointed to the academy staff. Learning that his mother was ill and family funds strained, he regretfully returned home in 1911. Before leaving London he gave a recital at the Bechstein Hall. The critic of the London *Musical Times* wrote, 'considering the youth of the performer his individuality is extraordinary'.

Hutchens found few opportunities in New Zealand as a concert pianist. In 1913 he decided to return to London via Sydney, but he remained in Sydney, where friends helped him. He gave a recital and soon made a name for himself as a teacher. In 1915, at the invitation of Henri Verbrugghen [q.v.], he became a foundation professor at the New South Wales State Conservatorium of Music. An influential and successful teacher, he was one of the first exponents of the Matthay method in Australia. He was rejected for military service in 1916.

His name also became a household word in Sydney through his association with Lindley Evans in a two-pianoforte partnership from 1924. Annual concerts, broadcasts and music club recitals were given. They were among the first composer-performer teams to be recorded commercially in Australia, when Hutchens's *Fantasy concerto* and Evans's *Idyll* were given their premières in the Sydney Town Hall on 4 September 1943 with the Sydney Symphony Orchestra under Edgar Bainton [q.v.7].

In 1932 Hutchens had returned to London, and gave three concerts at the Aeolian Hall. In 1939 he was made a fellow of the Royal Academy of Music. His extensive compositions were soundly professional and useful for teaching; they had qualities of charm and craftsmanship; the best-known were *Concerto symphonique* for pianoforte and orchestra, the *Concerto* for pianoforte and strings, *Quintet* for piano and strings and *'Air mail' Palestine* for baritone and orchestra set to the words of David McNicoll. He also made many recordings for the Australian Broadcasting Commission.

As an examiner for the Associated Board of the Royal Schools of Music and Trinity College of Music, London, Hutchens was admired throughout Australia. An organizer of the Australian Music Examinations Board as an indigenous body, he also helped to inaugurate demonstration recitals for teachers in country towns. He became a vice-president of the Musical Association of New South Wales in 1940, a member of the advisory panel that controlled the conservatorium in 1946, and was a director of the Australasian Performing Right Association in the 1950s.

On 2 June 1955 at St Peter's Anglican Church, Neutral Bay, Hutchens married Joyce White, granddaughter of R. H. D. White [q.v.6], whom he had met as one of his students in 1927. A keen musician herself, she gave him invaluable support in his career. In 1962 he was appointed O.B.E. Hutchens was still an able pianist and an active teacher when he died on 18 October 1965 in Mona Vale Hospital after a car accident. He was cremated after a service at St Martin's Church of England, Killara. He was survived by his wife. His estate was valued for probate at £142 634. Composition scholarships are awarded annually in his name, to students under 25. His portrait, by the Cornish painter Stanhope Forbes, is held by the State Conservatorium of Music, Sydney.

S. Jobson (ed), *Frank Hutchens* (Syd, 1971), and for compositions; *SMH*, 19 Oct 1965; *Australian*, 23 Oct 1965; Hutchens papers (NL).

HELEN BAINTON

HUTCHINSON, WILLIAM (1864-1924), watchmaker, jeweller and politician, was born on 31 May 1864 at Pleasant Creek (Stawell), Victoria, son of William Hutchinson, miner, and his wife Mary, née McKay, both from northern Ireland. Educated at Pleasant Creek State School, he worked on his uncle's farm before becoming a shop assistant at Murtoa where he attended night school. In 1885 he moved to Warracknabeal and established his own business as a watch-

maker and jeweller. On 7 September 1898 at Carlton, Melbourne, he married Janet MacKay, a schoolteacher; they had three sons and one daughter. After his wife's death in 1907 Hutchinson sold his business and moved to Melbourne, although maintaining wheat-farming interests in the Warracknabeal district in partnership with his brother Samuel.

In 1900 Hutchinson was narrowly defeated for the Legislative Assembly seat of Borung. He successfully recontested the seat in October 1902 with the backing of the National Citizens' Reform League. He became a leader of the Country Liberal group and was regarded as the principal parliamentary spokesman of the temperance lobby. An active Presbyterian, he was a prominent supporter of attempts to introduce Scripture readings into state schools. He voted for the overthrow of Sir Thomas Bent [q.v.3] in 1908 and chaired the royal commission of 1909 which condemned Bent's activities while minister of lands.

In 1913 Hutchinson refused to countenance moves by some Country Liberals to bring down the Watt [q.v.] government. He was rewarded with the portfolios of water supply and agriculture in the second Watt ministry from December 1913 to June 1914. He retained these posts under Sir Alexander Peacock [q.v.] until November 1915. From then until November 1917 he was minister of lands under Peacock and from March 1918 to November 1920 held the portfolios of public instruction and forests in the Lawson [q.v.] ministry. As a minister Hutchinson was an efficient rather than an imaginative administrator who was noted for the clarity of his explanations in introducing bills to the House. While minister of forests he successfully carried a bill establishing the Forests Commission.

A 'big and burly' man with a 'drooping tan moustache', Hutchinson was a popular and genial figure who, nevertheless, kept a strict moral code and 'would not indulge in intrigue of any kind'. He was defeated in October 1920 and became an agent for the agricultural machinery firm of his cousin H. V. McKay [q.v.]. He had suffered from angina for some years and died at his East Malvern home on 18 December 1924; he was buried in Brighton cemetery.

S. Priestley, *Warracknabeal* (Brisb, 1967); *Punch* (Melb), 5 Mar 1914; *Argus*, 19 Dec 1924; *Warracknabeal Herald*, 23 Dec 1924; family information.

GEOFF BROWNE

HUTCHISON, JAMES (1859-1909), printer and politician, was born on 20 April 1859 at Aberdeen, Scotland, son of James Hutchison, weaver, and his wife Isabella née Smith. After primary education at Dr Bell's school he worked in a carpet factory, a grocery and a bakery. He became an apprentice compositor on the *Daily Free Press* and attended the mechanics' institute. Later he worked on the *Aberdeen Weekly Journal* before following his workmate J. A. McPherson [q.v.] to South Australia in 1884.

They joined the South Australian Typographical Society and found work on the *South Australian Register*. On 28 October 1886 Hutchison married Mary Jane Trebilcock. Two years later McPherson and Hutchison were in a strike at the *Register* over its opposition to union labour. Both were sacked. In 1889, with two other dismissed compositors, Hutchison established the trades press, Hutchison, Craker & Smith. Early next year H. Congreve Evans and Alfred T. Chandler joined them as editors to publish a satirical paper, *Quiz*; it flourished and soon incorporated its rival the *Lantern*.

Hutchison supported the growing United Labor Party as an office-holder of the East Adelaide local committee and in public speaking in the Botanic Park and at the Adelaide Democratic Club. In 1896 he was president of both the club and of the U.L.P. In January 1898, following McPherson's death, Hutchison won a by-election for his friend's seat of East Adelaide in the House of Assembly. Next year he was re-elected. He was a member of the State Children's Council in 1898-1902 and sat on the 1899-1901 royal commission into the civil service.

Hutchison was a lively handsome man and his maiden speech was fervent and rhetorical. He supported Federation and White Australia, citing Queensland as a 'breeding-ground of piebalds'. He called for law reform; somewhat presciently, he described those 'who flocked around the rotten carcase of an insolvency' as wielders of a 'two-edged sword of craft and oppression'.

Hutchison attracted attention by his opposition to the electric tramways bill of 1901. Flouting the recommendations of a 1900 select committee, a private company was to take over many of Adelaide's tramways and convert them to electricity. In September Hutchison presented a petition of protest from the Public Tramways League. A 'firebrand' who lived on his nerves, he sustained pressure on the bill's supporters in and out of parliament and marshalled comprehensive evidence from interstate and overseas examples. But his opponents baited him into making rash claims about them in the press. Hutchison specifically attacked W. Charles Tucker [q.v.], a parliamentary supporter of the company, and C. G. Gurr. The bill was passed in December,

with important amendments secured by Hutchison, but Gurr doggedly pursued their differences in the press and Tucker sued for libel. Hutchison lost the case. Although only fined £50, he had to pay £762 in costs; by 2 April 1902 he was insolvent. On 3 May, following a redistribution of electorates, he lost his parliamentary seat. Having left *Quiz* in 1901, he now edited the Labor weekly, the *Herald*.

In 1903 he won the Federal seat of Hindmarsh and was unopposed in 1906. Having always been an enthusiastic volunteer soldier, from November 1908 till June 1909 Hutchison was a popular honorary minister representing the minister for defence in the House of Representatives. His death in Melbourne on 6 December 1909 from 'inflammation of the kidneys and gall bladder', was sudden and shocking; he left a widow and six children. His body was returned to Adelaide for a Presbyterian burial in West Terrace cemetery. He died in poverty.

H. T. Burgess (ed), *Cyclopedia of South Australia* 1 (Adel, 1907); *A'sian Typographical J*, Feb 1898; *Observer* (Adel), 5 Feb 1898; *Advertiser* (Adel), 15, 16, 19, 27, 30 Nov, 18 Dec 1901, 12, 14, 15 Mar 1902, 7, 8 Dec 1909; *Herald* (Adel), 7 Dec 1901, 11 Dec 1909; *Age* (Melb), 7 Dec 1909; GRG 66/5/6680 (SAA).   SUZANNE EDGAR

HUTTON, SIR EDWARD THOMAS HENRY (1848-1923), British regular soldier and first organizer of the Australian Army, was born on 6 December 1848 at Torquay, Devon, England, only son of Edward Thomas Hutton, banker, and his wife Jacintha Charlotte, née Eyre. Hutton was educated at Eton after which he joined the 60th Rifles as an ensign in 1867. He was promoted captain in 1879 and major in 1883. In 1879-85 he saw much active service in Africa, in the Zulu War (1879), the first South African War (1881), the occupation of Egypt including the battle of Tel-el-Kebir (1882) and the Nile Expedition (1884-85). During this period he became deeply interested in the training and employment of mounted infantry with which he thrice served on operations. At Aldershot, England, he raised and commanded mounted infantry units in 1888-92, becoming recognized as one of the leading proponents of this form of mobility. A good speaker with a flair for publicity, he was identified as one of the 'Wolseley Ring' of army reformers. He also founded the military society at Aldershot as a professional forum.

In 1889 Hutton was promoted lieut-colonel and on 1 June, at St Paul's Anglican Church, Knightsbridge, London, he married Eleanor Mary, daughter of Lord Charles

Paulet and granddaughter of the marquis of Winchester. His marriage and his appointment as aide-de-camp to Queen Victoria in 1892 afforded him a degree of influence unusual for an officer of his rank. Promoted colonel in 1892, 'Curly' Hutton became commandant of the New South Wales Military Forces with the local rank of major general in 1893. The advent of an able leader committed to military reform and with recent war experience revived the flagging spirit of the New South Wales forces. Hutton inspected units in every part of the colony, addressed public gatherings and brought the army before the community, beginning with a major review in Sydney in July 1893. On one of his inspections he travelled 680 miles (1090 km) in twenty days including 500 miles (805 km) on horseback. He visited training camps and exercises, delivered lectures to officers, fostered rifle clubs and supported the movement for raising national regiments such as the Irish Rifles.

Valuable as the public side of his work was, Hutton's reorganization of the New South Wales forces was even more important because it gave the colony an army capable of taking the field as part of a Federal force. He restructured the headquarters staff, persuaded the government to transfer the influential department of the military secretary from the chief secretary to his own command and organized administrative services to support the fighting arms. All this was achieved in a period of acute economic depression and in the face of political and military opposition. At the outset of his command he quarrelled bitterly with the premier, Sir George Dibbs [q.v.4], who had insisted on a reduction of £30 000 in the defence estimates, the practical result of which was the cancellation of the Easter training camps. When Hutton's views on this were reported in the press the premier publicly censured his commandant saying, *inter alia*, 'he is a good soldier but he writes and talks too much. He means well ... but he has much to learn in regard to his official duties'. There was substance in this criticism. Hutton from the start aroused suspicion in some quarters by his outspoken remarks on helping 'England in her hour of need'. He also vigorously supported the movement for Federal defence; in a speech at Bathurst in January 1894 he advocated one defence policy for the six colonies, a common organization of their forces while preserving their identity, a Federal regiment of artillery and a Federal council of defence.

At the intercolonial military conference of October 1894 Hutton recommended the establishment of a council of defence, composed of delegates from all the colonies, to take charge of the forces in time of war or general emergency. This was supported by the conference but its recommendations made little impression on the colonial premiers. However, the startling successes of the Japanese forces in the war with China in 1894-95 provided Hutton with a useful argument for greater preparedness which he placed before his government in March 1895. A second meeting of the commandants, chaired by him, in January 1896 reaffirmed their proposals for the employment of the forces of every colony in the joint defence of Australia under the control of a council of defence, while rejecting a suggestion from London that their field forces should be liable to serve beyond Australia. By this time the political movement for Federation was overtaking the military movement and political leaders were looking for Federation as the necessary preliminary to national defence.

Hutton returned to England in March 1896. By the end of his command he and his wife had won the esteem of the New South Wales forces and Hutton had become an important public figure. A convinced Imperialist, he quickly began to propagate his ideas on Australian defence, addressing members of parliament on the topic and the Aldershot Military Society on 'Our comrades of Greater Britain'. In that address the concept of the Australian soon to be popularized by C. E. W. Bean [q.v.7] was already discernible: 'The Australian is a born horseman. With his long, lean muscular thighs he is more at home on a horse than on his feet, and is never seen to a greater advantage than when mounted and riding across bush or a difficult country ... Fine horsemen, hardy, self-reliant, and excellent marksmen, they are the beau ideal of Mounted Riflemen ... Accustomed to shift for themselves in the Australian bush, and under the most trying conditions of heat and cold, they would thrive where soldiers unaccustomed to bush life would die'. This address was widely reported in Australia as well as in Britain. In April 1898 he read a paper on 'A co-operative system for the defence of the Empire' before the Royal Colonial Institute in London, using the Australian Federal defence scheme as the pattern for a scheme of Empire defence.

After a staff appointment in Ireland Hutton went to Canada in 1898 to command the Canadian Militia, a force which presented him with opportunities of reform as far-reaching as those in New South Wales. His aim was to build a national army for Canada which would also be available to serve abroad. Unwisely, he became involved in Canadian politics; his efforts to pursue a military policy of his own became known to the Canadian government and his public speeches at the time of the South African War in 1899, with other devious activities, led to a crisis in which he was forced to resign. He returned to his true sphere, serving in South Africa where, as a major general, he commanded a strong brigade of mounted infantry with great distinction in the advance to Pretoria. His brigade included Australian, New Zealand, Canadian and British units and he chose his staff largely from the colonial forces. His letters reveal his enthusiasm for the colonial citizen soldier and his awareness of a special responsibility in such a command which seemed to him as much political and Imperial as military. For his services in South Africa he was appointed K.C.M.G. in 1900.

In 1901 the first Australian government appointed Hutton to command and organize its land forces. He was recommended by Field Marshal Lord Roberts after several other officers had refused or were rejected by the government. He returned to Australia in January 1902 to tackle the congenial task of transforming the six colonial forces into a national army. He was warned by his friends about speech-making, his intemperate language and the need for tact when dealing with ministers, but such warnings were quickly forgotten. That year in Melbourne he published some of his addresses, *The defence and defensive power of Australia.*

Hutton came with high hopes and with the intention of organizing an army capable of supporting Australian and British interests beyond the Australian Commonwealth. His command began with personal frustrations owing to the refusal of the War Office to promote him lieut-general despite his much wider responsibilities and the refusal of the Australians to allow him to bring his own aide-de-camp. The government was without a defence policy, having withdrawn its first defence bill after it had been roughly handled in parliament. Confident and ambitious, Hutton submitted a minute in April 1902 outlining the strategic situation of Australia and the military organization he considered appropriate to it. He proposed a garrison force to defend the major coastal centres and ports and a field force which could be sent wherever Australian interests might require it. His proposals aroused adverse criticism not only in Australia but also in the Colonial Defence Committee in London. A new draft defence bill, prepared by Hutton at the request of the prime minister, was passed and finally proclaimed in March 1904 but it made no provision for sending Australian troops overseas. Nevertheless the general shape of the Australian Army as proposed by Hutton was preserved.

Meanwhile Hutton was merging the colonial militia forces into an Australian citizen army, although not without difficulty. He was furiously attacked in parliament and the press over the disbandment of small volunteer units whose disappearance was necessary to the development of a properly organized force. There was an alarming shortage of trained officers but the posting of a regular officer to a command in place of an elderly and inefficient militia colonel aroused a storm of protest. Similarly the transfer of instructors from one State to another caused a crisis between South Australia and the Commonwealth in 1902. Hutton fought a losing battle in trying to maintain a headquarters staff adequate for its task but reduction of the numbers of permanent officers and soldiers was a ready and popular way of saving money, especially as there were no pensions for those retrenched.

Hutton promoted efficiency, discipline and training in every department of the new citizen army. Much that he proposed had to wait for better times and the better atmosphere which the general officer commanding was incapable of creating. Among his proposals were a military college, an Army Service Corps, an Ordnance Corps, and superannuation for the permanent force. He was successful in creating the field force and the garrison force, with complete war and peace establishments. The cavalry and other mounted units he transformed into mounted infantry known as light horse. On the other hand he could not obtain funds for the equipment and rearmament of the forces. He instituted staff rides for the tactical training of officers and non-commissioned officers and began the process of producing an educated officer corps. These changes involved a degree of control and centralization which inevitably aroused resentment in the States. That some officers were also members of parliament or influential politically hindered his plans.

Hutton quarrelled frequently with his ministers, some of whose interventions were petty or foolish in the extreme. A more tolerant man would have made allowances for their inexperience and ignorance and for the very novelty of the experiment in which all were engaged. But Hutton the autocrat and fighter was in a hurry. He had insisted on a three-year appointment rather than the five he had been offered and there was still much to be done. Fortunately he had an eye for talent; chief among his protégés were Lieut-Colonel (Major General Sir) W. T. Bridges, Lieut-Colonel (General Sir) Harry Chauvel [qq.v.7] and Captain (General Sir) Brudenell White [q.v.], all of whom were to play important roles in the development of the army, especially in World War I. His constant battles with his ministers were Hutton's undoing. In 1904 a succession of ministers worked at revising the Defence Act along the lines of the recent reorganization of the War Office where the commander-in-chief had been replaced by an army council. No government wanted another G.O.C., whether British or Australian. Hutton strongly opposed this policy but the bill providing a military board in place of the G.O.C. was passed by the end of the year. By that time he had resigned after another furious quarrel over payment for a cable in cipher, the contents of which he refused to divulge.

The handicaps under which Hutton worked cannot be disregarded. He began his task in years of recession when weak governments were struggling to reduce expenditure. In three years he had to deal with four prime ministers and six ministers of defence. Parliament and the army itself included men of parochial outlook in military affairs and there was widespread popular suspicion of regular officers who were associated with 'militarism' and 'gold lace'. For all his soldierly qualities, professionalism, experience and zeal, Hutton was devoid of the tact which might have eased his relations with the ministers whom, too often, he despised. Perhaps his chief difficulty arose from his desire to serve two masters, the War Office and the Australian government. He saw the Australian Military Forces and the armies of other dominions as branches of one great British Army. He intended to give Australia an efficient citizen force for its own defence but he also wanted it to be ready to defend any part of the Empire. Despite the strength of the Imperial ties, Australian national sentiment and a growing appreciation of the country's proper interests were too strong for Hutton. However much he was disliked and distrusted by politicians, he was held in affection and admiration within the army and he left his mark on those who were to lead the Australian Imperial Force.

On his return to the United Kingdom he was given charge of administration in the Eastern Command and made G.O.C. of the 3rd British Division. At last in November 1907 he was promoted lieut-general on the eve of retirement. He was appointed K.C.B. in 1912. When Bridges was raising the Australian Imperial Force he suggested that it be commanded by Hutton. The government rejected the suggestion but Hutton was recalled by the War Office to organize and command the 21st British Division. A riding accident in 1915 brought about his final retirement.

During World War I Hutton corresponded with Bridges, Chauvel, White and others, rejoicing in Australian successes.

After the victory of Romani in August 1916 he congratulated Chauvel, commanding the Anzac Mounted Division. 'You and your men are establishing Australia as a Nation great by land and sea—which shall stand for British Freedom, Justice and Honour in the Southern Seas for all time.' Senior officers of the A.I.F. would visit the old soldier whose health was declining. He died on 4 August 1923 and was buried with full military honours at Lyne near his home at Chertsey, Surrey. He was survived by his wife; they had no children. Portraits by Tom Roberts [q.v.] are in the Royal Military College, Duntroon, and Victoria Barracks, Sydney.

N. Meaney, *A history of Australian defence and foreign policy, 1901-23*, 1 (Syd, 1976); R. A. Preston, *Canada and 'Imperial defense'* (Durham, NC, 1967); *PP* (Cwlth), 1901-02, 2 (A36), 1903, 2 (37), 1904, 2 (25); *Aust Q*, Dec 1956; *VHM*, 29 (1959), no 1; *Bulletin*, 15 July 1893; *SMH*, 24 Aug 1923; E. T. H. Hutton papers (NL) (British Lib, Lond).

A. J. HILL

HUTTON, GEORGE SAMUEL (1848-1913), accountant and Freemason, was born on 1 October 1848 at Sheffield, Yorkshire, England, son of George Hutton (1820-1902), civil servant, and his wife Mary, née Dowenend. Educated at Manchester Grammar School, he migrated to Queensland with his parents in November 1862 in the *Prince Consort*. After farming with his father he worked briefly in the railways, then joined Clark, Hodgson & Co., merchants at Ipswich and Brisbane.

From the late 1870s Hutton was confidential accountant with the Brisbane branch of S. Hoffnung [q.v.4] & Co. until in October 1893 he commenced practice as a public accountant. Specializing in insolvencies and liquidations which were so numerous at the time, his practice flourished. His audit clients included his old firm Hoffnung's and the Queensland National Bank, while he managed the Queensland business of the Manchester Assurance Co. A member of the Brisbane board of advice for the Federal Institute of Accountants, and founder and principal partner of G. S. Hutton & McFarlane, he was a prominent figure in the business world.

Hutton was initiated as a Freemason in 1871 and by 1898 had succeeded Sir Samuel Griffith [q.v.] as provincial grand master of Queensland under the Irish constitution. Although the other States had united their lodges formed under the English, Scottish and Irish constitutions, Queensland had failed to do so and in 1903 Hutton was asked to try again. Although he succeeded in achieving a measure of unity by 1904, most of the English and many of the Scottish lodges remaind aloof, and the three parent lodges in the British Isles withheld recognition from the new grand lodge of which Hutton had become grand master. The split became notorious in Freemasonry circles as the 'Queensland question'. In an effort to heal the rift he induced the governor, Lord Chelmsford [q.v.7], to accept nomination as grand master in his stead in 1906, but the union was not completed until 1919. The first building of the Freemasons' Homes at Sandgate was named after Hutton.

6 ft. 4 ins. (193 cm) in height, Hutton was commissioned in the Queensland Defence Force in 1876 and retired as a captain in 1897. Through his land order certificate granted to volunteers, in 1881 he acquired fifty acres (20 ha) of land in the Gympie district. He was a member of the Hamilton Town Council in 1902-11 and mayor in 1905-06. A government appointee on the committee of the Brisbane General Hospital in 1909-13, he was active in Liberal Party politics but never stood for parliament. He was a foundation member of the Brisbane Club.

On 13 October 1885 Hutton had married a widow Catherine Palmer, née Chapman, by whom he had two daughters and a son. They lived 'a gracious sort of life' at Bay View, a fine house in spacious grounds at Albion, with his aged parents living in a small house adjacent. He died of cancer on 4 August 1913 and was buried in Toowong cemetery with Masonic and Anglican rites. His estate was valued for probate at £5581.

Alcazar Press, *Queensland, 1900* (Brisb, nd); United Grand Lodge of Antient Free and Accepted Masons Qld, *The centennial story—the history of Freemasonry in Queensland* (Brisb, 1959); *A'sian Insurance and Banking Record,* 19 Oct 1898, 21 Aug 1913; *Brisbane Courier,* 12 Feb 1899, 12 June, 30 Nov 1906, 23 Jan 1912, 5, 6, Aug 1913; *Week,* 3 Nov 1893, 8 Aug 1913; Grand Lodge of Qld, Procs, 1904-21 (Masonic Temple, Brisb); information from Mr. T. B. Hutton, Buderim, Qld.

MERLE M. GYNTHER

HUXHAM, JOHN SAUNDERS (1861-1949), politician, was born on 14 May 1861 at Ivybridge, Devonshire, England, son of Simon Huxham, labourer, and his wife Agnes, née Chapman. She was illiterate. He was registered as Samuel John Chapman Huxham and adopted the names of John Saunders later. He was educated at Ivybridge at a 'harsh and desolate Dame School' where punishment consisted of 'confinement in a dark cellar', and in London. After occasional visits to Australia in six years as a merchant seaman, he settled in Sydney in 1879 as a bookseller's accountant. On 25 December 1884 at St Silas Anglican Church, Waterloo, he married Eliza Jane Bubb; they had five children.

Huxham went to Townsville, Queensland, in 1889 as accountant for Alfred Shaw & Co., general merchants, and transferred in April 1893 to their Brisbane office. He became manager of Pollard & Co., music and instrument retailers. When the firm closed, he and a partner, Alex McKenzie, in 1908 founded John Huxham & Co., importer and sporting and musical goods retailer. After his wife died in 1896 he married on 13 October 1897 a widow Helen Julia Meiklejohn, née Dougherty; they had one daughter.

Huxham contested the Legislative Assembly seat of South Brisbane for Labor in May 1907 and won it in February 1908. In November the party moved to direct opposition of the Kidston–Philp [qq.v.] coalition and at the October 1909 general election Huxham lost his seat. He returned to business life but won the adjacent suburban seat of Buranda in April 1912 and held it till 1924.

Teaching in Sydney 'ragged schools' in the 1880s gave Huxham a deep concern for welfare, especially that of the handicapped or disadvantaged. His daughter's blindness, caused by meningitis when 7, encouraged his active interest in the Queensland Blind, Deaf and Dumb Institute where his daughter taught; he was a life member by 1915. Quiet, moderate, a teetotaller and a Baptist lay-preacher, in parliament he would sit quietly for long periods, 'legs crossed, head bent slightly forward, arms folded'. He was not, he said, 'a straight from the shoulder man', and preferred conciliation. Quoting such philosopher-poets as Goethe, he often urged moderation and inter-party cooperation for 'the good of the people'. As a successful businessman he asserted that 'the friends of the workers' were not all in the Labor Party. This conciliatory trait was not a disguise for weakness. On 'Black Friday', during the general strike of February 1912, 'Honest John' was in the thick of the unionists and claimed to have lost friends and business in consequence.

Huxham was particularly interested in charitable institutions, hospitals, prisons and the Aboriginals, areas administered by the home secretary J. G. Appel [q.v.7] whom he admired. As early as 1912 he expressed interest in succeeding to this portfolio. Though not an original member of the Ryan [q.v.] ministry formed on 1 June 1915, on 10 July he was appointed minister without portfolio to assist home secretary David Bowman [q.v.7], and on Bowman's death became home secretary on 23 March 1916. Though Huxham was circumscribed by tight finances, the first baby clinics were created in March 1918. He secured public control of the Brisbane General Hospital in April 1917 and the transfer of the Blind, Deaf and Dumb Institute to the Department of Public Instruction in 1918. The achievements which satisfied him most were the opening in January 1919 of the Willowburn Epileptic Home at Toowoomba and in September of Westwood Sanatorium near Rockhampton which was designed mainly to cope with miner's phthisis.

Despite economic difficulties exacerbated by large salary increases for teachers in November 1919, as minister for public instruction from 9 September 1919 to 14 July 1924 Huxham encouraged important developments in vocational education and the treatment of disadvantaged children, especially of the isolated and handicapped. State education for the handicapped began at South Brisbane school in 1923. The primary correspondence school was introduced for rural children in 1922 and travelling vocational railway schools in 1923. Agricultural education was reorganized in 1923 by transfer of the Queensland Agricultural College to Huxham's department and the initiation of a Home Project Club scheme in schools.

Influenced probably by pressure to appoint a businessman and to create cabinet vacancies for younger members, E. G. Theodore [q.v.] chose Huxham in July 1924 to be agent-general in London; his wife died soon after their arrival. Returning to Brisbane in August 1929, Huxham lived quietly in retirement until his death on 4 August 1949. He was buried in South Brisbane cemetery with Baptist forms. His estate, valued for probate at £22 372, financed the Helen Huxham Hostel for blind girls in memory of his second wife. A pastel portrait by G. Harrington is held by the family and a plaster bust is in the collection of the Royal Historical Society of Queensland.

The Labour government of Queensland (Brisb, 1915); *Administrative actions of the Labour government in Queensland (1915-26)* (Brisb, c. 1927); *Morning Bulletin*, 8 Sept 1919; *Daily Mail* (Brisb), 15 Nov 1919; *Peak Downs Telegram*, 20 Mar 1920; *Brisbane Courier*, 3, 11 July, 19 Aug 1929; Newspaper cutting-books, 1915-24 (Qld Dept of Education Archives, Brisb); information from Mrs N. Bauld, Melb, Mrs O. and Mrs J. B. Huxham, and Mrs S. Gall, Brisb.   G. N. LOGAN

HYDE, SIR GEORGE FRANCIS (1877-1937), admiral, was born on 19 July 1877 at Southsea, Southampton, England, son of Ebenezer Hyde, a clerk with Grant and Madison's Bank, Old Portsmouth, and his wife Maria, née Alexander. He was educated until 16 at a private school at Portsmouth kept by a Dr Cody, his uncle by marriage. There was no naval or military tradition on either parent's side but local associations— Nelson's *Victory* moored in the harbour of the world's premier naval port, a close friendship with the son of a dockyard official—and a desire to serve his country seem to have inspired him with a love of the sea and also strengthened his ambition to enter the Royal Navy and attain high rank in it. His father could not afford to send him to H.M.S. *Britannia* to train for a commission, and the only channel open to him therefore was to join the merchant service, get a commission in the Royal Naval Reserve and thence a permanent commission through a 'supplementary list'.

After a few months in a bank at Ryde on the Isle of Wight, he persuaded his father in 1894 to allow him to enter the merchant service as an apprentice in the sailing ship *Mount Stewart*, a fine iron and steel woolclipper. Her normal voyage was with general cargo from London to Sydney via the Cape of Good Hope and home with wool via Cape Horn. On his first voyage, before the ship left Barry in Wales, young Hyde showed his mettle by jumping, with seaboots on, into the dock to save a boy from drowning. His apprenticeship completed in 1898 after four voyages in the *Mount Stewart*, he sailed as second mate in the barque *Amulree* from Rotterdam, The Netherlands, to Port Pirie in South Australia and home via Chile. This was his last voyage in the merchant service. He qualified, however, in 1902 as extra master, and in 1930 was to become a member of the Honourable Company of Master Mariners (London).

Hyde was a midshipman in the Royal Naval Reserve from 1896 but from 1899, instead of training with the Royal Navy in periods of up to twelve months as was customary, he contrived to maintain continuous service in the R.N. As a reserve officer he served successively in H.M. Ships *Tribune*, *Magnificent*, *Victorious*, *Bacchante* and *Leviathan*, being promoted sub-lieutenant, R.N.R., in 1901 and lieutenant in 1902. While in H.M.S. *Leviathan*, flagship of the 3rd Cruiser Squadron, Mediterranean Station, he gained his first great objective by being gazetted lieutenant in the R.N. in July 1905, with seniority from 19 July 1902. He had won a competition instituted by Admiral Lord Charles Beresford for the best essay on the Russo-Japanese War and it was on Beresford's thrice-repeated application on behalf of a 'brilliant' young officer that he was, as an exceptional case, 'elevated to join the list of Supplementary Lieutenants'.

After commanding *Torpedo Boat No. 6*

(1907-08), the destroyer *Rother* (1908-09) and the cruiser *Shannon* (1910), he left for Australia in December 1910 on loan to the Commonwealth Naval Forces to command the destroyer flotilla. Already an admirer of Australia, attracted by its bright future, the absence of class prejudice, better prospects of promotion in a young navy, and by higher pay in addition to retirement pay from the R.N., he transferred to the Royal Australian Navy in 1912 in the rank of commander with seniority from 1 January 1911. In 1913 he joined the new battle-cruiser H.M.A.S. *Australia* in England and sailed in her to Australia. After the outbreak of war in 1914 *Australia*, as a 'dreadnought', had the important objective of seeking out and destroying the German Pacific Squadron.

In July 1915 Hyde was appointed by the Admiralty to command the light cruiser H.M.S. *Adventure* in the Coast of Ireland Command. Here he spent two and a half hazardous and strenuous years as flag captain to Vice Admiral Sir Lewis Bayly. An unusual duty occurred during the Irish Easter Rebellion. From 24 to 29 April 1916 when it was feared that the British Army's commander-in-chief in Ireland might be unable to communicate with the outside world, *Adventure* was sent by Admiral Bayly to provide essential communications and generally to assist. Bayly reported to the Admiralty on 30 April that Hyde had 'performed his duties with great tact and ability'. A sequel to this duty was to convey Prime Minister Asquith from Queenstown back to England after he had visited Dublin and Cork. Duties such as this helped to develop Hyde's ability to appreciate complex political and military situations.

He was mentioned in dispatches and promoted captain on 1 April 1917. A captured German officer commended the courtesy and kindness shown him in the *Adventure* and the 'perfect discipline, order and cleanliness' in that ship. In December 1917 Hyde went to the Mercantile Movements Division at the Admiralty and on 6 June 1918 he became senior naval officer at Holyhead, England. There on 10 August, with Anglican rites, he married Alice Marjorie Trefusis, née Spicer, a widow; the marriage was dissolved in 1928 without issue. A few days after the wedding Hyde returned to Australia to become director of the war staff at the Navy Office, Melbourne. He remained in this appointment until August 1919.

Earl Jellicoe asked for him to be attached to his staff during his mission to Australia in 1919. Hyde was an aide-de-camp to the governor-general in 1919-24 and he commanded H.M.A.S. *Brisbane* in 1919-21. He was second naval member of the Australian Naval Board in 1923-24. In 1926 he became commodore commanding the Australian Squadron. During his three-year command he was appointed C.B.E. in 1926 and C.V.O. in 1927, and in 1928 became an honorary A.D.C. to King George V, the first Australian naval officer to be so appointed. Promoted rear admiral on 23 February 1928, he took over at Portsmouth two important additions to the R.A.N., the new 'County' class cruisers *Australia* and *Canberra*.

On 16 February 1929, in Sydney with Presbyterian forms, Hyde married Isla, daughter of Malcolm Robertson of Jandra Station, Bourke, New South Wales. At the London Naval Conference in 1930 Hyde was an adviser to the Australian delegate James Fenton [q.v.8]. From May 1930 to May 1931, because of his 'exceptional record', he held the Royal Navy command of the 3rd Battle Squadron of the British Home Fleet, first in *Emperor of India* and then in *Marlborough*. After three months at the Admiralty he returned to Australia to become first naval member on 20 October 1931. He became vice admiral in 1932, K.C.B. in 1934 and admiral in 1936.

When Hyde took over as its professional head in 1931 he found the R.A.N. in a much-reduced state as a result of the Depression. He expressed concern in public speeches, warning of the inadequacy of naval defence, deploring decreases in the navy and stressing the importance of British sea supremacy. He attended a conference of naval commanders-in-chief at Singapore and in 1935 visited England for technical discussions at the Admiralty. During this visit, as adviser to the Australian high commissioner S. M. (Viscount) Bruce [q.v.7], he participated in the discussions that led to the London Naval Treaty of 1936. After this era of disarmament had passed and international peace was being threatened again he bore as first naval member a major responsibility for the rebuilding of the R.A.N., insisting on the maintenance of the closest association with the R.N. He could see no alternative to this policy and was unshakeable about its wisdom. He continually stressed the need for regular exchanges of R.N. and R.A.N. ships, for special training of Australian officers in the R.N., and for keeping in close touch with British naval thought. He was convinced that all this was vital, as a small navy could not advance solely on its own resources. It was possible to realize many of his hopes, for the adverse attitude in Whitehall to Dominion navies had changed to one of encouragement.

Although Australian naval expenditure more than doubled during Hyde's tenure of office as first naval member, expansion had to be geared to the financial stringency of the Depression economy. It was therefore his difficult task, but one most ably performed, to choose what expenditure to recommend to the Australian government for building and maintenance of ships and equipment, recruiting and training and shore support. British naval weaknesses came to be recognized fully in Australia only after his time. It is a matter of conjecture whether an officer less Admiralty-minded than Hyde would have discerned these weaknesses and looked for alternative policies.

Throughout his life Hyde had enjoyed excellent health. He was treated for sub-acute pneumonia in 1915 but otherwise was in robust health until 1933 when he was operated on for cancer of the mouth. In April 1937, however, his health deteriorated and he had several falls. It was at this time, while he was concerned about his health, his lack of rapport with the minister for defence, Sir Archdale Parkhill [q.v.], and the prospect of retirement in October without a pension, that he suffered the shock of accidentally running down a pedestrian while driving his car on 20 June. The pedestrian died and, while a coronial inquiry absolved Hyde from blame, the distress which this accident caused him undoubtedly hastened his death. On 28 July 1937 while still in the appointment of first naval member, he died in Melbourne of pneumonia. The funeral service and cremation were private in accordance with the admiral's own wish; there was no ceremonial naval funeral. His wife and 4-year-old daughter survived him.

Many tributes were paid to his memory: by Prime Minister J. A. Lyons [q.v.], 'he has done so much for his country'; by Sir Maurice Hankey, 'he was such a splendid man, so full of courage and enthusiasm under all sorts of difficulties'; by the Melbourne *Sun*, 'he was known not only as a brilliant tactician but as a most able administrator, and he was loved by his men'. Captain P. E. Phillips, R.N., who had served as second naval member with him, wrote that Hyde's 'views on Empire Defence, which embraced all Services, were extraordinarily sound'.

When, two years after Hyde's death, war came again, Australia was able to call on a navy which within its limits was well equipped, well balanced, well trained and imbued with fighting spirit. This preparedness of the R.A.N. for war in 1939 is perhaps Admiral Hyde's best memorial and he was not the sort of man to seek any other. His single-minded devotion to the navy appears to have caused some lack of sympathy from the general public. But of his zeal and devotion to duty, and of his demands for the highest professional standards in himself and in others, there can be no question. His

energy, determination and decisiveness were outstanding.

Hyde had begun life without social advantages in the England of Queen Victoria at a time when to attain and sustain commissioned rank in the navy depended largely on class and family means. By ability and force of character he gained his commission in the R.N. through the side-door of the merchant service and the R.N.R. and, transferring to the young Australian navy, gained there the highest rank and filled its most senior appointments. He was its first officer to become a full admiral and its first sea-going officer to become first naval member of the Australian Naval Board.

H. J. Feakes, *White ensign—southern cross* (Syd, 1951); R. Hyslop, *Australian naval administration 1900-1939* (Melb, 1973); J. M. McCarthy, *Australia and Imperial defence 1918-1939* (Brisb, 1976); *Argus, Age, Sun-News Pictorial, SMH*, and *The Times*, 29 July 1937; B. N. Primrose, Australian naval policy 1919-1942 (Ph.D. thesis, ANU, 1974); Navy Office correspondence files (AAO, Melb).

ROBERT HYSLOP

HYETT, FRANCIS WILLIAM (1882-1919), trade unionist, was born on 9 February 1882 at Bolwarra, near Ballarat, Victoria, son of William Hyett, sawmill labourer from Tasmania, and his wife Annie Kingston, née Pearce, born at Bungaree. William Hyett died of pneumonia on 1 March 1883, two months after the birth of his second child, a daughter.

Frank's schooling began at Bolwarra but was punctuated by the family's moves, first to Brunswick and then to other inner suburbs of Melbourne in search of cheaper housing. He left school at 13 and began work as a grocer's boy, later becoming a clerk. His early interests were cricket and football and he played with Coburg Juniors and later Brunswick. He also read widely, at first technical subjects but increasingly economics and politics.

By 1902 he had become attracted to socialism, which, under the tutelage of Frank Anstey [q.v.7], became for him a way of life. Hyett acquired a facility for forceful oratory and persuasive pamphleteering from Anstey, who also instilled into him a hatred of Imperialism and militarism. John Curtin was a fellow protégé of Anstey and a close friend of Hyett from 1903. The other early influence in Hyett's political life was Tom Mann [q.v.]. Hyett followed him into the Social Democratic Party, of which he became secretary in 1905, and the Victorian Socialist Party of which by March 1906 he was deputy secretary.

The following years were halcyon days

for the V.S.P. and marked the height of Hyett's involvement. He was active in the party's lecture programme and Yarra Bank meetings and was prominent in its fight for the right to hold public meetings in Prahran. He was gaoled for fourteen days over this issue. However, the V.S.P. increasingly became divided over its relationship with the reformist Australian Labor Party. Hyett, who had been a delegate to the 1908 conference of the Socialist Federation of Australia, sided with Mann and other moderates who, while critical of the Labor Party, believed it was political suicide to cut their links with the only electorally viable working-class party.

In February 1910 Hyett became paid organizer with the Amalgamated Society of Railway Employees, a position he obtained largely through his prominence in the V.S.P., as he had no knowledge of railways. He proved a capable organizer and became general secretary of the A.S.R.E. in July. He was a strong advocate of industrial unionism. In 1911 he helped to form the Victorian Railways Union, becoming its first general secretary. His work in this capacity was particularly directed towards consolidating the V.R.U. as an industrial union, and gaining access to an independent wages board. The first was substantially achieved whilst Hyett also played a major role in the formation of the Australian Railways Union, eventually achieved in 1920. He was also involved in the One Big Union movement. Access to a wages board dominated by the Railways Commission was gained in 1917, and in 1919, shortly after Hyett's death, a totally independent wages board was established.

Hyett's style as general secretary was one of sensitivity towards the wishes of the rank and file, combined with a determination that the V.R.U. should be centrally organized and strongly led. Consequently, he asserted his power to the limit which union rules would permit, while cajoling the rank and file with suitably tailored socialist or moderate rhetoric. In his dealings with the railways commissioners he was a formidable debater and negotiator. However his charm and affability helped to induce an atmosphere of conciliation rather than confrontation, in keeping with his members' reluctance to strike—as public servants it was illegal for them to do so.

During 1916-18 Hyett was very prominent in the anti-conscription campaign. He was able to carry the V.R.U. with him, and the union's newspaper became a medium for the anti-conscriptionists. The Labor Party split left it to Hyett, and others on the Trades Hall Council's Anti-Conscription Campaign Committee, to organize opposition to the second conscription referendum in Vic-

toria. He was also prominent in supporting the Victorian Labor College, and was a member of the socialist 'Y Club'.

Hyett's cricket career developed late. He transferred from Brunswick to Carlton as a wicket-keeper and opening batsman and represented Victoria several times in 1914-15, scoring a century against Tasmania. He was vice-president of the Carlton Football and Cricket clubs.

Hyett was married on 19 May 1910 to Ethel Margaret, sister of John Gunn [q.v.], in one of the V.S.P.'s socialist weddings; they had two daughters and a son. Hyett's sister Elizabeth had married F. O. Barnett [q.v.7] in 1909.

Hyett died of pneumonia on 25 April 1919 after contracting 'Spanish' influenza while with the Victorian cricketers in Sydney. His funeral, at Box Hill cemetery, was attended by 5000 people, an indication of the affection and loyalty he had earned.

I. Turner, *Industrial labour and politics* (Canb, 1965); *Railway Union Gazette*, 1911-20; *Vic Railway News*, 1910; G. C. Hewitt, A history of the Victorian Socialist Party, 1906-1932 (M.A. thesis, La Trobe Univ, 1974); A. Scarlett, Frank Hyett, a political biography (B.A. Hons thesis, La Trobe Univ, 1979).   A. SCARLETT

HYMAN, ARTHUR WELLESLEY (1880-1947), solicitor and soldier, was born on 18 June 1880 at Tamworth, New South Wales, eldest child of Lewis Hyam Hyman, a London-born merchant, and his Sydney-born wife Sara, née Lev(e)y. He was educated at Tamworth and at The Armidale School where he played in the cricket and Rugby teams. He was articled to a Sydney solicitor Mark Mitchell in 1898 and was admitted on 21 November 1903; he practised in Sydney until 1914. At the Great Synagogue he married Zara Herrmann on 25 May 1904; they lived at Neutral Bay.

Commissioned in the 2nd Light Horse Regiment on 19 September 1910, Hyman enlisted in the Australian Imperial Force on the outbreak of World War I. He was transferred to the 7th Light Horse and in December 1914 was promoted captain. He took part in the landing on Gallipoli on 25 April next year and later served in Egypt and Sinai. Major from August 1916, he was claims officer at 4th Division Headquarters in France and Belgium for two years. Twice mentioned in dispatches, he was appointed O.B.E. on 1 January 1919. Early that year he served on Lieut-General Sir John

Monash's [q.v.] staff in London dealing with repatriation; from May he attended lectures of the Council of Legal Education, Lincoln's Inn.

In October 1919 Hyman embarked for Australia. He divorced his wife in March 1921 and on 31 August, at the Great Synagogue, Sydney, married Naida Elizabeth Solomon. In 1922-36 he practised with Bradley, Son & Maughan (Bradley, Son, Maughan, Hyman & Kirkpatrick from 1930) and thereafter on his own. He was a commissioner for affidavits in all States and for the High Courts of Australia and New Zealand.

A diligent worker for ex-servicemen, Hyman was for many years a vice-president, and in 1926-27 and 1940-44, president of the State branch of the Returned Sailors' and Soldiers' (and Airmen's) Imperial League of Australia. Moreover, he was a trustee of the Anzac Memorial, Sydney, a member of the Soldiers' Children Education Board, a council-member of the New South Wales branch of the Australian Red Cross Society and a vice-president of the Legacy Club of Sydney and of the United Service Institution.

Mindful that he belonged to an established Jewish family, Hyman was an active president of the Australian Jewish Historical Society in 1941-44 and delivered to it a paper on Barnett Levey [q.v.2], his maternal great-great-uncle. He was a member of the Board of the Great Synagogue and of the Board of Jewish Education and president and trustee of the Jewish War Memorial. He did much honorary legal work for the many organizations, ex-service and Jewish, that he served. He was also a member of Australia's 150th Anniversary Celebrations Council.

For many years Hyman, a keen surfer, was president of the North Bondi Surf Life Saving Club and a vice-president of the Surf Life Saving Association of Australia. His only son was drowned in 1930 while trying to rescue a girl in a dangerous surf: Hyman later founded a lectureship to his memory in the University of Sydney faculty of law.

Promoted lieut-colonel in 1924, Hyman was senior legal staff officer for the 1st Cavalry Division until 1941. In 1944 he retired from legal practice and went to Melbourne as chairman of the Repatriation Assessment Appeal Tribunal. On 31 December 1947 he died of heart disease at his Edgecliff home and was buried in the Jewish section of Rookwood cemetery. He was survived by his second wife and by a daughter of his first marriage.

Aust Jewish Hist Soc, J, 2 (1944-48), pt 8; Reveille, Feb 1948; SMH, 2 Jan 1948; Bulletin, 7 Jan 1948.

L. E. FREDMAN

HYNES, MAURICE PATRICK (1885-1939), politician and trade union organizer, was born on 29 September 1885 at Mackay, Queensland, son of Patrick Maurice Hynes, publican, and his wife Catherine Anges, née Ready. Educated at Mackay State School, he worked throughout north and western Queensland at a variety of occupations including railway navvy, stockman and waterside worker before returning to Mackay as a labourer in the sugar industry. On 20 September 1907 he married Margaret Josephine Hennessey; they had two sons and three daughters.

A founder and sometime president of both the Mackay Trades and Labor Council and the Workers' Political Organization, Hynes was employed in 1918 as a Mackay-based organizer for the Australian Workers' Union and quickly earned respect, particularly for his work in the Queensland Arbitration Court. Appointed northern district secretary in 1920, he was superseded at union elections later in the year but was reappointed in November 1921.

Hynes was active in the anti-conscription campaigns and was briefly a State councillor of the One Big Union movement. His political ambitions received a set-back when he failed to win the Legislative Assembly seat of Mirani in the 1918 and 1920 general elections; in 1922 he was again defeated for the Federal seat of Herbert. Locally prominent and willing to campaign for the cause, he could not be permanently overlooked; on 12 May 1923 he defeated the Northern Country Party incumbent of the Townsville seat, W. H. Green [q.v.], by 164 votes. He held the seat until his death.

A junior back-bencher in the administrations of E. G. Theodore, W. N. Gillies and W. McCormack [qq.v.], 'Mossy' Hynes characteristically chose to direct his energies towards extra-parliamentary Labor organization and diligent constituency work. In 1925 he was elected vice-president of the State branch of the A.W.U.; in 1926 he became a member of the executive committee (the 'inner executive') of the Labor Party's Queensland central executive. These two positions, which he retained until his death, ensured him an influential place in the Queensland Labor movement's most important industrial and political bodies.

When the party regained office after three years in opposition in 1932, Hynes became minister for labour and industry. While Queensland struggled out of the Depression, this proved an exacting portfolio. The overriding priorities of the Forgan Smith [q.v.] government were encouragement of primary industries which would generate employment, and the gradual restoration of reforms made by previous Labor governments, which had been withdrawn by their economy-minded opponents. The most important legislation introduced by Hynes was the Industrial Conciliation and Arbitration Act, 1932, which re-established a comprehensive arbitration system and reintroduced the forty-four-hour week; it was subsequently amended four times under Hynes. He also improved workers' accommodation provisions and extended unemployment relief work under award conditions. As a minister Hynes gave the impression of underrating his parliamentary duties. Although he was a very forceful speaker on the hustings, his speeches in parliament were direct and brief; even when introducing important legislation he rarely spoke for longer than ten minutes. Nevertheless, he enjoyed a reputation for competent administration and by 1938 was able to boast that Queensland had the highest basic wage, the shortest working week and the lowest percentage of unemployed unionists in Australia.

Hynes was never a radical: his commitment to gradual reform through parliament and the arbitration system made him an archetypal representative of moderate Labor orthodoxy in the 1930s. A physically large, warmhearted but retiring Roman Catholic, he was a personal friend of the premier, Forgan Smith, and of A.W.U. general secretary Clarrie Fallon at a time when these two men (both from Mackay) dominated Queensland Labor politics.

During 1938 Hynes's health deteriorated rapidly. In the State elections of April the Protestant Labor Party mounted an energetic but unsuccessful campaign against him including accusations (certainly false) of scabbing in the 1911 sugar strike. In hospital for some time in January 1939, he spent part of six months leave from cabinet on vacation in Tasmania but died on 27 March 1939 at his home in Kedron of atherosclerotic disease. After a state funeral from St Stephen's Roman Catholic Cathedral, he was buried in Toowong cemetery.

D. J. Murphy et al (eds), *Labor in power . . . Queensland 1915-1957* (Brisb, 1979); *Worker* (Brisb), 23 Nov 1922, 28 Mar 1939, 4 Apr 1939; *Courier Mail*, 28 Mar 1939; *Townsville Daily Bulletin*, 28, 29 Mar 1939; *Bulletin*, 29 Mar 1939; S. K. Young, The Protestant Labour Party (B.A. Hons thesis, Univ Qld, 1971); D. W. Hunt, Federal politics in the Herbert electorate, 1915-1925 (B.A. Hons thesis, James Cook Univ, 1974).

D. W. HUNT

I

IDRIESS, ION LLEWELLYN (1889-1979), author, was born on 20 September 1889 at Waverley, Sydney, son of Walter Owen Idriess, sheriff's officer from Wales, and his native-born wife Juliette Windeyer, née Edmunds. Registered as Ion Windeyer at birth, he liked to be known as 'Jack'. Fittingly for a great traveller, his earliest memories were of travelling with his family: Tenterfield, Lismore, Tamworth, then Broken Hill where he completed his education at the superior public school and the School of Mines and where he gained a job in the assay office of the Broken Hill Proprietary mine. Idriess claimed that when 15 he almost died in the typhoid epidemic which killed his mother. He was sent to his grandmother in Sydney and found work on a paddle-steamer on the run to Newcastle. After a typhoid fever relapse he went ashore and worked in the western districts of New South Wales as a rabbit poisoner, boundary rider and drover. Lightning Ridge drew the young man; but the several hundred pounds' worth of opal he found he 'blued' in three months before heading to North Queensland to search for gold, tin and sandalwood. He travelled extensively throughout Cape York Peninsula, often with Aboriginals, beginning his lifelong interest in their customs, and then on to the cattle stations of the Gulf of Carpentaria.

In 1914 Idriess enlisted in the 5th Light Horse, Australian Imperial Force, as a trooper. Specializing in sniping, he was wounded at Gallipoli, witnessed the charge at Beersheba, and was wounded again in the fighting after the battle of Gaza. He was invalided home in March 1918. His experiences were to form the basis of a series of pamphlets on sniping and guerilla warfare published in 1942 when an invasion of Australia was expected. After convalescence he surveyed and explored parts of Cape York, travelled with pearlers and missionaries in Torres Strait and then turned to gold in New Guinea, buffalo shooting in the Northern Territory, and exploration in Central and Western Australia.

In 1928 he settled in Sydney as a freelance writer. He had written short pieces for the *Bulletin* while at Lightning Ridge and published the first of forty-seven books, *Madman's island*, in 1927, in 1931 he had some success with a fossickers' guide *Prospecting for gold* and the same year wrote his first best-seller, *Lasseter's last ride*. From then on he published at least a book a year (apart from 1943) until 1964. His last book appeared in 1969. Works like *The cattle king* (1936) and *Flynn of the Inland* (1932) were to go through forty to fifty reprintings.

In 1932 Idriess was described as 'a slight, medium-sized man, with a narrow, pale face, slightly greying hair and remarkable hazel eyes; a soft-voiced man with a typical Australian drawl'. He was also a highly motivated writer. He said of himself that he wrote 'like stinking hell', spending two hours every morning covering quarto pages of white paper with large handwriting at a desk in Angus [q.v.7] & Robertson's [q.v.] old building in Castlereagh Street. It was said that he could write a book in two months, and he twice published three books in one year (1932 and 1940). About 1932 he married Eta Morris. He was appointed O.B.E. in 1968. Survived by his two daughters, Idriess died on 6 June 1979 at Mona Vale, and was cremated.

Idriess's contribution to Australian publishing and literature was profound. His combination of the bush yarn and historical or geographical subjects brought a new vision of Australia to its city-bound readers. He developed a number of Australian legends: the Light Horse, Flynn [q.v.8], Lasseter, Kidman [qq.v.], the survival skills of the Aboriginals of Northern Australia. Together with a belief in the heroic went a belief in the social and economic development of Australia, a vision which matched the aspirations of governments of the 1940s and '50s. Idriess was no stylist, but his writing was immediate, colourful, well paced and, despite the speed at which it was written, always well structured. The combination of an optimistic view of Australia's progress and the romance of its past with a style drawn from the spoken language ensured his popularity. Idriess contributed to a resurgence of Australian publishing and established a form of writing which continued to flourish in the work of such authors as Frank Clune and Colin Simpson.

Gems from Idriess, introd C. Roderick (Syd, 1949); *Meanjin Q*, Dec 1964, p 348; *Walkabout*, 1 Apr 1951, p 8; *Aust Author*, Oct 1979, p 17, *Aust Handbook*, Mar 1932, p 23, 25; *Age*, 17 Dec 1960.

JULIAN CROFT

IFOULD, WILLIAM HERBERT (1877-1969), librarian and floriculturist, was born on 28 August 1877 at One Tree Hill near Gawler, South Australia, son of Edward

Lomer Ifould, farmer, and his wife Marion Burn, née Cameron. Educated at Adelaide Collegiate School, he studied arts subjects at the University of Adelaide in 1902-07. He had entered the Public Library, Museum and Art Gallery of South Australia as a cadet in 1892 and in 1905 was appointed principal librarian. At St John's Church, Halifax Street, he married Carrie Eugene Foale (d. 1969) on 5 March 1907.

Appointed principal librarian and secretary of the Public Library of New South Wales in July 1912, over the next thirty years Ifould built up its staff and resources, making it the foremost library in Australia. He developed the country reference section and the country circulation department and provided a valuable service to industry by expanding the research department. He established staff-training, with a series of grade examinations, reputedly the first of their kind in Australia, and in 1939 the first library school. He persistently advocated the completion of the main part of the library building and exerted great influence on its interior design and decoration; he was made an honorary member of the Institute of Architects of New South Wales in 1921. While overseas in 1929 he bought at Sotheby's a collection of letters of Sir Joseph Banks [q.v.1] for £8600.

Appointed O.B.E. in 1928, Ifould received a Carnegie travel grant in 1936. Next year he was foundation president of the Australian Institute of Librarians and in 1939 was elected a fellow of the Library Association of the United Kingdom. As chairman of the Libraries Advisory Committee from June 1937, he helped to draft the Library Act of 1939; next year he became chairman of the Library Board. He retired as principal librarian on 1 March 1942 and served as deputy-director of the Department of War Organisation of Industry in New South Wales until 1945. A trustee of the National Art Gallery of New South Wales from 1921, he was vice-president in 1929-58, president in 1958-60 and several times was acting director.

An ardent floriculturist, Ifould had been twice president of the National Rose Society in Adelaide. In 1912 he founded the National Rose Society of New South Wales and was president until 1923. An orange orchard at Waikerie, South Australia, planned and developed by him at week-ends before leaving Adelaide, became a profitable enterprise, which he managed throughout his life. He contributed a weekly garden column to the *Sunday News* in 1919-29 and published numerous articles, speeches and lectures on librarianship, art, gardening and other subjects that interested him. He was a keen sportsman: in his earlier days a licensed amateur steeplechase rider and a good tennis player; later he took up golf and trout fishing in the Snowy streams. He was a member of the Australian and Elanora Country clubs and in 1927-28 president of the Rotary Club of Sydney. From about 1914 he lived at Ahwao, Turramurra.

Ifould died at his home on 6 April 1969 and was cremated with Anglican rites. He was survived by one of his three sons; his two younger sons were killed in action in World War II. A bronze bust by Arthur Fleischman is held by the State Library of New South Wales.

H. Fysh, *Round the bend in the stream* (Syd, 1968); F. M. B. Cass, *Libraries in New South Wales* (Adel, 1972); Public Library of NSW, Annual Report, *PP* (LA NSW), 1912-42; *Aust Library J*, 18 (May 1969), p 31; *Daily Telegraph* (Syd), 21, 25 June 1912; *Sun* (Syd), 7 Apr 1937; *SMH*, 4 Feb 1942, 8 Apr 1969; personal information from Mrs M. Ifould, Bayview, Syd.   JEAN F. ARNOT

ILIFFE, JOHN (1846-1914), dentist, was born on 19 November 1846 at Coventry, England, son of Francis Iliffe, ribbon manufacturer, and his wife Maria, née Simmons. He was educated at Stoneygate School, Leicester. At 14 he was apprenticed to a dentist, probably in London where he attended lectures at the Dental Hospital in Soho Square. As he never used letters after his name it may be assumed that he did not obtain a formal qualification. He later recalled attending meetings of the Odontological Society in England, thus stimulating a lifelong interest in the dental reform movement.

Iliffe arrived in Melbourne with his family in 1866. He obtained work as assistant to Charles Pardoe, dental practitioner of Collins Street, and in 1871 succeeded to the practice.

From the early 1880s Iliffe was active in efforts to achieve organizational and educational reforms in the dental profession in Victoria. In February 1884 he helped to form the Odontological Society, becoming treasurer in 1884-88, president in 1888-96 and treasurer again in 1896-1914. In November 1884 the society began to work for legislation along the lines of the English Dental Act of 1878. Iliffe helped to draft the bill by which, when it eventually came into force in March 1888, a Dental Board was set up to register dentists and to formulate a curriculum for new students; Iliffe was a member from 1890 until 1914. He was also prominent in the formation in August 1889 of a Dental Association which aimed to obtain educational facilities for dentists. In September 1890 a dental hospital opened in Lonsdale Street with Iliffe as vice-president and chairman of the honorary dental staff. With the formation of the Australian College of Dentistry in June 1897, and the transfer of the hospital and college to a new location in November, he was appointed special lecturer in dental prosthetics and metallurgy.

Iliffe became editor of the *Australian Journal of Dentistry* in 1898. Although not a noted scientific contributor, he produced a column, 'Notes by the Way', and many thoughtful editorials on the dental reform movement in Victoria and overseas. He also published several articles on prosthetic techniques. A paper which he gave to the Odontological Society was republished as a pamphlet; it raised important questions on the future direction of dental education.

In evidence to the royal commission on the University of Melbourne in 1903, Iliffe opposed amalgamation of the dental college with the university 'at the present time', arguing that the specialized mechanical and biological skills required for dentistry could best be taught through the existing autonomous institutions of the dental hospital and college. Others did not share his views, however, and further negotiations led to an agreement in 1904 which established a faculty of dentistry.

Iliffe was a leading figure in discussions which led to the formation of a national dental organization in 1911, and was first president. At a dinner in his honour on 11 July 1913 Dr A. Burne, a leading Sydney dentist, generously acknowledged Iliffe as 'the Father of Australian Dentistry'. Yet his dominating position within the various dental organizations was frequently challenged, especially by those who felt that in dealing with matters of controversy, Iliffe was wearing too many hats. Younger dentists, academically qualified, sought to emphasize scientific and biological training over the practical and mechanical skills which Iliffe was seen to represent. Yet his remarkable tenacity and clear vision were widely recognized as helping to create an independent and respected profession in the years 1885-1910.

Iliffe died of cerebro-vascular disease on 2 August 1914 at his home in Prahran, and was buried in Melbourne general cemetery. He was survived by his wife Lavinia Cook, née Edwards, whom he had married at Collins Street Independent Church on 17 November 1897; there were no children. His extensive library was donated to the dental hospital, and his estate, valued for probate at £7839, on the death of his wife was bequeathed to the faculty of dentistry for the establishment of scholarships in his name.

A. Sutherland, *Victoria and its metropolis*, 2 (Melb, 1888); J. Smith (ed), *Cyclopedia of Victoria*, 1 (Melb, 1903); R. W. Halliday, *A history of dentistry in New South Wales 1788 to 1945*, A. O. Watson ed (Syd, 1977); Roy Com on the University of Melbourne, *V&P* (LA Vic), 1903, 2 (20), p 319; *Scientific Australian*, 20 Mar 1908; *Aust J of Dentistry*, 8 Dec 1911, 31 July 1913, 31 Aug 1914; *Argus*, 8 Dec 1911; Dental Assn, Minutes, 1889-1890, *and* Dental Bd, Minutes, vol 1, 1890 (held at Dental Bd of Vic); Odontological Soc, Minute-books, 1884-87 (held at Dental Hospital Archives, Melb).

Susie Ehrmann

ILLINGWORTH, FREDERICK (1844-1908), speculator and politician, was born on 24 September 1844 at Horton, Yorkshire, England, son of James Illingworth, woolcomber, and his wife Sarah, née Irving. He migrated to Victoria with his parents in 1848 and as a youth worked in the ironmongery trade in Melbourne and Brighton. There he developed what became a lifelong advocacy of the temperance movement. He married Elizabeth Tarry at Carlton on 5 September 1867; they had one son and one daughter. In the late 1870s he became an estate agent in partnership with John R. Hoskins, a former mayor of Bendigo, and prospered enough to acquire a pastoral property at Yalook. Bad seasons ruined him and in 1883 he opened an ironmongery business, specializing in electroplated goods, in Melbourne.

In 1888, with support from his fellow teetotaller James Munro [q.v.5], Illingworth became a founder and major shareholder in the Centennial Land Bank. Having purchased suburban land at inflated prices and relied on further inflation to maintain profits, the bank was in serious difficulties when land values collapsed at the end of 1890. Illingworth had also been indulging in heavy private borrowing for speculation and by early 1891 his personal liabilities were estimated at £283 000. A member of the Legislative Council for Northern Province from July 1889, he obtained parliamentary leave of absence in June 1890, ostensibly for a business trip to Europe. In fact, he left the ship at Albany and settled in Western Australia as a land and estate agent; his council seat was declared vacant in 1891. The liquidation of his assets produced £600 to meet debts of nearly £300 000 but it was not until 1897 that a Melbourne court order resulted in his appearance before the Western Australian Bankruptcy Court. In December 1903 his remaining creditors agreed to release him from sequestration. None of this prevented him from pursuing an active and prominent career in Western Australian politics.

Making his way to the Murchison gold-field, Illingworth invested in several mines, including the Rose Pearl at Mount Magnet. On 18 November 1896 in Adelaide he married Jane McGregor; they had no children. In July 1894 he had been elected to the Legislative Assembly as member for Nannine. When the constituency was subdivided he represented Central Murchison from June 1897 and Cue from April 1901. He soon made a reputation as a tenacious if sometimes prolix critic of Sir John Forrest's [q.v.8] government, specializing in financial and constitutional questions. When George Leake [q.v.] resigned his seat in parliament in August 1900 Illingworth replaced him as leader of the Opposition and almost immediately moved a motion of no confidence in Forrest's government. It was lost by sixteen votes to twenty-two, but was by far the strongest challenge to Forrest until then.

Following Forrest's departure to Federal politics his party lost office at the 1901 election. Illingworth was invited to form a ministry but stood down in favour of Leake, serving in his two cabinets from May to November 1901 and December 1901 to June 1902 as colonial treasurer and colonial secretary. His only budget, an optimistic performance, summarized in the slogan, 'Go forward; go on and possess the land', earned praise from his old opponent Forrest. At odds with his colleagues over railway administration Illingworth was passed over for the acting premiership when Leake fell fatally ill in June 1902. The new premier (Sir) Walter James [q.v.] excluded him from the ministry. In December 1903 he became chairman of committees, but lost his seat to a Labor candidate in June 1904. He was reappointed chairman in November 1905 after becoming member for West Perth, but resigned his office and his seat because of ill health in August 1907. Despite allegations that, while treasurer, he had authorized the loan of government trust funds to a developer who was dummying for him, the Western Australian government granted him £1000 on the ground that the Victorian proceedings had almost ruined him. While Illingworth went to Melbourne, the auditor-general inquired into the charges but no action was taken against him before he died at Brighton, Melbourne, of arteriosclerotic heart disease on 8 September 1908. He was buried in Melbourne general cemetery with Church of Christ forms.

A diligent local member with a pawky sense of humour, Illingworth might have lived down his Victorian reputation in Western Australia if he had been a politician of sufficient calibre, but he was too much a man of detail to fill the vacuum left by Forrest.

W. B. Kimberley (comp), *History of West Australia* (Melb, 1897); P. W. Thiel & Co., *Twentieth century impressions of Western Australia* (Perth, 1901); M. Cannon, *The land boomers* (Melb, 1966); *PD* (WA), 1907, p 207, 514; *Table Talk*, 20 June 1901; *Truth* (Melb), 18 July 1903; *West Australian*, 28 Oct 1905.

G. C. BOLTON

ILLINGWORTH, NELSON WILLIAM (1862-1926), sculptor, was born in August 1862 at Portsmouth, England, son of Thomas Illingworth, plasterer, and his wife Sarah, née Harvey. With his parents he migrated as a child to the United States of America. At 14 he returned to England, was apprenticed to a plasterer at Brighton and studied drawing and modelling at the art school there. After completing his articles, he was employed as a model-maker and modeller in the art department of the Royal Doulton potteries, Lambeth, London, for nine years. He also studied at the City and Guilds of London School of Modelling, under the noted teacher of sculpture W. S. Frith. On 20 July 1884 at St Barnabas Church, Kensington, he married 16-year-old Hannah Elizabeth Martha Johnson.

Illingworth and his family arrived in Sydney on 28 February 1892. He was employed as instructor in modelling at Sydney Technical College but was retrenched in 1893 and set up his own studio. Unable to make a living by sculpture alone, he set up the Denbrae Fine Art Pottery at Forest Lodge to manufacture a large range of flowerpots, fernpots and statuettes. Among his early works were the figure-head for the pilot-ship *Captain Cook* and heads of Aboriginals. From 1895 he exhibited portrait busts, including a series of heads of Aboriginals, and statuettes with the Society of Artists, Sydney, and later with the (Royal) Art Society of New South Wales. Despite producing notable busts of Victor Daley [q.v.8] and Cardinal Moran [q.v.] in 1899, chronic rheumatism hampered his work and he was declared bankrupt in 1900. He had recovered his health by 1902.

From the 1890s Illingworth produced portrait busts of such notable men as (Sir) Edmund Barton [q.v.7], (Sir) George Reid, (Sir) Thomas Hughes, Archbishop W. Saumarez Smith, Lord Hopetoun and (Sir) Denison Miller [qq.v.]. His medallion portrait, statuette and life-sized figure of Sir Henry Parkes [q.v.5] were executed between 1895 and 1902. He was commissioned by the New Zealand government to produce a bust of R. J. Seddon and in February 1908 Illingworth accepted a commission for ten portrait busts of Maori chiefs at fifty guineas each. He lived with Maori tribes while working on the busts, but his commission was terminated after he had completed eight; this led to an acrimonious exchange on copyright with the New Zealand solicitor-general. Returning to Sydney, Illingworth produced, among others, the excellent bust of Henry Lawson [q.v.] in 1915 and the unorthodox informal life-size statue of J. C. Manifold [q.v.] erected at Camperdown, Victoria, in 1921. He held an exhibition at Anthony Hordern's [q.v.4] Fine Art Gallery in 1924.

A smallish, stocky man, Illingworth generally wore his unconventional 'long curly hair flowing over a poncho-like cape, and a turned down collar'. He was a genial, lively and notable Sydney Bohemian who enjoyed life to the full, but his reputation as a sculptor probably suffered as a result. Much of his portrait work is vigorous and very perceptive, although usually composed for a single viewpoint. He was preparing a design for the Lawson monument when he died suddenly of heart disease on 26 July 1926 at Harbord; he was buried in the Roman Catholic section of Northern Suburbs cemetery. His wife, two sons and two daughters survived him; Nelson, his elder son, was well known as a singer before going to the United States.

Illingworth's portrait by Dattilo Rubbo [q.v.] is held by the Art Gallery of South Australia and a bust by Paul Montfort [q.v.] by his family; his own work is represented in the major Australian galleries.

G. A. Taylor, *Those were the days* (Syd, 1918); K. Parkes, *Sculpture of today*, 1 (Lond, 1921); R. Lindsay, *Model wife* (Syd, 1967); K. W. Scarlett, *Australian sculptors* (Melb, 1980); Aust Soc for Hist Archaeology, *Newsletter*, 7 (1977), no 2, p 9; *SMH*, 22 May 1937; Bankruptcy file 10/23292 (NSWA).

NOEL S. HUTCHISON

IMLAY, ALEXANDER PETER (1885-1959), NORMAN GEORGE (1887-1973), soldiers, and ELLEN JEANIE (1881-1978), nursing sister, were the sons and daughter of Alexander William Imlay, station manager, and his wife Emma Carbery, née Woodlands. Ellen was born on 15 April 1881, at Toowoomba, Queensland, Alexander on 1 February 1885 at Comongin South station, Bulloo River, and Norman on 11 January 1887 at Croydon, Sydney. Alexander Imlay [q.v.2] was their grandfather. Their father, who had served in the Maori Wars as a naval surgeon, died in 1888.

Alexander, educated at Crown Street Superior Public School, Sydney, was a commercial traveller at the time of his marriage to Edith Henrietta Murray at the Marrickville Presbyterian Church on 22 December 1909. He soon went to Adelaide as a mercantile manager for Arthur Cook & Sons. Norman, also state school educated, became a clerk with John Hunter, Sydney, in April 1910 and then with Burns [q.v.7], Philp [q.v.] & Co. in 1910-13. In Papua he joined the public service as a customs officer.

Both Alexander and Norman showed an early interest in military affairs. They served in the New South Wales Scottish Rifles, Alexander in 1901-08 and Norman in 1904-06. In Adelaide on 1 July 1914 Alexander joined the 75th (Hindmarsh) Infantry, Australian Military Forces, as second lieutenant; he was commissioned second lieutenant, 16th Battalion, Australian Imperial Force, on 29 September. Norman served in Papua from October 1914 with the European Armed Constabulary and joined the 20th Battalion, A.I.F., on 8 October 1915. Ellen also evinced an interest in army work before the war: she trained as a nurse in Sydney and joined the Australian Army Nursing Service in 1912, transferring to the A.I.F. on 20 March 1915.

Alexander embarked for Egypt on 22 December 1914. Promoted lieutenant on 25 March next year, he landed at Gallipoli on 26 April, and was involved in heavy fighting. Seriously wounded on 2 May, he was evacuated to England, but rejoined his battalion on Gallipoli as company commander on 31 October. On 20 January 1916 in Egypt he was promoted captain and in March transferred to the 48th Battalion as second-in-command with promotion to major. Between March and June, as part of the Egyptian Expeditionary Force, he was involved in operations against the Turks in the Sinai Desert. Wounded on 13 May, he was hospitalized for two weeks before embarking for France on 2 June.

Between June and November in France and Belgium Imlay engaged in operations at Houplines, Fleurbaix, Pozières (where he was wounded but remained on duty), Mouquet Farm, Wytschaete, Flers and Gueudecourt. On 1 March 1917 he transferred to the 47th Battalion as second-in-command and after the 1st battle of Bullecourt on 11 April was awarded the Distinguished Service Order. He took command of the battalion on 20 April following the wounding of Lieut-Colonel Eric Lewis and was promoted temporary lieut-colonel. On 12 October at Passchendaele he was severely wounded by shell-fire and was evacuated to England; for his 'gallantry and conspicuous bravery' he was awarded a Bar to his D.S.O. Returning to France on 4 February 1918, he was again wounded on 5 April at Dernancourt but remained on duty. In

May the 47th Battalion was disbanded and Imlay, who had been four times mentioned in dispatches, was given command of the 12th Training Battalion at Codford, Wiltshire, England. He remained with this unit until it was disbanded in February 1919. His A.I.F. appointment was terminated in August after his return to Australia.

Alexander Imlay was promoted major in the A.M.F. in August 1920 and transferred to the reserve of officers as lieut-colonel in October. Next year he joined the Gordon Highlanders, British Army, as captain and in 1930, after a period of secondment, transferred to the Royal Indian Army Service Corps. Promoted major in 1935, he retired in 1937 but was reappointed in 1940 as major (honorary lieut-colonel) for service during World War II. He died on 23 April 1959 at Skene, Aberdeen, Scotland, survived by his wife and children.

Norman Imlay left Australia for Egypt with the 8th Reinforcements for the 20th Battalion on 17 December 1915. He joined the 12th Brigade Machine Gun Company on 27 March 1916, was promoted corporal on 23 May and arrived in France on 11 June.

On 19 August at Pozières Norman was commissioned second lieutenant and four days later transferred to Alexander's battalion (the 48th) as a platoon commander. On 8 December he was promoted lieutenant. He received the Military Cross in June 1917, probably for his splendid efforts during the 1st battle of Bullecourt when he was in charge of a bomb and ammunition carrying party.

After promotion to captain on 12 July 1917 Imlay served with the 12th Training Battalion from August until January 1918 when he returned to the 48th Battalion. Severely wounded in the assault on Monument Wood on 2-3 May when he commanded the left front company (and deliberately ignored orders he deemed foolish), he rejoined his unit on 18 September but saw no further action. He returned to Australia in November 1919.

In 1920 Imlay resumed his career in the New Guinea Customs Department as collector of customs at Samarai. On 31 March 1927 at the Pitt Street Congregational Church, Sydney, he married Jessie Mildred McMaster. After various New Guinea postings he moved in 1930 to Port Moresby as Treasury accountant and in 1934 became acting treasurer and member of the Executive Council. On his retirement in 1937 he returned to Australia to work until 1957 as postmaster at Willoughby, New South Wales. During World War II he saw further service in a training role but this was of a limited nature, his wound from May 1918 having resulted in the loss of a lung. He died

on 18 August 1973 at Balgowlah, survived by his wife and son, and was cremated.

Ellen Imlay embarked for Egypt on 10 April 1915 as a staff nurse reinforcement for the 1st Australian General Hospital at Heliopolis. She served there until 19 March 1916 when she re-embarked on a hospital transport for Sydney, returning to Egypt in May. On 20 May she was appointed sister and further promoted to temporary matron for another trip to Australia on 10 July. Leaving Sydney on 7 October as temporary head sister in the *Ceramic* for service in England, she worked at the 3rd Australian Auxiliary Hospital at Dartford, Kent, from 29 November until 8 January 1918 when she was transferred to France for service with the 2nd A.G.H. at Boulogne and later with various casualty clearing stations. In December she became ill and was invalided back to Sydney on 7 February 1919 and discharged in June. Miss Imlay retired from the A.A.N.S. Reserve in 1930 and later moved to Toowoomba, Queensland. She lived in Sydney after her marriage to a retired public accountant Harry Ninham Gooch on 10 July 1945 at Mosman. In old age, alert and good-humoured and wearing her medals on Anzac Day, she recalled the lighter moments of her nursing experience at Heliopolis where the hospital was a disused amusement park and the troops slid down the slippery dips on their pillows. Predeceased by her husband, she died in Sydney on 11 June 1978.

W. Devine, *The story of a Battalion* (Melb, 1919); C. E. W. Bean, *The story of Anzac*, 1917, 4 (Syd, 1933), 1918, 5 (Syd, 1937); C. E. W. Bean and H. S. Gullett, *Photographic record of the war*, 12 (Syd, 1923); C. Longmore, *The old Sixteenth* (Perth, 1929); A. G. Butler (ed), *Official history of the Australian Medical Services in the War 1914-18*, 2, 3 (Canb, 1940, 1943); *London Gazette*, 2 Jan, 1 May, 1, 15 June, 14, 25 Dec 1917, 25 May 1918; *Reveille* (Sydney), June 1934, p 18, Aug 1934, p 30, Nov 1934, p 27; *Bulletin*, 2 Mar 1922; *Daily Telegraph* (Syd), 26 Apr 1977; War diaries, 47th and 48th Battalion, AIF, *and* biographical file for A. P. Imlay (AWM).   K. R. WHITE

INGRAM, GEORGE MAWBY (MORBY) (1889-1961), soldier and carpenter, was born on 18 March 1889 at Bagshot near Sandhurst (Bendigo), Victoria, son of George Ronald Ingram, farmer, and his wife Charlotte, née Hubbard, both Victorian-born. Educated at Lilydale State School, he was apprenticed as a carpenter and joiner. He later went to Caulfield, Melbourne, and worked as a carpenter until 1914. On 19 January 1910, at East Prahran, he had married Jane Francis Nichols with Congregational forms. There were no children of the marriage which was dissolved in 1926 with Ingram as petitioner, the grounds being desertion by his wife.

In 1905-14 Ingram was a member of the militia forces and was attached to the Australian Garrison Artillery. On 10 December 1914 he enlisted as a private with the 3rd Battalion, Australian Naval and Military Expeditionary Force, and served in New Guinea until his discharge on 19 January 1916; he immediately enlisted in the Australian Imperial Force and was allotted to the 16th Reinforcements to the 24th Battalion. In January 1917 he joined his unit in France. Within the next nine months he received promotions from corporal to company sergeant major and was awarded the Military Medal for 'great courage and initiative as a member of a bombing section' at Grevillers, near Bapaume, in March. He was in hospital from April until June and again during September and October, after which he rejoined his battalion. On 20 June 1918 he was appointed second lieutenant but three days later he was evacuated with illness, resuming duty on 12 July. He was promoted lieutenant on 24 October.

Ingram was awarded the Victoria Cross for his part in the last Australian infantry action, the attack on Montbrehain on 5 October. In the advance which began at dawn the 24th suffered heavy casualties because of strongly defended enemy positions. Without hesitation Ingram, at the head of his platoon, rushed a post, captured nine machine-guns and killed forty-two Germans who had shown stubborn resistance. Later, after his company had suffered severe casualties and many officers had fallen, he took control of the situation once again, rallied his men under intense fire, and led them forward. He rushed another fortification and overcame serious resistance. Twice more that day he displayed great courage and leadership in the capture of enemy posts and the taking of sixty-two prisoners.

A tall man of robust physique and quiet and unassuming character, Ingram paid tribute to the bravery of the men in his company during the advance. In April 1919 he returned to Melbourne and on his discharge became general foreman with E. A. and Frank Watts Pty Ltd, building contractors. He married a widow, Lillian Wakeling, née Hart, on 10 February 1927 at the Methodist parsonage, Malvern, giving his occupation as farmer. After the completion of Melbourne's Shrine of Remembrance, he became a guard there. During World War II he served with the Royal Australian Engineers and attained the rank of captain.

Ingram's second wife died in May 1951 and on 24 December he married another widow, Myrtle Lydia Thomas, née Cornell,

at Brunswick Methodist Church. Survived by his wife and their son, and a son from his second marriage, he died of coronary vascular disease at his home at Hastings on 30 June 1961 and was buried in Frankston cemetery.

W. J. Harvey, *The red and white diamond* (Melb, 1920?); C. E. W. Bean, *The A.I.F. in France*, 1918 (Syd, 1942); L. Wigmore (ed), *They dared mightily* (Canb, 1963); *London Gazette*, 11 May 1917, 6 Jan 1919; *Mufti*, Nov 1937; War diary, 24th Battalion, AIF (AWM).   DARRYL MCINTYRE

INNES, REGINALD HEATH LONG (1869-1947), barrister and judge, was born on 17 November 1869 at Double Bay, Sydney, third son of (Sir) Joseph George Long Innes [q.v.4] and his wife Emily Jane(t), daughter of John Smith [q.v.6], pastoralist. In 1882 he was sent to Malvern College, Worcestershire, England, where he excelled in scholarship and sport, winning the Lea Shakespeare and Chance prizes and representing the school at cricket, boxing and rifle-shooting. In 1888 he went up to New College, Oxford (B.A., 1891; B.C.L. 1893). Like his father he entered Lincoln's Inn in 1889 and in 1892 read with W. M. Cann, a notable equity pleader. He was called to the Bar on 26 January 1893 and in July appeared before the Judicial Committee of the Privy Council as junior counsel for the respondent in the appeal case, *Makin* v. *Attorney-General of New South Wales*.

Upon his return to Sydney, Innes was admitted to the New South Wales Bar on 21 September and later joined Denman Chambers in Phillip Street. He was associate to his father, a Supreme Court justice, and from 1896 to Mr Justice A. H. Simpson [q.v.]. At St James Anglican Church, Sydney, he married Mary Louise McCartie on 18 December 1905.

After an early struggle Innes built up a flourishing practice, predominantly in the equity and bankruptcy jurisdictions, and was appointed K.C. in 1916. 'In Court his attitude was dogmatic to the point of arrogance'. Grave and rather austere, he had 'a proper sense' of his own dignity. He was a founder in 1923 and first honorary secretary and treasurer of the Barristers' Benevolent Association and donated many books to the Bar library. He was commissioned as a lieutenant in the Australian Military Forces and, too old to go overseas, served on the home front in 1916-19. A firm believer in the maxim *mens sana in corpore sano*, he was a good batsman, playing for I Zingari for many years, a keen tennis-player and a foundation member of Royal Sydney Golf Club.

He also belonged to the Union Club from 1908.

On 10 February 1925 Innes was appointed to the Supreme Court bench and judge in bankruptcy. Recognized as a sound lawyer and a hard-working judge, he became chief judge in equity in 1935. He found 'in Equity, while every case is difficult, every case is different, and every case is interesting: and ... some are amusing'. Innes regretted that age compelled him to retire in November 1939 and described his years on the bench as 'the happiest part of my life'.

Soon after retiring, Innes moved from Darling Point to the family holiday-home, Woodlands, at Medlow Bath in the Blue Mountains. During World War II he served as chairman of No. 1 Aliens Tribunal from 12 December 1940. His last years were tragically marred by the loss of his only son George Selwyn over Western Europe while serving with Royal Air Force Bomber Command. Innes died at Medlow Bath on 26 May 1947 and was cremated with Anglican rites. He was survived by his wife and three daughters, of whom Patricia had been his associate in 1929-35. His estate was sworn for probate at £15 484.

Cyclopedia of N.S.W. (Syd, 1907); J. M. Bennett (ed), *A history of the New South Wales Bar* (Syd, 1969); *Law Reports, Appeal Cases*, 1894; *NSW State Reports*, 1939, 1947; *Punch* (Melb), 19 Mar 1925; information from Malvern College, Worcs., UK; family papers (held by Mrs P. Watson, Medlow Bath, NSW).   PETER HOHNEN

INNES-NOAD, SIDNEY REGINALD (1860-1931), tea merchant and politician, was born on 12 May 1860 at Clerkenwell, London, son of Frederick Innes Noad, merchant and later ship-owner, and his wife Emma Matilda (formerly Clark), née Tennant. Educated in London at Highgate School and Braintree College, Essex, he reached Melbourne in 1883. A tea-taster, he married at Balaclava on 1 June 1886 Rosa Gertrude, the well-dowered daughter of William Howard Smith [q.v.6], and sister of Bruce Smith [q.v.]. Later Innes-Noad was a buyer for Lange & Thonemann and Joseph Webster & Co., tea importers, and by 1890 was in partnership with O. M. Malcolm. In the early 1890s he formed Innes-Noad, Price & Griffiths. The company expanded and also imported 'real Mountain Dew whisky'.

Selling out in 1897, Innes-Noad set up as a tea merchant in Brisbane. By 1903 he was living on independent means near Bowral, New South Wales, and for some years was secretary of the Berrima District (Cottage) Hospital at Bowral. In 1909 he moved to Sydney (though keeping their country house) and with his wife was on the executive of the Twilight League.

An independent Liberal, Innes-Noad unsuccessfully contested the Legislative Assembly seats of Wollondilly (1904) and, as a Liberal, Hartley (1910). In 1911 he established and was president of the Liberal Debating Club to train young men to join the 'Liberal Speaking Team', and was later president of the National Speakers' Association. He and his wife were councilmembers of the Liberal Association of New South Wales in 1913 and of the National Association of New South Wales in 1918-30 and he was vice-president in 1914-18 and 1930-31. During World War I, after a short visit to England, he was given to fighting the German menace at home by declaring that the Constitution should prevent people of 'alien blood' from ever holding a position in the public service or armed forces. Preselected for the Federal seat of St George in 1917, he stood down for William Bagnall, the ex-Labor candidate, and was nominated to the Legislative Council on 6 May.

Described by Sir Joseph Carruthers [q.v.7] as 'not only the best looking man in the House, but a man with the most motherly nature', Innes-Noad was foundation president of the Royal Society for the Welfare of Mothers and Babies in 1918-28. A voluntary organization, attracting donations from the wealthy as well as government funds, it established the Tresillian nursing homes for mothers and babies and training courses for mothercraft nurses, under the direction of Dr Margaret Harper [q.v.]. In 1925-26 he was attacked by supporters of Dr Truby King's methods used in New Zealand where infant mortality was lower than in New South Wales. He also served on the influenza committee in 1919, the State royal commission on lunacy law and administration in 1922-23 and the Commonwealth royal commission on health in 1925. His interest in health, welfare and housing always reflected the conservative beliefs of his peers that bonny babies for a beautiful Australia could be achieved by legislation and moral guidance from the state. He was appointed C.M.G. in 1929.

Survived by his wife and five daughters, Innes-Noad died at home at Beecroft on 11 February 1931 and was cremated with Anglican rites. His estate was valued for probate at £1792.

Roy Com on lunacy law and administration, *PP* (NSW), 1923, 1, p 651; *Aust Nurses' J*, 15 June 1927; *Fighting Line*, 19 Feb 1913, 18 Sept 1916, 19 June 1917, 21 Oct 1918; *Australasian*, 18 Aug 1917; *SMH*, 12 Feb 1931; M. J. Lewis, Populate or perish: aspects of infant and maternal health in Sydney 1870-1939 (Ph.D. thesis, ANU, 1976).
                                    MICHAL BOSWORTH

INWOOD, REGINALD ROY (1890-1971), soldier and miner, was born on 14 July 1890 in Adelaide, eldest son of Edward Inwood, labourer, and his wife Mary Ann, née Minney. He was educated at North Adelaide Public School and Broken Hill Model School. Inwood worked as a miner at Broken Hill.

In August 1914 he enlisted in the Australian Imperial Force and was allotted to the 10th Battalion. Embarking in October, he served at Gallipoli until November 1915. He was promoted lance corporal in August. By April 1916 the battalion was in France. Inwood, who had been promoted temporary corporal in August was in October reduced to private, owing to absence without leave.

In the battle of Menin Road in September 1917 the 10th Battalion attacked at Polygon Wood. 'During the advance to the second objective, [Inwood] passed through our barrage, and alone captured a strong post, killing several and capturing nine. He volunteered for a special night-long patrol. He went out 600 yards [550 m] and sent back the most valuable information. Early on the morning of 21 September Inwood went out alone and located and bombed a machine-gun. He killed the crew and brought in the one survivor with the gun'. He was awarded the Victoria Cross for 'most conspicuous bravery and devotion to duty'. Although the citation states that Inwood went out alone on this attack, the *Official History*, the unit history and Inwood's own statement confirm that he was assisted, however briefly, by another man. Promoted corporal in October 1917, and later sergeant, Inwood served with the 10th Battalion until May 1918. He embarked for Australia on 24 August and was demobilized in Adelaide in December.

Returning to a hero's welcome at Broken Hill in October Inwood contrasted, in a public speech, his departure when he was, he claimed, 'stoned by mongrels at the train', with his return when 'those mongrels were the first to . . . shake me by the hand . . . If the boys stick together like they did in France there will be no Bolshevikism in this town . . . I would like to be at one end of the street with a machine-gun and have them at the other end'. Departing recruits had been hooted and jeered by militant socialists at Broken Hill but there is no evidence of stone-throwing. M. P. Considine [q.v.8], member for Barrier in the House of Representatives, accused Inwood of trying 'to incite trouble between returned soldiers and the working classes'.

Broken Hill was not a comfortable place for Inwood. He soon moved to Adelaide and on 31 December 1918 married a widow Mabel Alice Collins, née Weber. Inwood had difficulty in finding work. After an assault charge by police, which resulted in a fine in 1919, and his divorce in 1921, he spent a short time mining at Queenstown, Tasmania, and at a eucalyptus distillery on Kangaroo Island. He returned to Adelaide and was employed by the city council as a labourer in 1928-55. During World War II he served as a warrant officer with the Australian Military Forces.

Inwood married Evelyn Owens in 1927 and after her death married Louise Elizabeth Gates in 1942. He had no children. A rugged, independent, well-built man, 'with the rough corners still on him', the years after his third marriage were spent happily and quietly. This loyal labourer, perhaps exploited by some at Broken Hill, gave the impression that 'his VC had not done him much good'. He never lost his pride in the 10th Battalion and always marched with them on Anzac Day. The Other Ranks Mess, 10th Battalion, Torrens Parade Ground, Adelaide, is called the Roy Inwood Club. His Victoria Cross hangs in the council chambers of the Adelaide City Council. He died on 23 October 1971, was given a military funeral and was buried in West Terrace cemetery. Two brothers, Harold and Robert, also served with the A.I.F.; the latter was killed in action at Pozières.

C. E. W. Bean, *The A.I.F. in France*, 1916, 1917 (Syd, 1929, 1933); C. B. L. Lock, *The fighting 10th* (Adel, 1936); L. Wigmore (ed), *They dared mightily* (Canb, 1963); R. H. B. Kearns, *Broken Hill*, 3 (Broken Hill, 1975); *Sydney Mail*, 2 Jan 1918; *SMH*, 28 Dec 1917, 23 Oct 1918, 26 Oct 1971; *Advertiser* (Adel), 24 Dec 1919, 6 July 1921; information from A. J. Dowd, Broken Hill, NSW, and F. and P. Fraser, Klemzig, SA.   JOYCE GIBBERD

IREDALE, FRANCIS ADAMS (1867-1926), cricketer and writer, was born on 19 June 1867 at Surry Hills, Sydney, son of Thomas Richardson Iredale, English-born ironmonger, and his Irish wife Margaret, née Adams. Like many great Sydney cricketers Iredale learned the game in the Domain, where after practice his stepfather would throw oranges to improve his catching: dropped oranges could not be eaten! The highlight of his successful junior career was his inclusion in a junior eighteen which played the English XI in 1884-85. As a batsman and medium-pace bowler he played for Balmain in 1885-86, the Oxford Club, Inverell, in 1887, the Albert and Belvedere clubs, and on the introduction of district cricket for Balmain again. He described himself as a surveyor and draughtsman when he married Edith Rebecca Brade on 24 February 1896 at Leichhardt.

In his début for New South Wales in 1888 Iredale played against the Australian XI and made 66 not out against a Queensland fifteen, but did not really shine as a batsman until the first Test against Stoddart's England XI at Sydney in 1894-95 when he made 81; in the third Test at Adelaide he hit a magnificent 140, finishing the series with 337 runs at 37.44. Iredale toured England in 1896 and 1899 and passed 1000 runs on both visits. After failing in the early part of the 1896 tour, he suddenly struck form, scoring 94 not out, 114, 106, 171, and 108 in the Test at Old Trafford: his tour batting average was 27.32. On the 1899 tour he scored 1039 runs at 29.68. In Tests against England he made 807 runs at an average of 36.68; in Sheffield Shield matches 2466 at 38.53 and in all first-class matches 6795 at 32.67.

On retiring from big cricket in 1902, Iredale devoted himself to administration and writing. He was a New South Wales delegate to the Australian Board of Control for International Cricket Matches and a State and Australian selector; in the latter capacity in 1912 he witnessed the famous fight between P. McAlister and Clem Hill [q.v.]. He wrote for the London *Sportsman* and in 1920 published *33 years of cricket*, illustrated by Arthur Mailey [q.v.]. In February 1922 Iredale's testimonial match in Sydney brought him £1740.

In 1914-26 he was secretary of the New South Wales Cricket Association. Ill health led to his resignation and he died of acute miliary tuberculosis on 15 April 1926 at the Mater Misericordiae Hospital, North Sydney. Survived by his wife, son and daughter, he was buried in the Anglican section of Northern Suburbs cemetery.

Tall and lean, 'Noss' Iredale was a stylish and attractive right-hand batsman. Although a bad starter, once settled he played all types of bowling with equal facility, being particularly brilliant behind the wicket where he cut to perfection, often with his left foot across. He combined sound defence with good hitting; a free and elegant forward player, he drove brilliantly on the off. He was also an excellent outfielder and fine slip.

C. B. Fry, *Book of Cricket* (Lond, nd); A. G. Moyes, *Australian batsmen* (Syd, 1954); R. Robinson, *On top down under* (Syd, 1981); C. Martin-Jenkins, *The complete who's who of Test cricketers* (Adel, 1980); *Lone Hand*, Nov, Dec 1913; *Wisden Cricketers' Almanack*, 1927; *T&CJ*, 8 Feb 1890; *Sportsman* (Lond), 13 Mar 1906; *SMH*, 14 Feb 1922, 17 Feb, 16, 19 Apr 1926; *Daily Telegraph* (Syd), 17 Apr 1926.

G. P. WALSH

IREDALE, TOM (1880-1972), conchologist and ornithologist, was born on 24 March 1880 at Stainburn, Cumberland, England, eighth child of John Iredale, market gardener, and his wife Ann Lamb, née Wilkinson. Educated at a private school, he suffered a tubercular infection at 17 and spent a year as an invalid; thereafter his education was informal. About 1899 he was apprenticed to a pharmacist, but in 1901 sailed for New Zealand, seeking a milder climate.

Arriving at Christchurch in 1902, Iredale worked as a clerk. On 16 April 1906 at nearby Addington he married Alice Maud Atkinson; they were divorced in 1923. In his spare time Iredale observed birds with W. R. B. Oliver, who introduced him to mollusca. In 1908 with four companions he spent eleven months on Kermadec Islands and, after visiting Queensland, returned to England in 1909.

As a freelance worker in the British Museum, Iredale met Gregory Mathews [q.v.]. As amanuensis to Mathews, he contributed to his twelve-volume *Birds of Australia* (London, 1910-27). In 1913 they began preparing notes on a handbook of New Zealand birds. Articles followed and in 1921 they published the first and only volume of *Manual of the birds of Australia*. Despite their long collaboration relatively little appeared under their joint names. Recent research has shown that Iredale wrote much that carried Mathews's name.

While in Mathews's employ, Iredale managed to study chitons, collect avian parasites in Hungary, assist C. Davies Sherborn with his massive *Index animalium*, and serve for four years on the British Ornithologists' Union's nomenclature committee. He was also a member of the Malacological and fellow of the Zoological societies of London. Gifted with extraordinary bibliographical ability, he enjoyed astounding scientific gatherings by quoting long references from memory.

At the St Giles registry office on 8 June 1923 he married an artist LILIAN MARGUERITE MEDLAND (1880-1955); they had met while working at the British Museum. The same year they settled in Sydney, and, with A. F. Basset Hull [q.v.], he published the first part of a *Monograph of the Australian loricates*. On 1 August 1924 he was appointed conchologist to the Australian Museum; he retired in 1944. He was to publish over 400 papers on shells, birds, books, naturalists, studies in ecology, zoogeography and the linking up of fossil molluscs with their living relations. He named many new genera and species of animals, and his own name is perpetuated in ornithology, conchology and ichthyology. He was a fellow of the Royal Zoological

Society of New South Wales (1931) and its president in 1937-38. In 1959 he was awarded the (W.B.) Clarke [q.v.3] medal of the Royal Society of New South Wales.

A controversial figure with a powerful personality, Iredale was of medium height and slight build, with brown eyes and hair; he was always affable, with a ready smile.

His wife Lilian Medland was born on 29 May 1880 at North Finchley, London, daughter of Lewis Medland, landed proprietor, and his wife Ada Emmeline, née Cranstone. Educated by a governess, she enjoyed sketching out-of-doors, mountain climbing, skiing and skating. As a girl she reared two lion cubs, induced salamanders to breathe through their lungs by gradually extending their time out of water, and kept a woodpecker in her studio. She belonged to that band of emancipated women who by about 1910 were bold enough to smoke and to wear knickerbockers when cycling. Brown-eyed, she was of medium height with a strong face and a luxuriant sweep of auburn hair.

She left home at 16 to train as a nurse at Guy's Hospital. Between 1906 and 1911 she completed 318 monochrome plates to illustrate Charles Stonham's five volumes on *The birds of the British Islands*—a remarkable achievement as an attack of diphtheria in 1907 left her almost completely deaf. Lively and independent, she continued nursing and painting. In 1911 she was invited to illustrate a revised edition of William Yarrell's *A history of British birds*; it was never completed, but in 1972 the 248 paintings she had done were discovered in immaculate condition.

In Australia Lilian painted thirty species of birds for the Australian Museum, which were issued as postcards in 1925. In the 1930s she completed 53 plates depicting 883 Australian birds for Mathews. She illustrated articles in various journals and painted plates for her husband's *Birds of paradise and bower birds* (Melbourne, 1950), *Birds of New Guinea* (Melbourne, 1956) and his proposed book on Australian kingfishers. Her lovely painting of the Providence petrel *Pterodroma solandri* was used on a Norfolk Island stamp issued in 1961.

Lilian Iredale died of cancer at her home at Queenscliffe on 16 December 1955 and was cremated; Tom Iredale died in hospital at Harbord on 12 April 1972 and was cremated with Anglican rites. He was survived by a daughter of his first marriage and by a son and daughter of his second.

G. P. Whitley, 'The life and work of Tom Iredale (1880-1972)', *Aust Zoologist*, 17 (1972), pt 2, p 65, and for publications; *Nautilus*, 86 (1972), p 61; *Emu*, 49 (1950), pt 4, p 257, 73 (1973), pt 2, p 74, 76 (1976), pt 4, p 183; T. Iredale, Notes (NL); Iredale

family papers (held by Mr R. Iredale, East Lindfield, and Mrs B. Page, Harbord, NSW).

TESS KLOOT

IRELAND, HORACE (1877-1938), solicitor and businessman, was born on 11 September 1877 at Newcastle, New South Wales, fifth son of Jesse Ireland, storekeeper, and his native-born wife Elizabeth Sarah, née Wolledge. His father had reached Melbourne in 1855 in the *Marco Polo* from Gloucestershire, England, and two years later moved to New South Wales. After operating stores at Baulkham Hills and Penrith, he settled at Newcastle in 1867. By the mid-1880s he was established as a grain and produce merchant, and owned a large store and warehouse in Hunter Street and, nearby, a large, ornate, four-storied warehouse. After he died in October 1887 trustees carried on and expanded the business, diversifying into food processing.

Horace was educated at Newcastle Grammar School and, in 1891-95, at Sydney Church of England Grammar School (Shore), where he captained the Rugby team and rowed in the second crew. He was articled to the Sydney legal firm W. H. Pigott & J. Stinson [qq.v.], and was admitted as a solicitor on 24 May 1902. By 1904, after an overseas trip, he had set up in practice in Australasia Chambers, Martin Place. He and Thomas Davis, an accountant practising in the same building, organized the incorporation of his father's firm as J. Ireland Ltd in 1905 as a family company. In close collaboration with Davis, he took over from the trustees and conducted the business from Sydney.

At St James's Church, Sydney, Ireland married Minnie Madge Reddell on 12 February 1912, and next year gave up practice as a solicitor and returned to Newcastle as full-time managing director and director of the firm's subsidiary and associated companies. Under his influence the firm expanded into manufacturing, wholesaling and retailing of foodstuffs. He established a cherished relationship with members of the family and the companies' senior officers; nevertheless he fell out with his once-insolvent brother Frank and with Davis. In late 1936 he resigned because of ill health. Next year the firm was reconstituted as J. Ireland Pty Ltd, with W. J. Cleary [q.v.8] as managing director. Ireland was a council-member of the Newcastle Chamber of Commerce in 1915-28 and president in 1919, and a member of the Newcastle and Newcastle Golf clubs.

Survived by his wife and three daughters, Ireland died of cerebral haemorrhage on 22 April 1938 at his home at Church Street and was cremated with Anglican rites. J. Ireland Pty Ltd, one of the 'big three' food wholesalers in northern New South Wales, was wound up in 1964.

Newcastle Morning Herald, 25 Apr 1938; Ireland family and business archives (Newcastle Public Library); 19th Century family register from Christ Church Cathedral (Univ Newcastle Archives); information from Mrs J. V. Mather, Newcastle.

DENIS ROWE

IRVINE, GERALD ADDINGTON D'ARCY *and* MALCOLM MERVYN D'ARCY; *see* D'ARCY-IRVINE

IRVINE, HANS WILLIAM HENRY (1856-1922), vigneron and politician, was born on 2 August 1856 in Melbourne, son of John William Henry Irvine and his wife Mary, née Gray. His father was a flour-miller of Irish parentage who established a business at Learmonth, near Ballarat. Hans was apprenticed to a printing firm to learn lithography, but being of 'exceptionally spirited enterprise' he became foreman and, aided by his father, acquired a share in the business; it would appear that his skills lay in sales and management. Sir Alexander Peacock [q.v.] remembered him as 'a solid worker' for the Australian Natives' Association. On 7 October 1885 at St Paul's Church, Ballarat East, Irvine married 36-year-old Mary Jane Robinson, daughter of a coppersmith; they had no children.

While still a young man he became wealthy, investing in land, mining and viticulture. He sold his interest in the printing trade and in 1888 acquired Joseph Best's [q.v.3] Great Western vineyard, cellars and winery, as well as some grazing land. Between 1888 and 1890 he acquired more vine-growing land at nearby Arawatta. He was also fortunate to obtain the services of the Frenchman Charles Pierlot, a former employee of the champagne house Pommery & Greno. Irvine was aware of the potential market for this popular and protected type of wine. In 1890 2000 bottles of sparkling wine were laid down in the cellars and another 52 acres (21 ha) planted for production of base material for sparkling wine. Irvine made the first of many journeys to Europe in 1891 to investigate the possibilities of an export market in Britain, and wine-making practices in France. Next year he entertained the Victorian governor, another potential market, in lavish style. He was also a pioneer of wine advertising.

In the early 1890s Irvine purchased two-thirds of the produce of local vignerons. Much of this was distilled into his brandy, which became quite as well known as his claret, hock, chablis, burgundy, hermitage, sparkling hock and sparkling burgundy. Keenly interested in wine science and the latest technology, Irvine maintained expert standards in his cellars. He employed for a time Leo Buring, son of T. G. H. Buring [q.v.3]. By 1906 he had 250 acres (101 ha) under vine at Great Western, cellars in Melbourne and a depot in London. By 1907 over one mile (1.6 km) of 'drives' had been excavated at Great Western for the underground maturation of wine.

Irvine's personal success stood in stark contrast to the difficulties faced by other Victorian wine-growers during the period. In 1894 he suggested a conference of vignerons to discuss problems facing the industry. He supported moves for a college of viticulture and the systematic introduction of phylloxera-resistant American root-stocks at a time when government policy opposed it. Although phylloxera never reached Great Western he maintained a nursery of American vines on his property. He also supported industry self-regulation by an elective board of viticulture, the establishment of regional wineries, and cheaper finance for investors in the industry. First president of the Viticultural Society of Victoria in 1905, he initiated the important mission of inquiry to Europe in 1907 by François de Castella, later Victorian government viticulturist. Irvine's *Report on the Australian wine trade* was produced at the request of the Victorian minister of agriculture in 1892.

His other interests included mining, especially in the Black Range in Western Australia; he earlier had used the cyanide process to yield rich profits from disused ore dumps. He owned Mininera Estate in the Hamilton district which he later subdivided. In July 1901 Irvine was elected to the Legislative Council for Nelson Province, acquiring a reputation as one of that chamber's most liberal members. He resigned in September 1906 to contest Grampians in the House of Representatives where, until defeated in 1914, he occupied a corner seat and supported Alfred Deakin [q.v.8]. While not particularly active or ambitious in parliament, he won respect as a 'robust, self-trained man of action and affairs'.

Described by *Punch* in 1910 as 'a man of about middle height, with a fair, ruddy face, a large white moustache, a large beaming smile, white hair sparse in places, and a large cigar', he was dubbed 'the wine king of Australia'. Both an entrepreneur and an innovator, he succeeded in the commercial production of a champagne style where others had failed.

In 1918 Irvine sold out to Benno Seppelt, son of J. E. Seppelt [q.v.6], bought a grazing property, Kerrisdale, and retired to South Yarra. He went to England in 1922 to seek medical attention for a gastric ulcer. He died in London on 11 July after an operation, and his body was returned to Victoria and buried in Great Western cemetery. His wife had predeceased him in 1915. He left his estate, valued for probate at £173 356, largely to relations, and to friends and employees.

L. R. Francis, *100 years of winemaking—Great Western 1865-1965* (priv pub, nd, Melb); *Wine and Spirit News and Aust Vigneron*, June 1894, p 25, 29, July 1894, p 43, Sept 1906, p 350, July 1910, p 271, 31 July 1922, p 289; *Punch* (Melb), 12 Dec 1907, 24 Mar 1910; *Ballarat Star*, and *Argus*, 13 July 1922; Irvine papers (LaTL).

DAVID DUNSTAN

IRVINE, ROBERT FRANCIS (1861-1941), economist, was born on 30 July 1861 at Scatsta, Shetland Islands, Scotland, son of William Irvine, farmer, and his wife Joan, née Sandison. The family migrated to New Zealand when he was a child. He was educated at Canterbury College (B.A., 1883; M.A., N.Z., 1884) where he won a senior scholarship in 1881 and the Bowen [q.v.3] prize for an essay on 'The influence of Latin civilization on the modern world'. In 1883-84 and 1888-89 he was on the staff of Christ's College, Christchurch. In between he toured England and Germany, acting as overseas correspondent for the Wellington *Evening Post*.

In 1891 Irvine came to New South Wales and in 1892-93 was headmaster of Moore College Grammar School, Liverpool. A widower, he married Florence Julia Herborn at Liverpool on 30 December 1892. By early 1894 he was headmaster of Springwood College in the Blue Mountains. Irvine moved in literary and artistic circles: with Arthur Adams, Christopher Brennan [qq.v.7], George Lambert and Thea Proctor [qq.v.], among others, he planned the ill-fated *Australian Magazine* in 1897 and in 1906 founded the Casual Club as a conversation group.

Originally intended as a minister of the kirk, Irvine broke with religion. On 26 March 1897 he was appointed examiner and inspecting officer to the Public Service Board and from July 1900 secretary to the board of examiners for the public service. He was a member of the board in 1910-12. As special commissioner appointed by Premier W. A. Holman [q.v.] he visited Europe and the United States of America; his *Report of the commission of inquiry into the question of the housing of workmen in Europe and America* was published in 1913 and used by A. B. Piddington [q.v.] in his inquiry into the basic wage in 1920.

From 1907 Irvine had lectured on economics at the University of Sydney, organized courses and invited prominent businessmen such as (Sir) George Allard and (Sir) Henry Braddon [qq.v.7] to lecture on special subjects. In 1912 he became the first professor of economics and built up the Sydney department which became a separate faculty in 1920. Widely read, he was described by an ex-student F. A. Bland as a 'magnificent instructor', who inspired his students 'with zeal for the Truth and zeal for the service of the commonweal'. He was a member of the University Extension Board and lectured widely at other universities, to town planning associations, tax-reform groups, primary producers and labour groups (including the Industrial Workers of the World). Among his controversial publications were *The place of the social sciences in a modern university* (1914), *The veil of money* (1916) and *The roots of our discontent* (London, 1922), in which he praised the role of labour and criticized Australian businessmen and orthodox economists on such questions as methodology, wages, depression and monetary policy. Sometimes in the 1920s Irvine adopted a syndicalist position on the organization of industry, a viewpoint which became much more uncompromising in a series of articles in the *Sunday Times* on the 'Financial system' (November 1920-January 1921 and July-August 1921), the 'Wages system' (March 1921) and the 'Industrial system' (April-June 1921). The post-war wave of anti-socialist hysteria that swept Australia probably contributed to his removal from the university.

Already unpopular in some university circles because of his radical political views Irvine was forced to resign in 1922 when his adultery was brought to the attention of the university authorities. He became a private consultant on finance and economics and a director of the Primary Producers' Bank of Australia (until government support was withdrawn in 1931-32). In 1929-32 he sketched proposals for a credit policy to assist the revival of Australia's agricultural sector. In December 1930 Irvine opposed Professor (Sir) Douglas Copland at the Federal basic wage hearing. He also ghosted a radical version of E. G. Theodore's [q.v. plan for reviving the Australian economy (16 January 1931), but his efforts were thwarted.

Irvine completed his last major work, *The Midas delusion*, in 1933. Another version (1935) was written for a Canadian publisher and largely endorsed Major Douglas's credit proposals. Irvine acknowledged here his intellectual debt to F. A. Soddy and stated his belief that 'the intrusion into the economics field of engineers, scientific men or humanists pure and simple is all to the good [and] it is particularly good for the economist who is apt to claim a too-exclusive knowledge, and to magnify over-much his office as expert'.

From 1933 Irvine lived quietly at Paddington; he died on 1 July 1941 at 215a George Street, Sydney, and was cremated with Presbyterian forms. His wife and three sons survived him. His eldest son had served overseas with the Australian Imperial Force in World War I.

B. McFarlane, *Professor Irvine's economics in Australian labour history, 1913-1933* (Canb, 1966); L. J. Louis and I. Turner (eds), *The depression of the 1930s* (Melb, 1968); F. H. G. Gruen, *Surveys of Australian economics*, 2 (Syd, 1979); A. Clark, *Christopher Brennan* (Melb, 1980); J. Mackinolty, *The wasted years?* (Syd, 1981); *Scottish A'sian*, 27 Aug 1920; *Hermes* (Syd), Nov 1922, p xxviii, 183; *New Outlook* (Syd), 15 Nov 1922; *Economics* (Syd), 1972; *SMH*, 2 July 1941; Univ Syd, Senate minutes, *and* registrar's records (Univ Syd Archives).

B. J. McFARLANE

IRVINE, SIR WILLIAM HILL (1858-1943), premier and chief justice, was born on 6 July 1858 at Dromalane, Newry, Down, Ireland, sixth of seven children of Hill Irvine, farmer and linen manufacturer, and his wife Margaret, née Mitchel. William, a nephew of John Mitchel [q.v.2] the Irish patriot, was educated at the Royal School, Armagh, and at Trinity College, Dublin (B.A., 1879), sharing college rooms with a cousin and leading 'a cheerful and rather riotous student life'. He won prizes in modern history and Italian and did well in mathematics. On graduation, achieved despite financial difficulties when Hill Irvine, overwhelmed by the failure of his linen mill, suffered a heart attack and died, William entered the King's Inns. But when his mother determined upon a new start overseas, he abandoned legal studies and persuaded her to go to Australia. Some of the family sailed for Melbourne in 1879 and set up house at Richmond.

Irvine undertook further degree courses at the University of Melbourne (M.A., 1882; LL.B., 1884; LL.M., 1886). He meanwhile derived a little income as a private tutor and, for a time, as a master at Geelong College—but he disliked teaching. After reading with (Sir) Henry Hodges [q.v.] he was admitted to the Victorian Bar on 8 July 1884. On 17 September 1891 at St Andrew's Presbyterian Church, Ballarat, he married Agnes Somerville, eldest daughter of T. D. Wanliss, member of the Legislative Council, and sister of D. S. Wanliss [q.v.] with whom Irvine shared a room in Selborne Chambers, Melbourne. There were three children of the marriage, but the first eight years were childless and spent with scrupulous regard for economy while Irvine struggled at the Bar. Yet they were able to entertain modestly, and found pleasure in music, gardening and the keeping of dogs. Irvine had, for a few years, a virtual obsession about goldmines and applied whatever cash he could spare in taking up mining leases. They came to nothing.

Irvine occupied idle moments in chambers writing a practice book on the powers of justices of the peace, published in 1888, and he worked up a reputation for his conduct of cases in the Gippsland County Courts. He also wrote with (Sir) Frank Gavan Duffy [q.v.8] *Law relating to the property of women* (1886). He sometimes examined for the law school at the university. But his work and income were erratic. 'Solicitors', he wrote, 'are very shy just at present, and I occasionally have a fit of a distinctly azure hue'. When a brief came he surmounted a disposition to indolence and applied himself to the task without reserve, severely draining mental and physical energy and requiring compensation in vigorous outlets like sculling, fitness exercises and bushwalking. He suffered from acute anxiety, sometimes of almost neurotic degree, possibly derived from the troubled years after his father's death.

In 1894 when his practice was solid but unspectacular, he stood for the rural Legislative Assembly seat of Lowan, representing the Free-trade Democratic Association; he advocated a land tax and claimed independence from both the Patterson and Turner [qq.v.] parties. Although virtually unknown in the electorate and opposed by the ministerialist Richard Baker, who also supported tariff reform, Irvine achieved a surprise victory which, ironically, may have been helped by the anti-Patterson public service vote which he personally distrusted.

Irvine found politics congenial. Through the offices of William Shiels [q.v.] he served in the 1899-1900 McLean [q.v.] ministry as attorney-general. He showed himself a man of absolute probity, clear vision and firm resolution and when McLean moved into Federal politics in 1901 Irvine, having lost his bid for the Federal seat of Wimmera, became leader of the Opposition. A Peacock [q.v.]-Irvine coalition was mooted, but in June 1902 Irvine carried a vote of no confidence in the Peacock ministry. Commissioned to form a government, he was remarked for his temerity in choosing a cabinet without consulting David Syme

[q.v.6]. The defeat of the members' reim-
bursement and public officers' salaries retrenchment bill secured him a double dissolution in September and he went to the polls
on 1 October. Prudently he had allied himself with the Kyabram movement and its
Citizens' Reform League which fought
drought and economic recession with demands for reduced government spending.
On a platform of parliamentary reform and
retrenchment within the public service as
the prerequisites for State economic development he won a resounding victory.

Irvine's ministry, unchanged after the
election, was essentially a country one. He
had appointed Shiels treasurer and kept the
post of attorney-general for himself; from
February 1903 he was also solicitor-general,
and treasurer from July. Irvine carried retrenchment and initiated major irrigation
programmes. His reform proposals, providing for reduction of the legislature by approximately one-third and reducing the
powers and widening the franchise of the
Legislative Council, were trimmed. But the
premier demonstrated his implacable will
by making acceptance of another provision,
separate parliamentary representation for
railway workers and public servants, a condition of his continuation in office.

In May 1903 the railway engine drivers
struck in a protest against working conditions and the humiliations of the retrenchment policy. Irvine's reaction to a crisis
which he had probably not deliberately provoked but which he had done nothing to
avoid was swift and crushing. A strike
suppression bill was introduced, accrued
financial and other benefits of strikers were
declared forfeit, the ringleaders were dismissed and strike-breakers engaged. The
strike was over within a week. Middle-class
interests applauded Irvine's stand, but
labour organizations were bitter in condemnation. 'Your turn will come, my smooth
beauty', yelled Dr Maloney [q.v.] across the
chamber: politically, Irvine had become a
'marked man'.

The strain of Irvine's dual position as
premier and treasurer began to show by
November when he announced his early intention of retiring as head of government;
already in September he had relinquished
the posts of attorney-general and solicitor-
general. His reduced income and sustained
criticism from the *Age* over his October budget were rumoured as explanations, but deteriorating health was probably the most
compelling factor. Under pressure from colleagues and with promises of relief from routine administration he rescinded his decision; but, suddenly, in February 1904,
under 'imperative orders' from physicians,
he resigned as premier.

In the premiership years his reputation as
'Iceberg' Irvine evolved. For one who
wished so much to succeed in politics he was
not helped by his appearance of cold aloofness and his reserve when among strangers.
He cultivated a 'thoughtful demeanour and
a monosyllabic, incisive method of speech'
that was primly logical. Even his choice of
thin-rimmed spectacles compounded an impression of austerity and detachment. He
did nothing to court popularity but convinced himself that 'the people trust me'.

Following his resignation a testimonial
fund of £2000 was raised by supporters and
presented to his wife. The Irvines travelled
overseas for seven months, and he was
awarded an honorary LL.D. at Trinity
College, Dublin. In a speech to citizens of
his birthplace he ostentatiously avoided reference to Home Rule. 'He would always be
proud to be a Newry man', he said, but 'his
fortunes and his work were cast in Australia, and to a large extent he belonged to
Australia'. On his return to Melbourne he
gave increasing time to his family and his
home Killeavey at Eltham. In 1906 he revealed his priorities by declining a seat on
the Supreme Court bench but taking silk on
23 October and moving on to Federal politics as member for Flinders from December.
He spoke out for strengthened Commonwealth powers, particularly in the fields of
taxation, immigration and defence. At the
same time his Bar career flourished and he
was senior counsel in many major cases before the High Court of Australia and the Victorian Supreme Court.

In the national parliament his continuing
sense of independence won him some admirers but few friends. He began nominally
as a member of the 'Corner-group' and
clashed often with Alfred Deakin [q.v.8] and
W. M. Hughes [q.v.] who called Irvine a
'mere phrasemaker' and taunted that
'Democracy asks him for reform, and he
gives it a speech'. He was left out of the
Fusion ministry in 1909: although (Sir)
Joseph Cook [q.v.8] desired his inclusion he
was anathema to Sir John Forrest [q.v.8];
moreover Hume Cook [q.v.8] reminded
Deakin of the railway strike and advised,
'This man MUST BE EXCLUDED at all costs'.
Irvine contested the leadership of the party
on Deakin's resignation in 1913, but had to
withdraw after the first ballot, thus losing
hopes he had begun to cherish of becoming
prime minister.

From June 1913 to September 1914 he was
attorney-general in the Cook ministry. But
as the government was enfeebled in its legislative programme by Senate obstruction his
term in office was frustrating. He survived
a censure motion in September 1913 by only
one vote, after allegations that he had al-

lowed himself to be placed in a position of conflict by accepting while a minister of the Crown a general retainer from the Marconi Co., then engaged in litigation against the Commonwealth. He was knighted in 1913 and raised to K.C.M.G. the following year.

When the Cook ministry fell in September 1914 Irvine's political career was all but over. Although he was described by Governor-General Sir Ronald Munro Ferguson [q.v.] three years later as the most statesmanlike man in parliament ('there is no public man who so often hits the right nail on the head'), he refused to join any ministry which was unprepared to legislate for conscription, an issue he pursued throughout the war years with typical single-mindedness. In July 1915 Irvine had called for compulsory registration of all men and next year he took a leading part in the referendum campaign. After the referendum was lost he helped to prepare the platform for a 'Win-the-War party' while hinting to Munro Ferguson of the efficacy of Imperial decree. Hughes seriously considered sending him as Australian representative to the Imperial Conference early in 1917. That year Irvine was prominent among his Nationalist colleagues in his refusal to accept Hughes's pledge not to introduce conscription without a special warrant from the people, and in October and November led the second conscription movement, decrying the need for referenda shackled to the 'sentiment' of women. He was still pushing for a conscription bill in March 1918 when on the death of Sir John Madden [q.v.] he accepted the chief justiceship of Victoria.

Irvine was sworn in on 9 April, some commentators likening his appointment to a consolation prize for his thwarted political aspirations. Preoccupation with politics had reduced his legal powers and, though he had many good judicial qualities, he was not a jurist and his judgments have little enduring legal merit. While clear and expeditious in his decisions, he was a slavish user of precedent and never commented on the state of the law. However in 1923 he set an important administrative precedent when he refused to nominate a Supreme Court judge to conduct a royal commission on a matter which had political implications.

Sir Robert Menzies considered him a 'first-class trial judge, dignified, upright, cold in manner . . . but perceptive, and devoted to justice'. Sir Arthur Dean recalled that Irvine 'presided over his court with great dignity and decorum, but with some degree of detachment from the case before him, particularly in the dangerous hours after lunch. He was not a profound lawyer, but usually an industrious one . . . He had a quiet and restrained sense of humour, a firm sense of justice, a high standard of duty and propriety, and great personal charm'. He did not transfer his 'Iceberg' reputation to his relations with the legal profession. But he confided that he felt lonely and isolated on the bench as he loved to be in affairs. He allowed himself to remain too long in office and had in his late seventies to be prompted by a colleague to resign; his inattention in the afternoons and his increasing forgetfulness had become excessively embarrassing. His resignation took effect on 30 September 1935.

From 1919 he administered the State as lieutenant-governor several times and was acting governor for nearly three years from June 1931. He and his wife moved with the presence and punctiliousness appropriate to ceremonial office and the community warmed to their enjoyment of touring and meeting people. His resonant and rich speaking voice helped to melt some of the chill of his formal bearing. He was raised to G.C.M.G. in 1934. His membership of the Royal Automobile Club of Victoria from 1909 and his position as patron from 1918 reflected his great enjoyment of motoring and of things mechanical; they, with mathematics, were his abiding forms of recreation.

His declining years were spent at Killeavey and then at Toorak where after suffering a progressively disabling disease that restricted movement and speech he died on 20 August 1943. Survived by his wife, two daughters and a son, he was accorded a state funeral. A portrait by Buckmaster won the Archibald [q.v.3] prize in 1933.

E. H. Sugden and F. W. Eggleston, *George Swinburne* (Syd, 1931); E. Scott, *Australia during the war* (Syd, 1936); T. Waters, *Much besides music* (Melb, 1951); F. M. Bradshaw, *Selborne Chambers memories* (Melb, 1962); R. G. Menzies, *Afternoon light* (Melb, 1967); L. C. Jauncey, *The story of conscription in Australia* (Lond, 1968); A. Dean, *A multitude of counsellors* (Melb, 1968); J. Iremonger et al (eds), *Strikes* (Syd, 1973); J. Rickard, *Class and politics* (Canb, 1976); R. Campbell, *A history of the Melbourne Law School, 1857 to 1973* (Melb, 1977); *VHJ*, 48 (1977), and for bibliog; F. W. Eggleston, Confidential notes (Menzies Lib, ANU); Deakin, Higgins and Symon papers (NL); Murray papers (SAA); Shiels papers (LaTL).   J. M. BENNETT
ANN G. SMITH

IRVING, GODFREY GEORGE HOWY (1867-1937), soldier, was born on 25 August 1867 at the University of Melbourne, son of Professor Martin Howy Irving [q.v.4] and his first wife Caroline Mary, née Bruyeres. He was educated at Hawthorn Grammar

School and was still attending school when he joined the 2nd Battalion, Victorian Rifles, as a private in June 1885. Next year he began work with McCulloch [q.v.5], Sellar & Co., a firm of Melbourne merchants. He gained a militia commission as lieutenant in the 2nd Battalion in 1887 and in 1891 was appointed captain in the permanent forces as battalion adjutant. For the next nine years he was adjutant of the 1st, 2nd, 3rd, 4th and 5th Battalions at various times. On 29 April 1896 he married Ada Minnie Margueritha, daughter of Frederick Thomas Derham [q.v.4], at the Catholic Apostolic Church, Melbourne.

In March 1900 Irving became adjutant of the Victorian Rangers and was promoted major in July; in March 1902 he was appointed to headquarters staff in Victoria. In May he left for South Africa in command of the 6th Battalion, Australian Commonwealth Horse, with temporary rank of lieut-colonel. Four days after arriving in Natal the unit received orders to return to Australia owing to the end of the war. Irving returned aboard the *Drayton Grange*; the poor conditions on the ship became the subject of a royal commission. He resumed duty on the Victorian staff, and in November 1903 was appointed to Army Headquarters staff. He left for England in June 1905 to undergo training and returned via India in January 1906. Next March he was posted to the Administrative and Instructional Staff in New South Wales where he remained until he was appointed commandant in Western Australia in September 1909. He was made substantive lieut-colonel in December 1909, temporary colonel in January 1911, and substantive colonel in May 1914.

Irving became commandant in South Australia a month before the outbreak of World War I. On 24 May 1915 he was appointed temporary chief of the General Staff; he relinquished this post in November to become 'General Officer Commanding Australian Troops in Egypt', with temporary rank of brigadier general. On arriving in Egypt he found that most reinforcements and other unallotted troops were being absorbed into the new divisions of the Australian Imperial Force. He was therefore given command of the 15th Infantry Brigade on 21 February 1916 but a week later was transferred to command the 14th Brigade. For a time he commanded the 5th Australian Division pending the arrival of Major General J. W. McCay [q.v.] from Australia.

On 20 March the division was ordered from Tel-el-Kebir to take over part of the Suez defences, with the bulk of the men to march across about forty miles (64 km) of desert. Irving's brigade began the march on 27 March and next day the unit virtually disintegrated as troops suffered the effects of thirst and exhaustion. Although physical unfitness of the troops, worn-out boots and recent inoculations contributed to the disaster, much blame was attached to Irving himself. There was a demonstration of feeling against him when the brigade was reviewed at Ferry Post by the prince of Wales on 29 March, and McCay, considering Irving's arrangements for the march to have been seriously defective, relieved him of command on 1 May. He returned to Australia where his A.I.F. appointment ended in June 1916.

Irving resumed the post of commandant in South Australia on 28 June; speculation concerning his recall forced an official statement by the minister for defence which disclaimed that he had been sent back as a result of the events of 28 March. Next February he became commandant in Queensland and remained there until May 1921 when he was appointed deputy quartermaster general at Army Headquarters. He was placed on the unattached list in 1922 and was made an honorary major general on the retired list in November 1925.

Irving died of coronary vascular disease on 11 December 1937 at his home in Kew, Melbourne, and was buried in Boroondara cemetery. He was survived by a son and two daughters; his wife had died in 1934. Sybil Howy Irving (1897-1973) was the founder and controller of the Australian Women's Army Service in 1941-47. Ronald Godfrey Howy Irving (1898-1965) graduated from the Royal Military College, Duntroon, in 1919 and retired from the Australian Military Forces in 1953 with the rank of brigadier. Freda Howy Irving (b. 1903) became a well-known Melbourne journalist.

Irving was a physically striking figure, being nearly 6 ft 5½ ins (197 cm) tall. He was active in his youth in the Victorian Rifle Association, took a keen interest in ex-servicemen's affairs and was an enthusiastic bowls player. Contemporary accounts indicate that he was a popular officer, respected for his military capacity as well as his personal qualities, but his ability as a commander, clouded by his performance on active service, must remain in doubt.

J. S. Battye (ed), *Cyclopedia of Western Australia*, I (Adel, 1912); A. D. Ellis, *The story of the Fifth Australian Division* (Lond, 1920?); C. E. W. Bean, *The A.I.F. in France*, 1916 (Syd, 1929); *V&P* (LA Vic) 1900, 1(3), p 67; *PP* (Cwlth), 1901-2, 2, p 119; *British A'sian*, 12 Oct 1916; *Listening Post*, Dec 1937; *Western Mail* (Perth), 3 July 1914; *Argus*, 25 May 1915, 26 June, 11 Aug 1916, 14 Feb 1934, 13, 14 Dec 1937; *Age*, 13 Dec 1937; Pearce papers, file 419/80/2, bundle 1, 106 (AWM).

C. D. COULTHARD-CLARK

IRVING, JAMES (1852-1910) and JAMES
WASHINGTON (1871-1948), veterinary
surgeons, were father and son. James was
born in 1852 at Rochdale, Lancashire,
England, son of John Irving, draper, and his
wife Sarah, née Holden. Educated at
Collier's Proprietary School, Rochdale, and
at Knaresborough Grammar School, Yorkshire, he was articled to a veterinary surgeon for two years, then studied at the Royal
(Dick) Veterinary College, Edinburgh, gaining his diploma in 1870. He was also awarded
the veterinary art diploma of the Highland
and Agricultural Society of Scotland. He
opened a practice at Oldham, Lancashire,
but, having married Charlotte Naomi Rothwell at Lancaster in 1868, soon entered a
partnership with his brother-in-law J. P.
Rothwell at Rochdale.

In 1873 Irving arrived in Brisbane and
began to practise in the Logan district. The
first qualified member of the profession to
practise privately in Queensland, he frequently treated human patients unable to
find a doctor. Settled in Brisbane from 1876
and appointed a government veterinary surgeon under the Diseases of Animals Act,
1881, he investigated a number of stock diseases, provided quarantine certificates for
imported stock and served as veterinary surgeon to the postal department, the police
force and the tramway company. As a major
in the Queensland Defence Force and later
a lieut-colonel, he supervised purchase of all
horses used by Queenslanders in the South
African War. He was honorary veterinary
surgeon and a councillor of the National
Agricultural and Industrial Association of
Queensland and of the Queensland Society
for the Prevention of Cruelty to Animals,
and was also president and patron of the
Queensland Kennel Club and inspector of
dairies for the City of Brisbane. An office-
bearer of the Royal Geographical Society of
Australasia (Queensland) for seventeen
years, he was also a director of the Brisbane
Permanent Building and Banking Co. Ltd.
Survived by his wife, three daughters and
a son, he died in Brisbane on 1 December
1910 of cirrhosis of the liver and was buried
in Toowong cemetery with Congregational
forms. His estate was valued for probate at
£16 173.

James Washington was born on 18 October 1871 at Oldham, Lancashire, and educated at the Brisbane Normal School. He
then went to Scotland and graduated at the
Royal (Dick) Veterinary College in 1893.
Later that year he joined his father's practice and was associated with most of the
same organizations as his father. He owned
ponies and horses which he successfully
exhibited in shows, and played polo.
Like his father, Irving was proud of his

profession and at the meeting to form a pro-
fessional veterinary body in Queensland on
11 June 1920 he was elected first president.
In June 1924 he became one of the four
Queensland councillors of the Australian
Veterinary Association which absorbed the
Queensland body. On 25 January 1911 in
Brisbane he had married Edith Mary
Thorpe Aulsebrook by whom he had one
daughter. Soon after his retirement he died
on 21 April 1948 and was cremated with
Anglican rites. His estate, valued for pro-
bate at £65 617, was left to his family.

Alcazar Press, *Queensland, 1900* (Brisb, nd);
Queenslander, 24 Oct 1874.   L. G. NEWTON

IRWIN, LEIGHTON MAJOR FRANCIS
(1892-1962), architect, was born on 9 November 1892 at Eastwood, Adelaide, son of Edward Henry Irwin, stock and station agent,
of Hagley, Tasmania, and his wife Helen
Mary, daughter of Major Francis Downes
[q.v.4]. He moved to Melbourne with his
family when he was 8. After education at
Haileybury College he undertook the
diploma of architecture course within the
University of Melbourne's engineering faculty.

Irwin was articled to F. L. Klingender in
1910-14; during this time R. H. Alsop [q.v.7]
had joined the partnership. Irwin then spent
some months with Bates, Peebles & Smart.
In November 1916 he joined the Australian
Imperial Force and on 1 December in Sydney married Freda Gwendolyn James. A few
days later he embarked with reinforcements for the 1st Field Artillery Brigade. He
was promoted lieutenant in August 1917. At
the war's end, from January to July 1919 he
attended the Architectural Association's
school in London.

Irwin returned to Melbourne in February
1920 and became assistant director under
Alsop of the newly opened Melbourne University Architectural Atelier. In 1925 he became director, retaining the position for
nearly twenty years, and served also on the
Royal Victorian Institute of Architects'
board of architectural education. The books
of photographs acquired by the atelier form
the basis of a library which now bears his
name at the school of architecture and building.

By 1931 he was vice-president of the
Working Men's College council and was
president in 1936-38. Irwin contributed
many articles to journals on architectural
subjects, notably to the R.V.I.A.'s *Journal,
The Australian Hospital* and *Australian
Home Beautiful*. He was elected to the

R.V.I.A. council by 1922, becoming assistant secretary and in 1931 president. Bitterly opposed to the federal body of the institute, Irwin launched an unexpected attack on its viability at the annual conference of 1931. That year he chaired the first Victorian Building Industry Congress. J. M. Freeland describes him as 'unvaryingly intense, fiercely serious and humourless . . . but with . . . intelligence, drive, capacity for work and ability beyond most men'.

In 1922 Irwin had formed a partnership with Roy Kenneth Stevenson. Their varied commissions included war memorials and ecclesiastical and domestic work: Irwin's own Spanish-flavoured, double-fronted villa at 3 Holmwood Avenue, Brighton (1927), won repute for the firm. However their success in the Melbourne Public Library competition of 1925 meant most to their immediate future and eventually established them as the library trustees' official architects.

In 1930 the firm undertook its first medical commissions. Mildura Base Hospital was an application of the northern European approach to hospital design, with its streamlined form, multi-storeyed construction, and continuous, north-facing sun balconies: a theme which was frequently repeated in hospital design. Before they dissolved their partnership in September 1934, Irwin and Stevenson designed the Royal Australasian College of Surgeons building and a factory complex for British Xylonite.

After 1934 Irwin's clients consisted almost entirely of hospital boards. His speciality was the reversal of the former clinical hospital atmosphere, and to this end he created an interior design section within his firm. He added a mechanical and electrical engineering section, and by 1946 had introduced structural engineers to his team. He also started a model-making shop, so convinced was he of the value of architectural models to explain the many facets of his schemes. In 1945 the firm became a limited proprietary company.

Irwin designed hospitals and hospital extensions in Melbourne, Sydney, Hobart and Launceston, as well as in country towns in New South Wales and Victoria. Perhaps his greatest triumph was Prince Henry's Hospital and Nurses' Home in St Kilda Road: its tall central block with its 'glass by the acre' was completed in 1940. Among the largest of his commissions was the Heidelberg Military (Repatriation) Hospital. His later hospitals included those at Box Hill, Caulfield, Portland and, in New South Wales, Marrickville and Blacktown, all designed in the mid-1950s.

Leighton Irwin died of hypertensive heart disease on 4 August 1962 at Epworth Private Hospital, Richmond. He was survived by his wife and daughter, and was cremated. His estate was valued for probate at £101 547.

R. Boyd, *Victorian modern* (Melb, 1947); J. M. Freeland, *The making of a profession* (Syd, 1971); *Age*, 6 Apr, 18 Aug 1956, 12 Apr 1957, 6 Aug 1962; *Box Hill Reporter*, 27 Apr 1956; *Herald* (Melb), 6 Aug 1962.   GRAEME BUTLER

ISAACS, SIR ISAAC ALFRED (1855-1948), governor-general, judge and politician, was born on 6 August 1855 at Elizabeth Street, Melbourne, eldest of six children of Alfred Isaacs, tailor, and his wife Rebecca, née Abrahams. Two sisters and a brother survived infancy. Alfred Isaacs had been born in what was then Russian Poland, which he left in the 1840s and settled in London. He married Rebecca in 1849 and they migrated to Victoria in 1854, arriving in September. Rebecca, who was London-born, had a powerful mind, wide-ranging intellectual interests, and the capacity to understand and discuss complex matters. She was an ambitious and dominating woman who exercised a very strong influence over her first-born.

In 1859 the family moved to Yackandandah in north-eastern Victoria where Isaac attended in turn a small private school and the state school. He was a bright and lively child with wide interests from an early age. When in 1867 the family moved to the larger neighbouring town of Beechworth, he went first to the Common school and then to Beechworth Grammar School of which he was dux. Having qualified as a pupil-teacher he taught at the Common school and the state school which replaced it from 1870 until 1875. That year, after a dispute with the headmaster about fees allegedly due to him, he resigned from the Education Department and taught for a few months at the grammar school. Through the good offices of the local member G. B. Kerferd [q.v.5] he then secured an appointment as a clerk in the prothonotary's office in the Crown Law Department in Melbourne, where he had extensive experience in practical legal matters. Necessarily a part-time student, he began law at the University of Melbourne in 1876 and graduated in minimum time in April 1880 with first-class honours and the exhibition (LL.M., 1883). A notebook of 1879 which survives is a model of precision and clarity in its brief statement of doctrine and principle, and in its excellent summary notes of decided cases. It is said that Isaacs had a photographic memory and in examinations could cite cases with reference to volume and page.

He remained in the Crown Law Office until 1882 when he decided to go to the Bar and took chambers in Temple Court. With no connexions and little financial backing, Isaacs found the going slow, but his qualities of persistence and determination, linked with great legal ability and capacity for hard work, brought him an increasing practice. By 1890 he was well established: that year he appeared nineteen times before the Full Supreme Court and was taking briefs on behalf of large corporate clients including banks, the stock exchange, land and finance companies and local authorities. The range of his practice was very wide: during the 1890s he appeared in various company law matters, in cases involving tort, contract, insurance, insolvency, mining and local government law. Sir John Latham [q.v.] recalled that Isaacs was noted at the Bar for 'the close and detailed attention which he paid to his cases, the completeness of the arguments which he presented and his pertinacity in advocacy. He had a remarkable equipment of legal knowledge'.

In 1886 Isaacs had brought his parents to Melbourne where from 1888 they lived in a substantial two-storey house at Auburn. On 18 July at the bride's home at St Kilda, he married 18-year-old Deborah (Daisy), daughter of Isaac Jacobs, a tobacco merchant who had been president of the St Kilda Hebrew Congregation and in 1889-90 was to be president of the Chamber of Manufactures. Daughters of the marriage were born in 1890 and 1892. The family shifted house frequently, but one lasting abode was a country house at Mount Macedon. Isaacs kept in close daily touch with his mother and, indeed, in the early years of his marriage sometimes left his family for short periods to stay with her. Even when over 50 and a justice of the High Court, he would write to 'My sweet darling Mammie': she yielded little of her hold over him before she died in 1912.

Throughout his life, Isaacs was a student of languages. He learned the rudiments of Russian, French, German, Italian and Greek from his parents and from miners in the north-east of Victoria, as well as a smattering of Chinese. He took every opportunity throughout his life to develop his proficiency by conversation with migrants and practice at the family table, and in carrying on correspondence. He continued to read widely in religion, science and literature, and ornamented his speeches with quotations from poets and prose writers. In his years at the Bar he was an active member of the Australian Natives' Association and as a Freemason was the first Grand Registrar of the United Grand Lodge of Ancient, Free and Accepted Masons of Victoria for the year 1889-90.

At the Victorian general election of April 1892, Isaacs was elected by a comfortable margin to the Legislative Assembly as member for Bogong, a district which included Yackandandah and Beechworth. His policy-speech, in the context of a severe depression, emphasized an equitable spread of retrenchment, introduction of income taxation rather than indirect taxes which unfairly hit the poor, reform of company law, conciliation machinery to resolve industrial disputes, railway reform and support for Federation. Isaacs initially supported the Shiels [q.v.] ministry but in January 1893 helped to vote it out of office and accepted the portfolio of solicitor-general in the new Patterson [q.v.5] ministry. Sir Matthew Davies [q.v.4] and another associated with the failed Mercantile Bank had been committed for trial on charges of conspiracy to defraud. The attorney-general, Sir Bryan O'Loghlen [q.v.5] decided not to proceed with the indictments, whereupon Isaacs announced that in the exercise of the independent authority vested in him as solicitor-general he proposed to consider instituting proceedings. After cabinet had resolved that it was unconstitutional for him to interfere with O'Loghlen's decision, he was still determined to proceed. At the premier's demand he resigned on 25 May. He won much political popularity over the incident: when he resigned his seat on the issue he was returned unopposed. O'Loghlen had been wrong in not proceeding but Isaacs's interpretation of the law was strained and his action was not in accord with the principles of cabinet government. Having challenged persons of standing and institutions of power and authority he was henceforth distrusted in these quarters, and his conduct as a member of the government gave rise to the feeling that he was not trustworthy as a colleague.

On the fall of the Patterson ministry Isaacs became attorney-general in the Turner [q.v.] Liberal ministry from 27 September 1894 to 5 December 1899 and again in Turner and Peacock [q.v.] ministries from 19 November 1900 until 4 June 1901. Described by the *Bulletin* as Turner's 'brilliant henchman', Isaacs served occasionally as acting premier. In November 1894 he introduced comprehensive legislation to reform Victoria's lax company law in an attempt to cleanse the colony's reputation after the numerous swindles of the land boom period. His announcement of each stringent new clause was vociferously cheered in the Legislative Assembly. But, after a two-year battle with the Legislative Council, only an emasculated, though still very useful, version was passed. On this and many other issues the radical *Age* lauded Isaacs and the conservative *Argus* reviled him. He strongly supported social reforms such as the Factories Act, which established wages boards and attempted to eliminate sweating, denounced plural voting and favoured women's suffrage. He struggled to control gambling but failed narrowly in 1898 to amend the Police Offences Act in an attempt to destroy John Wren's [q.v.] Collingwood 'tote'. Throughout his period as a minister he carried on an extensive Bar practice. His younger brother, John Alfred (1863-1944), a practising solicitor, represented Ovens in the Legislative Assembly from 1894 to 1902.

Alfred Deakin [q.v.8] describes Isaacs in the later 1890s as follows: 'A clear, cogent, forcible and fiery speaker, he set himself at once to work to conquer the methods of platform and parliamentary debate and in both succeeded. He was not trusted or liked in the House. His will was indomitable, his courage inexhaustible and his ambition immeasurable. But his egotism was too marked and his ambition too ruthless to render him popular. Dogmatic by disposition, full of legal subtlety and the precise literalness and littleness of the rabbinical mind, he was at the same time kept well abreast by his reading of modern developments and modern ideas'. These comments are not misleading: he was a man to be reckoned with. His unpopularity cannot wholly be dismissed as jealousy, anti-Semitism or other prejudice, although there was prejudice and ugly and unworthy things were said and written about him. He was a lone wolf and a determined, ambitious and unrelenting man. At the same time he retained wide popular support as a political leader articulating reformist ideas.

Isaacs had often spoken to A.N.A. meetings about 1893 on the obstacles to Federation and the need to arouse popular interest. He looked forward to the day when he could say, 'I am an Australian'. In March 1897 he was elected fifth, on the *Age* ticket, as a Victorian delegate to the Federal convention which assembled for five months in Adelaide, Sydney and Melbourne before concluding in March 1898. Isaacs was not elected to the vital drafting committee. Deakin says that this was due to 'a plot discreditable to all engaged in it', that Isaacs was antagonized and humiliated, and that his 'tendency to minute technical criticism was sharpened so as to bring him not infrequently into collision' with the drafting committee. In the long run, 'with magnificent self restraint [Isaacs] subordinated his sense of personal injustice'. He had mastered the American, Canadian and European literature of federation; no delegate could outdo him in learning. But his long expositions and analyses and his inability to

refrain from interjection wearied and irritated his colleagues. He spoke in the convention as a Victorian. He had a special interest in the position of the larger States; he was opposed originally to equal numerical membership for all States in the Senate, but finally yielded the principle. He was insistent on the primacy of the House of Representatives; he was a strong supporter of the referendum as an instrument of decision for constitutional change and for the resolution of deadlocks between the two Houses, and he did not favour joint sittings. He supported H. B. Higgins's [q.v.] proposal for the insertion of the industrial arbitration power among Federal powers. He favoured restriction of appeals from the High Court to the Privy Council of which he later spoke disparagingly. He was active in seeking to protect Victorian railway interests, and he warned of the dangers which might flow from the broad language of what became the much litigated section 92 of the Constitution. He was no supporter of the transcription of 'Bill of Rights' provisions from the American to the Australian Constitution.

Isaacs, Turner and the Victorian ministry had many reservations about the draft constitution which was to be put to the vote of the people; the *Age* went into outright opposition. At the A.N.A. banquet at Bendigo on 15 March 1898 Isaacs hesitantly pleaded for delay for further consideration. Deakin's famous speech following him roused the A.N.A. to confirm its full support. Public and parliamentary enthusiasm led the ministry to change course and the *Age* to give grudging consent. Isaacs campaigned forcefully in support of the measure. 'Every vote for the Bill is a brick that will help to raise the edifice of the Nation'. The referendum was passed sweepingly in Victoria but the majority in New South Wales was inadequate. Isaacs did not take any prominent part in the subsequent premiers' conference which modified the draft or in the second referendum campaign. He was in England in 1900 in order to appear before the Privy Council, but although Deakin recommended him to Premier McLean [q.v.] as the most suitable Victorian nominee to the Australian delegation to see the Constitution through the Imperial parliament, McLean insisted on Deakin going. Isaacs was guest of honour at a dinner of the Anglo-Jewish Society, his wife was presented to the Queen, and he watched with interest the successful conclusion of negotiations over the Constitution bill.

When Turner joined Barton's [q.v.7] first Commonwealth ministry early in 1901 Isaacs became acting premier and, although he had already stated his intention of standing for the House of Representatives, the Victorian cabinet and the *Age* encouraged him to remain as premier. He refused the offer, however, and was decisively elected for Indi, the north-eastern Victorian seat. Isaacs continued in broad alliance with Deakin as a radical protectionist Liberal and supported the Barton ministry. He was returned unopposed in 1903. A vehement advocate of the White Australia policy and the abolition of Melanesian labour, he also strongly supported Deakin's proposed notion of a High Court convening in all State capitals, as against a temporary court of State chief justices. He was equally vehement in favour of Deakin's conciliation and arbitration bill: 'This bill simply bids the wave of passion, prejudice, and partisanship to be still. It evolves order out of chaos. It is a national proclamation of peace. With equal voice to all, it commands that none shall ever lay down the implement of labour and take up the weapons of war'. He did not approve of the devices by which the Watson [q.v.] Labor government was brought down in 1904, and during the succeeding Reid [q.v.] administration he was prominent in manoeuvres by the radical wing of the Deakinites which reached an alliance with the Labor Party and its policies. While never a supporter of socialism, Isaacs saw the virtues of trade union organization, the justice of the demand for fair and reasonable wages and working conditions, and the need for state intervention to bring them about. He was especially aware of the threat to protectionist policies, and scathing in his attacks on Reid.

Isaacs was appointed attorney-general from 5 July 1905 in the second Deakin ministry and, as throughout his working life, displayed extraordinary energy in the post. Samuel Mauger [q.v.] enthused him with the policy of New Protection and Isaacs drafted and carried ingenious legislation which aimed to implement it, together with attempts to repress monopolies and introduce the trade union label. Much of this legislation was eventually subjected to successful constitutional challenge in the High Court. Sir Robert Garran [q.v.8], secretary of the Attorney-General's Department, recalled that Isaacs 'had a remarkably keen brain but it was apt to be sometimes too subtle for my liking. When we were drafting a bill whose constitutionality was not beyond doubt, his devices to conceal any possible want of power were sometimes so ingenious as to raise, rather than evade, suspicion'. While holding office as attorney, Isaacs maintained a large private practice; when criticized in parliament he defended his conduct with characteristic vehemence. According to Garran, 'Isaacs' capacity for

work was amazing. By day he carried on the biggest practice of the Victorian Bar; by night he did full justice to the duties of Attorney-General'. They would work on a draft of legislation which Garran would leave with the government printer about midnight; in the morning Garran might find the draft redone, Isaacs having had second thoughts and recovered the bill from the printer's office. Between 1901 and 1906 Isaacs appeared as leader in well over one hundred reported cases in the Victorian Supreme Court and in twenty-five in the High Court. Their range was very wide, including some of constitutional importance; he also argued will, trust and administration matters, liability to land tax, mining law, and matters of statutory construction.

Isaacs was appointed to the High Court of Australia on 12 October 1906 and remained on the Bench, in the full maturity of life, for almost twenty-five years. The chief justice, Sir Samuel Griffith [q.v.] and Sir Edmund Barton both strongly disliked him and were strongly opposed to the trend of his constitutional interpretations. For many years Isaacs and Higgins were frequently to find themselves a dissenting minority. Isaacs brought enormous energy and learning and very strong convictions to the task of judging. He was one of the earliest of Australian Federal judges to give explicit recognition to the social implications of decision-making and he spelled out social (and, where appropriate, economic) policies, often in detail, in his judgments. Family and divorce law, factory legislation and legislation designed to protect employees are examples. He spoke of the need for the courts to be 'living organs of a progressive community'. In his youth the deficiencies of Victorian company law during the boom and bust had been brought home to him; he had experienced the depression of the 1890s with its unemployment and exploitation of labour; he regarded gambling as an evil which struck primarily at the welfare of the working man and his family. He read widely in social and economic literature which he mustered, as well as copious legal authority, as a formidable artillery in support of his position. In the criminal jurisdiction he emphasized the protection which the law should assure to accused persons. Yet in administrative law he sometimes showed a perhaps disproportionate sympathy for the interest of public authority at the cost of the individual.

On constitutional issues he moved steadily to a position of strong and almost undeviating support for the exercise of national, central power. In a case touching the Federal arbitration power, he put it that the issue was whether the Commonwealth could deal with its most momentous social problems, unimpeded by the sectional policies of particular States. For almost a decade and a half he found himself dissenting in major constitutional cases but, with the departure of Griffith, the balance of the court shifted and the Engineers' Case of 1920 became a great monument to Isaacs's achievement. The precise issue of the Federal arbitration power in that case could have been decided on quite narrow ground, but the majority in the court, in a judgment which indisputably reveals Isaacs's hand, took much higher ground. Over a range of issues he asserted a wide reach for Federal power, especially during World War I and with regard to the migration and other powers. By 1920 he had reached the position that although section 92 of the Constitution had a broad scope it bound only the States, leaving the Commonwealth free from its far-reaching constraints. Once he reached that position he asserted that no other conclusion was credible. When, after his retirement from the court, the Privy Council held that section 92 bound both Commonwealth and States he denounced the decision as a palpable error. Surely there has never been on the Australian High Court bench a nationalist quite like him.

The style of his speaking and of his judgments, however, was often rhetorical and verbose. More objectionable was his appalling certainty, his unshakeable conviction of the rightness of his opinion and his utter inability to see merit in any other view. He was unwilling to confess error in those cases where he simply had to reverse course and retreat from a position dogmatically stated and wrong. Reading his judgments sometimes leaves a sense that a result has been achieved by a trick, by sleight of hand. He never ceased to be a committed advocate. We have it, however, on the testimony of a great lawyer that he was a courteous judge and could, in some circumstances, be persuaded to a change of view. Sir Owen Dixon who often appeared before him in the High Court recalled: 'To argue as counsel against a view he had formed was an exercise amounting almost to a forensic education. Always courteous, never overbearing or assertive, he met you point by point with answers drawn by a most powerful and yet ingenious mind . . . if you were able to bring to his mind an aspect of the case or an argument which he had not seen and struck his mind as new to him and as having substance he would give it due consideration and sometimes change his opinion entirely'.

Isaacs was sworn of the Privy Council in November 1921 while on long leave in Britain and became a member of its judicial committee three years later. He was appointed K.C.M.G. in 1928. He succeeded Sir Adrian Knox [q.v.] as chief justice of the High Court on 5 April 1930, but held the office for less than ten months. Early in December his appointment as governor-general was announced. On 22 January 1931 he took the oaths of office, the first native-born Australian to be appointed.

For months there had been great controversy. Early in 1930 the retiring governor-general, Lord Stonehaven [q.v.], had informed the Labor prime minister, J. H. Scullin [q.v.], that the United Kingdom government would welcome an indication of a suitable successor before consulting the King. According to Garran, cabinet in February or March, after considering Isaacs and Sir John Monash [q.v.], decided to recommend Isaacs and so informed Prime Minister Ramsay MacDonald. By April the rumoured appointment had produced violent opposition, based largely on party-political grounds, to preferment of an Australian. It was argued that a local man would inevitably have personal involvements and that a distinguished citizen of the United Kingdom would better secure the bonds of Empire; Isaacs, moreover, was in his mid-seventies. The constitutional position was uncertain in that it was not clearly established where the constitutional advice for the appointment of a governor-general should originate. While the Imperial Conference of 1926 had precluded the tendering of advice by the United Kingdom government, it did not then state that the source of advice for appointment was the prime minister of the relevant Dominion. Led especially by the advice of his private secretary, Lord Stamfordham, King George V was strongly opposed to the appointment of Isaacs because he was a 'local man', there had been no prior consultation and he was elderly and personally unknown to him. The Imperial Conference confirmed early in November 1930, however, that a governor-general should be appointed on the advice of the Dominion government concerned, though only after informal consultation. Late in November, in audience with the King, Scullin stood firm, the King reluctantly approved, and the announcement of Isaacs's appointment was made with a clear implication of the King's displeasure.

Isaacs attended to his duties with zest. His age was no impediment to great enthusiasm and he discharged the ceremonial duties of his office with obvious enjoyment. To his constitutional duties he brought not only great application and assiduity but also a unique learning and knowledge. In special cases, he furnished elaborate memoranda expounding the reasons for his action. Of these the most notable was his answer to the address of the Opposition-controlled Senate in 1931 praying that he should refuse to approve certain regulations under the Transport Workers Act. He also wrote at length to explain why he had accepted Scullin's request in November for a dissolution. No difficult constitutional issues emerged during his further period of office. By the time he retired on 23 January 1936 it was generally acknowledged that he had served as governor-general during harsh depression years with dignity and distinction. He had voluntarily surrendered one-quarter of his salary and declined to take his retired judge's pension while he held office.

Isaacs sailed for England early in 1936 in order to give a personal account of his stewardship to King Edward VIII. An ardent Empire and King's man, he greatly enjoyed the visit. In 1932 he was appointed G.C.M.G. and in 1937 the high honour of G.C.B. was conferred on him; he had also been appointed an Associate Knight of Grace of St John of Jerusalem in 1931. For the remaining years of his life he and Lady Isaacs lived at four addresses in South Yarra and Toorak and at Macedon. During these years of retirement he remained for the most part very vigorous and active, reading regularly at the Public Library and discussing books and their work with students, writing pamphlets and articles, making speeches, broadcasting, presiding at functions, and carrying on an extensive correspondence. In an oration in 1937 he reviewed in characteristically florid and rhetorical style the life and achievements of Sir John Monash. He campaigned consistently for constitutional reform and wider Commonwealth powers, notably in his pamphlets *Australian democracy and our constitutional system* (1939), *An appeal for a greater Australia* (1943) and *Referendum powers: a stepping-stone to greater freedom* (1946). In the last year of his life, 'in defence of the State Constitution', he supported the Cain Labor government of Victoria against coercion by the Legislative Council.

Isaacs also wrote widely on biblical and religious subjects for the Jewish press and frequently spoke at various Jewish functions. He did not observe religious practices and had taken little part in community affairs but was acutely aware of his Jewishness; his strong interest in religious doctrines and writings had probably been nurtured by his mother. In his public life he was very sensitive to anti-Semitic attacks and responded to them angrily, especially when there was any suggestion of a contradiction between Jewishness and British citizenship. Throughout his life he took immense pride in his British citizenship and its Imperial links, and insisted that Jewish-

ness was a matter of religion and not of race or nationality.

In the early 1940s Isaacs copiously attacked 'political Zionism', as he described it, mainly in the *Hebrew Standard*. It is an unhappy story which, allowing for his great age, once again reveals his inflexible dogmatism and his insensitiveness towards the differing beliefs of others. When Professor Julius Stone opposed him cogently, Isaacs reacted with great anger not only to the argument but against Stone personally. He threatened a body of Melbourne Jews that if they proceeded with a public protest meeting against the implementation of British policy in Palestine, he would publicly denounce them on the ground that 'our simple duty is to our King and country in this hour of trial', and he did so. During these years of holocaust, what Isaacs did was painful and divisive; both his writings and his actions were extravagant and left a blemish on his reputation in the Jewish community which had taken such pride in the splendour of his career.

Isaacs attributed his powers of endurance largely to his physical fitness and regular exercise. While he was not an athlete and had little interest in organized sport, he ran quite long distances until middle age, often swam, and continued to be a keen and assiduous walker. He was abstemious: he did not smoke and drank very little alcohol. His only excess was tea drinking.

In old age be became frail and deaf, but his mind was unimpaired to the end. After some weeks illness he died in his sleep, aged 92, on 11 February 1948 at his South Yarra home. After a state funeral and a synagogue service at which the eulogy was delivered by his old friend Rabbi Jacob Danglow [q.v.8], he was buried in Melbourne general cemetery. His wife and daughters survived him. His few memorials include the names of a Canberra suburb and a Federal electorate, and the title of a chair of law at Monash University. The centenary of his birth passed almost unnoticed. There are portraits by John Longstaff [q.v.] at Parliament House, Canberra, by Percy White at the High Court of Australia, Canberra, and by Bryan Westwood at Government House, Canberra.

Some of his contemporaries, especially his professional, political and judicial peers, disliked or distrusted Isaacs. Others such as his associate John Keating, his doctors and many simple people who knew him had the warmest affection for him and remembered him as invariably courteous, kind, thoughtful and warm. It is hard to find neutrals. But, as Sir John Barry said, 'his efforts were directed towards the amelioration of social misery and the uplifting of mankind'. He was a master lawyer and one of the greatest judges in our Federal history, and he brought to his work and to the whole of his public life an unflagging and almost inexhaustible energy and a mind of great strength, power and range.

A. Deakin, *The Federal story*, H. Brookes ed (Melb, 1944); R. R. Garran, *Prosper the Commonwealth* (Syd, 1958); M. Gordon, *Sir Isaac Isaacs, a lifetime of service* (Melb, 1963); Z. Cowen, *Isaac Isaacs* (Melb, 1967, *and* 1979); *Meanjin Q*, 26, 1967, no 4, p 443; Isaacs papers (NL).

ZELMAN COWEN

ISRAEL, JOHN WILLIAM (1850-1926), Commonwealth auditor-general, was born on 4 July 1850 at Launceston, Van Diemen's Land, son of John Cashmore Israel and his wife Adelaide Maria, née Cook. His father was probably the Cashmore Israel convicted of larceny and transported to New South Wales in 1818. Removed to Van Diemen's Land next year, he was granted a free pardon in 1841 and subsequently followed his own father's trades of baker, confectioner, jeweller and pawnbroker, in Launceston. By the 1850s he was a man of property, able to send his son to Abraham Barrett's private academy, where John William's extraordinary prowess in mental arithmetic provided entertainment on speech days, and to the Launceston Church Grammar School.

At 17 Israel became a storekeeper's clerk at Latrobe and then on the Waterhouse goldfields. In 1870, after competitive examination, he obtained a junior clerkship under R. M. Johnston [q.v.] in the audit branch of the Launceston and Western Railway Co. He was promoted to stationmaster at Perth and then Launceston. After the railway was taken over by the government in 1872 Israel returned to the accounts office where he succeeded Johnston as accountant in 1880. Two years later he again succeeded Johnston, as chief clerk in the government Audit Department, Hobart. He rose quickly to deputy auditor and, on 31 December 1894, to auditor.

Of medium height, bearded and bespectacled, the 'lightning calculator' was a man of high integrity. He instituted the travelling audit by which inspectors personally examined departmental and local accounts. He placed great stress on the independence of his office; after the ministry reduced his salary in February 1895 he annually drew attention to this as a contravention of the 1894 Audit Act. Israel was founding president of the Civil Service Association in 1897; in 1899 he became a commissioner of the Public Debts Sinking Fund. A Freemason, he was a master of Pacific Lodge (1894-95),

secretary of the Tasmanian Masonic Benevolent Fund and in 1897 first president of the Board of Benevolence, Grand Lodge. In Launceston he was for many years secretary of the musical union.

On 1 December 1901 Israel became the first Commonwealth auditor-general, with the crucial task of establishing procedure. He held the position not only for the formative years of the Commonwealth Public Service, but during World War I and the expansive post-war period when he was well past the usual retiring age. He was still able to ensure the continued independence of the office and competence of the work while retaining the respect of both ministers and public servants. He was appointed I.S.O. in 1916.

While in Melbourne Israel served as honorary treasurer of the Royal Geographical Society of Australasia (Victorian branch) and of St Paul's Cathedral. He kept his links with Tasmania, holidaying annually at Ulverstone, the birthplace of his wife Jane, née McDonald; they had married there on 1 November 1883 with Anglican rites. Israel died of cancer at Kew, Melbourne, on 30 May 1926, survived by his wife and son, and was buried in Box Hill cemetery. His estate was valued for probate at £16 814. 'His work', according to an obituarist, 'was the subject of much encomium, his prime object always being the safeguarding of the moneys entrusted to the care of the Government'.

Cyclopedia of Tasmania, 1 (Hob, 1900); *Examiner* (Launc), 9 July 1895, 29 Nov 1901, 31 May 1926; *Mercury*, 4 Aug 1898, 15, 30 Nov 1901; *Punch* (Melb), 21 Sept, 12 Oct 1916; *Weekly Courier* (Launc), 3 June 1926; M. P. Peck, The auditor-general of Tasmania 1826-1968 (Diploma of Public Administration, Univ Tas, 1971); H0/10/57, 11/3, 16/1.

R. J. K. CHAPMAN

IVES, JOSHUA (1854-1931), musician and university professor, was born on 2 May 1854 at Hyde, Cheshire, England, sixth son of John Ives, furniture broker, and his wife Hannah, née Goddard. He was educated in Manchester at the Commercial School and Owens College and studied music with (Sir) Frederick Bridge and Henry Hiles. From 1878 he was organist and choirmaster at Anderston Parish Church, Glasgow, where he married Janet Boyd on 3 December 1879. That year he began lecturing on music at the Glasgow Athenaeum; he was a successful and efficient teacher. From 1882 he studied music at Queen's College, Cambridge (Mus.Bac., 1884). He was soon appointed foundation professor of music at the University of Adelaide and arrived there in March 1885.

The chair of music, Australia's first, had been financed by public subscription and Ives's salary (£500) made him one of the lowest paid of the seven Adelaide professors. The university therefore persuaded the Adelaide City Council to appoint him city organist, a position he held in 1885-90 at £200. The university council, at Ives's request, also made an exception and allowed him to receive students' fees to a limit of £250 a year because of the temporary nature of the chair, and his contention that he had been promised a higher salary. As Ives had persuaded the council to make matriculation concessions for those enrolling in music, there were plenty of students, most of whom were women. By 1890 there were more undergraduates in music than in any other department. Yet during the sixteen-year period of Ives's tenure of the chair there were only seven graduates in music, and most of these had received outside tuition. In 1891 press comment suggested that he was spending an inordinate amount of time daily at the Stock Exchange.

In 1886 the council had agreed to Ives's proposal that the university institute local public examinations in music, similar to those conducted in England. Held from 1887 in Adelaide and in country centres, these were the first Australian university public examinations in the subject: it was a step which led to an Australia-wide system.

Following Sir Thomas Elder's [q.v.4] bequest for a school of music in 1897, and Ives's investigation of music teaching in England and Europe that year, council approved Ives's plan for a 'Conservatoire' within the university, obtained temporary premises, engaged staff and appointed him director of its Elder Conservatorium for three years from January 1898, at an additional salary of £200. A new building, with the Elder Hall, was opened in September 1900 at a ceremony which included compositions by Ives for the occasion. He was a prolific composer, especially of songs and works for the organ.

In 1898-1900 the university council received a stream of protests, mainly from music teachers, about the conduct of the conservatorium, Ives's competence as an examiner, and his bias in favour of conservatorium candidates. Ives alleged that the complaints were due to 'a jealousy and ill-feeling towards the Elder Conservatorium'. The council upheld his position and affirmed its confidence in him, and in return Ives offered to resign as examiner. He also intimated his intention not to apply for reappointment as director of the conservatorium after the expiry of his term. The council immediately took steps to replace him, whereupon he applied for a salary increase. A petition from conservatorium staff 'praying for the reappointment of Professor Ives as Director' was rejected, and in December 1900 the council informed him that his engagement as professor would not be renewed after December 1901.

Despite Ives's accusations of injustice, council was adamant. It stated that there were no charges against Ives, that the non-renewal of his appointment did not constitute dismissal, that it desired to make a change and would allow him to resign.

Late in 1901 a disagreement between Ives and the university's external examiners (who reported that none of the six candidates for the third year B.Mus. examination was fit to pass) was the subject of a parliamentary paper. Ives dramatically addressed the audience after the official party's departure at the conclusion of the annual commemoration proceedings. After this outburst in which he vilified the chancellor and vice-chancellor and defended himself, Ives left Adelaide. He settled in Melbourne where he taught music in Collins Street until 1920 and then at Brighton. He also became a small property-owner and engaged in moneylending.

Ives died at Kew on 16 June 1931, leaving the bulk of his estate of £2985 to a daughter and his 'dear partner' Sarah Howard. He was buried in Fawkner cemetery.

PP (SA), 1901 (139); Univ Adel, *Calendar*, 1886-1902; *Table Talk*, 18 July, 26 Dec 1901; *Observer* (Adel), 21 Dec 1901; D. M. Bridges, The role of universities in the development of music education in Australia 1885-1970 (Ph.D. thesis, Univ Syd, 1970); S. Way letter-book, PRG 30/5/9 (SAA); Council minute-books, vols 3-7, and letters (Univ Adel Archives).   DOREEN BRIDGES

IXIA; *see* PELLOE, EMILY

J

JACKA, ALBERT (1893-1932), soldier and merchant, was born on 10 January 1893 at Layard near Winchelsea, Victoria, fourth child of Nathaniel Jacka, a Victorian-born labourer, later a farmer and contractor, and his English wife Elizabeth, née Kettle. The family moved to Wedderburn when Albert was 5. After elementary schooling, Bert worked as a labourer with his father, then for the Victorian State Forests Department. He was a shy youth, but excelled at sports, especially cycling.

Jacka enlisted on 18 September 1914 as a private in the 14th Battalion, Australian Imperial Force, and trained at Broadmeadows camp. His unit embarked on 22 December and spent two months training in Egypt before landing at Anzac Cove, Gallipoli Peninsula, on 26 April 1915. Early on 19 May the Turks launched a massive counter-attack along practically the entire Anzac line. At about 4 a.m. they rushed Courtney's Post. Amid frenzied fighting some Turks captured a twelve-yard section of trench, one end of which was guarded by Jacka. For several minutes he fired warning shots into the trench wall until reinforcements arrived and, after shouting his instructions, he and three others sprang out into the trench. All but Jacka were immediately hit so he leapt back into the communication trench. A new plan was devised. Two bombs were lobbed at the Turks while Jacka skirted around to attack from the flank. Amid the smoke and the noise he clambered over the parapet, shot five Turks and bayoneted two as the rest hastily retreated. 'I managed to get the beggars, Sir', he reputedly told the first officer to appear. For this action he received the Victoria Cross, the first to be awarded to the A.I.F. in World War I.

Instantly Jacka became a national hero. He received the £500 and gold watch that the prominent Melbourne business and sporting identity John Wren [q.v.] had promised to the first V.C. winner. His image was used on recruiting posters and magazine covers. On 28 August 1915 he was promoted corporal, then rose quickly, becoming a company sergeant major in mid-November, a few weeks before Anzac was evacuated. Back in Egypt he passed through officer training school with high marks and on 29 April 1916 was commissioned second lieutenant.

The 14th Battalion was shipped to France early in June. Jacka's platoon moved into the line near Pozières on the night of 6-7 August and as dawn broke German troops overran a part of the line. Jacka had just completed a reconnaissance and had gone to his dugout when two Germans appeared at its entrance and rolled a bomb down the doorway, killing two men. Jacka charged up the dugout steps, firing as he moved, and came upon a large number of the enemy rounding up some forty Australians as prisoners. He rallied his platoon and charged at the enemy, some of whom immediately threw down their rifles. Furious hand-to-hand fighting erupted as the prisoners turned on their captors. Fifty Germans were captured and the line was retaken. Jacka was awarded a Military Cross for his gallantry. C. E. W. Bean [q.v.7] described the counter-attack 'as the most dramatic and effective act of individual audacity in the history of the A.I.F.' The entire platoon was wounded, Jacka seriously in the neck and shoulder; he was sent to a London hospital. On 8 September London newspapers carried reports of his death but Bert Jacka was far from done for. He had been promoted lieutenant on 18 August, rejoined his unit in November and was promoted captain on 15 March 1917 and appointed the 14th Battalion's intelligence officer.

Early in 1917 the Germans had retired to the Hindenburg line and on 8 April Jacka led a night reconnaissance party into no man's land near Bullecourt to inspect enemy defences before an allied attack against the new German line. He penetrated the wire at two places, reported back, then went out again to supervise the laying of tapes to guide the infantry. The work was virtually finished when two Germans loomed up. Realizing that they would see the tapes, Jacka knew that they must be captured. He pulled his pistol; it misfired, so he rushed on and captured them by hand. Jacka's quick thinking had saved the Anzac units from discovery and probable disastrous bombardment; for this action he was awarded a Bar to his Military Cross.

Captain Jacka was wounded by a sniper's bullet near Ploegsteert Wood on 8 July and spent nearly two months away from the front. On 26 September he led the 14th Battalion against German pill-boxes at Polygon Wood and displayed 'a grasp of tactics, and a military intuition that many had not given him credit for'. In May 1918 he was badly gassed at Villers-Bretonneux and saw no more action. In September 1919 he embarked for Australia aboard the *Euripides*. A large crowd, including the governor-

452

general, greeted the ship when it berthed at Melbourne and a convoy of eighty-five cars with Jacka at its head drove to the town hall where men from the 14th Battalion welcomed their famous comrade. He was demobilized in January 1920. Shortly after his return Jacka, R. O. Roxburgh and E. J. L. Edmonds (both former members of the 14th Battalion) established the electrical goods importing and exporting business, Roxburgh, Jacka & Co. Pty Ltd. Jacka contributed £700 of the firm's paid up capital. The company's other directors were John Wren and his associate 'Dick' Lean, while Wren's brother Arthur held over three-quarters of the company's shares. In 1923 the business name was altered to Jacka Edmonds & Co. when Roxburgh withdrew.

On 17 January 1921 at St Mary's Catholic Church, St Kilda, Jacka had married Frances Veronica Carey, a typist from his office. They settled at St Kilda and later adopted a daughter. In September 1929 Jacka was elected to the St Kilda Council and became mayor a year later. He devoted most of his energies on council to assisting the unemployed. His own business flourished until 1929 when the Scullin [q.v.] government increased import tariffs and the company went into voluntary liquidation in September 1930. It was rumoured that the company's difficulties stemmed in part from Wren removing his support after Jacka refused to follow his wishes. Jacka then became a commercial traveller with the Anglo-Dominion Soap Co.

He fell ill, entered Caulfield Military Hospital on 18 December 1931 and died on 17 January 1932 of chronic nephritis. Nearly 6000 people filed past his coffin when it lay in state in Anzac House. The funeral procession, led by over 1000 returned soldiers flanked by thousands of onlookers, made its way to St Kilda cemetery where he was buried with full military honours in the Presbyterian section. Eight Victoria Cross winners were his pallbearers.

At his funeral Bert Jacka was described as 'Australia's greatest front-line soldier'. Few would challenge this assessment. Bean and the men of the 14th Battalion ('Jacka's Mob') shared the belief that he had earned three V.C.s. He might have risen higher in the A.I.F. but his blunt, straightforward manner frequently annoyed his superiors. 'He said what he meant, and meant what he said', recalls one friend. As an officer he invariably won respect by his example. It was claimed that he preferred to punch an offender than to place him on a charge. 'His methods could not have been adopted generally in the A.I.F. without disaster', Bean noted. Nevertheless Jacka seemed to epitomize the Anzac creed of mateship, bravery,

fairness and an absence of pretentiousness. Many sought to exploit his fame. In 1916 and 1918 he spurned offers from Prime Minister Hughes [q.v.] to return to Australia and assist with recruiting campaigns. His name was also used by (Sir) Keith Murdoch [q.v.] in the 1916 conscription referendum. His father promptly stated publicly that Bert had never declared himself in favour of conscription. The anti-conscriptionists made much of this denial but on balance it seems probable that Jacka did support conscription. His standing remained so high that a memorial plaque and sculpture for his grave was paid for by public subscription while £1195 was raised towards buying his widow a house. His portrait, by G. J. Coates [q.v.8], is in the Australian War Memorial. Two of his brothers had A.I.F. service.

C. E. W. Bean, *The story of Anzac*, 2 (Syd, 1924), and *The A.I.F. in France*, 1916-17 (Syd, 1929, 1933); N. Wanliss, *The history of the Fourteenth Battalion A.I.F.* (Melb, 1929); E. J. Rule, *Jacka's mob* (Syd, 1933); L. Wigmore (ed), *They dared mightily* (Canb, 1963); *London Gazette*, 23 July 1915, 14 Nov 1916, 15 June 1917; *Reveille* (Syd), Mar, Apr 1931, Jan 1932, Jan, May 1933, Jan 1939, July 1950; *Mufti* (Melb), Aug, Sept 1964; City of St Kilda, Council minute-books, 1929-32; file 932/6982 (PRO, Vic); R. Cooper and N. Buesst, *Jacka, V.C.* (documentary film), and film-makers' notes (lent to author, Monash Univ, Melb); A. Jacka, Biographical files, *and* C. E. W. Bean diaries (AWM).

KEVIN J. FEWSTER

JACKSON, ARCHIBALD (1909-1933), cricketer, was born on 5 September 1909 at Rutherglen, Glasgow, Scotland, only son of Alexander Jackson, brickyard foreman, and his wife Margaret, née Gillespie. Alexander came to Australia in 1912 and his wife, two daughters and Archie arrived in Sydney on the *Themistocles* on 1 August 1913. They lived in a terrace-house at Balmain ('the 'main').

Jackson was educated at Birchgrove Public and Rozelle Junior Technical schools. He was captivated by sport when young and was dubbed 'Champ'; he excelled at soccer and cricket and represented Public Schools' Amateur Athletic Association at both. He loved cricket and his delicate skill at the intricate game gave joy to his youth. Balmain was an ambiguous suburb in 1919-30, predominantly working class with some poverty; a coal-mine provided unstable work and pollution. But the district spread downhill to meet Sydney Harbour; Birchgrove Oval, near the Jackson home, edged the water. 'The 'main' was a golden place for juvenile cricketers. Jackson and his mates, especially Bill Hunt, sometimes 'crashed' the oval but often played on the streets, defying horse-drawn traffic and newfangled motor vehicles, breaking windows, and blocking drains to save the loss of precious balls. Of the carefree and talented team, Jackson and Hunt became Test players and two others first-class cricketers.

In the 1923-24 season Jackson, in short trousers and sandshoes, played in lower-grade sides of the Balmain Cricket Club. Next season, fitted out by Dr H. V. Evatt, he was promoted to first grade. He had gone to work as a messenger boy in 1924. A. A. Mailey [q.v.] helped to polish his natural batting artistry and he had long been attracted to A. F. Kippax's [q.v.] flowing style, with some worshipful contemplation of the legendary Victor Trumper [q.v.]. Jackson's 879 runs at 87.9 in 1926-27 was a club record. He was selected for the State side and his cricketing was facilitated by employment at Kippax's sports store. He scored his maiden century in first-class cricket against Queensland. Next season he scored a century in each innings against South Australia, and he toured New Zealand with the Australian team.

At 18 Jackson was a celebrated strokemaker at a time when big crowds savoured delicately placed late cuts and leg glances. He was the flowering of the 'Sydney school of batsmanship' founded by W. Caffyn in the nineteenth century. He was fair complexioned and good looking, gentle and modest. A Methodist, he neither smoked nor drank. Yet he was a sunny companion. The grace and precision of his batting matched his medium height and slender physique. His life rotated around cricket, but he had his off days, even when playing. There were early, furtive, signs of the tuberculosis that wasted his life.

Jackson reached his peak at 19 when, in Adelaide against England in February 1929, he played in his first Test match and scored a chanceless 164 runs in 368 minutes. He had opened the first innings with W. M. Woodfull [q.v.]; at one stage the score was 3 for 19. P. G. H. Fender said he made 'every conceivable stroke, [with] perfection of timing'. He was the toast of Australia. By then he had become the star of Anthony Hordern [q.v.4] & Sons' sports department. Testimonials enabled him to buy a De Soto car and he helped his family to move up the harbour to a detached cottage at Drummoyne.

He was selected for the 1930 tour of England, but the weather and ill health constricted him, though he scored 1023 runs. The disease stalked him; he failed in the 1930-31 series against the West Indies and was dropped from the Australian side. Lung ravage was diagnosed in 1931 and Jackson went to a sanatorium in the Blue Mountains,

later to a cottage there to be looked after by his sister Margaret. Seeking warmer weather, he went to Queensland in 1932, played some cricket and looked forward to the 1934 tour of England. But he died in Brisbane on 16 February 1933 and was buried in the Field of Mars cemetery, Sydney. He was unmarried.

Jackson's first-class batting average was 46.31; in Sheffield Shield 54.65; and against England (4 Tests) 58.33. His fourth-wicket partnership of 243 with (Sir) Donald Bradman at The Oval in 1930 still stands as an Australian Test record for that ground. He remains the youngest batsman to have scored a century in his first Test in Australia-England matches.

H. Buchanan (comp), *Great cricket matches* (Lond, 1962); D. Frith, *The Archie Jackson story* (Ashhurst, Eng, 1974); *Daily Telegraph* (Syd), 18 Jan 1929, 16 Feb 1933; *Sun* (Syd), 16 Feb 1933; *SMH*, 16 Feb 1933, 18 Feb 1983; *Sun Herald* (Syd), 24 Feb 1974; information from W. A. Hunt, Balmain, Miss M. Jackson, and C. M. Winning, Drummoyne, Syd.

BEDE NAIRN

JACKSON, CLEMENTS FREDERICK VIVIAN (1873-1955), public servant and mining engineer, was born on 24 April 1873 at Double Bay, Sydney, son of London-born Frederick Jackson, insurance underwriter, and his Australian wife Mary Josephine Teresa, née Macnab. Eucated at Royston College, he performed brilliantly at the University of Sydney where he graduated B.E. with first-class honours in civil engineering in 1895, then entered the engineering shops of Mort's [q.v.5] Dock. Appointed field assistant to the chief engineer of the Queensland Government Railways, he designed and constructed steel bridges over the Bremer River near Ipswich and the Fitzroy River at Rockhampton. As an assistant engineer from May 1897 his major achievement, the work of two years, was the bridge across the Burdekin River near Charters Towers. A thesis based on this work won him membership of the Institution of Civil Engineers, London, and their Telford prize.

Inspired by the Charters Towers area, he returned to Sydney University and graduated as a mining engineer in 1900, then went back to Queensland as an assistant government geologist. His major tasks in the next three years were an investigation of the Queensland opal-mining industry and a geological reconnaissance of the west coast of Cape York; he was the first to record the presence at Weipa of bauxite.

Jackson worked for the Geological Survey of Western Australia in 1903-04, then returned to Queensland as its first chief inspector of mines. On 11 May 1904 in Brisbane he had married Effie Doris, daughter of F. H. S. Hart, a member of the Legislative Council. Promoted in 1911 to State mining engineer, he retired in 1940. He played a significant part in major changes in Queensland's mineral history and was one of the government's most respected advisers. His most important task was the drafting of the Mines Regulation Act, 1910, and its associated regulations which were for some time a model for other States and countries. During the early years of Labor government he was heavily involved in supervising the design and construction of state-owned projects such as mines, batteries, smelters and treatment works. Some of them, such as the iron and steel works proposed in the early 1920s, proved abortive. When the government decided to leave petroleum exploration to private enterprise, he drafted the Petroleum Act, 1923, and its regulations, which were once again widely copied. In the 1920s Jackson was deeply involved in the establishment of Mount Isa as a world-class mine and in the closure of the Mount Morgan Gold Mining Co. Ltd. In 1929-30 he was a member of the important royal commission on the mining industry; he conducted several other inquiries.

Clements Jackson was tall, slight, taciturn and self-effacing; his face would light up with kindness when interested or amused. His father had been a member of the Royal Sydney Yacht Squadron and Jackson had been a constant sailor on the harbour when young. He did not race in Brisbane but the yacht in which he cruised on Moreton Bay was moored on the river beneath his home at Kangaroo Point. His house and furniture bespoke his enthusiasm for carpentry. A practising Anglican, he was a close friend of the architect Robin Dods [q.v.8] and was his adviser and collaborator in designing the foundations for the Cathedral of St John the Evangelist in Brisbane.

Jackson died on 27 February 1955 in Brisbane and was cremated. His wife, daughter and son survived him.

Geological Survey of Qld, pub 177, *The opal mining industry and distribution of opal deposits in Queensland*, and pub 180, *Report on a visit to the west coast of Cape York Peninsula* . . . (Brisb, 1902); Inst of Civil Engineers (Lond), *Minutes of Procs*, 142 (1900), p 253; A'sian Inst of Mining Engineers, *Trans*, 15 (1910), pt 2, p 471; *Qld Government Mining J*, 20 Mar 1955; C. F. V. Jackson papers (held by Dr D. Jackson, Brisb).

I. W. MORLEY

JACKSON, SIR CYRIL (1863-1924), inspector-general of schools, was born on 6 February 1863 at Kentish Town, London, son of Laurence Morris Jackson, stock-broker, and his wife Louisa Elizabeth, née Craven. Educated at Charterhouse and New College, Oxford (B.A., 1885), he was called to the Bar in 1893 at the Inner Temple but never practised law. Instead, he studied post-primary education with the object of improving educational opportunities for the socially disadvantaged. In 1885-95 he worked for the Universities' Settlement Association in London's East End and lived at Toynbee Hall. He was simultaneously on the management board of the Northey Street Boys' Club, central secretary of the Children's Country Holiday Fund and, from 1891, a member of the London School Board.

Influenced by the Liberal reform programme in the 1890s, Jackson explored the 'New Education' movement, studied Hebartian logic and was attracted by the ideas of Pestalozzi and Froebel, accepting the proposition that children learn better by reason and understanding than by repetitive memorization. By 1895, with his wide theoretical and practical background, Jackson was known as a gifted educator. Despite promise of a brilliant London career, he accepted appointment in December 1896 as inspector-general of schools in Western Australia. His educational philosophy was not original but he insisted that his practical ideas were experimental and sought 'an opportunity of putting into practice ideas, untrammelled by any vested interests worth speaking of, and no old system to break down'.

Jackson reached Western Australia at the peak of an economic boom that had attracted continuing immigration. As school enrolments had doubled in 1896 more buildings and vigorous recruitment of teachers were imperative. During 1897 he travelled through Western Australia and to the eastern colonies to make comparative evaluations of schools. He concluded that too many were cramped and uncomfortable. Besides inferior buildings, uneven teaching standards revealed a disquieting lack of understanding of basic pedagogical principles. In his reports he denounced the outmoded 'pupil teacher' training system, deplored inadequate teacher salaries, expressed dismay at the absence of state secondary schools, technical colleges and continuation classes, and was appalled at the paucity of government scholarships to private secondary schools. In short he roundly damned the existing system and proposed guide-lines for reform. He clashed immediately with the Education Department's permanent secretary O. P. Stables on the issue of direct access to the minister and resigned when E. H. Wittenoom [q.v.], as minister, reprimanded him for outspoken public criticism of state schools. The resignation was only withdrawn after the intervention of Premier Sir John Forrest [q.v.8]. When Wittenoom was replaced as minister in May 1897, the office of permanent secretary was abolished and Jackson became actual permanent head of the department. His relations with succeeding ministers, particularly George Randell [q.v.6], were cordial and productive but he was reported to have stood up to Forrest in 1898 over impending cuts in the education vote.

Jackson's 1898 curriculum reformed the methods of teaching rather than the subjects taught. He commended the 'object lesson' of Pestalozzi and recommended the Froebelian principles of harmonizing the child's 'sense, perception and bodily activity'. His detractors thought him too radical and one critic deplored the 'spasmodic somersaults' of his 'aerobatic department'. The Teachers' Union conference of 1899 condemned the new arithmetic syllabus and in 1900 pressed for uniform textbooks, but Jackson refused to yield. By now, he had won over public opinion and his scheme had been published in the English *Teachers' Aid*.

The major reforms launched by Jackson included the reorganization of elementary education with special provisions for infant teaching; the establishment of Perth Technical School, Claremont Teachers' Training College and continuation classes; and the promotion of James Street School as a teaching model-school. Compulsory school-age legislation was passed, the salaries and status of teachers were improved and the *Education Circular* was published regularly. Jackson succeeded in enticing well-qualified teachers from England and the eastern States and sought specialists to supervise manual training, needlework and domestic science. Although prepared to listen to 'grass-roots' lobbies and to delegate to specialists when appropriate, Jackson believed firmly in central authority and sometimes generated strong opposition. His early attempt to form a commercial and agricultural college at Katanning was obstructed in 1902 by professional agriculturalists J. M. A. Despeissis, A. Crawford [qq.v.8] and P. Wicken. His bid to control the proposed Coolgardie School of Mines was likewise frustrated by the political machinations of the minister for mines Henry Gregory [q.v.]; Jackson withdrew from the committee to select the school's first principal.

Keenly analytical and boundlessly energetic, Jackson subscribed to the Protestant ethic of rewarded effort and, although he possessed substantial private means, abhorred any form of financial speculation. A devout Anglican, he yet never swerved from his commitment to secular education. Widely remembered for his camaraderie, he

could still administer a swift, stinging rebuke when provoked by a subordinate speaking out of turn in his cups. Although given himself to occasional impulsiveness, he was a strict disciplinarian and a stickler for protocol. He remained intensely loyal to his colleagues, as Bishop Gibney [q.v.8] discovered in 1900 when he cast aspersions on the capability of the departmental inspectors.

In later years, plagued by insomnia, Jackson became increasingly difficult to work with. At Bassendean he lived in style at Daylesford, a commodious, if architecturally curious, house where he was attended by a team of domestic servants, including an Indian valet and a Chinese gardener. He was financially generous to those less fortunate and was well known in his local community as a member of the West Guildford Road Board. Physically slight, Jackson wore a thick moustache and was always well groomed. A connoisseur of porcelain and fine furniture and an accomplished organist and pianist, he delighted in a rollicking singsong with a group of young people. Determined that his work should be continued in the same vein, Jackson took exhaustive steps before his departure to secure the appointment of C. R. P. Andrews [q.v.7] as his successor.

It was a timely coincidence for Jackson personally that he was on leave in England during the passage of the British Education Act of 1902. His Western Australian contract, due to expire, would undoubtedly have been renewed but he had achieved his colonial goal by establishing a sound state system and had other aspirations at home. Refusing an attractive South African offer, he finally left Western Australia on 3 March 1903 in the *Indic*, bearing a gold watch presented by the Teachers' Union in recognition of his contribution to the profession. Chief inspector to the Board of Education in London until 1906, he became an investigator for the royal commission on the Poor Law. His briefs then multiplied: many appointments to commissions and statutory committees followed. His interest in local government continued as representative for Limehouse on the London County Council in 1907-13, and as alderman in 1913-16 and 1919. He chaired the council in 1915, twice chaired its education committee and also led the municipal reform party. For services during World War I he was appointed K.B.E. in 1917. His publications included *Unemployment and trade unions* (1910), *Outlines of education in England* (1913), *The religious question in public education* (1911) (with M. Sadler and A. Riley) and many articles in encyclopaedias and journals.

Jackson was often consulted by the Western Australian government and obligingly acted briefly as agent-general in 1910-11. He also lent weight to the advisory committee which selected Hugh Gunn as organizer of the University of Western Australia. Only two days before his death he discussed with the agent-general, (Sir) Hal Colebatch [q.v.8], a project of the Young Australia League in Western Australia. Despite many sea trips, he had long been ill and died suddenly from cerebral haemorrhage on 3 September 1924 at his country house, Ballards Shaw, Limpsfield, Surrey, where he was buried. He was unmarried. His portrait hangs in the Royal Academy of Arts, London. The Cyril Jackson Senior High School at Bassendean, Western Australia, was named in his honour in 1964.

Jackson claimed that his success in welding the best elements of contemporary educational systems into a cohesive whole and creating a viable scheme for Western Australia was his proudest achievement. Having steeled himself to be firm and hard-hitting and to ignore personal inclinations to let things be, he fulfilled his role with distinction.

C. Turney (ed), *Pioneers of Australian education*, 2 (Syd, 1972); D. Mossenson, *State education in Western Australia, 1829-1960* (Perth, 1972); *PP* (WA), Education Department annual report, 1897-1902; *Education Dept* (WA), *Education Circular*, July, Dec 1900, May 1901, and *Education*, 1 (1952); *West Australian*, 8 Mar 1898, 7 July 1899, 2 May, 4 Sept 1900, 28 Feb, 2 Mar 1903, 13 Sept 1924; *The Times*, 5, 6, 8 Sept 1924; Education Dept (WA), File 97/843, 1903, 2790, 1900/504, 635, 1902/419, 647.   WENDY BIRMAN

JACKSON, ERNEST SANDFORD (1860-1938), medical practitioner, was born on 18 July 1860 at Sandford, Victoria, son of John Henry Jackson, Tasmanian-born grazier, and his wife Mary Ann, née Bowtell; Samuel Jackson [q.v.2] was his granduncle. Educated at Geelong Church of England Grammar School and Trinity College, University of Melbourne (M.B., Ch.B., 1881), he served as resident medical officer at the Melbourne and Brisbane hospitals and was appointed medical superintendent of the latter in February 1883. A strict disciplinarian, he considered patient care paramount and founded Queensland's first training school for nurses in 1886.

Jackson entered private practice as a surgeon in 1898 with a visiting, later consulting, appointment at the Brisbane Hospital. He bought St Helen's private hospital in 1900. A foundation member of the Queens-

land branch of the British Medical Association, he was its president in 1895, 1911 and 1926. He was a founding father of the medical school at the University of Queensland and a vice-president of the Brisbane Ambulance Committee. In evidence at the bar of the Legislative Council in 1911 he argued for continuation of the controversial venereal diseases legislation directed mainly at prostitutes.

In November 1914 Jackson left Australia with the Australian Imperial Force as a major in the 1st Australian General Hospital but after serving in Egypt was invalided home in November 1915. Early in 1926 he launched a campaign which led eventually to the Queensland Cancer Trust over which he presided. He was a member of the royal commission into public hospitals of 1930 and of inquiries into lead poisoning and the repatriation of soldiers. He was also a founder of the (Royal) Australasian College of Surgeons in Queensland.

Tall and well-built, with a moustache and clear blue eyes, Jackson had a magnificent presence, a fine speaking voice and a deep sense of honour. A councillor of the Church of England Grammar School, Brisbane, in 1914-38, he was president of the Queensland Club in 1914. He had rowed for Trinity College and Melbourne University and was a splendid horseman. From the family estate in Victoria, he brought blood horses to Queensland and won many show prizes.

Late in life Jackson began to research the history of sea exploration and of medicine. Accepting an invitation in 1931 to deliver the first annual Jackson oration established in his honour by the B.M.A.'s Queensland branch, he entitled it 'Some voyages connected with the discovery of Australia; their medical history'. His historical papers are preserved in the Roberts Centre at Brisbane Grammar School. As a vice-president of the (Royal) Historical Society of Queensland he contributed actively to its proceedings. He retired in 1934 to Koorakooracup, a house at Victoria Point named after a station owned by his family in Victoria, where he indulged his love of horses, history and gardening.

At Brisbane on 14 August 1890 Jackson had married with Baptist forms the Scots nurse Christina Bain; they had seven children. He died of hypertensive heart disease at St Helen's Hospital on 29 June 1938 and was buried with Anglican rites in Toowong cemetery.

W. P. F. Morris, *Sons of Magnus* (Brisb, 1948); *MJA*, 15 Oct 1938, p 659, 20 Dec 1969, p 1271; Brisb Hospital Cttee, 17 Jan 1899 (HOS 1/D13, QA); personal information from N. E. S. Jackson, Brisb, *and* P. R. S. Jackson, Longford, Tas.

ROSS PATRICK

JACKSON, JOHN WILLIAM ALEXANDER (1897-1959), soldier, hotelkeeper, farmer and clerk, was born on 13 September 1897 at Gunbar near Hay, New South Wales, son of John Jackson, labourer, and his wife Adelaide Ann, née McFarlane. He worked as a drover in the Merriwa district before enlisting as a private in the 17th Battalion, Australian Imperial Force, on 20 February 1915 and embarking in May. After training in Egypt the battalion landed at Gallipoli on 20 August and immediately fought in the battle for Hill 60. On 3 October Jackson was evacuated with dysentery and rejoined his unit on 8 March 1916 in Egypt. Shortly afterwards the battalion left for the Western Front and relieved the Northumberland Fusiliers at Bois Grenier, near Armentières, France, on 10 April.

An intensive training programme was arranged for a raid on enemy trenches; 18-year-old Jackson volunteered for the operation. On the night of 25-26 June the raiding party of 9 officers and 73 other ranks, under cover of artillery fire, assaulted the forward trenches of the 231st Prussian Reserve Infantry Regiment. Jackson was a member of the scout group which reconnoitred the approaches to the enemy positions. The raiding party moved out in the face of withering machine-gun fire. After the scout group had neutralized the enemy listening posts the raiders, supported by a box barrage, entered the enemy trenches, encountering only token resistance. Five minutes later the Australians withdrew under heavy shelling.

Jackson brought a prisoner back and returned to bring in a wounded man. Again he went out and with a sergeant was carrying in another man when his right arm was shattered by a bursting shell and the sergeant was rendered unconscious. He returned for help, disregarding his own condition, and went out again to help bring back the sergeant and the wounded man; one was recovered. For this act of courage he was immediately awarded the Distinguished Conduct Medal. This was cancelled, however, and he was awarded the Victoria Cross for his 'splendid example of pluck and determination'. The citation stated: 'his work has always been marked by the greatest coolness and bravery'.

Jackson was evacuated and his arm was amputated. He embarked for Australia on 4 May 1917 and was discharged on 15 September. He became a hotelkeeper at Wollongong, then returned to Merriwa but after almost seven years of drought he left the land and moved to Sydney for employment. He had several jobs, including clerical work with the Metropolitan Water, Sewerage and Drainage Board. On 12 January 1932 he married a dressmaker, Ivy Muriel Alma Morris, at St Paul's Anglican Church, Kogarah; there was one daughter of the marriage which was dissolved in 1955. During World War II he served as an acting sergeant in Eastern Command Provost Company, 1941-42. In 1953 he moved to Melbourne and became commissionaire and inquiry attendant at the Melbourne Town Hall.

In 1956 Jackson visited England to attend the Victoria Cross centenary celebrations. Survived by his daughter, he died of arteriosclerotic heart disease on 4 August 1959 at the Austin Hospital, Heidelberg, Melbourne, and was cremated. Jackson was the youngest Australian to be awarded the Victoria Cross in World War I and his was the first V.C. to be awarded to a member of the A.I.F. in France.

C. E. W. Bean, *The story of Anzac* (Syd, 1921, 1924), and *The A.I.F. in France*, 1916 (Syd, 1929); K. W. McKenzie, *The story of the Seventeenth Battalion A.I.F. in the Great War 1914-1918* (Syd, 1946); L. Wigmore (ed), *They dared mightily* (Canb, 1963); *London Gazette*, 8, 22 Sept, 20 Oct 1916; *Reveille* (Syd), Jan 1932, Feb 1933, Jan 1960, July 1964, Oct 1966; *Age*, 5 Aug 1959; War diary, 17th Battalion A.I.F., *and* records (AWM); records, Dept of Veteran's Affairs (Syd); information from Mrs J. W. Parkes, West Como, *and* Mrs A. E. Jones, Hurstville, Syd.   R. SUTTON

JACKSON, PETER (1861-1901), boxer, was born on 3 July 1861 at Christiansted, St Croix, Virgin Island, West Indies, son of Peter Jackson, warehouseman, and his wife, and grandson of Jackson's freed slave Peter. He was well educated to primary level before going to sea. Landing in Sydney about 1880, he worked on the waterfront and in hotels before drifting into boxing in 1882 under the tuition of Larry Foley [q.v.4].

Between 1883 and 1886 Jackson fought seven times, once with bare knuckles, only losing to the Australian champion Bill Farnham in 1884. After two years as an instructor at Foley's, he easily won the Australian heavyweight championship from Tom Lees in thirty rounds on 25 September 1886. Jackson's magnificently trained and proportioned physique, 6 ft. 1½ ins. (187 cm) tall and weighing 190 lbs. (86 kg), gave him a rare combination of speed and strength. An intelligent boxer rather than a slugger, he possessed a marvellous feint, strong jabs and a masterly left-right combination. On 18 April 1888 he left for the United States of America and Britain.

Jackson fought twenty-eight of the best men of England and America between 1888 and 1892, losing to none. The nearest he came to defeat was an eight-round draw in Melbourne on 21 October 1890 against Joe Goddard—he was undertrained and on a lightning visit to his adopted country, where he was fêted and accepted as an Australian. His most memorable fights were the 61-round, four-hour draw with James J. Corbett on 21 May 1891 at San Francisco and the hectic ten-round victory over fellow Australian Frank Slavin on 30 May 1892 in London. Jackson was one of the finest boxers never to fight for a world championship: John Sullivan refused to defend his title against a black and Corbett avoided Jackson once he gained the heavyweight crown in 1892.

Termed the 'darkey' or worse early on, Jackson became known as 'Peter the Great' or 'The Black Prince'. He was always deemed a 'gentleman' and a 'real whiteman'. His great sportsmanship and modesty reflected his nature, and also was a role forced on him in a white world. His deference, good looks, fine speaking manner and skill made him universally popular: he was one of the few boxers, black or white, allowed to move freely in the National Sporting Club rooms in London.

After 1892 Jackson was unable to obtain fights. Past his prime, he was debilitated by fast living and probably even then tubercular. He taught boxing, worked as a publican, toured as an actor in *Uncle Tom's cabin* and boxed exhibitions. In March 1898 he was sacrificed to Jim Jeffries, who flattened him in three rounds, and next year suffered the third of his losses in thirty-seven fights at the hands of a fourth-rater at Vancouver. Money was raised to send him to Australia, where he toured with Fitzgerald's circus but he was too ill to box. After several benefits he was sent to Queensland where he died of tuberculosis at Roma on 13 July 1901. He was buried with Anglican rites and pomp in Toowong cemetery. A magnificent tomb was later erected by subscription with the words, 'This was a man'.

N. Fleischer, *The 1965 ring record book and boxing encyclopedia* (NY, 1965); T. Langley, *The life of Peter Jackson* (Leicester, UK, 1974); *Sportsman*, 27 Aug, 10 Sept 1890, 16 July 1901; *Brisbane Courier*, 15 July 1901; *Australasian*, 20 July 1901.

RICHARD BROOME

JACKSON, SIDNEY WILLIAM (1873-1946), naturalist, was born on 12 June 1873 in Brisbane, son of Irish parents Francis Daniel Jackson, draper, and his wife Frances, née Martin. He was educated at Toowoomba Grammar School and at Grafton, New South Wales, where his father was in business. As a boy he was interested in bird-watching and egg-collecting. On leaving school he worked as a clerk at Grafton and began recreational study of natural history, particularly of birds.

By 1907 Jackson had amassed a unique collection of Australian birds' eggs, which he described in *Egg collecting and bird life of Australia: catalogue and data of the Jacksonian zoological collection* (1907) and illustrated with his own photographs. He sold the collection that year to the prominent collector H. L. White [q.v.], a pastoralist of Scone. (This constitutes a major part of the H. L. White egg collection now in the National Museum of Victoria.) In 1907-27 Jackson was employed by White as curator of his collections and one of his chief field-workers.

Jackson carefully recorded his field expeditions to different parts of Australia in diaries. Before modern transport and camping equipment, these journeys were lengthy and arduous, involving hard living in the bush. Although described as portly or corpulent he more than held his own with experienced bushmen. With his brother Frank he developed techniques for climbing trees, involving the use of leg-spikes and rope-ladders, and often reached nests 100 feet (30 m) above the ground. One of his major ornithological achievements was to obtain a specimen of the female Rufous Scrub-bird in Queensland in 1919 'after four weeks of most constant and diligent searching' in thick bush.

A meticulous observer, Jackson had a penchant for minute detail. He sketched well, his handwriting was of copperplate neatness, and he had considerable skill as a photographer, going to endless trouble to secure negatives of the highest quality and detail. He was also an expert taxidermist. A member of the Royal Australasian Ornithologists' Union he reported most of his serious ornithological work in its journal, *Emu*. He was also an authority on land mollusca and collected much valuable botanical material. Entirely self-trained he achieved distinction and recognition as a versatile and highly competent field naturalist before professional interest in this field became widely established. After White's death in 1927 Jackson lived in Sydney and wrote newspaper and magazine articles.

Devoted and generous to his parents and family, Jackson was 'full of idiosyncrasies and odd little vanities' and given to melancholy and hypochondria. He could however be amusing and light hearted. He delighted in practical jokes and was something of a ventriloquist, a skill he used as an amateur entertainer and, in the field, as a mimic of bird-calls. About 1912 he married, but by 1916 he had parted from his wife.

Jackson died in hospital at Neutral Bay on 30 September 1946 and was buried in the Church of England section of Northern Suburbs cemetery.

J. White, *The White family of Belltrees* (Syd, 1981); *Wild Life* (Melb), 6 (May 1944), no 5, p 147, 8 (Dec 1946), no 12, p 426; *Emu*, 46 (Jan 1947), pt 4, p 315, 58 (May 1958), pt 2, p 101; S. W. Jackson papers (NL).   GUY B. GRESFORD

JACOB, CAROLINE (1861-1940), headmistress, was born on 18 January 1861 at Sevenhill, South Australia, daughter of John Jacob, pastoralist, and his wife Mary, née Cowles. Well-educated by her mother and at Mrs Woodcock's School, North Adelaide, Caroline gained a first-class certificate in general education from the South Australian Institute in 1877, then taught at Winnold House, Mount Gambier, her mother's school, until she joined the South Australian Education Department and began part-time university study in 1879; she won the Thomas Elder [q.v.4] prize for physiology in 1886. From 1885 she taught at the Advanced School for Girls under headmistress Madeline Rees George [q.v.8].

Determined to extend girls' higher education, she bought Tormore House, which she and her sister Annie reopened on new lines in 1898; they intended to prepare girls for university examinations. The excellent response soon enabled them to build new premises in pleasant grounds in Childers Street, North Adelaide.

Caroline Jacob designed Tormore's balanced curriculum to stretch students' capabilities, including, as compulsory subjects, English, Latin, mathematics, French or German, class singing and calisthenics, and encouraging botany, physiology and sport. Some boarders learned domestic subjects. Staff included botanist Ellen Benham [q.v.7], artist Rosa Fiveash [q.v.8] and old scholars whom Caroline trained through tutorials. She delighted in her students' academic and public attainments, while applauding those who undertook 'woman's highest work, the training of their own children'.

In 1907-11 she owned Unley Park School, bicycling eight miles between her schools several times weekly. In 1912 an educational tour of England reinforced her admiration of English girls' public schools. Her innovations at Tormore included school diaries to facilitate parental understanding, school uniform to eliminate frippery, Swedish physical training in a fine gymnasium donated by her father, rowing and cricket, and a badge and motto, *Aspice finem* (Look to the goal). She worked for the Collegiate Schools Association, the Headmistreses' Union (which she founded), the Kindergarten Union and its Training College, and the South Australian Advisory Council on Education. Many of her students became teachers, five being headmistresses.

A dedicated Anglican, in 1913 Miss Jacob was appointed to the council of the Adelaide Diocesan Missionary Association. Tormore had close links with the Church, and when enrolments declined in World War I, she approached Bishop A. Nutter Thomas [q.v.] to take it over. Both strong-minded, they 'failed to come to terms'. In 1920 she reluctantly closed Tormore.

She taught at Launceston Church of England Girls' Grammar and Adelaide High schools and travelled abroad in 1926-27; later she devoted herself to the Girl Guide movement and her Old Scholars' Association. Miss Jacob died at her home on the Esplanade, Henley Beach, on 4 November 1940. Tormore old scholars gave the Caroline Jacob memorial wing in the Erora, New Guinea, mission hospital and erected a memorial plaque in Christ Church, North Adelaide.

D. Angove, *Tormore* (priv print, North Adel, 1962); *Tormorean*, 1899-1920; *Register* (Adel), 21 Dec 1900; Tormore Old Scholars' Assn, Minutes (SRG 196/1) and Teachers' records (GRG 18, Tsf 450/6, 1876-1887), and C. Jacob by H. Jones, taped ABC radio broadcast, Personalities remembered, SRG 196/25 (SAA); letters from C. Jacob to her mother (Jacob papers, held by Miss N. Jacob, Kensington, SA).   HELEN JONES

JACOBS, JOSEPH (1854-1916), scholar and historian, was born on 29 August 1854 in Sydney, sixth surviving son of John Jacobs, a publican who had migrated from London about 1837, and his wife Sarah, née Myers. Entering Sydney Grammar School in 1867, he won the (Sir Edward) Knox [q.v.5] prize twice and was school captain in 1871. Next year, on a scholarship, he studied arts at the University of Sydney and won many prizes. In October 1873 he was admitted as a pensioner at St John's College, Cambridge (B.A., 1877, senior moralist).

In an essay, 'Mordecai', in *Macmillan's Magazine* in 1877, Jacobs had replied to criticisms of the Jewish part of George Eliot's *Daniel Deronda*; later Eliot became a close friend. That year Jacobs studied in Berlin under the famous Jewish scholars Moritz Steinschneider and Moritz Lazarus. Returning to England he was secretary of the Society of Hebrew Literature in 1878-84. At the St Pancras registry office, London, on 3 April 1880 he married Georgina Horne, daughter of a livery-stable keeper; she bore him two sons and a daughter. In January 1882 he wrote articles for *The Times* on the persecution of the Jews in Russia and became honorary secretary until 1900 of what became the Russo-Jewish Committee. This connexion led him to investigate the general Jewish question in articles to the *Jewish Chronicle* and the *Journal* of the (Royal) Anthropological Institute of Great Britain and Ireland.

With Lucien Wolf, Jacobs prepared the *Catalogue* of the Anglo-Jewish Historical Exhibition of 1887 and *Bibliotheca Anglo-Judaica*, on which all future work in Anglo-Jewish history was based. In 1893 his important work, *The Jews of Angevin England*, appeared and that year he was a founder of the Jewish Historical Society of England (president, 1898-99). His anthropological studies had led him to folklore; he edited several books of fables and in his generation became one of the most popular writers of fairy tales for English-speaking children. He edited the magazine *Folk-lore* and the *Papers and transactions* of the 1891 International Folk-Lore Congress in London. He even wrote a novel on the life of Jesus, *As others saw him*, published anonymously in 1895.

A master of many languages, Jacobs translated Hebrew, Italian and Spanish works, and brought out new editions of English classics. For many years he was a member of the executive committee of the Anglo-Jewish Association and of its joint foreign committee with the Board of Deputies of British Jews. In 1896-99 he published the first issues of the *Jewish year book*.

In 1896 Jacobs visited the United States of America to lecture on philosophy and returned in 1900 as revising editor of *The Jewish encyclopaedia*; he was responsible for its style and contributed several hundred articles. On completing the *Encyclopaedia* in 1906, he became registrar and professor of English at the Jewish Theological Seminary of America in New York. He retired in 1913 to become chief editor of the *American Hebrew and Jewish Messenger*. His incomplete *Jewish contributions to civilization* was published posthumously in 1919.

Jacobs died of heart disease at his home at Yonkers, New York, on 30 January 1916 and was buried in Temple Emanuel cemetery, Mt Hope. Australian Jewry can claim this great and gentle scholar, whose versatile ability knew no bounds, as an outstanding son; yet because his contribution to his people was intellectual and his life spent far from his homeland, he is nearly forgotten in Australia.

Dictionary of American biography (New York, 1928); Jewish Hist Soc of England, *Trans*, 8 (1915-17); American Jewish Hist Soc, *Publications*, 25 (1917); Aust Jewish Hist Soc, *J*, 3 (1949) no 2; *New York Times*, 1 Feb 1916; *American Hebrew and Jewish Messenger*, 11 Feb 1916.

G. F. J. BERGMANN*

JACOBS, SAMUEL JOSHUA (1853-1937), lawyer, merchant and brewer, was born on 28 March 1853 in Adelaide, third son of Charles Jacobs, storekeeper, and his wife Elizabeth, née Joshua, whose marriage in 1844 was the first celebrated in the Jewish faith in South Australia. He was educated at John L. Young's [q.v.6] Adelaide Educational Institution and Geelong College, Victoria, where he was dux in 1870. He studied law at the University of Melbourne, and on 4 April 1876 was admitted to the Bar in Victoria on the motion of George Higinbotham [q.v.4] and later in the year to the South Australian Bar. With W. F. Stock he formed the partnership Stock & Jacobs. On 3 December 1878 in Melbourne he married Caroline Ellis, sister of Dr Constance Ellis [q.v.8].

His legal career was short. In 1884 he joined his father's firm of sugar importers, Charles Jacobs & Sons. In 1888 he was an original subscriber to the South Australian Brewing, Malting & Wine & Spirit Co. Ltd, of which he was chairman and managing director in 1903-37. He was also the founding chairman of Castle Salt Co. Ltd, which refined lake salt from Edithburgh, Yorke Peninsula, and chairman of the Timor Development Co. These activities led him to sever his association with his father's firm whose Australian activities ceased in 1914.

The S.A. Brewing Co. prospered under his guidance and absorbed several smaller breweries, although not its principal rivals for Jacobs valued competition as a cornerstone of free enterprise. He became a well-known and respected public figure. He was president of the Adelaide Chamber of Commerce in 1901-03 and of the General Council of the Associated Chambers of Commerce of Australia in 1903-04. In 1904 and 1905 he stood unsuccessfully for the Torrens seat in the House of Assembly. For a time he was on the University of Adelaide's council as chairman of the finance committee. For thirty-four years he was a committee-member of the South Australian Jockey Club Ltd and he served long terms as chairman of Tattersalls Club and of the Society for the Prevention of Cruelty to Animals. Although well read and educated in the classics, he had little interest in art, music or drama.

Jacobs was a tall, upright figure of commanding personality and appearance, but gentle, even tempered and free of ostentation. These qualities, with his integrity and ability, made him the confidant and adviser of many younger men who sought his guidance in the early days of their business careers. He died on 4 January 1937 at his Glenelg home, survived by his wife, four daughters and a son; his elder son had died young in South Africa in 1914. His younger son, (Sir) Roland Jacobs (d. 1981), inherited many of his father's talents and interests. The daughters achieved some note by marrying four brothers of the wife of (Sir) Isaac Isaacs [q.v.], the first Australian-born governor-general.

Jacobs was buried in the old Jewish cemetery at West Terrace, Adelaide. His portrait was painted posthumously by William Dargie and hangs in the board room of the S.A. Brewing Co.

H. T. Burgess (ed), *Cyclopedia of South Australia* 1 (1907); H. Munz, *Jews in South Australia, 1836-1936* (Adel, 1936); *Quiz* (Adel), 29 Jan, 21 Oct 1904, 19 May 1905; *Observer* (Adel), 8 Dec 1928; family papers (held by author, Adel).

S. J. JACOBS

JAGEURS, MORGAN PETER (1862-1932), monumental mason and Irish patriot, was born on 10 October 1862 at Tullamore, King's (Offaly) County, Ireland, only son of Peter Jageurs, monumental mason, and his wife Mary, née Casey. The family migrated to Queensland in 1865, moved to Sydney in 1868 and finally to Melbourne two years later. Morgan was educated at St Brigid's School, Fitzroy, and Christian Brothers' College, East Melbourne, of which he was joint dux. He was apprenticed to several trades and in 1883-84 attended the National Gallery Art School. He travelled extensively in Europe before joining his father in 1892 in Jageurs & Son, monumental sculptors, marble and granite merchants, Sydney Road, Parkville. The business carried on a large trade in ecclesiastical furnishings as well as monumental work. On 17 February 1892 he married a teacher, Bridget Maria Bartley, at St Patrick's Cathedral where he had been an altar boy.

Jageurs was prominent in almost every Irish cause. In 1881 he joined the committee of the Victorian branch of the Irish National (Land) League, later the United Irish League, and became its very active secretary, working closely with Joseph Winter [q.v.6] and Dr N. M. O'Donnell [q.v.] in support of the Home Rule movement. He was on close terms with the Irish leaders Michael Davitt (who was godfather to his elder son), John Dillon and the Redmond brothers [q.v.6]. Jageurs was a student of Irish language and literature and an enthusiast for Irish music, art and sports; professionally he was noted for his Celtic memorials. A founder of the Celtic Club, he encouraged close relations between the Celtic societies. He was an exemplary Catholic, worked vigorously for the Catholic Young Men's Societies movement and was president of the St Patrick's Society in 1889-1900. He wrote widely for the Irish-Catholic press and was a doughty controversialist. During the South African War he was a member of the Peace, Humanity and Arbitration Society of Victoria, founded by Professor J. L. Rentoul [q.v.].

The events of 1916 and after were to cause Jageurs much distress. That year he succeeded O'Donnell as president of the United Irish League and waged a vigorous defence of John Redmond and the constitutional party against the Sinn Fein 'wreckers'. At the same time he was charged under the War Precautions Act regulations for such offences as protest against denial of free speech to Sinn Feiners and pleading for Sir Roger Casement's life. The Celtic Club, of which he was president, stood firm in defence of Dominion Home Rule, but it was a losing battle within the Irish-Catholic community. Writing to H. B. Higgins [q.v.], whom he revered, Jageurs deplored 'the sinister and powerful influence of Dr Mannix' [q.v.]. He welcomed the Irish treaty of 1922 but, 'weary and sick after 41 years hard work' dropped out of communal politics. However he never lost faith in the spirituality of the Irish people and their comparative lack of materialism.

Survived by his wife, three daughters and a son, Jageurs died at Brighton on 28 April 1932 and was buried in Melbourne general cemetery. His elder son had died in World War I.

J. Smith (ed), *Cyclopedia of Victoria*, 1 (Melb, 1903); P. S. Cleary, *Australia's debt to Irish nation-builders* (Syd, 1933); *Advocate* and *Tribune* (Melb), 5 May 1932; H. B. Higgins papers (NL); J. Dillon papers (National Library of Ireland).

GEOFFREY SERLE

JAMES, SIR CLAUDE ERNEST WEYMOUTH (1878-1961), politician and agent-general, was born on 24 February 1878 at Launceston, Tasmania, son of John Abraham James, clerk, and his wife Helen, née Weymouth. Educated at Launceston High School, he worked as a clerk for the local firm, Walch Bros & Birchall. In 1894 he became a junior clerk at the town hall and advanced to accountant in the electric light department. From 1913 he was city treasurer and accountant, resigning in 1918 to take up a directorship of W. & G. Genders Pty Ltd, merchants. An alderman of the city council in 1921-28, he was mayor in 1924 and a justice of the peace from 1928. He was member for Bass in the House of Assembly in 1925-37 and served as chief secretary and minister for railways and mines in the J. C. McPhee [q.v.] government from June 1928 until June 1934. He had also been president of the Launceston chambers of Commerce and Manufactures. He was a member of the Commonwealth Board of Trade in 1927 and chairman of the committee to prepare *The case for Tasmania*, which argued for greater financial allocations by the Commonwealth, in 1930, 1934 and 1935.

In 1937 James, although a leading figure in the Nationalist Opposition, was appointed Tasmanian agent-general in London by the Labor premier A. G. Ogilvie [q.v.]. On the outbreak of World War II he chose to remain in London; he was unceasing in his care for his fellow Australians on service and was prominent in setting up the Boomerang Club. Knighted in 1941 for his outstanding efforts, James chose the motto 'I try to serve'. He was given the freedom of the City of London and that of the borough of Launceston, Cornwall.

James's wife Alice Mary, née Wilkins, whom he married on 15 December 1900 at Launceston died there on 4 August 1949. Subsequently, in London, he married Barbara Ellen Taylor. After completing the longest term to that time as Tasmanian representative in London, James returned in 1950 to Launceston where he was unsuccessful in the House of Assembly elections of September 1951.

James was a fellow of the Australian Institute of Secretaries and of the Federal Institute of Accountants. A Rotarian, he was president of the Launceston Club in 1927 and of the London Club in 1942. A Freemason from 1901, initiated in the Tasmanian St Andrew Lodge, he was grand master of the Grand Lodge of Tasmania in 1926-28 and founder and first master of the Australian Masonic Lodge, London, 1947. He was co-founder and treasurer of the Northern Tasmanian Home for Boys, secretary of the Launceston section of the Belgian Relief Fund and president of the Tasmanian Rights League; he was a member of the Tasmanian and Launceston clubs. An Anglican, he died on 27 August 1961 at Launceston and was cremated, survived by his second wife and their son and two daughters, and by four sons of his first marriage.

History of Freemasonry in Tasmania 1828-1935 (Launc, 1935); *Weekly Courier*, 29 Aug 1928; *Examiner*, 28 Aug 1961; information from R. J. Bain, Launceston, Tas.   R. A. FERRALL

JAMES, DAVID (1854-1926), contractor, mining promoter and politician, was born at Nantyglo, near Abergavenny, Mon-

mouthshire, Wales, son of Rees James and his wife Mary. He worked in the coal-mines as a youth. After Rees's death, James migrated to Adelaide in 1877 with his mother and family. They settled at Kapunda where James became a contractor and worked at fencing and well and dam-sinking. At Semaphore on 19 February 1883 he married Emily Davies, a servant from Abergavenny.

That year, with his partner Jim Poole, James was sinking dams at Mount Gipps sheep-station in western New South Wales. In September Charles Rasp [q.v.6] persuaded them to join him in pegging a mineral claim there. James drove the first peg in the hill—which was to become Broken Hill—containing the world's richest lead-silver-zinc deposit. The 'syndicate of seven' under the leadership of George McCulloch [q.v.5] pegged additional leases and formed the Broken Hill Mining Co. During the uncertain prospecting period before the discovery of rich silver chlorides in 1885, James sold one half of his syndicate share for £110, and another quarter for £1800. He retained the remaining quarter-share interest and thus, in August 1885, was entitled to an initial allotment of 500 shares in the Broken Hill Proprietary Co. Ltd.

He returned to Kapunda where he was elected to the municipal council next year, and was mayor in 1888-89 and 1900-05; he always directed that his mayoral allowance be distributed to charitable causes. He was prominent in the local agricultural societies, racing club and Anglican church, and was several times chairman of the hospital board. In 1909 he bought into the *Kapunda Herald*. In 1894 James had bought an estate near Kapunda which he renamed Coalbrook Vale after a mining locality near his birthplace. He established a stud, producing horses which won races in Adelaide and Melbourne; in 1895 his three-year-old filly Auraria won the Melbourne Cup at odds of 50/1. In 1902 he was elected to the House of Assembly, representing the new constituency of Wooroora. He supported all legislation effecting pastoral and agricultural reforms, and the introduction of the Warren water scheme. An unobtrusive man, he was opposed to extremes, but was broadminded and progressive. Because of his part in the discovery of the famous Broken Hill mining field, James was associated with the development of other silver and gold-mining enterprises in South Australia and Western Australia. He continued to trade in B.H.P. scrip and in 1890 held shares valued at approximately £100 000 but by 1901 had disposed of his entire holding.

Emily James died in March 1925 and James married Ada Mullen at Kapunda in

August. Having been diabetic for some years, he died in Ru Rua Hospital, Adelaide, on 21 July 1926 and was buried at Kapunda. His wife and two daughters and a son from his first marriage survived him.

R. Bridges, *From silver to steel* (Melb, 1920); Lord Casey, *Australian father and son* (Lond, 1966); R. H. B. Kearns, *Broken Hill 1883-1893* (Broken Hill, 1973); *Advertiser* (Adel), 22 July 1926; *Kapunda Herald*, 23 July 1926; *Observer* (Adel), 24 July 1926; MS biog of D. James prepared by family and correspondence of Mrs M. E. James (held by author, Wattle Park, Adel); information from Corporate Archivist, Broken Hill Pty Co. Ltd, Melb, *and* Christ Church Rectory, Kapunda, S.A.

R. H. B. KEARNS

JAMES, FREDERICK ALEXANDER (1884-1957), merchant and litigant, was born on 17 December 1884 at East Marden, South Australia, second son of Thomas James and his wife Emily, née Pitt. Thomas had an extensive trade in fresh and dried fruit, marketed under his 'Trevarno' label. After intermittently attending various state schools and Muirden College for Business Training in 1900-01, Frederick entered the family business which he and his brother Charles carried on after their father's retirement in 1910. On 19 October 1910 in the Moseley Street Methodist Church, Glenelg, Frederick married Rachel May Scarborough who gave him three daughters and two sons.

The James brothers were financially embarrassed when, during the severe drought accompanying the start of World War I, they received no payment for a shipment of fruit to Germany. The partnership was dissolved in 1915, but Frederick set up as a wholesaler on his own and paid his debts. He also bought land at Berri where he established orchards and vineyards. From 1920 his business as a dried fruit dealer grew rapidly. The National Bank of Australasia Ltd lent him up to £12 000 each year to purchase from other growers vine fruits which he processed, packed and marketed using the 'Trevarno' mark. He ensured supplies by advancing money to or guaranteeing the overdrafts of needy ex-servicemen settled on Riverland blocks, the borrowers being obliged to offer him their entire crop.

By 1923-24 the soldier-settler schemes had led to over-production, just when the world market was depressed. The Australian Dried Fruits Association, comprising most growers and dealers, attempted to restrict output voluntarily so all producers could share in the more profitable Australian and New Zealand markets. When this failed, the association persuaded the Commonwealth and four State governments to set up boards to regulate domestic and overseas sales. To keep the home price artificially high, each grower was permitted to sell in Australia only a prescribed proportion of his produce. The remainder was to be sold abroad under the direction of the Commonwealth Dried Fruits Control Board. This irked James. He had never joined the A.D.F.A. His strict quality controls meant Australian demand for 'Trevarno' products was still rising. Many smallholders preferred to sell their fruit to him because he offered fixed prices and could pay cash on delivery. Those who consigned fruit to A.D.F.A. dealers had to wait about a year for payment and sale was not guaranteed. James believed that if the weak went to the wall, the governments whose policies had created the overproduction crisis should not solve it by depriving efficient producers of their just rewards.

When learning typing and shorthand, James had practised by repeatedly copying the Commonwealth of Australia Constitution Act. His familiarity with it now led him to suspect that vital provisions of the marketing-scheme legislation were in conflict with section 92, guaranteeing freedom of interstate trade. He obtained a licence for his packing-shed and registration as a dealer, but resolved to obey the directives of the dried fruits boards only when they suited him. In 1925, without prior notice to the Commonwealth board, he managed to sell most of his export quota in New Zealand where prices averaged £16 a ton more than in London. When he tried to do the same in 1926, the board annulled the contracts.

James was then advised that his Australian quota for 1926 was a mere 68 tons, and that he could send 5 tons a month on consignment to London. Compliance with these decrees would have ruined him, as he had just purchased over 400 tons of dried fruit from smallholders. In June his Australian quota was raised to 136 tons. However, after consulting a young Berri solicitor Kevin Ward, who agreed that some of the enabling legislation might be invalid, James sold an additional 240 tons to brokers in New South Wales and Victoria. In September the South Australian board instituted proceedings against him, and thus began a series of twenty-eight lawsuits with governments and statutory bodies. Several of these cases dragged on for years, but ultimately he was wholly or partially successful, and was awarded costs, in all but one.

His most famous cases have generated an extensive literature. In *James* v. *South Australia* (1927) the High Court of Australia held that the State Act empowering the South Australian Dried Fruits Board to control sales beyond the State was an infringement of s.92 of the Constitution. The State then tried to stop him selling fruit interstate by invoking its board's powers of compulsory acquisition. In *James* v. *Cowan* (1930), a majority of the High Court upheld these powers, but on appeal (1932) the Judicial Committee of the Privy Council reversed the judgment. Anticipating this outcome, in August 1928 the Commonwealth had begun to try to control the domestic dried fruits market as well as the export market, relying on the High Court's judgment in McArthur's case (1920) that s.92 bound the States only. However in *James* v. *The Commonwealth* (1928) the High Court accepted James's contention that the Commonwealth regulations were invalid because they discriminated between the States and thus contravened s.99 of the Constitution.

New regulations were proclaimed, and when the Federal board refused James a renewal of his dealer's licence and began seizing his fruit without compensation he challenged the Commonwealth's power to prevent him from engaging in interstate trade. In *James* v. *The Commonwealth* (1935) the High Court confirmed its previous declaration that s.92 did not bind the Commonwealth, but a majority indicated that they adhered to the doctrine mainly because they felt bound by the court's previous decisions. James again appealed to the Privy Council which ruled in 1936 that s.92 bound the Commonwealth as well as the States. This immediately nullified legislation governing the marketing of a wide range of primary products. A referendum to amend s.92, held in March 1937, was defeated; in South Australia only 18.25 per cent of the electors voted 'Yes'.

James won the legal battles but the politicians and boards won the war, for they invented new means of gaining their objects as quickly as he found loopholes. His schemes for outwitting government inspectors, including the use of other producers' packing-sheds and 'border-hopping' by land and sea, so vexed his opponents that they behaved vindictively. He planned to market 3000 boxes of seeded raisins in 1927, but the State board abolished his raisin quota and by compulsory acquisitions prevented him seeding more than 50 boxes. The initial Dried Fruits Acts covered only vine fruits; when he developed a substantial trade in dried stone fruits, the legislation was extended to cover them. In 1930-33 and 1935-36 he was denied the use of the railways, and ship and lorry owners were informed their would lose their carriers' licences if they carried his fruit. There were some bizarre incidents as when in 1929 the South Australian minister of agriculture, (Sir) John

Cowan [q.v.8], having been subpoenaed, took refuge in parliament for a fortnight. Twice when James had decided to accept a quieter life and obey the rules, bureaucratic bungling prompted him to renew the struggle.

The real victors in James's cases were the lawyers, whose fees sometimes totalled over £10 000. His twenty-eighty years association with Kevin Ward brought the latter fame, fortune and silk. Yet it was always James who did the lateral thinking; Ward clothed his client's ideas in legal language. The National Bank, which financed James's litigation, was equally satisfied, for his cases had led the courts to declare that s.92 of the Constitution has the effect of protecting private enterprise from State and Commonwealth interference. This enabled the private banks to escape nationalization in the 1940s.

In December 1927 James had moved back to Adelaide, where he diversified by establishing a fruit cannery and jam and sauce factories at Southwark. He also purchased 4000 acres (1620 ha) of timbered country near Second Valley, on Fleurieu Peninsula. He cleared it, became a beef, lamb and wool producer, and grew tomatoes for his sauce factory. In 1937 he sold his dried fruit business for £20 000. He claimed he had lost sales of 6500 tons of dried fruit because of Commonwealth intervention, but when he sued for damages in 1938-39, Justice (Sir Owen) Dixon's strict legalism saved the day for the government, and James was awarded only £878.

An early member of the Country Party, James resigned when it espoused organized marketing. Failing to gain United Australia Party endorsement for the 1937 Federal elections, he stood as an Independent for the Senate, campaigning for removal of controls on road transport. He won 7.9 per cent of the valid votes, a record for a South Australian Independent in Senate elections.

Diminutive yet robust, a go-getter who was ruthless with his debtors, James made few friends but enjoyed overseas travel, motoring and race meetings. The strain of the long war of nerves took its toll, especially on his wife, who had managed his undertakings during his frequent absences. In 1936 his marriage finally broke down and his wife instituted divorce proceedings. She dropped the suit when James settled out of court, but the extent of her alimony demands had surprised tax inspectors who promptly wrought vengeance on her spouse. He lost one private suit in 1937 when a dried fruits inspector sued him for damages for slander.

James's wife died in 1949. On 19 April 1950 he married Constance Winifred

Timothy-Keighley, who survived him. He died at Toorak Gardens on 19 March 1957. His estate was sworn for probate at £90 359.

D. B. Copland and C. V. Janes, *Australian marketing problems* (Syd, 1938); H. H. Pitt and M. N. Wicks, *The Pitt family of Payneham* (Adel, 1977); *SA State Reports*, 1929, 1931; *Round Table*, 27 (1936-37), p 194, 651; *Cwlth Law Reports*, 40-43, 52, 55, 62; *SMH*, 23 June 1932, 18, 20-25 July 1936, 16 Mar 1938; *Age* (Melb), 18-24 July 1936; *Advertiser* (Adel), 21-23 Oct, 13 Nov 1937, 26 Feb, 15, 16 Mar 1938, 3 Nov 1949, 20 Mar 1957; family papers (held by Prof A. T. James, and Judge G. Ward, Adel, and Mr L. James, Victor Harbor, SA).

P. A. HOWELL

JAMES, TRISTRAM BERNARD WORDSWORTH (1883-1939), soldier, was born on 4 March 1883 in Hobart, son of Charles Wordsworth Scantlebury James, civil engineer, and his wife Maude Turton Balfour, née Crabbe. Both parents appear to have used the surname 'Wordsworth James' but their son went by the name 'James' throughout his army career.

Educated at The Hutchins School, Hobart, and Guildford Grammar School, Western Australia, James began his military service by enlisting in the volunteer artillery in Western Australia in 1899. He was commissioned second lieutenant in the Goldfields Infantry Regiment in January 1904 and promoted lieutenant in December. In February 1906 he obtained a permanent appointment in the Royal Australian Garrison Artillery and after attending courses at the School of Gunnery in Sydney in 1908 was transferred to Queensland in August 1909.

In February 1911 James was appointed the first adjutant of the Royal Military College at Duntroon—one of the few Australian officers on its staff—and was promoted captain in May 1911. Cadets later recalled him as a busy and inquisitive figure, moving briskly about the college in performance of his duties. His short, slightly tubby build, high-pitched voice and quick movements earned him an 'unflattering insectivorous name' but he was generally recognized as an efficient adjutant, meticulous in attention to detail.

James's term at R.M.C. was extended for two years in 1915 owing to the departure of most officers from the staff for the war. In April 1916, however, he was released for active service. He enlisted in the Australian Imperial Force as a battery commander in the 7th Field Artillery Brigade with the rank of major, and after six months training in England arrived in France in December 1916 with the 25th Battery. In 1917 he won the Distinguished Service Order for extinguishing a fire in a gun-pit under heavy shell-fire. He was wounded in action on 22 July but remained on duty. In December he was transferred to the 2nd Divisional Artillery but in January 1918 was given command of the 3rd Divisional Ammunition Column. On 1 April 1918 he was appointed to command the 7th Field Artillery Brigade with the rank of lieut-colonel; he was mentioned in dispatches on 7 April and gassed on 24 April. Next month James took over the Reserve Brigade, Australian Artillery.

Returning to Australia at the end of 1919, he was allotted for duty with the garrison artillery in New South Wales, but in August 1920 was transferred to command the garrison artillery at Fremantle, Western Australia. In May 1921 he was moved to Victoria to the 2nd Battery, Australian Field Artillery, and in August 1922 he was placed in command of the 1st Coast Artillery Brigade and the garrison artillery in New South Wales. He went to England in November 1923 for two years exchange and on returning resumed his previous appointment in Sydney. He was promoted lieut-colonel, Australian Military Forces, in August 1926. On 30 May 1931 he retired, reportedly because of war injuries, and went to live in North Adelaide with his widowed mother.

James never married. After his mother's death in October 1936 he went on several trips abroad and died of chronic asthma and emphysema at Battersea, England, on 15 September 1939.

J. E. Lee, *Duntroon* (Canb, 1952); Roy Military College, Duntroon, *Annual Report*, 1910/11-1915/16, and *Journal*, 1969; *Reveille* (Syd), Dec 1939; *Mercury*, 10 Mar 1883; *Advertiser* (Adel), 30 Oct 1939; records (AWM); information from Major General R. N. L. Hopkins, Walkerville, Adel, *and* Brigadier W. J. Urquhart, Everard Park, Adel.

C. D. COULTHARD-CLARK

JAMES, SIR WALTER HARTWELL (1863-1943), lawyer and politician, was born on 29 March 1863 in Perth, son of Edward Senior James of the Colonial Commissariat and his wife Lucy, née Francisco, both of whom later were publicans. Educated at government schools and Perth High School, he spent three years jackerooing on De Grey station; then, helped by his stepfather George Randell [q.v.6], he was articled to George Leake [q.v.] in 1883. He studied in Perth and served six months in a barrister's office in London before he was called to the Western Australian Bar in 1888. He had difficulty establishing himself before forming James & Darbyshire in 1896. At the Anglican church, Albany, on 21 June 1892 he married Welsh-born Eleanora Marie Gwenyfred Hearder.

Convivial, urbane, generous with money and racy in humour, James combined personal charm with intensity on social and political issues. On these he spoke rapidly, reflecting a volatile temperament. England opened his eyes to urban squalor and confirmed a commitment to the underdog born of his upbringing: he had played Australian Rules football, the working-class sport, which he identified with egalitarianism and Australian nationalism. These remained his political values. Western Australia's land, wealth and power were concentrated in a few families. James determined to break the hold of this coterie, but was disappointed by the conservative Constitution of 1890 establishing responsible government. Aiming to democratize the electoral process and correct social injustice, he became active in reform groups, and co-operated with trade union leaders such as (Sir) George Pearce [q.v.].

Municipal experience led James into politics. A Perth city councillor in 1890-96, he also served on the Central Board of Health and the Perth Hospital Board. He was a member, then chairman, of the South Perth Roads Board in 1892-98. After serving on the Perth District Board of Education he opposed grants to church-schools and promoted state education. The issue featured in the 1894 elections in which James won the Legislative Assembly seat of East Perth; he supported the moves which saw grants to denominational schools cease next year and the emergence of free, compulsory, secular education by 1899.

James had campaigned on a platform of protectionism, cautious rural development and social reform including secular education, payment of parliamentarians, the eight-hour day and workers' compensation. A parliament unhampered by party discipline gave opportunities for initiatives: James occupied a cross-bench reflecting his Burkeian independence. He simplified and codified existing legislation; put the views of the Municipal Conference; and amended government bills to satisfy trade unions. Quoting W. P. Reeves, he was dubbed 'member for New Zealand' as he transformed the employers' liability bill (1894) to ensure that workers were not contracted out of compensation for injury. He failed to exclude cheap coloured labour through his Chinese immigration restriction bill (1894).

Re-elected for East Perth in 1897, James declined Sir John Forrest's [q.v.8] offer of the attorney-generalship, preferring independence. He admired the premier but not his reluctance to embrace social improvement. During 1898-99 James's supporters formed a faction of five and success came with his Early Closing Act (1898) requiring shops to close at 6 p.m. He was proud of Western Australia being the first colony to enforce this. Important too was his successful work for female suffrage as parliamentary spokesman for feminist groups in 1897-99.

James participated in Federal convention sessions in Adelaide, Sydney and Melbourne in 1897-98, serving on the judiciary committee. His suggestion that State courts be given Federal jurisdiction was adopted. Overall, he was less States-rightist than fellow Westralians. Nevertheless he worked hard for Western Australian finances to be protected by the retention of its customs revenue for ten years, but had to be content with the sliding scale provisions of section 95. He was impressed by Alfred Deakin [q.v.8], with whom he maintained an amiable correspondence; Deakin enjoyed his 'hypernervous untameable temperament'. Back home he chaired the Federal League meeting in May 1898 launching the Federal campaign. He wanted Forrest to take the presidency of the league and resented moves by him and (Sir) J. W. Hackett [q.v.] in 1899 designed, it seemed, to make it impossible for Western Australia to federate. He campaigned for referral of the question to a referendum and opposed the Forrest government on the issue. In welcoming Federation in 1901 he did not appreciate fully the difficulties a 'small' State would experience. His work had been important but not crucial to the Western Australian Federal movement.

Payment of members of parliament from 1901 helped James; although his legal firm did well in the gold rush, he had a family and expensive tastes, and gave generously to relatives and friends including Labor parliamentary candidates. When George Leake's Liberal government emerged in 1901 James again declined a portfolio but was spokesman on social legislation, steering through parliament in 1902 the Act to legalize trade unions, and the Workers' Compensation Act so that an employer's negligence was no longer an essential element in compensation cases. He introduced the industrial conciliation and arbitration bill (1902) which replaced the existing unworkable measure. He had achieved nearly all his original political ambitions, but his future was uncertain because of his avoidance of ministerial responsiblity.

Leake's sudden death changed the situation. James vetoed other attempts to take the helm and emerged as premier and attorney-general on 1 July 1902 with Labor support. He was soon embroiled with the Commonwealth in disputes: occupancy of transferred buildings; channels of communication; disentanglement of governmental functions; State debts; refunds of customs revenue to the State. Section 95 of the constitution caused concern: it disadvantaged local traders and permitted the Commonwealth to retain part of the revenue, leading to clashes between James and Federal ministers Deakin and C. C. Kingston [q.v.]. Submissions to the 1903 premiers' conference and 1904 treasurers' conference achieved little. James remained committed to Federation but concerned at the failure of co-operative federalism and the tendency to 'exalt the Commonwealth'. His views were unchanged thirty years later when he opposed Western Australian secession but wanted pressure put on the Commonwealth for increased grants to the State.

The James government continued Forrest's policy of settling the gold-rush population on the land: railways were constructed and agricultural loans liberalized. A transcontinental railway was planned. The conservative Legislative Council mutilated social initiatives including a far-reaching shops and factories bill, linking early closing with health and safety rules. But two significant social measures were enacted in 1903: the Lunacy Act which reformed mental health care and the Prisons Act which sought to humanize prisoners' treatment. James removed government insurance from private companies, established a state hotel and advocated state insurance, banking, coal-mines and abbatoirs. Opponents of his state socialism were labelled 'fat, selfish monopolists'. He strove also to establish free secondary education, but had more success in opening schools of mines in Coolgardie and Kalgoorlie and in passing the University Endowment Act (1904).

Challenging the 'Hippopotami of the upper house', James decided to amend the Constitution and electoral acts to secure control of both houses of parliament by the democratic majority. Bills sought to end plural voting, to extend the lower house franchise and to redistribute electorates for the better representation of the populous mining and metropolitan regions. The Constitution bill provided machinery to overcome disagreements between the houses— requiring the Lower House to go to the people twice before a joint sitting could break a deadlock. After acrimonious wrangling the Upper House, led by Hackett, threw out the reforms, leaving only minor amendments and a redistribution.

Labor members, chafing at slow progress, drifted into opposition in 1903-04 and, in the campaign for the 1904 election, James appealed for a choice to be made between his progressive government and the Labor Party, which he criticized for its sectional interests and caucus control. The result was indecisive: 22 Labor, 18 James's party and 10 conservatives. Labor combined with the conservatives to turn out the government in August. James was shattered and bitter that Labor had ended his bid for liberal reform based on working-class co-operation. He went as agent-general to London where from 1904 he worked hard for two years promoting immigration and, upon returning to Perth, was knighted in 1907. He had been appointed K.C. in 1902.

With the rise of party politics James had become an anachronism lacking the necessary pragmatism. He could not stomach Labor. Nor was he comfortable with anti-Labor's conservatism, although he stood as a Liberal for Beverley in 1910 and supported Nationalist-conscriptionist policies in 1917. As an old man he chaired the State National Party in 1935. Otherwise, he devoted the rest of his life to the law and education.

Rebuilding his legal career in 1907, after five years absence, became complicated when B. H. Darbyshire resigned leaving James in debt. However he was a capable, versatile lawyer; he lacked flair in examination but was a fine appeals advocate. In partnership with R. R. Pilkington, a skilful barrister, success was consummated by amalgamation with the firm of (Sir) Edward Stone [q.v.] and Septimus Burt [q.v.7] in 1919. Stone James & Co. became one of the largest law firms in Perth with James the leader of the Bar until his retirement in 1937.

Service to the University of Western Australia capped his long interest in state education. Having set aside land for the university in 1904, he served on the 1909 royal commission which led to its establishment in 1911; next year he was appointed senator. He was pro-chancellor in 1929-30 and chancellor in 1930-36, and received an honorary doctorate of laws in 1936. His posthumous portrait by W. Boissevain hangs in the university.

James gradually merged into the Establishment; he was president of the Weld Club in 1931-32 and was appointed K.C.M.G. in 1931. He relied on his legal income but invested profitably in Stanley Brewery, later Swan Brewery, and in the West Australian Newspaper Co. of which he was a director. His youthful brashness mellowed, leaving the likeable wit, humility and social concern. The nickname 'Nutty' James persisted—mocking the ideals of the most significant social reformer in Western Australia. He died in Perth on 3 January 1943, and was cremated with Anglican rites; three sons and a daughter survived him.

Lady James (d. 1938) had been prominent in feminist causes through the Karrakatta Club and the Women's Service Guild. She had been a president of the National Council of Women (Western Australia) and represented Australia at the British Empire Red Cross Conference in London in 1930. At the time of her death she was State president of the Girl Guides.

F. Alexander, *Campus at Crawley* (Melb, 1963); D. J. Murphy (ed), *Labor in politics* (Brisb, 1975); P. Loveday et al (eds), *The emergence of the Australian party system* (Syd, 1977); L. Hunt (ed), *Westralian portraits* (Perth, 1979); C. T. Stannage, *The people of Perth* (Perth, 1979), and (ed), *A new history of Western Australia* (Perth, 1981); *Aust Q*, Dec 1949; *Studies in W.A. Hist*, 2, March 1978; *Aust Economic Hist Review*, 8 (March 1968), no 1; *West Australian*, 4 Jan 1943; *Bulletin*, 6 Jan 1943; R. Gore, The Western Australian Legislative Council 1890-1970 (M.A. thesis, Univ WA, 1975); L. Hunt, A political biography of Walter Hartwell James 1894-1904 (M.A. thesis, Univ WA, 1974); F. M. and A. W. Robinson, Unpublished manuscript concerning the history of Stone James & Co. (held by authors, Perth); I. S. Emanuel correspondence, held by Emanuel brothers, West Perth; W. H. James, Letter-books, 1887-88 (Battye Lib), and papers (ML, and RHSV); Deakin papers (NL).

LYALL HUNT

JAMES, WILLIAM EDWARD (1882-1954), soldier and farmer, was born on 12 April 1882 at Harcourt, Victoria, son of Joseph James, farmer, and his wife Mary Anne, née Frost, both Victorian born. His father died two years later and his mother remarried. As a boy he had difficulties with his stepfather Robert Martin, and lived at Harcourt with his widower grandfather Isaac James. Having completed primary schooling he worked with his grandfather and uncle, who were orchardists and beekeepers. Influenced by his deeply religious grandfather, who was a Methodist and Rechabite, he grew up in a loving but strongly disciplined environment.

James began his military career by joining the militia in 1901; he was commissioned second lieutenant in the 8th Australian Infantry Regiment, Australian Military Forces, in 1904 and was promoted captain in 1911. On 15 April 1908, with Methodist forms, he married Edith Mary Eagle (1884-1970) at her parents' home at Harcourt. In 1914 James was an area officer involved in the A.M.F.'s universal training scheme and was therefore discouraged from joining the Australian Imperial Force. He eventually enlisted in the A.I.F. on 1 May 1915 as a captain and company commander in the 24th Battalion and embarked for active service a week later. After training in Egypt, where he was promoted major, his battalion reached Gallipoli on 5 September and moved into the trenches at Lone Pine. In November James contracted paratyphoid and was evacuated to Malta and then to Australia, arriving in Melbourne in May 1916. After recovering he embarked for England in October.

On 5 February 1917 James rejoined his unit at Fricourt, France, and that month was appointed second-in-command of the 24th Battalion which had experienced heavy fighting and losses at Pozières and Mouquet Farm. After being wounded in action on 3 March at Grevillers, he resumed duty in May and was promoted lieut-colonel commanding the battalion in July. He showed fine leadership and courage in the 3rd battle of Ypres and was awarded the Distinguished Service Order for gallantry when his battalion captured the key objective of Broodseinde Ridge. He earned a Bar to his D.S.O. for his conduct in the attacks on Beaurevoir and Montbrehain in October 1918, and was mentioned in dispatches twice in 1918-19. From February 1919 he commanded A.I.F. demobilization camps in England and returned to Australia in March 1920; his A.I.F. appointment ended in May.

James continued service in the A.M.F. in the 1920s, reaching the rank of colonel in 1929. His family lived modestly at Harcourt, relying on subsistence farming and pig husbandry; they were widely known and respected in the Castlemaine-Harcourt district. James went on to the A.M.F. unattached list in 1932 but returned to active duty during World War II, commanding the Infantry Training Brigade, Southern Command, at Wangaratta in 1940-41. He was placed on the retired list in April 1942.

Survived by his wife, daughter and two sons, he died at Whittlesea on 26 September 1954 and was buried in Harcourt cemetery after a Methodist service. Billy James was a strict Rechabite but, except for his immediate family, he did not impose on others his views on the evils of drink. Strong self-discipline was his outstanding characteristic. His 1915 passport shows him as 5ft. 10ins. (178 cm) with grey eyes and brown hair, and photographs reveal a strong, fresh face. He had a rare understanding of the strengths and weaknesses of men, and his sincere manner, his cool, brave demeanour in the face of adversity and his readiness to help anyone in need inspired affection and respect.

W. J. Harvey, *The red and white diamond, 24th Battalion, A.I.F.* (Melb, 1920); C. E. W. Bean, *The story of Anzac* (Syd, 1921, 1924), and *The A.I.F. in France, 1916-18* (Syd, 1929, 1933, 1937, 1942); *London Gazette*, 28 May, 3 June 1918, 2 Apr, 11 July 1919; Report on the Department of Defence 1914-17 (AWM); War diary, 24th Battalion, AIF (AWM); Family papers held by, and personal information from, Mr C. H. James, Harcourt, Vic.

MICHAEL MIGUS

JAMES, WINIFRED LLEWELLYN (1876-1941), writer, was born on 20 March 1876 at Prahran, Melbourne, ninth surviving child of Thomas James, Wesleyan minister from Cornwall, and his wife Gertrude, née Peterson, from Yorkshire, England. She was educated privately at St Kilda. After running a teashop in King William Street, Adelaide, in 1901-03, she returned to Melbourne and began writing short stories, several of which were published in the *Australasian*. Their success encouraged her to go to London.

She arrived there in 1905 and a year later her first book, *Bachelor Betty*, was published; it ran into four editions in four weeks. This was followed by *Patricia Baring* (1908), *Saturday's children* (1909) and the extraordinarily successful *Letters to my son* (1910), sentimental essays couched in the form of letters addressed by a young mother-to-be to her unborn son. The seventeenth edition (1913) was dedicated to the Boy Scouts and had a foreword by Sir Robert Baden-Powell. *More letters to my son, Letters of a spinster* and a novel appeared in 1911. In 1912 she visited the West Indies and Panama. She returned to England, completing a travel book before her marriage on 30 April 1913 at St George's, Hanover Square, London, to Henry De Jan, a merchant of Panama.

Winifred James's next book, which described setting up house in the 'wilderness' of Panama, was written in her customary first-person style: chatty, familiar, yet never carelessly crafted. She had claimed in 1908 that while her stories almost wrote themselves—'they bubble out so spontaneously'—she worked extremely hard at the technique. When World War I broke out she organized a huge junk-fair to raise money for the British Red Cross Fund. She visited London in 1916 and for an Economy Exhibition arranged a 'working girls' room' furnished on £3 which she also showed in provincial centres. Back in London in 1922 she took a replica of this exhibit to south-west England for a year. She managed an antique shop in London and her knowledge of furniture, china, pictures, brass and curios was reflected in the furnishing of her Chelsea home. Another interest was the cuisine of countries in which she had lived.

In 1927, after unsuccessful suits in New York and New Jersey and three years of dispute, De Jan divorced his wife in Panama. They had no children. Now regarded under English law as an alien, Winifred James turned her energy to publicizing the need for laws to protect the nationality of women who married foreigners. Her case became famous in February 1933 when she went to court for refusing to register with the police as an alien; there were street demonstrations in her support. Eventually in 1935 she was granted a naturalization certificate.

As a writer, Winifred James maintained a rigorous work schedule. In the 1920s and 1930s she contributed articles to the *Yorkshire Post, London Daily Chronicle* and *Evening Standard* and published three novels, volumes of essays and travel books. In 1939, ill and alarmed by the onset of war, she returned to Australia, arriving in Sydney on 26 December. She brought with her the manuscript of her last novel, *The gods arrive* (published in 1941), and a half-finished autobiography. She died from cerebral thrombosis in Newington hospital, Sydney, on 27 April 1941 and was cremated.

British A'sian, 10 Sept 1908, 15 May 1913; *Home*, 1 Dec 1923; *New York Times*, 26 July 1924, 5 Aug, 5 Sept 1925, 3 May 1927, 7 Feb 1933; *Argus*, 6, 7 Feb 1933, 9 July 1935; *Herald* (Melb), 20 Jan, 7 Mar 1940; *SMH*, 16 Jan 1940; publisher's note to *The gods arrive*.   SALLY O'NEILL

JAMIESON, WILLIAM (1853-1926), surveyor and businessman, was born in 1853 at Aberdeen, Scotland, son of George Jamieson, minister of the Church of Scotland, and his wife Jane, née Wallace. Educated at Aberdeen, he arrived in Adelaide in 1869 as an apprentice on a sailing-ship and made his way to the Victorian goldfields. As a protégé of his father's friend (Sir) John Hay [q.v.4] he later worked in New South Wales as a jackeroo at Thurrulgoona station near Bourke and Grangle station in the Lachlan district, and studied surveying. In 1881 he joined the New South Wales public service as a surveyor and in 1883 was in charge of the Bourke district. He was tenacious and resourceful, but severe drought brought work to a standstill and he left for a visit to New Zealand, returning next year to survey the Barrier silver-mining region.

Jamieson arrived at Silverton just as the long drought broke: one story tells how his bushcraft and canny sense of danger saved his party from a flash flood. An early visit to the Broken Hill lease, held by George McCulloch [q.v.5], Charles Rasp [q.v.6] and five others, aroused his interest and soon after the shares were divided into fourteen he bought three for £320, though he was forced to sell two of them. His entry into the Broken Hill Mining Co. preceded by a few months that of W. R. Wilson, the manager of the Barrier Ranges Silver Mining Association, Harvey Patterson and Bowes Kelly [q.v.], all of whom were to play an important part in the development of the 'big mine'.

Jamieson probably provided the first serious opposition McCulloch encountered in running the mine. One rather dramatic story accepted by Roy Bridges [q.v.7] has it that McCulloch was about to persuade a meeting of shareholders to sell half the mine when Jamieson announced discoveries of rich chlorides of silver. Unfortunately no records of this meeting (11 April 1885) exist; but Jamieson must have done something to impress shareholders because on 25 April 1885 they offered him the management of the mine at a salary of £500. He accepted their offer and promptly resigned from his government post. Within a month the decision was taken to attract capital by registering the company in Melbourne as the Broken Hill Proprietary Co. Ltd. J. S. Reid of the *Silver Age* printed the first prospectus and Jamieson, wearing a new suit borrowed for the occasion, travelled by coach to Adelaide taking copies with him. After a revision of the prospectus the company was floated in August.

During the following months Jamieson felt himself increasingly inadequate as manager. 'The fact is old boy', he confided to William Knox [q.v.] 'I am . . . a new chum at the game of mining generally and feel that the Company. . . would very likely have to pay dearly for my inexperience'. However in spite of limited experience and occasional ill health, he carried out the early developmental work, visited the only other silver mine in Australia at Sunny Corner, New South Wales, and began the erection of smelters along the line of lode. With the government surveyor T. H. N. Goodwin, Jamieson selected the site of the town of Broken Hill and the first house erected was his; he also became a director of the Barrier Ranges and Broken Hill Water Supply Co.

At the end of 1885 he resigned as manager and returned to his native Scotland but the 'roaming spirit' and business interests drew the six feet (183 cm) tall 'moralising ruffian' back to Melbourne. In England again in 1890, he married Helene Matilda Meyer on 10 July at Little Chesterford, Essex, and served as chairman of the London board of B.H.P. until 1892. A director on the Melbourne board in 1906-26, he and his fellow 'Broken Hillionaires' played two-up with gold sovereigns after meetings.

Persuaded by Bowes Kelly to invest in Mount Lyell, Tasmania, Jamieson sat on the board of the Mount Lyell Mining & Railway Co. Ltd in 1893-1926 and was chairman in 1911-14. In 1897 he and Kelly became directors of the controversial Emu Bay Railway Co. which, if it had proceeded according to its prospectus, would have been in direct competition with the Mount Lyell railway. Jamieson was also a director of the Broken Hill Proprietary Block 10 Co. and the Blythe River Iron Co., Tasmania, and had pastoral interests in New South Wales. He died of cancer at St Kilda, Melbourne, on 8 May 1926, survived by his wife and son. His estate was valued for probate at £25 194.

R. Bridges, *From silver to steel* (Melb, 1920); G. Blainey, *The peaks of Lyell* (Melb, 1954), and *The rise of Broken Hill* (Melb, 1968); *BHP Recreation Review*, Feb, Apr 1926, Oct 1932; B. Kennedy, 'Regionalism and nationalism: Broken Hill in the 1880's', *Aust Economic Hist Review*, 21 (1980), no 1; *Punch* (Melb), 29 Aug 1918; BHP Archives, Melb.   B. E. KENNEDY

JARVIS, ERIC ROY (1896-1967), soldier and postmaster, was born on 2 August 1896 at Mount Gambier, South Australia, son of Arthur Jarvis, policeman, and his wife Eliza Jane, née James. He attended Victor Harbor Public School, and at 13 joined the Port Elliot Post Office as a telegram boy. Two years later he was transferred to Adelaide General Post Office as a telegraphist.

In July 1915, after eighteen months in the 75th Battalion cadets, Jarvis enlisted as a private in the 10th Battalion, Australian Imperial Force, but his telegraphic skills were soon recognized and in March 1916 he was transferred to the 5th Divisional Signal Company in Egypt. Soon afterwards his unit sailed for France. He was promoted lance corporal in May 1917 and temporary corporal next August. On 4 April 1918, at Hamelet near Corbie, he led a party of linesmen to establish a forward station under fierce shelling. This action earned him the Military Medal and promotion to sergeant. On 8 August, at Villers-Bretonneux, for 'continuously . . . repairing lines under heavy shell fire' and displaying 'courage', 'cheerfulness' and 'total disregard for danger', he received a Bar to his M.M. He won a second Bar on 29 September, at Bellicourt, when he again established an advanced post under heavy fire and gasattack. Later, as one of Australia's most decorated soldiers, he was presented to King George V.

Discharged in July 1919, Jarvis returned to the Adelaide Post Office. On 23 August 1920 at the Holden Memorial Methodist Church, Adelaide, he married Alice May Scott. In 1923, and again in 1929, he was posted for three-year terms in Darwin, the second time in charge of the telegraph. During the Depression he operated the repeater station at Cook on the Nullarbor Plain, before becoming postmaster at Orroroo and, in 1940, Port Augusta. In 1942 he was commissioned lieutenant in the Australian Corps of Signals and organized the vital communications link with Darwin for the rest of World War II. After the war he was postmaster at Port Pirie, then from 1950 at

Glenelg whence he retired to Victor Harbor in 1961.

Roy Jarvis was a 'livewire', totally involved in all he did. He was active in the returned servicemen's association, the Masonic lodge, golf and bowls clubs, and helped to form the Victor Harbor Progress Association. He was vice-president of the Commonwealth Postmasters' Association and its representative on the P.M.G. appeals board. During World War II, he ran the local recruitment campaigns and comforts fund. Verses by an Orroroo colleague described him as 'always . . . up and doing', a man 'who can touch the people's hearts' and their 'pockets'. Modest about his achievements, he often told his grandchildren that he won his medals for 'milking cows under shell fire'. However, he did boast the world's longest golf drive: at Cook he drove a ball into a passing railway-truck and it was returned to him from Kalgoorlie, 1100 miles (1770 km) away.

Survived by his wife, son and daughter, Jarvis died at Victor Harbor on 13 November 1967 and was cremated with Anglican rites in Adelaide.

A. D. Ellis, *The story of the Fifth Australian Division* (Lond, 1920?); C. E. W. Bean, *The A.I.F. in France, 1918* (Syd, 1942); *London Gazette*, 6 Aug 1918, 24 Jan, 14 May 1919; J. H. Thyer, Royal Australian Corps of Signals: Corps history, 1906-18 (MS, 1974, AWM); information from, and press clippings held by, Mrs A. M. Jarvis, Frewville, SA.

CARL BRIDGE

JAUNCEY, LESLIE CYRIL (1899-1959), economist and author, was born on 7 November 1899 at Norwood, Adelaide, son of George Jauncey, clerk, and his wife Agnes Binnie, née Davis. With his three elder brothers he was educated at Prince Alfred College. Jauncey's father had died in December 1899 and when his mother, a leading Methodist and prominent member of the Woman's Christian Temperance Union, died in 1916 he completed his schooling and joined his brother Eric in the United States of America. He graduated from Washington University, St Louis, Missouri (B.A., 1926), and from Harvard University (M.A., 1927; Ph.D. economics, 1929). In 1929-30 he was associate professor and head of the department of economics of the University of New Mexico and in 1930-32 was research assistant in business economics at the Harvard Business School.

In 1932 Jauncey returned to Australia and met King O'Malley [q.v.] to whom he had dedicated his doctoral thesis and who was to become a lifelong friend. With O'Malley's encouragement he published this thesis as *Australia's government bank* (London, 1934) attributing the major role in the founding of the Commonwealth Bank of Australia to O'Malley. On his way to England in 1933 Jauncey met Beatrice Eva Fripp, née Edmonds, from New Zealand, a divorcee he later described as 'in no way economically depressed'. They were married on 17 January 1934 in London where Jauncey had begun writing *The story of conscription in Australia* (London, 1935), a lively, partisan narrative that was to be as controversial as his first book. He wrote privately on the anniversary of the defeat of conscription in October 1917 that 'I always spend two minutes in silence on that anniversary'. His book emphasized the role of the religious pacifists and he acknowledged his debt to the Quakers John P. Fletcher and J. F. Hills [q.v.].

Jauncey led a peripatetic existence and admitted cheerfully that 'Most reformers seem to lose money rather constantly and I am afraid I am no exception'. The Jaunceys returned to Australia and visited New Zealand and South Africa in 1934. An enthusiastic radical from his boyhood, Jauncey returned to London fired with 'the spirit of Eureka' to be further inspired by a visit to Russia at the end of 1935 when he embarked on 'a great history of finance in Soviet Russia'. After brief visits Jauncey and his wife travelled in the U.S.A. after 1936 from San Diego to New York, unable to decide where to settle. In ill health for some of the time Jauncey pondered whether to return to Australia, dabbled mildly in radical politics and contributed articles to, among other journals, the Sydney *Labor Daily*.

In 1940 the Jaunceys invested in property in San Diego, California, and lived there until they visited Australia and New Zealand in 1947-48. In 1949 Jauncey's first book, revised, was published in Melbourne as *Modern banking*. He died of cancer on 12 March 1959 at San José, California, and was cremated. His wife survived him.

P. O'Farrell, introduction to L. C. Jauncey, *The story of conscription in Australia* (Lond, 1968); King O'Malley papers (NL).

MARGARET STEVEN

JEFFERIES, RICHARD THOMAS (1841-1920), musician, was born probably on 2 November 1841 at Hoxton, Middlesex, England, son of Alfred Thomas Jefferies, embosser, and his wife Anne, née Walters. Seven years a chorister at Lincoln's Inn Chapel under Alfred Novello, he was educated at the school conducted jointly by the chapel and the choir of the Temple Church.

He later studied violin at the Royal Academy of Music with William Watson and, while still very young, became choirmaster at the Alhambra Music Hall. A violinist in leading London orchestras, he formed and conducted the Saturday Orchestral Union about 1870. Concerts conducted by him at the Queen's Concert Rooms, Hanover Square, and the Music Hall in Store Street received favourable reviews.

Jefferies married Arena Mary Massie, a harpist, at Trinity Church of England, Marylebone, on 3 June 1871 and they sailed for Brisbane soon after. He farmed briefly and unsuccessfully near Gatton and made his first professional appearance as a violinist in Brisbane on 1 February 1872 with Henrietta Mallalieu as accompanist. The two later started the long-lived Monday Popular Concerts which introduced new music to Brisbane. In 1876 Jefferies formed a string quartet and, when his children grew up, a family quartet. With James Brunton Stephens [q.v.6] he published an Australian national anthem which won some acceptance.

Soon after his arrival Jefferies had become conductor for the new South Brisbane Harmonic Society, the success of which led to the establishment of the Brisbane Musical Union; he conducted its first concert on 18 December 1872. With (Sir) Charles Lilley [q.v.5] as president and William Hemmant [q.v.4] as vice-president, the society offered, within its first four years, the initial Brisbane performances of Handel's *Messiah, Judas Maccabeus* and *Israel in Egypt,* Mendelssohn's *Elijah* and *St Paul* and Haydn's *Creation* and *Seasons.* Jefferies also founded the Brisbane Musical Union Orchestra and guided both organizations in 1872-78, 1880-86 and 1895-98.

He had soon begun importing music and instruments as R. T. Jefferies & Co. The partnership of Kaye, Paling [q.v.5] & Jefferies was established in 1876 and, when it dissolved in 1881, he resumed independent management with branches in Ipswich and Toowoomba. He conducted the Ipswich Musical Society in 1876 and the Toowoomba Musical Choir in 1884. As organist of St John's Pro-Cathedral in 1873-78 and 1880-82 he introduced sung services in the English cathedral tradition. He was organist of St Mary's, Kangaroo Point, in 1893 and All Saints, Wickham Terrace, in 1882 and 1896-97.

Jefferies gradually retired from the public platform about the turn of the century, because of indifferent health. He was small and heavily bearded with a bad squint in the right eye. He had great organizing ability, high standards, energy, patience and tact. Retiring and shy of publicity, he

was a martinet as a teacher. Of his six children, Mary (d. 1949) and Vada (d. 1952) taught and performed on the cello and violin respectively. His sons Felix Mendelssohn Bartholdy and Richard Beethoven were musically undistinguished. Jefferies died in Brisbane on 4 August 1920 and was buried in the graveyard at Christ Church, Tingalpa. Despite a flirtation with Christian Science, he was buried as an Anglican. Much of his music library was bequeathed to the Queensland Conservatorium.

Government Gazette (Qld), 1876, 19, p 541, 1881, 28, p 432; *Brisbane Courier,* 17 Mar 1872, 2 May 1891, 6 Jan 1896; *Week,* 27 May 1876; R. K. Boughen, An account of the music of St John's Cathedral Brisbane from 1843-1887 (M.Mus. Qual. thesis, Univ Qld, 1974); B. J. Hebden, Life and influence of Mr Richard Thomas Jefferies (M.A. Qual. thesis, Univ Qld, 1980); P. Brier, One hundred years and more of music in Queensland (Oxley Lib); IMM 114, p 164 (QSA).

ROBERT K. BOUGHEN

JEFFERY, WALTER JAMES (1861-1922), journalist and author, was born on 20 August 1861 at Portsmouth, Hampshire, England, son of James Jeffery, warrant officer in the Royal Navy, and his wife Rosina, née Wright. At 15 Walter entered the navy but after two years transferred to the merchant marine, visiting India and Australia. He was also employed on a lightship in the English Channel, as a fireman in London, as a farmworker, and as a newspaper reporter at Portsmouth. At Portsea, Hampshire, on 19 December 1881 he married Ellen Martha Elizabeth Wilson (d. 1934).

Settling in New South Wales in 1886, Jeffery worked on the Illawarra coalfields, but by October 1887 he had begun a long career with the newspaper empire founded by Samuel Bennett [q.v.3]. Employed as a reporter on the Sydney *Evening News,* he became in 1891 sub-editor of the weekly *Australian Town and Country Journal* and in 1893 editor. In the thirteen years that he presided over its fortunes the journal circulated widely in New South Wales and was a significant competitor of the more strident *Bulletin.* From 1906 until his death Jeffery was manager and editor of the *Evening News.* Under his management the paper made more effort to entertain its readers but did not altogether lose its nickname, the 'Evening Snooze'. In 1918 he played a leading part in the negotiations which transferred control of the *News* and the *Journal* from the Bennett family to a public company, S. Bennett Ltd. Widely respected in Australian newspaper circles, he was committed to the Anglo-Australian connexion, and attended the Imperial Press Conference in Ottawa in 1920.

In the early 1890s Jeffery met George Lewis ('Louis') Becke [q.v.7], a writer of sea stories. Between 1896 and 1901 they collaborated on three novels, *A First Fleet family* (1896), *The mystery of the Laughlin Islands* (1896) and *The mutineer* (1898), the last focused on the *Bounty* mutineer Fletcher Christian; a biography of Arthur Phillip [q.v.2] (1899); a history, *The naval pioneers of Australia* (1899); and a miscellany, *The tapu of Banderah* (1901), which reprinted some of the many sketches and stories contributed to the *Fortnightly Review*, the *Pall Mall Gazette* and other journals in London, where Becke was based in 1896-1902. Their correspondence reveals that the partnership was uniformly and unusually harmonious, with Jeffery completing most of the research and preparing initial drafts which Becke reworked and sold to London publishers. On his own account Jeffery also published a novel, *The King's yard* (London, 1903), and *A century of our sea story* (London, 1901), in which solid research and the telling anecdote are fruitfully combined.

In addition to his writings Jeffery compiled for (Sir) William Dixson [q.v.8] indexes of references to Australasia in the journals and debates of the House of Commons and to other historical sources. He also campaigned vigorously for a statue of Phillip to be erected and for rescue of the anchor of the *Sirius*, a First Fleet ship, from the waters around Norfolk Island. He was a trustee of the Public Library of New South Wales in 1908-22. He died of Bright's disease at North Sydney on 14 February 1922 and was buried in the Church of England section of Rookwood cemetery. His wife and one daughter of their seven children survived him.

The Evening News, 1867-1926 (Syd, 1926); A. G. Day, *Louis Becke* (New York, 1966); R. B. Walker, *The newspaper press in New South Wales, 1803-1920* (Syd, 1976); *SMH*, 15 Feb 1922; *Bulletin*, 16 Feb 1922; G. L. Becke papers (NL).

B. G. ANDREWS
SANDRA BURCHILL

JEFFRIES, CLARENCE SMITH (1894-1917), soldier and mining surveyor, was born on 26 October 1894 at Wallsend, New South Wales, only child of Joshua Jeffries, colliery manager, and his wife Barbara, née Steel, both born at Wallsend. After attending Dudley Primary School, where he excelled at cricket, and the Newcastle Collegiate and High schools, he was apprenticed to his father as a mining engineer. A young

man of high standards and ideals, he strove to excel in all he did. Jeffries had a particular interest in the study of breeding thoroughbreds, although not in racing them, and always kept fine horses.

His military service began in the militia when he was 14. He joined the 14th (Hunter River) Infantry Regiment as a private in July 1912 under the compulsory training scheme, and was promoted sergeant a year later. Commissioned second lieutenant on 22 August 1914, he was mobilized for home defence duties and instructed volunteers for the Australian Imperial Force at Newcastle and Liverpool camps. He was promoted lieutenant in July 1915. On 1 February 1916 Jeffries, then in charge of the Abermain Collieries surveying department, was appointed second lieutenant in the 34th Battalion, A.I.F., and three months later embarked for England. In August he was promoted lieutenant and in November his battalion moved to the Western Front where he spent the early months of 1917 on frontline service in the Armentières sector, France. Highly respected by those serving under him and by his superiors, his first major action was at Messines where, on 9 June, he was wounded in the thigh while leading a reconnaissance patrol. Promoted captain on 26 June, Jeffries rejoined his unit in September.

On 12 October, in the attack on Passchendaele during the third phase of the battle of Ypres, his company's advance towards its first objective was held up by two pill-boxes. He organized and led a bombing party which eliminated the obstacle and captured thirty-five prisoners and four machine-guns. He then led his company forward, under an extremely heavy enemy artillery barrage and enfilade machine-gun fire, to the objective. Later that morning the battalion's advance to its second objective was delayed by a machine-gun post. Jeffries led another party to capture the position, enabling the advance to continue, but was killed during the operation. For his service that day he was posthumously awarded the Victoria Cross, for 'most conspicuous bravery in attack'.

Jeffries was buried near Passchendaele, in the Tyne Cot military cemetery. His headstone is inscribed:

> On Fame's eternal camping ground
> Their silent tents are spread.

Upon his mother's death, his Victoria Cross was presented to Christ Church Cathedral, Newcastle. Elsewhere, he is commemorated by photographic portraits in the Abermain Memorial and Citizens' Club, a carved chair presented to Abermain Holy Trinity Anglican Church by his uncle and aunt, and by the Jeffries-Currey Memorial Library at

Dudley Primary School where William Currey, V.C. [q.v.8], had also been a pupil.

C. E. W. Bean, *The A.I.F. in France*, 1917 (Syd, 1933); *Short history of the 34th Battalion, AIF* (Carlton, NSW, 1957); L. Wigmore (ed), *They dared mightily* (Canb, 1963); *London Gazette*, 14 Dec 1917; *Reveille* (Syd), Feb 1929, May 1933; *Newcastle Morning Herald*, 17 Dec 1917, 26 June 1919; *SMH*, 22 Dec 1917, 28 Apr 1954; *Sydney Mail*, 2 Jan 1918; war diary, 34th Battalion (AWM); information from Mrs E. Jakeman, Maitland, NSW.

J. B. HOPLEY

JEFFRIES, LEWIS WIBMER (1884-1971), medical practitioner and soldier, was born on 9 August 1884 at Derby, England, son of William Jeffries, Wesleyan minister, and his wife Mercy, née Wibmer. After his family migrated to Australia he attended schools at Toowoomba, Queensland, and Broken Hill, New South Wales, completing his education at Prince Alfred College, Adelaide (1900-02), and the University of Adelaide (M.B., B.S., 1907). While at university he was awarded a blue for lacrosse and represented South Australia.

After graduation Jeffries assisted Dr Arthur Powell at Kadina, then worked at Johns Hopkins Hospital, Baltimore, United States of America, with the great Harvey Cushing, 'doing faithful work, particularly in surgical pathology'. A period at the Children's Hospital, Great Ormond Street, London, was followed by study at Breslau, Germany, then a year in Kashmir at a Church Missionary Society hospital, carrying out any and every form of surgery. In 1912 he resumed at Great Ormond Street until his return to Australia in 1914. At this time the famous surgeon, Lockhart Mummery, wrote of him 'I have been very much impressed by Mr Jeffries' ability . . . He is tactful, courteous and considerate for his patients, and as a surgical colleague is all that can be desired'.

Jeffries enlisted in the Australian Imperial Force as a captain in the Australian Army Medical Corps on 2 October 1914, embarking with the 4th Field Ambulance. He was involved in operations in Egypt before and after Gallipoli, where he served from April to December 1915, and was slightly wounded on 9 May. In May 1916, in France, he was appointed medical officer to the 50th Battalion and was awarded the Distinguished Service Order for tending the wounded and reorganizing stretcher-bearers in the front line at great personal risk. When only a few bearers were left he carried back wounded under heavy fire. He was promoted major in November, was transferred briefly to the 12th Field Ambulance and from December 1916 to January 1918 was deputy assistant director of medical services, 4th Australian Division. He was then appointed assistant director of medical services at A.I.F. Headquarters, London, where he was responsible for medical arrangements for transport and hospitalization of wounded. Promoted lieut-colonel in November 1918, he was twice mentioned in dispatches for his service in France and Belgium and in 1919 was appointed O.B.E. His A.I.F. appointment ended in July 1920.

On his return to South Australia Jeffries joined the Citizen Military Forces, filling several important service appointments. He was placed on the reserve of officers in 1939 and the retired list in 1944, but in 1951 returned to full-time duty as officer commanding a camp hospital during national service. In 1920-32 he was successively in partnership with Dean Dawson, Charles Turner and Charles Yeatman, outstanding Adelaide general practitioners, doing most of his own surgery and delivering up to 200 babies annually, most in homes. He was a senior vice-president of Legacy, active in the St John Ambulance Brigade, and a member of several Adelaide clubs. There is constant evidence throughout of a good doctor, a capable administrator, and a man loved by his patients and respected by his colleagues, medical and military.

In 1933 Jeffries was appointed inspector-general of hospitals in South Australia, a position held until 1947, which also entailed chairmanship of the Royal Adelaide Hospital Board and membership of the State Medical Board and of the faculty of medicine, University of Adelaide. This was probably the most difficult period of his life, divorcing him from direct patient care and including the Depression, wartime and early post-war years with their problems of shortages of doctors, nurses and hospital equipment. He returned to clinical practice, performing relieving work in country areas, including the Woomera and Maralinga Weapon Ranges and for the army, as well as acting as medical officer to the Red Cross Blood Transfusion Service until his death.

The biographer remembers him as a big, slow-moving gentleman, with very kind eyes. He was officially a Methodist, but his family say he was an atheist. On 20 December 1917 in St George's Church, Bloomsbury, London, he had married Shirley Frances Singleton, born in South Africa. They had three sons who served in World War II in different services, the eldest, John Singleton Jeffries, being an outstanding army field medical officer.

Lew Jeffries's youngest brother, Shirley Williams, was a South Australian attorney-general and minister for education, and was knighted. The eldest of his three sisters,

Elsie, was decorated for her Army nursing service in France. Survived by his sons, Jeffries died in the Royal Adelaide Hospital on 6 October 1971 and his ashes lie in Centennial Park cemetery.

A. G. Butler (ed), *Official history of the Australian Army Medical Services... 1914-19*, 2 (Canb, 1940); *London Gazette*, 14 Nov 1916, 2 Jan, 1 June 1917, 3 June 1919; L. W. Jeffries personal narrative, A. G. Butler collection (AWM); Family papers and information supplied by Dr J. S. Jeffries, Woodforde, SA.

C. M. GURNER

JEFFRIES, MAUD EVELYN CRAVEN (1869-1946), actress, was born on 14 December 1869 at Willow Farm, near Lula, Mississippi, United States of America, daughter of James Kenilworth Jeffries, cotton planter, and his wife Elizabeth Field, née Smith. At Miss Higbee's school at Nashville, Tennessee, she took part in amateur theatricals. In 1889 she went to New York where she played bit parts at Daly's Theatre for a year. On 4 December 1890 she made her London début in Wilson Barrett's production of *The people's idol*. With a speed that she found disconcerting she became his leading lady. Returning to U.S.A. she created the part of Mercia in Barrett's melodrama, *The sign of the Cross*, at St Louis on 28 March 1895 and next year took it to London where her 'grace, ... spiritualized beauty and ... air of youthful innocence' were admired.

Barrett's company visited Melbourne and Sydney in 1897-98 for J. C. Williamson [q.v.6]. Maud Jeffries starred in such established favourites as *Claudian*, *The Manxman*, *Virginius*, *The silver king*, *Othello* and a production of *Hamlet* that divided the critics. On her return to London she played two more seasons with Barrett before joining Herbert Beerbohm Tree's company.

By an arrangement between Williamson and Tree a company headed by Julius Knight and Maud Jeffries visited Australia in 1903-06. In their first production, a dramatization of Tolstoy's novel *Resurrection*, which opened at Her Majesty's Theatre, Melbourne, on 12 September 1903, her performance as Katusha was described as 'a very great triumph', 'an excellent combination of realism and restraint'. It was followed by a romantic drama, *Monsieur Beaucaire*, and *The Eternal City*, a melodrama in which she played a courtesan.

After a short Sydney season the company returned to Melbourne with a new play, *The darling of the gods*, followed by revivals. From June 1904 to February 1905 the Knight-Jeffries company toured Australia and New Zealand. At Papanui, Christ-

church, on 25 October 1904, Maud Jeffries married James Bunbury Nott (1878-1934), fifth son of Pat Hill Osborne [q.v.5]; he was a pastoralist who had recently joined the company after admiring Maud across the footlights. Despite rumours of her imminent retirement Maud Jeffries completed her touring engagements with Williamson in Melbourne and on tour. When Knight contracted typhoid fever in Sydney in May 1905, Maud's husband played Monsieur Beaucaire to her Lady Mary Carlyle, a partnership which drew repeated curtain-calls. The company gave its final performance in Adelaide on 4 May 1906 and disbanded, to the regret of its large audiences.

A tall woman with fine features, expressive eyes and long brown hair, Maud Jeffries was acclaimed by critics for her versatility, grace, sincerity, good taste and restraint. Such was her popularity by 1906 that an English company selling mortuary statuary offered photographs of her in the role of Mercia for the embellishment of gravestones. She visited U.S.A. before settling on her husband's property, Bowylie, Gundaroo, New South Wales, where she chose a secluded life, devoted to her garden and her son born in 1908; a daughter died in infancy. She returned to the stage only once in a charity performance of *Pygmalion and Galatea* in Sydney in August 1910. She died of cancer at Gundaroo on 26 September 1946 and was buried in the Anglican section of Waverley cemetery with Presbyterian forms.

Home Queen, 18 Jan, 18 Feb 1904; *The Times*, 5 Dec 1890, 6 Jan 1896; *Australasian*, 11 Dec 1897, 4 June 1898, 6 Oct 1900, 16 Apr 1904, 1 July, 14 Oct 1905, 3 Feb 1906; *Bulletin*, 7 Apr 1904; *SMH*, 19 June 1905, 2 Oct 1946, 18 May, 7 Sept 1963; information from Mr J. Osborne, Bowylie, Gundaroo, NSW.

DIANE LANGMORE

JENKIN, JOHN GRENFELL (1865-1966), Methodist minister, was born on 4 August 1865 at Kerrow Madron, Penzance, Cornwall, England, son of John Jenkin, shoemaker, and his wife, Elizabeth, née Grenfell. At 12 he came to Australia with his parents who, after a short period in New South Wales, settled at Daylesford, Victoria, as storekeepers. Educated locally, Jenkin worked as a clerk.

His family was closely associated with the Wesleyan Methodist Church and in 1890 Jenkin became a candidate for the ministry. He transferred to South Australia and after brief terms as assistant in four churches, he was in 1892 the first Methodist minister at Renmark, the new irrigation settlement. His first services were held under a gum-tree but he soon built a galvanized-iron church. After five years' probation and the completion of his studies Jenkin was ordained minister in 1895. A year as pioneer minister at Elliston, Eyre Peninsula, followed and then he volunteered for service in Western Australia.

In 1897-99 he was on the Menzies goldfields north of Kalgoorlie. Conditions were difficult: he lived in a tent and, with dogged tenacity, cycled seventy miles (113 km) over camel pads between the two centres. With iron will and spirit he established a congregation and built the first church at Menzies. He then served in five Western Australian circuits, including Perth and Fremantle and twice at Kalgoorlie. He presided over the State conference in 1913. On 30 March 1904 at South Fremantle he had married Roberta Claudine Bernier De La Grange; they had two sons. Jenkin is remembered in the family as a rather severe but concerned family man. He was interested in youth work: the young men's club he established at Boulder had 200 members and he was a chaplain to the military forces in Western Australia in 1911-17.

In 1918 Jenkin returned to South Australia and spent three years at Kapunda. In 1921 he moved to Pirie Street which for the first six years of his ministry was part of the Adelaide Central Mission. Pirie Street was the leading church of South Australian Methodism; his predecessor had been the great preacher Henry Howard [q.v.] who had drawn huge congregations. Jenkin ministered here for twelve years and maintained the church's primacy as a preaching centre. He formed a young people's institute with spiritual, literary, music and recreation branches and was president of the South Australian Conference in 1931. Strongly evangelical, he fostered the Church's missionary work in the Pacific region. He retired in 1936 but took services for another twenty years. He was a keen artist, caricaturist and photographer and a collector of minerals and gem stones.

His ministry had been distinguished for its vigorous, purposeful preaching; his congregations were always large. He was also active in several community groups, notably Rotary and the South Australian Cornish Association: in the 1920s he was a popular speaker on Cornish subjects and singer of Cornish songs. Jenkin died on 7 November 1966 at 101 and was buried in Payneham cemetery. He had said that his long life was due to 'the goodness of God, the great devotion of his wife and . . . good ancestors'. He never 'sought anyone's favour nor feared anyone's frown'.

Methodist Church of A'sia (SA), *Conference minutes*, 1967; *Aust Christian Cwlth*, 7 Apr 1933; *Mail* (Adel), 8 March 1958; *Advertiser* (Adel), 6 July 1960, 31 July 1965, 5 Aug, 8 Nov 1966; information from Mr J. Jenkin, La Trobe Univ, Melb; family scrapbooks held by Mr T. W. Jenkin, Prospect, SA.

ARNOLD D. HUNT

JENKINS, SIR GEORGE FREDERICK (1878-1957), politician and grazier, was born on 24 June 1878 in the South Australian country town of Terowie, son of George Kirkhouse Jenkins, farmer, and his wife Mary Ann, née Gordon. After education at Terowie Public School and Roseworthy Agricultural College, he was active as a debater in literary societies and began a pastoral career in the north and north-west of the State. By 1918, when he finally won the seat of Burra Burra in the House of Assembly, his pastoral holdings were considerable. He owned Neath Vale merino stud and had a part interest in Wirraminna station. He was re-elected in 1921, defeated in 1924, elected in 1927, defeated in 1930 and re-elected in 1933. He later looked back on himself as extremely conservative, but defeat taught him to take a broader view and, following the 1936 redistribution, he won Newcastle in 1938. He held it until his resignation from parliament in 1956.

Jenkins showed 'rare ability' as minister of agriculture and town planning and as assistant minister of repatriation in the Barwell [q.v.7] ministry in 1922-23. For six months in 1923-24 he held the portfolios of public works, local government and marine. On returning to parliament in 1927, he was commissioner of crown lands and minister of local government in 1927-30; in 1929 he secured the passage of the important Pastoral Amendment Act. For the first four months of 1930 he also held railways and marine; these were all in the R. L. Butler [q.v.7] government. He held the portfolios of agriculture and forests in 1944-54 in the Playford ministries. Jenkins described his record as a 'good innings'; he thought personality and persistence the most important qualities for a politician.

He played a key role in the South Australian Liberal Federation. He was president in 1924-27 and assisted in the protracted negotiations with the Country Party which led to the formation of the Liberal and Country League in 1932. He was chairman of the L.C.L.'s parliamentary party in 1933-44.

Jenkins was a moderate and practical minister who fostered research into soil conservation and passed the crucial Soil Conservation Amendment Act (1945) which controlled   indiscriminate   clearing.   He developed an advisory service within the Department of Agriculture and extended educational programmes and facilities for rural industries, including annual farmers' schools in country towns. Farmer and grazier interest-groups received his support. Jenkins was also a driving force in the rapid growth of the State's softwood forests. He was president of the Stockowners' Association of South Australia in 1931 and president of the Graziers' Federal Council of Australia in 1932.

On 2 April 1907 he had married Ruby Vera Bowen at the Southwark Baptist Church; they had three sons and two daughters. Jenkins was knighted in 1946. He died in Calvary Hospital, Adelaide, on 25 July 1957 and was buried in Centennial Park cemetery. On his retirement, Premier (Sir) Thomas Playford had said: 'his magnificent service to the State has seldom been equalled and never excelled. The fact that S.A. enjoys an agricultural advisory service second to none in Australia is due to his work and practical knowledge'.

Observer (Adel), 30 Aug 1924, 9 Apr 1927; *Advertiser* (Adel), 17 Sept 1955, 16 July 1957.

DEAN JAENSCH

JENKINS, JOHN GREELEY (1851-1923), premier, was born on 8 September 1851 at Clifford, Susquehanna, Pennsylvania, United States of America, fourth son of Evan Jenkins and his wife Mary, née Davis. His Welsh parents had migrated in 1834. After education at Wyoming Seminary, he worked on his father's farm and studied at night school until 1872 when he became a publisher's traveller. He arrived in South Australia in 1878 to represent his company and, at the end of his contract, established his own successful book-importing business. He sold this and became South Australian manager of the *Picturesque atlas of Australasia* (1886). In 1886 with C. G. Gurr he formed the firm Jenkins & Gurr, agents and auctioneers. A member of the Adelaide Literary Society, Jenkins sharpened his debating skills in its mock parliament and in 1886 was elected to the Unley City Council; in 1888 he was mayor. On 4 January 1883 he had married Jennie Mary Charlton; they had a son and a daughter.

From 1887 Jenkins, a protectionist, was a member for Sturt in the House of Assembly; after a redistribution he represented Torrens in 1902-05. He was seen as a clever, 'shrewd long-headed' Yankee and there was said to be no 'back-wounding calumny' about him. First appointed to a ministry when Thomas Playford [q.v.] re-

shuffled his 1890-92 administration, Jenkins dealt with education and the Northern Territory in 1891-92 and was commissioner of public works for six months in 1892. When C. C. Kingston [q.v.] formed his ministry in 1893, political parties had emerged. The conservative National Defence League formed an Opposition and the United Labor Party occupied the cross-benches. Jenkins was ministerialist party whip until he was again commissioner of public works in Kingston's ministry in 1894-99. Jenkins then was chief secretary in (Sir) Frederick Holder's [q.v.] ministry of December 1899-May 1901.

In 1901 Holder was elected to the Federal House of Representatives, and in May Jenkins became premier and chief secretary. Although he had been reputedly one of the more radical political figures of the 1880s and close to Kingston, Jenkins now looked elsewhere for support. He approached the Australasian National League (formerly the National Defence League) and accepted its views against franchise reform of the Legislative Council as a concession in return for support. A. H. Peake [q.v.] spoke for most former Kingstonian Liberals when he warned that the Jenkins government must not be surprised if not only Labor but other members who favoured liberal legislation turned their backs on it. The 1902 election saw Jenkins win government but, curiously, he was dependent on the votes of the A.N.L. Opposition! A critic described him as a 'political acrobat' and A.N.L. leader John Darling said: 'as the policy of the Government had been mainly taken from that of the Opposition the duty of the Opposition was to support the Ministry'. In 1904 the anomaly was formalized by Jenkins's incorporation of A.N.L. members in his ministry, with dissident Liberals forming the Opposition. In 1905 Jenkins resigned to become South Australian agent-general in London until 1908. The once ardent democrat was now passionately respectable.

As minister and premier he had been responsible for important legislation, including free education (1891), the provision of Happy Valley water to supply Adelaide, and South Australia's participation in the transcontinental railway. He also played a major role in an agreement between the States about the River Murray, and in continuing attempts to develop the Northern Territory. As chief secretary in Holder's government, he was also minister for defence and had responsibility for the four South Australian contingents to the South African War. Jenkins was a Congregationalist and a zealous teetotaller; he neither smoked nor swore. A Freemason, he was deputy grand master of Leopold Lodge in 1897-1901.

In London he was a popular agent-general with a facility for repartee; he relished his responsibilities. He argued effectively for ending double income tax for colonials in England and was vice-president of the Royal Colonial Institute where he was regarded as one of those 'most helpful men who hold others together . . . who look for avenues of agreement not difference'. He published pamphlets on Australian products and social conditions and edited the Australasian section of the *Encyclopedia Americana*. In 1908 he represented Australia at the International Telegraphic Conference, Lisbon. Next year he returned to South Australia, reportedly interested in contesting his old seat, but he arrived too late. He then attempted unsuccessfully to negotiate with Prime Minister Deakin [q.v.8] for a subsidy for his company, Papuan Lands Ltd, to develop a telegraphic link between Australia and Papua.

Jenkins returned to live in London where he became a steel importer. He was also treasurer of the London Chamber of Commerce, vice-chairman of the British Imperial Council of Commerce and a director of the International Chamber of Commerce. He attended international trade conferences in Boston (1912) and Atlantic City, U.S.A., and in Paris (1914, 1920). Survived by his wife and children, he died of pulmonary embolus following surgery on 22 February 1923 and, after a memorial service in St Clement Danes Church, was buried in Kensal Green cemetery.

J. J. Pascoe (ed), *History of Adelaide and vicinity* (Adel, 1901); *PD* (SA), 1901, p 590, 1903, p 87; *Quiz* (Adel), 20 June 1890, 24 Mar 1898, 24 May, 7 Nov 1902, 12 Feb 1904; Roy Cwlth Soc, Lond, *United Empire*, 14 (1923), p 209; *Observer* (Adel), 11 July 1891; *Australasian*, 10 July 1909; *The Times*, 23 Feb 1923; *Advertiser* (Adel), 24 Feb 1924; A1 10/330 (AAO, Canb).　　　　　DEAN JAENSCH

JENKS, EDWARD (1861-1939), professor of law, was born on 20 February 1861 at Lambeth, London, son of Robert Jenks, upholsterer, and his wife Frances Sarah, née Jones. He was educated at Dulwich College (1874-77) and King's College, Cambridge (B.A., LL.B., 1886; M.A., 1890) where he was scholar (1886) and in 1889-95, fellow. He gained the Le Bas and Thirwall prizes and was chancellor's medallist. In 1887 he was called to the Bar and for the next two years lectured at Pembroke and Jesus colleges, Cambridge.

In March 1889 Jenks was appointed first professor of law at the University of Melbourne and successor to W. E. Hearn [q.v.4] as dean of the faculty of law. But he soon felt his position at the university untenable and resigned early in 1892 after sharp confrontations with leading members of the administration, particularly the vice-chancellor (Sir) John Madden [q.v.] and Dr T. P. McInerney. In an article 'The government of universities', published in the *Centennial Magazine* in May 1890, Jenks arraigned the university council for being lax, interfering, suspicious and irritating to the teachers, who were not represented on it.

Jenks's intransigence has sometimes been blamed for the disputes; but he was not the only university teacher at loggerheads with the authorities and many of the desired changes were recommended by the investigating royal commission of 1902-04. Brilliant, sincere and fearless, in articles and public lectures he had been a vehement social critic in a time of unprecedented stress.

Though in Melbourne so briefly, Jenks left his mark. He was the first secretary, and the mainstay, of the University Extension Board. Within the faculty of law he introduced the moot. 1891 saw the publication of his book *The government of Victoria*, one of the first legal text-books in Australia to be specifically produced for students, and that year Jenks won the Yorke prize from Cambridge for his essay 'The history of the doctrine of consideration in English law'. On 14 June 1890 in Queen's College Chapel he married Annie Ingham who had followed him from England; she died after childbirth in May next year leaving a son subsequently killed in action in 1917.

On returning to England in 1892 Jenks held distinguished posts successively at University College, Liverpool, Oxford University, the Law Society, London, and the University of London. He achieved renown as a prolific writer of legal works of distinction and great diversity and as one of England's most significant legal educators. He published in 1895 *A history of the Australasian colonies*. In 1927 in the *Cambridge Law Journal* he argued that appointment of a governor-general of a British dominion should be on the advice of the relevant prime minister. With historical as well as legal talent Jenks was a notable researcher into the English Civil War, although his most provocative essay, in the *Independent Review* 1904-05, challenged the interpretation of Magna Carta. He was elected a fellow of the British Academy in 1930 and received many other academic honours.

Jenks died at Bishop's Tawton, Devonshire, on 10 November 1939, survived by his second wife Dorothy Mary, née Forwood, whom he had married in 1898, and by their son and daughter.

E. Scott, *A history of the University of Melbourne* (Melb, 1936); G. Blainey, *A centenary history of the University of Melbourne* (Melb, 1957); R. Campbell, *A history of the Melbourne Law School, 1857 to 1973* (Melb, 1977); *Independent Review*, 4 (1904-05); Society of Public Teachers of Law, *J*, 1947-51, 1959-61; *Melb Univ Law Review*, May 1973; *Argus*, 12 Apr 1890, 8 Dec 1891; Records, Univ Melb; information from Mr P. H. Northcott, Geelong, Vic.

RUTH CAMPBELL

JENNER, ISAAC WALTER (1837-1902), artist, was born on 18 March 1837 at Brighton, Sussex, England, son of Thomas Jenner, blacksmith, and his wife Harriet, née Walter. Without known formal education, he worked on oyster and crab smacks and signed on for a voyage in Arctic waters. In March 1855 he joined the Royal Navy, serving during the Crimean War in the Black Sea and in H.M.S. *Retribution* at the Dardanelles. In 1864 he was present at the bombardment of Shimonoseki, Japan. Discharged in 1865, he learned to paint and worked as a landscape and marine painter in 1873-79 at Brighton and at Hove in 1880-83; he exhibited at Brighton, Lewes and once at the Royal Academy. After trouble with picture dealers, he decided to migrate and reached Brisbane by R.M.S. *Roma* on 19 September 1883.

Jenner made a living by selling paintings, holding art unions and teaching at Miss O'Connor's School, Oxley, and at the Brisbane Technical College in 1887-89. Although he travelled in New South Wales and New Zealand in 1889, he exhibited only in Brisbane and at the Centennial International Exhibition of 1888-89 in Melbourne. He had helped to found the Queensland Art Society in 1887. He considered Brisbane lacking in taste and civilized pursuits and he felt unrecognized by the art world, even to the extent of victimization. For this reason, perhaps, he moved his studio in 1890 to Montrose Road, Taringa. There he lived and worked for the rest of his life.

A self-taught marine and landscape painter of considerable ability and technical skill, Jenner painted much local scenery but continued all his life to paint English scenes from memory. His most popular subjects were the Sussex and Cornish coasts and large historical seascapes, such as his 'H.M.S. Agamemnon in the Great Gale in the Black Sea, October 14th 1854', shown at the Queensland International Exhibition of 1897. In 1895 he gave one of his large seascapes, 'Cape Chudleigh, Labrador' (1890) to the Queensland National Gallery soon after its opening.

Stylistically, Jenner was steeped in the romantic English landscape tradition with a strong preference for dawns and sunsets. He in fact taught oil and crayon drawings (sunsets) as his special subject at the Brisbane Technical College. His own art jottings underline his interest in picturesque subjects and the importance he attached to light and harmony. His 'Precept for a Painter' has, in parts, strong Ruskinian leanings. Although his contribution to art in Brisbane was considerable, his claim to be the founder of art in the colony was at least dubious. He died at Taringa on 1 March 1902 and was buried in Toowong cemetery. He was survived by his wife Mary, née Jenkins, whom he had married on 23 May 1860 at Anthony, Cornwall, and by three sons and three daughters.

Art and Aust, 15 (Winter 1978), no 4, p 393; Jenner papers (Queensland Art Gallery); ADM 139/195 (PRO, Lond).

MARGARET MAYNARD

JENSEN, HARALD INGEMANN (1879-1966), geologist and socialist pamphleteer, was born in 1879 at Aarhus, Jutland, Denmark, son of Niels Georg Oscar Jensen, farmer and clerk, and his wife Clara, née Nielsen, who claimed descent from Bernhard Severin Ingemann (1789-1862), Denmark's great romantic poet. Migrating with his parents to Queensland at 6, Jensen attended public schools at Irvinebank, North Queensland, and Caboolture, then won a scholarship to the Brisbane Boys' Grammar School. After employment at Clement Wragge's [q.v.] Mount Kosciusko observatory in 1898, he entered the University of Sydney, withdrew to teach in Sydney and North Queensland in 1900-01 and returned in 1902, graduating B.Sc. in 1904 with honours in geology. An assistant demonstrator in geology and chemistry under (Sir) Edgeworth David [q.v.8] in 1904-05, he was appointed first Macleay [q.v.5] fellow of the Linnean Society of New South Wales in 1905. Before resigning in 1908 he travelled in Fiji, Samoa, Tonga and New Zealand and published many professional papers. Awarded a D.Sc. and the university medal in 1908, he worked in 1908-11 as a soil scientist with the New South Wales Department of Agriculture and wrote *Soils of New South Wales* (1914).

A convinced socialist from childhood, Jensen was an active member of the Labor Party and wrote *The rising tide. An exposition of Australian socialism*, which extolled New Protection as an historic compromise between capital and labour. Printed serially in the *Worker* in October 1908-March 1909, it was published separately in 1909. He continued to write regularly for Labor and union journals on politics, economics and mining. In August 1912 he was appointed director of mines in the Northern Territory in order, he believed, 'to carry out the platform and objectives of the Labor movement as far as mining is concerned'. He took with him his wife Jane Elizabeth Ellen, née England, whom he had married in Sydney on 26 September 1906, and their three children.

Soon at loggerheads with the administrator, J. A. Gilruth [q.v.], Jensen was demoted in March 1915 from his directorship of mines but remained chief geologist. Incensed, he wrote to the minister for external affairs preferring forty-three charges against the administration. The report of the subsequent royal commission in June 1916 found no justification for the allegations. Following assertions that he had made disloyal statements while the country was at war, a public service inquiry found that although the statements were improper Jensen was not disloyal. When Gilruth recommended dismissal, however, the Federal government insisted in September on his resignation.

In 1917-22 Jensen was a government geologist in Queensland. His application in 1919 for the general managership of the Chillagoe smelting plant failed. He recommended consideration of purchase of the nearby Mungana mines by government and, at a later royal commission, revealed that he knew of the private interests held in Mungana by E. G. Theodore and W. McCormack [qq.v.]. (Jensen is 'Dr Jenner' in Frank Hardy's *Power without glory*.)

Jensen was defeated as a Labor Party candidate for the Federal seat of Lilley in 1917 and again as a Senate candidate for Queensland in 1922 and 1925. Following his article in *Stead's Review* in August 1926 attacking the party's neglect of socialism, the Queensland central executive expelled him. A close friend of the elusive Daniel Green [q.v.], he published a eulogy of him after his death in 1948.

Working as a consultant geologist in 1923-38, Jensen was principally engaged in seeking oil in the Roma basin, Queensland, and in the Mandated Territory of New Guinea. In 1938-40 he led the Queensland section of the Aerial Geological and Geophysical Survey of North Australia. An excellent bushman, 6 ft. 4 ins. (193 cm) tall, he is remembered by team-mates for his ability to live hard off the land on stews brewing continuously for days, and for his love of 'geology, grog and women'.

Jensen returned to his early interest in weather prediction in 1943-56 and worked with Inigo Jones [q.v.] at his Crohamhurst laboratory. His book *Seasonal forecasting* (1956) expressed his disappointment that an interesting hypothesis could not be proved. He died after accidental electrocution in Brisbane on 13 July 1966 and was cremated. He had been divorced in 1937. Two sons and three daughters survived him.

Jensen did notable pioneering work on the petrology of the Glasshouse, Nandewar and Warrumbungle volcanic regions. He produced a useful series of geological reports on the Northern Territory and played an important part in the oil search of the 1920s. Described as 'a geologist of outstanding ability and quick perception', he was prolific in publication and internationally respected, although his restless mind sometimes jumped to conclusions without sufficient detailed investigation.

Jensen's political and geological 'visions' were combined in his advocacy of a network of state-owned railways bringing a mining surplus and cattle exports out of a North Australia where public ownership and control of land and mining would have been established. To this end, large absentee pastoral holdings would be broken up and reasonable royalties paid to the Crown by graziers as mere custodians of the wealth of the state. Economic development of Australia would then be assured by the formula, 'railways, cattle, minerals, and control of the public estate'.

K. H. Kennedy, *The Mungana affair* (Brisb, 1978); J. H. Kelly, *Struggle for the north* (Syd, 1966); R. K. Johns (ed), *History and role of government geological surveys in Australia* (Adel, 1976); A. Powell, *Far country* (Melb, 1982); Roy Soc of NSW, *J*, 45 (1912); Dansk Geol Foreningen, *Meddelelser*, 17 (1967); *Records of the Aust Academy of Science*, 2 (1970), no 1; *Worker* (Syd), 18 Feb 1909; *Bulletin*, 20 June 1912; *Daily Standard*, 6 Sept 1916; Fisher papers (NL); Jensen papers (Oxley Lib); A2 item 17/2032, A3 items NT 15/1197 16/1305, 3564, CRS A3832 RC 19 item 1 (AAO). B. J. McFARLANE

JENSEN, JENS AUGUST (1865-1936), publican and politician, was born on 2 May 1865 at Sebastopol, Ballarat, Victoria, third son of Danish gold-rush immigrants, Anthon Jensen, carpenter, and his wife Anna Marie Christine, née Peterson. Educated at Ballarat, he left school at 11 to work as a stable-boy. When he moved to Beaconsfield, Tasmania, in 1878 he found employment as rabbit-hawker and miner; in 1893 he gained a certificate of service as a mining engine driver. On 1 July 1885 at Beaconsfield he married Elizabeth Frances Broadhurst with Primitive Methodist forms. She died in 1894 leaving him with one son and four daughters. On 18 August 1896 he married Bertha Hopton, a domestic servant, at the York Street Baptist Manse, Launceston. That year Jensen built a hotel and theatre at Beaconsfield and was so successful as a publican that he was able to invest the profits in a large establishment at Beauty Point. The Beauty Point Hotel was acclaimed as 'one of the best and prettiest country hotels in the colony'. Jensen, who also acquired an orchard in the district, was a member of the Beaconsfield Town Board in 1899 and became a justice of the peace in 1908.

In 1903 he won the House of Assembly seat of George Town, identifying himself with the 'Opposition' group of liberal-democrats led by W. B. Propsting [q.v.]. In 1906 he was re-elected for George Town as an endorsed Labor candidate and in 1909 was a member for Wilmot; in October when the Labor Party briefly held office he was chief secretary. Jensen left State politics in 1910 to stand successfully for the Federal seat of Bass. Described by Melbourne *Punch* a few years later as a 20-stone (127 kg) 'giant' with 'protuberant girth and wealth of watch-chain', he impressed observers with his easy, confident manner. He often spoke in support of the Fisher [q.v.8] government's efforts to 'bring about legislation that will benefit the masses' and pressed for increased financial assistance for Tasmania. He argued that the State needed compensation for its loss of customs duties; he was chairman of a select committee on Tasmania customs leakage in 1910 and a royal commission on the same subject in 1910-11, the findings of which persuaded the government to grant the State an additional £500 000 over ten years.

Following the September 1914 elections, Jensen was appointed assistant minister for defence in the third Fisher government and in July next year was elevated to the newly created navy ministry. A pro-conscriptionist, he followed Hughes [q.v.] when the Labor Party split in November 1916 and retained his portfolio in the second Hughes government. He was appointed minister for trade and customs when Hughes formed his National ministry in 1917 and next year was president of the Board of Trade. However, in December 1918 when the report of a royal commission on navy and defence administration was released, Jensen was relieved of his ministerial post. The commissioner found that during his period as navy minister Jensen had incurred expenditure 'either without reference or in opposition to the Naval Board, and with unsatisfactory and costly results to the Commonwealth' in the purchase in 1916 of the [A.J.] Shaw [q.v.]

Wireless Works at Randwick, Sydney, and of two unsuitable small vessels, S.S. *Emerald* and S.S. *Togo*. Jensen withdrew his support from the Nationalists after this and was defeated as an Independent at the 1919 elections.

In 1922, having campaigned against the Lee [q.v.] government's conservative financial policy, Jensen was elected to the Tasmanian House of Assembly as member for Bass. He was defeated in 1925 but, following readmittance to the Labor Party in 1927, won a seat for Wilmot next year and held it until 1934. Of placid demeanour in public, Jensen was at times violent at home and showed his second wife little affection. In 1934 he gave away most of his considerable wealth to Miss Maggie Jane Gilbert, his alcoholic cousin and for thirty-seven years his mistress. He had suffered from diabetes for many years and died on 16 November 1936 of cerebro-vascular disease at South Caulfied, Melbourne. Survived by his wife and their son and daughter, he was buried in St Kilda cemetery. His remaining estate, valued at £394, was bequeathed to Miss Gilbert; the provisions of the will were unsuccessfully contested in 1937 in a much publicized case by four of the children of Jensen's first marriage.

Cyclopedia of Tasmania (Hob, 1900); E. Scott, *Australia during the war* (Syd, 1936); *British A'sian*, 6 Jan 1916; *Punch* (Melb), 4 Jan 1912, 4 Mar 1915; *Australasian*, 14 Dec 1918; *Argus*, 5-8 Oct 1937.   QUENTIN BERESFORD

JENSEN, JOERGEN CHRISTIAN (1891-1922), soldier, was born on 15 January 1891 at Loegstoer, Denmark, son of Joergen Christian Jensen, farmer and wool merchant, and Christiane, known as Jensen. Nothing is known of his childhood. He migrated to Australia alone in March 1909, having spent the previous year in England. After disembarking in Melbourne he worked as a labourer at Morgan, South Australia, and at Port Pirie, and was naturalized on 7 September 1914 in Adelaide.

Jensen enlisted as a private in the Australian Imperial Force on 23 March 1915, was posted to the 6th Reinforcements for the 10th Battalion and joined his unit at Gallipoli in August. The battalion left the peninsula on 22 November for a rest period at Lemnos and did not return before the evacuation. Jensen moved from Egypt to France in March 1916. On 14 August he was wounded in action and after recovering was transferred to the 50th Battalion on 28 January 1917.

Jensen won the Victoria Cross for 'most conspicuous bravery and initiative' on 2

April at Noreuil, one of the 'outpost villages' of the Hindenburg line. During its long advance towards the village the 50th Battalion came under enfiladed fire from a German forward machine-gun post which caused heavy casualties. Jensen, covered by another private, rushed the post with bombs. After eliminating the machine-gun crew with one of his bombs he threatened to throw the others and bluffed the German position into surrendering, taking about forty prisoners. Later that day, after a fierce fight, Noreuil was captured. Jensen served from July to October with the 13th Training Battalion and returned to the 50th on 6 October; he had been promoted lance corporal on 4 April, corporal on 4 July and temporary sergeant on 5 October. He was seriously wounded on 5 May 1918 while on patrol near Villers-Bretonneux and was invalided to Australia on 26 August.

Jensen was discharged from the A.I.F. in Adelaide on 12 December 1918 with the rank of corporal. After demobilization he worked as a bottle-oh. He married a divorcee Katy Herman, née Arthur, at the Adelaide Registry Office on 13 July 1921. Admitted to Adelaide Hospital in alcoholic mania, Jensen died shortly afterwards on 31 May 1922. His wife later remarried.

C. E. W. Bean, *The A.I.F. in France*, 1917 (Syd, 1933); C. B. L. Lock, *The fighting 10th . . . A.I.F., 1914-19* (Adel, 1936); L. Wigmore (ed) *They dared mightily* (Canb, 1963); *London Gazette*, 8 June 1917; *Advertiser* (Adel), 1 June 1922; *Observer* (Adel), 3 June 1923.   H. J. ZWILLENBERG

JEPHCOTT, SYDNEY WHEELER (1864-1951), poet and farmer, was born on 30 November 1864 at Nariong, Upper Murray, Victoria, fifth child of Edwin Jephcott and his wife Susannah, née Sansome, ribbon weavers from Coventry, Warwickshire, England. On his cattle-farm at Ournie, Upper Murray, Edwin established an arboretum of diverse species of exotic trees grown from seeds provided by (Sir) Ferdinand Mueller [q.v.5] on a visit in 1874. Sydney and his family collected rare native specimens, including *grevillea Jephcottii*, for Mueller, who in 1886 sent Charles French [q.v.8] on an alpine botanical expedition with Sydney as guide.

Jephcott, who never attended a school but read widely from his father's library, claimed that living alone in a tent in the mountains from the age of 12 was the 'chief formative influence' on his mind. He began to write verse in the late 1870s, after meeting Henry Kendall [q.v.5]; the first of his poems in the Sydney *Bulletin* appeared in December 1889. The poet John Farrell [q.v.4] introduced him to several writers, including Francis Adams [q.v.3] who in England saw Jephcott's *The secrets of the south: Australian poems* (London, 1892) through the press. Jephcott then completed an unpublished critical selection of Adams's poems. Through Rose Scott [q.v.] he became an avuncular confidant of the young Stella Miles Franklin [q.v.8]. A novel in progress about the Monaro, discussed with her in 1905, was never published. His poems *Penetralia* (Melbourne) appeared in 1912.

Bardic and meditative, Jephcott's verse pursues ethical and metaphysical speculations in a mood of solitary, sensuous loftiness frequently evoked in relation to mountainous Australian landscape. Despite poetic overcrowding and crudity, at its best it is urgent and vital and, in the tradition of Charles Harpur [q.v.1] and Francis Adams, seeks to open 'new avenues of sensation to . . . Truth and Beauty' in order to cultivate public awareness of 'the vital Ideal in our national existence'. A democrat and Federationist, Jephcott discerned a prevailing Australian spiritual and political complacency, and to his long-time correspondent Alfred Deakin [q.v.8] castigated 'the besotted worship of selfishness in national affairs'.

Jephcott remained a cattle-farmer throughout his life. On 29 January 1896 he had married Rebecca Snadden Dickson (d. 1935) at Richmond, Melbourne, in a service of the Australian Church performed by Rev. Charles Strong [q.v.6]. The couple lived first on the Upper Murray's Victorian bank, moved across to Ournie, then after the 1902 drought to Crewar in the southern Monaro, New South Wales, returning to Ournie in 1914 after the theft of their cattle. Jephcott campaigned for Deakin's Liberal Protectionists, and wrote political leaders for the Albury press. He served on the Towong Shire Council (Victoria) for one term and on the Tumbarumba Shire (New South Wales) for two. At Ournie he fondly maintained and extended his inherited arboretum, and contributed articles on trees and pasturage to the *Sydney Morning Herald*. Described by Nettie Palmer [q.v.] as 'full of humour and vision', he wrote verse and kept up literary friendships until he died at Albury on 3 July 1951. Survived by three sons and two daughters, he was buried in the Anglican section of Corryong (Victoria) cemetery.

B.P. Mag, Sept 1941; *Aust Q*, Mar 1944; *Southerly*, 13 (1952); *Riverlander*, Dec 1963, Jan, Feb, Mar 1964; *Corryong Courier*, 31 July, 7 Aug 1968; Deakin papers (NL); S. M. Franklin papers (ML); information from Mrs Lois Jephcott, Corryong, Vic.   KEN STEWART

JERGER, CHARLES ADOLPH (1869-1927), Catholic priest, was born on 5 January 1869 at St Blasien, Baden, son of Philip Jacob Morlock (d. 1869), land surveyor, and his wife Wilhelmina, née Ellenwohn, a Catholic, and was baptised in his father's Evangelical faith. In 1870 or 1871 his mother married John Jerger, born at Niedereschach in 1842. They moved about 1875 to Plymouth, England, where Charles was educated at Beaconsfield College, and migrated to Sydney in 1888. He finished his schooling at Parramatta, worked in a jeweller's shop at Goulburn and there joined the Roman Catholic Congregation of the Passion on 10 April 1893. He made his profession on 9 May 1894 and was ordained priest at Goulburn on 21 May 1899. While based at Goulburn and, after April 1915, at Marrickville, Sydney, he preached in many parts of Australia.

After a sermon at Marrickville on 24 September 1916 a parishioner officially complained that Jerger had expressed disloyal sentiments calculated to discourage enlistment in the Australian Imperial Force. On investigation by the police he denied making any such statements and visited Melbourne to seek help from Hugh Mahon and explain his position to the minister for defence (Sir) George Pearce [qq.v.]. He was interviewed by Major E. L. Piesse [q.v.], head of military intelligence, and registered as an alien. Jerger had mistakenly believed himself to be a naturalized British subject: but his mother had not been naturalized when a widow and he was not covered by his stepfather's naturalization.

Late in 1917 Jerger was again accused of conducting an anti-British campaign and interned on 15 February 1918 under the War Precautions Regulations (1915). The charges against him were never specified. Leading churchmen, especially Archbishops Mannix and Kelly [qq.v.], made efforts, and the Catholic Federation organized popular agitation, to secure his release; it was opposed by Protestant groups and the Loyalty League. P. M. Glynn [q.v.] repeatedly brought his case before cabinet and the Department of Defence. At the Holsworthy internment camp (where he was Catholic chaplain) Jerger was aggressive and volatile, claiming that he was persecuted and thwarted. His tactlessness and obstinacy did not help his cause.

A stipendiary magistrate, sitting as the Aliens Board, recommended that Jerger's internment be continued. In 1919 the royal commission on the release of internees twice considered Jerger's case and twice reported that the magistrate's decision should be upheld. Cabinet approved and the solicitor-general Sir Robert Garran [q.v.8] advised deportation on 29 March 1920. In June Garran heard evidence from Fr Jerger, but reported that his attitude was German and that during the war he had expressed his German sympathies. Jerger's counsel T. J. Ryan [q.v.] was not allowed to appear. The failure to examine witnesses heightened the feeling that Jerger had been unfairly treated. Demonstrations were organized and court actions and the threat of strikes were used in an attempt to keep him in the country. The full bench of the High Court of Australia found that he had failed to establish that he was a British subject. John Wren [q.v.] and other supporters unsuccessfully challenged the validity of the War Precautions Act and issued writs of habeas corpus.

Jerger had been released on 30 April 1920 but was rearrested on 7 July. He was eventually deported from Adelaide in July. The issue was no longer a simple sectarian dispute: the labour movement protested at the deportation and there were bitter divisions in both Catholic and Protestant groups on the question of Jerger's loyalty and his right to remain in Australia.

After his deportation Jerger lived in Holland, Chicago, United States of America (where his brother was a doctor), Dublin and in England at Herne Bay, Kent. He died in London, after an operation, on 11 September 1927 and was buried in the grounds of the Passionist Monastery, Highgate.

E. Scott, *Australia during the war* (Syd, 1936); P. J. O'Farrell, *The Catholic Church and the community in Australia: a history* (Melb, 1977); *PD* (Cwlth), 1917-19, p 4152 ff, 1920-21, p 2833 ff, 2918, 3723, 4921; *PP* (NSW), 1918, 1, p 627 ff; *Cwlth Law Reports*, 27, 28; *Labour Hist*, Nov 1976, no 31; P. L'Estrange, Alien and alienated: the case of Charles Jerger 1916-1920 (B.A. Hons thesis, Univ Melb, 1974); PM's correspondence files, items 1920/496, 3319, S.C. H25/1, F42/1 *and* Attorney-General's Dept, correspondence files, items W8/4[163], [208] *and* Governor-General's Office, general correspondence, item 1920/1025 (AAO, Canb); Dept of Defence, general correspondence, MP 367/1, items 512/3/1109, 567/3/3432, 567/8/2239 *and* Common Law Files, MP 401/1, items CL 1126, 1126A (AAO, Melb); Passionist Fathers, Archives (St Ives, NSW); Glynn *and* Hughes *and* Mahon papers (NL).

P. L'ESTRANGE

JERSEY, SIR VICTOR ALBERT GEORGE CHILD-VILLIERS, 7th EARL OF (1845-1915), governor, was born on 20 March 1845 at Berkeley Square, London, eldest son of George Augustus Frederick Villiers, 6th Earl, and his wife Julia, eldest daughter of Prime Minister Sir Robert Peel. An Eton schoolboy when in 1859 he succeeded to the earldom and great landhold-ings of about 20 000 acres (8090 ha), he matriculated at Balliol College, Oxford, in April 1864. Prodigality in his minority led to racing debts and he abandoned the turf. On 19 September 1872 at Marylebone he married Margaret Elizabeth, daughter of William Henry, 2nd Baron Leigh of Stoneleigh. A Conservative, Jersey was lord-in-waiting to the Queen in 1875-77 and paymaster-general in 1889-90. Selected as governor of New South Wales in July 1890, he was appointed G.C.M.G. He arrived in Sydney on 15 January 1891, reputedly bring-ing 'a large supply of drinking water' and 'a number of bathtubs'. His wife, delayed by a bout of typhoid fever, arrived in March.

The *Argus* reported that Jersey had a 'commanding presence, standing fully 6ft. [183 cm] tall'; but to a *Bulletin* correspon-dent he was 'small and somewhat baggy'. His nose was large and aquiline, he had mutton-chop whiskers and red hair which he combed 'cranewise over his globe-shaped cerebrum'. Sir Henry Parkes [q.v.5] found the new governor 'amiable and well-intentioned', but 'very much occupied with his own family'. Jersey 'did not excel as a public speaker', unlike his wife. A supporter of Federation, he was official host at the 1891 Australasian National Convention in Sydney. No major political difficulty dis-turbed his term.

To the vexation of the Colonial Office, Jersey prematurely tendered his resig-nation in November 1892 on the grounds of pressing business affairs. He wrote to the secretary of state: 'the duties and responsi-bilities of a governor can hardly be called serious nowadays being chiefly of a social character'. Lord Salisbury [q.v.3 Cecil] be-lieved Jersey had found that there was 'less individual power to his office than he im-agined'. Jersey left Sydney on 2 March 1893.

Next year he represented the United Kingdom at the colonial economic confer-ence in Ottawa. He was appointed G.C.B. in 1900. In 1903-05 he acted as New South Wales agent-general in London: his close connexion with banking institutions (he was principal proprietor of Child's Bank) helped the State's loan negotiations. He revisited Australia in 1905. Deakin [q.v.8] contem-plated appointing Jersey first Australian high commissioner in London. An active Freemason, he was senior grand warden of England and provincial grand master of Ox-fordshire.

Invalided by a stroke in 1909, Jersey died at his beautiful home, Osterley Park, Middlesex, on 31 May 1915, survived by his wife, two sons and three daughters. Lady Jersey, founding president (1901-14) of the Victoria League, an opponent of women's suffrage, and author of travel articles, chil-dren's plays, verse and *Fifty-one years of Vic-torian life* (1922), was appointed D.B.E. in 1927. She died at Middleton Park, Oxford-shire, on 22 May 1945, aged 95.

DNB, 1912-21 and 1941-50; V. Powell, *Margaret: Countess of Jersey* (Lond, 1978); A. W. Martin, *Henry Parkes* (Melb, 1980); *Argus*, 28 July 1890; *Bulletin*, 27 Sept 1890, 17, 24 Jan, 14 Feb 1891; *The Times*, 1 June 1915; *SMH*, 2 June 1915; Hopetoun House MSS (AJCP, NL); Ripon papers (British Lib, Lond).
　　　　　　　　　　　　　　　　　　CHRIS CUNNEEN

JESS, SIR CARL HERMAN (1884-1948), soldier, was born on 16 February 1884 at Sandhurst (Bendigo), Victoria, one of nine children of George Jess, a master painter from Schleswig-Holstein, and his Irish-born wife Mary, née Talty, who was illiterate. He was educated at the Violet Street State School, Bendigo, and taught there in 1899-1906.

In parallel with his career as a teacher Jess displayed an interest in military life, joining in 1899 the 1st Battalion, Victorian Volun-teer Cadets, in which he became a colour sergeant, and beginning a lifelong hobby of making coloured sketches of regimental uniforms. In February 1902 he enlisted in the militia 5th Battalion, Victorian Infantry, and over the next four years reached the rank of sergeant. Resigning his position with the Victorian Education Department in June 1906, he joined the permanent staff of the Australian Military Forces as an in-structor with the rank of staff sergeant, be-coming staff sergeant major next year.

After qualifying in 1908 as an officer on the Administrative and Instructional Staff, Jess was appointed lieutenant on 1 July 1909 and allotted for duty in New South Wales. Granted the temporary rank of captain in January 1911 (confirmed July 1912), he be-came brigade major to the 5th Infantry Brig-ade until transferred to Victoria in Novem-ber 1911 to become staff captain responsible for administering the new national scheme of compulsory military training in that State. In 1912 he attended the diploma course conducted by the department of mili-tary science at the University of Sydney. He was appointed to the instructional staff in Victoria in July 1913 and a year later was transferred to South Australia as deputy as-sistant adjutant general. He married Mar-jory Mary McGibbon at St Luke's Anglican Church, North Fitzroy, Melbourne, on 15 July 1914.

When Colonel (Sir) John Monash [q.v.] was appointed in September 1914 to com-mand the 4th Infantry Brigade, Australian Imperial Force, he selected Jess as staff captain on his headquarters. Despite a whispering campaign concerning his German origins in October, Jess embarked on active service in December. He served throughout the Dardanelles campaign and, during fighting on 2-3 May 1915 and on 7 August, showed himself to be a tireless front-line organizer. From 23 May he was brigade major of the 2nd Brigade with the rank of major. He was mentioned in dispatches in June and in 1916 the Serbian Order of the White Eagle was conferred for his Gallipoli service.

With the return of the A.I.F. to Egypt Jess took command of the 7th Battalion on 28 February 1916 and was promoted lieut-colonel from 12 March. He retained command until March 1917 and temporarily led the 2nd Brigade for two months from late November 1916. He was awarded the Distinguished Service Order in December for his work during the battle of Pozières, when he was gassed but remained on duty; a second mention in dispatches followed next month.

In March 1917 Jess was seconded for duty in England as an instructor at the Senior Officers' School, Aldershot, the first Dominion officer to hold such an appointment. In September he was appointed general staff officer, grade 2, Headquarters, 1st Anzac Corps, after which he became general staff officer, grade 1, in Major General Monash's 3rd Division on 20 January 1918. Monash declared Jess to be 'easily the best man in sight for the job'.

Promoted colonel and temporary brigadier general in October, Jess assumed command of the 10th Brigade—at 34 one of the youngest brigadiers in the British service. He was mentioned in dispatches again on 31 December and next day was appointed C.M.G. for his service during the battle of Amiens. From March 1919 he commanded the A.I.F. Training Depot at Codford, England, and in July he became commandant at A.I.F. Headquarters, London. He additionally acted as director general of repatriation and demobilization, vice Monash, and officiated as general officer commanding, A.I.F., relieving General Sir William Birdwood [q.v.7], for several months until January 1920. For his work in winding up A.I.F. affairs overseas he was appointed C.B.E. in October.

Jess's A.I.F. appointment was terminated on 21 January and he reverted to peacetime rank of lieut-colonel, A.M.F., but instead of returning to Australia he joined the Staff College at Camberley, completing the course with an 'A' class certificate and a grading as an 'officer of Exceptional Merit'. Returning to Australia in February 1921 he resumed instructional duties in Victoria until May when he became a staff officer

on the headquarters of the militia 4th Division. Early in 1925 he was transferred to Tasmania as commandant of the 6th Military District and in April 1926 was promoted colonel. He was also State marshal during the royal visit to Tasmania by the duke and duchess of York in May 1927.

Next August Jess was appointed district commandant in Western Australia, being promoted brigadier in January 1929 and made aide-de-camp to the governor-general for four years from June 1931. From January 1932 he commanded the 4th Division and also became base commandant in Victoria. After his organizational involvement in centenary celebrations in Western Australia he was invited in 1933 by the premier, Sir Stanley Argyle [q.v.7], to organize Victoria's centenary celebrations. The army released him from May 1933 to November 1934; he was knighted in the 1935 New Year honours.

In December 1934 Jess had been appointed adjutant general of the A.M.F. and second member of the Military Board. He was promoted major general in July 1935. Reputedly because of a personality clash on the board between Jess and the chief of the General Staff, Major General J. D. Lavarack, the government decided to re-establish the post of inspector general of the forces and to offer the appointment to Lieut-General E. K. Squires of the British Army in 1938. In May 1939 Jess, on advice of the judge advocate general, challenged the legality of Squires's appointment as acting chief of the General Staff but was overruled by the minister for defence on the advice of the solicitor-general. In August he was notified that by government decision he was to be retired, but this notification was cancelled next month when war began. At the request of the minister he became chairman of the manpower committee within the Department of Defence with local rank of lieut-general on 12 October.

Jess, as adjutant general, was initially appointed chairman of the manpower committee when it was established in September 1938 but, because of his preoccupation with increasing the militia to 70 000, it had been decided in November to appoint Major General Sir Thomas Blamey. He resumed chairmanship when Blamey was appointed to command the 6th Division of the 2nd A.I.F. His work in the expansion of the forces and completion of mobilization arrangements was recognized when he was appointed C.B. in June 1939.

The main duties of the services' manpower committee were absorbed by the manpower priorities board of the Commonwealth Department of Labour and National Service in August 1941, but Jess retained the chairmanship of the committee until March 1944 and additionally became deputy chairman of the new body. He was seconded from the army to become Services adviser to the director general of manpower and was promoted lieut-general on 1 September 1942. During the year he also organized the Australian Women's Land Army and in 1943 assumed additional duties as director of women's national services in the Department of Labour and National Service.

After relinquishing his position on the manpower committee in March 1944 Jess commenced special duty in connexion with the survey and classification of army records, during which he compiled a report on the activities of the A.M.F. from 1929 to 1939. This work lasted until July 1945 and was unfinished when he went on sick leave. On 1 April 1946 he was placed on the retired list because of invalidity.

Jess died intestate, of pulmonary tuberculosis, at the Heidelberg Repatriation Hospital, Melbourne, on 16 June 1948 and was cremated with full military honours. He was survived by his wife, a son John David Jess who was a member of Federal parliament in 1960-72, and a daughter. His elder son Carl McGibbon, a lieutenant in the 2nd A.I.F., was killed in action at Tobruk in 1941.

In 1945-46 the Australian War Memorial, acting on a suggestion by C. E. W. Bean [q.v.7], purchased part of Jess's unique collection of original water-colours featuring British and Australian Army uniforms from 1853. Bas-relief models of military figures, carved and hand-painted by Jess, are displayed at the Royal Military College, Duntroon. His portrait, painted in 1919 by John Longstaff [q.v.], is in the Australian War Memorial collection.

Described by Sir Sydney Rowell as a 'striking figure', Jess was largely self educated; 'he had a most inventive brain, was a master of expediency and had an ability to teach quite above the normal. He was steeped in the tradition of the army and had hardly an interest outside the service'. He had a deep admiration for Monash, with whom he associated the 'happiest and best' periods of his service in the A.I.F. Monash wrote in July 1921 that 'out of regard for our personal friendship of many years I rejoice that you, at least, belong to that meagre minority who achieved, by their sterling performances, what they were justly entitled to'.

Although Jess reputedly had some rough autocratic ways, it was said of him that he always manifested a remarkable aptitude for throwing himself whole-heartedly into whatever position demanded his attention. His rise from the bottom rank is one of the more remarkable personal stories of Australia's army.

C. E. W. Bean, *The story of Anzac* (Syd, 1921, 1924), and *The A.I.F. in France* 1916-18 (Syd, 1929, 1933, 1937, 1942); A. Dean & E. W. Gutteridge, *The Seventh Battalion, A.I.F.* (Melb, 1933); F. M. Cutlack (ed), *War letters of General Monash* (Syd, 1934); S. F. Rowell, *Full circle* (Melb, 1974); G. Serle, *John Monash: a biography* (Melb, 1982); *London Gazette*, 3 Aug 1915, 29 Dec 1916, 2 Jan, 13 Feb 1917, 27, 31 Dec 1918, 19 Oct 1920, 1 Jan 1935, 8 June 1939; *Herald* (Melb), 1 Feb 1919, 9 Mar 1934, 17 Aug 1939, 17 June 1948; *Australasian*, 10 Sept 1927; *Table Talk*, 25 May 1933; *Argus*, 19 May 1933, 12 Dec 1934, 1 Jan 1938, 18 June 1948; *Age*, 30 Nov 1934; *Sun* (Syd), 29 July 1939; *SMH*, 11, 14 Nov 1941; *Bulletin*, 30 June 1948; Monash papers (NL); records (AWM), also AWM file 895/3/9; information and family papers from Mr J. D. Jess, Hawthorn, Vic.

C. D. COULTHARD-CLARK

JESSEP, THOMAS (1848-1916), fruit merchant and politician, was born on 1 November 1848 at Gooderstone, Norfolk, England, son of Thomas Jessep, farmer, and his wife Jane, née Cooper. He reached Hobart Town in 1854 with his mother and elder brother James; his father had died on the voyage. In 1861 he began work as a farmhand and five years later left for the Victorian diggings. Unsuccessful, he arrived in Sydney in 1869.

Starting as a carrier, in 1874 Jessep moved into the fruit trade and by the early 1880s was a well-established wholesale fruit merchant, operating as a commission agent for intercolonial, New Zealand and, particularly, Fijian producers. His speciality was bananas, and he later encouraged their cultivation in the New Hebrides and Papua. When in 1890 the Sydney Municipal Council proposed moving the fruit market from the Queen Victoria site to the Haymarket, many merchants and growers formed a cooperative and established their own market, the Fruit Exchange, in Bathurst Street. Jessep was, until his death, its chairman. For many years he was president of the Fruit Merchants' Association of New South Wales and appeared as an expert witness before several inquiries into the industry. By the late 1880s prosperity had enabled him to build a large residence, Norfolk House, at Waverley.

An alderman on Waverley Municipal Council in 1889-90 and 1892, he represented Brisbane Ward on Sydney Municipal Council in 1893-1900. In 1896, at a by-election, he was elected to the Legislative Assembly for Waverley as a free trader, holding the seat in 1898, 1901 and 1904 as a Liberal. Although defeated in 1907 (by liquor and sporting interests) and again in 1910 (for Camperdown), he remained active in party matters.

A committed evangelical Methodist, Jessep became experienced in public speaking as a lay preacher. For nearly twenty-eight years he was superintendent of the Waverley Methodist Sunday School. His was an evangelical rather than a denominational Christianity. His arrival in Sydney had coincided with an outburst of sectarianism and the formation of Catholic and Protestant sectarian subcultures. In 1870 he joined the Loyal Orange Institution of New South Wales; he was grand secretary (1883-85 and 1911-12), deputy grand master (1886-88) and grand master (1889). In 1915 he was president of the grand council of the Loyal Orange Institution of Australasia. For many years he was a chairman of the Protestant Hall Co. Ltd and in 1901 was a foundation member of the Australian Protestant Defence Association and a member of the Evangelical Council of New South Wales. He had been secretary of the New South Wales Total Abstinence Society in 1871 and was prominent in local option campaigns in 1907 and 1916. Temperance organizations endorsed him in his election campaigns. His main political interest was moral reform: local option, control of music halls, prevention of gambling. Although he never returned 'Home' he retained a British identity: 'I am a loyal Britisher, not a loyal Australian', he once testily remarked. Both his commercial interests and his sectarianism pushed him to the Liberal side of politics, but he placed his commercial interests before parliamentary duties. He was, however, an important link between Protestant sectarianism, wowserism and commerce that provided the Liberal party with its main electoral base in the first decade of the twentieth century.

On 7 November 1916 Jessep died of cancer and was buried in Waverley cemetery. He was survived by his wife Louisa, née Drury, whom he had married in Sydney on 10 April 1873, and by four daughters and three of their four sons.

W. A. Stewart (ed), *Early history of the Loyal Orange Institution, N.S.W.* (Syd, 1926); R. L. Broome, *Treasure in earthen vessels* (Brisb, 1980); *PP* (NSW), 1913, 3, p 467, (Cwlth), 1913, 4 (59), p 1111; *SMH*, 8 May 1871, 8 Nov 1916; *Protestant Standard*, 25 Aug 1883, 5 Aug 1885, 11 Feb 1888; *Methodist* (Syd), 18 Nov 1916; M. Lyons, Aspects of sectarianism in New South Wales circa 1865 to 1880 (Ph.D. thesis, ANU, 1972).   MARK LYONS

JOBSON, ALEXANDER (1875-1933), public accountant, soldier and financial writer, was born on 2 April 1875 at Clunes, Victoria, son of Christopher Jobson, English-born merchant, and his second wife Elizabeth Cameron, née McColl, from Scotland. Educated at Clunes State School and Eton (Queensland) Public School, at 14 Jobson started as a junior clerk with the Australian Mutual Provident Society in Melbourne. He studied accountancy and in 1896 qualified as Associate of the Institute of Actuaries (London).

Jobson moved to Sydney in 1902 and became actuary for Australasia for the Equitable Life Assurance Society of the United States of America. On 5 September 1905 he married Madaline Ruth, daughter of Judge Alfred McFarland [q.v.5], at St Thomas Anglican Church, North Sydney, and next year began his own business as a consulting accountant and actuary. In 1910-16 he also wrote on company finances in his column 'Profit and loss' which appeared weekly in the Sydney *Sun*. He was noted for his frank analysis; indeed, his criticisms of the Co-operative Assurance Co. resulted in the *Sun* and Jobson being sued for £50 000 damages for libel in 1914. The action was unsuccessful, Jobson's article being considered 'fair comment on a matter of public interest'.

Jobson devoted much time to military activities. He had joined the Victorian Scottish Regiment in August 1898, was commissioned in December 1899 and promoted captain in August 1902. On moving to Sydney he transferred to the New South Wales Scottish Rifles with the rank of lieutenant and was promoted captain in 1903 and major in 1909. He transferred in that rank to the 25th Infantry Regiment in July 1912, and next July was promoted lieut-colonel and appointed to command the 34th Infantry Regiment, Australian Military Forces. In July 1915 he took command of the 35th Infantry Regiment but on 10 February 1916 he was appointed to the Australian Imperial Force with the rank of colonel to command the 9th Infantry Brigade. He was promoted temporary brigadier general and in May embarked at Sydney.

Jobson's brigade reached France in November after training in England and saw action first in the Armentières sector in November-December 1916, then at Houplines, Le Touquet, Ploegsteert and Messines. Jobson was mentioned in dispatches on 1 June 1917 and recalled the preparations for, and participation in, the battle of Messines as the most interesting part of his war service. Twice during the earlier months of 1917, during Major General (Sir) John Monash's [q.v.] absence, he temporarily commanded the 3rd Division. Although Monash had praised his 'active mind and great industry' and placed great trust in his leadership at Messines, Jobson was not by nature suited for active command. C. E. W. Bean [q.v.7] commented that he was 'a man of many fine and endearing qualities, of marked ability and absolute probity, but constitutionally incapable of facing battle conditions'. Offered the opportunity to resign by Monash, Jobson accepted. On 25 August he relinquished command of the 9th Brigade and on 9 December his A.I.F. appointment was terminated. That month he was again mentioned in dispatches and was awarded the Distinguished Service Order in the 1918 New Year honours.

After returning home Jobson became State president of the New South Wales branch of the Returned Sailors' and Soldiers' Imperial League of Australia in 1918. In October that year he was given command of the 2nd Battalion, 53rd Infantry Regiment, A.M.F., with the rank of lieutcolonel and honorary brigadier general, and in December 1919 was promoted colonel. In February 1921 he was transferred to the reserve of officers. In January 1918 he had resumed his financial writing in Sydney newspapers and in 1920 he began publication of the *Australian investment digest* (later to be called *Jobson's investment digest of Australia and New Zealand*), a monthly publication summarizing and criticizing latest company reports. A fellow of the Australasian Corporation of Public Accountants, and generally acknowledged as one of the keenest and most searching of financial critics, he established a considerable professional reputation. He held numerous business directorates; in particular he was appointed a director of the A.M.P. Society in 1925 and vice-chairman in 1932.

Survived by his wife and only child Alexander, Jobson collapsed and died in King Street, Sydney, from coronary artery occlusion on 7 November 1933 and was cremated with Presbyterian forms. His estate was sworn for probate at £11 102. One of his sisters, Nancy Jobson [q.v.], was a prominent educationist and another, Isabella Kate Jobson, saw active service as a nursing sister in World War I.

C. E. W. Bean, *The A.I.F. in France*, 1916-18 (Syd, 1929, 1933, 1937, 1942); *London Gazette*, 1 June, 25, 28 Dec 1917; *SMH*, 7 Apr 1906, 2-4 July 1914, 2 Jan 1918, 21 June 1923, 8, 11 Nov 1933; *Sun* (Syd), 6 July 1914, 24 Apr 1916, 10 Jan, 22 Mar 1918; *Punch* (Melb), 4 May 1916; A. Jobson file, war records section (AWM).

COLIN FORSTER

JOBSON, NANCY (1880-1964), headmistress, was born on 17 April 1880 at Clunes, Victoria, daughter of Christopher Jobson, merchant from Northumberland, England, and his second wife Elizabeth Cameron, née

McColl (d. 1926). Educated at Presbyterian Ladies' College, Melbourne, in 1897 she entered the University of Melbourne (B.A., 1900; M.A., 1902). Later she became senior resident and sports mistress at P.L.C. In 1910-18 she was headmistress of Southland Girls' High School, Invercargill, New Zealand, and in 1919 first principal of the Presbyterian, Queen Margaret College in Wellington. After two years she moved to Queensland to become headmistress of Fairholme Presbyterian Girls' College, Toowoomba. In 1921 she was appointed principal of the Presbyterian Ladies' College, Pymble, Sydney.

Part of a new wave of Australian headmistresses, Miss Jobson partly abandoned the traditional goals of academic attainments and examination success, and hoped to interest her girls in 'excellence' in home management and the cultivation of refined manners and artistic sense. Emphasizing the differences between the schooling of boys and girls and the importance of 'woman's sphere' in the family and home life, she introduced courses in domestic science and music. She tried to instil a female ethic of service to the community: the school supported welfare work in hospitals and most senior girls joined the Christian-based Toc H. In November 1924 she outlined her views in an article, 'The education of girls', in the *Australian Teacher*. She visited Italy, 'that land of art, history and beauty' in 1928.

Enrolment grew from 256 in 1921 to 414 in 1929 and the number of boarders from 95 to 161. However the Depression brought a crisis: by 1932 enrolment was only 208. Among other economies, the school council wished to close Grey House where Miss Jobson had lived with a few senior boarders. She resisted the move strongly and in November 1932 the council gave her six months notice. In what became a matter of public knowledge and legal dispute, she appealed to the Presbyterian Assembly, but finally accepted a settlement and resigned in mid-1933. Next year Miss Jobson founded Hopewood House, a finishing school for girls which concentrated on homecraft and secretarial studies; it closed in 1943. Her last active years were spent at the International Correspondence Schools, teaching Latin, Greek, English and logic. She was appointed M.B.E. in 1955.

Tall, rather impressive, but aloof, Miss Jobson depended often on others for support and help: her mother lived with her, and her sister Jeanie, who had earlier taught at Ballarat High School and whose letters to the troops were published in 1917, assisted Nancy at Toowoomba and at P.L.C., before being killed in an Italian railway accident in 1925. Her companion at P.L.C. Winifred

Wilson and Florence Suiter, a domestic science teacher, accompanied her to Hopewood House. They lived together in retirement at 10 Hope Street, Pymble, where Nancy Jobson died on 22 June 1964; she was cremated. Her brother Alexander [q.v.] was a soldier and financial reporter.

J. Jobson, *Cheering letter to the Australian troops at the front...* (Melb, 1917); M. O. Reid, *The ladies came to stay* (Melb, 1960); M. D. Gambrill, *A history of Queen Margaret College* (Wellington, 1969); Hopewood House, *Prospectus and booklet of photographs* (np, nd); Presbyterian Church of NSW, *Minutes of proceedings of General Assembly*, 1921-33; Presbyterian Ladies' College, Pymble, *Magazine*, 1921-33; *SMH*, 9 June 1955, 23 June 1964; Presbyterian Ladies' Colleges, Council minutes (Presbyterian Library, Assembly Hall, Syd); information from Miss A. Gorst, Chatswood *and* Mrs N. C. Sherratt, Killara, NSW.

G. E. SHERINGTON

JOHN, CECILIA ANNIE (1877-1955), singer, feminist and pacifist, was born on 5 November 1877 in Hobart Town, daughter of Welsh parents Daniel Bevan John, blacksmith, and his wife Rosetta, née Kelly. In her early teens she left home to study music and singing in Melbourne under Mrs Trantham Fryer. She had a fine contralto voice and became a successful performer with the Metropolitan Liedertafel, the (Royal) Melbourne Philharmonic Society and with George Musgrove's [q.v.5] German Opera Company. To pay for her musical training Miss John started a poultry farm at Deepdene; of necessity her own labourer, she built the poultry sheds and carried out farm chores with great resourcefulness. By 1911 she was a poultry expert as well as a successful teacher of singing and voice production.

A relation of Dr L. D. Bevan [q.v.7] and a member of the Collins Street Independent Church, Cecilia became interested in social questions. She distributed early anti-conscription literature for the Australian Freedom League and became a passionate friend of Vida Goldstein [q.v.], supporting Vida in her bid for Federal parliament in 1913. She joined the Women's Political Association and wrote for the *Woman Voter*. In July 1915 Cecilia John and Vida Goldstein created the Women's Peace Army which called for the abolition of conscription and militarism, for equal rights for women and control of production by the people. The new organization, of which Cecilia was financial secretary, attracted the more radical of Melbourne's feminists and boasted Adela Pankhurst [q.v.] among its members. In 1918 at a celebration to mark the anniversary of the Russian Revolution Cecilia

shared the platform with Siminoff, the unofficial Russian consul.

Concerned about the indoctrination of children with militaristic ideas, she formed the Children's Peace Army. She also campaigned on behalf of unemployed women and with Ina Higgins, sister of H. B. Higgins [q.v.], she ran a women's farm at Mordialloc, the Women's Rural Industries Co. Ltd. In 1916 the *Woman Voter* reported Cecilia's attendance at a rape trial in support of the victim. She also combined her musical talents with her politics and in 1918 with Mrs Stewart Macky set up the People's Conservatorium. *Stead's Review* of 1924 described her as having a strength of character and breadth of vision 'rare in a member of the fair sex'.

Cecilia's pacifist activities were carefully monitored by military intelligence. Although she was never arrested, her letters were opened and her home searched. She often sang at anti-war meetings and was once charged and convicted for failing to keep the aisles clear. She sang 'I didn't raise my son to be a soldier' to such effect that the song was banned. The *Woman Voter* suffered heavy censorship and armed soldiers once threatened to seize the printing equipment of the Women's Peace Army.

In 1919 Cecilia John and Vida Goldstein attended the Women's International Peace Conference at Zurich. Cecilia also worked with the International Red Cross in Geneva and the Save-the-Children Fund in London. She was profoundly moved by Europe's starving children and on her return to Melbourne formed an Australian Save-the-Children Fund. She had also become interested in the Dalcroze Eurhythmic system of dancing and in 1921 returned to London to study it further. Next year she took charge of the overseas department of the London Save-the-Children Fund.

Miss John became an enthusiastic exponent of Dalcroze Eurhythmic dancing. She toured Australia in connexion with the method in 1923 and 1927-28 and was principal of the London School of Dalcroze Eurhythmics from 1932 until her death. Her critics accused her of using 'bulldozer tactics' and having a 'constitutional inability to compromise', but acknowledged her boundless energy and determination. She died at Godalming, Surrey, on 28 May 1955.

L. M. Henderson, *The Goldstein story* (Melb, 1973); N. Tingey (comp), *A record of the London School of Dalcroze Eurhythmics ... 1913-1973* (Lond, nd); E. Windschuttle (ed), *Women, class and history* (Melb, 1980); *Stead's Review*, 14 June 1924; Dept of Defence, Intelligence Reports (AAO, Melb); Roy Philharmonic Soc, Records (Univ Melb); S. Merrifield collection (LaTL); Palmer papers (NL).

PATRICIA GOWLAND

JOHN, MORGAN BEVAN (1841-1921), metalworker and businessman, was born on 21 January 1841 at Hirwaun, Glamorganshire, Wales, son of Isaac John and his wife Sarah, née Bevan. Young Morgan learned his trade as a moulder and set up his own iron and brass foundry at Pontardulais, near Llanelly, producing varied types of agricultural machinery upon request.

However when one of his major debtors went bankrupt, John found himself in financial difficulty. He decided to migrate either to San Francisco or Victoria. The toss of a coin favoured Australia, so John took his wife Louisa, née Owen, whom he had married on 16 November 1861, and his young family to Victoria in 1874-75. They went straight to Ballarat where deep quartz-mining required much foundry-produced heavy equipment.

John invested his capital in a mining company, but disaster soon struck and he found himself almost penniless. For a while he earned a precarious living as a piano tuner. Fortunately he soon found employment as a moulder and in 1878 joined the Phoenix Foundry. He soon rose to be in charge of the brass shop, and for eighteen years he turned out the brass work for more than three-quarters of the locomotives delivered by the Phoenix to the Victorian Railways. As his financial circumstances improved, he was able to pay to have his son William apprenticed as a fitter and turner at the foundry.

In 1896 John decided to establish his own business, the Ballarat Brass Foundry. It opened in a very small way in Armstrong Street South, employing three men, but business was brisk and within three months he moved to Lydiard Street South, where extensive workshops were built. William had by 1900 completed his course in mechanical engineering at the Ballarat School of Mines. He joined his father's business and made the momentous decision for the foundry to concentrate on the manufacture of all types of valves. The fortunes of the foundry and the family rose rapidly with this decision: the company of M. B. John Ltd, incorporated in 1927, became one of the largest industries in Ballarat and one of the most important valve manufacturers in the world. The Ballarat foundry and associated plant by 1960 employed 850 men, with a total of almost 2000 employees at its branches and other plants throughout Australia. William's five sons all became involved in the company. Morgan John also invested in other companies, and in 1912 he bought the old Ballarat firm of J. B. Cowley's; his youngest son Bevan became manager of Cowley's Eureka Ironworks.

Morgan John's special love was music,

and for many years he was a member of the Philharmonic Society. He conducted the St John's Presbyterian Church choir, and also took part in Ballarat's famed Welsh Eisteddfod by conducting the massed choir in its performance of the *Messiah* at the Alfred Hall.

John's first wife died of typhoid on 17 March 1880, survived by five of their ten children. On 1 June 1881 at Geelong he married Emily Arnott (1858-1950); they had two daughters and a son. In old age he suffered a stroke, but attended board meetings of the company until his death at his residence, Fernside, on 18 February 1921. He was buried in the old Ballarat cemetery. His estate was valued for probate at £47 963.

J. Smith (ed), *Cyclopedia of Victoria*, 2 (Melb, 1904); *Ballarat Courier*, 19 Feb 1921; G. S. Cope, Some aspects of the metal trade in Ballarat, 1851-1901 (M.A. thesis, Univ Melb, 1971); information from Mr M. B. John, Ballarat, Vic.

ANNE BEGGS SUNTER

JOHN, ISABELLE; *see* BEAN, ISABELLE

JOHNS, FREDERICK (1868-1932), journalist and biographer, was born on 22 March 1868 at Houghton, Michigan, United States of America, son of Ezekiel Johns. After his father's death, Fred was taken as an infant to West Cornwall, England. He was educated there before migrating at 16 to join an uncle at Mount Gambier, South Australia. He worked briefly on the Adelaide *Advertiser* and, from 1885, for thirty years on the *South Australian Register* where he became a sub-editor. In 1914 he was appointed to lead the newly established parliamentary Hansard staff where he remained for the rest of his life. He was sparing of copy paper: it was said he could inscribe the Lord's Prayer on paper the size of a sixpence. On 14 March 1894 at Mount Gambier Wesleyan Church he had married Florence Susanna Renfrey who had one daughter before her death two years later.

As a development from a monthly column in the Sydney *Bulletin*, in 1906 Johns compiled and published a biographical dictionary that was to become a national institution, *Johns's notable Australians*. Three features characterized this and later editions: painstaking accuracy, information obtained directly from the individuals concerned, and apolitical, factual entries with no comment or eulogy. It was republished in 1908 and in 1912-14 appeared as *Fred Johns's annual*. The series revived in 1922 as *Who's who in the Commonwealth of Australia* and in 1927 as *Who's who in Australia*.

In 1920 Johns had published a collection of his patriotic poems, *In remembrance*, and two years later *A journalist's jottings*. This included ardent praise for the Anzacs and described significant Australian events and people; it was written in an intense, florid prose unlike that of the dictionaries whose dry brevity reflected Johns's reserved personality. He believed that difficulty helped 'to make the joy of life'. For biographical work he had 'a passion and a love' allied with 'persistent plodding'. His happiest times were spent in his well-stocked library, 'detached from the busy, bustling, worrying world, calm and refreshed'. In 1908 he became a fellow of the Institute of Journalists, London.

Johns was a devout Christian and a Freemason; in 1920-25 he also edited the *South Australian Freemason* and the *Victorian Craftsman*. His biographical books brought him influential contacts all over Australia but travel made him restless with the knowledge of all he had yet to do to complete his work. He was active in the Public Service Association and secretary of the South Australian branch of the Royal Society of Saint George (in 1919-32) and of the Flinders [q.v.1] memorial statue committee.

In his eighteen years as Hansard reporter Johns never missed a parliamentary sitting. In 1926, perhaps conscious of overwork, he spent a month's leave at Hepburn Springs Sanatorium in Victoria. By 1928 he had lymphatic leukaemia which necessitated exhausting radium treatment. In 1931 he considered retirement: 'My billet, one of the most strenuous in the service, has been totally responsible for the shattering of my health'. Although his illness had drastically altered his appearance, Johns still hoped to finish his current dictionary; but on 3 December 1932 he died and was buried in Glen Osmond cemetery. His daughter helped to complete the very useful *An Australian biographical dictionary* (1934), which included entries on the dead as well as the living and one on Johns himself. He had left £1500 to the University of Adelaide to found the Fred Johns scholarship for biography. The Herald and Weekly Times Ltd, Melbourne, bought the rights to continue publication of *Who's who in Australia*.

Newspaper News, 1 Dec 1932; *Mail* (Adel), 15 Apr 1916; *Sun* (Syd), 3 June 1917; *Bulletin*, 27 May 1926, 27 May 1931, 7 Dec 1932; *Advertiser* (Adel), 5 Dec 1932; *SMH*, 10 Dec 1932; information from Mrs E. S. Hookney, Rose Park, Adel.

SUZANNE EDGAR

JOHNSON, EDWARD ANGAS (1873-1951), medical practitioner, was born on 15 January 1873 at Angaston, South Australia, second son of James Angas Johnson, accountant and pastoralist, and his wife Cath-

erine, née Williams. His grandmother was Rosetta French Johnson, eldest daughter of George Fife Angas [q.v.1]. After education at Whinham College and the Collegiate School of Saint Peter, Johnson studied medicine at the University of Adelaide from 1893. In 1896 a dispute between the government and the honorary medical staff of the (Royal) Adelaide Hospital over an appointment to the nursing staff led to suspension of clinical instruction at the hospital. Johnson and other 'exiled' students had to transfer to either the University of Melbourne or of Sydney. He graduated in Melbourne next year, returned to Adelaide and was admitted to the corresponding degrees (M.B., Ch.B.) at its university.

Johnson was house-surgeon at the Adelaide Children's Hospital before setting out in 1898 for Europe to undertake postgraduate work in pathology and bacteriology at the University of Göttingen (M.D., 1899). He also studied at the universities of Berlin and Strasbourg and at the Pasteur Institute, Paris, and worked in London and at Cambridge. On returning to Australia he found that he disliked private practice and was in 1902 appointed honorary assistant physician to the Adelaide Hospital. In 1909-24 he was honorary physician and in 1926-42 the hospital's honorary sanitary adviser.

In 1903 Johnson sat on the Adelaide City Council; he then resigned to attend the London School of Tropical Medicine. He stood unsuccessfully for the Legislative Council in 1905. In 1907 he was again elected to the city council and remained a councillor until 1924 when he resigned to become medical officer of health for Adelaide, an appointment he held until 1938. At the same time he was chairman of the Adelaide Board of Health, a member of the Metropolitan County Board and the Metropolitan Abattoirs Board and represented the government on the Central Board of Health. He was a governor and benefactor of the Botanic Garden and published many papers on the history of plants. He was the South Australian editor for Virchow's (Berlin) *Jahresbericht*.

Johnson was an opinionated man and this sometimes led to conflict with his colleagues, as when he reported adversely on diphtheria immunization in 1937, but he was respected for having the courage of his convictions. His hobby was collecting curios and historical relics, especially those relating to South Australian history. This remarkable collection and his library were distributed to public institutions before his death. He was commissioned in the Australian Army Medical Corps in 1902 and served until 1920, reaching the rank of major.

Johnson married twice. His first wife Margarethe Friedericke Charlotte Klevesahl, sister-in-law of Charles Rasp [q.v.6], whom he had married in London on 27 September 1900, was German; she died in 1936, leaving a son. On 3 January 1939 he married Dorothy Muriel Brandt who survived him. Johnson died at his Glenelg home on 19 June 1951 and was cremated after an Anglican service.

Universal Publicity Co., *The official civic record of South Australia* (Adel, 1936); *Honorary Magistrate*, May 1920; *Register* (Adel), 2 May 1905; *Mail* (Adel), 8 Feb 1913; *Advertiser* (Adel), 4 Nov 1947, 21 June 1951.   J. ESCOURT HUGHES

JOHNSON, FLORENCE ETHEL (1884-1934), feminist and educationist, was born on 26 March 1884 at Port Melbourne, daughter of Victorian-born parents Henry Johnson, boilermaker, and his wife Minnie, née Johnson. Florence began her career in 1900 as a pupil-teacher at South Preston State School. Her considerable aptitude led to appointment as head of Arcadia South State School in April 1906 and to a further thirteen years highly regarded work in various Victorian schools. She joined the Victorian Lady Teachers' Association in 1908 and later the Sixth Class L.T.A.; in 1915 she organized the Junior Teachers' Association.

During World War I Miss Johnson fought for a return to the pre-1892 pay scale for women of four-fifths the male wage, a principle granted in 1918. She attempted to improve the career prospects of women teachers and was several times on deputations to the Education Department. A delegate to the first Victorian State Service Federation council-meeting in January 1917, she was elected an honorary secretary to the Sixth Class L.T.A. in May. She then helped to form the Victorian Women Teachers' Association and was elected president; in December when the L.T.A. merged with the W.T.A. she became vice-president.

By 1918 Florence Johnson's 'great talent for organisation' was generally acknowledged. In November she was appointed to a V.S.S.F. review committee and in July next year she resigned her teaching post at Mount Waverley to become secretary of the V.S.S.F.'s women's division. She took up the cudgels for equal pay for women teachers but also sought, with some success, improved conditions for members of the Mental Hospital Nurses' Association, and for female typists and clerks in the public service. In March 1921, however, she resigned to become assistant secretary of the reorganized Victorian State Teachers' Union. She worked furiously to improve union membership and was disheartened by her apparent demotion in October to organizer. A growing dissatisfaction with union policy 'not in the best interests of women teachers' led to her resignation in March 1924 and the re-forming, with herself as paid secretary, of the W.T.A.

After the Teachers' Act of 1925 Miss Johnson urged the promotion rights of teachers with a long service record but minimal qualifications. With a colleague, Ida Body, she formed the supportive Victorian Federation of Mothers' Clubs. In 1927, miffed by the omission of the W.T.A. from the departmental organizing committees for the visit of the duke and duchess of York, she clashed with the minister, Sir Alexander Peacock [q.v.]; he accused her of preaching 'the doctrine of discontent' but was no match for her clever repartee.

In 1927 Florence Johnson stood as an Independent Labor candidate for St Kilda, the only woman in the Legislative Assembly elections. Concentrating her campaign on health, welfare and education, she unwisely relied on the female vote. Her defeat necessitated her re-entry into the Education Department as teacher at isolated Mirboo North. In Melbourne again from 1928 she campaigned through the W.T.A. for a women teachers' welfare officer; during the Depression she promoted teachers' and students' work to assist the unemployed.

In 1932 *en route* to Ceylon Florence made a surprise marriage to a marine engineer Frederick Arthur Ingram on 24 December at St George's Cathedral, Perth. Idealistic (but also pragmatic), courageous, a 'little "live-wire" ', 'the Emily Pankhurst of Victorian teachers', she continued her work with the W.T.A. after her marriage. She died at Malvern of complications of mitral valve disease on 6 November 1934, and was cremated.

W. J. McDonald, 'Florence Ethel Johnson', *VHJ*, no 201 (Aug 1980), and for bibliog; Education Dept of Vic, History section, MS 79/18.

JOHNSON, GEORGE (1868-1952), sugar-grower, was born on 7 February 1868 at Stillington, County Durham, England, son of Thomas Johnson, farmer, and his wife Isabella, née Robinson. Educated at Houghton-le-Spring High School, Durham, he left England with a brother in 1889, hoping to acquire a western Queensland grazing run, but because of drought took employment in the sugar industry. Two years later he and his brother selected 320 acres (130 ha) at Mia Mia, about thirty miles from Mackay, on which they began to grow sugar. Johnson was soon giving active encouragement to English migration to the sugar districts.

Johnson soon became involved in sugar affairs. He was particularly impressed by the Sugar Works Guarantee Act of 1893. In 1906-07 and 1911-14 he was president of the Pioneer River Farmers' and Graziers' Association and was president of the Mackay District Show Association in the same years.

In 1913 the P.R.F.G.A. sponsored action which led to the formation at Mackay of the United Cane Growers' Association in December 1914. Johnson was first president of the association until 1917; maintenance of cohesive membership and adequate finance were always problems. In 1915 he contested the Legislative Assembly seat of Mackay unsuccessfully against W. Forgan Smith [q.v.]. Johnson represented the association in the Industrial Court in 1914-17, was active in the agitation preceding the Co-operative Sugar Works Act of 1914 and the Regulation of Sugar Cane Prices Act of 1915, and gave evidence for the U.C.G.A. to the board of inquiry into the sugar industry of 1916.

The Queensland Primary Producers Organization and Marketing Act of 1922 provided for compulsory membership and brought most Queensland farmers into industry groupings. The sugar industry did not easily conform to this general pattern, primarily because of special circumstances related to the phasing out of black labour from the cane-fields in 1901-12, the establishment of the Central Sugar Cane Prices Board in 1915 and of the Queensland Sugar Board in 1923. The Queensland Cane Growers' Association, with the Queensland Cane Growers' Council as its governing body, was inaugurated following a State conference of sugar men at Mackay in January 1926. Though Forgan Smith, minister for agriculture, presided, Johnson was the actual leader of the proceedings. When the council was set up a few days later, he became inaugural chairman and held the position until he retired in 1946.

Johnson supplied cane to North Eton mill, established since 1887 as Australia's first central mill owned by growers and sponsored by government. From 1927, when North Eton became a co-operative under the Primary Producers' Co-operative Associations Acts of 1923-26, until 1940, Johnson was its chairman. He was also a member of Pioneer Shire Council in 1907-14 and chairman in 1911-13, chairman of Mirani Shire Council in 1914-17 and 1920-39 and chairman of the agriculture section of the Queensland Society of Sugar Cane Technologists in 1940-41.

Johnson lived in retirement at Mackay, died there on 2 May 1952 and was buried in Mackay cemetery with Presbyterian forms. His estate, valued for probate at £28 958, was left to his wife Elizabeth, née Dumma, whom he had married at Mackay on 23 July 1906, and to their three sons and two daughters.

R. E. Easterby, *The Queensland sugar industry* (Brisb, c. 1934); *Queensland and Queenslanders* (Brisb, 1936); *PP* (Qld), 1911-12, 2, p 1158, 1915-16, 2, p 1053, 1916-17, 2, p 904; *Sugar J and Tropical Cultivator* (Mackay), 15 Feb 1895; *Aust Sugar J*, 1952, p 165, Oct 1976, p 344; *Qld Educational J*, Mar 1915; *Daily Mercury* (Mackay), 21, 29 Jan 1926, 14 Dec 1914, 5 May 1952.   K. W. MANNING

JOHNSON, JOHN ANDREW (1861-1933), educationist, was born on 27 October 1861 at Clisbow, Unst, Shetland Islands, Scotland, son of James William Johnson, fisherman, and his wife Andrina Ross, née Henderson. The family migrated in 1870 to New Zealand, where John attended school at Waipori and became a pupil-teacher at 14. He then attended the Dunedin Teachers' Training College and Otago University (B.A., N.Z., 1890; M.A., 1891). After various teaching posts he became headmaster of Timaru School in 1896 and was also literary editor of the New Zealand *Journal of Education*.

In 1905, following the enquiry conducted by W. L. Neale [q.v.], a reconstruction of the Tasmanian education system was begun. Improvements included the establishment of a teachers' training college in Hobart. Johnson was appointed principal and began work in 1906, at first in the Technical School, then in the new Philip Smith [q.v.2] buildings on the Domain, opened in 1911. He took a keen interest in changing ideas in education, especially the 'New Education', which he saw as placing the teacher in the role of elder brother whose task was to perfect the mental growth and development of the pupil, not just to impart knowledge. Johnson disliked reliance on rote learning and examinations; he advocated that the pupil learn by observation; that handwork should be taught as well as headwork; and that the child be seen as an individual with rights and a personality to be respected. He imparted his ideas with great success, giving his students a sense of the greatness of the vocation of teaching. At first the college was little more than a secondary school, but after the inception of high schools in 1913 it assumed its proper role. Johnson was an able administrator and from the start the college ran smoothly.

Johnson's great love was literature, especially poetry, and although he lectured in other subjects, including Latin and mathematics, and supervised practice teaching, he excelled in his English lectures. He aimed to make his students love and appreciate poetry through inspiration: he would read a poem aloud and leave this to make an impact. He possessed a warm personality; each month all the students were invited to his home for an evening, while he encouraged walks and picnics, properly chaperoned (sometimes by himself), socials, dancing, singing, swimming and football. He preferred to influence by praise rather than by criticism, and his quiet, dignified, courteous and occasionally stern manner commanded respect. However, he had some difficulty dealing with crises: once when students engaged in forbidden, riotous initiation ceremonies which outraged public opinion Johnson suspended them, only to have to rescind this decision the next day. He also had occasional clashes with the Education Department, and, as a romanticist, enjoyed a prolonged newspaper debate in the *Mercury* with the rationalist professor of English at the university, A. B. Taylor; Johnson aimed for untrammelled appreciation of literature by students.

His students included the later prime minister, J. A. Lyons [q.v.] and his wife (Dame) Enid. On his retirement in 1931 the *Bulletin* commented that Johnson was one of the most successful teachers of teachers in Australia, with not only 'sound scholarship, wide experience and a passionate enthusiasm for his job', but also the asset of 'a speaking voice of that peculiarly sympathetic, almost caressing, quality' typical of Shetland and Orkney Islanders. Johnson wrote the Tasmanian section of G. S. Browne's *Education in Australia* (London, 1927) and, with C. E. B. Fletcher, edited an anthology of poetry for use in schools. In 1906 he was elected a fellow of the Royal Society of Tasmania, before which he read a paper on the 'New Education' (1906) and another on developments in experimental pedagogy (1913). For seventeen years Johnson lectured in education at the University of Tasmania and until 1932 he was a member of the university council. Other interests included tennis, golf, and bushwalking. A Presbyterian, he was conservative in both religion and politics. His wife, Laura Elizabeth, née Kingston, whom he had married on 23 December 1889 at South Dunedin, New Zealand, died in 1919; she was musical, artistic, patriotic and an enthusiastic philanthropist. Johnson died on 21 January 1933 in Hobart, survived by a son and two daughters. A portrait by Lucien Dechaineux [q.v.8] is displayed in the Southern Teachers' Centre, Hobart.

Mercury, 23 Jan 1933; *Otago Daily Times*, 24 Jan 1933; *Bulletin*, 1 Mar 1933; information from Dr J. H. B. Walch, and Mr and Mrs T. Jacobs, New Town, Mrs G. Donnelly, Lenah Valley, Miss K. Gordon, Taroona, Mr W. Perkins, South Hobart, and Mr H. Swift, Claremont, Tas.

ALISON ALEXANDER

JOHNSON, JOSEPH COLIN FRANCIS (1848-1904), journalist, mining promoter and politician, was born on 12 February 1848 at King William Street, Adelaide, son of Henry Johnson, solicitor, a migrant of 1838 and prominent Roman Catholic, and his wife Wilhelmina Colquhoun, née Campbell. In the 1850s the family moved to Victoria. Johnson attended the Geelong National Grammar School, then took to bush life. He was correspondent for metropolitan papers before returning to Adelaide in 1868. Joining the staff of the *South Australian Register*, he wrote well on commerce, mining, viticulture and the theatre.

In 1872-73 Johnson published brief collections of stories and verse (*On the wallaby, Christmas on Carringa* and *Over the island*); though ordinary in style, they anticipated Lawson [q.v.] and others in depicting bush life. In 1880 he went to the Mount Browne, New South Wales, diggings, a visit which was financially successful and was described in his press articles and book, *Moses and me* (1881). He became proprietor and editor of the satirical weekly *Adelaide Punch*, then turned his attention increasingly to mining. Publicly urging more enterprise, he privately developed promising mines near Mannahill and Woodside, and employed prospectors. He fostered better prospecting and mining practice through lectures and his books *Practical mining* (Adelaide, 1889), which sold 10 000 copies, and *Getting gold* (London, 1897). He successfully negotiated the sale of the Maritana mine in Western Australia in 1896. A founding member of the Australian Institute of Mining Engineers, he was also an honorary life member of the Australian Mine Managers' Association and a fellow of the Geological Society, London. The choicest of his fine auriferous specimens were presented to Queen Victoria, the remainder to the British Museum.

In 1884 Johnson won the seat of Onkaparinga in the House of Assembly. A staunch protectionist, he preferred the term 'productionist' to explain his position. He became one of three members ('The Triumvirate') who were effective watchdogs on government expenditure. In 1887-89 he was minister of education and responsible for the Northern Territory. He drafted and introduced useful mining legislation, encouraged the study of drawing and the natural and physical sciences in state schools and supported Federation; his later parliamentary career was undistinguished. In 1895-97, financially independent, he travelled in Britain and America with a commission from the government to report on new methods of mining and the treatment of ores. He had retired from parliament in 1896.

Beyond parliament Johnson was more effective; he promoted the Australian National Union which later amalgamated with the Australian Natives' Association, in which he was also active. In 1900 he raised funds for the Bushmen's Contingent in the South African War by sponsoring repeated sales of the horse Bugler and, later, of a bullock, a mare and a donkey. His suggestion of a statue of heroic proportions commemorating the South Australian Bushmen led to the fine memorial erected outside Government House, Adelaide, in 1904.

Johnson's interests included literature, art, music and travel. He was on the council of the South Australian School of Mines and Industries and the board of the Public Library, Museum and Art Gallery of South Australia. Known as 'Alphabetical' to his friends, one critic found him disputatious and showy, but he was acknowledged as a mining pioneer. After falling down stairs, he died on 18 June 1904 at North Adelaide, where he had lived with his mother, and was buried in the Catholic section of West Terrace cemetery. Johnson was survived by an adopted son.

J. J. Pascoe (ed), *History of Adelaide and vicinity* (Adel, 1901); P. Depasquale, *A critical history of South Australian literature, 1836-1930 with subjectively annotated bibliographies* (Adel, 1978); W. F. Morrison, *The Aldine history of South Australia*, 2 (Syd, 1890); *Advertiser* (Adel), and *Register* (Adel), 20 June 1904.   R. M. GIBBS

JOHNSON, WILLIAM DARTNELL (1870-1948), carpenter and politician, was born on 9 October 1870 at Wanganui, New Zealand, son of George Groheim Johnson (Johnston), plumber, and his wife Elizabeth Ann, née McCormish. He was educated at Turakina State School until, aged 13, he began three years work at the local post office. He then became a carpenter. He migrated to Western Australia in 1894, and next year went to the goldfields. He founded and was first president of the Kalgoorlie branch of the Amalgamated Society of Carpenters and Joiners and for two years was secretary of the Kalgoorlie, Boulder and District Trades and Labor Council, whose establishment owed much to his efforts. He

was the *Westralian Worker*'s first business manager. On 27 November 1901 he married Jessie Elizabeth Stewart, née McCallum, a widow.

In 1901 Johnson won for Labor the Kalgoorlie seat in the Legislative Assembly. He continued his trade, going as far afield as the North-West, and soon became a leading speaker in the assembly, mainly on industrial issues. He sat on a select committee which recommended the construction of railway workshops at Midland Junction.

In August 1904 Johnson joined the State's first Labor cabinet as minister for works. He later became minister for mines and railways. He was involved in the controversial proposal to buy the Midland Railway Co., which caused the Daglish [q.v.8] government's fall in August 1905. Johnson became party leader, only to lose his seat in October.

Next July Johnson won the Guildford seat. From August he sat on a select committee which recommended measures to reduce sweating in Perth industries. In October 1911 he became minister for works in John Scaddan's [q.v.] cabinet, and from November 1914 was minister for lands and agriculture. He was now a farmer, and seemed more interested in developing the State's resources than in working-class issues. His proposals for a standing parliamentary committee to report on significant, planned public works, and to build a railway line north from Esperance, were defeated in the Legislative Council. In January 1915 he had passed legislation to help settlers who had been hurt by the severe drought, the Industries Assistance Act.

Johnson also shared credit for the government's vigorous establishment of state enterprises, which he saw as helping to protect the 'masses' from the 'exploiters'. But he admitted that cabinet had made a bad appointment as manager of the State Agricultural Implement Works, and he pleaded with employees of the enterprises to do a fair day's work. Johnson's involvement with one state instrumentality harmed his career. In 1914 cabinet reversed an earlier decision and announced it would build a meatworks at Wyndham, as many people had long urged. Scaddan and Johnson awarded the contract to S. V. Nevanas, a London-based financier, without calling tenders, and against the advice of Johnson's department that Nevanas could not build the works for the price quoted. This prediction proved correct. The contract was cancelled and Nevanas received compensation. In 1915 a select committee investigated the fiasco. The Nevanas case was the occasion, if not the cause, of one Labor man (E. B. Johnston [q.v.]) switching sides. This, and a working arrangement between the Liberal and

Country parties, resulted in the government being voted out of office in July 1916.

Johnson was one of the first State parliamentarians to oppose conscription and consequently lost his seat at the 1917 elections. Though he regained Guildford in 1924, he never again held ministerial rank. Of the anti-conscriptionists who had been ministers under Scaddan, he had the least successful subsequent career.

In 1924 Johnson was appointed to a royal commission which recommended improvements in the administration of the Group Settlement Scheme in the south-west. He was Speaker from August 1938 to August 1939, remained a leading Labor spokesman, and was chairman of the parliamentary party in 1924-48. He was still a 'state socialist', for example welcoming governmental entry into the insurance field, but his main concern was with developmental politics. He was worried at eastern Australia's domination of the State's commercial and mining life, but he opposed secession as impractical. In 1933 he clashed with Premier Collier [q.v.8] over the appointment of Sir James Mitchell [q.v.] as lieut-governor; Johnson later criticized Collier for allowing a delegation to go to London to seek support for secession.

Johnson remained a member of parliament until his death on 26 January 1948. He was cremated after an Anglican ceremony at Karrakatta cemetery. His wife, a son and three daughters survived him. His estate was sworn for probate at £963. Johnson had seen sound economic management of the State as the basis for improvements in the lot of ordinary people, but had not always been a judicious administrator. He had a long association with the co-operative movement and had been a Freemason.

PD (WA), 1905, p 779, 1917, p 1485, 1929, p 682, 1933, p 1401, 1934, p 243; *Western Mail* (Perth), 8 May, 26 June 1914; *Morning Herald* (Perth), 11 Aug 1901; *Westralian Worker*, 6 Oct 1905; *West Australian*, 9 Oct 1911; J. R. Robertson, The Scaddan government and the conscription crisis 1911-1917 (M.A. thesis, Univ WA, 1958).

J. R. ROBERTSON

JOHNSON, SIR WILLIAM ELLIOT (1862-1932), politician, was born on 10 April 1862 at Newcastle-on-Tyne, Northumberland, England, son of John Ellis Johnson, scene painter, and his wife Mary, née Nutsforde. After an adventurous life as a youth, which included some telegraphy and scene painting in London, he came to Sydney as a ship steward and on 29 June 1881 married Marie McLachlan, a dressmaker from Scotland.

Johnson divided his time for the next few years between scene painting, journalism and politics. Four times president of the Newtown branch of the Labor Electoral League, he was a faithful contributor to the *Labour Defence Journal* and a devoted disciple of Henry George [q.v.4] whom he escorted on his 1890 lecture tour. In 1894 he stood unsuccessfully as pledged L.E.L. candidate for Marrickville in the Legislative Assembly. He left the Labor Party when, in his view, it turned wrongly towards socialism and state interference, to become honorary secretary of the Free Trade and Liberal Association of New South Wales. Though he had opposed Federation, in 1903 he was elected as a Free Trade Liberal to the Federal seat of Lang which he held until 1928.

Parliament was a natural forum for the loquacious Johnson. His politics were to remain unusual, maintaining a mixture of radicalism and conformism through changing party titles and creeds. As a populist and a democrat committed to 'equal opportunity, justice and liberty for all', he attacked impartially socialism, collectivism, government intervention, employers' federations and capitalist concentrations of wealth and opportunity. Strongly opposed to 'sweating', he fought tenaciously for better conditions for the lower grades of postal, telegraphic and clerical workers and for old-age pensions. He believed that the land value tax would promote a sturdy yeomanry through whom Australian freedom and individualism would flourish. A rigorous free trader he was at his best demolishing either the Labor Party or protectionist iniquities with prolific quotations, examples and figures. He opposed the Fusion, but supported the Liberal Party under Deakin [q.v.8].

In 1911 Johnson attended the coronation as a member of the parliamentary delegation to England and became one of the founders of the Empire Parliamentary Association and honorary secretary of the Australian branch. A strong advocate of White Australia, he was concerned with defence and Imperial policies in the Pacific, especially with regard to the New Hebrides and Papua. He was a member of royal commissions on the pearling industry (1913) and the New Hebrides mail service (1915).

Johnson was parliamentary party secretary in 1912-13 and a deputy chairman of committees in the House of Representatives. He was twice Speaker, in 1913-14 and 1917-23. Under his old companion, later political foe and eventual benevolent prime minister, W. M. Hughes [q.v.], the experienced and hard-working Johnson found his political place. His decisions were fair, he battled for the parliamentary staff and resisted parliamentary inquiries such as the economies commission (1919) with gusto. He was appointed K.C.M.G. in July 1920, adopting the style Elliot. When summarily replaced as Speaker by W. A. Watt [q.v.], he retained his political exuberance and continued as vice-president of the National Association in 1923.

A firm, orthodox Christian he was a leading teetotaller and a successful campaigner against licensing in the Capital Territory, the import of opium and lesser evils like starting-price betting. He had been closely associated with the choice of Canberra as the capital site and with a range of minor improvements to communications and electoral administration. An amateur artist and photographer himself (the National Library of Australia holds a collection of his works), he supported the development of public art-collections.

The protectionist policies of the 1920s remained obnoxious to Johnson. He left parliament as he had entered it, quoting Henry George, when defeated in 1928 by the Labor Party he had so long resisted and by the 'working man of Lang' upon whom he had proudly relied. Johnson was distinguished in appearance by a full moustache, sported since early days. Popular and an engaging conversationalist, he was full of tales of the sea and distant lands. His political ideas predated the parties with which he was perforce associated and he became accustomed to working with those with whom he was in only partial sympathy. Though his radical instincts for the aspirations of the less well-off left him isolated he was admired for his personal warmth, candour and tolerance. He lived his principles and left no followers.

He died of cerebro-vascular disease on 8 December 1932 at Geelong, Victoria. Born an Anglican he was buried at Rookwood cemetery, Sydney, as a Presbyterian. He was survived by his only daughter. A portrait by Florence Rodway [q.v.] hangs in Parliament House, Canberra.

J. A. La Nauze, *Alfred Deakin* (Melb, 1965); B. Nairn, *Civilising capitalism* (Canb, 1973); L. Fitzhardinge, *The little digger* (Syd, 1979); *Daily Telegraph* (Syd), 26 June 1894; *Punch* (Melb), 21 Aug 1913, 29 Dec 1921; *SMH*, 9 Dec 1932; Deakin papers (NL).   G. N. HAWKER

JOHNSTON, CHARLES MELBOURNE (1892-1941), soldier and company director, was born on 12 May 1892 in South Melbourne, son of Adolf Charles Johnston, a Swedish-born engineer, and his wife Bertha Selvince Taglinoi Mignonneete, née Turner, from South Australia. He attended Melbourne Church of England Grammar School

in 1907-11 and at the outbreak of war in 1914 was a law student.

After two previous commissions in the cadets he was again commissioned in December 1914 as a lieutenant in the Senior Cadets, 3rd Military District. He was seconded to the Australian Imperial Force on 16 April 1915 as a second lieutenant and that day embarked from Brisbane with the 5th Reinforcements for the 15th Battalion, reporting for duty at Gallipoli on 2 June. From the outset he emerged as a leader and on 13 September he was posted to command 'C' Company as a temporary captain. His battalion was evacuated from Gallipoli on 13 December. In Egypt, on 20 January 1916, Johnston's rank was confirmed. In the reorganization of the A.I.F. he remained with the 15th Battalion, and embarked for France on 31 May. In northern France, on 10 July, he was promoted major and retained command of his company.

Johnston became brigade major, 4th Brigade, on 14 December and retained this post until February 1918 though on 6 July 1917 he was seriously wounded at Messines. From February to June 1918 he served temporarily in the 14th Battalion, at first as commanding officer and then as second-in-command. On 1 July, as a temporary lieut-colonel, he was appointed to command the 45th Battalion. He took part in the battle of Hamel in July and the battle of Amiens in August.

On 2 September Johnston was transferred to the 15th Battalion and from 21 October held the substantive rank of lieut-colonel. He took command on the night of 16-17 September, in time for the 15th's 'last fight, and their best' on the 18th when an outpost of the Hindenburg line was taken. He retained this command until the battalion was disbanded in March 1919. He embarked for Australia on 9 July as officer commanding troops on the *Prinz Ludwig* and on 13 November his A.I.F. appointment ended. His war service as an infantry officer in regimental and staff appointments was outstanding. He had risen from a junior subaltern to a lieut-colonel and, aged 26, had commanded battalions in action with distinction. For his services he was awarded the Distinguished Service Order and mentioned in dispatches three times.

After the war Johnston returned to Melbourne and became a manufacturer. On 15 March 1923 at the Presbyterian church in Mosman, Sydney, he married Winefred Amelia Wyllie; they had two sons. At the time of his death on 10 April 1941 in East Melbourne he was managing director of Pearlite Manufacturing Co. Pty Ltd, Burnley. Survived by his wife and sons, he died of hypertensive cerebro-vascular disease and was buried in Box Hill cemetery after a Presbyterian service. Major General C. H. Brand [q.v.7], one of his wartime brigade commanders, was a pallbearer.

J. B. Kiddle (comp and ed), *War services of Old Melburnians 1914-1918* (Melb, 1923), and *Liber Melburniensis 1848-1936* (Melb, 1937); J. E. Lee, *The chronicle of the 45th Battalion, A.I.F.* (Syd, 1924); N. Wanliss, *The history of the Fourteenth Battalion, A.I.F.* (Melb, 1929); T. P. Chataway, *History of the 15th Battalion A.I.F.* (Brisb, 1948); *Argus*, 12, 14 Apr 1941; C. M. Johnston file, war records section (AWM).   WARREN PERRY

JOHNSTON, EDWARD BERTRAM (1880-1942), politician, was born on 11 January 1880 at Geraldton, Western Australia, eldest son of HARRY FREDERICK JOHNSTON and his wife Maria Louisa (Minnie), née Butcher. H. F. Johnston had been born at Bunbury on 24 April 1853, a grandson of M. W. Clifton [q.v.3] and son of a surveyor. Entering his father's profession he joined the Western Australian Lands and Surveys Department in 1883, conducting important surveys in the Kimberleys in 1883-84 and 1901. He became surveyor-general in 1896 and, during a period of rapid expansion of land settlement, oversaw the mapping of most of Western Australia's goldfields and the opening of the agricultural south-west. He was first chairman of the Workers' Homes Board created in 1912. He died following a shooting accident at his home in Swan View on 14 June 1915, survived by his wife and six sons.

Bertie Johnston entered his father's department as a clerk in 1895 after education at the High School, Perth. In 1904-09 he was government land agent at Narrogin. He resigned, went to Kalgoorlie and, as honorary secretary of the Esperance Land and Railway League, gained experience as a lobbyist and land speculator. In 1911, flouting his family and class traditions, he was returned as Labor member for Williams-Narrogin. He first made his mark in 1912 by carrying a resolution that no fees should be charged for university or government school education in Western Australia. In 1914 he was returned with a much increased majority; he was the only Labor member ever to achieve this feat in a Western Australian farming electorate.

A genial bachelor with a taste for the good things of life, he was an indefatigable local member. 'Whenever any voter in his consitituency wanted some shopping done in Perth Johnston was the man to do it; whenever any elector desired some service to be performed, their trusty member was only too willing to oblige.' He lobbied vigorously for local railways and developed remarkable foresight in anticipating the best locations for hotel properties alongside them. A restive back-bencher, he clashed with the premier, John Scaddan [q.v.], over land policy and the management of a contract for the Wyndham meatworks. Failing to topple Scaddan in caucus, in December 1915 he resigned and was returned unopposed at a by-election as an Independent. This left the Scaddan government in a minority of one in the Legislative Assembly. In July 1916 Johnston combined with the Liberal and Country parties to oust the government.

In February 1917, anticipating Johnston's support, Labor moved a motion of no confidence in the new Liberal ministry; but when the Labor Speaker M. F. Troy resigned to support the motion, Johnston was elected in his place. His three weeks in the chair were uniquely turbulent. After summoning the editor of the *West Australian* to the bar of the House to apologize for casting aspersions on his negotiations for the Speakership, Johnston showed such zeal for suspending his former Labor colleagues that uncontrollably rowdy scenes ensued. He resigned in March and chose the unveiling of a war memorial at Darkan to regale his electors with such a provocative account of the manoeuvres over the Speakership that the government and Opposition combined to pass a resolution of strong censure on him in the Legislative Assembly. Undaunted, in June Johnston joined the Country Party, but at the October election he had to share the party's endorsement with another candidate. His rival's prospects looked promising until, just before the election, Johnston issued a well-publicized libel suit against him. This swung sympathy to Johnston, although after his return a jury assessed his damages at a farthing and the judge passed some caustic comments on him.

When the Country Party split in 1922 Johnston became deputy-leader of that section opposed to coalition with Sir James Mitchell [q.v.]. He resigned in 1928 to enter the Commonwealth Senate, where he remained from 1929 until his death. An uninhibited advocate of State-rights, during the Depression he pushed the sectional interests of wheatgrowers, at times annoying colleagues by his urging. In his last year he consistently broke party discipline to vote with John Curtin's Labor government; but for his vote at a critical stage, uniform tax legislation could not have passed the Senate. He was under stress because his substantial investments in hotels and real estate had attracted the unfavourable attention of the Federal taxation authorities. On 6 September 1942 he was found drowned near his brother's home at the Melbourne suburb of Black Rock. He was taken home to be buried in the Anglican cemetery at Guildford. A negotiated taxation settlement avoided bankruptcy proceedings against his estate. On 18 February 1931 he had married Hildelith Olymphe Lethbridge who survived him with three daughters.

A maverick politician who treated the decorous conventions of public life with adventurous disregard, Johnston never lost an election because voters responded to his gusto and his willingness to prime the parish pump. His younger brother Frederick Marshall Johnston (1885-1963) was Commonwealth surveyor-general in 1944-49.

J. S. Battye (ed), *Cyclopedia of Western Australia*, 1 (Adel, 1912); F. M. Johnston, *Knights and theodolites* (Syd, 1962); W. E. Greble, *A bold yeomanry* (Perth, 1979); *West Australian*, 1 Dec 1917, 7 Sept 1942; *Herald* (Melb), 4 June 1942; J. R. Robertson, The Scaddan government and the conscription crisis 1911-17 (MA thesis, Univ WA, 1958).

G. C. BOLTON

JOHNSTON, GEORGE JAMESON (1868-1949), soldier, administrator and businessman, was born on 24 October 1868 in East Melbourne, son of Charles Johnston from Cork, Ireland, and his English-born wife Elizabeth, née Jameson. He was educated at the Model School and entered the family firm of Charles Johnston & Co., furniture manufacturers and warehousemen, Fitzroy. In 1887 he joined the militia as a gunner in the Victorian Field Artillery, was commissioned lieutenant in 1889 and promoted captain in 1895. His love of horses was an integral part of his life: he always kept good stables, played polo and rode to hounds until his sixties. On 24 October 1894, at Holy Trinity Anglican Church, East Melbourne, he married Margaret Hobson, a granddaughter of Dr Edmund Hobson [q.v.1]. He was a member of the Fitzroy City Council in 1896-99.

Johnston volunteered for active service in the South African War and was attached to the 62nd Battery, Royal Field Artillery, as a special service officer. He left Australia in November 1899 as a captain and was promoted major in March 1900. He served at Modder River, did regimental duty with the 62nd Battery as a section commander, and saw action at Klip Drift, Paardeburg and Osfontein before the march on Bloemfontein; he was then attached to a howitzer brigade with the Royal Field Artillery before being invalided home with fever in July 1900. He re-enlisted in March 1902 as a temporary lieut-colonel commanding the 4th Battalion, Australian Commonwealth Horse, but by the time he reached South Af-

rica peace negotiations had begun and his unit returned without seeing active service. His brother Lieutenant Alfred Gresham Johnston was killed in action at Rhenoster Kop. Johnston resumed his business activities in Melbourne, was promoted lieut-colonel, Australian Military Forces, in 1910 and commanded the Victorian Brigade, Australian Field Artillery.

On 18 August 1914 Johnston was appointed to the Australian Imperial Force as lieut-colonel commanding the 2nd Field Artillery Brigade, 1st Australian Division. His 4th Battery landed the first 18-pounder field-gun at Anzac on 25 April 1915. The guns of 'Johnston's Jolly', situated near Lone Pine, were used, in the current slang of the troops, to 'jolly up' the Turks. Johnston remained at Anzac until the evacuation; he was temporary commander of the 1st Divisional Artillery from August to October and from then until late November commanded the 3rd Infantry Brigade; he was promoted colonel and temporary brigadier general in December. In January 1916, in Egypt, he was appointed commander of the 2nd Divisional Artillery and sailed for France in March. From 27 April, when his artillery placed its first barrage on the enemy parapet near Armentières, the division's infantry felt 'a sure reliance' upon its own gunners. Johnston commanded the 2nd Divisional Artillery in all its engagements from 1916 until late 1917, including the battles of Pozières, Bullecourt and 3rd Ypres. He relinquished command on 1 November 1917 and returned to Australia to attend to urgent commercial affairs. For distinguished war service he was appointed C.B. and C.M.G. and was mentioned in dispatches four times.

Early in 1918 Johnston's wife died after a riding accident and on 16 March he was appointed military administrator of German New Guinea. During his term several of the outlying parts of the Territory were brought under more effective control, and he was the first administrator to propose a training scheme for New Guinea district officers. His administration received some public criticism and his appointment was terminated in May 1920 but he was appointed C.B.E. in recognition of his work. The *Encyclopaedia of Papua and New Guinea* (1972) states that he 'conscientiously did his best in an appointment for which he was suited by neither temperament nor training'. On returning to Melbourne he resumed his position of governing director of Johnston's Pty Ltd and continued his service with the citizen forces, commanding the 3rd Division in 1922-27 with the rank of major general from 1 October 1923. Survived by two sons and a daughter, he died on 23 May

1949 and was buried in Brighton cemetery after a military funeral. His estate was sworn for probate at £81 363.

W. T. Reay, *Australians in war: with the Australian Regiment from Melbourne to Bloemfontein* (Melb, 1900); Aust Defence Dept, *Official records of the Australian military contingents to the war in South Africa*, P. L. Murray ed (Melb, 1911); C. E. W. Bean, *The story of Anzac* (Syd, 1921, 1924), and *The A.I.F. in France*, 1916 (Syd, 1929); S. S. Mackenzie, *The Australians at Rabaul* (Syd, 1927); C. D. Rowley, *The Australians in German New Guinea* 1914-1921 (Melb, 1958); *Encyclopaedia of Papua and New Guinea*, I, (Melb, 1972); *London Gazette*, 5 Nov 1915, 2 Jan, 1 June, 25 Dec 1917; *Brisbane Courier*, 26 Feb 1902; *SMH*, 6, 9 Nov 1915, 4 June 1917, 18 Mar 1918, 9 Aug 1919, 17 Mar, 15 May, 16 Oct 1920; *Argus*, 24 May 1949; G. Johnston papers, war records section (AWM).

PHYLLIS ASHWORTH

JOHNSTON, THOMAS HARVEY (1881-1951), biologist and parasitologist, was born on 9 December 1881 at Balmain, Sydney, son of Thomas Johnston, Irish-born foreman mason, and his Australian-born wife Mary, née McLeod. After schooling Johnston joined the education department, won the Jones memorial medal and went to the University of Sydney (B.A., 1906; B.Sc., M.A., 1907; D.Sc., 1911). On 1 January 1907 at Petersham he married Alice Maude Pearce.

Johnston taught at Fort Street Public School in 1903-06, lectured in zoology and physiology at Sydney Technical College in 1907-08 and became assistant director of the Bathurst Technical College in 1908. He was appointed assistant microbiologist at the newly established Bureau of Microbiology of the New South Wales Health Department in 1909. Lecturer in charge of the department of biology in the new University of Queensland from 1911, he was appointed professor in 1919.

Johnston was chairman of a committee formed in 1912 to investigate control measures for the introduced pest, prickly pear, and worked overseas in 1912-14 with Henry Tryon [q.v.]. The two men, known as 'the prickly pair', succeeded in introducing *Dactylopius ceylonicus*, the cochineal insect which controlled one species of the pear *Opuntia monacantha*. In 1920 Johnston was appointed controller of the Commonwealth prickly pear laboratories and went overseas again in 1920-22. He had twice collected and introduced unsuccessfully the insect *Cactoblastis cactorum* in 1914, when it did feed on the pear but died out in 1921. The eventual devastation of the prickly pear by it followed a later introduction in 1924.

Johnston was keenly interested in the marine ecology of Caloundra and the southern Barrier Reef islands. He was president of the Royal Society of Queensland (1915-16) and of the Queensland Field Naturalists' Club (1916-17). He was a foundation member of the Great Barrier Reef Committee and a member of the Australian National Research Council until his death.

Johnston was appointed professor of zoology at the University of Adelaide in 1922, creating a new department, and acted also as professor of botany in 1928-34. Specializing in descriptive parasitology, he was also a world authority on helminthology; he added much new material to the extensive collection of the South Australian Museum. At the invitation of Sir Douglas Mawson [q.v.] he served as chief zoologist with the British, Australian and New Zealand Antarctic Research Expedition of 1929, went on two cruises of the *Discovery* in 1929-31 and was editor of the zoological and botanical reports. In 1929-37 he participated with (Sir) John Cleland [q.v.8] in many expeditions to Central Australia.

Active in many scientific and cultural institutions and societies, Johnston won numerous honours including the David Syme [q.v.6] prize in 1913, the first Walter and Eliza Hall [qq.v.] fellowship in economic biology in the University of Queensland, the Sir Joseph Verco [q.v.] medal and, in 1939, the Mueller [q.v.5] medal of the Australian and New Zealand Association for the Advancement of Science. He wrote or co-authored 299 papers.

Affectionately known as 'T.H.J.', Johnston was gentle, kindly, hard working, clear thinking and sensitive, with a slow, quiet sense of humour. He lived up to a high ethical code and was in the sense of the Greek philosophers 'a complete man'. He died in Adelaide of coronary thrombosis on 30 August 1951, survived by his wife and daughter; his son predeceased him. He was cremated.

D. J. and S. G. M. Carr, *Plants and man in Australia* (Syd, 1981); Roy Soc SA, *Trans*, 75 (Nov 1952), and for publications; Roy Soc Qld, *Procs*, 64, Mar 1954; *Queenslander*, 25 Dec 1920; T. H. Johnston notes 1914-1930 (SA Museum, Adel).

DOROTHEA F. SANDARS

JOHNSTON(E), ROBERT MACKENZIE (1843-1918), civil servant, scientist and statistician, was born on 27 November 1843 at Connage, Invernesshire, Scotland, son of Lachlan Johnstone, crofter, and his wife Mary, née Mackenzie. His mother died in his infancy, and he was raised by his eldest sister. He early showed an aptitude for study and became an avid reader, especially of biographies of humble boys rising to eminence by their own exertions; he also developed an interest in natural history, encouraged by Hugh Miller, a neighbouring stonemason and geologist. After village schooling he worked on a local farm but became discontented with country life and ran away from home in 1859.

At first he combined manual labour in Edinburgh with wide reading; then as a worker on railway construction in north Scotland he was able to study rocks, soil and vegetation. After he became a ticket-clerk the company promoted him to its head office in Glasgow where he attended evening classes in botany, geology and chemistry at Anderson's University. In 1870 he sold most of his possessions and sailed to Melbourne. He went on to Tasmania and that year was given charge of the accounts section of the Launceston and Western Railway; he became accountant and storekeeper when it passed into public ownership in 1872. In 1880 Johnston became chief clerk in the government Audit Department. After a composite Statistical and General Registry Department was created in 1882 he was appointed government statistician, registrar of births, deaths and marriages and registrar of trade marks and letters patent; he held these offices for thirty-six years.

With new opportunities to develop his scientific interests Johnston was soon involved in expeditions to little-known parts of the island. He published his *Field memoranda for Tasmanian botanists* in 1874. After compiling a descriptive catalogue of Tasmanian fishes in 1882 he was appointed a member of the 1883 royal commission on Tasmanian fisheries; later he joined the Salmon Commission and its successor, the Fisheries Board. He contributed many papers on palaeontology, geology, zoology and botany to the Australasian Association for the Advancement of Science, and the Royal Society of Tasmania; the society also received his large collection of fossils, Aboriginal flints and natural history specimens which he had collected with Ronald Campbell Gunn [q.v.1]. But his greatest claim to scientific fame was his monumental *Systematic account of the geology of Tasmania* (1888). Its treatment of the island's Permian, Triassic and Tertiary rocks and fossils demonstrated outstanding scientific skills and laid firm foundations for the serious study of Tasmanian geology.

Johnston also lectured and published widely on economics and social science. He was a powerful opponent of radical and collectivist economic writing. While sympathizing with the poor and unemployed and an enthusiastic supporter of old age pensions, he insisted that workers' welfare could be improved more effectively by gov-ernment planning of private activity, including scientific allocation of labour, than by government ownership. In the applied field of statistics he won high repute. President of the economic and social science and statistics section of the A.A.A.S. in 1890, he was often invited to move from Hobart to more important statistical posts in other Australian colonies.

Under Johnston the scope and detail of Tasmanian statistics were broadened and methods of collection and presentation improved. He superintended the censuses of 1891 and 1901, introduced statistics of factory activity and had the finances of friendly societies placed on a sound footing. He was a major influence on the Australia-wide design of the censuses of 1891 which made radical reforms in methods, including introduction of an industrial classification to complement the traditional occupational one. In 1890-92 he published the first three issues of the *Tasmanian official record*, yearbooks designed to offer a more popular descriptive account of the colony and its economy than annual statistical tables could provide. Lack of funds ended the venture, but Johnston's work was acknowledged when the Tasmanian official year-books resumed in 1967. He attended all the intercolonial conferences of Australian government statisticians, and was well aware of the pressures for centralization of statistical services, especially after the Commonwealth Bureau of Census and Statistics was created in 1906. As a stout defender of State rights he opposed these moves.

Johnston also figured prominently in discussions about how surplus revenues of the new Commonwealth government should be distributed among the States, in the 1890s issuing 'showers of figures' to show how Tasmania would be disadvantaged by the arrangements originally proposed. He was from the outset a staunch advocate of distribution of the surplus on a *per capita* basis, with special treatment for the small States, and although his arguments were not at first accepted, he lived to see the principle adopted.

He was before his time in his ideas on municipal districts. In giving evidence to a parliamentary select committee in 1888 Johnston advocated larger municipal units, a standing board to advise the government on boundaries, and the harmonizing of the divisions so formed for all administrative purposes. In 1890-1902 he was chairman of a boundaries board of advice, although this was ineffective. He was active in the formation of the Civil Service Association in 1897 and was chairman of the newly created Civil Service Board from 1901 until its replacement in 1906 by a Public Service Board with an appointed full-time chairman. He also became a persistent advocate of the Hare-Clark [q.v.3] system of proportional representation adopted for city electorates in the House of Assembly in 1896 and for all Tasmania in 1907; his belief in its virtues stemmed partly from his views on intrastate divisions and boundaries, and his interest was sustained by the mathematical challenge the new system presented.

Despite his great achievements, Johnston was quiet, unassuming and kindly. He never married but was almost fatherly towards his friends' children, many of whom were remembered with his Scottish nephews and nieces in his will. A fellow of the Linnean Society of London and the Royal Geographical Society of Australasia and honorary fellow of the Royal Statistical Society of London, he was awarded the Imperial Service Order in 1903. He was a member of various Anglican choirs and examined for the Royal College of Music, London. He was a member of the Hobart Committee of Technical Education in 1888-90, and in 1894-1918 served on the Council of the University of Tasmania. He died in Hobart of heart disease on 20 April 1918 and was buried in Queenborough cemetery. The statistical and administrative operating systems he advocated are as much his monument as the writings he left behind him, some of which were assembled in a memorial volume in 1921.

The R. M. Johnston memorial volume (Hob, 1921); E. W. Skeats, Some founders of Australian geology (Syd, 1934); C. D. W. Goodwin, Economic enquiry in Australia (Durham, N.C., 1966); Roy Soc Tas, Papers, 1918; Mercury, 22, 23 Apr 1918; D. N. Allen, The development of official statistics in Tasmania (Diploma of Public Administration dissertation, Univ Tas, 1965); Hunt Inst biogs (Basser Lib, Canb).   R. L. WETTENHALL

JOHNSTONE, JOHN LORIMER GIBSON (1881-1968), soldier and solicitor, was born on 4 March 1881 at Armidale, New South Wales, seventh child of Scottish-born Dr Thomas Johnstone, Presbyterian minister, and his wife Eliza, née Glass, from Singleton. Educated at The Armidale School, he was later prominent in its development, becoming treasurer, president of the old boys' union, member of council and honorary vice-president.

Johnstone was articled in 1899 to Albert Whitby Simpson, founder of Armidale's oldest law firm. After World War I he became a partner in A. W. Simpson & Co., solicitors, with Eustace and A. W. (Jack) Simpson. He retired from the partnership and active work on 16 November 1962. 'J.L.G.' had been a foundation member and early

president of the Tamworth and North-West Law Association.

From the school cadets Johnstone had enlisted as a bugler in the New South Wales Lancers. In 1905 he was commissioned second lieutenant, 6th Australian Light Horse Regiment, which became the New England Light Horse in 1906 and the 5th Light Horse (New England) in 1912; he was promoted lieutenant in 1906 and captain in 1912. Johnstone enlisted in the Australian Imperial Force on 25 August 1914 as a sergeant and embarked from Sydney with the 1st Field Artillery Brigade Ammunition Column; his unit served with the British artillery at Cape Helles, Gallipoli, from April to December 1915. He then served on the Western Front from March 1916 until the Armistice. Commissioned second lieutenant in May 1916, he was transferred to the 1st Divisional Artillery's Heavy Trench-Mortar Battery. He was promoted lieutenant next September and temporary captain in June 1917 and commanded the battery after being mentioned in dispatches. While still serving with the A.I.F. he was confirmed as captain, 12th Light Horse, Australian Military Forces. His A.I.F. appointment ended in April 1919.

On 10 August 1920 Johnstone married a masseuse, Noémi Marie Genevieve de Lepervanche at Neutral Bay, Sydney. Johnstone resumed his legal practice and continued service with the 12th Light Horse; he was promoted major in 1923 and lieut-colonel in 1927 and was commanding officer of the regiment in 1927-33. In 1936-40 he commanded the 2nd Cavalry Brigade and was granted temporary rank of brigadier in 1938. Taken on strength, 2nd Australian Motor Brigade, in 1941, he retired with the honorary rank of brigadier in June 1942.

The interest of this gentle, slightly built man in his fellow ex-servicemen was shown in his inaugural presidency of the Armidale and Dumaresq Shire Repatriation Committee, a position he held until 1964, and in his foundation membership and presidency (1952) of Armidale Legacy Club. He was director in 1921-66 and for many years chairman of the New England Mutual Building and Investment Society. Cricket, golf, tennis and shooting were among his active interests. Survived by his wife, one son and four daughters, he died at Armidale on 27 July 1968 and was cremated after a service at St Paul's Presbyterian Church.

E. Rolls, A million wild acres (Melb, 1981); Armidale Hist Soc, J and Procs, no 25, 1982; London Gazette, 1 June 1917; Armidale Express, 29 July 1968; Johnstone family records, New England Historical Resources Centre, Armidale; information from Messrs P. L. and I. M. Johnstone and Miss J. L. Johnstone, Armidale, NSW.   JOHN ATCHISON

JOLLIE-SMITH; *see* SMITH

JOLLY, NORMAN WILLIAM (1882-
1954), forester, was born on 5 August 1882
at Mintaro, South Australia, son of Henry
Dickson Jolly, storekeeper, and his wife
Annie, née Lathlean. Educated at Mintaro
State School, Prince Alfred College, Adelaide, (where he was dux) and the University
of Adelaide (B.Sc., 1901), he taught at
Townsville Grammar School, Queensland,
before proceeding to Balliol College, Oxford, in 1904 as South Australia's first
Rhodes Scholar. His sporting ability
matched his intellectual brilliance: he
played A-grade cricket, rowed in the Adelaide university eight and three times represented South Australia in Australian
Rules football. After graduating B.A. from
Oxford with a first in natural science (1907)
he studied under (Sir) William Schlich, and
briefly in Europe, to obtain the Oxford
diploma of forestry. He joined the Indian
Forest Service in Burma in 1907 but returned to Australia in 1909 to teach at Geelong Church of England Grammar School.
  Next year, as instructor in forestry for the
South Australian Department of Woods and
Forests, Jolly founded the first course in
higher forestry training in Australia; he was
also assistant conservator of forests in 1911.
On 18 August at Parkside Methodist Church
he married a widow, Mary Clyatt Gellert,
née Colebatch, and that month moved to
Queensland as director of forests, remaining there until 1918 when he became one of
the forestry commissioners in New South
Wales. An appointment as the first professor of forestry at the University of Adelaide followed in 1925. However, when that
school was closed after the formation of the
Australian Forestry School by the Commonwealth government in 1926, Jolly resigned
to return to New South Wales as sole forestry commissioner. He retired in October
1933 with impaired health after continual
conflicts with the government over policy,
and returned to Adelaide. In 1937 Jolly
undertook consultancy work with New Zealand Perpetual Forests Ltd and in 1939 he
became forestry consultant to the South
Australian Woods and Forests Department
and a member of the South Australian Forestry Board. He was elected an honorary
member of the Institute of Foresters of Australia in 1953.
  Reticent about his personal achievements, Jolly commanded the enduring respect of students and subordinates. He is
credited with the establishment of proper
forest management in Queensland and his
'Silvicultural notes on forest trees in
Queensland' and 'The structure and iden-

tification of Queensland woods', published
by the Public Lands Department in 1917,
were pioneering technical forestry publications in that State. The authorship of the
first manual of Australian silviculture, published by the Forest Commission of New
South Wales in 1920, is also attributed to
Jolly. Yet he was a reluctant author and his
sixteen papers do not fully indicate his contribution to Australian forestry. Regret-
tably he restricted publication of his adaptation to South Australian conditions of
German mensuration work on the volume
line theory to internal manuscript only,
although that work was the corner-stone of
South Australia's subsequent high international standing in the forecasting and
management of the yield from plantation
forests.
  Jolly's outstanding characteristic was his
professional integrity; in all matters of administrative judgement he was first and
foremost a forester. This led, on the one
hand, to implementation of sound forestry
practice in both *Eucalyptus* forests and
Pinus plantations, and, on the other, to some
difficulty in compromising over conjoint
matters.
  Jolly died in Adelaide of pyelonephritis on
18 May 1954 and was cremated; he was survived by a daughter. In 1954 the Institute
of Foresters established the N. W. Jolly
medal as its highest award and in 1957 a
cairn to his memory was unveiled in a 180
ft. (55 m) high stand of virgin *Eucalyptus
microcorys* (tallow wood) in Moonpar State
Forest, near Dorrigo, New South Wales.

N. B. Lewis, *A hundred years of state forestry*
(Adel, 1975); *PD* (NSW), 1933-34, p 383; *Australian
Forestry*, 17 (1953), no 2, p 31; *Empire Forestry Review*, 33 (1954), no 3, p 200; *Advertiser* (Adel), 1
July 1904, 19 May 1954; *Observer* (Adel), 19 Sept,
3 Oct 1925; *SMH*, 8, 9, 11, 12, 13 Sept 1933; personal, *and* family information.   N. B. LEWIS

JOLLY, WILLIAM ALFRED (1881-
1955), accountant, mayor and politician,
was born on 11 September 1881 at Spring
Hill, Brisbane, son of Alexander Jolly, gardener, and his wife Mary, née Kelly. Educated at Ashgrove State School, he worked
as a clerk for the law firms Hamilton &
Graham, and Atthow & MacGregor before
starting to study accountancy. Later, he
worked for the National Cash Register Co.,
as secretary of the Synchronome Electrical
Co. and as accountant to the Lowood
Creamery Co. Once qualified (F.C.A., 1913),
he joined A. J. Robinson in the accountancy
firm Robinson & Jolly in 1914. He became
a local authority auditor and served on the
State council (chairman 1934-36) and the

general council of the Federal Institute of Accountants for several years. When the Institute of Chartered Accountants in Australia was established in 1928, he was elected to the first board and to the general council for three years. He was a director of the Queensland National Bank and, subsequently, of the National Bank of Australasia when it absorbed the Queensland bank in 1948.

After serving an apprenticeship as secretary of the Wooloowin Progress Association, Jolly was an alderman of the Windsor Town Council in 1912-25 and mayor in 1918-23, but his interest in municipal affairs extended beyond his own suburb. He represented metropolitan local authorities on the Brisbane and South Coast District Hospitals Board for several years and the north Brisbane councils on the Brisbane Tramways Trust in 1923-25. Under his leadership as mayoral candidate in the first elections for the Greater Brisbane City Council in 1925, the United Party won the mayoralty and thirteen of the nineteen wards. Though renamed the Nationalist Civic Party, Jolly's team repeated its success in 1928 when he expanded his personal vote as mayor. He resigned just before the end of his second term to groom the vice-mayor as a mayoral candidate for the next election. He himself turned later to national politics, won Lilley for the United Australia Party in 1937, increased his majority in 1940 and was narrowly defeated in 1943. He then retired from politics.

President of the Brisbane Rotary Club, Jolly was also a board member of the Young Men's Christian Association and several times president. A keen golfer, he was largely responsible for the establishment of the Victoria Park Golf Club, was its first president and later a life member. As an active and prominent Methodist layman, he attended both State and general conferences and was a councillor of King's College in the University of Queensland. Jolly was reported to have declined an offer by the McCormack [q.v.] government of a knighthood because it might interfere with his family life and gardening, but he was appointed C.M.G. in 1927 and, in his second civic term, was elevated to lord mayor.

Jolly was genial, unassuming and respected and popular for his civic work. Direct election of the mayor and the strong executive powers granted by the City of Brisbane Act suited his personality. Despite initial reservations he became a firm believer in the Greater Brisbane scheme. He was clearly a prime mover in developing high-grade arterial road systems, the expansion of drainage, the purchase of extensive parklands and the construction of the Grey Street Bridge (now renamed the William Jolly Bridge). He was particularly proud of his role in deciding the university site. His determination that Greater Brisbane should succeed inspired his every action.

Jolly married Lillie Maude Moorhouse on 8 January 1907; they had seven sons. He died at his Windsor home on 30 May 1955 from hypertension and coronary occlusion and was buried in Toowong cemetery. A portrait by Caroline Barker is held by the Brisbane City Council's art gallery.

Men of Queensland (Brisb, 1929); G. Greenwood and J. Laverty, *Brisbane 1859-1959* (Brisb, 1959); *Daily Mail* (Brisb), 23 Apr 1927; *Courier Mail*, 31 May 1958; W. A. Jolly, unpublished biographical summary (held by Mr S. Jolly, Brisbane); City Council Minutes, 1925-31 (Town Hall, Brisb).

JOHN LAVERTY

JONES, ALFRED JAMES (1871-1945), politician and mayor, was born on 4 October 1871 at Gayndah, Queensland, son of Joseph Jones, bushman and selector, and his wife Ann, née Stevens. Educated at the Burnett State School, Jones drifted as pupil-teacher, selector, drover, coach driver, storekeeper and goldminer before turning to politics. He won the Legislative Assembly seat of Burnett for the Labor Party in 1904, lost it after the Kidston [q.v.] split in 1909, and failed to regain it in 1912. A partner in a Maryborough mining and investment firm, he won Maryborough in the landslide Labor victory of 1915. He resigned the seat in 1917 to become leader of the government in the Legislative Council and was appointed to the cabinet as secretary for mines. He resigned in 1920 to contest Carnarvon but when he failed to secure election was reappointed to the council. In 1922 he won Paddington, abandoned by J. A. Fihelly [q.v.8], and held it until Labor was defeated in 1929.

Jones was secretary for mines almost continuously from 1917 to 1929. Indeed, mining and oil exploration became almost an obsession with him. Though himself an eminently unsuccessful miner, he displayed a sound working knowledge of the industry in his speeches and press articles. Nevertheless most of the numerous government mining ventures launched by him proved to be white elephants. Bernays [q.v.3] accused him of 'a Micawber-like hope of something turning up'. Though deeply committed to the Chillagoe and Mungana mines, Jones was never associated with the unsavoury financial aspects of these ventures. He took the government into them simply from excessive zeal and optimism.

After a political hiatus during the Depression, Jones successfully contested the lord mayoralty of Brisbane for the Labor

Party in 1934. His team won fifteen of the twenty-one wards and immediately set about reinstating the original Greater Brisbane concept after the disastrous subversion of metropolitan administration by the conservative Moore [q.v.] government. More importantly, they began an extensive programme of loan-financed civic works. Although the party was re-elected for a second term in 1937 with a reduced but still substantial majority, rumours of patronage at city hall had induced the central executive of the Labor Party to withdraw the endorsement of half the former Labor aldermen including five committee chairmen. Public accusations of continued patronage, unorthodox or improper financial practices and increasing evidence of maladministration alarmed the State government. The McCracken-George commission, appointed at Jones's request by the government in 1937, found clear evidence of patronage, inefficiency, a lack of effective co-ordination between departments, wastage of resources and inadequate planning. Despite Jones's attempts at reform, the weaknesses of the civic Labor administration became a growing embarrassment to the Forgan Smith [q.v.] government. The collapse of the civic budget in 1939 when the loan market dried up forced the hand of the government and a public servant was provided to overhaul the council's administrative system. At the 1940 election Jones and his team were routed.

Bernays described Jones as 'kindly and genial, though heavy and somewhat slow-thinking . . . a loyal man both to his King and country and his party'. He was 'honest and well meaning but optimistic to a fault. As a politician, too trustful'. He failed largely because he could not discipline his team and had neither capacity nor will for reform. In 1922 the *Daily Standard* described him as 'parliamentarian, philosopher and poet' and pointed out the versatility which enabled him to work as miner, auctioneer, stock and station agent, journalist and mining agent when out of parliament. He took great pride in his work as a commissioner for Queensland to the British Empire Exhibition at Wembley in 1924.

A dedicated family man, Jones had married Martha Elizabeth Leggett at Reid's Creek, Gayndah, on 1 May 1895. He died in Brisbane Hospital on 7 October 1945 and was cremated. He was survived by his wife, four sons and four daughters. He had been a practising Anglican.

Jones was an inveterate speechmaker and a regular contributor to the press on topics such as mining, oil exploration, politics, immigration, Australian parochialism and the unnecessary profusion of parliaments in Australia. He occasionally wrote poems for the Sydney *Bulletin* under the pseudonym 'Shrdlu Etaoin'.

The Labour government of Queensland (Brisb, 1915); C. A. Bernays, *Queensland politics during sixty years (1859-1919)* (Brisb, 1919), and *Queensland—our seventh political decade 1920-1930* (Syd, 1931); G. Greenwood and J. Laverty, *Brisbane 1859-1959* (Brisb, 1959); D. J. Murphy et al (eds), *Labor in power . . . Queensland 1915-1957* (Brisb, 1979); *Telegraph* (Brisb), 25 Sept 1931; *Worker* (Brisb), 24 Mar 1932; *Daily Standard*, 22 June 1932; *Courier Mail*, 8 Oct 1945; Central Executive of the ALP, Qld Branch, Minutes, 1918-40 (Brisb Labor House); City Council minutes, 1934-40 (Town Hall, Brisb).

JOHN LAVERTY

JONES, ALLAN MURRAY (1895-1963), airman and company director, was born on 25 February 1895 at Caulfield, Melbourne, son of John Albert Jones, a pharmacist from Wales, and his English-born wife Emily Gertrude, née McIsaac. Preferring to be known as Murray Jones, he was educated at Melbourne High School and then began study at the Melbourne College of Pharmacy.

Jones joined the Victorian Cadet Corps as a second lieutenant in the 47th Battalion in June 1912 and just before World War I interrupted his pharmacy course to join the army. On 16 June 1914 he was commissioned as a second lieutenant, 46th Infantry, Australian Military Forces. He applied for training at the Central Flying School, Point Cook, Victoria, and received his pilot's certificate on 15 June 1915. On 1 July he was seconded to the Australian Flying Corps, A.M.F., as a lieutenant. With Lieutenant (Air Marshal Sir Richard) Williams [q.v.] he completed an advanced flying course in preparation for service in Mesopotamia. The posting did not eventuate and on 5 January 1916 Jones, as a lieutenant in the Australian Imperial Force, joined the newly formed No. 1 Squadron, A.F.C.

The squadron arrived in Egypt in April and between June 1916 and November 1917 Jones was constantly in action against German and Turkish forces in the Sinai Desert. In B.E. 2c, 2e, 12a and Martinsyde aircraft, he developed a reputation for flying prowess and daring and aggressive tactics. In 1916 he was mainly involved in desert reconnaissance and was promoted captain and flight commander in December. In February 1917 he was in a bombing raid on Beersheba, destroying three German aircraft, and next month near Gaza took part in the squadron's first serious aerial combat. On 6 April while escorting a patrol after the 1st battle of Gaza he fought off five enemy planes before his own machine was damaged and forced to land; although the Germans bombed his grounded aircraft he escaped unhurt. After an engagement with a German scout over Rafa in May he was again forced to land and this time was hospitalized in Cairo where 'large pieces of petrol tank' were removed from his leg. He was awarded the Military Cross in April for 'carrying out a raid on a hostile aerodrome. He descended to a height of 500 ft [150 m] under very heavy fire and destroyed two hangars'. He was twice mentioned in dispatches for his Middle East service.

Jones took over as commanding officer, No. 2 Squadron, A.F.C., in France in May 1918. 'If we had one officer outstandingly suited for such an appointment, it was Murray Jones', Williams recalled in his autobiography. Under Major Jones's inspired leadership the squadron emerged as one of the finest on the Western Front. It was equipped with S.E. 5a fighters, and was one of seven squadrons comprising the 80th Wing, Royal Air Force. Lieut-Colonel L. A. Strange, the officer commanding the wing, recorded in his *Recollections of an airman* that Murray Jones was 'a quiet, unassuming fellow, but a most resolute leader . . . No. 2, A.F.C., accounted for over 100 machines in one way or another in four months'. Jones was awarded the Distinguished Flying Cross in June 1918. No. 2 Squadron operated until the Armistice and Jones was again mentioned in dispatches and awarded a Bar to his D.F.C. for service on 10 November when 'he led his whole squadron on a low bombing raid against an enemy railway station. Descending to 100 feet [30 m] he remained at this low altitude till all his machines had completed the attack, though subject to heavy fire from machine-guns'. He was officially credited with shooting down seven enemy aircraft.

Returning to Melbourne in May 1919, Jones was registered as a pharmacist on 14 April 1920. On 9 March 1921 he married Phyllis Adelaide Brown at Christ Church, South Yarra. When invited by Williams, he gave up pharmacy and on 31 March was commissioned in the (Royal) Australian Air Force as a flight lieutenant and honorary squadron leader. In January 1922 he was appointed commanding officer, No. 1 Station, R.A.A.F., Point Cook, a position he retained until he resigned his commission on 30 June 1924. For the next five years he was an orchardist, then on 10 May 1929 joined the Department of Civil Aviation as superintendent of flying operations. 'He was an excellent pilot and able administrator', recalled Arthur Butler, adding that during Jones's term of office 'the greatest expression of flying activities, up to that date, occurred in Australia'.

Jones resigned from the department on 21 July 1931 to become general manager of de Havilland Australia Pty Ltd. Thirty-two years later he was still with the company, having progressed to chairman in 1953 and deputy chairman of Hawker de Havilland Australia Pty Ltd in 1960. 'Murray Jones firmed and widened greatly the de Havilland spheres of service to Australia, and made possible manufacturing developments which vitally helped our war effort, and added an important industrial echelon to our Air Arm', Norman Ellison commented in *Aircraft*, March 1957.

Survived by his wife, son and two daughters, Jones died of cancer at his Double Bay home, Sydney, on 8 December 1963 and was cremated after an Anglican service. His estate was valued for probate at £54 788. Sir Hudson Fysh [q.v.8] observed that 'If anyone lived a full life it was Allan Murray Jones and none of us will forget his infectious laugh with which he would preface the suggestion for a party or some dare, or some shrewd observation on a business topic. He was a kindly, friendly soul, a characteristic which cloaked shrewd judgement and efficiency'.

F. M. Cutlack, *The Australian Flying Corps . . . 1914-1918* (Syd, 1923); L. A. Strange, *Recollections of an airman* (Lond, 1933); L. W. Sutherland and N. Ellison, *Aces and kings* (Syd, 1935); C. A. Butler, *Flying start* (Syd, 1971); K. Isaacs, *Military aircraft of Australia, 1909-1918* (Canb, 1971); *Reveille* (Syd), Nov 1934, Feb 1938; *Aircraft* (Melb), Mar 1957, Jan 1964; King Cole, Merry old souls (MS held by Mrs S. Clerehan, Sth Yarra, Melb).   KEITH ISAACS

JONES, SIR CHARLES LLOYD (1878-1958), merchant and patron of the arts, was born on 28 May 1878 at Burwood, Sydney, son of native-born parents Edward Lloyd Jones (d. 1894), draper, and his wife Helen Ann, née Jones, and grandson of David Jones [q.v.2]. He was educated at the Manor House School, London, and Homebush Grammar School, Sydney, but showed little academic aptitude. In 1895 he attended Julian Ashton's [q.v.7] art school and later the Slade School of Fine Art, University College, London. Failing in his ambition to exhibit at the Royal Academy of Arts, he gave up hopes of an artistic career, and qualified as a tailor and cutter in London. On 16 November 1900 when visiting Sydney he married Winifred Ethelwyn (d. 1916), daughter of Dr Frederick Quaife and granddaughter of Rev. Barzillai Quaife [q.v.2], at Trinity Congregational Church, Strathfield; they were childless.

On his return to Sydney in 1902, Jones worked in David Jones' clothing factory before transferring to the advertising department. His creative flair and awareness of American trends were recognized and by 1905 he was advertising manager. When David Jones Ltd became a public company in 1906, he was appointed a director and was chairman in 1920-58. Under his guidance the firm prospered and expanded: a second store in Elizabeth Street was completed in 1927 (which benefited from the nearby St James station) and a third on the corner of Market and Castlereagh streets was opened in 1938 to mark the firm's centenary. The first interstate extension came in 1953 with the acquisition of Bon Marché in Perth.

A staunch advocate of free enterprise, Jones prided himself that David Jones was a 'store with a soul', dedicated to customer service, responsible to its shareholders (who regularly received a ten per cent dividend) and to its staff. Strict when necessary, Jones was approachable and a ready listener; his paternalistic care for staff and his quiet courtesy won him respect and loyalty.

Among other public positions Jones was treasurer of the Sydney Chamber of Commerce (1915-16), president of the Retail Traders' Association of New South Wales (1915), the Australian division of the Chartered Institute of Secretaries and of the Kindergarten Union of New South Wales, a founder and director of the board supervising the Australian National Travel Association, chairman of the Cancer Appeal Fund and member of the University Cancer Research Committee. A director of radio station 2BL, he was appointed first chairman of the Australian Broadcasting Commission in May 1932. He hoped to found a national orchestra and wanted the A.B.C. to follow 'in the footsteps of the British Broadcasting Corporation' with programmes that would be popular as well as cultural. Educational broadcasts and concerts began, but striking a balance between ideals and resources proved difficult. Conflict over content and disunity in the administration, coupled with the death of his brother and Depression business worries, led him to resign in 1934.

A man of medium build, with silver hair, thin lips and shrewd humorous blue eyes, Jones was described as 'that rare combination of artist and businessman'. Much influenced by the French Impressionists he continued to paint landscapes and regularly exhibited with the Society of Artists, Sydney, of which he was sometime treasurer. He built up a notable private collection of paintings including the works of Conder, Bunny [qq.v.3,7], Streeton [q.v.] and Maurice Utrillo. He was an early patron of William Dobell. In 1916, with Sydney Ure Smith and Bertram Stevens [qq.v.], he foun-

ded the quarterly journals, *Art in Australia* and the *Home*. He was a trustee of the National Art Gallery of New South Wales in 1934-58 and in 1944 established the David Jones' Art Gallery. He occasionally contributed articles to the press and also encouraged music and the theatre.

At Auckland, New Zealand, on 29 October 1917 Jones had married Louise Violet Multras (d. 1973). He divorced her at Reno, Nevada, United States of America, on 19 July 1929 and at Chicago on 25 July he married Hannah Benyon Jones (d. 1982) of Sydney. From the early 1930s they lived at Rosemont, Woollahra, where they frequently entertained politicians and overseas visitors. (Sir) Robert Menzies was a close friend.

A veteran sailor and member of the Royal Sydney Yacht Squadron from 1903, Jones was rear-commodore in 1906-08 and commodore in 1949-55. He was a founder of the Rotary Club of Sydney in 1921 and a member of the Australian, Athenaeum and Royal Sydney Golf clubs and the Royal Automobile Club, London. Knighted in 1951, he was appointed officer of the Légion d'honneur in 1954.

Sir Charles died at Rosemont on 30 July 1958 and was cremated after a service at St Andrew's Cathedral when Menzies gave the funeral oration. He was survived by a daughter of his second marriage and by his third wife and their two sons. His estate was valued for probate at £235 768. Portraits of Jones by Dobell (1951) and Ivor Hele (1958) are held by the family. His own paintings are represented in the Art Gallery of New South Wales and the National Gallery of Victoria.

P. R. Stephensen (ed), *Sydney sails* (Syd, 1962); *PD* (Cwlth), 1952, p 106, 130; *Newspaper News*, 8 Aug 1958; *Art and Australia*, Sept 1971; *SMH*, 25 Apr, 19, 22, 31 July 1929, 28 May 1932, 9 May 1952, 31 July 1958; *Daily Telegraph*, 25 May 1946; *Smith's Weekly* (Syd), 1, 8, 18 May 1948; *People* (Syd), 1 June 1955; R. M. Thompson, David Jones' in war and peace (B.A. Hons thesis, Macquarie Univ, 1980); personal and business records, David Jones Ltd archives (Syd).   RUTH THOMPSON

JONES, DORIS EGERTON (1889-1973), writer, was born on 23 December 1889 at Mitcham, Adelaide, daughter of John Elias Jones, accountant, and his wife Emma Marie, née Fischer. The family moved around Victorian and Western Australian goldfields when Doris was young, but she later attended Glenelg Public School and, in 1901-05, the Advanced School for Girls in Adelaide. At 14 she wrote her first play, 'Ned Kelly, bushranger', and next year a novel, *Peter Piper*. The heroine of this romance dressed as a boy until she was 18 when her 'womanliness' asserted itself; it was published in London in 1913.

From 1909, while living with her mother, sister and uncle Dr Fischer, Doris Jones attended the University of Adelaide (B.A., 1911). After graduating she began to study law, although women were not allowed to practise in South Australia. She protested to Premier John Verran [q.v.] and later in 1911 an enabling law was passed, but she became ill and abandoned study. She resumed writing and contributed to the war effort; her story 'Burnt offerings' in the *Lady Galway Belgium book* (1916) shows a youth in conflict over whether to enlist.

In 1915 Jones had published the novels *Time o' Day* and *Green eyes*. Next year, *The coconut planter*, in which she utilized material gathered on holiday in New Guinea, appeared; its heroine struggled to establish her independence. In 1918 Jones travelled to London where she sold her first play, 'Uncle Buncle'. On 28 March at St Matthew's, Bayswater, she married Reginald Callaghan, a clerk who had served with the Australian Imperial Force. She also published her last book, *The year between*. Like her other novels it was mostly narrated in the first person by a rather breathless heroine who begins life as an innocent tomboy. There are excellent descriptions of the Australian bush, maltreatment and misunderstanding of Aboriginals by whites, and the Anzac landing at Gallipoli; but the sentimental plot moves slowly to an improbably delayed happy ending. The novel belongs to the romance fiction genre.

Doris Jones, who kept her maiden name for writing, returned with her husband to Sydney in 1922 where she collaborated with the actress Emelie Polini to write *The flaw*. Her first play to be performed, it was staged by J. C. Williamson [q.v.6] Ltd at the Criterion Theatre from 27 January 1923. Although criticized as 'the rawest melodrama', it proved popular. Her next play, produced in August 1930, was a three-act historical comedy, *Governor Bligh*. The author portrayed Bligh [q.v.1] as an Australian patriot, 'a hot-headed, hard-shelled, warm hearted, kindly disciplinarian'.

Jones now had a daughter and two sons and she gave up writing to rear them. 'I do not think it is possible to write and mother a family at the same time', she said. Her later writing failed to find a publisher. Her recreations were mothercraft, bridge and charity causes and she read Shaw, Wilde and Galsworthy. A tall, vital woman who preferred to dress in mauve, she remained enthusiastic and strong minded, although often unwell. In 1944 her eldest son was shot down flying over Germany. In 1963

Reginald Callahan (they had changed the name's spelling) died. Survived by her daughter and younger son, Doris Egerton Jones died on 30 September 1973 at Wahroonga and was cremated.

P. Depasquale, *A critical history of South Australian literature, 1836-1930 . . .* (Adel, 1978); N. Krauth (ed), *New Guinea images in Australian literature* (Brisb, 1982); *Stage and Society*, 11 Jan 1923; *Woman's World*, 1 Feb 1923; *Aust Woman's Mirror*, 23 Sept 1930; Pioneer Books of Adel, *In-House*, June, Sept 1982; *Sunday Sun* (Syd), 28 Jan 1923; information from Mr Terry Callahan, Wahroonga, Syd.   SUZANNE EDGAR

JONES, ERNEST (1869-1943), cricketer, was born on 30 September 1869 at Auburn, South Australia, son of Joseph Jones, stonemason, and his wife Mary, née Williams. After attending the local school he worked with his father as a painter and mason on government contract works around Quorn and at Broken Hill, New South Wales. He began his cricketing career as a deadly tearaway bowler on indifferent country pitches, then joined North Adelaide Cricket Club where he had considerable success. He first played for South Australia in December 1892 and for Australia against England in 1894.

Jones toured England in 1896, 1899 and 1902 taking 121, 135 and 71 wickets at 19 runs apiece. His English début was sensational. In the first match against a top England XI Jones put a ball through W. G. Grace's beard and to W.G.'s imperious 'What do you think you're at, Jonah?', replied 'Sorry, Doctor, she slipped'. He hit Grace in the chest, broke F. S. Jackson's ribs and took 7 for 84—only Ranjitsinhji mastered the terrific pace. Thereafter 'Whar be Jones?' was the first question asked everywhere the Australians went. Other successes included 8 for 39 against an England XI and 6 for 74 and 7 for 36 against Yorkshire. Inevitably some asserted that he threw, but Jones was never 'called' in England. Although he was less successful in the Tests, W. L. Murdoch [q.v.5] and Sussex offered him £350 a year to qualify for residence, but he declined.

In Australia in 1897-98 he took 22 Test wickets at 25.13 apiece and a record 14 for 237 for South Australia against an England XI at Adelaide. In the five Tests in England in 1899 Jones was more destructive than H. Trumble or M. A. Noble [qq.v.] taking 26 wickets at 25.26; his 10 for 164 at Lords clinched the rubber. In 1902 the wet weather told against fast bowlers and he took only three Test wickets.

In the 1900s Jones played several games

for Western Australia, ending his first-class career in 1907. In 19 Tests he took 60 wickets at 29.28 apiece; in Sheffield Shield and first-class cricket he took 209 at 26.35 and 645 at 22.75 runs respectively. In 1912 he joined the shipping branch of the Department of Trade and Customs as a searcher and watchman at Fremantle where he rowed out to barrack visiting English teams aboard ship. He transferred to Port Adelaide in 1924 and was promoted in 1927.

Australia's first express bowler, 'Jonah', tallish, barrel-chested and very strong, always attacked the stumps; from a comparatively short run he made the ball lift sharply on a good length. He was a magnificent off-side fieldsman, but a slogger with the bat. When introduced to the prince of Wales, who asked if he had gone to St Peter's College, Adelaide, he facetiously replied, 'Yes, I take the dust cart there regularly!'. He was also a professional runner and fine Australian Rules footballer, playing for South Australia, and for South, Port and North Adelaide clubs, captaining the last to its first premiership.

Jones died on 23 November 1943 in Royal Adelaide Hospital and was buried in West Terrace cemetery. He was survived by his wife Eliza, née Matthews, whom he had married in Adelaide on 12 September 1893, and by a daughter; two sons and two daughters predeceased him.

F. Iredale, *33 years of cricket* (Syd, 1920); A. G. Moyes, *Australian bowlers . . .* (Syd, 1953); *Wisden Cricketers' Almanack*, 1943; *Sporting Globe*, 22 Jan 1941, 27 Nov 1943; information from Mr M. W. Jones, Reid, ACT.   G. P. WALSH

JONES, FREDERIC WOOD (1879-1954), anatomist, naturalist and anthropologist, was born on 23 January 1879 at Hackney, London, only son and youngest of three children of Charles Henry Jones, builder, slate merchant and architect, and his wife Lucy, née Allin. The family moved to Enfield where he attended local schools and showed enthusiasm for natural history. In 1897 he entered the London Hospital Medical College which in 1900 became part of the University of London where he graduated (B.Sc., 1903; M.B., B.S., 1904; D.Sc., 1910). In 1904 he became a member of the Royal College of Surgeons; he was made a fellow in 1930.

At the university he began a lifelong friendship with the anatomist (Sir) Arthur Keith whose encouragement influenced him to make his career in anatomy, but, as a young graduate, Wood Jones found medicine 'cramped and small when compared to biology' and jumped at the chance of a post

as medical officer to the Eastern Extension Telegraph Co. on the Cocos-Keeling Islands (1905-06). There his duties left him time for studies in natural history which earned him a doctorate, published as *Coral and atolls* (London, 1910). There, too, he met his future wife Gertrude, daughter of George Clunies-Ross, governor of Cocos-Keeling. Married in London on 11 June 1910, they had no issue but his wife brought to the union five children by an earlier marriage. Wood Jones dedicated almost all his books to her.

The foundation of his work in anthropology was laid when, granted leave as demonstrator at the 'London', he obeyed a summons from (Sir) Grafton Elliot Smith [q.v.], professor of anatomy, Cairo, to join the archaeological survey of Nubia, made urgent because the raising in height of the Aswan Dam would soon flood important sites. Elliot Smith had academic duties in Cairo and, after a few weeks training, Wood Jones was left as his deputy to examine, in the trying conditions of desert camps, the human relics from thousands of burials of widely ranging antiquity. The quality of his work won Elliot Smith's admiration, and their results were published in the second volume of *The archaeological survey of Nubia: report for 1907-1908* (Cairo, 1910).

Wood Jones gained experience as an academic anatomist through teaching posts at the medical schools of the London, St Thomas's and the Royal Free hospitals, and at the University of Manchester. At the Royal Free (London School of Medicine for Women) he was appointed lecturer and head of department (1912) and professor of anatomy (1915). He gave the Arris and Gale lectures at the Royal College of Surgeons (1914, 1915, 1916, 1919), some of which formed the nucleus of *Arboreal Man* (London, 1916) which addressed one of his central interests, the evolution of man. Early in 1918 he joined the army as captain, Royal Army Medical Corps. As he was posted to the Special Military Surgical Hospital, Shepherd's Bush, London, he was still able to fit in some lectures for the school. His anatomical masterpiece, *The principles of anatomy as seen in the hand* (London, 1920), had its origin in lectures given at Shepherd's Bush.

On the recommendation of Keith, Wood Jones was offered the (Thomas) Elder [q.v.4] chair of anatomy at the University of Adelaide in 1919 and took up his duties in January 1920. These, he discovered to his dismay, had to be carried out in cramped quarters without adequate technical assistance or anatomical specimens. With his usual energy, and skill in presenting a case, he persuaded the university to build him a lecture theatre and provide a skilled technician with whom he could begin to assemble a museum. That Wood Jones was a brilliant teacher had been demonstrated in London. In Adelaide as, later, in Melbourne, his lectures were widely acclaimed for their infectious enthusiasm, absorbing interest, wit, clarity of exposition and superb blackboard draughtsmanship. Academic considerations apart, the Australian appointment had attracted him because of the opportunities it promised for study of the native fauna; and almost all his vacations, and spare money, were spent on field excursions to the inland and islands. He became an active member of the Royal Society of South Australia and the first of his many articles to appear in its *Transactions* was published in 1920. Later he was commissioned to write a handbook, *The mammals of South Australia*, which was illustrated with his own drawings and published in three parts (Adelaide, 1923-25). He also published *Unscientific essays* (London, 1924), typical of his many writings in lighter vein. He was elected a fellow of the Royal Society in 1925. Wood Jones also became very interested in the Aboriginals both as an anthropologist and as a humanitarian. He was a prime mover in 1926 in founding the Anthropological Society of South Australia. He liked and admired the Aboriginals and was appalled by the conditions under which the detribalized so often had to exist and by public indifference to their plight. He did what he could with his pen to arouse public awareness of the problem in Adelaide and later supported their cause even more vigorously in Melbourne.

In 1920 Wood Jones, as Adelaide's delegate to the Pan-Pacific Scientific Congress in Honolulu, had entered a wider anthropological community, and in 1927 he accepted an invitation to the Rockefeller chair of physical anthropology at the University of Hawaii. There he wrote *The matrix of the mind* (Honolulu, 1928) with the psychologist S. D. Porteus [q.v.] and *Man's place among the mammals* (London, 1929), a sequel to *Arboreal Man*, in which he set out his unorthodox views on the evolution of man whom he considered to be more nearly related to *Tarsius* than to the great apes. At first he rejoiced in the freedom from teaching; but he came to miss it, and was easily persuaded to accept the chair of anatomy at the University of Melbourne in 1930. A drop in salary was at first a stumbling-block, but several Melbourne citizens, mostly medical practitioners, guaranteed an additional £200 a year.

In Melbourne, under the restrictions of the Depression, Wood Jones laboured to build up a department which would embody his ideals. The resulting institution won a high reputation not only for the excellence of its undergraduate teaching but for its encouragement of research. At first there was little time for outside interests, but in 1935 he helped to found the McCoy [q.v.5] Society for Field Investigation and Research, became its first president and took part in its ecological surveys of various offshore islands. He renewed an interest in birds and, in addition to more learned writings, published his delightful book of verse for children, *Sea birds simplified* (London, 1934). He was in great demand as a public speaker and became known to a wider public through contributions to press and radio. In 1932-33 he acted as temporary director of anatomy, Peiping Union Medical College, China. An honorary fellowship of the Royal Australasian College of Surgeons was conferred on him in 1935. He had already received the honorary degree of D.Sc. from the universities of Adelaide (1920) and Melbourne (1934).

Wood Jones had planned to retire and return to England at the end of 1938 but instead he accepted the chair of anatomy in Manchester where his success with students again became legendary. In 1945, to his delight, he was appointed Sir William H. Collins professor of human and comparative anatomy and conservator of the anatomical museum at the Royal College of Surgeons of England. It became a labour of love to restore the Hunterian collection, extensively damaged by an enemy bomb in 1941. In 1951, owing to a change in regulations, Wood Jones, then 72, had to retire. However, the college made him honorary curator of the Hunterian collection and he continued to work there until a few months before his death. He died in London of cancer on 29 September 1954, survived by his wife.

If he made no one dramatic discovery or theoretical advance, Wood Jones's contributions to the sciences were numerous, and impressive in the aggregate; but his genius undoubtedly lay in his powers as a teacher, something of which can still be felt in the vivid prose of his books. He brought to any subject a refreshing originality of approach, seeing new and surprising connexions within it and beyond. He never considered an anatomical structure in isolation from its function in the living animal, or from its embryological or evolutionary development. His standpoint was essentially comparative and evolutionary; but, never afraid of unconventionality, he became a Lamarckian evolutionist. Most people found him a man of great charm and humanity; sometimes unnecessarily scathing in debate with his peers, he was consistently patient and friendly with students who, everywhere, regarded him with affectionate admiration. He rejected orthodox religion and a personal, anthropomorphic deity, but believed that there was mind or spirit of some kind behind Nature. He discussed his metaphysical position in works of his later years such as *Design and purpose* (London, 1942). There is a portrait at the Royal Australasian College of Surgeons, Melbourne, by W. B. McInnes [q.v.] and another by A. Egerton Cooper at the Royal College of Surgeons, London.

B. E. Christophers (comp), *A list of the published works of Frederic Wood Jones, 1879-1954* (Melb, 1974); *MJA*, 2 (1954); Roy College of Surgeons of England, *Annals*, 15 (1954), 25 (1959), 34 (1964); *Adel Medical Students' Review*, May 1955; *J of Anatomy* (Lond), 89 (1955); *Biographical Memoirs of Fellows of the Roy Soc*, 1 (1955); Roy Anthropological Inst, *Man*, 56 (1956); Manchester Univ Medical School, *Gazette*, 37 (1958); *The Times*, 30 Sept 1954; Arthur Keith papers (Roy College of Surgeons of England); information from Rt Rev. M. A. Hodson, Lond, and Miss J. Dobson, Ashford, Middlesex, England.   M. MacCallum

JONES, HAROLD EDWARD (1878-1965), intelligence officer, was born on 22 August 1878 at Beveridge, Victoria, seventh child of George Jones, railway platelayer from Liverpool, England, and his Melbourne-born wife Margaret, née McColl. Educated at state schools, and the Working Men's College, Melbourne, in 1896 he joined the engineering department, Victorian Railways. In 1904 he transferred to the Crown Solicitor's Office as a conveyancing clerk and in 1911 became chief clerk and senior assessor in the Federal Taxation Department. He served as a militiaman in the Australian Corps of Engineers Submarine Mining and Field Troop and in May 1910 as a lieutenant joined the Australian Intelligence Corps (Victoria) under (Sir) John Monash [q.v.]. He was promoted captain in June 1914.

In November 1914 Jones was appointed to head the Intelligence Section, General Staff, operating from the Attorney-General's Department. In January 1916 the section's internal security intelligence responsibilities were largely assumed by Australia's first civil intelligence body, the Counter Espionage Bureau, a branch of the British Counter Espionage Bureau (forerunner of MI5). Jones was promoted brevet major in October 1916 and when the Special Intelligence Bureau was created in February 1917 he was appointed assistant to the director, (Sir) George Steward [q.v.]. Steward's withdrawal later in the year coincided with an emphasis on counter-subversion, particularly surveillance of critics of the Hughes [q.v.] government, and a marked increase in Jones's influence. In November 1919, after a contest with the Department of Defence for control of internal security, the bureau was reorganized as the Commonwealth Investigation Branch and Security Section, with Jones as director. He was to create an agency independent of the States to deal with claims and other matters arising from the war and to investigate offences against the Commonwealth. He was also to continue, under cover of the C.I.B., the Special Intelligence Bureau.

In the tense aftermath of the war Jones deployed his agency in surveillance of communists and Irish nationalists who it was feared would manipulate the unemployed and returned soldiers to revolution. In 1921 he proposed that influential private enterprise be enlisted in an anti-communist propaganda campaign, primed with confidential intelligence in return for financial and organizational support. Extensive files were developed on left-wing individuals and bodies and on militant trade unionists to provide material for government prosecutions. The law was exploited to its limits to root out 'dangerous' elements. The C.I.B. was an integral part of the Attorney-General's Department, supported there by Sir Littleton Groom [q.v.], Sir Robert Garran [q.v.8] and (Sir) John Latham [q.v.]. Jones was the central authority for Australia (under the League of Nations convenants) for white slave traffic, protection of women and children and for obscene publications. He was responsible for investigating and recommending on applications for immigration and naturalization and developed a thorough system of literature surveillance. During the late 1920s European political refugees of the right and the left as well as criminal groups such as the Camorra Society attracted Jones's attention. From 1925 Jones (as chief of police) organized and controlled the Commonwealth Peace Officer Guards, transferring in 1927 to Canberra with the Attorney-General's Department. In 1925-33 he was attached for special duties to the chief of General Staff's branch.

Jones investigated right-wing paramilitary groups in the early 1930s when, alarmed by their potential danger to order, he advised the prime minister that military officers should be ordered to dissociate themselves. During the later 1930s surveillance was extended to the political activities of Nazi Germans and Italians and an interest was taken in the Japanese. Rivalry with military intelligence grew bitter after 1934 when the army mounted an extensive domestic security campaign. When the army took responsibility for internal security in 1939, Jones battled to preserve his territory. In March 1941 the Commonwealth Security Service, a wartime organization, was established in the Attorney-General's Department, leaving C.I.B. with non-security work. Jones, still reporting to MI5, refused to co-operate. He continued his inquiries and refused to relinquish security files and the London codes, transferred eventually in 1942 during his absence.

When Jones retired on 1 January 1944 he held the rank of honorary lieut-colonel on the retired list (1933). He was known as an unpretentious, methodical man who spent his leisure in rose and fruit cultivation, who kept his own counsel and shunned personal publicity or recognition beyond the O.B.E. he was awarded in 1925. In his youth he had won the Victorian amateur 100-yard sprint title and played interstate lacrosse for Victoria and football and cricket for Essendon. He was an honorary member of both the Canberra and Narooma Rotary clubs and served as a district governor of Rotary. He was twice married: to Elizabeth Amelia McKinery on 12 September 1905 in Melbourne, and to Beryl Olivia Dooley on 12 December 1957 at Bega, New South Wales. He died on 20 September 1965 at Moruya and was buried in Narooma cemetery with Anglican rites. He was survived by his wife and two sons and a daughter of his first marriage.

A. Laughlin, *Boots and all* (Melb, 1951); C. D. Coulthard-Clark, *The citizen general staff* (Canb, 1976); R. Hall, *The secret state* (Syd, 1978); G. Cresciani, *Fascism, anti-fascism and Italians in Australia, 1922-1945* (Canb, 1980); *Canb Times*, 25 June 1978; F. M. Cain, The origins of political surveillance 1916-32: reactions to radicalism during and after the First World War (Ph.D. thesis, Monash Univ, 1979).   JACQUELINE TEMPLETON

JONES, SIR HENRY (1862-1926), jam manufacturer, was born on 19 July 1862 in Hobart Town, eldest son of John Jones, clerk in Alexander McGregor's [q.v.5] mercantile and shipping office, and his wife Emma, née Smith. Both parents were Welsh; his father was known as an amusing 'good fellow', but Henry was more influenced by his mother's devout Wesleyanism. He was educated at Mr Canaway's school where he excelled in commercial subjects. After beginning work, aged 12, at George Peacock's [q.v.5] jam factory on the Old Wharf, pasting labels on tins, within a few years he had become an expert jam-boiler. On 21 April 1883 at St David's Anglican Cathedral, Hobart, Jones married Alice Glover, a capable, striking, auburn-haired woman who bore him three sons and nine daughters and who became one of the principal supporters of art in Hobart.

In 1885, at a time when the viability of the Tasmanian intercolonial jam trade was threatened by mainland competition, Jones was promoted factory foreman; and in 1889 when Peacock retired he took control as H. Jones & Co. in partnership with A. W. Palfreyman [q.v.] and Peacock's son Ernest. With Jones as manager the firm slowly recovered: by 1898 'splendid' new premises had been built, the range of canned products had been diversified, and the partners had entered the hop-production business and the overseas export trade. During the partnership period Jones adopted the brand name IXL (a play on 'I excel') and was himself popularly dubbed 'Jam Tin Jones'.

In 1902 the partnership was dissolved and a limited liability company was formed in July 1903. Jones, as chairman and managing director, was joined by (Sir) Alfred Henry Ashbolt [q.v.7] and George Bertrand Edwards, a former football team-mate who had become Federal member for South Sydney and an expert on tariff matters. The need for strong united policies to deal with the new system of national wage fixation and the conditions required by tariff legislation relating to protection of industries led to the formation in Melbourne in November 1909 of a confederation of companies, Henry Jones Co-Operative Ltd. The group organization received much public criticism; yet it was in fact a rare example of 'horizontal monopoly' which did not result in policies harmful to the consuming public. The company eventually extended to all Australian States, New Zealand and South Africa.

Jones was a shrewd investor in promising Tasmanian undertakings. His greatest profits came not from jam, but from the Thailand tin-dredging industry whose promoter was Hobart-born E. T. Miles [q.v.]. The IXL Prospecting Co. was formed about 1903, followed by the Tongkah Harbour Tin Dredging Co. (1906) and Tongkah Compound (1910). The word 'Tongkah' entered the Hobart vocabulary as an adjective denoting good financial luck. Jones became a leading Australian financier and one of the early advisers to the Commonwealth Bank. During World War I he advised British government authorities on their Tasmanian investments. His support for the war effort also included the gift of an aeroplane to the British Army. He was knighted in 1919.

Caricatured as the 'Knight of the Jam Tin', Jones confronted post-war difficulties with his customary energy. He was influential in the formation in Hobart of the Growers' Export Pool in 1919; his part in the operation of the scheme entailed securing steamers to carry the fruit to England. He also tried, with limited success, to improve the cargo shipping services between Tasmania and the mainland by a programme of wooden ship-building at Tasmanian ship-yards. On a visit to England in 1921 he arranged for the erection of woollen mills in Launceston by the English firms of Paton & Baldwins Ltd and Kelsall & Kemp Ltd. The rival Hobart jam manufactory, W. D. Peacock & Co., was acquired by purchase after World War I, but an attempt to establish branch factories in California failed. In 1922 Jones retired and was succeeded by Frederick H. Peacock.

Jones accepted appointment to the Executive Council in 1924, although he was characteristically a man who shunned public office. A teetotaller, he liked to entertain his few cronies over billiards in his home, Glenora, and supported with quiet generosity such institutions as the Methodist Church, the Nurses' Home, the Girls' Industrial School and various sporting bodies. In his youth an active Australian Rules player, he was a lifelong supporter of the North Hobart Football Club. His factory manager of the 1890s, William Leitch, was a star player, and many a promising young footballer was assured of a job with the firm. Jones was also a member of the Hobart Chamber of Commerce and Hobart Rotary and consul for Denmark. He died on 29 October 1926 in Melbourne of coronary thrombosis while negotiating for the establishment in Launceston of a British tyre-manufacturing industry. Survived by his wife and children he was buried in Cornelian Bay cemetery. His estate was valued for probate at £112 646.

PTHRA, 20 (1973), no 1, and for bibliog.

JOHN REYNOLDS

JONES, HOOPER JOSSE BREWSTER (1887-1949), musician, was born on 28 June 1887 at Black Rock Plain, South Australia, son of William Arthur Jones, schoolmaster, and his wife Rebecca, née Williams. He was educated at country schools at Armagh and Bute largely by his father who taught him music until he left home at 13 to board in Adelaide. From 1901 he studied piano at the Elder [q.v.4] Conservatorium of Music. In 1905 a review of one of his concerts described him 'as the most promising student' who had ever entered the conservatorium. He won the overseas Elder scholarship, giving him three years at the Royal College of Music, London, where he studied composition, chamber music and piano.

Jones returned to Adelaide in 1909 to teach piano, singing and composition. Teaching, he believed, should be a 'psychological study of the student's possibilities'. He gave recitals, played chamber music, and appeared with visiting musicians. Next year, on 11 June, he married Gerta Homburg, an amateur singer and authority on German lieder. In 1914 he was president of the new Adelaide Chamber Society. In July 1915 Jones conducted his first orchestral concert in the Exhibition Hall; he later formed the Brewster Jones Symphony Orchestra at Queen's Hall. By 1920 it numbered seventy players; during World War I it was South Australia's only symphony orchestra.

Jones introduced contemporary French music to both Adelaide and Melbourne; as a composer he was prolific, original and unacademic. His symphonic poem *Australia Felix*, 'thoroughly professional' programme music, has been played throughout Australia by Australian Broadcasting Commission orchestras. His love of bush and bird-life resulted in many songs and seventy-three piano pieces of South Australian bird-calls. Of his string quartet performed in 1977 at the old Hahndorf Academy, a critic wrote that its 'ideas and textures stamp it firmly as belonging to the 20th century and the thematic workings show the composer's sound training and impeccable ear, as well as a lively invention and intense energetic drive'.

Jones worked with the A.B.C. as a pianist, lecturer on radio, and conductor of the State studio orchestra in the 1930s. He was music critic for the Adelaide *Advertiser* in 1935-40 and, later, for the *News* until shortly before his death. In 1936 his 'Pioneers and Problems', South Australia's musical history, appeared in *Australian Musical News*. He adjudicated at many eisteddfods and competitions in other States and was an examiner for the Australian Music Examination Board.

By the late 1940s Jones had retired. His son Arthur in 1947 formed a string orchestra and on 8 July 1949 his father was soloist with it, playing the D minor Mozart piano concerto. It was a fine performance, but fifteen minutes later he died from a heart attack. Jones's wife and two of their three sons survived him. He was buried in Centennial Park cemetery.

A handsome, popular man, Jones once related proudly how he had left Sir Charles Stanford's class in London. Jones's composition, *An Indian serenade*, contained several tonal and duodecuple effects, ending on the chord of the added 6. Stanford 'threw his fingers anywhere' on the piano and asked if 'that' was melody. By accident, the performance was tonal and good. Jones had the courage to reply 'That was splendid melody, sir'. He was expelled.

J. Glennon, *Music and musicians* (Adel, 1968); *Quiz* (Adel), 30 June 1905; *Aust Letters*, Mar 1960; *Advertiser* (Adel), 9 Sept 1909, 19 July 1915, 10 Oct

1977; *Mail* (Adel), 10 Apr 1915; information from Dr W. Galusser, and Prof A. McCredie, Elder Conservatorium, Adel, A. Brewster-Jones, Encounter Bay, and N. Penalurick, Montacute, SA.

JOYCE GIBBERD

JONES, INIGO OWEN (1872-1954), meteorologist, was born on 1 December 1872 at Croydon, Surrey, England, son of Owen Jones, civil engineer, and his wife Emilie Susanne, née Bernoulli, of a famous scientific family. Emilie's mother Dorothy Inigo-Jones was descended from the architect Inigo Jones (1573-1652). A family likeness between the two Inigos has been claimed.

In 1874 his parents migrated to Queensland where his father designed roads and railways. When 11 Inigo obtained a scholarship to the Brisbane Grammar School. Interested in astronomy and meteorology, he had an observatory at his parents' Kangaroo Point home and was a student member of the Royal Society of Queensland. In 1888 the colonial meteorologist Clement Wragge [q.v.] persuaded Jones to serve a cadetship in his office rather than attend the University of Sydney. When Wragge became interested in Edouard Bruckner's investigation of the changing levels of the Caspian Sea, comparing Bruckner's 35-year rainfall cycle with the 11-year sunspot cycle, Jones began to develop a special interest in long-range forecasting on the basis of sunspots.

In 1892 his parents bought a farm about sixty miles (97 km) north of Brisbane and named it Crohamhurst after a property near Inigo's birthplace. Inigo joined them there and on 2 February 1893 recorded an Australian record for one day's rainfall of 37.714 inches (958 mm). For the next thirty years he lived in relative obscurity, helping his father with pioneering work on the farm and continuing meteorological research as a hobby stimulated by first-hand experience of the farmer's dependence on weather forecasts.

In 1923 Jones successfully predicted the end of a dry spell and the resulting press publicity created demands for his forecasts. Urged on by scientific and other friends, he became a full-time forecaster—lecturing, writing and seeking sponsorship in 1927-34 from his home in suburban Dutton Park. The Queensland government appointed him director of the Bureau of Seasonal Forecasting of the Council of Agriculture, and with contributions from governments and industry, the Inigo Jones Seasonal Weather Forecasting Trust was formed in October 1928. From 1929 he wrote forecasts for many Australian newspapers.

The observatory building at Croham-hurst, financed by the trust and the Colonial Sugar Refining Co., was opened on 13 August 1935 by Governor Sir Leslie Wilson [q.v.], a friend and supporter; the Queensland government helped with operating expenses and declared the site of the observatory a reserve for scientific purposes. Jones henceforth divided his time between work on the farm and work in the observatory. In 1942 Sydney grazing interests provided further support through the Long Range Weather Forecasting Trust.

A fellow of the Royal Astronomical and the Royal Meteorological societies, London, and a member of the Société Astronomique de France and the American Meteorological Society, Jones had a fertile imagination, read widely and corresponded with reputable scientists in many countries. He had a scientist's commitment to demonstrable truth and an aversion to astrology, 'that master of delusion'. Although, in the light of modern knowledge, his faith in sunspot activity as a predictive tool was well founded, his evidence was largely anecdotal and he did not prove his hypothesis. The Commonwealth Bureau of Meteorology reported adversely on his methods in both 1939 and 1953. He dreamed nevertheless of seasonal forecasting and tried to forecast sunspot activity several years ahead. Testing the hypothesis that the magnetic fields of the planets, especially Jupiter, influenced sunspot activity, he sought connexions between planetary positions and the weather since the first century and was unfairly branded by opponents as an astrologer. His hypothesis is now disproved, but in the 1930s Jones was ahead of his time in recognizing the importance of magnetic fields in space.

A member of the Anglican Diocesan Synod, Jones was also, while living in Brisbane, president of the Queensland Astronomical Society and of the (Royal) Historical Society of Queensland and vice-president of the Town Planning Association. An accomplished artist and musician, he was a vice-president also of the Queensland Authors' and Artists' Association. On 11 January 1905 at Crohamhurst he had married Marion Emma Comrie; they had three surviving daughters. Jones died at Crohamhurst on 14 November 1954 and was buried in the nearby Peachester cemetery. His meteorological work was continued by Lennox Walker.

Inigo Jones Research Weather Forecasting Trust (nd, Brisb); *People* (Syd), 21 June 1950; *Queenslander*, 31 Jan 1885, 7 Feb 1935; *SMH*, 15 Nov 1954; *Courier Mail*, 16 Nov 1954; Series 9, item G25/37 (CSIRO Archives, Canb); personal information from Mrs U. Koroloff, Bardon, Brisb.

JOHN STEELE

JONES, JOHN PERCY (1872-1955), businessman and politician, was born on 22 October 1872 in Hobart Town, son of Thomas John Jones, coachman, and his wife Bridget, née Costello, both Irish Catholics. Jones's mother and two siblings died before he was 3 and he was brought up by his father and elder brother while friends took care of his two sisters. From 8 he worked in stables at Oatlands and delivered chemists' prescriptions before and after school. At 11 he became a rouseabout and boundary rider on R. Q. Kermode's [q.v.2] sheep-station, Mona Vale, near Ross, and determined to 'get on'. In 1888 his father died; Jones sold a pony and saddle given to him by Kermode and left for Melbourne.

He worked there for a butcher, became an early member of the Butchers' Union and attended the Working Men's College. Rejecting Catholicism he joined a variety of progressive and labour associations and developed an admiration for Henry George [q.v.4] whom he met in 1890; but Ruskin's ideas and Fabianism attracted him most. After spending the early 1890s as a drover and as a canvasser of his own brand of brass polish he established Melbourne's first pay-as-you-wear tailoring business in 1893: his Eureka-inspired motto was 'Be true to the Southern Cross'. At the same time, for both health and advertisement he took up cycling, competing in the Austral Wheel Race against Charles Kellow [q.v.] and 'Plugger Bill' Martin. Later he exchanged cycling for boxing and wrestling and was knocked out in a practice round with Bill Squires. Late in the 1890s he employed a team of cyclists to collect money owing to him, using some of his profits to subsidize the weekly *Tocsin* of which he was founding secretary in 1897. That year he became secretary of the North Melbourne branch of the Political Labor Council and on 22 December, at Charles Strong's [q.v.6] Australian Church, married Mary Ann Worrall, daughter of an ink manufacturer.

Jones helped to sponsor the visit of Ben Tillett to Australia in 1897, and in 1901, when he took his first trip to England, he met other European socialists. He also arranged to bypass the Flinders Lane cloth merchants by setting up a direct cloth supply from Bradford, Yorkshire. On his return to Melbourne he met Tom Mann [q.v.] and subsequently supported him financially. With Mann he established the Social Questions Committee (soon the Victorian Socialist Party) in 1905 and was president until June 1907. Jones influenced the committee to aim for an investigation of poverty in Victoria. Meanwhile, as his business boomed, he bought tenement housing, built a factory and acquired rural property. In 1907 he was chairman of the Australian Manufacturing Exhibition.

Jones left the V.S.P. in 1910 to stand successfully against William Pitt [q.v.] for the Legislative Council seat of East Melbourne as a Labor candidate, admitting to those suspicious of his business practices that 'whilst a Socialist on the outside he was a Capitalist on the inside'. In the council he soon became leader of the Labor contingent. His main concern was with common diseases such as the tuberculosis from which he had himself suffered, and gonorrhoea. In December he was a minister without portfolio in the ephemeral Elmslie [q.v.8] administration; and in 1924 he was commissioner of public works, minister of public health and in charge of immigration and vice-president of the Board of Land and Works under Prendergast [q.v.]. In the Hogan [q.v.] ministry of 1927-28 he exchanged public health for mines, holding the same offices in Hogan's second ministry (1929-32). He was acting treasurer in 1931-32.

Jones travelled to Europe in 1911, represented Victoria at a conference on tuberculosis at Westminster, London, in 1921, and attended the King George V jubilee celebrations in London in 1935. He bought a country estate, Ruskin Park, at Croydon in 1911 and lived there until 1921 when he purchased a mansion at Kew, Ruskin Hall. A cultured man whose collection of Labor literature was highly rated, he was the Legislative Council representative on the Council of the University of Melbourne from 1923. He was a justice of the peace, and a director of the Eagle Star Insurance Co. and the Great Ocean Road Trust.

Gradually his political views changed. A strong supporter of the Melbourne (financial) Agreement of August 1930, Jones was one of only five Victorian Labor parliamentarians who refused to sign a pledge to maintain government spending. At the 1931 Premiers' Conference, in a move which he saw as the pinnacle of his career, he called for an urgent conference to find ways to maintain Commonwealth solvency. He chaired the sub-committee which produced the Copland plan, the basis for the Premiers' Plan which he saw as promising economic salvation. After the government was forced to election in 1932 Jones resigned from cabinet, claiming it supported repudiation. Although not due for re-election until 1934, he campaigned for the Premiers' Plan on United Australia Party platforms and was expelled from the Labor Party.

Reallocated his portfolios in the Argyle [q.v.7] ministry, Jones remained a minister until March 1935 when he resigned along with the Country Party members. In 1940, having represented South-Western Province from 1934, he retired from the council, whose abolition he now advocated, to rule over a family empire of real estate and grazing properties. In his later years his ideas seemed confused: he claimed both Tory and radical sympathies. Jones died on 12 October 1955, his death unnoticed in parliament. Survived by his wife, two sons and a daughter, he was buried in Box Hill cemetery, leaving an estate valued for probate at £160 541.

Labour Hist, May 1975, no 28; *Advance Aust*, 15 Sept 1904; *Punch* (Melb), 27 Mar 1924; *Labor Call*, 30 Oct 1924; *Smith's Weekly*, 6 June 1931; *Herald* (Melb), 8 Mar 1934, 15 May 1938; *Argus*, 28 Mar 1939; Industrial Workers of the World, Correspondence (NL); Central Executive, Political Labor Council (Melb), Minutes, book 4, 17 Oct 1909 to 12 Nov 1910, *and* Democratic Labor Party papers, *and* J. P. Jones papers (LaTL).   BRUCE PAULE

JONES, KATHLEEN ANNIE GILMAN (1880-1942), educationist, was born on 30 September 1880 at Fazeley, Staffordshire, England, daughter of Charles Jones, smallware mill manager, and his wife Harriett, née Gilman. Kathleen was educated at Hiatt Ladies' College, Wellington, Shropshire, and at Newnham College, Cambridge, where in 1903 she gained a second class in the mathematical tripos. After obtaining her Cambridge Teachers' Diploma, she taught in Birmingham and Salford, before proceeding to South Africa as vice-principal of the Queenstown High School for Girls. In 1914 she came to Australia as joint headmistress of Ascham School, Sydney, and in 1916 became headmistress of Melbourne Church of England Girls' Grammar School.

Besides administering a leading boarding and day-school in wartime, she was engaged on building projects: a hall, laboratory and classrooms were completed in 1919. Her educational and feminist activities included membership in 1917-38 of the Council of Public Education (vice-president, 1922-23), the Schools Board in 1922-25 and 1927-36, and of the body which became the Incorporated Association of Registered Teachers of Victoria (president 1925 and 1935). She was especially involved in the establishment of the I.A.R.T.V.'s teacher-training institute (later Mercer House). Her main concerns were teacher qualifications, educational standards, superannuation and salary inequities: her school's salary scale was used in the 1940s by women teachers in their struggle for a wages board. She employed married teachers, contrary to custom, always upholding the status of professional women.

As a member of the Headmistresses' As-

sociation of Victoria (president 1923-24), Miss Gilman Jones worked to maintain the Homecraft Hostel (later Invergowrie) as 'an educational experiment' in a tertiary home-making course. Vice-president of the National Council of Women of Victoria in 1925, she supported the appointment of women principals for girls' high schools and the promotion of women as municipal and parliamentary candidates. She was vice-president of the Victorian Women Citizens' Movement in 1930-34 and president of the Australian Women Voters' Association in 1922. She was a ready and fluent speaker, holding her own amicably on male-dominated committees.

As a headmistress who understood how to delegate responsibility and obtain co-operation, Kathleen Gilman Jones introduced educational experiments. She inaugurated parent-teacher conferences; mathematics and science were strengthened, as were music and musical appreciation (with Dr A. E. Floyd [q.v.8]); public speaking and drama were encouraged; some sport was compulsory and also annual medical inspection; a 'Home-making Fifth' gave status to less academic programmes; speakers and artists of repute visited the school regularly; and the use of libraries was taught, especially for new studies in civics and international affairs.

She affirmed the Church character of M.C.E.G.G.S., with its parish role, and she herself taught divinity, took boarders' Sunday School classes and conducted daily assemblies, stressing direct giving, social service and missionary work. Her own generosity to deserving young students was known to few but the recipients. In the chapel she planned, but never saw, her memorial was dedicated in 1967.

The Aileen Dent portrait at the school conveys the impressive dignity of Kathleen Gilman Jones: her letters, in their distinctive handwriting (she had no personal secretary until 1933), reveal her directness and her humanity. Her recreations were walking, swimming, golf, music and reading. Before she left, in 1938, a university scholarship was founded in her name. She retired to Merton Cottage, Etchingham, Sussex, England, and died at Kent & Sussex Hospital, Tunbridge Wells, on 16 September 1942, of burns after a house fire, having endured prolonged suffering with characteristic fortitude.

G. Lloyd, *Melbourne Church of England Girls' Grammar School* (Melb, 1928); Melb C of E Girls' Grammar School, *Jubilee History* (Melb, 1953) and *School Magazine*, 1915-42; Melb C of E Girls' Grammar School Archives; information from friends and former staff and students.

L. M. M. MITCHELL

JONES, LESLIE JOHN ROBERTS (1886-1970), aeronautical engineer, was born on 4 June 1886 at Bathurst, New South Wales, second son of William Henry Jones, picture-framemaker, and his wife Rosina, née Dumbrell. He was educated at St Stanislaus College and worked in his father's shop. His family later moved to Sydney, where Jones was apprenticed to Edge and Edge Ltd, electrical and mechanical engineers. He later worked as an engineer for several firms.

While a hospital X-ray operator, in 1907 Jones turned his attention to aeronautics, trying to design a steam engine. With his brother William he constructed a frame and engine, which he entered (on paper) in the Commonwealth military aircraft competition in 1910. After much testing at Penrith the aircraft flew short distances, but was damaged in a storm. Next year he constructed a lighter machine also powered by steam; it was wrecked, rebuilt with a petrol engine, but abandoned after further damage.

On 16 October 1916 Jones enlisted in the 4th Squadron, Australian Flying Corps and served in France; he was discharged in London with the rank of corporal mechanic on 20 March 1919. At Birmingham on 30 April he married Pretoria Eugesta Hinchcliffe; they were childless and were divorced in 1936. Remaining in England, Jones joined General Electric Co. Ltd and A. V. Roe & Co. Ltd, aircraft manufacturers. Back in Australia in 1921 he worked for Edgar Percival [q.v.] at Richmond, Aviation Service Co. Ltd and Larkin [q.v.] Aircraft Supply Co., then set up as an aeronautical engineer and consultant. From February 1923 he was one of the few to hold aircraft-engineer licences in all categories.

Commissioned in 1927 to design and construct an aircraft for the Australian market, and crossing the Tasman Sea, Jones designed an all-steel welded framework. A contemporary report referred to it as a 'chrysallis', concealing 'many strange innovations in the business of aircraft construction'. Usually known as the 'Wonga', it had a Curtiss engine. After successful flight tests it was damaged by a storm in August 1930 and was rebuilt using the Harkness Hornet engine. On 16 June 1932 it crashed, killing both occupants.

In the early 1930s Jones lectured on aeronautical engineering at the East Sydney Technical College, and was a foundation member of the Hargrave [q.v.] Institute. From May 1933 he helped to design and construct an all-Australian aircraft for the 1934 London to Melbourne centenary air race; however time and money expired and it was abandoned.

Jones for a time worked with Tugan Aircraft Ltd on the Gannet, and with (Sir) George Julius [q.v.]. In World War II he was project engineer for the State division of the Department of Aircraft Production, and worked on the Mosquito bomber. After the war he left the aircraft industry, and retired altogether in 1962. He died at Windsor on 28 July 1970 and was buried in the Field of Mars cemetery with Methodist forms. He was survived by his second wife Olive Marion, née Love, whom he had married at Killara on 7 November 1936, and by their son. A contemporary claimed that Jones's contribution to aeronautical design in Australia had been outstanding.

J. Goode, *Wood, wire and fabric* (Melb, 1968); R. J. Gibson, *Australia and Australians in civil aviation*, 1 (Syd, 1971); *Aircraft* (Melb), 15 May 1923, p 316, 20 Oct 1924, p 2; *A'sian Engineer*, 30 (Dec 1930), no 174, p 4, 36; Inst of Engineers, Aust, *J*, 9 (June 1937), no 6, p 247; *SMH*, 11 Dec 1931; L. J. R. Jones papers (held by J. R. Jones, Freeman's Reach, NSW); MP 1849/8/132 (AAO).

E. D. DAW

JONES, NINA EVA VIDA (1882-1966), racing motorist, was born on 30 January 1882 at Livingstone House, Harris Street, Ultimo, Sydney, youngest daughter and seventh child of Sydney-born parents William Henry Harris, gentleman, and his wife Susan Mary, née Clarke, and niece of John [q.v.4] and (Sir) Matthew Harris [q.v.]. Vida was educated at home with a sister.

At St John's Church of England, Darlinghurst, on 2 April 1910 Vida Harris married JOHN ALEXANDER STAMMERS JONES (1870-1933), brewer of Lithgow. He was born on 28 November 1870 at Currawang near Lake George, son of William Watkin Jones, Welsh mining surveyor, and his wife Eliza, née Mills. Educated at Cooerwull Academy, Bowenfels, he was a notable cyclist and a daring horseman in his youth. He won many races as an amateur rider and, an early member of the Sydney Hunt Club, gained many prizes in shows with his famous hunter Viking. He was a member of the Australian Jockey Club, Royal Automobile Club of Australia, Sydney Bicycle and New South Wales Light Car clubs.

They visited England, returning late in 1910 to live at Lithgow near the Zig Zag Brewery. Next year they built Nia Heymo (Esperanto for 'our home') at Darling Point, thereafter alternating between their two homes where they entertained liberally. A daughter and son were born at Lithgow in 1912 and 1913.

Mrs Jones started driving at Lithgow where her husband had two Darracq cars with which they practised climbs on their freak hill (with a gradient of one in two). In

1923 she toured northern New South Wales and Queensland and in Brisbane entered a reliability trial to Sydney. She took part in many events and trials organized by the R.A.C.A. In 1925 the Maroubra Speedway opened: in 1925-26 Mrs Jones drove her new 20/70 horsepower Crossley in events from scratch, winning the 'Weekender Trophy', averaging 78 miles (126 km) per hour in the heavy touring car. In a 24-hour event in 1927 she was one of the few women ever to win a gold medal.

The Zig Zag Brewery was sold in 1928 and the Jones family visited France and Italy looking at sports cars. At Milan they bought a 6-cylinder 1750cc supercharged Alfa Romeo. Mrs Jones drove it successfully, gaining the fastest time in 1929 at Sydney Bicycle and Motor Club's hill climb at Prospect and in the R.A.C.A. Kurrajong hill climb. At the Light Car Club's acceleration test on Bondi Promenade in June 1930 she gained the fastest time of 18.4 seconds for the quarter mile, beating sixty-seven male rivals. As soon as they were old enough her children also took part in motor sporting events.

After her husband died of cancer at Darling Point on 5 May 1933, Mrs Jones gave up competition driving. A colourful personality, she had become one of the legends of Australian motor sport. She died at her Darling Point home on 2 March 1966 and was buried in the Presbyterian section of Rookwood cemetery. Her estate was valued for probate at $149 875. She was survived by her daughter Vidie, who had married William Branthwaite Clarke, great-grandson of Rev. W. B. Clarke [q.v.3]. Her son Jack had been killed in an aircraft accident at Mascot in 1939.

Motor Life, 22 Feb 1930; *Wheels*, Feb 1954; *SMH*, 16 Aug 1927, 9 July 1929, 5 May 1933; information from Mrs W. B. Clarke, Waverton, NSW.

K. A. JOHNSON

JONES, REES RUTLAND (1840-1916), solicitor, was born on 12 February 1840 in Sydney, son of Rees Jones, then a grocer and subsequently a grazier and mayor of Yass, and his wife Ann, née Thompson. The merchant David Jones [q.v.2] was his uncle. Precocious and exceptionally gifted, Rees received his primary education at Yass. In 1852 he attended Dr John Dunmore Lang's [q.v.2] Australian College, Sydney, moved to St James Grammar School in 1853, and in 1854 was tutored by William Timothy, son of William Cape [q.v.1], for the matriculation examination which he passed when not yet 15. He went to the University of Sydney in 1855 on a general proficiency scholarship, won the Barker [q.v.1] scholarship for

mathematics in 1857 and graduated B.A. in 1858 (M.A., 1872).

Jones was employed by the Commercial Banking Co. of Sydney until in 1861 he was articled to James Norton [q.v.5]. Admitted as a solicitor in New South Wales on 4 June 1864 and in Queensland on 3 September, he arrived at Rockhampton, Queensland, on 10 September and spent the rest of his life there. On 12 December 1865 he married Matilda Jane, daughter of W. J. Brown, called 'Brown the Magnificent'; they had thirteen children. An alderman in 1870, he was a town solicitor in 1871-96, an original trustee of the Rockhampton Grammar School and chairman in 1885-98, and president of the Rockhampton Club for thirty years.

Jones established a legal business in Rockhampton in partnership with his brother-in-law William John Brown. When Brown died in 1889 he was replaced by Charles Sydney Jones (no relation). More than ninety years later the firm was still entitled Rees R. & Sydney Jones. He represented the Mount Morgan syndicate in the appeal to the Privy Council over the 'jumping' cases, and in 1886 when the Mount Morgan Gold Mining Co. Ltd was registered, acquired shares and drafted its memorandum and articles of association. In his criminal practice he defended the murderer T. J. A. Griffin [q.v.4] and appeared for the prisoner Palmer in the Halligan murder case of 1869. In the latter case his defiance of the magistrate in defence of his client's interests enhanced his reputation.

After failure in Clermont and Rockhampton in 1883 Jones won the North Rockhampton seat in the Legislative Assembly in 1888 as a member of the McIlwraith [q.v.5] faction. He supported the separation of central Queensland in the 1891 debate on the provincial legislatures bill but usually spoke only on matters of interest to lawyers or to his electorate. He resigned just before the 1893 general election. Jones was a bon vivant and a brilliant conversationalist, whose chief interests were mathematics and Australian history. He published pamphlets entitled *Gold mining in central Queensland and the Mount Morgan mine* (1913), *The merino sheep in Australia* (1914), and *Souvenir of Emu Park, Emu Park and its early history* (1915), which moved the (Royal) Queensland Historical Society to confer life membership upon him. Before it could be granted, he contracted cancer, went to Sydney for an operation and died there on 30 December 1916. He was buried in Waverley cemetery with Presbyterian forms.

Alcazar Press, *Queensland, 1900* (Brisb, nd); *JRHSQ*, 30 Nov 1916; *Brisbane Courier*, and *Morning Bulletin*, 1 Dec 1916, 15 Oct 1964; *Bulletin*, 7

Dec 1916; *Capricornian*, 9 Dec 1916; Autobiographical notes held by E. R. Baker, Hackett, ACT.

J. P. SHANAHAN

JONES, WILLIAM (1842-1907), master mariner, industrialist and civic leader, was born at Newborough, Wales, second son of Robert Jones, hotelier and farmer, and his wife Margaret, née Griffiths. Educated at Newborough County School and Caernarvon Maritime College, he worked as a lad on ferries across Menai Strait. In 1861 he became a deck-hand on the barque *Prince Consort* bound for Australia where his uncle, Captain William Jones, and elder brother were already engaged in the intercolonial shipping trade; for two years he sailed with his uncle. On 5 March 1863 at Table Cape, Tasmania, he married Martha Maria Dowling, member of a local pioneering family. Jones then became master of his uncle's ketch *Margaret Chessell* but, wanting his own ship, engaged William Mollison to build at Burnie the *Onward*, a schooner with which he traded until he 'came ashore' in 1872 to begin an enterprising mercantile and industrial career.

Jones became a principal in most steps to stimulate Burnie's development and for his devotion to community life and his business zeal he earned the title 'King of Burnie'. He began as licensee of the Ship Inn, Marine Terrace. Alongside he built a store which became chandlery, grain-store, auction-mart and supplier of mining equipment to the developing Mt Bischoff and other mines. In 1875 he built Jones's (later the Bay View) Hotel and in 1878 his mansion, Menai.

In 1876 he bought Uplands, a farming property on Cooee Creek, and began a range of primary and secondary industries. He used water-power for a sawmill and built stables for a team of horses which dragged logs to the mill on a wooden-rail tramway. He found good clay in the creek-bed and built brick kilns. Then, establishing his own harbour at the mouth of the creek, he engaged William Mollison to build north-west Tasmania's first steamer, the *Cambria*, for exporting the bricks and timber. He built a soft-drink factory; used power from his water-wheel to churn butter at Emu Bay Butter Factory, of which company he was chairman of directors; grew pigs, slaughtered them at his own abattoir and cured them at his Brookside Bacon Factory.

Such enterprise was typical of Jones's interests for thirty years. He became a shipping and estate agent as well as a property developer in his own right; a mining entrepreneur sponsoring prospectors on the west coast; and promoter of Blythe River Iron Mines Ltd. He was chairman of the Emu Bay Road Trust from 1879, first chairman of the Burnie Town Board in 1898, several times chairman of the licensing bench, a justice of the peace from 1889 and a foundation trustee of Burnie Institute, a group which built the first town hall. A warden of the Table Cape (later Burnie) Marine Board from 1875, Jones was harbourmaster in 1878-98. He was a member of the Poulett Masonic Lodge, Wynyard.

He died on 21 April 1907 at Burnie and was buried in Wivenhoe cemetery, survived by his wife, a daughter and seven sons. A clock tower was erected on the town hall, demolished in 1976, to honour his memory, and Old Jones Pier, built in 1901, and a more recent general cargo berth, are named after him. A fine crayon portrait is displayed at Burnie Pioneer Village Museum.

W. Winter, *Onward—Burnie historical sidelights in a biography of Capt Wm Jones* (Burnie, 1975); *Cyclopedia of Tasmania*, 2 (Hob, 1900); *Examiner* (Launc), 8 Feb 1896, 22, 25 Apr 1907; family information. W. G. WINTER

JONES, WILLIAM ERNEST (1867-1957), psychiatrist, was born on 14 July 1867 at Upper Gornal, Dudley, Staffordshire, England, son of Alfred Jones, surgeon, and his wife Caroline Maria, née Noott. Supported by a Clothworkers' medical scholarship, he attended Epsom College, and then Middlesex Hospital (M.R.C.S. (Eng), L.R.C.P. (Lond), 1890). Early in his career he was attracted to the study of lunacy, partly through interest and partly because by remaining in asylums he could avoid the high cost of buying into private practice. A series of appointments culminated in his becoming medical superintendent of the new Brecon and Radnor County Asylum in Wales.

In 1905 Ernest Jones was appointed inspector-general of the insane in Victoria. Notwithstanding later suggestions that he was selected through confusion with his namesake, the friend and biographer of Freud, he owed his position to references which highly commended his energy and administrative skills, and to a successful interview with the former Victorian premier (Sir) William Irvine [q.v.]. The initial appointment was for five years: in the event he held office until 1937.

Soon after his arrival in Melbourne, Jones visited the six Victorian asylums. In a report to cabinet he criticized severe overcrowding, inadequate staffing and outmoded attitudes, and recommended building improvements totalling £250 000. His early achievements included construction of a modern asylum at Mont Park and amendment of the Lunacy Act to allow the admission of patients at their own request. After wartime service within Australia as an honorary lieut-colonel in the Australian Army Medical Corps, he chaired a 1921 commission of inquiry into lunacy in Western Australia. In 1933 he advised the Tasmanian government on the rebuilding of New Norfolk Asylum and, following his retirement, he acted briefly as inspector-general of the insane in Western Australia. Jones remained active during World War II, medically examining recruits and servicemen about to be discharged, and in 1947, aged 80, chaired a government inquiry into his old department. He was appointed C.M.G. in 1935.

For Jones, the psychiatrist was 'the apostle of common sense', whose proper concerns ranged from the imbecile and psychopath to the delinquent and degenerate. In 1929 he conducted a Federal government inquiry into the mentally deficient, which concluded that a little under 3 per cent of the Australian population fell into this category. Jones saw this as a grave threat to national efficiency and advocated eugenic ideals as a remedy, partly through the Council of Mental Hygiene which he helped to establish. At his instigation, the name of the Lunacy Department was changed to the Department of Mental Hygiene, and his own title altered to director of mental hygiene. Although he rejected as impractical compulsory sterilization and doubted whether society would act to prevent the mentally defective from marrying, he proposed eugenic research and urged the 'inculcation of good hygiene in our matings'.

A man of strong opinions, Jones disliked the 'yellow press', 'professional philanthropists' and 'self-appointed guardians of Public Liberty', and was contemptuous of various non Anglo-Saxon races, especially 'low class Roman Catholic Irish' in whom he detected an 'inherent lunacy'. On 1 November 1905 at St Patrick's Cathedral, he had married Kathleen Mary Mahony with whom he lived in 'almost cloudless harmony' until her death in 1952. Of medium height and slight build, bespectacled and well-groomed, he was at home at the Melbourne Club and Sandringham golf links. Jones died, sane but cantankerous about the moral deterioration of the world, on 1 May 1957, and was cremated. His son and daughter survived him.

MJA, Feb 1939, 13 July 1957; *Punch* (Melb), 18 Jan 1917; *Herald* (Melb), 7-11 Sept 1936; *Canb Times*, 7 Mar 1934; W. E. Jones papers and diaries (Charles Brothers Museum, Parkville, Vic).

S. G. FOSTER

JONSSON, NILS JOSEF (1890-1963), cartoonist, was born on 13 December 1890 at Halmstad, Sweden, eldest of three sons of Carl Alfred Jönsson, a blacksmith turned farmer, and his wife Augusta Bernhardina, née Karlsdotter. As a lad he worked behind a plough on a neighbour's farm and at 18 went to sea. Sailing in windjammers, he developed a skill painting seascapes inside the lids of sailors' sea-chests for a few shillings each. He jumped ship in New Zealand in 1915 and worked in cold stores, before arriving in Australia in March 1917.

While working at a variety of jobs, including timber-cutting in Queensland and as a high-rigger on Sydney's White Bay wheat silos, Jonsson saved the fees to attend J. S. Watkin's art school full time. Within a year he was appointed as an assistant instructor, then succeeded as a commercial artist and freelance cartoonist. Some of his earliest comic drawings appeared in *Aussie* in the early 1920s. In 1924 he joined *Smith's Weekly*.

Jonsson's technique was perhaps the most deceptive drawing style of any comic draughtsman working for the Australian press. Compared with the work of his contemporaries, his drawings looked from the start—for he never changed his style—as if instead of a pen, they had been drawn with a toothbrush. Yet these brilliant pen-drawings were outstanding for their skill and humour, drawn always with tremendous dash and zest. His humour fitted *Smith's Weekly* perfectly: it was tough, sometimes cynical, and uninhibited. His rollicking depictions of burglars, card-sharps, punters, jockeys, shipwrecked sailors and, needless to say, his 'blottos' were characters from a vaudeville world, reflecting a low-life continuity recorded by the earlier *Bulletin* artists Alfred Vincent [q.v.] and Ambrose Dyson [q.v. 8 W. H. Dyson].

After *Smith's Weekly* closed in October 1950, Jonsson was engaged by Sir Keith Murdoch [q.v.] of the Herald & Weekly Times Ltd to create a weekly comic strip in colour. From February 1951 until March 1963 he drew his popular, nationally syndicated comic strip, 'Uncle Joe's Horse Radish', an outlandish racehorse owned by a battling rural family—the answer, when he was not occupied with light duties around the farm, to the punter's dream.

Known among his fellow artists and journalists as 'The Bletty Blutty Gentle Swede', Jonsson had sandy hair and was short in build but enormously thick through the chest, partly as a result of being noticeably humpbacked. His physical strength was enormous. Although gentle and retiring, he was not one to back off from a challenge and was known to have once butt-thrown four bullying larrikins over a hotel bar. With his friends George Finey, 'Unk' White, Lennie Lower [q.v.], Kenneth Slessor and others, Jonsson was one of the legendary Bohemians of Sydney in the late 1920s and early 1930s.

At the Bondi manse, Jonsson had married with Presbyterian forms a Sydney-born art student Agnes Mary McIntyre on 14 February 1927. They lived at Wahroonga with a dog, horse and numerous cats. Joe liked gardening and wood-carving. He died of cardiovascular disease at home on 19 March 1963 and was cremated. His wife and their son and daughter survived him. The poets, artists and journalists of Sydney honoured him with a traditional form of wake reserved only for those they considered a worthy, loved and respected person.

V. Lindesay, *The inked-in image* (Melb, 1970); G. Blaikie, *Remember Smith's Weekly?* (Adel, 1975); *People* (Syd), 21 Apr 1954; *Journalist*, Apr 1963; *Sunday Mail* (Brisb), 4 Feb 1951.

VANE LINDESAY

JORDAN, SIR FREDERICK RICHARD (1881-1949), chief justice, was born on 13 October 1881 in London, son of Frederick Jordan of Marsworth, Buckinghamshire, hay and straw merchant, and his wife Sarah, née Nobel. His parents migrated to Sydney when he was 5 and set up a modest home at Balmain. Educated at Balmain Superior Public School and Sydney Boys' High School, he showed intellectual promise, but university education was then financially out of reach.

Employed as a clerk at the Master in Lunacy's office in 1898-1900, Jordan was a clerk, shorthand writer and typist in the Public Library of New South Wales from 1900 and joined the State's Intelligence Department in January 1906. He saved enough to begin evening studies in arts at the University of Sydney, winning scholarships that carried him on to law (B.A., 1904; LL.B., 1907). His second-class honours in law were surprisingly humble for one of his ability. But, at the time, his great love was for classical and modern languages. And he was inclined to cynicism about education—'Schools and universities', he later said, 'are valuable institutions ... It is good to have passed through them, provided one has emerged on the other side'.

On 19 August 1907 Jordan was admitted to the New South Wales Bar and practised from Selborne Chambers. He was a versatile counsel but became best known for success in equity matters. The range of his interests was better shown in his accomplishments as a part-time lecturer in the university's law school for a decade from 1911. He was the Challis [q.v.3] lecturer in equity, probate, bankruptcy and company law. He also lectured in Admiralty law. Some of his lecture notes were published and used as practice books.

At St Stephen's Presbyterian Church Jordan married Bertha Maud Clay on 9 January 1928; the marriage was childless. The same year he took silk. A man of bookish tastes, he was respected rather than liked by most of his colleagues who, while recognizing his brilliance as a lawyer, found him cold as a person. He, in turn, despised the narrowness of many of his fellows, writing that 'those who are constrained to think for the purposes of their professions refrain in general from thinking about anything else'. He delighted to relax in his vast library, indulging his voracious appetite for Romance languages, and committing to memory the entire contents of many literary works. Physical recreation did not extend beyond swimming and, for a time, fencing. But there was a less withdrawn side to his character. He was a connoisseur of food and wine and a devotee of the arts, particularly literature and the live theatre. With those who shared his interests he 'expanded genially', as Sir Lionel Lindsay [q.v.] put it, becoming the antithesis of his austere and aloof legal *alter ego*. Lindsay further assessed him as a 'humanist and good European'. Jordan was very critical of things that obtruded upon the purity of the theatre. 'Cinematography', he wrote, 'is used to provide entertainment of the most debasingly vulgar type, with deplorable results to standards of public taste'. The radio was worse. He thought it 'an organization some branches of which succeed each week in achieving the impossible, that of broadcasting a programme worse even than that of the previous week'.

On 1 February 1934 he gave up his leadership of the equity Bar to become chief justice in succession to Sir Philip Street [q.v.]. He was appointed K.C.M.G. in 1936. As chief justice Jordan stood in a class of high judicial excellence. His pronouncements on all aspects of the law were succinct, commanding and technically refined. A fitting compliment was paid to him by Sir Owen Dixon, on retiring as chief justice of the High Court of Australia, when he described it as a 'tragedy in the life of the High Court' that Commonwealth governments had not elevated Jordan to that bench. 'At all events', said Dixon, 'he was not appointed, and by one of those curious twists which seem to touch the finest natures, this highly scholarly man and very great lawyer eventually took some queer views about federalism'. The last was a tilt at Jordan's strenuous support for the powers and rights of the States as against the Commonwealth, and his harsh judicial treatment of direct and delegated Commonwealth legislation, not least the National Security Regulations during World War II.

Jordan was an efficient administrator of his court especially when wartime stringency made abnormal demands and, after the war, when the court outstripped its accommodation and staff resources. On the bench he was a daunting figure. 'He adopted a manner in his robes that was not merely cold, but chilling. He had a high-pitched voice of frosty intonation, and his thin-rimmed spectacles added to the severity of his demeanour'. He became lieut-governor in 1938 and administered the government for nearly a year from June 1945. His public aspect was always bleak and he seemed to have no enthusiasm for any service outside the strict call of duty.

In August 1949 he underwent surgery from which his recovery was only briefly successful. Survived by his wife, he died of hypertensive cardiovascular disease on 4 November at his home at Vaucluse; he was accorded a state funeral, and was cremated. His remarkable collection of essays and an anthology of parallel passages in the writings of diverse authors were published posthumously in 1950 in a limited edition entitled *Appreciations*, illustrated by Lindsay.

T. R. Bavin (ed), *The jubilee book of the law school of the University of Sydney* (Syd, 1940); O. Dixon, *Jesting Pilate*, comp Judge Woinarski (Syd, 1965); J. M. Bennett, *A history of the Supreme Court of New South Wales* (Syd, 1974), and *Portraits of the chief justices of New South Wales, 1824-1977* (Syd, 1977); D. Marr, *Barwick* (Syd, 1980); *Aust Law J*, 23 (1949), p 395; *NSW State Reports*, 49 (1949).

J. M. BENNETT

JOSE, ARTHUR WILBERFORCE (1863-1934), journalist and historian, was born on 4 September 1863 at Clifton, Bristol, England, eldest son of William Wilberforce Jose, merchant and alderman, and his wife Sarah Maria, née Woodward. His father was a governor of University College, Bristol, and chairman of the Bristol School Board's technical education committee. Arthur was educated at Clifton College. After a year at Balliol College, Oxford (scholar 1881-82), his health broke down. Recuperating in Australia in 1882, he learned of the loss of his father's fortune and spurned the offer of a clerical position at Bristol, choosing to go bush in Australia. Often living rough, he cut wood for the Victorian Railways, picked

hops and apples, made bricks and tutored in Tasmania.

In 1885-87 Jose was assistant master at All Saints' College, Bathurst, New South Wales—he had met the headmaster Edwin Bean [q.v.3] in Hobart. He edited the *Bathurstian* and wrote several school songs. In 1888 he became a university extension lecturer and as 'Ishmael Dare' wrote *Sun and cloud on river and sea* (1888), a collection of verses. He was a reader for his publishers Angus [q.v.3] & Robertson [q.v.] for many years and, although he never practised, was admitted to the Bar on 28 August 1891. Temporary lecturer in modern literature at the University of Sydney in 1893, he was organizing secretary of the University Extension Board in 1894-99.

Jose's first major work, *The growth of the Empire*, was published in Sydney in 1897 (John Murray later produced enlarged English editions). His *A short history of Australasia* appeared in 1899; with an added chapter on literature it became his *History of Australasia*, ran to fifteen editions by 1929 and was translated into French. Briefly editor of the *Australian Magazine*, Jose went to South Africa as war correspondent in 1899. After a spell in London, he was sent to India in 1901 to promote Murray's books and next year was acting professor of English and modern history at the Mohammedan Anglo-Oriental College at Aligarh. In England in 1903, he lectured for the Imperial Tariff and Tariff Reform leagues. He returned to Sydney in 1904 as correspondent for *The Times*, having had published in London *Australasia* (1901) and *Two awheel and some others afoot in Australia* (1903), illustrated by George Lambert [q.v.]. At St James's Church he married Evelyn Agnes Absell (d. 1967) on 2 November 1905; her sister Amelia had married Lambert.

As *Times* correspondent Jose sought confidential information from governors, ministers of the crown and officials. He corresponded at length with Alfred Deakin [q.v.8], who became a close friend, and advocated the political centre where Deakin and Labor sometimes joined and sometimes jostled—a position destroyed by the Fusion of 1909. A disciple of Joseph Chamberlain, Jose believed wholeheartedly in the unity of the Empire and also in White Australia and Imperial preferential tariffs. His dispatches (not always welcome to his employers or to Whitehall), with Deakin's letters to the *Morning Post*, gave Australia publicity abroad on a hitherto unknown scale. In 1909-11 he also wrote a bi-monthly letter for the *National Review*. An early member of the (Royal) Australian Historical Society, he frequently contributed to its *Journal and Proceedings* and wrote for other magazines.

Almost half of *New South Wales—historical and economic* (1912) was his.

A Sydney founder of the Australian National Defence League in 1905, Jose was appointed provisional lieutenant in the Australian Intelligence Corps in July 1909 and was promoted honorary captain. In March 1911 he went to Britain to spend a year with *The Times*. He parted company with the newspaper in 1915 when as honorary captain in the Australian Military Forces he was attached to the intelligence branch of the Royal Australian Navy to compile a history of naval operations and to analyse intelligence about China, Japan, the Philippines and the Dutch East Indies. At C. E. W. Bean's [q.v.7] request he was released in 1920 to write the naval volume of the Australian official war history. Owing to many delays and the determination of the Naval Board to censor it, *The Royal Australian Navy 1914-1918* did not appear until 1928. The largely uncensored revision was done by Bean on the basis of new material, some of which Jose had located in Paris.

Appointed editor-in-chief of *The Australian encyclopaedia* (1925, 1926) in 1920, Jose left for England in 1926 leaving volume two, according to Robertson, 'in a state of chaos'. Disillusioned by politics and in pecuniary difficulties, he turned increasingly to historical scholarship—his publications included *Builders and pioneers of Australia* (London, 1928), and *Australia, human and economic* (London, 1932). In 1932 he returned to Australia, settling in Brisbane, and reviewed books, lectured, and wrote articles and his autobiographical *Romantic nineties* (Sydney, 1933).

Bespectacled and with a soldierly moustache, Jose had an astonishing memory and was quick witted and rigidly independent, oblivious of financial gain. If to some his cocksure manner appeared arrogant, he was quick to admit and correct his own errors. His vivid prose was easily recognizable and had a 'didactic and often contentious flavour'. His history was scholarly. Jose was passionately interested in cricket, on which he often wrote for *The Times*, and intensely musical. 'To see him seated at the piano' wrote Bean, 'head thrown back, nostrils dilated, body swaying, and the long sensitive fingers tearing from the keys one rolling arpeggio after another, was to see a picture of the Spanish ancestor who, many generations ago, had settled in Cornwall'.

Jose died in Brisbane Hospital of peritonitis on 22 January 1934 and was buried in Toowong cemetery with Anglican rites. His wife and son survived him.

His younger brother GEORGE HERBERT JOSE (1868-1956), was born on 15 December 1868 at Bristol and educated at Clifton College, Monkton Combe School, Bath, and Worcester College, Oxford (B.A., 1903; M.A., 1906). He came to Australia in 1888, married Clara Ellen Sturt (d. 1925) in 1890 and went with her to China as a lay missionary next year. He was ordained in 1893 and was a missionary at Taichow until 1899. He was Davis Chinese scholar at Oxford in 1900 and in 1903 went to Adelaide where he had charge of several churches until in 1906 he was appointed rector of Christ Church, North Adelaide, where he remained until 1933. During World War I he was chaplain in the Australian Military Forces and from 1916 deputy senior chaplain.

A canon of St Peter's Cathedral in 1918-29, Jose was archdeacon of Mount Gambier in 1927-29, archdeacon of Adelaide in 1929-32 and dean of Adelaide in 1933-53. He compiled a three-volume history of *The Church of England in South Australia* (1937, 1954, 1955); his other writings include *Annals of Christ Church* (1921) and *The story of Jesus Christ* (1930). He died in Adelaide on 26 November 1956, survived by one of his three sons; another had been killed in action in France in 1917.

H. Newbolt, *My world in my time* (Lond, 1932); W. A. Steel and J. M. Antill, *The history of All Saints' College, Bathurst, 1873-1963* (Syd, 1964); A. W. Barker (ed), *Dear Robertson* (Syd, 1982); *Hist Studies*, 20 (Apr 1983), no 80; *SMH*, 23 Jan, 8 Feb 1934; *The Times*, 23 Jan 1934; C. E. W. Bean papers (AWM); Deakin papers (NL); Jose papers (ML); Navy Dept files (AAO); family papers (held by D. A. Jose, Nunawading, Melb).   R. LAMONT

JOSELAND, RICHARD GEORGE HOWARD (1860-1930), architect, was born on 14 January 1860 at Claines, Worcestershire, England, son of Richard Joseland, wine merchant, and his wife Elizabeth Katherine, née Voss. Howard Joseland was articled to Haddon Bros at Hereford before going to London in 1881 as assistant to George Robinson, art director of the architectural firm George Trollope & Sons. Robinson was an exponent of Pugin's principles of design; this influence was important in Joseland's Australian work.

Because of ill health attributed to overwork, Joseland went to New Zealand in 1886, seeking a better climate, and for six months worked on the Auckland railways. After visiting Australia, in 1888 he settled in Sydney where he married Isabella Alice Taylor (d. 1891) on 13 September. Soon after arrival he met Walter Vernon [q.v.] with whom, in 1889, he entered and won a competition to design a model suburb; they worked jointly on other projects. In 1890 when Vernon became government architect he invited

Joseland to take over his practice. The depression years were difficult for Joseland. He had little or no work in 1897, although on 6 April he married Blanche Augusta Hay at Coolangatta near Berry; her family was connected with the (David) Berry [q.v.3] estates, on which Joseland had first done work in 1892. With a commission for F. Lassetter's [q.v.5] hardware store in George Street in 1898, the practice began to revive.

In 1903 Joseland took into partnership his former pupil Hugh Vernon [q.v.], Walter's son. Although Joseland's work always included a variety of building types, the greater part of his practice was domestic architecture. He built many houses on Sydney's developing North Shore, particularly on the Berry estates at North Sydney and Wahroonga, where for twenty-two years he lived in a house built for himself in 1900. He was in sole practice from 1914 until 1919, when he formed a partnership with Frederic Glynn Gilling, a young English architect. Thereafter he became less active and retired in 1929, selling out to Gilling, who retained the name—Joseland & Gilling is still an important architectural firm.

Joseland was among the first to reject the excesses of late Victorian architecture in Australia. In an article, 'Domestic architecture in Australia', in *Centennial Magazine* (August 1890), he advocated design for climate, using appropriate materials undisguised, and excluding irrelevant embellishment. These principles contributed to the development of the 'Queen Anne' or 'Federation' style in Australia. A fashionable architect, he had many clients among the prosperous people who were then building substantial houses on the upper North Shore. He had helped to found the Sydney Architectural Association in 1891 and was elected president in November 1893, but the association did not survive the depression and was disbanded next year. In 1906 he became a fellow of the Institute of Architects of New South Wales. Joseland took part in community activities, and belonged to musical societies, including the Sydney Liedertafel. He was a keen angler—which also afforded opportunities for sketching—and was among the first to introduce fly-fishing on New South Wales trout streams; his book, *Angling in Australia and elsewhere*, was published in 1921. In 1907 and 1927 he and his wife visited England.

Joseland died of cancer at Darlinghurst on 20 July 1930, survived by a daughter of his first marriage and by a son and daughter of his second, and was buried in South Head cemetery with Anglican rites.

Cyclopedia of N.S.W. (Syd, 1907); J. M. Freeland, *Architecture in Australia* (Melb, 1968); A. J. Allen, R. G. Howard Joseland (architect), 1860-1930 (B.Arch. thesis, Univ NSW, 1978), and for bibliog; information from R. E. Apperly, Cremorne, Syd.

PATRICIA CHISHOLM

JOWETT, EDMUND (1858-1936), pastoralist, businessman and politician, was born on 6 January 1858 at Bradford, Yorkshire, England, son of Joseph Jowett, stuffmaker in a woollen mill, and his wife Sarah, née Craven. Edmund was educated at Mr James Ward's Classical School, Clapham Common, London, and learned the wool trade at his uncle's mill at Thornton, Yorkshire. With his elder brother Charles he followed his father to Australia in 1876 and settled in Melbourne, working on the *Argus*, contributing articles to the *Australasian Banking Record* and becoming the wool expert of the Australian Mercantile Land and Finance Co. Ltd. On 24 November 1883 at St George's Presbyterian Church, East St Kilda, he married Annette Rose McCallum.

Though he had arrived in Australia without capital, Jowett gradually acquired pastoral properties (mainly in Queensland, where he began with Kynuna station about 1886, but a few in New South Wales and Victoria) until he controlled over forty, covering more than six million acres (2 400 000 ha). He greatly increased the carrying capacity of his sheep-stations and specialized in developing unimproved properties. At his death he was credited by the *Bulletin* with having owned more sheep than anyone else in the world. Jowett also promoted woollenmanufacturing, instituted 'Wool Week', and headed a 'Use More Wool' committee. A well-dressed man, he boasted that he always wore woollen suits made in Australia. In 1916 he was appointed growers' representative on the wartime Central Wool Committee and subsequently served in a similar capacity on the Commonwealth Bureau of Commerce and Industry and on the Victorian Meat Advisory Committee.

As a young man Jowett came under the influence of Sir Frederick Sargood [q.v.6] and was a member of the Young Victorian Patriotic League. He seems to have taken no active part in politics until October 1916 when he campaigned on the Darling Downs for conscription; his younger son, of the Royal Flying Corps, had been killed in action in July. On the formation of the National Party in January 1917 Jowett became Victorian vice-president. Unsuccessful at the Federal election in May as a 'win the war' candidate for Maribyrnong, in October he won Grampians at a by-election. In 1919 he was re-elected with the endorsement of the Victorian Farmers' Union and, in January 1920, was chosen as deputy leader of the new parliamentary Country Party. In 1922 when a redistribution abolished his seat he unsuccessfully contested Bendigo. 'A wiry-looking man' with a penetrating glance and a square jaw, he was an active member of the Country Party for the remainder of his life.

Jowett frequently wrote and lectured on economic questions. Before the turn of the century he argued against the gold standard and in later years strongly opposed any return to it. In and out of parliament he advocated electoral reform and proportional representation, particularly for Senate elections. He also worked to encourage Britons to settle on the land in Australia. He was Australian president of the British Immigration League from 1916 and representative in Australia of the Royal Colonial Institute. His publications included *The unnatural fall in prices due to currency legislation* (1895), *The ruinous fall in the prices of produce and the prevailing scarcity of money* (1894), *Electoral reform for Australia* (1917) and *Proportional representation for the Senate* (1919). He was a director of several companies, including the Norwich Union Insurance Society, and a member of the advisory board of Australian Estates and Mortgage Co. He belonged to the Melbourne, Australian and Queensland clubs and enjoyed tennis, polo, ballroom dancing and poetry.

Jowett died suddenly on 14 April 1936 at Strathane, one of his Queensland properties, and was buried in the Presbyterian section of St Kilda cemetery, Melbourne. His wife, a son and three daughters, one of whom was daughter-in-law to Sir George Fairbairn [q.v.8], survived him. His estate was valued for probate at £56 399. The *Argus* obituary described him as not only a grazier but a 'politician, economist, writer, sportsman and wit'.

E. J. Brady, *Australia unlimited* (Melb, 1918); *Punch* (Melb), 19 Apr 1917, 27 May 1920; *Farmers' Advocate*, 20 Nov 1919; *Argus*, 15 Apr 1936; *Countryman* (Melb), 17 Apr 1936; *Bulletin*, 22 Apr 1936; *Kyneton Guardian*, 29 Nov 1956; *Aust Financial Review*, 14 Dec 1981; family papers held by *and* information from Mr E. Jowett, Broadford, Vic.   JOAN RYDON

JOYCE, EDMUND MICHAEL (1889-1961), Christian Brother and educationist, was born on 2 April 1889 at Hampden, Otago, New Zealand, fifth child of Michael Joyce, police constable, and his wife Mary, née Casey, both Irish born. Edmund was educated at Hampden Primary School, Christian Brothers' College, Dunedin, and the University of Tasmania (B.A., 1921). He represented his school at cricket, soccer and Rugby. In 1906 he passed the civil service examination and joined the Treasury in Wellington. An 'A' grade cricketer who represented the North Island, he also excelled at tennis and was a crack shot.

In 1909 he entered the Congregation of the Irish Christian Brothers and in May 1910 began training at Mount St Mary, Strathfield, Sydney, taking the religious name of Edmund Dominic. On completion of his novitiate he was appointed to St Joseph's Primary School, Abbotsford, Melbourne, and in 1916 was transferred to St Virgil's College, Hobart. Though his days and evenings were fully occupied by teaching, he began studies at the University of Tasmania. Contemporaries recalled that from late at night till the early hours of the morning, Joyce pursued his studies in the boiler-room by candlelight. A gifted teacher and sports coach, the excellent results from his pupils, especially in mathematics and science, won him a growing reputation. Dedicated to his religious life, he devoted himself completely to his God, and to his pupils. His discipline was legendary, but so was his absolute fairness. He never sought eminence and though he was headmaster and local superior from 1927 to 1931 and again from 1935 to 1937, he much preferred to be vice-principal and sub-superior, posts which he occupied almost to the end of his life.

Joyce soon became an educational authority in the State, as well as official spokesman for the Catholic sector. In 1930 he was appointed to the Teachers and Schools' Registration Board on which he served for thirty years, being chairman from 1942 until 1960. From 1931 to 1959 he was a member of the bursaries board of the Education Department. In May 1935 he was appointed to the Soldiers' Children's Education Board of the Repatriation Department, as representative of the non-state secondary boys' schools, and remained on this board until his retirement owing to ill health in June 1960. He also served on numerous syllabus committees for university entrance exams. In May 1960 he celebrated the golden jubilee of his entry to the Congregation, but refused to have any public acknowledgment. Generous donations and gifts to St Virgil's were sent to him. In appearance 'Old Ted' was tall and gaunt with piercing blue eyes in an 'aescetic countenance'; later years added a pronounced limp from a knee injury.

He died on 2 March 1961 in Calvary Hospital, and was accorded one of the largest funerals the State has known. At the requiem Mass held in St Mary's Cathedral Archbishop (Sir) Guilford Young described Joyce in his panegyric as a man of towering principle and a great schoolmaster. A portrait hangs in the library at St Virgil's College, Hobart.

Univ Tas, *Calendar*, 1917-21, 1961; *Christian Brothers' Educational Record*, 1962; *Mercury*, 3, 6 Mar 1961; *Standard* (Hob), 10 Mar 1961; information from family and the Congregation of the Irish Christian Brothers.   CHRISTINE WOOD

JOYNTON-SMITH, JAMES JOHN; *see* SMITH, JAMES JOHN JOYNTON

JUDKINS, WILLIAM HENRY (1869-1912) and GEORGE ALFRED (1871-1958), Methodist reformers, were the sixth and seventh children of Henry Judkins and his wife Eliza, née Ward, both devout Methodists from Aylesbury, Buckinghamshire, England.

William was born on 26 February 1869 at Franklinford, Victoria, where his father was a schoolteacher. William taught briefly at Creswick Grammar School, but his ambition was to join the Methodist ministry. The conference transferred him to New Zealand where he studied as a probationer, fought for temperance causes and threw himself into local option battles with such devotion that he became ill and abandoned the idea of being ordained. However, he remained a lay preacher.

At Palmerston North on 2 September 1896 he married Myra Elizabeth Carty; they came to Melbourne in 1902. Judkins was mild and friendly to meet but had a florid style in the pulpit and was vigorous with the pen. He became editor of the journal, *Review of Reviews*, and set about attacking the 'social evils' of the day—prizefighting, gambling, racing, drinking, dancing, and even barmaids. As secretary of the Criminology Society he convened a conference on 20 October 1905 as part of the successful campaign for legislation to establish a children's court.

His campaigns came to a climax in 1905 and 1906 when he sought permission from the Methodist Committee on the Amendment of the Betting Laws to stage a campaign against John Wren [q.v.] and gambling. Wren and Judkins were of a similar age and build, small with sharp features, and to their mutual embarrassment were frequently mistaken for each other. Judkins saw Wren, drink, gambling and Catholicism all combined into one terrible evil. He accused Wren of using known criminals to staff his Collingwood tote, he openly charged the police with corruption, and

attacked Chief Secretary Sir Samuel Gillott [q.v.] for weak and ineffective administration.

'Juddy', although often ill, was indefatigable. He preached all over Melbourne, and particularly for Pleasant Sunday Afternoon audiences at Wesley Church in Lonsdale Street. Some meetings turned into near riots and once he was pelted with eggs. He told reporters: 'A very small thing to suffer in the cause of righteousness. Ten thousand blows like that will not stop me'. Although he helped to push through the Licensing Act of 1906 which began the reduction in the number of hotels, his main object was stricter gambling laws which might wipe out Wren's pony tracks. On 13 June 1906 John Wren and six others were fined £100 for having used the City Tattersall's Club for betting on horse-racing. When Judge Neighbour [q.v.] upheld Wren's appeal and wiped out the convictions, Judkins was aghast. At the Pleasant Sunday Afternoon of 16 September he told the large audience: 'If I were to tell you all I could you would hold your breaths . . . matters are so serious in some departments of our public life you would shiver'.

Wren, who was about to leave for America, cancelled his trip. Judge Neighbour protested at the innuendoes and Premier (Sir) Thomas Bent [q.v.3] offered Judkins a royal commission. Next Sunday at the Wesley Church the congregation was so huge a thousand people could not get inside. However, Judkins backed away from a royal commission and would not specify those grave matters that would make the public shiver. Yet on 2 December he did have something to say. He revealed at the Pleasant Sunday Afternoon that Sir Samuel Gillott was registered as the mortgagee of 36 Lonsdale Street, which housed the most notorious brothel in Melbourne. Gillott immediately resigned, protesting that he had no personal knowledge of what went on at 36 Lonsdale Street. Even so, Judkins had scored an impressive victory. The Gillott affair gave a push to the languishing gambling suppression bill, which became law early in 1907. Wren quietly closed his Collingwood tote.

Judkins was a force at a time of extreme moral uprightness. He continued his fiery preaching but he never again gained the publicity of 1906. His health became so bad he had to support himself in the pulpit on sticks. In 1910 he was seriously ill with cancer and he had one kidney removed. When it was obvious he would not recover, his friends opened a testimonial fund for his family. Many of his old enemies were among the subscribers. He died on 3 September 1912, survived by his wife and a 13-year-old daughter, and was buried in Boroondara cemetery.

George Alfred Judkins was born on 13 March 1871 at Glendaruel, near Clunes. He probably attended Sheepwash (Tourello) School where his father was headteacher and his mother and eldest sister also taught. George 'made the choice of Christ' on his thirteenth birthday, not long before he entered the telegraph office of the Railways Department in Melbourne. He temporarily lost his spiritual bearings but at 17 he returned to the goldfields to lead Saturday night evangelistic meetings at Ballarat, an experience which confirmed his call to the ministry.

After short trials as a local preacher at Coleraine and Katamatite he enrolled for theological studies at Queen's College in 1892. His first appointment, in 1897, was to the raw Tasmanian mining town of Queenstown, where he practised an earnest open-air evangelism and supervised erection of the first church. His Victorian ministry followed, with short stays at Richmond (1899-1900), Yarram (1901-03), Bendigo (1904-07), Echuca (1908-10) and Horsham (1911-13).

From 1914 minister of the Ballarat Neil Street Methodist Church, Judkins came to the forefront of the moral reform movement as successor to his more famous brother and throughout World War I was conspicuous in defence of God and country. During the 1917 conscription campaign he aligned himself with the Orange cause, claiming that 'Romanism and nationalism were irreconcilable'. He supported the campaign for local option and six o'clock closing and in the early 1920s pressed the Methodist Conference to establish a specialized department to voice its 'unswerving hostility to the liquor traffic'. In 1925, the year he became secretary of the Federal Council of Churches, he was appointed director of the newly formed Methodist social services department.

During the next fourteen years Judkins toured the State in a crusade against social evil. By a combination of fiery oratory and adroit lobbying of Spring-street politicians, he largely succeeded in preserving Victoria from the iniquities of the totalizator, the lottery, the immoral book and the 'Continental Sunday'. At his election as president of the Victorian and Tasmanian Conference in 1937 he even dared to prophesy a spiritual revival to match the incipient economic recovery.

Judkins had little sympathy with co-religionists who questioned the prohibitionist approach to social questions; in 1937 he opposed state ownership of the liquor industry and the totalizator, and the intro-duction of sex education in state schools. In his *Red raiders—the ruthless attack of communism on civilisation* (1933) he acknowledged the seductive power of communism to those destitute 'in a land of plenty', but scorned its atheistic premises and its 'impractical and lying' promise of secular salvation.

In 1939 'Juddy', in poor health, resigned from the social services department, acting in retirement as chaplain to Epworth Hospital and as a pastor to congregations at Malvern and Canterbury. He was short and balding, with a square jaw and bristling moustache, his pulpit manner was fervent and pugnacious; yet he was loved as a kindly and understanding pastor. His marriage, to Aline May Giroud at Richmond on 8 April 1901, was happy and Judkins was proud that their four children all 'walked in the way of the truth'. Survived by his family he died at Box Hill on 8 October 1958 and was cremated.

K. Dunstan, *Wowsers* (Melb, 1968); N. Brennan, *John Wren* (Melb, 1971); E. H. Buggy, *The real John Wren* (Melb, 1977); Methodist Church (Vic), *Minutes of the annual conference*, Melb, 1939, 1959; *J of Religious Hist*, June 1978; *Argus*, 14, 21, 23 June, 24 Sept, 17 Dec 1906, 4 Sept 1912, 10 Sept 1917, 1 Mar 1932; *Spectator* (Melb), 1 Apr 1925, 3 Mar 1937, 2 Mar 1938, 15 Oct 1958; *Age*, 9 Oct 1958; *Herald* (Melb), 3 Sept 1912; E. M. Wilson, The campaign for national righteousness. The Methodist Church and moral reform in Victoria 1900-1916 (B.A. Hons thesis, Univ Melb, 1957).

KEITH DUNSTAN
GRAEME DAVISON

JULIUS, SIR GEORGE ALFRED (1873-1946), mechanical engineer and inventor, was born on 29 April 1873 at Norwich, England, eldest son of Churchill Julius, clerk in holy orders, and his wife Alice Frances, née Rowlandson. His father was mechanically minded and encouraged George to spend many hours in his workshop. Appointed archdeacon of Ballarat in 1884, Churchill Julius took his family to Victoria and in 1890 to New Zealand when he became bishop of Christchurch and later primate. George was educated at Melbourne Church of England Grammar School and at Canterbury College (B.Sc. (mechanical engineering), N.Z., 1896).

Employed as an assistant engineer by the Western Australian railways in 1896-1907, Julius married Eva Droughsia Odieuna, daughter of C. Y. O'Connor [q.v.], on 7 December 1898 at St John's Church, Fremantle. In 1906-07 he published three important works on the physical characteristics and economic uses of Australian hardwoods, and in 1907 moved to Sydney as consulting engineer to Allen Taylor [q.v.] & Co. Ltd, timber merchants, at a salary of £550 and the right of private practice. Next year he invented the racecourse totalizator; it was first used at Auckland, New Zealand, in 1913. He continually improved the keyboard machine that printed tickets and recorded issues; by 1929 it showed dividends after the deduction of tax. An expert craftsman in his home workshop, he built a model railway with steam locomotives for his sons, and a model city which was later exhibited for charity and presented to a technical museum.

Julius was president of the Engineering Association of New South Wales for three terms in 1910-13 and of the Electrical Association of Australia in 1917-18. A founder of the Institution of Engineers, Australia, in 1919, he was on the preliminary committee, a council-member in 1919-40 and fifth president in 1925; he was awarded the (Sir) Peter Nicol Russell [q.v.6] memorial medal in 1927. Julius fostered the formation of the Australian Commonwealth Engineering Standards Association in 1922; while he was serving as vice-chairman and chairman in 1926, Australia-wide rules were adopted for electrical safety. He was chairman of the Standards Association of Australia in 1929-39 and president of the Australian National Research Council in 1932-37.

About 1914 Julius was joined in partnership by William Poole and in 1922 by A. J. Gibson [q.v.8]; he remained senior partner of Julius, Poole & Gibson until his death. The firm's clients included the Commonwealth and State governments. Julius served on a committee to inquire into electricity supplies (1925) and reported upon a water conservation scheme for the northwest of the State (1937) and the break of gauge in the railway (1939). He widely promulgated his personal views on fiscal policy, unemployment during the Depression, industrial standardization and professional qualifications.

The prime minister, S. M. (Viscount) Bruce [q.v.7], in 1926 sought his advice on the bill to establish the Council for Scientific and Industrial Research and appointed Julius chairman—a position he held until 1945. He quickly appreciated that the most pressing problems facing the council related to primary production. With (Sir) David Rivett and A. E. V. Richardson [qq.v.], he helped to fight prickly pear, to investigate diseases affecting sheep, dairy cattle and food supplies, and set up a division of forest products. He could quickly assess a proposed course of action and 'form a shrewd estimate of its cost'.

In the 1930s he realized the need for more research work in secondary industry. Despite strong opposition from the Depart-

ment of Defence to any extension of the activities of C.S.I.R., Julius was appointed chairman of the important Commonwealth Committee on Secondary Industries Testing and Research in 1936. Under his leadership the committee worked fast and in 1937 recommended the establishment of the National Standards Laboratory, a technical information service, and research into aero and automobile engines. During World War II he also served on the Central Inventions Board, the Australian Council for Aeronautics (as chairman) and the Army Inventions Directorate.

Knighted in 1929, Julius was a member of the Commonwealth Board of Trade (1927), president of the Rotary Club of Sydney in 1932, a trustee of the Public Library of New South Wales from 1937, a director of Automatic Totalisators Ltd and Imperial Chemical Industries of Australia and New Zealand Ltd and a trustee of the Mutual Life & Citizens Assurance Co. Ltd. He was a member of the Australian Club, Sydney, and of the Institution of Mechanical Engineers, London. In 1939 he was awarded the Kernot [q.v.5] medal, also a D.Sc. in 1940 by the University of New Zealand.

Julius died of coronary vascular disease and cancer at his Killara home on 28 June 1946 and was cremated. He was survived by his wife and two sons—another son had been killed in an air crash in 1939. A portrait by Norman Carter [q.v.7] is held by the Commonwealth Scientific and Industrial Research Organization, Melbourne.

With 'his rather gaunt face, his crop of curly brown hair, and his very luminous blue eyes', Julius was slight in build. He was always mentally alert and spoke in a staccato manner. He 'could be autocratic, impatient, even choleric, but those qualities were disciplined by his sense of fair play, his quick sense of humour, his objectivity in scientific judgement and his keen political sense'.

DNB, 1941-50; D. P. Mellor, *The role of science and industry* (Canb, 1958); G. Currie and J. Graham, *The origins of CSIRO* (Melb, 1966); A. H. Corbett, *The Institution of Engineers, Australia* (Syd, 1973); Inst of Engineers (Aust), *Trans*, 1 (1920), 6 (1925), and *Q Bulletin*, 5 (1928), *J*, 12 (1940), 15 (1943); Engineering Assn of NSW, *Memoirs*, 35 (1920); *Records of the Aust Academy of Science*, 2 (Nov 1970), no 1; *SMH*, 2 July 1946, 6 Dec 1964; Allen Taylor & Co. Ltd, Letter-books (ANU Archives).   ARTHUR CORBETT

JULL, MARTIN EDWARD (1862-1917), public servant, was born on 18 January 1862 at Horsham, Sussex, England, son of Thomas Jull, pharmacist, and his wife Elizabeth Vincent Float, née Burtenshaw. Educated at Brighton Grammar School, he was apprenticed in 1879-82 to T. G. Warden & Co., auctioneers, valuers and estate agents of London; he was subsequently employed by Weatherell & Green. After a prolonged sea voyage including Ceylon, Japan, New Zealand and 'unfrequented places in the South Seas', a voyage taken on medical advice, he returned to Weatherell's until 25 March 1886 when he migrated to Western Australia.

Employed first by the Perth *Daily News*, Jull joined the Department of Public Works and Railways, nominally as a draughtsman but actually as private secretary to the director J. A. Wright [q.v.]. In 1887 he was attracted to Melbourne, then in the late phases of its land boom, and worked for the Coburg Reserve Estate Co. Ltd, managing suburban branches and deputizing for the manager during an absence from the colony.

In May 1891 Jull returned to Perth as chief clerk in the Department of Public Works and Railways. With Charles Yelverton O'Connor [q.v.], who arrived in June to become engineer-in-chief and acting general manager of railways, he formed an association which extended through a period of unprecedented expansion and activity caused by the gold rushes and Sir John Forrest's [q.v.8] determined policies. Their official association and personal friendship, lasting until O'Connor's death in 1902, was said by J. S. Battye [q.v.7] to be the reason for the 'forward condition of public works and useful services throughout the State'. In 1895-96, works and railways became separate departments. O'Connor remained as engineer-in-chief for public works while Jull became under-secretary with responsibility for all but the engineering branches. They made a superb team. Both were forward thinkers concerned that the department should give the best possible service in rapidly changing circumstances, and both recommended, as prerequisite, improved methods of recruiting, training and promoting staff.

On 12 November 1898 Jull married a young Scottish doctor, then practising in Perth, Roberta Henrietta Margaritta Stewart [q.v. R. Jull]. They settled at Brookside in the Armadale district, a property including orchards and vineyards where Jull shared with his colleague, friend and best man, Ernest E. Salter, a keen interest in horticultural experiments; he was credited with importing several new types of vines. Although they had not succeeded in selling this property, the Julls and their daughter, later the distinguished author Henrietta Drake-Brockman, in 1909 moved from Brookside to Longviews at Cottesloe.

Jull left the Department of Works in April 1905 to become the first public service commissioner under the terms of the Public Service Act, 1904. An admirable choice for his proven administrative capacity, personal integrity and wide experience, he became responsible in 1905-06 for 'the biggest reform yet attempted in this State', the reorganization of the entire public service, commencement of the formidable task of classification, provision of guide-lines for the service and establishment of machinery for recruiting, training and promotion. In his initial report covering the first fourteen months of the operation of the commission Jull declared that 'selection by examination . . . combined with reasonable security of tenure is the safest method in the long run of building up an efficient and honest permanent civil service. The incentive being to serve the country apart from any particular party'. Responsible public servants acknowledged that these principles were an excellent basis for classification. Despite political instability and shortage of funds for appropriate salaries, Jull was determined to complete the creation of an effective service free of patronage, and twice accepted extension of his term.

Jull was a handsome man of distinguished bearing, wide interests and cultivated tastes. A devout Anglican, he was a member of the diocesan council and an honorary lay reader. With a wide circle of friends both in and out of Western Australia, some of them from his schooldays, he was actively interested in cricket, boating, swimming, sailing, and cycling. He worked actively in the Young Men's Christian Association from its foundation in the State. Though his position as commissioner made him appear remote to many in the public service, those who worked with him as chairman of the Civil Service War Distress Committee during the last two years of his life recognized his compassion for those facing suffering.

Jull died of cerebral haemorrhage on 14 March 1917 at his home, following a diving mishap. He was buried in Karrakatta cemetery.

J. S. Battye (ed), *Cyclopedia of Western Australia*, 1 (Adel, 1912); *PP* (Cwlth), 1904-05, 2 (27), p 1819; *Civil Service J* (Perth), 11 (1917), no 105, p 1, 12, 19 (1929), no 217, p 71; *West Australian*, 15 Nov 1898; M. E. and (Dr) R. Jull papers (Battye Lib).

MERAB HARRIS TAUMAN

JULL, ROBERTA HENRIETTA MARGARITTA (1872-1961), medical practitioner, was born on 16 August 1872 in Glasgow, Scotland, second of four children of Robert Stewart, minister of the Free Church in Lisbon, and his wife Isabella Henrietta, née Fergusson. Educated at schools in London and Scotland, Roberta returned to Portugal to nurse her mother (d. 1890). Encouraged by her father, a 'follower of John Stuart Mill and believing in equal opportunities for men and women', she realized her ambition to study medicine and with her brother Fergusson began a medical course at Glasgow University, following their elder brother Mitchell. Excluded from lectures for men students, the women attended Queen Margaret College and the Royal Infirmary. Such experiences of discrimination were powerful influences in Roberta's work for women. In 1896, after an extra year studying diseases of the eye, she graduated M.B., C.M. In November 1896 she joined her brothers' practice at Guildford, Western Australia, and was dismayed by the living conditions and high infant mortality among her patients.

In 1897 she joined the Karrakatta Club for Women in Perth and formed lasting friendships with women dedicated to social reform, including Edith Cowan [q.v.8] and M. Phoebe Holmes [q.v.]. She set up a practice in Perth, the first woman to do so. In 1898, with Dr H. Horrocks, Roberta initiated moves which established a branch of the British Medical Association in Perth. On 12 November at Guildford Roberta married Martin Edward Jull [q.v.]. Their only child (b. 1901), became the writer Henrietta Drake-Brockman. Ill health took her to Britain for treatment in 1910. She was centred at St Andrews, Scotland. Dr Jull increased her medico-social knowledge, studied botany and socialism, and attended a conference in Glasgow of the National Union of Women Workers of Great Britain and Ireland. She returned to Western Australia in 1913.

Roberta Jull became a respected force for social reform, with education and health of women and children paramount. From 1909 she was a foundation member of the Children's Protection Society (its honorary medical adviser and parent counsellor) and of the Women's Service Guild; from 1913 a member of the Western Australian National Council of Women (president, and delegate to the International Council of Women in Vienna in 1930). She campaigned effectively for the early closing bill and for conscription in the referenda 1916-17. In 1915, having originally opposed it, she supported legislation for compulsory notification and treatment of venereal diseases, for reasons typically far sighted and informed. An authority on this subject and prostitution, Roberta was adviser to the 1938 royal commission on the administration of Perth City Council; she opposed licensing of brothels. Her association with students had begun in 1896 as local supervisor of public examin-

ations for the University of Adelaide. After the University of Western Australia opened in 1913 she became a member of Convocation (warden 1925-30) and of the Senate (1914-42). Roberta acted to form the Association of University Women in 1923, was its first president and initiator of the prolonged efforts to establish the residential university women's college (St Catherine's); she was a member of its first council in 1946.

After her husband's death she became in 1918 the first medical officer of schools in the Public Health Department. Her reports drew attention for the first time to the widespread health defects of children, especially in outback areas. She took a leading part in the extension of infant health centres of which she was superintendent, and studied child welfare programmes in Britain, New South Wales and New Zealand in 1921 and 1925. Before royal commissions on education (1921) and health (1925) Dr Jull pressed for child endowment and facilities for the mentally defective. She retired from the department in 1928. Her last report recorded significant reductions in infant mortality.

She was devoted to the cause of peace and disarmament, she represented the N.C.W. in the local League of Nations Union. In 1922 she attended a league summer school at the Oxford University and was an alternate delegate for Australia at the 1929 league assembly in Geneva, Switzerland, presenting a paper on traffic in women and children.

Roberta Jull was a prolific writer, lecturer and broadcaster on subjects ranging from ante-natal education and the higher education of women to the promotion of international peace; her influence was widespread over thirty years. Internationalist and practical, she envisaged women as coworkers with men in effecting politico-social reforms, with education as the instrument. In recognition of her work, especially 'in the cause of women', the university conferred an honorary doctorate of laws in 1943, and St Catherine's College its first honorary fellowship in 1951—its Jull common room has a bronze plaque in her likeness by Edgar Steitz.

From 1945 increasing deafness caused her withdrawal from public affairs. She died at Subiaco on 6 March 1961 and was cremated with Presbyterian forms; her ashes were scattered over her husband's grave.

N. Stewart, *St. Catherine's College* (Perth, 1978); F. Alexander, *Campus at Crawley* (Melb, 1963); F. K. Crowley, *Australia's western third* (Melb, 1960); Commissioner of Public Health, Annual Report, *V&P* (LA WA), 1929; *Western Mail* (Perth), 25 Dec 1915; *West Australian*, 2 June 1921; R. Jull papers (Battye Lib).   PATRICIA SHOLL CHURCH

K

KAEPPEL, CARL HENRY (1887-1946), educationist, was born on 13 January 1887 at Nattai, Mittagong, New South Wales, son of Carl William Herbert Kaeppel, merchant, and his wife Emily Annette, née Edwards. Educated at Sydney Grammar School, he was school captain in 1905 and Salting [q.v.2] exhibitioner in 1906. After graduating B.A. from the University of Sydney in 1910 with first-class honours in Greek and Latin he travelled to Europe on a Cooper [q.v.3] graduate scholarship, returning to teach at Sydney Church of England Grammar School (Shore) and The Armidale School. On 8 January 1916 at St Peter's Church, Neutral Bay, he married Muriel Beatrice Bailey; he divorced her in 1920.

Kaeppel had been active in the Sydney University Scouts and in 1914 was a lieutenant in the Sydney senior cadets. He enlisted in the Australian Imperial Force in December 1915, was soon commissioned and during service in France and England with the 18th Battalion and the 5th Training Battalion gained 'a reputation for grim soldiering and hard drinking'. He won the Military Cross in September 1916 and was promoted captain in July 1917. By the time of his appointment as adjutant of the 18th Battalion in December next year the once handsome, curly-haired, athletic student had become a balding, thickset figure with lined face and missing teeth.

After the Armistice Kaeppel studied archaeology in England, his researches in the British Museum laying the foundation for his profound knowledge of ancient geography. He returned to Australia in August 1919 and next year was appointed classics master at Melbourne Church of England Grammar School where the headmaster R. P. Franklin [q.v.8], a former fellow teacher at Shore, was a close friend.

A voracious reader with a photographic memory, Kaeppel excelled as scholar and teacher. Although he lacked an ear for phonetics (and could not pronounce an r), he had not only an intimate knowledge of Greek and Latin but 'explored with indefatigable thoroughness' the lesser-known ancient languages. A short man, in grey slacks and a well-worn sports jacket, he was a firm disciplinarian in the classroom; he carried an ash walking-stick which he banged on the ground to emphasize points and reputedly could inspire even the recalcitrant idler. His 'lads' greatly respected him.

He lived in the school lodge, made generous, impulsive gifts to his friends from his extensive library, and was an *habitué* of the Savage and Naval and Military clubs. He was a spell-binding conversationalist. However, his heavy drinking increased with the years and in 1931 he was forced to leave Melbourne Grammar. He moved to Sydney where he lived by coaching and by freelance journalism. In 1932 he wrote *A short history of Latin literature* and in 1935 the fascinating *Off the beaten track in classics*.

A. R. Chisholm, who considered him 'one of the three or four most eminent scholars that Australia has produced', described him as 'exuberant, but moody; purposeful, but nostalgic; almost blatant at times, but fundamentally shy'. Nominally a Protestant and in practice an atheist, he was converted to Catholicism during his later Sydney years. He died of cancer at Lewisham Hospital on 6 December 1946 and was buried in Waverley cemetery. His estate was valued for probate at £20.

A. R. Chisholm, *Men were my milestones* (Melb, 1958); Melb C. of E. Grammar School, *Liber Melburniensis*, (Melb, 1937).   ANN G. SMITH

KALESKI, ROBERT LUCIAN STANISLAUS (1877-1961), dog expert, bushman and author, was born on 19 January 1877 at Burwood, Sydney, son of John Stanislaus Kaleski, insurance agent and native of Posen (Poznan), Prussia, and his English wife Isabel, née Falder. For health reasons, aged 9 to 12 and for other long periods, he lived with a relation at Holsworthy where he dodged school and gained much knowledge of the bush. With access to a good library and making up his education in Sydney, he began legal studies but at 21 went in for droving and general bush work. After working for a year on a station at Grenfell, two years timber-getting on the Dorrigo plateau and a year housebuilding at Mosman, he took up a small selection at Holsworthy in 1904. Henry Lord, an agriculturalist at Sydney Technical College, was an early and valued educational influence.

Beginning as a dog owner at 6 and coaxing dogs into school ('I'm sure there's a dog somewhere, Kaleski, do you know anything of this?'), Kaleski was a lifelong student of the dog and dingo (Canis familiaris dingo). In 1893 he and others began improving the blue heeler breed of cattle-dog and in 1903 he drew up and published the first standard for that breed in the *Agricultural Gazette of New South Wales*. In 1904 he published the first standards for the kelpie and also the barb 'variety' of sheepdog. These standards were approved by leading breeders and adopted by the Kennel Club of New South Wales and the Cattle and Sheep Dog Club of Australia (founded by Kaleski in September 1907) and became standard almost Australia-wide. An energetic breeder, worker, exhibitor and judge of dogs, Kaleski with Nugget (1908-12) founded the noted Nugget strain of blue heeler prizewinners which included such champions as Clovelly Mavis and Clovelly Biddy.

Under various pen names, including 'Falder', Kaleski wrote on a variety of practical subjects for the *Sydney Mail, Sydney Morning Herald, Bulletin* and *Worker*; his articles on dogs and other animals were featured in A. G. Stephens's [q.v.] *Bookfellow*. He prepared *The Australian settler's complete guide*, published by Anthony Hordern [q.v.4] & Sons Ltd in 1909, and in 1914 some of his articles and stories appeared as *Australian barkers and biters*. Kaleski also patented several improvements for farm implements and had devised a scheme to offset the effects of drought. A self-styled 'soil expert', in 1918 he bought a run-down 300-acre (121 ha) farm, Thorn Hill, at Moorebank, near Liverpool, which he restored by applying his theories. In 1926 he contributed the authoritative article on 'Sheep-and-Cattle Dogs' to the *Australian Encyclopaedia*.

In 1933 Kaleski published a completely revised and expanded edition of *Australian barkers and biters* which embodied his theories on the origin of the dog. An admirer, breeder and champion of the dingo, Kaleski regarded it, probably erroneously, as the primal dog of the world. He was a fellow of the Linnean Society of New South Wales.

Kaleski, true bushman and environmentalist, was the first serious writer on Australia's working dogs; his powers of observation were likened by Sir Joseph Carruthers [q.v.7] to those of the naturalist Jean Henri Fabre. An interesting conversationalist he wrote as he talked, with 'wit and brevity'. A bachelor, Kaleski spent most of his life on his farm at Moorebank. He died on 1 December 1961 at Hammondville and was cremated with Anglican rites.

Agricultural Gazette (NSW), Aug 1903, p 752, Feb 1904, p 133; *SMH*, 11 Sept 1907, 15 Jan 1908, 1 Sept 1972; *Aust Worker*, 28 Jan 1909; *Sun-Herald*, 1 Dec 1957.   G. P. WALSH

KASHIWAGI, TAIRA (1868-1954), was born on 23 June 1868 at Shioya, Wakayama prefecture, Japan, son of Heibei Kashiwagi and his wife Ito, née Nishikaze. He is known to some as the Japanese catechist who, even in midsummer, would never address his Maker in his shirtsleeves; and to others as one of the witnesses who drew to the attention of the Mackay royal commission (1908) the unpalatable fact that the viability of the pearling industry rested on the courage and perseverance of the Japanese diver. He represents those among the Japanese community in Queensland (3247 in 1898) who remained after the enactment of the Immigration Restriction Act and made Queensland their home. About 550 of these remained in Queensland in 1921.

On graduating from Wakayama Teachers' College Kashiwagi taught for some years at Izumo primary school at Shionomisaki and then joined the stream of younger sons from that village emigrating to Thursday Island, where he arrived on 2 March 1895. After two years as a shop-assistant he established a general store for the Japanese community. Meanwhile under the tutelage of 'The Little Deaconess', Florence Buchanan [q.v.7], he gained a good command of English and was able to derive additional income as an interpreter. Later he also acquired a boat-building yard. His influence among the local Japanese steadily increased and by 1908 he had become president of Thursday Island Japanese Club, a powerful body which among its other activities negotiated the annual contracts between the Japanese divers and the Caucasian master-pearlers. He was a member of the Anglican parish council and under his leadership his compatriots raised the funds to erect a school building in the church grounds, in which they received religious instruction in English.

About 1910 Kashiwagi left Thursday Island, intending to become a planter in Papua. When, however, a personal reconnaissance of the Oriomo and Fly rivers failed to reveal suitable land, he withdrew to Brisbane where he opened a Japanese fancy-goods store and on 13 June 1914 married an Australian, Marguerite Kilner. By 1927 he had become one of the mainstays of Brisbane's Japanese Association of which he was president in December 1941 when, together with all other Japanese in Australia, he was interned. He was released in December 1943, having suffered three heart attacks. He died at Rockdale, Sydney, on 2 July 1954, and was cremated.

In Kashiwagi's life some of the difficulties implicit in membership of two societies are visible. At Thursday Island, as a Japanese, he was associated with measures to make the Japanese community commercially self-sufficient and to strengthen the voice of the Japanese Club. He supported those divers who on Japanese national holidays flew Japanese ensigns on the luggers (British vessels) *above* the British flag. In Brisbane, in the years preceding the outbreak of war he contributed not only to Australian charities but also to Japanese patriotic funds which solicited from Japanese residents overseas. In May 1942, when the Aliens Tribunal asked him 'Is it that you have lost all your interest in Japan?', he replied 'I am still interested in my own country'. On the other hand when, three months later, he was offered immediate repatriation to Japan, he elected to remain in internment.

Kashiwagi was atypical of the other Japanese settlers in that he achieved more than a bare subsistence. As well as putting his daughter through the University of Queensland, he was able to amass some savings: at the time of his internment his wife owned real estate worth about £3000.

Wakayama-ken, *Wakayama-ken iminshi* (Wakayama-shi, 1957); A367 34044, BP 242/1 Q24602, BP 4/3, MP529/3 (AAO, Canb).

D. C. S. SISSONS

KATER, SIR NORMAN WILLIAM (1874-1965), medical practitioner, grazier and politician, was born on 18 November 1874 at Brush Farm, Ryde, New South Wales, second son of native-born parents Henry Edward Kater [q.v.5] and his wife Mary Eliza, daughter of William Forster [q.v.4]. He was educated at All Saints' College, Bathurst, in 1886-88 and Sydney Grammar School in 1889-91, where he excelled at rifle-shooting.

Resident in St Paul's College while he studied medicine at the University of Sydney (M.B., Ch.M., 1898), he won the Haswell [q.v.] prize (1893) and Renwick [q.v.6] scholarship (1894), and rowed for the university. He was resident medical officer at Royal Prince Alfred Hospital in 1898, then worked his way to Britain as ship's surgeon. He spent three months studying midwifery at the Rotunda Hospital, Dublin, and his spare time hunting. Later he attended courses at specialist hospitals in London.

On his return to Sydney, Kater bought a practice at College Street. He married Jean Gaerloch Mackenzie on 25 February 1901 at St James' Church. After the death of his elder brother in 1902 he reluctantly abandoned his practice and bought Nyrang near Molong. He was a member of the Boree Shire Council in 1906-11.

When his father and uncle divided the Mumblebone stud in 1906 he joined his father in H. E. Kater & Son and supervised the Egelabra merino stud, near Warren. By 1911 he had virtually exterminated rabbits there and at Nyrang.

Late in 1915, Kater went to Egypt to assist the Australian Red Cross commissioner

(Sir) Adrian Knox [q.v.]. He soon departed for France and joined the French Service de Santé Militaire, working at the St Rome base hospital near Toulouse. Unable to enlist in the Australian Imperial Force in London, he returned to Sydney in 1917 and in October joined the Australian Army Medical Corps. He worked at the Military Hospital, Randwick, and, promoted captain and temporary major, from January 1918 to February 1919 as A.A.M.C. adjutant at Victoria Barracks. For his services in France he was appointed chevalier of the Légion d'honneur and awarded the Médaille de la Reconnaissance Française.

After the war Kater returned to pastoral pursuits. He sold Nyrang in 1920 and bought a house in Sydney; in 1924 he inherited Mount Broughton near Moss Vale, where he spent most weekends. In 1915-64 he was a council-member of the Graziers' Association of New South Wales. As president in 1922-24, he successfully opposed Sir John Higgins's [q.v.] attempt to turn the British Australian Wool Realisation Association Ltd into a permanent central organization for the stabilization of the wool industry. In 1923 he had to contend with a long and bitter strike by shearers for shorter hours. In the summer of 1927-28 he was chairman of the Federal Pastoral Advisory Committee. Knighted in 1929, he was appointed to the State committee of the Commonwealth Council for Scientific and Industrial Research that year.

With the aid of his expert classer E. H. Wass, Kater kept the Egelabra flock pure, despite the popularity of 'wrinkley' sheep in the early twentieth century. At the Sydney Sheep Show he won the Stonehaven [q.v.] cup for pens of five in 1933, 1938, 1939 and 1940 and bred the grand champion merino ram in 1938 and 1940. About 1939 he took his sons into partnership and later formed H. E. Kater & Son Pty Ltd, with himself as governing director. He was president of the New South Wales Sheepbreeders' Association in 1940-44. From the 1920s Kater had developed important business interests—he was chairman of the Co-operative Wool and Produce Co. Ltd, and a director of the Colonial Sugar Refining Co. (1924-49), the Graziers' Co-operative Shearing Co. Ltd (Grazcos) (from 1919), Globe Worsted Mills Ltd (from 1927), Newcastle-Wallsend Coal Co. (from 1933) and a local director of the Liverpool and London and Globe Insurance Co. Ltd.

A member of the central council of the Progressive Party, Kater was nominated to the Legislative Council in 1923. Elected to the reconstituted council in 1933 and 1942, he did not seek re-election in 1954. In the council he spoke briefly and to the point and strongly opposed J. T. Lang's [q.v.] governments.

'Austere in his speech and in his dress', Sir Norman was tall, handsome, clean shaven, with smooth silver hair and 'very piercing blue eyes'. Shy and unable 'to stand fools lightly', he sometimes gave the impression of arrogance. He played polo as a young man, enjoyed tennis, golf, bowls and bridge, and loved the theatre and ballet. His first wife died in London in 1931. At St Mark's, Darling Point, on 14 January 1938 he married Mary (d. 1969), daughter of L. A. B. Wade [q.v.], but they later separated. He was president of the Australian Club in 1945-49 and belonged to the Union Club, Sydney, the Queensland Club and the Junior Carlton in London. Appointed to the State advisory committee of the Australian Broadcasting Commission in 1949, he was chairman of the Institute of Public Affairs in 1951.

Sir Norman died in St Luke's Hospital, Darlinghurst, on 18 August 1965, and was cremated with Anglican rites. He was survived by four sons and two daughters of his first marriage, who inherited his estate, valued for probate at £238 801. Fluent in French and widely read, Sir Norman gave outstanding service to the pastoral industry and to the wider community. His portrait by an unknown artist is held by the family.

NSW Sheepbreeders' Assn, *The Australian merino* (Syd, 1955); D. S. Macmillan, *The Kater family 1750-1965* (Syd, 1966); *Pastoral Review*, 18 May 1962; *SMH*, 25 Sept 1915, 8 July, 31 Dec 1918, 8 Dec 1920, 3 June 1922, 1 Mar 1929, 19 Mar 1941, 19 Aug 1965; *Aust National Review*, 20 Aug 1923; *Land* (Syd), 29 Apr 1955; *Daily Telegraph* (Syd), 29 May 1956; Kater family papers (NL); information from (Lady) Catherine Kater, Syd.

MARTHA RUTLEDGE

KAUFFMANN, JOHN (1864-1942), photographer, was born on 29 December 1864 at Truro, South Australia, second son of Alexander Kauffmann, merchant, and his wife Therese, née Victorsen; theirs was an orthodox Jewish household. At 17 Kauffmann was articled to the architect John H. Grainger, father of Percy [q.v.]; in 1886 he attended H. P. Gill's [q.v.] classes at the Art Gallery of South Australia's school of design. Next year he went to England, and abandoned architecture for chemistry. In Zurich in 1890-93 he studied chemistry at the Swiss Federal Institute of Technology. He was fascinated by new photographic reproduction processes such as photogravure, worked in a Viennese portrait studio and studied zinc etching and the collotype process in Bavaria. In about 1896 he spent a year at the Vienna Imperial Technical and Research Institution for Photography and Reproduction Processes.

In 1897 Kauffmann returned to Adelaide and appears to have imparted the ideals of a European pictorial style of art photography to the South Australian Photographic Society. He exhibited enlargements on pearl bromide paper in Adelaide and Sydney in 1897; a critic found his 1898 show 'exquisite in the delicacy and gradation of the tones, giving a depth and softness'. Next year Kauffmann won prizes at the Photographic Society of New South Wales's intercolonial exhibition. He continued showing his impressionistic work in Adelaide and in London where it won silver medals. Kauffmann's trademark became soft focus. He was one of the leading Australian exponents of the 'pictorialist' style in which the camera's lens was opened up to focus on the subject's chief feature while inessential details were diffused. Harold Cazneaux [q.v.7] was inspired by Kauffmann.

In 1909 he moved to Melbourne and, later, a studio in Collins Street. Next year the Photographic Association of Victoria mounted its first one-man show of seventy-four of his photographs. Kauffmann's status rose in 1914 when his influential second one-man show in Melbourne was repeated in Sydney. Critics preferred his naturalistic approach to the extremists of 'the fuzzy-wuzzy school'. His best work was done with gums and tea-trees near Healesville.

In 1919 a monograph, *The art of John Kauffmann*, appeared containing twenty landscapes and urban scenes and an essay by Leslie H. Beer. But low-key tonal Impressionism was becoming unpopular. Kauffmann was sometimes criticized for artificiality and 'fakery', implying a manipulation of the prints: photographers were adopting a style truer to Australian sunlight. Although he illustrated a book on the Sunraysia district in 1920, and contributed to a Sydney Ure Smith [q.v.] book on Melbourne in 1931, he felt bitter that by 1934 his romantic treatment was considered dated. Possibly due to poor eyesight, he now made close-up studies of Australian flora which were bold and modern in composition and unusual as subjects at that time. In 1936, old and sick, he gave up his studio, but continued to paint and play the violin.

Kauffmann was a shy man, and frugal, but his style was that of an aesthete and a Bohemian. He 'was usually off to an art exhibition, a chamber music recital, or an alfresco lunch in the Botanical Gardens' with artist friends, including Septimus Power [q.v.]. Known as Jack, he was attractive to women and dressed with yellow gloves, cane, spats and pince-nez on a silk cord.

Kauffmann was living at his sister's South Yarra boarding-house when he died, unmarried, on 29 November 1942. After a service at the Chevra Kadisha, Carlton, he was buried in Fawkner cemetery. The Australian National Gallery, Canberra, holds eighty-eight of his photographs.

G. Newton, *Silver and grey: fifty years of Australian photography* (Syd, 1980); J. Mollison and L. Murray (eds), *The Australian National Gallery* (Canb, 1982); G. Newton, 'John Kauffmann 1864-1942 art photographer', *A'sian Antique Collector*, 1980, p 114; information from Mr A. Marcus, SA.

G. NEWTON
SUZANNE EDGAR

KAUPER, HENRY ALEXIS (1888-1942), aviation and radio engineer and inventor, was born on 12 March 1888 at Hawthorn, Melbourne, son of Charles Henry Kauper, carpenter and later orchardist, and his wife Rosa Victoria, née Francis. Harry's father, an Estonian seaman, landed at Port Melbourne in 1877.

After education in state schools Kauper entered the motor engineering trade, specializing in electrical and ignition systems. In 1910 he was a chauffeur at Willaura but in May 1911, with his mechanic friends H. G. Hawker [q.v.] and Harry Busteed (they were known as 'The Three Harry's'), Kauper went to England to study aviation. After working in the Sunbeam and other engineering works he became a mechanic in June 1912 with T. O. M. Sopwith who was building his first aeroplane at Brooklands, Surrey. Through Kauper's influence Hawker was also employed and when the Sopwith Aviation Co. was formed in 1913 at Kingston-upon-Thames, Kauper became foreman of works and Hawker chief test pilot.

On 25 August Kauper, as engineer-mechanic, accompanied Hawker, the only entrant in the £5000 *Daily Mail* seaplane flight around the British coast. Hawker brought Kauper, as chief mechanic, to Melbourne in January 1914 to demonstrate to the Defence Department the new Sopwith Tabloid biplane. Both men had contributed significantly to the design of this plane, the prototype of the Sopwith war-plane, the 'Pup'. They returned to England in June and, with the outbreak of war, Kauper became works manager for Sopwiths, in charge of 3800 employees turning out 45 planes a week. An inventive genius, he is best known for the patented Sopwith-Kauper interrupter gear which synchronized the firing of a machine-gun through a rotating aeroplane propeller. First used in

April 1916, 3950 were fitted to Sopwith planes during the war.

Kauper joined the Royal Air Force on 25 October 1918 as a second lieutenant (administration) engaged in experimental research. On 12 May 1919, at All Saints Anglican Church, Kingston-upon-Thames, he married Beatrice Minnie Hooper who had also worked at Sopwiths. With the two planes of Captain H. J. Butler [q.v.7] Kauper reached Adelaide next July and in August they flew to Minlaton, carrying the first air mail over water in South Australia. In October they formed the Harry J. Butler & Kauper Aviation Co. Ltd which pioneered commercial aviation in South Australia but went into voluntary liquidation in 1921.

Kauper had turned to radio. Under experimental licence S643 (1919) he established station 5BG at Dulwich in 1920. In 1922 he participated in the first radio telephony tests in South Australia, gave helpful advice to crystal set enthusiasts on his popular 'Dulwich Calling' broadcasts, and addressed radio clubs and the Wireless Institute of Australia. As an experimenter he was important in developing radio for broadcasting. He was a partner in the Adelaide Radio Co., manufacturing radio equipment, and was a part-time operator from 12 June 1924 when the company, under contract, loaned its call sign 5DN and equipment to Edward James Hume's experimental station at Parkside.

Kauper's station was one of the earliest low-powered, crystal-controlled transmitters in Australia; in November 1925 his signals were picked up in New York and California—a world record. In June Kauper and George Towns, an invalid soldier, built the first compact radio for Rev. John Flynn [q.v.8]. Operated by a generator off the rear wheel of Flynn's truck, it proved an outstanding success but Flynn wanted a set workable under all outback conditions. In 1926 Kauper introduced Flynn to Alfred Traeger [q.v.] who ultimately developed the pedal wireless used by the Flying Doctor Service of Australia.

On 7 June 1926 Kauper was appointed chief engineer of 5CL, Adelaide (Central Broadcasters Ltd). When in January 1930 5CL was taken over by the National Broadcasting Service, he did not transfer but became chief engineer for 5AD (The Advertiser Broadcasting Network Pty Ltd), designing the transmitter and establishing the station. In 1931, after a world tour, he became consulting engineer to 3DB, Melbourne.

At the invitation of the director, Group Captain Eric Harrison [q.v.], Kauper accepted appointment, as a civilian, to the Aeronautical Inspection Directorate in

1940, in charge of the radio electrical and instrument section. Responsible for inspection of equipment being manufactured or repaired for the Royal Australian Air Force by civilian contractors, although in ill health he contributed greatly in those formative years of the directorate, particularly in his specialist field of radio. He died suddenly at his Richmond home on 22 April 1942 of coronary vascular disease and was cremated. He had no children and his wife later returned to England.

Kauper was a modest man with deep-set, thoughtful blue eyes, rugged features and sandy hair. 'He went out as quietly as he had lived', but his death lost to radio and aviation 'another of the pioneering spirits' whose constructive work so advanced rapid development in these fields. 'Nothing mechanical held any problems for him and, in all things pertaining to radio, he stood alone'.

F. M. Cutlack, *The Australian Flying Corps* (Syd, 1923); H. C. Miller, *Early birds* (Adel, 1968); R. J. Gibson, *Australia and Australians in civil aviation, an index to events 1823 to 1920* (Syd, 1971); G. R. Copley, *Australians in the air* (Adel, 1978); J. F. Ross, *A history of radio in South Australia, 1897-1977* (Adel, 1978); Aviation Hist Soc of Aust, *J*, 4 (1963), no 4; Institute of Radio Engineers, Australia, *I.R.E. Bulletin*, Feb 1943; *Age*, 4 May 1911, 23 Apr 1942; *Argus* (Melb), 26-30 Aug 1913, 14 Jan-6 May 1914, 23 Apr 1942; *Observer* (Adel), 9 Aug 1919, 11 Sept 1920; *Advertiser* (Adel), 4 Sept 1920, 27 Apr 1942; *Register* (Adel), 4 Sept 1920, 4 Oct 1924; *Herald* (Melb), 23 Apr 1942; papers held by author, Paynesville, Vic; C. H. Kauper papers (AAO, Canb).   JEAN P. FIELDING

KAVANAGH, EDWARD JOHN (1871-1956), trade unionist, politician and public servant, was born on 30 October 1871 in Sydney, eleventh child and second surviving son of William Kavanagh, publican, and his wife Ellen, née Carty. His parents, both Irish, died when he was 2 and he was reared by an elder sister. Educated at Gladstone Public School, Balmain, and Marist Brothers' College, North Sydney, he excelled in amateur boxing as a featherweight. At 16 as a steward he shipped to the Pacific Islands and San Francisco. He boxed in the United States of America but his variable weight division was a handicap. He went to England, worked his passage to Sydney and was briefly a boxing instructor.

In 1888 Kavanagh became an apprentice presser and joined the Pressers' Union; he eventually held every union office including that of delegate to the Trades and Labor Council. Among the issues for which he fought was that of a minimum wage for children. In 1902 he won the legal right for apprentices to articles of indenture—it was the union's first case and the second in the New South Wales Court of Industrial Arbitration. The experience influenced him and he consistently urged arbitration rather than strike action. In 1905 he was elected president of the Labor Council and in 1906-18 was its full-time secretary. He established an arbitration section within the council to help affiliated unions present their cases. In 1915-18 he was a government nominee to the Senate of the University of Sydney.

During the transport strike of August-September 1917 which began in the railway and tramway workshops in protest at the introduction of the Taylor job-card system, Kavanagh was a leading member of the strike defence committee. The National government quickly carried repressive legislation and Kavanagh with three others, including A. C. Willis [q.v.], was arrested and charged with conspiracy. When apprehended Kavanagh had a notebook containing in a form of shorthand the points he had made in speeches about the strike. The police paid £200 to have the notes translated, hoping they would assist in securing Kavanagh's conviction; instead they recorded his opposition to general strike action and ensured his acquittal. Next year Kavanagh was appointed a commissioner representing the unions on the New South Wales Board of Trade.

Kavanagh had been a member of the Legislative Council since 1912. Under the Storey [q.v.] government of 1920-21 he became leader in the Upper House and vice-president of the Executive Council. Following Storey's death he served in addition in 1921-22 as minister for labour in the Dooley [q.v.8] cabinet. He remained on the Board of Trade after Labor's defeat in 1922 and in 1926 was appointed by the Lang [q.v.] government to the State Industrial Commission as deputy industrial commissioner—the first layman in a judicial position able to act alone and to make determinations from which there was no appeal. He had long argued for lay participation in industrial arbitration, believing that 'laymen having practical knowledge and experience and a closer touch with the people . . . should be in a better position to give a decision likely to satisfy both sides without legal hair-splitting'. He held the office for five years. In 1931 after he had lost the support of the 'Jock' Garden [q.v.8] Trades Hall group Lang did not reappoint him.

In 1931-37 Kavanagh practised privately as an industrial advocate and adviser, retained by both employers and unions. Unsuccessful in the reformed Legislative Council elections of 1934, he was permitted to retain the title 'Honorable'. In 1937 he became an apprenticeship and conciliation commissioner in the Federal Department of Labour and Industry and in 1941 succeeded J. B. Chifley as director of labour in the Department of Munitions, responsible for the allocation of manpower during World War II. He retired in 1948.

Kavanagh had married Agnes Jane Cousins in the Glebe Congregational Church on 31 December 1894. He died a widower on 10 October 1956 at Concord, and was cremated. Of his three sons and three daughters, one daughter survived him. His estate was valued for probate at £636. He was a good example of an underprivileged man whose innate skills and compassion were developed for the benefit of the community by his experience as a trade unionist.

V. G. Childe, *How Labour governs*, F. B. Smith ed (Melb, 1964); J. Iremonger et al (eds), *Strikes* (Syd, 1973); *NSW Industrial Gazette*, 13 (1918), 30 (1926); *Aust Worker*, 17 Nov 1910; *SMH*, 15 May 1920, 15 May 1926, 19 June 1931, 23 May 1941, 18 Oct 1956; *Smith's Weekly* (Syd), 7 June 1941; information from Sir W. McKell, Double Bay, Syd.

BARRIE UNSWORTH

KAY, ALICK DUDLEY (1884-1961), Domain orator, was born on 3 October 1884 at Petersham, Sydney, eldest child of Edward Kay, storeman, and his wife Bridget, née Murphy. Educated at Stanmore Superior Public School, he worked in a warehouse and was a clerk when, on 7 June 1913 at Hawksburn, Melbourne, he married Mary Elizabeth Purves, née Robertson, a 37-year-old widow with five children. He was a clerk with the New South Wales railways when he joined the army in July 1915. As Sergeant Kay, he was attending the National Party Debating Club in Sydney in 1917-18. He contested the safe Labor, Federal seat of South Sydney for the Nationalists in 1917.

Kay severed formal connexions with the National Party in 1918. He began regular appearances in Sydney Domain as an anti-Communist speaker and his flair and wit attracted large crowds. He founded the Citizens' Democratic Association through which his backers channelled funds to him. He issued a pamphlet, *The ideal social system*, and in 1924-25 published *Kay's News*. Its contents were devoted to crude individualism and the promotion of himself and a few conservative businessmen. He travelled alternate weeks to Melbourne to deliver anti-communist homilies beside the Yarra.

Unexpectedly in 1925 Kay as an Independent was elected to the Legislative Assembly as fifth member for North Shore. He supported Labor in the first censure motion. In parliament he spoke with more restraint than on the platform: 'a sane Labor Government is the best barrier against Bolshevism'. He favoured a 44-hour week and approved of Labor's controversial arbitration bill.

His apostasy riled his erstwhile supporters. He was under attack from them before J. T. Lang [q.v.] appointed him to the Metropolitan Meat Industry Board as a consumers' representative. Under electoral law his replacement in parliament was a Labor candidate at the last election and the Opposition alleged Kay had been bought. Following the National and Country parties' victory in the 1927 elections Kay was removed from the Meat Board by Act of parliament. He was irrepressible. In 1929 again campaigning against socialism, he sought financial assistance from the Graziers' Association of New South Wales.

Restored to his position on the Meat Board after Labor's return to office in 1930, he was ousted again with the next change of government. In 1933, unemployed, Kay went to England and spoke at least once on Hyde Park Corner. A widower, he married Dorothy Edith Gamson at Islington on 15 June 1943. In World War II he may have been employed by the Department of Information, as he claimed in 1951, after his return to Australia. He was eligible by then for an Australian aged pension. In an interview he lied about his age and boasted that while in England he 'had talked down the Cliveden set and talked up Lloyd George and Anthony Eden'. On Sundays he returned to the Domain.

Survived by his wife, Kay died on 4 February 1961 without issue and was cremated after a service at St John's Anglican Church, Milsons Point. At most a shrewd eccentric, Kay is perhaps better described as a 'harmless ratbag'.

People (Syd), 7 Nov 1951; *Fighting Line*, 20 Apr 1917, 20 July, 21 Dec 1918; *SMH*, 29 July 1926, 26 Jan 1928; Graziers Assn of NSW (E256/250, ANU Archives).

HEATHER RADI

KAY, WILLIAM ELPHINSTONE (1888-1941), surgeon, was born on 3 January 1888 at Glen Innes, New South Wales, second son of Robert Kay, Presbyterian minister, and his wife Christina, née Elphinstone, both born in Sydney of Scottish parents. He was educated at Sydney Boys' High School and graduated in medicine from the University of Sydney (M.B., 2nd class honours, 1911; Ch.M., 1919). He was a fine athlete representing St Andrew's College in various sports and gaining a rowing blue. In 1912 he became a resident medical officer at Sydney Hospital; next year he was medical and surgical registrar and in 1914 assistant medical superintendent. Having been a member of the University Scouts, he was appointed captain in the Australian Army Medical Corps in 1913.

On 20 August 1914 Kay enlisted in the Australian Imperial Force and was appointed captain in the 1st Field Ambulance. He served in that unit at Gallipoli, landing at approximately 9.30 a.m. on 25 April 1915. Except for a short period acting as regimental medical officer to the 1st Battalion in June, he remained with the 1st F.A. on Gallipoli, displaying great courage throughout. Evacuated on 1 September with enteric fever, he rejoined his unit at Lemnos in October when he was promoted temporary major. In December he returned to Egypt where he remained after his unit's departure for France in March, working with the 3rd Australian General Hospital. He rejoined the unit at Buire in November 1916.

Kay was promoted major in June 1916, temporary lieut-colonel and officer commanding the 2nd F.A. in April 1917 and lieut-colonel in September 1917. He made an enormous impression on the officers and men of the 2nd F.A. as well as with his superiors. One of his officers wrote: 'He had the efficiency of the unit at heart and the well-being and comfort of his men constantly in the fore-front of his mind' and especially so when conditions were severe. His outstanding service at Gallipoli, on the Somme and in Flanders was recognized by a mention in dispatches, and in June 1918 by award of the Distinguished Service Order 'for marked ability, zeal and devotion to duty' between 22 September 1917 and 24 February 1918. 'When in charge of the Advanced Dressing Station at Ypres, Lieutenant-Colonel Kay was constantly up and down the line, working continually under bad weather conditions and heavy enemy shelling. His disregard of personal danger and his constant attention to the maintenance of all posts and lines of evacuation were responsible for the speedy evacuation and comfort of the wounded.' In September 1918 he left the 2nd F.A. to join the 2nd A.G.H. of which he became acting officer-in-charge in November. He returned to Australia in December in the *Argyllshire* as senior medical officer.

On return to civilian life Kay commenced practice at Glen Innes. On 19 January 1921 at St Stephen's Presbyterian Church, Sydney, he married Margaret Mitchell McLeod, daughter of Scottish immigrants Dr James and Christina McLeod. Kay returned to Sydney in 1923 to general medical practice at Waverley and in 1930 to surgical practice in Macquarie Street. In 1923 he was appointed honorary assistant surgeon at the Sydney Hospital and in 1931 clinical tutor. In 1931 he gained his fellowship of the Royal Australasian College of Surgeons. During World War I Kay had developed a great admiration for the Australian soldier which he carried into civilian practice, earning him the esteem of all his patients. At Sydney Hospital, 'big Bill Kay' was held in respect by staff and students alike for his ability, cheerfulness and humanity.

Kay remained with the A.A.M.C., Australian Military Forces. In 1934 he became assistant director of Medical services, 1st Division, with the rank of colonel. In the midst of his busy professional life and his outside interests, he managed to play golf, was fond of surfing and was a warm-hearted family man.

In May 1940 in the rank of colonel Kay was posted to command the 2/5th A.G.H., A.I.F., and had the responsibility for establishing and training it. His charm, personality and ability to command ensured that it was 'a happy and contented unit'. The 2/5th A.G.H. arrived in the Middle East in December 1940 but in March 1941 Kay was ordered to prepare the unit to move. They embarked at Alexandria, Egypt, on 10 April, four days after Germany had invaded Greece and, arriving in Athens on 12 April, proceeded to establish a hospital at Kephissia. Kay ensured that the 'unit worked with all possible speed and the day after arrival at the site was able to accommodate fifty patients'.

It was soon apparent that the campaign in Greece was failing but throughout the confusion of the next week Kay's hospital continued to receive, treat and evacuate casualties. On 18 April Major General (Sir) Samuel Burston, director of medical services, A.I.F., informed Kay that he was the senior medical officer of the Australian medical services in Athens. On the night of 21 April Kay learned that the original plan for the 2/5th A.G.H. to remain and become prisoners of war, except for the nursing staff who were to be evacuated, had been abandoned: he was to be sent to Egypt because of his great experience. Kay arranged for a small party to stay and maintain the hospital while the rest were evacuated. On 24 April Kay went to Piraeus to board the *Neon Hellas* which was embarking wounded and others. Late in the afternoon the ship was hit by a bomb. Kay was severely wounded in the head and his right arm was severed below the elbow. He died of his wounds on 26 April 1941 at Kephissia and was buried there. His wife, son and three daughters survived him.

A. S. Walker, *Medical services of the R.A.N. and R.A.A.F.* (Canb, 1961); Univ Syd Medical School, *Senior Year Book*, 1938, and *Medical J*, Nov 1941; *Reveille* (Syd), 1 July 1941; *SMH*, 15 Sept 1915, 15 Oct 1941; War diaries, 1st and 2nd Field Ambulance, AIF and 2/5th Aust General Hospital; W. E. Kay file, War Records Section (AWM); records (AWM).   W. D. REFSHAUGE

KAW, CHIN; *see* CHIN KAW

KEANEY, PAUL FRANCIS (1888-1954), Christian Brother, was born on 5 October 1888 at Corralskin, Kiltyclogher, Leitrim, Ireland, son of Terance Keaney, farmer, and his wife Mary, née McGowan. He helped on the farm before migrating in 1911 to Australia where he worked on the land in northern New South Wales and probably as a policeman in Queensland. His sister Christina, a Dominican nun, influenced him to become a novice with the Christian Brothers in Sydney in 1916. Keaney chafed under the rigid rules of the novitiate, but next year was appointed to St Vincent's Orphanage, South Melbourne. Here he advocated more enlightened methods of training orphans.

In 1919 Keaney moved to Perth, to the St Peter's Intermediate Orphanage and farm for boys at Clontarf. He then taught at Christian Brothers' College, Fremantle, before returning to Clontarf as superior in 1924. In 1927 he helped to develop St Mary's Agricultural Farm School at Tardun, 300 miles (480 km) to the north, for the boys' further training. He lived primitively, on black tea, damper and kangaroo meat, while building and labouring. Of his clothes he remarked, 'Well you can't expect me to run a farm and build a monastery dressed up like a model'. Keaney was a 'big stout man with the neck of a bull', a mop of white hair and rosy face. Building materials were improvised: old tram and train rails, sweepings from the cement works. During the Depression he enlisted the help of wage-earners, who gave small donations and voluntary work, and of the wealthier who provided money, skills and influential contacts. Though abstemious, Keaney was a jovial host and raconteur.

In 1930-35 he taught again at the Brothers' colleges in Perth and Fremantle. He then returned to Clontarf as superior. When the property was requisitioned by the Royal Australian Air Force in World War II, most boys were evacuated to Tardun, but a few went to a property near Bindoon to begin the new St Joseph's Farm School. This site was the gift of Katherine Musk. In 1942

he began building there; his pupils, of all religions, now included refugees. Finances were minimal. State wards often stayed on to work on the farm and buildings and some, at Tardun, were assisted to buy nearby farms.

To Keaney there were no bad boys; his success with the troublesome ones was widely recognized; often they came to him from the courts. He trusted them whatever their record: doors were left unlocked, responsibility was delegated. The peculiarities of a strict, hard-working father endeared him to them. So did his highly picturesque sayings, impatient outbursts and humour. An enthusiast, Keaney was easily depressed by criticism.

In 1945 he went to Tasmania and Melbourne to recuperate from ill health. In 1948 he was back as superior over the pupils at 'Boys' Town', Bindoon. He was appointed M.B.E. and I.S.O. in 1953. Next year he planned to visit Ireland but died at Subiaco on 26 February, two days after a farewell dinner. He was buried at 'Boys' Town', Bindoon, where the chapel has been named for him.

A. D. Scott (comp), *Biography. Reverend Brother Paul Francis Keaney* (Perth, nd); H. Sutherland, *Southward journey* (Lond, 1942); D. F. Bourke, *The history of the Catholic Church in Western Australia* (Perth, 1979); *People* (Syd), 13 Jan 1954; *West Australian*, 26, 27 Feb 1954, 7 Oct 1957; PR 1810 B/KEA (Battye Lib).   F. D. SHORTILL

KEARTLAND, GEORGE ARTHUR (1848-1926), naturalist, was born on 11 June 1848 at Wellingborough, Northamptonshire, England, second of ten children of William Keartland, draper, and his wife Martha, née Morris. He was brought to Melbourne by his parents in 1850 and, by all accounts, was educated at George Street Public School, Fitzroy.

By a childhood accident he was lamed for life. Nevertheless he developed a strong affinity with the outdoors and interest in shooting and nature. After some training as a photographer he completed an apprenticeship to a printer and became a compositor with the *Age*, where he was employed for over fifty years. He joined the Melbourne Typographical Society in 1871 and was twice president of the Australasian Typographical Union. Anglican by birth, he married with Wesleyan forms on 11 June 1873 at Brunswick, Margaret Jane Nicol who had been born in Manchester, England, and educated at Mrs James's Academy for Girls, Fitzroy. They settled at Collingwood.

In 1886 he attended his first meeting of

the Field Naturalists' Club of Victoria and was immediately inspired to study all branches of natural history. However, he was especially drawn to ornithology. His latent ability emerged in the guidance he provided on club excursions, and such instruction continued as late as 1907 when he taught bird-skinning to fifty teachers at the club's Mornington camp.

Keartland became a field ornithologist of national standing on the Horn [q.v.] and Calvert [q.v.] expeditions. On the former, from Oodnadatta to the MacDonnell Ranges in May to August 1894, Keartland, as naturalist-collector, preserved some 200 bird-skins, representing 78 species including 5 previously undescribed. A. J. North, of the Australian Museum, Sydney, regarded the collection as the most important after Sturt's [q.v.2] of 1839 for its information on species distribution. North's published account includes Keartland's valuable field notes.

On the ill-fated Calvert expedition to north-west Australia 1896-97, Keartland was again a naturalist-collector but had to abandon over 300 bird-skins including a 'new' and possibly still unknown pigeon, returning with 167 specimens of 59 species excluding nests and eggs. This significant collection was also accompanied by excellent field notes, including early details of the Night Parrot.

Keartland's enthusiasm and dedication overcame all physical disabilities. In 1926 Professor Sir Baldwin Spencer [q.v.] recalled the cold winter nights of the MacDonnell Ranges when 'hour after hour [Keartland] used to work away [skinning birds] by the light of the flickering lamp, with a rug wrapped round him and the water frozen in the billy-can'. On the Calvert expedition the heat was intense by mid-October and on one night the water in the casks 'almost scalded one's fingers'. The collection, equipment and all personal effects had to be abandoned for survival; but Keartland, it is said, continued day after day to carry across the sand-hills the gun lent by a friend, later to hand it back without a word about the burden it had been.

Keartland's private ornithological collection is divided. Sir Malcolm McEacharn [q.v.] purchased from him bird-specimens and notes representing some 140 species and an egg-collection of 398 clutches dating from 1884 to 1902. These were later presented to the Royal Scottish Museum, Edinburgh. A further 464 clutches of eggs for the period 1878-1914 are in the South Australian Museum. Historically Keartland's species-notes in Edinburgh are of considerable ornithological interest.

Keartland's published notes on birds are found chiefly in the *Victorian Naturalist*. They exemplify careful observation including his early recognition of the two Australian Teal species and his timely plea for biologically sound Quail seasons. His 'Birds of the Melbourne district', 1900, treats 185 species personally observed and provides a useful historical view for comparison with contemporary avifaunal accounts. He also made observations on native bird-species in his aviaries.

In 1900 Keartland was prominent in the founding of the (Royal) Australasian Ornithologists' Union. He was president of the Field Naturalists' Club of Victoria in 1907-09. His name is commemorated in *Lichenostomus (Meliphaga) keartlandi*, Grey-headed (Keartland's) Honeyeater, named by North from the Horn expedition collection, and in *Keartlandia*, a now synonymized generic name, created by Mathews [q.v.], for the Orange Chat. The name Keartland Hills in Western Australia commemorates his part in the Calvert expedition as does the name *Gardenia keartlandii* for a plant collected near the Fitzroy River.

Keartland was of kindly and family-loving disposition. He died of cancer at his home at Preston on 21 May 1926 and was buried in Coburg cemetery. He was survived by his wife, two of his five sons and four of his six daughters.

W. B. Spencer (ed), *Report on the work of the Horn Scientific Expedition to Central Australia* (Melb, 1896); H. M. Whittell, *The literature of Australian birds* (Perth, 1954); *A'sian Typographical J*, June 1897, p 7; Roy Soc SA, *Trans*, 22 (1897-98); *Emu* (Melb), 26 (1926), p 87, 58 (1958), p 123; *Vic Naturalist*, June 1926; *Age*, 13, 23 May, 5 Dec 1896, 23 Sept 1908, 22 May 1926, 17 Feb 1962; *Australasian*, 30 Jan 1897; *Leader* (Melb), 19 June 1897, 5 Jan 1907; *Preston Leader*, 26 June 1926; *Advertiser* (Adel), 26 June 1937.   ALLAN McEVEY

KEATING, JOHN HENRY (1872-1940), politician and lawyer, was born on 28 June 1872 in Hobart Town, son of James Keating, carpenter and later furniture manufacturer, and his wife Mary, née Cronley. Educated at Officer College, Hobart, and at St Ignatius' College, Riverview, Sydney, he obtained the Tasmanian Council of Education's degree of associate of arts in 1890 before attending the University of Tasmania (LL.B., 1896); he supported himself with scholarships and exhibitions. He was admitted to the Tasmanian Bar in August 1894 and after practising for two years in the gold town of Lefroy established himself in Launceston where he became known as a brilliant advocate; by 1902 he was in partnership with J. R. Rule. A leader of the Australian Natives' Association while in Hobart and later secretary and organizer of the Northern Tasmanian Federation League, he campaigned enthusiastically for Federation in the 1898 and 1899 referenda. He was unsuccessful as an Independent candidate for George Town in the House of Assembly elections of 1900, but topped the poll for Tasmania in the Senate elections next year to become the youngest member of the first Commonwealth parliament.

Noted as a disciple of R. E. O'Connor [q.v.], Keating was government whip in the Senate in the first Barton [q.v.7] and Deakin [q.v.8] governments. During this period he supported moves towards a compulsory conciliation and arbitration system and a Commonwealth old-age pension scheme, and, espousing White Australia, showed particular interest in the passage of the 1901 immigration restriction bill; in 1924 he wrote a series of articles for the Launceston *Examiner* and published them as a booklet, *White Australia: men and measures in its making*. Mindful of the needs of his home State, he was chairman in 1901-02 of a select committee on steamship communication between Tasmania and the mainland; a daily mail service to and from the island resulted.

In July 1905 Keating was given an honorary place in Deakin's second ministry and next year became vice-president of the Executive Council. He was responsible for the framing and drafting of the Copyright Act (1905) and was a member of the select committee (1905) and royal commission (1906) on the tobacco monopoly. As minister for home affairs from January 1907 to November 1908 he oversaw the passage of the bounties bill, the first attempt by the Commonwealth to use its jurisdiction to assist industry, and the quarantine bill, which sought to establish a uniform system of quarantine regulations. A back-bencher after the fall of the Deakin government, he sat on the 1913 select committee on the general election and the standing committee on public works (1914-17).

Keating actively supported Australia's involvement in World War I and in 1916 visited England and the Western Front at the invitation of the Empire Parliamentary Association. However, with Senator T. J. K. Bakhap, he withheld support from the Hughes [q.v.] government in March 1917, thereby precluding the extension of parliament and forcing the government to an election. This was in protest against the circumstances under which John Earle [q.v.] replaced the ailing Tasmanian Labor senator, R. K. Ready.

In 1922 Keating was defeated as a Nationalist and, after twenty-two 'conspicuously useful' years in the Senate, took up legal practice in Melbourne. Widely read, a dedicated Shakespearian and an accomplished French speaker, he was appointed officier de l'instruction publique, Ordre des Palmes Académiques, by the French government in 1924 for wartime services. He annotated and was managing editor of the 1936 consolidation of the Tasmanian statutes, published by Butterworth & Co. (Australia) Ltd. He retained links with Federal government: in 1932-33 he was counsel assisting the royal commission on performing rights; in 1934 he sat on the Federal committee which prepared the case for union in reply to the secessionist movement in Western Australia; and in 1940 he was an adviser to the Federal Department of Information.

Keating had married a Launceston girl, Sarah Alice (Lallie) Monks, on 17 January 1906 at St Mary's Catholic Church, East St Kilda, Melbourne. Lallie was an accomplished pianist, having studied at the Melbourne Conservatorium, and was author of the first government-published travel book on Queensland, *Up north; a woman's journey through tropical Queensland* (n.d.). She inaugurated the Bush Nursing Association in Tasmania, under the auspices of Lady Dudley [q.v.8], and was a principal in the Tasmanian child welfare movement and World War I comforts fund. She died on 29 October 1939. Keating died in Melbourne from the effects of a duodenal ulcer on 31 October 1940, leaving an estate valued for probate at £743. He was buried next to his wife, with Catholic rites, in the family vault in Cornelian Bay cemetery, Hobart; they were survived by a son and daughter.

E. Scott, *Australia during the war* (Syd, 1936); *Table Talk*, 18 Apr 1901; *Punch* (Melb), 5 Apr 1906; *SMH*, 16 Feb 1924, 1 Nov 1940; *Examiner* (Launc), 30 Oct 1939; *Mercury*, 1 Nov 1940; Deakin Papers (NL).

QUENTIN BERESFORD

KEATINGE, MAURICE BARBER BEVAN (1887-1952), soldier, was born on 8 October 1887 in South Brisbane, son of Eldred Pottinger Keatinge, master mariner, and his wife Julia Maria, née Willis. After attending Brisbane Grammar School, he studied mechanical engineering at Sydney Technical College. He was later an associate member of the Institution of Engineers, Australia, his career as a civil engineer centreing on railway construction. He also pursued a strong military interest. Commissioned second lieutenant in the Australian Garrison Artillery (New South Wales) on 26 October 1905, he was promoted lieutenant in January 1908 and captain in November 1909 and served as adjutant in

1910-11. On 23 April 1912 at St John's Church of England, Ashfield, Sydney, he married Myra Christina Cameron; they had a son and daughter.

Keatinge joined the Australian Imperial Force as lieutenant in December 1915 and, promoted captain the following February, embarked in June for Europe with the 3rd Pioneer Battalion. His service in France and Belgium included special railway construction work in March-April 1917. On 6 September 1918 near Tincourt he made a personal reconnaissance and led a successful attack on wooded and waterlogged ground heavily defended by machine-guns and snipers. Next month he was appointed major and on 1 February 1919 was awarded the Military Cross for his 'conspicuous gallantry and devotion to duty'. At Tincourt, his citation reads, he 'set an example of coolness and disregard of danger at a critical time'.

After his return to Australia in July 1919 Keatinge published a *History of the 3rd Australian Pioneer Battalion* (1922) and resumed his A.M.F. career. From November 1923 to June 1925 he was staff officer, 1st Heavy Brigade, Australian Garrison Artillery, before commanding the 1st Medium Brigade; he was promoted lieut-colonel in 1927. As temporary colonel he took charge of the 2nd Divisional Artillery in 1932-35 and then the 1st Divisional Artillery until 1938 when he was appointed temporary brigadier commanding the 8th Australian Infantry Brigade. He was an outstanding artillery leader, quietly efficient, with a fine understanding of gunnery. Of medium height, dark, his voice finely modulated, he displayed courtesy, tenacity and a sense of humour. He sat on the District Inventions Board and was for many years a devoted member of the United Service Institution of New South Wales.

Keatinge had always placed training in the forefront of a regiment's programme and during World War II he held various training commands; in 1942 he was seconded to the A.I.F. to take charge of the New South Wales lines of communication training depots. He joined the reserve of officers in 1944 and retired in 1950. From about 1946 Keatinge worked for the New South Wales branch of the Commonwealth Department of Works and Housing. At his death in London from rupture of the aorta on 23 December 1952 he was an executive officer (plant and material) at Australia House.

W. Perry, 'Brigadier M. B. B. Keatinge, M.C., V.D.', *United Service Q*, Apr 1953.

KEATS, HORACE STANLEY (1895-1945), composer and accompanist, was born on 20 July 1895 at Mitcham, Surrey, England, son of Charles William Keats, commercial traveller, and his wife Mary, née Clifford. He was a boy soprano at the Oratory, Brompton Road, South Kensington, and briefly learned the piano, but ran away to sea aged 13 and worked as a ship's pianist. He returned to England after the outbreak of World War I in 1914 to enlist in the army, but was rejected for poor eyesight. Engaged as an accompanist by a singer, Nella Webb, on her tour of American and Pacific variety theatres, he arrived in Sydney with her in 1915.

Keats accompanied Ella Caspers and Peter Dawson [q.v.8] in 1915, played incidental music to silent films for J. C. Williamson [q.v.6] Ltd in 1916 and Greater Union Theatres in 1918-20, and led a restaurant trio at Farmer's [q.v.4] department store, Sydney, in 1920-23. After Farmer's radio station 2FC opened in December 1923, he was heard on air regularly with his trio and as accompanist to the radio eisteddfods; by 1929 he was conducting a sixteen-piece broadcast ensemble.

In January 1930 Keats went to England to work for the British Broadcasting Corporation but ill health forced him to return to Sydney within six months. In 1932 he joined the Perth staff of the new Australian Broadcasting Commission but was dismissed next year; from 1934 he worked as a freelance accompanist in Sydney, sometimes for the A.B.C.

Married on 9 November 1918 to soprano Janet le Brun Brown, Keats described his wife as his 'critic' and 'guide'. As 'Barbara Russell' she also became the principal performer of his songs.

Keats's first published composition was for piano, *Three Spanish dances* (1922), but most of his work was for voice, and dates from the last twelve years of his life. He wrote at least 115 songs, two choral works, incidental music for films and radio plays, and a musical, *Atsomari* (1935). Thirty of his songs were published (chiefly in Sydney by W. H. Paling [q.v.5] & Co.) and some were recorded by Dawson, Harold Williams [q.v.], Lionel Cecil and Anthony Strange; all are now rare. Keats believed that 'real music must first of all have a melody' and he wrote attractive, fluent tunes with economical, evocative accompaniments. His best-known work, *She walks in beauty* (1939), uses a Byron text, but he concentrated on setting Australian poetry, notably by Christopher Brennan [q.v.7], Hugh McCrae [q.v.] and early manuscript poems of Kenneth Mackenzie.

A tall and rather thickset man, Keats 'tended to "huddle" over the piano, as if he were "savouring" every sound'. Described by contemporaries as modest, amiable and gentle, he had a lifelong love for Australia and faith in Australian culture. He died of cerebral haemorrhage on 21 August 1945 at his Mosman home and was cremated with Christian Science forms. He was survived by his wife and by a son and daughter; his elder son Russell had been killed in action in H.M.A.S. *Canberra* in 1942. An anonymous etching of Keats, commissioned by Paling's, appears on the title pages of much of his published music.

W. Stone, *A McCrae miscellany* (Syd, nd); I. Moresby, *Australia makes music* (Melb, 1948); *ABC Weekly*, 1 Sept 1945; A'sian Performing Right Assn, *APRAJ*, 2 (1981), no 9; *Punch* (Melb), 9 Dec 1915; *SMH*, 12 Nov 1940, 22 Aug 1945, 22 June 1946; *Bulletin*, 29 Aug 1945; K. I. Mackenzie papers (ML); Keats musical MSS (NL); H. Keats family papers (held by B. Keats, Mosman, NSW); information from E. Todd, Darling Point, Syd.

WARREN A. BEBBINGTON

KEEGAN, JOHN WALTER (1867?-1941) and THOMAS MICHAEL (1878?-1937), trade-unionists and politicians, were probably born on 30 June 1867 at Bulldog, Victoria, and on 29 May 1878 at Ararat, sons of John Walter Keegan, miner, and his wife Mary, née Flood, both Irish born. John was at Broken Hill, New South Wales, in 1892; a widower with a son, he married Mary Alice Cummins on 2 July 1893 at Parkes. The brothers were at Wyalong in the 1890s, John working as a navvy and local agent for the Australian Workers' Union and Tom at the Lighthouse mine and organizing for W. A. Holman [q.v.].

Tom was sacked for supporting Holman's stand against the South African War and left Wyalong. He represented Parkes at the 1901 Labor conference and, finding work with the Sydney Municipal Council, became active in the United Labourers' Union of New South Wales and the Glebe Labor League. On 7 August 1904 he married Mary Hallam at St Mary's Cathedral; they were divorced in 1923. At the 1910 elections he won Glebe and except briefly in 1920-21 represented it (Balmain in 1921-27) until his retirement in ill health in 1935. He attended to the particular concerns of his inner city electorate, repeatedly pressing ministers on public transport and the working conditions of State and municipal employees. He secured the appointment of a select committee on rents and a bill to establish a fair rents tribunal which finally passed during World War I. On conscription, Tom Keegan stayed with the party and in defence of the 1917 transport strikers spoke with rare eloquence; he supported the war, but was anxious that industrial conditions were not altered while 'our men' were at the front. When faction fighting led J. T. Lang [q.v.] to reconstruct his ministry in 1927, Tom's brief reward was the portfolio of local government.

In 1925 the Labor Party caucus elected John Keegan among additional appointments to the Legislative Council. For twenty years John had built bridges under contract to the government railways and tramways, as a member, and sometime official, of the Amalgamated Society of Carpenters and Joiners. Again widowed, he had married a widow Agnes Benna Brown (d. 1932), née Delaney, on 15 December 1912; her illness brought him to Sydney in 1925. He was employed as a joiner by the Sydney Municipal Council until he fractured an elbow. He voted in vain for abolition of the Legislative Council and took a special interest in child endowment and workers' compensation.

After twelve months without employment, John became a temporary carpenter with the Department of Public Works and, on gaining permanency, worked in the Botanic Gardens. In 1927 his political enemy became his employer; H. V. C. Thorby [q.v.], the minister for agriculture, inspected work in the gardens and allegedly found workers leaning on their tools listening to political speeches. Several were dismissed including John who had been speaking at Labor rallies in his lunch hours.

The brothers were typical of the trade unionists who had been influential in creating the Labor Party: they expected it to protect labour and fight obvious hardship; they required it to make no distinction between Protestant and Catholic. They neither attempted to shape it to more radical use nor had they sympathy for any such endeavour. Twice Tom brought relief to the least fortunate in the community: he had the ten-shilling maximum fine on parents, whose children failed to attend school regularly, reduced to five shillings; and he obtained the withdrawal in child welfare legislation of 1923 of a provision to gaol state wards who absconded. Tom fell silent and was often absent from the assembly during Lang's 1930-32 radical ministry, and John gradually was driven to oppose Lang. As an exponent of industrial unionism, he objected to Lang's industrial legislation and to the altered pledge requiring loyalty to Lang himself.

In the landslide defeat of 1932, Tom held his seat. John, facing opposition from Lang's faction in the election in 1934 for the reconstituted council, did not nominate. He stood unsuccessfully as a Federal Labor candidate for Parramatta in 1934 and Annandale in 1935.

Tom died of tuberculosis on 14 September 1937, survived by two sons and a daughter of his first marriage, and by his second wife Doris Vera Cains, née Martin, a divorcee whom he had married on 3 November 1923. John died on 25 August 1941 and he, too, was buried in the Roman Catholic section of Rockwood cemetery, survived by five sons and three daughters, and by his fourth wife Edith Lilley, née Morgan, a widow whom he had married on 1 October 1938. It would have pleased him to be remembered as the union official who wrote out a ticket for his first born at birth and kept him financial until he came of age.

SMH, 18 Oct 1910, 22 Dec 1925, 15 Sept 1937, 26 Aug 1941; *Labor Daily*, 22 Dec 1925; *Bulletin*, 31 Dec 1925; Molesworth papers, uncat MS 71 (ML); information from Syd City Council.

HEATHER RADI

KEENAN, SIR NORBERT MICHAEL (1864-1954), lawyer and politician, was born on 30 January 1864 in Dublin, son of (Sir) Patrick Joseph Keenan, then chief of instruction of the Board of National Education, and his wife Elizabeth Agnes, née Quin. Educated at Downside School, Somerset, England, and Trinity College, Dublin, he read law at King's Inn, Dublin, and the Middle Temple, London, becoming a barrister in both Ireland and England.

Migrating to Western Australia in 1895, Keenan practised at Kalgoorlie where he became prominent as attorney for many British investors, vice-president of the chamber of mines and mayor in 1901-05. Having unsuccessfully contested the Kalgoorlie seat in the Legislative Assembly as an Independent in 1904, he accepted Liberal endorsement in October 1905 and defeated the sitting Labor member W. D. Johnson [q.v.]. As attorney-general in the Newton Moore [q.v.] ministry from May 1906, he pursued electoral reform and in 1907 put through bills for preferential voting and improvements in the compilation of electoral rolls. One of the few Liberals to defend Federation during the secession agitation of 1906-07, he represented the State at the 1907 Premiers' Conference. Disagreeing with Moore's financial policy, he resigned office in May 1909, and later criticized the government's redistribution plan of 1910-11. He was defeated in the Labor landslide of October 1911.

Like most goldfields members Keenan lived and practised in Perth; he took silk in 1908. An advocate of the foundation of the University of Western Australia, he served on its senate in 1912-18. A keen yachtsman, he was long president of the Perth Flying Squadron. After preparing and presenting the Western Australian case to the Commonwealth Disabilities Commission in 1925, he supported secession.

In April 1930 Keenan returned to the assembly as Nationalist member for the new suburban seat of Nedlands, and chief secretary and minister for education in Sir James Mitchell's [q.v.] second administration. He is remembered mainly for his decision to close the State's only teacher training college for three years as a Depression economy. Incensed at Mitchell's failure to consult his cabinet before selling the State Savings Bank to the Commonwealth Bank, he resigned office again in September 1931. When the whole Nationalist ministry was swept out of parliament in April 1933, Keenan, as the only surviving Nationalist with ministerial experience, became party leader, yielding the leadership of the Opposition to the larger Country Party. The coalition remained out of office for fourteen years. Keenan resigned as leader in April 1938 but retained his seat until March 1950. Although he achieved the distinction of becoming Western Australia's oldest parliamentarian and was knighted in 1948, he failed to make a timely retirement and was defeated after losing pre-selection. He died at Subiaco on 24 April 1954 and was buried in the Roman Catholic portion of Karrakatta cemetery.

Throughout his life Keenan bore the characteristics of his 'Dublin Castle Catholic' background. A lucid administrator and able speaker, courteous but quick-tempered in debate, he had a high sense of honour which sometimes verged on the cantankerous and hampered his effectiveness in parliament. On 17 February 1900 at a Perth registry office he had married Rose Elizabeth, daughter of (Sir) Stephen Henry Parker [q.v.]; she survived him with one of their sons. Keenan's estate was sworn for probate at £80 176.

Western Argus, 26 Sept 1905; *Catholic Press*, 30 Nov 1905, 31 May 1906; *West Australian*, 14 Apr 1930, 26 Apr 1954.

G. C. BOLTON

KELLAWAY, CECIL LAURISTON (1890-1973), actor, was born on 27 August 1890 at Cape Town, South Africa, son of Edward Kellaway, engineer from Devon, England, and his wife Rebecca, née Brebner. A godson of Cecil Rhodes, he was educated at the Normal College, Cape Town, and in England at Bradford Grammar School. He studied engineering and on his return to South Africa was employed in an engineering firm. He had, however, taken part in amateur theatricals from childhood, and soon left to go on the stage, touring for three years through China, Japan, Siam, Borneo, Malaya, North and South Africa and Europe. In Johannesburg on 15 November 1919 he married 17-year-old Doreen Elizabeth Joubert.

Well-known as a comedian in South Africa, Kellaway came to Australia in 1921 under contract to J. C. Williamson [q.v.6] Ltd. On 21 January 1922 he appeared as the comic father of four daughters in *A night out* at Melbourne's Theatre Royal. He made a hit and performed in revivals in 1924, 1926 and 1931. For sixteen years he played character roles in musical comedies with Williamson's New Musical Comedy Company and became a favourite with audiences in such roles as Count Orpitch in *Katja* (1925), the polite lunatic in *The belle of New York* and the British major in *Sons o'guns* (1931). In 1932 he played in *Blue roses* and *Hold my hand* with Madge Elliott and Cyril Ritchard and in 1936-37 in *The gipsy princess, A southern maid* and *The merry widow* with Gladys Moncrieff [q.v.]; in the last as Baron Popoff he gave 'the audience a mild attack of convulsions with his gait, and his red boots and yellow pants'. Whatever his part, Kellaway played it with 'aplomb and careless grace'. Sometimes an inferior piece was partly redeemed by his acting--the *Bulletin* claimed that in a revival of *Floradora* (1931) Kellaway gave 'a depth and humanity to Tweedlepunch that even the author could not suspect was there'.

In 1933 Kellaway made his first screen appearance as Dad Hayseed in *The Hayseeds* but his performance derived from Bert Bailey's [q.v.7] and lacked spontaneity. However he wrote the story for *It isn't done* (1937) for Cinesound Productions and played an Australian squatter who inherited an English title with such success that he was given an American contract by RKO Radio Pictures, Inc. and went to Hollywood. He returned briefly to Sydney next year to make *Mr Chedworth steps out* (1939) for Cinesound.

At Hollywood he appeared in over seventy-five feature films including Earnshaw in *Wuthering heights* (1939) with Laurence Olivier and Merle Oberon, *I married a witch* (1942), *The postman always rings twice* (1946) and *Harvey* (1950). He was twice nominated for Academy awards for his roles in *The luck of the Irish* (1948) and *Guess who's coming to dinner* (1967). Occasionally he appeared in New York in Broadway musicals and later on television. Experienced, professional, polished and versatile, he always researched his parts deeply, endeavouring to play the man not the type, and had a 'passion for accuracy' in his scripts.

An 'eccentric roly-poly' weighing sixteen stone (102 kg) with a 'round-faced, cherubic' countenance, Kellaway was an 'incurable gambler' who pored over racing papers. He always regarded Australia as his country by adoption and kept open house for Australian servicemen at his home at Saltair. He also owned a ranch in Arizona. He died on 28 February 1973 at Los Angeles; his ashes were buried in Westwood Memorial Park. His wife and two sons survived him. Of his brothers, Alec (d. 1973) appeared in Australian feature films and Leon, a ballet dancer known as Jan Kowsky, became ballet-master for Edouard Borovansky and the Australian Ballet.

J. Cargher, *Opera and ballet in Australia* (Syd, 1977); A. Pike and R. F. Cooper, *Australian film 1900-1977* (Melb, 1980); *J. C. Williamson Ltd Mag*, 1 Aug 1931; *Australasian*, 26 Dec 1925, 2 Jan 1937; *Bulletin*, 11 Mar, 14 Oct 1931, 9 Sept 1936; *Argus*, 2 Apr 1934; *SMH*, 9 Oct 1936, 2, 8, 31 Mar 1937, 4 Aug, 24 Oct 1938, 26 Mar 1943, 3 Mar 1973; *People*, 19 Dec 1951; *New York Times*, 2 Mar 1973.

MARTHA RUTLEDGE

KELLAWAY, CHARLES HALLILEY (1889-1952), medical scientist, was born on 16 January 1889 in the parsonage attached to St James's Old Cathedral, Melbourne, second of five children and first son of the curate Rev. Alfred Charles Kellaway, from Dorset, England, and his wife Anne Carrick, née Roberts, who was born at Longford, Tasmania. With his elder sister Charles was taught at home by his father up to the age of 11. After a year at Caulfield Grammar School he went with a scholarship to Melbourne Church of England Grammar School (1902-06), crowning a good scholastic record with first-class honours in physics and chemistry in the Senior Public Examination. He did a brilliant medical course at the University of Melbourne, heading each year's honours list and graduating M.B., B.S. (1911), M.D. (1913) and M.S. (1915).

Kellaway's professional career falls into four phases. In the years after his graduation he held the usual hospital appointments and junior teaching posts; he was tutor in physiology at Trinity College, and in the early months of 1915 acting professor of anatomy at the University of Adelaide. In 1915-18 he served in various capacities in the Australian Army Medical Corps in Egypt, France where he was awarded the Military Cross, and England where he was promoted major in September 1918. Then came four years of physiological research in London and in 1923 the call to become director of the Walter and Eliza Hall [qq.v.] Institute of Medical Research, Melbourne, where he remained until 1944. The last phase began when, in the midst of his wartime activities, he moved to London to take over from Dr C. R. Wenyon the post of director of scientific policy for the Wellcome Foundation Ltd, which he held until 1952.

Kellaway's induction into the field of experimental physiology began in 1918 after his service in France had been cut short by phosgene poisoning in a German gas attack. Sent to London to convalesce and attached to the Australian Flying Corps, he was seconded to the newly formed Medical Research Committee to work on the problems of oxygen lack in air crew flying in unpressurized machines at high altitude. A close association began with (Sir) Henry Dale which continued to the end of Kellaway's life. The work on anoxia was published in the *Journal of Physiology*, 1919, and was his first significant contribution to science.

During a brief sojourn in Australia in 1919 he was acting professor of physiology at the University of Adelaide and on 12 December at Trinity College Chapel, Melbourne, married Ethel Eileen Scantlebury, the daughter and sister of medical practitioners. He was then appointed as a Foulerton research student of the Royal Society. His work with Dale, which resulted in two classic papers that firmly established the nature of anaphylaxis, determined the general direction of almost all Kellaway's subsequent research. He continued such work in collaboration with S. J. Cowell in T. R. Elliot's department of clinical medicine at University College Hospital. Here they studied the anti-histamine effect of extracts of the adrenal gland. Kellaway also found opportunities to develop a variety of physiological techniques and to gain the good opinion of his seniors; in 1923 he was unanimously recommended as the institute's London advisers as successor to S. W. Patterson at the Walter and Eliza Hall Institute.

The new director found the still very immature institute a challenge. Its building was shared with the clinical laboratories of the (Royal) Melbourne Hospital; Kellaway himself was the only member of the staff with any research experience and, apart from some very small research grants, the £2800 provided by the Walter and Eliza Hall Trust was its only financial support. Kellaway's first task therefore was to find funds and begin to build up his research staff. From the beginning he envisaged three research groups—in physiology, biochemistry, and microbiology—but the Depression delayed progress and World War II was looming before his plans came to fruition. Nevertheless, by 1939 the institute had an established position in the world of science and a steady stream of significant research was being published. Kellaway was elected a fellow of the Royal College of Phys-

icians in 1929 and was foundation fellow of the Royal Australasian College of Physicians in 1938; he received the Walter Burfitt [q.v.7] prize and medal from the Royal Society of New South Wales in 1932 and in 1940 became a fellow of the Royal Society of London.

Soon after the outbreak of war, Kellaway's personal research career virtually ended. He had advised the Federal government on several occasions, in particular in 1928 as chairman of the royal commission into the fatalities attending the immunization of children against diphtheria at Bundaberg, Queensland. In 1923-36 he had served as army director of hygiene in Victoria. In 1940-42, as colonel, he was the first director of pathology at Army Headquarters and later became scientific consultant to the medical services of all the Australian armed forces. He was deeply involved in the development of transfusion services and, when war moved to the Pacific theatre, with the physiological problems of tank crews in tropical war zones. As scientific director for the Wellcome Foundation from 1944 his main task was the difficult one, characteristic of the times, of converting the pattern of war-directed research activities to new peacetime aims. This he achieved successfully. Kellaway's scientific work was directed mainly to the study of the effects on certain organs and tissues of the body, of natural poisons of animal origin, and of toxic substances generated in the body itself by injury or immune reaction. His place in the history of physiology will probably be as one of the workers who extended and clarified the fields that Dale had opened up at the borderland of physiology and pharmacology. Kellaway's application of the techniques he had learned in London to analyse the pharmacological actions of Australian snake venoms was probably his most important contribution. The papers on snakes and snakebite in Australia that he published in association with (Sir) Hamilton Fairley were masterly. In modern physiology laboratories he is probably best remembered for his discovery, with E. R. Trethewie, of a 'slow reacting substance' produced by a variety of tissue injury.

Kellaway is also remembered for having a 'genius for friendship'. He was a keen fisherman and in the 1920s a birdphotographer. He died of cancer at St Pancras, London, on 13 December 1952, survived by his wife and three sons.

F. M. Burnet, *Walter and Eliza Hall Institute 1915-1965* (Melb 1971); *MJA*, 1 (1953), p 203; Roy Soc Lond, *Obituary Notices of Fellows of the Roy Soc*, 8 (1953), p 503; *Age* and *The Times*, 16 Dec 1952.   MACFARLANE BURNET

Kellermann

KELLERMANN, ANNETTE MARIE SARAH (1886-1975), swimmer, aquatic performer and film actress, was born on 6 July 1886 at Marrickville, Sydney, daughter of Australian-born Frederick William Kellermann, violinist, and his French wife Alice Ellen, née Charbonnet, pianist and music teacher. A weakness in Annette's legs necessitated the wearing of painful steel braces and at 6, to strengthen her legs, she learned to swim at Cavill's [q.v.7] baths in Sydney. By 13 her legs were practically normal and by 15 she mastered all the swimming strokes, using F. Lane [q.v.] and Percy Cavill as her models for the trudgen and single overarm strokes, and won her first race. She also gave diving displays.

In 1902 Annette took up swimming in earnest and won the ladies' 100 yards and mile championships of New South Wales in the record times of 1 minute, 22 seconds and 33 minutes, 49 seconds. The family moved to Melbourne and while a pupil at Simpsons' School, Mentone, where her mother was music teacher, she was active in theatricals. As a schoolgirl she gave exhibitions of swimming and diving at the main Melbourne baths, performed a mermaid act at Princes Court entertainment centre and did two shows a day swimming with fish in a glass tank at the Exhibition Aquarium. In June-July 1903 she performed in the Coogee scene of Bland Holt's [q.v.4] spectacular, *The breaking of the drought*, at the Theatre Royal.

In 1905 after a long-distance swim in the Yarra and exhibitions throughout Australia she and her father went to England where Annette, holder of all the world 'records' for ladies' swimming, began giving demonstrations. On 30 June she swam the Thames from Putney bridge to Blackwall pier (over thirteen miles (21 km)) in 3 hours, 54 minutes. The *Daily Mirror* sponsored her in an attempt to swim the English Channel and she made her first unsuccessful attempt on 24 August. In France, on 10 September Annette, the only woman competitor, was placed third in a seven-mile race down the Seine.

In June 1906 she beat Baroness Isa Cescu in a twenty-two mile (36 km) challenge race down the Danube and on 7 August made a second unsuccessful attempt on the Channel. On her third attempt she swam three-quarters of the distance and stayed in the water ten and a half hours. 'I had the endurance', she said, 'but not the brute strength'. Her one-piece swim suit made by stitching black stockings into a boy's costume and her epic and often risky swims made her a sensation and attracted attention in the United States of America.

After a few more races Kellermann re-tired from long-distance swimming and concentrated on the stage. Following a winter season at the London Hippodrome she went to U.S.A. in 1906 where she performed her vaudeville aquatic act at Chicago and Boston and then in New York where she earned $1250 a week. In 1907 she was arrested on a Boston beach for wearing a brief one-piece swimsuit: the publicity helped to relax laws relating to women's swimwear. She married her American-born manager, James Raymond Louis Sullivan, probably on 26 November 1912 at Danbury, Connecticut.

In a long career as a vaudeville headliner Annette Kellermann, the 'Australian Mermaid' and 'Diving Venus', played in the leading theatres in Europe, U.S.A. and Australia with a routine which, apart from aquatic feats, included ballet-dancing in front of mirrors, wire-walking, acrobatics, singing and male impersonations. In May 1912 she appeared in London in *Undine*, an 'idyll of forest and stream' and, returning to America, made films including the very successful *Neptune's daughter* (1914), *A daughter of the gods* (1916), *The honor system* (1916), *Queen of the sea* (1918) and *The art of diving* (1920). She did her own stunts including diving from ninety-two feet (28 m) into the sea and sixty feet (18 m) into a pool inhabited by crocodiles! In New Zealand in 1924 she made *Venus of the South Seas*.

Judged the 'perfect woman' (though, as she quipped, only 'from the neck down') from 10 000 contestants in U.S.A., Kellermann was a strong advocate of swimming for physical health, fitness and beauty and in 1918 published *Physical beauty, and how to keep it* and the partly autobiographical *How to swim*. She travelled widely, especially in America and Germany, lecturing on health and fitness. She visited Australia several times and during World War II lived in Queensland where she assisted Sister Elizabeth Kenny [q.v.], worked for the Australian Red Cross Society and entertained troops. A teetotaller and lifelong vegetarian, she ran a health food store for some years at Long Beach, California. Golf, tennis and horse-riding were other interests and she published a book of children's stories *Fairy tales of the South Seas* (London, 1926), illustrated by her sister Marcelle Wooster. A film of her life, *Million dollar mermaid*, starring Esther Williams, appeared in 1952.

In 1970 Annette and her husband returned to live in Australia. In 1974 she was honoured by the International Swimming Hall of Fame at Fort Lauderdale, Florida, U.S.A. Predeceased by her husband, she died in hospital at Southport, Queensland, on 6 November 1975 and was cremated with Roman Catholic rites. She had no children.

Breezy, unaffected and full of vibrant energy (she could still do a high kick well into old age) Annette Kellermann did much to make women's swimming popular and socially acceptable; she regarded her part in emancipating women from the neck-to-knee costume as her greatest achievement. Her large collection of costumes and theatrical memorabilia was bequeathed to the Sydney Opera House.

F. Taylor, *Schooldays with the Simpsons 1899-1906* (Tirau, NZ, 1964 ?); *People* (Syd), 23 May 1951; *The Times*, 20 June, 27 July, 25 Aug, 11, 27 Sept 1905, 8 Aug 1906, 7 Nov 1975; *Daily Mirror* (Lond), 3, 20, 31 July, 1, 4, 12 Aug, 12 Sept 1905; *Sportsman* (Lond), 12, 20 June 1905; *Sun* (Syd), 14 Jan 1913; *Sun-Herald* (Syd), 9 Sept 1962; *Age, Australian* and *Courier Mail* (Brisb), 7 Nov 1975.

G. P. WALSH

KELLETT, ADELAIDE MAUD (1873-1945), hospital matron, was born on 1 September 1873 at Raglan near Bathurst, New South Wales, daughter of Charles Henry Kellett, post office clerk, and his wife Sarah, née McClintock. Maud Kellett entered Sydney Hospital as a probationer in January 1898 and was granted her certificate in September 1901. From October 1910 she was deputy to Rose Creal [q.v.8]. She joined the Australian Army Nursing Service in 1907 and embarked with 'Nellie' (Ellen Julia) Gould [q.v.] in October 1914, having enlisted in the Australian Imperial Force in September. She was theatre sister with the 2nd Australian General Hospital, Cairo, for ten months, served on the hospital ship *Gascon* during the Gallipoli evacuation, and on return to Egypt became temporary matron of Choubra Military Infectious Hospital. In August 1916 as matron she opened the 2nd Australian Auxiliary Hospital at Southall, England, where work with limbless patients was satisfying and her staff content.

In July 1917 Matron Kellett took charge of the 2400-bed 25th British General Hospital, Hardelot, France, which was mainly under canvas and for skin patients who were otherwise well, and thus hard to manage. Her Australian nurses also resented Royal Army Medical Corps doctors and 'skins' (mostly scabies). Hardelot closed in March 1919 and she helped Colonel A. G. Butler [q.v.7] in London to gather personal narratives from Australian nurses awaiting transport home. She returned to Sydney in October having been twice mentioned in dispatches (1916, 1919), awarded the Royal Red Cross, 1st class (1917) and appointed C.B.E. (1919).

Maud Kellett became matron of the 4th A.G.H. (Randwick) and principal matron of the 2nd Military District. In December 1921 she returned to Sydney Hospital, succeeding Rose Creal as matron. The organization of the A.A.N.S. was then under review but her appointment as principal matron was confirmed on 1 January 1924. She retired from that post on 31st August 1929. She was first president of the Returned Army Nursing Sisters' Association, New South Wales. (1920).

She had joined the Australasian Trained Nurses' Association in 1903 and was a member of its council from 1920. She was the first nurse to be elected president in 1929-30 and was re-elected in 1933-34, part of 1937, and 1941-42. Among numerous A.T.N.A. duties she was a nominee to the National Council of Women (from 1931), the Nurses' Registration Board (1934-43) and the Australian Nursing Federation. She was honorary treasurer of the A.N.F. from 1930 and president in 1937-45. Her last public duty was to chair a crisis session of the A.N.F. held at Sydney Hospital in November 1943. She was long the dominant force in New South Wales nursing, but her pride suffered when her hospital deputy Elsie Pidgeon [q.v.] was awarded the Florence Nightingale medal by the International Red Cross in 1935. Miss Kellett had to wait two years for similar recognition.

Within Sydney Hospital her brilliance as an administrator was acknowledged. Her memory was superb; she knew all the in-patients and whose responsibility they were. There was no set pattern for her ward rounds—a porter would signal when she left the Nightingale Wing and the entire hospital would stiffen to attention. She commanded respect and not affection. Her rage over trivial lapses was the more cutting for the lisped venom of her alliteratives. Her nurses feared her but they were proud of her as well, and often forgave her tantrums years afterwards, when they recognized the professionalism behind their training. From 1923 Matron Kellett sponsored the first regular reunions of Sydney Hospital nurses.

Short and heavily built, she was vain about her appearance and always beautifully turned out. Her white hair and fine skin were her best features, her eyes were blue. In 1939 she broke an arm and in October 1942 a more serious fall resulted in a fractured femur. In June 1944 she retired. She died in the War Memorial Hospital, Waverley, on 12 April 1945. Maud Kellett was cremated after a funeral service 'full to overflowing' at St James Anglican Church, Sydney; her family memorial is at St Stephen's, Penrith. Her estate, valued for probate at £4958, was left to her sister Daisy. The Sydney Hospital preliminary training school bore the name of Kellett until absorbed into the Lucy Osburn [q.v.5] School of Nursing from 1968. The directors also placed a memorial tablet in the hospital chapel. The A.T.N.A. established the A. M. Kellett prize, a badge awarded from 1946 to the nurse obtaining the highest marks in the written section of the registration examination.

A'sian Nurses' J, Mar 1903, p 24, May 1920, p 164, Mar 1930, p 82, Dec 1943, p 142, May 1945, p 57; *SMH*, 15 July 1937, 3 June 1944, 14 Apr 1945; *Sun* (Syd), 29 Dec 1942; War narratives by A. M. Kellett et al, A. G. Butler collection, boxes 5 and 6 (AWM); Syd Hospital, Annual Report, 1945, p 12, and House Cttee minutes and Matrons' minute-books 1898-1945; H. M. Woolston, Series guide to the minute-books of the Council of the A'sian Trained Nurses Assn, 26 May 1899 to 19 Dec 1972 (Syd, MS 1980, copy ML); information from Miss L. Breakell, Miss L. Dowell, Mrs D. Greive and Mrs Z. Waldon, Syd.   ANN M. MITCHELL

KELLOW, HENRY ARTHUR (1881-1935), headmaster and literary critic, was born on 8 July 1881 at Guard Bridge, Fifeshire, Scotland, son of Henry Edward Kellow, railway stationmaster, and his wife Agnes, née Macgregor. Educated at Airdrie Academy and Glasgow University (M.A.), he won honours in English and history and was a university prizeman. From 1904 he taught briefly at Calderbank Public School at Airdrie, moved to Airdrie Academy, then settled down as head of English at Allan Glen's School, Glasgow. Kellow travelled widely, as far south as Morocco and north as Scandinavia. In 1912 he was offered three choices: a position as principal in India, an inspectorship in the Scottish Education Department and the headship of Rockhampton Grammar School, Queensland. Perhaps his passion for travel inspired his decision to migrate to Queensland. On 8 May he married Mary Hope and the couple left Scotland, which he was never to see again.

In Rockhampton, as headmaster of the grammar school, Kellow for many years faced unceasing demands on his resources in managing finance, staff and school organization. With the reduction of state subsidies to non-government schools, all Queensland grammar schools were struggling and for a time they seemed doomed. For some years Kellow was obliged to teach full time as well as perform his administrative duties. A man of considerable personality, he exercised discipline with a mere glance. As a teacher he could be luminous and cut to the heart of a question. He played an active role in the community as a university extension lecturer, an advocate of a women's college in the university and as a participant in the fight to revive the Mount Morgan mine.

In 1911 Harrap had published in its 'Poetry and Life' series Kellow's *Burns and his poetry*, a very popular booklet. His *A practical training in English* of the same year ran through several revised editions. With its heuristic methods it was something of a pioneer work. His anthology, *A treasury of Scottish verse*, appeared in 1912. He had in mind a volume on Dr Johnson, but the notes which he had intended to take to Queensland were stolen and he never resumed the undertaking. Apart from some newspaper articles and public lectures, Kellow let his pen lie idle for some fifteen years before writing *Queensland poets* (1930). Although his subjects were minor poets, perhaps only two or three of whom were likely to be considered in a national context, the book was important, both as the first coverage of the area completed at a very early date and as a perceptive and stylish essay. In 1931 Kellow was made a fellow of the Educational Institute of Scotland in recognition of his services to education by example, practice and writing.

Kellow died of pneumonia on 6 September 1935 and was buried in North Rockhampton cemetery. His wife and three of their four children survived him.

L. McDonald, *Henry Arthur Kellow* (Townsville, 1981), and for bibliog; family information.
                                      CECIL HADGRAFT
                                  LORNA L. McDONALD

KELLOW, HENRY (CHARLES) BROWN (1871-1943), motor car dealer, was born on 24 October 1871 at Sutton Grange, Victoria, son of Joseph Kellow, grazier, and his wife Elizabeth, née Patterson. He changed his name to Charles by deed poll. Educated at Kings' College, Clifton Hill, Melbourne, he soon escaped to clerical work, for a time in the real estate firm of his uncle (Sir) James Patterson [q.v.5], before exploiting the bicycle boom of the 1890s as a racing cyclist and salesman. A dashing performer on the new safety-bicycle, he won the Austral Wheel Race (the 'Melbourne Cup' of cycling) in 1896 and some £800 in prize-money in 1897. In business, he and his partner W. H. H. Lewis [q.v.] prospered in their Swanston Street bicycle shop, despite an unprofitable interlude Kellow spent on the goldfields of Western Australia in 1894.

Kellow married Florance McRae Coles at Richmond on 10 August 1898 and, having assumed sole ownership of the bicycle shop, began thinking about branching out into motor cars, cranky and commercially unpromising contraptions though they appeared to be. Although not as mechanically gifted as Harley Tarrant and Herbert Thomson [qq.v.], he imported and demonstrated a Darracq early in 1901 and captured headlines with spectacular advertising and sporting stunts in the improved cars of later years. During the railway strike of 1903 he delivered Melbourne newspapers to country towns and in 1905, with Harry James, set a 24-hour endurance record of 556 miles (895 km) in a 12 horsepower Humber. They made a record-breaking Melbourne to Sydney run of 25 hours 40 minutes in 1908, driving a 15 horsepower Talbot.

By 1910 the Kellow Motor Co., established in Exhibition Street, was importing a large range of both popular and expensive vehicles from England, Europe and the United States of America, selling them to Melbourne's developing truck and taxi services and to a rapidly growing motoring public. At the first Melbourne Motor Show in 1912 the Kellow stand was among the most prominent, with a display in which lesser breeds like Wolseley, Minerva, Albion (lorry) and Renault (van) paid court to the regal splendour of a Rolls-Royce.

A big man—13 stone (83 kg) in cycle-racing trim—Kellow was enormously energetic, personally popular and commercially audacious to the point of illegality. In 1910 he was fined £1980 by the High Court of Australia for manipulating invoices to evade customs duty. In his forties he looked for opportunities to diversify his interests and expand his wealth and found them in the traditional Australian fields of sheep-grazing and horse-racing. While continuing to develop his motor business, he invested in Gundaline, a Riverina sheep-station to which he travelled by private plane in later life, and also in Hall Mark, Heroic, Nuffield and many less notable gallopers, trained by Jack (Michael) Holt [q.v.]. Hall Mark won the 1933 Melbourne Cup, Heroic justified the very high price of 16 000 guineas Kellow paid for him in 1925 by winning more than twice that amount, while Nuffield won the Sydney and Melbourne Derbys in 1938.

Kellow's first wife died in 1923. On 27 March 1926 at Kew he married a widow Lucy Maude Sommerville Coles, née Hutchings. Kellow died of heart failure at his South Yarra home on 2 July 1943 and was cremated. He was survived by his second wife and three of the four daughters of his first marriage. His estate was sworn for probate at £147 229.

H. H. Painting (ed), *The James Flood book of early motoring* (Melb, 1968), and *The second James Flood book of early motoring* (Melb, 1971); *Tatler* (Melb), 30 Apr 1898; *Punch* (Melb), 22 Apr 1909; *Argus*, 31 Aug 1912, 9 Mar 1929; *Herald* (Melb), 9 Mar, 25 Oct 1929, 6 Dec 1935, 2 July 1943.

H. S. BROADHEAD

KELLY, ALICIA MARY (1885 ?-1942), nurse, was born in Mayo, Ireland, daughter of Richard Kelly, farmer, and his wife Jane, née Bell. Nothing is known of her childhood or migration. She completed nursing training at the (Royal) Melbourne Hospital in 1910, nursed at the Eye and Ear Hospital, then worked at a private hospital run by Dr Kent Hughes.

On 29 March 1915, aged 29, Alicia Kelly enlisted as a staff nurse in the Australian Army Nursing Service, Australian Imperial Force, giving her mother, who lived at Mount Dandenong, as next-of-kin. In April she embarked from Sydney with reinforcements for the 1st Australian General Hospital and reached Egypt in time to receive the thousands of wounded who poured into the hospital after the landing at Gallipoli. From 28 August until the evacuation of Gallipoli she made at least two trips on *Euripides*, transporting severely wounded men home to Australia. Her feelings about this sudden introduction to mass human destruction remain unknown, Alicia having been quiet and retiring by nature. In April 1916 she was posted to France with the 1st A.G.H. and served with it until December when she joined the 29th Casualty Clearing Station, Rouen. On 3 April 1917 she was promoted sister, and on 31 July was transferred to the 3rd Australian C.C.S.; while there she became one of only seven Australian nurses to win the Military Medal.

The usual method of recognizing an army nurse's service was to award her the Royal Red Cross or its associate; the Military Medal was reserved for 'conspicuous gallantry under fire'. Sister Kelly was on duty at the 3rd A.C.C.S. during an air raid. Orders sent the rest of the medical staff running for their lives as bombs fell. A padre discovered Sister Kelly sitting in one of the hospital tents holding a patient's hand. When he asked why she had not left with the rest she answered 'I couldn't leave my patients'. She had covered their heads with enamel washing basins or urine pots to give them some feeling of security; she knew that the basins would be useless against flying shrapnel or a direct hit but there were no helmets. Her quiet courage enabled her patients to come through the bombardment 'with confidence'. Her medal was presented to her at Buckingham Palace on 16 October 1917.

From August Sister Kelly worked at the 3rd A.G.H. before returning to England in March 1918 for transport duty and then to Australia in May. She was also awarded the Royal Red Cross, 2nd class (A.R.R.C.), on 1 January 1918. She was sister-in-charge on the voyage home and on their arrival at Fremantle the men she had cared for presented her with a silver cup which they had made.

Soon after her discharge Alicia Kelly married on 7 August in Perth Arthur Rupert Chipper, a corporal in the 10th Light Horse, A.I.F., and a farmer at Bullaring. After many years at Bullaring the Chippers moved to a farm at Narrogin before retiring for health reasons. They had no children.

At the outbreak of World War II, despite poor health deriving from her 1914-18 war experiences, Mrs Chipper (whose nickname was 'Loll') returned to nursing and was appointed matron of the Old Women's Home, Woodbridge, Guildford. She died of pneumonia on 16 April 1942 at Midland, Perth, and was buried in Karrakatta cemetery with Anglican rites.

A. G. Butler (ed), *Official history of the Australian Army Medical Services ... 1914-1919*, 3 (Canb, 1943); *London Gazette*, 17 Oct 1917, 1 Jan 1918; *Aust Nurses' J*, 15 May 1915; *Herald* (Melb), 23 Oct 1917, 29 July 1919; information from K. Chipper and V. Hobbs, Perth, WA; records (AWM).

SUZANNE WELBORN

KELLY, ANTHONY EDWIN BOWES (1852-1930), company director, was born in 1852 at Ballinasloe, Galway, Ireland, son of John Kelly and his wife Louisa, née Daly. In 1854 John with three children migrated to New South Wales where he became sub-collector of customs at Albury and from 1856 police magistrate at Deniliquin; the rest of the family, including Bowes, joined him in 1860. Educated by a tutor at Deniliquin, Bowes worked as a jackeroo on Riverina sheep-stations and as a drover. He became manager of Billilla Station on the Darling River near Wilcannia about 1875 and was eventually a partner. About 1881 he joined a Melbourne syndicate speculating in land around the Paroo River and made the basis of his fortune. He next fitted out a party to explore the Nullarbor plain region, and subsequently joined a group taking stock by ship to the Kimberleys, Western Australia, for the King Sound Pastoral Co.

In 1884, hearing of silver discoveries in the Barrier Ranges, Kelly journeyed to Silverton and on behalf of himself, his brother George (father of Sir George Dalziel [q.v.]), and William Weatherly bought a one-fourteenth share in the new Broken Hill mine which, however, he did not visit. The share had belonged to James Poole, one of the syndicate of seven who began digging at Broken Hill in 1883. Poole had swapped his share with (Sir) Sidney Kidman [q.v.] for four steers; Kelly bought it for £150 and within ten years it was worth £1.5 million.

In 1885 Kelly was a member of the committee asked by the syndicate (then number-ing fourteen) to draw up a prospectus for the new Broken Hill Proprietary Co. Ltd. He was a member of the board of directors which held its first meeting on 15 August and served until his death. He was chairman of the board from 29 April to 2 August 1892, while a great strike saw Broken Hill armed and barricaded, and from 23 March 1893 to 1 February 1895. His longest period as chairman, however, was from 9 March 1917 to 27 October 1922 when he oversaw the most difficult period of B.H.P.'s development: the company's steelworks had opened in 1915 and the organization faced both external competition and internal strain as it moved from mining and smelting at Broken Hill and Port Pirie, South Australia, to steelmaking at Newcastle.

Kelly's association with B.H.P. in 1884 sparked off an interest in mining which absorbed him over several decades. Although he lacked technical mining knowledge he was ever willing to invest, in particular in large fields which were either under capitalized or poorly managed. He was one of a group of B.H.P. directors which included William Jamieson, William Knox, Duncan McBryde [qq.v.], W. R. Wilson and James Reid, who between them invested in all the main base-metal fields in Australia before 1914. Kelly's brothers, Herbert and Aloysius, followed him into mining investment.

His second fortune was based on the copper mine at Mount Lyell, Tasmania, discovered in 1883 and worked for gold with little success. Kelly and William Orr [q.v.] in 1891 sent ore samples to Broken Hill for analysis, and a decision was made to mine for copper. The Mount Lyell Mining Co. N.L. was formed with Kelly as principal shareholder having some 27 000 shares purchased for £3500. This company was superseded by the Mount Lyell Mining and Railway Co. Ltd in 1893; Kelly was a director until his death and in 1914-24. Enormous capital expenditure—approximately £400 000—was required for the building of a railway to Strahan and a smelter, but with excellent management the mine made substantial profits for Kelly and other shareholders by 1910.

In 1897 Kelly was one of four directors of the Emu Bay Railway Co. Ltd, floated to connect the copper fields with the port of Burnie. Following the huge success of Broken Hill's Silverton Tramway, the Emu Bay Co. was rushed for shares. But there were two other competing lines, including Mt Lyell's own line to Strahan, and no dividends were paid. In 1912 Kelly, with Tasmanian entrepreneur Lindsay Tulloch [q.v.], bought up shares in the Hercules and Primrose silver-lead-zinc mines at Mount

Read and Rosebery. A planned merger with the German owners of the Zeehan smelters, the Tasmanian Smelting Co., was thwarted by World War I. But in 1915 Mount Lyell acquired the Hercules and Primrose shares as well as the Tasmanian Copper Co.'s Mount Read mine and formed the subsidiary Mount Read and Rosebery Mines Ltd. In 1920 this was sold to the Electrolytic Co. of Australia Ltd. Not all Kelly's Tasmanian ventures were successful. He lost money on Zeehan and Dundas enterprises, a cement works at Maria Island and the Sea Elephant Tin Mining Co. on King Island.

In 1902 Kelly bought the historic Tasmanian station Norton Mandeville. He also invested in city and rural properties around Melbourne; at his mansion Moorakyne in Glenferrie Road, Malvern, the family reputedly dined off gold plate. He was a member of the Malvern Shire Council in 1892-96. A director of the Colonial Bank of Australasia from 1907, and chairman from 1914, until its merger with the National Bank of Australasia Ltd in 1918, Kelly remained a director of the National Bank, and from 1909 of Union Trustees, Executors and Agency Ltd. He was president of the Australian Club in 1903-05 and of the Athenaeum Club in 1925-26. Kelly was over 6 feet (183 cm) tall, 'a massive man with a bone-crushing handshake', ginger-haired. The story of board meetings ending with a two-up game played with sovereigns, clings to his name. When he died at Moorakyne on 16 October 1930, little remained of his original fortune: his estate was valued for probate at £36 589 in Victoria and £1895 in New South Wales. He was survived by his wife Mary Fanny, née Hawley, whom he had married at Christ Church, South Yarra, on 14 February 1888, and by six of his nine children. He was buried in St Kilda cemetery with Anglican rites.

For at least four decades Bowes Kelly enhanced Australian mining and manufacturing. He combined financial daring with shrewd appreciation of mining or industrial possibilities and gave extraordinary time to running Australia's main manufacturing venture, B.H.P. Skilled in manipulating the stock-market, he never speculated for his own financial gain in mines which lacked a solid basis for mineral wealth. His investments instead encouraged the growth of companies which both gave employment to thousands and broadened the base of Australian economic life.

G. Blainey, *The peaks of Lyell* (Melb, 1954), and *The rise of Broken Hill* (Melb, 1968), and *The steel master* (Melb, 1971); P. Mawson, *A vision of steel* (Melb, 1958); A. Trengove, *What's good for Australia...* (Syd, 1975); BHP *Recreation Review*, May 1927, Oct 1930; *Argus*, 17 Oct 1930; BHP Board, Minutes, 1885-1930 (BHP Archives, South Melb); Malvern Council (Melb), Minutes, 1879-1930; family information.   DOREEN WHEELER

KELLY, CECILIA MAY; *see* GIBBS

KELLY, ETHEL KNIGHT (1875-1949), actress and author, was born on 28 January 1875 at St John, New Brunswick, Canada, elder daughter of Scots parents William Knight Mollison, merchant, and his wife Margaret, née Millen. She was brought up partly in Britain, but her education was sketchy, consisting of piano, elocution and French lessons twice a week at St John. She loved reading, especially the novels of 'Ouida' and Rider Haggard.

From childhood Ethel 'enjoyed dramatic action'. In December 1893 she played the lead when her three-act play, *A mischievous miss*, was staged at St John. It was a roaring success as she had satirized the 'local society in general and one or two families in particular'. While very young she married a Mr Moore and lived in New York. Widowed within a year, she was engaged to play with Olga Nethersole and Maurice Barrymore in *Camille* in 1894. For some eight years she was associated 'with the best companies in the United States', using her maiden name. Her favourite roles were Roxanne in *Cyrano de Bergerac* and Katharina in *The taming of the shrew*.

Engaged by J. C. Williamson [q.v.6], Miss Mollison arrived in Sydney on 14 March 1903 and opened in the farcical comedy, *Are you a Mason?*, on 11 April. In June the company left for Newcastle and New Zealand. In Sydney she played Cio-Cio San in David Belasco's *Madame Butterfly* at the reopening of Her Majesty's Theatre on 1 August, before going to Melbourne. At Christ Church, Hawthorn, she married Thomas Herbert Kelly [q.v.] on 29 August. She left the professional stage in October.

Between 1904 and 1913 Mrs Kelly bore two sons and two daughters. An Edwardian beauty, with a vibrant personality, wit and boundless energy, she soon established a reputation for 'original ideas'. She helped to arrange elaborate fancy-dress balls and acted in matinées to raise money for the Women's Hospital, St Vincent's Hospital and Lady Dudley's [q.v.8] Australian Bush Nursing Scheme. She visited India and on her return wrote a book, *Frivolous peeps at India* (1911).

During World War I Mrs Kelly, among her many fund-raising activities, organized a dolls' carnival for which she 'reproduced in miniature a whole theatre of Russian ballet'. She acted in matinées, notably as Lady Teazle, with Cyril Maude, in *The school for scandal* (in September 1917) and in her own play, *Swords and tea* (February 1918). On several occasions with Margaret Gordon [q.v.], she was the 'speaking voice' in Henri Murger's 'La Ballade du Désespéré'. In May 1918 she played Mrs Manners, the 'match-making mother', in the amateur film, *Cupid camouflaged*. She organized the Elizabethan musical water pageant on 16 October 1918 and, as Queen Elizabeth accompanied by her court and madrigal singers, travelled slowly down the harbour on the royal barge (a brilliantly lit ferry). Ethel Kelly loved clothes and always ensured that every detail was historically correct.

From 1919, while their sons were at Eton and Oxford, the Kellys made frequent visits to Britain and Europe. In November 1922 Mrs Kelly was asked by (Sir) Joynton Smith [q.v.] to conduct the woman's page of *Smith's Weekly* at a salary of £1040. Late in 1923 she was allowed as a journalist to visit Tutankhamun's tomb in Egypt and sent reports to *Smith's*. It also inspired her to write a novel, *Why the Sphinx smiles* (London, 1925).

From about 1925 Mrs Kelly lived mainly at Florence, Italy, while supervising her daughters' education. She wrote another novel *Zara* (London, 1927) and her memoirs, *Twelve milestones* (London, 1929). While in Italy she became a Roman Catholic. She returned to Sydney in 1934 at her husband's request; they built an Italianate villa at Darling Point. In 1937 she was president of the Pageant of Nations advisory committee for Australia's 150th Anniversary Celebrations.

During World War II Ethel Kelly was president of the French-Australian League of Help and the Victoria League, a vice-president of the St John Ambulance Association and the French Red Cross Societies, honorary treasurer of Colonel de Basil's Ballet Russe de Monte Carlo, a committee-member of the Actors' Benevolent Fund and a trustee of the Women's and St Vincent's hospitals and the Kindergarten Union of New South Wales. She helped to raise money for all of them—and for many other causes.

All her life Ethel Kelly enjoyed meeting and entertaining 'interesting people' and shared her husband's love of music. She collected antique furniture, Persian rugs and rare Venetian wine glasses. She died in her flat at Darlinghurst on 22 September 1949 and was buried in the Catholic section of Northern Suburbs cemetery. A son and two daughters survived her. In the early 1920s Longstaff [q.v.] painted her wearing a Spanish shawl, a pose that accented her small stature, dark hair and eyes, and determined chin (she always liked a definite answer) and the faintly exotic aura that always clung to her.

Theatre Magazine, 1 May 1913; *Home*, Dec 1920, 1 Sept 1921; *Daily Sun* (St John, Canada), 2 Dec 1893; *SMH*, 28 Mar, 13 Apr 1903, 25 Sept 1909, 1 June, 4 Dec 1918, 29 Sept 1921, 22 Aug 1938, 4 Aug 1948, 29 Jan 1949; *Australasian*, 15 Aug 1903, 19 Dec 1914, 9 Feb, 22 June, 26 Oct 1918; *West Australian*, 2 May 1934; *Truth*, 18 Sept 1910; *Bulletin*, 11 Jan 1912; *Smith's Weekly*, 2 Dec 1922; F. S. Kelly diaries (NL); information from, and newspaper cuttings held by, Mrs B. McPhillamy, Sydney.

MARTHA RUTLEDGE

KELLY, FREDERICK SEPTIMUS (1881-1916), oarsman, musician and soldier, was born on 29 May 1881 in Sydney, fourth son of Irish-born Thomas Hussey Kelly [q.v.5], and his native-born wife Mary Anne, née Dick. He was educated at Sydney Grammar School and, like his brothers Thomas Herbert and William Henry [qq.v.], in England at Eton (1893-99). He went up to Balliol College, Oxford (B.A., 1903; M.A., 1912), as a Lewis Nettleship musical scholar and graduated with fourth-class honours in history.

Possessing a rare combination of outstanding sporting and musical ability, Kelly had rowed in the Eton eight in 1897 and stroked that crew to victory in the Ladies' Plate at Royal Henley Regatta in 1899. He began to scull at Oxford and won the Diamond Sculls at Henley in 1902, 1903 and in 1905—in the last setting a record that stood until 1938. In 1903 he also rowed in the Oxford eight and won the Wingfield Sculls. From 1903 he rowed for the Leander Club: in the eight which won the Grand Challenge Cup at Henley in 1903-05; in the coxless four that took the Stewards' Cup in 1906; and in 1908 in the veteran eight that won the gold medal at the Olympic Games. Contemporary reports of his oarsmanship were glowing: 'his natural sense of poise and rhythm made his boat a live thing under him'.

His musical abilities were apparent as a child: long before his hands could span an octave, Kelly played Mozart and Beethoven piano sonatas. At Eton he was taught by Dr Charles Harford Lloyd and at Oxford studied under (Sir) Donald Tovey. He often performed at the Oxford Musical Club (of which he was president) and in the Balliol Sunday evening concerts. In 1903-08 he studied piano under Ernst Engesser and composition and counterpoint with Ivan Knorr at the Dr Hoch Konservatorium, Frankfurt am Main, Germany. He dedicated himself to fulfilling his dual ambition to become 'a great player and a great composer'.

On his return to England in 1908 Kelly played at numerous private and semi-public concerts. From 1909 he advised Sir Edgar Speyer on programmes of the Classical Concert Society, London, and in 1912 succeeded him as its chairman. In 1911 he visited Sydney and between June and August, to the delight of the Sydney critics, gave three solo recitals (with programmes ranging from Bach, Mozart, Beethoven, Liszt, Schumann and Brahms, to recent works of Scriabin and Debussy and his own *Cycle of lyrics*). He also gave two chamber music concerts, performed the Beethoven G major concerto with the Sydney Symphony Orchestra, and conducted a chamber orchestra concert when Melba's [q.v.] flautist John Lemmone [q.v.] played Kelly's *Serenade* for flute and small orchestra.

Back in London, Kelly gave three recitals in February and March 1912. The critics referred to his 'crisp, clear enunciation', his 'equable and melodious touch' and to his 'intellectual grasp of the music': that they objected to his giving the audience 'credit for nerves as strong as his own' in loud passages, suggests that his interpretation was in advance of its time. Later that year he played concertos by Beethoven, Schumann, Mozart and Brahms with the London Symphony Orchestra under (Sir) George Henschel. He also played chamber music and duo-sonatas with such notable instrumentalists as the violinist Jelly d'Aranyi (who was long deeply in love with him) and the cellist Pablo Casals.

His comparatively few compositions include some effectively written and charming piano pieces and later, more substantial works such as *Theme, variations and fugue* for two pianos and a *Violin sonata*, written for Jelly d'Aranyi and first performed by her and Kelly's close friend, the pianist Leonard Borwick at the memorial concert at the Wigmore Hall, London, on 2 May 1919.

In September 1914 Kelly joined the Royal Naval Division and was soon involved in the unsuccessful defence of Antwerp, Belgium. Early next year he sailed for the Dardanelles with the *Hood* Battalion with such scholar-soldiers as Rupert Brooke, Arthur Asquith and Patrick Shaw-Stewart; they were known on the ship as the 'Latin Club'. He landed on Gallipoli in April. While recovering from wounds he wrote the poignant *Elegy* for string orchestra, in memory of Brooke whose burial on Skyros he had attended. Promoted lieutenant in June, Kelly returned to Gallipoli in July and was among the last to leave. He was awarded the Distinguished Service Cross for 'conspicuous gallantry' there. In May 1916 he went with the *Hood* Battalion to France, in command of 'B' Company. His strict standards of discipline 'were not generally palatable', but his 'unfailing fearlessness and scrupulous justice', and activities as director of the regimental band, won him enormous respect. He was killed on 13 November 1916 while leading an attack on a machine-gun emplacement at Beaucourt-sur-Ancre.

Kelly was a man of extraordinary vitality and physique. Speyer wrote that while one might on first acquaintance 'be struck by an apparent bluntness of manner and a disregard for some of the conventions of polite society', one soon realized this resulted from his 'transparent honesty . . . and contempt for anything like pretentiousness or insincerity'. His estate was valued for probate at nearly £20 000. Unmarried, he had lived at his home Bisham Grange, near Marlow, Buckinghamshire, with his sister Mary (Maisie). In 1915 at Malta she married Captain (Admiral Sir John) Kelly, after whom the famous destroyer, commanded by Mountbatten, was named.

DNB, 1912-21; *Balliol College War Memorial book*, 1 (Oxford, 1924); E. Speyer, *My life and friends* (Lond, 1937); M. Grierson, *Donald Francis Tovey* (Lond, 1952); C. Hassall, *Rupert Brooke*, and R. Pound, *The lost generation* (Lond, 1964); G. Keynes (ed), *The letters of Rupert Brooke* (Lond, 1968); J. Macleod, *The sisters d'Aranyi* (Lond, 1969); *SMH*, 4 June 1881, 19 June, 5, 10, 14, 22 July, 5, 9 Aug 1911, 22, 26 May 1943; *Daily Telegraph* (Syd), 25 Mar, 19 June, 5, 7, 10 July, 5 Aug 1911; *The Times*, 21, 28 Feb, 6, 20 Mar, 16 May, 4 June, 13 Dec 1912, 7 May 1913, 28 Apr, 3 May 1919; F. S. Kelly diaries, Oct 1907-Apr 1915 (NL).

JOHN CARMODY

KELLY, SIR GEORGE DALZIEL (1891-1953), pastoralist and company director, was born on 27 July 1891 at Brighton, Melbourne, third child of George Colman Kelly, grazier, and his wife Agnes Dalziel, née Wilson. His uncle was Bowes Kelly [q.v.]. He was educated for a year at Edinburgh Academy, Scotland, while his parents toured Europe, and at Melbourne Church of England Grammar School and the University of Melbourne (LL.B., 1914).

In 1915 he became manager of Barwidgee, a 13 500-acre (5470 ha) sheep property near Caramut, Victoria. His father bought the property in 1908 at the instigation of Dalziel's elder brother Charles. It passed to a partnership of Dalziel and Charles and their sister Mabel, wife of (Sir) Russell Grimwade [q.v.], when their father died. Charles, the pastoralist of the family, joined an English cavalry regiment in 1915. Advised to recuperate in the country after surgery for tubercular glands, Dalziel took his place on the station. On 10 April 1918 he married

Beryl Gwendolene, daughter of St Kilda doctor Robert Louis McAdam, and in that year returned to Melbourne to serve his articles, being admitted to the Bar in 1920. In 1924 the family partnership purchased Caramut North, with about 16 000 sheep on 16 000 acres (6480 ha), and Kelly managed it until 1934.

Before he returned to the land, Kelly had already evinced a keen interest in grazier politics. In 1923 he was a Victorian delegate to the Graziers' Federal Council of Australia of which he became an executive member in 1924-37 and president in 1929 and 1933-34. From 1923 he was an executive member (acting as vice-president for a time) of the Pastoralists' Association of Victoria (from 1929 the Graziers' Association of Victoria) and president from 1925 until 1937. He was also a member of the Australian Woolgrowers' Council in 1925, its vice-president from 1930 to 1935 and chairman from 1935 until 1939. From 1931 until 1952 he was a co-opted member of the Victorian State Advisory Committee of the Council for Scientific and Industrial Research and was vice-chairman of the Australian Pastoral Research Trust (later the George Aitken [q.v.7] Research Trust) for many years.

By the end of the 1920s Kelly was convinced that grazier organizations should pursue two political ends. One was to reduce costs of pastoral production by securing reductions in land taxes and in import duties on goods used by pastoralists. The other was to stimulate the use of woollen goods by reducing tariffs on finished goods, especially in Australia, and by promotion to a mass market. After lengthy lobbying and a strongly worded recommendation from a joint committee of the Australian Woolgrowers' Council and the Graziers' Federal Council, in 1936 the government established the Australian Wool Board to finance publicity and research with funds levied from wool-growers. Kelly was one of the six initial appointments recommended by the industry (the seventh, representing the government, was Senator J. F. Guthrie [q.v.]) and was chairman until he retired in 1943. His skills as a committee-man and negotiator, already shown in his official capacities and his vice-chairmanship of the 1931 Empire Wool Conference, were evident in his chairmanship of the January 1937 conference between representatives of Australian, New Zealand and South African wool-growers that decided to establish a jointly funded International Wool Secretariat in London. A force in the appointment of (Sir) Ian Clunies Ross as Australian representative on I.W.S., Kelly was chairman of the international executive until 1943. He had a direct hand in creating I.W.S. publicity. Some stunts,

such as putting wool back in the Woolsack in the House of Lords, were widely acclaimed; others, including mannequin parades of woollen summer garments and above all proposals that nylon heels and toes be used in woollen socks, aroused opposition from conservative wool-growers.

Though knighted in 1938 for services to the pastoral industry, Kelly had already severed his personal link with wool-growing, selling his share in the family partnership to his sister in 1934. Urbane, dapper and charming, Kelly was a townsman at heart. Practical pastoral life left habits—he preferred to do things himself rather than call in others, whether it was repairing his car, fixing household equipment or building a shed. Yet he was entirely at home with Melbourne's business and political elite, and soon found scope to extend his interests. In 1936 he became a director of the Argus & Australasian Ltd, newly reconstituted under Staniforth Ricketson, senior partner in the stockbroking firm of J. B. Were [q.v.2] & Son. Next year he joined the board of the Colonial Mutual Life Assurance Society Ltd, chaired by A. B. Were. After Ricketson retired from the Argus company in November 1940, Kelly moved to the board of the Herald and Weekly Times Ltd, and by 1941 he was director of the four investment companies comprising the Capel Court group that J. B. Were & Son operated. Ten years later he was a director of thirteen major companies, liked and respected as much by office staff and lift attendants as by his colleagues.

Increasing complexity of business commitments led Kelly to retire from grazier politics in 1939 and from the Wool Board in 1943. In April 1945 his wife died of cancer; he had visited her thrice daily during the long periods in hospital. This utterly changed the pattern of his life. After her death, childless, he took up residence with the family of his brother-in-law, Dr C. G. McAdam, adopting it as his own, and immersed himself almost entirely in city affairs. He died on 18 February 1953 of coronary vascular disease, leaving his estate of £121 789 to his sister-in-law and her children.

Pastoral Review, 16 May, 15 Sept 1923, 16 May 1924, 16 Sept 1925, 16 July 1929, 16 Sept 1930, 16 Mar 1936, 16 Mar 1953; *Herald* (Melb), 2 July 1938; *Stock and Land*, 25 Feb 1953; personal information from Mr J. A. Kelly, Caramut, Vic, and Mrs D. M. McAdam, Melb.   ALAN BARNARD

KELLY, MICHAEL (1850-1940), Roman Catholic archbishop, was born on 13 February 1850 at Waterford, Ireland, son of James Kelly, of Camlin Woods, New Ross, and his wife Mary, née Grant, of Glenmore, Kilkenny. He was educated at the Christian Brothers' College, Waterford, and the Classical Academy, New Ross, receiving clerical education at St Peter's College, Wexford, and the Irish College, Rome. After his ordination on 1 November 1872, Kelly spent the next twenty years attached to the House of Missions, established in 1866 at Enniscorthy, Wexford, by Bishop Furlong of the diocese of Ferns, to conduct missions for the suppression of intemperance. Kelly became a leader in a revival of this campaign, which was to lead on to the formation in 1901 of the Pioneer Total Abstinence Association of the Sacred Heart, the most famous and longest-lived of Irish temperance organizations.

His preaching and writing on temperance matters brought him prominence within the Irish Church, and in 1891 Kelly was appointed rector *pro tempore* of the Irish College in Rome, to assist the aged rector Archbishop Tobias Kirby and to rescue the college from a decline. He had some success in restoring proper order and financial solvency and was confirmed as rector when Kirby died in 1895, but his rectorship lacked the stature of his famous and adroit predecessor. In matters of authority and discipline, he tended towards the arbitrary and the petty. He was not popular, and although his administration was efficient, his decisions were usually extremely cautious as well as occasionally politically inept: these characteristics were all evident in his later Australian career. In Ireland he was credited with 'great piety, but a small share of wisdom'.

On 20 July 1901 Kelly was preconized coadjutor archbishop of Sydney, with right of succession to Cardinal Moran [q.v.], who treated him with coldness and arbitrary command, a situation which Kelly accepted with uncomplaining humility until Moran died in 1911. He succeeded to the see on 16 August. Having lived in Moran's shadow for ten years, Kelly at 61 had nothing original to offer by way of Church policy, save a much heavier accent on piety and a continuance in Australia of his lifelong crusade against intemperance. His piety was central to his episcopal rule and typified a form of religious life then common in Australia. It was narrow, austere and rigidly disciplined, emphasizing mortification. The result was a strict spirituality of intense, at times tormented, self-questioning in long hours of meditation. Kelly kept detailed spiritual diaries which reveal a man constantly at war with himself and temptation. With Milton a favourite author, he shared that sombre Puritan vision, seeing himself personally besieged by pride, anger, gluttony, avarice.

A short, portly man, Kelly fought against the desire to eat too much. He strove to suppress his inclination to ready anger. He craved riches, worldly honour and popularity, and set out deliberately to crush these yearnings. What emerged from this internal struggle, this merciless self-discipline, came across to others as a colourless evisceration of personality, as chill remoteness and inhumanity. His acute sense of episcopal dignity often appeared to be stiff pomposity, and his stilted habit of referring to himself in the episcopal plural 'we' seemed ludicrous and was the basis for many jokes. Even within his Church he had a reputation for insensitivity and tactlessness, which resulted in much needless alienation and resentment. In part, this unfortunate public image reflected the fact that he regarded the daily affairs of men, social problems and the like, as vanities and trifles, distraction from the crucial business of holy living, but it was also a result of his rigorous repression of self.

Kelly's episcopacy spanned nearly thirty years of major events and changes—World War I, Irish rebellion, conscription referenda, social changes of the 1920s, Depression, Catholic Action and the outbreak of World War II. In relation to all of these his position was invariably conservative and hierarchical and, particularly as he moved into his eighties, often uncomprehending. He continued to champion vigorously the claims of Catholic education to state aid, but he was unsympathetic to, and suspicious of, university education and intellectual life generally. He initially supported the war in 1914, but his enthusiasm rapidly waned as it raised divisive issues—particularly conscription—and as the Irish situation worsened after the 1916 rebellion: his uncertain reactions in that regard suggest an inability to cope with complex social problems, particularly when his deep conservatism was in conflict with his genuine Irish nationalism. In these areas, the radical and confident Archbishop Mannix [q.v.] was much more prominent, although Kelly supported Mannix from time to time, particularly when he was visiting Ireland in 1920.

Kelly was much more at home responding belligerently to the wave of anti-Catholic agitation which swept over New South Wales from 1916 to 1925, culminating in the State government legislation seeking to declare illegal Catholic canon law on mixed marriages: in these sectarian engagements Kelly was a strident, uncompromising, but often inept and unnecessarily narrow Catholic leader. The high point of his episcopacy was the International Eucharistic Congress held in Sydney in 1928, a triumphant public demonstration of Catholic numerical growth and piety, centring on the newly completed St Mary's Cathedral and its archbishop.

The 1930s saw Kelly gradually retiring from public view, overtaken by age and ill health. He continued his habit of issuing frequent pastoral letters, usually on matters of spiritual improvement and devotion: his few pronouncements on unemployment counselled Christian resignation, and he saw Catholic Action as meaning greater piety. He was increasingly out of touch with the problems of the day, and the social orientation of his own Church. In 1922 he had taken as coadjutor bishop the distinguished Maynooth catechetical scholar, Dr Michael Sheehan. After fifteen years of waiting for the succession while Kelly moved into his late eighties, Sheehan resigned in July 1937 to return to Ireland; another coadjutor archbishop, (Cardinal Sir) Norman Thomas Gilroy was appointed, who succeeded when Kelly died at Manly on 8 March 1940. He was buried in the Kelly Memorial Chapel in the crypt of St Mary's Cathedral.

By virtue of longevity and the limitation of his own perception, Kelly carried well into twentieth-century Catholic New South Wales the attitudes and style of nineteenth-century clerical Ireland. Immensely strong in areas of simple piety and individual religion, Kelly's was essentially a fortress Church, at war with the world and Protestantism. It was hostile to any lay initiative and insistent on total clerical control. Its concept of Catholicism was Irish separatist and belligerent, opposed to novelty or change and largely impervious to the difficulties posed by new social developments. Set against its strengths in the areas of faith, devotion and certainty, were its weaknesses in failure to accommodate the growing Australian character of the Church and to engage the problems of the day. Kelly's own repressed inner warfare, between absolute certainties and the manifold problems of daily living, was reflected in the ambivalent character of the Church on which he placed his stamp.

Archbishop Kelly had been created count of the Holy Roman Empire and assistant at the Pontifical Throne in 1926. His bronze statue by Bertram Mackennal [q.v.] is on the south-east side of the steps leading to the main entrance of St Mary's Cathedral. A small portrait in oils (artist unknown) of Kelly as a young priest, is held by the Church of Mary Immaculate, Manly.

P. O'Farrell, *The Catholic Church and the community in Australia* (Melb, 1977); F. S. L. Lyons and R. Hawkins (eds), *Ireland under the union* (Oxford, 1979); P. O'Farrell, 'Archbishop Kelly and the Irish question', *J of the Aust Catholic Hist Soc*, 4, 1974, part 3; Kelly papers (St Mary's Cathedral, Syd).

PATRICK O'FARRELL

KELLY, NICHOLAS WILLIAM (1851-1907), soldier, auctioneer and estate agent, was born on 1 October 1851 in Dublin, son of Christopher Kelly and his wife Honoria, née Moran. He began school in the west of Ireland but, aged 14, accompanied his parents to Melbourne where he completed his studies at Archibald Millie's private academy.

In May 1866 Kelly began work with the Victorian Railways as a fuel clerk in the locomotive division. He enlisted as a gunner for part-time military service with the Melbourne Artillery Corps in 1868, thus beginning a steady climb up the promotion ladder. Commissioned lieutenant in April 1875 in the Victorian Volunteer Artillery, he was promoted captain in April 1880. Upon the formation of the Victorian Militia in 1884 he was appointed to 'C' Battery, Field Artillery, at South Melbourne. There he captained its champion rifle team and led many teams which competed in intercolonial shooting contests. In April 1888 Kelly was promoted battery commander with the rank of major. In May he left the railways to open an auctioneering business in partnership with Thomas Carney in Swanston Street. Promoted lieut-colonel in 1895 he went to England in 1897 as adjutant and coach to the rifle team, captained by Colonel Templeton [q.v.6], which won the Kolapore Cup. In England he underwent a course of instruction while attached to the Royal Artillery.

'Keen eyed and slightly grizzled', Kelly left on 1 May 1900 for service in the South African War in command of the 4th Victorian (Imperial Bushmen's) Contingent. Disembarking at Beira, Kelly's regiment crossed Rhodesia, reaching Mafeking on 20 August. There they entered the Transvaal as part of Brigadier General Lord Erroll's brigade, commanded by Lieut-General Sir Frederick Carrington. Later Kelly's force was attached to a flying column under direct orders from Lieut-General Lord Methuen. Kelly was a popular and trusted leader who constantly attempted to improve mounted infantry tactics in an effort to match the Boer commandos. At Hartebeestfontein on 16 February 1901 he received a thigh wound which necessitated convalescence in England where he was presented to King Edward VII. For his work in South Africa Kelly was appointed C.B. and was twice mentioned in dispatches (16 April and 7 May 1901).

Invalided home in August he returned to his business, becoming sole proprietor after

Carney's death in 1902. In April he was awarded the Volunteer Officers' Decoration and in July was placed on the reserve of officers. He was posted to the unattached list in 1905, but was next year appointed to command the 4th Light Horse Brigade in the rank of colonel. During 1906 he suffered a haemorrhage of the brain, but ignored the instructions of his medical adviser, Colonel (Sir Charles) Ryan [q.v.], to retire and live more quietly. On 9 June 1907 Kelly died, unmarried, of apoplexy at his home in Smith Street, Collingwood, and after a requiem Mass in St Patrick's Cathedral was buried with military honours in Melbourne general cemetery.

J. Smith (ed), *Cyclopedia of Victoria*, 1 (Melb, 1903); J. Stirling, *The colonials in South Africa, 1899-1902* (Edinb, 1907); Aust Defence Dept, *Official records of the Australian military contingents to the war in South Africa*, P. L. Murray ed (Melb, 1911); R. L. Wallace, *The Australians at the Boer War* (Canb, 1976); *London Gazette*, Apr, May, June 1901; *Argus*, 14 Apr 1900; *Age*, 14 Apr 1900, 10, 12 June 1907; *Australasian*, 14 Apr 1900, 15 June 1907; *Table Talk*, 28 Feb 1901, 21 Sept 1905, 13 June 1907; *Weekly Times* (Melb), 2 Mar, 27 Apr 1901, 15 June 1907; *Herald* (Melb), 13 June 1907.

JOHN E. PRICE

KELLY, ROBERT (1845-1920), pastoralist and politician, and WILLIAM STANLEY (1882-1969), sheep-breeder and agriculturalist, were father and son. Robert was born on 6 May 1845 at Cudlee Creek in the Adelaide Hills, third son of William Kelly, farmer and pioneer settler of 1838, and his wife Jane Christian, née Caley. He was educated at Montague Ambrose's school at Hartley and J. L. Young's [q.v.6] Adelaide Educational Institution. He became a grazier and farmer in the Riverton district in the mid-north of South Australia, taking up Merrindie station, Giles Corner.

In 1891-93 he represented Wooroora in the House of Assembly where he succeeded his brother Hugh Craine Kelly (1848-91). Robert had been a member of the pastoral lands royal commission in 1891. In 1893 the government passed the Pastoral Act and set up the Pastoral Board to which Kelly was appointed, at a salary of £450, to mediate between the Crown and pastoralists. Although the Kingston [q.v.] government was dubious, the board successfully and usefully recommended lowering rents. In 1905 Kelly became a member of the newly inaugurated Land Board and, also, the Advances to Settlers Board. From about 1915 he administered the Drought Relief Act, which prevented the wholesale abandonment of much of the mallee country. In 1917 he retired.

Robert Kelly died of cancer in Adelaide on 26 October 1920, survived by one son and five daughters; his wife Mary, née Goldsack, whom he had married on 21 July 1870, had died in 1893. Kelly was buried in Payneham cemetery.

William Stanley was born on 24 August 1882 at Merrindie and educated at East Adelaide Public School and Prince Alfred College. From 1901 he was in charge of the property. On 10 February 1909 at North Adelaide he married Ada May Dawson. With the development of the frozen meat trade, Kelly and his father bred sheep and lambs for export. William studied the lamb trade in New Zealand and imported from there selected English Leicesters which became the basis of a pure-bred stud. Some years later a Dorset Horn stud was added. The English Leicester stud was sold in the 1920s, and the famous Merrindie stud now consists of Poll Dorsets.

Encouraged by Professor G. C. Henderson [q.v.], for six years Kelly studied arts by correspondence at the University of Adelaide. In April 1917 he enlisted as a private in the 48th Battalion, Australian Imperial Force, seeing active service in France in 1918 where he was wounded. He later lectured, as a lieutenant, for the A.I.F. Education Service, writing the textbook *Beef, mutton and wool* (London, 1919). He returned to Australia in 1919 and next year had 'a serious breakdown'.

In 1922-24 he was chairman of the South Australian Advisory Board of Agriculture. In 1929 he became a member of the Commonwealth Tariff Board in Melbourne. Kelly steadily supported the board's opposition to the high duties on imported goods imposed by the Federal government; he believed that extreme protection artificially propped up inefficient industries, invited retaliation from overseas buyers of Australian primary produce, and increased farmers' expenses.

In May 1940 Kelly and his wife arrived in England to do war work. He arranged the distribution of blankets, the gift of Australia, to air raid victims, and in 1940-41 represented the Australian Wool Board on the International Wool Secretariat in London. From his return to Australia in 1942 Kelly was in Canberra as an adviser on primary products to the Commonwealth prices commissioner Professor (Sir) Douglas Copland, and was his representative on the Agricultural Standing Committee and the Australian Meat Commission.

On the advice of the commission, he recommended to Copland the regulation of the price of meat per pound. This was rendered partly ineffective by butchers selling meat at excessive prices on the black market;

both Copland and the commission backed Kelly in a controversy with butchers. He also secured a government subsidy of £6½ million for the troubled dairy industry.

In 1945-53 he was a co-opted member of the advisory council of the Council for Scientific and Industrial Research and its successor, and in 1950 he reported for the Western Australian government on price control difficulties; in 1951-53 he was chairman of the Joint Dairying Industry Advisory Committee. He was appointed O.B.E. in 1951.

When the Australian Mutual Provident Society began to develop the Ninety Mile Desert in the upper south-east of South Australia by the addition of trace elements in the late 1940s, it benefited from Kelly's expertise in developing similar country on Kangaroo Island. For three years he was chairman of the society's land development committee. In 1952-60 he represented Australia's rural industries on the Consultative Committee on Import Policy. He continued to deplore the excessive protection of secondary industry and advocated massive expansion of rural industries.

His travels as a member of the Commonwealth Tariff Board until 1940 had alerted Kelly to the dangers of soil erosion. For over thirty years he advocated the planting of trees; on his own property he placed thousands of native and other trees, and influenced many to do the same. After retiring Kelly published in Adelaide *Rural development in South Australia* (1962), his autobiography, *Remembered days* (1964), and a biography of his wife who died in 1955.

Kelly died on 5 June 1969 and was buried in Riverside cemetery. He had been a devout Methodist. He was survived by two daughters and two sons, one of whom, Charles Robert Kelly, was a member of the House of Representatives for Wakefield and minister for the navy and for works. In 1977 he endowed the Stan Kelly Memorial Lecture to be delivered biennially at the Australian National University, Canberra.

H. T. Burgess (ed), *Cyclopedia of South Australia*, 1 (Adel, 1907); *Pictorial Aust*, March 1891; *Pastoral Review*, 16 Nov 1920; *Observer* (Adel), 30 Oct 1920; *Advertiser* (Adel), 17 June 1960, 14 Nov 1961, 6 June 1969.   DIRK VAN DISSEL

KELLY, ROBERT VANDELEUR (1843-1913), medical practitioner and army officer, and ROBERT HUME VANDELEUR (1878-1951), army officer, were father and son. Kelly senior was born on 26 July 1843 at Glencara, Westmeath, Ireland, son of Robert Hume Kelly, barrister, and his wife Isabella Olivia, née Isdell. He was educated at Bonn, Prussia, and in 1855-60 at The King's School, Parramatta, New South Wales; the headmaster of the school, Rev. F. Armitage [q.v.3], was his brother-in-law.

Kelly studied medicine in Edinburgh (L.M., L.R.C.P., 1873) and worked as a dispensary medical officer for six months in Glasgow and four years in Ireland where he was also assistant surgeon to the Westmeath (Rifles) Militia. After his marriage on 13 June 1877 at Horseleap, Westmeath, to Anne Holmes Fetherstonhaugh according to the rites of the Church of Ireland, he moved to Warwickshire, England, as medical officer, Castle Bromwich District, Aston Union, and as surgeon to the Militia Medical Department. Appointed F.R.C.S. in 1880, he joined the South Staffordshire Regiment as surgeon in 1883. In 1885 he returned to Westmeath.

In 1889 Kelly migrated to Sydney. He established a city practice and for nearly five years was an 'outdoor' surgeon to Sydney Hospital; he often acted for Dr Paton, the government medical officer. He was commissioned as a partially paid surgeon captain in the Military Forces of New South Wales on 12 October 1889 and promoted surgeon major on 9 January 1896.

Kelly was a founder of the St John Ambulance Association in New South Wales in 1890 and later a Knight of Grace of the Order which he served strenuously all his life. In April 1894 he delivered a paper on army ambulance organization to the United Service Institution of New South Wales, proposing recruitment of a special force from civilian ambulance services, including surgeons, nurses and stretcher-bearers equipped with sprung, mule-drawn, covered wagons like 'those used for carrying Grand Pianos' and independent of Army Service Corps transport. The proposal was commended by Lieut-Colonel (Sir) William Williams [q.v.] and was probably the origin of the field ambulances which made the New South Wales Army Medical Corps impressively mobile in the South African War. It may also have been the origin of the Army Nursing Service Reserve which Kelly helped Williams, Colonel R. E. Roth and Miss E. J. Gould [qq.v.] to organize.

With the temporary rank of lieut-colonel Kelly commanded two contingents of the N.S.W.A.M.C., embarking with the Second Contingent on 17 January 1900 and with the Third Contingent on 17 March 1901. He served in the Transvaal and the Orange River Colony, including actions at Johannesburg, Pretoria, Diamond Hill and Bethlehem. He was mentioned in dispatches and appointed C.B. in 1902. A junior colleague described him as 'a fairly witty Irishman with a pretty taste in literature', and 'a gentlemanly, kindly figure-head [who] really knew nothing of actual management'.

After the war Kelly practised medicine at Auburn. He died of cerebral haemorrhage at Balmoral on 15 October 1913. Survived by his wife and their son and daughter, he was buried in the Anglican section of Thirlmere cemetery.

His son Robert was born at Erdington, Warwickshire, on 13 April 1878. Educated at Sydney Grammar School, he was commissioned second lieutenant, Mounted Rifles, Military Forces of New South Wales, on 21 March 1896 and left for South Africa with the First Mounted Rifles on the same day as his father, 17 January 1900. He served till April in the Orange River Colony in actions at Poplar Grove and Dreifontein.

On 23 May 1900 Kelly obtained a commission as second lieutenant, Royal Artillery, British Regular Army; he was promoted lieutenant in 1907, captain in 1911 and major in 1914. He served with the Royal Artillery Ordnance Corps in World War I, from 14 February 1917, when he was promoted lieut-colonel, as assistant director of ordnance services. For eight months in 1917 he was attached to 1 Anzac Corps, Australian Imperial Force.

Twice mentioned in dispatches, he retired on 6 December 1922 and returned to Sydney. It is believed he never married. Kelly died at Cremorne on 23 January 1951 and was cremated.

Aust Defence Dept, *Official records of the Australian military contingents to the war in South Africa*, P. L. Murray ed (Melb, 1911); A. G. Butler (ed), *Official history of the Australian Medical Services in the war 1914-18*, 1 (Melb, 1930), 3 (Canb, 1943); L. M. Field, *The forgotten war* (Melb, 1979); *V&P* (LA NSW), 1899, 5; United Service Inst (NSW), *J*, 6 (1894); *T&CJ*, 29 Oct 1913; R. Scot Skirving, Memoirs (Basser Lib, Canb); E. Gould papers (AWM).   PATRICIA MORISON

KELLY, THOMAS HERBERT (1875-1948), metal merchant, and WILLIAM HENRY (1877-1960), politician, were born on 17 May 1875 and on 1 December 1877 in Sydney, second and third sons of Irish-born Thomas Hussey Kelly [q.v.5] and his native-born wife Mary Ann, née Dick. Thomas, known to his friends as Bertie, was educated at Sydney Grammar School and in England at Eton (1890-95) and Magdalen College, Oxford (B.A., 1898). William went to All Saints' College, Bathurst, and Eton (1893-96).

Thomas returned to Sydney in 1898. On the death of his father in 1901, he became managing director of the family firm, the Sydney Smelting Co., and chairman of the Australian Alum Co. Like his youngest brother Frederick Septimus [q.v.], he was musical and had some lessons from Joachim. He played with the first violins in Roberto Hazon's [q.v.] Sydney Amateur Orchestral Society, but preferred chamber music, playing the violin or viola in several quartets. He became very knowledgeable about music and its history.

Handsome, clean-shaven, with smoothly parted dark hair and large, wide-set eyes, the brothers were dashing young men about town—Willie was known for his physical courage and love of motor cars. They belonged to fashionable clubs: Thomas to the Australian and Royal Sydney Golf clubs and the Royal Sydney Yacht Squadron of which he was a committee-member; Willie was a member of the Melbourne Club, the Australian and Union clubs, Sydney, and the Marlborough Club, London. Both married actresses. At Christ Church, Hawthorn, Melbourne, Thomas married a widow Ethel Knight Moore [q.v. Kelly], née Mollison, on 29 August 1903; they lived in the family home, Glenyarrah, Double Bay, until it was sold in 1913. In London William married Olive Miller, better-known by her stage name Olive Morrell, on 25 January 1908; a great beauty, she had toured Australia in 1906 for J. C. Williamson [q.v.6].

The brothers also shared an interest in politics and defence matters. Thomas was defeated for the State seat of Hawkesbury in 1904, but represented Bourke Ward on the Sydney Municipal Council in 1906-19. He had joined the Australian Field Artillery in 1905 and, commissioned in 1907, was promoted captain in May 1908; transferring to the Australian Intelligence Corps in October, he was appointed major in 1910. Stationed in Sydney, he commanded the A.I.S. (N.S.W.) from 27 May 1913 until 1919, as lieut-colonel from 1 July 1914.

From the 1920s Thomas Kelly was chairman of the Perpetual Trustee Co. and a director of Tooth [q.v.6] & Co. Ltd and the Bank of New South Wales. He helped to establish Koala Park at Pennant Hills as a sanctuary and advocated the use of Australian plants and trees in town planning. A committee-member of the Royal Philharmonic Society of Sydney, he was a lavish host to visiting musicians and a friend of Melba and Verbrugghen [qq.v.]. When he built a house at Darling Point in the 1930s he included a large music-room designed by his daughter Beatrice. A good linguist, he was a member of the Dante Alighieri Art and Literary Society. He had a ponderous and didactic manner of speaking at times, but also 'that rare determination to make the best of things'. His brother Frederick (with whom he was very good friends) found him 'a complete philistine about literature & especially poetry'.

Thomas died of cancer in St Vincent's Hospital on 12 May 1948 and was cremated with Anglican rites. He was survived by his wife, two sons and two daughters. His estate was valued for probate at £58 944: his wife presented his important musical reference library to the University of Sydney.

William represented Wentworth in the House of Representatives as a Liberal (later Nationalist) in 1903-19. A perpetrator of practical jokes, he at first 'gained a reputation for levity and irresponsibility'. Nevertheless, despite his 'Eton drawl', his party found his 'skill in argument and mordant wit were of incalculable value in a party fight. In baiting a Minister or upsetting the composure of a dangerous opponent he was without equal in the House'. He spoke frequently on defence matters and in 1905 drew attention to German naval expansion; he constantly urged the necessity to contribute to the cost of Imperial naval defence, while strongly criticizing (Vice-Admiral Sir William) Creswell's [q.v.8] recommendations for an Australian navy. In 1906 he became Opposition whip and in May 1909 moved the adjournment of the debate on the address-in-reply that led to the fall of the Fisher [q.v.8] government.

From June 1913 to September 1914 Willie Kelly was honorary minister and acting minister for home affairs in (Sir) Joseph Cook's [q.v.8] cabinet. He was responsible for bringing Walter Burley Griffin [q.v.] to Canberra in 1913 as Federal capital director of design and construction, reversing King O'Malley's [q.v.] decision to use the departmental plan—thereby laying the seeds of future disagreements. Kelly's scheme for a uniform railway gauge, on a basis of the Commonwealth and States concerned contributing to the cost proportionally to the benefit its people would receive, was endorsed by the 1914 Inter-State Conference, but was scrapped by the succeeding Fisher government. In opposition for most of World War I he could do little but encourage recruiting. He retired from politics in November 1919.

For the next forty years Kelly travelled widely, kept an eye on his investments, played bridge at his clubs, and wrote a novel, *Winifred wakes up* (Sydney, 1933), 'a skit on modern foibles'. Separated from his wife, who returned to England with their daughter, he became bitter and very lonely. He died in Royal Prince Alfred Hospital on 27 January 1960 and was cremated with Anglican rites. His estate was valued for probate at £149 545.

Cyclopedia of N.S.W. (Syd, 1907); C. D. Coulthard-Clark, *The citizen general staff* (Canb,

1976); *PD* (Cwlth), 1905, p 1987; *PP* (Cwlth), 1914, 2, p 261; *Vade Mecum*, 25 July 1934; *Punch* (Melb), 20 Feb 1908, 17 July 1913; *SMH*, 27 Oct 1919, 13 Apr 1920, 4 Aug 1922, 6, 8 Dec 1932, 13 May, 6 July 1948; *Canberra Times*, 14 Nov 1964; Jose papers (ML); F. S. Kelly diaries (NL); information from Mrs B. McPhillamy, Syd.

MARTHA RUTLEDGE

KEMP, HENRY HARDIE (1859-1946), architect, was born on 10 March 1859 at Broughton, Lancashire, England, son of Alexander Kemp, woollen merchant, and his wife Mary, née Hardie, both from Scotland. He was educated privately at Bowden, at the Academy Fairfield and the Victoria University, Manchester, and the Royal Academy, London. From an early age he aimed to be an artist. In 1875 he was articled in the office of Manchester architects Corsen & Aitken, then in London with R. W. Edis and, just before his migration to Melbourne in 1886, with Paull & Bonella. Drawings from his student days show the development of his later architectural style—his interest in the half-timbered vernacular of Cheshire and Manchester, in Gothic work, and in that of the contemporary English architects E. Nesfield and R. N. Shaw. He gained many prizes, and after becoming travelling student and medallist of the Architectural Association, London, in 1881, made the first of a number of sketching tours of France.

In Melbourne he was chief assistant with the firm of Terry & Oakden [qq.v.6,5], and in 1887 became a partner in the firm, restyled Oakden, Addison & Kemp. Before the financial collapse of 1892 greatly reduced the practice, Kemp was associated with a number of substantial projects: Queen's College, University of Melbourne; the Queen's Coffee Palace, Carlton (1889, demolished); the twelve-storey Australian Property and Investment Co. Building, corner of Elizabeth Street and Flinders Lane (1887, demolished); the Workingmen's College (1888); and Woodlands for Alexander McCracken [q.v.], North Essendon (1888). He also designed three distinctive brick buildings: a manse, Highbury Grove, Kew, where on 12 December 1888 he married Charlotte Wilhelmina Harvey; a pair of residences at 117 Princess Street and 1 Fellows Street, Kew; and a bank, now the shire office, Kerang.

In 1895-97 Kemp is believed to have been in Sydney, but he returned to Melbourne where in 1899 he entered into a brilliant partnership with Beverley Ussher (1868-1908). The practice specialized in domestic work and their houses epitomize the Marseilles-tiled Queen Anne (or Federation style) houses characteristic of Melbourne, and considered now to be a truly distinctive Australian genre. At the time of their creation they were a break with the use of cement render, applied stucco ornament, cast iron, slates, and double hung windows. Their designs use red bricks, terracotta tiles and casement windows, avoid applied ornamentation and develop substantial timber details. The picturesque character of the houses results from a conscious attempt to express externally with gables, dormers, bays, roof axes, and chimneys, the functional variety of rooms within. Dalswraith for William Gibson [q.v.8], 99 Studley Park Road, Kew (1906) and a house for A. Norman, 7 Adeney Avenue, Kew (1908) are superb examples of his designs.

Ussher died in 1908 while Professional Chambers, Collins Street, was being built. Kemp continued alone in practice until 1911 when he joined George Charles Inskip in a partnership lasting until 1913. Between 1918 and 1929, when he retired, he was in partnership with his nephew F. Bruce Kemp. A number of interesting designs survive from these years, including his own house, Heald Lawn, Kew (1913). An associate of the Royal Victorian Institute of Architects, Kemp was a quiet, reserved man with a stern manner, an exacting and admired master devoted to architecture as an art and craft. He was a founder of the Fellowship Association of Victoria and an elder of the Presbyterian Church. He died at Kew on 22 April 1946, survived by his wife, four daughters and son. His estate was valued for probate at £41 216.

Historic Environment, 2 (1982), no 2, p 4; J. R. Ingram, H. H. Kemp, research essay, 1961, *and* A. Trollope, H. H. Kemp, research report, 1970, Dept of Architecture, Univ Melb; H. H. Kemp drawings (LaTL), *and* collection (held by R. H. Kemp, 1 Balcombe Park Lane, Beaumaris, Melb); architectural index (Univ Melb).

GEORGE TIBBITS

KENDALL, WILLIAM TYSON (1851-1936) and ERNEST ARTHUR (1876-1938), veterinary surgeons, were father and son. Kendall senior was born on 10 February 1851 at Sunny Bank, Torver, Lancashire, England, son of William Kendall, medical practitioner, and his wife Elizabeth, née Jackson. He graduated at the Royal College of Veterinary Surgeons, London, in 1873. On 8 September 1875 at Lowick, Lancashire, he married Elizabeth Park (d. 1904).

Kendall arrived in Melbourne in 1880 *en route* for New Zealand. Finding a city with only four veterinary surgeons, he stayed to establish a practice first at Sandridge (Port Melbourne), then at Fitzroy; his wife and three infants followed him out. He founded a veterinary association and several journals and in 1884, when he published *The diseases of Australian horses*, he succeeded in obtaining a royal commission on bovine tuberculosis. Next year he established a veterinary hospital at Fitzroy. In January 1888, after enactment of the veterinary surgeons bill (1887) which Kendall had drafted and which provided for the registration of qualified veterinary surgeons, he opened the Melbourne Veterinary College with government assurances of legal protection for its graduates, but without a subsidy. The college, offering a four-year course with examinations conducted by the Veterinary Board of Victoria (of which Kendall was president in 1897-1906 and 1912-24), was absorbed into the University of Melbourne in 1908 under J. A. Gilruth [q.v.]. Kendall, who graduated D.V.Sc. from the university in 1909, remained on the staff as lecturer until 1918; from 1914 he was sub-director of the Stock Diseases Research Institute.

Kendall was an honorary associate of the Royal College of Veterinary Surgeons (1891) and had an oration established in his honour in Canberra in 1930. He died at West Brunswick on 11 August 1936 survived by five children from his first marriage, and by his second wife Elizabeth, formerly Todd, née Coward, whom he had married on 29 June 1905 at the Australian Church, Melbourne. He was buried in Melbourne general cemetery. A portrait by Frederick McCubbin [q.v.] is held by the veterinary clinical centre of the University of Melbourne, Werribee, and the student residential hall there is named after him.

His eldest son Ernest was born on 30 August 1876 at Ambleside, Westmorland, England, and was educated at Scotch College, Melbourne, the Melbourne Veterinary College whose teaching staff he joined in 1897, and the University of Melbourne (B.V.Sc., 1911) where he was a temporary lecturer in veterinary medicine and obstetrics in 1909-10. In 1901 he joined the public service as a veterinary officer in the Department of Agriculture, becoming assistant chief veterinary officer in 1908. On 9 February 1910 he married Alma Cresswell Connelly at All Saints Pro-Cathedral, Bendigo.

Kendall was keenly interested in the volunteer forces of Victoria. Joining the Victorian Mounted Rifles as a private in April 1897, he was commissioned captain in the Australian Army Veterinary Corps and as veterinary officer, Victorian Mounted Rifles, in October. During the South African War he was responsible for the creation and organization of the veterinary section of the 5th Victorian contingent, 1st Australian Regiment, and saw active service. Promoted major, A.A.V.C., in January 1904, he was appointed principal veterinary officer, 3rd Military District, in April. In November 1913 he was promoted lieut-colonel.

On the outbreak of World War I Kendall became acting director of veterinary services in the central administration; in October 1915 he joined the Australian Imperial Force as lieut-colonel and senior veterinary officer, 2nd Australian Remount Unit. He served in Egypt and France. Promoted deputy director of veterinary services and temporary colonel in February 1916 (confirmed in February 1918), he was mentioned in dispatches and appointed C.M.G. in December 1917. He returned to Australia in 1919.

Resuming his career in the Department of Agriculture, Kendall succeeded W. A. N. Robertson [q.v.] as chief veterinary officer in August 1926. After considerable criticism of the Melbourne milk supply, in 1933 Kendall chaired an investigating committee and as first chairman of the resulting Milk Board made his outstanding contribution as a public servant in Victoria.

Kendall helped to form the Veterinary Association of Victoria in 1913, was secretary until 1924 and president in 1928 and 1929. A leading Freemason, he enjoyed golf and gardening. He died at North Brighton of coronary vascular disease on 21 March 1938 and was buried in Melbourne general cemetery, survived by his wife, three daughters and two sons.

Ernest's brothers, William Augustus (1878-1949?) and John (1882-1945) also combined veterinary and military careers. Both were graduates of the Melbourne Veterinary College: William established a veterinary practice at Prahran, John at Seymour. They were both commissioned in the A.A.V.C., and promoted captain in 1913. Both joined the A.I.F. as captains on 20 August 1914 and served as veterinary surgeons in Egypt and France. John, who was also present at Gallipoli, was appointed O.B.E. Both continued service with the A.A.V.C. and were promoted lieut-colonel on 1 August 1924. Their sister, Eleanor Jane (b. 1880), served in World War I with the Australian Army Nursing Service. Another brother was a civil engineer.

William Tyson's fifth son and successor to his Fitzroy practice, HECTOR (1885-1961) was educated at Wesley College, the Melbourne Veterinary College and the University of Melbourne (B.V.Sc., 1917). For thirty years he was veterinary surgeon to the Royal Society of Victoria, the Victorian Society for Protection of Animals and the Victorian Trotting and Racing Association. In 1933 he was appointed assistant director of the Royal Zoological and Acclimatisation Society with the right of succession to the director Andrew Wilkie—an agreement reluctantly ratified by the Legislative Assembly when, on Wilkie's retirement late in 1936, a Zoological Board was formed.

Kendall's association with the board remained uneasy; he publicly blamed the board for the death of 100 monkeys after alterations to their enclosures, and other disagreements led to his dismissal in September 1945. He developed a practice at Sunbury and died in Melbourne on 3 October 1961.

A. Sutherland, *Victoria and its metropolis*, 2 (Melb, 1888); *PP* (LA Vic), 1901, 3 (36), p 242; A'sian Assn Advancement of Science (Section K), *Report of Meeting*, 1913; *Aust Veterinary J*, 12, 1936, 14, 1938, 52, 1976; Aust Veterinary Assn, *Annual Conference Handbook*, May 1970; *Argus*, 12 Aug, 23, 24 Oct, 6, 19 Nov 1936, 22 Mar 1938, 23 Jan, 28 Sept 1945; W. T. Kendall papers (Univ Melb Archives).   HAROLD E. ALBISTON

KENNEALLY, JAMES JOSEPH (1879-1954), politician, was born on 15 May 1879 in Sydney, son of Patrick Kenneally, engine-driver, and his wife Charlotte, née Young. He was educated by the Christian Brothers and moved to Western Australia in 1899 where he became a locomotive cleaner, then engine-driver, with the railways. He was president of the West Australian Locomotive Engine-drivers', Firemen's and Cleaners' Union of Workers in 1914 and secretary in 1919. On 15 November 1911 in Adelaide he had married Mary Anne Flaherty, a teacher.

In 1927 Kenneally was president of the State branch of the Australian Labor Party and was elected member of the Legislative Assembly for East Perth. Next year he became federal president of the A.L.P., and was later a central participant in the bitter struggles which eventually destroyed the Scullin [q.v.] Federal government and split the party. At one level Kenneally's vigorous opposition to J. T. Lang [q.v.] can be seen as an assertion of the final authority of the federal branch. At another, his attack on Lang partly reflected Kenneally's basic fiscal 'respectability' and the fact that Lang, in his efforts to secure control of the New South Wales branch, had been engaged in a savage factional dispute with the Australian Workers' Union, an organization with which Kenneally was closely associated. At the 1930 federal conference he asserted that conference 'should be strong enough to say that those who did not observe [its decision] should go outside' the party.

Kenneally was urging that, although the

consequences might be grave, the party's rules could not be ignored. However, in 1931 and 1933 Kenneally, as chairman of the federal executive, made two extraordinary decisions. He ruled that the Premiers' Plan was not in conflict with Labor's official policy, and that members of the Parliamentary Labor Party 'are at liberty to use their own discretion when dealing with the Premiers' Plan'. The latter implied a free vote in parliament in conflict with party rules.

Within the State labour movement Kenneally was a leader of the dominant moderate group and showed skill and firmness in maintaining its control. His important role was most clearly demonstrated during his time as a minister in the Collier [q.v.8] government in 1933-36. Although he was without ministerial experience, Kenneally's seniority and his ability ensured him a leading place. His principal portfolio in this Depression period was employment; he was also minister for industrial development and child welfare until March 1935, then minister for a year for public works and labour.

He had the primary responsibility for applying the policy of preference to unionists on government relief works. Leaders of unions covering government employees urged that relief workers be compelled to join the relevant union. But officials of other unions whose members were being forced out of their normal occupations on to these projects, urged that they should be permitted to remain in their original unions. Kenneally applied the former policy although the government could not obtain approval for it from the party executive.

Kenneally's role was even more apparent in the destruction of the newly formed 'Relief and Sustenance Workers' Union' led by T. J. Hughes, the previous Labor member for East Perth. This union was successful in attracting members—many felt it unfair to expect men on part-time work to pay the full union fee, which in the case of the A.W.U. was 25 shillings, and it was claimed that the A.W.U. had insufficient sympathy for part-time workers' problems. Recognition for the new union was bluntly denied by Kenneally.

The major effect of the government's policy was the strengthening of the A.W.U.: between the A.L.P.'s 1932 and 1935 general councils A.W.U. membership almost trebled. This meant that the union's voting strength rose from under 10 per cent in 1932 to 20 per cent in 1935. The A.W.U. was a strong backer of the State Labor government when its policy was being criticized within party conferences. Clearly this support was a major reason why there was little opposition within Labor ranks in this diffi-

cult period, despite the government's cautious policies.

Kenneally also alienated many by his alleged policy of moving 'militants' on government relief works to areas where their effect was diminished. By his firmness and vigour, particularly against those whom he saw as threats to party stability, Kenneally won both friends and opponents. Many of the latter campaigned against him at the February 1936 State election. The Labor government was returned but Kenneally lost his seat to his old rival Hughes.

Kenneally was a man who, when not working, enjoyed literature, cricket and the races. Shortly after his defeat he was appointed chairman of the Lotteries Commission. Later the Curtin Federal government appointed him to the Commonwealth Grants Commission and he was reappointed to this by the Menzies government. He retained both positions until his death of hypertensive heart disease on 9 October 1954. Survived by his wife and two of their five children, he was buried in Karrakatta cemetery with Catholic rites.

L. F. Crisp, *The Australian Federal Labour Party 1901-1951* (Lond, 1955), and *Ben Chifley* (Melb, 1961); *Labour Hist*, Nov 1970, no 19; *West Australian*, 11 Oct 1954; R. F. Pervan, The Western Australian Labor movement, 1933-47 (M.A. thesis, Univ WA, 1966).   RALPH PERVAN

KENNEDY, JOHN JOSEPH (1881?- 1957), priest and military chaplain, was probably born on 28 October 1881 at Dingle, Kerry, Ireland, son of John Kennedy and his wife Johanna, née Lynch. He was educated at the Christian Brothers' School at Dingle, went to a seminary at Killarney, and studied for the priesthood at All Hallows College, Drumcondra. Ordained on 24 June 1904 he volunteered for the Australian mission and became assistant priest at Wangaratta, Victoria. He later worked in several north Victorian towns including Heathcote, Shepparton and Yarrawonga.

Kennedy was appointed a chaplain captain in the Australian Imperial Force on 1 December 1915, saying that 'his duty called upon him to offer his services'. He sailed on 29 December from Melbourne and was posted to the 14th Infantry Brigade headquarters in Egypt. He was attached to the 53rd Battalion and, as was the case with many other chaplains, identified closely with 'his' battalion even though his duties extended to the whole brigade. He reached France in June 1916. The battalion's first engagement was at Fromelles on 19-20 July when severe losses were suffered. Kennedy wrote of 'scenes of carnage'. He worked with the doctors in an aid-post and was astonished by the bravery and generosity of the wounded. The battalion, he wrote, 'failed to see the meaning of the task allotted to us at Fromelles. It was hopeless from the very outset'.

For his part in the battle Kennedy was awarded the Distinguished Service Order 'for conspicuous gallantry and devotion to duty. He carried wounded men from the front trenches to the dressing station under very heavy shell-fire throughout the whole night, returning repeatedly to the firing-line'. He also assisted in dressing wounded men and, with Chaplain Maxted who was killed doing similar duties, was a conspicuous example of practical Christianity. Kennedy absorbed the Australian soldier's hatred of sectarianism and made no distinction between men. Of a Methodist in the battalion he wrote: 'I say of him most sincerely that he is one of the most perfect Christians I have ever met'. In December 1917 ill health forced him to leave the 53rd Battalion and he was posted to the 3rd Training Brigade. In April 1918 he returned to Australia; his A.I.F. appointment was terminated on 31 May.

Kennedy honoured the gallantry of the men with whom he had served in *The Whale Oil Guards* (Dublin, 1919). One of the first battalion histories published, it was far from the best, concentrating on one or two officers and containing no detailed accounts of operations or of the life of the battalion. He had previously written three novels: *Carrigmore* (Wangaratta, 1909), *The inseparables* (Wangaratta, 1910) and *Gordon Grandfield* (Melbourne, 1912). *Carrigmore, or light and shade in West Kerry*, is a sentimental, melodramatic story written by an apparently homesick author about Ireland and its saintly people.

Kennedy continued to work in Victorian country parishes until in 1936 he migrated to the United States of America. He died at Augusta in Georgia, on 18 February 1957.

M. M. McKernan, *Australian churches at war* (Syd, 1980); *London Gazette*, 26 Sept 1916; *Advocate* (Melb), 27 Nov 1915, 30 Sept, 23 Dec 1916; *Freeman's J* (Syd), 12 Oct 1916, 29 July 1920.

MICHAEL MCKERNAN

KENNEDY, MALCOLM (1858-1944), JOHN (1862-1937) and COLIN (1868-1936), engineers and shipbuilders, were brothers. Malcolm was born on 1 July 1858 at Anderston, Glasgow, Scotland, first son of eight sons and three daughters of Robert Kennedy, ship carpenter, and his wife Florinda, née Aitken. In 1860 the family migrated to Melbourne where Kennedy senior set up as a shipwright and where his second son John was born on 4 April 1862 and his fourth son Colin on 5 December 1868. In 1879 Malcolm and John, who trained as a naval architect, joined their father as Robert Kennedy & Sons, shipbuilders and shipsmiths. On 27 December 1883 at North Melbourne, Malcolm married Ann White with Presbyterian forms. Next year Robert Kennedy & Sons removed to Hobart where with John W. Syme and W. J. Duffy, partners until 1889, they took over the Derwent Ironworks & Engineering Co., a foundry formerly owned by the (Alexander) Clark [q.v.1] family. The Kennedys also acquired the patent slipyard, formerly Ross's, at Battery Point.

The firm's first major undertaking was the construction under government contract of the dredge (Sir James Wilson) *Agnew* [q.v.3]. The shipyard workers were trained from scratch by the Kennedys and the *Agnew* was launched on 26 March 1887 amid acclaim as the first iron ship built in Tasmania. The Kennedys also built the steam launch *Tarrina* for the Launceston Marine Board, made ironwork for bridges, and towards the end of Robert's life began operating a fleet of interstate trading vessels. Robert Kennedy died in Hobart on 15 May 1903.

Colin joined the business about 1901 after education at St James's School, Melbourne, and experience on the Tasmanian railways, at the Lefroy and west coast mines and as mine-manager in Western Australia. After the shipbuilding industry in Hobart began to flag John also turned to mining: he attended the Ballarat School of Mines in Victoria and reopened the Hobart smelters which had been an adjunct of the Derwent Ironworks in the 1870s. He made several voyages overseas on smelting business and as mining promoter, and was a member of the London Stock Exchange. In 1913-14 he was manager of Tongkah Compound (1910); Robert Kennedy & Sons was reputed to have contributed to the success of the Hobart-run Tongkah Harbour, Thailand, tin mines by developing a suitable dredge. The brothers also held shares in the Irrawaddy Burma Co. John was a member of the Australasian Institute of Mining Engineers and from 1932 an honorary life member of the American Institute of Mining & Metallurgical Engineers. He and Colin both owned and raced trotting horses. Colin died in Hobart on 2 June 1936, survived by his wife Amy Naomi, née Wilkinson, whom he had married on 18 September 1895 at Hobart, and by a daughter. John died in Hobart on 10 January 1937; his second wife Helen and two sons survived him.

Malcolm succeeded his father as head of the family business in 1903 and when this was incorporated as a limited liability company in 1926 was managing director. His interests extended to fur-trading, mining and general hardware; he succeeded (Sir) Alfred Ashbolt [q.v.7] as chairman of directors of Tongkah Harbor Tin Dredging Co. in 1919 and as a director of Charles Davis Ltd in 1920. President of the Economic Society in 1911 and vice-chairman of the Hobart Chamber of Commerce in 1918-20, Kennedy contributed substantially to the founding of the faculty of commerce at the University of Tasmania in 1918. He served the government in the 1920s on the Public Service Salaries, the Bursaries, the Commonwealth Carbide Co. and the State Development boards. Once active in athletics, rowing and football, in 1912 he was president of the Royal Hobart Bowling Club. Like John a member of the Independent Order of Oddfellows, he was grand master of Buckingham district in 1895; he was a Rotarian and a manager of Scots (Chalmers) Church. He died, childless, in Hobart on 28 July 1944, leaving an estate valued for probate at £34 999. The Kennedys were all buried in Cornelian Bay cemetery.

J. Reynolds, *Men & mines* (Melb, 1974); Univ Tas, *Calendar*, 1920; *Mercury*, 26, 28 Mar 1887, 18 May 1903, 3 June 1936, 12 Jan 1937, 29 July 1944; Kennedy family scrap-books (SLT).

ANN G. SMITH

KENNEDY, THOMAS (1876-1943), soldier and labourer, was born on 5 July 1876 at Rossmore, near Liverpool, New South Wales, son of James Kennedy, farmer, and his wife Mary, née Kennedy. He served for three years in India with the Devonshire Regiment, and for nine years in the Garrison Artillery in Australia. Describing himself as a labourer, he enlisted in the Australian Imperial Force on 17 August 1914 and was allocated to the machine-gun section of the 1st Battalion. On 18 October he embarked for Egypt and from 8 December his battalion trained at Mena Camp.

On 10 April 1915 the unit embarked for Mudros and on the morning of 25 April landed on Gallipoli, and took part in the operations that day on Baby 700, the 400 Plateau and MacLaurin's Hill. During the first days of fighting Kennedy was wounded but had displayed great coolness and courage while collecting stragglers, regrouping them and leading them back into the firing line. For his conspicuous gallantry he was awarded the Distinguished Conduct Medal and was mentioned in dispatches. After hospitalization Kennedy returned to his unit on 15 August. On 22 October he was promoted

lance corporal and on 7 November temporary corporal. After the evacuation from Gallipoli on 20 December the 1st Battalion returned to Egypt and on 9 January 1916 at Tel-el-Kebir he was promoted sergeant.

With the expansion of the A.I.F. Kennedy, after attending a school of instruction, was transferred to the newly established 1st Machine-Gun Company on 12 March. On 22 March the company embarked for France and entrained at Marseilles for Steenbecque, the 1st Anzac Corps concentration area in Flanders. In April the company experienced its first shelling by the Germans. During the 1st Australian Division assault on Pozières in July-August, when the 1st Brigade suffered very heavy casualties, Kennedy's outstanding performance earned a mention in dispatches. On 18 November he was promoted warrant officer, class 2, and was appointed company sergeant major. In January 1917 he was mentioned in dispatches again.

In the second attempt to capture Bullecourt in April-May 1917 Kennedy was wounded. During the operations in the Ypres sector from September to November, regardless of enemy shelling and despite being wounded again on 5 October, he worked day and night to supervise the movement forward by work-parties of ammunition, rations and other supplies. His men suffered no casualties and for his excellent work he was awarded a Bar to his D.C.M.

From January to July 1918 Kennedy attended the Machine-Gun Training Depot at Grantham, England. He returned to his unit on 9 July and on 29 August, in the operations preceding the attack on Mont St Quentin, was wounded for the fourth time. On 8 October he embarked at Taranto, Italy, for Australia and on 3 February 1919 was discharged from the A.I.F. in Sydney.

Giving his occupation as wireman, on 24 September 1925 at St Joseph's Catholic Church, Woollahra, Kennedy married Kathleen Floyd (d. 1936). In the post-war years he engaged in a range of labouring jobs; as a result of his wounds, and his having been gassed several times, this period was marred by bad health. Kennedy died at Paddington, Sydney, on 25 September 1943 and was buried in the Catholic section of Botany cemetery. The epitaph on his headstone reads: 'His duty nobly done'.

B. V. Stacy et al, *The history of the 1st Battalion, A.I.F. (1914-1919)* (Syd, 1931); C. E. W. Bean, *The story of Anzac* (Syd, 1921, 1924) and *The A.I.F. in France*, 1916-18 (Syd, 1929, 1933, 1937, 1942); *London Gazette*, 2 July, 3 Aug 1915, 2 Jan, 16 Nov, 25 Dec 1917; *SMH*, 27 Sept 1943; War diaries, 1st Battalion and 1st Machine-Gun Company AIF; records, Dept of Veterans' Affairs, Syd, and AWM.

R. SUTTON

KENNEDY, THOMAS JAMES (1859-1929), farmer and politician, was born on 14 June 1859 at Moonee Ponds, Victoria, third child of James Kennedy, labourer, and his wife Margaret, née Reilly, both from Tipperary, Ireland. His early years were spent at Gisborne where he worked as a rural labourer before establishing his own farm at Cobram in 1877. On 2 February 1887 at Yarrawonga, with Catholic rites, he married Bridget Hanrahan.

Kennedy served on the Yarrawonga Shire Council (1889-94) and was president in 1892-94. In 1893, campaigning as a Liberal protectionist, he contested the Legislative Assembly seat of Benalla and Yarrawonga at a by-election. Kennedy and his conservative opponent, J. M. Templeton [q.v.6], both polled 753 votes; the returning officer's casting vote gave the seat to Templeton. Kennedy successfully appealed against the result and in a new poll won by sixty votes. He retained the seat until 1901.

In parliament Kennedy was regarded as a 'Lib-Lab' man. He supported the concept of a state bank, advocated a compulsory arbitration system and admired the Labor Party's 'splendid discipline'. However, he could not countenance a land tax. He considered himself bound by 'measures not men' and, although sympathetic to the Turner [q.v.] government, voted in 1899 for the no confidence motion which brought in the McLean [q.v.] ministry. After the 1900 election he urged both Liberal factions to heal the 'unjustifiable rift' between them. He served on enquiries relating to the establishment of a state bank, the failure of the Mildura settlement, law reform, locomotive spark arresters and (as chairman) the Leongatha labour colony.

In 1901 Kennedy resigned from State parliament and was elected to the House of Representatives for Moira. He was a 'singularly loyal' Protectionist and a forthright exponent of White Australia but retained his reputation for independence, voting against his party's proposals for establishment of the High Court of Australia and the East-West Transcontinental Railway. A colleague, R. A. Crouch [q.v.8] recalled him as a 'fine, homely man', tall, bearded and usually wearing a slouch hat. He maintained his leaning towards 'state socialism', declaring that 'no section of the community has derived more benefit from it than have the farmers of Victoria'. In 1906, following a redistribution, Kennedy failed by thirty-two votes to win the seat of Echuca. He petitioned against the result and, as in 1893, succeeded in having the poll voided. At the subsequent by-election he was soundly defeated.

Kennedy was appointed chairman of the Victorian Closer Settlement Board in 1910. In 1915 a royal commission condemned the activities of the board, finding that it had paid excessive prices for unsuitable land. Kennedy's lack of administrative experience was emphasized by the commission's discovery of 'hundreds of sheets of minutes' written by him on matters which should have been attended to by others. Kennedy defended himself, claiming that ministerial interference was the 'curse of the Board'. Nevertheless he was not reappointed and his public career was blighted. Two years later he stood for his old State seat, Benalla, and lost his deposit.

About 1919 Kennedy took up farming and grazing at Buffalo and died there on 16 February 1929. Predeceased by his wife, he was buried in Cobram cemetery. Three daughters and a son survived him.

V&P (LA Vic), 1915, 1 (C2), p 785, 2 (21), p 39; *Cobram Courier*, 21 Feb 1929.

GEOFF BROWNE

KENNIFF, PATRICK (1863-1903) and JAMES (1869?-1940), cattle duffers, were sons of Irish-born James Kenniff, selector, and his wife Mary, née Stapleton. Patrick was born at Main Creek, near Dungog, New South Wales, on 28 September 1863. James's birth was not registered. After convictions for stock stealing in northern New South Wales, they overlanded in 1891 with their father to the Springsure district of Queensland, being joined later by their younger brothers Thomas and John. Living by bush work, they also raced horses and opened books on the local race meetings.

Moving to the Upper Warrego in 1893, they occupied blocks in the Hoganthulla and Killarney resumptions and later the Ralph block which adjoined William Collins and Sons' Carnarvon-Babbiloora consolidation. With convicted cattle duffers Thomas Stapleton, John and Richard Riley and others, they launched a reign of 'mild terror' from their base on Ralph, stealing cattle from Carnarvon and other neighbouring stations. During this period both brothers served prison terms. When neighbouring cattlemen protested, the government terminated the Kenniffs' lease of the Ralph block and established the Upper Warrego police station thereon.

The Kenniffs now assumed a more truculent attitude, riding armed through the district, and moved their base across the Dividing Range to Lethbridge's Pocket. They developed a special animosity towards the manager of Carnarvon, Albert Christian Dahlke.

When the charred remains of Dahlke and

Constable George Doyle of the Upper War-rego police station, who had set out during Easter 1902 to arrest the Kenniffs for horse-stealing, were found in Lethbridge's Pocket, strong suspicion fell on Patrick and James Kenniff. Although he did not see the actual murders, Doyle's Aboriginal tracker, Sam Johnson, heard shooting and when he neared the arrest scene the Kenniffs pursued him, but he escaped. Despite a reward of £1000 and a large police manhunt, they were not taken until 23 June at Arrest Creek, south of Mitchell.

Chief Justice Sir Samuel Griffith [q.v.] presided over the trial in Brisbane. Found guilty of wilful murder, both prisoners were sentenced to death but execution was deferred, pending an appeal. Even before the trial there was much public sympathy for the Kenniffs. This was partly a manifestation of public discontent with unemployment and a drought, and partly a revival of the old antipathy between squatter and cockatoo farmer among New South Wales expatriates. The appeal, financed by funds contributed by supporters, was dismissed by a full bench of the Supreme Court; the only dissenter was Mr Justice Real [q.v.] who was not convinced of James's guilt. Patrick was executed on 12 January 1903 and buried in South Brisbane cemetery with Catholic rites; the sentence of James was commuted to life imprisonment.

Exacerbated by sectarianism, public controversy over the case gave a strong impetus to moves for the abolition of capital punishment in Queensland. Sympathy for the Kenniffs was greatly stimulated by the appearance of two ballads, 'The Kenniffs' and 'The hanging of Paddy Kenniff'. James eventually served only twelve years. After working on cattle-stations in the north-west he fossicked in the ranges north of Charters Towers and died there of cancer on 8 October 1940. He was buried in Charters Towers cemetery.

Qld Heritage, 1 (1968), no 9, p 3, 2 (1969), no 1, p 3.   GRENFELL HEAP

KENNY, AUGUSTUS LEO (1863-1946), surgeon and Catholic layman, was born on 29 July 1863 at Salford, Lancashire, England, son of Irish parents John Kenny, grocer, and his wife Mary, née Naughton. He migrated to Melbourne with his parents in 1870 and, educated by the Christian Brothers at Victoria Parade, East Melbourne, and by the Jesuit Fathers at St Patrick's and Xavier colleges, graduated from the University of Melbourne (M.B., 1885; Ch.B., 1886).

In 1886 Kenny was appointed first resident surgeon at the Eye and Ear Hospital, Melbourne. He proceeded to England in 1888 for further studies, becoming a member of the Ophthalmological Society of the United Kingdom. Returning to Melbourne, he was first honorary ophthalmic and aural surgeon at St Vincent's Hospital from 1893 until his retirement to private practice in Collins Street in 1908.

Kenny's influence on medical affairs in Victoria was profound. In 1899 he was a founder of the Ophthalmological Society of Melbourne and that year was elected president of the Victorian branch of the British Medical Association; he was re-elected in 1914. Honorary general secretary of the Australasian Medical Congress in 1923, he was a founder in 1927 of the (Royal) Australasian College of Surgeons, serving as first honorary secretary and treasurer and, until 1944, as a council-member. He was a member of the Medical Board of Victoria and official visitor to Melbourne mental hospitals.

Kenny was a sincere and pious Catholic devoted to the advancement of his Church. A prefect of the Professional Men's Sodality, he welcomed the second Catholic archbishop Dr Thomas Carr [q.v.7], a distant relation, to Melbourne in 1887. A confidant and adviser of Carr, he continued this close association with Archbishop Mannix [q.v.] despite publicly revealed differences of opinion during World War I on conscription and Irish independence. Kenny received the papal order of St Gregory the Great in 1888 and the grand cross of the order in 1929. He was an outstanding secretary of the Australasian Catholic congresses in 1900 and 1904 and in 1907 was appointed a papal chamberlain of cape and sword. Kenny was elected first president of the Cathedral Club for Men in 1903. He was a founder of the Victorian Catholic Federation and helped to found Newman and St Mary's colleges at the University of Melbourne. In 1939, as his last official role for the Church, he chaired the peace demonstration in May in the Exhibition Building.

Charitable, energetic and intelligent, Kenny lent his services to the general community. He was long a member of the Lord Mayor's Fund for Metropolitan Hospitals and Charities and in 1934 an executive member of the committee established for the centenary of Victoria celebrations. He was a long-standing member of the Melbourne Club. Interested in horse-riding and cricket, he also valued literature, painting, sculpture and music, being himself an accomplished pianist. He was appointed C.M.G. in 1938.

On 13 January 1892 at St Patrick's Cathedral Kenny had married Frances Monica O'Connor. She died, childless, in 1901, and on 10 July 1912 at St Patrick's Kenny married Olga Constance Mary Zichy-Woinarski, a well-known violinist. Kenny died at Kew on 27 September 1946, survived by the two sons and two daughters of this marriage. A portrait by John Hennessy is in the collection of the Historical Commission of the Archdiocese of Melbourne and another, by Violet Teague [q.v.], is held by Dr Elizabeth Kenny. An alabaster bust by J. W. Elisher is at Newman College.

College of Surgeons of A'sia, *J*, 1, 1928-29, 2, 1929-30; St Patrick's College, East Melb, *Patrician*, 1946; Ophthalmological Soc of Aust, *Trans*, 6, 1946; *Aust J of Ophthalmology*, 1980.

T. A. HAZELL

KENNY, ELIZABETH (1880-1952), nurse, was born on 20 September 1880 at Warialda, New South Wales, daughter of Michael Kenny, farmer from Ireland, and his native-born wife Mary, née Moore. She received limited education at small primary schools in New South Wales and Queensland. There is no official record of formal training or registration as a nurse. She probably learned by voluntary assistance at a small maternity hospital at Guyra, New South Wales. About 1910 Kenny was a self-appointed nurse, working from the family home at Nobby on the Darling Downs, riding on horseback to give her services, without pay, to any who called her. In 1911 she used hot cloth fomentations on the advice of Aeneas McDonnell, a Toowoomba surgeon, to treat symptomatically puzzling new cases, diagnosed by him telegraphically as infantile paralysis (poliomyelitis). The patients recovered. Kenny then opened a cottage hospital at Clifton.

During World War I, using a letter from McDonnell as evidence of nursing experience, she enlisted on 30 May 1915 and was appointed staff nurse in the Australian Army Nursing Service, serving on troopships bringing wounded home to Australia. On 1 November 1917 she was promoted Sister, a title she used for the rest of her life. Her army service terminated in March 1919. After the war she resumed her home nursing and became the first president of the Nobby chapter of the Country Women's Association. In 1927 she patented the 'Sylvia' ambulance stretcher designed to reduce shock in the transport of injured patients.

In 1932 Sister Kenny established a backyard clinic at Townsville to treat long-term poliomyelitis victims and cerebral palsy patients with hot baths, foments, passive movements, the discarding of braces and callipers and the encouragement of active movements. At a government-sponsored demonstration in Brisbane doctors and masseurs ridiculed her, mainly because they considered her explanations of the lesions at the site of the paralysis were bizarre. Thus began a long controversy at a time when there was no vaccination for poliomyelitis. The strong-willed Kenny, with an obsessional belief in her theory and methods, was opposed by a conservative medical profession whom she mercilessly slated and who considered her recommendation to discard immobilization to be criminal. Despite almost total medical opposition, parental and political pressure with some medical backing resulted in action by the Queensland government which was influenced by Home Secretary E. M. Hanlon and his public service adviser, C. E. Chuter. In 1934 clinics to treat long-term poliomyelitis cases were established in Townsville and later in Brisbane. The Brisbane clinic immediately attracted interstate and overseas patients. Kenny clinics in other Queensland cities and interstate followed.

In 1937 she published in Sydney *Infantile paralysis and cerebral diplegia*, with a foreword by Herbert Wilkinson, professor of anatomy at the University of Queensland. Grateful parents having paid her fare to England, she was given two wards at Queen Mary's Hospital at Carshalton, Surrey. She shocked English doctors with her recommendations to discard splinting used to prevent deformities and her condemnation of the orthodox treatment of poliomyelitis cases. Returning to Australia, she was greeted with the report of a royal commission of leading Queensland doctors which damned her methods. However, she was given a ward at the Brisbane General Hospital and early cases of the disease to treat. Aubrey Pye, medical superintendent, stated that her patients recovered more quickly and that their limbs were more supple than those treated by the orthodox method. But the medical profession largely ignored her.

In 1940, armed with an introduction to the Mayo Clinic, Rochester, Minnesota, signed by six Brisbane doctors and her fare paid by the Queensland government, she arrived in the United States of America. At first most doctors rejected her theories of 'spasm', 'mental alienation', and 'incoordination' by which she explained the disability caused by poliomyelitis. However, orthopaedists Miland Knapp, John Pohl and Wallace Cole arranged for her to be given beds in the Minneapolis General Hospital. Her methods became widely accepted. She began courses for doctors and physiotherapists from many parts of the world.

The Sister Kenny Institute was built in Minneapolis in 1942 and other Kenny clinics were established.

Kenny became a heroine in America and was awarded many honours. She accepted numerous invitations to lecture in other countries and received honorary degrees. Her autobiography, *And they shall walk*, written in collaboration with Martha Ostenso, was published in New York in 1943. In 1946 she was eulogized in the film, *Sister Kenny*. Abraham Fryberg, Queensland director-general of health and medical services, and Thomas Stubbs Brown, orthopaedic specialist, after an overseas visit recommended in 1947 that treatment based on the Kenny method be used in the early stages. They argued, however, that her concept that the disabilities in poliomyelitis were caused by the virus invading peripheral tissues, and not the central nervous system as traditionally taught, was not proven. In 1950 Congress gave her the rare honour of free access to the United States without entry formalities. Despite this success, she remained the centre of bitter controversy, partly because of her intolerance of opposition, and returned to Australia several times with little acclaim.

A big woman, with white hair which she often covered with large hats, Elizabeth Kenny was an imposing figure. She could speak gently to a patient one minute and harshly criticize a doctor the next. She gained basic knowledge as she progressed and, at times, submitted other people's ideas as though they were her own. Although her views on the pathology of the disease were generally not accepted, she made a significant contribution towards the treatment of poliomyelitis and stimulated fresh thinking. Developing Parkinson's disease, she retired to Toowoomba in 1951 and died there of cerebro-vascular disease on 30 November 1952. After a service in the Neil Street Methodist Church, she was buried in Nobby cemetery. Unmarried, she was survived by an adopted daughter. Her estate, valued for probate at £17 117, was left mainly to relatives, but a collection of memorabilia was left to the Kenny Foundation in the United States and a desk and prayer-book, belonging once to Florence Nightingale, were left to the United Nations Organization. Her book, *My battle and victory*, was published posthumously in London in 1955. A bust by L. Randolph is displayed in the Toowoomba City Art Gallery.

V. Cohn, *Sister Kenny: the woman who challenged the doctors* (Minneapolis, Minn, USA, 1975); Reports on concepts and treatment of poliomyelitis, *PP* (Qld), 1947-48, 2, p 1021; *MJA*, 1, 1938, no 5, p 187; *Toowoomba Chronicle*, 1 Dec 1952; Elizabeth Kenny papers (held by Qld Country Women's Assn, Nobby Branch); information from M. McCracken, Caloundra, Qld, and Sir A. Fryberg, Clayfield, Bris.   ROSS PATRICK

KENNY, THOMAS JAMES BEDE (1896-1953), soldier and salesman, was born on 29 September 1896 at Paddington, Sydney, son of Austin James Kenny, butcher, from Auckland, New Zealand, and his wife Mary Christina, née Connolly, of New South Wales. Bede Kenny was educated at the Christian Brothers' College, Waverley. He began to train as a chemist's assistant at Bondi but after three months he enlisted in the Australian Imperial Force on 23 August 1915—a fortnight after the major Australian actions at Lone Pine and The Nek, Gallipoli. On 20 December he embarked with the 13th Reinforcements, 2nd Battalion and, after arriving in Egypt, served with the 54th Battalion before joining the 2nd on 27 February 1916. In March he went to France and in the second phase of the battle of Pozières fought in the battalion bombing platoon.

In spring 1917, as British and Australian forces captured the 'outpost villages' of the Hindenburg line, Kenny won the Victoria Cross. In the attack on Hermies, mounted by the 2nd and 3rd battalions on 9 April, his platoon came under heavy fire from a machine-gun post which caused severe casualties. Kenny, single-handed, rushed the enemy, hurling three bombs, the last of which knocked out the post. He then made prisoners of the surviving Germans and his action contributed significantly to the success of the operation.

Kenny was immediately promoted lance corporal and soon afterwards was evacuated to England with trench feet. He rejoined the battalion at Hazebrouck and on 26 June 1918 was wounded during fighting in the Merris sector. Though he described his injuries as 'nothing to write home about' he was invalided to Australia in August, having become a corporal that month. He arrived in Sydney on 9 October to a tumultuous welcome. He rejected an offer to join the military police, whom he disliked intensely, and was discharged on 12 December.

Returning to civilian life, Kenny first worked for Clifford Love & Co., manufacturers, importers and merchants, as their northern New South Wales traveller. He then joined the *Sunday Times* newspaper in Sydney, and shortly after became a traveller for Penfolds Wines Ltd. He married Kathleen Dorothy Buckley, a florist, at St Mary's Cathedral, on 29 September 1927; they had three children and their home is remembered as a happy one. Kenny repeatedly suffered the effects of trench feet; the war had also made him partially deaf. He never recovered from the deaths of his elder daughter in 1943 and his only son in 1948 (both from rheumatic fever). Survived by his wife and one daughter, he died in Concord Repatriation Hospital, Sydney, on 15 April 1953 and was buried in Botany cemetery. It was a bitter irony that the pall bearers at his funeral were military policemen.

Kenny was a staunch Catholic, a vital man of immense character and physical stature. He had no shortage of friends and was often involved in good-natured pranks. Though he never talked openly of his wartime experiences, he always led the V.C. winners in the Sydney Anzac Day march. In 1957 the Bede Kenny Memorial Ward was opened at Wentworth Private Hospital, Randwick, to provide beds for ex-servicemen ineligible for repatriation hospital treatment.

C. E. W. Bean, *The A.I.F. in France*, 1917-18 (Syd, 1933, 1937, 1942); F. W. Taylor and T. A. Cusack, *Nulli secundus: a history of the Second Battalion, A.I.F., 1914-19* (Syd, 1942); L. Wigmore (ed), *They dared mightily* (Canb, 1963); *Reveille* (Syd), Oct 1930; *Sydney Mail*, 20 June 1917, 23 Oct 1918; *Bulletin* (Syd), 22 Apr 1953; A.I.F. nominal roll, *and* War diary, 2nd Battalion (AWM); information from Mrs P. Sparkes, Portland, and Mr E. Kenny, Cronulla, N.S.W.   MATTHEW HIGGINS

KENYON, ALFRED STEPHEN (1867-1943), engineer, ethnologist and historian, was born on 7 December 1867 at Homebush, Victoria, third son of Alfred Henderson Kenyon, storekeeper from Manchester, England, and his Scottish wife Agnes Fleming, née Agnew. In 1869 the family shifted to Avoca, where A. H. Kenyon established a general store, followed by others at Ararat, Beaufort, Buangor, Stawell and Horsham. In 1875, because of ill health, he took up farming at Bulgana.

Alfred was educated mostly at home, by his father, mother and uncle, until the drought of 1878-81 drove the family to Melbourne. There the elder Kenyon set up in Richmond, as bookseller, librarian, stationer and purveyor of artists' materials. Alfred attended St Stephen's Grammar School. In 1884 he matriculated at the University of Melbourne, beginning an arts degree as a preliminary to engineering. At the end of his third year he entered the Public Works Department, in order to gain the required practical experience, and remained there as a pupil engineer, chiefly at the drawing table. Kenyon lived at home, influenced by the Bohemian group, which included Arthur Streeton [q.v.] and G. R. Ashton [q.v.7], centred on his father's Richmond

shop and home. He also played baseball, cricket and football.

In August 1888 Kenyon was appointed draughtsman in the Department of Victorian Water Supply, and a year later junior engineering draughtsman, passing the departmental examination for the hydraulic engineers' certificate. His duties related to stream gauging and other measurements of water supply. In 1899 his section was reorganized as a branch of the Department of Mines and Water Supply and his professional duties were stated as 'supervising loan expenditure on Trust works and on Mallee Water Supply Works'. On 27 December 1900 he became an assistant engineer. In January 1906 Dr Thomas Cherry [q.v.7] persuaded him to join the Department of Agriculture as engineer of agriculture. In his specially created position Kenyon superintended irrigation and water-supply activities for farmers, boring for water, and construction of silos. He went on to open up the interior of the Mallee, being responsible for road construction and the provision of local water-supply by bores and tanks. He was concerned with large-scale methods of clearing and cultivation by the use of mechanical plant—steam traction engines—in place of horse teams. He contributed to the *Journal of Agriculture* on many topics, lectured in all the agricultural districts and explored much of the western Mallee.

In 1896 Kenyon was elected as a member of the Australasian Institute of Mining Engineers (later, of Mining and Metallurgy) and at once became assistant honorary secretary. He delivered his first paper to the Field Naturalists' Club of Victoria in 1906 and joined the Royal Society of Victoria, of which he was for a time librarian. In 1911 he was elected to the council of the recently formed Historical Society of Victoria. In his first paper in August he urged legislative action to preserve Aboriginal relics. His own collection of stone implements, which he had begun in 1898 and which by 1907 numbered over one thousand objects, had been purchased by the National Museum; he had set about building another, while continuing to help the museum with acquisitions and advice.

In 1910 the responsibility for crown lands improvement in the northern Mallee was transferred to the State Rivers and Water Supply Commission, and the staff with it. Kenyon was appointed engineer-in-charge, North-West Mallee, and opened wide tracts to farming. He also supervised large flood reclamation works at Kooweerup and Cardinia in western Gippsland, and stream improvements in all parts of Victoria. In 1915 he published his first major literary work, *The story of the Mallee*.

Despite his lack of an academic qualification Kenyon had become influential in the Melbourne University Engineering Society which he represented at the conference in Melbourne in February 1918 in furtherance of the amalgamation of the professional engineering institutions. He became an associate member of the Institution of Engineers, Australia, in 1920, and a member two years later.

In 1918 Kenyon was asked to report on land settlement for the dried fruits industry, needed for the placement of former soldiers. He recommended the development of Red Cliffs, the extension of Merbein, and the establishment of what was to become the Robinvale Irrigation District, all on the Murray River. He was placed in charge of developing the Red Cliffs District, which before long became prosperous. He maintained his headquarters in Melbourne. While distracted by his many outside interests, he still gave proper attention to the special problems of his area and displayed originality in solving them. For example, it was he who devised the 'ironclad catchment' for conserving the scanty rain for domestic and stock supplies.

In 1932 Kenyon was at last appointed a commissioner. Meanwhile, he had published *Pastures new* (1930), followed two years later by *Pastoral pioneers of Port Phillip*, both written with R. V. Billis. He had served his turn as chairman of the Melbourne division of the Institution of Engineers, Australia, in 1927, and as president of the Australasian Institute of Mining and Metallurgy in 1928. From 1931 to 1935 he was president of the (Royal) Historical Society of Victoria, and thereafter edited its journal. He collaborated with Charles Barrett [q.v.7] in writing two books dealing with Aboriginals, published in 1932 and 1934, and he was closely concerned with the historical aspects of the 1934 celebration of Victoria's centenary. Early in 1935 Kenyon retired from the Public Service. He dispersed his ethnological collection, and thereafter wrote more on historical subjects. He gave his card index of pioneers to the Public Library of Victoria. Before the war he had joined the Victorian Numismatic Society; he now spent more time as numismatist with the Public Library, and in 1938 he added the responsibilities of keeper of antiquities when that department was set up in the National Museum. He continued to write and lecture actively until shortly before his death at his home in Heidelberg on 14 May 1943. On 2 April 1895 he had married, with Australian Church forms, Alexandrine Aurélie Leontine Augustine Délépine from St Hélier, Jersey. She died in 1940. Their only daughter survived them.

Not everyone liked Alfred Kenyon. He was a man of strong opinions, and he expressed them without reserve, never withholding due criticism. However, the closer the association, the greater the respect and affection he inspired. His was an original mind, and his interests covered an extraordinarily wide field. He spoke French and read German, and moved widely in diverse cultural circles. He is remembered not only as a unique personality, but for his work in opening up the northern and western Mallee and extending the districts irrigated from the Murray, and for his pioneer studies in the ethnology of Victorian Aboriginals and pastoral history.

A portrait of Kenyon by Graham Thorley hangs in the Council Chambers at Red Cliffs.

Inst of Engineers, Aust, *Trans*, 1919; A'sian Inst of Mining and Metallurgy, *Procs*, 121, Feb 1941; *Vic Naturalist*, 60, June 1943; *Aqua*, Aug, Oct 1957; Kenyon papers (Royal Hist Soc of Vic, and LaTL).

RONALD MCNICOLL

KERNOT, WILFRED NOYCE (1868-1945) and MAURICE EDWIN (1852-1934), engineers, were the fifth and second sons of Charles Kernot [q.v.5] and his wife Mary Wright, née Archer. Charles Kernot had a fine home workshop and many of his descendants became prominent in the engineering profession, notably his eldest son William Charles [q.v.5], foundation professor of engineering at the University of Melbourne.

Wilfred was born on 18 July 1868 at Newtown, Geelong, Victoria, and attended the Flinders School. He matriculated at the university in 1885, and graduated B.C.E. in 1894 (M.Mech.Eng., 1918), meanwhile being appointed in 1891 as a lecturer in applied mechanics at the Working Men's College, Melbourne (Royal Melbourne Institute of Technology). On the establishment of the important day-diploma courses in 1898 Kernot became head of the college's engineering department, a position he retained with distinction; in 1901 he was one of the two highest-paid members of staff, on £380 a year.

In 1904-05 Kernot travelled to the United States of America and to Europe, investigating high-voltage transmission and engineering education. From about 1909 conditions at the Working Men's College became increasingly unpleasant, with internecine strife and attacks on the administration from the reinforced 'business' element on the college's council, and in 1911 Kernot resigned to join the staff of the engineering school at the university, where he had for some time been undertaking responsible part-time work. His departure from the Working Men's College was regretted in technical education circles.

Kernot became associate professor in engineering in 1923, and from 1932 to 1936 was professor, in succession to Henry Payne [q.v.]. Kernot's appointment to the chair came just fifty years after his brother's appointment to the same position.

At the university Kernot specialized in the teaching of graphics and engineering design, with a reputation as an able teacher and administrator. His lecture on 'Mechanical Paradoxes', employing ingenious home-made devices, is still remembered, as is his nick-name 'Crunch', from his mannerism of muttering and grinding his teeth. He had strong extramural interests. He was a director of the New Australian Electric Co., of which his brother William had been chairman from its foundation in 1882 until 1900, and where he was known as the 'trouble man'; with A. G. Thomas he won a competition for the design of a swing-bridge over the Yarra at Spencer Street, and he designed several other bridges and irrigation works; he was employed as a consultant by such instrumentalities as the Metropolitan Gas Co., the Defence Department, the Commonwealth Public Works Department and the Council for Scientific and Industrial Research. Kernot was recognized as an expert on patents, electric tramways and power generation, but worked widely over the fields of mechanical, civil and electrical engineering. Professor Charles Moorhouse, one of his students, has called him 'one of the last of the general engineers'.

Kernot was also active in the organization of the engineering profession, and was president of the Institution of Electrical Engineers of Australia (Melbourne) in 1917, as well as acting federal president; president of the Working Men's College (1920); and was administratively associated with C.S.I.R., the Royal Society of Victoria, the Institution of Civil Engineers (London) and Caulfield Technical School. At the university he was dean of the faculties of engineering and architecture.

After retirement Wilfred Kernot acted as examiner to Melbourne technical colleges and spent much time in his well-equipped home workshop at Malvern, where his interest in clocks led to his constructing gearing for time signals from the Melbourne Observatory. His personality was regarded as humorous, patient, kindly and jovial. He died, unmarried, of coronary vascular disease on 17 May 1945 and was cremated, leaving the considerable fortune of £71 943, spread over a number of careful investments.

Maurice Edwin Kernot was born on 10 June 1852 at Geelong and educated at the Gheringhap Street State School and the High Church School, of which he was dux.

Matriculating in 1869, he did not complete his engineering course at the university but worked 'on the job' with the Water Supply Department, the Mines Department, and from 1874 the Railways Department. Kernot married Caroline Grace Home in 1880. He achieved some distinction in his career as a railway engineer, being 'the first to apply the principles of technical analysis to railway location in Victoria', and achieved large savings through his administration of the 'butty gang' or 'direct labor' system, which replaced the letting of large contracts in the 1890s. While he was engineer-in-chief of the Victorian Railways from 1907 to 1923, over 1000 miles (1600 km) of railways were built.

In 1914 Maurice Kernot investigated railway practice in Europe and America and he was active, especially after retirement, in the affairs of the Institution of Engineers, Australia, being awarded its Peter Nicol Russell [q.v.6] medal in 1933; he was also awarded the Kernot memorial medal in 1928.

Kernot was an active member of the Presbyterian Church, a methodical man with a sense of humour and simple tastes. He died on 13 January 1934 and was cremated. He was survived by his wife, a daughter and a son Charles Home Kernot (1885-1963), who became chief engineer of the State Electricity Commission of Victoria.

Another brother, Frederick Archer Kernot (1854-1920), dentist, actively aided the transition of dentistry from a trade to a profession, served on the Dental Board of Victoria and the council of the Australian College of Dentistry, and took some part in the establishment of the original Dental Hospital in Melbourne. He was also a well-known amateur photographer.

J. Smith (ed), *Cyclopedia of Victoria*, 1 (Melb, 1903); *Scientific Aust*, 20 Mar 1906; Inst of Engineers, Aust, *J*, 8, 1936, p 277; *Punch* (Melb), 25 Apr 1918; *Argus*, 18 May 1945; letter from H. Payne, 21 June 1923, Monash papers (NL); W. N. Kernot papers (LaTL).   S. MURRAY-SMITH

KERR, DAVID McFARLANE McLACHLAN ('ANDY') (1867-1955), bookmaker, was born on 30 December 1867 in Edinburgh, son of Dickson Kerr, lathsplitter, and his wife Catherine, née Kerr. Migrating to Sydney in 1885 as footman to Lord Carrington [q.v.3], he married Sydney-born Annie Elizabeth Butler, daughter of a schoolteacher, on 8 February 1893 at St Thomas's

Roman Catholic Church, Lewisham. He showed an early interest in Labor politics and made good as a grocer at Newtown, Marrickville and Erskineville.

Kerr began his career as a bookmaker at the pony tracks of Sydney and in 1903 advanced to the major metropolitan racecourses. He established his reputation by offering to take bets on any sporting event, whatever and wherever, and his style earned him the title, which he adopted as his slogan, the 'Longest Odds Bettor on Earth'. He once laid a bet of £300 to nothing and another of £50 to a cigar and won them; in the 1913 Melbourne Cup he laid odds of 1000 to one against Golden Shore and bet the punter who accepted £10 to £1 that the horse would run last; it finished second-last. In 1923 he paid out £15 000 to £45 on the Epicure-David Doncaster-Sydney Cup double.

His betting stand resembled a sideshow: his bagmen bore his name emblazoned in bold block letters on their leather satchels and, bedecked in straw boaters, his team of clerks noted the bets while Kerr walked among the punters engaging in badinage while laying the odds—he teased female punters for being 'pests personified'. He had a rule that, on taking silver or gold in payment of a wager, if he missed when he flipped the coin into the assistant's bag the crowd might scramble for the money. Nicknamed 'Andy' and known for most of his life as 'The Coogee Bunyip' because of his fondness for swimming there, he was generous to charities and owned such diverse interests as the Gaiety Theatre, the *Variety Magazine*, a jewellery shop in Market Street and the Bondi Casino nightclub. In his heyday from 1903 to 1930 Kerr was a natty dresser with a three-piece suit, wing-collar and striped tie; blue-eyed, 6 ft. 3 ins. (191 cm) tall, slim and clean-shaven with spruce fair hair, he smoked cigars and flaunted diamonds in his tie-pin, ring and cuff-links. He belonged to Tattersall's Club, enjoyed cricket, fishing and motoring, and treasured an illuminated address presented to him in 1911 by Sydney's leading sportsmen. His fortunes collapsed utterly during the Depression, he became a commission agent and, though he retained his dignity and wit, he never regained his place as a dashing leader of Sydney's turf world. He adopted a philosophical attitude, saying that 'Lady Luck' could give 'a lift or a raspberry'.

In 1941 Kerr wrote a series of 'Random reminiscences' for Sydney *Truth* and *Sportsman*; after his wife died he married a widow, Charlotte Elizabeth Weston-Campbell, née Parker, cakeshop proprietress, on 6 April 1942. He frequently revisited Coogee, recalling past times with other old identities, and indulged his hobby of cooking at the home of a granddaughter at Kirribilli. Predeceased by his three sons and three daughters, Kerr died there on 9 October 1955 and was buried in the Presbyterian section of Northern Suburbs cemetery.

Newspaper Cartoonists' Assn of NSW, *Sydneyites as we see 'em 1913-14-15* (Syd, 1915?); J. Holledge, *The great Australian gamble* (Syd, 1966); W. F. Wannan (comp), *Australian folklore* (Melb, 1970); *People* (Syd), 24 May 1950; *Grit*, 30 Oct 1941; *Sun* (Syd), 18 Dec 1954, 29 Oct 1975; *Sun-Herald*, 16 Oct 1945; *Daily Examiner* (Grafton), 13 July 1977; information and newscuttings from Mrs P. Ryan, Coffs Harbour, NSW.   JOHN RITCHIE

KERR, GEORGE (1853-1930), blacksmith, politician and grazier, was born on 7 February 1853 at Beadnell, Northumberland, England, son of John Johnson Kerr, farm-labourer, and his wife Catherine, née Atcheson. He trained as a blacksmith and migrated to Queensland in 1877.

At the new Croydon goldfield in 1888-90 Kerr acquired a reputation as a mining speculator. In 1891 he set up his forge at Tambo in the Barcoo electorate and in 1893 won the seat for the Labor Party. From October 1895 to June 1896 and from July 1901 to September 1907 Kerr was a member of Labor's central political executive; he was president in 1904-05 and treasurer in 1905-07. Leader of the Parliamentary Labor Party from May 1904 to May 1907, he joined the Kidston [q.v.] faction after the 1905 split and was minister for railways in July-November 1907 and minister for railways and public works in February-October 1908. He earned a reputation for humane administration. In October 1908 Kidston formed a coalition with (Sir) Robert Philp [q.v.]. Unable to deny so completely his labour origins, Kerr resigned his portfolios. He stood as an Independent at the October 1909 election but was defeated by the endorsed Labor candidate for Barcoo, the formidable T. J. Ryan [q.v.].

Kerr believed that parliamentary representatives were 'the reflex of the people' and that their brief was 'to frame a political programme that is possible of attainment within a reasonable time'. Thus he had supported Kidston's proposal for coalition with Morgan [q.v.] Liberals in 1903 in the hope of achieving adult suffrage and other electoral reforms and opposed, as impracticable, the socialist objective adopted at the 1907 Labor-in-Politics convention. As parliamentary Labor leader he supported continuation of the coalition but was decisively defeated when the convention resolved that Labor should fight the next election alone.

Industrious and moderate despite his suspension with others in September 1894, Kerr was noted for his unassuming tenacity and responsible approach to parliamentary matters. He rejected the popular Labor view that a member is a delegate rather than a representative, but his frequent trips throughout his large electorate, his regular attendance at and reports to Australian Workers' Union meetings and his close attention to local deputations assisted his political survival; however, his majorities declined at the elections of 1907 and 1908 against endorsed Labor candidates. The *Western Champion* depicted him as St George defending the Barcoo maiden against the dragon of extremism. Kerr's faith in Queensland's potential overrode his reservations about capitalism and he was party to Kidston's 'apostasy' on land sales and private railways because of their developmental emphasis. A Methodist and a Freemason with a firm belief in the human potential for self-improvement, Kerr was particularly interested in friendly societies. He was compared frequently to Longfellow's village smith. The *Western Champion* reported that 'he left his peaceful smithy under the gidyea tree at Tambo to become a political angel and Minister of Grace in the Councils of the Nation'. His faith and somewhat plodding tenacity were best conveyed by a *Worker* rhymester:

> His brow was wet with honest sweat
> He earned six quid per week
> And looked the whole House in the face
> When he began to speak.

Married in May 1882 to Florence McCulloch at Bogantungan, he was left a widower in February 1883. On 17 February 1891 at Tambo he married with Church of England rites a widow, Susan Jane Moore, née Deacon; they had one daughter. After leaving public life he acquired grazing properties at Longreach and Cloncurry. Kerr retired to Brisbane and died there on 18 January 1930. He was buried in Toowong cemetery.

D. J. Murphy et al (eds), *Prelude to power* (Brisb, 1970); *Worker* (Brisb), 22 Jan 1930; *Brisbane Courier*, 15 Mar 1907; *Western Champion* (Barcaldine), 27 Apr 1907, 1 Apr 1908; *Queenslander*, 23 Jan 1930.

RODNEY SULLIVAN

KERR, JAMES SEMPLE (1836-1915), schoolteacher, was born on 29 August 1836 at Stewarton, Ayrshire, Scotland, son of John Kerr, butcher, and his wife Agnes, née Semple. Attending lectures at Glasgow and Anderson's universities in 1852-53, he trained as a teacher at the Glasgow Free Normal School in 1854-55 and taught at

Gourock Free School for six years. In 1863 he joined the teaching staff of the Queensland Board of General Education and spent five years as headmaster at Warwick and fifteen months at Fortitude Valley. In 1870 he was promoted to inspector and training master.

Becoming headmaster of the Brisbane Boys' Normal School in 1874, Kerr used his impressive physical presence, strength of character and awesome energy to fashion an institution renowned for its strict discipline upon pupils and teachers alike and for its academic standards, demonstrated each year by the long list of grammar school scholarship winners.

Kerr's devotion to the Protestant work ethic sprang from his firm Presbyterian convictions. Believing in the teacher as a moral example, he scorned laziness or shirking and was himself painstaking about school management. Parental concern over the length of home lessons and the daily two hours of extra tuition for scholarship candidates together with the jealousy of other schools caused an official inquiry in 1892. Kerr defended his policy vigorously. Despite a cramped urban environment with overcrowded classrooms and makeshift buildings alongside the girls' and infants' central schools and opposite the noisy and dusty road to Brisbane Central Railway Station, the Normal School boasted 1132 boys on the roll in 1888. Only 282 came from the immediate vicinity of the school.

He offered the substance of his educational convictions in evidence to royal commissions on education (1874), the civil service (1888) and a university (1891). A firm supporter of the British national system with its teaching of 'common Christianity', he regretted Queensland's move to purely secular education in the 1875 Education Act. He continually urged the foundation of a teachers' training college linked to a university. He preferred indirect to direct compulsion of attendance in a young colony heavily dependent on juvenile labour. An early believer in women teachers for young boys, he advocated equal pay for equal work and criticized the requirement for teachers' wives in rural schools to serve as unpaid assistants. 'The female mind', he said, 'is the clear mind of the colony'. As a representative of the East Moreton Teachers' Association before the civil service commission, he boldly criticized the bureaucratic high-handedness of Chief Inspector David Ewart and told of teachers' grievances over low salaries, uneven classifications, demoralizing transfers and poor rural housing. To the commission on a university he urged that state-subsidized grammar schools should be replaced by primary schools upgraded to matriculation level. He retired from the department in 1906 and, with his wife, ran a private school in the suburbs until 1912. He died in Brisbane on 18 February 1915 and was buried in Toowong cemetery.

Kerr was married four times: at Gourock in September 1859 to Margaret Black who left one daughter; at Warwick in January 1865 to Jane Twatt who left three daughters; to Wilhelmine Scott in Brisbane in April 1877; and to schoolmistress Jane Anne McLeod in September 1888.

V&P (LA Qld), 1875, 2, p 171, 1888, 1, p 500, 1891, 3, p 873; J. S. Kerr testimonials (History Unit, Dept of Education, Brisb); Brisb Boys' Central School files, EDU/Z326-27 (QSA).   T. WATSON

KERR, WILLIAM WARREN (1864-1949), businessman and government adviser, was born on 21 December 1864 at Kilmore, Victoria, eleventh child of John Wilson Kerr, head teacher at Kilmore National School and later town clerk of Fitzroy, and his wife Ellen, née Gardiner, both Irish born. He was educated in 1877-79 at Melbourne Church of England Grammar School. In 1885 with Henry Richardson he formed Richardson & Kerr, insurance brokers. He married Jane Buchanan, daughter of Rev. Alexander Gosman [q.v.4], at Augustine Congregational Church, Hawthorn, on 7 April 1887. Kerr became a deacon and chairman of trustees of the Independent Church, Collins Street, Melbourne. In 1905-06 he was chairman of the Congregational Union of Victoria and was later treasurer of the Congregational Union of Australia and New Zealand. He was a member of Kew Borough Council in 1904-12 and mayor for the year 1907-08.

During World War I Warren Kerr became a prominent adviser of governments, serving as chairman of the Commonwealth War Savings Council and of the Victorian War Savings Committee. He was president of the Melbourne Chamber of Commerce in 1916-18 and of the Associated Chambers of Commerce of Australia in 1918-20. After the war he optimistically accepted 'new ideals of social justice', encouraged employers to face industrial disharmony 'on the lines of equity and justice and humanitarianism' and deplored 'useless party strife'.

In 1920 Kerr was appointed chairman of a Commonwealth royal commission which was intended generally to overhaul the taxation system. In the first twelve months from October, 118 public sittings were held and 191 witnesses examined. The final, fifth report was presented in February 1923.

Meanwhile, important amendments to taxation law, based on the commission's recommendations, had been made in the Income Tax Assessment Acts of 1921 and 1922: boards of appeal were established and businessmen, as well as primary producers, were allowed to average income over five years. Kerr's advice influenced the shape of the Commonwealth-States Financial Agreement of 1927. That year he represented Australia at the World Economic Conference, Geneva, Switzerland. He had been appointed C.B.E. in 1918 and C.M.G. in 1924.

In his later years Kerr bore a heavy load of institutional commitments. From 1923 he was a commissioner of the State Savings Bank of Victoria and chairman in 1931-48. He was president of the Charity Organisation Society from 1923 to 1945 and important in shaping State relief policies during the Depression. He was also grand master of the United Grand Lodge Freemasons of Victoria in 1932-35, an international Rotary delegate, sometime president of the Constitutional Club, a director of the Mutual Store Ltd, and a founding council-member of Swinburne [q.v.] Technical College from 1908. He was active in the Scouting movement and Toc H; bowls was his chief pastime.

Kerr died on 2 July 1949 at his home in Kew, survived by a daughter and a son, and was buried in Box Hill cemetery. His estate was sworn for probate at £25 696. At the memorial service Judge Book singled out Kerr's 'remarkable humility', 'inspiring and persuasive eloquence' and 'great capacity for true brotherliness'. Another son had been killed on Gallipoli. In her grief Jane Kerr dedicated her remaining life to the abolition of war. In 1915 she issued a leaflet, 'An appeal to women', and later became vice-president of the Sisterhood of International Peace. She died in 1945.

C. A. Grant, *500 Victorians* (Melb, 1934); E. M. Moore, *The quest for peace as I have known it in Australia* (Melb, 1950); J. A. Maher (comp), *Tale of a century: Kilmore 1837-1937* (Melb, 1938); *Southern Congregationalist*, 2 Aug 1949; *SMH*, 29 Jan, 16 Mar 1920; *Age, Argus*, 4 July 1949.

GEOFFREY SERLE

KERRY, CHARLES HENRY (1857-1928), photographer, was born on 3 April 1857 at Bombala, New South Wales, son of Samuel Kerry, commissioner's orderly and later grazier from Derbyshire, England, and his native-born wife Margaret, née Blay. Educated at Bombala and in Sydney, at 17 he joined Alexander Henry Lamartiniere's photographic studio and about 1883 became a partner. Soon afterwards Lamartiniere absconded with Kerry's small capital, but he carried on in partnership with C. D. Jones, paid off the firm's debts and turned a small portrait studio into the colony's largest photographic organization.

Kerry sold albums of high-quality pictures of the countryside; he filled his shop window with news pictures of the latest funeral, cricket match or vice-regal garden party and sold prints to the public. In 1885 he was asked to prepare an exhibit of Aboriginal portraits and corroboree pictures for the 1886 Colonial and Indian Exhibition in London. In 1891 he was commissioned by the government to photograph the Jenolan and Yarrangobilly caves. The project, carried out by candlelight and magnesium flashes, was hazardous. At Yarrangobilly he found and named the Jersey [q.v.] cavern after the governor. He also visited leading pastoral stations in New South Wales professionally.

At St Mark's Church, Darling Point, Kerry married Delphine Hilda Vivian on 20 January 1897. Next year his luxurious three-storied studio was opened and he used electric arc lights to photograph guests at a ball. By 1900 Kerry & Co. handled the major illustrations for the local press. In 1908 he photographed the visit of the American fleet and the Burns-Johnson fight, when he rushed the exposures of each round to the studio to be printed and put in his show-window within minutes of their arrival.

Long interested in mineralogy, Kerry floated tin-mining companies in the Federated Malay States and Siam, and was chairman of the Malayan Tin Corporation and of the Ratrut Basin and Takuopa Valley tin-dredging companies until his death. He handed over his studio to a relation in 1913 to concentrate on his mining interests and twice visited the East. A keen angler and bushman, Kerry had joined the Sydney Lancers in the 1880s and in five years won twenty-five prizes in cavalry sports. In the 1890s he took up clay pigeon shooting, in 1893-94 won the New South Wales open handicap and was a founder of the New South Wales Gun Club. He pioneered snow sports at Kiandra and in the winter of 1897 led a party from Jindabyne to the summit of Mt Kosciusko, which led to the opening up of the area for skiing and the naming of a run after him. He was president of the Kosciusko Alpine Club.

Soon after his return from a visit to the Great Barrier Reef, Kerry died suddenly at his home at Neutral Bay on 26 May 1928 and was cremated with Anglican rites. He was survived by his wife and son who inherited his estate, valued for probate at £8303.

J. Cato, *The story of the camera in Australia* (Melb, 1955); *A'sian Photo-Review*, Mar 1952; *ISN*, 11 Apr 1891; *Sydney Mail*, 23 Sept 1903; *SMH*, 19 Dec 1924, 24, 29 Oct 1927, 28 May 1928.

KEAST BURKE*

KERSHAW, JAMES ANDREW (1866-1946), scientist, was born on 13 April 1866 at Fitzroy, Melbourne, son of William Kershaw, taxidermist, and his second wife Elizabeth, née Boyde, both from the north of England. He was educated at Alma Road State School, St Kilda, and later at East St Kilda Grammar School.

On 1 October 1883 Kershaw was appointed to the National Museum as assistant taxidermist, helping his father who for many years had been in charge of preserving and mounting the museum's 'unstuffed collection' of insects, skeletons, fossils and shells. The director, (Sir) Frederick McCoy [q.v.5], later made James his first assistant, giving him technical training in general zoology and museum administration.

Kershaw's training took place during an exciting new era of taxonomic zoology centrally linked with the museum. Under the leadership of McCoy, Sir Ferdinand Mueller and A. W. Howitt [qq.v.5,4], he worked with enthusiastic naturalists such as C. J. Gabriel, Charles French [qq.v.8], T. S. Hall, (Sir) Baldwin Spencer, George Lyell [qq.v.] and O. A. Sayce. With the help of French and Lyell he branched out into the broader fields of entomology, a subject in which he continued to specialize.

In July 1890 James Kershaw was promoted to taxidermist; his father retired a year later. On McCoy's death in 1899 the museum was transferred to the Public Library site and Professor Spencer was appointed honorary director. Kershaw was made curator of the zoological collection. He succeeded Spencer as director in 1929 and on retirement in 1931 was appointed first honorary curator of zoology.

Kershaw travelled widely on collecting trips for the museum, accompanying the Royal Australasian Ornithologists' Union to Bass Strait in 1908. He visited the Bass Strait islands again in 1909, accompanied Dr W. Macgillivray to the Barrier Reef in Queensland in 1913, undertook a special investigation into the habits of the platypus in the Hopkins River, Victoria, in 1911, and in 1921 visited Ooldea in Western Australia, collecting ethnological and zoological material.

With others, Kershaw was responsible in 1908 for the reservation of Wilson's Promontory as a national park and sanctuary for native fauna and flora; he was honorary secretary to the park's committee of management in 1908-46. He became a member of the Royal Society of Victoria in 1900, a councillor in 1902, president in 1918, honorary secretary in 1920-23, honorary librarian in 1924-25 and trustee in 1922. He was also a fellow of the Royal Entomological Society of London and a corresponding member of the Zoological Society of London. An active member of the Field Naturalists' Club of Victoria from 1888 and later president, he published extensively in the *Victorian Naturalist*, including ten papers on entomology.

On 23 April 1889 at Windsor he had married Elsie Charlotte Brown with Church of Christ forms. He died on 16 February 1946 at his home in Windsor, predeceased by his wife and survived by three sons. He was buried in Brighton cemetery. Kindly and sincere, he was always encouraging to young people, with whom he was very popular. However, when necessary he could be firm and forceful.

Kershaw's most outstanding contributions to the National Museum were the acquisition by donation of the H. L. White [q.v.] collection of Australian birds and eggs in 1927, and the George Lyell collection of Australian Lepidoptera in 1931.

A. Musgrave, *Bibliography of Australian entomology 1775-1930* (Syd, 1932); R. T. M. Pescott, *Collections of a century* (Melb, 1954); *Vic Naturalist*, 62 (1945-46), p 243. R. T. M. PESCOTT

KESTEVEN, HEREWARD LEIGHTON (1881-1964), medical scientist, was born on 16 January 1881 at Levuka, Fiji, son of Leighton Kesteven, district medical officer, and his wife Caroline Elizabeth, née Eames. In the 1880s the family moved to Brisbane and in 1891 to Sydney where he attended Sydney Church of England Grammar School until he left because of his father's bankruptcy. In 1903 Kesteven was appointed technical assistant to the curator of the Australian Museum.

Married to Ivy Valentine Smith, a professional musician, on 18 October 1905 at Randwick Registry Office, he attended the University of Sydney (B.Sc., 1909; D.Sc., 1911; M.B., 1914; Ch.M., 1916). His doctoral thesis was on 'The constitution of the gastropod protoconch'. From 1908 to 1913 Kesteven was lecturer-in-charge of the department of physiology at Sydney Technical College. For the benefit of students he published *A manual of practical bio-chemistry* (1912).

Entering general practice in 1915 at Belmore, Kesteven later moved to Queensland where he practised at Gin Gin and Gladstone. In 1919 he returned to Sydney where he gained his M.D., receiving the University medal for his research in comparative anatomy. At Maroubra, where he set up practice,

he used the local cinema as his surgery during the influenza epidemic.

Kesteven soon abandoned the pressures and restrictions of a suburban practice for Bulahdelah where he remained from 1920 to 1936. Patients unable to pay cash plied him with local produce instead. Deprived of regular research facilities, Kesteven added a laboratory and dissecting room to his house. The locals, knowing of his research interests, provided lizards and snakes for dissection. Appointed honorary zoologist to the Australian Museum, Sydney, in 1926, he wrote for its publications and for those of the Linnean Society of New South Wales and the Royal Society of New South Wales of which he was a member.

A person of great energy and varied interests, Kesteven was largely responsible for providing Bulahdelah with a hospital, which he helped to build. He assembled the town's first radio set. He played tennis, cricket and billiards enthusiastically and thumped out Gilbert and Sullivan with particular relish. A keen farmer and botanist, he acquired and worked a property near Bulahdelah. Kesteven had opinions on economic matters which he was good enough to share with John Maynard Keynes. In the Federal election of 1934 Kesteven stood against Sir Earle Page [q.v.] on a Douglas Credit platform and lost. He took a keen interest in the opening of the Myall Lakes and was a vociferous advocate of northern development.

Returning in 1936 to Sydney, where most of his family were now living, Kesteven became medical director of Goodyear Tyre and Rubber Co. (Australia) Ltd. After some wartime work in armament factories in the Lithgow area, in 1942-46 he was director of medical services to the Allied Works Council and organized the provision of medical services to the civilian work force. In this period Kesteven wrote a series of articles for the *Australasian Manufacturer*, later published as *An industrial medical-efficiency service*. His attempt in 1946 to establish an industrial medical service at Richmond, Melbourne, failed.

Between 1942 and 1946 the Australian Museum published his 'The evolution of the skull and the cephalic muscles: a comparative study of their development and adult morphology', the result, in Kesteven's words, of 'half a life-time devoted to the small portion of comparative anatomy and embryology it deals with'. He won the Walter Burfitt [q.v.7] prize in 1944 and the David Syme [q.v.6] prize in 1946.

Kesteven's first wife had suffered a cerebral haemorrhage in 1936 and, after a long and agonizing illness, died in 1943. On 24 June 1944 at St Mark's Church of

England, Darling Point, he married Louise Ray Smith, a nurse. Ill health and the need for a warmer climate took him in 1948 to Queensland. He practised at Cooktown, Palmwoods, Maroochydore and Brighton where he died suddenly on 18 May 1964. Survived by his wife, and four sons and four daughters of his first marriage, he was cremated with Anglican rites.

MJA, 3 Oct 1964; Bankruptcy file 10/22858 (NSWA); family information.   D. R. WALKER

KETHEL, ALEXANDER (1832-1916), seaman, timber merchant and politician, was born on 2 November 1832 at Perth, Scotland, son of William Kethel, carpenter, and his wife Mary, née Watson. Briefly attending village schools, at 10 he became an errand boy for his grandfather and in 1845 was apprenticed to the master of a schooner engaged in the Baltic trade. After many adventures at sea, he jumped ship in Sydney in March 1853, worked on coastal vessels under an assumed name and visited the Victorian goldfields. Back in Sydney he obtained his master's certificate but a third shipwreck led him to abandon the sea in 1857.

Employed by John Booth [q.v.3] at his sawmill at Balmain, Kethel soon became foreman of the timber-yard and in 1870, when Booth retired, leased the business with two partners. The mill was destroyed by fire in 1874 and Kethel went into business as a wholesale timber merchant, wharfinger and commission agent, and in 1877 leased the Market Wharf. He prospered, leased other wharves and acquired several ships, including steamers, engaged in the coastal trade. Late in life he was briefly engaged in the coal trade. He retired from active business about 1900; before and after, he made several long visits to Britain.

Outgoing and optimistic, Kethel was a voracious reader; if undisciplined, his mind was sharp and logical. He had a fund of experience which he could draw upon to illustrate a point, and was an entertaining and forceful speaker. In middle age he had bushy white eyebrows and a neat curly beard. On 1 August 1861 in Sydney he had married Mary Anne Yeates (d. 1913) from Dublin, with Presbyterian forms. For many years he was an elder of St Andrew's Presbyterian Church. A council-member of the Caledonian Society in the mid-1870s, he helped to found the Highland Society of New South Wales in 1877; he was a council-member and vice-president and contributed frequently to its publication, the *Scottish Australasian*. He became president of the Burns' Anniver-

sary Club in 1892 and helped to arrange Sydney's Highland Games.

Kethel never forgot the poverty of his childhood and supported associations designed to advance the self-improvement of working men. In 1856 he had joined the Manchester Unity Independent Order of Odd Fellows (grandmaster, 1876) and was active in the Sydney Mechanics' School of Arts. He became a vice-president of the technical college it established in 1878 and in 1881 with Norman Selfe and Edward Dowling [qq.v.6,8] recommended greater funding for technical education. He was a member of the Board of Technical Education in 1883-89, a trustee of the Public Library of New South Wales in 1901-16 and a member of the executive of the National Shipwreck Relief Society of New South Wales and of the local League of Ancient Mariners.

Elected to the Legislative Assembly in 1885 and 1887, Kethel was firmly committed to free trade and supported Sir Henry Parkes [q.v.5]. He did not stand for re-election in 1889 but was nominated to the Legislative Council in 1895. He spoke in parliament on shipping, coastal ports, friendly societies, technical and agricultural education and forestry. In 1888 he carried resolutions proposing the establishment of an agricultural college and a system of experiment farms. He served on the Parliamentary Standing Committee on Public Works in 1888-89 and 1901-04 and on the royal commissions on the extension of the railway into the city (1890-91) and into the charges against E. M. G. Eddy [q.v.8] (1892). In 1892-94 he was a member of the Council of Arbitration and later chairman of the Board for Exports.

Kethel devoted much of his energy to forest conservation. In 1889 he persuaded Parkes to bring the ineffective forestry branch under the premier's control and to appoint J. Ednie Brown [q.v.3] to head it. He crusaded for permanent reserves, listing the variety of native timbers and evoking the spectre of their disappearance. He urged appointment of properly trained staff, establishment of a forestry school and placement of forestry management under an independent commission. In 1907 he chaired a royal commission which extensively investigated the State's forest resources and practices.

Predeceased by his wife and two sons, he died at Castle Hill on 23 June 1916 and was buried in Rookwood cemetery. Two sons and three daughters survived him.

Scottish A'sian, Sept 1911, Aug-Dec 1913, Jan-Apr 1914, July 1916, Feb, Apr, June, July 1918, May 1924; *T&CJ*, 29 Oct 1892, 14 Sept 1895, 6 Oct 1909; *SMH*, 24 June 1916; newspaper cuttings, vol 145, p 102 (ML).   MARK LYONS

KEYNES, JOSEPH (1810-1883), and RICHARD ROBINSON (1857-1928), sheep-breeders, were father and son. Joseph was born on 29 July 1810 at Blandford, Dorset, England, eldest son of Richard Keynes, Congregational minister, and his wife Harriet, sister of the evangelical Congregational preacher John Angell James. Joseph was educated by his father and decided to be a farmer. At 28 he was renting land at Blandford and noted as a talented sheep-breeder. Richard Keynes wrote to George Fife Angas [q.v.1] in 1838 seeking information on South Australia for Joseph and his brother William. Quick to notice a Dissenter with practical skills, Angas offered William a workman's job and Joseph the position of overseer of his stock and land in South Australia in the partnership, Joseph Keynes & Co.

Joseph accepted, arrived in 1839 and managed the farm at Flaxman's Valley for Angas. In 1841 he leased the property north of Adelaide near Angaston which became Keyneton Estate and remains in the family. However his performance was not promising. His partnership with Angas was marred by inexperience and gullibility in commercial dealings and an inability to adapt to colonial life; it was dissolved in 1843 and Keynes declared his bankruptcy in 1846, leaving Angas with £9000 in debts, great resentment and injured pride.

But by 1850 the once despairing farmer had become a member of the 'squattocracy', with land in the Barossa Ranges, the Wakefield Survey and at Mount Remarkable and a high reputation as a merino sheep-breeder. From 1840 he had been a committee-member of the (Royal) Agricultural and Horticultural Society. In March 1850 he married Ellen Robinson; they had three daughters and one surviving son. But in 1862 Ellen deserted him for the local doctor and they were divorced in November. The scandal forced Keynes to England next year.

However, he returned in 1864 and on 8 March 1866 married Anne Taunton Stephenson, née Scammell, a widow. While offspring of his first marriage went to England for their education and protection from colonial gossip-mongers, Keynes systematically amassed thousands of acres, wealth and social respect, being a member of the North Rhine District Council from its formation in 1873 to 1883. He died on 14 May 1883 at Lockleys, Adelaide, and was buried in the Congregational cemetery at Keyneton, the town named for him.

Richard Keynes, born on 15 April 1857, returned to South Australia at 20 after education at Parkstone, Dorset, and an apprenticeship to London woolbrokers. Unlike his zealous father, Richard seemed disinclined to work Keyneton station and became overfond of Adelaide's social life and playing polo.

But his father's death brought the property's management on to his shoulders and he too became a notable sheep-breeder. He expanded the station's business to include the breeding of draughthorses and Shorthorn cattle. He too was on the North Rhine District Council, for thirty-seven years, twenty-nine as chairman. On 27 August 1884 Keynes had married Margaret Ruth Shannon; they had three sons and two daughters. The stud's wool had won prizes at the Philadelphia Centennial Exhibition in 1876 and the Colonial and Indian Exhibition in 1886, as well as at local and interstate shows. Richard Keynes died on 25 November 1928 and was buried next to his father in Keyneton cemetery.

R. Cockburn, *Pastoral pioneers of South Australia*, 1 (Adel, 1925); Angas family and Keynes family papers (held by R. W. Linn, Dept of Hist, Univ Adel).   R. W. LINN

KEYS, CONSTANCE MABEL (1886-1964), nurse, was born on 30 October 1886 at Mount Perry, Queensland, seventh child of Irish-born James Keys, schoolteacher, and his wife Margaret, née Pelham, who was English. She trained at the Brisbane General Hospital and enlisted as a staff nurse in the Australian Army Nursing Service, Australian Imperial Force, on 21 September 1914; she embarked three days later.

On arriving in Egypt Nurse Keys was posted to a British military hospital at Abbassia and then to the 1st Australian General Hospital at Heliopolis where she treated casualties from Gallipoli. She was promoted sister on 21 November 1915. On 4 December she joined the hospital ship *Themistocles* which was filled with wounded, and after arriving in Sydney re-embarked on 1 March 1916 for Egypt. There she briefly joined the 3rd A.G.H. at Abbassia, then went to England and on 5 October took up duty at the Kitchener Hospital, Brighton. She served in hospitals in England until 15 November 1917 when she was transferred to the 3rd A.G.H. at Abbeville, France. By this time she had been promoted head sister, A.A.N.S. On 9 February 1918 she went up the line as sister-in-charge of the 2nd Australian Casualty Clearing Station at Trois Arbres near Bailleul.

For most of 1918 Constance Keys was seldom far from the front line. During the German offensive in March she and her staff were ordered to transfer the 2nd A.C.C.S.

to Hazebrouck. On 12 April Hazebrouck was shelled and the station was transferred to St Omer which that night was heavily bombed. Five days later Sister Keys and her nurses rejoined their unit at Blendecques near St Omer and remained there until 4 September when the station was moved forward again to Hazebrouck. Conditions throughout this period were appalling. The retreat from Bailleul took place in cold, wet weather which made movement difficult and increased the suffering of the wounded and the escaping civilians. By the time Sister Keys had reached St Omer she and her staff had become, in her own words, 'refugees'. At Blendecques they had to treat many gassed patients, cope with an outbreak of influenza in June, and deal in July and August with casualties suffering from exhaustion as well as from wounds.

After their advance to Hazebrouck in September the 2nd A.C.C.S. staff still had to nurse large numbers of sick and wounded. Two weeks later Sister Keys moved south with her staff to St Venant and then to Estaires, near Armentières, where many wounded civilians were admitted to the station. On 15 November the 2nd A.C.C.S. received cases at Tournai, Belgium, and after three weeks work there, opened again at Ath near Brussels. In January 1919 work slackened but in February influenza again broke out. Early in March the work of the station was handed over to the Royal Army Medical Corps Field Ambulance, and Sister Keys returned to England, where she spent some months with the 1st A.G.H. at Sutton Veny. She left England on 1 November and was discharged from the A.I.F. on 17 February 1920 in Melbourne.

Sister Keys was one of the most highly decorated nurses in the A.A.N.S. She was twice mentioned in dispatches (1 December 1916 and 31 December 1918), received the Royal Red Cross, second class (29 December 1916) and first class (3 June 1919), and was awarded the Médaille des Epidémies in recognition of work for French refugees.

After her return to Queensland Miss Keys became matron of a convalescent hospital for returned soldiers at Broadwater, Brisbane. While there she met and married on 3 December 1921 at Galloways Hill, Lionel Hugh Kemp-Pennefather, a Gallipoli veteran, who was in charge of the farm section at the hospital. Mrs Pennefather ceased her professional career after marrying but during World War II did voluntary work for service organizations. The Pennefathers lived in Brisbane until the 1950s when they moved to Southport. Survived by her husband, a son and a daughter, she died there on 17 March 1964 and was cremated with Anglican rites.

Connie Keys was a gentle, compassionate and fearless woman whose courage is amply attested to by her decorations. She was also an accomplished pianist. Her citations, medals and other records are in the Medical Corps Museum at the Australian Army School of Health, Healesville, Victoria.

A. G. Butler (ed), *Official history of the Australian Army Medical Services. . . 1914-19*, 3 (Canb, 1943); *Aust Nurses' J*, July 1920; *Aust Women's Weekly*, 19 April 1972; *South Coast Bulletin*, 10 Nov 1961; Report by Sister C. Keys, Butler collection (AWM); information from Mrs M. G. Thorsborne, Caldwell, Qld.   P. H. AND R. S. MERRILLEES

KEYSOR, LEONARD MAURICE (1885-1951), soldier and businessman, was born on 3 November 1885 at Maida Vale, London, son of Benjamin Keysor, a Jewish clock importer. The name was sometimes spelt Keyzor. After education at Tonnleigh Castle, Ramsgate, Keysor spent ten years in Canada. He migrated to Sydney, where he found employment as a clerk, about three months before the outbreak of World War I. On 18 August 1914 he enlisted in the 1st Battalion, Australian Imperial Force, and embarked for Egypt on 18 October. Keysor landed at Gallipoli on 25 April 1915 and was promoted lance corporal on 20 June. His deeds during the second (and last) great effort to take the peninsula are among the most spectacular individual feats of the war.

At 5.30 p.m. on 6 August the 1st Australian Infantry Brigade launched a diversionary attack at Lone Pine and by nightfall had seized the Turkish trenches; but bitter fighting with bayonets and bombs continued for three days and nights as the Turks retaliated. Keysor, a master of bomb-throwing, scorned danger. As Turkish bombs lobbed into his trench he would leap forward and smother the explosions with sandbags or coat. If time allowed he would throw a bomb back; he caught several in flight and smartly returned them as though playing cricket. Twice wounded, he nevertheless maintained his efforts for fifty hours. His bravery saved his trench and removed the enemy from a temporarily commanding position. C. E. W. Bean [q.v.7] recorded that 'the battalions of the 1st Brigade lost so heavily that few witnesses of its efforts remained. Consequently of the seven Victoria Crosses awarded after this fight, four went to a reinforcing battalion'. Of the other three, one was awarded to Keysor.

After Lone Pine Keysor went to England suffering from enteric fever. Rejoining his battalion in France in March 1916, he took part in the fighting at Pozières. On 17 November he was transferred to the 42nd Battalion and promoted sergeant on 1 December. Commissioned second lieutenant on 13 January 1917, he was promoted lieutenant in July. He was wounded on 28 March 1918 while fighting on the defensive Méricourt-Sailly-Le-Sec line and evacuated. Back with his unit, he was again wounded on 26 May in a gas bombardment near Villers-Bretonneux.

In October 1918 Keysor, an uncompromising advocate of conscription, returned to Australia with other veterans and assisted in the recruiting campaign. Discharged from the army as medically unfit on 12 December, he resumed clerical work but in 1920 he entered business in London. There, on 8 July at the Hill Street Synagogue, he married Gladys Benjamin.

Keysor was persuaded to re-enact his bomb-throwing exploits in a film, *For valour*, in 1927, but he was essentially a shy man who shunned publicity. White-haired and deaf when interviewed in the 1940s, he described himself as 'a common-or-garden clock importer' and remarked that 'the war was the only adventure I ever had'. Keysor was rejected for military service in 1939 on medical grounds. He died in London of cancer on 12 October 1951, survived by his wife and daughter, and was cremated after a memorial service at the Liberal Jewish Synagogue, St John's Wood. His Victoria Cross is held at the Australian War Memorial, Canberra.

L. Wigmore, *They dared mightily* (Canb, 1963); C. E. W. Bean, *The story of Anzac*, 2 (Syd, 1924); *Sydney Mail*, 16 Oct 1918; *The Times*, 13 Oct 1951; *Sun* (Syd), 29 July 1977; War diary, 42nd Battalion, AIF, 1916-18 (AWM).   DUDLEY MCCARTHY

KIBBLE, NITA BERNICE (1879-1962), librarian, was born on 8 June 1879 at Denman, New South Wales, younger daughter of George Augustus Frederick Kibble, Scottish postmaster, and his wife Eliza, née McDermott. Brought up as an Anglican, she was educated at Denman Public School and St Vincent's College, Potts Point, Sydney. For a short time she was a pupil-teacher at the Sacred Heart College, Darlinghurst.

On 3 October 1899 Nita Kibble successfully answered an advertisement for a junior assistant, Public Library of New South Wales, her signature having been taken for that of a male. Having the necessary educational qualifications and having topped the library test for forty-two candidates, she was appointed on probation junior attendant in the lending branch on 20 November at the male salary of £26 a year. In 1903 she became a library assistant and rose steadily,

passing the various grades of Public Service Board examinations and undertaking special courses at the University of Sydney. In December 1915 she was promoted to the professional division.

With the appointment of W. H. Ifould [q.v.] as principal librarian in 1912, Miss Kibble began a long and loyal association with him, first in the reorganization of the cataloguing department, of which she became senior cataloguer in July 1916, and later in the research department. In order to publicize the resources of the library, in 1919 she organized an exhibition of technical and commercial literature. Because of the success of this venture and the great expansion in secondary industries taking place, the research department of the library was established. Miss Kibble was appointed principal research officer on 19 June. On her retirement in 1943, the trustees resolved: 'The establishment and development of the Research Department of the Library were largely due to her efforts, knowledge and skill . . . The industries of the State were particularly assisted in a formative period by the bibliographical research work done by her and under her direction'. This department became the prototype for similar services in libraries of other States.

During her long and outstanding career Miss Kibble keenly participated in efforts to raise the status of the library profession; she was a foundation member of the Australian Institute of Librarians. She read widely, was a devotee of the theatre and collected period furniture, fine china and glass. Unmarried, she died on 4 February 1962 and was buried in the Church of England section of Northern Suburbs cemetery.

Lib record of Australasia, 1 (1901); papers held by Miss N. M. Dobbie, Lane Cove, NSW.

JEAN F. ARNOT

KIDMAN, SIR SIDNEY (1857-1935), pastoralist, was born on 9 May 1857, probably at Athelstone near Adelaide, third son of George Kidman, farmer, and his wife Elizabeth Mary, née Nunn, who were married in St Mary's Church of England at Bury St Edmunds, Suffolk, England, in 1848. Next year they migrated to South Australia. George Kidman died about six months after Sidney's birth. His son was educated at private schools in suburban Norwood but left home with five shillings in his pocket and riding a one-eyed horse which he had bought with laboriously acquired savings. He stole away by night and made his way to Poolamacca station in the Barrier Range where his brother George found him a job with George Raines, a landless bushman who roamed about with his stock, squatting on the unfenced runs wherever he found good feed. This 'corner' country of New South Wales later became the heartland of Kidman's pastoral empire.

The boy shared a dug-out in the bank of a dry creek with an Aboriginal known among whites as Billy. Treating him seriously as a friend and equal, Sidney learned from him tracking and other bush skills and so became a better bushman than most white adults. He learned also to admire and exploit Aboriginals: for the rest of his life he rarely travelled in the back-country, where he was most at home, without an Aboriginal guide and offsider. When Raines moved on, Kidman worked for a year or two as a rouseabout on Mount Gipps station, the site of the fabulous silver-lead-zinc discovery at Broken Hill a decade later. When he asked for a rise he was sacked, but found work as a stockman for a neighbouring shanty-keeper, German Charlie. Here he saved enough money to buy a bullock-team. Thenceforth he worked for himself and soon employed others.

Kidman contracted to cart supplies in the country between the isolated settlements at Mount Gipps, Wilcannia, Swan Hill (Victoria), Menindee, Bourke, Tibooburra, Louth and Cobar. He also drove mobs of horses and cattle, sometimes to market in Adelaide. Following the discovery of copper at Cobar in the early 1870s he set up a butcher's shop and, like James Tyson [q.v.6] at the Bendigo gold rush twenty years earlier, made enough money to establish himself as a large squatter. In 1878 he inherited £400 from his grandfather and traded with it successfully. He increased his capital by setting up coaching businesses in western New South Wales and in Western Australia. He supplied them with horses and began providing the British army in India with remounts. He grew richer still by continually buying cattle and selling them to his brother Sackville, who conducted a large butchering business at Broken Hill.

These activities were a means to an end. In 1886 Kidman bought his first station, Owen Springs on the Hugh River, southwest of Alice Springs. Long before his thirtieth birthday he had conceived the idea of buying a chain, later two chains, of stations stretching in nearly continuous lines from the well-watered tropical country round the Gulf of Carpentaria, south through western Queensland to Broken Hill, and across the border into South Australia within easy droving distance of Adelaide. Many stations on this 'main chain' were watered by Cooper's Creek and the Georgina and Diamantina rivers which sometimes brought northern tropical rain-waters to the centre even during droughts. By the 1890s he had begun to acquire his second chain of stations strung along the Overland Telegraph line from the Fitzroy River and Victoria River Downs in the north to Wilpena station in the Flinders Ranges near Adelaide. Thus, by moving stock from drought-stricken areas to others, by selling in markets where the price was highest, by his detailed knowledge of the country, and by his energy and bushcraft he withstood the depression of the 1890s and the great drought of 1902. By the time of World War I he controlled station country considerably greater in area than England or Tasmania and nearly as great as Victoria.

By the war's end he had become a national institution, having given fighter aeroplanes and other munificent gifts to the armed forces. In 1920 he gave to the Salvation Army £1000 and a half share in one of his cattle-stations. In 1921 he gave his country home at Kapunda, the scene of his annual horse-sales, to the South Australian government for a district high school. It may have been mere coincidence that he was knighted next day. He grew richer still by bilking the government of taxes. In August 1924 the Federal treasurer, Dr Earle Page [q.v.], issued a writ for recovery of £166 067. Kidman was fined £10 with four guineas costs for having failed to furnish land tax returns, the magistrate remarking with breathtaking disingenuousness that 'a heavier penalty would serve no purpose to a man in Sir Sidney Kidman's position'. Three years later, after High Court of Australia litigation, the government accepted £25 132 in settlement of his land tax debts. By this time 'Kidman' meant in fact a complex of interlocking companies, partnerships and agencies with branches in all the mainland capital cities and some country towns. Kidman and his children seem to have controlled the whole apparatus from Adelaide. In 1927 he retired.

On 30 June 1885 he had married at Kapunda Isabel Brown Wright, a schoolteacher; they had three daughters and a son. His wife taught him much and they travelled overseas four times. Kidman was six feet (183 cm) tall and well built, with an affable manner and an easy smile. He made friends readily and was a good judge of people. Like Churchill, Napoleon and some other great achievers, he could go to sleep anywhere and in almost any position. He never touched alcohol or tobacco or was profane, even his bullock teams being abused only as 'jolly tinkers'. In the Kidman country stories of his meanness still circulate today, but in fact he was a generous employer and benefactor to many institutions. His reputation for meanness sprang from his hatred of wastefulness; he was known to sack employees he considered guilty of it. His strength had been as a dealer rather than a breeder: he exploited the pastoral areas rather than developed them. In old age he suffered from increasing deafness and rheumatism, but otherwise retained his faculties unimpaired until his death in Adelaide on 2 September 1935; he was buried in Mitcham general cemetery. Kidman's estate, amounting to some £300 000, was mostly left to his family, but much went to charities.

E. J. Brady, *Australia unlimited* (Melb, 1918); I. L. Idriess, *The cattle king* (Syd, 1936); *A hundred famous Australian lives* (Syd, 1969); *Pastoral Review*, 15 Jan, 16 Sept 1903, 15 Aug 1910, 16 Jan 1911; *Observer* (Adel), 5 Sept 1903, 17 July 1920, 4, 11 June 1921, 2 Feb 1924, 21 Mar 1925, 17 July 1926, 5 May, 23 June, 18, 28 Aug 1928; *Catholic Press*, 3 Nov 1904; *Punch* (Melb), 1 May 1913; *T&CJ*, 27 July 1910, 22 May 1918; *Australasian*, 4 June 1921; *Freeman's J* (Syd), 11 Aug 1921; *Chronicle* (Adel), 6 Nov 1930; *The Times*, 3 Sept 1935; *Argus*, 9 Sept 1935; *Aust Worker*, 11 Sept 1935; Business records of S. Kidman & Co. Pty Ltd 1886-1928 (SAA).   RUSSEL WARD

KIDSTON, WILLIAM (1849-1919), bookseller and premier, was born on 17 August 1849 at Falkirk, Scotland, son of Richard Kidston, ironmoulder, and his wife Janet, née Reid. Apprenticed to his father's trade at 13, he later completed a certificate in chemistry, declined a position as a chemist in England and returned to his trade. On 22 January 1875 he married Margaret Scott of Falkirk with Free Church of Scotland forms; they had five sons and one daughter.

To escape the Scots industrial environment, Kidston migrated to Sydney in 1882 and nine months later settled at Rockhampton, Queensland, as a bookseller and stationer. A supporter in Britain of the Liberal Party and Home Rule for Ireland, he soon became involved in local politics. One of the founders of the Workers' Political Association and a sergeant in the local Volunteers, he was court-martialled and dismissed for refusing to be enrolled as a special constable in the 1891 shearers' strike. Kidston was Rockhampton's principal Labor figure throughout 1891, defending gaoled strikers and addressing public meetings.

In August 1892 Kidston represented the W.P.A. branches of Rockhampton, Mount Morgan and Clermont at the Labor-in-Politics convention in Brisbane; his proposals for electoral reform and for central and northern separation were adopted. He lost the contest for the two-member Rockhampton electorate in 1893, but demonstrated his loyalty to the Labor Party and

to central Queensland separatism. Kidston worked hard for election at his second attempt in March-April 1896, emphasizing local loyalty and standing as a democrat rather than a Labor candidate. He won and was accepted as a Labor member.

Practical politics, Kidston soon found, was more difficult than he had envisaged. He could not see Labor soon taking office but foresaw the possibility of Liberal and Labor progressives coalescing to remove 'the continuous government'. Pursuing the alliance tenaciously, he was one of three Labor representatives appointed by the 1898 convention to confer with the Liberal Opposition. He judged Federation by its possible effect on central Queensland separation, the influence of interstate free trade on Queensland industries and by whether the referendum would be taken under adult franchise. His attempts to have a referendum on central Queensland separation with the Federation referendum and to introduce white adult male suffrage into the Federation enabling bill were both defeated, but his campaign against Federation led to a 'No' vote in Rockhampton.

In December 1899 Kidston was treasurer and postmaster-general in the brief minority Labor government of Anderson Dawson [q.v.8]. It taught him that a Labor-Liberal alliance was possible. Albert Hinchcliffe [q.v.] referred to Kidston as 'the most tenacious': the next three years proved him right. Visiting Scotland briefly in 1901, Kidston returned to Queensland for the 1902 election. Because clause 124 of the Federal Constitution left the question of separation to the State parliament, he concentrated on securing a Labor government. Robert Philp's [q.v.] ministerial party won easily in 1902, but eighteen months later they were in Opposition and Kidston was treasurer. Though only deputy to Labor leader William Browne [q.v.7], he had grasped a favourable opportunity and was the architect of the plot which brought down the Philp ministry.

Kidston had envisaged a moderate centre coalition that would attract Labor support for electoral reform and workers' compensation, and Liberal support for electoral reform and efficient administration of the State's finances. For an acceptable leader he chose (Sir) Arthur Morgan [q.v.], who had publicly admired Kidston's 'shrewd, clearsighted and far-seeing . . . qualities', and succeeded in replacing the thirteen-year-old 'continuous ministry' with a Liberal-Labor coalition. Seven years in politics had changed Kidston. He was plumper, he wore spectacles, his well-kept beard showed traces of grey and the old uncertainty as a speaker was gone. Despite his success he was not gregarious and preferred to spend spare time at home with his extensive library of English literature.

Queensland's first full-time treasurer without outside business commitments, Kidston managed well and improved the efficiency of government. He financed the clearing of scrub lands by the unemployed but lost in the Legislative Council a bill to reduce tax on incomes below £52 a year. In April 1904 Browne died and Kidston became party leader and deputy to Premier Morgan. Despite Kidston's emphasis on Labor moderation, the coalition remained tenuous and lost defectors to Philp, particularly over Kidston's demand for electoral equality. Having barely survived a division, the government went to an election in August which proved a triumph for Kidston. Labor won 34 seats, the Morganites 21 and the Opposition only 17. As leader of the larger partner, Kidston could have claimed half the portfolios and the premiership for his party but chose to do neither, because without electoral reform Labor's electoral base remained weak. He preferred a judicious alliance with Morgan.

Dominant in cabinet, Kidston took a leading part in the deportation of Pacific Islanders, sorting out Commonwealth-State relations and reorganizing the State's finances while altering the incidence of taxes. In January 1905 an elections Act amendment bill, which introduced votes for women and abolished plural voting, was finally passed by the Legislative Council under threat of swamping. Dissatisfied with the financial treatment of his State under Federation, Kidston sought at premiers' conferences to have the Commonwealth take over State debts and make fixed annual payments to the States from customs and excise revenue.

Once electoral reform had been achieved, both parties were uneasy about the future of the coalition. The Liberals feared Labor's reforming zeal. Kidston felt hampered by the party objective of 1905 which called for 'collective ownership of the means of production, distribution and exchange' and by party policy to stop further sales of Crown land. He and George Kerr [q.v.], who led the party outside cabinet, sent a statement to newspapers calling for the Labor-in-Politics convention to recommit the objective and the Crown land sales policy. The first large split in the Queensland Labor Party had begun.

Following the passage in 1905 of some reform legislation, Morgan resigned and Kidston became premier on 19 January 1906 after unsuccessfully proposing that Digby Denham [q.v.8] should accept the succession. Outsiders, including the governor-

general Lord Northcote [q.v.] and Alfred Deakin [q.v.8], expressed respect for Kidson's ability. Inside Queensland he was seen by some of his Labor colleagues as an autocrat, determined to go his own way. A break between Kidston and his party seemed likely through 1906 and when the Labor vote fell by 13 per cent in Queensland in the December Federal election, Kidston saw a rejection of Labor's socialist policies. He decided to leave the party and form his own party in which candidates would be bound to him personally. For the May 1907 election he unfolded his 'gang forrit' policy speech in Rockhampton and invited candidates to join him. All but fourteen members of the Labor Party did so and in the ensuing election he won 24 seats to Labor's 18. Philp's party won 29. Kidston reconstructed his ministry. As in the Federal parliament, there were now three parties in the field with Kidston's in the middle.

After the Legislative Council had rejected elections and wages board bills, in November 1907 the governor Lord Chelmsford [q.v.7] refused to agree to Kidston's request to appoint government supporters to the council in order to pass the legislation. Kidston resigned, whereupon Chelmsford commissioned Philp to form a ministry and, after complicated manoeuvres, granted him a dissolution. The subsequent election in February 1908 resulted in three almost even parties in the assembly, and Kidston returned to office. His alliance with Labor produced the Parliamentary Bills Referendum Act providing that bills rejected by the council in two consecutive sessions could be made law by passage in a referendum.

Once his Old Age Pension and Wages Board Acts were passed, Kidston and Labor finally parted. After a trip to Scotland he fused his party with Philp's. As a disillusioned contemporary wrote, 'he rose by cursing Philp and died embracing him'. Not all his party accepted the fusion and he was left with a parliamentary majority of one. He was still returned easily in October 1909. His final achievement was an electoral Act based on 'one vote, one value'. The new university, established in 1911, gave him an honorary doctorate of laws. He used the title but neither sought nor accepted the knighthood usually offered to non-Labor premiers.

Kidston's loneliness in government was exacerbated by the deaths of his wife in July 1910 and of his friend John Blair [q.v.7]. In February 1911 he left politics for the presidency of the Land Court. He died of heart disease in his home at Greenslopes on 25 October 1919 and was buried in Rockhampton cemetery with Presbyterian forms after a state funeral. Three sons survived him.

In that period in Queensland politics between Griffith and Ryan [qq.v.], Kidston stood out as the dominant figure and the principal reformer. He was certainly self-assured and perhaps conceited, but his ability was well above that of his colleagues. His reforms in Queensland and his political methods mark him out as a similar politician to Deakin in a period in Australian politics which precedes the simple division between Labor and non-Labor.

H. V. Evatt, *The king and his dominion governors*, (Lond, 1967); D. J. Murphy and R. B. Joyce (eds), *Queensland political portraits 1859-1952* (Brisb, 1978); V. R. de Voss, Separatist movements in Central Queensland in the nineteenth century (B.A. Hons thesis, Univ Qld, 1952); B. A. Knox, The Honourable Sir Arthur Morgan, Kt: his public life and work (B.A. Hons thesis, Univ Qld, 1956); K. J. Wanka, William Kidston: a political biography (B.A. Hons thesis, Univ Qld, 1962).

D. J. MURPHY

KIEK, EDWARD SIDNEY (1883-1959) and WINIFRED (1884?-1975), Congregational ministers, were husband and wife. Edward was born on 5 August 1883 in London, elder son of Sidney Kiek, theological bookseller and publisher, and his wife Susannah, née Berry, who was of the Moravian Brethren. Sidney Kiek, son of a Congregational minister William Kick, changed his name and repudiated his father's strict Calvinism, but remained a liberal Congregationalist. Edward was educated at the Central Foundation School, City Road, London. He left at 16 to become an Admiralty clerk, but joined the Sidcup Congregational Church in 1900 and prepared for the ministry, matriculating at King's College, London. From 1903 he studied at the University of Oxford (B.A., 1906; M.A., 1910) and Mansfield College from which he graduated in 1908. In 1912 he obtained the B.D. from the University of London.

On 21 October 1910 Kiek was ordained at Newcastle-under-Lyme, Staffordshire. Next year, on 28 August in Manchester, he married Winifred Jackson. In 1913 he moved to Square Congregational Church, Halifax, Yorkshire. He preached liberal evangelical Christianity and socialism as 'the gospel in action', and denounced militarism; but his enthusiasm for Fabianism waned. During World War I he lectured widely for the Young Men's Christian Association and under the university extension scheme.

In 1919 Kiek succeeded L. D. Bevan [q.v.7] as principal of Parkin College, Adelaide, a small Congregational theological institution. Kiek arrived next year. Critical of traditional theological training, he modelled his courses on his Oxford experience, aiming to produce graduates in arts and theology. Although he raised standards, few obtained the two degrees. Baptist and Presbyterian students attended his lectures in the 1920s and in 1937 a co-operative lecture scheme with Wesley College began; Kiek taught New Testament and Church history. He also gave courses for the Workers' Educational Association.

Kiek revitalized the South Australian theological world in the 1920s. He founded the interdenominational Adelaide Theological Circle and restated Christian doctrine in the light of modern knowledge. His espousal of higher criticism and denial of the verbal inspiration of the Bible soon provoked controversy and earned him the reputation of an arch-modernist; he called himself 'a progressive evangelical'. He was equally critical of liberal rationalism. His summer schools lectures were published in *The modern religious situation* (Edinburgh, 1926). He also wrote *An apostle in Australia* (London, 1927), a generous biography of J. C. Kirby [q.v.5], who had opposed Kiek's liberalism.

Kiek was chairman of the Congregational Union of South Australia in 1929-30 and 1950-51. He founded the Round Table Christian Sociological Society and was its president for thirty-seven years. A temperance reformer and opponent of gambling, he was president of the South Australian Council of Churches in 1927-28 and its successor, the United Churches Social Reform Board, in 1946-47. He was also a Freemason.

Some of Kiek's meditations in the college chapel were published in *The battle of faith* (London, 1938). He contributed to the *Australian Christian World* and from 1937 wrote the Saturday leader for the Adelaide *Advertiser*. He wrote books and pamphlets on psychological, theological and social questions and on Congregational polity. For his thesis on the early church father Lactantius, the Melbourne College of Divinity conferred the D.D. in 1950. In 1943-46 he had lectured under the Army Educational Scheme; he continued to work for peace and world federation and was chairman of the State regional committee of the United Nations Relief and Rehabilitation Association in 1946-48.

Kiek was president of the Congregational Union of Australia and New Zealand in 1946-48. In 1949 he attended the International Congregational Council in America. Next year he wrote *Our first hundred years*, a history of Congregationalism in South Australia. An advocate of church union and ecumenism, Kiek was vice-president of the State committee of the World Council of Churches for several years and its president in 1954.

Gradually he became more conservative, and disliked the more pessimistic neo-orthodox theology which flourished in post-war Australia. His theology was unchanged: 'I am a Ritschlian. I've always been a Ritschlian', he confided to a student, and continued to lecture from outdated notes. In 1957 he retired.

Although not original, Kiek was well read and fluent; he was over fond of alliteration and mouthing words, but was a lucid and popular preacher. A genial, rotund man with spectacles, he detested morbidness, especially in religion. Survived by his wife, a daughter and two sons, he died from a heart attack on the Overland Express on 24 April 1959. His ashes were interred in Centennial Park cemetery. A portrait by G. P. Rayner hangs in Parkin-Wesley College, Adelaide.

Winifred Kiek was born in Manchester, second child of Robert Jackson, tea sales-man, and his wife Margaret, née Harker, frugal Quakers. Educated at private schools and Urmston Higher Grade School, at 16 she won a scholarship to Manchester Pupil Teacher Training Centre. In 1904 she entered the Victoria University of Manchester (B.A., 1907) where she won the university prize in logic; she became a schoolteacher. After marrying Kiek she embraced Congregationalism and her husband's church work.

In Adelaide she studied theology and in 1923 was the first woman to graduate B.D. from the Melbourne College of Divinity. In 1929 she took an M.A. in philosophy at the University of Adelaide. A devoted mother, she described her child-rearing theories in *Child nature and child nurture* (London, 1927).

Conscious of a divine vocation, she had begun public speaking in Quaker meetings and then in Congregational churches. From 1926 she preached in the new Colonel Light Gardens Congregational Union Church and became its pastor next year, the first woman in Australia to be so ordained. She relinquished this in 1933. Her only other charge was Knoxville Congregational Church, where she ministered in 1939-46, but she preached frequently in Congregational and other churches. Several of her sermons were published in the *Christian World Pulpit*; they were thoughtful, clear expositions of liberal theology. Some expressed her views on the status of women, from whom she held that Christ had removed 'the curse' of inferiority.

Though never a militant feminist, Winifred Kiek championed sexual equality and the women's movement from her arrival in South Australia, joining the newly founded National Council of Women. She was convenor of its committee on equal moral standards in 1927-31 and of the committee for peace and arbitration in 1938-50. She held office in the Women's Non-Party Association (later League of Women Voters), and in the Australian Federation of Women Voters. A member of the Pan-Pacific and Southeast Asia Women's Association, she was a delegate to women's conferences in New Zealand (1952), Sri Lanka (1955), Iran (1960) and Japan (1966).

After World War II Kiek became the World Council of Churches' liaison officer in Australia for work among women; in 1950 she joined the council's commission on the work of women in the Churches and attended its Oxford meeting in 1952. In 1953-56 she was convenor of the Australian Council of Churches' commission on the co-operation of men and women in the Church, about which she wrote in *We of one house* (Sydney, 1954). This work was recognized in 1965 by the foundation of the Winifred Kiek scholarship, to provide Christian training in Australia for Asian women. She was twice vice-chairman of the Congregational Union of South Australia and acting chairman in 1944-45. She supported her husband on social questions, especially peace and world federation; they both learned Esperanto.

Slight, unassuming and softly spoken, with a trace of a Lancashire accent, Winifred Kiek retained a quiet spirituality. Her upbringing made her disdain comfort; she managed the domestic affairs of Parkin College parsimoniously. She was a proficient puppeteer, presenting performances around South Australia. She had domestic help for most of her married life as well as her husband's support. After his death she retired. She still preached occasionally and also attended the Society of Friends, without separating from Congregationalism. She died at Victor Harbor on 23 May 1975; her ashes were interred with her husband's. Her children survived her.

M. L. Knauerhase (ed), *The larger hope* (Adel, 1959), and *Straight on till morning* (Adel, 1963), and *Winifred* (Adel, 1978); W. Phillips, *Edward Sidney Kiek* (Adel, 1981); *Register* (Adel), 20 May 1920; *Advertiser* (Adel), 14 June 1927, 27 Apr 1959; E. S. Kiek *and* W. Kiek papers (SAA).

WALTER PHILLIPS

KIERAN, BERNARD BEDE (1886-1905), swimmer, was born on 6 October 1886 in Sydney, sixth child of Irish parents Patrick Kieran (d. 1891), seaman and labourer, and his wife Annie, née Mackin. He attended the local convent school, learned to read and write, but at 13 became delinquent. In March 1900 his mother had him committed to the nautical school-ship *Sobraon* where, under the influence of his mentor W. Hilton Mitchell, he took up swimming and at 16 became a carpenter's apprentice.

Barney Kieran's brilliant swimming career began in 1904 when swimming for the *Sobraon* Club he finished four times a close second to the champion Dick Cavill [q.v.7] and beat him in the Australasian 880 yards and mile championships in record time. Coached by Robert Robertson Craig, by April 1905 Kieran had won six State and six Australasian freestyle titles, equalled F. C. V. Lane's [q.v.] 220 yards freestyle world record and set 'world' record times for 200, 300, 400, 500 and 1000 yards and mile, the last in the astonishing time of 23 minutes 16.8 seconds.

Invited to England by the (Royal) Life-Saving Society to compete in the King's Cup, Kieran, accompanied by Mitchell, arrived in London on 17 June. On 26 June at the Bath Club, Piccadilly, 'the Sobraon Boy' began a sensational record-breaking tour by easily lowering the record time for 600 yards by 17.6 seconds in an exhibition swim. 'He is a fish, not a man', shouted one spectator. Though Kieran lost his first two races to the great David Billington and was as unsuccessful as he was unfamiliar with the King's Cup lifesaving events, he thereafter won every race he entered, including handicaps.

In August Kieran beat Billington in the 440 yards salt-water and 880 yards freestyle titles, the latter in the world record time of 11 minutes, 28 seconds. At an international meeting in Sweden he won four events and set a world record for 500 metres. On the 28th at Leeds he defeated Billington for the 500 yards title in the world record time of 6 minutes, 7.2 seconds. In September he won the 220 yards title and his third English record medal, for the 300 yards. Kieran also gave diving displays and set new records in Scotland and Ireland in addition to 'newspaper' records over unrecognized distances. His modesty and sportsmanship won him many admirers and on his return to Australia in November he was accorded a hero's welcome.

After winning three Australasian titles in Brisbane he became ill on 8 December and after an appendicectomy he died in hospital on 22 December 1905. Amid widespread expressions of public grief—many recalled Henry Searle [q.v.6]—he was buried in the Catholic section of Gore Hill cemetery, Sydney. A monument to the 'Champion Swimmer of the World' was erected by public subscription.

Barney Kieran was of a happy and retiring disposition and altogether unspoiled by success. Solidly built and dark-com-plexioned with large bright eyes, he stood 5 ft. 6½ ins. (169 cm) tall and weighed 158 pounds (72 kg). He swam the double overarm (trudgen) stroke, characterized by a greater roll of the body which gave him both a longer reach and time to breathe; his powerful kick was timed as the corresponding arm pulled down.

Kieran was the greatest swimmer that the world had seen, yet despite his phenomenal times, not approached until years after his death, the Fédération Internationale de Natation Amateur in 1908 only accorded him retrospective recognition for his 500 yards world record. Kieran's numerous medals and trophies were acquired by the New South Wales government and he is commemorated by the Kieran memorial shield awarded annually to the champion State in the Australian championships. In 1969 he was honoured by the International Swimming Hall of Fame at Fort Lauderdale, Florida, United States of America.

W. W. Hill (comp), *N.S.W. Amateur Swimming Association Annual: Season 1905-6* (Syd, 1905); *Forbes Carlisle on swimming* (Lond, 1963); *Sportsman* (Lond), 29 Sept 1904, 23 Mar, 26 Apr, 8 May, 19 June, 2, 4 Oct, 25, 26 Dec 1905, 20, 27 Jan 1906; *Nordisk Idrottslif*, 16 Aug, 2, 9, 11, 16, 20, 27 Sept 1905; *Scottish Referee*, 4 Sept 1905; *Ireland's Saturday Night* (Belfast), 16 Sept 1905; *SMH*, 23 Nov, 23, 25, 27 Dec 1905; *Referee* (Syd), 29 Nov, 27 Dec 1905; *T&CJ*, 27 Dec 1905, 3 Jan, 13 June, 22 Aug 1906; *Freeman's J* (Syd), 30 Dec 1905; 8/1747 (NSWA).

G. P. WALSH

KIERNAN, ESMOND LAURENCE (1881-1967), furniture dealer and politician, was born on 26 December 1881 at Fitzroy, Melbourne, eighth child of Irish-born John Joseph Kiernan and his wife Margaret, née MacDonald of Hobart, both schoolteachers. He was educated at state schools in the Avoca district and at Gordon and began work in a Collingwood furniture store. He soon transferred to a nearby store, became a partner and by 1917 sole proprietor. The firm, Kiernan & Co., eventually had several Melbourne and country branches. He also established a money-lending business, the K-Cash Order Co.

A founding member of the Clerks' Union, Kiernan joined the Labor Party in 1909, campaigned strongly against conscription in 1916-17 and was a member of the Collingwood City Council in 1916-19. At this time he was known as an associate of John Wren [q.v.] but they fell out later. In June 1919 he was elected as Labor member for Melbourne North Province in the Legislative Council.

That year he carried a rating reform bill, enabling municipal councils to introduce rating on unimproved values. He made regular attempts to have the school leaving age raised to 15 and pioneered moves to abolish capital punishment in Victoria, introducing the first of six unsuccessful bills in 1922.

In December 1929 Kiernan became an honorary minister in the Hogan [q.v.] ministry. From June 1930 to February 1931 he had an onerous task as the State's first minister of sustenance. He defied his party by his outspoken support of the Premiers' Plan, arguing that Hogan was a 'greater and more sincere Laborite than most of the pack that were continually barking at his heels'. After Labor's downfall at the 1932 elections he was expelled by the State executive on 1 July.

The experience of serving in a Depression government shocked Kiernan, destroying his faith in conventional political solutions. His health had broken down early in 1931 and he spent eight months in Europe. He returned as an admirer of Mussolini, and came to believe that, as the parliamentary system had failed, the only way to overcome 'vile and vulnerable' capitalism was the establishment of a corporate state in which employer and employee would combine to bring about a 'planned economy'. His beliefs eventually led him to become the president of a short-lived Melbourne branch of the Australia First Movement. Surprisingly, he was not opposed at the 1934 council elections and, in 1939, initiated moves which led to a royal commission into bribery allegations against four Labor politicians; in June 1940 he lost his seat.

Kiernan's public career was relatively unsuccessful, yet his intellectual bent and independent spirit were qualities rarely seen in inter-war Victorian politics. Gentle and soft-spoken, he greatly admired Dante, organized lectures on European culture and entertained visiting Italian opera singers. He was a trustee of the Henry George [q.v.4] Foundation, a founding director of radio station 3AR and an active Catholic, being president of the Catholic Young Men's Society in 1914.

Kiernan died on 19 April 1967 at St Vincent's Hospital and was buried in Melbourne general cemetery of which he had been a trustee. He was survived by his wife Eileen Mary, née Harrison, a music teacher, whom he had married at St John's Catholic Church, Heidelberg, on 31 January 1917, and by two sons and two daughters.

L. J. Louis, *Trade unions and the Depression* (Canb, 1968); *Labor Call*, 7 Jan 1926; *Age*, 20 Apr 1967; information from P. B. Kiernan, Toorak, and J. J. Kiernan, Hawthorn, Vic.   GEOFF BROWNE

KILBURN, JOHN GEORGE (1876-1976), bricklayer, trade unionist and politician, was born on 2 July 1876 at Middlesborough, Yorkshire, England, son of George Kilburn, bricklayer, and his wife Ellen, née Horner. He left school at 12 and followed his father's trade. At Middlesborough on 20 January 1898 he married Elizabeth McNamara, a domestic servant. He was a member of the Independent Labour Party from 1905 but, frustrated by the lack of continuous work, in 1912 he and his family migrated to New South Wales.

On arrival he worked as a bricklayer, probably at the Hoskins' [q.v.] steelworks at Lithgow. A tall and commanding figure, Jack Kilburn soon made his mark as a rank and file trade unionist. In 1917 he became an organizer for the Bricklayers' Union and represented it on the Labor Council of New South Wales. He was a member of the Marxist Australian Socialist Party in 1912-17 and twice contested State seats, but abandoned that party to become a leading advocate of the One Big Union.

Kilburn then was active in attempts to create a non-sectarian revolutionary socialist labour party and became one of the key figures in the group of unionists known as the 'Trades Hall Reds' who followed J. S. Garden [q.v.8], though he was also fiercely independent and suspicious of any attempts to substitute the ideas of a political élite for the interests of the working class. During a speech by Kilburn in the Sydney Domain on May Day 1921 angry ex-soldiers started a series of mêlées that were strikingly similar to (and probably the basis for) the scenes of violence described by D. H. Lawrence in his novel *Kangaroo*.

In 1922 Kilburn joined the Australian Labor Party but was soon expelled, then readmitted. He was a member of the State executive in 1923-24, 1938-39 and 1940-41, and vice-president of the party in 1927 when annual conference reappointed J. T. Lang [q.v.] as parliamentary leader and brought into force the 'Red Rules'. In the late 1920s he was a delegate to numerous interstate trade union conferences and an executive member of the Australasian Council of Trade Unions. A delegate to the A.L.P.'s federal conference in 1930 and 1940, he was a member of the federal executive in 1927-31. He was a member of the executive of the International Class War Prisoners' Aid in 1929-30. In 1931 he was nominated to the Legislative Council on the advice of Lang.

At the Easter conference of the State party in 1930 Kilburn successfully moved for a committee 'to devise ways and means to propagate socialisation' and became chairman of the party's socialisation units, which were disbanded in 1933. That year

Kilburn was expelled for supporting A. C. Willis [q.v.] in his candidature at the Bulli by-election against a Lang nominee. Readmitted, then expelled in 1936, next year he was readmitted to the Belmore branch with the support of the federal executive after a campaign by left-wing unions on his behalf. In 1939 he was unsuccessful as a Labor candidate for the Legislative Council.

After retiring as secretary of the Bricklayers' Union in 1943, Kilburn and his wife lived quietly at their home at Belmore. In 1973 they celebrated their seventy-fifth wedding anniversary . In October they moved to Hammondville retirement village. Predeceased by his wife, Jack died on 2 April 1976 and was cremated. He was survived by two sons and two daughters. He had been upset by the dismissal of the Whitlam government, but had also been keenly looking forward to celebrating his hundredth birthday.

R. Cooksey, *Lang and socialism* (Canb, 1971); M. Dixson, *Greater than Lenin?* (Melb, 1977); F. Farrell, *International socialism and Australian labour* (Syd, 1981); *SMH*, 18 Mar, 7 May 1931, 20 July 1933, 7 Mar 1934, 30 June 1937.

FRANK FARRELL

KILGOUR, ALEXANDER JAMES (1861-1944), headmaster, was born on 29 May 1861 in Edinburgh, son of Alexander James Kilgour, watchmaker, and his wife Mary Jane, née Henley. He accompanied his parents and sister to Sydney about 1868 and was educated at Fort Street Model School, becoming a pupil-teacher. His first teaching appointment was in 1882 at Brombin Public School on the north coast. At Ennis, Port Macquarie, he married Elizabeth Dawes on 23 July 1884. After six months training that year, he was sent to Goodooga. Transferred to Bowenfels in April 1886, he was promoted by examination in July and took charge of Braidwood Public School in September.

His first city appointment was to Plunkett Street, Woolloomooloo, in January 1901, where the previous headmaster had 'reigned by means of anarchy'. Kilgour promptly transformed the school: 'the pupils there learned manners and everything else' and he established his reputation as a rigid disciplinarian who, unconventionally, did not use the cane. His became the champion school for military drill. Kilgour attended evening classes at the University of Sydney (B.A., 1894; LL.B., 1904) and in 1900 achieved the top teaching classification. He was headmaster of Neutral Bay in 1901-03 and of Chatswood in 1904. Early next year Kilgour was chosen against strong competition to succeed J. W.

Turner [q.v.] as headmaster of Fort Street. Although in charge of the primary and both boys' and girls' secondary schools, with little time for teaching, he concentrated on the senior boys' classes preparing for the public examinations. He was 'fundamentally a Latinist', and 'his teaching was excellent, though his standards were inflexible'—he had 'no tolerance for slackers and dullards'. Professor A. R. Chisholm described him in his mid-forties: 'He wore spectacles whose lenses were sliced horizontally along the middle; and, being moderately tall, he looked down over these with a quiet dignified authority that made any resort to corporal punishment inconceivable. His dark hair, like his beard and moustache, was closely cropped; his forehead rather receding and his head rather small for a man with such good brains'. With Peter Board's [q.v.7] reorganization, he became headmaster in 1911 of Fort Street Boys' High School, and in 1916 supervised its move to a new building on Parramatta Road at Petersham.

Kilgour became a legend in his lifetime for the scholastic excellence of Fort Street and for his dedication to discipline and hard work. He was able to build and hold a staff of outstanding men including Walter Selle, George Mackaness, C. B. Newling [qq.v.] and Samuel Lasker. Closely interested in all his pupils, he urged the ablest into law and medicine and for others found places in commerce. Those who testified to his inspiration and influence include Professor John Hunter [q.v.], H. V. Evatt, Sir Garfield Barwick, Sir Percy Spender and Chisholm.

On retiring from Fort Street in 1926, Kilgour was headmaster of Strathfield Grammar and Preparatory School for Boys for five years; when it amalgamated with Trinity Grammar School he became classics master. He visited Britain in 1936. On his eightieth birthday his portrait by Norman Carter [q.v.7] was unveiled at Fort Street. He died in hospital at Newcastle on 26 December 1944 and was cremated with Anglican rites. Two sons and three daughters survived him.

L. E. Gent, *The Fort Street centenary book* (Syd, 1949); A. R. Chisholm, *Men were my milestones* (Melb, 1958); C. B. Newling, *The long day wanes* (Syd, 1973); C. Morris, *'The school on the hill'* (Syd, 1980); Teachers records (NSW Dept of Education, Syd), and school files (NSWA).

BRUCE MITCHELL

KILLIAN, ANDREW (1872-1939), Catholic archbishop, was born on 26 October 1872 at Edenderry, Offaly, Ireland, son of Nicholas Killian and his wife Eliza Josephine, née Ryan, who were school teachers. His grandfather Nicholas Killian had conducted a 'hedge school'. Andrew was educated at Mungret Jesuit College, Limerick, and St Patrick's College, Carlow. He graduated B.A. from the Royal University of Ireland, in 1894, and was ordained priest on 4 June 1898; he came to Australia later that year. His younger brother Patrick and sister Mary also worked in the Australian Catholic Church.

Killian's first appointment was as an assistant priest in the parish of Bourke in western New South Wales. In 1907 he visited Ireland and next year was transferred to Broken Hill. He subsequently filled the offices of parish priest, administrator of the cathedral, dean and vicar-general (1919). In 1919 he was designated a domestic prelate of the Holy See. At Broken Hill his talents as an administrator were recognized. He cleared the parish of debt, extended the bishop's house and built St John's School at Broken Hill North. Elected bishop of the neighbouring South Australian diocese of Port Augusta, he was consecrated on 15 June 1924 in the pro-cathedral at Peterborough. Between 1924 and 1933 the bishop travelled thousands of miles visiting the scattered parishes of his vast diocese which stretched from the eastern to the western border of South Australia. In 1926 he attended the Eucharistic Congress at Chicago; on this journey he was received by the Pope in Rome and visited Ireland again. In July 1933 Killian was appointed coadjutor archbishop of Adelaide to assist the ailing Archbishop Spence [q.v.]. When Dr Spence died next year Killian became archbishop.

It was an era of expansion for the Church despite the Depression. Archbishop Killian cited as the achievements of which he was proudest: the reopening of the historic school at Penola, originally founded by Mother Mary McKillop [q.v.5], the opening of the juniorate of the Sisters of St Joseph at Cowandilla, the arrival of the Carmelite Sisters in the diocese and the National Catholic Education Congress of 1936.

He is most remembered for the congress. The first such gathering in Australia, it was arranged to mark the State's centenary. In announcing the event the archbishop said: 'The Education Congress will enable us to consolidate our forces behind the movement and enable us to acquaint our fellow-citizens of the sacrifices made by us. Catholics should know and understand the sacrifices made for Catholic Education'. Papers were presented by leading Catholic educationists about the work of Catholic schools and the congress ended with a Eucharistic procession of 100 000 people through Adelaide's streets.

In his last year Archbishop Killian was afflicted by cancer. He died on 28 June 1939 in the Mercy Hospital, East Melbourne, and was buried in West Terrace cemetery, Adelaide. He is remembered as a large, kindly, paternal man. His acceptance by Catholics and others was evidenced by the thousands of mourners who lined the path of his funeral cortège.

Australian Catholic Education Congress (Melb, 1936); *Southern Cross* (Adel), 7 July 1939; R. Morrison, Summary notebook, B3 (no 13), E2 (no 4), (Adel Diocesan Archives of the Catholic Church).

R. J. EGAR

KING, ALICE ROSS-; *see* ROSS-KING

KING, COPLAND (1863-1918), missionary, was born on 24 June 1863 at Parramatta, New South Wales, son of Rev. Robert Lethbridge King [q.v.5], and his wife Honoria Australia, née Raymond. A twin, he was great-grandson of Philip Gidley King and grandson of both Phillip Parker King and James Raymond [qq.v.2]. Educated at home until 15, he later attended Sydney Grammar School and the University of Sydney (B.A., 1885; M.A., 1887). A lay catechist at Holy Trinity Church, Sydney, from 1885, he was ordained in September 1887 and served curacies at Castle Hill, Rose Hill and Dural.

King heard an address in 1890 by Rev. Albert Maclaren who had just been appointed to launch an Anglican mission in New Guinea. When they met King accepted Maclaren's challenge to join him. Arriving at Wedau on the eastern end of New Guinea on 10 August 1891, they established their headquarters at nearby Dogura. Having lost many of their Papuan and European workers by sickness and desertion, the two leaders also fell sick. King was sent back to Sydney to recover and Maclaren died late in the year.

Against the advice of his family and friends, King insisted on returning to New Guinea and in March 1892 was appointed head of the mission. The following month he resumed his work and concluded it twenty-six years later. In 1897 he declined an invitation to become the first bishop of New Guinea, believing that his talents were more suited to subordinate positions. With his flair for languages, he soon mastered the Wedauan tongue used around Dogura. He spent his time mainly in missionary journeys and translating the Scriptures and educational material.

King was with Sir William MacGregor [q.v.5] when he discovered the mouth of the Mambare River in 1898. The discovery of gold in the upper reaches by MacGregor's party resulted in a rush of miners to the Gira and Yodda goldfields. After violent clashes between miners and the local Papuans with much loss of life on both sides, an uneasy peace was established. At MacGregor's prompting, the Anglican mission opened a station near the government post at Tamata Creek which served the goldfields. King took charge of the station in 1900 and remained in the north-east for the rest of his time in the country, becoming the first, and one of the very few Europeans ever, to master the difficult Binandere language. He was at odds with resident magistrate C. A. W. Monckton [q.v.] and most of the miners on the field, and was one of the few Evangelicals in a largely High Church diocese. He made accurate and valuable anthropological observations, collected plant specimens and corresponded with botanists abroad. He donated his botanical library and specimens to the Botanic Gardens, Sydney; after his death his photograph was placed in the fern herbarium at the gardens. He was awarded the diploma of scholar of theology by the Australian College of Theology in 1914.

Unmarried, King died of chronic nephritis and heart disease in Sydney on 5 October 1918 and was buried in the churchyard at Camden where his brother was rector. In 1972 his portrait was published in a series of the stamps of Papua New Guinea honouring early missionaries.

F. M. Synge, *Albert Maclaren* (Lond, 1908); A. K. Chignell, *Twenty-one years in Papua* (Lond, 1913); G. White, *A pioneer of Papua* (Lond, 1929); H. Nelson, *Black, White and gold* (Canb, 1976); D. Wetherell, *Reluctant mission* (Brisb, 1977); Bishop M. Stone-Wigg, Diaries and papers (Bishop's House, Port Moresby); Dogura papers (New Guinea collection, UPNG Lib); Publications of the Aust Bd of Missions (ABM Lib, Syd).

IAN STUART

KING, SIR GEORGE ECCLES KELSO (1853-1943), businessman, was born on 30 December 1853 in Sydney, seventh child of Rev. George King [q.v.5] and his wife Jane, née Mathewson. He was educated at Calder House, leaving school young because of his father's financial difficulties. After working briefly as a jackeroo in Queensland, he returned to Sydney and joined the Bank of New South Wales in 1870. Transferring to the Commercial Banking Co. of Sydney as a clerk on 27 November 1872, he served at Parkes, Carcoar, Bathurst, Cootamundra and elsewhere. He acted as gold-buyer for the bank and once was chased by bushrangers whom he managed to outride. In 1876 he became managing clerk of Henry

Beit & Co., Sydney stock and station agents. On 9 April 1879 he was married, by his father, to Irene Isabella Rand in St John's Church, Wagga Wagga.

In December 1877 Kelso King had become secretary, with a salary of £350, of the new Mercantile Mutual Insurance Co. Ltd which opened for business in Pitt Street on 10 January 1878. During its first six months King was the company's only employee: as well as setting up the office he issued 971 policies. He had a lifelong willingness and ability to work long hours at high pressure. Within a year he had established branches in Brisbane, Melbourne and Adelaide but, proving unprofitable, they were closed by 1882; the company confined its operations to New South Wales until a branch was reopened in Melbourne in 1901. He took a personal interest in the staff and established an officers' provident fund. To mark his seventieth birthday, he eventually donated shares and government bonds to the value of £3000 to create an endowment fund to assist staff members in personal difficulties.

In 1880-81 King managed the Anglo-Australian Investment, Finance & Land Co. Ltd at a salary of £400. He was early associated with Walter and Eliza Hall [qq.v.], whom he met travelling in a Cobb [q.v.3] & Co. coach. Later he acted for Walter Hall in many of his business activities, and was his executor. He assisted his widow with her affairs and to plan the Walter and Eliza Hall Trust of which he was an original trustee.

King also became a director of many companies including Mount Morgan Gold Mining Co. Ltd, the Electrolytic Refining & Smelting Co. of Australia Ltd, Metal Manufacturers Ltd, Australian Fertilizers Pty Ltd, Illawarra & South Coast Steam Navigation Co. Ltd, the Colonial Mutual Life Assurance Society Ltd, Beale [q.v.7] & Co. Ltd and the Bank of New South Wales (1929-40), chairman of Mort's [q.v.5] Dock & Engineering Co. Ltd and Brisbane Theatres Ltd, and first managing director of the Australian General Insurance Co. Ltd from 1912.

A prominent Anglican, King was a lay canon of St Andrew's Cathedral and churchwarden of All Saints, Woollahra, a member of the Church of England Property Trust and Sydney Diocesan Board of Finance, honorary treasurer of a number of church funds, and a governor of The King's, Trinity Grammar and Canberra Grammar schools. He was chairman of the executive committee of the State branch of the Boy Scouts' Association in 1922-43, a trustee of Royal Naval House, honorary treasurer of the New South Wales branch of the Navy League, president of the Royal Life Saving Society, commander of the Order of St John of Jerusalem and, from 1937, president of the New South Wales branch of the St John Ambulance Association. He was a foundation member of the Australasian Pioneers' Club (president, 1928-43) and belonged to the Australian and Union clubs. He was president of the Royal Empire Society and a benefactor of the Royal Australian Historical Society. Knighted in 1929, he was known as Sir Kelso.

An active Freemason, King had been initiated on 7 June 1878 in the Prince of Wales Lodge, Sydney, and became worshipful master in 1885. He was influential in establishing the Provincial Grand Lodge of Mark Master Masons in 1889 and became grand mark master mason of New South Wales (1892-95).

After the death of his first wife in 1900, King lived in a flat in Macquarie Street until he purchased Quambi, Edgecliff, in 1917. On 13 November 1907 at Christ Church, South Yarra, Melbourne, he had married Alicia Martha Kirk (d. 1956); she was a cousin of Eliza Hall, who had become her guardian when she had been orphaned at 14. Like her husband Alicia King was active in charitable and community organizations. She was assistant State commissioner for the Girl Guides' Association in 1925-31.

When young, King belonged to a rowing club and rode a 'bone-shaker' bicycle. Throughout his life he regularly walked part way to work. Fond of the theatre, he was a regular 'first nighter' and an opera subscriber whenever companies visited Sydney. He enjoyed choral music and was a patron of the Royal Philharmonic Society of Sydney. In his later years increasing deafness prevented his enjoying such pleasures. Abstemious in habit, he drank no spirits but enjoyed wine; Australian wine was served at his table long before it became fashionable. A patriotic Australian, he was at the same time intensely loyal to Britain, sentiments in which he saw no incompatibility.

Far from being stuffy and self-righteous, King was invariably courteous and had a sense of fun and a charm of manner which endeared him to many friends. He died in his sleep at his home Kilbronae, Point Piper, on 7 February 1943, and was cremated after a service in St Andrew's Cathedral, where his ashes were interred. He was survived by his wife, their son and daughter and by two daughters of his first marriage; one, Olive King [q.v.] drove an ambulance in World War I. His portrait by Longstaff [q.v.], commissioned in 1928 to mark its jubilee, is held by the Mercantile Mutual Insurance Co.

His elder sister Georgina King (1845-1932) published pamphlets and articles in the press on geology and anthropology and dissipated much energy in waging in vain a long and bitter campaign for recognition. She was a fellow of the Royal Anthropological Society of Australia and a friend of Daisy Bates [q.v.7] and of Rose Scott [q.v.], with whom she was a founder of the Women's Club and the Women's Literary Society.

A. de Brune (ed), *Fifty years of progress in Australia 1878-1926* (priv print, Syd, 1929); H. Mayfield, *Servant of a century* (priv print, Syd, 1978); *Century*, 12 Feb 1943; U. Bygott *and* D. Branagan, *Univ Syd Archives Record*, Jan, Sept 1982; Mercantile Mutual Insurance Co. Ltd Archives, Syd; ML printed cat; family papers held by author, Darling Point, Syd; information from R. W. McKay, Artarmon, Syd.   HAZEL KING

KING, GEORGE RAYMOND (1872-1950), architect and educationist, was born on 16 October 1872 at Ballarat, Victoria, son of George Joseph King, blacksmith from Ireland, and his wife Annie, née Mercer, from Scotland. From an early age he lived in Geelong, for most of his life with his widowed mother, and he never married. After primary schooling at Ashby he was articled to A. J. Derrick, architect, and attended classes at the Gordon Technical College, then joined Thomas F. Seeley in a partnership which later became Seeley, King & Everett.

King served the Gordon Technical College (named after General Gordon of Khartoum) as secretary and director from 1898 and, in addition, as instructor in architectural subjects from 1902. In 1908 the people of Geelong sent him to England to study educational developments and discuss with British manufacturers the provision of machinery for the college's projected courses on textiles; on his return he gave up private practice to become principal of the college (Gordon Institute of Technology from 1921) and head of its architectural section from 1909 until his retirement in 1935.

King's initial appointment as secretary at a time when the college was being stultified by lack of funds allegedly prompted his question: 'Am I to preside at the funeral of the corpse, or be the doctor to put life into it?'. He had the staunch backing of G. M. Hitchcock [q.v.4], president of the college. The resuscitation and expansion of the institution, which was to produce leading scientists, engineers and architects, as well as hundreds of skilled technicians, was the result of King's optimism and his persistent and effective lobbying for government money. The establishment of the Textile College in 1951 also owed much to King's years of endeavour. His design of courses and supervision of standards influenced technical education throughout Victoria.

King is credited with being the first educationist in Victoria to provide for the complete training of the architect. He 'has indirectly fostered more good architecture than any other man in Australia', Robin Boyd wrote of him in 1947. Although classical and conservative, he trained many who became leading modernists and his students, as teachers or advisers, carried on his influence at the Gordon.

Among King's strengths were his constant aim for excellence, his purpose being to give boys and girls not only practical but cultural training; his flair for vocational guidance; and his ability to recruit strong senior staff and lead them in a tradition of placing the interests of the students above all else. In pursuing his ideals he was pragmatic, ever ready to bend rules and cut red tape. This and his very human foibles gave rise to many anecdotes about him as 'the last of the Bohemians'; but former students still revere the memory of one who inspired them to accomplish more than they thought possible and who then secured jobs for them.

A founding local Rotarian, King held at retirement twenty-six public appointments including membership of the Council of Public Education and the Architects' Registration Board of Victoria. But he influenced community affairs even more through the significant people who came unbidden to seek his common-sense advice. One whom he helped thus was Rev. J. J. Booth, later archbishop of Melbourne; another was R. G. (Lord) Casey.

He wrote little for publication, but much of his outlook on education can be read in records held by the Gordon Technical College in its historical museum. Appointed O.B.E. in 1935, he was a serving brother of the Order of St John of Jerusalem, held fellowships of the Royal Australian Institute of Architects and the Victorian Institute of Town Planning, and was a member of the T-Square Club, Melbourne. He died on 11 September 1950 at Geelong and was cremated. His portrait by Charles Wheeler [q.v.] is held by Gordon Technical College on permanent loan from the Geelong Art Gallery.

R. Boyd, *Victorian modern* (Melb, 1947); D. F. Wild, *The tale of a city: Geelong 1850-1950* (Melb, 1950); W. R. Brownhill, *The history of Geelong and Corio Bay* (Melb, 1955); *PP* (LA Vic) 1901, 3 (36), p 282; *Argus*, 3 June 1935; *Geelong Advertiser*, 12 Sept 1950; K. M. Sillcock, The Gordon of Geelong—a history of the Gordon Institute of Technology, 1887-1980 (MS, 1981, held by Gordon Technical College, Geelong, and by author, Kew, Vic); Gordon Institute papers *and* collection of tributes to G. R. King (Gordon Technical College, Geelong).
K. SILLCOCK

KING, GIFFARD HAMILTON MAC-ARTHUR-; *see* MACARTHUR-KING

KING, HENRY (1855 ?-1923), photographer, was born at Swanage, Dorset, England, son of William Isaac King, stonemason, and his wife Eliza, née Toms. He came to New South Wales with his family about 1857 and as a lad worked with the Sydney photographer J. Hubert Newman [q.v.]. On 27 November 1878 he married Elizabeth Laing in Sydney with Congregational forms. In 1880 King established a photographic studio at 316 George Street in partnership with William Slade and by 1884 was sole proprietor. For the rest of his life he worked from studios in George Street, although much of his reputation was derived from work done outside.

King travelled widely through eastern Australia photographing Aboriginals. His portraits, mostly half length and identically posed, were often taken against a painted studio backdrop of the bush. At the World Columbian Exposition at Chicago in 1893 he was awarded a certificate and a bronze medal for the size, technique and artistic finish of his Aboriginal portraits. As his career progressed, and with the invention of dry-plate techniques, King turned more to landscape photography, producing as well as popular scenic views a series of Sydney street scenes, now valued for their historic as well as their artistic interest.

During the first decade of the twentieth century King carried out photographic work for the National Art Gallery of New South Wales and for several art societies. He counted many artists among his friends. His photograph of the 1907 selection committee of the Society of Artists, Sydney, featuring Julian Ashton, Will Dyson [qq.v.7,8], Norman Lindsay, Sydney Long, D. H. Souter [qq.v.], Rose Soady (Lindsay) and Harry Weston, has often been reproduced.

In 1901 the *Australasian Photographic Review* described King as 'one of the oldest and . . . most successful photographers in New South Wales' and three years later illustrated an entire issue with his work: 'Mr King is a photographer of the old and new schools combined, and stands high in the esteem of the craft, and by amateurs he is regarded as a true and valued friend'. His name, it concluded, had become 'a household word'.

Bearded and bespectacled, King was a self-effacing man. He died aged 68 in Waverley War Memorial Hospital on 22 May 1923 following abdominal surgery and was buried on 24 May in the Congregational section of Waverley cemetery. He was survived by his son and three daughters. After his death King's studio collection of glass negatives was purchased by J. R. Tyrrell [q.v.] and eventually by Consolidated Press Holdings. In 1975 an exhibition of his Aboriginal portraits was held at the Australian Centre for Photography. Factual and uncluttered by artistic effect, they were appreciated for their ethnological significance and the dignity of his subjects.

W. T. Tyrrell (comp), *Early Sydney postcards*, 3 (Syd, nd); National Art Gallery of New South Wales, *Catalogue* (Syd, 1906); *A'sian Photo-Review*, 21 Feb 1901, 21 Dec 1904, 15 Oct 1923; *Australian*, 4 Jan 1975; *SMH* 30 Jan 1975.

RICHARD KING

KING, JAMES HAROLD (1889-1959), Congregational minister, was born on 21 May 1889 at Warren, New South Wales, son of William Henry King, English-born draper, and his Australian wife Mary, née Jones. After schooling at Woollahra, Sydney, Harold became a candidate for the ministry at Camden College, Sydney. His studies were interrupted when he enlisted in the Australian Imperial Force in 1916. He rose through the ranks of the 30th Battalion and was commissioned on 2 February 1918; he was wounded in France in August and returned to Australia in November 1919. His post-war studies were influenced by the distinguished Hebraist G. W. Thatcher [q.v.] and by Rev. Samuel Angus [q.v.7]. The historical-critical method shaped King's liberal views on the creeds, but his message stressed God's love in Christ and avoided public dispute.

At Woollahra on 22 October 1921 King married Elsie Marie Fancourt, who was five years his senior. That year he was ordained and inducted to the charge of Kurri Kurri on the coalfields. Many of his people there were of Welsh mining stock and strengthened his regard for organized labour and socialist reform. His second pastorate (1925-36) in the more affluent and fashionable Woollahra Church, Sydney, showed he was nevertheless attuned to all social classes and a counsellor for seekers and those in trouble. His preaching, meticulously prepared and phrased, appealed from the text to the will, without emotional frills. He ministered personally to youth through the Congregational Young Men's Companionship; many young men were drawn by him to the ministry or gained a lifelong sense of lay vocation. In 1931-32 he was chairman of the Congregational Union of New South Wales. In two subsequent charges—Strathfield-Homebush (1936-38) and the city church at Brown Street, Newcastle (1938-44)—King pursued his honorary work as secretary of the Camden College

council, upholding standards of pastoral and academic excellence set by his mentor Thatcher.

Moving to Queensland in 1944, King served the important Ipswich Church until 1958 and gave leadership in many capacities to the small Congregational Union of Queensland. He became a co-founder and chairman of the board of governors of Cromwell College in the University of Queensland. Though he did much personal research to justify the choice of the controversial name, his ecumenical sense of humour savoured the situation when Reginald Halse, Anglican archbishop of Brisbane, remarked at the laying of the foundation stone that he had recently dedicated a church to King Charles the Martyr. In 1948-49 King was chairman of the Queensland Congregational Union and in 1952-54 was president of the Congregational Union of Australia and New Zealand.

Deeply marked by his war experiences, King became a pacifist. Convinced that war was incompatible with the mind of Christ, he resigned his commission in 1936 and worked for the Peace Pledge Union and the Fellowship of Reconciliation. He helped many conscientious objectors during World War II. He never wore a clerical collar, but his grave and wise manner, relieved by a memorably compassionate smile and by his penetrating eyes, conveyed immediate authority. He was honoured and admired in many parts of Australia and New Zealand for his personal influence among non-believers and Christians of all parties. King died at Fairfield, Queensland, on 1 October 1959 and was cremated. He was survived by his wife and daughter.

J. A. Garrett and L. W. Farr, *Camden College, a centenary history* (Syd, 1964); G. L. Lockley, *Grads and undergrads and fellows; Cromwell College . . .* (Brisb, 1964); sermons and broadcasts in possession of Mrs M. Mayne, Bundaberg, Qld.

JOHN GARRETT

KING, JOSEPH (1839-1923), Congregational minister, was born on 30 July 1839 at Downend near Bristol, England, son of James King, schoolmaster, and his wife Mary Ann, née Kitchen. He grew up in a nonconformist home in Oxfordshire and in 1853 was apprenticed at Reading. He attended a school run by his pious employer which nurtured five missionaries for the London Missionary Society including himself and his lifelong friend W. G. Lawes [q.v.5]. In 1857 he became a member of Trinity Congregational Church, Reading, volunteered as a missionary in 1860, and entered Bedford Missionary College. He married Miriam Walkington in London on 6 February 1863, and was ordained on 11 February before embarking in the *Wellesley* for Melbourne. Arriving on 6 June, the missionaries travelled in Victoria, Tasmania, South Australia and New South Wales on a promotion campaign, before leaving Sydney in the *John Williams* for Apia, Samoa. King served as a missionary on Upolu until 1865 and on Savai'i until 1872 except in 1869-70 when he was in charge of the training institution for Samoan pastors at Malua. In November 1872 King and his family left for England. On 27 July 1874 he resigned from the society because of his wife's ill health.

Having 'fallen in love' with Australia in 1863, King returned to Victoria where he continued to promote the Protestant missionary cause in the Pacific. He was Congregational minister at Sandhurst (Bendigo) in 1874-81 and at South Melbourne in 1881-89. From 1883 he gradually assumed much of the work of the L.M.S. in Australia, particularly in Melbourne as the president of its Victorian auxiliary, and revisited Samoa on deputation in 1887. While in London in 1889 he was invited by the directors to become their organizing agent for Australasia. For twenty-two years, until his resignation in 1911, King was an important link between missionaries in the field, the home society and government, particularly the administrations of British New Guinea and Papua. He was on terms of close friendship with George Brown, James Chalmers [qq.v.3], Sir William MacGregor [q.v.5] and Albert Maclaren. He claimed that his annual journeys in Australia and New Zealand averaged about 12 000 miles (19 000 km) and that he had 'the largest speaking acquaintance of any man in Australia'.

In June 1893 King chaired the committee of the first united missionary conference held in Melbourne and in 1896 he organized the centenary celebrations of the L.M.S. in Sydney. He accompanied the society's deputation to New Guinea and Torres Strait in 1897. In April 1900 he attended the Ecumenical Conference in New York as delegate for the New Guinea and Polynesia missions and some of the Australian auxiliaries. As sole member of a deputation to New Guinea and Torres Strait, early in 1905 he visited thirteen stations including Kwato, Port Moresby and Thursday Island. His ecumenical contacts no doubt helped in the eventual easy transfer of the Torres Strait mission to the diocese of Carpentaria.

King amassed a collection of original documents, including the papers of L. E. Threlkeld [q.v.2] and other early missionaries; these are now held in the Mitchell Library, Sydney. From them he wrote *Ten decades: the Australian centenary story of the London Missionary Society* (London, 1895),

Christianity in Polynesia: a study and a defence (Sydney, 1899), and *W. G. Lawes of Savage Island and New Guinea* (London, 1909). His 'Congregationalism in Australasia' was serialized in the *Victorian Independent* in 1917-18. He was also a regular correspondent and contributor to the newspapers. A life deacon of Kew Independent Church, King continued to preach and lecture until his death at Kew on 18 September 1923. He was buried in Boroondara cemetery, survived by his wife, two sons and five daughters. He was noted for his genial disposition, made friends readily, and had a remarkable ecumenical vision.

R. W. Thompson, *My trip in the John Williams* (Lond, 1900); R. C. Blumer and E. C. Rowland, *The Pacific and you* (Syd, 1943); *Vic Independent*, 1 Oct 1923; *Australasian*, 15 Apr 1911; *Argus*, 19, 20, 21 Sept 1923; *SMH*, 20 Sept 1923; J. King letter-books, 1866-1912 (LaTL).   NIEL GUNSON

KING, OLIVE MAY (1885-1958), ambulance driver, was born on 30 June 1885 at Croydon, Sydney, youngest daughter of Sir (G.) Kelso King [q.v.] and his first wife Irene Isabella, née Rand. Educated at home, at Sydney Church of England Grammar School for Girls and in Germany, she travelled widely and had a taste for adventure. In 1910, with three male companions, she climbed Mount Popocatapetl in Mexico.

On a visit to England when World War I broke out, Olive King supplied her own vehicle and went to Belgium as a driver with a volunteer field ambulance service. The organizers were suspected of spying and returned hastily to England, leaving her and two other drivers to be arrested; they were released just in time to escape the invading German army. She then joined the Scottish Women's Hospitals for Foreign Service and went to France in spring 1915 with the Girton and Newnham Unit. After some six months the unit was sent to Serbia.

They landed at Salonika, Greece, on 3 November and moved up to Gevgelija on the Greco-Serbian border where they established a hospital. After six weeks they were forced to dismantle it hurriedly before the advancing enemy. The three women drivers were left behind when the medical and nursing staff were evacuated but managed to get themselves and their vehicles on to the last train just before the station was bombed.

With Serbia occupied by the enemy, allied forces regrouped at Salonika where Olive King remained until 1918. In 1916 she joined the Serbian Army as a driver attached to medical headquarters. She mastered their difficult language and lived in a hut made from an aeroplane case. For a time her large ambulance was the only vehicle available to transport hospital stores, take equipment and reinforcements to the front line twelve miles away and return with patients. She made many such journeys over hazardous roads and was promoted sergeant in April 1917. In August when fire destroyed much of Salonika, she drove for twenty hours at a stretch, often in danger, transporting civilians, medical personnel, patients and hospital records to safety. For this she was awarded the Serbian silver medal for bravery; a year later she received the gold medal for zealous conduct.

Long distressed at the plight of Serbian soldiers, Olive King appealed to her father for money to set up canteens. The committee he formed quickly raised £10 000; she administered the first Australian-Serbian canteen in devastated Belgrade late in 1918 and opened seventeen canteens to sell food, blankets, clothing and other necessities at cost price or below. Obtaining and transporting supplies presented great problems, for the railway system was in chaos, many roads were impassable and bridges destroyed. Often she slept on top of the stores in railway trucks, lorries and wagons to fend off marauding thieves. The last canteen closed in June 1920. For this work Olive King was awarded the Samaritan Cross and the cross of the Order of St Sava, personally bestowed upon her by King Alexander. She returned to Belgrade in 1922 as a special guest at his wedding.

Back in Sydney in 1920, Olive King was active in the Girls Guides' Association of which she was State secretary in 1925-32 and assistant State commissioner in 1932-42. She received King George V's silver jubilee (1935) and George VI's coronation (1937) medals. During World War II she studied inspection at a Commonwealth government aircraft school and was an examiner at de Havilland Aircraft Pty Ltd in 1942-44.

Physically energetic, she particularly enjoyed ice skating, tennis and surfing. She wrote verse and short stories prolifically, but published little; as a hobby she took up bookbinding in leather. She was devoted to her father and family. Moving to Melbourne in 1956, she died there on 1 November 1958 and was cremated.

M. Krippner, *The quality of mercy* (Newton Abbot, Devon, 1980); *Scottish A'sian*, 30 Nov 1920; *Australasian*, 3 Nov 1917; ML printed cat; family papers in possession of author, Darling Point, Syd.
HAZEL KING

KING, REGINALD MACDONNELL (1869-1955), solicitor and politician, was born on 9 April 1869 at South Brisbane, son of Thomas Mulhall King, public servant,

and his wife Jane Maria, née MacDonnell. His father was to hold several senior positions in the Queensland Public Service, including under secretary to the Treasury. Educated at the South Brisbane State School and Brisbane Grammar School, Reginald decided to take up law, was articled to A. G. Unmack and admitted to practice on 14 March 1893. After early partnerships with Romido Francis Alwyne Sachse and Harold Morton Rutledge, both of whom went to country practices but retained King as their town agent, he formed a partnership on 1 January 1911 with his former articled clerk George Roydon Howard Gill which survived for the rest of King's professional career.

Elected to the Coorparoo Shire Council in 1894, he remained a member until the shire was absorbed in Greater Brisbane and was chairman nine times from 1898. With a considerable reputation as an authority on local government law, he served as president of the Local Authorities' Association of Queensland and acted as secretary and solicitor to the association for some eighteen years until 1929. He also had some part-time semi-governmental service on wages boards and on the Victoria Bridge Board.

In 1918 King contested unsuccessfully the rural seat of Logan in the Legislative Assembly for the National Party. On 9 October 1920 he stood again and won. He became prominent and was appointed deputy leader of the Opposition in the new United Party of 1924 with A. E. Moore [q.v.] as his leader. When, in 1929, Labor lost power for the first time since 1915, King became deputy premier to Moore with the portfolios of public instruction and public works. The Moore government won power just as the great Depression swept the world and it was defeated in 1932. Owing to the strains of office in a period of great stress for all, King was seriously ill in the latter part of 1932 but recovered and again became deputy leader of the Opposition. A redistribution of 1935 turned his once rural seat of Logan into a collection of Brisbane suburbs and King was immediately defeated. He did not contest the seat again.

He resumed practice with Gill and his son Stephen in King and Gill, retired in 1951 and died in Brisbane on 7 September 1955. After a state funeral with Church of England rites, he was cremated. He was survived by his Irish-born wife, Helena Maria Hewson, whom he had married in Brisbane on 7 September 1895, and by two sons and two daughters.

A useful citizen, a sound lawyer and a creditable legislator, King was a sincere and kindly friend. Despite opportunities, he never used his official positions for his personal enrichment; he was that now rare being, an honest gentleman.

S. Stephenson (comp), *Annals of the Brisbane Grammar School, 1869-1922* (Brisb, 1923); C. A. Bernays, *Queensland—our seventh political decade 1920-1930* (Syd, 1931); C. L. Lack (ed), *Three decades of Queensland political history, 1929-1960* (Brisb, 1962); *JRHSQ*, 19 (1971-72), no 3; *Courier Mail*, 8 Sept 1955.   J. C. H. GILL

KINGSFORD SMITH, SIR CHARLES EDWARD (1897-1935), aviator, was born on 9 February 1897 in Brisbane, fifth son and seventh child of William Charles Smith, banker, and his wife Catherine Mary, née Kingsford. The name Kingsford was added to the family surname in Canada; William went into real estate business there in 1903 and later became a clerk with the Canadian Pacific Railways. The family returned to Sydney in 1907. Charles was educated at Vancouver, Canada, at St Andrew's Cathedral Choir School, Sydney, and at Sydney Technical High School. At 16 he was apprenticed to the Colonial Sugar Refining Co. Ltd.

In February 1915 after three years with the Senior Cadets Kingsford Smith enlisted in the Australian Imperial Force. He embarked with the 4th Signal Troop, 2nd Division Signal Company, on 31 May as a sapper and served on Gallipoli and, as a dispatch rider, in Egypt and France. In October 1916, as sergeant, he transferred to the Australian Flying Corps. After training in England he was discharged from the A.I.F. and commissioned as second lieutenant, Royal Flying Corps, in March next year; he was appointed flying officer in May and in July joined No. 23 Squadron in France. Wounded and shot down in August, he was awarded the Military Cross 'for conspicuous gallantry and devotion to duty'; he had brought down four machines during his first month at the front and done valuable work in attacking ground targets and hostile balloons. After promotion to lieutenant in April 1918 he served as an R.F.C. flying instructor.

Barred from participating in the 1919 England to Australia air race because of supposedly inadequate navigational experience, Kingsford Smith and his friend Cyril Maddocks piloted joy-flights in England as Kingsford Smith, Maddocks Aeros Ltd. 'Smithy' then went to the United States of America where he failed to attract sponsors for a trans-Pacific flight and was briefly a stunt flier in a flying circus. Back in Australia in January 1921 he worked first in Sydney with another joy-riding organization, the Diggers' Aviation Co., and then as a salaried pilot for Norman Brearley's Western Australian Airways Ltd. On 6 June 1923 at Marble Bar, Western Australia, he married Thelma Eileen Hope Corboy.

Realizing the great potential for air transport in Australia, Kingsford Smith formed a partnership in 1924 with fellow pilot Keith Anderson. They raised the capital to buy two Bristol Tourers by operating a trucking business from Carnarvon, the Gascoyne Transport Co., and in 1927 they returned to Sydney to operate with Charles Ulm [q.v.] as Interstate Flying Services. After tendering unsuccessfully for an Adelaide-Perth mail service, the partners launched a series of important demonstration flights.

On the first of these in June 1927 Kingsford Smith and Ulm completed a round-Australia circuit in 10 days, 5 hours, a notable achievement with minimal navigational aids. Kingsford Smith at once sought support for a trans-Pacific flight and obtained a grant of £9000 from the New South Wales government as well as backing from Sidney Myer [q.v.] and the Californian oil magnate G. Allan Hancock. In a three-engined Fokker plane, the *Southern Cross*, with Ulm and two American crewmen, Harry Lyon and Jim Warner, he took off from Oakland, California, on 31 May 1928 and flew via Hawaii and Suva to Brisbane, completing the historic crossing in 83 hours, 38 minutes, of flying time. The fliers received subscriptions of over £20 000; Kingsford Smith was awarded the Air Force Cross and appointed honorary squadron leader, Royal Australian Air Force. Anderson, no longer a partner, sued unsuccessfully for part of the prize-money.

In August Kingsford Smith flew the *Southern Cross* non-stop from Point Cook, Victoria, to Perth. In September-October with Ulm and an Australian crew he piloted the plane from Sydney to Christchurch, New Zealand, demonstrating the feasibility of regular passenger and mail services across the Tasman Sea. He then set out to fly the *Southern Cross* to England to place orders for a fleet of four aircraft with which he intended to begin an inter-capital air service in Australia. However, on 1 April 1929, losing radio contact with the ground and meeting bad weather over north-west Australia, he was forced to land on the flats of the Glenelg River estuary. Before help reached the stranded party on 17 April, Keith Anderson and Robert Hitchcock had perished in the search. After an official inquiry exonerated Kingsford Smith and Ulm from a charge of having staged the incident for publicity, the flight to England was resumed in June and completed in the record time of 12 days, 18 hours.

Kingsford Smith's airline, Australian National Airways, began operations in January 1930 with Kingsford Smith piloting one of the new Avro Ten planes, the *Southern Cloud*, on the Sydney-Melbourne route. But 'Smithy' was far from ready to settle down. Collecting his 'old bus', *Southern Cross*, from the Fokker Aircraft Co. in Holland where it had been overhauled, in June 1930 he achieved an east-west crossing of the Atlantic, from Ireland to Newfoundland, in 31½ hours. New York gave him a tumultuous welcome. He then returned to England to take delivery of an Avro Avian biplane, *Southern Cross Junior*, and attempt a record-breaking solo flight to Darwin in October. This he accomplished, within ten days, beating four competitors who had left England ahead of him and breaking Hinkler's [q.v.] time by 5½ days.

He was now 34 and world famous. Divorced in May 1929, he married Mary Powell on 10 December 1930 at Scots Church, Melbourne. A little later he joined Eric Campbell's [q.v.] New Guard. He had been made honorary air commodore in November, and the future of his airline appeared bright.

However, on 21 March 1931 the *Southern Cloud*, flying from Sydney to Melbourne with pilot, co-pilot and six passengers, was lost in severe storms over the Snowy Mountains. There were no survivors and the wreckage was not discovered until 1958. This loss and the deepening Depression crippled the airline. Yet to a man with Kingsford Smith's ambitions the pressure to continue flying was constant. In April 1931 he flew the *Southern Cross* on an emergency mission to pick up mail for Australia from a damaged Imperial Airways plane in Timor. In September he made a solo flight to England in a new Avro Avian biplane, *Southern Cross Minor*, intending to gain publicity with an immediate return flight. But his health was showing the strains of an arduous career and the return trip was abandoned on medical advice. In November, however, when one of his company planes under contract to fly Christmas mail to England was damaged in Malaya, he took off in another plane to collect the stranded mail, flew it to England in time for Christmas delivery, and returned with mail for Australia.

In 1932, when he was knighted for services to aviation, Kingsford Smith was almost back to where he had started, selling joy-flights at ten shillings a trip. A flight to New Zealand in 1933 added to this precarious income but failed to persuade the New Zealand government to give him a charter for passenger and mail services between Auckland and Singapore. That year he established a flying training school in Sydney, Kingsford Smith Air Service, but sold out at a loss in 1935.

Towards the end of 1933 prospects brightened. After travelling to England by sea in September, he achieved a brilliant success in October, flying solo from London to Wyndham, Western Australia, in a Percival Gull, *Miss Southern Cross*, in just over seven days. After the feat the Commonwealth government granted him £3000 and he was appointed aviation consultant to the Vacuum Oil Co.

Inevitably, he was attracted by the announcement that a London to Melbourne air race, sponsored by Sir Macpherson Robertson [q.v.] with a prize of £10 000, would be a feature of Victoria's centenary celebrations. With financial help from friends and sponsors, he bought a fast two-seater Lockheed Altair, which he named *Lady Southern Cross*, and invited (Sir) P. G. Taylor [q.v.] to accompany him in the race. The plan had to be dropped when modifications to the aircraft could not be completed in time. Kingsford Smith and Taylor then flew *Lady Southern Cross* from Brisbane to San Francisco in October-November 1934 in order to sell it and reimburse sponsors. This west-east trans-Pacific flight was another first in aviation history.

Leaving the *Lady Southern Cross* to find an American purchaser, Kingsford Smith and Taylor returned to Australia to the long-awaited authorization for a trans-Tasman airmail service. They began the inaugural flight on 15 May 1935. The result was failure in a setting of spectacular courage. Before dawn and some 500 miles (800 km) out over the Tasman, a damaged propeller blade had put one of the three motors out of action, and a second motor threatened to seize as it rapidly burned oil. Taylor, climbing out of the cockpit, succeeded at great hazard in collecting enough oil from the sump of the dead motor to replenish the other. By jettisoning cargo, and finally most of the mailbags, Kingsford Smith nursed the *Southern Cross* back to Sydney.

He was a tired man of 38; but he was impelled to go on demonstrating that the future of world transport was in aviation. He arranged for the still unsold *Lady Southern Cross* to be shipped to England. From there, with J. T. Pethybridge, he took off on 6 November 1935, aiming to make one more record-breaking flight to Australia. It was the end of the long endeavour. The plane and both fliers were lost. It is assumed they crashed into the sea somewhere off the coast of Burma while flying at night towards Singapore. Kingsford Smith was survived by his wife and son and left an estate valued for probate at £12 875.

His contribution to civil aviation was an effort of faith and stamina and places him among the world's notable pioneers. Lean, with 'cool blue eyes', generous mouth and terse manner, he is featured on the Australian $20 note. Sydney's airport is named after him and there is a memorial to him, Taylor and Ulm at Anderson Park, Sydney. The *Southern Cross* is on view at Brisbane airport. Kingsford Smith was the author of *The old bus* (1932) and, with Ulm, *Story of 'Southern Cross' trans-Pacific flight* (1928). His autobiography *My flying life* was published posthumously in 1937 and the story of his life was filmed in Australia in 1946.

N. Ellison, *Flying Matilda* (Syd, 1957); F. J. Howard, *Charles Kingsford Smith* (Melb, 1962); P. G. Taylor, *The sky beyond* (Boston, 1963); E. Campbell, *The rallying point* (Melb, 1965).

FREDERICK HOWARD

KINGSMILL Sir WALTER (1864-1935), politician, was born on 10 April 1864 at Glenelg, South Australia, son of Walter Kingsmill, pastoralist, and his wife Jane Elizabeth, née Haslam. He was educated at the Collegiate School of St Peter and the University of Adelaide (B.A., 1883). In 1883-86 he was employed by the Geological Department of South Australia. He then went prospecting in the Teetulpa and Manna Hills districts and the Barrier district of New South Wales, moving to Western Australia in 1888 and next year to the Pilbara gold rush. He remained on the Pilbara for eight years, managing several mines and serving on the Pilbara Roads Board. From November 1894 to October 1895 he was mining registrar at Marble Bar.

In 1897-1903 Kingsmill was member of the Legislative Assembly for Pilbara. Originally a supporter of Sir John Forrest [q.v.8] he joined the Opposition in 1899, became junior whip, and was appointed by George Leake [q.v.] as minister for public works in his first ministry (May-November 1901) and commissioner of railways in his second ministry (December 1901-July 1902). During Leake's fatal illness he was chosen as acting premier in preference to his senior colleague Frederick Illingworth [q.v.], but after Leake's death Kingsmill yielded the premiership to (Sir) Walter James [q.v.] under whom he served from July 1902 to August 1904 as colonial secretary and minister for education. From February 1903 he became member of the Legislative Council for Metropolitan-Suburban Province and led the government in the Upper House. After a period in Opposition he resumed his old portfolios under C. H. Rason [q.v.] from August 1905 to May 1906, but when Rason resigned was ousted from cabinet by the new premier (Sir) Newton Moore [q.v.], probably because Kingsmill supported a rival aspir-

ant. Contemporaries considered Kingsmill too gentlemanly and easygoing for the cut and thrust of party politics, and his administrative style lacked drive. He was consoled by the chairmanship of committees in the Legislative Council.

The remnants of ambition nudged Kingsmill into standing for the Commonwealth Senate in March 1910, but the Liberals lost and in May he re-entered the Legislative Council as member for Metropolitan Province, retaining the chairmanship of committees. A useful private member, he became a member of the King's Park Board and president of the Lawn Tennis Association of Western Australia, but his main interest was the conservation of native fauna and flora. In 1911-12 he initiated amendments to the Game Acts so as to extend protection to many species of native birds and animals. He was a council-member of the Zoological and Acclimatization Society, acted as director of the Zoological Gardens in 1916-17 and was president of its board, 1916-22. In 1917 he undertook an eleven-week journey to Malaya and the Dutch East Indies (Indonesia) for zoological specimens and also carried out an investigation for the Western Australian government on the prospects of improved trade in South-east Asia; but no steps were taken to act on his recommendation that trade commissioners should be appointed with joint funding from private enterprise and government. In 1918-19 he was appointed to the Senate of the University of Western Australia. In July 1919 he was unanimously chosen president of the Legislative Council.

Then at the elections of May 1922 he suffered defeat by another Nationalist. Kingsmill may have suffered because of his lack of partisan zeal (he deplored the custom of branding all anti-conscriptionists as unpatriotic), though he defended the Upper House staunchly against attempts at mild reform. At the Commonwealth Senate elections of December 1922 he was returned on the Nationalist ticket. He served as a temporary chairman of committees from 1926 to 1929 and was on the Joint Committee of Public Accounts as vice-chairman, 1926-27, and chairman, 1927-29. In 1929 he was unanimously elected president of the Senate and won respect by his dignified and impartial conduct of business during the Scullin [q.v.] Labor ministry. He relinquished the presidency in 1932 and was knighted next year. Once again he neglected his grass roots. He was out of sympathy with the clamour for secession in Western Australia, and was denied pre-selection for the 1934 elections, but before the expiry of his term died of coronary occlusion at his home at Elizabeth Bay, Sydney, on 15 January 1935. After a state funeral with Anglican rites, he was cremated. On 20 December 1899 at St Patrick's Catholic Church, Fremantle, Kingsmill had married Mary Agatha Fanning who survived him. They had no children.

W. B. Kimberly (comp), *History of West Australia* (Melb, 1897); J. S. Battye (ed), *Cyclopedia of Western Australia*, 1 (Adel, 1912); *V&P* (LA WA), 1918 (A4); *West Australian*, 16 Jan 1935; Kingsmill papers (NL).   G. C. BOLTON

KINGSTON, CHARLES CAMERON (1850-1908), lawyer and politician, was born on 22 October 1850 in Adelaide, younger son of Sir George Strickland Kingston [q.v.2] and his second wife Ludovina Catherina da Silva, née Cameron. He was educated at J. L. Young's [q.v.6] Adelaide Educational Institution and later articled to (Sir) Samuel James Way [q.v.]. He was admitted to the Bar in 1873, after the elder brother of Lucy May McCarthy unsuccessfully opposed his application on the alleged ground that Kingston had seduced Lucy. Later in the year, on 25 June, they married. When Way became chief justice of South Australia in 1876, Kingston began to practise on his own account, and in 1888 was appointed Q.C. Over six feet (183 cm) in height and possessed of tremendous strength, Kingston was a formidable athlete in his younger days and was president of the South Adelaide Football Club in 1880-1908. He also joined the Volunteer Military Force of South Australia and attained the rank of sergeant.

Kingston's parliamentary career began in 1881 as member for the House of Assembly seat of West Adelaide. He was re-elected for the same constituency six times until his resignation in 1900. He was attorney-general from June 1884 to June 1885 in the ministry of (Sir) John Colton [q.v.3], but the faction leader he most respected and admired was Thomas Playford [q.v.]. Kingston was attorney-general in the first Playford ministry from June 1887 to June 1889, and he played an important part in the introduction of legislation for the protective tariff and payment of members of parliament.

Kingston represented South Australia at the Australasian conference held in Sydney in June 1888 and, as a strong advocate of a White Australia and opponent of Chinese immigration, had much to do with framing the formula for its regulation. After Kingston's death the Federal Labor parliamentarian Dr William Maloney [q.v.] described him as the originator of the White Australia policy. He did not join the second Playford ministry when it was formed in 1890. However, as a favour to the premier, and at considerable monetary sacrifice, he became chief secretary for its last six months of office from January to June 1892. Playford was absent in India for most of this period and Kingston was acting premier.

The most dramatic and colorful episode in Kingston's political career occurred in 1892. After a prominent conservative member of the Legislative Council, (Sir) Richard Baker [q.v.7], denounced him as a coward, a bully and a disgrace to the legal profession, Kingston responded by describing Baker as 'false as a friend, treacherous as a colleague, mendacious as a man, and utterly untrustworthy in every relationship of public life'. Kingston did not stop there. He procured a pair of matched pistols, one of which he sent to Baker accompanied by a letter appointing the time for a duel in Victoria Square, Adelaide, on 23 December. Baker wisely informed the police who arrested Kingston shortly after he arrived, holding a loaded revolver. Amidst widespread publicity he was tried and bound over to keep the peace for twelve months. The sentence was still in force when he became premier in June 1893.

Victoria Square was the scene of another disturbance in 1895, when the Adelaide manager of the South Australian Co., provoked by remarks made by Kingston, thrashed him with a riding whip and drew blood. The powerfully built Kingston wrested the weapon away from his assailant and proceeded to chastise him. He later told the press: 'Who can now say that I have not shed my blood for South Australia? "What a pity", my capitalistic friends will say, "that there was not more of it" '.

The election of April 1893, conducted while the South Australian economy was in a depressed state, radically altered the composition of the House of Assembly through an influx of new Labor members and rural reformers. Kingston skilfully welded together the liberal factions led by Playford, (Sir) John Cockburn [q.v.8] and (Sir) Frederick Holder [q.v.] and, with the support of the Labor members, defeated the conservative Downer [q.v.8] ministry. The Kingston ministry was in office until December 1899, then the longest-serving ministry in South Australia. Kingston continuously held the portfolio of attorney-general and was also minister of industry from January 1895.

The Kingston ministry is popularly credited with the following reforms: extension of the franchise to women, a legitimation Act, a conciliation and arbitration Act, establishment of a state bank, a high protective tariff, regulation of factories, and a progressive system of land and income taxation. The sheer volume of work accomplished is striking. Not all these reforms; however, were innovations of the Kingston ministry. For example, a land tax and a graduated income tax were already on the statute book, introduced by Kingston in 1885 when attorney-general in the Colton ministry; his own ministry merely increased the rates of taxation. Kingston had opposed adult suffrage during the 1893 election but was persuaded to change his views under pressure from two of his ministerial colleagues, Cockburn and Holder, and from the Woman's Christian Temperance Union. Persuaded that votes for women would be politically advantageous, he proceeded to enforce Sunday closing of hotels, which had been legislated for by the Playford ministry but had remained a dead letter. In December 1894 South Australia became the first Australian colony to enact adult suffrage.

Kingston's industrial arbitration and conciliation legislation of 1894 was the first attempt in Australia to impose arbitration by law as a means of preventing and settling industrial strife. The trade unions did not care to register under the Act and remained outside its jurisdiction. Thus the Act was not a success. The Kingston ministry also established co-operative settlements along the banks of the River Murray in an attempt to alleviate high unemployment in the metropolitan area.

The (Royal) Adelaide Hospital dispute, developing from a comparatively trivial administrative conflict in 1894, plagued the ministry during its term of office and brought the government and the medical profession into open opposition. Kingston's intemperate remarks kept the row at fever pitch. The exchange of letters between (Sir) Josiah Symon [q.v.] and Kingston in the columns of the *South Australian Register* in July 1896 were so vituperative, according to Alfred Deakin [q.v.8], that they 'would have justified half a dozen duels'. In 1896 Kingston also described Dr E. W. Way, a member of the hospital's honorary staff and a brother of the chief justice, as 'medical Jack the Ripper'. A senior official of the Colonial Office, in a minute dated 24 June 1896, despaired of the dispute and dismissed Kingston as 'perhaps the most quarrelsome man alive'. Kingston's transfer to Federal politics in 1901 was an important factor in bringing about settlement of the imbroglio.

Kingston's vindictive streak also came out in his savage cuts to the salary and allowances of the governor, the earl of Kintore [q.v.5], in 1893. He attempted to restrict the vice-regal office further by sending documents needing approval in executive council so near to the time of the meeting that the governor had no hope of reading them.

In all his dealings with Kingston, Kintore scrupulously observed the correct constitutional and social conventions and in his official correspondence never commented on Kingston's personality. However, in a private letter to the permanent head of the Colonial Office, he warned that 'in dealing with Kingston you are dealing with an able but absolutely unscrupulous man. His character is of the worst; he is black hearted and entirely *disloyal*'.

One of Kingston's enduring preoccupations was to reduce the powers of the Legislative Council which heavily amended or rejected the more radical legislation passed in the Lower House. Successive attempts to reform the council's constituency by widening the franchise were defeated in the Upper House. Kingston's obsession with the council continued after the April 1899 election and caused some of his supporters to fear that his uncompromising attitude would lead him to seek a dissolution of the House of Assembly, with unpredictable consequences. In December 1899 a group of members including Playford, his political mentor who looked upon him almost as a son, crossed the floor and the Kingston ministry was defeated by one vote. Kingston requested the governor, Lord Tennyson [q.v.], to dissolve the parliament so that he could appeal to the people. The governor did not act on Kingston's advice but sent for the mover of the adverse motion, Thomas Burgoyne [q.v.7], who declined the offer, and then for V. L. Solomon [q.v.] who succeeded in forming a ministry. This is the last-known occasion on which a governor of South Australia refused a premier's request for a dissolution of the House of Assembly. Ironically, Tennyson, in a letter to Queen Victoria of 19 September 1899, had written of Kingston that we 'work admirably together, & I greatly value his absolute straightforwardness'. But a letter written by Lady Tennyson in July 1903 revealed that her husband 'has always said he thinks [Kingston] is a terrible bully and frightfully obstinate'. Kingston resigned his seat in the assembly in February 1900. After unsuccessfully contesting a seat for the Legislative Council in May he eventually was elected at a by-election in September. He resigned on 3 December to enter Federal politics.

Kingston's major achievement was the contribution that he made to the Federation movement. As attorney-general in 1888 he took charge of the bill for securing the entry of South Australia into the Federal Council of Australasia. With Playford he represented South Australia at the session of the Federal Council held in Hobart in February 1889 and piloted through resolutions for enlarging membership of the council. At the National Australasian Convention in Sydney in 1891, he was appointed to assist Sir Samuel Griffith [q.v.] and A. I. Clark [q.v.3] to prepare the original Commonwealth bill. The South Australian delegates to the second convention of 1897-98 were elected directly by the people. Kingston headed the poll. He was elected president of the convention when it assembled in Adelaide in March 1897. His old political foe Baker lobbied successfully to keep him off the drafting committee. Such a move was regrettable; (Sir) George Reid [q.v.] later praised Kingston as the best parliamentary draftsman he ever knew. Under Kingston's chairmanship, the convention made considerable progress towards a draft constitution. Kingston and the Victorian radical H. B. Higgins [q.v.] were responsible for the clause relating to the arbitration powers of the Commonwealth. Division between small and large States over the financial powers of the Senate was avoided when Kingston dramatically announced that he would vote with the delegates from New South Wales and Victoria to curtail these powers.

The convention was adjourned later in 1897 to enable the colonial representatives to attend Queen Victoria's diamond jubilee celebrations. While in England Kingston was appointed to the Privy Council and received an honorary D.C.L. from the University of Oxford. He also refused a knighthood. Playford, who had resigned from the Kingston ministry in 1894 to become agent-general in London, wrote to his daughter: 'Mrs. K. did not like it . . . and she made herself as disagreeable as she knew how. Poor Kingston had a fearful time of it with her'.

Kingston returned to London in 1900 with Deakin and (Sir) Edmund Barton [q.v.7] to ensure that the Commonwealth of Australia bill passed through the Imperial parliament with as few changes as possible. The delegation gained several peripheral concessions from the British colonial secretary, Joseph Chamberlain, but lost the most important point when Chamberlain insisted that appeals to the Privy Council not be deleted from the bill. After tenaciously arguing their case Kingston and the others had no choice but to give in, though Deakin called the whole affair 'A Drawn Battle'.

At the first Federal election in 1901 South Australia voted as one electorate for House of Representatives seats. Standing on a strong protectionist platform, Kingston topped the poll. He emphasized the social consequences of protection: the goods produced overseas by cheap labour had to be excluded to protect employment and living standards. Protection, he believed, would integrate nation-building and the interests of

the working-class, and was the essential prerequisite for factory regulatory acts and the system of conciliation and arbitration he desired to establish.

The *Bulletin* would have liked to see Kingston become the first prime minister. Barton gave him the demanding portfolio of trade and customs. Kingston guided the first tariff through parliament; it took a whole year of untiring effort before the legislation was passed. As an autocrat he insisted upon personally making all decisions affecting the administration of the department, no matter how trivial. As a result he was a bad administrator. Moreover, he was ill from 1902 and subject to moods of great depression. Barton wrote to Deakin about his fears for Kingston's mental balance and the overworking of customs officials. In applying the Customs Act and its regulations, Kingston fell foul of business interests, notably chambers of commerce, for his meticulous checking of duties liable on imports; many importing firms were prosecuted for breaches of the law. It would appear that the dividing line between inadvertent error and wilful fraud was not always recognized. Predictably, Kingston enjoyed a fight with his enemies, despite the embarrassment caused to some of his ministerial colleagues, and refused to make any concessions. Nevertheless, his tyrannical style of administration abolished many anomalies and laid the foundations for a department with high standards of probity.

The last issue that Kingston threw himself into was the conciliation and arbitration bill of 1903. As the pioneer of such measures in Australia, he drafted the bill but disagreement broke out in cabinet over whether the proposed legislation should apply to British and foreign seamen engaged in the Australian coastal trade. Sir John Forrest [q.v.] was intransigent in his opposition, Barton sided with him and Kingston resigned from the ministry in July 1903. Shortly afterwards his health broke down completely. Political unsettlement and the intervention of an election delayed the bill from gaining the royal assent until December 1904.

In December 1903 Kingston was elected unopposed for the new seat of Adelaide. When the first Labor ministry was formed by J. C. Watson [q.v.] in 1904, he was invited, with the concurrence of the Labor caucus, to join the ministry. Unlike his colleague Higgins he did not accept, probably because ill health was already causing frequent absences from parliament. It is unlikely that Kingston ever considered joining the Labor Party; his scorn of caucus tyranny suggests that he remained a nineteenth-century radical and individualist. The Labor Party gave him immunity at the November 1906 election and he was re-elected unopposed, although by this time clearly too ill to carry out his parliamentary duties. Kingston died of cerebro-vascular disease in Adelaide on 11 May 1908, and was accorded a state funeral. In earlier days he had profited from mining interests in Western Australia and at Silverton, New South Wales, but he was devoid of all money sense and left an estate of less than £2200. However, his wife, who died in 1919, left an estate of some £30 000.

Kingston was the dominant and outstanding figure in late colonial politics in South Australia. He was also one of the leading figures in the Federation movement and left his stamp on the early Commonwealth. A passionate and explosive personality, he was a warm and generous friend. But he was also a bullying and vindictive foe. In 1898 he insisted that his former friend turned critic, E. Paris Nesbit, Q.C. [q.v.], be kept in a lunatic asylum, despite the medical superintendent's opinion that Nesbit should be released.

Kingston's almost total preoccupation with politics may possibly be linked to the tragedy of his family life. His marriage was not a happy union and he soon returned to lechery. He was widely believed to be the father of the firebrand Labor politician A. A. Edwards [q.v.8]. His talented elder brother, Strickland George Kingston, to whom he was close and who had been his legal partner until receiving six months imprisonment in 1884 for shooting at a cabman, became an alcoholic and eventually suicided in 1897. Disputes with his family over the terms of his father's will dragged on through the courts for many years. There was no issue from his marriage and his adopted son died in 1902. His wife's behaviour became increasingly eccentric.

For radicals and Labor supporters, the *Bulletin*'s obituary of Kingston summed it all up: he was 'Australia's Noblest Son . . . a good Australian all the time, and a good Democrat all the time'. He is still regarded in radical circles as one of the greatest Australians, a tremendous reformer, and a wild man to boot. However, the tribune of the people was also an autocrat with a titanic ego, and the passions which often motivated him were not those of a gentle idealist. Deakin, admiring his 'great ability' and 'indomitable will', noted that 'No man more enjoyed the confidence of the masses'. Yet he regretted that 'Kingston's courage verged upon unscrupulousness' and observed: 'Strong passions had crippled his self-development'. Beatrice Webb had mixed feelings when she met him in 1898. She admired him as 'an industrious, upright and capable administrator, with great Parliamentary powers'. At the same time she was disturbed by his 'spite' and 'demagogic dislike of any distinction or superiority', epitomized by his 'war with "Society", the University and his colleagues in the legal profession'. More recently Douglas Pike, in his *Australia: the quiet continent*, had similar qualms: 'he liked to champion the weak as a lawyer, but as Premier he preferred to bully the opposition. His support for arbitration in industrial disputes and votes for women won him repute as a Democrat, but most of his reforms were designed to hurt his enemies more than to help the people'. A bronze statue by A. Drury of Kingston in the uniform of a privy councillor was unveiled in 1916 in Victoria Square, Adelaide, a portrait by Ambrose Patterson is held at Parliament House, Canberra, and a bust is held in Parliament House, Adelaide.

H. G. Turner, *The first decade of the Australian Commonwealth* (Melb, 1911); T. A. Coghlan, *Labour and industry in Australia*, 4 (Oxford, 1918); F. Johns, *A journalist's jottings* (Adel, 1922); A. J. McLachlan, *McLachlan* (Adel, 1948); E. L. French (ed), *Melbourne studies in education 1960-61* (Melb, 1962); A. Deakin, *The Federal story*, J. A. La Nauze ed (Melb, 1963); B. Webb, *The Webbs' Australian diary 1898*, A. G. Austin ed (Melb, 1965); C. P. Trevelyan, *Letters from North America and the Pacific 1898* (Lond, 1969); J. A. La Nauze, *The making of the Australian Constitution* (Melb, 1972); R. Norris, *The emergent Commonwealth* (Melb, 1975); P. Loveday et al (eds), *The emergence of the Australian party system* (Syd, 1977); *Audrey Tennyson's vice-regal days*, A. Hasluck ed (Canb, 1978); M. Blencowe and R. van den Hoorn (eds), *Historical essays: South Australia in the 1890's* (Adel, 1983); *Observer* (Adel), 31 Dec 1892, 3 Aug 1895, 16 May 1908; *Advertiser* (Adel), 12 May 1908; *West Australian*, 16 May 1908; *Mail* (Adel), 27 May 1916, 8 July 1922; *Register* (Adel), 24 Mar 1873, 25 Feb 1927; R. L. Reid, South Australia and the first decade of federation (M.A. thesis, Univ Adel, 1953); E. J. Wadham, The political career of C. C. Kingston (1881-1900) (M.A. thesis, Univ Adel, 1953); C. Campbell, Charles Cameron Kingston: radical liberal and democrat (B.A. Hons thesis, Univ Adel, 1970); M. A. Heaney, The Adelaide hospital dispute (1894-1902) (B.A. Hons thesis, Univ Adel, 1980).
JOHN PLAYFORD

KINGSTON-McCLOUGHRY; *see* McCLOUGHRY

KINNEAR, EDWARD HORE (1874-1965) and HENRY HUMPHREY (1876-1936), businessmen, were born on 27 October 1874 and 15 April 1876 at Moonee Ponds, Melbourne, sixth and seventh of nine children of George Kinnear (1826?-1902) from Nottinghamshire and his second wife Susannah Hamlyn, née Hore, from Devon, England. George Kinnear migrated to Melbourne in 1864 to establish a rope plant for James Miller & Co. He established his own Colonial

Rope Works at Moonee Ponds in 1874, a small but lucrative business, specializing in lashings, clothes-lines and hayband. George Kinnear imported and designed advanced machinery and acquired a reputation for technical innovation, a quality shared by all four of his sons. But it was to Edward and Henry that the business was sold in 1899, for £340.

Edward left Essendon State School at 13 to help in the business. A teetotaller, he became an accomplished gymnast, cricketer, cyclist and footballer. Between 1894 and 1903 he played 159 games for Essendon Football Club, and was in three premiership teams. On 18 September 1901 at Essendon he married Jessie Frew Connelly. Henry was employed by a local newsagent and was later a station book-keeper before entering the family business. On 8 July 1902 at Essendon he married Charlotte Ethel Thrussell (d. 1907) by whom he had a son and a daughter. On 19 January 1909 in Melbourne he married Linda Wilhelmina Alderson; they had one son.

Edward, the senior partner, superintended the manufacturing; Henry managed the office, later established a city headquarters and store, and specialized in buying raw materials and handling sales. Trading as George Kinnear & Sons, in 1902 they transferred the works to a larger site at Footscray. The enterprise expanded steadily through the Kinnears' innovative and aggressive organization and marketing, tariff protection and wartime demands. The workforce grew to some 200 in 1915. John McKellar's novel *Sheep without a shepherd* (Melbourne, 1937) contains an astringent portrait of the brothers in this pioneering phase. Kinnears' entered into price-fixing agreements with the other major Victorian ropemakers, Donaghy's [q.v.4] and James Miller; these three with A. Forsyth [q.v.4] & Co. of Sydney and an Adelaide firm acquired the West Australian Rope & Twine Co. Pty Ltd in 1914-15.

The Kinnears kept abreast of overseas advances: Edward travelled abroad, and his son Edward Hore (1902-1949) spent several years with James Mackie & Sons of Belfast. For a time the Kinnears enjoyed an Australian monopoly of Mackie's designs. The latest machinery was installed at Footscray, serviced, improved and duplicated by a modern engineering and fitting shop. By 1934 Kinnears had a soft fibre spinning mill and advanced plant for manufacturing industrial yarns and twists, sewing and shop twines and cordage; products were sold throughout Australia, New Zealand, the Pacific islands, the Straits Settlements and South Africa. When sanctions were imposed against Italy in 1935 Henry successfully encouraged partnership with James Miller in the reconstruction of the Australian flax growing and milling industry (Flax Fibres Pty Ltd). During World War II Kinnears' supplied the allied forces in the South-West Pacific, and the machine shops made gun, artillery and tank parts. After 1945 expansion occurred into synthetic fibres.

Edward and Henry's sons all served in the factory. From 1925 Henry junior understudied his father, and he and Edward junior joined the board. Henry senior died at St Kilda on 24 February 1936, survived by his children and second wife. A keen golfer and punter, he was regarded affectionately in business circles. Upon the death of Edward junior in 1949, Edward senior relied more on his sons James, sales manager, and George, factory manager. Members of the fourth generation now entered the business. Edward Kinnear senior retired as chairman of Kinnear Ropes (Australia) Ltd when he was 89. Aside from his business interests, which extended beyond ropemaking, he was an Essendon city councillor in 1911-34, a Melbourne Rotarian, and sometime vice-president of the Victorian Amateur Boxing and Wrestling Association.

Widowed in 1944, Edward in 1953 married Chrysanthe Pendergast. He died at his Essendon home Tooronga on 3 March 1965, survived by six children and his second wife, and was buried in Fawkner cemetery. He left an estate valued for probate at £77 580. In recent years Kinnears' became the major ropemaker in Australia.

H. Michell (ed), *Footscray's first fifty years* (Melb, 1909); *Footscray's first 100 years* (Melb, 1959); *Advance Australia*, 15 Mar 1916; *A'sian Manufacturer*, 25 Sept 1920; *Advertiser* (Footscray), 3 May 1902, 9 Mar 1907, 26 Dec 1908, 13 Nov 1915, 10 Mar 1934; *Leader* (Melb), 26 Dec 1908; *Essendon Gazette*, 9 Mar 1922, 19 Dec 1929; *Mail* (Footscray), 27 Oct 1934; *Argus*, 25 Feb 1936; family and business papers (held by Kinnears Ltd, Melb); information from Mr H. Kinnear, Buderim, Qld, and Mrs E. Payne, Currabubula, NSW.

JOHN LACK

KIPPAX, ALAN FALCONER (1897-1972), cricketer, was born on 25 May 1897 at Paddington, Sydney, third son of Arthur Percival Howell Kippax, cashier, and his wife Sophie Estelle, née Craigie, both born in Sydney. Educated at Bondi and Cleveland Street Public schools, he began playing at 14 with Waverley District Cricket Club and by 1914-15 was an established first-grade batsman. When the Sheffield Shield competition was resumed in 1918-19 he was twice chosen to play for New South Wales; the return to Australia, however, of H. L. Collins's [q.v.8] Australian Imperial Force side restricted his opportunities until 1922-23, when he topped the Australian averages with 491 runs at 98. Next season he toured New Zealand with a State team and in 1924-25 played in the last Test against England.

The omission of Kippax from the 1926 Australian team to England, despite a Sheffield Shield average of 112 in 1925-26, is a celebrated blunder in Australian cricket history. After scoring heavily for New South Wales in 1927-28, including one innings of 315 not out, Kippax returned to the Australian side next season; he remained a Test regular until 1932, playing all five Tests against England in 1928-29, on the 1930 tour of England, and against the West Indies in 1930-31. A head injury in 1931, which caused him to miss one of the Tests against South Africa, made him susceptible to 'bodyline'; dropped after the first Test in 1932, he broadcast accounts of later matches for the British Broadcasting Corporation, and with E. P. Barbour [q.v.7] wrote the polemical *Anti bodyline* (Sydney, 1933). He made a second tour of England in 1934 when, although hampered by illness, he played in the final Test. In 22 Test matches, he scored 1192 runs at 36, with two centuries.

A right-hand, impeccably correct and elegant batsman, Kippax had an upright, easy stance at the wicket; like his schoolboy idol Victor Trumper [q.v.], he rolled his sleeves between wrist and elbow and excelled with the late cut. Captain of New South Wales in 1926-34, 'Kip' welded with wit, kindness and some practical joking a raw team into a formidable unit, nurturing such youngsters as Archie Jackson, Stan McCabe [qq.v.] and (Sir) Donald Bradman; through him the Trumper style passed to Jackson. Kippax's 6096 runs at 70 for New South Wales in Sheffield Shield competition, has remained a record since his retirement in 1935. His most famous innings was at Christmas 1928, when he made 260 not out against the traditional enemy Victoria, sharing a world record last-wicket partnership of 307 with H. L. Hooker. In first-class matches Kippax scored some 12 750 runs at 58, with 43 centuries; for Waverley he made over 7000 runs at 53. Elected a life member of the New South Wales Cricket Association in 1943-44, he shared a benefit with Bert Oldfield [q.v.] in 1949 which realized almost £6100.

In 1926 Kippax, then a clerk, had opened a sports store at Martin Place which he built into a successful business. A prominent lawn bowler after his retirement from cricket, he died of heart disease at his home at Bellevue Hill on 5 September 1972, survived by his wife Mabel Charlotte, née Catts, whom he had married at St Stephen's Presbyterian Church on 20 April 1928. His estate was sworn for probate at $302 160. The Kippax Centre in the Canberra suburb of Holt is named after him.

G. Tebbutt, *With the 1930 Australians* (Lond, 1930); A. G. Moyes, *A century of cricketers* (Syd, 1950); R. Barker and I. Rosenwater, *England v Australia . . . 1877-1968* (Melb, 1969); D. Frith, *The Archie Jackson story* (Ashhurst, Eng, 1974); NSW Cricket Assn, *Annual Report and Year Book*, 1913-14 to 1936-37, 1941-42, 1948-49; *Wisden Cricketers' Almanack*, 1919, 1925, 1927, 1973; *Parade*, no 140 (Mar 1964); *Aust Cricket*, Oct 1972; Waverley District Cricket Club, *Annual Report*, 1980-81; *SMH*, 8 Jan 1926, 23 Dec 1932, 11, 12 July 1934, 30 Dec 1941, 25 Sept 1963, 6 Sept 1972, 27 Feb 1973; *Sunday Herald*, 20 Feb 1949.

B. G. ANDREWS

KIRK, MARIA ELIZABETH (1855?-1928), temperance advocate and social reformer, was born probably on 9 December 1855 in London, daughter of Alfred Peter Sutton, salesman's assistant, and his wife Maria Elizabeth. On 14 September 1878 she married Frank Kirk, an ironmonger's assistant and later a bootmaker.

Reared in the Quaker faith, Marie Kirk worked as a missionary in London's slums, and in her late twenties became active in the British Women's Temperance Association. She represented it in 1886 at a meeting held in Toronto, Canada, to organize the World's Woman's Christian Temperance Union. Later that year the Kirks migrated to Victoria and settled first at Warragul before moving to Camberwell late in 1888.

In November 1887 Mrs Kirk played a large part in establishing the Woman's Christian Temperance Union of Victoria, an offshoot of the American organization founded in 1874 by Frances E. Willard to fight the liquor traffic and promote social and moral reforms. After serving briefly as recording secretary of the new union and president of a short-lived Warragul branch, in February 1888 Kirk became colonial (later general) secretary of the W.C.T.U. of Victoria. She also edited the W.C.T.U. journal, *White Ribbon Signal*, from its inception in 1892, and later served for many years as president of the union's Melbourne branch. In May 1891 she became secretary of the newly formed W.C.T.U. of Australasia, and in 1897 represented the Victorian body at temperance conventions in Britain and the United States of America. In 1902, as a delegate of the W.C.T.U., she helped to establish the National Council of Women of Victoria, and served on its executive committee until 1913. Kirk resigned the secretaryship of the W.C.T.U. of Victoria late in 1913, because of ill health, but remained an active member for some years longer.

In appearance Mrs Kirk was a 'rather fragile, delicate little woman', yet her 'passionate earnestness', 'winning manner' and 'more than ordinary' organizing ability made her 'the heart of the movement'. Her wide-ranging activities included founding new branches of the union, managing its headquarters, raising funds, and running a club for working-girls. She imbued the *White Ribbon Signal* with her ardent Christian piety, together with lively feminist views and a keen interest in social reform, preoccupations which reflected the W.C.T.U.'s commitment to 'Home Protection'.

In 1891 she organized and presented to parliament a huge Women's Petition for enfranchisement; and in 1894 was a founding committee-member of the Victorian Women's Franchise League. During the 1890s she also led the W.C.T.U.'s successful defence of a higher age of consent for girls. Her visits among women prisoners made her advocate appointment of female gaol attendants, and her own efforts contributed greatly to the introduction of police matrons in 1909. With both the W.C.T.U. and the N.C.W. Kirk did much to bring into being the Children's Court Act of 1906. She was also actively interested in free kindergartens for children of inner suburbs; in 1909 she founded the W.C.T.U.'s South Richmond kindergarten, which later bore her name as a memorial to her work. At her death, Kirk's W.C.T.U. colleagues paid eloquent tribute to her 'wisdom, courage, tact and ability', and her 'splendid pioneer service' for temperance and social reform, setting upon her grave the epitaph: 'Her works do follow her'.

She died on 14 January 1928 at Malvern, Melbourne, and was buried with Presbyterian forms in Box Hill cemetery. She was survived by her husband and their daughter.

I. McCorkindale (ed), *Pioneer pathways* (Melb, 1948); A. M. Norris, *Champions of the impossible* (Melb, 1978); *PD* (Vic), 1906, p 603, 3201; WCTU (Vic), *Annual Report*, 1888-1913; *White Ribbon Signal* (Melb), Apr 1894, 1 Nov 1913, 8 Feb 1928; *Aust Woman's Sphere*, 10 Oct 1902, 8 Apr, 10 May 1903; National Council of Women (Vic), *Annual Report*, 1903-13; *T&CJ*, 31 Mar 1894; *Argus*, 17, 18, 19 Jan 1928; information from Mrs H. E. L. Patton, Melb.

ANTHEA HYSLOP

KIRKBY, SYDNEY JAMES (1879-1935), Anglican bishop, was born on 24 January 1879 at Sandhurst (Bendigo), Victoria, eleventh (and fifth surviving) child of Joseph Kirkby, clerk, and his wife Alice Maude, née Paine, both English born. Educated at Gravel Hill State School, Kirkby was strongly influenced by Rev. Herbert Begbie and became a lay reader at White Hills in 1902. He was sent by Bishop Langley to Moore Theological College, Sydney, where he blossomed as a student. Abbott scholar and senior student for 1905, he took a rare first in the Oxford and Cambridge preliminary examination.

Returning to Bendigo, Kirkby was made deacon on 24 December 1905 and placed at Pyramid Hill. At Bendigo on 17 October 1906 he married Victoria Ethel Godfrey. Priested by Archbishop Clarke [q.v.8] on 21 December, he became rector of Malmsbury. A vigorous pastor, imbued with a deep spirituality, he remained a scholar. In 1911 he returned to Moore College to be acting principal of Moore College. Taking advantage of the recent affiliation to the University of Durham, England, to proceed to a theology diploma, he spent 1912 there and graduated B.A. In 1914 he became rector of St Anne's, Ryde.

A firm Evangelical, Kirkby had a keen interest in promoting his school of churchmanship through the activities of the Anglican Church League and similar agencies, but he also perceived that the Evangelicals had a part to play in specialized missions to the outback. The Bush Church Aid Society for Australia and Tasmania was formed in Sydney in 1920 with promised support from the Colonial and Continental Church Society in England, and Kirkby became executive officer. Archbishop Wright [q.v.] of Sydney was among the few bishops to countenance the scheme.

A man of plain habits and considerable physical strength, Kirkby 'carried his swag' and underwent much hardship on his outback tours. While thus conforming to the bush image, he knew that only good organization and the use of modern technology could make the mission effective. Missioners were trained in Sydney and Melbourne and nurses recruited; bush nursing sisters were organized in 1922 and bush deaconesses in 1925; hospitals and hostels were opened in the far west of New South Wales and in South Australia and mission vans pressed into service; and an 'aeroplane mission' began in 1928. From his base in Sydney, Kirkby conducted a steady publicity campaign, editing the society's journal, *Real Australian*, and writing in 1930 a vivid account of its work, *These ten years*.

In 1932 Kirkby was recalled to diocesan affairs. Already part-time archdeacon of Camden, he was now appointed bishop coadjutor of Sydney. Consecrated on 24 August, he found himself in charge of the diocese when Wright died next February. He applied himself vigorously to the financial and social problems of the Church, still suffering from the Depression, and to the apparently perennial difficulty of constitutional reform. As bishop coadjutor he was also rector of the city church of St Philip. Here he maintained a popular ministry, his weekday lunchtime services attracting large crowds. It fell to Kirkby to preside over the election of the new archbishop. Although nominated against his wishes, he avoided serious candidature and steered the synod through an exhausting session wherein a carefully orchestrated movement for the election of Bishop H. W. K. Mowll of West China succeeded. Despite Kirkby's popularity and robust good sense, he was unable to heal the resulting split in Evangelical ranks.

After Mowll's enthronement in March 1934, Kirkby continued as assistant to the archbishop and, with more enthusiasm, as minister at St Philip's. Suffering from chronic nephritis, he died in Royal Prince Alfred Hospital on 12 July 1935 and was buried in the grounds of St Philip's. His wife, two sons and two daughters survived him.

C of E, Diocese of Syd, *Yearbook*, 1932-36; *Church Standard*, 19 July 1935; *Aust Church Record*, 25 July 1935.   K. J. CABLE

KIRKCALDIE, DAVID (1848-1909), railway commissioner, was born in December 1848 near Kirkcaldy, Fifeshire, Scotland, son of William Kirkcaldie, farmer, and his wife Katherine, née Methuen. In 1861 after local schooling, he joined the Leven and East of Fife Railway as a cadet. He spent nearly fifteen years with that company and with the North British Railway which absorbed it, slowly climbing the ladder on the traffic side.

Kirkcaldie arrived in Sydney in 1876 and was appointed as a clerk in the New South Wales railways. Promoted chief clerk in 1880 and office superintendent next year, in 1883 he became assistant traffic manager for the southern and western lines at a salary of £550 a year. In 1889, after the southern and western system was connected to the northern line by the new Hawkesbury River bridge, he became chief traffic manager for the combined system at a salary of £1000, increased in 1891 to £1100.

In October 1897 Kirkcaldie was appointed a railway commissioner after the death of E. M. G. Eddy [q.v.8]. He brought to his new position a thorough grounding and wide experience in all traffic matters, especially rates and rating, but a clash of personalities with the chief commissioner C. N. J. Oliver [q.v.] led to the appointment of the royal commission into railway administration in 1905. Part of its brief was to examine the 'inharmonious relations' between the commissioners. The royal commission concluded that the term 'inharmonious relations' was a euphemism, and that the cause of the conflict was Oliver's autocratic style and his long-standing personal antipathy to Kirkcaldie, who had opposed him on a number of issues. The result of the inquiry was the abolition of the system of three commissioners. Kirkcaldie became assistant commissioner for railways under the new commissioner, T. R. Johnson.

Bearded, with a dignified and rather austere countenance, Kirkcaldie had a strong capacity for friendship. Although quick-tempered and at times impatient, he had a rigid sense of justice, and was quick to admit fault if one of his decisions was proven wrong. It was this quality, combined with a courteous attitude to his juniors, an instinctive leadership and a commanding presence which enabled him to control with conspicuous success a large and expanding staff at a time of increasing union militancy. His contemporaries recognized his commercial and technical ability. In 1901 he was offered the commissionership of the Victorian Railways and, to keep him, the New South Wales government carried a special Act to increase his salary.

Kirkcaldie had married Alice Angela Mountain at Petersham on 5 June 1884; they lived at Homebush. He died in hospital at Summer Hill on 5 September 1909 from septicaemia following an operation for appendicitis, and was buried in the Anglican section of Enfield cemetery.

He was survived by his wife and three daughters, the second of whom, Rosa Angela Kirkcaldie [q.v.] served as a nursing sister overseas in World War I.

Cyclopedia of N.S.W. (Syd, 1907); *PP* (NSW), 1906, 4, p 295; *Pastoral Review*, 15 Sept 1909; *T&CJ*, 11 Apr 1906, 30 Jan 1907, 8 Sept 1909; *SMH*, 6 Sept 1909.   J. D. WALKER

KIRKCALDIE, ROSA ANGELA (1887-1972), hospital matron and army nurse, was born on 3 June 1887 at Homebush, Sydney, second daughter of Scottish-born David Kirkcaldie [q.v.] and his English wife Alice Angela, née Mountain. She entered Royal Prince Alfred Hospital, Sydney, as a probationer in March 1910, gained her nurse's certificate in March 1914 and won the Sir Alfred Roberts [q.v.6] medal. With the outbreak of World War I, she resigned on 21

August to join the *Grantala*, the hospital ship accompanying the Australian Naval and Military Expeditionary Force to German New Guinea.

Kircaldie returned to Sydney with the *Grantala* in December. Impatient to enlist, she went to England and in May 1915 joined Queen Alexandra's Imperial Military Nursing Service Reserve. In mid-May she began work at the Hospital of the Knights of St John, Valetta, Malta. Casualties from Gallipoli, many of them Australians, were pouring in. 'So many were brave beyond belief', she recalled in a narrative of her war experiences. In October she volunteered for duty on hospital ships, joining the *Panama* which was taking wounded from Malta to England. In November it went to Gallipoli to evacuate wounded and Kirkcaldie recorded: 'They came to us straight from the trenches, their muddy, filthy clothing frozen on them. They were famished, gaunt, and weary, and suffering intolerable pain'. Her sympathy was mingled with anger: many frostbitten limbs were gangrenous and required immediate amputation. In mid-February 1916 the *Panama* was ordered to England to transport wounded across the Channel and after the battle of the Somme began in July its nursing staff suffered 'continuous and intense' strain.

In the autumn Rosa Kirkcaldie was transferred to the 8th General Hospital at Rouen, France; in March 1917 she was posted first to the 5th Stationary Hospital, Abbeville, then to the 8th Casualty Clearing Station at Arras. On 9 April, during the Arras offensive, Kirkcaldie and her colleagues 'commenced to know work as we had never known it, and to face sights the tragedy of which no words can tell'. For the next few days the C.C.S. was filled with the remnants of the splendid Scottish regiments she had seen marching up to the front only days before. In May she received three weeks leave in England—her first leave in two years. She was then posted briefly to the 10th Stationary Hospital at St Omer, France, and to the 6th C.C.S. at Barlin. Here, in July 1917, she first saw 'the deadly effects of poison gas'. After only a few weeks there she was recalled to England and reprimanded for returning to France without the prescribed medical examinations. She worked in military hospitals in Lancashire and at Warrington but when her contract ended in November she resigned. For her service she received the Queen Alexandra's Imperial Military Nursing Service Medal.

Back in Sydney by early 1918, Kirkcaldie was acting assistant matron at Royal Prince Alfred Hospital in 1918-19 and then became matron of Canonbury Hospital. Her book, *In gray and scarlet*, written with clarity and sen-

sitivity, was published in 1922. From 1922 she was secretary of the New South Wales Bush Nursing Association, but resigned in 1924 to become the 'very celebrated' matron of the Royal Alexandra Hospital for Children, Camperdown. In 1979 the hospital's historian wrote: 'she was one of the Hospital's greatest matrons, intelligent, competent, making great demands of herself and expecting those under her to do their best'. A 'high-minded idealist', she was generous, sensitive and inspired firm loyalties. In 1932-33 she was president of the Australasian Trained Nurses' Association and in 1935 was appointed C.B.E. The hospital's new nurses' home, completed in 1941, was later named Kirkcaldie House. She resigned her matronship in July 1945.

Kirkcaldie died, unmarried, on 4 August 1972 at Collaroy and was privately cremated. Most of her estate, sworn for probate at $56 969, was left to her sisters and ultimately to the Royal Alexandra Hospital for Children. Part of this bequest funds the R. A. Kirkcaldie medal awarded annually to the most promising trainee. Petite, with delicate features but great stamina, Rosa Kirkcaldie was a gracious, courageous woman totally dedicated to her profession. Her portrait, by Norman Carter [q.v.7], hangs in Kirkcaldie House. Her elder sister, Katherine Vida Kirkcaldie, served abroad with the Australian Army Nursing Service in World War I.

A. G. Butler (ed), *Official history of the Australian Army Medical Services . . . 1914-19*, 3 (Canb, 1943); D. M. Armstrong, *The first fifty years* (Syd, 1965); D. G. Hamilton, *Hand in hand* (Syd, 1979); *A'sian Nurses' J,* July 1923, Aug 1935, Aug 1945; *SMH,* 7 Aug 1972; nursing registers and records, Royal Alexandra Hospital for Children, Sydney, *and* Royal Prince Alfred Hospital, Sydney; records (AWM).   MERRILYN LINCOLN

KIRKPATRICK, ANDREW ALEXANDER (1848-1928), printer and politician, was born on 4 January 1848 in London, son of Patrick Alexander Kirkpatrick, an Irish railway policeman, and his wife Mary Ann Gildin, née Stinton, a nurse who later accompanied Florence Nightingale to the Crimean War. His father died when he was 1, leaving thirteen children; the boy began work on a farm at 9. In 1860 he migrated with his mother to Adelaide and was apprenticed as a printer while attending night school. Later he worked on the *Advertiser* and at the Government Printing Office before forming his own printing firm. He was a foundation member (1874) and, in 1882, president of the Typographical Society of South Australia and in 1883 was president of the National Liberal Reform League of South Australia. He helped to form the United Trades and Labor Council (1884) and the Eight Hours' Celebration Union, of which he was chairman for several years from 1886.

When the unions endorsed and supported candidates for election in the late 1880s, Kirkpatrick was on the parliamentary committee of the U.T.L.C.; and when it formed the United Labor Party in 1891, he was one of three endorsed candidates that year at the first election the party fought, for the Legislative Council. In 1887 he had unsuccessfully contested the assembly seats of Port Adelaide and West Torrens with U.T.L.C. support. He represented the Southern council district, not a 'natural' Labor area, for his six-year term, but was defeated in 1897. His special interest was constitutional reform and the most radical private bill introduced by a U.L.P. member was his unsuccessful franchise extension bill of 1894. In 1899 he tried again to enter the House of Assembly but lost.

In 1900 he returned to the Legislative Council as representative for Central district and was re-elected in 1902 and 1905. In 1902 he battled for the establishment of wages boards. As a pioneer Labor parliamentarian Kirkpatrick set a high standard and provided a model for those who followed. He resigned in 1909 to be the State's first Labor agent-general in London. He returned to South Australia in 1914 and resumed political life as member for Newcastle in the House of Assembly in 1915-18, and as a member for Central No. 1 in the Legislative Council from 1918 until his death. Quick-witted and holding strong views, he was always a cool and fluent debater.

He had been chief secretary and minister for industry in the Tom Price [q.v.] government of 1905-09 and leader of the government in the Upper House. He held the portfolios of mines, marine, immigration and local government in the Gunn [q.v.] ministry of 1924-26 and in the Hill [q.v.] ministry of 1926-27. Following the 1917 Labor split over conscription, he had been Opposition leader in the assembly in 1917-18.

A faithful and devoted Labor leader, 'Kirk' was 'a wonderful old man, honest, and as straight as a die'. In old age his thick snowy beard and hair gave him a venerable appearance. He was a Protestant. He had married Catherine Maria Cooper in Adelaide on 4 April 1878; they had four daughters and three sons. Unwell from 1925, he died on 19 August 1928 and, after a state funeral, was buried in Payneham cemetery.

H. T. Burgess (ed), *Cyclopedia of South Australia*, 1 (Adel, 1907); J. Churchett, *One hundred years of the Printing Union in South Australia, 1874-1974* (Adel, 1974); *Quiz* (Adel), 4 Sept 1891; *Printing Trades J*, 9 Oct 1928; *Observer* (Adel), 6 June 1891, 25 Aug 1928; *Advertiser* (Adel), 20 Aug 1928; J. Scarfe, The Labour wedge: the first six Labour members of the South Australian Legislative Council (B.A. Hons thesis, Univ Adel, 1968).

DEAN JAENSCH

KIRKPATRICK, JOHN (1856-1923), architect, was born on 12 September 1856 at Albury, New South Wales, first of eight children of John Hunter Kirkpatrick, carpenter from Scotland, and his Bathurst-born wife Margaret, née Jones. His father, influential in the Hume district, used his political connexions for his son's benefit when Kirkpatrick commenced practice in Sydney at 17. Like many aspiring architects of the time, he was articled to Edmund Blacket [q.v.3], and worked for him until, energetic and ambitious, he set up his own practice in 1880. At 23 he had already been responsible for constructing approximately fifty-six buildings, including shops and warehouses, housing projects, insurance buildings and Masonic halls. Typical of the period is the famous Carrington Hotel at Katoomba, the first of many hotels he designed.

Between 1880 and 1890 Kirkpatrick was awarded first premium in at least ten major competitions. His initial success was in a competition for the New Holy Trinity Church at Grenfell. Notable among the commissions he won is the Mutual Life Insurance Co. of New York building, Martin Place, Sydney, constructed in the early 1890s. He completed Sydney Hospital, replacing the original architect, Thomas Rowe [q.v.6], in 1891, and designs for public hospitals at Goulburn and Bathurst followed. In 1887 Sir Henry Parkes [q.v.5], an acquaintance of Kirkpatrick, had held a competition for a state house to be constructed in what was to be called Centennial Park, Sydney, to commemorate the centenary of Australian settlement. Kirkpatrick also won this competition, although because of political wrangling related to the potentially excessive cost the building was never constructed. (Sir) George Dibbs [q.v.4] claimed in parliament that although the budget was £150 000 it would finally cost £800 000. £200 000 had already been spent on purchasing the land.

Kirkpatrick was criticized by fellow architects and others who claimed that he had undue influence among parliamentarians, particularly with the secretary for public works, (Sir) William Lyne [q.v.], and that this accounted for his uncanny success in acquiring commissions for major public buildings. Parliamentary records indicate that Lyne did indeed give Kirkpatrick exceptional support in the debates related to these buildings. (Sir) John Sulman [q.v.] also recorded his belief that Kirkpatrick systematically corrupted competition judges by withholding repayments on loans.

On 24 May 1887 in Sydney Kirkpatrick married Annie Elizabeth Douglas Morris; they had nine children, of whom the eldest and youngest sons became architects. Kirkpatrick's practice survived the 1890s depression despite petitions against him in the bankruptcy court. In this period he constructed the original five stands at the Sydney Cricket Ground which are among his finest buildings. He joined the Institute of Architects of New South Wales in 1891 and was a fellow by 1904 but he was never on good terms with the institute.

In 1894 Kirkpatrick proposed a 'Marine Drive' to run along the foreshores of Port Jackson, preventing waterfront development and preserving a green belt for public use. It never eventuated. In 1903 he was selected as chairman of the royal commission appointed to recommend a site for the national capital. The commission originally recommended the site of Albury but Canberra was later chosen for political reasons. Kirkpatrick was not only closely involved in the initial investigations but, as one of the judges, recommended the acceptance of Walter Burley Griffin's [q.v.] design for the city.

Kirkpatrick was a cousin of (Sir) Denison Miller [q.v.], governor of the Commonwealth Bank. When it was decided in 1912 to construct major buildings in each State Kirkpatrick became official bank architect, commencing with the commission, completed in 1916, for the large Commonwealth Bank on the corner of Martin Place and Pitt Street, Sydney. Banks in Melbourne, Newcastle and Geelong followed. Kirkpatrick was also commissioned to design warservice homes and, in partnership with his eldest son Herwald, constructed 1777 houses in all States over three years, from 1918. In 1920 Kirkpatrick recommended that Sydney's Martin Place be widened and extended to Elizabeth Street, culminating in a large war memorial. Although patriotic fervour was strong among Australians wishing to honour their war dead, and the proposal was argued for years after Kirkpatrick's death, the financial implications proved an insurmountable barrier.

Kirkpatrick died of cancer at Woollahra on 14 May 1923, survived by his wife and children, and was buried in South Head cemetery with Presbyterian forms. His estate was valued for probate at £5944. His practice, continued for a time by Herwald, was later incorporated into the firm of Robertson & (T. J.) Marks [q.v.], with whom Kirkpatrick had been involved in ventures dating back to 1912. A good, but not exceptionally gifted architect, Kirkpatrick owed his success, extending over forty years and involving several hundred buildings, more to outstanding drive and political connexions than to creative skill.

J. M. Freeland, *Architect extraordinary* (Melb, 1970); S. W. Malone, The life and work of John Kirkpatrick (B.Arch. Hons thesis, Univ NSW, 1969).
                                                STEPHEN MALONE

KIRKPATRICK, JOHN SIMPSON (1892-1915), soldier, 'the man with the donkey', was born on 6 July 1892 at Shields, County Durham, England, son of Robert Kirkpatrick (d. 1909), merchant seaman, and his wife Sarah Simpson. After attending the Barnes and Mortimer Roads schools he became a milkboy for four years and at 17, after a brief association with the local Territorial Army, joined the merchant navy.

In May 1910 Kirkpatrick deserted at Newcastle, New South Wales. After humping his bluey ('about the best life that a fellow could wish for') and briefly trying cane-cutting and station work in Queensland, he worked his passage from Cairns to Sydney and became a coalminer at Coledale, Corrimal and Mount Kembla in the Illawarra district. In 1911 he went briefly to the Yilgarn goldfield in Western Australia and for the next three and a half years worked as a steward, fireman and greaser on vessels around the Australian coast. Deeply attached to his mother and sister, he wrote regularly and sent a generous portion of his wages to his mother. On 25 August 1914 as John Simpson he joined the Australian Imperial Force at Blackboy Hill Camp, Perth, believing like many others that he would be going directly home to England. Allotted to the 3rd Field Ambulance, Australian Army Medical Corps, he embarked from Fremantle on 2 November for Egypt.

Private Simpson (Kirkpatrick) landed on Gallipoli with the covering force at dawn on 25 April 1915 and quickly befriended a donkey (called variously 'Abdul' or 'Murphy' but usually 'Duffy') to carry leg wound casualties to the dressing station. Day and night he worked cheerfully and unconcernedly amid fierce shrapnel and rifle-fire, carrying the wounded from the head of Monash valley down Shrapnel gully to the beach. So valued was his work that he was allowed to operate separately, camping with his donkey at the Indian mule-camp. He was known to his fellow diggers as 'Murphy', 'Scotty', 'Simmie', or simply 'the bloke with the donk'. His name immediately became a byword for courage: the Indian troops called him Bahadur—'bravest of the brave'. His inspirational work and good fortune, however, were to be short lived. On 19 May he was shot through the heart in Monash valley and buried on the beach at Hell Spit. He was mentioned in orders of the day and in dispatches and though recommended he received no bravery award.

John Simpson Kirkpatrick, perhaps the best-known and most famous Anzac of all, was 5'8" (173 cm) tall, stockily built and weighed 12 stone (76 kg); his complexion was fair with blue eyes and brown hair. He was a typical digger: independent, witty and warm-hearted, happy to be indolent at times and careless of dress. He loved all kinds of animals. Though others after him also used donkeys to bring in the wounded, Simpson and his donkey became a legend—the symbol of all that was pure, selfless and heroic on Gallipoli.

'The man with the donkey' is commemorated by Wallace Anderson's bronze statue at the Shrine of Remembrance in Melbourne and by paintings by H. Moore-Jones in Canberra and Auckland, New Zealand. In 1965 the theme was depicted on three Australian postage stamps marking the golden jubilee of the landing at Anzac Cove.

C. E. W. Bean, *The story of Anzac* (Syd, 1921); I. Benson, *The man with the donkey* (Lond, 1965); *London Gazette*, 5 Nov 1915; *Reveille* (Syd), May 1929, Nov 1930, Nov 1955, Aug 1961; *Sydney Mail*, 3 Nov 1915, 26 Apr 1916; *Age*, 22 June 1936; records (AWM).   G. P. WALSH

KIRKPATRICK, MARY (1863?-1943), midwife, was born at Belfast, Ireland, daughter of George Magee, poulterer, and his wife. She married Hugh Kirkpatrick, butcher, on 19 October 1881 at Ballymacarrett, Belfast. They arrived in Sydney as migrants in the *Cambodia* on 4 April 1884 with an infant son David. A second son George was born at Armidale in June 1889. Mary and Hugh soon separated, and she moved with her children to Kempsey on the Macleay River. In 1902-03 she trained in midwifery in Sydney at the Home Training School and Lying-in Hospital, Newtown.

Mary Kirkpatrick established the first maternity hospital at Kempsey in 1905 and sometime before 1910 managed another institution called The Poplars. She opened a private maternity hospital, Hollywood, at West Kempsey in 1913 and two years later established her last hospital, Down, named after her birthplace, County Down. She worked closely with local doctors and in early years travelled with them to attend deliveries in outlying villages.

Known simply as Nurse Kirk by family, friends and patients, she performed a fine service in her hospital which was unblemished by high mortality rates for mothers or infants. She was 'a fanatic when it came to cleanliness', and there was always washing drying on the hospital verandah, fresh from the boiling copper. While on duty Mary Kirkpatrick dressed formally in a long white uniform, black boots or shoes, a navy blue cloak, a navy pillbox hat on her wavy fair hair and a blue scarf reaching from her hat to the edge of her gown.

Although Nurse Kirk acquired a modest competence from her midwifery work, she readily gave it away. A member of the Church of England, she had strong personal views about moral and social behaviour, but at the same time cared deeply about the unhappiness of others to whom her door and her purse were always open. Nurse Kirk was in her sixties when she discontinued her licence to own a registered private hospital in 1926. She was crippled with arthritis and could only walk with the aid of a stick. Her son George had been killed in action in France in 1917. Her elder son was farming at Nulla Creek. Alone in her last years, she died at West Kempsey on 16 February 1943 and was buried there with Anglican rites.

Remembered as a woman of strong character, single-minded purpose and stern, uncompromising ways, Mary Kirkpatrick became a legend. In the Macleay valley she began a tradition of skilled and careful midwifery practice and impeccable hospital care that continued throughout her career, and that others followed.

Aust Trained Nurses Assn, *Register of members* (Syd, 1907); Armidale Hist Soc, *J and Procs*, Mar 1981, p 83; *Macleay Argus*, 14 Sept 1907, 8 Aug 1913; register of licensed private hospitals, 1913-26 (NSWA).   NOELINE WILLIAMSON

KIRTON, JOSEPH WILLIAM (1861-1935), auctioneer, politician and secretary, was born on 23 November 1861 at Ballarat East, Victoria, son of Emanuel Kirton, bootmaker, and his wife Jane, née Milburn, both from Cumberland, England. After attending Oldham's National School and its successor, the Dana Street State School, he was apprenticed to a trade and then worked in the Post and Telegraph Department. He continued his studies with a tutor from the

School of Mines and became an auctioneer and commission agent. On 20 April 1893 at Williamstown he married a Ballarat girl, Annie Elder Thomas (d. 1897). He married Violette Hillas Finnis with Congregational forms at Ballarat on 26 August 1899.

A teetotaller and Sabbatarian, Kirton also expressed the concern of goldfields society for social justice and economic opportunity. His ideas matured within three powerful Ballarat institutions, the Lydiard Street Wesleyan Church Mutual Improvement Association, the Australian Natives' Association and the South Street Debating Society. He was president of the A.N.A. at Ballarat in 1890 and Victorian president in 1895.

Elected to the Legislative Assembly in April 1889, Kirton represented Ballarat West until May 1904 (except briefly in 1894), and again from July 1907 to December 1908. He chaired the 1897-98 royal commission on old age pensions, was a member of royal commissions on gold mining (1889-91) and the factories and shops laws (1900-02), and served as minister without office under Irvine [q.v.] from June 1902 to April 1903 when he became chairman of the Ballarat Water Commission.

Kirton condemned privilege and fought single-handed against the abuse of free railway passes. As well as pioneering old age pensions he passionately supported the income tax, abolition of plural voting and votes for women. A strong Federationist, he hoped for strictly limited Senate powers. In the 1890s he championed the poor, particularly through village settlement schemes; he openly supported strikers, accepted the socialist rhetoric of the workers as the true producers of wealth and advocated salary cuts for top public servants. As a minister, however, he seemed to forget lifelong principles and by calling the rail strike of May 1903 a rebellion he so alienated the *Ballarat Courier* and his working-class support that he lost his seat.

In 1911 Kirton moved to Melbourne where he established a Collins Street estate agency. He also became secretary of the Victorian Master Bakers' Association. (His younger brother Alfred James, later member of the Legislative Assembly for Mornington, was a Melbourne baker from 1913.) In 1914 Kirton, representing the Federal Master Bakers' Association in the Commonwealth Court of Conciliation and Arbitration, blocked a call for day baking and in 1921 he fought for changes to the day baking bill. He resigned his secretaryship in May 1921, his brother selling his bakery about the same time. In an emotional farewell the Master Bakers' Association praised Kirton as much for his dissemination of culture as for the improvements he had

wrought in the trade, while Kirton acknowledged friendships which only the 'grim Reaper' could break.

He died at Balwyn on 12 October 1935 and was buried in Burwood general cemetery, survived by his wife, two daughters and a son.

M. M. McCallum, *Ballarat and district citizens and sports at home and abroad* (Ballarat, 1916); Associated Bread Manufacturers of Aust and NZ, *The first sixty years, 1904-1964* (Adel, 1967?); *A'sian Baker and Millers' J*, 13 Apr 1921, 10 May 1921, 30 July 1921; *IAN*, 1 May 1895; *Ballarat Courier*, 14 Oct 1935; M. Aveling, A history of the Australian Natives' Association, 1871-1900 (Ph.D. thesis, Monash Univ, 1970); information from Mr E. C. Kirton, Wendouree, Vic. WESTON BATE

KIRWAN, Sir JOHN WATERS (1869-1949), journalist and politician, was born on 2 December 1869 in Liverpool, England, son of Nicholas John Kirwan, gentleman farmer, formerly of Woodfield, Galway, Ireland, and his wife Mary, née Waters, granddaughter of Garrett Byrne, a rebel leader in 1798. After leaving school Kirwan worked for two years for the Dublin *Morning Mail* and *Evening Mail* while doing some freelance work. He wrote 'Our Dublin Letter' for the *Drogheda Argus* whose editor considered him 'one of the most promising and talented journalists of the Dublin press'. On 25 May 1889 he sailed with his sister for Australia to join his brother Edmund, a journalist on the *Brisbane Courier*.

Employed for several months on the *Courier*, Kirwan resigned and travelled via Sydney to Melbourne, arriving in December 1889. He briefly worked for the *Daily Telegraph*, then for rural bi-weekly newspapers at Kerang and Casterton. By 1893 he was back in Sydney, moving to New Zealand later in the year to write commissioned articles for Australian newspapers. He accepted there an invitation to become editor of the *Port Augusta Dispatch* in South Australia. Under him, the paper supported the Kingston [q.v.] ministry and he was publicly thanked by the premier for services to the Liberal cause. A municipal farewell was tendered to Kirwan on the eve of his departure in November 1895 to become editor of the *Western Argus* and *Kalgoorlie Miner* in Western Australia. (Sir) Hal Colebatch [q.v.8], who held the position temporarily, later described Kirwan as 'the ideal journalist, of tireless energy, making himself familiar with all the needs and aspirations of the community and unsparing in his advocacy of what he believed to be right'.

Shortly after his arrival in Kalgoorlie, Kirwan became part-owner with the Hocking [q.v.] brothers of the two papers. The *Kalgoorlie Miner* soon became the sole daily paper in Kalgoorlie and Boulder and a political force respected by parliament and government. It spoke for the most volatile third of the population, a politically conscious and vocal section which Kirwan kept informed on issues affecting their well-being and future prosperity of the goldfields.

By 1898 he had become a harsh critic of the Forrest [q.v.8] ministry, contending that it discriminated against the goldfields population by inadequate parliamentary representation and in other ways. During the year an action for an alleged breach of parliamentary privilege brought against the *Kalgoorlie Miner* failed and Kirwan's criticism of the government continued unabated. He argued for more goldfields members, campaigned successfully for withdrawal of the 'ten foot' regulations which had led to exaggerated reports of near-riots, and perhaps most importantly he played a key part in the Western Australian Federation movement. The reluctance of the Forrest government to hold a referendum on Federation, after the Constitution had been accepted by that method in the eastern colonies, provoked Kirwan to campaign in the *Miner* for separation. Goldfields and Esperance residents, he urged, should petition the Queen for separation from Western Australia in order to join the Commonwealth as an independent State. The campaign culminated in December 1899 in the formation of the Eastern Goldfields Reform League and its presentation of a petition to the Queen signed by 27 733 male residents. The government reconsidered its position and, in the ensuing referendum, 44 800 voted 'Yes' and 19 691 'No'; more than half the 'Yes' vote came from the goldfields.

Kirwan had failed to win the Legislative Council seat of North-East Province in 1898 by ninety votes. When he stood for Kalgoorlie in the first Federal election he won comfortably: the vote reflected his efforts for the Federation movement and the standing of his paper. In the House of Representatives he supported free trade, opposed compulsory military service overseas but favoured the creation of a military college. Like all West Australian members, he urged a transcontinental railway but with a link with Esperance to counteract the Forrest government's deliberate centralization of trade and services in Perth. He was deputy chairman of committees, a member of the Elections and Qualifications Committee and a member of the royal commission on the bonuses for manufacturers bill in 1902-03.

Defeated in the election of December 1903 by a local Labor Party grown strong, Kirwan returned to his editorial chair but was soon forced by poor health to take a long vacation in Britain and Europe. In 1908 he entered the Western Australian Legislative Council as an Independent member for South Province; he retired from the seat in 1946. He continued to support the building of the Esperance railway link (eventually completed in 1927) which he believed would prolong the life of many of the mines, lower prices and introduce thousands of farmers to the area between Esperance and Norseman. In 1923-26 he was chairman of committees and was president of the council from 1926 until he retired.

During his parliamentary career Kirwan took considerable interest in the Empire Parliamentary Association as a foundation member and senior president of the Western Australian branch. In 1931 he was Australian delegate to the seventeenth Conférence Parliamentaire Internationale du Commerce at Prague and in 1933 to the eighteenth conference at Rome, where he was considerably impressed by the achievements of Mussolini. His outstanding position in the newspaper industry was recognized in his appointment as a delegate from Western Australia to the first Empire Press Conference in London in 1909, to the second in Ottawa in 1920 and to the third in Melbourne in 1925. In 1912 he was appointed a foundation member of the Senate of the University of Western Australia and remained a member until 1924.

In 1896 Kirwan had been appointed a justice of the peace and in 1906-23 was a member of the East Coolgardie Licensing Bench. In 1904 he had become the first Federal parliamentarian to have conferred on him for life the title of Honourable. He was knighted in 1930 and appointed K.C.M.G. in 1947. On 2 May 1912 in Sydney he had married Teresa Gertrude, daughter of Timothy Francis Quinlan, a Western Australian politician. They had three sons, one of whom was killed in action in World War I.

Sir John Kirwan was a member of the Western Australian Historical Society and contributed articles to its journal *Early Days*. He was also a frequent contributor to *The Times, Empire Review, Review of Reviews* and *Nineteenth Century*, and author of *The financial and economic structure in Australia* (London, 1931), *A hundred years of the Legislative Council in Western Australia* (Perth, 1932), *An empty land* (London, 1934) and his genial and generous reminiscences, *My life's adventure* (London, 1936).

Kirwan died at Subiaco on 9 September 1949 after a short illness and was buried in the Catholic section of Karrakatta cemetery. His estate was sworn for probate at £14 138.

J. S. Battye (ed), *Cyclopedia of Western Australia*, 2 (Adel, 1913); J. Raeside, *Golden days* (Perth, 1929); *Government Gazette* (WA), 9 Nov 1906; *West Aust Mining and Commercial Review*, Nov 1938; *SMH*, 31 Dec 1889; *Morning Herald* (Perth), 4 Apr 1901; *West Australian*, 12 June 1902, 14 May 1908, 10 Sept 1949; D. Mossenson, Gold and politics: the influence of the eastern goldfields in the political development of Western Australia, 1890-1904 (MA thesis, Univ WA, 1952); J. S. Bastin, The West Australian Federation movement (MA thesis, Melb, 1952); Kirwan papers (NL and Battye Lib).

PAT SIMPSON

KIRWAN, MICHAEL JOSEPH (1873-1941), politician and public servant, was born on 26 April 1873 at Jinbah, Mary River, Queensland, son of Michael Kirwan, sugar worker, and his wife Sarah, née Costello, both from Tipperary, Ireland. After primary education at Yengarie and Petrie Terrace (Brisbane) state schools, Mick entered a bootmaking apprenticeship in 1884, but in 1907 transferred to the Railways Department as a porter based in Brisbane. His considerable vocal power made him a notable train-caller.

Active in the Australian Railways Union which was at the centre of the Brisbane general strike of 1912, Kirwan was sacked after the strike and at the election of 27 April attempted the seemingly hopeless task of wresting the seat of Brisbane from the long-time sitting member E. B. Forrest [q.v.8]. Labor, however, polled particularly well in the metropolitan area and Kirwan won by a slender majority. He retained the seat until 1932. At Tenterfield, New South Wales, on 29 September 1912 he married Catherine Swift; they had one son.

Kirwan approached his new profession with dedication and enthusiasm. His genial personality was well suited to a parliamentary career and he became an impressive speaker and debater. Elected chairman of committees in 1920, he harboured ministerial ambitions and in 1924 was one of those elected to cabinet during the brief and abortive rebellion against Premier E. G. Theodore [q.v.]. Kirwan believed that this indiscretion would ruin his political career, but in July he was made minister without portfolio. Promoted to public works in February 1925, he held this position until Labor's defeat in 1929.

Kirwan's ministerial career was solid rather than spectacular. He never ranked higher than seventh in a cabinet of ten and his legislative initiatives were largely of a housekeeping nature. Nor was he a high-

flier in the organizational wing of the Labor Party. He attended the Labor-in-Politics convention in 1913 and was the parliamentary party's delegate to the central executive in 1916-18. Thereafter he played a minor role in the high councils of the party.

At the 1929 election Kirwan just retained his seat. He was not so fortunate in 1932 when he narrowly lost pre-selection to an Australian Workers' Union organizer. When Labor returned to office in 1932 Premier Forgan Smith [q.v.] appointed Kirwan to the Tourist Bureau. In 1938 he was transferred to the Department of Agriculture and Stock and retired later that year.

Kirwan was a member and office-bearer of the Queensland Irish Association (and was a vehement anti-conscriptionist in 1916-17). He also maintained a long-term interest in the lifesaving movement and was first president of the Surf Life Saving Association of Australia (Queensland centre) in 1931-41. He died of cerebral haemorrhage on 13 February 1941 in Brisbane and was buried with Catholic rites in Nudgee cemetery.

C. A. Bernays, *Queensland politics during sixty years* (Brisb, 1919), and *Queensland—our seventh political decade 1920-1930* (Syd, 1931); J. Larcombe, *Notes on the political history of the Labor movement in Queensland* (Brisb, 1934); *Courier Mail*, 14 Feb 1941; *Worker* (Brisb), 18 Feb 1941.

B. J. COSTAR

KITAMURA, TORANOSUKE (1866-1930), merchant, was born on 12 April 1866 in Kyoto, Japan, eldest son of Kitamura Uhei, druggist, and his wife Kishi, née Fujita. His father died during his childhood. In 1876 he began work as an office-boy with S. Nagoaka, wholesale druggist at Osaka, and in 1885 he went to Hong Kong to gain a practical grounding in foreign commerce. There in 1887 he met and impressed Kanematsu, Fusajirō, the owner of the *Osaka Mainichi* newspaper and former managing director of the Osaka Shōsen shipping company. Two years later, when Kanematsu set up a firm at Kobe to open direct trade with Australia, he prevailed on Kitamura to accompany him to Sydney to establish an office there and manage it after his return; they arrived in the *Tsinan* on 16 February 1890.

The early years in Sydney were not easy. Kitamura later recalled: 'for three years our meals morning and evening consisted of a dish of beef or mutton with a piece or two of bread. For lunch we had bread and water. We tried to economize expenses, attending to labourers' work ourselves, moving the goods in and out of the office'. At Woolwich on 24 March 1894 he married Riku Yasuda;

the marriage was registered at the Japanese consulate on 5 March 1903. She later returned to Japan with their three children.

It was in the station produce industry that Kitamura's influence was first felt. Finding that many items such as sinews, hooves, and leg-bones, for which there was a market in Japan, were discarded in Australia, Kitamura toured boiling-down establishments and, armed with American samples that he had procured from Chicago, gave full directions for the preparation of each product. In this manner he turned what had been an annual waste into a lucrative trade.

In order to gain a practical grounding in the technicalities of the wool trade, Kitamura worked for a time in the wool store of Harrison, Jones & Devlin Ltd. There he made trial purchases of small lots and shipped them to London for resale. In his forty years as head of the Sydney office the number of bales of wool shipped by the firm from Australia rose from 200 in 1890-91 to 2000 in 1904-05, to 10 000 in 1909-10 to 100 000 in 1930 (the year in which Japan supplanted France for second place in the Australian wool market). He first bought wheat in 1900; annual shipments reached 13 000 tonnes in 1919 and 60 000 tonnes in 1925.

When the parent firm in Japan became a public company in 1918, Kitamura was its largest single shareholder, owning 18 percent of the issued capital. From 1922 when the Sydney office became a separate company, F. Kanematsu (Australia) Ltd, he was its managing director. Throughout, it was his custom to have his midday meal with the rest of the Japanese staff at an old table covered with a sheet of newspaper in a corner of the wool sample room. New arrivals saw this as his method of passing on his experience and expertise and impressing upon them that it was economy that saw the firm through its initial difficult years.

It was in 1929, when he was still at the helm, that the firm endowed the Kanematsu Memorial Institute of Pathology and Biochemistry at Sydney Hospital.

Kitamura's principal residence was at Woodford in the Blue Mountains. During the week he lived at 60 Blue's Point Road, North Sydney. He was unusual among the local Japanese community in that he was a permanent resident (only possible for those who arrived before 1901) and raised an Australian family. He had a great regard for Britain and sent two of his daughters to school there.

He was a keen race-goer. One of the most popular and respected figures in the Sydney wool trade, Kitamura made regular visits to Japan and owned a residence and other real estate at Kyoto. He developed bronchitis at sea *en route* to Japan and died at Kobe on 6 June 1930, a few days after his arrival. In accordance with his wishes his ashes were returned to Sydney and buried in South Head cemetery. His estate in New South Wales was valued for probate at £9535. He was survived by a son and two daughters in Japan and by one son and three daughters in Australia.

Kanematsu Ltd, *Kanematsu Rokujūnen no Ayumi* (Kobe, 1961); *Dalgety's Annual Wool Review*, 1929-30; *Kanematsu Geppō*, June 1954, Aug 1959; Official municipal family register (*koseki*) of Kitamura, Toranosuke of 309 Shinnyodō-chō, Nijōnoborou, Kuruma-chō, Kamikyō-ky, Kyoto.

D. C. S. SISSONS

KITSON, SIR ALBERT ERNEST (1868-1937), geologist, was born on 21 March 1868 at Manchester, England, son of John Kitson, schoolmaster, and his wife Margaret Wishart, née Neil. Albert received his early education in India where his father ran a school. The family migrated to Victoria probably in 1878; both parents took up teaching posts at Enoch's Point State School and transferred to Winton North State School near Benalla next year. After John Kitson's death in 1879 Margaret succeeded him as head-teacher; her own children were among her pupils. Albert in 1886 entered the clerical division of the Victorian Public Service by examination.

Initially a clerk with the Postmaster-General's Department at a yearly salary of £80, in 1889 Kitson transferred to the Department of Lands and Survey where he was responsible for keeping rent-roll registers. A further transfer in 1896 took him to the Department of Mines and Water Supply. He undertook part-time studies in geology, mining, and surveying at the Working Men's College and the University of Melbourne. Kitson's success in these studies together with his scientific competence and enthusiasm attracted the attention of the geological survey branch of his department. While still employed as a clerk at £200 a year he carried out geological field work from 1899 until September 1904 when he was appointed senior field geologist at £300.

A member of both the Royal Society and the Field Naturalists' Club of Victoria and of the Australasian Institute of Mining Engineers, Kitson participated in all the meetings of the Australasian Association for the Advancement of Science between 1898 and 1907. In 1897 he was elected fellow of the Geological Society of London. As well as the many reports he prepared for the Victorian Geological Survey he published scientific papers in various Australian journals on geology and natural history. His work in-

Kitson

cluded a survey of Victorian coal deposits and inspection of gold and coal mining. In 1900 he surveyed the Buchan Caves in East Gippsland and recommended the creation of a reserve; one of the caves now bears his name. He was a keen collector of natural history specimens, sending many to Victorian and overseas institutions. He compiled a catalogue of the Tertiary fossils of Australia and had a fossil mollusc, a fossil eucalypt and a living eucalypt named after him.

In 1906-11 Kitson was principal of the Mineral Survey of Southern Nigeria and in 1913 was appointed director of the Gold Coast Geological Survey. Upon retirement to England in 1930 he acted as a geological adviser to the Colonial Office and joined the boards of several mining companies. The author of numerous reports and papers on geology, mining, water power, and geography, Kitson is credited with the discovery of economically important deposits of coal in Southern Nigeria and manganese, diamonds, and bauxite in the Gold Coast. The Geological Society, London, awarded him the Wollaston fund in 1918 and the Lyell medal in 1927. He was president of Section C (Geology) of the British Association for the Advancement of Science in 1929 and of the Geologists' Association in 1934-36. Appointed C.B.E. in 1918 and C.M.G. in 1922, he was knighted in 1927.

Kitson ('Kittie' to his friends), a 'serious' man, religious and an abstainer, clearly enjoyed the field work involved in geology; he was an energetic worker and a strict disciplinarian. A facility in handling snakes, acquired in the Australian bush, earned him a reputation on the Gold Coast as a fetish doctor.

In 1910 Kitson married Margaret Legge, née Walker, who died in 1920. In 1927 he married Elinore Almond Ramage. He died of respiratory disease at Beaconsfield, Buckinghamshire, England, on 8 March 1937, survived by his second wife, their two sons and a stepson of his first marriage.

Nature (Lond), 139, 3 Apr 1937, p 576; *Vic Naturalist*, 54 (1937-38), p 9; *Mineralogical Mag*, 25 (1938-40), p 294; *The Times*, 9 Mar 1937.

LYNDSAY FARRALL

KNEEBONE, HENRY (1876-1933), printer, journalist and politician, was born on 17 March 1876 at Wallaroo, South Australia, son of Cornish miner and engine driver, Henry Kneebone, and his wife Elizabeth Ann, née Tonkin. Elizabeth had taught her husband to read and write and inspired in her son a love of literature. He was educated at Kadina Public School and when 12 began work in the Wallaroo copper-mines. A year later he was apprenticed as a compositor with the *Kadina and Wallaroo Times*, gaining journalistic and typographical skills. Lured in 1894 to the Murchison goldfields, Western Australia, he failed as a prospector but found work on the *Coolgardie Miner*. He became its printer and publisher in 1899 and managing editor in 1906.

In socially militant Coolgardie Kneebone's beliefs and vigorous journalistic and debating styles matured. He was a foundation member of the local branch of the Typographical Society of Australia and joined the Western Australian Workers' Association. He was also active in the Labor Party and sat on the Coolgardie Council in 1906-09. On 4 November 1903 with Methodist forms he had married Henrietta Whitta, a dressmaker from Bendigo, Victoria.

In 1910 Kneebone returned to Adelaide to the Labor paper, the *Daily Herald*; next year he became editor. In 1912 the Federal Labor government appointed him press officer to the new High Commission in London. Kneebone helped to popularize Australia, a series of his pamphlets was translated into German, French and Italian, and he founded a London branch of the Australian Natives' Association. In 1914 and 1915 he represented Australia at the British War Press Bureau and was the founder and first secretary of the Anzac Buffet, which provided free meals and entertainment to Australian soldiers in Britain.

Kneebone returned to Adelaide in 1916 to a Labor Party riven by the conscription crisis. He replaced E. H. Coombe [q.v.8] as editor of the *Daily Herald*. Initially the paper maintained a neutral, impartial stance on conscription but, after control by the Labor Party was confirmed in 1917, it became strongly anti-conscriptionist. In the following years Kneebone used the *Herald* to give a new sense of reconciliation, direction and vigour to the party. But commercially it never recovered from the crisis and its survival till 1924 may have been secured through funds from liquor interests.

Kneebone rose quickly in the party. From 1920 till his death he was on the State executive; he was party president in 1922 and 1930 and regularly attended federal conferences and federal executive meetings in the 1920s and early 1930s. He was also the delegate of the State branch of the Printing Industry Employees' Union of Australia to the United Trades and Labor Council and a delegate to the Australasian Council of Trade Unions. In 1924 he won the House of Assembly seat of East Torrens but resigned next year to contest unsuccessfully the Federal seat of Boothby. He then returned to journalism as industrial roundsman for the conservative daily, the *Advertiser*.

As president of the State Labor Party in 1930 he deprecated the Hill [q.v.] government's 'policy of taxation, dismissals and deflation', but strove to contain the fissiparous forces spilling over from the Federal sphere which were ultimately to wreck the State party. In April 1931 he was appointed to a casual Senate vacancy and announced that he would vote against every measure introduced under the Premiers' Plan; but he lost his seat in the conservative landslide in December.

Next year, although unwell with diabetes, Kneebone threw his energies into creating the weekly newspaper, the *Labour Advocate*, and his work as vice-president of the A.C.T.U. He was also a member of the Advisory Council on Education and the Board of Industry. On 30 November 1933 he collapsed on his way home from work and died of heart disease on 22 December. He was buried in Mitcham general cemetery, survived by his wife, three daughters and two sons, both of whom worked on newspapers.

Kneebone had been a prolific polemicist, a lively populist orator and a hard-working Labor official. Burly in figure, genial and generous in spirit, with the passion of the largely self-taught for education, Kneebone represented the best of that Nonconformist strand which so enriched the early South Australian Labor Party.

F. S. Wallis, *Labour's thirty years record in South Australia* 1893-1923 (Adel, 1923); *Printing Trades J* (Syd), 13 Feb 1934; *Univ Studies in History*, 1963-64, p 47; *Labour Hist*, May 1975, no 28; *Advertiser* (Adel), 23 Dec 1933; *Labour Advocate*, 5 Jan 1934; D. Hopgood, A psephological examination of the South Australian Labor Party from World War One to the Depression (Ph.D. thesis, Univ Adel, 1974).   NEAL BLEWETT

KNEESHAW, FREDERICK PERCIVAL (1883-1955), engineer and company director, was born on 6 August 1883 at Leeston, Canterbury, New Zealand, son of John Kneeshaw, stationmaster, and his wife Annie Elena, née Glasson, both Victorian born. His father's appointment in 1890 to the New South Wales railway service, where he became in 1900 tramway manager, brought the family to Sydney. Frederick was educated at Sydney Technical College and as a cadet in the tramways, where he became assistant engineer in 1904.

After Kneeshaw joined Noyes Bros (Sydney) Ltd in 1909 he was chief engineer for several years before enlisting as a gunner in the Australian Imperial Force in October 1914. Commissioned in January 1915 and promoted captain in the 5th Field Artillery Brigade in October, he served in Egypt, France and Belgium. In January 1917 he was mentioned in dispatches and promoted major in the 6th Field Artillery Brigade. After being wounded in Belgium in July, he was invalided to Australia in November. His appointment with the A.I.F. terminated in February 1918.

Kneeshaw was appointed general manager of Kandos Cement Co. Ltd in 1922, and was also general manager of Kandos Collieries and of Australian Portland Cement Co. Pty Ltd. His directorships included Australian Portland Cement Pty Ltd, Cable Makers Australia Pty Ltd, Colonial Mutual Life Assurance Society Ltd and Parkinson (Australia) Ltd. Active in support of the development and protection of local industry, he was a councillor of the Employers' Federation of New South Wales, president of the New South Wales Chamber of Manufactures in 1935-37 and of the Associated Chambers of Manufactures of Australia in 1937. During this period he was a persistent critic of the clauses of the Ottawa Agreement that gave concessions to British manufactures. Elected president of the Australian Cement Manufacturers' Association in 1938 and appointed to the Commonwealth Advisory Panel on Industrial Organization in 1939, Kneeshaw was also on the council of the Standards Association of Australia. A council-member of the United Australia Party in 1932-34, he was elected in December 1933 to the reconstituted Legislative Council of New South Wales where he spoke frequently on a wide range of issues until his retirement in 1949.

Kneeshaw represented the New South Wales section of the Electrical Association of Australia at the first council-meeting which formed the Institution of Engineers, Australia, in 1919 and in January 1920 was elected the first chairman of the Sydney division. He served on the council in 1923-44 and as president in 1938. Appointed O.B.E. in 1938, he was chairman in 1941-43 of the Australian Shipbuilding Board which was attached to the Department of Munitions.

A solidly built, gregarious bachelor, Kneeshaw accepted any forum which gave him an opportunity to express his carefully formulated opinions. He took a keen interest in the Boys' Brigade. A member of the Australian Club, Sydney and the Athenaeum Club, Melbourne, he lived at Turramurra. He died on 3 February 1955 of hypertensive heart disease and was cremated with Presbyterian forms. His estate, valued for probate at £45 440, was left to his sister and her family.

Inst of Engineers Aust, *Trans*, 1 (1920), and *J*, 10 (1938), 27 (1955); *NSW Railway and Tramway Mag*, Dec 1920; *SMH*, 18 Dec 1933, 5 Sept 1935, 17 Dec 1937, 9 June 1938, 7 Mar 1941, 5 Feb 1955.   ARTHUR CORBETT

KNETES, CHRISTOPHOROS (1872-1958), Greek Orthodox bishop, was born on 17 December 1872 and baptised Charidemos at Vathi, Samos (then under Ottoman suzerainty), son of Charidemos Knetes, merchant, and his wife Fioritsa, née Phoka. He was educated at the Pythagoreion Gymnasion at Vathi, the University of Athens and the Theological School at Halki, Constantinople (Istanbul), graduating in 1898. Made deacon on 19 July, with the monastic name of Christophoros, he taught at his old school on Samos for some years.

In 1905 Christophoros spent a year studying theology and improving his English at the University of St Andrews, Scotland. With financial support from the Greek community in London he transferred to the University of Oxford (B.Litt., 1909). His thesis, 'The sacred ministry and its relation to marriage in the Holy Eastern Orthodox Church', was published in the *Journal of Theological Studies* next year. Returning to Constantinople, he served as archivist and editor of *Ekklesiastike Aletheia*, the official journal of the patriarchate. Ordained priest on 23 April 1910, he was raised to the rank of archimandrite and on 12 December consecrated titular bishop of Stauropolis. In 1918 he was raised to the vacant metropolis of Serrai (Macedonia), where he organized assistance for thousands of refugees from Turkey.

In March 1922 the ecumenical patriarchate in Constantinople resumed jurisdiction over the Greeks of the diaspora (who had been with Athens since 1908) and in March 1924 established the metropolis of Australia and New Zealand. Christophoros, with his fluent English, was appointed hierarch. Tall, with a King Edward beard 'shot with grey' and restless 'deep-set brown eyes', he arrived in Australia on 8 July, to begin what was to become a very stormy episcopate.

Discontent soon crystallized into open confrontation—in Melbourne the priest, the consul and the Ithacan party combined against him. On 12 October the priest Archimandrite Irenaios (Kasimatis) ignored Metropolitan Christophoros in his church and also wrote inflammatory articles in the local Greek press. Although the metropolitan defrocked this priest and appointed another, the rebel and his supporters held rival services for some years. In February 1925 attempts to exclude the metropolitan from his church were frustrated, but the division continued.

In Sydney in February 1926, in the face of accusations of immorality, Knetes charged four young Greeks with conspiring to accuse him falsely of 'infamous conduct'. The case was dismissed but nevertheless exacerbated the situation. The *Hellenic Herald* conducted 'an incessant tirade against the Metropolitan' as a person rather than the authority and institution he represented. In November the priest in Sydney, Archimandrite Athenagoras (Waraklas), transferred himself to another jurisdiction and the metropolitan was excluded from his church. Christophoros retaliated by building a new church, St Sophia, at Paddington in 1927. In view of the untenable situation in Sydney and Melbourne, he was recalled in February 1928. He had ordained at least two priests in Australia and left six 'official' communities.

Granted the title of metropolitan of Bizya (East Thrace) Knetes spent most of his remaining life at Vathi, where he died on 7 August 1958. Factional rivalry and bitterness among the Greeks of Australasia had prevented him achieving much and set unfortunate precedents for future disputes.

S. Zervopoulos (ed), *Enkyklopaidikon Emerologion*, A (Constantinople, 1934); *O Sevasmiotatos Metropolites Bizyes Vizyes Kyrios Christophoros Knetes* (Samos, 1953); *Threskeutike kai Ethike Enkyklopaideia*, 12 (Athens, 1980); *SMH*, 12 Feb 1926; *Truth* (Syd), 14 Feb, 27 June 1926; M. P. Tsounis, Greek communities in Australia (Ph.D. thesis, Univ Adel, 1971).   H. L. N. SIMMONS

KNIBBS, SIR GEORGE HANDLEY (1858-1929), statistician, was born on 13 June 1858 at Redfern, Sydney, son of John Handley Knibbs, foreman, and his wife Ellen, née Curthoys. Nothing is known of his early education but in December 1877 he joined the public service and in January 1878 was appointed a licensed surveyor. On 2 January 1883 in Sydney he married Susan Keele James with Baptist forms. He joined the Royal Society of New South Wales in 1881 and was honorary secretary and editor of its *Journal and Proceedings* for nine years and president in 1898-99. In 1889-1905 Knibbs was an independent lecturer in geodesy, astronomy and hydraulics in the engineering school of the University of Sydney. In 1902 he represented the university on the board composing regulations for administering Rhodes scholarships and in 1902-03 travelled through Europe and North America as a member of the two-man commission on primary, secondary, technical and other branches of education (1902-06). In 1905 he became acting professor of physics at the university, concurrently with his appointment as New South Wales superintendent of technical education.

In 1906 Knibbs was appointed first Commonwealth statistician, directing the work of the newly established Commonwealth Bureau of Census and Statistics. That year he presided over a conference of State statisticians to secure uniformity of State returns. 1908 saw the issue of the highly praised first *Commonwealth year book*. Knibbs visited Europe in 1909, representing Australia at the International Congress on Life Insurance (Vienna), on the special committee revising the nomenclature of diseases (Paris), at an International Congress on the Scientific Testing of Materials (Copenhagen), at the International Institute of Statistics (Paris) and at the Geodetical Congress in London.

In 1911 the first Commonwealth census was taken, followed by the war census of 1915 under the War Census Act. Knibbs sat on the board reporting on the Federal capital site and was a member of the royal commissions on life, fire and other insurances (1909-10) and on food supplies during war (1914). He sat on several wartime committees and was a consulting member of the 1915 committee on munitions in war. He was chairman of the royal commission on taxation of Crown leaseholds in 1918-19. In 1919 he represented Australia at the conference on double income tax and war profits (London) and in 1920 attended the British Empire Statisticians' Conference (London), chairing the census committee. A past-president (1903-05) of the Society for Child Study in New South Wales, in 1921 he was elected vice-president of the International Eugenics Congress, New York. He resigned as Commonwealth statistician to become director of the newly constituted Commonwealth Institute of Science and Industry in 1921. Knibbs's indefatigable planning was rendered abortive by government economies and lack of initiative. His appointment terminated in 1926 after a period of leave of absence due to illness.

With ability and confidence evident in all his work, Knibbs won considerable prestige for the office of Commonwealth statistician, confounding those who had criticized his appointment. His major interest was in vital statistics and it was here that he won his international reputation. One of Knibbs's major contributions as statistician was his organization of the labour and industrial branch of his bureau. His failure to concern himself with current economic questions, coupled with his self-assurance and didacticism bordering on pomposity, may eventually have rendered him unpopular. His written expression, however, may have belied his reputed charm of manner and unvarying kindness of heart. He talked quickly and quietly in a high-pitched voice about his extraordinarily wide interests; one interviewer observed that 'an hour's conversation with him is a paralysing revelation'. He was the author of numerous monographs and even turned his talents to verse; his de-

scriptive works repay perusal for the detailed portraits they draw of his times. In 1928 he published *The shadow of the world's future or the earth's population possibilities* (London). In his later years he embraced a doctrine which he called the 'new Malthusianism'.

Knibbs received various honours of which he was perhaps inordinately proud. He was president of the Institution of Surveyors (1892, 1893, 1900), honorary fellow of the Royal Statistical Society, a fellow of the Royal Astronomical Society, an honorary member of the American Statistical Association and of the statistical societies of Paris and Hungary, and a member of the International Institute of Statistics, the British Science Guild and the International Association for Testing Materials. In 1921 he presided over the social and statistical section of the Australasian Association for the Advancement of Science and in 1923 was its general president. He was appointed C.M.G. in 1911 and was knighted in 1923. He died on 30 March 1929 of coronary vascular disease at his home at Camberwell, Melbourne, and was cremated with Anglican rites. His wife, three sons and a daughter survived him.

S. Bambrick, 'The first Commonwealth statistician Sir George Knibbs', Roy Soc NSW, *J*, 102 (1969), p 127, and for bibliog; *Punch* (Melb), 13 Jan 1911, 20 Feb 1913, 31 Mar 1921; *Herald* (Melb), 30 Mar 1929; *SMH*, 1 Apr 1929; S. Bambrick, Australian price indexes in historical perspective (Ph.D. thesis, ANU, 1970).   SUSAN BAMBRICK

KNIGHT, ALBERT (1894-1973), soldier and bushman, was born about March 1894 on Toorale station near Louth, New South Wales, son of John Knight and his wife Elizabeth, née Keagan. Albert grew up as an Aboriginal, probably went to school briefly, and then worked on the stations behind Bourke until he joined the Australian Imperial Force on 4 November 1915. He was the second of three brothers to enlist: Bill joined the 10th Battalion in 1914, transferred to the 43rd Battalion in 1916, won a Military Medal and lost an arm at Broodseinde on 4 October 1917, and returned home in 1918; Joe died of illness on 16 February 1917, a month after reaching England as a 13th Battalion reinforcement.

Albert joined the 13th Battalion near Ypres, Belgium, in October 1916, and was slightly wounded in the fierce fighting at 1st Bullecourt on 11 April 1917. He rejoined his battalion shortly afterwards, serving with it until Bill 'claimed' him into the 43rd Battalion in September. He was promoted lance

corporal after outstanding service in the
Passchendaele fighting, and by this time
was a bombing specialist and a noted scout,
'always crawling about No Man's Land, just
like a bloody Gurkha'. On the Somme in May
1918 Albert put his foot on a Mills bomb
which had fallen fizzing among his mates:
it exploded, and he spent two months conva-
lescing before returning to the front in July.
He was promoted temporary corporal in August, and on 30 September took part in the
attack on Bony village in the Hindenburg
line. The attack was stopped by heavy
machine-gun and trench-mortar fire, but in
broad daylight Knight and a mate advanced
over 200 yards (183 m) in the open under
heavy fire, located the enemy weapons, and
had them destroyed by artillery. He won a
Distinguished Conduct Medal, the award
second to the Victoria Cross for non-officers.
The next day his battalion quit the front for
the last time, and in July 1919 Knight returned to Australia.

He went back to bush work around
Bourke, probably married, and died at Bre-
warrina, New South Wales, on 15 October
1973. He was buried in the Roman Catholic
section of Bourke cemetery. In 1968 his
brother Bill remembered the war as
'alright', and Albert may well have too, for
it was one of the few activities in which part-
Aboriginals such as they could be accepted
as equal to white men.

E. J. Colliver and B. H. Richardson, *The Forty-
Third* (Adel, 1920); C. E. W. Bean, *The A.I.F. in
France*, 1917 (Syd, 1933); *London Gazette*, 3 June
1919, supplement; *Bourke and District Hist Soc*, 5
(1975); information from D. Huggonson and B.
Cameron, Bourke, NSW.   BILL GAMMAGE

KNIGHT, HATTIE; *see* LECKIE, JOHN
WILLIAM

KNIGHT, JOHN JAMES (1863-1927), editor, was born on 7 June 1863 at Shelton, Staffordshire, England, son of James Knight,
potter and printer, and his wife Louisa, née
Blagg. Taken to New Zealand early, he left
school at 11 to learn printing on the *Bruce
Herald*, returned to England at 17 and joined
William Owen and Henry Broadhurst in
starting the *Staffordshire Knot*, a paper supporting trade unionism. Migrating to
Queensland in 1884, he found work with the
Brisbane Newspaper Co. Ltd as a printer. He
was soon a reporter on the *Brisbane Courier*
and became chief parliamentary reporter in
the 1890s.

Knight's political and industrial enthusiasm disappeared rapidly. He had won the
confidence of Andrew Fisher [q.v.8] and
Thomas Glassey [q.v.] and when William
Lane [q.v.] left for Paraguay in 1893 Knight
was offered but declined the editorial chair
of the Queensland *Worker*. During the industrial turmoil of the 1890s he preferred
to investigate local history. His works included *In the early days* (1895), *Australian
pioneers and reminiscences* (1896), completed after the death of Nehemiah Bartley
[q.v.3] from Bartley's notes and diaries, and
*Brisbane: a historical sketch of the capital of
Queensland* (1897). The historical stream
dried up when he became editor in 1900 of
the *Courier*'s evening publication, the *Observer*.

Editor-in-chief of all the company's publications in 1906-16, Knight then became
managing director and later chairman. His
years in command saw such abrasive events
as Brisbane's tram strike of 1912, the Labor
government's introduction of state enterprises in 1915 and the abolition of the Legislative Council in 1922. The *Courier* was
Labor's fiercest critic on these and other
counts, yet the recrimination evoked
seemed never to touch Knight personally.
Like William Morris Hughes [q.v.], he replaced his youthful fervour for unionism
with an ultra-patriotic Imperialist stance
during World War I. He represented
Queensland on the Imperial Mission to the
War Fronts of pressmen in 1918 and returned to publish *The true war spirit*, praising the British role.

A founding member and president of the
Queensland Aero Club with a belief in the
future of aviation, Knight was discussing
aeroplanes for medical transport with Rev.
John Flynn [q.v.8] long before the creation
of the Australian Inland Mission and had a
company formed to deliver copies of the
Courier by air to the country. His sympathy
with country people led to practical support
of the Country Women's Association and
the Bush Book Club. As he grew older, he
became very remote from his staff who occasionally saw a white-haired, mild-
mannered man wearing rimless spectacles.
Regular national and international press
conferences which he relished took him on
visits to Europe and North America.

When he died of pneumonia on 24 November 1927 in his home at Kangaroo Point,
Knight left the whole of his estate, valued
for probate at £2884, to his wife Kitty, née
Dutton, whom he had married at Shelton on
2 August 1884; they had two daughters.
Hundreds attended his Anglican funeral at
Toowong cemetery. The Labor government
which his papers had berated for years was
represented by the minister for works at the
express wish of Premier McCormack [q.v.];

former Labor premier William Neal Gillies [q.v.] was seen weeping at the graveside.

N. Bartley, *Opals and agates* (Brisb, 1892); R. S. Browne, *A journalist's memories* (Brisb, 1927); *JRHSQ*, 4 (1951), no 4; *Brisbane Courier*, 22 June 1926 (jubilee supplement), 25, 26 Nov 1927.

H. J. SUMMERS

KNOWLES, SIR GEORGE SHAW (1882-1947), solicitor-general, was born on 14 March 1882 at Toowong, Brisbane, son of George Hopley Knowles, postmaster from Staffordshire, England, and his Brisbane-born wife Mary Maria, née Cocks. From Warwick West Boys' School he won a scholarship to Toowoomba Grammar School where he was a day-boy from 1894. In 1898 he joined the Queensland Public Service as a clerk, working first in the Stock Department and then, after attending evening classes in accountancy at the Brisbane Technical College, in the Auditor-General's Department. In 1902 he transferred to the Federal Audit Office, Melbourne, moving to the Patents Office in 1904. An evening student at the University of Melbourne, he graduated LL.B. (1907), LL.M. (1908), B.A. (1910) and M.A. (1912). On 10 November 1908 at the Methodist Church, Albert Street, Brisbane, he married Eleanor Louisa, daughter of John Smith Bennett, registrar of the Queensland Land Court.

In 1907 Knowles joined the Attorney-General's Department. Induced by 'the personal spell and inspiration' of (Sir) Robert Garran [q.v.8] to abandon plans of returning to Queensland, he became chief clerk (termed assistant secretary from 1921) and assistant parliamentary draftsman in 1913. A member of the Patent Attorney's Examination Board from 1915, he was admitted as a barrister and solicitor of the High Court of Australia next year and of the Supreme Court of Victoria in 1927. Garran later recalled: 'Sir George was my right hand . . . I relied entirely on him for the organization and discipline of the Department'. Knowles succeeded Garran as solicitor-general, secretary of the department and parliamentary draftsman in 1932.

Described as 'quiet in manner and speech', Knowles was a relentless worker. He produced an annotated edition of the Commonwealth Acts 1901-11 in 1913 and of the Australian Constitution in 1937. He was adviser to the Australian delegates attending the League of Nations assemblies in 1920 and 1924 and the Imperial Conference in 1937, and secretary for Australia in the British Empire delegation to the Washington Conference on the Limitation of Armaments in 1921-22. He was a member of the

National Debt Commission from 1932. Appointed O.B.E. in 1920 and C.B.E. in 1928, he was knighted in 1939. World War II was a strenuous time for him, not least because H. V. Evatt, with whom he had little rapport, was a most active attorney-general. In 1946 he accepted appointment as first high commissioner to South Africa.

In Canberra Knowles was secretary of the University Association in 1929-32 and represented it on the Council of Canberra University College in 1930-46. The Canberra circuit of the Methodist Church was constituted at the Knowles's Mugga Way home in 1929 and the Church's annual garden parties were held there for the next eleven years. After Sir George's death, following surgery, at Pretoria on 22 November 1947 his body was brought back to Canberra for burial. He was survived by his wife, who died in 1981 aged 100, a daughter and two sons; his second son, a fighter-pilot in the Royal Australian Air Force, was killed in World War II. The George Knowles memorial prize for law was instituted at Canberra University College in 1950 and the Canberra law courts are situated in Knowles Place.

R. R. Garran, *Prosper the Commonwealth* (Syd, 1958); A. Dalziel, *Evatt the enigma* (Melb, 1967); J. S. Udy, *Living stones* (Syd, nd); *Aust Law J*, 14 June 1946; *Courier Mail*, 22 Apr 1907; *SMH*, 16 Jan 1932, 2 Jan 1939, 10 Apr 1946, 24 Nov 1947, 2 May 1950; *Herald* (Melb), 14 Feb 1939.

E. G. WHITLAM

KNOWLES, MARION (MILLER) (1865-1949), writer, was born on 8 August 1865 at Woods Point, Victoria, eldest child of Irish immigrants James Miller, storekeeper, and his Catholic wife Anne Maria, née Bowen. She was educated privately until, the family's prosperity declining, she became a pupil-teacher at the local state school in December 1878. In 1886 she began a long period of relief teaching in Melbourne, in various country towns, and in remote and lonely one-teacher schools. In January 1893 she became junior assistant at Box Hill, remaining there until her marriage on 19 September 1901 at St Patrick's Cathedral to a widower, Joseph Knowles, a Melbourne city valuator.

In childhood Marion Miller learned to love poetry and soon attempted her own. Thereafter, verse came 'most naturally' to express her feelings toward Nature, children, love and death. When teaching isolated her from family and friends, she also wrote sketches of country life and characters observed and remembered. First writing as 'John Desmond', she contributed poems and sketches to the *Australasian*, then edited by D. Watterston [q.v.] whose advice and encouragement she gratefully remembered. In 1896 she published her first novel, *Barbara Halliday*, and two years later a book of collected verse, *Songs from the hills*, both to run to four editions; in 1900 *Shamrock and wattle bloom*, a collection of tales and sketches, appeared.

In September 1899 Marion Miller commenced a women's column in the *Advocate* and in 1900 became 'Aunt Patsy' of the 'Children's Corner'. When a legal separation from her husband left her with a small allowance on which to bring up two boys (a daughter had died at birth), her friend Joseph Winter [q.v.6] appointed her to the *Advocate* staff. Working at home but leaving household matters to a housekeeper (as she would do for the rest of her life), she remained with the *Advocate* after his death until obliged to retire in April 1927. Then, through the paper, a committee raised a testimonial of £334, a deposit on a house in Kew, her home thereafter.

Marion Miller Knowles played a leading part in the organization of the Catholic laity before World War I, becoming foundation president of the Catholic Women's Club in 1913, later chairing the board of directors of its hostel. Also in 1913, through the *Advocate*, she helped to form a social club for single Catholics. During the war she organized the dispatch of parcels to Catholic soldiers, and in 1919 chaired the committee responsible for welcoming them home. From early in the century she was honorary secretary of the committee for St Joseph's Home for Destitute Children, Surrey Hills, and after World War II, its patron. She was appointed M.B.E. in 1938.

While running her women's and children's pages, soon considerably expanded, Marion Miller Knowles published a second collection of verse, *Fronds from the Blacks' Spur* (1911), and further gift booklets of verse between 1913 and 1923. She continued to write serial stories for the *Advocate* and other Catholic papers, including the *Irish Catholic* (Dublin), publishing some in Melbourne in book form: *Corinne of Corrall's Bluff* (1912), *The little doctor* (1919), *The house of the garden of roses* (1923) and *Meg of Minadong* (1926). On retirement she issued through Pellegrini in Sydney *Pretty Nan Hartigan* and *Pierce O'Grady's daughter* (1928), *The wonder find at Power's Luck* (a mining tale) and a second edition of *The little doctor* (1929).

In celebrating Catholicity these romances with country settings, their characters chiefly Irish-Australian, attracted only a small readership; even Catholic reviews could be lukewarm. Despairing of promotion by booksellers and critics, she advertised and distributed her books from home with some success. In retirement, her name no longer before the Catholic public, and unable to attend functions of the Australian Literary Society of which she was a longstanding member, she feared herself forgotten. However, in 1931 she was granted a Commonwealth Literary Fund pension of ten shillings a week, and in 1935 a committee of friends arranged publication of her *Selected poems*, which in 1937 reappeared in two volumes: *The harp of the hills* and *Lyrics of wind and wave*.

In good health but with failing eyesight, Marion Knowles, stout and bespectacled, remained in her home until shortly before she died on 16 September 1949. Survived by her sons, she was buried in Brighton cemetery.

J. R. Stevens (comp), *Adam Lindsay Gordon and other Australian writers* (Melb, 1937); *Weekly Times* (Melb), 18 June 1910; *Advocate* (Melb), 23 June 1927, 22 Sept 1949; J. Booth *and* J. Howlett Ross papers (LaTL); A3753 72/2760 (AAO); records, History Section, Dept of Education (Vic).

CECILY CLOSE

KNOX, SIR ADRIAN (1863-1932), barrister and chief justice, was born on 29 November 1863 in Sydney, fourth surviving son and youngest of eight children of Sir Edward Knox [q.v.5], founder of the Colonial Sugar Refining Co., and his Irish wife Martha, sister of William Rutledge [q.v.2]. He attended Waverley House, Sydney, and H. E. Southey's school at Mittagong. In 1878 he went to England to continue his education at Harrow and Trinity College, Cambridge (LL.B., 1885). He was admitted to the Inner Temple in May 1883 and called to the Bar on 19 May 1886. On his return to Sydney, Knox was admitted to the colonial Bar on 26 July. He read with his eldest brother George (1845-1888) at Lyndon Chambers. On George's death he succeeded to much of his practice and was briefed by leading solicitors. In 1888-90 he reported equity cases for the *New South Wales Law Reports*. From the early 1890s he had rooms in Northfield Chambers.

Standing on a platform of free trade and non-payment of members, Knox was elected to the Legislative Assembly for Woollahra in 1894. He was 'an excellent speaker... precise, easy, deliberate' and supported (Sir) George Reid [q.v.], favouring direct taxation, civil service reform and Federation. Disillusioned with politics, he did not seek re-election in 1898. At Christ Church, Bong Bong, near Moss Vale, on 5 February 1897 he had married Florence Lawson, a descendant of the explorer William Lawson [q.v.2].

'No mean cricketer' when young, Knox played for I Zingari in Australia and later enjoyed golf, sailing, and fishing on the south coast. He handled a motor car 'in expert fashion', but his great interest was the turf in all its forms. As a young man he was a gambler. From 1896 he served on the committee of the Australian Jockey Club and owned several good horses—Crown Grant, Popinjay and Vavasor, winner of the 1910 Sydney Cup—but gave up racing his own horses during World War I. The 'iron discipline' that he imposed as chairman of the A.J.C. in 1906-19 'had much to do with lifting the tone of racing' in New South Wales to a high level. While he was in office, Randwick racecourse was 'practically rebuilt' and the totalizator introduced. At the same time added prize money increased from £23 000 a year to over £80 000, much of it for weight-for-age events. He revised the rules and encouraged country racing associations.

By the 1900s Knox was a leader at the Bar and took silk in February 1906. Except in 1910 and 1916, he served on the Council of the Bar of New South Wales from its foundation in 1902 until 1919. He was a director of the Australian Mutual Provident Society and an original member of the Walter and Eliza Hall [qq.v.] Trust. A 'brilliant thinker', he found it 'more congenial to argue abstruse issues in the placid atmosphere of Equity' than to browbeat an untruthful witness, but his all-round knowledge of the law was 'unusually deep and wide' and his 'capacity for hard work was enormous'. From 1903 the High Court of Australia provided a new arena for leading barristers: before it Knox enhanced his reputation, becoming known as an outstanding constitutional lawyer. His practice became largely appellate. He was briefed by Commonwealth and State governments, taking part in most of the major constitutional cases including the steel rails, wire netting and musicians' cases. In 1911-12 he appeared for the defendants in *R.* v. *Associated Northern Collieries*, known as the Vend case, when the Commonwealth tried to suppress an alleged monopoly and price fixing.

A foundation member of the executive of the New South Wales division of the British (Australian from 1916) Red Cross Society, in August 1915 Knox and (Sir) Norman Brookes [q.v.7] went to Egypt as Australian Red Cross commissioners; they 'flung themselves with the greatest zeal into the work'. Knox showed great organizing ability and worked 'amid many difficulties and not a few risks' (when he took stores to Gallipoli) to allocate comforts for the wounded, stores and medical supplies. Returning to Sydney early in 1916, Knox was an official visitor to internment camps and served on a Commonwealth advisory committee on legal questions arising out of war problems. He was appointed C.M.G. in 1918. On 10 December he made a celebrated appearance at the bar of the Legislative Assembly to defend the members of the Public Service Board against charges arising out of the report of a royal commission.

On 18 October 1919 Knox succeeded Sir Samuel Griffith [q.v.] as chief justice of the High Court and was sworn in on 21 October. He immediately resigned as chairman of the A.J.C. (which thereupon instituted a classic race for three-year-old fillies, the Adrian Knox Stakes), and sold all his shares, including his inheritance in C.S.R., lest he should be involved in a conflict of interest. His elevation to the High Court bench coincided with the disappearance of the original justices who had established, mainly from American precedents, a 'balanced' theory of interpretation of Commonwealth and State powers. A second generation of justices, headed by (Sir) Isaac Isaacs and H. B. Higgins [qq.v.] favoured a view which gave maximum scope to the Commonwealth's express powers without any assumptions about effects on the States' residuary powers. There is no evidence that Knox shared the political enthusiasms of Isaacs, but the new views were more consistent with a literal interpretation of the Constitution in accordance with received English principles of statutory interpretation, wholly congenial to Knox, than with Griffith's reliance on American doctrines. The opportunity for establishing the new view as accepted doctrine came in the Engineers' case, dealing with the question of the extent to which Commonwealth laws made under the trans-State industrial arbitration power (sec. 51 (xxxv)) could bind State governments. In a joint judgment written by Isaacs, he and Knox, (Sir) George Rich and (Sir) Hayden Starke [qq.v.] (Higgins agreeing separately) emphatically rejected the older principles and adopted the new, and upheld the application of the Commonwealth industrial awards in question to State activities.

This view has since remained the dominant principle of the Court's Federal jurisprudence. Some other pro-Commonwealth initiatives of Isaacs in which Knox at first joined have been less influential, and Knox's apparent intellectual affinity with Isaacs waned in later years. The court's ordinary appellate work increased and, as a 'considerable body of precedents' was established, 'argument and decision could and did become far more a matter of syllogistic or casuistical reasoning from dogmatic jural postulates'. Knox was a competent exponent of settled doctrines, but apart from his share in the 1920 events made little individual mark on the evolution of Australian law. Vigilant in guarding the High Court from encroachments on its independence, Knox firmly resisted repeated requests that other Commonwealth tribunals should use its leased premises in Sydney and Melbourne. He also refused requests in 1919, 1921, 1923 and 1928 to nominate or to permit a justice of the High Court to act as a royal commissioner lest they should be drawn into political controversy. In 1927 he advised (Sir) John Latham [q.v.], the Federal attorney-general, on proposed amendments to the Judiciary Act and questioned the wisdom of a single justice hearing constitutional cases at the first instance as this would reduce the appellate Full Court to six and render an even decision possible. Knox was appointed to the Privy Council on 2 March 1920 and K.C.M.G. in 1921. In 1924 he visited England to sit on the Judicial Committee of the Privy Council dealing with the disputed border between the Irish Free State and Northern Ireland.

In impaired health, Sir Adrian resigned as chief justice on 30 March 1930 on learning that he was a residuary legatee under the will of his 'old and intimate friend' John Brown [q.v.7], 'the acceptance of which involved a direct, if not an active participation by me in a business carried on in Australia [that] was incompatible with the retention by me of any judicial office'. The bequest included racehorses—one, Balloon King, won the 1931 Victoria Derby. He became a director of the Bank of New South Wales and the Commercial Union Assurance Co. Ltd, rejoined the board of the A.M.P. Society and in 1931 was chairman of the Primary Producers' Advisory Council. He strongly disapproved of the governor, Sir Philip Game [q.v.8], acceding to J. T. Lang's [q.v.] demand for nominations to the Legislative Council. His likely appointment as governor-general was widely reported in the press before the government nominated Isaacs.

Clean-shaven, Knox had a long, straight nose, brown eyes, and a firm mouth and chin. Although his practice was lucrative, unlike his brothers Edward [q.v.] and Tom he never built a large house, living after his marriage at eight different addresses at Woollahra and Potts Point; nor did he speculate in real estate, but he did give his wife beautiful jewellery. He liked entertaining, and frequenting the Union Club (which he had joined in 1886) and, from 1915, the Melbourne Club; he was an excellent bridge player. 'As fierce as his brothers were mild', he was held in affection by his family: his sister-in-law always had a whisky and soda waiting for him when he came to afternoon tea. He loved Australian and Sydney silky terriers and would often return from Melbourne with a pup in his pocket. In his later years he spent much time in his garden and would not permit anyone else to prune his roses. Knox died of heart disease at his home at Woollahra on 27 April 1932 and was cremated after a service at All Saints. His wife, son and two daughters survived him; his younger daughter Elizabeth married Lewis Joseph Hugh, 12th baron Clifford of Chudleigh.

To some Knox appeared 'brusque in manner': Sir Ronald Munro Ferguson [q.v.] recorded that he was an 'ill-tempered person ... a worthy man, but sees the disagreeable side of things first'. To others, especially juniors at the Bar, he was helpful and patient. R. C. Teece [q.v.] thought Knox a 'man of strong opinions', who always listened 'with attention and courtesy to the arguments of others'. According to G. E. Flannery [q.v.8] he was in argument 'suave, persuasive, clear and short. Before Courts of Appeal, he had no equal in his generation'. As chief justice at a time of consolidation, he conducted his court with dignity and brought to it common sense and 'a wide knowledge of the world' and of men. His judgments were 'almost without exception short and to the point. Neither at the Bar nor on the Bench was he discursive: he reduced a problem to its simplest terms with a marked facility'. To a later chief justice, Sir Owen Dixon, he was 'a conspicuous advocate' but 'a type you do not often meet: a highly intellectual man without any intellectual interests'.

Portraits of Knox by Florence Rodway [q.v.] are held by the A.J.C. and the Mitchell [q.v.5] Library, Sydney, and a copy is in the High Court, Canberra.

E. Scott, *Australia during the war* (Syd, 1936); G. Sawer, *Australian Federal politics and law, 1901-29* (Melb, 1956); O. Dixon, *Jesting Pilate*, comp Judge Woinarski (Syd, 1965); J. M. Bennett, *Keystone of the Federal arch* (Canb, 1980); *PD* (NSW), 1918, 74, p 3670; *Cwlth Law Reports*, (1908), vol 5, p 789, 818, (1912), vol 15, p 65, 636, (1920), vol 20, p 128, (1932), vol 47, p v; *Daily Telegraph* (Syd), 18 June 1894; *Punch* (Melb), 29 July 1915, 7 May 1925; *SMH*, 15, 21 Oct 1915, 3 June 1918, 18, 20, 22 Oct, 28 Nov 1919, 1 Jan, 24 Mar 1921, 5, 7 June, 24 July 1924, 28 Apr 1932; *Bulletin*, 6 Jan 1921; *The Times*, 28 Apr 1932; Game papers, and Knox papers (ML); Latham papers (NL); A432 38/322, 50/482 (AAO); information from Elizabeth, Lady Clifford, Lond and Spain, Mrs T. L. F. Rutledge, Syd, and Prof. G. Sawer, Canb.

MARTHA RUTLEDGE

KNOX, EDWARD WILLIAM (1847-1933), industrialist, was born on 1 April 1847 in Sydney, second of four surviving sons of Sir Edward Knox [q.v.5], founder of the Colonial Sugar Refining Co., and his Irish wife Martha, sister of William Rutledge [q.v.2]. Educated at Sydney Grammar School, in 1863 he won the senior Knox prize. He refused a university education and joined C.S.R. in April 1864 as a junior clerk.

In 1870 Knox took charge of the company's crushing mills on the Clarence. Inheriting 'his father's drive, his integrity and his uncanny intuition', he sought many improvements in management and encouraged the cane-farmers to improve their agricultural methods and to grow sweeter cane. In 1876 he visited the West Indies to study milling: next year double crushing was adopted. He later visited sugar-beet factories in Germany and France. At St Matthew's Church, Manly, he married Edith (d. 1942), daughter of J. S. Willis [q.v.6] on 30 January 1878.

Appointed general manager of C.S.R. in 1880, Knox 'surrounded himself with able lieutenants'. During his first five years C.S.R. expanded its operations into Queensland and Fiji, and built seven new mills and a refinery at Auckland, New Zealand. He realized that profits depended on increased efficiency through the application of science to every aspect of the industry.

In the early 1880s the company recruited chemists from Scotland and Germany and, after the slump of 1884, Knox introduced a system of chemical book-keeping. In 1890 he addressed the Australasian Association for the Advancement of Science 'On an application of chemical control to a manufacturing business'.

The company's size, efficiency and tendency to absorb competitors laid it open to criticism, particularly by politicians raising the cry of monopoly, especially after Federation and the payment of the Commonwealth sugar bounty. The attacks culminated in the royal commission on the sugar industry in 1911-12. Knox categorically refused to answer questions about costs or to produce the company's books, as he believed publication would damage the company. He was vindicated when C.S.R. successfully challenged an amendment to the Royal Commissions Act in the High Court of Australia and was upheld by the Privy Council. A stubborn free trader, he desired 'a uniform absence of [government] interference in industrial matters'. (He was again to refuse to give information to the royal commission chaired by A. B. Piddington [q.v.] in 1920.)

However, in May 1915 W. M. Hughes [q.v.] and Knox met to draft the principles of the Commonwealth's wartime control of the industry. In 1920 Knox became chairman and managing director of C.S.R. He visited London in 1922 at the request of the British government to discuss the problem of Indian labourers in Fiji. He resigned as managing director in December 1932.

Although diffident about his 'inability to speak in public' and his civic achievements, he served on four royal commissions, including the Sydney water supply (1902), and as an alderman on Woollahra Municipal Council in 1887-1902. A member of the Board of Health in 1888-1902, he found its work interesting and varied.

He was a fellow of the Senate of the University of Sydney in 1894-1919 and a trustee of Sydney Grammar School in 1884-1924 and of the National Art Gallery of New South Wales from 1907. He served on the committee of the Union Club for forty years (president in 1908-21) and was a member of the Australian Jockey Club.

His gabled stone house, Rona, on Bellevue Hill, was completed in 1883. His great pleasure was sailing: in 1875 he and his brother Tom bought and raced *Pleiades*. In 1881 he had built *Sirocco*, a ten-ton cutter, won many races in her over twenty years, and continued to be a familiar sight on the harbour until he sold her in 1927. He was commodore of Royal Sydney Yacht Squadron in 1883-84. Ned, as he was known in the family, enjoyed dancing, attending the theatre and opera, and frequent foreign travel from which he brought home many *objets d'art*. He was guided by his friend George, son of S. K. Salting [q.v.2], in buying Chinese porcelain and ivories, but paintings 'he chose for himself'. A shy man, who would never speak on the telephone, he was happiest among his relations.

In old age Knox wrote some random recollections. He resigned from the board of C.S.R. in February 1933, died at Rona on 26 June and was buried in Waverley cemetery after a service at All Saints Anglican Church, Woollahra, where he had worshipped all his life. He was survived by his wife and four daughters; the eldest Dorothy married (Sir) Colin Stephen [q.v.]. His younger brothers were Thomas Forster (1849-1919), managing director of the Sydney branch of Dalgety [q.v.4] & Co. Ltd for many years, and Sir Adrian [q.v.], chief justice of the High Court.

Knox's 'intuitive knowledge of the course to be taken in emergencies' enabled the 'Sugar Company' to surmount the crises and fluctuations in price that beset the industry. As a salaried man he thought it wrong to speculate and his fortune derived from shares in the company. His estate was valued for probate at £223 701 in New South Wales and £4066 in Victoria. His portrait by Longstaff [q.v.], in the Union Club, emphasized his glistening white hair and beard, 'the face so full of health and open air vitality', and his piercing china-blue eyes. Portraits of him and Mrs Knox by McInnes [q.v.], painted for their golden wedding in 1928, are held by the family.

Colonial Sugar Refining Co., *Account of the proceedings at the presentation to E. W. Knox* (Syd, 1914); A. G. Lowndes (ed), *South Pacific enterprise* (Syd, 1956); P. R. Stephensen (ed), *Sydney sails* (Syd, 1962); L. F. Fitzhardinge, *William Morris Hughes, 1-2* (Syd, 1964, 1979); *PP* (LA Vic), 1902-03, 2 (31); *PP* (Cwlth), 1912, 3, p 1035, 1913, 4, p 1169, 1920, 4, p 960; *Cwlth Law Reports*, 1912, vol 15, p 182, 1914, vol 17, p 644; *Aust Sugar J*, Jan 1977, p 492; *SMH*, 6 Sept 1921, 28 Mar 1928, 4 May, 27 June 1933; C.S.R. Co. records (ANU Archives); information from and typescript by Mrs T. L. F. Rutledge, Syd, and E. W. Knox letters in her possession.   MARTHA RUTLEDGE

KNOX, SIR ERROL GALBRAITH (1889-1949), newspaperman, was born on 25 June 1889 at Glebe, Sydney, eighth child of Joseph Knox, a grocer from County Tyrone, Ireland, and his native-born wife Elizabeth Jane, née Drew.

Knox was educated at Fort Street Public School (where he was known as 'Knocker') and began an arts course at the University of Sydney, completing two years full-time study and a third year of evening classes. A clever debater, he seemed destined for a career in law. Instead, in 1910 he went into journalism. He worked as a sub-editor for the *Sunday Times* and in 1914 travelled to the United States of America and Canada for the paper. In July 1915 he enlisted as a private in the 12th Reinforcements for the 2nd Battalion, Australian Imperial Force; he was commissioned a second lieutenant in September and in January 1916 embarked for Egypt. In January 1917 he joined No. 69 Squadron, Royal Flying Corps, as recording officer and was promoted captain next year and major in late 1918. He served as air staff officer with the British Army of Occupation on the Rhine until July 1919. He was twice mentioned in dispatches and in June 1919 was appointed M.B.E. On 4 September at Thakeham, Sussex, he married with Roman Catholic rites Gertrude Mary Coore.

Knox returned to Sydney early in 1920 and joined *Smith's Weekly* before becoming news editor of the *Daily Telegraph*. In 1922 he was appointed managing editor of the *Evening News*. Within a year the paper had doubled its circulation and by 1928 Knox was dubbed 'one of the shrewdest newspaper administrators in Australia'.

In 1929 he became a director of the newly formed Associated Newspapers Ltd, but three years later he resigned when Sir Hugh Denison [q.v.8] closed down the *Evening News*. For the next five years he pursued a variety of publishing interests. For a short time he edited *To-Day*, a monthly, and he also had a hand in the production of *Newspaper News*. He edited two editions of *Who's Who in Australia*—the 1933-34 volume and an enlarged version in 1935—and produced and published three editions of the *Medical Directory for Australia*. Another project was the *Australian year book*, 1933-34.

In September 1937 Knox moved to Melbourne to be managing editor of the Argus & Australasian Ltd; he became managing director in 1940. It was hoped that his enterprise and energy would give the *Argus* a new lease of life. One of the first and most noticeable changes he made was to replace advertisements with news on the front page. Knox's influence was soon felt right through the organization. He knew each member of his staff personally and kept himself informed about the welfare of their families. Every aspect of newspaper production interested him and he was fascinated by machinery and technical innovation.

Even before the outbreak of World War II Knox was preoccupied with questions of Australian defence. In December 1942 he was appointed director-general of public relations with the temporary rank of brigadier, and in this capacity he visited New Guinea, Britain and the United States in May-November 1943. Ill health, however, forced him to retire from active service in January 1944.

Dynamic was the word most frequently used to describe Knox. A. R. Chisholm, who had known him from schooldays, remembered him as 'violently argumentative', clever, self-assertive but basically modest. 'No man had a greater inability to endure bad work patiently' but he never bore rancour. He loved poetry, especially Australian poetry which he could quote at length. He was interested in the development of a national opera and in March 1946 he was appointed as a trustee of the National Museum of Victoria. In Sydney he had been a director in 1925-30 of the Royal Prince Alfred Hospital; in Melbourne he was a member of the board of advice of St Vincent's Hospital. Boating had been a favourite recreation in Sydney. He was a member of all Melbourne metropolitan racing clubs and was chairman of Hanging Rock Racing Club. At nearby Woodend he had bought a cattle and sheep stud-farm.

Knox was knighted in January 1949. Later that year the London *Daily Mirror* bought a controlling interest in the *Argus*. Still nominally managing director, Knox went overseas to look at a new colour printing plant for the paper but became critically ill. He was flown back to Melbourne where he died in hospital of coronary vascular disease on 17 October 1949, survived by his wife, two daughters and a son. After a service at St Patrick's Cathedral, he was buried in Woodend cemetery.

A. R. Chisholm, *Men were my milestones*(Melb, 1958), R. B. Walker, *Yesterday's news* (Syd, 1980); *Newspaper News*, 1 June 1928; *Bulletin*, 8 Apr 1926; *Argus*, 9, 18 Oct 1949; *Herald* (Melb), 17, 19 Oct 1949; information from R. T. M. Pescott, Camberwell, Melb.   SALLY O'NEILL

KNOX, SIR GEORGE HODGES (1885-1960), orchardist, soldier and politician, was born on 17 December 1885 at Prahran, Melbourne, eldest son of William Knox [q.v.] and his wife Catherine Mary, née MacMurtrie. (Sir) Robert Knox [q.v.] was a brother. Educated at Scotch College and the Working Men's College, George was employed as an electrical engineer and spent two years in Manchester, England. Returning to Victoria, he married Kathleen Purves MacPherson on 4 February 1909 at Christ Church, South Yarra, and became an orchardist at Beaconsfield.

In May 1909 Knox was commissioned lieutenant in the Australian Volunteer Automobile Corps; in November he transferred as second lieutenant to the 1st Battalion, Victorian Scottish Regiment, and after promotion to captain moved to the 52nd Infantry Regiment in 1912. Appointed captain in the 23rd Battalion, Australian Imperial Force, on 29 March 1915 and major on 1 April, he commanded the battalion from August at Gallipoli and in Egypt and France with the rank of lieut-colonel. In July 1916 he was blown up at Hardecourt and evacuated to England where in November he took charge of No.1 Command Depot. Twice mentioned in dispatches, he was appointed C.M.G. in 1917. He returned to Melbourne in April 1918 and his A.I.F. appointment was terminated.

Knox's brother William Johnstone, who served with the 3rd Field Artillery Brigade, A.I.F. and was awarded the Military Cross, died of wounds in 1917. Another brother in the A.I.F., MacPherson, who was also awarded the Military Cross, was permanently incapacitated.

In April 1918 Knox was appointed aide-de-camp to the governor of Victoria and in November was given temporary command of the 2nd Battalion, 5th Infantry Regiment, Australian Military Forces. He spent August 1919 to February 1920 overseas on special service as lieut-colonel, A.I.F., after which he settled on his new property Greenlaw at Ferntree Gully. He had been divorced in June 1919 and on 19 August 1921 at Malvern Presbyterian Church he married Ada Victoria Harris.

Knox continued his army career, his concern for his men making him a popular leader. He was lieut-colonel commanding the 48th Battalion from March 1921 and the 52nd Battalion in 1922-27. In 1939 he was appointed commander of the 5th Battalion and next year was temporary colonel commanding the 2nd Infantry Brigade. Promoted temporary brigadier in 1941, he had charge of the Queenscliff-Nepean Covering Force in March-August 1942 when he retired with the rank of honorary brigadier.

Late in 1918 Knox had been an unsuccessful Nationalist candidate at a by-election for the Federal seat of Corangamite. Five years later he was elected to the Ferntree Gully Shire Council and in 1927 he won the Legislative Assembly seat of Upper Yarra for the Nationalists. A diligent local member, he was unopposed in 1929-40; from 1945 until his death he represented Scoresby. In 1928 Knox carried a motion directing the assembly to open its sittings with the Lord's Prayer. (His father had persuaded the Federal parliament to adopt this procedure in 1901). Knox was secretary to cabinet in the McPherson [q.v.] ministry of 1929 and that year served on a royal commission into the dairying industry. In December 1929 and in March-April 1935 he was honorary minister in the McPherson and Argyle [q.v.] governments respectively, but in 1936-37 as one of the Liberal-Country Party faction in the United Australia Party he was critical of Argyle's leadership.

Knox was an effective and impartial Speaker in 1942-47 and was knighted in 1945. Throughout 1947 he was pressed by the Liberal Party to resign the Speakership and support a no confidence motion against the vulnerable Cain ministry. He refused, maintaining that the Speaker should be above party politics; he disapproved of the refusal of supply in October. In later years he persistently advocated the use of simple language in the drafting of legislation.

Described as 'tall, broad-shouldered with rugged features', Knox was admired for his integrity and kindness. He was president of the Melbourne Hunt Polo Club and a life member of the Polo Association of Victoria. He was an honorary forest officer and inspector of fisheries and native game in Victoria.

Lady Knox was an active philanthropist. Chief among her interests was the Australian Red Cross Society with which she was associated for over forty years. She was a life governor of the Eye and Ear Hospital and also worked for the St John Ambulance

Association, the Royal Victorian Institute for the Blind, the Good Neighbour Council, the Girl Guides' Association and mental hospitals. She was appointed C.B.E. in 1961 for social welfare services in the Ferntree Gully area.

Sir George died of coronary vascular disease on 11 July 1960 at Ferntree Gully and was cremated after a state funeral. He was survived by his wife and by a son from both marriages, a daughter of his first marriage having predeceased him. His estate was valued for probate at £40 741. The city of Knox commemorates his name.

H. Coulson, *Story of the Dandenongs, 1838-1958* (Melb, 1959); *PD* (Vic), 1960, p 17; *Geelong Advertiser*, 5 Apr 1929; *Smith's Weekly* (Syd), 18 Oct 1947; *Sun-News Pictorial*, 12 July 1960, 10 June 1961; *Age*, 12 July 1960; *Mountain District Free Press*, 14 July 1960.   GEOFF BROWNE

KNOX, SIR ROBERT WILSON (1890-1973), businessman, was born on 17 May 1890 at South Yarra, Melbourne, fourth son of William Knox [q.v.] and his wife Catherine Mary, née MacMurtrie. (Sir) George Knox [q.v.] was his eldest brother. Educated at Melbourne Church of England Grammar School, where he excelled at athletics and was a lieutenant in the Cadet Corps, he joined his father's mining firm Knox, Schlapp [q.v.] & Co. in 1908. He was a member of the Old Melburnians Council from 1912 to 1924. On 11 November 1914 at the school chapel he married Victoria Ivy, daughter of Sir William and Lady (Janet) Clarke [qq.v.3].

During World War I Knox was an executive member of the Victorian central council of the Australian Red Cross Society and served as a commissioner in Egypt and France. After the war his career in commerce and insurance burgeoned. He was the first federal president of the Australian Association of British Manufacturers (1919-20) and in 1928 was elected president of the Melbourne Chamber of Commerce and vice-president of the Associated Chambers of Commerce of Australia (president, 1934-36). In 1929-34 he was chairman of the Australian national committee of the International Chamber of Commerce. A consultant to the Australian delegation to the Ottawa conference on tariffs and trade in 1932, he was knighted in 1934. In 1936 when he was an executive member of the central council of the Employers' Federation of Australia he represented the Australian employers at the International Labour Organisation in Geneva.

Knox's business links included at various times directorships of Dunlop (Australia) Ltd, Vickers Australia Pty Ltd, Vickers Commonwealth Steel Products Ltd, the Bank of New Zealand, the Commercial Banking Co. of Sydney (he was chairman of its Victorian board), Noyes Bros. Ltd and the Mount Lyell Mining and Railway Co. Ltd. He was chairman of directors of Knox Schlapp Ltd (1950-69), N.K.S. (Holdings) Ltd (1958-69) and the National Mutual Life Association of Australasia Ltd (1953-65). He was appointed a foundation director of the Victorian Gas & Fuel Corporation in 1951, having been on the board of the Metropolitan Gas Co. since 1938.

Unlike his father and brother, Sir Robert did not seek a parliamentary career, but he was nevertheless influential in politics. Early in 1931 as president of the National Union, the Nationalists' chief fund-raising body, he held discussions with 'the group', a conclave of Melbourne businessmen who, concerned to re-establish 'sound finance' in government, were endeavouring to unify the anti-Labor forces under the leadership of Joseph Lyons [q.v.]. Knox's role, resting on informality, is imprecisely defined; but he appears to have been deeply involved in persuading the Nationalist leader (Sir) John Latham [q.v.] to throw in his lot with Lyons and in formulating a new conservative policy statement. On 19 April he attended a meeting to form the United Australia Movement; this led in May to the establishment of the United Australia Party which won power in November. In subsequent years Knox continued to meet with and advise Lyons who became a firm friend.

A 'tall, big-framed figure', Knox played golf and tennis and ran a stud farm near Gisborne. He was a member of the Alfred Hospital Board of management and president of the Melbourne-based National Theatre Movement. Generous and friendly, he took a deep interest in the employees of the firms with which he was associated. He belonged to the Adelaide, Melbourne and Australian clubs and for many years his mansion Greenknowe was a centre of Toorak social life.

Predeceased by his wife, Knox died on 14 April 1973 in the Freemasons' Hospital, East Melbourne. After a funeral at Toorak Presbyterian Church, where he had been an elder, he was buried in the family vault at Boroondara cemetery. His estate of $633 369 was left to his daughter, surviving son and grandchildren. He had revoked small bequests to the Presbyterian Church in 1973.

A century of life (Melb, 1969); *Labour Hist*, no 17, 1970, p 37; *Age*, 16 Apr 1973.
D. H. BORCHARDT

KNOX, WILLIAM (1850-1913), business-man and politician, was born on 25 April 1850 in Melbourne, son of George Knox, schoolteacher, and his wife Mary, née John-son, his parents having arrived two months earlier from Berwickshire, Scotland. The family moved to Horsham, then Ballarat. After schooling at Scotch College, Mel-bourne, where he excelled at athletics, Knox was employed by Robert Harper [q.v.] & Co. as an office boy, before joining the Bank of Victoria in 1866. He served at Beechworth, Kilmore, Daylesford and several other country centres before returning to the Mel-bourne office as confidential secretary to the general manager. In 1882 he resigned to set up a private accountancy practice.

On 27 June 1885 Knox accepted Harvey Patterson's offer of the secretaryship of the newly formed Broken Hill Proprietary Co. Ltd, Patterson having noted Knox's work for the Pioneer Tin Mining Co., Tasmania. In 1888 his yearly salary of £75 was in-creased to £1500, conditional on his relin-quishing work for companies other than B.H.P. and its offshoot the British Broken Hill Proprietary Co. Ltd.

Generally regarded as the brains behind B.H.P., which quickly became Australia's wealthiest enterprise and the world's most successful silver-mine, Knox threw great energy and talent into resolving the com-pany's increasing complexities. The mine and its technical staff were located at Broken Hill, New South Wales, the refinery and shipping outlet at Port Pirie, South Aus-tralia; the board of directors was part time and based in both Melbourne and Adelaide where there were large and vocal share-holder groups; while London agents com-municated weekly the world metals prices and arranged sales of the company bullion. Knox was the co-ordinator, and also ar-ranged liaison with the New South Wales and South Australian governments regard-ing railway, water, land and mineral leases. He organized branch offices in Adelaide, Sydney and London, floated Broken Hill Proprietary Block 14 Co. Ltd in 1887, Broken Hill Proprietary Block 10 Co. Ltd in 1888 and that year travelled to London to float British B.H.P. He revisited London in 1890 to open a register for British share-holders in the parent company, with a separ-ate board of London directors. London nego-tiations in particular involved delicate handling of brokers, financiers and publicists, and intimate knowledge of Eng-lish and colonial share markets.

During the 1892 strike at Broken Hill Knox represented the combined employers as honorary secretary of the Barrier Ranges Mining Companies Association. When he resigned as B.H.P. secretary on 17 March

next year to become managing director of Mount Lyell Mining and Railway Co. Ltd he was immediately offered a seat on the B.H.P. board, which he held until 1910; in 1907-09 he was vice-chairman.

In June 1893 Knox visited London to in-terest English investors in Mount Lyell, but was thwarted by depression, coal strikes and a fall in metals prices. In 1899 as acting chairman of Mount Lyell he began negotia-tions with the North Mount Lyell Copper Co. and in 1903, after discussions with the North Lyell board in London, succeeded in arrang-ing a merger described as 'the greatest in Australian mining history'.

Knox was also a shareholder in Mount Morgan (Queensland) and Kalgoorlie (Western Australia) gold-mines, and a direc-tor of the Tharsis Co. (Tasmania) and the Chillagoe Mining and Railway Co. (Queens-land). In 1888 he helped form the Silverton Tramway Co. which became the second most profitable enterprise in New South Wales; and in 1894 he established, with H. H. Schlapp [q.v.], the mine agent and ma-chinery firm, Knox, Schlapp & Co.

From 1888 Knox was a member of the Melbourne Stock Exchange; in 1889 he was on the committee of the Victorian Associ-ation of Legal Managers and Secretaries of Mining Companies; and in 1896 he took a leading part in establishing the Chamber of Mines and was its first president. He was president of the Melbourne Chamber of Commerce in 1904-07, and of the Associated Chambers of Commerce for several years (including 1909 when he chaired the organ-izing committee for the Victorian meeting of the Imperial Congress of Chambers of Commerce). He was president of the Aus-tralasian Institute of Mining Engineers in 1900. In 1901 when Professor W. C. Kernot [q.v.5] made a personal donation of £1000 to the University of Melbourne for a school of mining engineering, Knox attempted to raise £2000 from the State government and prominent mining men; but he failed to in-terest the government.

Knox was a Malvern Shire councillor in 1892-1910 and president in 1892-95. In 1898 he was elected to the Legislative Council for South-Eastern Province and in 1900-02 was a member of the royal commission on local government laws. A keen advocate of Feder-ation, Knox became member for Kooyong in the 1901 House of Representatives where, although he moved from a free-trade to a protectionist position, he remained un-waveringly opposed to Labor. On his motion parliament decided to commence each day's sitting with prayers. He was an enthusiastic supporter of Deakin's [q.v.8] Defence Act of 1903 and afterwards produced valuable work on State and Federal finances. In

1904-06 he served on the royal commission on navigation laws. Never an orator but notable for solid, painstaking work, Knox resigned his seat in 1910 after a stroke left him partially enfeebled.

Photographs show Knox as large and moustached, with curly hair middle-parted, alert eyes and pugnacious jaw. His manner was commanding, affable with friends and disdainful with enemies. An ardent supporter of the cadet and rifle movements, Knox was president of the Malvern Rifle Association. He was a founder of the Royal Melbourne Golf Club, a member of the Australian Natives' Association and the Old Scotch Collegians and in 1906 chairman of the Protestant Electors' Committee. He was an enthusiastic Freemason. His imposing estate, Ranfurlie, in East Malvern, was annually used by the Melbourne Hunt Club for its opening meet.

On 24 January 1884 at Carlton, Knox had married Catherine Mary McMurtrie; they had five sons and two daughters. In March 1913 with his wife and younger children he again visited England. He died on 25 August 1913 at Folkestone, Kent; his body was returned to Melbourne for burial in Boroondara cemetery after a Presbyterian service. He left an estate valued for probate in Victoria at £49 411. Knox had declined a knighthood, but two of his sons, George Hodges and Robert Wilson [qq.v.], were so honoured.

William Knox with Bowes Kelly, William Jamieson, Duncan McBryde [qq.v.] and others was one of the 'mining magnates' of the period 1885 to 1914. All made fortunes, but the investment was honest and not based on market-rigging. Knox in particular backed his financial contribution with outstanding zeal and administrative ability and a broad grasp of public and financial affairs.

J. Smith (ed), *Cyclopedia of Victoria*, 1-3 (Melb, 1903-05); R. Bridges, *From silver to steel* (Melb, 1920); J. B. Cooper, *A history of Malvern* (Melb, 1935); P. Mawson, *A vision of steel* (Melb, 1958); G. Blainey, *The peaks of Lyell* (Melb, 1967), and *The rise of Broken Hill* (Melb, 1968); A. Trengove, *What's good for Australia...* (Syd, 1975); *Scientific Aust*, 20 June 1901; *Bulletin*, 12 Nov 1892; *Table Talk*, 28 Apr 1893; *Punch* (Melb), 11 Aug 1904, 16 Nov 1905; *Age*, *Argus*, 27 Aug 1913; R. A. Crouch memoirs, *and* W. C. Kernot papers (LATL); BHP, Minutes of board meetings, 1885-1910, and half-yearly reports of general meetings, 1893, 1910, 1913, and correspondence, 1885-95 (BHP Archives, Melb); Malvern Shire Council, Minutes, 1892-1910 (PRO, Vic).   Doreen Wheeler

KOCH, JOHN AUGUSTUS BERNARD (1845-1928), architect, was born on 27 August 1845 in Hamburg (Germany), son of Johann Christian Koch, joiner, and his wife Friederike Henriette, née Ernst. In 1855 the family migrated to Melbourne where the father worked as a dyer. By 1870 Koch was listed in the Melbourne directory as an architect at Richmond, having served articles with F. M. White [q.v.6] and become his assistant. On 26 October 1871 at the Melbourne Lutheran Church he married Anna Püttmann from Switzerland. Over sixty buildings, mainly in Richmond where he was appointed city architect in 1887, and Hawthorn where he lived from 1896, can be attributed to Koch; most were completed in the 1880s and 1890s and display distinguishing German and European motifs.

Appointed architect to the City of Melbourne in 1873, he designed the hay, horses, cow and pig markets and the corn exchange. Later institutional buildings included the two Richmond libraries, the German Club in Alfred Place, and projects associated with the Women's, Melbourne (of which he was honorary architect and life member) and Castlemaine hospitals. Two of his Richmond hotels, the Spread Eagle and the Prince Alfred, survive in addition to some warehouses, factories and stables. These latter utilitarian structures are praiseworthy for their sound construction, firm lines and sparing use of decorative brickwork.

Koch's versatility was considerable. He was at home with the Gothic style while executing plans for the Lutheran Church at Doncaster and for the parsonage next to the East Melbourne Lutheran Church of which he was a member. With commercial buildings he could embrace the Renaissance style: his award-winning Flinders Lane warehouse built for L. Stevenson & Sons has been demolished, but his smaller four-storied Collins Street Record Chambers remains complete, adorned with doric pilasters, dentil cornice, panelled frieze, floriated scrolls and caryatids. His houses and shops can invariably be identified by his use of Hellenistic motifs, including the Greek key pattern, sculpted classical masks, caryatids, acroteria and foliated scrolls and consoles. They were frequently prominently located on parapets and skylines. Labassa at Caulfield represents his most striking achievement in domestic architecture.

Koch was a justice of the peace from 1866, a Richmond city councillor in 1877-85 and mayor in 1883. While a councillor he was chairman of a board to adjudicate on designs for improvements to the Swan Street crossing and station buildings and chairman of the school district board of advice. In 1903-04 he was president of the Royal Victorian Institute of Architects to which he delivered papers on professional standards and the need for well-trained craftsmen. He represented the institute at the 1901 Melbourne Congress of Engineers, Architects and Surveyors where the design for a Federal capital was discussed. In 1910 he took his fifth son (Oscar) Bernard into partnership. After serving in World War I with the Australian Flying Corps Bernard carried on the practice under his own name from 1922.

Koch had ceased practice about 1913 to concentrate on his hobbies of carpentry, cabinet-making and inventing. A paper he delivered in 1904 suggests he was a pioneer in the new science of heating and ventilation and in 1912 he patented a combined road-sweeper and watering machine. He was an important member of the Melbourne German community. Short in stature, shock-headed, with rosy complexion and piercing blue eyes, he is remembered by grand-children as an awesome pipe-smoking figure, clad in smoking-jacket and matching cap, who set up detailed working models of his buildings and inventions. They loved him for his family dinners, German food and customs. His colleagues respected him for his progressive attitudes, ideals, imagination and distinctive work. He died on 30 August 1928 at Hawthorn, survived by his wife, six sons and three daughters, and was buried in Boroondara cemetery.

A. Sutherland, *Victoria and its metropolis*, 2 (Melb, 1888); J. Smith (ed), *Cyclopedia of Victoria*, 1 (Melb, 1903); Roy Vic Inst of Architects, *J of Procs*, Apr 1903, Mar 1906, Jan 1913; *IAN*, Nov 1869, Mar 1884, Nov 1885; *Weekly Times* (Melb), Aug 1906; *Argus*, 1 Sept 1928; S. Forge, John A. B. Koch *and* W. Forge, The buildings of J. A. B. Koch (MSS held by S. and W. Forge, Hawthorn, Melb); letters from C. Koch and L. Gleadwell also held.   W. FORGE

KODAK; *see* O'FERRALL, ERNEST FRANCIS

KOERSTZ, CHRISTIAN CHRISTIANSEN (1847-1930), manufacturer and inventor, was born on 23 July 1847 at Kolding, Denmark, son of Christian Kortz, tailor, and his wife Anne Pouline Augusta Johanne, née Flerong. At 20, after being an apprentice mechanic in a Dutch firm of windmill-makers, he went to New Zealand and settled at Waverly, North Island. After twelve years spent making butter-boxes, and in building and bridge construction, he visited Denmark where at Kolding on 12 June 1887 he married Christina Petra Kors (1868-1907).

In August they reached Sydney where Koerstz met and became a business associate of Frederick Mason, grain and produce merchant of Sussex Street, who held patent rights to a woolpress and was agent for the Deering Harvester Co. Describing himself as a carpenter, Koerstz was granted provisional protection certificates by the Patents Office for an improved bundle-press in February 1890 and in 1891 for certain improvements in woolpresses, water pump and motor, and with Mason for an improved rotary pump. He thus began a long series of inventions and patents and a manufacturing firm which became well known in the pastoral industry in Australia and overseas.

Realizing the great potential market for more efficient and labour-saving wool-presses, Koerstz designed and made presses for both the large and small sheep-owner. By 1898 Mason, Koerstz's sole agent, had sold hundreds of the 'New Koerstz Selectors' and Homestead Lessees' Press', which was claimed to have 'practically annihilated all competition'. Keenly priced at £15 and originally designed for the smallholder, it weighed 12 cwt (610 kg), could be worked by one man and handle the pressing of wool from flocks of over 20 000 sheep. By 1910 Koerstz was a large and successful exhibitor at the Royal Agricultural Society's Sydney Show and his woolpresses—'Little Wonder', 'Squatter', 'Station', 'Bosker', 'Conqueror' and 'Improved Langley'—ranging in price from £12 10s to £35, were standard equipment in a large and increasing number of shearing-sheds. His factory at Pyrmont also produced hay, skin, cotton and wine-presses, quartz-crushers, pumps and a wide range of other agricultural implements. The expanded factory moved to Mentmore Avenue, Rosebery, in 1925.

Koerstz, whose inventiveness and high standard of workmanship did much for Australia's wool industry, was naturalized in 1907. At 65 he retired in favour of his children who continued the business as a partnership. He died at his residence, Kolding, Ryde, on 9 May 1930, survived by three sons and three daughters, and was buried in the Anglican section of the Field of Mars cemetery. His estate was sworn for probate at £14 167.

F. Wheelhouse, *Digging stick to rotary hoe* (Melb, 1966); *Pastoral Review*, 15 June 1898, 15 Apr 1910, 15 May 1911, 15 Apr 1912, 16 Sept 1933; *Government Gazette* (NSW), 5 Mar 1890, 5 Feb, 6 Apr, 4 Dec 1891; *SMH*, 16 May 1930.   G. P. WALSH

KOMINE, ISOKICHI (1867-1934), planter and trader, was born on 17 July 1867 at Shimabara, Japan. He migrated to Thursday Island, Queensland, in 1890 and soon advanced from pump-hand to diver, leasing his own pearling lugger. By 1894 he had also acquired an interest in a boat-building yard. He ascended the Binaturi and Fly rivers in Papua in 1895 in search of agricultural land; but was unable to attract Japanese capital to exploit his discoveries.

In 1901, when his plan to purchase land on behalf of Japanese investors to grow sugar near Cairns was frustrated by his failure to secure naturalization, he moved to German New Guinea. There his first employment was to operate his cutter for the government at Rabaul. In time he expanded his operations to include recruiting, planting, ship-building, retail and overseas trade, and sawmilling. In 1910 by borrowing from the New Guinea Co. he was able to acquire a thirty-year lease from the government of plantation land on Manus, Los Negros and Rambutjo islands. In 1911 he built a shipyard and general store at Rabaul. By 1919 he was employing 163 (including 8 Japanese) on the plantations and 144 (including 35 Japanese) at the shipyard. His success was not achieved without risk. In 1909 when trading at Loniu he was enticed into an ambush but managed to recover his pistol from his assailants and escape. In 1910 his plantation at Kali was attacked and its labourers killed.

On the outbreak of war in 1914 Komine acted as pilot for the Australian expeditions sent to occupy the Admiralty and Western islands and to capture the steam-yacht *Komet* at Talasea. He also reported that H. R. Wahlen & Co. was passing military information to the enemy; the Australian administration showed its appreciation by transferring Wahlen's pearling rights to Komine.

With the intention of expanding his existing activities and engaging in direct trade with Japan and Australia using Japanese vessels, Komine in 1917 formed a company in Japan, the Nanyō Sangyō Kaisha, to which in return for a 40 per cent shareholding he surrendered his New Guinea interests, valued at £70 000. The policy of the Hughes [q.v.] government, however, was to keep Japan and Japanese interests as far away from Australia as possible; and to use the military occupation to ensure that in New Guinea foreign enterprises could not expand and that, when the peace conference eventually ceded the Territory to Australia, Australian firms would be able to enter an arena in which there were no strongly entrenched foreign rivals. The Military Administration, largely by its controls over exports, shipping, immigration and mortgages successfully countered Komine's attempts at expansion and diversification. By 1921 (when civil administration was established) the damage had been done: British shipping had returned from the war and, in

this and other fields of activity, there were many competitors.

In 1930 financial difficulties forced Komine to transfer the management of his properties to Burns [q.v.7], Philp [q.v.] & Co. to permit profits being applied to pay off his debts. He died at Rabaul on 3 October 1934 of food poisoning and was buried in the botanic gardens with Japanese rites. His wife survived him.

Gaimushō, Takumukyoku, *Gōshū inintōchiryō nyuginia jijō* (Tokyo, 1938, copy in NL); T. Irie *Hōjin kaigai hattenshi*, 1 (Tokyo, 1942), p 401; C. D. Rowley, *The Australians in German New Guinea 1914-21* (Melb, 1958); P. Biskup, 'Foreign coloured labour in German New Guinea', *J of Pacific Hist*, 5, 1970; *Rabaul Times*, 5 Oct 1934; Piesse papers, Series 6/752, PM's Dept 650/19A/40 *and* Japanese Foreign Ministry Archives, 4.2.5.240, microfilm G16166 (NL); COL/73, file 98/11159 (QA).

D. C. S. SISSONS

KOPSEN, WILLIAM (1847-1930), manufacturer and ship-chandler, was born on 29 December 1847 and baptized Gustaf Wilhelm at Vaxholm, Sweden, only son of Erik Gustav Kopsen, marine customs house porter, and his wife Anna Greta, née Ohrstrom. His early childhood was marred by family discord and straitened circumstances. Orphaned at 15 he lived in 1862-64 on a farm at Osteraker where he was tutored by the rector Dr Samuel Ponten who encouraged Kopsen to study geography and anthropology.

From 1864 Kopsen worked as a shop assistant and book-keeper in Stockholm. He migrated in 1868, reaching Sydney on 10 September. After working as a cook and shepherd on sheep-stations near Bathurst, he went next year to the Clarence River where he bought a small boat and traded. But, 'seized by a longing to see the Fiji Islands', he joined the missionary ship *John Wesley* and reached Levuka in May 1870. For two years he transported cargoes round the islands and early in 1873 became a book-keeper in Levuka, while acting as commission agent for Swedish planters. In 1875 he established W. Kopsen & Co., with J. C. Smith, to import and trade in textiles and general merchandise. By the late 1870s he was a member of the hospital board, secretary of the yacht and rifle clubs, and consul for Sweden and Norway from 1881.

Britain had annexed Fiji in 1874 and in 1877 Kopsen was naturalized. In Levuka on 20 October he married Laura Theresa Turner from Sydney. He had sent articles about native customs, flora and fauna to a Stockholm newspaper, and donated artefacts from the South Pacific to a Swedish museum—in 1882 he was elected to the

Swedish Society for Anthropology and Geography. When the capital was moved to Suva that year, Kopsen moved too and in 1883 became an alderman and mayor. He was a member of the Marine Board and in 1885 formed and was chairman of the Fiji Fire and Marine Insurance Co. Ltd.

In 1889 Kopsen settled in Sydney, carrying on business at 70 Clarence Street as Smith & Kopsen, ship-chandler. After Smith retired the firm of W. Kopsen & Co. Ltd was registered in December 1905. On a cycling tour of the Snowy Mountains he became interested in a timber which locals called 'mountain ash'. Foreseeing its commercial potential, Kopsen in 1906 built a plant at Auburn, where tests indicated its suitability for oars and implement handles. When transport of the timber proved difficult and costly, a factory was built at Laurel Hill, near Batlow, where 'Pioneer' oars and handles were made. By 1927 W. Kopsen & Co. Ltd were contractors to government departments and always had 10 000 oars ready for delivery within Australia and shipment to the Pacific Islands. He did much to revive the Australian timber industry and to reduce domination by American imports.

From 1911 Kopsen served as foundation senior vice-president of the Swedish Chamber of Commerce for Australia, New Zealand and South Sea Islands, and in 1923-28 was honorary vice-consul for Sweden. In 1914 he was largely responsible for erecting a monument at Kurnell to Daniel Solander [q.v.2].

Described as 'a giant, elegant both in appearance and manners', Kopsen had great personal charm, humanity and optimism, with the ability to organize, act quickly and take command. He had been brought up as a Lutheran, believing in the virtues of thrift, industry and self-discipline; in Australia he was a Congregationalist. He visited Sweden in 1910 and afterwards said that 'a good wind blew over my head the day I travelled away from the old country'. Kopsen retired in 1928 and died at his home at Strathfield on 15 August 1930; he was cremated. His estate was valued for probate at £34 092. His wife, two sons and three daughters survived him. In 1983 William Kopsen & Co. was carried on by a grandson.

Sydney Chamber of Commerce, *Commerce in congress* (Syd, 1909); L. Nordstrom, *William Kopsen* (Stockholm, 1933); *A'sian Manufacturer*, 30 July 1927, p 28, 39; *Swedish-A'sian Trade J*, 18, June 1931, p 363; *SMH*, 18 Aug 1930.

B. DALE

KRAEGEN, EDWARD CHARLES (1864-1943), union organizer and public servant, was born on 3 August 1864 at Albury, New South Wales, son of Carl Wilhelm Immanuel Kraegen, telegraph officer, and his wife Emma Wilhelmina Dorothea, née Lassen, both German born. In 1872 Edward and his two younger sisters were orphaned and dependent on the care of their maternal grandparents. In 1878 the largely self-taught Edward became a telegraph messenger at Parramatta post office, and next year was promoted to cadet telegraph operator at the General Post Office, Sydney. Kraegen became a member of the committee elected to form the New South Wales Electric Telegraph Society in 1855. In 1887 he was elected secretary and when it was reformed in 1889 as the Post and Telegraph Officers Association became president. He helped to found the association's journal the *Transmitter* in 1891 and was its editor in 1895-1900.

The association was almost certainly the first industrial organization to be formed among government employees in Australia and reputedly the first among post and telegraph employees anywhere. When delegates from the seven colonial associations met to form the Australian Commonwealth Posts and Telegraphs Officers' Association in October 1900 it was largely because of Kraegen's efforts. As the president of the first federal industrial conference he took its programme to mass meetings in four States. He resigned his union positions when appointed clerk to the Commonwealth public service inspector in New South Wales in December 1902. He was promoted to inspector in March 1910, an appointment he held until 1923. On 22 December 1903 at Oakleigh, Victoria, he married Louisa Margaret Dunkley [q.v.8], a leader of the Victorian Women's Post and Telegraph Association.

Kraegen was one of the first to organize public service and white collar unions and to support the movement for new and uniform industrial rights within Commonwealth employment. He proved a talented pioneer and architect, avoiding royal commissions and conciliation and arbitration proceedings in a pattern of personal negotiation that earned him respect and recognition and the affectionate title of 'Trusty' Kraegen. In the reorganization initiated by the newly constituted Public Service Board, in 1923 Kraegen was appointed public service inspector for South Australia. By mid-1924 he completed the reclassification of the Commonwealth Department of Trade and Customs and later reported creatively on the service in New Guinea, Papua and the Northern Territory. He travelled widely and when one of his last official journeys took him across central Australia to Darwin he attempted to locate the grave of his father in the desert. On his retirement in 1926 the

Federal Public Service Journal recorded his impartiality and regretted the loss of 'one of the ablest, most clear-headed and most diligent' members of its association.

Kraegen was well known in rowing and bowling circles: he was a member of the Glebe Rowing Club and the Old Oarsmen's Union and president of the Lane Cove Bowling Club. He died on 25 July 1943 at his home at Longueville and was cremated with Anglican rites. A son and daughter survived him.

G. E. Caiden, *Career service* (Melb, 1965); Aust Cwlth Post and Telegraph Assn, *Transmitter*, 17 Jan 1903; *SMH*, 27 July 1943.   J. S. BAKER

KROME, OTTO GEORG HERMANN DITTMAR (1863-1917), educationist, was born on 27 October 1863 at Dorum, Hannover, eldest son of Rev. Christian Wilhelm Ferdinand Krome, Lutheran minister, and his wife Helene Maria Mathilde, née Kröger. Educated at gymnasia at Verden and Hameln, he was sent in 1880 to South Africa to avoid Prussian military service. He taught at Panmure Public School, East London, where his uncle, Pastor Müller, was principal, and from 1884 at Dale College, King William's Town, becoming vice-principal in 1885 when he graduated B.A. from the University of Cape Town. He may also have engaged in diamond prospecting.

In 1890 Krome migrated to Victoria where he worked for another German immigrant, the architect William Vahland, at Bendigo until his papers arrived; he then taught at two local colleges, St Andrew's and Girton. In 1893 he left to teach German at Oberwyl, Kalymna, Newnham College and Wesley College, Melbourne. He also lectured at the university colleges, Ormond, Trinity and Queen's.

In 1894 Krome and Thomas Palmer [q.v.] in partnership leased Melbourne Teachers' College, Carlton, from the Education Department and opened University High School, a private, co-educational secondary school which quickly became one of the largest and most successful in Melbourne. Accepted into Melbourne cultural circles, Krome in June became with Palmer a foundation member of the Wallaby Club. In 1895 he became vice-principal of University High School, supervising the girl boarders with his wife, Vahland's eldest daughter, Eleanor Mary, whom he had married at Bendigo on 24 March 1894. That July he was naturalized. He also joined the Melbourne University Masonic Lodge and became senior grand warden in Grand Lodge in 1912-13, remaining a Freemason until his death.

After Palmer became headmaster of Wesley College in 1897, Krome was co-principal of University High School with L. A. Adamson [q.v.7] until 1901 when Adamson returned to Wesley. In 1902-06 Krome was sole principal. In 1904 as secretary of the Schools' Association of Victoria, he initiated with Adamson the formation of the Associated Independent Secondary Teachers of Victoria, and remained an active council-member until his death. In 1905 he was one of the deputation to the minister of education opposing the establishment of state secondary schools.

In 1906 Krome succeeded J. R. Corr as headmaster of Methodist Ladies' College, Kew, and inaugurated a period of outstanding academic achievement and strong school spirit—among day-girls as well as boarders. He introduced the prefect system and a sports club to encourage team games, inter-form competition, swimming sports and lifesaving. He maintained close contact with Adamson, discussing educational matters by telephone most evenings.

Described as 'a tall, plump, chubby-faced man, good-humoured, hospitable, fond of good cheer and of singing German songs', Krome, although a loyal supporter of the British Empire, suffered anti-German persecution during World War I. He was strongly defended by W. H. Fitchett [q.v.8], Adamson and the school council but the harassment hastened his death at Hawthorn on 19 December 1917. Survived by his wife and five daughters, he was buried in Brighton cemetery. His daughter Eleanor Victoria became headmistress of Queen's College, Ballarat, and of The Hermitage, Geelong.

A posthumously painted portrait is in the assembly hall of Methodist Ladies' College; a school house is named after him and the wrought iron Krome Memorial Gates were opened in 1923.

A. G. T. Zainu'ddin, *They dreamt of a school* (Melb, 1982); MLC, *Old Collegian*, 1 (1917), no 1; *Looking Back/Kykies in die Verlede*, 12 (Mar 1972), no 1, p 21; W. H. Fitchett, The headmaster of the Methodist Ladies' College (1916, copy in MLC history collection); MS 8577 (LaTL).
A. G. THOMSON ZAINU'DDIN

KRUTTSCHNITT, JULIUS (1885-1974), mining executive, was born on 7 May 1885 in New Orleans, Louisiana, United States of America, son of Julius Kruttschnitt, railway engineer, and his wife Wilhelmina, née Kock. Educated initially at Belmont, California, he went on to Yale University (B.Phil., 1906) and, after a year of postgraduate work, took up an appointment as a mine surveyor with the Arizona Copper Co. He joined the mining department of the American Smelting & Refining Co. as superintendent of the Reforma lead-mine in Mexico. He moved later to Asientos to superintend a silver-mine. Years later, his Spanish-style house at Mount Isa was named Casa Grande, probably commemorating his Latin American sojourn.

Recalled to U.S.A. to manage the company's mining department of the south-west with headquarters in Arizona, he was responsible for mine examination, exploration and operation over a wide area. In September 1930 Kruttschnitt accepted appointment as general manager of Mount Isa Mines Ltd, Queensland, arriving in December. He wrote later: 'To my consternation I found on my arrival a condition bordering on bankruptcy with creditors being importuned to await a none-too-certain influx of capital'. The financial situation and serious technical problems presented a challenge to the quietly spoken American, particularly since his directors were pressing for early production. Additional financial backing came from the American Smelting & Refining Co. and by July 1931 the mine and smelters were producing their first lead bullion. Although the operation showed a profit by 1937, no dividend was paid until 1947.

Kruttschnitt joined Mount Isa Mines long before the days of air-conditioning but he always dressed immaculately in a suit and tie even in very high temperatures. J.K., as he was known, even wore a tie when playing golf. With a high level of financial and technical skills Kruttschnitt, though small in stature, commanded respect. Remarkably in tune with the community, he involved himself in a wide range of social and sporting activities. While seeking to restore the ailing mining company, he showed an interest in the welfare of miners and their families, particularly in housing. The unique Mount Isa tent house, initially a tent to which was added a corrugated iron wall designed to create a ventilation channel, was developed while Kruttschnitt was general manager.

In 1931 Kruttschnitt was appointed a director of Mount Isa Mines Ltd and he became chairman in 1937. He retired as chairman in 1953 but stayed on the board until 1967. During his twenty-two years at Mount Isa he held other directorates with Big Bell Mines Ltd, Anglo-Westralian Mining Pty Ltd, the Mining Trust Ltd, New Guinea Goldfields Ltd and several other companies. For fourteen years he was president of the Queensland Chamber of Mines and was president of the Australasian Institute of Mining and Metallurgy in 1939 and 1952. In 1962 the English Institute of Mining and Metallurgy awarded him its gold medal. He was awarded the Australasian Institute of Mining and Metallurgy's medal in 1946 in recognition of his outstanding services to the industry in Australia. He was also a member of the American Institute of Mining and Metallurgical Engineers. In 1953-60 Kruttschnitt was a member of the Australian Atomic Energy Commission's advisory committee on uranium mining. He was a board-member of the faculty of engineering at the University of Queensland in 1954-62 and was granted an honorary doctorate of engineering in 1971. In the same year Mount Isa Mines Ltd presented the Julius Kruttschnitt Mineral Research Centre to the university in his honour.

On 24 September 1907 in San Francisco, California, Kruttschnitt had married Marie Rose Pickering (d. 1940); they had two sons and two daughters. On 3 June 1944 at Cloncurry, he married his secretary Edna May Roger, née Maxted. Shortly before his death he visited Mount Isa and spoke to senior students of the high school. 'Although he was by now a frail old man approaching 90', an observer commented, 'Dr Kruttschnitt held the normally restless teenagers spellbound for more than half an hour as he talked to them about mining'. He lived in retirement at Indooroopilly within sight of the Julius Kruttschnitt Mineral Research Centre and, predeceased by his wife in 1967, died in St Andrew's War Memorial Hospital on 23 September 1974. He was cremated.

G. Blainey, *Mines in the spinifex* (Syd, 1960); *Courier Mail*, 5 Feb 1944, 5 May 1960, 15 May 1967, 11 Sept 1968, 24 Sept 1974; *Telegraph* (Brisb), 10 May 1971, 24 Sept 1974; *Sunday Mail*, color magazine, 6 Jan 1974.
                     A. J. Lynch
                     J. R. Hopper

KWAILIU, JOHN; *see* FATNOWNA, JOHN

KWOK BEW (GUO BIAO) (1868-1932), merchant, was born in January 1868 in Chung Shan district near Canton, China, son of Chap Hing, farmer, and his wife Fung Size. After the death of his father, Kwok left for New South Wales in 1883, working as a door-to-door salesman at Grafton and later as a produce merchant in Sydney. Known in Australia as George Bew, he married 16-year-old Darling Young, daughter of Ma Tin Young, a Bourke merchant, at the Presbyterian Chinese Church in Foster Street, Sydney, on 16 September 1896; he became a Christian.

Through his Wing Sang & Co. he expanded from general produce into a marketing agent for fruit and vegetables supplied by Chinese gardeners in northern New South Wales, Queensland and the Pacific. The Wing Sang grew rapidly and with several other Chinese enterprises managed to control the wholesale banana market in New South Wales and Queensland. By 1899 the Wing Sang had an annual turnover of some £36 000 from the Queensland banana trade and next year the firm started importing bananas from Fiji. In the early 1900s Bew was a founder of Wing On & Co., an expanding commercial conglomerate.

As proprietor of one of the Chinese community's outstandingly successful firms, George Bew emerged as a business leader of considerable influence. He played a leading role in negotiations which led to the formation of the China-Australia Mail Steamship Line in November 1917. His strongest support within the Chinese community came from merchants of Chung Shan origin, who looked upon him as their leader, and in 1904 Bew became a vice-president of the Chinese Merchant's Defence Association, formed to counter the propaganda of 'White Australia' merchants. He had also been a founder of the Chinese Empire Reform Association in 1901, but a decade later became a supporter of Sun Yatsen, the Chung Shan revolutionary leader, and helped to establish the *Chinese Republic News* in Sydney in February 1914. The paper circulated extensively in Australasia, the South Pacific, the Straits Settlements, Hong Kong and China itself. Sydney began to emerge as a centre of the republican movement among Nanyang Chinese and in April 1916 a Chinese Nationalist League of Sydney (Kuomingtang) was established with Bew as president.

Late in 1917 he returned to China to found the Wing On emporium in Shanghai. Kwok continued to show creativity and business acumen. The emporium specialized in quality local and imported goods and became the largest department store in China. Sales staff were trained in English and French and encouraged to become Presbyterian Christians. Kwok sought to ensure that his entrepreneurial role would be conducted in a safe political environment: he became quite prominent in the Kuomintang through his financial contributions and successful fund-raising activities; while his home and business enterprises, by the early 1920s expanding into banking, retail and manufacturing, were located in the foreign concessions in Shanghai and Canton.

Kwok died on 3 January 1932 in Shanghai, survived by his wife, four sons and four daughters. At the time of his death he was a director of the Chinese Government Mint as well as managing director of the Wing On Co. Ltd.

C. F. Yong, *The new gold mountain* (Adel, nd); J. H. C. Sleeman, *White China* (Syd, 1933); Roy Com on the fruit industry, *PP* (Cwlth), 1913, 4, p 1; *SMH*, 6 Feb 1932.   FRANK FARRELL
                                           ADRIAN CHAN

KYNGDON, LESLIE HERBERT (1860-1923), regular soldier, was born on 10 July 1860 at Exeter, Somerset, England, son of Boughton Kyngdon, medical practitioner, and his wife Elizabeth Maria, née Cobb. Fourth child in a family of five sons and three daughters, he was educated at Whitgift School, Croydon, Surrey. The family migrated to Sydney in 1878. They were then in comfortable circumstances but their fortune was later embezzled by a lawyer.

Kyngdon was commissioned as a second lieutenant in the artillery of the New South Wales Volunteer Forces on 30 June 1880 and promoted lieutenant in 1881 and captain in 1884. He served as captain commanding 'D' Company, New South Wales Infantry Battalion, in the Sudan campaign of 1885, taking part in the advance on Tamai. He transferred to the permanent forces, New South Wales Artillery, on 12 November 1885 as a lieutenant and was promoted captain in 1891. In 1896 he was sent to England for six months attachment to the Royal Artillery and on his return was appointed adjutant, 2nd Garrison Division. Released for active service in the South African War, he was a special service officer with the Royal Artillery from January to December 1900 and later served in Cape Colony and the Orange River Colony.

In 1902-05 Kyngdon was staff officer, Artillery, in Queensland, Western Australia and New South Wales and was promoted major in February 1905. Commander of Thursday Island in 1906-08, he was company officer in the Royal Australian Artillery in New South Wales in 1908-09. From February 1910 he commanded the Royal Australian Artillery (coastal defences) in Queensland, then Victoria, and in 1912-16 New South Wales, being promoted lieut-colonel in November 1910. Promoted colonel in April 1916, he was inspector of coast defences until June 1919 when he became temporary chief of ordnance. He was placed on the retired list in November 1919 with the honorary rank of brigadier general.

Although, apparently, Kyngon 'had an eye for the ladies' he never married. After retirement, he lived at the Athenaeum Club, Melbourne, until his death from cancer on 11 April 1923 at Mount St Evins Hospital,

Fitzroy. He was buried in Brighton cemetery with Anglican rites. Kyngdon was much respected and known in the army as 'Gruffy'. His bitch Nettle, feared by junior officers, slept at the entrance to the officers' mess until the last officer came home. Nettle would then go to 'Gruffy's' bed, wake him and he would note the time. Next day Kyngdon would pick the officer who showed the most obvious signs of tiredness and ask what had kept him out so late.

Kyngdon's service in the Australian Army spanned forty years and three conflicts in which Australian troops were involved. Apart from his campaign medals for service in the Sudan and South Africa he received a mention for 'meritorious service' on the home front in World War I.

F. Hutchinson and F. Myers, *The Australian contingent* (Syd, 1885); Aust Defence Dept, *Official records of the Australian military contingents to the war in South Africa*, P. L. Murray ed (Melb, 1911); *Argus*, 19 Sept 1912; information from Mr C. W. T. Kyngdon, Melb, and Mr R. Kyngdon, Bowral, NSW.   RICHMOND CUBIS

L

LABY, THOMAS HOWELL (1880-1946), physicist, was born on 3 May 1880 at Creswick, Victoria, youngest child and only son of Thomas James Laby, flourmiller, and his wife Jane Eudora, née Lewis. About 1883 the family moved to New South Wales, Laby senior establishing a ropeworks at Toongabbie. His death in 1888 left the family in straitened circumstances. After education at various country schools, supplemented by private study, Laby obtained Senior Public Examination mathematics and history, but was unqualified to matriculate. In 1898 he joined the Taxation Department in Sydney, but with brief coaching in chemistry won a position in the Department of Agriculture's chemical laboratory. In 1901 he became junior demonstrator in chemistry at the University of Sydney on the recommendation of his chief F. B. Guthrie [q.v.].

Laby attended university evening classes in chemistry, physics and mathematics, and undertook research resulting in two papers published by the Royal Society of New South Wales: 'The separation of iron from nickel and cobalt' (1903) and, with (Sir) Douglas Mawson [q.v.], 'Preliminary observations on radio-activity and the occurrence of radium in Australian minerals' (1904). In 1905 he left for England with an Exhibition of 1851 science research scholarship. He intended to work in chemistry at the University of Birmingham, but was advised instead to pursue his interest in radio-activity at the Cavendish Laboratory, Cambridge, under (Sir) J. J. Thomson. Here he received in 1907 the B.A. degree by research for theses on the ionization produced by alpha-particles and on the supersaturation and nuclear condensation of organic vapours. Supported by a renewal of his scholarship, a research exhibition from Emmanuel College and the Joule studentship of the Royal Society of London (he also won the Sudbury Hardyman research prize) he remained to pursue further investigations. At this time he met Ernest (Lord) Rutherford, later a valued friend.

In 1909 Laby took up the new chair of physics at Victoria (University) College, Wellington, New Zealand, imbued with an enthusiasm for Cambridge and a conviction that a university would be judged by its research. For this Wellington offered little opportunity, but Laby established his laboratory, campaigned to reform the University of New Zealand, and completed work begun in Cambridge with G. W. C. Kaye leading

to the publication of their *Tables of physical and chemical constants with some mathematical functions* (London, 1911) which ran to fourteen editions. In 1910 he became a foundation member and treasurer of the Wellington Round Table group, thus entering upon a lifelong interest in Imperial affairs. He presided over section A of the Australasian Association for the Advancement of Science in Melbourne in 1912, and on 17 February 1914 married, in London, Beatrice Littlejohn, daughter of a Wellington jeweller and optician.

In 1915 Laby moved to the Melbourne chair of natural philosophy. He promptly joined the Melbourne Round Table group, to become its secretary until his death, and acting Dominion secretary in 1916-19, expressing through this movement and elsewhere his concern for Australia's Imperial war effort. He developed valves for an antigas respirator (accepted by the military authorities but not used in action) designed with W. A. Osborne and (Sir) D. O. Masson [qq.v.]; he undertook radiographic testing of fuse for the Defence Department and inspected X-ray equipment for military hospitals; but he chafed at the shortage of scientific war-work. In 1918 Mr Justice Higgins [q.v.] engaged him to report on the training and classification of Commonwealth Public Service professional officers.

Laby had on arrival taken his place on several university faculties, and later on the technical colleges and schools boards; he served as dean of science in 1926-28 and professorial representative on council in 1927-31. After the war he sought improved accommodation and apparatus for his department, developed its practical teaching and promoted research. The most promising of his research students, twelve of whom received 1851 Exhibition scholarships, were encouraged to proceed to the Cavendish Laboratory.

Awarded a Cambridge Sc.D. for research in 1921, Laby continued working chiefly in the fields of heat and X-ray spectroscopy, the former culminating in his precise determination, with E. O. Hercus, of the mechanical equivalent of heat. His experience with X-rays and radium directed him towards problems in their medical use. He assisted in introducing radiology in the medical course. In 1925 he inquired into methods of cancer treatment during his visit to Europe and the United States of America, urging the foundation of a Melbourne centre modelled on the Paris Cancer Institute. In 1929 the Commonwealth Radium Laboratory was formally established in university premises with Laby as Commonwealth adviser in radium. He assisted in implementing Australian Cancer Conference resolutions, supporting the movement to establish the Victorian Anti-Cancer Council, and promoting university diplomas in radiology in Melbourne. He made strenuous efforts to secure facilities to investigate and advise on regulation of X-ray dosage, and standardization of dosage measurement. In 1935 the Department of Health agreed to locate its new X-ray laboratory within Laby's department of natural philosophy. The arrangement, however, foundered on problems arising from shortage of space and equipment, and from a divided authority. Laby resigned as Commonwealth adviser in 1937, and the Commonwealth laboratory was re-sited in the university grounds.

Always deeply interested in the organization of science, Laby had taken part in the early deliberations of the Advisory Council of Science and Industry and joined its Victorian committee. When the Council for Scientific and Industrial Research was formed in 1926, however, he found himself excluded from it. Further, he resigned from its maintenance of standards committee when not appointed chairman. Nevertheless, in 1927 he joined C.S.I.R.'s Australian Radio Research Board which from 1929 funded research into field strength of radio signals, a subject already investigated under Laby's supervision for the Broadcasting Co. of Australia. The Melbourne group moved on to study atmospherics, Laby helping to design equipment and producing with his students a paper showing that atmospherics are reflected by the ionosphere. But when the board turned its attention to radar, centreing this activity in Sydney, Laby resigned. In 1928 he joined the executive committee of the Imperial Geophysical Experimental Survey, to which his laboratory gave technical assistance, and in 1929 helped edit its final report, *Principles and practice of geophysical prospecting* (Cambridge, 1931).

In 1931 Laby was elected a fellow of the Royal Society. He continued research other than that sponsored by C.S.I.R., undertaking studies in measurement including (with V. D. Hopper) that of the electronic charge. He travelled regularly to Europe and U.S.A. and in 1936 he attended the Congress of the Universities of the British Empire at Cambridge, and Round Table discussions during which he tried to assess Britain's likely attitude to Imperial defence in the event of European war.

A fellow of the Institute of Physics since 1923, Laby became in August 1939 foun-dation president of its Australian branch. In May 1940 he began contributing articles to the *Argus* on World War II. In July he became chairman of the Optical Munitions Panel (later Scientific Instruments and Optical Panel) appointed to draw up optical specifications for lenses for telescope sights and other military instruments. The panel co-ordinated work in several laboratories and was administered from Laby's own, where all unrelated research was set aside.

A tall, thin figure, Laby had long suffered from recurring low blood pressure and asthma. Never of equable temperament, he many times demonstrated his readiness to resign rather than yield a point he deemed essential. As his health declined, he showed increasing inability to accommodate the difficulties inseparable from co-operative enterprises. In 1941 he resigned as president of the Australian Institute of Physics and late in 1942 he relinquished his department ('by far the best in the Southern Hemisphere', (Sir) Mark Oliphant had told him). In 1944 he resigned from the Scientific Instruments and Optical Panel. He died on 21 June 1946 of arteriosclerosis, survived by his wife and two daughters, the elder of whom later became a senior lecturer in his old department. He was cremated.

Many testified to Laby's essential diffidence, his helpfulness and generosity as well as to his tenacity in pursuing the advancement of his discipline. A collection of his published papers is held by the physics school of the University of Melbourne.

J. C. Beaglehole, *Victoria University College* (Well, 1949); D. P. Mellor, *The role of science and industry* (Canb, 1958); G. Currie and J. Graham, *The origins of CSIRO* (Melb, 1966); W. F. Evans, *History of the Radio Research Board, 1926-1945* (Melb, 1973); J. F. Richardson, *The Australian Radiation Laboratory* (Canb, 1981); Aust Cancer Conference, *Report*, 1930-37; *Aust Physicist*, 17 (Dec 1980); *Hist Studies*, 20 (Apr 1983); *Obituary Notices of Fellows of the Roy Soc*, 5 (May 1948); *Records of the Aust Academy of Science*, 3 (Mar 1975), no 1.   CECILY CLOSE

LACEY, ANDREW WILLIAM (1887-1946), trade unionist and politician, was born on 19 October 1887 at Terowie, South Australia, son of George Lacey, labourer, and his wife Mary Ellen, née McLean. He attended the Terowie Public School. As an adult he worked in the smelters at Port Pirie and became an active trade unionist. In 1916-22 he was the Australian Workers'

Union organizer at the works and in 1920-22 and 1932-35 a member of the Port Pirie Municipal Council. Port Pirie was the major population centre for the Federal electorate of Grey and had been held since Federation by A. Poynton [q.v.] who left the United Labor Party in 1916 over his support for conscription. Lacey, who opposed conscription, defeated him in 1922. He held the seat for Labor until 1931 and the end of the Scullin [q.v.] Labor government. Lacey was a member of a select committee on the operation of the Navigation Act in 1924. He was also a member of the Public Works Committee in 1925-28 and its chairman in 1929-31.

In 1933 Lacey won the State seat of Port Pirie. In this parliament Labor was split into 'Official', 'Premier's Plan' and 'Lang' factions. The official group was the largest and as its head Lacey, who had voted against the Premier's Plan in the Federal parliament, became leader of the Opposition. A year later the three factions reunited. He remained leader until 1938 and was deputy leader till his death.

Lacey was representative of the generation of Labor men who replaced those who had left the party with Hughes, Holman [qq.v.] and the South Australian wartime leader Crawford Vaughan [q.v.]. Like his contemporaries John Gunn and L. L. Hill [qq.v.], he was identified with the industrial wing of the party. His union, the A.W.U., was through the 1920s almost as influential in the South Australian branch of the party as it was in Queensland. Though not a Catholic, he was of Irish stock and was attracted to the Australian nationalism which inspired the anti-conscription movement in World War I and so changed the course of Labor history. During the Depression he advocated nationalization of the banks. It was his misfortune to achieve prominence at a time when the Labor Party was deeply divided over the best means to counter the Depression. He exercised a moderating and healing influence within the party in the years of rehabilitation after 1933. An affable 'people's man', Lacey was never acrimonious in dispute.

He was prominent in the Justices' Association and was a trotting enthusiast, the owner of several horses. When young, he had been a keen sprinter. On 13 October 1908 he had married Helene Clara Welke. She and two sons and a daughter survived him when he died of heart disease on 24 August 1946. He was buried in Centennial Park cemetery.

SMH, 8 Aug 1934, 4 Apr 1938; *Advertiser* (Adel), 26 Aug 1946, 11 Oct 1948; PRG 455 (SAA); information from C. Cameron, Tennyson, SA, and J. Lacey, Kenmore, Qld.

DONALD J. HOPGOOD

LADE, FRANK (1868-1948), clergyman, was born on 21 December 1868 at Kilmore, Victoria, son of Stephen Lade, farmer, and his wife Anne, née MacConchie. He was educated at state schools and worked on the farm before in 1890 beginning training for the Methodist Church. He attended Queen's College, University of Melbourne (B.A., 1903; M.A., 1905), and began his ministry with two years in Tasmania. In 1895 he was transferred to the Toorak Methodist Church, Melbourne, where he met Lillian Frances Millard, the church organist, whom he married there on 17 March 1898; they had four daughters and two sons. That year they visited England where British preachers impressed the young Australian minister.

After ministries in Victoria and Tasmania, in 1911 Lade transferred from Hobart to the historic Kent Town Methodist Church in Adelaide for five years; then followed three years at the Archer Street, North Adelaide, pulpit. He was active in the South Australian Temperance Alliance and led the successful fight for a referendum that resulted in 6 o'clock closing of hotel bars by the Licensing Act of 1915. This was followed, after further agitation led by Lade, by the 1917 Licensing Act which stipulated that a local option poll must be held before any additional liquor licence could be granted for a defined local area. In 1919 Lade was seconded to the Temperance Alliance for two years as a field officer and public lecturer on abstinence. He maintained an influential and fiery attack on drinking and gambling throughout his life. In retirement he edited the *South Australian Patriot*, the alliance's journal. His articles showed clarity and zeal. He desired prohibition, but only if decreed by the 'will of the people'. His opponents argued that alcohol was a stimulant, but Lade reiterated 'It is a narcotic'. In this he was fifty years ahead of his time. His argument reflected a deliberate shift in strategy from the doctrinal to the dietary.

Lade was scholar, preacher, social reformer: for him all were compatible and complementary. All his work was marked by masterful logic, yet his fundamental message was always delivered with striking simplicity. He was tall, dignified, immaculately dressed, yet ready to preach in Victoria Square, or wherever people could be gathered. Though intensely evangelical, he was sensitive and respected by his adversaries. His repartee was spontaneous and entertaining: an interjector once called, 'You're not a producer, Lade, you haven't produced anything'. 'Yes, I have', replied Lade. 'I've produced this crowd, and I doubt if you could do that.'

In 1922 he became the first principal and

revered pastor of his Church's theological college, an institution which began as Brighton College and, upon moving to North Unley, became Wesley College. Lade belonged to the Adelaide Theological Circle and read several papers to it. He retired in 1939. In 1916 and 1936 he had been president of the South Australian Methodist Conference and, in the latter year, delivered an occasional address as part of the State's centenary celebrations. As president-general of the Methodist Conference of Australia in 1929-32 he visited missions in the South Pacific.

Lade's wife had died in 1933 and on 18 September 1940 he married Amy Maud Dunstan at Malvern, Melbourne. Survived by his second wife and five children, he died of cancer in Adelaide on 9 October 1948 and was buried in Payneham Methodist cemetery.

General Conference of the Methodist Church of A'sia, *Methodist Ministerial Index*, 1936, and SA branch, *Conference Minutes*, 1939, 1949; Temperance Alliance of SA, *S.A. Patriot*, Jan 1944-Dec 1945 (copies SAA); *Mail* (Adel), 9 May 1914; *Aust Christian Cwlth*, 24 May 1929; *Advertiser* (Adel), 11 Oct 1948; S. Close, Social attitudes to liquor and liquor legislation in South Australia, 1876-1917 (B.A. Hons thesis, Univ Adel, 1961); family records held by Mrs C. Duguid, Kent Town, Adel.

A. E. VOGT

LAFFER, GEORGE RICHARDS (1866-1933), fruit-grower and politician, was born on 14 September 1866 at Coromandel Valley, South Australia, son of Philip Frederick Laffer and his wife Elizabeth Jane, née Brown. His father, born in Cornwall in 1834, arrived in Australia in 1840 and went to the Victorian goldfields in 1852. In South Australia in 1854 he began fruit-growing at Belair and sent one of the first shipments of Australian apples to London four years later.

George Laffer was educated at Mitcham Public School and Prince Alfred College. In 1883 he too became a fruit-grower at Belair. On 15 June 1892 at Blackwood he married Adelaide Annie Maria Kelsey; they had no children. He served on the Mitcham District Council for nine years, becoming chairman in 1901 for four years.

Laffer was a member of the local Druids' Lodge and interested in cricket, football and shooting. However, his main interest was agriculture. He was a founder of the South Australian Fruitgrowers' Association, a life member of the Agricultural Bureau, founding member and chairman of the Advisory Board of Agriculture and a member of the Royal Agricultural Society.

He joined the Liberal Union and, on his third attempt, in 1913 was elected to the House of Assembly for Alexandra. Over the next twenty years he served on numerous parliamentary committees, and in 1918-20 was chairman of committees. From 8 April 1920 he was commissioner of Crown lands and immigration and minister of repatriation in the Barwell [q.v. 7] government. He supervised all soldier settlement schemes on the Murray River and elsewhere. Town planning was under Laffer's control and in 1920 South Australia became the first State to pass a town planning act. It set up a department, a permanent head with control of all new towns, and an advisory board. He was also minister for irrigation from 3 November 1922.

Although the Barwell government was defeated in the April 1924 election, Laffer retained his seat and when the Liberal-Country coalition won office in 1927 he was Speaker of the House of Assembly until 1930. In 1932-33 he was a member of a royal commission which examined the controversial subject of illegal betting, and whether bookmakers should be licensed. The commission recommended the establishment of State-wide, off-course, totalizator facilities controlled by a board, and drafted a bill to this effect. Laffer, who had a reputation for straightforwardness and sincerity, exhausted himself by fighting tenaciously in parliament to ensure that the bill was passed. He was successful, and the resulting laws were applauded by the sporting community. But he died unexpectedly of coronary vascular disease at Belair on 7 December 1933. He received a state funeral before being buried at Mitcham Anglican cemetery. His wife survived him.

Associated Publishing Service, *The civic record of South Australia 1921-1923* (Adel, 1924); Universal Publicity Co., *The official civic record of South Australia* (Adel, 1936); *Observer* (Adel), 30 Apr 1921; *Advertiser*, 8 Dec 1933.

MARYANNE McGILL

LAHEY, FRANCES VIDA (1882-1968), painter, was born on 26 August 1882 at Pimpama, Queensland, daughter of David Lahey, Irish-born farmer and timber-miller, and his wife Jane Jemima, née Walmsley. Educated at Goytelea School, Southport, she learned painting from Godfrey Rivers [q.v.] at Brisbane Technical College, then studied at the National Gallery School, Melbourne, in 1905-06 and in 1909 under Bernard Hall and Frederick McCubbin [qq.v.]. In 1910 she taught privately in Brisbane and consolidated an official association with the (Royal) Queensland Art Society begun in 1908.

In 1915 Vida Lahey went to London for

family reasons and unofficially to further her studies but became heavily involved in war-work. On a visit to the Continent in 1919, she saw seventeenth century paintings in the Netherlands which probably helped to turn her eventually to still life. She studied briefly at Colarossi's in Paris and returned to Australia in 1920. She began to exhibit regularly in all major Australian cities in 1923 and subsequently participated in exhibitions in Paris, London and the United States of America. Her early subjects included genre, landscape and portraits but still life, especially floral pieces in water-colour, became predominant. Most successful in water-colour, she believed that her still life work had developed its uses in a new way. By the mid-1920s she had won a firm place among Australian women artists and she was well regarded for her vivacious and sensitive treatment of light and colour.

Returning in 1927 from a short stay in Europe where she saw something of the modern movement, she established what became one of the three dominant studios in Brisbane. Her public involvement in artistic affairs helped to lift Brisbane from the cultural doldrums and make the 1930s one of its liveliest artistic periods. In 1929 she and her close friend, the much younger Daphne Mayo, were co-founders of the Queensland Art Fund. In its name, they helped to raise £10 000 in 1934-35 to secure the important John Darnell bequest for the Queensland National Art Gallery and to maintain the city council's Randall Collection. For several years from 1936 she acted as custodian of the Q.A.F.'s art reference library. She was also on the gallery's board of advice in 1923-30, was a member of the art advisory committee in 1931-37 and was a trustee of the Godfrey Rivers [q.v.] Trust.

In children's art classes established at the Art Gallery in 1941 she applied her philosophy of a universal language of art, explaining her views in the University of Queensland Duhig [q.v.8] lecture, 'The rudiments of the language of art', delivered by her in 1940. Her pamphlet, *Art for all* (c.1946), made an urgent plea to combat the ugliness and monotony of the modern world through imagination and a pleasing environment. Short, slight and very shy, Vida Lahey believed strongly in the dignity of labour and herself laid much of the brickwork around her St Lucia home, designed by her brother Romeo [q.v.].

Aware of the need to record the history of local art, she began a catalogue of the Darnell Collection in 1948 and in 1959 published on behalf of the Art Gallery the only general history of Queensland art to date, *Art in Queensland 1859-1959*. Acknowledged by the Society of Artists' (Sydney) medal in

1945 and appointed M.B.E. in 1958, Vida Lahey was a sensitive and pleasing painter but her main contribution lies in her role as teacher and public spokeswoman in a State not noted for its interest in culture. She died unmarried in Brisbane on 29 August 1968 and was cremated. She is represented in most State galleries and the Australian National Gallery.

Courier Mail, 30 Aug 1968, 26 June 1982; V. Lahey papers (held by John Oxley Lib).

MARGARET MAYNARD

LAHEY, ROMEO WATKINS (1887-1968), engineer, timber merchant and national parks advocate, was born on 2 June 1887 at Pimpama, Queensland, third son of David Lahey, arrowroot merchant, and his wife Jane Jemima, née Walmsley. Educated at Pimpama and Junction Park State schools, the Normal School and Brisbane Grammar School, he was a clerk with the Australian Mutual Provident Society in Brisbane before entering the University of Sydney (B.E., 1914; M.E., 1921). In World War I he served with the Royal Australian Engineers, from July 1915 in the 11th Field Company, Australian Imperial Force. Commissioned second lieutenant in December, he was wounded in action in December 1916 and promoted lieutenant next month. In 1919 he attended a town planning course at the University of London, winning the Lever prize.

An imaginative engineer, Lahey worked mainly in south-east Queensland in a private capacity and for the extensive Lahey saw-milling enterprises. A considerable achievement was the Mount Cainbable road, depicted in Chauvel's [q.v.7] film *Heritage*. A director of Brisbane Timbers Ltd and its Fiji-based subsidiary from 1924 until after the Depression, he was then chairman of directors of Laheys (1934) Pty Ltd until 1949. He managed Laheys' activities at Canungra including banana-growing, dairy-farms and a successful Jersey stud. Well aware of the conflict between conservation and exploitation, he initiated reafforestation and reduced wastage in milling. He was a compulsive buyer of land, usually in areas of scenic beauty, but restless energy and lack of capital often prevented him from waiting for a favourable return. Lengthy litigation followed the Commonwealth's resumption in 1942 of his Bulimba land for the Brisbane Graving Dock.

In evidence to the 1931 royal commission on the development of North Queensland, he supported a timber industry. His ambitious 'Lahey Scheme' for timber-cutting near Cardwell was denied approval in 1932 by both the Moore and Forgan Smith [qq.v.] governments: the latter ignored Lahey's contention that E. G. Theodore [q.v.] had first put up the proposition. Percy Pease [q.v.], Labor's secretary for public lands, attacked Lahey's rebuilding of the Yarraman State Sawmill in the November 1932 supply debate, and again rebuffed Lahey when, with J. A. Fihelly [q.v.8] and William McCormack [q.v.], he resubmitted the plan in November 1933.

In World War II Lahey served with the Royal Australian Engineers in Northern Command in 1940-43, reaching the rank of major. He then joined the Allied Works Council as an engineer, transferring in 1945 to the Commonwealth Department of Works and Housing. In 1950-52 he was technical assistant, lands requisition branch, Queensland State Housing Commission.

Four years dedicated work by Lahey as a young man had culminated in the proclamation in July 1915 of Lamington National Park. In 1932 he took an option on adjoining Mount Roberts, and with Arthur Groom [q.v.] and others established Queensland Holiday Resorts Ltd which built Binna Burra Lodge. Resigning as director in 1946 in protest at tree-felling on the property, he rejoined the board in 1954. He was a founder of the 'Save the Trees' campaign in 1946 and chairman until 1949.

Largely at Lahey's instigation, the National Parks Association of Queensland was formed in April 1930. Although he had been a Nationalist candidate for Fassifern in 1923 (not contesting the seat because of a leg injury), as president of the association he eschewed politics and maintained amicable relations with ministers (including Pease) in charge of national parks. He designed graded tracks to minimize ecological disturbance, often at his own expense surveyed suitable areas, and in his seventies completed field work for a Windsor Tableland park, paying for aerial surveying and a field trip. He was appointed M.B.E. in 1960. A plaque was unveiled in 1967 by Premier (Sir) Francis Nicklin on land Lahey gave for incorporation in Lamington National Park, one of several gifts to the national estate.

Small but dynamic, modest but self-assured, quiet but tenacious, Lahey was in Arthur Groom's words 'a thorny problem to many who have not seen eye to eye with him'. Lahey had married Alice Sybil Delpratt on 13 February 1920 in St John's Cathedral, Brisbane. He died on 26 October 1968 at his Yeronga home and was cremated with Anglican rites. He was survived by his wife, two daughters and a son, David Delpratt Lahey, prominent in the national parks movements of Victoria and South Australia. The National Parks Association

of Queensland sponsored the Romeo Watkins Lahey memorial lectures and the minister for lands opened a lookout in his memory at Mount Cainbable in 1970. A house designed by Lahey, and for many years the home of his elder sister Frances Vida Lahey [q.v.], has been classified by the National Trust of Australia (Queensland).

A. Groom, *One mountain after another* (Syd, 1949); D. Jones, *Cardwell Shire story* (Brisb, 1961); M. Curtis, *Canungra heritage 1879-1979* (Brisb, 1979); R. W. Lahey memorial lectures, 1-7, 1969-1981 (National Parks Assn, Brisb); A. S. Drake, Biographical sketch of R. W. Lahey (MSS, held by ADB, Canb); R. W. Lahey diaries in possession of and information supplied by D. D. Lahey, Cremorne, NSW; PRE/A1086 no 6902/1933 (QA).

BETTY CROUCHLEY

LAIDLER, THOMAS PERCIVAL (1884-1958), socialist propagandist and bookshop manager, was born on 19 November 1884 at Corindhap, Victoria, son of William Laidler, an English miner and later selector, and his wife Annie, née Ross. Second of seven children, he was educated at local schools and at 14 worked in a Ballarat mining office. He later moved to a similar position in Melbourne and was also a junior reporter on the *Argus*.

Lodging with a socialist family at Carlton served to introduce Laidler to the Victorian Socialist Party and its secretary Tom Mann [q.v.]. He became a noted local speaker and organizer, schooled by Tom Tunnecliffe [q.v.] and described by *Melbourne Punch* as 'about the best mob orator that has struck Melbourne for many years'. Laidler assumed a leading role in unemployed demonstrations, acted as secretary of the Socialist Co-operative Society and organized Ben Tillett's 1907 Victorian tour. Next year, when he became Mann's assistant, he stood for the Legislative Assembly as a socialist against Martin Hannah at Collingwood, receiving 85 votes.

Under Mann's influence, Laidler became increasingly disenchanted with the V.S.P. and by 1909 was a convinced syndicalist, arguing that revolutionary industrial organization was more important than political action. He found ample scope to expound these views at Broken Hill, New South Wales, where, having resigned as the V.S.P.'s assistant secretary, he became an organizer of mine workers during the aftermath of the bitter 1909 strike. Here he mixed syndicalism with a potent brand of provocation; in July he proposed an occupation of the British Mine unless the State government provided unemployment relief.

On 24 June 1911 in a civil ceremony at

South Melbourne Laidler married Christiane Alicia Gross, a tailoress active in the Clothing Trades Union and an executive member of the V.S.P. That year he became manager of Will Andrade's [q.v.7] Bourke Street bookshop. It was Laidler rather than Andrade who made the shop the Australasian centre for importing, publishing and distributing radical, free-thought and socialist literature. The shop was a meeting-place for socialists, and Laidler helped to shape the political regrouping that culminated in the establishment of the Communist Party of Australia in 1920.

Although a sympathizer, it is not clear whether Laidler ever became a member of the Industrial Workers of the World. While he later claimed membership, it is likely that his rejection of their ideology of sabotage and 'bummery' prevented his joining them. However, his 1912-14 street meetings did promote syndicalism and other I.W.W. theories and he later became Melbourne secretary and organizer for the I.W.W. Prisoners Release Committee. He was also prominent in the anti-conscription campaigns of 1916 and 1917.

Laidler, like so many of his contemporaries, was profoundly influenced by the Russian Revolution. In 1918 he wrote his major theoretical contribution to Australian socialism, *Arbitration and the strike*, an attack upon H. B. Higgins's [q.v.] concept of the living wage and a denunciation of arbitration as repressive of working-class militancy. The pamphlet represented a transitional stage in Laidler's politics. He went on to sponsor the first Australian publications, under Andrade's imprint, of writings by Lenin, Bukharin, and Trotsky, and in 1920, with Guido Baracchi, he began publication of the *Proletarian*, a Marxist review promoting the establishment of a Communist party in Australia.

Laidler chaired the inaugural meeting of the Melbourne branch of the Communist Party of Australia in 1921, but it soon collapsed. 'Its membership', he later wrote, 'contained too many of the old school and too few new men. Communist philosophy was not widely understood'. After the collapse Laidler became absorbed in Trades Hall Council activity. He represented the Shop Assistants and Warehouse Employees' Federation of Australia in 1921-25 and served on the T.H.C. executive and subsidiary committees. His daughter Bertha Walker remembered him going to the Trades Hall every night whether he had a meeting there or not. He also became president of the Victorian Labor College. He again became a prominent supporter of strike action, particularly the 1923 Melbourne police and the 1925 British seamen's strikes which the

labour movement had hesitated to endorse.

Although he was an avowed Marxist, Laidler's lack of sectarianism and his readiness to support publicly any cause he believed worthwhile ensured the trust and respect of erstwhile opponents. His unique position found expression in the Victorian Labor Propaganda Group which he formed in March 1922 to promote within the T.H.C. a programme of industrial reform, child endowment and social security. The group also sought to revitalize both Eight Hours' Day and May Day as working-class celebrations and seems to have provided the ideological basis for Communist reformation in Melbourne during 1924. Laidler did not rejoin the Communist Party but he was relied upon for advice and for a period acted as the party's Victorian banker.

During the Depression Laidler became a sponsor of the Friends of the Soviet Union and a speaker on behalf of the Unemployed Workers' Movement. The Communist Party's promotion of a popular front after 1935 appealed to him and, once more identified as a communist, he spoke for anti-Fascist organizations, including Spanish Relief and the Movement Against War and Fascism. However, like many of the socialists from pre-war days whom he brought together to celebrate Tom Mann's eightieth birthday in 1936, he was not fully at ease with the Communist Party's 'Bolshevism'.

At Prime Minister Curtin's suggestion Laidler undertook educational work for the army during World War II, lecturing on Soviet Russia and socialist society. He was divorced in 1946 and on 2 July 1947 at the North Fitzroy Methodist parsonage he married fellow bookseller Caroline Isabella Kate Bradford. Laidler died of cerebro-vascular disease at Preston on 21 February 1958. He was survived by his wife and a son and daughter from his first marriage. At a secular service, orations were delivered by members of the Labor and Communist parties.

B. Walker, *Solidarity forever* (Melb, 1972); *Communist Review*, Oct 1936, June 1937; *Guardian* (Melb), 27 Feb 1958; B. Walker papers (LaTL).

ANDREW REEVES

LAKE, GEORGE HINGSTON (1847-1900), administrator, newspaper proprietor and politician, was born on 10 December 1847 in London, youngest child of Henry Lake, plasterer, and his wife Ann, née Trehane. He arrived in Adelaide from Devon in 1853 with his family and was educated at public and private schools.

In the 1860s the Lakes took up pastoral

land in south-west New South Wales. George Lake is reputed to have been the first to take a team through the Barrier Ranges, reaching Menindee via Cumbummbuck Creek on which the later town of Silverton developed. Five years of drought discouraged him, and he returned to South Australia to study law while articled to his brother James.

Lake abandoned law to work for four years as an accountant with the Port Adelaide timber merchants and contractors, Lake & Reynolds. In 1878 he moved to the rapidly growing frontier settlement of Jamestown in the northern highlands of South Australia where he became an insurance agent, general merchant and manager of a Clare solicitor's office. When the corporation of Jamestown was formed that year Lake was appointed town clerk, with (Sir) John Cockburn [q.v.8] as mayor. Cockburn later said of him, 'He was as good a Town Clerk as was ever found in S.A. He performed his duties with an intelligence and vigilance unsurpassed'. He was a genial, unassuming man who was an active Anglican. In 1881 he bought the *Jamestown Review*, resigned as town clerk, and changed the paper's name to the *Agriculturist and Review*. Country readers expected a wide reportage of news and editorials of 'fire and brimstone'. They got both from Lake.

Seven years later he became the first secretary, and later manager, of the South Australian Farmers' Co-operative Union, formed at Jamestown by a determined band of producers seeking better returns. Lake's newspaper office became the headquarters of an organization which grew from being a pioneer co-operative enterprise, to a large-scale business with branches throughout the colony. Of that difficult formative period, a leading bank manager later said, 'The Farmer's Union was the best managed little company in the colony'.

Spurred on by his friendship with Cockburn, by this time premier and chief secretary, Lake won the junior seat of Burra, as a 'moderate Protectionist', in the 1890 House of Assembly election. Handing over as editor (but retaining the ownership of his paper), Lake continued as secretary-manager of the rapidly expanding Farmers' Union until 1895. By 1896 his health was failing and he declined to re-contest the Burra seat. During his six years as a politician he had been a comparatively undistinguished back-bencher. The *South Australian Register* described him as 'painstaking', following in the footsteps of his solicitor brother who had represented Barossa in 1871-75.

Lake died of cerebro-vascular disease on 31 October 1900 at Malvern. His wife Marion, daughter of William Rogers, a member of the Upper House, and one son survived him.

W. F. Morrison, *The Aldine history of South Australia*, 2 (Adel, 1890); *The South Australian Farmers' Co-operative Union Limited* (Adel, 1919); N. Robinson, *Change on change* (Leabrook, SA, 1971); *PD* (SA), 1890, p 183; *Pictorial Aust*, 1890, p 62, 141; SA Farmers' Union, *Farm*, 1 Sept 1932, 5 June 1963; *Agriculturist and Review*, 25 July 1883, 4 July, 10 Oct 1888, 16 Apr 1890, 7 Nov 1900, 4 June 1909; *Register* (Adel), 1 Nov 1900; information from Mr R. H. Lake, Torrens Park, Adel; SA Farmers' Union files, Robinson Collection (National Trust Museum, Jamestown, SA).

NANCY ROBINSON WHITTLE

LALOR, VIVIAN WILLIAM (1895-1960), soldier and carpenter, was born on 29 November 1895 at Healesville, Victoria, eldest of nine children of William James Lalor, labourer and later a Melbourne Metropolitan Board of Works ranger, and his wife Ann Matilda, née Madden, both native born. He attended school at Gruyere and became a labourer.

Lalor enlisted in the Australian Imperial Force in Melbourne in February 1916 and embarked for service on the Western Front on 4 May. In January 1917 he was taken on strength of 'Jacka's [q.v.] Mob', the 14th Battalion. Courageous and level-headed, he was made lance corporal in May and corporal in October. He won his first Military Medal in the battle of Polygon Wood, Belgium, on 26 September when he engaged enemy machine-guns with his Lewis-gun, thereby allowing his company to consolidate its defence after taking an objective.

His second Military Medal was awarded for a similar action near Morcourt, east of Corbie, France, on 8 August 1918 when he covered the advance of his platoon and 'neutralized enemy fire on three separate occasions'. At the end of the great advance that day he inflicted heavy casualties on the retiring enemy. He received his last major decoration in the fighting for the Hindenburg outpost line, being awarded the Distinguished Conduct Medal for 'conspicuous gallantry' near Ascension Wood on 18 September. Although his company was suffering heavy casualties and three men of his section were wounded, he rushed ahead and brought his Lewis-gun into action, covering the company's advance. Pushing ahead, he then silenced two enemy machine-guns and late in the advance displayed great tactical skill in the use of his gun. He worked forward several times into shell-holes to engage enemy machine-guns and was largely responsible for his company reaching its objective with relatively few casualties. Lalor suffered a gunshot wound in the intestine that day.

Invalided to Australia in December he was discharged from the A.I.F. on 11 March. Returning to Healesville, he trained as a carpenter, and later worked for a local builder. He then moved to Eaglehawk and took over a mixed retail business. He married Annie Grace, née Benfield, a confectioner and a widow with three children, on 25 September 1930 at St Kilian's Catholic Church, Bendigo. In the 1950s he moved to Canberra, working as a carpenter with the Department of the Interior, and then to Ingleburn, New South Wales. He died there of heart disease on 29 May 1960 and was buried with Catholic rites in Campbelltown cemetery. His wife had predeceased him.

Vivian Lalor was a typical digger who did not stand much on ceremony. He did not receive the 'promised' pension despite many appeals; he stayed away from Anzac Day parades and like so many diggers seldom, if ever, spoke about his war experiences. His medals are held by the Australian War Memorial, Canberra.

N. Wanliss, *The history of the Fourteenth Battalion, A.I.F.* (Melb, 1929); E. J. Rule, *Jacka's mob* (Syd, 1933); *London Gazette*, 14 Dec 1917, 24 Jan, 18 Feb 1919; War diary, 14th Battalion, AIF (AWM); records (AWM); information from Mr A. Lalor, Canberra.   J. G. WILLIAMS

LAMARO, JOSEPH (1895-1951), politician and judge, was born on 27 July 1895 at Redfern, Sydney, son of Sicilian parents Dieco Lamaro, fruiterer, and his wife Maria Guiseppa, née Taranto. After attending St Patrick's College, Goulburn, on a scholarship, he worked from 1912 as a clerk in the Department of Public Instruction while attending evening classes at the University of Sydney (B.A., 1915). Although rejected because of defective eyesight when he first tried to join the Australian Imperial Force, he was accepted in January 1916; as a signaller in the 18th Battalion he saw action in Belgium and France at Ypres and on the Somme before being discharged through illness at the end of 1917. Returning to the department and his university studies, he graduated LL.B. in 1922 and was admitted to the Bar on 1 June. In the 1925 Federal elections he stood unsuccessfully for Labor against W. M. Hughes [q.v.] for North Sydney.

Elected to the Legislative Assembly for Enmore in 1927, Lamaro was a staunch supporter of J. T. Lang [q.v.], and took part in attempts to obstruct the Bavin [q.v.7] government. When Lang took office in October 1930, Lamaro became minister of justice, transferring to the office of attorney-general nine months later. Liberal in his views, he drew some press criticism for releasing a number of life-prisoners who had served over twenty years of their sentences, in particular the notorious Eugenia Fallini. More serious was indiscreet criticism of the judiciary after the High Court's decision on the validity of the Financial Agreements Enforcement Act of 1932, which led to protests from the Incorporated Law Institute of New South Wales and seriously damaged his later prospects at the Bar.

Although defeated in May 1932, Lamaro won Leichhardt at a by-election in December, but resigned to contest the Federal seat of Watson in August 1934. When he lost, he found himself prevented, perhaps through a misunderstanding or perhaps as a result of internal party manoeuvres, from obtaining the 'Lang Labor' nomination for his former constituency.

In October Lamaro had his name removed from the roll of barristers and practised as a solicitor, in partnership with Abram Landa, until 21 November 1941, when he was readmitted to the Bar. In 1943 he became crown prosecutor for the Western district and in 1947, after four months as an acting judge, was appointed to the District Court bench. He became, in October 1949, the object of some press hysteria because he took the sensible view that the ameliorative provisions of the Crimes Act regarding first offenders could reasonably be applied to persons charged with driving under the influence of alcohol. The attorney-general C. E. Martin accused him of trying to 'annul' the law against drink-driving, and he was transferred to the South-Western circuit. In poor health since undergoing emergency abdominal surgery in September 1944, he suffered a cerebral haemorrhage while sitting at Hay and died on 22 May 1951; he was buried in Botany cemetery with Roman Catholic rites. He was unmarried.

Bespectacled and 'shortish and thickset in build', Lamaro had been a competent footballer in his youth, and was for several years chairman of the Australian Rugby League Board of Control. Cheerful and sociable by nature, he could nevertheless be stubborn, and even passionate, in defence of his convictions.

H. T. E. Holt, *A court rises* (Syd, 1976); *Aust Worker*, 22 Oct 1930; *SMH*, 23 Oct 1949, 23 May 1951.   W. G. McMINN

LAMBERT, ADA MARY; *see* à'BECKETT

LAMBERT, GEORGE WASHINGTON THOMAS (1873-1930), artist, was born on 13 September 1873 at St Petersburg (Leningrad), fourth child and posthumous son of George Washington Lambert, an American railway engineer, and his English wife Annie Matilda, née Firth. Soon after his birth the family moved to Württemburg, Germany, with his maternal grandfather, and then to England where George was educated at Kingston College, Yeovil, Somerset. The family decided to migrate and George, reaching Sydney with his mother and three sisters in the *Bengal* on 20 January 1887, soon went to Eurobla, near Warren, a sheep-station owned by his great-uncle Robert Firth.

After eight months Lambert returned to Sydney to work as a clerk with W. and A. McArthur [q.v.5] & Co., softgoods merchants, and in 1889-91 in the Shipping Master's Office. He attended night classes conducted by Julian Ashton [q.v.7] for the Art Society of New South Wales but returned to the country and worked as a station-hand for about two years. These two relatively brief experiences of bush life gave him an enduring love for horses and rural themes. Back in Sydney he met the illustrator B. E. Minns [q.v.] who advised him to consider becoming an artist and he returned to Ashton's classes, while working by day as a grocer's assistant. Ashton's teaching emphasized draughtsmanship, studying casts from the antique, then drawing from life. At this time American illustrators such as W. T. Smedley and Charles Dana Gibson were also popular. These several influences are seen in Lambert's early work, including pen-and-ink cartoons for the *Bulletin*, to which he began to contribute in 1895, and illustrations for three books published by Angus [q.v.7] & Robertson [q.v.]. His earliest extant portrait, of A. W. Jose [q.v.], belongs to this period.

From 1894 Lambert had exhibited with the Art Society and the Society of Artists, Sydney, but his first interesting, if sentimental, painting 'A Bush Idyll' dates from 1896. His important picture, 'Across the Black Soil Plains', which modestly expressed a nationalist sentiment through the honest labour of horses, won the 1899 Wynne prize and was bought by the National Art Gallery of New South Wales for 100 guineas. Lambert had a growing appreciation of the 'excellence of craftsmanship' of old masters, albeit observed secondhand in 'Judgment of Paris' by his English contemporary Maurice Grieffenhagen at the Art Gallery. In 1900 he won the first travelling art scholarship awarded by the Society of Artists from funds made available by the government.

Receiving in return for contributions an income of £2 a week from the *Bulletin*, Lambert married Amelia Beatrice (Amy) Absell, a retoucher, on 4 September 1900 at St Thomas Church, North Sydney. Two days later the Lamberts sailed for England; a fellow-passenger was the artist Hugh Ramsay [q.v.]. Finding London expensive and its atmosphere 'too forbidding', in February next year they moved to Paris where, with Ramsay, Lambert studied at Colarossi's art school and at the Atelier Delécluse. In Paris he particularly admired seventeenth-century artists such as 'Rubens the rollicking and Vandyke the irreproachable', Velasquez, and such of his contemporaries as J. M. Whistler and John Singer Sargent whom he felt had preserved the qualities of old masters. Lambert was to emulate Titian in 'The Sonnet' (Australian National Gallery) and Whistler in one of his own favourite works of this period, 'La Blanchisseuse'.

In November the Lamberts returned to London with their infant son. Briefly in a studio in Lansdowne House, Holland Park, Lambert moved in 1904 to Rossetti Studios, Chelsea, and in 1913 to 25 Glebe Place, Chelsea. He contributed illustrations to *Cassell's Magazine* (1900) and the *Pall Mall Magazine*, and for Jose's *Two awheel* (1903) and W. H. Lang's *Australia* (1907). He supplemented his income by work as a riding instructor and, succeeding Frank Brangwyn, as a teacher at the London School of Art.

Before World War I Lambert's principal work was in portraiture, both paintings and drawings. The paintings, often large uncommissioned studies of his family and friends, are invariably characterized by a sober palette, generalized landscape background, and a self-conscious treatment of hands, but a fine evoking of the tone of flesh and texture of costume. Several of these portraits were hung in exhibitions of the Royal Academy of Arts—the first, in 1904, was a half-length of Thea Proctor [q.v.]. Of his commissions, the most important were of (Sir) George Reid [q.v.] and an equestrian portrait of King Edward VII. His more numerous drawings, usually bust length in profile or three-quarter view with summarily treated drapery, are an advance on his illustrative work, cool in presence and more sophisticated tonally.

Also interested in murals and decorative painting, Lambert designed some of the interior decorations for the liner *Alsatian*. This interest was the basis for 'Important People' (Art Gallery of New South Wales), a rather self-important allegory in high colour. By 1914 he was coming into prominence —he was a frequent exhibitor, and a member of the Chelsea Arts Club, an associate of the Société Nationale des Beaux-Arts (New

Salon), Paris, a council-member of the International Society of Sculptors, Painters and Gravers and a founder of the Modern Society of Portrait Painters. He was elected an associate of the Royal Academy, London, in 1922.

On the outbreak of World War I Lambert, unable to enlist in the Australian Imperial Force in London, joined a Voluntary Training Corps, became a divisional works officer and supervised timber-getting in Wales. In December 1917 he was appointed an official war artist, A.I.F., with the honorary rank of lieutenant, and commissioned to execute twenty-five sketches and to paint 'The Charge of the Light Horse at Beersheba' on 31 October 1917. He arrived at Alexandria, Egypt, in January 1918. Despite contracting malaria, he embarked for Marseilles, France, in May with over 130 sketches, many of which were exhibited later that year at the Royal British Colonial Society of Artists' War and Peace Exhibition.

In January 1919, as honorary captain, he visited Gallipoli on the historical mission with C. E. W. Bean [q.v.], who described 'Lambert, with the golden beard, the hat, the cloak, the spurs, the gait, the laugh and the conviviality of a cavalier'. He also noted that Lambert 'was, I think, more sensitive than the rest of us to the tragedy—or at any rate the horror—of Anzac'. Lambert impressed on Bean that he wanted 'a clear military "operation order" setting out the work to be done'.

After recovering from dysentery in Cairo he visited Palestine, returning to London in August. His many meticulous and often spirited sketches made at a time when he was 'ridiculously happy' were to serve as the foundation for four other large battle-pictures now in the Australian War Memorial, Canberra, and a fine portrait 'A Sergeant of the Light Horse' (National Gallery of Victoria). His war drawings 'possess the impersonality and brevity of a good military dispatch'—he saw himself as an 'Artist Historian' recording 'events precious to the history of the nation'. His A.I.F. appointment was terminated on 31 March 1920.

Lambert returned to Australia in 1921, arriving in Melbourne where a retrospective exhibition was held in May at the Fine Arts Society Gallery, before he settled in Sydney. Portraiture was again to predominate, from the mannered 'The White Glove' (Art Gallery of New South Wales) and the quieter double portrait of Leigh and Beatrice Falkiner, 'Weighing the Fleece' (Australian National Gallery), to 'Mrs Murdoch' (winner of the 1927 Archibald [q.v.3] prize). Portraits of the 1920s tend to reflect with their generally dry colour and muted characterization an increasing disenchant-

ment with this aspect of his art. He also painted rural landscapes, often of the Monaro, and an occasional urban landscape or still life. He exhibited annually with the Society of Artists and from 1926 with the Contemporary Group which he formed with Thea Proctor. With Sydney Ure Smith [q.v.] he helped to keep the Society of Artists liberal in outlook and supported such younger artists as Roy de Maistre [q.v.8]. As a draughtsman he influenced among others William Dobell and Douglas Dundas.

Tall and athletic, Lambert had been a good boxer in his youth. He was fond of music and had a good baritone voice. With great charm, he moved easily in fashionable circles, but behind his 'slightly theatrical manner' were loneliness, ill-health and overwork. To Bernard Smith he was 'essentially a talented craftsman who gave his greatest love to his work and his horses'.

In the 1920s Lambert became interested in sculpture and received several large commissions—a war memorial for Geelong Church of England Grammar School, Victoria, an unknown soldier for St Mary's Cathedral, Sydney, and a statue of Henry Lawson [q.v.] for Mrs Macquarie's Chair, Sydney (1930). In executing the last two he had the assistance of Arthur Murch. He was inexperienced, however, and 'performed great physical labours in handling the clay', which proved too much for his constitution. He had suffered from mitral valve disease for some time before his sudden death on 29 May 1930 at Cobbity, near Camden. He was buried in the Anglican section of South Head cemetery.

A Lambert memorial fund was quickly established and two memorial exhibitions held before the end of the year. His wife (in England at the time of his death) and two sons survived him. His elder son Maurice (1901-1964) was a distinguished sculptor and an associate of the Royal Academy; the younger Constant (1905-1951), a prominent composer and conductor, was musical director of the Vic-Wells Ballet until 1947.

A portrait by Longstaff [q.v.] and George Lambert's self-portrait are in the Art Gallery of New South Wales.

J. S. MacDonald, *The art and life of George W. Lambert* (Melb, 1920); C. E. W. Bean, *Gallipoli mission* (Canb, 1948); Bernard Smith, *A catalogue of Australian oil paintings in the National Art Gallery of NSW* (Syd, 1953), and *Australian painting 1788-1970* (Melb, 1971); A. Lambert, *Thirty years of an artist's life* (Syd, 1977); The art of George W. Lambert A.R.A., *Art in Aust*, 1924, and Lambert Memorial Number, Aug-Sept 1930; *Aust Q*, Sept 1930; *SMH*, 30 May 1930, 16 July 1938; Lambert *and* A. W. Jose *and* J. L. Mullins papers (ML).

MARTIN TERRY

LAMBERT, WILLIAM HENRY (1881-1928), politician and union leader, was born on 24 March 1881 at Swallow Creek, near Orange, New South Wales, son of James Lambert, Irish-born stonemason, and his native-born wife Elizabeth, née O'Brien. He attended primary school and as a young man worked as a shearer. Soon involved in the Australian Workers' Union, in 1903 he helped to convert the Yacannia shed (north-west of Broken Hill) to the union. He married Bertha Anne McConnell, a 19-year-old waitress, at Dubbo on 9 October 1909. That year he became an organizer for the A.W.U., and in 1915 secretary of its central branch, a post he held until 1921.

Like many union officials, Lambert did not enlist during World War I but became active in the anti-conscription movement. This brought him to prominence in the Labor Party and he served as State president in 1917-21; the party then was later described by J. T. Lang [q.v.] as an 'AWU dictatorship' with control shared by Lambert and Jack Bailey [q.v.7]. In December 1918 Lambert was elected to Sydney Municipal Council for Denison Ward and was lord mayor in 1921. Holding the balance of power with his casting vote, Lambert enforced Labor policy—the promised 'Greater Sydney' plan degenerated into a scheme to amalgamate the city with inner working-class suburbs to enable permanent Labor domination of the council. Various sharp practices, such as letting contracts through negotiations instead of open tender, were perpetrated and created great mistrust. He also gave precedence to the Australian flag over the Union Jack.

Lambert won a House of Representatives by-election for the safe Labor seat of West Sydney in September 1921. In parliament he had remarkably little to say, except for occasional statements about juvenile labour, employment conditions, the threat of 'coolie labour' and the rights of trade unionists. Reflecting his early days as a shearer and union organizer he regarded the farmer as a 'loafer upon the State'. Lambert continued to pursue fierce faction politics. In the early 1920s he was accused of staging 'crook ballots' for the A.W.U.'s central branch elections, and was allegedly involved with Bailey, who apparently had considerable influence over him, in a scheme to misappropriate funds and to inflate membership of the branch to obtain extra delegates at the 1921 party conference. The A.W.U. convention found that the charges could not be sustained; nor was Lambert implicated when Bailey was expelled from the party in 1923, but with Lang now leader of the State Labor Party his political fortunes waned.

Furious at losing pre-selection for the seat of West Sydney in 1928, and apparently egged on by Bailey, Lambert told the *Daily Telegraph Pictorial* that in 1925 he had been offered £8000 if he would resign his seat in E. G. Theodore's [q.v.] favour. The same allegation had been published in the *Evening News* in December 1925, but Lambert had specifically denied it. His 1928 revelations led the Bruce [q.v.7]-Page [q.v.] government to appoint a royal commissioner, who discounted Lambert's accusations, because of his denial in 1925, but found that another member, W. G. Mahoney, had been compensated for resigning in Theodore's favour.

It was a last-ditch stand by Lambert, now in failing health, against a Labor Party in which he and the A.W.U. now had little influence. He died of heart disease on 6 September 1928 and was buried in Randwick cemetery with Catholic rites. A quiet and shy man, who had no children, he had remained a 'sterling laborite'.

A. B. Berry, *Lambert and Co. Ltd. secrets exposed* (Syd, nd); J. T. Lang, *I remember* (Syd, 1956); V. G. Childe, *How Labour governs*, F. B. Smith ed (Melb, 1964); I. Young, *Theodore* (Syd, 1971); F. A. Larcombe, *The advancement of local government in New South Wales, 1906 to the present* (Syd, 1978); *PP* (Cwlth), 1926-28, 4, p 1235; *Labor Daily*, 7 Sept 1928; *Aust Worker*, 12 Sept 1928, 29 Jan 1936, supp; *SMH*, 7, 10 Sept 1928.

PETER SPEARRITT

LAMBIE, CHARLES GEORGE (1891-1961), professor of medicine, was born on 24 July 1891 in Port of Spain, Trinidad, West Indies, son of Lieut-Colonel George Lambie, merchant and commanding officer of the Trinidad Light Infantry Volunteers, and his wife Sophia Agnes Theresa, née Stollmeyer. By 8 he was composing for the piano and had given concerts. He went to boarding-school in Scotland at Ayr Academy and Stanley House, Stirlingshire, and attended the University of Edinburgh (M.B., Ch.B., 1914; M.D., 1927). He was president of the Royal Medical Society while serving as a resident physician in the Royal Infirmary, 1914-15, and was awarded a Murchison scholarship in clinical medicine. In 1915 he enlisted in the Royal Army Medical Corps and was commissioned. Invalided from Mesopotamia to India, he spent a year as a pathologist at Poona. Promoted captain in November 1916, he commanded mobile laboratories in France and in 1918 was awarded the Military Cross.

After demobilization Lambie lectured in pharmacology in Edinburgh with Professor Cushny and carried out clinical research with Professors Meakins and Lyon. Visiting North America in 1921 he undertook research at the University of Toronto, Canada, where Frederick Banting and Charles Best had just produced the first insulin. On his return to Edinburgh in 1922 Lambie became the first person in Europe to use it for the treatment of diabetic patients. Appointed assistant physician at the Royal Infirmary and lecturer in clinical medicine at the university, he published papers on insulin, diabetes and kidney function and was a Beit memorial fellow in 1923-26. From 1926 he also lectured at the school of medicine of the Royal Colleges of Edinburgh.

On 15 April 1925 Lambie married Elizabeth Anne Walton (1892-1965) according to the rites of the Episcopal Church in Scotland; they had two daughters. In 1927 he became a fellow of the Royal Society of Edinburgh and of the Royal College of Physicians of Edinburgh, which next year awarded him the Lister fellowship. His doctoral thesis 'On the locus of insulin action' (1927) gained him a gold medal.

In 1929 Lambie applied for the chairs in medicine in the universities of Aberdeen and Sydney. Offered both, he chose the G. H. Bosch [q.v.7] chair in Sydney, taking up his post on 21 January 1931. By the end of 1932 he and Professor H. R. Dew, the first Bosch professor of surgery, had completely recast the clinical curriculum, into a form which remained unchanged until 1974.

Affectionately known as the 'Wee Mon' by students, Lambie was an excellent teacher. His approach was theoretical rather than practical, in accord with his belief that the inculcation of attitudes and basic skills was more important for students than a facility with routine procedures. His lectures and addresses, always scholarly and well-adorned with classical allusions, were orations. Lambie campaigned for a broad-based secondary curriculum to enable students to enter the university equipped with a liberal education. He also pressed for a university course of 120 lectures for all students, covering the sciences and humanities.

Aloof from the established medical hierarchy, Lambie was, in some of his ideas, ahead of his time. An honorary physician at Royal Prince Alfred Hospital, he failed to achieve the unity between the university and the hospital that he believed desirable, but most of his ideas were later carried out. At a council-meeting of the newly founded Association of Physicians of Australasia in May 1931, he proposed that a college of physicians be established. Although the council rejected his proposal the Royal Australasian College of Physicians, when inaugurated in 1938, had essentially the same aims as those which he proposed. Lambie was a foundation fellow but took no further part in its development.

Owing to a shortage of staff and money, Lambie's research in Sydney was limited, but he collaborated in studies on the purification and actions of thyrotropic hormone. He published some thirty papers in which he described rare diseases, reviewed scholarly works and expressed his ideas on medical education. His chief work was *Clinical diagnostic methods* (1947), written with Dr Jean Armytage. He contributed a chapter reviewing French contributions to medicine to *Light out of France* (1951). After a serious illness in 1940-42, Lambie was rarely seen outside his university department or hospital ward. Suffering from diabetes and arterial disease, he visited Edinburgh in 1950 for surgical treatment, returning next year. After retiring in 1957 he assisted a committee of the New South Wales branch of the British Medical Association, chaired by (Sir) William Morrow, inquiring into medical education. At the time of his death he was writing a scholarly medical history.

Lambie was the first full-time academically trained professor of medicine in Australia and profoundly influenced the discipline. Eighteen professors of medicine appointed to Australian universities were his students or graduates of the school which he founded. His meticulous drill-like clinical teaching also had a major influence on many practising doctors.

Reserved, idealistic and punctilious, Lambie was a frugal man who neither smoked tobacco nor drank alcohol and seldom attended social functions other than those connected with music. His most treasured possession was his grand piano. Of wide musical interests, he studied composition with Edgar Bainton [q.v.7] and received favourable notices from Sydney critics. He learned Italian, German, and French and had some familiarity with Hindustani and Arabic. A committed Christian, he translated the New Testament from Greek into English. He died of coronary vascular disease on 28 August 1961 in the Royal North Shore Hospital and was cremated with Presbyterian forms. His wife and two daughters survived him. A portrait by Nora Heysen is held by the University of Sydney.

London Gazette, 16 Sept 1918; *MJA*, 27 Jan 1962; *Bulletin of the Postgraduate Committee in Medicine, Univ Syd*, 25 Sept 1969; *Bulletin*, 13 Nov 1957; Univ Syd Archives; Roy A'sian College of Physicians Archives (Syd); information from W. Lambie, Wondalga, Dr P. Cambourn, Cammeray and Sir J. Kempson Maddox, Syd.

C. R. B. BLACKBURN

LAMBLE, GEORGE EDWIN (1877-1939), Anglican clergyman, was born on 19 February 1877 at Durham Lead near Ballarat, Victoria, second child and eldest son of George Robert Lamble, state school headmaster, and his wife Catherine Mary, née Mullins. As a boy he enjoyed the outdoor life and recalled that after the family moved to Kew, Melbourne, he and his brother explored 'every inch of the Yarra, from Dight's Falls to Warrandyte'. He matriculated from Scotch College in 1892. He was ordained deacon on 10 June 1900 and priest on 2 June 1901 by Bishop Goe [q.v.], serving curacies at Cunninghame (Lakes Entrance) in 1900 and at St Columb's, Hawthorn, in 1900-02. On 22 October 1904 at St Columb's he married Louisa Clark.

Lamble's work was important in the formative years of the diocese of Wangaratta. He was locum tenens of Glenrowan in 1902, then minister of Mooroopna and Tallygaroopna. In 1903 he undertook diocesan responsibilities at Wangaratta as registrar (until 1907), warden of St Columb's Hall and rector of its dependent centres, and chaplain to Bishop Armstrong [q.v.7]. While at Wangaratta he graduated Th.L. from the Australian College of Theology (1908).

In 1910 he returned to the diocese of Melbourne, until 1912 as incumbent of St Barnabas', South Melbourne. That year he enrolled at the University of Melbourne but did not complete his degree. For the next thirteen years he was rector of St Stephen's, Richmond, where he showed keen awareness of the difficulties faced by people in industrial suburbs.

Lamble's Richmond ministry was interrupted by the war. As chaplain in the Australian Imperial Force from October 1916 he served in France from March 1917 to March 1918. His appointment was terminated at his own request after the deaths of his father and brother, and the recall of his wife's missionary sisters to China, left his wife, his five children and two spinster sisters in need. His wife died on 8 August 1919 after the birth of their sixth child and on 22 September 1921 at St Mark's, Camberwell, he married Winifred Jessie Bainbridge.

Lamble began his most significant work in 1925 when he was appointed missioner of the district of St James and St John, Melbourne. This was founded in 1919 to care for those in need in these two Melbourne city parishes; under Canon Lamble the emphasis widened to the establishment and maintenance of 'homes for the homeless' and the provision of 'means for the reclamation of the fallen'. The St Agnes' Home for Girls and the St Nicholas' Home for Boys were opened at Glenroy in 1926. A few months later the mission purchased The Horseshoe at Carlton and transformed it into a home for girls suffering from venereal disease and next year the Kadesh Maternity Home for unmarried mothers was opened at Carlton. Appointed archdeacon of Carlton in 1927 by Archbishop Harrington Lees [q.v.] and rector of St John's and St Martin's homes for boys in Canterbury, Lamble continued his work for the mission for another twelve years. In April 1928 the St Paul's and St Barnabas' Training School for Boys began operation at Newhaven, Phillip Island. The St Gabriel's Babies' Home was opened at Balwyn in February 1935.

Archdeacon Lamble took a leading part in Freemasonry and was grand chaplain in Victoria. He was on the councils of the Melbourne Church of England Girls' Grammar School and of the Phillip Island Shire. He died on 4 June 1939 at East Melbourne of pulmonary embolism following surgery for hernia and was buried in Burwood cemetery. He was survived by his second wife and by the three daughters and three sons of his first marriage. At his funeral service Archbishop Head [q.v.] emphasized his own dependence on Lamble and described him as 'a true man of God, a forceful leader with a wonderful capacity for organization'. An old boy of St Nicholas' Home later wrote of him as 'truly a father to the fatherless and father-forsaken; always approachable and sympathetic; a wise counsellor; and in correction or encouragement, one who made himself loved by all'.

K. Cole, *Commissioned to care* (Melb, 1969); *Sun-News Pictorial*, 1 Dec 1926; *Argus*, 5, 6, 7 June 1939; *Herald* (Melb), 6 June 1939; Dioceses of Melb and Wangaratta, Records (1900-39); Mission of St James and St John, Records (1919-40); St Stephens, Richmond, Records (1912-25).   KEITH COLE

LAMINGTON, 2nd BARON (1860-1940), governor, was born CHARLES WALLACE ALEXANDER NAPIER COCHRANE-BAILLIE on 29 July 1860 in London, son of the politician and author Alexander Baillie-Cochrane, later 1st Baron, and his wife Annabella Mary Elizabeth, née Drummond, granddaughter of the Duke of Rutland. He was educated at Eton and Christ Church, Oxford (B.A., 1881). Assistant private secretary to Lord Salisbury [q.v.3, Cecil] in 1885, he was narrowly defeated as Conservative candidate for North St Pancras but won the July 1886 'Home Rule' election contest. According to the *St Pancras Guardian*, 'nothing has been left undone that money could accomplish to secure his election'. His rare appearances in the Commons were said to be 'a good augury of an impending dissolution'. The death of his father in February 1890 removed him to the House of Lords. On 13 June 1895 at St Michael's Church,

Pimlico, he married Mary Houghton Hozier; they had two children.

Chosen in October 1895 to succeed Sir Henry Norman [q.v.] as governor of Queensland, Lamington served from 9 April 1896 to 19 December 1901 including six months leave in England in 1899-1900. In his dispatches he demonstrated his conservatism and declined to forward a Labor address 'advocating extreme socialism because it was so crude [and] wanting in sense'. He found class divisions more accentuated than in England and feared that Federation might lead to extreme socialism.

Concerned at the unsatisfactory treatment of Aboriginals and Melanesians, Lamington visited British New Guinea in 1898 and travelled extensively in Queensland. He confided in Chief Justice Sir Samuel Griffith [q.v.], although they clashed when Griffith deputized for him in 1898. He supported Griffith's attempts to retain appeals from federated Australia to the Privy Council and hoped that the status of State governors would not diminish under Federation so that Britons 'of recognized appeal or high social standing' would still apply. He came eventually to realize that governors needed other qualities; 'mere show appeals but little to Australians'.

As governor of Bombay in 1903-07, Lamington found that he had more power than in Australia where he had only the royal prerogative to administer. He and his wife retained an interest in Australia, corresponding with Governor-general Lord Northcote [q.v.] and Griffith. He spoke on Queensland at the Royal Colonial Institute and in the House of Lords. In 1919 Lamington served as commissioner of the British Relief Unit in Syria. He died on 16 September 1940 at Lamington House, Lanarkshire, Scotland. He had been appointed G.C.M.G. in 1900 and G.C.I.E. in 1903.

Lamington's name is remembered in Australia by place names, particularly the Lamington Plateau in Queensland and Mount Lamington in Papua-New Guinea. It is claimed that a cake covered in chocolate and coconut is named after him.

DNB, 1931-40; Lamington papers, XVIIIE 6666-68 (Duke Univ Lib, Durham, NC); MSS EUR 13 159/1-11-111 (India Office Lib); Lamington correspondence 1896-1913 in Griffith papers (Dixson Lib); CO 234/63-71, 418/12 (PRO microfilm, NL).

R. B. JOYCE

LAMOND, HECTOR (1865-1947), journalist, publisher and politician, was born on 31 October 1865 at Broughton Creek, Shoalhaven, New South Wales, son of Scottish-born Allan Lamond, farmer, and his wife Charlotte, née Day, born in London. He was educated at public schools and at 14 was apprenticed as a printer to the Carcoar *Chronicle* where he learned to publish and write for newspapers. By 25 he was editor of the *Chronicle*. Lamond was the unsuccessful Free Trade candidate for Cowra at the 1894 elections and next year left Carcoar for Sydney.

In 1895-1916 he was editor and subsequently manager of the *Australian Worker*, published by the Australian Workers' Union. Its success was attributed largely to Lamond whose terse, lively editorials established a house style and confirmed him as one of the most vigorous and capable journalists of the day. He had been associated with reformist politics since his boyhood, and became a socialist after the William Morris model. He supported the Labor Party as an extension of the trade union movement, and was active in its development in 1895-1900. But he accepted the A.W.U.'s policy of attempted domination of the party. He was a loyal and close friend of the union's president William Guthrie Spence [q.v.6], and on 10 July 1902, at Petersham, he married Spence's daughter Gwynetha. Lamond helped Spence write and publish *Australia's awakening* (1909) and the *History of the A.W.U.* (1911) as well as many articles.

In 1911 Lamond was president of the Homebush Political Labor League and was a leading exponent of increased Federal powers, using the *Worker* and the A.W.U. to oppose W. A. Holman [q.v.]. He unsuccessfully contested the Federal seat of Lang as a Labor candidate in 1913 and 1914. During World War I he became disturbed by radical labour and such manifestations as the Industrial Workers of the World. In 1916 he became a staunch ally of W. M. Hughes [q.v.] as honorary general secretary in New South Wales for the first conscription campaign. The council of the *Worker* already opposed conscription and demanded that its staff 'go with the majority'. Lamond, with his own convictions strengthened ('I have been compelled to choose between speaking the Truth as I see it, or losing my job'), resigned from the *Worker* regretfully ('God alone knows who is right and who is wrong in the great controversy'). His reputation in Labor circles was to be clouded by the bitter charge that he had used his influence also to identify the failing Spence with conscription.

Lamond joined the Nationalists and captured the Federal seat of Illawarra in May 1917. He was joint honorary secretary of the National Federation in 1917 and a member of the New South Wales council of the National Association in 1917-23. He remained loyal to Hughes and was appointed assistant minister for repatriation from 21 December 1921. In parliament, and outside it, he was a forcible speaker, widely read and alert who was perceived as a strong man who could 'balance the Conservative element' in the party. He battled conscientiously and effectively with repatriation and war homes complexities and, as a member of the Federal Capital League, to see a start made on building the national capital at Canberra. He was defeated when he stood for Barton in December 1922 as a balanced alternative to conservatism or communism.

In 1923 Lamond purchased the *Southern Mail* and three other country newspapers which he edited and published from Bowral. He died on 26 April 1947 at Bowral and was cremated with Anglican rites. His wife, two sons and a daughter survived him.

B. Nairn, *Civilising capitalism* (Canb, 1973); *Daily Telegraph* (Syd), 11 July 1894; *Bulletin*, 7 July 1904; *Aust Worker*, 28 Sept 1916; *SMH*, 9, 16 Oct 1916, 24 Oct, 18 Dec 1922, 28 Apr 1947; V. Molesworth papers (ML).   CORAL LANSBURY

LANCASTER, G. B.; *see* LYTTELTON, EDITH JOAN

LANCASTER, SAMUEL (1852-1918), farmer and politician, was born on 6 August 1852 at Wigglesworth Hall, Wigglesworth, Yorkshire, England, son of Thomas Lancaster, farmer, and his wife Elizabeth Bowers, née Anderton. The Lancasters migrated to Victoria in 1860. Samuel was educated at Lancefield and spent two years in a general business at Echuca. When 21 he selected land with his father and uncle at Kyabram. Among the earliest settlers in the Goulburn Valley, they began with mixed farming but turned to fruit-growing when the area was irrigated in the 1880s. At Darraweit Guim on 12 March 1879 Samuel married Annie Amelia Francis with Wesleyan forms.

Lancaster's public activities centred on the Goulburn region. He was a member of the Rodney Shire Council in 1886-1918 and president in 1894-95, 1902-03 and 1911-12. He was a founding member of the Rodney Irrigation Trust and a commissioner of the Kyabram Urban Water Trust. He was for twenty-five years a justice of the peace. In 1900 he unsuccessfully contested the Legislative Assembly seat of Rodney. Then in November 1901, after Federation and a severe drought had revived demands for a smaller State parliament and retrenchment in government spending, he helped to found the Kyabram Reform League; its retrenchment and reform policy quickly gained popularity throughout Victoria. In April 1902 Lancaster chaired a large reform conference in Melbourne which set up the National Citizens' Reform League, backed by Melbourne conservative and free-trading interests, with Lancaster as president. After initial rebuffs from the Peacock [q.v.] government, a new ministry led by (Sir) William Irvine [q.v.] agreed in May 1902 to implement a policy satisfactory to the league. When Irvine called an election in October the league fully supported him. Lancaster again contested Rodney and was easily elected, as were a number of other league candidates.

In parliament Lancaster proved a faithful government supporter. He rarely spoke, and then only to urge greater retrenchment. When the drought broke, however, government finances improved and retrenchment became less popular. The league continued to co-operate with (Sir) Thomas Bent [q.v.3] who succeeded Irvine in February 1904, but much of its force was gone. Lancaster's political career similarly declined: he was defeated in the election of June 1904 and again in 1907 and 1911.

Lancaster came from a strongly Methodist family. He was a prominent lay preacher and president of a local temperance organization, the Gilgila Band of Hope. He lived on his property, Gilgila, at Lancaster, a settlement named after his father, and was highly esteemed in the district for his active interest in local welfare schemes. He died of pneumonia on 26 December 1918. Survived by his wife, four daughters and two sons, he left an estate valued for probate at £32 157. He was buried in Kyabram cemetery.

W. H. Bossence, *Kyabram* (Mclb, 1963), and *Tatura and the Shire of Rodney* (Mclb, 1969); J. Rickard, *Class and politics* (Canb, 1976); *Weekly Times* (Melb), 19, 26 Apr 1902; *Australasian*, 26 Apr 1902; *Argus*, 28 Dec 1918; K. Rollison, Groups and attitudes in the Victorian Legislative Assembly, 1900-1909 (Ph.D. thesis, La Trobe Univ, 1972).   KAY ROLLISON

LANDSEER, ALBERT HENRY (1829-1906), merchant and politician, was born on 10 February 1829 in London, only son of Henry Landseer, soldier, and his Canadian wife Lucy, née Barker. He attended Mr Hill's Academy in Swan Street: 'I hope the improvement I have made this half year will be equal to your most sanguine expectations', he wrote dutifully to his parents at 9. In keeping with family tradition—his cousin was the painter (Sir) Edwin Landseer, and his father was an artist also—

Albert studied sculpture before migrating to South Australia in 1848. It was a decision possibly opposed by his parents, for he did not write home for twelve years. By then he was well established in the colony.

After working as a small building-contractor, he was successful on the Victorian goldfields until 1858—Landseer later looked back on this period with considerable affection. He then moved into Murray River shipping, which was opening up. It was a timid venture at first, a small office at Port Elliot with the agency for Francis Cadell's [q.v.3] River Murray Navigation Co. But it proved to be a shrewd move. As the river trade boomed in the 1860s and 1870s business grew apace. Hard work, honesty and reliability (he once fined himself £10 for delivering goods a day late) ensured his success. By about 1870 he was one of the colony's principal river merchants whose opinion was sought regularly on the river trade and its future. Steamers and barges carried his name to Bourke, Wilcannia and Hay, New South Wales. Milang, a township on Lake Alexandrina and his base after 1860, was jocularly known as 'Landseer's town' and Landseer as 'the Duke of Milang'. He had large woolsheds at Goolwa and Port Victor and flour-mills at Morgan, Milang and Lake Alexandrina. This massive investment in the lower Murray district in 1875 secured his election as member for the seat of Mount Barker in the House of Assembly. Although he had declared his candidacy late there were distinct advantages, one newspaper noted, in being represented by the owner of 'one of the largest businesses in the colony'. Initially conservative, he grew more liberal with age.

Landseer held the seat continuously till 1899. A member of four royal commissions, he never held ministerial office. The demands of business may have deterred him, though he was 'a most perplexing and prolix speaker'. He was probably too inflexible on matters of principle to succeed in government: his private correspondence reveals distaste for the sharp practices of politics and a refusal to countenance underhand activity on his behalf. His support for Kingston's [q.v.] ministry of 1893-99 was tempered by doubts about the premier's personal integrity. Barely veiled contempt for the landowning gentry of Strathalbyn and Mount Barker almost certainly cost his business dearly.

After Landseer's resignation from parliament in 1899, his health was undermined by rheumatism and, later, heart disease; and his fortune by the decline of the river trade and reckless speculation in the Western Australian gold boom. An Anglican, he had married twice and had eight children: two by his first wife Rosina, née Masson, and six by his second wife Harriett Sarah, née Taylor, whom he married at Goolwa on 15 August 1872. He died on 27 August 1906 and was buried in Milang cemetery. His estate was sworn for probate in Victoria and South Australia at £15 716.

Quiz (Adel), 10 July 1891, 23 June 1898; *Southern Argus* (Strathalbyn), 25 Feb 1875, 31 Mar 1881, 10, 24 Apr 1884; *Observer* (Adel), 7 July 1883, 11 Oct 1884, 5 Dec 1885, 10 May 1890, 27 May 1893, 1 Sept 1906; Letter-books, 1890-99 and family records (held by E. M. and P. J. Landseer, Leabrook, Adel).   A. J. STIMSON

LANE, ERNEST HENRY (1868-1954), journalist, was born on 26 December 1868 at Bristol, England, son of James Lane, nurseryman and florist, described by his son as 'an active Tory politician', and his wife Caroline, née Hall. A small, aesthetic-looking youth, he probably based his image of himself as a rebel on the poetry of Shelley. Major influences on his development were his elder brother William [q.v.], accounts of the Paris Commune of 1871 and the trial of Chicago anarchists in 1886. Migrating to Brisbane in 1884, he worked briefly on a dairy farm at German Station (Nundah) before sailing to San Francisco. He returned to Australia in 1890 and worked for two years in a grocery store in Sydney, mixing privately with the socialists E. J. Brady [q.v.7], J. D. Fitzgerald [q.v.8], S. A. Rosa and A. G. Yewen [qq.v.] and the Scottish anarchist Larry Petrie. Too poor to join the first contingent for New Australia, Paraguay, in 1893, he worked his way back to Brisbane where he met Mabel Gray whom he married on 8 January 1895; they had two daughters and two sons.

Employed in a store at West End and subsequently at Five Ways, Woolloongabba, Lane became a propagandist for socialism. With John Bond and Harry Turley, he reformed the Socialist League, distributing pamphlets and arranging street-corner meetings. In 1899, with Albert Hinchcliffe, Charles Seymour [qq.v.] and Francis Kenna, he formed the Social Democratic Vanguard and became its secretary. He was repeatedly sacked because of his political work and ultimately blacklisted among employers.

In 1903 Lane with his wife and three children went to Cosme, the breakaway colony from New Australia in Paraguay, but left it in 1904 in disgust at its drift from communistic principles. Before returning to Australia he spent two years at the Puerto La Plata meatworks. Back in Brisbane he worked at Foggitt Jones', bought a house at Highgate Hill and began his involvement with the Amalgamated Workers' Association and, after 1913, with the Australian Workers' Union. He held office in the Brisbane branch of the A.W.A. and was a conference delegate in 1912 and 1913. He moved the motion which led to the Brisbane general strike of 1912. As a delegate of the Queensland branch of the A.W.U., he went to the annual conventions in Sydney in 1918, 1920 and 1923 and to national trade union congresses in Melbourne in 1919, 1921 and 1922. Vice-president of the A.W.U. in 1916, he secured some support for the purchase of socialist literature and was able to distribute among members hundreds of volumes imported from Kerr's Publishing House in New York. When he tried to extend eligibility for membership of the A.W.A. to coloured workers, he was soundly defeated partly perhaps because of articles written by William Lane expressing the strong racist attitudes of many workers.

An A.W.U. delegate on the Queensland central executive of the Australian Labor Party in 1916-23, Lane attended the Labor-in-Politics Convention in 1918 and the federal conference in 1921 as a proxy delegate for Tasmania. He contributed to a manifesto designed to consolidate the political and industrial wings during difficulties in 1919 but resigned from the A.L.P. in 1926 when required to sign an anti-communist pledge. In *Dawn to dusk* (1939) he expressed his lifelong dedication to communist ideals and his disappointment with the defection of many old colleagues; however, he had never joined the party.

In 1915 Lane had been appointed industrial editor of the Labor-controlled *Daily Standard* and wrote sometimes controversial articles under the non-de-plume 'Jack Cade'. Some of these were published by R. S. Ross [q.v.] in *The One Big Union and reconstruction in the light of the war* (1918). Active in the fight against conscription in 1916-17, Lane believed that reform could be achieved only by the industrial section of the labour movement, not by politicians who had ceased to be workers. He became unpopular again by urging the cause of members of the Industrial Workers of the World whom he believed to have been wrongly convicted of sedition, arson and conspiracy. His dismissal from the *Daily Standard* in 1931, ostensibly as a financial retrenchment, was strongly criticized at the annual meeting of shareholders but the decision was not reversed. Engaged by the *Daily Mail*, merged later with the *Courier Mail*, to report union affairs, he was dismissed in 1937. Spiritually tired and disillusioned though physically active, he

spent some time at Currumbin where he enjoyed surfing.

Lane died at Annerley on 18 June 1954 and was cremated. A funeral notice asked mourners to send red flowers. The service was attended by many old political friends and the valedictory address was given by the secretary of the Queensland Trades and Labor Council. Gentle and kindly, Lane was a revolutionary activist in a reformist labour movement. His influence was limited by his refusal to join the power structures established by his more pragmatic colleagues.

G. Souter, *A peculiar people* (Syd, 1968); D. J. Murphy et al (eds), *Prelude to power* (Brisb, 1970); *Advocate* (Brisb), 15 May 1931; *Qld Guardian*, 23, 30 June 1954; information from Mr C. Beckingham; BP 4/1, 66/4/2165 (AAO, Brisb).

JOY GUYATT

LANE, FREDERICK CLAUDE VIVIAN (1880-1969), swimmer, was born on 2 February 1880 in Sydney, son of John Stoneman Lane, ship's chandler, and his wife Muriel, née Frederick. When 4 he was saved by his brother from drowning in Sydney Harbour and took up swimming. On 2 April 1892 he won the All Schools' handicap race and, after several other wins, the 100 yards championship of St Ignatius College, Riverview, in 1894. Next year he joined the East Sydney Amateur Swimming Club where he was coached by George Farmer. He completed his schooling at Sydney Grammar School where in December 1896 he won the 100 and 200 yards handicap events as well as the All Schools' 100 yards championship.

In 1897-98 Lane set an Australasian record of 64.8 seconds for 100 yards, won the 200 and 440 yards freestyle championships of New South Wales and the Australasian 100 yards title at Christchurch, New Zealand. In 1898-99 he won all but one State freestyle titles and in winning the mile championship in the Murrumbidgee at Wagga Wagga performed the unprecedented feat of swimming the whole distance recovering each arm over the water. Sponsored by Mark Foy [q.v.8] in the English championships in 1899, Lane won the 220 yards freestyle title in the record time of 2 minutes, 38.2 seconds and the 440 yards salt-water title.

Australia's first Olympic swimmer and the only one at the Paris Olympics in 1900, Freddy Lane won the 200 metres freestyle title in 2 minutes, 25.2 seconds, winning by 5.8 seconds, and the 200 metres obstacle race title.

Lane swam two more seasons in English championships and worked in a legal firm at Blackpool. In September 1900 he dead-heated in the 220 yards in record time. In July 1902 he won the 100 yards and became the first to clock one minute flat for the distance; in August he won the 220 yards in 2 minutes, 28.6 seconds, ratified in 1974 by the Fédération Internationale de Natation Amateur as the first world record for 200 metres. At Leicester in October he astounded the swimming world and established the first magic mark in swimming history when he broke the minute for 100 yards (59.6 seconds). After a highly successful European tour he returned to Australia and retired.

Lane became a master printer and partner in the printing and stationery firm Smith & Lane, Bridge Street, Sydney. On 14 September 1908 at St Mark's Church, Darling Point, he married Rosemund Pearle Atkinson Lord. His hobbies were art, literature, model-building and collecting stamps, cigarette cards and newspaper cuttings. He had a fine collection of the works of the marine artists Jack Spurling and John Allcott as well as paintings and literary works by his friend Norman Lindsay [q.v.]. He wrote and printed a book on Lindsay's bookplates. He died at Avalon on 14 May 1969 and was cremated with Anglican rites. His son and daughter survived him.

Slim, muscular and smallish in stature Freddy Lane swam a modified trudgen stroke; swimming on his left side he rode high in the water and used a small flutter movement of his legs in between a narrow scissors kick. Although often exhausted after races, Lane dispelled the widely held view that the trudgen was unsuitable for longer distances. His name is engraved on the Helms World Trophy in the Helms Museum of Sport, Los Angeles, United States of America, and in 1969 he was honoured by the International Swimming Hall of Fame at Fort Lauderdale, Florida. He won about 350 trophies, including over 100 medals.

Forbes Carlisle on swimming (Lond, 1963); P. Beresford, Encyclopaedia of swimming, (Lond, 1976); ANZ Bank, Chequerboard, Aug 1968; Referee, 27 Jan 1897, 14 Dec 1898; Australasian, 8, 22 Jan 1898; People, 24 Oct 1951; Sportsman (Lond), 7 Aug 1899, 18 Sept 1900, 25 July, 19 Aug 1902, 7 Jan 1903.   G. P. WALSH

LANE, LAURA; see LUFFMAN, LAURA BOGUE

LANE, WILLIAM (1861-1917), journalist, trade unionist and Utopian, was born on 6 September 1861 at Bristol, England, eldest son of James Lane, an Irish Protestant, and his English wife Caroline, née Hall. His father was a landscape gardener whose drunkenness impoverished the family and made the boy a lifelong abstainer.

After proving himself a gifted pupil at Bristol Grammar School, William worked his passage to Canada at 16. At Montreal his right foot, deformed since birth by talipes (club-footedness), was operated on with partial success. In that time of widespread strikes and brutal repression, Lane worked at odd jobs and as a linotype operator, discovered the social thought of Henry George [q.v.4] and Edward Bellamy, and by 24 was a reporter in Detroit, United States of America. On 22 July 1883 at Algonac, Michigan, he married 19-year-old Anne Mary Macguire, born in Edinburgh. In 1885 the Lanes and their first child sailed for England, only to re-embark for Australia with Will's 19-year-old brother John. Two younger brothers, Frank and Ernest [q.v.], had preceded them.

Lane's luggage included copies of Smith's Wealth of nations, Marx's Das Kapital and Gronlund's Co-operative commonwealth. With this foundation he became one of Australia's foremost radical journalists, addressing himself mainly to the bushworkers of Queensland, whom he idealized. Settling in Brisbane, the limping reporter with 'a slight Yankee twang'—a delicate-looking man with drooping moustache and clear blue eyes behind gold-rimmed spectacles—wrote under the pseudonyms of 'John Miller', 'The Sketcher' and 'Lucinda Sharpe'. He was also an active participant in Queensland's developing trade union movement. In 1887 he founded a Bellamy Society, devoted to ideas advanced by the author of the Utopian romance Looking backward (1887), and helped to launch the weekly Boomerang, which he co-edited. His first novel, a racist polemic, entitled White or yellow? A story of the race-war of A.D. 1908, appeared in the Boomerang as a twelve-part serial by 'The Sketcher'.

Lane was largely responsible for the formation in 1889 of the Australian Labour Federation, an organization of Queensland unions which replaced the Trades and Labor Council in Brisbane. In 1890 he became first editor of the Worker, which was financed by the A.L.F. and other Queensland labour bodies. He covered the Rockhampton conspiracy trial during the 1891 shearers' strike, though some Brisbane newspapers said he should more properly have been charged as 'the arch-conspirator' and 'the man behind the curtain'. His ironically titled novel The working man's paradise (Brisbane, 1892) was written by 'John Miller' to raise funds for the families of the convicted Rockhampton prisoners. While the defeat of the shearers and other strikers helped to turn the labour movement towards the political action from which the Australian Labor Party emerged, it turned Lane into a Utopian by-road.

As early as 1889 he had corresponded with a communal settlement in Mexico, Topolobampo, and he was familiar with the North American Utopian community, Icaria, founded by followers of Robert Owen. On 2 May 1891 the *Worker* announced that the New Australia Co-operative Settlement Association had dispatched an agent, Alf Walker, formerly business manager of the *Boomerang*, to seek in South America the suitable land which the association had been unable to obtain in Australia. Lane and his friends chose remote South America in order to discourage the weak. His hypnotic speaking style was a factor in attracting more than 600 subscribing members.

The promised land, 463 000 acres (187 000 ha) unsettled and free of charge, was found in Paraguay. Under Lane's leadership a first batch of 220 colonists, including Lane's wife, their four children and John Lane and his wife, sailed from Sydney on 16 July 1893 aboard the *Royal Tar*, bound via Cape Horn and Montevideo to Asuncion. New Australia, 109 miles (176 km) southeast of Asuncion, was bound by rules of temperance and racial exclusiveness with which some settlers refused to comply. Lane would not compromise. His puritanism contained no tact, and little human sympathy; for him, New Australia's articles of association were 'the Code of the Medes and Persians'. He was autocratic, and under pressure his simplistic communism and mateship developed a non-denominational but distinctly religious tinge. The result, after the arrival of a second contingent, was schism. 'The crooked ones will have to go', he wrote.

On 7 July 1894, sixty-three settlers loyal to Lane made, as he said, 'a quiet, safe start on bedrock' at a new site called Cosme, 45 miles (72 km) south of New Australia. They were joined by other true believers from Australia and a few families recruited by Lane during his strangely protracted visit to England in 1896-98. Cosme's bedrock was not as sound as Lane had hoped, though the collapse occurred more gradually there than at New Australia.

As the colony never became more than barely self-sufficient, a growing number of settlers sought a better standard of living elsewhere, or were expelled for breaches of communal practice. Lane felt betrayed. Weakened by illness and hardship, and disillusioned by human nature, he resigned as chairman in June 1899. Leaving Cosme with his family on 1 August, he sailed for New Zealand. The colony retained some of its original character and then, like New Australia, became increasingly Paraguayan.

Lane revealed nothing of his feelings about New Australia and Cosme in later life but his career on Auckland's conservative *New Zealand Herald*, from 1900 as leader writer and from 1913 as editor, clearly demonstrated a political volte-face. The radical of the 1890s had become a conservative Imperialist. His writings under the pseudonym of 'Tohunga' (the Maori word for prophet) made almost as big an impression on New Zealand as those of 'John Miller' had made on Queensland, though in very different vein. He denounced industrial lawlessness, advocated the introduction of universal military training, and when war came showed himself a master of patriotic rhetoric.

Lane died on 26 August 1917, as the result of bronchitis and a serious weakness of the heart, and was buried in Purewa cemetery, Auckland. He was survived by his wife, a son and five daughters. Three other children had predeceased him; one son had been killed at Gallipoli.

Lane's obituaries in Australia's labour press were a mixture of loyalty and recrimination. The Brisbane *Worker* excused his failure in Paraguay and said that the memory of his earlier days in Queensland would last as long as the labour movement. The *Australian Worker*, which Lane had edited briefly in 1900, found him guilty of egotism and arrogance in Paraguay, and *Ross's Monthly* lamented: 'Billy Lane is dead—dear old Billy Lane. And he died in the camp of the enemy!'. Although by going to Paraguay Lane in one sense opted out of Australian history, his essay at Utopia remained part of the national experience. Lane appeared as a character in two theatrical works, Vance Palmer's [q.v.] play *Hail tomorrow!* (1947) and George Hutchinson's musical drama *The ballad of Billy Lane* (1982).

L. R. M. Ross, *William Lane and the Australian labour movement* (Syd, 1937); E. Lane, *Dawn to dusk* (Brisb, 1939); G. Souter, *A peculiar people* (Syd, 1968); New Australia and Cosme (newspaper and manuscript material, Series 9, May 1965, held by NL).

GAVIN SOUTER

LANE, ZEBINA (1829-1906) and ZEBINA BARTHOLOMEW (1856-1912), mining engineers, were father and son. Zebina senior was born on 5 November 1829 at St Stephens, New Brunswick, Canada, son of Mathew Lane, farmer, and his wife Dorcas, née Lumbard. The family moved to Maine, United States of America, during his infancy. Leaving school at 15 he became an engineer. Then in February 1850 he left New York in a group, sponsored by Cornelius Vanderbilt, which blazed a short direct route through Nicaragua to the Californian goldfields and, surviving Indian attacks and fever, arrived there in May.

After little success at the diggings, Lane and other Canadians joined the Victorian gold rush in 1853 at Bendigo. At Eaglehawk, then Canadian Gully, their luck improved. In 1856 he discovered the rich Lane's reef at Wedderburn, then turned to blacksmithing at Sandhurst (Bendigo). He soon returned to mining for many years in the Huntly, Lauriston and Malmsbury districts. At St Arnaud in 1887, initially opposed by miners and owners, he proved the efficacy of his methods by reviving the run-down Lord Nelson mine which remained profitable through the 1890s. On 18 April 1855 in Melbourne with Anglican rites he had married Mary Kearney, from Galway, Ireland. At St Arnaud Lane became increasingly involved in community and civic affairs; rifle-shooting and brass bands were major interests. After suffering a stroke in 1904 he retired to Caulfield, Melbourne, where he died on 12 April 1906.

The eldest of his five children, Zebina Bartholomew, was born on 27 January 1856 at Moliagul. When 15 he managed a mine at St Arnaud. He then joined the Colonial Smelting Co. at Kyneton, later moving to New Zealand for eight years and visiting California. In Sandhurst, Victoria, on 12 February 1878 he married Euphemia Leslie. Lane arrived at Broken Hill, New South Wales, in 1885 where, determined not to be 'a miner today, mine manager tomorrow and miner the day after', his tough management brought promotion but resulted in confrontation with the miners. In July 1892, during the 'big strike', he was hanged and burned in effigy in Argent Street. As manager of the Block 14 mine he obstructed the inquiry into lead-poisoning in Broken Hill, although his infant daughter had died of the disease in 1890. An active participant in the Mine Managers' Association and in civic affairs, he was mayor in 1889-90.

In November 1893 Lane visited Coolgardie, Western Australia, and seized opportunities there, floating mining companies including the Great Boulder and the Iron Duke in London in mid-1894. He remained consultant engineer and attorney to the Great Boulder until 1899, but avoided management; his frequent promotional trips to London brought him wealth. He formed the British Westralia syndicate which floated the Great Boulder Persever-

ance mine in 1895. Later he invested in urban development and the jarrah timber trade, and floated the Collie Proprietary Coalfields Co. By 1901 he had reputedly introduced capital worth over £15 million into Western Australia.

From January 1902 Lane lived in Perth and was elected to the Legislative Council in 1903-08. At first a promising participant in debates, he retreated into silence after criticism from the royal commission into the Great Boulder Perseverance mine in 1904. He left Perth, later acquiring mines in America and the Flowerdale estate at Broadford, Victoria, for his two sons. After abdominal surgery in London in 1910 he quipped, 'I once managed a silver mine, but I am one myself now', referring to the woven silver plate inserted in him. While on his travels he wrote of his experiences for the Perth *Sunday Times* which he helped J. Mac-Callum Smith [q.v.] to purchase in 1901. He adopted the title 'Colonel', being honorary colonel of the 1st Battalion of the West Australian Infantry. He was a member of the Perth Club. After more operations he faced major surgery to remove the then unravelling plate and admitted that 'I am putting things in order in case of fire, and for the first time I am funking it'. He did not survive the operation, died in Berlin on 20 October 1912 and was cremated, leaving an estate of about £155 000.

Twentieth century impressions of Western Australia (Perth, 1901); Truthful Thomas, *Through the spy-glass* (Perth, 1905); A. Reid, *Those were the days* (Perth, 1933); Y. S. Palmer, *Track of the years* (Melb, 1955); B. Kennedy, *Silver, sin and sixpenny ale* (Melb, 1978); C. T. Stannage, *The people of Perth* (Perth, 1979); *V&P* (LA NSW), 1892-93, 4, 1250; *PP* (SA), 1888 (90); *V&P* (WA), 1904, 2 (A13), 1905, 1 (3).   ANNE PORTER

LANE-POOLE, CHARLES EDWARD (1885-1970), forester, was born on 16 August 1885 at Easebourne, Sussex, England, youngest son of Stanley Edward Lane-Poole, Egyptologist and professor of Arabic at Trinity College, Dublin, and his wife Charlotte Bell, née Wilson. He was educated at St Columba's College, Dublin, and at the Ecole Forestière, Nancy, France. After a year at the South African Forest School in 1906-07 he served until 1910 as district forest officer in the Transvaal. In Dublin on 20 July 1911 he married Ruth Pollexfen by special licence in the chapel of St Columba's College. In 1911-16 he was conservator of forests, Sierra Leone, and a member of the Legislative Council. On the recommendation of Sir David Hutchins, who had reported on forestry in Australia, Lane-Poole was appointed conservator of forests for Western Australia in 1916 and vigorously set about providing a sound forest policy and a school to train foremen and rangers. The Forests Act (1919) which he formulated was regarded as a model in professional circles, but lack of support and opposition to its implementation prompted his resignation in 1921.

In 1922 he was commissioned by the Commonwealth government to report on the forest resources of Papua and New Guinea and recommend a programme for their development. In his mainly solo surveys of hazardous terrain Lane-Poole indulged a taste for living dangerously, surviving disease and the attentions of hostile inhabitants. He was dexterous in the handling of his equipment, despite the substitution of a steel hook for his left hand, and he was also an expert horseman. In 1925-27 he was forest adviser to the Commonwealth government. At his prompting, the States and the Commonwealth finally agreed to establish an Australian Forestry School which was set up temporarily in Adelaide in 1926. In 1927 Lane-Poole became inspector-general of forests and acting principal of the Australian Forestry School (1927-44) in Canberra. He was also the administrator of the Forestry Bureau which he had proposed to co-ordinate education, research and policy (not formally established until 1930). The research section which he first promoted in Western Australia to include research into making paper from eucalypts was developed in Melbourne as the division of forest products, Council for Scientific and Industrial Research. The forestry research section of the bureau eventually developed as the division of forest research, C.S.I.R., in Canberra.

Lane-Poole represented the Commonwealth government at the Empire Forestry conferences of 1920, 1923 and 1928. At the first conference (London) he proposed the resolution which led to the formation of the Empire Forestry Association. He was one of the great pioneers of forestry in Australia, working tirelessly to promote a national policy. Of strong personal and professional principles, he exerted considerable influence through his teaching and administration and as the author of over fifty papers covering both scientific and general aspects of forestry. He was a foundation member of the Royal Society of Australia (Royal Society of Canberra). After his retirement as inspector-general in 1945 he carried out consulting work in Sydney. He died on 22 November 1970 in Sydney, and was cremated. His wife and three daughters survived him.

His brother, Vice-Admiral Sir Richard Hayden Owen Lane-Poole (1883-1971), joined the Royal Navy as a cadet in 1897 and was appointed O.B.E. in World War I. In 1924-27 he commanded the Royal Australian Naval College at Jervis Bay. In 1929-31 he was captain of the Royal Navy College at Greenwich and in 1936-38 rear-admiral commanding the Australian Squadron. He came out of retirement in England to serve as commodore of convoys and director of demagnetization in World War II. In 1957 he settled at Armidale, New South Wales.

Cwlth Forestry Review, 50, 1971; *SMH*, 26 Mar 1971; *The Times* (Lond), 3 Apr 1971; Lane-Poole papers (NL); A457 I521/1 (AAO).   L. T. CARRON

LANG, JOHN THOMAS (1876-1975), estate agent and politician, was born on 21 December 1876 in George Street, Sydney, son of James Henry Lang, watchmaker of Edinburgh, and his wife Mary, née Whelan, of Galway, Ireland. His father's illness and financial problems in the mid-1880s forced him to live with an uncle at Bairnsdale, Victoria, where he went to the local convent school. Back in Sydney Jack sold newspapers and attended St Francis Marist Brothers' School, Haymarket. In 1889 he worked on a poultry farm; later he drove a horse-bus, and served in H. J. Douglass's bookshop; at 17 he became an office-boy in an accountant's office. He was a gangling youth, darkly handsome.

On 14 March 1896 at St Francis Church Lang married 17-year-old Hilda Bredt, step-daughter of W. H. McNamara [q.v.] who kept a well-known socialist bookshop in Castlereagh Street. Henry Lawson [q.v.] married Hilda's sister. The Langs lived with the McNamaras and their first child was born in June.

By 1899 Lang was an accountant's clerk in R. Harley's real estate office at Auburn. In 1901 he and H. H. Dawes became land agent and auctioneering partners there. Lang lived at first in Carnarvon Street, from 1912 in a stately house in Adderley Street where he remained for most of the rest of his life. Beginning as a pinched, semi-rural, western suburb, Auburn grew slowly as a mainly working-class district with some home ownership but much absentee investment for needy tenants; it slowly became industrialized. Lang became absorbed in the area, nourishing its middle-class aspirations and adjusting to its growing radical tinge.

In 1901-13 Lang consolidated his contrary traits of uncouthness and a yearning for respectability. He grew into a large, solid, man, 6 ft. 4 ins. (193 cm) tall. His black moustache spread as his hair receded, making him more striking in appearance, formidable to men and not unattractive to women. His auctioneering produced a crude but effective public speaking style: rasping voice, snarling mouth, flailing hands, sentences and phrases punctuated by long pauses. Increasing wealth did not disturb or surprise him, and he wore the uniform of the successful Edwardian man—three-piece suit, watch and chain, stiff collar, sober tie, polished boots, obtrusive felt hat. He was not a punctilious churchgoer, but he was religious and had a good Catholic faith, which, however, he regarded strictly as part of his private life. He denounced sectarianism.

Lang seldom laughed; his rare smiles highlighted his jutting jaw. He was insecure with people, but they were attracted by his appearance of strength. He gained many followers but no real intimates, and in the 1920s T. D. Mutch [q.v.] said he would die without a friend. He was ruthless, calculating and shrewd, adept at short-term judgements that fostered his own interests, the model of the self-seeking house and land agent. In 1906 he became secretary of the Starr-Bowkett Ballot and Sale Society, a workers' co-operative home-buying group. But he had no view of integrated improvement. His reading had been desultory. His social ideas were meagre. But he was determined, tireless and ambitious, if more than a little suspicious, cautious and defensive. He liked walking and punctuality. He came to loathe gambling and affected a horror of elegant hotels.

In 1903 Lang was secretary of the Granville Labor League, in 1906 of the Nepean Federal Council of the party, and in 1913 president of the Granville Electoral Council. He was also secretary of the Newington Progress Association. He was associated with St Joseph's Hospital and took part in Catholic social life. In 1907-14 he represented Newington Ward on the Auburn council and was mayor in 1909-11. By 1910 W. A. Holman's [q.v.] great organizing was bringing suburban areas within the Labor Party's ambit and, after a conflict with G. Cann [q.v.7] over pre-selection had been settled, Lang took the local seat of Granville in 1913.

For a while Lang was out of his depth in parliament and revealed his chagrin and envy of Holman by unruly behaviour. He was a good local member, exhibiting his habitual persistence, becoming a justice of the peace in 1914. He shrewdly waited on events in 1915-16 as the premier's difficulties with the party increased. From 1911 Lang had noted the resentment towards Holman of some trade unions, led by the Australian Workers' Union; he observed the opposition of organized 'industrialists' at the 1916 Labor conference, though he had little

understanding of or sympathy with unions. But he supported the conference's ban on conscription for overseas war service; the consequent mass expulsions, including Holman who formed a National ministry, enabled Lang to become caucus secretary in 1916-17 and whip in 1917-18, favourable positions from which to judge the new groups contending for party power in the post-Holman era.

Lang perceived the rising strength of trade union influence though it was riven by conflict between the A.W.U., led by J. Bailey [q.v.7], and a divided extremist section in which A. C. Willis [q.v.] of the miners' federation and J. S. Garden [q.v.8], secretary of the Labor Council of New South Wales, were prominent. By 1919 Bailey had won, but he failed to control the parliamentary party—it comprised mainly middle-class reformists; Lang fitted in nicely, his ambition gradually tuning into the new factionalism.

Labor narrowly won the 1920 general election, held under proportional representation. Lang gained one of the Parramatta seats and became treasurer in the Storey [q.v.] ministry; he continued in office until the fall of the Dooley [q.v.8] government in 1922. He failed to win the deputy leadership in 1921. Stressing his own rectitude, he managed the State's finances as he had his Auburn business. His tight-fistedness riled some trade unions, but Sir John French [q.v.8] of the Bank of New South Wales described him 'as one of the best Treasurers'.

The A.W.U. and Bailey still influenced the State executive and were powerful in the Federal party. In 1923 Dooley defied the executive which replaced him with J. J. G. McGirr [q.v.]. Lang distrusted the A.W.U., backed Dooley, and with P. Loughlin's [q.v.] support, sought Federal intervention. Overcoming his distaste for the Trades Hall, Lang found that he could attract devotees even there: two powerful moderates, E. C. Magrath of the printers' union, and T. J. Tyrrell [q.v.] of the municipal workers', supported him and helped to keep Garden in check. With Willis's help Lang partially manipulated the 1923 conference, and he liked the experience. This was real power. Bailey was expelled, the A.W.U.'s dominance shaken. In July caucus elected Lang as leader and Loughlin as his deputy.

Lang knew that members of the Communist Party of Australia had infiltrated the Labor Party, and he was determined to eliminate them. He was always implacably opposed to communism. But he also argued that 'Capitalism must go'. Conservative forces, already fearing him, responded with a constant attack linking Labor with revolution, even after communists were banned in 1924.

Lang's abrasiveness and pugnacity increased with his new assurance. He was irked by caucus restrictions and by 1924 had seen the opportunity of increasing his power by gaining the backing of conference and executive. He became a director of the *Labor Daily*, the party's official organ, founded by Willis's union. But his unsubtle deceit alienated many of his colleagues and in June he defeated Mutch, supported by the A.W.U., by only one vote for the leadership. Willis, president, and Tyrrell, vice-president, of the party executive later went to Parliament House to rally caucus behind Lang.

Garden's 'Trades Hall Reds' also proved difficult for Lang. In a speech in June he promised a 44-hour week, preference to unionists, and socialization of industry. Garden responded next month with a trade union conference which demanded Lang's expulsion. Lang scorned it, was supported by Willis, and attacked Garden and other communists. Meanwhile, he continually scored against the government. The press, especially the *Sydney Morning Herald*, intensified its bitter campaign against him. Nevertheless, he led Labor to a two-seat victory at the May 1925 general election.

Lang became premier and treasurer, after defeating Loughlin by one vote for the leadership. At once he forced the resignation of (Sir) B. S. B. Stevens [q.v.], a senior officer of the Treasury, whose actions and politics had displeased him. To the dismay of many Labor parliamentarians he quickly appointed Willis to the Legislative Council and ministry. Magrath, now president of the executive and Tyrrell, vice-president, were also put into the council. Lang increased his support from unionists, the party machine and branches as the government reinstated the 1917 transport strikers and restored the 44-hour week. But he remained a loner and a hater. Nor was he a good administrator: cabinet work was unbalanced. The council rejected and mutilated legislation, including the death penalty abolition bill, and Lang gained wide party agreement when he decided to abolish it. After much opposition from the governor, Sir Dudley de Chair [q.v.8], twenty-five Labor members were appointed in December but, at the crucial vote in January 1926 some of them reneged on their pledge, and the council survived. In March Lang sent the attorney-general, (Sir) E. A. McTiernan, to London to complain about de Chair. (Sir) T. R. Bavin [q.v.7], leader of the Opposition, said Lang wanted to pose as 'a strong man' at the next Labor conference.

At the April conference Magrath and Tyrell were under fire from the A.W.U. and various radical unionists. Lang stood aloof and was rapturously received. J. A. Beasley,

president of the Labor Council, said that the trade unions 'would stand solidly behind' him. The majority of unionists, whatever their ideologies, now appreciated the premier's apparent strength and welcomed the Widows' Pensions and Workers' Compensation Acts; many sought his patronage. In September even Garden embraced Lang, but was not yet readmitted to the party. But the agitation of many caucus members intensified; Loughlin said that they would not tolerate communists in the party; they were further alarmed by conference's decision that Lang rather than caucus select Labor candidates for the Upper House.

The Nationalists and their newspaper allies now claimed that Lang was subverting the State's constitution. Their fury increased when Lang announced that he would extend 'a hearty welcome' next year (1927) to the duke and duchess of York. The premier attempted to improve his position by appointing A. D. Kay [q.v.], a member for North Sydney, to the Metropolitan Meat Industry Board and having one of his own supporters replace him. In the turmoil in September 1926 Loughlin resigned his portfolio and opposed Lang for leadership; he objected to 'Red' infiltration and subversion of the party's rules; he also said that the government's legislation was based on the party's platform and caucus pressure and not solely on Lang. The vote was tied and Lang remained premier. The *Labor Daily* published wild allegations that certain caucus members had been open to Nationalist bribery to oust Lang. H. V. Evatt chaired a select committee on it and later criticized Lang's evidence, his vanity, his apathy towards sport, and his 'resorting to abuse and insult'.

Most unions and party branches supported Lang, but the A.W.U.'s hostility was sharpened by the intervention of E. G. Theodore [q.v.] from Queensland. Garden's strong, if often embarrassing, backing was helpful. In November a special conference confirmed Lang as parliamentary leader. Loughlin again resigned from the ministry and with R. T. Gillies and V. W. E. Goodin threatened to bring down the government. But in the censure debate the premier made a stirring defence; the dissident trio did not vote and Lang survived. The government held on tenuously, bringing in family endowment after further conflict with the Legislative Council in March 1927. But there was more cabinet strife, centred on Willis and the April conference chaired by W. H. Seale; in May the governor approved Lang's reconstructed ministry subject to an early election.

The April conference had chilled the Labor caucus. It had expelled Loughlin, Gillies and Goodin, consolidated Lang as leader, or 'dictator' as his opponents put it, provided for regional conferences, and arranged future conference and executive representation by a group-elective system—a blow to communists and the A.W.U. but a boon to Lang. Despite its reaffirmation of the communist ban, it was dubbed the 'Red Rules' conference; Lang re-emerged as the 'Red Terror' and the press's 'song of hate' grew louder. This obscured his personal defects and administrative deficiencies and, as Evatt claimed, ensured him undue credit for the government's legislation. Labor's non-parliamentary section had capitulated to him. The A.W.U., Theodore and caucus rebels had favoured a rival executive under F. Conroy, but a 'unity' conference in July 1927, organized by the federal executive, recognized the Seale regime, after a strong campaign by Lang had won more votes for his candidate than the Conroy-federal nominee at the Warringah by-election. He soon commanded the 'Inner Group', based on the Trades Hall, which ran the State party machine. The end of the industrialists' drive for power since 1916 was the ascendancy of a maverick parliamentarian, 'the Big Fella'. But he lost the October elections.

Caucus was now cowed and Lang dominated the 1928 conference. He kept up his campaign against communists and insisted that Labor alone could achieve social justice. Garden rejoined the party in 1929 and continued as an acolyte, helping to repel renewed aggression from the A.W.U. Lang criticized the Commonwealth financial agreement bill, 1928, arguing that the Loan Council it set up gave the Commonwealth excessive power over State development, but in November the Loan Council became part of the Australian Constitution. He welcomed the Scullin [q.v.] Labor Federal government in October 1929, but next year again castigated Theodore, now Commonwealth treasurer; it was suggested that Lang should enter the Federal parliament.

The Depression was now biting, with severe unemployment and balance of payments problems forcing orthodox deflationary policies. Lang ignored its social dangers and took the opportunity not only to attack the Bavin State government, but also the Scullin government, especially when it sought advice from the Bank of England and the Sir Otto Niemeyer mission arrived in July 1930. His policy for the October general election included extensive public works to reduce unemployment, restoration of reductions in public service salaries, markets for farmers' produce, and double payment for each family's first child. He also promised to balance the budget and rejected repudiation. He won the election by twenty seats.

In December Lang's legislation gave relief to mortgagors and tenants, and restricted evictions and the sale of tenants' furniture. But his request for forty to fifty new members of the Legislative Council was refused by the governor, Sir Philip Game [q.v.8]. Hard-pressed for revenue, he introduced a State lottery, a 10 per cent tax on winning bets, and increased the unemployment tax on wages and salaries from threepence to one shilling in the pound. He appealed for help to the banking system, but Sir Robert Gibson [q.v.8], chairman of the Commonwealth Bank of Australia and of the Bankers' Conference, insisted that all borrowings by governments should be handled by the Loan Council. Lang argued in January 1931 that the need to free 'ourselves from the power of the money-ring transcends everything else confronting Australian governments'. He was assisted by several 'publicity officers', including H. R. McCauley and J. H. C. Sleeman.

At a Federal-States conference in Canberra in February it was agreed that budgets should be balanced within three years. Lang proposed 'the Lang Plan', that interest payments to British bondholders should be suspended, that interest on Australian government borrowings should be reduced to 3 per cent, and that a new form of currency should be based on 'the goods standard'. The scheme was opposed by Scullin and Theodore and soon divided the Australian Labor Party, with the New South Wales executive ruling that all party members should support it. A Federal cabinet spill backed the Scullin-Theodore line and Lang's henchman Beasley lost his portfolio of assistant minister of industry. But Lang's supporter E. J. Ward won the March East Sydney by-election. The conflict between State and Federal Labor branches hardened. Lang's policy, now being represented as mainly repudiation, received some nation-wide party approval.

In March 1931 Lang announced that interest due in London on 1 April would not be paid; he said dole commitments should come first. Scullin met the debt. The State party conference endorsed the Lang Plan and Lang and Garden campaigned interstate for its adoption and split Labor further. Lang's ultimate objective was the leadership of the Federal parliamentary party. In May the Government Savings Bank of New South Wales was forced to close. Next month the Premiers' Conference in Melbourne with Lang's agreement adopted a severe deflationary policy, including cuts in wages and pensions. Lang proposed that public servants' salaries should not exceed

£500. The *Herald* asked 'Are we to be driven to desperation . . . before the Governor dismisses him?' The governor still refused additional appointments to the Legislative Council which continued to obstruct Lang; Willis, now agent-general in London, was discussing it with the Dominions Office. In November Game agreed to twenty-five new members.

Lang renounced 'the Premiers' Plan' and his five Federal parliament followers, led by Beasley, harried Scullin about it. Lang had left the Loan Council but, as the State Treasury became depleted, requested Federal aid to meet his commitments. A huge Labor rally in the Domain responded enthusiastically to his justification of his actions. The New Guard, under E. Campbell [q.v.7.], organized counter-demonstrations. On 6 August 1931 public servants' salaries were not paid. 'Socialisation Units' in the State party were saying Lang was not radical enough. At last he began to wilt: he rejoined the Loan Council which provided him with £500 000 of Treasury bills, but his budget deficit was £11.5 million. Recovering his confidence, he told the eight-hour day dinner in October that 'the revolution has come . . . by Act of Parliament'.

Two Labor parties had emerged in New South Wales. In November 1931 Beasley brought down Scullin, and at the December elections the government lost disastrously. Theodore was defeated by a Lang candidate: only three Federal Labor candidates were returned in New South Wales. Lang Labor lost three seats, but won two. F. S. 'Judge' Swindell, who wanted a licence for 'tin (mechanical) hare' coursing, paid for the party's electioneering advertising. Lang had engineered the defeat of a Labor government, but the voting figures showed his own electoral support had been seriously sapped, following soon after defeat in country local elections, and preceding losses in metropolitan council voting in January 1932.

The new prime minister, J. A. Lyons [q.v.], indicated that the Commonwealth would use the law to check Lang. New South Wales was being isolated from the national attempt to alleviate the Depression, and Lang's 'State rightism' and fitful populism produced no viable alternative. The fearsome newspaper image of Lang seemed at last correct, but he was powerless to change events. 31 per cent unemployment prevailed in 1932. The party's metropolitan conference in February told him that 'socialisation of industry [must be] the main issue at the next State elections'. In parliament he faced charges of corruption in the operation of the 'tin hares'. Lyons's Financial Agreements Enforcement Act pro-

voked Lang to withdraw more than £1 million in cash from two Sydney banks. His opening of the Sydney Harbour Bridge on 19 March was an exciting solace. But next month the Federal government used its new powers to take over the revenues of New South Wales, depriving Lang of banking facilities. Massive demands were made on the governor to dismiss him. Trades Hall rumours were that a 'Red Army' would defend him, and a great multitude gathered at the Town Hall to hear him vindicate himself. The High Court upheld the validity of the Commonwealth's financial enforcement legislation. His response on 12 May was a law requiring mortgagees to pay to the Treasury 10 per cent of every mortgage, 'an act of war and pillage'.

Governor Game had been examining Lang's circular instructing public servants not to pay money into the Federal Treasury as required by law. He judged it was illegal. Lang refused to withdraw it and on 13 May the governor dismissed him. Constitutionally the grounds were dubious as the courts had the duty to determine illegality; but socially and politically Game was justified. Civil disorder threatened; Lang's inner resources were exhausted, his policies as bankrupt as his Treasury, his popular backing decimated. There were surreal aspects to his offensive on 'the secret money power', for he was trapped in constitutional realities and contemporary economic orthodoxy which at heart he accepted. He took his dismissal with relief: 'I must be going', he said, 'I am no longer Premier but a free man. I have attempted to do my duty'. Loughlin claimed he had sought dismissal. At the June elections Lang Labor seats fell from 55 to 24; but it polled 40 per cent of the vote while Federal Labor gained only 4 per cent, with no seats. Swindell again paid for Lang's advertising. Stevens became premier.

Lang never regained his electoral appeal as leader. In 1931-38 he lost 3 Federal elections, 3 State, 3 Sydney Municipal Council, and the Legislative Council reform referendum. These failures only gradually eroded his entrenched power in the New South Wales Labor Party. At the 1933 conference Garden, in helping to eliminate the Socialisation Units, proclaimed him 'greater than Lenin'. J. B. Chifley headed the Federal Labor group in 1934 but, after receiving much interstate, especially Victorian, help at that year's Federal poll, Lang won nine seats in New South Wales to Federal Labor's one. But he regarded the national results as unfavourable to his plans to become Federal Labor leader. In 1935 John Curtin replaced Scullin and Lang's chances had gone. Curtin wanted unity in New South Wales, and in February 1936 the State's Federal party was abolished and Lang's group became the official branch of the Australian Labor Party: the Langites oppressed many of their former opponents.

In 1933 Lang had broken with Willis, calling him 'a top-hatted gentleman'. In 1936 he fought Garden for control of the Labor Council's radio station 2KY, and lost: their struggle accentuated growing industrial opposition to Lang and in May a Trades Hall meeting of union secretaries condemned the *Labor Daily*'s attacks on them and sought its control from Lang. Magrath parted from him. R. A. King secretary of the Labor Council, O. Schreiber of the furniture workers' and J. J. Maloney of the bootmakers' were the chief organizers against Lang. They wanted basic reform of the State party. The disaffection spread to the wavering Labor caucus and in July W. F. Dunn [q.v.8], R. J. Heffron and (Sir) W. J. McKell were mentioned as possible leaders: Lang's response to the sustained defiance was a special conference in August that expelled Heffron, three other parliamentarians and sixteen union leaders, including King and Maloney. Next year King said, 'If I have been a fool for 10 years in indulging in hero-worship . . . I am not going to do it any longer'.

In February 1938 Lang at last lost the *Labor Daily*, and was paid £17 889 for his debenture over it, plus interest. In April he began another paper, the *Century*. He lost the State elections. Party turmoil increased. Next year Heffron's Industrial Labor Party won by-elections at Hurstville and Waverley, and precipitated a major caucus revolt in which federal intervention was demanded. The federal executive organized a unity conference in August at which all the pent-up opposition to Lang exploded on the floor and a free fight broke out in the gallery. The conference decided to revise the party's rules and directed that caucus should elect its leader and other officers: on 6 September McKell defeated Lang by twenty votes to twelve.

Lang retained many followers in the party, especially as communists had penetrated the State executive. At the 1940 conference a motion in effect demanded 'Hands off Russia', and in April Lang formed the Australian Labor (Non-Communist) Party, with supporters in both the Federal and State parliaments. The new party demanded home defence as World War II developed. Curtin again sought unity and the New South Wales executive was replaced. The Langites rejoined the official party in February 1941; Labor won the May State elections. In October Curtin formed his first wartime ministry including Beasley, whose defence views now diverged from Lang's, favouring Curtin's policy of modified con-

scription, with Japan threatening Australia; next year the *Century* attacked the policy and Lang was expelled in March 1943. He ran for the Federal seat of Reid but lost and was re-elected for Auburn in October. Next year he started a new Lang Labor Party (he labelled it the 'Australian Labor Party' and added 'Non-Communist' in 1948).

At the 1946 Federal elections Lang won Reid. He began in parliament by describing the government as 'the right wing of the Conservative Party', and remained a trenchant critic, solitary, bitter, aloof, resentful of Chifley, now prime minister. In 1947 he attacked the government's immigration scheme; he said it endangered the White Australia policy, which he had always defended. He opposed Chifley's plan for the nationalization of banking and the 1948 referendum on rent and price control; and claimed that communists were permeating government departments. He slaked his envy on the eve of the 1949 elections by accusing Chifley of lending money in Bathurst at exorbitant interest rates, hoping in vain to prevent him rebutting the charge before the poll. Lang lost his seat. He failed to win a Senate place in 1951.

He continued to make pronouncements, opposing compulsory unionism in 1953, Labor's 'industrial groups' in 1954, and the extension of legalized gambling in 1958. But in 1951 he had supported Evatt's campaign against the referendum to ban communism. In the late 1960s and early 1970s he emerged as a 'folk hero', addressing schools and universities on his career and current topics. When a bank opened on the site of the Lang and Dawes office at Auburn in 1967, a plaque paid 'tribute to a distinguished man of the people'. After a rebuff in 1970, next year he was readmitted to the Labor Party.

Lang's articles in the *Century* were reputedly written by A. C. Paddison. His other publications (probably ghosted) included *Why I fight* (1934), *Communism in Australia: a complete exposure* (1944), *I remember* (1956), *The great bust* (1962) and *The turbulent years* (1970).

He died in St Joseph's Hospital, Auburn, on 27 September 1975, survived by three of his four daughters and one of his three sons. After a requiem Mass at St Mary's Cathedral he was buried in Rookwood cemetery. His estate was valued for probate at $38 594.

The *Century*'s last issue was on 30 January 1976.

H. Radi and P. Spearritt (eds), *Jack Lang* (Syd, 1977) and for bibliog; F. Farrell, *International socialism and Australian labour* (Syd, 1981); *SMH*, 16 June 1925, 21 Oct 1926, 29 May, 16 June 1927, 28 Oct 1930, 3 June 1932, 12 Dec 1933, 12 Aug 1970, 29 Sept 1975; *Truth* (Syd), 5 June 1927.

BEDE NAIRN

LANGDON, THOMAS (1832-1914), grain merchant and politician, was born on 13 May 1832 at Roadwater, Somerset, England, son of John Langdon, carpenter, wheelwright and innkeeper, and his wife Prudence, née Bindon. Educated at Bristol, he worked for four years in a Bristol solicitor's office before deciding to migrate. He arrived in Melbourne in 1853 and quickly joined the gold rushes, working mainly in the Bendigo district as a carter and miner. In 1858 he took up farming at Laanecoorie, later becoming a grain merchant at Kangaroo Flat and Inglewood. He selected land at Boort in 1874. On 18 July 1855 at St Peter's Church of England, Melbourne, Langdon had married Esther Mary Temlett, also from Somerset. She died in December 1860 and on 29 November 1862 he married Sarah Ann Coventry of Gloucestershire at Dunolly.

Elected to the Marong Shire Council in 1871, Langdon served as president in 1877-79; he also spent three years on the Swan Hill Shire Council. In 1880 he won the Legislative Assembly seat of Avoca. A close friend of (Sir) Thomas Bent [q.v.3], he was a director of Bent's Heights of Maribyrnong Estate Co. Ltd. In 1888 in Melbourne he established T. Langdon & Co., grain merchants and general brokers, but next year his fortunes collapsed. Declared bankrupt, he was defeated for the new seat of Korong and in 1890 for Dunolly.

Ever energetic, Langdon re-established his business and, winning Korong in 1892, retained the seat for the rest of his life. In parliament he was an independently minded member of the 'Country' faction. Although resident in Melbourne he assiduously guarded the interests of his farming electorate: water conservation, closer settlement, road and rail extensions, cheaper grain freights and the establishment of local schools were his main concerns. In 1894-96 he was a member of a royal commission on water supply and in 1905 chaired a royal commission on locomotive construction. His most enduring work was done as president of the Council of Agricultural Education in 1901-14 and as chairman of two royal commissions (1902-03 and 1912-13) on the marketing, transportation and storage of grain. The second royal commission report, written by Langdon, led to the introduction of the bulk-handling system into Victoria.

A short, rotund, bustling figure with a self-important air, likened to 'a football on legs', Langdon reached the zenith of his political career as an honorary member of the Bent ministry in 1904-07. In January 1907, following the resignation of Sir Samuel Gillott [q.v.], he was appointed chief secretary and minister of labour. However, embittered by his exclusion from the reconstituted ministry in February, he helped to drive Bent from office next year.

In December 1913, aged 81, Langdon was elected chairman of committees on a combination of Labor and 'Country' faction votes. He still held that post when he died at his Albert Park home on 27 May 1914. Buried in Box Hill cemetery, he was survived by his wife and their two sons and three daughters. His estate was valued for probate at £276.

A. Sutherland et al, *Victoria and its metropolis*, 2 (Melb, 1888); J. Smith (ed), *Cyclopedia of Victoria*, 1 (Melb, 1903); M. Cannon, *The land boomers* (Melb, 1966); *PD* (Vic), 1907, p 862, 1914, p 20; *Punch* (Melb), 22 Nov 1906; *Age*, *Argus*, 27 May 1914; K. Rollison, Groups and attitudes in the Victorian Legislative Assembly, 1900-1909 (Ph.D. thesis, La Trobe Univ, 1972). GEOFF BROWNE

LANGLER, SIR ALFRED (1865-1928), journalist, was born on 5 May 1865 at Ipplepen, Devon, England, son of William Langler, master carpenter, and his wife Susanna Hext, née Colton. His awkward gait, caused by talipes (clubfoot), precluded Alfred from active occupations and at an early age he joined the literary staff of the *Western Daily Mercury*, Plymouth, as an apprentice journalist. He later contributed to other journals until he migrated to South Australia where he joined the Adelaide *Register* early in 1890. On 21 February 1893 he married Josephine Laverton; they had one son and a short-lived daughter.

In July 1895 Langler moved to Perth to become sub-editor on the enlarged *West Australian*. When J. L. Nanson [q.v.], the assistant editor and leader-writer, resigned in 1902 Langler, by then the paper's 'sheet anchor', replaced him. Langler's frugal and unequivocal use of language, his general knowledge and his detachment from Australian politics complemented the interests of the owners Charles Harper [q.v.4] and (Sir) John Winthrop Hackett [q.v.] who were both active in public affairs. Hackett, the editor, became Langler's friend and confidant. The deaths of Harper in 1912, Hackett in 1916, and of Hackett's executor G. H. Wickham in 1917 resulted in all responsibility devolving upon Langler as sole executor, editor and chairman of directors of the small limited liability company. When probate was declared on Hackett's estate in April 1916 the assets totalled less than the legacies and bequests, but Hackett had stipulated a delay in winding up his estate, giving Langler the opportunity to increase the value of the company, which stood at £93 230 in September 1917.

Langler drove himself and his staff to fulfil Hackett's ambition to endow the University of Western Australia. Wartime restrictions on newsprint necessitated succinct news coverage but allowed a rise in advertising rates. In 1920 the paper's price was raised to twopence. A printers' strike in 1922 left the presses idle for five weeks, but Langler withstood pressure to publish while the men were out. No inkling of the increased value of the company emerged until 1926 when Melbourne interests led by W. S. Robinson [q.v.] and W. L. Baillieu [q.v.7] purchased it for about £625 000. Langler became chairman of the board of directors of the new West Australian Newspapers Ltd. The share of the estate to Hackett's family was fixed, and when the residual estate was distributed the university's share was capitalized at £425 000 while the Anglican Church received £140 000 to build St George's College. Langler was knighted in 1927.

Langler's work filled his life. In 1920 he attended the Empire Press conference in Canada. A member of the Weld Club, a justice of the peace, amicable but not very sociable, he progressively became more retiring, eventually returning home as early as 6 p.m. where a junior reporter took the proofs of the leading article to be checked by him. He retired in 1927, suffering from senile dementia, and died of bronchopneumonia on 26 March 1928. His contribution to the university as executor of Hackett's estate is memorialized in a mosaic in the entrance to Winthrop Hall.

Truthful Thomas, *Through the spy-glass* (Perth, 1905); F. Alexander, *Campus at Crawley* (Melb, 1963); P. Hasluck, *Mucking about* (Melb, 1977); O. K. Battye, 'Notable men in the company's history No 2: Sir Alfred Langler'; *WA Newspaper Q*, 2, May 1962; *West Australian*, 27 Mar 1928; O. K. Battye, History of West Australian newspapers (MS with author, Nedlands, Perth).

ANNE PORTER

LANGLEY, GEORGE FURNER (1891-1971), educationist and soldier, was born on 1 May 1891 at Port Melbourne, son of English-born Jabez Langley, grocer, and his wife Fanny, née Furner, from South Australia. He was educated at Melbourne Continuation (High) School before attending Melbourne Teachers' College and the University of Melbourne (Dip.Ed., 1914; B.A., 1926). He excelled at Australian Rules football and athletics.

Langley taught at Williamstown High School before being transferred to Mans-

field Agricultural High School where he was teaching at the outbreak of World War I. A lieutenant in the Senior Cadets from October 1913, he enlisted as a private in the Australian Imperial Force in December 1914 and was commissioned lieutenant in the 21st Battalion on 24 March 1915. His unit embarked for Egypt in May and after training embarked on the *Southland* for Gallipoli. The ship was torpedoed on 2 September and Langley, who had been promoted captain that day, was blown into the air, falling back through a hatch into the bilge. Although badly shaken he organized the disembarkation of his men until he collapsed. The battalion was established on Gallipoli by 8 September and Langley, despite jaundice, served until the evacuation in December.

On returning to Egypt Langley was seconded to the Imperial Camel Corps on 26 January 1916 to raise and train the 1st Australian Company. During 1916 he led his company on six months of prolonged, exhausting and wide-ranging patrolling against the Senussi in the Western Desert. He was promoted major on 11 September and mentioned in dispatches after the advance on El Arish. In December the companies of the Imperial Camel Corps were brigaded; Langley was transferred to the 1st (Anzac) Battalion, appointed commanding officer and promoted lieut-colonel on 24 January 1917.

He led his unit until May 1918, taking it through the Sinai Desert and Palestine to the Jordan valley. They fought at Rafa, in the three battles for Gaza, the Amman raid where Langley was wounded, the defence of the Jordan valley, and the raid on Es Salt. In February 1917 he was awarded the Serbian Order of the White Eagle. In June 1918 the 1st (Anzac) Camel Battalion was reformed as the 14th Australian Light Horse. Langley commanded this regiment in the advance to Damascus where he won the Distinguished Service Order for 'skilful leadership and conspicuous gallantry'. He was later mentioned three times in dispatches for outstanding leadership. The regiment was *en route* to Aleppo when the Armistice was signed.

In Cairo in December Langley married Edmee Mary Plunkett. He was appointed in January 1919 to officiate in command of the 5th Light Horse Brigade to help suppress the Egyptian rebellion. He returned to Australia in August and his A.I.F. appointment terminated on 2 November; he was then appointed lieut-colonel on the reserve of officers, Australian Military Forces.

In 1920 Langley became headmaster of Mansfield Agricultural High School and then, in 1924, of Warrnambool High School where he remained for sixteen years. He retained his army links by commanding the 20th and then the 4th Light Horse Regiments but he was first and foremost a teacher and educational administrator. To those roles he brought the military virtues of briskness, efficiency and devotion to the ideas of courage and honour. At the same time he was a man of warm affections, civilized values and largeness of view. His students remember his infectious enthusiasm, the passion he brought to the teaching of French, and the morning assemblies when he spoke of the issues of the day, condemning small-mindedness and introducing, on occasion, radical perspectives on such questions as the Italian invasion of Abyssinia or the Spanish Civil War. In 1940 he moved to Bendigo High School and was appointed commanding officer of the 38th Battalion, A.M.F., in September. Promoted temporary brigadier in April 1942, he took the 2nd Infantry Brigade to Western Australia, then to Darwin, raising it to a high level of efficiency.

As war wounds precluded active service abroad Langley retired from the A.M.F. on 10 March 1944 as honorary brigadier. He joined the Australian Red Cross Field Force as commissioner in England and the Middle East, serving until 1946. He was appointed an officer of the Order of St John of Jerusalem. In 1946-47 Langley was headmaster at Mordialloc High School. He moved to Box Hill High School in 1948 before being appointed headmaster of Melbourne High School in 1949. During his eight years there he inspired unselfish service. His dedication, enthusiasm and energy influenced all associated with the school.

After retirement Langley became a director of Robertson & Mullens bookshop, a Victorian film appeal censor, a foundation fellow of the Australian College of Education and a member of the Melbourne City Development Association. He was a life member of the Victorian High School Headmasters' Association, having been president for seven years. He was appointed C.B.E. in 1958.

In 1970 the Langleys moved to Sydney. Survived by his wife and two daughters, he died at Killara on 24 August 1971 and was cremated with Presbyterian forms. The later years of his life were spent preparing a history of the Australian Camel Corps; his wife completed the task and published *Sand, sweat and camels* in 1976.

C. E. W. Bean, *The story of Anzac*, 1, 2 (Syd, 1921, 1924); H. S. Gullett, *The A.I.F. in Sinai and Palestine* (Syd, 1923); Univ Melb, *Record of active service* (Melb, 1926); D. McCarthy, *South-West Pacific area—first year* (Canb, 1959); *London Gazette*, 22 Sept 1916, 13 Feb 1917, 12 Jan 1918, 21 Jan, 8 Mar 1919, 11 June 1920; Melb High School, *Unicorn*, Dec 1955; Melb High School Old Boys' Assn, *Old Unicornian*, Nov 1971; *Age*, 3 Sept 1958, 25 Aug 1971; *SMH*, 25 Apr 1976; information from Lieut-Colonel R. Honner, Syd, J. C. Elden, Melb, and Prof J. D. Legge, Monash Univ; correspondence with Mrs E. M. Langley and Miss D. M. Langley, Avalon, Syd; personal information.

A. W. HAMMETT

LANGLEY, HUDSON JOHN WATSON (1894-1919), soldier, was born on 10 April 1894 at Kew, Melbourne, son of John Hudson Keys Langley, farmer, and his wife Eda Jane, née Rosier, both native born. His parents separated during his infancy and he was raised by his aunt Louisa Elizabeth Langley.

Langley, a Bendigo electrician, enlisted in the Australian Imperial Force on 5 July 1915, was promoted sergeant on 1 November and in April 1916 joined the 1st Australian Armoured Car Section. This section (afterwards renamed No. 1 Australian Light Car Patrol) arrived in Egypt in August and for the next eight months was mainly engaged in operations against Senussi raiding parties along a line of blockhouses extending over 100 miles (160 km) through the Libyan Desert.

The patrol arrived in Palestine in May 1917 and quickly distinguished itself in operations against the Turks, carrying out reconnaissance and other tasks, frequently well in advance of the mounted troops. John Langley, a vigorous leader and a man of splendid physique, was conspicuous as a car commander in the battle of Beersheba and afterwards in the pursuit of the Turks along the coastal plain to Jaffa. In 1918 he took part in the advance to Jericho, and in March did good work leading a patrol on foot over rugged country to re-establish contact with the Anzac Mounted Division after the first abortive attack on Amman.

On 14 July when the enemy mounted strong attacks on the Desert Mounted Corps' positions in the Jordan valley, Langley led a patrol of two cars across the river, dismounted his two Lewis-guns and took them forward to a position commanding the approach of an enemy column. He held the fire of his guns until the enemy were within close range when he opened up with telling effect. The column's pack-horses were stampeded or killed and a duel developed between the Australian and Turkish machine-gunners. One machine-gun was captured and the enemy fled. For his 'gallantry and devotion to duty' that day, Langley was awarded the Distinguished Conduct Medal.

Langley left the Jordan valley in September when his unit took part in the exhilarating drive of the Desert Mounted Corps along the coast to the plain of Esdraelon, to Nazareth and thence to Damascus. In October his unit was part of a mobile group of three armoured car batteries and three light car patrols which led the advance on Aleppo. On the 22nd the mobile group bested a fleet of enemy motor vehicles after a running fight—'probably the first occasion on record of a battle between two fleets of motor vehicles'. Next day Langley, in an armoured car, pursued over very rough ground an enemy patrol which approached the mobile group's positions. His quickness and dash enabled him to kill one of the enemy and capture four. His 'determination and initiative' that day won him a Bar to his D.C.M.

According to the unit's commander, 2 January 1919 was 'a day of gloom' for the Light Car Patrol. That day Langley, 'the gallant N.C.O. who had led his car into numerous fights and who was the admiration of the whole unit', died in Aleppo Hospital from malaria. He was buried in Aleppo cemetery and afterwards reinterred in the British War Cemetery at Beirut, Lebanon. He was unmarried.

H. S. Gullett, *Sinai and Palestine* (Syd, 1937); E. H. James, History of the 1st Australian Armoured Car Section in Egypt, Sinai, Palestine, Syria and Asia Minor (AWM); War diary, No. 1 Aust Light Car Patrol (AWM); records (AWM).

A. J. SWEETING

LANGWELL, HUGH (1859?-1933), politician and public servant, was born in Belfast, Ireland, son of Hugh Langwell, farmer, and his wife Matilda, née McCully. The family migrated to Victoria in 1861 and he was educated at Warrnambool. Moving north in 1880 Hughie worked as a station-hand, shearer, fencer and well-sinker on western stations in New South Wales and Queensland. About 1886 he settled at Bourke, New South Wales. After a win in Tattersall's sweep, he bought into a tobacco and hairdressing business, of which he soon became sole owner, later adding a licensed billiard saloon. On 28 October 1890 he married Sarah Jane Brooks at St Stephen's Presbyterian Church, Bourke.

An original member of the second branch of the Amalgamated Shearers' Union of Australasia, formed at Bourke on 2 October 1886, Langwell was its representative in 1888 at the union's annual conference. In 1891 he participated in abortive negotiations with the pastoralists for a stay of proceedings on importing outside labour after local shearers had struck in response to pressure to register with the Pastoralists'

Union of New South Wales. He played little further part in the A.S.U. although he was a member of the 1894 committee which drew up the Australian Workers' Union rules.

A short, stocky, jolly man, Langwell was an ardent protectionist who became president of the Bourke Labor Electoral League, which in 1891 selected him as candidate for Bourke in the Legislative Assembly. He won, but was not admitted to the Labor caucus because of the Bourke league's modifications of the official platform; but he voted with the party, and as it divided he joined the seventeen 'solids', the only protectionist to do so except McGowen [q.v.]. Labor candidate for Bourke in 1894, he was beaten decisively by a free trader, E. D. Millen [q.v.].

Appointed to the Legislative Council on 12 June 1900, Langwell moved his family next year to Sydney. In 1902 he resigned upon appointment to the new Western Land Board by the See [q.v.] government. In 1912, as royal commissioner inquiring into the control of the Kentia palm seed industry on Lord Howe Island, he recommended preserving the islanders' rights while placing the industry on a secure footing. He later became a member of the Lord Howe Island Board of Control.

The only member of the Western Land Board with continuous service from its formation until 1931, Langwell became chief commissioner and chairman in 1922. The Western Lands (Amendment) Act (1930), allowing forty-year renewable leases, and its repeal in 1931 created a confusing workload for the commissioners. In May 1931 a royal commission was appointed by the Lang [q.v.] government to inquire into the management, control and administration of the western division of New South Wales. The commissioner, E. A. Prior, found the board guilty of professional misbehaviour and incompetence, responsible for inaccurate and misleading advice to the minister and negligent in enforcement of the obligations of landholders. Despite their denials the three commissioners were dismissed by cabinet in December.

Langwell died, aged 73, at his home at Bondi, on 15 May 1933. After a service with Anglican rites he was cremated. His wife, four sons and three daughters survived him.

W. G. Spence, *Australia's awakening* (Syd, 1909); *Papers presented by members of the Bourke and District Historical Society . . . on the history of Bourke*, 2, 4, 5, 6 (Bourke, NSW, 1968, 1974, 1975, 1977); B. Nairn, *Civilising capitalism* (Canb, 1973); D. J. Murphy (ed), *Labor in politics* (Brisb, 1975); Report of Western Lands Board, *PP* (LA, NSW), 1902, 1915, 1919, 1923, 1927, 1931, 1932; Roy Com into the administration of the Western Division of New South Wales, Report, *PP* (NSW), 1930-32, 1, p 151; *PP* (Cwlth), 1926-28, 4, p 1235; *PD* (LA NSW), 1930-32, p 125; *Bulletin*, 7 Jan 1926; *SMH*, 21 Aug 1926, 12 Nov, 29, 30 Dec 1931, 16 May 1933; information from Mrs C. G. Bayliss, Wahroonga, Mrs P. Walker, Turramurra, Syd, Mrs W. J. Cameron, Bourke, and Dr J. Merritt, Canb.

JOHN ATCHISON

LANSELL, SIR GEORGE VICTOR (1883-1959), businessman, politician and philanthropist, was born on 3 October 1883 in London, elder son of George Lansell [q.v.5], the Bendigo 'Quartz King', and his second wife Harriet Edith, née Bassford. George was educated at St Andrew's College, Bendigo, and Melbourne Church of England Grammar School. On 20 January 1910 at All Saints Pro-Cathedral, Bendigo, he married a skiing champion, Edith Florence Gwendoline Frew; they had three daughters.

As a young man Lansell excelled in revolver shooting, boxing and swimming but his militia interests endured longest. First commissioned in the 8th Australian Infantry Regiment in 1904, he was a captain in 1909. In May 1916 he was commissioned captain in Bendigo's 38th Battalion, Australian Imperial Force. Entering the front line in France on 1 December he was wounded two days later and invalided back to Australia next March for discharge in August. After the war he rose in 1923 to major commanding the 38th Battalion, Australian Military Forces. Lieut-colonel in 1927, he retired as honorary colonel in 1942 after having organized the north-west Victorian group of the Volunteer Defence Corps early in World War II.

Lansell's major contribution was his service to returned soldiers. He was president of the Bendigo sub-branch of the Returned Sailors' and Soldiers' Imperial League of Australia for nearly thirty years. His work extended beyond grand gesture and he is remembered affectionately for his personal generosity to ex-servicemen and their dependants.

Lansell was director of the powerful Sandhurst Trustees' Co., the Bendigo Mutual Permanent Land & Building Society and many other local companies. He brought to Bendigo the overseas-based Hanro Knitting Mills and the Australian Swiss Watch Co. Early in his business career he acquired the *Bendigo Independent* and amalgamated it with the *Bendigo Advertiser* in 1918. He had interests in the *Riverine Herald*, the *Rochester Irrigator*, the *Stock and Station Journal* and Central Victorian Broadcasters Ltd, and was a delegate to Empire press conferences in Canada (1920), England (1923) and Australia (1925).

Shy and retiring, Lansell was the opposite of his swashbuckling father, but his philanthropy was no less extensive. With his mother he built a clinic at the Bendigo Hospital; he donated an X-ray plant, pathological and electro-surgical equipment and a radio system for patients. He supported the Bendigo Benevolent Home and the art gallery. He was president of the council of the School of Mines and had fifty years association with the Young Men's Christian Association. He was a Freemason, a Rotarian and a justice of the peace.

Despite twenty-four years in the Legislative Council as member for Bendigo Province, Lansell did not enjoy politics. He averaged about a comment a year and had little commitment to party. First elected in 1928 as a Nationalist, he joined the Country Party in 1944 and the Liberal-Country Party alliance in 1949. In 1950-51, however, he supported the J. G. B. McDonald Country Party government; his vote ensured supply and Legislative Council reform including adult suffrage. Appointed C.M.G. in 1937 he was knighted in 1951.

Predeceased by his wife, Lansell died at Bendigo on 9 January 1959 and was buried in Bendigo cemetery, leaving an estate valued for probate at £133 271.

J. A. Allan (ed), *The Victorian centenary book* (Geelong, Vic, 1936); *Mufti*, 7 Feb 1959; *Herald* (Melb), 1 Jan 1951; *Sun-News Pictorial*, 20 Mar 1951, 10 Jan 1959; *Bendigo Advertiser*, 10 Jan 1959.

KEVIN PEOPLES

LAPSLEY, JAMES McFARLANE (1856-1931), fire brigade officer, was born on 14 February 1856 at Beaufort, Victoria, son of John Henry Lapsley, Scots miner, and his wife Jean, née McFarlane. Reared in Scotland he was educated at the Highlanders' Academy, Greenock, and apprenticed to a firm of engineers. He returned to Australia in 1877, living first in Adelaide. Moving to Perth in 1885, he briefly taught dancing and deportment, then set up his own plumbing business.

An ingenious plumbing engineer, he is remembered for his invention of the Lapsley condenser, made from the black iron tanks in which groceries were transported to the goldfields. Portable by horse or camel, it ensured the survival of prospectors who only had access to limited supplies of salt water. Mining at Kurnalpi in the hot summer of 1894 was possible because of Lapsley's invention.

He also distinguished himself as a public-spirited citizen. He joined the Volunteer Fire Brigade of the Perth City Council in 1888 and served as engineer and foreman. He was appointed superintendent of fire brigades under the Fire Brigades Act of 1898, which gave the newly created board control of the Municipality of Perth. Fremantle came under the board's management in 1905. The West Australia Fire Brigades Board, created by the District Fire Brigades Act of 1909, appointed him chief officer and in this position he gained effective control of the State's fire brigades. Lapsley used his practical engineering experience: firemen employed at the Perth station were required to be mechanics with the result that all the requirements of the brigade could be manufactured on the premises. The service included a free accident ambulance van, named after Lapsley by his men. His contribution to ambulance work was recognized by his appointment as an honorary serving brother of the Order of St John of Jerusalem in 1905, and by his promotion to officer brother in 1912 and commander brother in 1927. Awarded the King's Police Medal in 1910 for his organization of the fire brigades in the State, he retired as chief officer in 1922.

In 1886 he had moved the motion that set up an association to seek the eight-hour day in Western Australia. He also helped to establish Scottish Freemasonry in the colony in 1897, being district grand master from 1907 until his death. He was one of the founders of the Caledonian Society, Druidism, and Sons of Temperance in the State and the principal office-bearer of many sporting organizations. In 1905 he was appointed a justice of the peace.

Lapsley was a settler in Perth at a time of growth when men of vision and good character were well rewarded with public office. He is remembered by an associate in the fire brigade as having a dominant personality and being a shrewd tactician. Photographs show him as having a long keen face, a stylish moustache, a lengthy nose and deep perceptive eyes.

Lapsley married Evelyn, daughter of George Bell, on 23 November 1887 at Wesley Church, Perth. He died at his home in South Perth on 9 January 1931 and was buried in the Presbyterian section of Karrakatta cemetery. His wife, two sons and a daughter survived him.

J. S. Battye (ed), *Cyclopedia of Western Australia*, 2 (Adel, 1913); *Western Mail* (Perth), 19 Feb, 27 Aug 1910; *West Australian*, 3 June 1886, 22 Mar 1901, 22, 29 Dec 1951; *Daily News* (Perth), 28 Dec 1886; *Sun* (Kalgoorlie), 3 Feb, 3 Mar 1901; *Western Argus*, 13 Jan 1931; *Sunday Times* (Perth), 9 Jan 1966.
SALLY ANNE HASLUCK

LARCOMBE, JAMES (1884-1957), butcher and politician, was born on 25 April 1884 at Rockhampton, Queensland, son of James Larcombe, butcher, and Mary Lee. He was educated at Jenkins's private school at Rockhampton. He then worked with his father, who had failed to win Rockhampton in the Legislative Assembly elections of 1893, and joined him in the activities of the local labour movement, becoming successively president, vice-president and secretary of the Rockhampton Workers' Political Organization. He failed to win party pre-selection in 1907 and 1911, but in 1912 was elected to the assembly for Keppel.

Larcombe continued to represent Keppel until the defeat of the Labor government in 1929. In 1916-18 and 1943-44 he was a member of the party's Queensland central executive. He was opposed to conscription and in 1916 was elected one of six delegates to a special interstate conference on conscription called by the federal executive. In 1932 he was returned as member for Rockhampton and held the seat until he retired before the 1956 election as the longest-serving member of the assembly. His period of almost twenty-three years in the ministry was also unequalled in Queensland. He was minister without portfolio from 9 September to 22 October 1919, secretary for public works to 7 April 1920, then secretary for railways until 21 May 1929.

He did not rejoin the ministry until 1939, partly because in 1932 he had beaten Premier W. Forgan Smith [q.v.] and C. G. Fallon in caucus with a proposition that Labor should legislate directly to restore awards and other rights removed by the Moore [q.v.] government; moreover some party leaders had scorned his handling of the 1927 railway strike and he had lost seniority by his electoral defeat. Gossip said that he regained his position by shameless flattery of Forgan Smith in his writings on the Labor Party. He was secretary for mines from April to August 1939, minister for transport from 4 August 1939 to 27 April 1944, then minister for public instruction to 7 March 1946. He was treasurer to 10 May 1950, then attorney-general and minister for prices to 10 March 1952 when he resigned from the ministry because of ill health.

Larcombe was an administrator rather than an initiator. He was attacked by the Australian Railways Union during the 1925 railway strike because of an order-in-council exempting gatekeepers from the provisions of the award and for allowing the employment of non-union labour. Nevertheless he managed both the 1925 and 1927 strikes well until Premier W. McCormack [q.v.] pushed him aside and assumed personal control of the Railway Department, taking a very hard line against the A.R.U.

Larcombe was physically small; he was of independent mind, widely read in poetry and economics and given to embellishing his speeches with quotations from his reading. He based much of his philosophy on the writings of Shelley and Robert Burns. With a florid style in writing and speaking, he was a prolific publicist for Labor. His nine studies of the A.L.P. between 1925 and 1944 included *Notes on the political history of the Labor government in Queensland* and *The case for Labor*. For many years he was the only chronicler of the labour movement in Queensland and his writings gave to the A.L.P. and the trade unions a sense of where they had been and where they were going. He was a great admirer of T. J. Ryan [q.v.], an early patron, and his lecture to the Lower East Street, Rockhampton, branch of the party on Ryan's life and work was published in 1937.

Larcombe had played Rugby League well, took a continuing interest in the welfare and development of the game and was president of the Queensland Rugby League in 1919-32. A teetotaller, non-smoker and bachelor, he worked long hours in Parliament House and the Windsor Hotel where he stayed when in Brisbane. Early aspirations for the Bar were abandoned when he reached the ministry. A legend in Rockhampton, he was generally known as 'Old Jimmy'. He died in Brisbane on 21 June 1957 and, after a service in St Paul's Anglican Cathedral, Rockhampton, was buried in Rockhampton cemetery after a state funeral.

The Labour government of Queensland (Brisb, 1915); C. A. Bernays, *Queensland—our seventh political decade, 1920-1930* (Syd, 1931); D. J. Murphy, *T.J. Ryan* (Brisb, 1975); D. J. Murphy et al (eds), *Labor in power . . . Queensland 1915-1957* (Brisb, 1979); *JRAHS*, Nov 1952, p 225; *Labour Hist*, Nov 1976, p 7; information from F. J. Waters and D. J. Murphy (St Lucia, Brisb).   JOY GUYATT

LARKIN, EDWARD RENNIX (1880-1915), football administrator and politician, was born on 3 January 1880 at North Lambton, Newcastle, New South Wales, third child of William Joseph Larkin, quarryman and miner, and his wife Mary Ann, née Rennix, both native born. Ted Larkin was educated at St Benedict's School, Chippendale, Sydney, and St Joseph's College, Hunters Hill, passing the junior and senior public examinations. He became a journalist on the *Year book of Australia*. On 24 July 1903 he married May Josephine Yates at St Joseph's Catholic Church, Newtown. They had two sons. Larkin had played Rugby Union foot-

ball at school, and then with the Endeavour Club, Newtown. Later he played first grade for Newtown and was captain in 1903. That year as a forward he played for the State against New Zealand and Queensland and for Australia against New Zealand. He was an able cricketer, swimmer and boxer. A 'ready and eloquent speaker', he was a member of St Joseph's (Newtown) Literary and Debating Society.

When Larkin joined the Police Force in October 1903 he was described as 5 ft. 10½ ins. (179 cm) in height, weighing 13 stone (83 kg), with blue eyes, brown hair and a fresh complexion. He was a foot-constable in the Metropolitan Police District until promoted ordinary constable in January 1905. Having parliamentary aspirations, he found the political restrictions of the force irksome, and in June 1909 resigned to become first full-time secretary of the newly formed New South Wales Rugby Football League. An excellent organizer, he quickly remedied the disordered administration and was a prominent advocate for the new code, believing in 'honest professionalism as against quasi amateur football'. He persuaded Marist Brothers' schools to play Rugby League in 1913. Under his guidance the code came to be the dominant winter sport in Sydney.

In 1911 Larkin became a justice of the peace. He was a 'keen student of social problems, and was seldom without a Socialist book or pamphlet in his pocket'. On 13 December 1913 to general surprise he won the seat of Willoughby in the Legislative Assembly for the Labor Party. He was appointed government representative on the board of Royal North Shore Hospital. On 17 August 1914 he enlisted in the 1st Battalion, Australian Imperial Force, and became a sergeant. After showing 'conspicuous gallantry' Larkin was killed in action at Pine Ridge, Gallipoli, on 25 April 1915. A memorial service was held in St Mary's Cathedral.

Larkin was an important figure in Rugby League: his career was an early indication of the link between it and the Labor Party. His enlistment and death helped to counteract accusations that the code was unpatriotic for continuing grade competition during World War I. A tablet commemorating him and Lieut-Colonel George F. Braund [q.v.7], who also died on Gallipoli, was unveiled in the Legislative Assembly in November 1915.

C. E. W. Bean, *The story of Anzac* (Syd, 1921, 1924); R. Cashman and M. McKernan (eds), *Sport in history* (Brisb, 1979); *Referee* (Syd), 23 June 1915; *Daily Telegraph* (Syd), 17 June 1915; *SMH*, 17, 18, 21 June 1915; *Aust Worker*, 24 June 1915.
          CHRIS CUNNEEN

LARKIN, HERBERT JOSEPH (1894-1972), aviator and aircraft manufacturer, was born on 8 October 1894 at South Brisbane, eldest child of Herbert Benjamin George Larkin, a clerk with the Australian United Steam Navigation Co., from Kent, England, and his Queensland-born wife Annie Mary Frances, née McHugh. About 1901 the family moved to Melbourne where Larkin's father (d. 1944) was appointed manager of the new Commonwealth Shipping Line in 1916; in 1923-26 he was chairman of the Commonwealth Shipping Board.

'Jimmy' Larkin, educated at St Thomas's Grammar School, Melbourne, worked as a junior clerk for the Union Steam Ship Co. In August 1914 he enlisted in the Australian Imperial Force as corporal, 1st Signal Corps, Royal Australian Engineers. He was signals clerk to Generals Monash [q.v.] and Chauvel [q.v.7] in Egypt and on Gallipoli before being wounded in September 1915 and invalided to England. In April 1916 he transferred to the Royal Flying Corps as temporary second lieutenant and, promoted captain, was posted to No. 5 Squadron in France where in March 1917 for 'conspicuously valuable photography and reconnaissance work in connection with the German retreat from Bapaume' he earned the Croix de Guerre avec palme. After a period in England as instructor he joined No. 87 Squadron and, returning to France in 1918, brought down eleven enemy aircraft and was awarded the Distinguished Flying Cross.

After the war Larkin, with his brother Reg and other members of 87 Squadron, formed a Sopwith & Engineering Co. Ltd agency, the Larkin Sopwith Aviation Co. of Australia Ltd. He arrived in Melbourne in July 1919 with his wife Vera Grace Russell, née Doman, whom he had married in St Saviour's Church, London, on 15 March, and concentrated initially on giving 'educational flights' in a Sopwith Dove and on the manufacture of petrol storage systems at his Glenhuntly workshop. On 25 October he claimed the first night flight in Australia when he piloted the Dove over Henley Regatta and in 1920 he organized Victoria's first aerial Derby. Next year when Sopwith went into liquidation he continued as Larkin Aircraft Supply Co. Pty Ltd.

In its heyday LASCO had over 100 employees. In 1925 it produced an Avro 405K and from its Coode Island factory, established in 1927, emerged the Lascoter (1929), probably the first Australian all-metal aircraft, and the three-engined Lasconder (1933), both designed by W. S. Shackleton. The company manufactured gliders (the Australian-designed Lark in 1931), several DH 9A and DH 50A type aircraft and in 1932-33 thirty-two DH Moths. In 1931 a flying school was opened. The Depression, however, was crippling.

Larkin was severely tried over his airline operations. In December 1921 he had won the government airmail contract between Sydney and Adelaide. However, difficulties in raising money and finding suitable aircraft led him into partnership with F. L. Roberts, the successful contractor for the Sydney-Brisbane service. The resulting Australian Aerial Services Ltd began the Adelaide-Sydney run on 2 June 1924 but the Sydney-Brisbane operation was stillborn. In February 1930 Larkin founded the unsubsidized Murray Valley Aerial Services Ltd and in March also commenced a run between Melbourne and Adelaide. But in comparison with Qantas and Western Australian Airlines Larkin's operations did not prosper and his subsidies for the southern mail services were withdrawn in June, leaving him with only the isolated and unprofitable Camooweal (Queensland)-Daly Waters (Northern Territory) service for which he had undercut Qantas in 1928.

Larkin was described by *Smith's Weekly* as having 'eyes deep set and a little close together, a hard, straight mouth, and a way of glaring hard at the person he is addressing'. The intense competition between the airline companies exacerbated his tactless, impatient temperament. His complaints against the civil aviation authorities erupted in headlines in February 1929 when he accused the former secretary for defence M. L. Shepherd [q.v.] of seeking bribes. The subsequent inquiry held the charges to be unfounded.

In 1932 Larkin antagonized his competitors by establishing the Australian Air Convention to formulate an aviation policy. On 26 February 1934 Western Mining Corporation sued the convention for suggesting that W.M.C. might gain a privately negotiated government subsidy for aerial survey work. Larkin conducted the defence, and lost. In liquidation, his companies' assets were sold to New England Airways, later incorporated into Airlines of Australia for whom he was traffic manager before leaving for Europe in 1937.

Larkin served with the American forces during World War II and, divorced from his wife, he married a widow Hélène Merley, née Castan, on 6 June 1945 in Paris. Little is known of his subsequent career in Germany, Switzerland and France but, divorced a second time in 1956, he next year retired to the Channel Islands from where he campaigned for human rights. A gardener since boyhood, in 1968 he published *Bonsai culture for beginners*. He died at St Martin's, Guernsey, on 20 June 1972, survived by a son and daughter from his first marriage and a son from his second.

Who's who in Australia, 1 (Melb, 1922); S. Brogden, *The history of Australian aviation* (Melb, 1960); H. Fysh, *Qantas rising* (Syd, 1965); G. R. Copley, *Australians in the air* (Adel, 1976); *Sea, Land and Air*, Aug 1919; *Wings* (Melb), June-Sept 1934; *Aircraft* (Melb), 1 May 1936; *Aust Manufacturer*, 12 May 1938; *Daily Standard*, 4 July 1916; *Argus*, 24 Aug 1916, 7 Dec 1926, 18 Sept 1944; *Table Talk*, 14 Apr 1927; Ellison papers (ANL); family papers held by Mrs O. Larkin, Turramurra, NSW.   ANN G. SMITH

LASERON, CHARLES FRANCIS (1887-1959), naturalist and connoisseur, was born on 6 December 1887 at Manitowoc, Wisconsin, United States of America, third and youngest child of English parents the Rev. David Laseron, Episcopalian clergyman, and his wife Frances, née Bradley. The Laserons were of eastern German origin and Moravian in religion. Late in 1888 the family returned to London but again migrated, reaching Sydney in January 1891. In June 1892 David Laseron was shot while travelling in a train near Redfern. His injuries led to severe nervous disorders and bouts of acute depression. In 1896 he was given charge of a parish at Lithgow, where Charles (or Carl as he was then known) received early schooling before his mother brought him to Sydney to attend St Andrew's Cathedral Choir School as scholar and chorister.

Self-reliance was forced on Charles by the difficult circumstances of his boyhood. He attended evening classes at Sydney Technical College where he came under the influence of Carl Sussmilch [q.v.] and gained the diploma in geology; he later served the college as a part-time lecturer. His first scientific paper, on the geology of the Shoalhaven district, appeared in July 1906, the month he joined the staff of the Technological Museum in Sydney as a collector; he also worked on eucalypts with R. T. Baker [q.v.7]. Further study of geology and palaeontology led to more papers, some published by the Royal Society of New South Wales which he joined in 1911.

That year Laseron joined the Australasian Antarctic Expedition under (Sir) Douglas Mawson [q.v.], officially as taxidermist and biological collector but in fact as general scientific assistant. He spent from January 1912 to February 1913 in Adelie Land, taking part in two major sledging journeys and making discoveries in geology as well as biology. His account of his Antarctic experiences, for which he received the Polar Medal, was eventually published in 1947 as *South with Mawson*.

On his return to the museum, Laseron was put in charge of its geological collections, but in September 1914 he enlisted in the Australian Imperial Force. Wounded on the second day of the Gallipoli landings while serving as a sergeant with the 13th Battalion, he returned to Sydney and was discharged in 1916. That year extracts from his war diaries appeared in a slim volume, *From Australia to the Dardanelles*. Part of the text had already been printed by a Sydney newspaper, the first of his many contributions to journalism. At Albury on 22 March 1919 he married with Presbyterian forms Mary Theodora Mason, a bank clerk.

After the war Laseron entered a new field at the museum, that of applied art of which he became officer-in-charge on 1 January 1926. His published guides to the collections of old pottery, porcelain and other artefacts drew attention to what he felt were sadly neglected subjects. Publicly and at the museum, he argued for an applied art collection, appropriately funded and suitably housed. Much later developments at the old Ultimo power house and elsewhere in Sydney have realized part of Laseron's vision, but with little acknowledgement to a man out of season. Beyond setting up the New South Wales Applied Art Trust to promote the cause, he could make no headway and, frustrated by attitudes within the museum, resigned in 1929. He set up in business as an antique-dealer and auctioneer of books, coins and stamps; he made a living despite the Depression and came to be a noted authority on philately.

During World War II Laseron returned to the A.I.F. as a map-reading instructor until severe bronchitis and consequent heart trouble led to his discharge as unfit in 1944. For some years he worked as a clerk with the Colonial Sugar Refining Co. Ltd in Sydney. Even before his retirement, however, Laseron devoted much time to writing and will be most widely remembered as a popular and effective exponent of science. *The face of Australia* (1953) and *Ancient Australia* (1954) have fostered lay understanding of geomorphology and geology. A more limited group esteems Laseron for his notable contributions to Australian malacology published from 1948 onwards, many of them by the Australian Museum, Sydney, which now houses his type collections.

Survived by his wife, a son and a daughter, Laseron died on 27 June 1959 in Concord Repatriation General Hospital and was cremated with Anglican rites. He had sought no honours, and few came his way, although colleagues have given his name to various new genera and species of molluscs.

He was an honorary correspondent of the Australian Museum and in 1952 the Royal Zoological Society of New South Wales, of which he had been a councillor, conferred on him its fellowship. As one obituarist wrote: 'Never a rich man, he nevertheless enjoyed a rich life'.

D. Laseron, *An autobiography* (Syd, 1904); D. Mawson, *The home of the blizzard* (Lond, 1915); N. Hall, *Botanists of the eucalypts* (Melb, 1978); *Aust J of Science*, 22, 1959; Roy Zoological Soc NSW, *Procs*, 1958-59, and for publications; *Stamp News*, 22 (1975), no 4; *SMH*, 19 Apr 1955, 1 July 1959; uncat MSS (ML).   T. G. VALLANCE

LASSETER, LEWIS HUBERT (HAROLD BELL) (1880-1931), gold-seeker, was born on 27 September 1880 at Bamganie, near Meredith, Victoria, second son of English parents William John Lasseter, labourer, and his wife Agnes, née Cruickshank. His mother died when he was young and his father remarried. His boyhood and youth are obscure but he claimed to have served four years in the Royal Navy, being discharged in 1901. He then went to the United States of America where, describing himself as a labourer, he married Florence Elizabeth Scott at Clifton Springs, New York State, on 29 December 1903.

About 1908 Lasseter returned to Australia and took up a small leasehold farm at Tabulam, New South Wales, worked as a maintenance man and wrote a little for a local newspaper. In 1913 he submitted a design for an arch bridge over Sydney Harbour and in 1915 lodged a provisional specification for a patent disc plough. On the outbreak of war he sold out, moved to Melbourne and unsuccessfully tried to enlist. On his second attempt, however, describing himself as a 'bridge engineer' he enlisted in the Australian Imperial Force in February 1916, only to be discharged as medically unfit on 17 October. In August 1917 he re-enlisted in Adelaide but after an unspecified illness was discharged in November. In 1919 he was granted a patent for an improved method in the treatment of wheat for storage: the patent lapsed when the fee was not paid.

On 28 January 1924 describing himself as 'Lewis Harold Bell Lasseter, bachelor', he married Louise Irene Lillywhite, a nurse, at Middle Park Methodist Church, Melbourne. Settling in Kogarah, Sydney, in 1925-30 Lasseter worked as a carpenter in Canberra and on the Sydney Harbour Bridge, feuded with the local council over his house, worked on another patent for pre-cast concrete construction and managed a pottery at Redfern. In September 1929 he publicly claimed to be 'the original designer of an arch bridge for Sydney Harbour' and unsuccessfully solicited payment for six months labour spent on it.

On 14 October 1929 Lasseter wrote to A. E. 'Texas' Green [q.v.], Federal member for Kalgoorlie, outlining what he called an 'out of the ordinary suggestion' to develop the mining, pastoral and agricultural industries. He claimed that eighteen years previously he had discovered 'a vast gold bearing reef in Central Australia' which over fourteen miles assayed three ounces to the ton and which could be developed with an adequate water-supply and capital of £5 million. Claiming to be 'a competent surveyor and prospector' he offered to survey an 800-mile (1287 km) pipeline route from a projected dam on the Gascoyne River to the reef for £2000. He sent a copy of his letter to the Western Australian minister for mines and suggested that State and Federal governments share the cost of the survey. In November Lasseter was interviewed by (Sir) Herbert Gepp [q.v.8], chairman of the Development and Migration Commission, and geologist Dr L. K. Ward who were sceptical of Lasseter's alleged reef which he vaguely located near the western edge of the MacDonnell Ranges. The government decided to take no action.

'Expecting the bailiff', as he put it in February 1930, the following month Lasseter approached John Bailey [q.v.7] of the Australian Workers' Union and told him of his find—this time thirty-three years previously, when he was 17! Travelling west from the MacDonnell Ranges his horses had died and he was rescued by a surveyor named Harding who took him to Carnarvon, Western Australia, whence they returned three years later and relocated the reef. Lasseter also told Bailey he was 'a qualified ship's captain' and that he had worked for years on coastal boats. In subsequent interviews with Fred Blakeley [q.v.7], Errol Coote, Charles Ulm [q.v.] and others the story varied in detail and aroused suspicion; nevertheless, the lure of gold in a time of economic depression led to the formation of a company to send out a search expedition for the reef.

The well-equipped expedition which left Alice Springs, Northern Territory, west for Ilbilba on 21 July comprised Blakeley, leader, George Sutherland, prospector, Philip Taylor, engineer and driver, Fred Colson, driver, Errol Coote, pilot of the aeroplane, Captain Blakeston-Houston, the governor-general's aide as 'explorer', and Lasseter as guide, paid £10 per week and insured for £500.

Lasseter's behaviour was peculiar, in turn unco-operative, suspicious and sulky; he passed his spare time singing Mormon hymns and writing up his diary. No trace of a reef was found and when accidents and rough terrain forced the party back in September, Lasseter carried on his search with Paul Johns, an English dogger, who had a string of camels. They quarrelled and parted company and Lasseter, after his two camels had bolted, lived for about sixteen weeks with Aboriginals and died apparently of starvation at Shaws Creek in the Petermann Ranges. Bob Buck [q.v.7], engaged to search for Lasseter, attested that he found his body and buried it in March 1931: a death certificate was issued giving the date of death as 30 January. His wife, their son and two daughters, and two daughters of his first marriage, survived him. Lasseter claimed in his diary, later recovered, that he had 'rediscovered' his reef and pegged his claim.

Lasseter, nicknamed 'Das' or 'Possum', was stocky, about 5 ft. 3 ins. (160 cm) in height, dark-complexioned with brown eyes; his partly bald scalp was deeply scarred. Self-educated, but literate and well-spoken, Lasseter was a *poseur* who had little regard for the truth. To Blakeley he was 'a man of jumbled moods' lacking 'a credible story about anything in all his reminiscences'. Coote wrote that he was 'a man of most eccentric nature', Taylor called him a 'humbug', and an old friend wrote that 'he was more or less of a crank, very aggressive, very self-opinionated and full of large, hopeful visions'.

It is clear from Lasseter's lack of knowledge of both bushcraft and prospecting, his conflicting and vague statements and his peculiar conduct during the expedition that he had never before been in that part of Central Australia, let alone found a gold reef. The myth of a cave or reef of gold (Earle's)

in the Centre long predated Lasseter's story which is remarkably reminiscent of an incident in Simpson Newland's [q.v.] novel *Blood tracks of the Bush* (1900). David Hennessey's *An Australian bush track* (1896) and Conrad Sayce's *Golden buckles* (1920) also deal with fabulous gold finds in the Australian desert, while the American Harold Bell Wright's *The mine with the iron door* (1923) was a popular contemporary novel and photoplay on much the same theme. Lasseter's addition of 'Harold Bell' to his names on his second marriage followed publication of Wright's novel. Given the existence of the myth, Lasseter may well have been suffering from an hallucination; or given his dire financial situation, he may have been hopeful of accidentally stumbling on a gold find once in the Centre.

The myth of 'Lasseter's Lost Reef' has persisted and excited numerous further expeditions largely as a result of Ion Idriess's [q.v.] romantic novel *Lasseter's last ride*, first published in September 1931, which ran to seventeen editions by 1935. Blakeley's much more reliable account *Dream millions* (Sydney, 1972), published posthumously, is highly critical of Lasseter but adds to the myth by suggesting that he did not die in the Centre but somehow made his way out, ultimately to U.S.A.

E. Coote, *Hell's airport* (Syd, 1934); C. T. Madigan, *Central Australia* (Oxford, 1936); F. Clune, *The red heart* (Melb, 1940); E. Hill, *About Lasseter* (Priv print, Adel, 1968); A. Stapleton, *Lasseter did not lie!* (Adel, 1981); *V&P* (LA WA), 1937, 1; *Aust Coal, Shipping, Steel and the Harbour*, 2 Sept 1929; *Walkabout*, 1 Aug 1936; *People* (Syd), 9 Feb 1955, 23 Dec 1959, 2 Aug 1961; *SMH*, 4, 5 Mar 1931, 1, 8 Feb 1958, 15 May 1977; *Bulletin*, 2 Mar 1932, 15 July 1936; J. Bailey, History of Lasseter's reef, *and* F. Blakeley, Dream millions (MSS, ML); A3043, A6964 (ML) and AI 30/512, 48/1143, C 64/7 (AAO).   G. P. WALSH